THE SCIENCE AND HISTORY PROJECT BOOK

THE SCIENCE AND HISTORY PROJECT BOOK

300 step-by-step fun science experiments and history craft projects for home learning and school study

CHRIS OXLADE, RACHEL HALSTEAD AND STRUAN REID

Contents

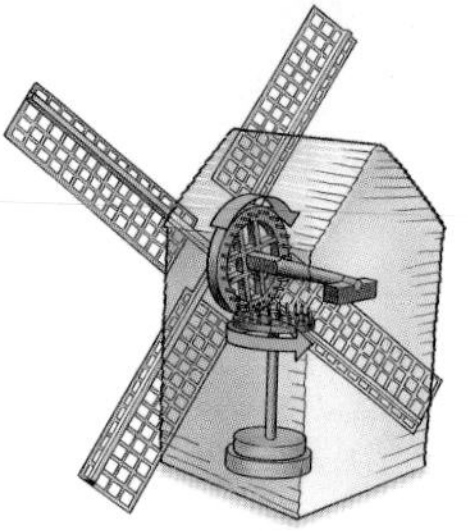

Great History Projects 252

Houses and Homes 256

Fashion and Accessories 310

Science and Technology 368

Customs, Arts and Entertainment 424

Introduction

This book is packed full with hundreds of exciting, entertaining and informative projects and experiments for you to do at home. They will help you to understand both the fascinating world of science and technology, and how people lived in the past and how their lives changed through history. The first half of the book contains a huge range of experiments on science and technology. For example, you can find out why the Moon seems to change shape and how rockets that journeyed to the Moon work, learn how plants need water to live, and how we use water to produce energy.

Projects about the Earth look at the rocks and minerals that the Earth is made of, the Earth's surface features, such as oceans and mountains, how the surface is changed by volcanoes and earthquakes, and weather. There are experiments which look at the matter from which our Universe is made, and how it can change. Discover how plants and animals share the world with us, and how they grow and live. Learn about technology and how we apply our knowledge of science in different areas of our modern lives. We use this knowledge to build cars, ships, aircraft, spacecraft and amazing structures such as skyscrapers and bridges, and to engineer tools and machines such as can openers and computers. Many more important inventions in the world of technology are demonstrated in this section of the book.

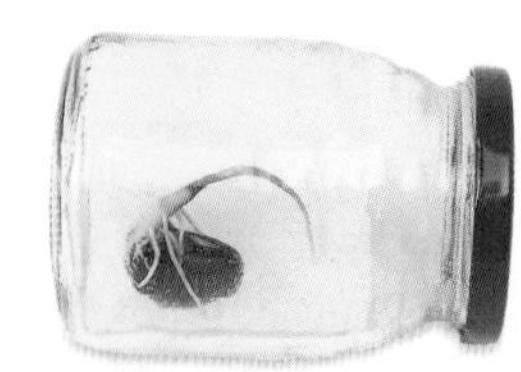

All history, from the ancient past to the 21st century, is littered with important scientific discoveries and technological innovations that people have used in all areas of their lives, from building homes and making clothes to creating weapons and new forms of transport.

The second half of this book is full of projects examining history. From these we learn about many different ages in history, as well as about a variety of cultures from all over the world. For example, there is a project that shows how ancient hunters used bones to make shelters, and another that shows how the Greeks made a game out of bones; we also discover how Ancient Egyptians built houses, and how, thousands of years later, the Vikings made bracelets.

Find out how homes and shelters – from mud huts to towering castles – were built, and how people decorated, furnished and lit their homes. Projects about food show you how people prepared and cooked the crops they grew in their fields, and how they made them tasty with spices. Fascinating facts about clothes and fashions tell you how people made fabrics and turned them into clothes to protect themselves from the weather, and how they made adornments and other decorations for themselves. This superb collection of exciting projects and experiments will give insights into how people lived and how things work; try them all and discover how amazing our world is.

Before getting to work on the projects, read the hints on pages 11 and 255. These will tell you how to have fun without making too much mess or having an accident. So use your imagination and have some fun.

GREAT SCIENCE EXPERIMENTS

Science at Home

Science is the search for truth and knowledge. It is the process of finding information about the world around us. It tries to answer questions about how it works. Scientists are people who gather this knowledge of the world. They develop techniques for investigating how things work. They work in controlled environments, such as laboratories, so that they can study results. We call this experimentation.

Why experiment?

Experiments help you discover and understand how things work and why things happen. When you try ideas out, concepts that seem hard to grasp become easier to understand. This is why scientists experiment – to test their ideas. By experimenting, people invent and perfect machines and processes that make our lives easier. Today, the quality of our lives depends on science for everyday comfort, health and entertainment, transportation and communication.

Innovation and change

The scientific experiments in this book demonstrate many of the breakthroughs and discoveries that have had an impact on our lives. The technique of asking questions and trying to answer them through observation and experiment is important to science. The continuous process of discovery and experiment means that scientists come up with different answers. This is why science is always changing. Innovations and inventions change the way we look at the world, so we see it differently. Imagine, for example, what people must have thought the stars were before the telescope was invented to help them see the heavens more clearly.

Finding your way around the first part of this book

The first half of this book is divided into four sections of experiments. Each section explores various specialized areas of science within an everyday theme:

Our Restless Earth looks at the Earth's formation. You will see how weather and geological activities, such as volcanoes and earthquakes, affect the shape of the land.

Natural Wonders Close to Home explores nature and the environment by discovering the habitats in your own garden or in nearby woods and parks.

Physical and Material Marvels investigates the basic principles of physics and chemistry, from how machines work to construction and building. This section focuses on power and energy, chemical change, light and cameras, electricity and magnets.

Finally, *Travel and Transport* explores how trains, cars, airplanes, rockets and ships have developed through history to the present day. This section will also explain how each of these machines work.

EXPERIMENTING HINTS

- Before you start, tell an adult what you are going to do. Show him or her the experiment and explain where and how you intend to do it.
- Make sure you have all the necessary items required for the project and that the materials and equipment are clean. You should be able to find everything you need either in your home or from a local shop.
- Read the whole project first. Then read each step and make sure you understand it before you begin. All the experiments are safe as long as you follow the instructions exactly, and ask for adult help when advised to do so.
- When you have finished a project, clear everything away safely, especially breakable items, such as glass. Remember to wash your hands!
- Take extra care with experiments that involve electricity, heating things up, handling chemicals, soil and glass. If you are using any food, make sure you have permission to use it and throw it away after you have finished. If a project advises using gloves, be sure to do so.
- Do not worry if an experiment doesn't work or you miss what happens. Try to work out why it has gone wrong and do the experiment again. It's all part of the fun!

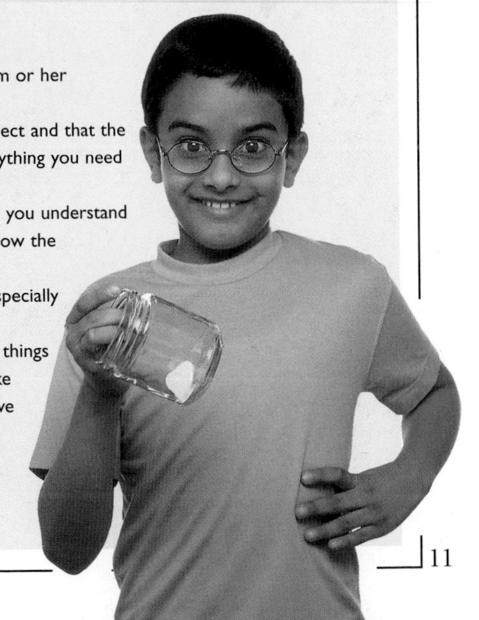

Our Restless Earth

Earthquakes and volcanoes are a reminder that the Earth's surface is constantly and dramatically changing. Fossils reveal how many kinds of plants and animals that were once alive have now disappeared. Scientists realize that it is part of the Earth's nature to undergo violent changes caused by natural processes that act over billions of years. In the following pages, you can discover how some of these natural processes, such as wind erosion, rivers and mountain formation, affect the Earth.

Spinning planet

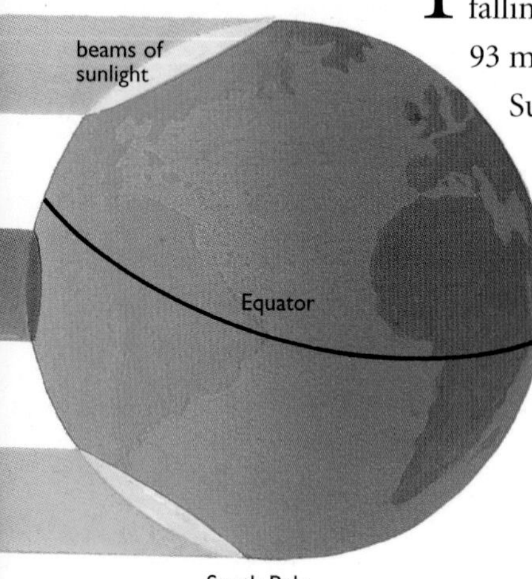

The Earth is like a giant ball spinning in Space. The only light falling on it is the light of the Sun, glowing 150 million km/ 93 million miles away. The Earth turns once a day, and it orbits the Sun once a year. The experiments on these pages investigate the two ways of moving, and explain why night and day, and the seasons, occur. The ball represents the Earth and the torch (flashlight), the Sun. In the final project, you can make a thermometer using water to record changes in temperature from night to day, and from season to season.

▲ Variable sunlight
The Sun's light does not fall evenly over the Earth, because our planet is round. Imagine three identical beams of sunlight falling on the Earth. One falls on the Equator, and the others on the North and South Poles. The beam falling on the Equator covers a much smaller area, so its energy is more concentrated and the temperature is higher.

YOU WILL NEED

Night and day: Felt-tipped pen, plastic ball, thin string, non-hardening modelling material, torch (flashlight).

The seasons: Felt-tipped pen, plastic ball, bowl just big enough for the ball to sit on, torch (flashlight), books or a box to set the torch on.

Make a thermometer: Water, bottle, food dye, clear straw, reusable adhesive, thin card, scissors, felt-tipped pen.

Night and day

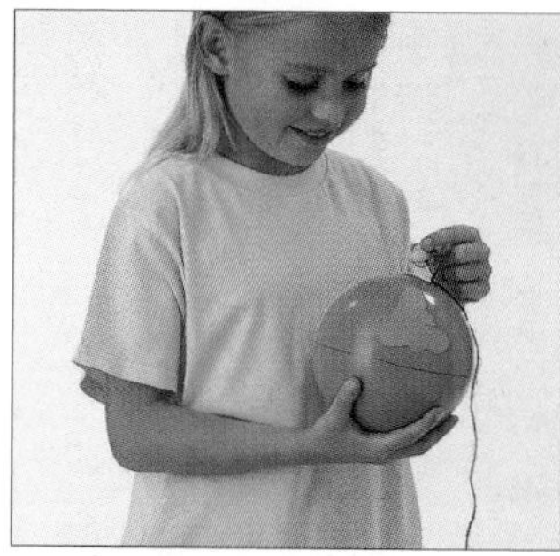

1 Draw or stick a shape on the ball to represent your country. Stick the string to the ball with modelling material. Tie the string to a rail, such as a towel rail, so that the ball hangs freely.

2 Shine the torch on the ball. If the country you live in is on the half of the ball in shadow on the far side, then it is night, because it is facing away from the Sun.

3 Your home country may be on the half of the ball lit by the torch instead. If so, it must be daytime here because it is facing the Sun. Keep the torch level, aimed at the middle.

4 Turn the ball from left to right. As you turn the ball, your country will move from the light half to the dark half. You can see how the Sun comes up and goes down as the Earth turns.

The seasons

1 Use the felt-tipped pen to draw a line around the middle of the ball. This represents the Equator. Sit the ball on top of the bowl, so that the Equator line is sloping gently.

2 Put the torch on the books so that it shines just above the Equator. It is summer on the half of the ball above the Equator where the torch is shining, and winter on the other half of the world.

3 Shine the torch on the Equator. It sheds equal light in each half of the ball. This is the equivalent of spring and autumn, when days and nights are a similar length throughout the world.

Solar power ▸

The Sun pours energy on to the Earth as heat and light. The amount of energy received in any one place on the Earth changes with the seasons. This is because the Earth's axis is tilted. In the summer, one half of the Earth tilts toward the Sun, and is warmer. In the winter, it tilts away from the Sun and is colder.

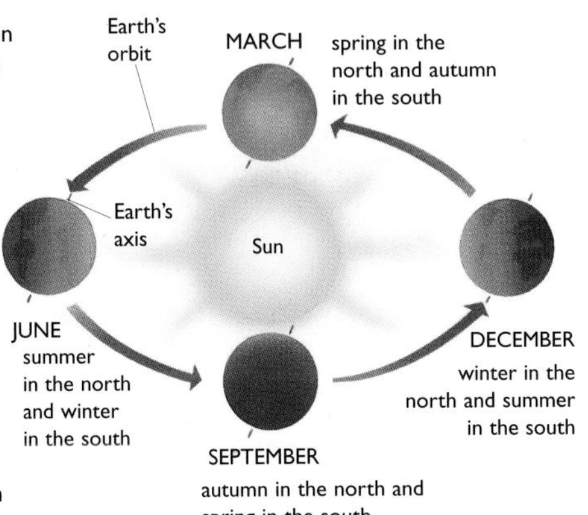

Make a thermometer

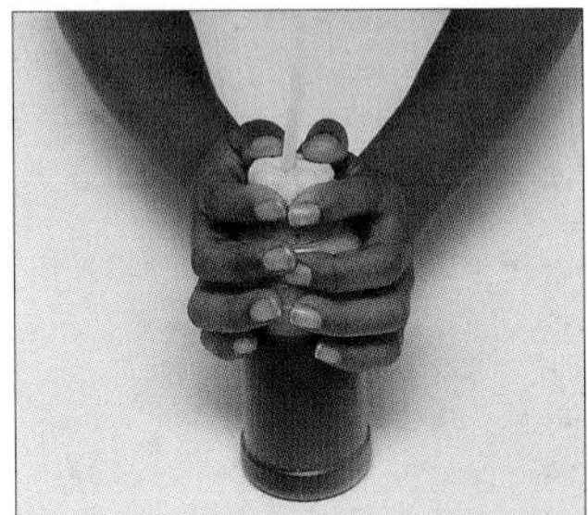

1 Pour cold water into the bottle until it is about two-thirds full. Add some food dye. Dip the straw into the water, and seal the neck tightly with reusable adhesive.

2 Blow down the straw to force some extra air into the bottle. After a few seconds, the extra air pressure inside will force the water level to rise up the straw.

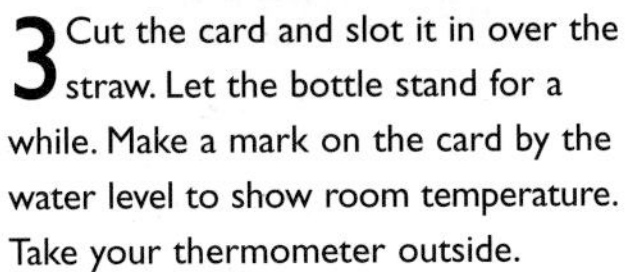

3 Cut the card and slot it in over the straw. Let the bottle stand for a while. Make a mark on the card by the water level to show room temperature. Take your thermometer outside.

4 On a hot day, the Sun's heat will make the air and water expand, forcing the water level in the straw above the room temperature mark. Cool the thermometer in the refrigerator. Mark the different levels with a pen.

Phases of the Moon

The Moon is the closest celestial entity to Earth. We know more about the Moon than about any other heavenly body because astronauts explored its surface. The Moon is Earth's only satellite. It measures 3,476km/2,160 miles across, about a quarter of the size of the Earth. It circles the Earth at a distance of about 385,000km/239,000 miles, and makes the journey about once a month. The Moon does not give out any light of its own. We see it because it reflects light from the Sun. The sunlight illuminates different parts of the Moon as the month goes by. This makes the Moon seem to change shape. The Moon spins around slowly as it circles the Earth, so the same side is always turned toward the Earth.

We only see the Moon lit up completely once a month, but you do not have to wait a month to see the changes in its shape or phases. The project here will show you in just a few minutes how the Moon goes through its phases!

▲ Face of the Moon
This picture shows a view of the Moon from the Earth. When the whole of the Moon is lit up like this, we call it a full Moon. The darker regions on the surface are great, dusty plains called seas, or maria. The lighter areas are highlands. These are pitted with craters that can be hundreds of kilometres/ miles across. Mountains on the Moon rise to more than 6,000m/18,000ft.

Make your own Moon

YOU WILL NEED
Inflatable ball, glue, glue brush, glass, foil, scissors, reusable adhesive, torch (flashlight).

1 Make sure that you have washed and dried your ball thoroughly before using! Paint glue all over the ball. Rest it on a glass or something similar, to keep it still.

2 Carefully cut the tinfoil into large square sheets. Wrap up the ball in the foil. Try to make sure that the wrapping is as smooth as possible. You now have your Moon!

3 Place your Moon on a table. Wedge a small ball of reusable adhesive under the ball. This will hold it firm and stop it from rolling off the table.

4 Get your friend to stand at one side of the table to shine a torch with a strong beam on your Moon. Go to the opposite side of the table. Look at your Moon with the main lights out.

5 Gradually move around the table, still looking at your Moon, which is lit up one side by the torch. You will see the different shapes it takes. These shapes are the Moon's phases.

Going through the phases ▸
When you are opposite your friend in the project, the side of the ball facing you is dark. This is what happens once a month in the night sky. We can only see a thin sliver of light, which we call a new or crescent Moon. As you move around the table, more of the ball is lit by the torch. All of it will be lit when you are behind your friend. When this happens to the real Moon, we describe it as full. As you continue moving around, the ball gradually fades into darkness. When you are opposite your friend again, you will see a new Moon again.

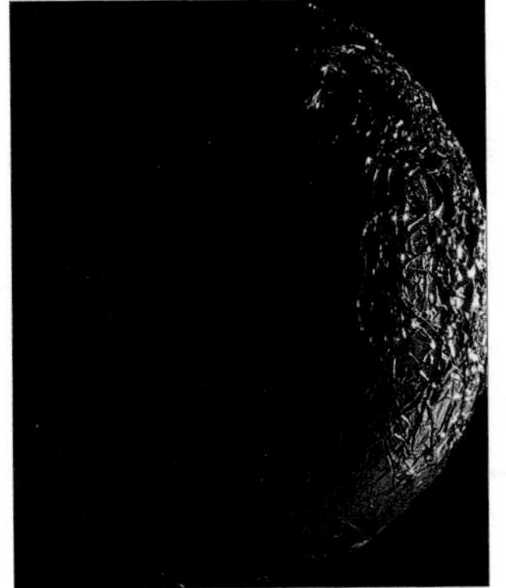

crescent Moon

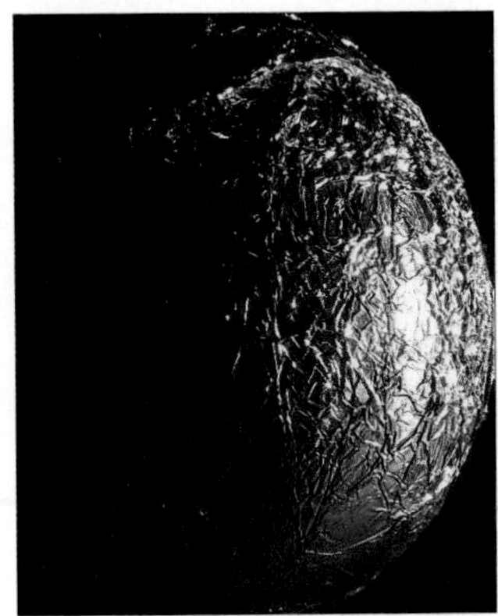

first quarter phase

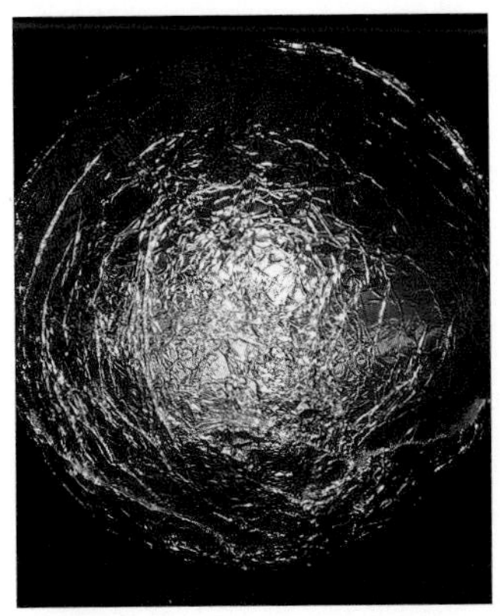

full Moon

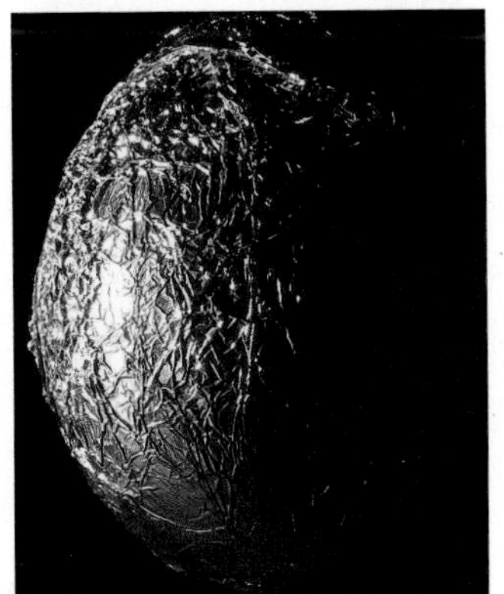

last quarter phase

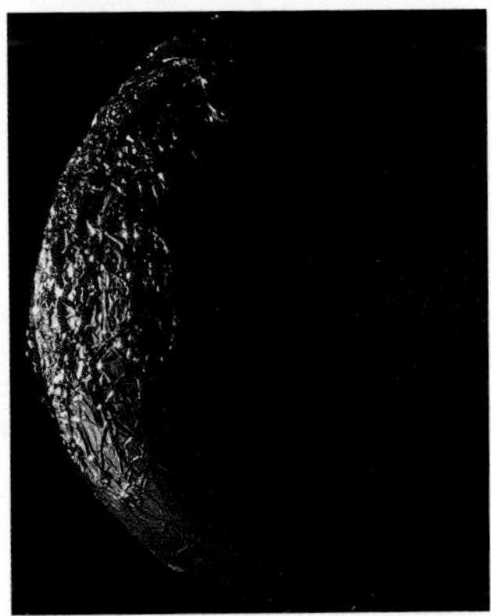

crescent Moon

The rise and fall of tides

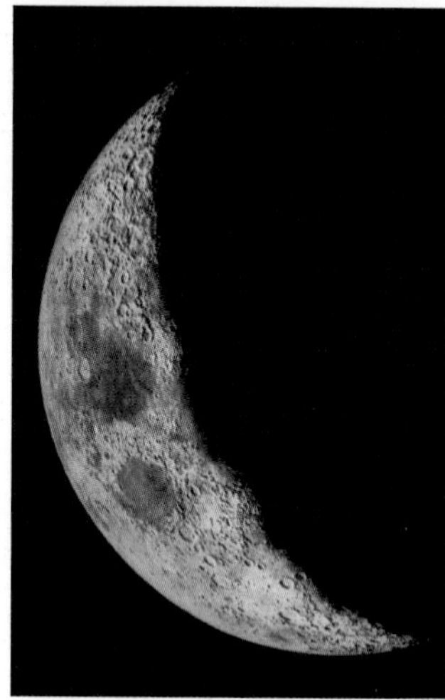

▲ The lunar cycle
The Moon is a lifeless desert of rock. It has no atmosphere to protect it from the Sun's dangerous rays, and no water to sustain life. The shape of the Moon appears to change during the month. We call these changes in shape the Moon's phases. It takes the Moon 29½ days to change from a slim crescent to a full circle and back again.

The Earth appears blue from the darkness of Space. This is because more than 70 per cent of its surface is covered with oceans. The seas make up more than one million million million tons of seawater.

Every 12 hours or so, the seawater rises, then falls back again. These rises and falls are called the tides. When the water is rising, we say the tide is flowing. When it is falling, we say the tide is ebbing. The movement of the ocean waters is caused by the Moon and by the Earth spinning. Gravity pulls the Moon and Earth together. As the Earth turns, the Moon pulls at the ocean water directly beneath it, causing the water to rise. A similar rise in sea level occurs on the opposite side of the Earth, where the water bulges out as a result of the Earth spinning. At these places, there is a high tide. Some six hours later, the Earth has turned 90°. The sea then falls to its lowest point and there is a low tide.

The two experiments opposite explain how the oceans rise and fall without any change in the amount of seawater, and how the tidal bulges of water stay in the same place below the Moon, as the Earth spins beneath it.

How tides occur

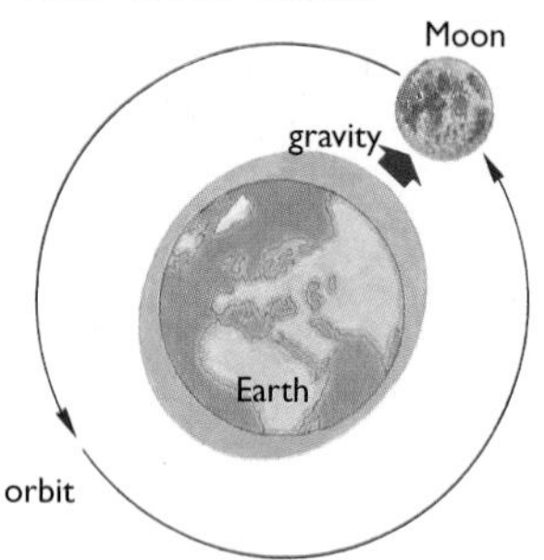

Tides rise beneath the Moon as the Earth turns. The gravity of the Moon tugs at the oceans, pulling the water around with it.

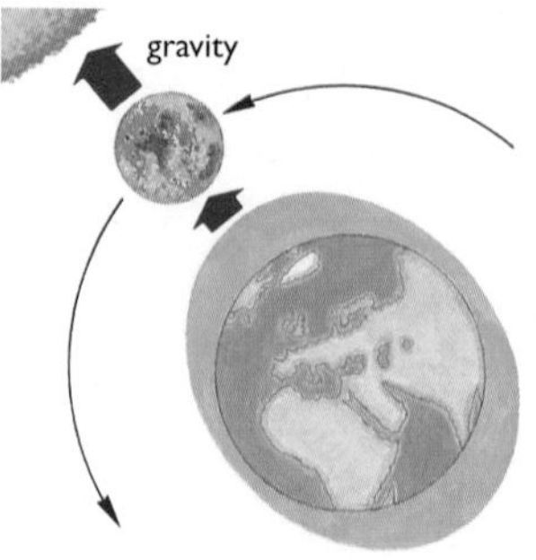

Once every two weeks, the Sun and the Moon line up with the Earth. Their combined pull creates a spring tide, where the tides are higher than usual.

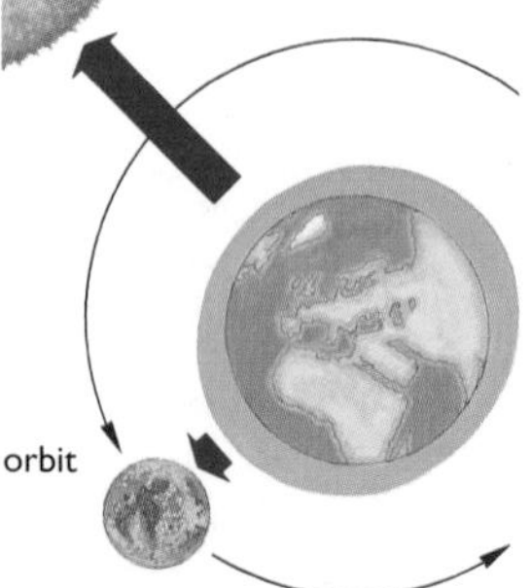

One week later, the Sun and the Moon are at right angles to each other. Pulling in different directions, they create a lower tide than usual, called a neap tide.

High and low tide

1 Place the bowl on a firm, flat surface, then half fill it with water. Place the ball gently in the water so that it floats in the middle of the bowl, as shown in the picture.

2 Place both hands on top of the ball, and push it gently but firmly down into the water. Look what happens to the level of the water. It rises in a 'high tide'.

3 Let the ball gently rise again. Now you can see the water in the bowl dropping again. So the tide has risen and fallen, even though the amount of water is unchanged.

The tidal bulge

YOU WILL NEED

High and low tide: Plastic bowl, water, plastic ball to represent the world.

The tidal bulge: Strong glue, one 20cm/8in length and two 40cm/16in lengths of thin string, plastic ball to represent the world, plastic bowl, hand drill, water.

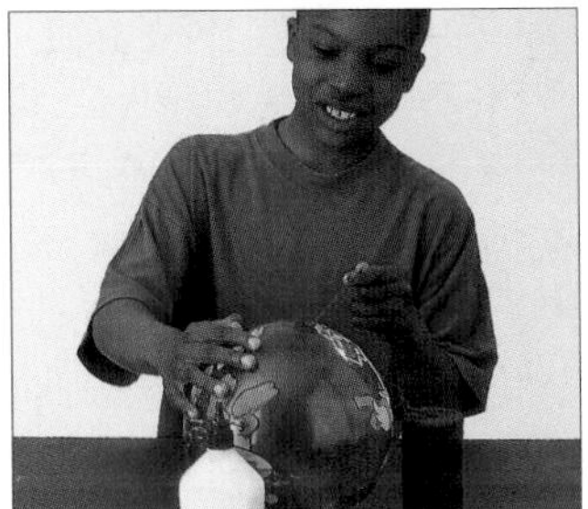

1 Glue the 20cm/8in length of the string very firmly to the ball and leave it to dry. Meanwhile, ask an adult to drill two holes in the rim of the bowl, one on each side.

2 Thread a 40cm/16in length of string through each hole, and knot the string around the rim. Half fill the plastic bowl with water and float the ball in the water.

3 Ask a friend to pull the string on the ball toward him or her. There is now more water on one side of the ball than the other. This is called a tidal bulge.

4 The Moon pulls on the water as well as the Earth. So now ask the friend to hold the ball in place, while both of you pull out the strings attached to the bowl until it distorts.

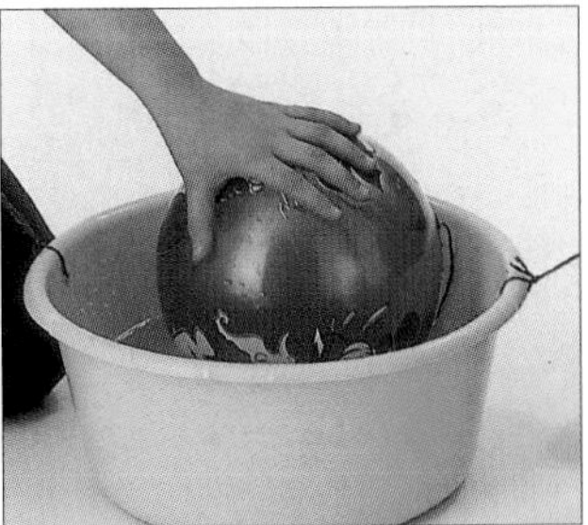

5 There is now a tidal bulge on each side of the world. One of you slowly turn the ball. Now you can see how, in effect, the tidal bulges move around the world as the world turns.

Ocean waves and currents

▲ **Powerful seas**
In stormy weather, giant waves rear up and crash down, turning the sea into a raging turmoil.

The sea is rarely still. Even on a calm day, you will see ripples on the surface. Waves move over the ocean's surface. They are driven mainly by the wind. The stronger the winds, and the longer the fetch (the distance they have travelled), the bigger and higher the waves are. Waves usually only affect the surface of the water. As they travel, the water itself does not move. It just moves up and down as the wave passes through it. At a very deep level in some oceans, the water does move in giant streams called ocean currents. These can be hot or cold, and can affect the world's climate. Ocean currents are usually caused by differences in the water's saltiness or temperature, rather than by the wind.

The first project shows how waves are made, and the second, how currents are set up by the wind blowing. Currents such as the ones in the third project happen on a much larger scale in the world's major oceans.

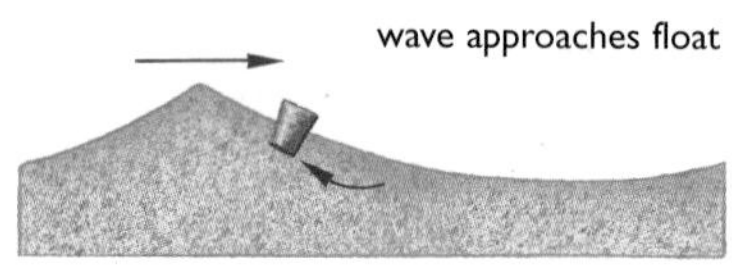

float maintains position

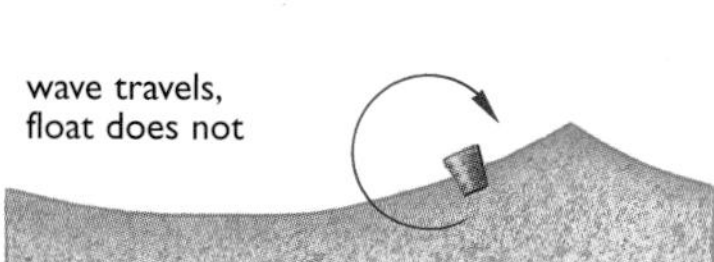

▲ **Wave goodbye**
The diagrams above show how waves travel across the water surface, while objects floating on the water hardly move at all.

Making waves

YOU WILL NEED
Rectangular plastic bowl, jug (pitcher), water, bathtub or inflatable pool, non-hardening modelling material.

1 Place the bowl on the floor or on a table. Choose a place where it does not matter if a little water spills over. Fill the bowl with water until it almost reaches the brim.

2 Blow very gently over the surface of the water. You will see that the water begins to ripple where you blow on it. This is how ocean waves are formed by air movement.

3 Fill the bathtub or pool with water. Blow gently along the length of the bath or pool. Blow at the same strength as in step 2, and from the same height above the water.

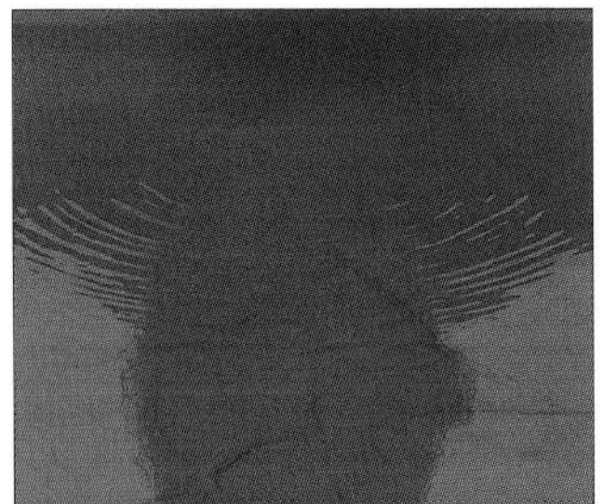

4 Keep blowing for a minute or so. Notice that the waves are bigger in the bathtub or pool, even though you are not blowing harder. This is because they reach farther across the water.

5 Now drop a small piece of modelling material into the water. Watch how it sets up waves. Ripples travel out in circles from where the modelling material entered the water.

Ocean currents

YOU WILL NEED

Rectangular plastic bowl, jug (pitcher), water, talcum powder.

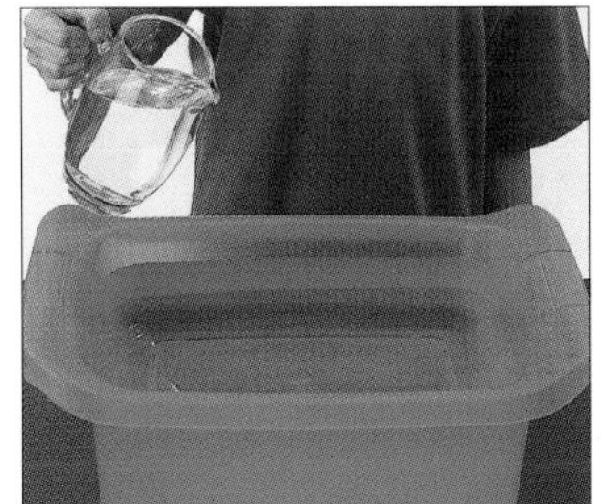

1 Place the bowl on the floor or on a table. Choose a place where it does not matter if a little water spills over. Fill the bowl with water until it almost reaches the rim.

2 Scatter a small amount of talcum powder over the water. Use just enough powder to make a very fine film over the water's surface. The less you use, the better.

3 Blow very gently across the water from the middle of one side of the bowl to the other. You will see how the water starts to move. Ocean currents begin to move in the same way.

4 Keep blowing, and the powder swirls in two circles as it hits the far side. This is what happens when currents hit continents. One current turns clockwise, the other turns anticlockwise.

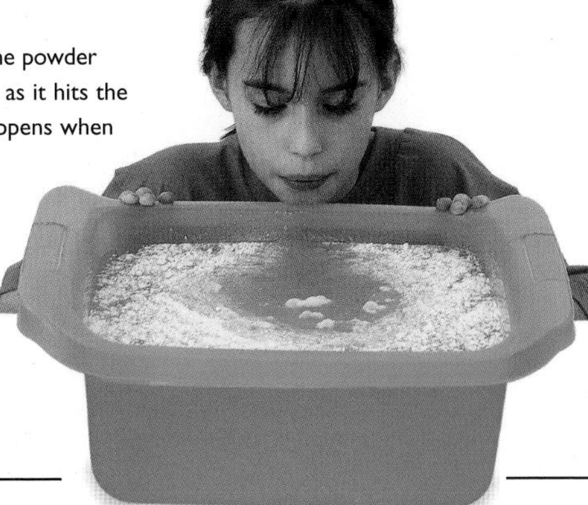

Changing coastlines

Of all the natural forces that erode (wear away) the land, the sea is the most powerful. It carries sand particles that act like a grindstone on the shore. Waves are forced into cracks in the rocks. They widen the cracks, eventually breaking up the rock face. Huge cliffs are carved out of mountains, broad platforms are sliced back through rocks, and houses are left dangling over the edges of the land.

New land can also be created at the ocean's edge. Where headland cliffs are being eroded by waves, the bays between may fill with sand. On coasts where the sea is shallow, waves build beaches of shingle, sand, and mud. The first experiment demonstrates the destructive effect of the sea when it hits the shore. The second project shows how waves make ripples on sandy beaches.

▲ Everchanging landscape
The sea's power to build and destroy a coastline can be seen in this picture. Coastal areas that are exposed to the full force of the waves are eroded into steep cliffs. Headlands are worn back, leaving behind stacks, stumps, and arches. In more sheltered places, the sand piles up to form beaches, or waves may carry material along the coast to build spits and mudflats.

▲ Relentless assault
The sea is at its most spectacular at the edges of big oceans, where the waves are big and powerful. In time, their continuous assault on the land will break up the toughest rocks into tiny pieces.

Attacking the shore

1 Mix a little water with the sand in a bucket, until it is very wet and sticks firmly together. Then pack the sand into a wedge shape at one end of the tank.

2 Carefully pour water into the empty end of the tank, so as not to disturb the sand too much. Fill the tank until the water level comes about two-thirds of the way up the sloping sand.

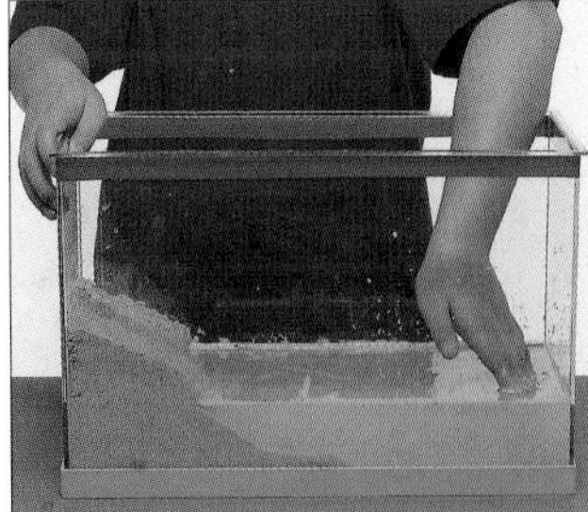

3 Make gentle waves in the water on the opposite side of the sand. Notice how the waves gradually wear away the sloping sand. This is what happens on a sandy seashore.

YOU WILL NEED

Making waves: Sand, plastic bucket, water tank, water, jug (pitcher).

How ripples are formed in sand: Heavy filled round can, round dishwashing bowl, jug (pitcher), water, fine, clean sand, spoon.

How ripples are formed in sand

1 Place a heavy can in the middle of the dishwashing bowl, then fill the bowl with water to at least half way. The water should not cover more than two-thirds of the can.

2 Sprinkle a little sand into the bowl to create a thin layer about 5mm/¼in deep. Spread the sand until it is even, then let it settle into a flat layer at the bottom of the bowl.

3 Stir the water gently with the spoon. Drag the spoon in a circle around the can. As the water begins to swirl, stir faster with the spoon, but keep the movement smooth.

4 As you stir faster, lift the spoon out and let the water swirl around by itself. The sand will start to develop ripples. As you stir faster, the ripples become more defined.

Water on the move

Rivers start high in the hills and wind their way down toward the sea, or sometimes, a lake. At its start, a river is a tiny stream tumbling down the slopes. It is formed by rain running off a mountainside, or by water bubbling up from a spring. As the water flows downhill, it is joined by other streams and grows bigger.

The first project shows how water shapes the landscape by physically eroding (wearing away) the rock. The second experiment demonstrates how in some places, erosion can be a chemical process, in which water dissolves the rock and carries it away.

Over millions of years, a river can carve a gorge deep through solid rock, or deposit (lay down) a vast plain of fine mud called silt. The great rivers of the world take millions of tons of mud, rock, and sand from the land every day and carry them into the sea. If the river meets a low-lying shoreline, the sediment is dropped. It may spread out into a fan-shaped muddy plain called a delta. When this happens, the river is forced to branch out into smaller streams as it flows into the sea. You can see how this happens in the third experiment.

upper reaches

middle reaches

lower reaches

◂ The course of a river
As it moves across the land, a river changes in character. In the upper reaches, it is a fast-flowing, tumbling stream that cuts down through steep, narrow valleys. Lower down, it broadens and deepens into a river. Eventually, it moves across a broad floodplain before reaching the sea.

The destructive power of water

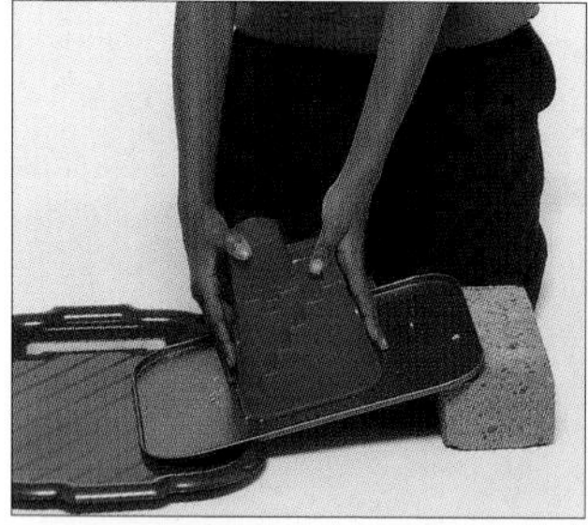

1 Put one end of a baking sheet on a brick. Put the other end of the baking sheet on a lower tray or bowl, so that it slopes downward. Make a sandcastle on the baking sheet.

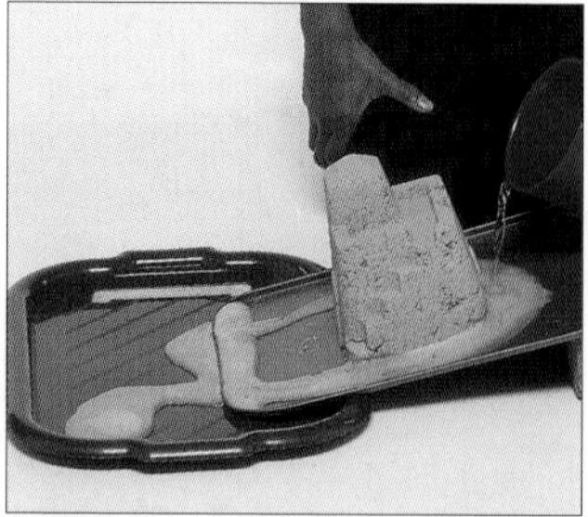

2 Slowly drip water over the sandcastle. Watch the sand crumble and form a new shape. This happens because the sand erodes away where the water hits it.

3 Make sure that the water flows down the middle of the baking sheet. This way, the water hits the middle of the sand castle, eroding the middle to form a natural stack.

Chemical erosion

YOU WILL NEED

The destructive power of water: Baking sheet, brick, tray or bowl, sand, sandcastle bucket, jug (pitcher), water.

Chemical erosion: Baking sheet, brown sugar, jug (pitcher) of water.

Making a delta: Scissors, long cardboard container, two garbage bags, adhesive tape, trowel, sand, woodblock, jug (pitcher) of water.

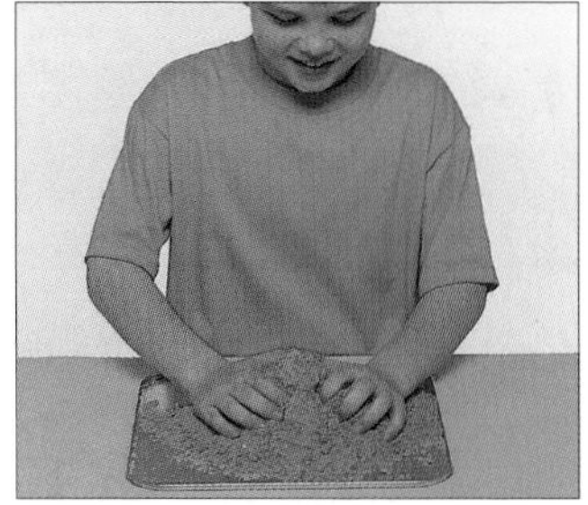

1 Build a pile of brown sugar on a baking sheet. Imagine it is a mountain made of a soluble rock (that dissolves in water). Press the sugar down firmly, and shape it to a point.

2 Drip water on your sugar mountain. It will erode as the water dissolves the sugar. The water running off should be brown, because it contains dissolved brown sugar.

Making a delta

1 Use scissors to trim the top of the cardboard container so that it is about 10–15cm/4–6in deep. Now take the two plastic garbage bags to make the box waterproof.

2 Cover the inside of the box with the garbage bags and tape them securely at each end of the box. Make sure that the seal between the garbage bags is secure.

3 Using the trowel, carefully spread a layer of sand over the bottom of the sheet until the sand is about 4–5cm/1½–2in deep. Flatten the sand with the trowel until it is smooth.

4 Rest one end of the container on a woodblock or something similar, to make a slope. Pour water from the jug on to the sand in the middle of the higher end.

5 If you continue pouring, you will find that the water gradually washes away a gully through the sand. It deposits sand it has washed away at the lower end in a delta region.

Cloud and rain

Water moves around the Earth and its atmosphere in a continuous process called the water cycle. Heat from the Sun causes water from oceans, lakes, and rivers to evaporate into water vapour. Water is also released into the atmosphere from plants in a process called transpiration. Flowers and trees take up water from their roots. They use some and release the rest back out through their leaves – water vapour rises into the atmosphere. It cools as it rises, and changes back into tiny droplets of liquid water. This is called condensation. The droplets gather together and form clouds. When the water in the atmosphere becomes too heavy to be held in the air, it returns to the Earth's surface as precipitation (dew, rain, sleet and snow). The land has a fresh supply of water, and so the water cycle continues.

The first experiment shows you how water changes to vapour and back again, when a cold surface makes the water vapour condense into water droplets. In the second project, you can make a simple rain gauge to measure the amount of rain you get where you live. If you live in a desert region, you may have to wait a long time!

cloud of ice crystals

cloud of water droplets

water vapour rises

▲ **Forming clouds**
Clouds form when warm air containing water vapour rises into the air and cools. The vapour turns into droplets of water, forming clouds. If the air is very cold, the vapour turns into a cloud of tiny ice crystals.

YOU WILL NEED
Heat-proof jug (pitcher), water, pan, oven gloves, plate.

Water vapour

1 Fill up the jug with water from the hot water tap. Pour the water into the pan. Switch on one of the rings on the stove and place the pan on it.

2 Heat the water until it is boiling and steam is rising. Lift the plate with the oven gloves. Hold it upside down above the pan. After a few minutes, turn off the heat.

3 Take the plate away, using the oven gloves. You will see that the plate is covered with drops of water. This is vapour that has cooled and turned back into liquid.

Measuring rainfall

YOU WILL NEED

Scissors, masking tape, large straight-sided jar, ruler, ballpoint pen, large plastic funnel, notebook, tall narrow jar or bottle.

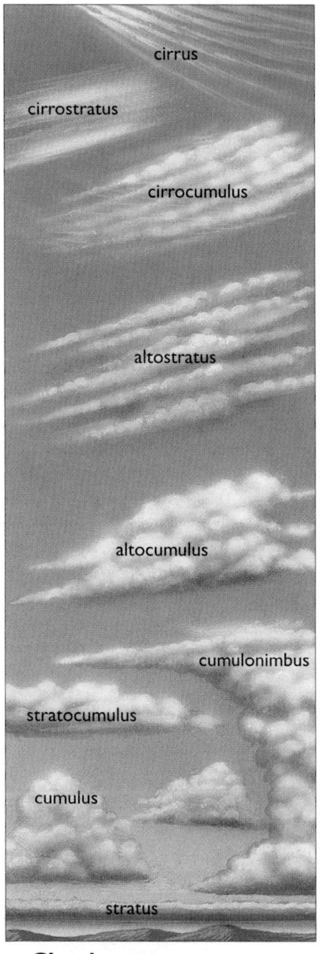

▲ **Cloud spotter**
The main kinds of clouds in the sky can be grouped according to how far they are above the Earth's surface. High clouds include cirrus clouds. Altostratus and altocumulus are middle clouds. Stratus and cumulus clouds are low ones.

1 Cut a strip of masking tape the same height as the jar. Stick it on the outsideof the jar. Use a ruler and pencil to mark 1cm/½in intervals on the masking tape.

2 Place the funnel in the jar. Put the gauge outside in an open space away from trees. Look at the gauge at the same time each day. Has it rained in the last 24 hours?

3 If it has rained, use the scale to see how much water is in the jar. This is the rainfall for the past 24 hours. Make a note of the reading. Empty the jar before you return it to its place.

4 You can measure rainfall more accurately if you use a separate, narrower measuring jar. Stick another strip of masking tape along the side of this jar. Pour water into the large collecting jar up to the 1cm/½in mark. Then pour the water into the narrow jar. Mark 1cm/½in where the water level reaches. Divide the length from the bottom of the jar to the 1cm/½in mark into 10 equal parts. Each will be equivalent to 1mm/1⁄16in of rainfall. You can now extend the scale past the 1cm/½in mark to the top of the narrow jar. Use this jar to measure the rainfall you collect to the nearest 1mm/1⁄16in, just as professional meteorologists do.

What is humidity?

The temperature of a place is mainly controlled by the amount of heat it absorbs from the Sun. Another factor is altitude (how high the land is). Areas at very high altitudes are colder than areas at sea level. The distance from the sea also affects temperature. The sea has a moderating effect. You can see how this works in the first project. Water takes more time to heat up than the land, but it holds its heat for much longer. Therefore, summers are cooler and winters milder on the coast than inland.

A temperature of 21°C/70°F in the Caribbean feels much hotter than 21°C/70°F in Egypt. This is due to humidity – the amount of water vapour in the air. When there is high humidity, the air feels moist and sticky. The perspiration on our skin cannot evaporate, since there is too much water in the air already. When there is little water vapour in the air, the air feels dry. The perspiration on our skin escapes more easily and cools us down. The second experiment shows you how to measure humidity using a simple device called a hygrometer. When the air is very humid, there is more of a chance that it will rain.

▲ Water from plants
Plants play a vital role in creating humidity. A plant's leaves give off water vapour in a process called transpiration. Cover a plant with a clear plastic bag. Seal the plastic around the pot with adhesive tape. Put the plant in direct sunlight for two hours. Notice that the bag starts to get misty, and droplets of water form on the inside. They form when the water vapour given off by the plant turns back to a liquid.

Measuring temperature changes

YOU WILL NEED

Measuring temperature changes: Two bowls, jug (pitcher) of water, sand, watch, thermometer, notebook, pen.

Measuring humidity: One sheet of red and one sheet of green thin card, scissors, ruler, pen, glue, toothpick, used matchstick, straw, reusable adhesive, blotting paper, hole punch.

1 Pour water into one bowl and sand into the other bowl. You do not need to measure the exact quantities of sand and water – just use roughly equal amounts.

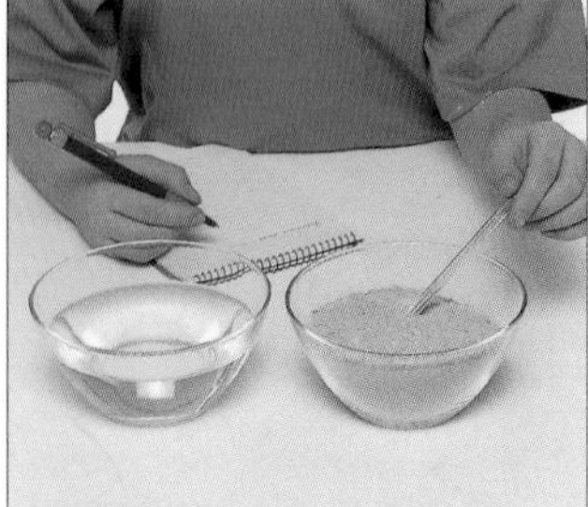

2 Place the bowls side by side in a cool place. Leave them for a few hours. Then note the temperature of the sand and water. The temperature of each should be about the same.

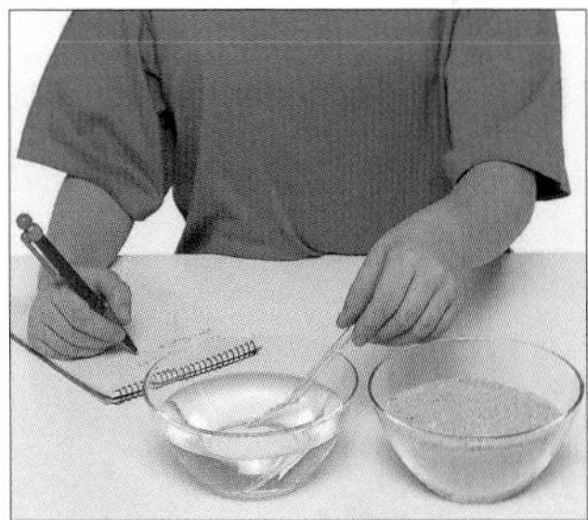

3 Place the bowls side by side in the sunlight. Leave the bowls for an hour or two. Then measure and record the temperatures of the sand and water in each bowl.

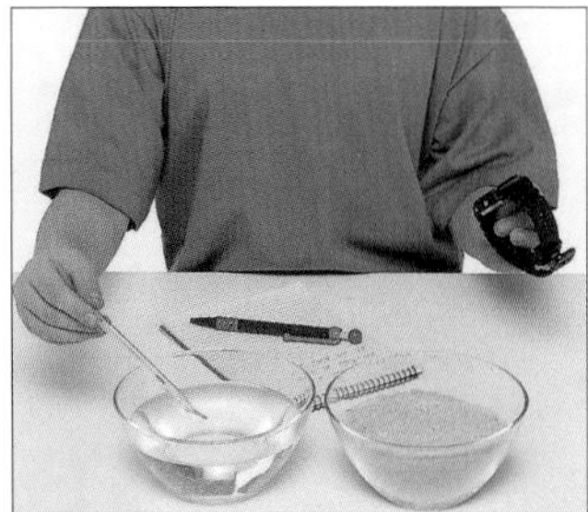

4 Put each bowl in a cool place indoors. Measure and record the temperature of the sand and water every 15 minutes. The sand cools down faster than the water.

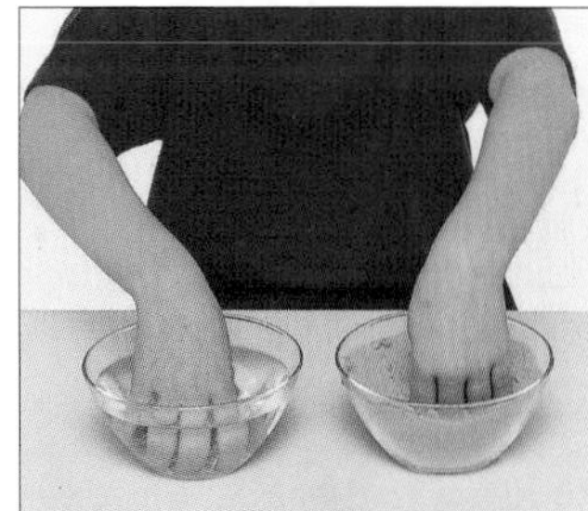

5 In this experiment, the sand acts like land and the water acts like the ocean. The sand gets hot quicker, but the water holds its heat longer. Dip your hands in to feel the difference.

Measuring humidity

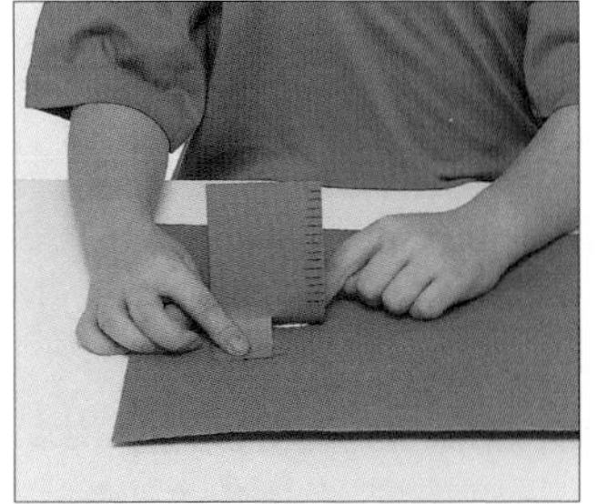

1 Cut out a rectangle from green card. Mark regular intervals along one side. Cut a 2cm/¾in slit in one short side. Split the parts and glue them to a red card base.

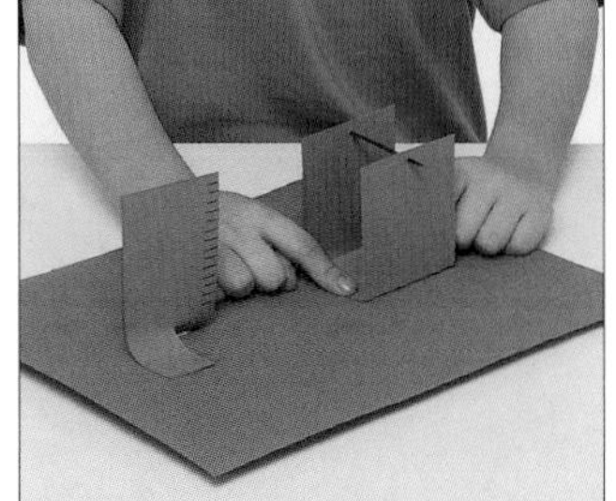

2 Cut another long rectangle from the green card. Fold it and stick it to the card base, as shown above. Pierce the top carefully with a toothpick to make a pivot.

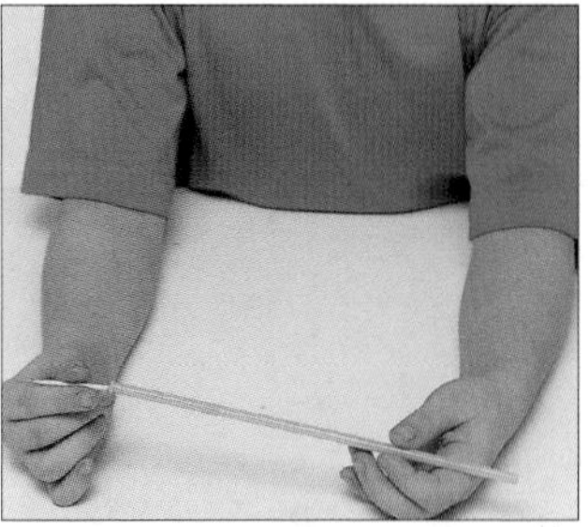

3 Attach the used matchstick to one end of the straw using some reusable adhesive, to make a pointer. Both the matchstick and the adhesive give the pointer some weight.

4 Carefully cut out several squares of blotting paper. Use the hole punch to make a hole in the middle of each square. Slide the squares over the flat end of the pointer.

5 Now carefully pierce the pointer with the toothpick pivot. Position the pointer as shown above. Make sure that the pointer can swing freely up and down.

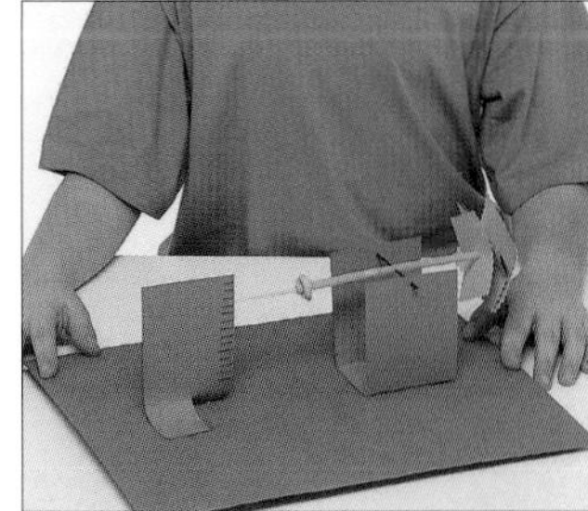

6 Adjust the position of the toothpick so that it stays level. Take the hygrometer into the bathroom and run a bath. The humidity makes the blotting paper damp. The pointer tips upward.

The way the wind blows

The wind is moving air. Wind can move dust, sand and other small items. The first experiment shows how the weight of a particle affects how far it travels. The wind also causes changes in the weather. Meteorologists study the wind to help them predict these changes. They use a weather vane to find out its direction. The second project shows how to make a simple weather vane. Wind speed is measured using an anemometer. This device consists of a circle of cups that spin when the wind blows, like a windmill. The faster the wind blows, the faster the anemometer spins.

YOU WILL NEED

How wind sorts sand: Two empty ice cube trays, piece of thin card large enough to fit over an ice cube tray, spoon, mix of fine and coarse sand, hair dryer.

Make a weather vane: Reusable adhesive, plastic pot and its lid, scissors, garden stick, two plastic straws, thin blue card, pen, adhesive tape, pin, plywood, compass.

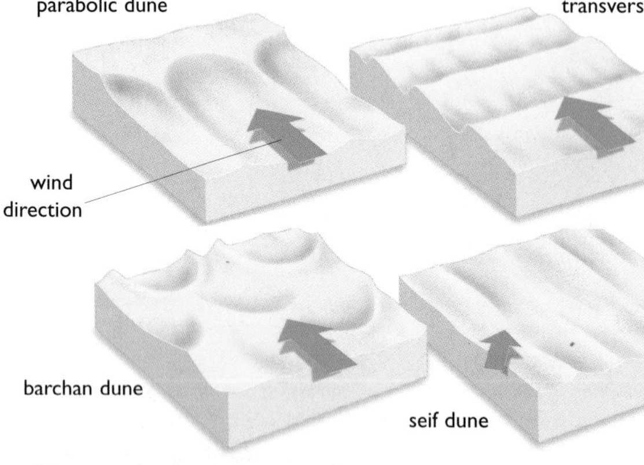

◂ Name that dune
Some deserts contain vast seas of sand, called ergs, where the wind piles sand up into dunes. The shape of the dune depends on the amount of sand and changeability of the wind direction. Crescent-shaped dunes, called parabolic dunes, are common on the coasts. The ones with narrow points facing away from the wind are called barchans. These dunes creep slowly forwards. Transverse dunes form at right angles to the main wind direction. Seifs occur where there is little sand, and wind comes from different directions.

How wind sorts sand

1 Turn one ice cube tray over, and lay it down end to end with another ice cube tray. Place the card over the upturned tray, and spoon the sand over it to make a sand dune.

2 Hold a hair dryer close to the upturned tray, pointing it towards the other tray. Turn the hair dryer on, so that it blows sand into the open ice cube tray.

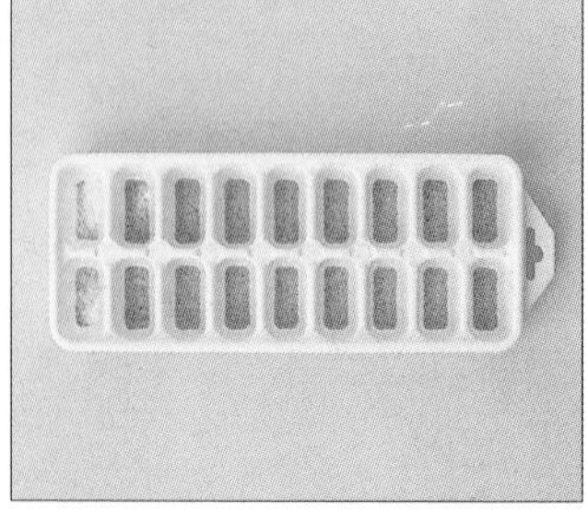

3 Look at the grains in each box. The distance a grain travels depends on its weight. Heavy grains fall in the end of the tray nearest to you. Light grains are blown to the farthest end.

Make a weather vane

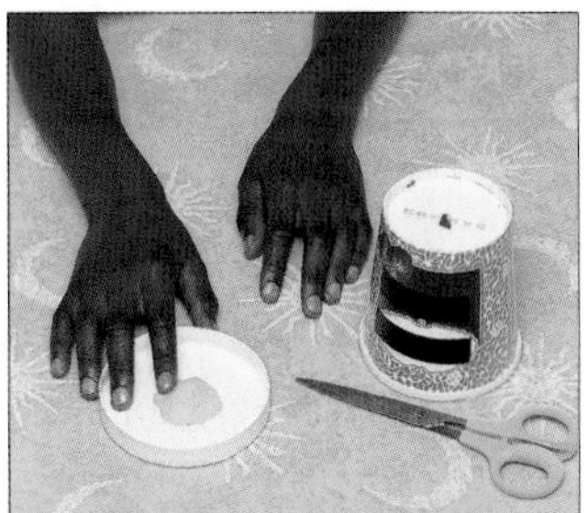

1 Stick a ball of reusable adhesive to the middle of the lid of the pot. Ask an adult to pierce a hole in the bottom of the pot with the scissors. Place the pot on top of the lid.

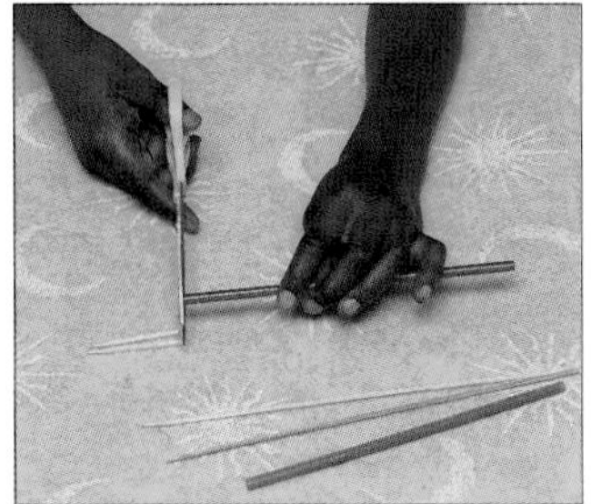

2 Slide the stick into one of the straws. Trim the end of the stick so that it is a little shorter than the straw. Push the straw and stick through the hole in the pot and into the adhesive.

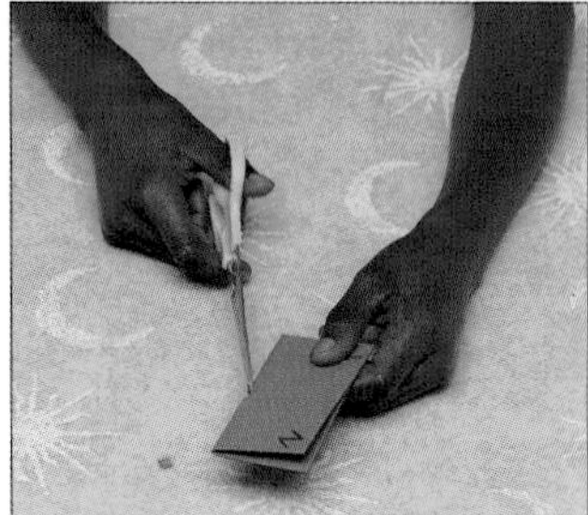

3 Cut out a square of card. Mark each corner with a point of the compass – N, E, S, W. Fold in half and snip a hole in the middle. Carefully slip the card over the straw.

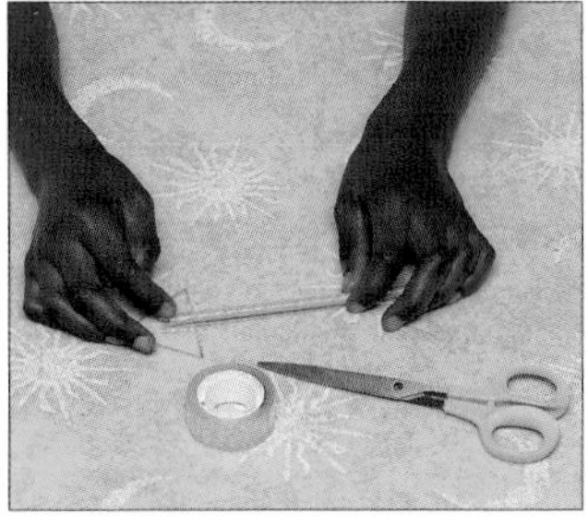

4 Cut out two card triangles. Stick them to each end of the second straw to form an arrow head and tail. Put a ball of reusable adhesive in the top of the first straw in the pot.

5 Push a pin through the middle of the arrow. Stick the pin into the reusable adhesive in the first straw. Be careful not to prick your finger when you handle the pin.

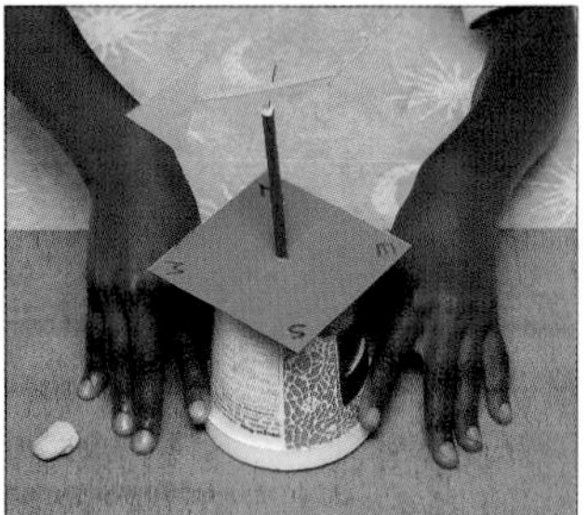

6 Attach your weather vane to a plywood base using a piece of reusable adhesive. Test it for use – the arrow should spin around freely when you blow on it.

7 Take your weather vane outside and use a compass to point it in the right direction. You can now discover the direction the wind is blowing.

Turning the sails ▸
The miniature windmills on this toy spin faster the harder you blow on them. The sails of real windmills also spin faster as the speed of the wind increases. As a result, windmills need a 'governor'. This device regulates the speed of the sails' rotation, so they are not damaged in very windy weather.

Recording weather

Meteorologists gather information about the weather from satellites, balloons, and other instruments. Powerful computers help them to analyze the data. Using this information, meteorologists draw weather maps. These can show the state of the weather at any one time, or they can be a forecast of weather in the future. The maps use symbols to represent conditions such as rainfall and wind direction.

You can set up your own weather station to record daily conditions with a few simple devices. You will be able to use some of the instruments you have made in other projects, such as the weather vane, hygrometer and rain gauge. You will also need to buy a thermometer to measure the temperature. Take measurements with your weather instruments every day. Write them down in a special weather book. Also, make a note of what the weather is like in general – fine, cloudy, drizzly, frosty and so on. Don't forget to make a note of the date!

Meteorologists look at records from the past to discover changes in climate. The project opposite shows you how to make your own discoveries about climate changes, by looking at the record of tree growth.

▲ Forecasting rain

A hygrometer will gauge the amount of moisture in the air. When the pointer tilts up on the scale, the air is moist and rain may be on the way.

▲ Measuring rainfall

A rain gauge will tell you how much rain has fallen. Rainfall is collected over a set period in a jar or measuring bottle, and the amount is recorded.

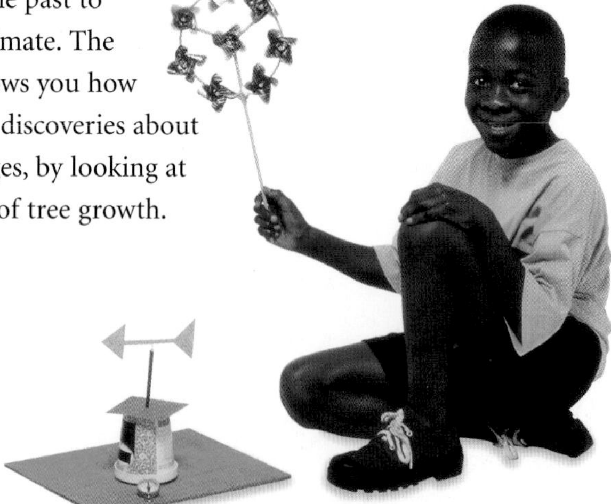

▲ Wind direction

A windmill shows how hard the wind is blowing. A weather vane will tell you the wind's direction. The arrow points in the direction that the wind is blowing from. So if the arrow points west, the wind is a west wind.

The wooden weather record

YOU WILL NEED

Newly cut log, decorating paintbrush, ruler with 1mm/1/16in measurements, graph paper, pen or pencil.

1 Ask a tree surgeon, the local council or a sawmill for a newly cut slice of log. Use the paintbrush to brush away the dust and dirt from the slice of wood.

2 When the log slice is clean, examine it closely. Look at the pattern of rings. They are small in the middle, and get bigger and bigger toward the outer edge of the log.

3 Each ring is a year's growth. So count the rings out from the middle carefully. This tells you how old the tree is. If there are 105 rings, for instance, the tree is 105 years old.

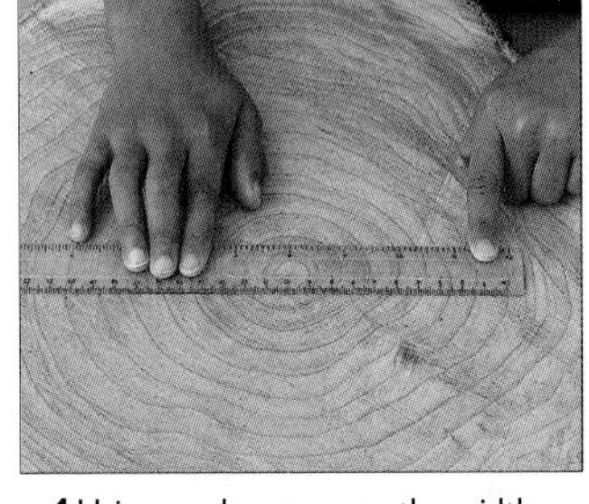

4 Using a ruler, measure the width of each ring. Start from the middle and work outward. Ask a friend to write down the widths as you call them out.

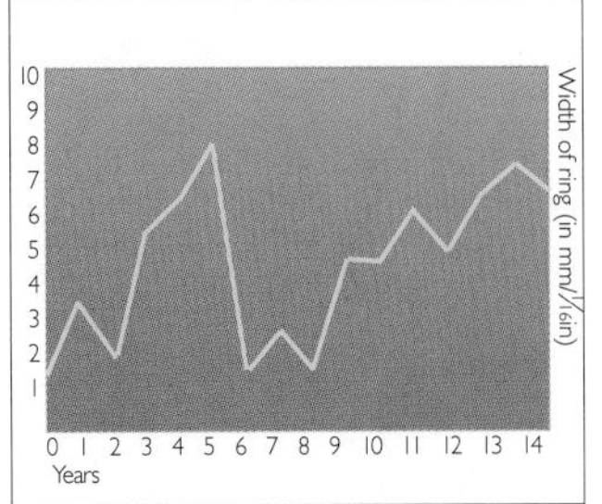

5 On graph paper, mark five squares for each year along the bottom. Mark widths for the rings up the side, five squares for each 1mm/1/16in. Plot your measurements as dots for each year.

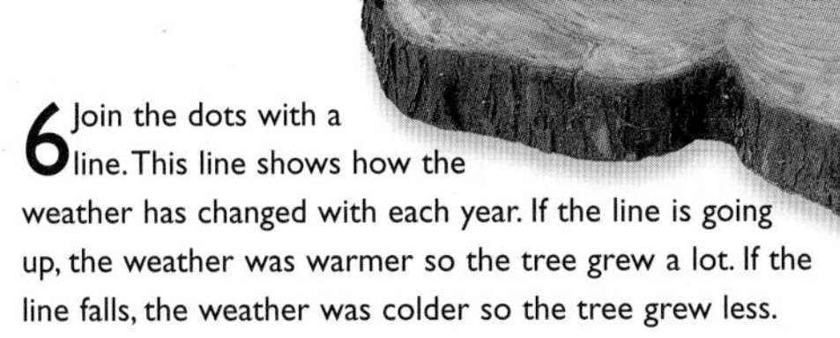

6 Join the dots with a line. This line shows how the weather has changed with each year. If the line is going up, the weather was warmer so the tree grew a lot. If the line falls, the weather was colder so the tree grew less.

Broken Earth

The surface of the Earth is not one piece but cracked, like a broken eggshell, into giant slabs. There are about 20 of these huge pieces of rock which are called tectonic plates. Tectonic plates are not held in one place, but slide around the Earth. They move very slowly – at about the pace of a fingernail growing. But tectonic plates are so gigantic that their movement has dramatic effects on the Earth's surface. Earthquakes and volcanoes happen where plates slide apart or past each other, or collide. Colliding plates also push up mountain ranges.

The continents drift around the world on tectonic plates. Once, they were all joined together in one huge continent called Pangaea. Around 200 million years ago, the tectonic plates beneath Pangaea began to move apart, carrying fragments of the continent with them. These fragments slowly drifted into the positions they are in now. The experiment opposite demonstrates how the continents may have once been, and how they move.

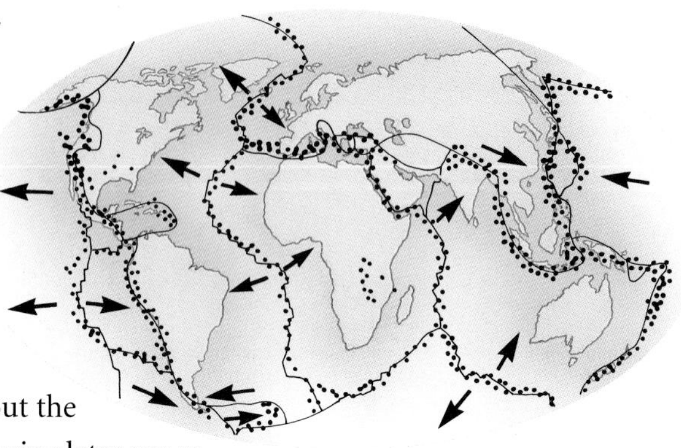

▲ Patterns of earthquakes
The Earth's rigid shell is called the lithosphere, from the Greek word lithos (stone). It is broken into the huge fragments shown on this map. The African plate is gigantic, underlying not only Africa, but half of the Atlantic Ocean too. The Cocos plate under the West Indies is much smaller. Black dots mark the origins of major earthquakes over a year. See how they coincide with the plate margins.

▲ Pulling apart
Right down the middle of the sea bed in the Atlantic Ocean, there is a giant crack where the tectonic plates are pulling apart. Molten (melted) rock from the Earth's interior wells up into the crack. As it cools, it solidifies (becomes solid) to form the mid-ocean ridge.

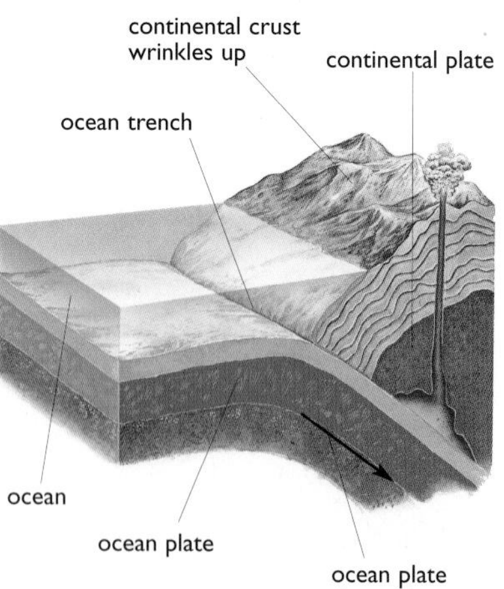

▲ Pushing together
In many places, tectonic plates slowly crunch together with enormous force. As they collide, one plate may be forced under the other. Earthquakes and volcanoes are often the result.

A continental jigsaw

YOU WILL NEED
Atlas, pencil, sheets of tracing paper, tape, sheets of green, purple and red thin card, scissors, paper clips, two boxes.

1 Find the continents of North and South America, Europe, and Africa in an atlas. Trace the outlines of the shape of these continents on to tracing paper.

2 Stick the tracing paper on to green, purple and red sheets of card. Then carefully cut around the outlines of the continents you have drawn from the atlas.

3 Move the eastern (right-hand) coasts of North and South America up to the western (left-hand) coasts of Europe and Africa to see how well they fit together.

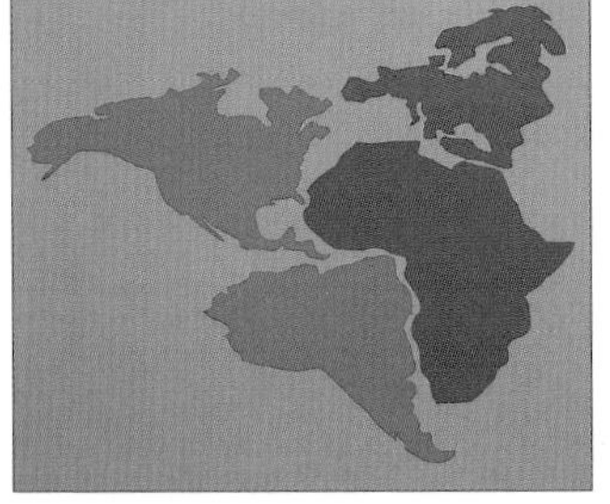

4 You will find that the coastlines of the Americas, Europe, and Africa fit together very well. Scientists believe that these continents were once joined together in this way.

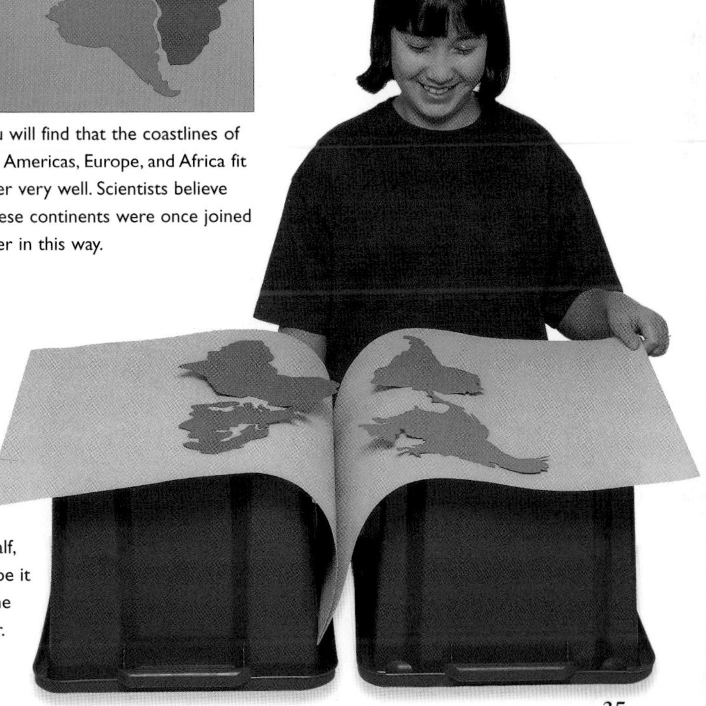

5 The continents of the Americas, Europe, and Africa sit on plates that are moving in opposite directions. Use the continent cards you have made in the above project to see how they drift apart. Fold a large sheet of card in half, and attach paper clips along the fold. Drape it over two boxes. Stick the Americas on one sheet, and Europe and Africa on the other. Push upward on the fold, and see the continents move apart.

Restless Earth

The movement of rocks that causes earthquakes usually occurs deep inside the Earth's crust. The exact point at which the rocks start to break is known as the focus. This can lie as deep as hundreds of km/miles or as close as tens of km/miles down. The most violent disturbance on the surface occurs at a point directly above the focus, called the epicentre. The closer the focus is, the more destructive the earthquake. San Francisco, in California, sits near a line of weakness in the Earth's crust known as the San Andreas Fault. The fault marks the boundary of the eastern Pacific plate and the North American plate. As they try to slide past each other, they make the ground shake violently. Earthquakes and volcanoes occur around the boundaries of all the plates on the Earth's surface.

▲ **Earthquake alert**
Most earthquakes originate many kilometres/miles below the surface, at the focus. The most intense vibrations on the surface are felt immediately above the focus, at the epicentre.

YOU WILL NEED

Tremors: Set of dominoes, card.

Quakes: Scissors, strong rubber band, ruler, plastic seed tray (without holes), piece of thin card, salt.

Tremors

1 This project investigates how energy in earthquake waves (tremors) varies with distance. Near the end of a table, build a simple house out of dominoes. Stand them up on their edges.

2 Place the cardboard on the dominoes to make the roof of your house. Many people in earthquake zones live in the simplest of houses, built not too differently from this one.

3 Go to the opposite end of the table and hit it with your hand, but not too hard. Your domino house probably shakes, but still stays standing. Now hit the table at the other end.

4 The waves you create when you hit the table are strong enough to knock down the house. When you hit the other end of the table, the waves are too weak to knock it down.

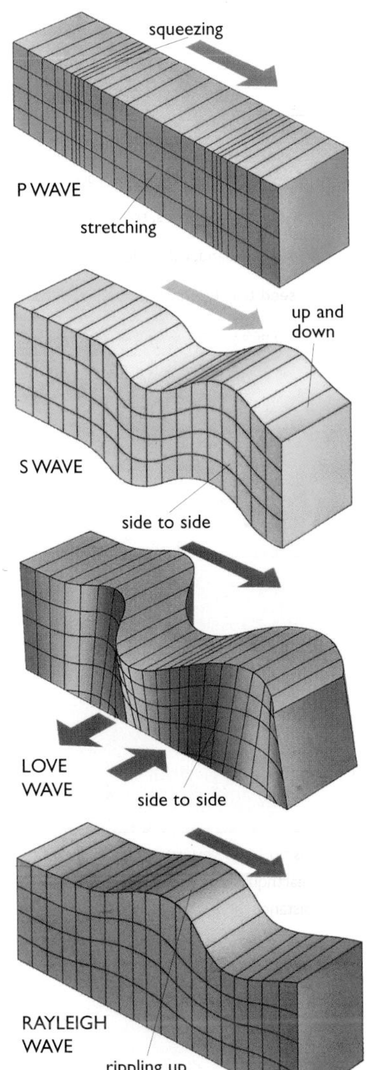

▲ How earthquakes move
The enormous energy released by an earthquake travels through the ground in the form of waves. The P (primary) wave compresses, then stretches rocks it passes through. The S (secondary) wave produces a side-to-side and up-and-down action. Love waves travel on the surface, making the ground move from side to side. Rayleigh waves are surface waves that move up and down.

Quakes

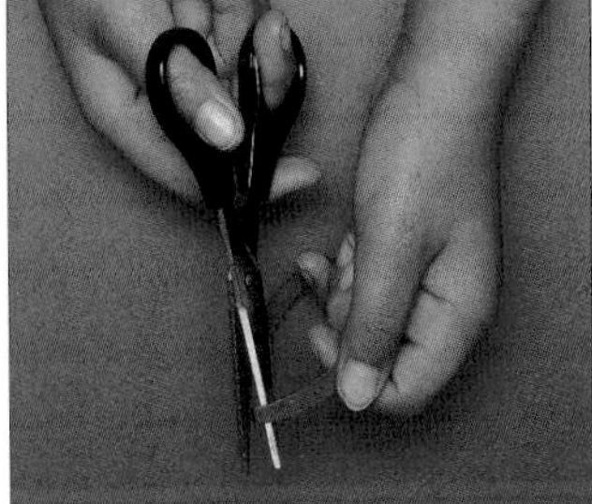

1 With the scissors, cut the rubber band at one end to make a long strip. This represents a layer of rock inside the Earth before it is affected by an earthquake.

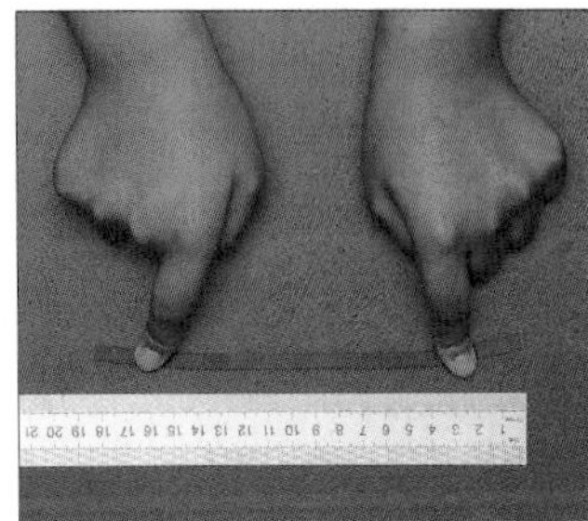

2 Measure the rubber strip with a ruler. This represents the original length of the rock in the ground. Make a note of how long the rubber is at this stage.

3 Stretch the rubber band and hold it tightly above the tray. In the same way, rocks get stretched by pulling forces inside the Earth during an earthquake.

4 Ask a friend to hold the card on top of the rubber strip and sprinkle some salt on it. The salt on the card represents the surface of the ground above the stretched rock layer.

5 Now let go of the ends of the rubber strip. Notice how the salt grains on the card are thrown around. This was caused by the energy released when the rubber shrank.

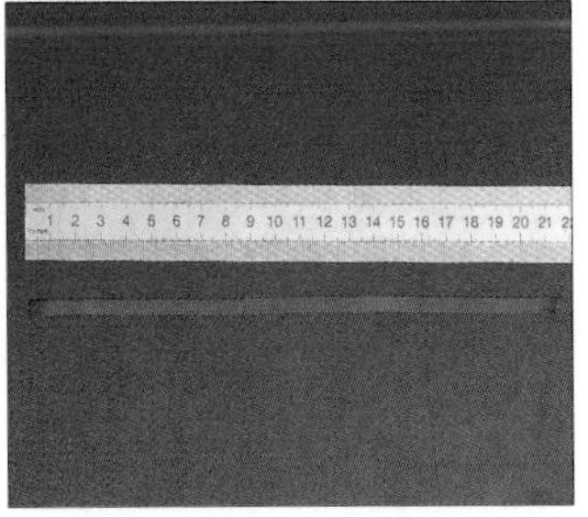

6 Finally, measure the rubber strip again. You will find that it is slightly longer than it was at the start. Rocks are often permanently stretched a little after an earthquake.

Measuring earthquakes

Scientists who study earthquakes are called seismologists. They have a variety of instruments to gather data. The Newton's cradle experiment below explains how waves (tremors) work. The other projects show two ways in which seismologists detect how the ground moves at the beginning of an earthquake. A gravimeter measures small changes in gravity. The tiltmeter detects whether rock layers are tilting.

YOU WILL NEED

Newton's cradle: Large beads, wool, adhesive tape, cane, wooden blocks.

Gravimeter: Masking tape, ruler, pen, large jar, non-hardening modelling material, rubber band, toothpick, pencil.

Newton's cradle

1 Tie the beads to the ends of the wool threads. Tape the other ends to the cane. Make sure the threads are all the same length, and that the beads just touch when they hang down.

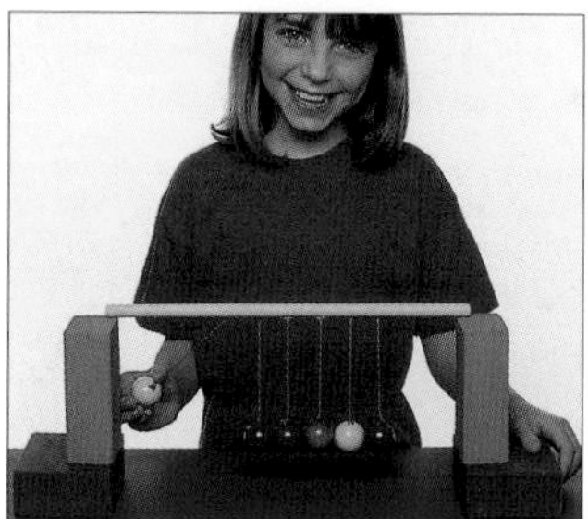

2 Prop up the cane at both ends on a pair of woodblocks supported by more blocks underneath. Secure the ends of the cane with tape. Lift up the bead at one end of the row and let go.

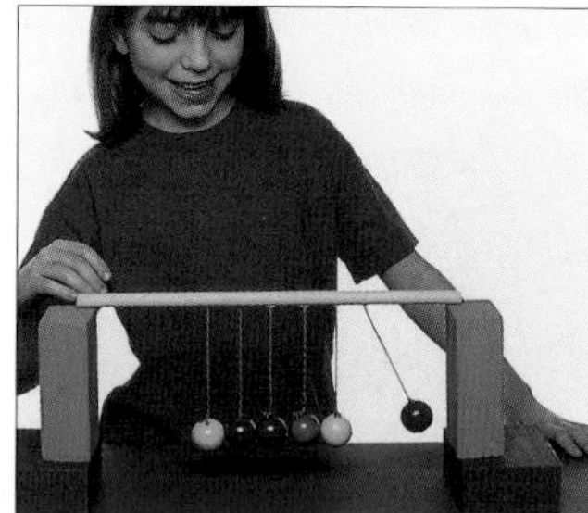

3 The bead at the other end flies up. The energy of the falling bead at one end travels as a pressure wave through the middle ones. It reaches the bead at the other end and pushes it away.

Gravimeter

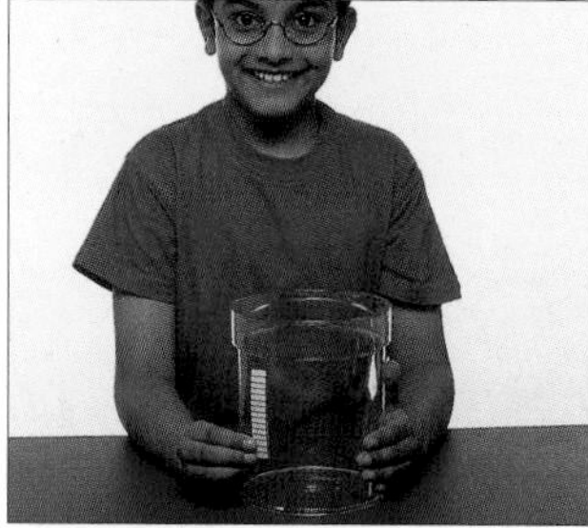

1 Draw a scale on a strip of masking tape using a ruler and pen. Stick the scale on the jar. On a real instrument, this would measure slight changes in gravity.

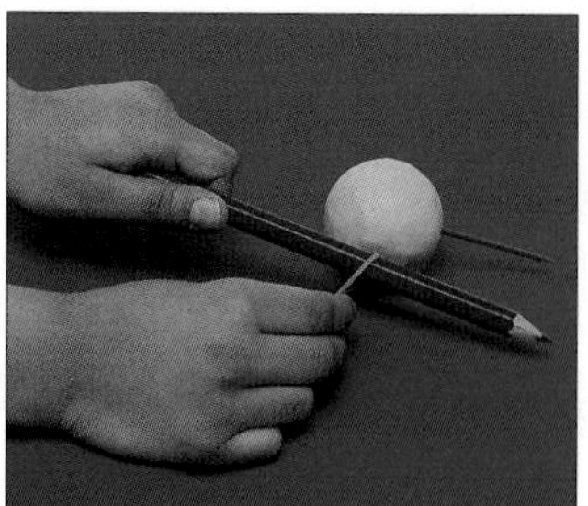

2 Bury one end of a rubber band in a ball of modelling material. Stick a toothpick in at right angles to the band, to act as a pointer. Pass the pencil through the loop of the band.

3 Lower the ball into the jar, so that the pointer tip is close to the scale. Attach the pencil on top with modelling material. Move the jar up or down, and the pointer moves down or up the scale.

Tiltmeter

YOU WILL NEED

Hole punch, two transparent plastic cups, transparent plastic tubing, non-hardening modelling material, pen, masking tape, ruler, wooden board, adhesive, food dye, jug (pitcher) of water.

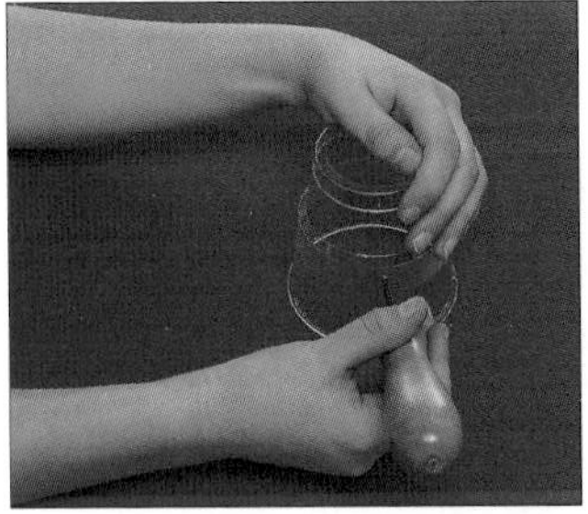

1 Use the hole punch to make a hole in the side of each plastic cup, just about halfway down. Be careful not to prick your fingers. Ask an adult to help you if you prefer.

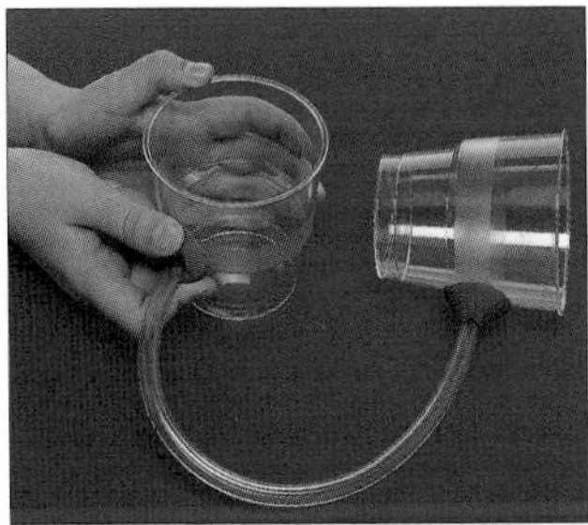

2 Push one end of the tubing into the hole in one of the cups. Seal it tight with modelling material. Put the other end in the hole in the other cup, and seal it as well.

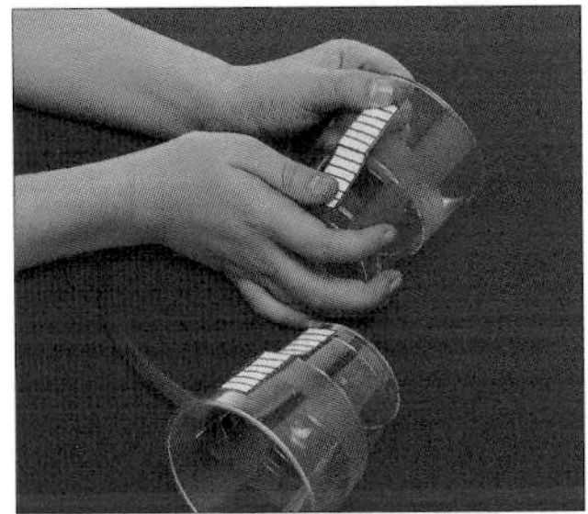

3 Using the pen, draw identical scales on two strips of the masking tape. Use a ruler and mark regular spaces. Stick the scales at the same height on the side of the cups.

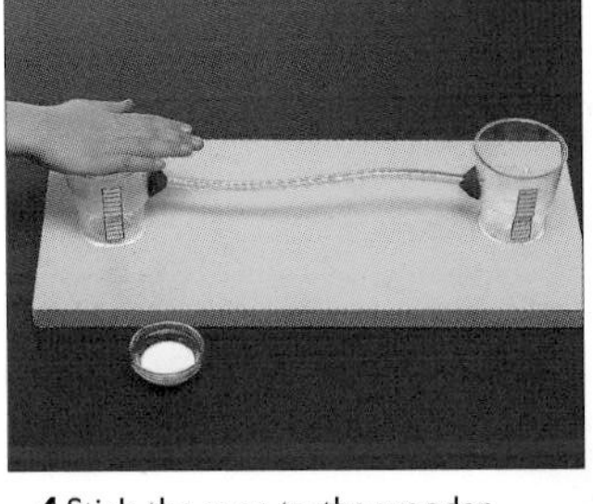

4 Stick the cups to the wooden baseboard with adhesive. Arrange them so that the tube between is pulled straight, but make sure it doesn't pull out.

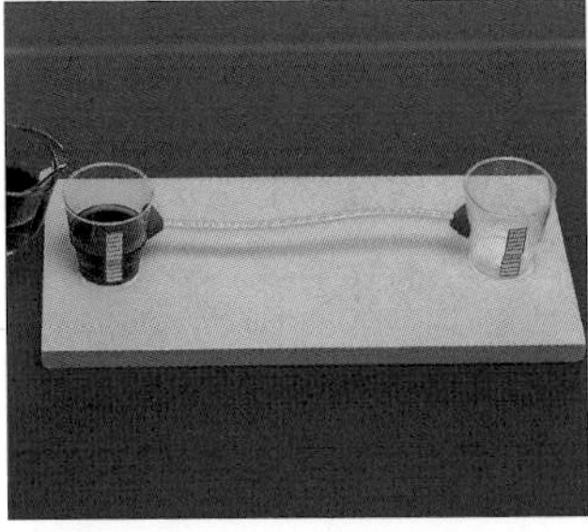

5 Add food dye to water in the jug, and pour it into each of the cups. Make sure to fill the cups, so that the water level reaches over the openings to the tubes.

6 Your tiltmeter is now ready for use. When it is level, the water levels in the cups are the same. When it tilts, the water levels change as water runs through the tube from one cup to the other. Scientists use tiltometers to detect whether rock layers are moving by comparing the water levels in two connected containers.

Do-it-yourself seismograph

There are hundreds of seismic (from the Greek word *seismos*, meaning earthquake) laboratories around the world. Within minutes of a quake, scientists begin analyzing data from their seismographs. They then compare notes with scientists in other countries.

The Italian scientist, Luigi Palmieri, built the first seismograph in 1856. All seismographs work on the same principle. They have a light frame attached to the ground, and a heavy weight attached to the frame by a spring. The heavy weight has a high inertia, which means it is more difficult to set in motion than a light object. When an earthquake happens, the frame shakes with the ground, but the heavy weight stays in the same place because of inertia. The movement of the frame around the steady weight is recorded by a pen on a roll of paper, which draws a wavy line. The same principle of the inertia of a heavy weight is used to detect tremors in the seismograph shown here.

▲ **Catching the tremors**
The Chinese invented a type of seismograph in AD132. When there was an earthquake, a ball was released from one of the dragons and fell into a frog's mouth. This showed the direction of the vibrations. The instrument detected a earth tremor 500km/300 miles away.

Building a seismograph

YOU WILL NEED
Cardboard box, bradawl, tape, non-hardening modelling material, pencil, felt-tipped pen, string, piece of thin card.

1 The cardboard box will become the frame of your seismograph. It needs to be made of very stiff cardboard. The open part of the box will be the front of your instrument.

2 Make a hole in what will be the top of the frame with the bradawl. If the box feels flimsy, strengthen it by taping around the corners, as shown in the picture.

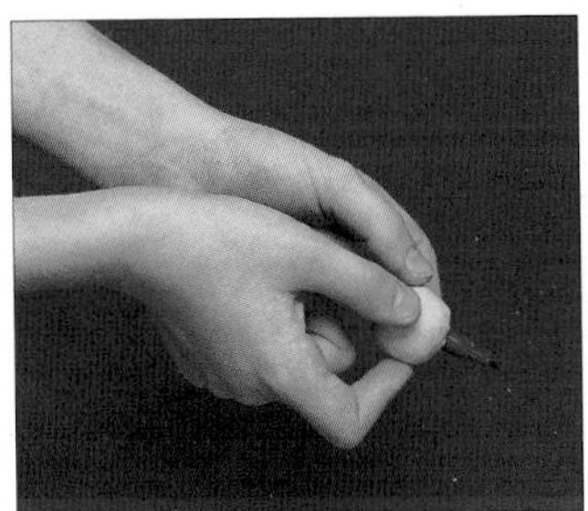

3 Roll a piece of modelling material into a ball, and make a hole in it with the pencil. Push the felt-tipped pen through the modelling material to reach a little way beyond the hole.

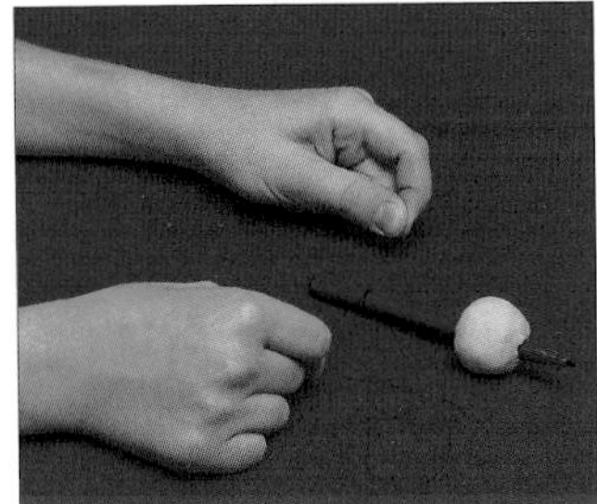

4 This will be the pointer of your seismograph and make a record of earthquake vibrations. Tie one end of the piece of string to the top of the pen.

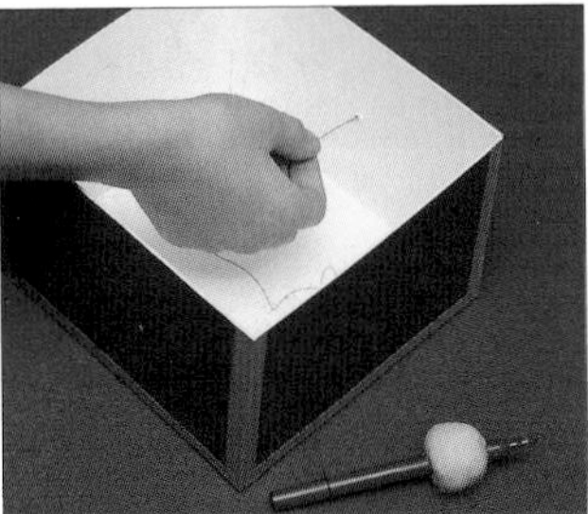

5 Thread the other end of the string through the hole in the top of the box. Now stand the box upright and pull the string through until the pen hangs free.

6 Tie the top end of the string to the pencil, and roll the pencil to take up the slack. When the pen is at the right height (just touching the bottom), tape the pencil into place.

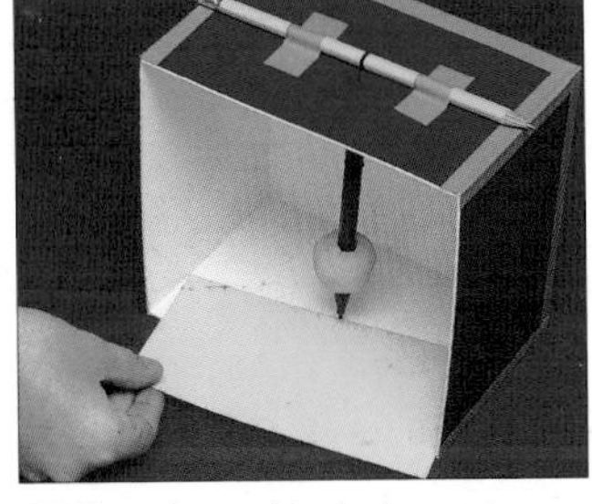

7 Place the card in the bottom of the box underneath the pen. If you have adjusted it properly, the tip of the pen should just touch the card to mark it.

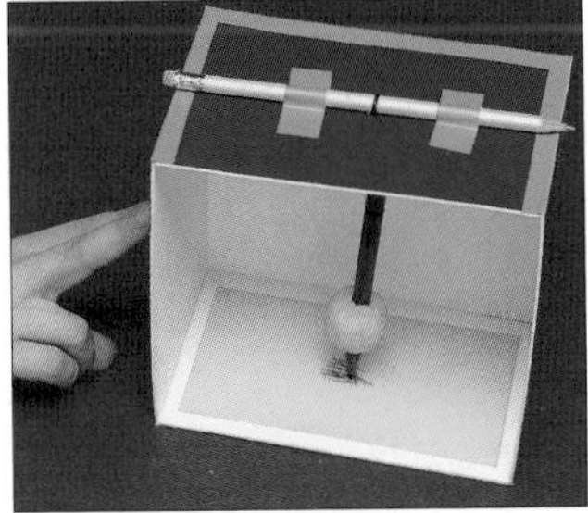

8 Your seismograph is now ready to use. It uses the same principle as a proper seismograph. The heavy bob, or pendulum, will be less affected by shaking motions than the frame.

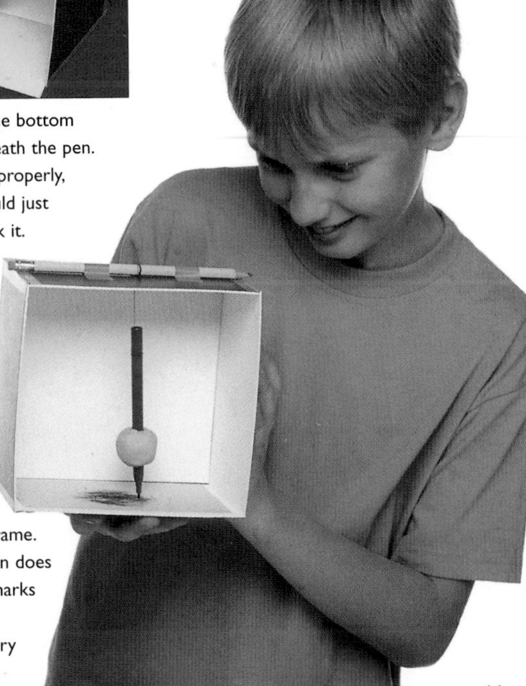

9 You do not have to wait for an earthquake to test your seismograph. Just shake or tilt the frame. The suspended pen does not move, but it marks the piece of card, giving you your very own seismograph.

Slips and faults

Every earthquake, from the slightest tremor to the violent shaking that destroys buildings, has the same basic cause. Two plates of rock grind past each other along a fault line where the Earth's crust has fractured. Friction between the plates means they do not slide past each other smoothly, but jam and then jump. The first experiment on the opposite page shows how friction at fault lines causes great destructive energy.

Crustal plates float on top of the mantle beneath. The oceanic crust is heavier and denser than the continental crust so it sits lower down. The experiment below demonstrates this.

There are several kinds of fault. When blocks slide past each other horizontally, it is called a transform, or strike-slip fault. In a normal fault, the rocks are pulling apart, and one block slides down the other. In a thrust fault, the blocks are pressing together, causing one to ride up above the other. The second project on the opposite page shows how these movements create landforms, such as mountains and valleys.

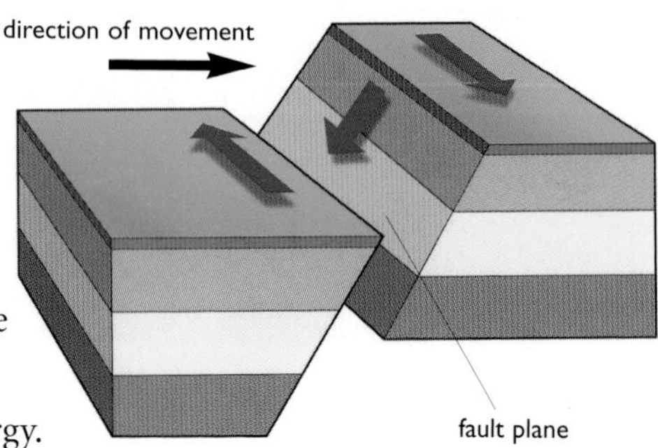

▲ **Making mountains**
Fault mountains form by the slow, unstoppable movement of tectonic plates. This puts rocks under such huge stress that they sometimes crack. Such cracks are called faults. Where they occur, huge blocks of rock slip up and down past each other, creating cliffs. In places, a whole series of giant blocks may be thrown up together, creating a new mountain range. The Black Mountains in Germany are an example of block mountains formed in this way.

Floating plates

YOU WILL NEED
Woodblock, polystyrene block, bowl of water.

1 The two blocks should be about the same size and shape. Polystyrene represents the continental crust, wood the oceanic crust, and water the fluid mantle.

2 Place the blocks in the water. The polystyrene floats higher, because it is less dense, just as the continental crust floats higher on the mantle. Which of the two blocks weighs more?

Fault movements

1 Hold a block in each hand so that the sides of the blocks are touching. Pushing gently, try to make the blocks slide past each other. You will find this easy.

2 Wet the sides of the blocks with the oil, and try to slide them again. You should find that it is easier, because the oil has lessened the friction between the blocks.

3 Pin sheets of sandpaper on the sides of the blocks, and try to make them slide now. You will find it much harder. The sandpaper is rough, and increases friction between the blocks.

Building mountains

YOU WILL NEED

Fault movements: Two woodblocks, baby oil, drawing pins (thumb tacks), sheets of sandpaper.

Building mountains: 20cm/8in square sheet of paper, non-hardening modelling material in various shades, rolling pin, modelling tool.

1 On the sheet of paper, roll out several flat sheets of modelling material, each one a different shade. The sheets should be about the same size as the sheet of paper.

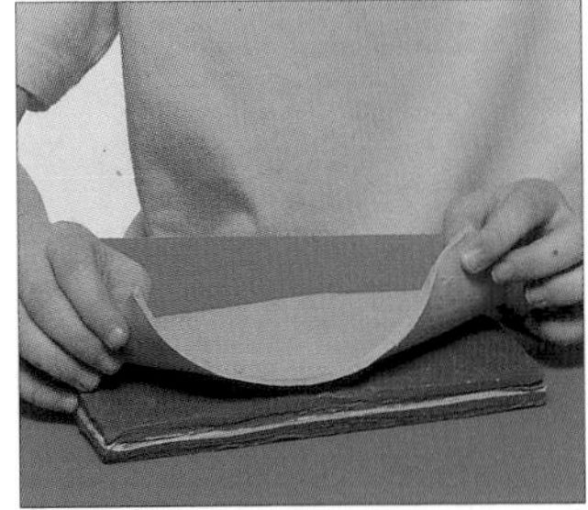

2 Place the square, flat sheets of modelling material on top of each other to make a layered block. The different layers are like the layers of rock strata in the Earth's crust.

3 Lay the layered block flat on the table. With a modelling tool, carefully make two cuts in the clay – one toward the left, and the other toward the right, as shown above.

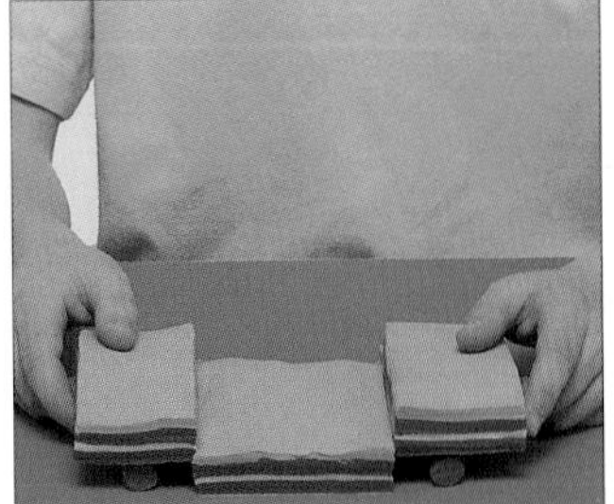

4 Make two small balls. Lift each of the outside pieces that you have cut on to a ball, as shown above. This forms a block mountain separated by a rift valley.

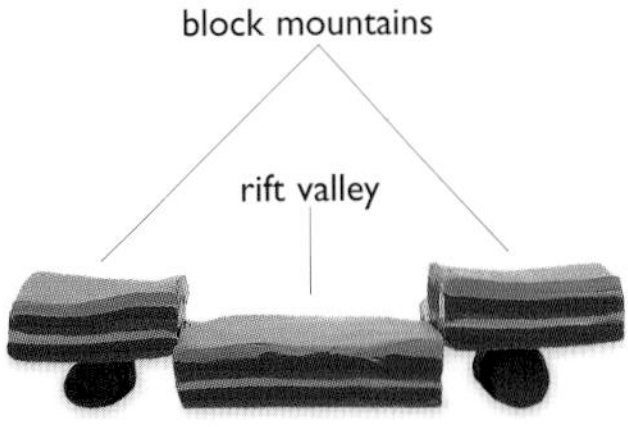

The crust breaks away at a rift zone where the plates are moving apart. Uplifted rock strata form block mountains, and a descending mass of rock creates the valley.

Building fold mountains

Most high mountains are a part of great ranges that stretch for hundreds of kilometres/miles. They may look as though they have been there forever, but geologically they are very young. They have all been thrown up in the last few hundred million years.

The biggest – and youngest – mountain ranges in the world, such as the Himalayas and the Andes, are fold mountains. They started life as flat layers of rock called strata. Layers of rock are laid down over millennia. Some strata form as successive layers of sediments, such as sand, mud and seashells, settle on the ocean floor. Other strata may be made up of molten rock thrown up from the heart of the Earth by volcanoes.

Fold mountains are layers of rock that have been crunched up by pressure – in a similar way to the pressure you will be exerting in these two projects. In real mountain formation, two of the tectonic plates that make up the Earth's surface push against each other, forcing the rock layers along their edges into massive folds. As the layers of rock are squeezed, the folds become more exaggerated.

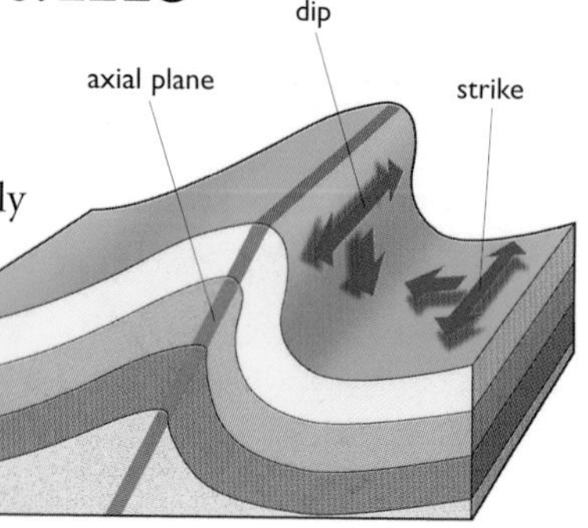

▲ Anatomy of a fold
Geologists describe an upfold as an anticline, and a downfold as a syncline. The dip is the direction the fold is sloping. The angle of dip is how steep the slope is. The strike is the line along the fold. The axial plane is an imaginary line through the middle of the fold – this may be vertical, horizontal, or at any angle in between.

YOU WILL NEED
Thin rug.

Simple folds

1 Find an uncarpeted floor, and lay the rug down with one short, straight edge up against a wall. Make sure the long edge of the rug is at a right angle to the wall.

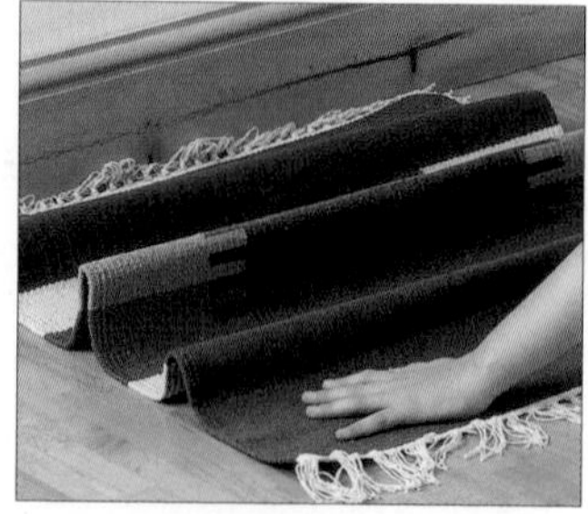

2 Now push the outer edge of the rug toward the wall. See how the rug crumples. This is how rock layers buckle to form mountains, as tectonic plates push against each other.

3 Push the rug up against the wall even more, and you will see some of the folds turn right on top of each other. These are like folded-over strata or layers, called nappes.

Complex folds

YOU WILL NEED

Rolling pin, non-hardening modelling material in various shades, modelling tool, two blocks of 5cm/2in square wood, two bars of 10 x 5cm/4 x 2in wood.

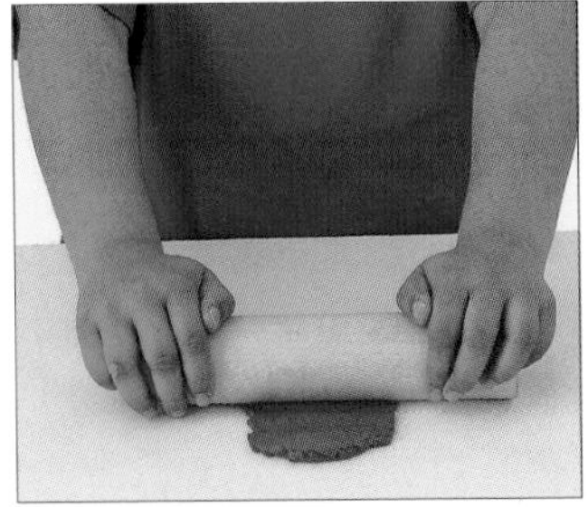

1 Roll out the modelling material into flat sheets in different shades, each about 5mm/¼in thick. Cut into strips about the same width as the woodblocks. Square off the ends.

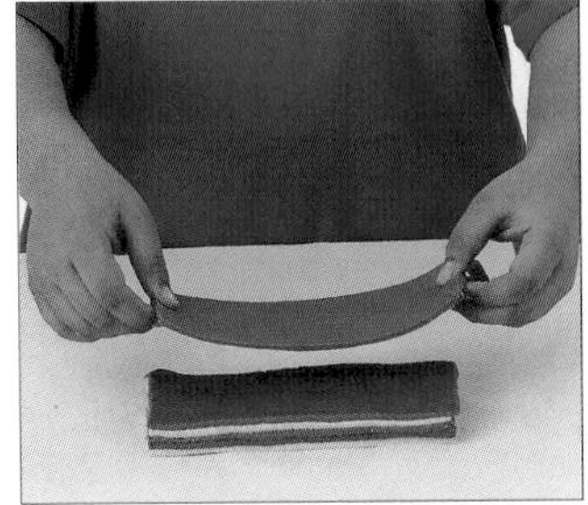

2 Lay the strips carefully on top of each other, in alternating hues or in a series of hues. These strips represent the layers or strata of rock.

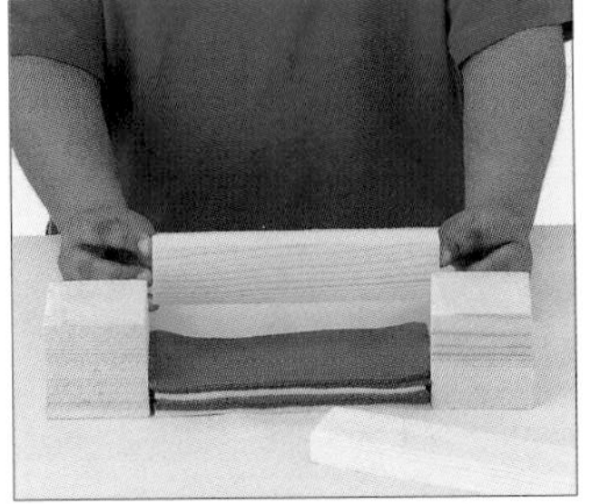

3 Place the woodblocks at either end of the strips. Lay the bars of wood down on either side of the strips to prevent them from twisting sideways.

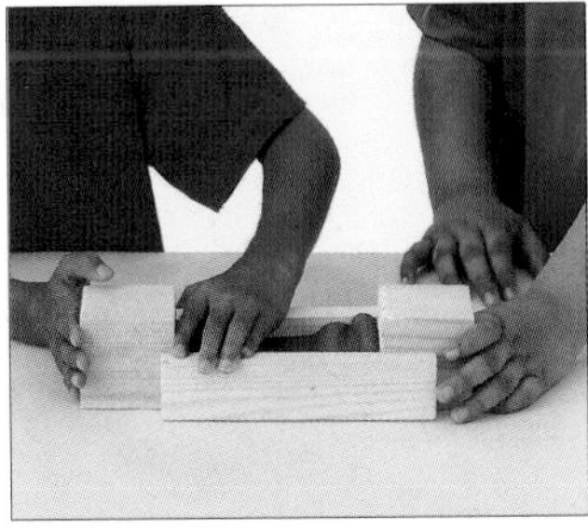

4 Ask a friend to hold on to one block, while you push the other towards it. As you push, the effect is similar to two tectonic plates slowly pushing together.

5 From time to time, stop and pull the bars of wood away, so that you can have a look at what is happening. As you push harder, see how the layers crumple increasingly and start to turn over themselves. Overlapping folds like this are called nappes.

Fire down below

Volcanoes begin many kilometres/miles beneath the Earth's surface. The landscape that makes up the surface of our planet is only a thin 'crust' of hard rock compared with what lies beneath. First, there is a thick layer of semi-liquid rock called the mantle. Then comes an intensely hot core of iron and nickel. This reaches temperatures of 3,700°C/6,700°F, but the surrounding pressure is so great it cannot melt.

Heat moves out from the core to the mantle. Here, rocks are semi-liquid and move like thick honey. They cannot melt completely because of pressure.

In some parts of the upper mantle, though, rocks do melt and are called magma.This collects in chambers, and it may bubble up through gaps in the crust via a volcano. You can watch how solids such as magma react to heat – become soft, then melt, and finally flow – in this project.

Most of the world's volcanoes lie along fault lines, where plates (sections of the Earth's crust) meet. A few, however, such as those in Hawaii, lie over hot spots beneath the Earth's crust. A hot spot is an area on a plate where hot rock from the mantle bubbles up underneath. The plate above moves, but the hot spot stays in the same place in the mantle. The hot spot keeps burning through the plate to make a volcano in a new place. A string of inactive (dead) volcanoes is left behind, as the plate moves over the hot spot. Some form islands above the ocean surface. Others, called sea mounts, remain submerged.

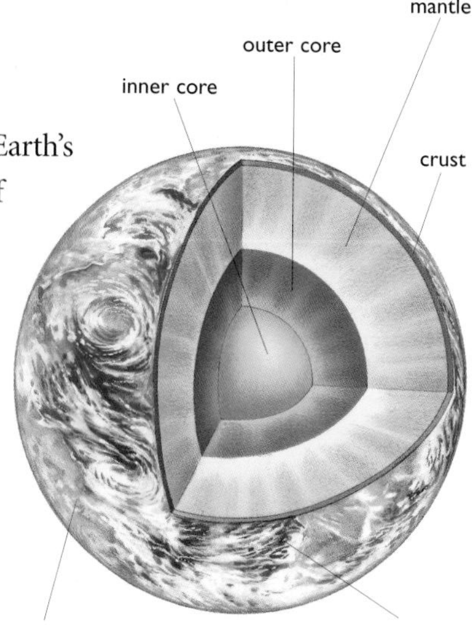

▲ **Inside the Earth**
Our planet is made up of different layers.The top layer is the hard crust. It is thinnest under the oceans, where it is only about 5–10km/3–6 miles thick. Underneath the crust is a thick layer of semi-liquid rock called the mantle. Beneath the mantle is a layer of liquid metal, mainly iron and nickel, that makes up the Earth's outer core.The inner core at the middle is solid, and is made up of iron and other metals.

chains of dead volcanoes

active volcano

ocean plate

hot spot

Volcano chain ▶
Magma breaks through the surface plate. As the plate moves, a new part moves over the hot spot.A new volcano forms and the old one dies.

Magma temperature

YOU WILL NEED
Solid margarine, jam jar, jug (pitcher), hot water, large mixing bowl, stopwatch.

1 Make sure the jar is clean and dry. Scoop out some margarine and drop it on to the bottom of the jar. For the best results, use solid margarine, rather than a soft margarine spread.

2 Pick up the jar and tilt it slightly. See what happens to the margarine. The answer is, not very much. It sticks to the bottom of the jar and does not slide down.

3 Fill the jug with hot water and pour some into the bowl. Shake it around to heat the bowl, then pour it out. Now pour the rest of the hot water into the bowl.

4 Pick up the jar and tilt it again. The margarine still will not move. Now place the jar on the bottom of the bowl. Keep your fingers well clear of the hot water.

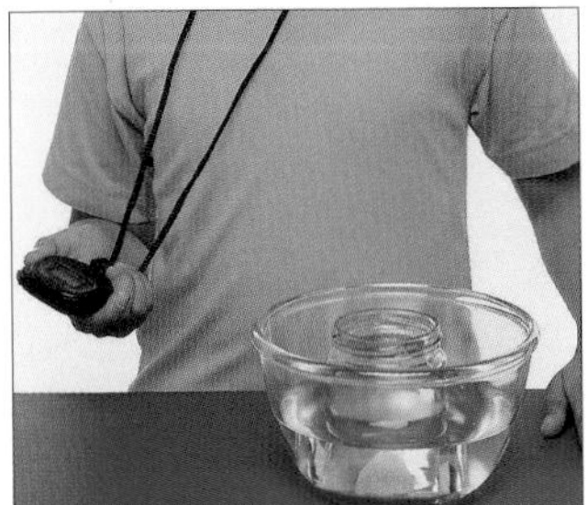

5 Start the stopwatch, and after one minute, take out the jar. Tilt it and see if the margarine moves. Return it to the bowl, and after another minute, look at it again.

6 Continue checking the jar for a few more minutes. After even a minute, the margarine will slide along the bottom as it warms and starts to melt. After several minutes, it is very fluid. Rocks in the upper mantle of the Earth react to heat in a similar way as the margarine.

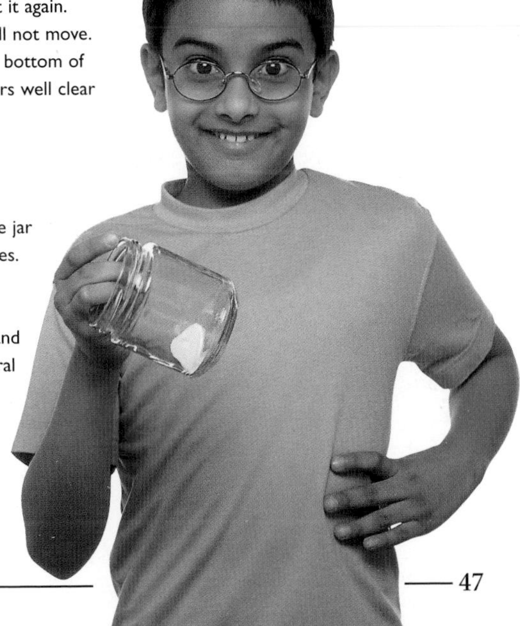

Moving magma

The temperature of the rocks in the Earth's mantle can be as high as 1,500°C/2,700°F. At this temperature, the rocks would usually melt, but they are under such pressure from the rocks above them that they cannot melt completely. However they are able to flow slowly. This is rather like the solid piece of modelling material in the experiment below, which flows slightly when you put enough pressure on it. This kind of flow is called plastic flow. In places, the rocks in the upper part of the mantle do melt completely. This melted rock, called magma, collects in huge pockets called magma chambers. The magma rises because it is hotter and lighter than the semi-liquid rocks. Volcanoes form above magma chambers when the hot magma can rise to the surface. The second project demonstrates this principle using hot and cold water.

▲ **Surprise eruption**
Mount St. Helens, in the north-east USA, lies in a mountain range that includes many volcanoes. Until 1980, Mount St. Helens had not erupted in 130 years.

◂ **Flowing like rock**
Underneath the Earth's hard crust, the rock is semi-liquid and moves slowly. It flows in currents. Hot rock moves upward and cooler rock sinks down.

YOU WILL NEED
Non-hardening modelling material, wooden board.

Plastic flow

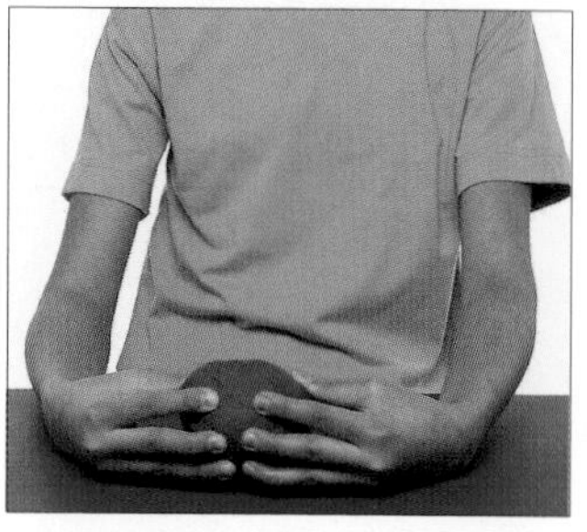

1 Make sure that the table is protected by a sheet. Knead the lump of modelling material in your hands until it is soft and flexible. Make it into a ball and place on the table.

2 Place the board on top, and press it down. The modelling material flattens and squeezes out. It is just like semi-liquid rock flowing under pressure. Make it into a ball again.

3 Press it with the board. Push the board forward at the same time. The modelling material will flow and allow the board to move forward like the plates in the Earth's crust.

Rising magma

YOU WILL NEED

Dark food dye, small jar, small jug (pitcher), transparent plastic food wrapping, scissors, strong rubber band, sharp pencil, large jar, oven gloves, large jug (pitcher).

1 Pour some of the food dye into the small jar. You may need to add more later, to give your solution a deep hue. This will make the last stage easier to see.

2 Fill the small jug with water from the hot tap. Pour it into the small jar. Fill it up to the brim, but don't let it overflow. Wipe off any water that spills down the sides.

3 Cut a circular piece from the plastic food wrapping a few centimetres/inches bigger than the top of the small jar. Place it over the top and secure it with the rubber band.

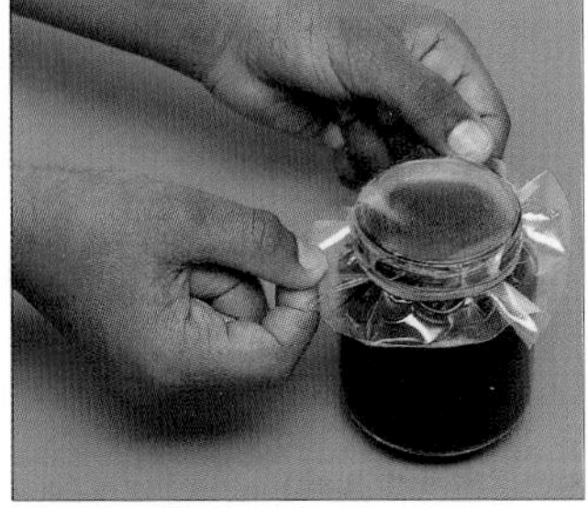

4 With the sharp end of the pencil, carefully make two small holes in the plastic that is covering the top of the jar. If any dyed water splashes out, wipe it off.

5 Now place the small jar inside the larger one. Use oven gloves because it is hot. Fill the large jug with cold water, and pour it into the large jar, not into the small one.

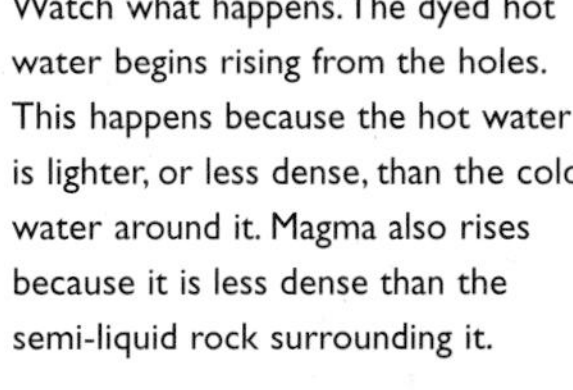

Watch what happens. The dyed hot water begins rising from the holes. This happens because the hot water is lighter, or less dense, than the cold water around it. Magma also rises because it is less dense than the semi-liquid rock surrounding it.

Erupting volcanoes

Volcanoes are places where molten (liquid) rock pushes up from below through splits in the Earth's crust. The word volcano comes from Vulcan, the name of the ancient Roman god of fire. Vulcanology is the term given to the study of volcanoes, and the scientists who study them are known as vulcanologists.

People usually think of volcanoes as producing molten rock. But volcanoes emit much more than just lava. The hot rock inside volcanoes produces many kinds of gases, such as steam and carbon dioxide. Some of these gases go into the air outside the volcano, and some are mixed with the lava that flows from it. The project opposite shows you how to make a volcano that throws out lava mixed with carbon dioxide. As you will see, the red, floury lava from your volcano comes out frothing, full of bubbles of this gas. In a real volcano, it is the gas that is mixed with the lava that makes the volcano suddenly explode.

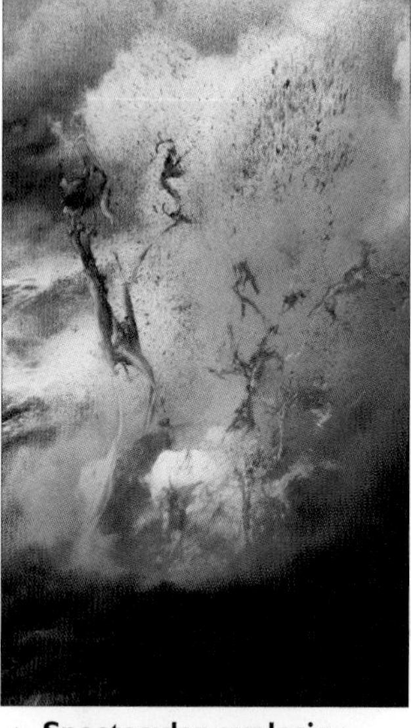

▲ Spectacular explosion
This gigantic volcano has erupted with explosive violence. Huge clouds of rock and ash have been blasted into the air and rivers of red-hot lava cascade down its slopes. Explosive volcanoes have magma inside them that is full of gas. Gas bubbles swell inside the volcano and violently push out a mixture of lava and gas.

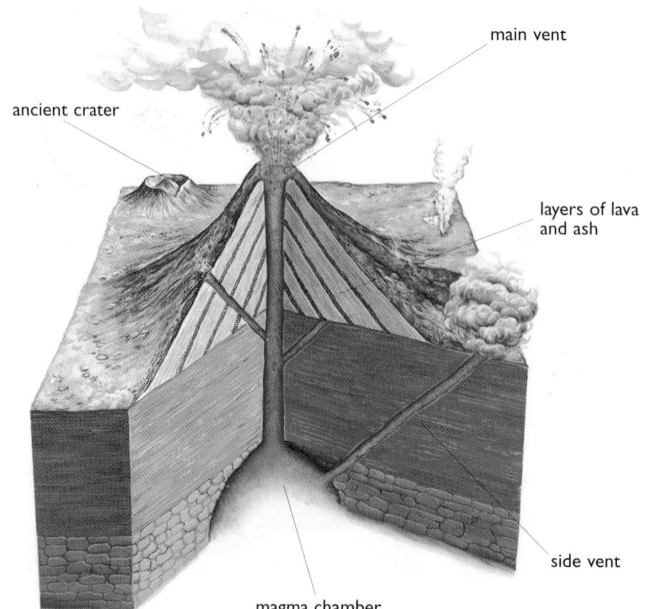

◄ Forming a cone
When an explosive volcano erupts, magma (red-hot, molten rock) forces its way to the Earth's surface. It shoots into the air along with clouds of ash and gas, and runs out over the sides of the volcano. In time, layers of ash and lava build up to form a huge cone shape. Quiet volcanoes (those that do not explode because their magma contains very little gas) form a different shape.

Eruption

YOU WILL NEED
Jug (pitcher), bicarbonate of soda (baking soda), flour, stirrer, funnel, plastic bottle, sand, seed tray (without holes), large plastic tray, vinegar, red food dye.

1 Make sure the jug is dry, or the mixture will stick to the sides. Empty the bicarbonate of soda into the jug and add the flour. Mix the two thoroughly using the stirrer.

2 Place the funnel in the neck of the plastic bottle. Again, first make sure that the funnel is perfectly dry. Now pour the mixture of soda and flour from the jug.

3 Empty sand into the tray until it is half full. Fill the jug with water and pour it into the tray to make the sand sticky, but not too wet. Mix together with the stirrer.

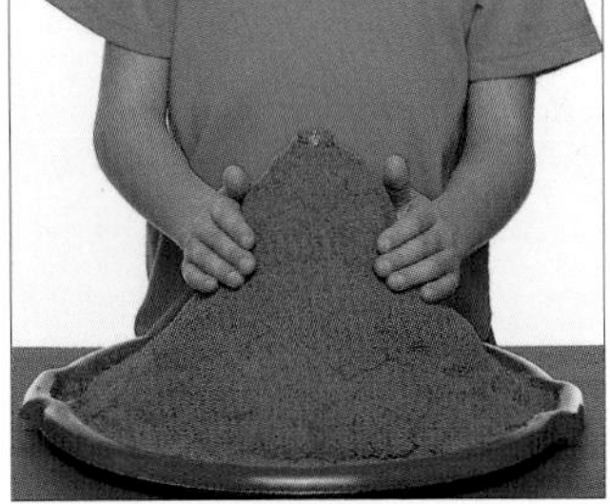

4 Stand the bottle containing the flour and soda mixture in the middle of the plastic tray. Then start packing the wet sand around it. Pat the sand into a cone shape.

5 Pour the vinegar into the jug. Then add enough food dye to make the vinegar a rich red. White wine vinegar will make a richer red than malt vinegar.

6 Place the funnel in the mouth of the plastic bottle, and quickly pour into it the red vinegar in the jug. Now remove the funnel from the bottle.

The sandy volcano you have made will begin to erupt. The vinegar and soda mix to give off carbon dioxide. This makes the flour turn frothy, and forces it out of the bottle as red lava.

Volcanic shapes

Some parts of the world have ancient lava (molten rock) flows that are hundreds of kilometres/miles long. Flows such as these have come from fissures (cracks) in the crust, which have poured out runny lava. This lava is much thinner than the lava produced by explosive volcanoes, which is sometimes called pasty lava. Scientists use the term viscosity to talk about how easily a liquid flows.Thin, runny liquids have a low viscosity, and thick liquids a high viscosity. The project shows the viscosities of two liquids, and how quickly they flow.

Heating solids to a sufficiently high temperature makes them melt and flow. Rock is no exception to this rule. Deep inside a volcano, hot rock becomes liquid and flows out on to the surface as lava. Its temperature can be as high as 1,200°C/2,200°F. Volcanoes grow in various shapes, depending on how runny or thick the lava is.

Submarine (undersea) volcanoes may grow in size until they rise above the surface of the sea.

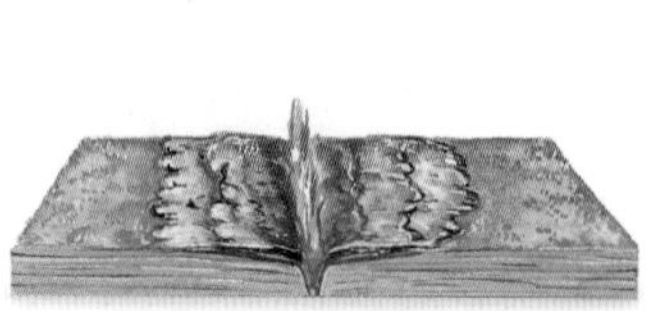

Fissure volcanoes are giant cracks in the ground from which lava flows.

Shield volcanoes have runny lava and gentle slopes.

Vulcanian volcanoes produce thick, sticky lava and erupt with violent explosions.

Strombolian volcanoes spit out lava bombs in small explosions.

Plinian volcanoes produce thick, gassy lava and shoot columns of ash high into the air.

Lava viscosity

YOU WILL NEED

Two paper plates, pen, saucer, jar of clear honey, tablespoon, stopwatch, jug (pitcher) of dishwashing detergent.

1 Mark a large circle on each plate by drawing around the edge of a saucer. Pour a tablespoon of honey from the jar into the middle of one of the circles. Start the stopwatch.

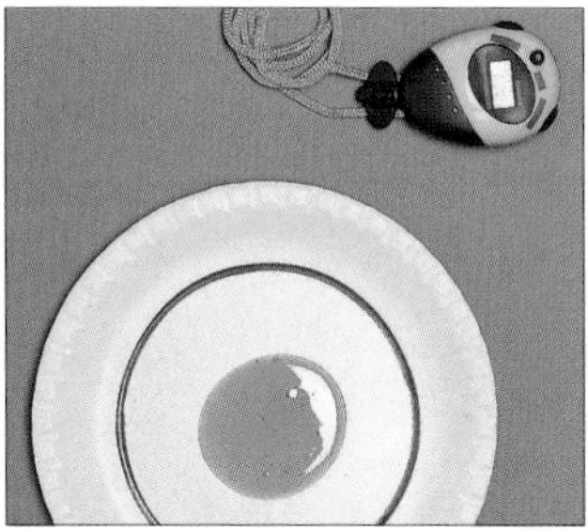

2 After 30 seconds, mark with the pen how far the honey has run. After another 30 seconds mark again. Stop the watch when the honey has reached the circle.

3 Part-fill the jug with dishwashing detergent and pour some into the middle of the other plate. Use the same amount as the honey you poured. Start the stopwatch.

After 30 seconds, note how far the liquid has run. You will probably find that it has already reached the circle. It flows faster because it has a much lower viscosity than honey.

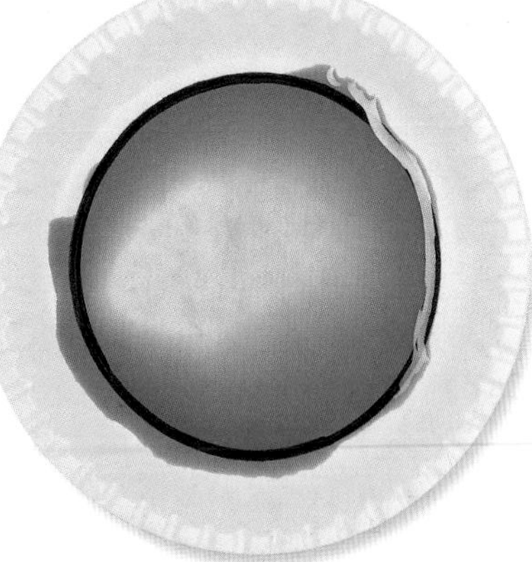

◂ Fast-flowing river

A river of molten lava flows down the slopes of the volcano Kilauea on the main island of Hawaii. Like the other volcanoes on the island, Kilauea is a shield volcano. It pours out very runny lava that flows for long distances, usually at speeds up to about 100m/330ft an hour. The fastest lava flows are called by their Hawaiian name of pahoehoe.

Vicious gases

▲ **Blast off**
An enormous cloud of thick ash billows from the top of Mount St. Helens, in Washington. The volcano erupted on May 18, 1980. The ash cloud rose to a height of more than 20km/12½ miles.

The experiments here look at two effects that the gases given out by volcanoes can have. In the first project, you can see how the build up of gas pressure can inflate a balloon. If you have put too much gas-making mixture in the bottle, the balloon may explode. Be careful! When the gas pressure builds up inside a volcano, an enormous explosion takes place, often releasing a deadly, hot gas cloud.

Volcanoes often give out the gas carbon dioxide. This is heavier than air, so a cloud of carbon dioxide descends, pushing air out of the way. Carbon dioxide can kill people and animals. They suffocate, because the cloud of carbon dioxide has replaced the air, so oxygen cannot reach their lungs. The second project shows the effect of carbon dioxide. The candle needs oxygen to burn, just as we need it to breathe. Carbon dioxide replaces the air, so the candle goes out.

YOU WILL NEED
Funnel, soft drink bottle, bicarbonate of soda (baking soda), vinegar, jug (pitcher), balloon.

Gas pressure

1 Place the funnel in the top of the bottle, and pour in some bicarbonate of soda. Make sure the funnel is dry or the soda will stick to it. Pour the vinegar into the bottle using the funnel.

2 Remove the funnel. Quickly fit the neck of the balloon over the top of the bottle. Notice that the vinegar and soda are fizzing as they give off bubbles of gas.

The balloon starts to blow up, because of the pressure, or force, of the gas in the bottle. The more gas there is, the more the balloon fills. Don't pop the balloon!

Suffocating gas

YOU WILL NEED

Funnel, bottle, bicarbonate of soda (baking soda), vinegar, jug (pitcher), non-hardening modelling material, pencil, long straw, tall and short candles, large jar, matches.

1 Place the funnel in the bottle and add the bicarbonate of soda. Pour the vinegar in from the jug. This bottle is your gas generator. The gas produced is carbon dioxide.

2 Knead a piece of modelling material until it is soft, then push it into the mouth of the bottle. Make sure it fits tightly. This will keep the gas from escaping.

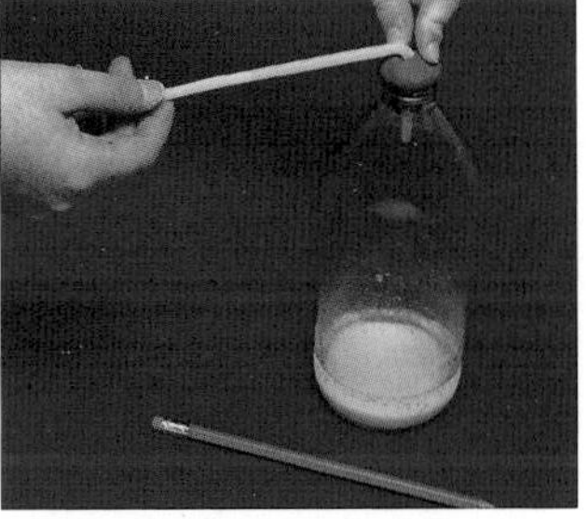

3 Make a hole in the clay stopper with the pencil. Carefully push the straw through the hole, so that it hangs down into the bottle. Press the modelling material around the straw.

4 Stand both candles in the bottom of the large jar. Ask an adult to light them. Light the short one first, to avoid the danger of being burned if the tall candle were lit first.

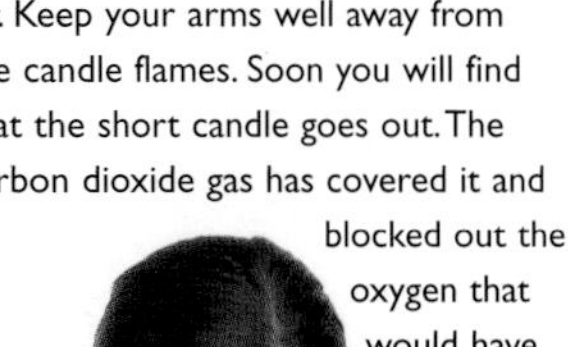

5 Direct the straw of your gas generator into the bottom of the jar. Keep your arms well away from the candle flames. Soon you will find that the short candle goes out. The carbon dioxide gas has covered it and blocked out the oxygen that would have let it burn.

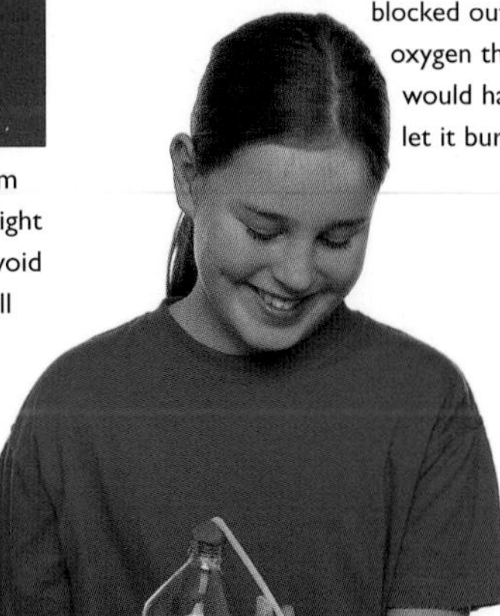

▲ **A record of the past**

Gas killed many of the victims at the Roman town of Pompeii. In AD79 Pompeii was buried by avalanches of hot ash and rock from the erupting Vesuvius. Archaeologists have recreated the shapes of people and animals who died there. They filled hollows left by the bodies with wet plaster of Paris and let it harden. Then they removed the cast from the lava that had covered the bodies.

Steaming hot

In some places in the world, often near plate boundaries, there is magma (hot molten rock) very near to the Earth's surface. This causes other volcanic features such as geysers and hot springs, called geothermal features. The word comes from geo, meaning the Earth, and thermal, meaning heat.

Water from the Earth's surface trickles down through holes and cracks in the land. Geothermal features are almost always caused by magma that affect underground water. The most spectacular geothermal feature is the geyser. This is a fountain of steam and water that erupts from holes in the ground. Vents (holes) called fumaroles, where steam escapes gently, are more common. Geysers and fumaroles may also give out carbon dioxide and sulfurous fumes.

Hot water can also mix with cooler water to create a hot spring, or with mud to form a bubbling mud hole. Water becomes heated in underground rocks to a temperature above body heat (about 37°C/98.6°F). Some hot springs can be twice this hot. Many are rich in minerals. For centuries, people have believed that bathing in these springs is good for health.

The first experiment on the opposite page shows you how to make a geyser using air pressure to force out water. Blowing into the top of the bottle increases the air pressure there. This forces the dyed water out of the bottle through the long straw. In the second project, you can create a mud hole and discover the sort of bubbles that form in them.

YOU WILL NEED

Geyser eruption: Non-hardening modelling material, 3 bendable straws, jug (pitcher), food dye, large plastic bottle, large jar.

Mudbaths: Cornflour (cornstarch), unsweetened cocoa powder, mixing bowl, wooden spoon, measuring cup, milk, pan, oven glove.

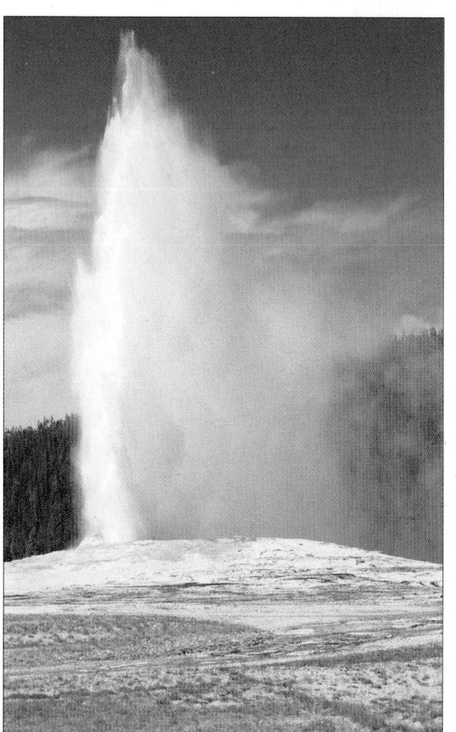

◂ Regular show

One of the most famous geysers in the world is Old Faithful, in Yellowstone National Park in Wyoming. This geyser erupts regularly about once every 45 minutes. Yellowstone is the most significant geothermal region in the USA. The National Park also boasts the world's tallest geyser, known as Steamboat. Its spouting column has been known to reach more than 115m/380ft.

Geyser eruption

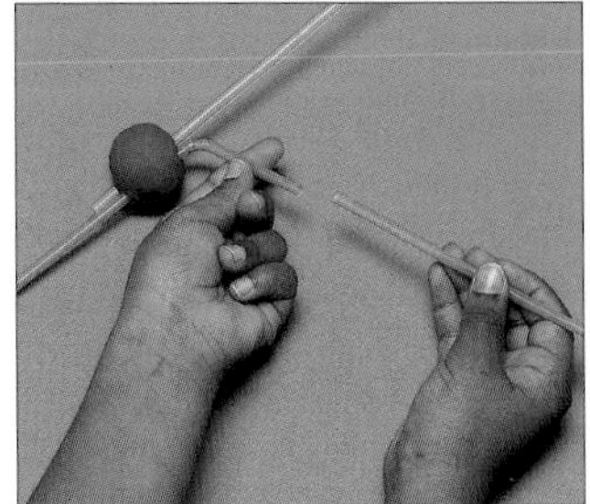

1 Make two holes in a little ball of modelling material and push two bendable straws through it, as shown. Push another straw through the end of one of the first two straws.

2 Pour water into the jug and add the dye. Then pour it into the bottle. Push the stopper into the neck, so that the elongated straw dips into the dyed water.

3 Place the jar under the other end of the elongated straw, and blow into the other straw. Water spurts into the jar. If the long straw was upright, the water would spout upward like a geyser.

Mudbaths

1 Mix together 30ml/2 tbsp of cornflour and two of cocoa powder in the bowl, using the wooden spoon. Stir the mixture thoroughly until it is evenly blended.

2 Pour about 300ml/10fl oz of milk into the pan, and heat it slowlywith adult supervision. Keep the ring on a low setting, to make sure the milk does not boil. Do not leave it unattended.

3 Add some cold milk, bit by bit, to the mixture of cornflour and cocoa in the bowl. Stir vigorously until the mixture has become a thick smooth cream.

4 Carefully pour the mixture into the hot milk in the pan. Hold the handle of the pan with the oven glove, and stir to stop the liquid from sticking to the bottom of the pan.

5 If you have prepared your flour and cocoa mixture well, you will now have a smooth, hot liquid that looks something like liquid mud. Soon it will start sending up thick bubbles.

The thick bubbles in the mixture will pop with gentle, plopping sounds. This is exactly what happens in hot mud pools in volcanic areas.

Volcanic rocks

The lava that flows out of volcanoes eventually cools, hardens, and becomes solid rock. Different types of lava form different kinds of rocks.

In the first project, we see how keeping a liquid under pressure stops gas from escaping. The magma (molten rock) in volcanoes usually has a lot of gas dissolved in it. As it rises through the volcano, the gases start to expand. They help push the magma up and out if the vent is clear. If the vent is blocked, the gas pressure builds up and eventually causes the volcano to explode. The lava that comes from volcanoes with gassy magma forms rock riddled with holes. In some explosive volcanoes, the lava contains so much gas that it forms pumice. This rock is so frothy and light that it floats on water.

When rising magma becomes trapped underground, it forces its way into gaps in the rocks and between the rock layers. This process is known as intrusion, and it is demonstrated by the second project. The rocks that form when the magma cools and solidifies are called intrusive rocks. Granite is the most common intrusive rock. Often, the heat of the intruding magma changes the surrounding rocks. They turn into metamorphic (changed form) rocks.

YOU WILL NEED

Dissolved gas: Small jar with tight-fitting lid, bowl, jug (pitcher), antacid tablets.

Igneous intrusions: Plastic jar, bradawl, pieces of broken tiles, non-hardening modelling material, tube of toothpaste.

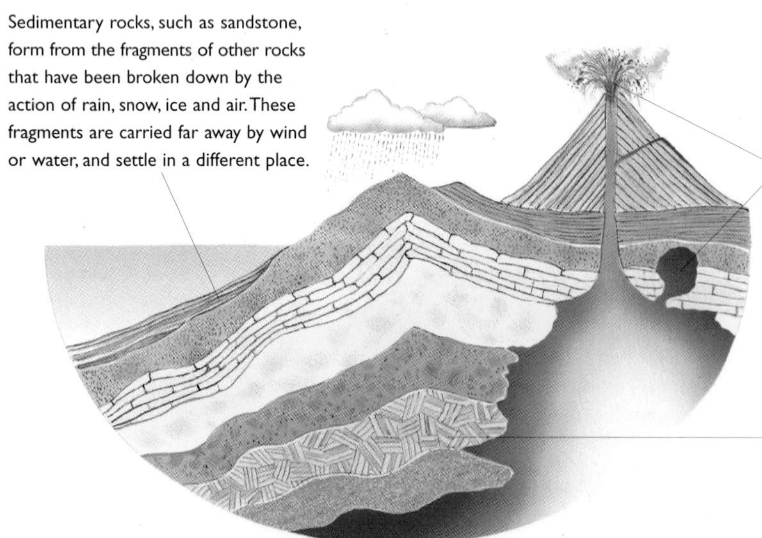

Sedimentary rocks, such as sandstone, form from the fragments of other rocks that have been broken down by the action of rain, snow, ice and air. These fragments are carried far away by wind or water, and settle in a different place.

At some hot parts of the Earth beneath the crust, huge pockets of liquid rock (magma) form. The magma rises, cools and solidifies to form igneous rocks such as granite. If magma reaches the surface of the Earth, it erupts as lava.

Within the Earth, the heat and pressure sometimes become so great that the surrounding rocks are changed. The new rocks are called metamorphic rocks. Marble is formed this way. It comes from limestone rock.

Dissolved gas

1 Stand the jar in the bowl. Pour cold water into the jar from the jug until the jar is nearly full to the top. Break up two antacid tablets and drop them into the jar.

2 Quickly screw the lid on the jar. Little bubbles will start to rise from the tablets, but will soon stop. Pressure has built up in the jar, and this prevents any more gas from escaping.

3 Now quickly unscrew the lid from the jar and see what happens. The whole jar starts fizzing. Removing the lid releases the pressure, and the gas in the liquid bubbles out.

Igneous intrusions

1 Make a hole in the bottom of the plastic jar with a bradawl, big enough to fit the neck of the toothpaste tube in. Keep your steadying hand away from the sharp end of the bradawl.

2 Place the pieces of broken tiles on the bottom of the jar. Keep them as flat as possible. They are supposed to represent the layers of rocks that are found in the Earth's crust.

3 Flatten out the modelling material into a disk as wide as the inside of the jar. Put the disk of modelling material inside the jar. Push it down firmly on top of the tiles.

4 Unscrew the top of the toothpaste tube, and force the neck into the hole you have made in the bottom of the bottle. You may have to widen it a little to get the neck in.

5 Squeeze the toothpaste tube. You will see the toothpaste pushing, or intruding, into the tile layers and making the disk on top rise. Molten magma often behaves in the same way. It intrudes into rock layers and makes the Earth's surface bulge.

Making crystals

Everything around you is made up of tiny particles called atoms. Crystals consist of atoms that are arranged in a regular repeating pattern. This gives the crystal its fixed outer shape. Most solid substances, including metals and minerals found in rocks, are in crystal form.

Igneous rocks are usually made of crystals that form as hot magma (molten rock) cools and solidifies. Crystals may also grow when a water solution containing minerals on the surface of the Earth evaporates. These two ways are demonstrated in the first two experiments.

The type of crystals that form depend on the substances that are dissolved in the liquid. Each mineral forms crystals with a characteristic shape. You can compare the crystals from the first two projects, which use two different solutions. The final experiment demonstrates how atoms are arranged in a crystal. In a liquid, the atoms are loosely joined together and can move around, which is why a liquid flows. As a liquid solidifies, the atoms join together in a regular pattern, like a pyramid, to form a crystal. When atoms are arranged in a disorderly way, they produce a gas.

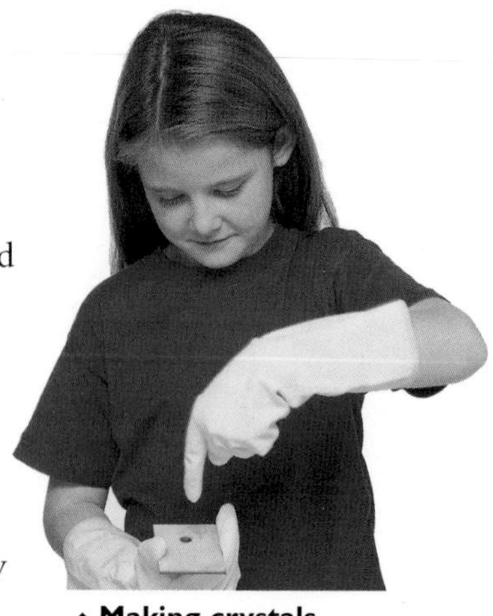

▲ **Making crystals**
Place a drop of water on a small, dry mirror and then put it in the freezer. The water will freeze into crystals, which can be seen with a magnifying glass.

YOU WILL NEED
Water, measuring cup, pan, sugar, tablespoon, wooden spoon, glass jar.

Growing crystals from sugar solution

1 Ask an adult to heat 600ml/1 pint/2½ cups of water in a pan until it is hot, but not boiling. Using a tablespoon, add sugar to the hot water until no more sugar will dissolve in the solution.

2 Stir the solution well, then allow it to cool. When it is completely cold, pour the solution from the pan into a glass jar, and put it somewhere where it will not be disturbed.

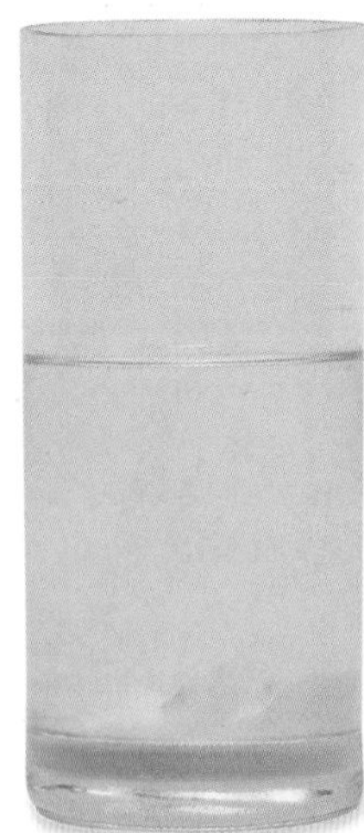

After a few days or weeks, the solution starts to evaporate and the sugar in the solution will gradually begin to form crystals. The longer it is undisturbed, the larger your crystals will grow.

Growing crystals from sodium carbonate

YOU WILL NEED

Growing crystals from sodium carbonate: Sodium carbonate, spoon, bowl, straw, cotton thread, paper clip, magnifying glass.

Make a model crystal: Small, shallow tray (such as the lid of a shoe box), five different marbles.

1 Get an adult to pour 250ml/8fl oz/1 cup very hot water into a jug. Add a spoonful of sodium carbonate. Stir until it all dissolves. Add more sodium carbonate until no more will dissolve.

2 Dissolving a solid in a liquid makes a solution. Your solution is said to be saturated, because no more solid will dissolve. Pour the solution into a bowl, leaving undissolved solids in the jug.

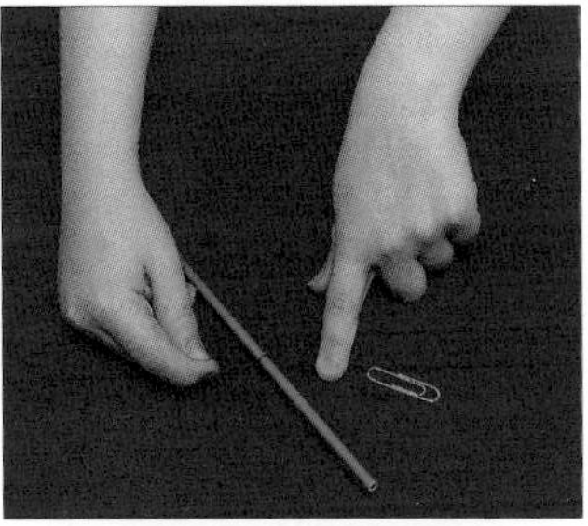

3 A crystal needs somewhere to start growing. Use a piece of thread to attach the paper clip to the straw. The distance from straw to clip should be about two-thirds the depth of the bowl.

4 Balance the straw on top of the bowl to let the paper clip dangle in the water. As time goes by, water evaporates, leaving crystals on the paper clip.

5 After several days, remove the clip and crystals from the solution, and wash them under the cold tap. Look at the crystals through a magnifying glass. The shapes of your crystals are identical.

Make a model crystal

1 Fit a layer of blue marbles into the tray in a square pattern. Each central atom is surrounded by eight others. (In some substances, atoms are arranged in a hexagon – a six-sided shape.)

2 Add a second layer. Each marble sits in a dip between four marbles in the layer below. Add a third layer. Each marble is directly above a marble in the first layer.

3 Add two more layers of marbles to make up a complete model crystal. The model crystal you have made is the shape of a square pyramid, because you used a square tray.

Glass and bubbles

Igneous rocks begins deep within the Earth as magma (molten rock). The word igneous means 'of fire'. Magma rises toward the surface where it may erupt as lava from a volcano, or cool and solidify within the Earth's crust as igneous rock. Rocks formed in this way are a mass of interlocking crystals, which makes them very strong and ideal as building stones.

The size of the crystals in an igneous rock depends on how quickly the magma cooled. Lavas that cool quickly contain very small crystals. Basalt and andesite are two common kinds of fine-grained igneous rocks, with small crystals. Other rocks, such as granite, cooled more slowly because they solidified inside the Earth's crust. These have a grainy texture because the crystals had time to grow.

The experiments opposite show how igneous rocks can be grainy or smooth and glassy. They use sugar to represent magma. Sugar melts at a low enough temperature for you to experiment with, but it will still be very hot, so ask an adult to help you do these projects. To make real magma, you would need to heat rock up to around 1,000°C/1,830°F until it melted! You can also make the sugar solution into bubbly honeycomb, a form similar to pumice stone.

▲ **Basalt**
Dark, heavy basalt is one of the most common volcanic rocks. It is formed from the thin, runny lava that pours out of some volcanoes. This sample is called vesicular basalt because it is riddled with vesicles (holes).

▲ **Andesite**
Lava from explosive volcanoes is thicker and less runny. It can form andesite, which is less dark than basalt. Andesite is so-called because it is the typical rock found in the Andes Mountains in Peru.

▲ **Pumice**
The bubbles in honeycomb are like those in pumice. Pumice is a very light rock that is full of holes. It forms when lava that contains a lot of gas pours out of underwater volcanoes.

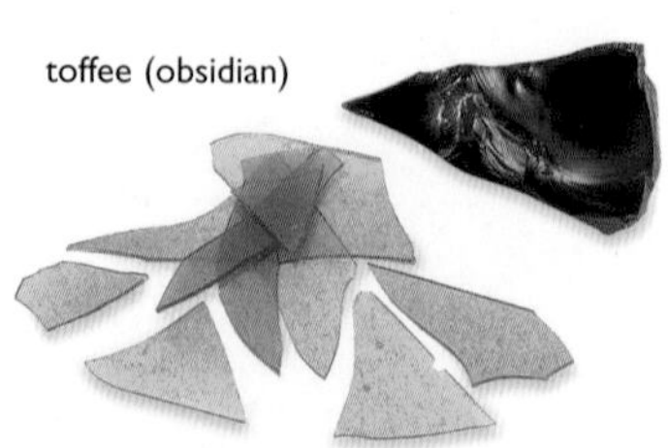

▲ **Obsidian**
Glassy toffee cools too rapidly to form crystals. Obsidian is a volcanic rock that is formed when lava cools very quickly. It looks like black glass and is often called volcanic glass.

▲ **Granite**
Fudge's grainy texture is similar to granite. The crystals are large, because they grew slowly as the magma cooled slowly. Rhyolite is a kind of granite with smaller crystals and sharp edges.

Crystalline rock

YOU WILL NEED

Crystalline rock: Sugar, water, pan, safety glasses, wooden spoon, milk.

Glass and bubbles: Waxed paper, butter, baking tray, oven gloves, sugar, water, pan, wooden spoon, safety glasses, bicarbonate of soda (baking soda).

1 Ask an adult to heat 500g/1¼lb/2½ cups of sugar with a little water in a pan. Continue heating until the mixture turns brown, but not black, then add a splash of milk. Leave to cool.

2 After an hour, you should see tiny crystal grains in the fudge mixture. Once it is completely cool, feel its grainy texture in your hands. The texture is similar to granite.

Glass and bubbles

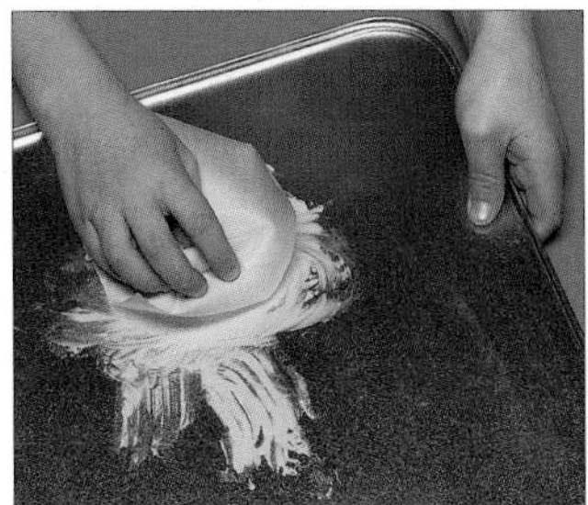

1 Use waxed paper to spread the butter on a metal baking tray. Put it in the freezer for at least an hour to get cold. Use oven gloves to take the tray from the freezer.

2 Ask an adult to heat about 500g/2½ cups of sugar with a little water in a pan. The sugar dissolves in the water, but the water soon evaporates, leaving only sugar.

3 Stir the sugar mixture with a wooden spoon while it is heating. Make sure that the sugar does not burn and turn black. It should be golden brown.

4 Pour the mixture on to the cool baking tray. After 10 minutes, the glassy and brittle toffee will be cool enough to pick up. Like obsidian, toffee cools too rapidly to form crystals.

◂ Holey honeycomb
To make honeycomb, stir in a spoonful of bicarbonate of soda in Step 3, just before you pour the sugar on to the tray. This will make tiny bubbles of gas in your 'magma'.

Layers on layers

Many of the most familiar rocks around us are sedimentary rocks. Particles of rock, shells and bones of sea creatures settle in layers, and then harden into rock over thousands of years. Rock particles form when other rocks are eroded (worn down) by the weather and are carried away by wind, rivers, and ice sheets. They become sediments when they are dumped and settle. Sediments may collect in river deltas, lakes and the sea. Large particles make conglomerates (large pebbles cemented together), medium ones make sandstones, and fine particles make clays.

To understand the processes by which sedimentary rocks are made, and how they form distinct layers called strata, you can make your own sedimentary rocks. Different strata of rock are laid down by different types of sediment, so the first project involves making strata using various things found in the kitchen. The powerful forces that move parts of the Earth's crust often cause strata to fold, fault or just tilt, and you can see this, too. In the second project, you can make a type of sedimentary rock called a conglomerate, in which sand cements pebbles together.

▲ **Cracks in the rockface**
Once they have formed, sedimentary rocks may be subject to powerful forces caused by the movement of the Earth's crust. Splits in the ground reveal how this strata has folded and cracked.

YOU WILL NEED
Large jar, non-hardening modelling material, spoon, flour, kidney beans, soft dark brown sugar, rice, lentils (or a similar variety of ingredients of different tones and textures).

Your own strata

1 Press one edge of a large jar into a piece of modelling material, so that the jar sits at an angle. Slowly and carefully spoon a layer of flour about 2cm/¾in thick into the jar.

2 Carefully add layers of kidney beans, brown sugar, rice, lentils and flour, building them up until they almost reach the top of the jar. Try to keep the side of the jar clean.

3 Remove the jar from the clay and stand it upright. The different toned and textured layers are like a section through a sequence of natural sedimentary rocks.

Making conglomerate rock

YOU WILL NEED

Rubber gloves, old plastic container, plaster of Paris, water, fork or spoon, pebbles, sand, earth, spare paper.

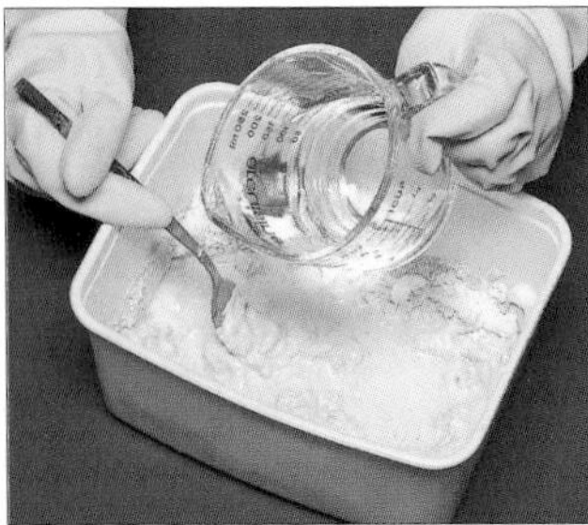

1 Put on a pair of rubber gloves. In an old plastic container, make up some plaster of Paris with water, following the instructions on the packet. Stir with a fork or spoon.

2 Before the plaster starts to harden, mix some small pebbles, sand, and earth into the plaster of Paris. Stir the mixture thoroughly, to make sure it is all evenly distributed.

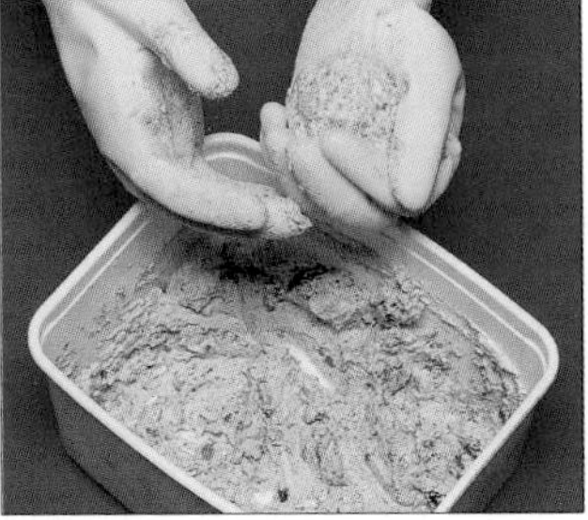

3 Leave the mixture for 10 minutes, until the plaster begins to harden, then take a small lump of it in your hand and form it into a ball shape to look like conglomerate rock.

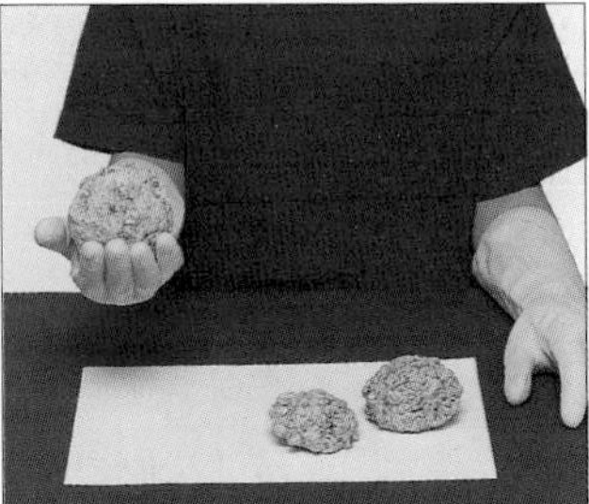

4 Make more conglomerate rocks in different sizes containing different amounts of pebbles. Place the rocks on a spare piece of paper so that they can harden and dry out completely.

▲ **Natural cement**

Conglomerates in nature can be found in areas that were once under water. Small pebbles and shells become rounded and cemented together by the water.

◀ **Clues in the cutaway**

The 1.6km/1 mile-deep Grand Canyon, in Arizona, was cut by the Colorado River. The cliff face reveals strata (layers of rock). The strata at the bottom are more than two billion years old. Those at the top are about 60 million years old. Each layer is a different type of rock, suggesting that conditions in this region changed many times in the past. For this reason, sedimentary rock strata can provide valuable clues about the distant history of the Earth.

What's a fossil?

The remains of some plants and animals that died long ago can be seen in rock as fossils. After an animal dies, it may become buried in sediments – rock particles ground down by wind and water. Slowly, over thousands of years, the sediments compact together to form sedimentary rock. The shape or outline of the plant or animal is preserved.

The study of fossils, called palaeontology, tells us much about how life evolved, both in the sea and on the land. Fossils give clues to the type of environment in which an organism lived, and can also help to date rocks.

These projects will help you to understand how two types of fossil came to exist. One type forms when sediment settles around a dead animal or plant. It hardens to rock, and the plant or animal rots away. This space in the rock is an outline of the dead animal or plant. This is usually how the soft parts of an animal, or a delicate leaf, are preserved. You can make this kind of fossil using a shell. In this case the shell does not decay – you simply remove it from the plaster.

The second project shows you another kind of fossil. Here, the skeleton of a decaying animal is filled with minerals. The minerals gradually become rock. This gives a solid fossil that is a copy of the original body part.

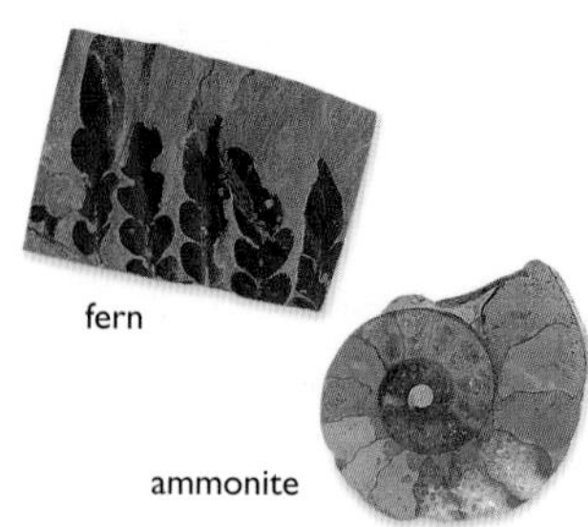

▲ Turned to stone
Two common fossils are shown here. Fossils of sea creatures are often found, because their bodies cannot decay completely underwater. Ammonites were hard-shelled sea creatures that lived between 60 million and 400 million years ago. Fernlike fossils are often found in coal.

YOU WILL NEED

Fossil imprint: Safety glasses, plastic container, plaster of Paris, water, fork, strip of paper, paper clip, non-hardening modelling material, shell, wooden board, hammer, chisel.

Solid fossil: Spare paper, rolling pin, modelling material, shell, petroleum jelly, paper clip, strip of paper, glass jar, plaster of Paris, water, fork.

How fossils are formed

An animal or plant dies. Its body falls on to the sand at the bottom of the ocean, or into mud on land. If it is buried quickly, then the body is protected from being eaten.

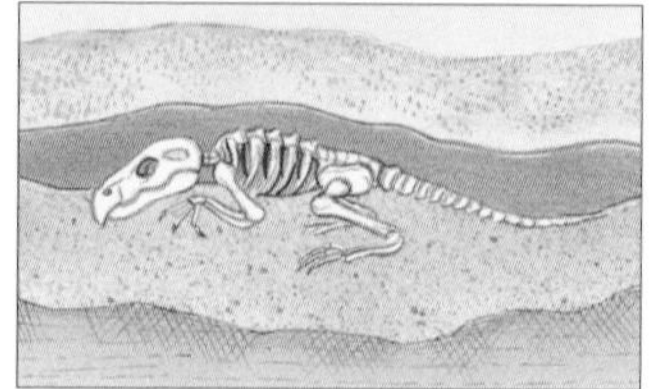

The soft parts of the body rot away, but the bones and teeth remain. After a long time, the hard parts are replaced by minerals – usually calcite, but sometimes pyrite or quartz.

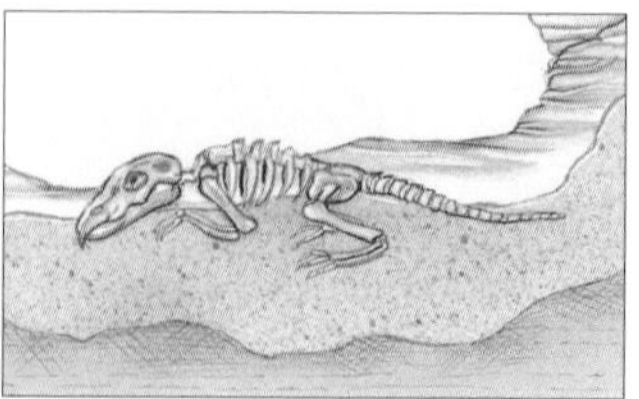

After millions of years, the rocks in which the fossils formed are eroded and exposed again. Some fossils look as fresh now as the day when the plant or animal was first buried.

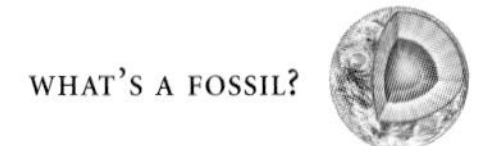

Fossil imprint

1 In a plastic container, mix up the plaster of Paris with some water. Follow the instructions on the packet. Make sure the mixture is fairly firm and not too runny.

2 Make a collar out of a strip of paper fastened with a paper clip. Use modelling material to make a base to fit under the collar. Press the shell into the clay. Surround the shell with plaster.

3 Leave your plaster rock to dry for at least half an hour. Crack open the rock and remove the shell. You will then see the imprint left behind after the shell has gone.

Solid fossil

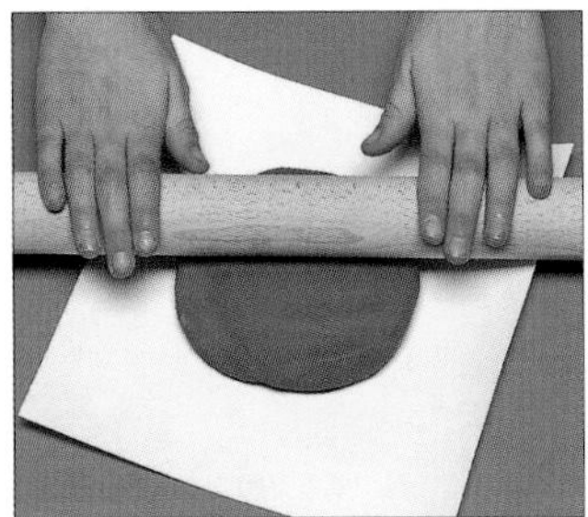

1 Put a spare piece of paper down on your work surface to protect it. Using the rolling pin, roll out some modelling material into a flat circle, about 2cm/¾in thick.

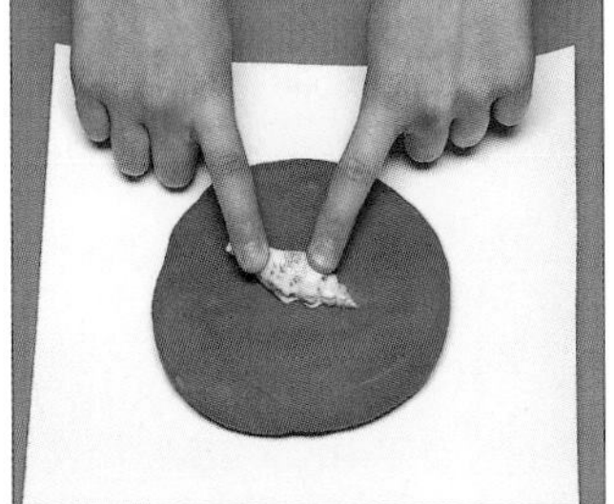

2 Press your shell, or another object with a distinctive shape, deep into the clay to leave a clear impression. Do not press it all the way to the paper at the bottom.

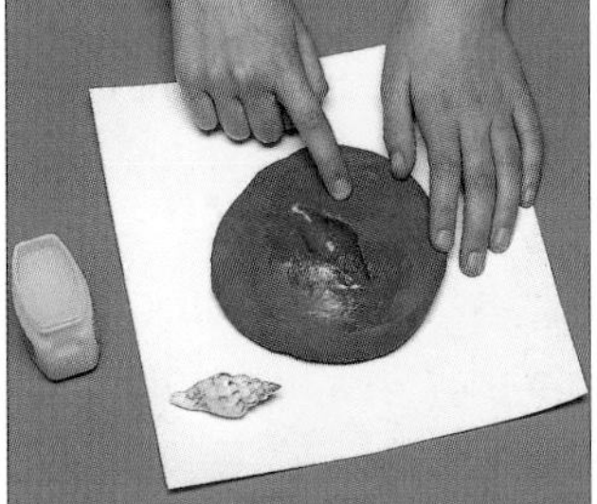

3 Remove the shell and lightly rub some petroleum jelly over the clay circle, which is now the shell mould. This will help you to remove the plaster fossil later.

4 Use the paper clip to fasten the paper strip into a collar for the mould. Mix up some plaster of Paris according to the instructions, pour it in, and leave it to set for half an hour.

5 Remove the solid plaster from the mould. In order not to damage them, palaeontologists have to remove fossilized bones or teeth, from rock or earth, very carefully.

These are the finished results of the two projects. Real fossils are imprints of organisms that lived millions of years ago.

Hard as nails!

The best way to learn about rocks is to look closely at as many different types as you can find. Look at pebbles on the beach and the stones in your garden. You will find that they are not all the same. Collect specimens of different pebbles and compare them. Give each stone an identification number and record where you found it, and its characteristics. A magnifying glass will help you see more details than can be seen with the naked eye. Look for different tones, shapes and hardness. Ask an adult to take you to a geological museum to compare your stone with the specimens there.

You can try simple versions of tests that geologists use on the following pages. They will help you identify some samples that you have collected. The first test involves rubbing a rock on to the back of a tile to leave a streak mark. The colour of the streak can give a clue to what minerals are present in the rock. The second test shows you how to discover a rock's hardness, by seeing how easily a mineral scratches. Hardness is measured on a scale devised in 1822 by Friedrich Mohs. He made a list of ten common minerals called Mohs' scale, which runs from 1 (the softest) to 10 (the hardest). The hardest natural mineral is diamond, with a hardness of 10. It will scratch all other minerals.

▲ Be a detective
Clean a rock with a stiff brush and some water. Stand in plenty of light and experiment to find the correct distance to see the rock's details clearly with a magnifying glass.

▲ Wearing away
Look at the different sizes of pebbles on a beach. The constant to-and-fro of the waves grinds the pebbles smaller and smaller. Eventually these particles will form sedimentary rock.

copper

▲ What is a mineral?
All rocks are made up of one or more minerals. Minerals, such as copper and quartz, are natural, solid, nonliving substances. Each mineral has definite characteristics, such as shape and colour, that distinguish it from other minerals.

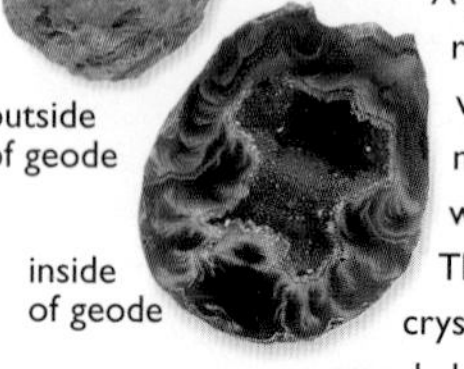

◀ Hidden inside
When mineral-rich water fills a crack or cavity in a rock, veins and geodes form. A geode is a rounded rock, with a hollow middle lined with crystals. The beautiful crystal lining is revealed when it is split open. Geodes are highly prized by mineral collectors.

Streak test

YOU WILL NEED

Streak test: White tile, several samples of different rocks or minerals, field guide.

Testing for hardness: Several rock samples, bowl of water, nail brush, coin, glass jar, steel file, sandpaper.

1 Place a tile face down, so that the rough side is facing upward. Choose one of your samples and rub it against the tile. You should see a streak appear on the tile.

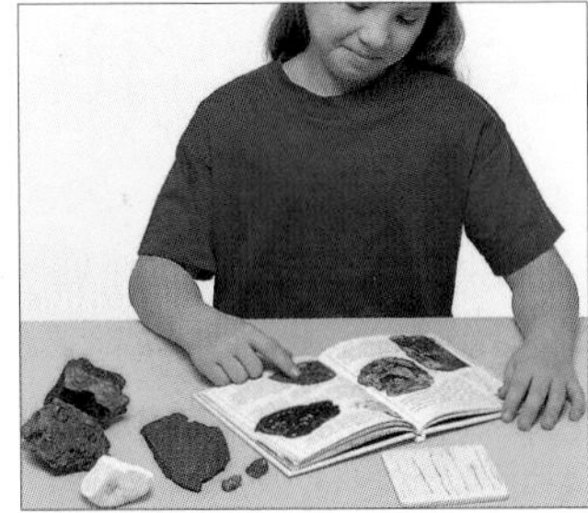

2 Make streaks using the other samples and compare the colours. Rocks made of several minerals may leave several different streaks. Try to identify them in your field guide.

Testing for hardness

1 Clean some rock samples with water using a nail brush. Scratch the rocks together. On the Mohs' scale, a mineral is harder than any minerals it can make scratches on.

2 A fingernail has a hardness of just over 2. Scratch each rock with a fingernail – if it scratches the rock, the minerals out of which the rock is made have a hardness of 2 or less.

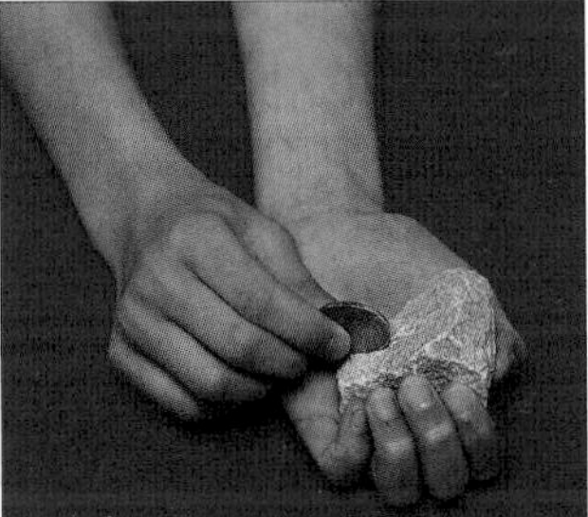

3 Put aside those rocks scratched by a fingernail. Scratch those remaining with a coin. A coin has a hardness of about 3, so minerals it scratches are less than 3.

4 Now scratch the remaining rocks on a glass jar. If any of the rocks make a scratch on the jar, then the minerals they contain must be harder than glass.

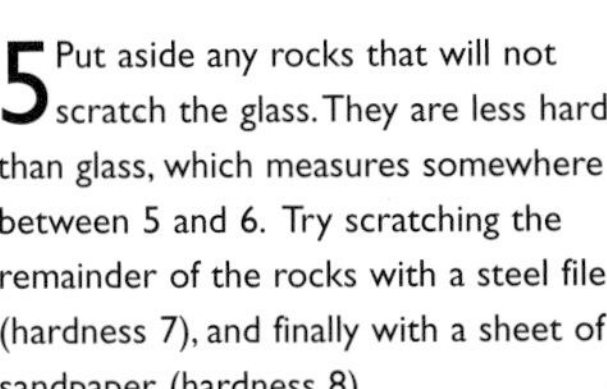

5 Put aside any rocks that will not scratch the glass. They are less hard than glass, which measures somewhere between 5 and 6. Try scratching the remainder of the rocks with a steel file (hardness 7), and finally with a sheet of sandpaper (hardness 8).

Testing for minerals

Rocks and minerals are the naturally occurring materials that make up planet Earth. Rocks are used for buildings, and many minerals are prized as jewels. Most people think of rocks as hard and heavy, but soft materials, such as sand, chalk and clay, are also considered to be rocks. Different rocks are made up from mixtures of different minerals. The minerals inside a rock form small crystals that are locked together to form a hard solid.

Geologists (scientists who study the Earth and its rocks) use many different methods to identify minerals that make up rocks. These experiments will help you to discover which minerals are in a rock sample. You can also identify rocks with a magnifying glass or from their hardness.

The acid test demonstrates if a gas is given off by the mineral. The second experiment is used to discover a rock sample's specific gravity. It compares a mineral's density to the density of water. Density measures how compact the particles are that make up a sample. Every mineral has a different density, which means that samples of the same mineral will have the same density.

▲ Weighing up the evidence
These two bricks are the same size and shape, but do not weigh the same. The materials they are made of have different densities.

YOU WILL NEED

Vinegar, bowl, spoon, samples of different stones, magnifying glass, reference book.

Acid test

1 Pour some vinegar into a bowl. Drop rock samples into the vinegar. If gas bubbles form, then the rock contains minerals called carbonates (such as calcite).

2 Alternatively, you can put a few drops of vinegar on each rock sample. Watch them carefully for clues to what they might be. Chalk, marble and limestone make vinegar fizz.

3 Limestone reacts with vinegar. Like chalk and marble, it reacts because it is a type of calcium carbonate. Common rocks such as flint, granite and sandstone are unaffected.

4 Now scratch one sample with another. Harder rocks leave marks on softer ones. Hardness also helps you to identify rocks. Think how difficult it might be to carve the harder ones.

5 Arrange your rocks in order of hardness. Igneous rocks, such as granite, are usually the hardest. Sedimentary rocks, such as sandstone, are usually the softest.

6 Use a lens to examine your rocks. There are sharp crystal minerals in igneous rocks. Metamorphic rocks look smooth and sedimentary rocks have layers and tiny bits in them.

Density or specific gravity test

YOU WILL NEED

Mineral or rock samples, accurate food scales, notebook, pen or pencil, measuring cup, water.

1 Choose a rock or mineral sample, and weigh it as accurately as you can to find its mass. The figure should be in grams or ounces. Make a note of the mass in your notebook.

2 Fill a clear measuring cup to the 250ml/8fl oz mark with cold water. Choose your first rock or mineral sample and carefully place it in the water.

3 Look at the scale on the cup to read the new water level. Make a note of the level of the water in your notebook. Now subtract 250ml/8fl oz from that figure.

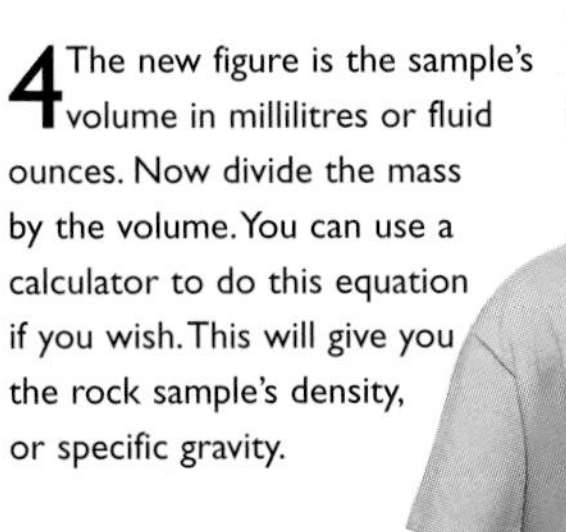

4 The new figure is the sample's volume in millilitres or fluid ounces. Now divide the mass by the volume. You can use a calculator to do this equation if you wish. This will give you the rock sample's density, or specific gravity.

Natural Wonders Close to Home

When forests are cut down, the plants and animal habitats that depend on the trees in those forests are put at risk. This section focuses on the natural habitats near your home, to explore the importance of plants, insects and birds in the way nature works on Earth.

What is soil?

Soil is formed from decayed vegetable matter (dead leaves and plants), mineral grains and larger pieces of rock. Creatures, such as earthworms, help the decomposition process by mixing the soil. The process by which rocks are often broken down into smaller pieces is called weathering. Chemical weathering occurs when minerals are dissolved by water. Some minerals break down or dissolve quickly. Others, such as quartz, are not dissolved but stay behind in the soil as stones. The action of burrowing animals, insects and growing plants is called physical weathering. Attrition (grinding down) is another kind of physical weathering and it occurs when wind-blown particles rub against each other. This kind of weathering occurs mainly in dry areas, such as deserts. You can see how attrition works, simply by shaking some sugar cubes together in a glass jar.

In the first experiment, you can examine what makes up the soil. The second shows you the range of sizes of mineral and rock particles in a soil sample. In the last project, you can find out how sediments form in rivers, lakes, and seas. First large, and then finer, particles of sediment are deposited.

▲ On the horizon
Soil occurs in layers, called horizons. There are four main horizons. The top horizon (also known as topsoil) is a layer of fine particles that supports the roots of plants and trees. The next two layers, beneath the topsoil, have larger soil particles. The bottom layer is partly solid rock.

Wormery

1 Cut the top off the large, clear plastic bottle, as shown. Place the smaller bottle inside the larger one. Make sure the gap is evenly spaced all the way around the smaller bottle.

2 Fill the gap with layers of soil and sand to within 5cm/2in of the top. Press the soil down lightly. Gently place the worms on top of the soil, and cover them with rotting leaves.

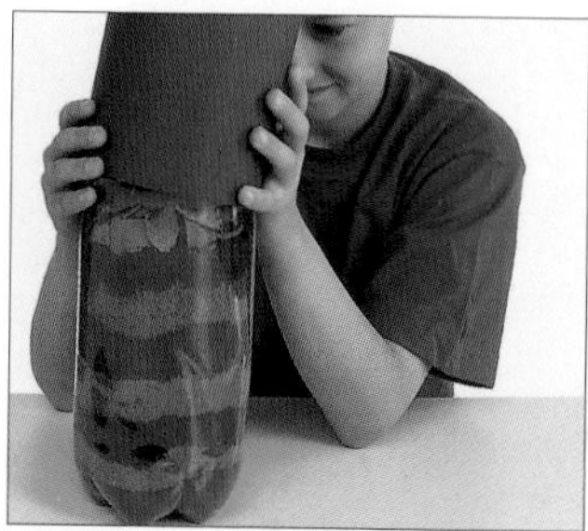

3 Cover the sides with black paper. Keep the soil moist. After a few days, remove the paper to see how the worms have tunneled away and dragged leaves into their burrows.

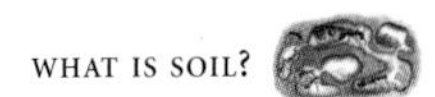

What is in soil?

1 Put on a pair of gardening gloves and place a trowel full of soil into the strainer. Shake the strainer over a piece of paper for about a minute or so.

2 Tap the side of the strainer gently, to help separate the different parts of the soil. Are there chunks that will not go through the strainer? Can you see if any of the chunks are rock?

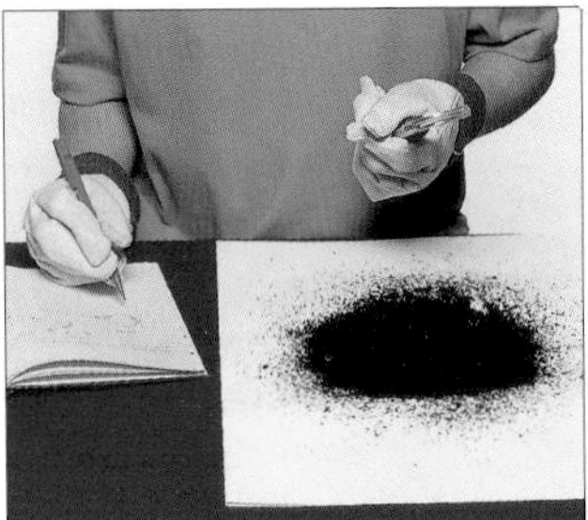

3 Use a magnifying glass to examine the soil particles that fall on to the paper. Are there any small creatures or mineral grains? Make a note of what you see in your notebook.

YOU WILL NEED

Wormery: Large and small plastic bottles, scissors, funnel, gloves, damp soil, sand, six worms, rotting leaves, black paper, adhesive tape.

What is in soil?: Gloves, trowel, soil, strainer, paper, magnifying glass, notebook, pen.

Big or small?: Scissors, large clear plastic bottle, wooden spoon, gravel, earth, sand, water, jug (pitcher).

Big or small?

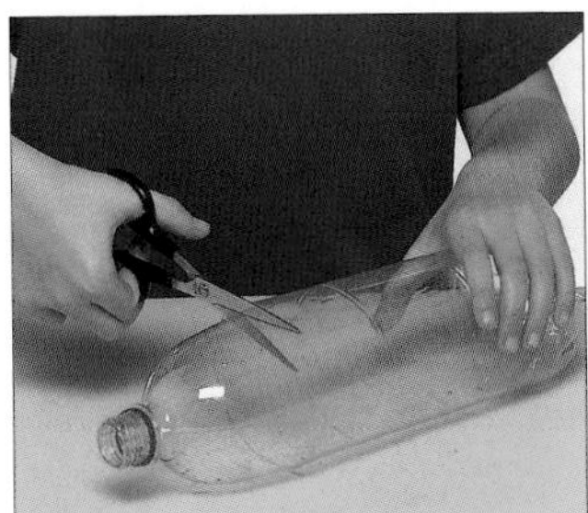

1 Use a pair of scissors to cut the top off a large, clear plastic bottle. Ask an adult to help, if you need to. You can recycle the top part of the bottle.

2 Use a spoon to scoop some gravel, earth and sand into the bottom of the bottle. Add water to the mixture, until it nearly reaches to the top of the bottle.

3 Stir vigorously to mix the stones, earth and sand with the water. In a river, soil and rock particles are mixed together and carried along by the moving water.

Leave the mixture to settle. You should find that the particles settle into different layers, with the heaviest particles at the bottom, and the lightest at the top.

Examining soil

Beneath the ground, the soil teems with life. Worms, slugs, millipedes and beetles live there, feeding on decaying matter. Tiny living creatures, called decomposers, break down everything that remains. Decomposers include microscopic bacteria, fungi, woodlice, mites and small insects. They digest organic material such as dead animals, leaves and plants, and break it down into nutrients. This process, called decomposition, creates a rich fertilizer for plants growing in the soil. As organic material rots, its nutrients or goodness are returned to the soil. The nutrients dissolve in rain water and trickle down to tree and other plant roots below.

The first experiment demonstrates the best conditions for decomposing plants. It shows that plant material decays quickest in warm, moist areas. You can take a closer look at the decomposers themselves in the second project, which shows how to separate creepy-crawlies from the rotting leaves they live in. You could repeat the experiment with leaves from a different area, and see if the insects you find are the same.

▲ Feast for woodlice
Rotting, in nature, does not happen by itself. Dead leaves are food for decomposers, such as woodlice. They eat the fallen leaves and pass many of the nutrients back into the soil, to be taken up again by the trees' roots.

Watching decay in the soil

YOU WILL NEED

Gardening gloves, trowel (optional), two clean plastic containers, soil, dead leaves, water in a watering can, one container lid.

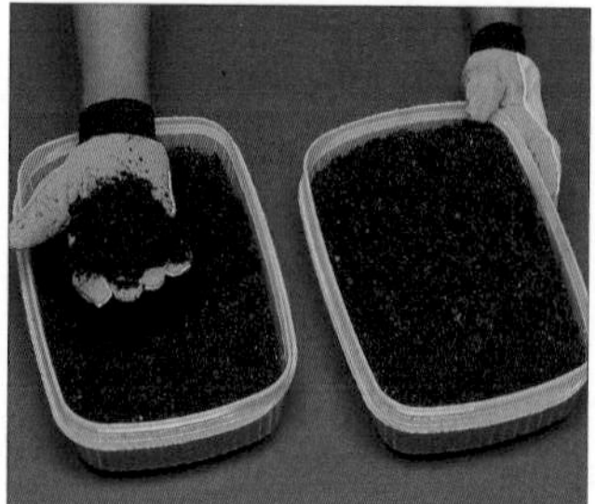

1 Be sure to wear a pair of gardening gloves for this project. Use your hand, or a trowel if you prefer, to fill two plastic containers with plenty of dry soil.

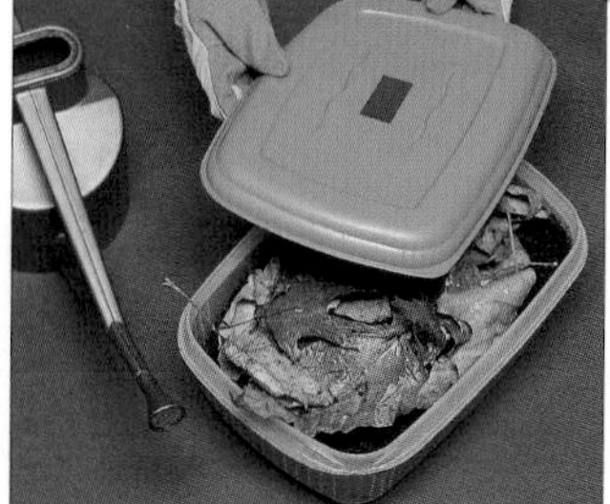

2 Put a layer of dead leaves on top of the soil in one of the containers. Water the leaves and soil thoroughly, then press the lid on to the container to cover it.

3 Place a layer of leaves on the dry soil in the other container. Do not water it and do not cover the container. Store both containers in a dry place.

After a few weeks, the leaves in the wet soil (*above left*) will have begun to rot, and those in the dry soil (*above right*) will have shrivelled.

Studying decomposers

YOU WILL NEED
Plastic funnel, large clear jar, gloves, rotting leaves from a compost heap, black paper, adhesive tape, desk lamp, magnifying glass, field guide.

1 Rotting leaves are covered in insects and other creepy-crawlies. You can separate them by using a lamp, a funnel and a large jar. Put the funnel inside the jar, as shown.

2 Wearing a pair of gardening gloves, loosely fill the funnel with rotting leaves. Tape a sheet of black paper around the sides of the jar to block out the light.

3 Place the lamp so that it shines on the leaves. The creatures will move away from the heat and the light of the lamp, and fall down the slippery funnel into the jar below.

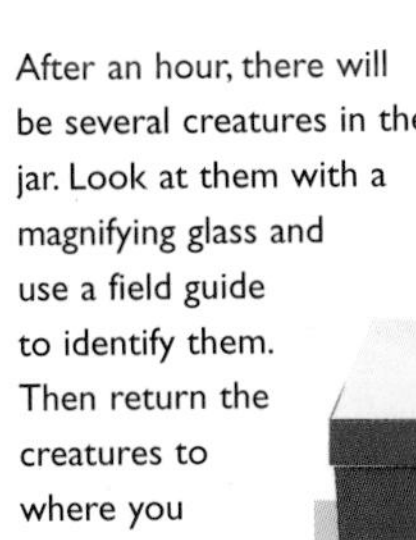

After an hour, there will be several creatures in the jar. Look at them with a magnifying glass and use a field guide to identify them. Then return the creatures to where you found them.

Tree study

There are several kinds of trees. In tropical rainforests, where it is warm and wet all year, most trees are evergreen and keep their leaves the entire year. Tropical rainforests are found near the Equator, where there is little difference between the seasons. In countries with a temperate (moderate) climate, deciduous, broad-leaved trees shed their leaves in fall. Losing leaves reduces evaporation. This helps the tree conserve energy and water when the ground water is frozen, and reduces damage by frost.

Trees can be identified by looking at such characteristics as bark, leaves and flowers, and in fall by their fruits and nuts, some of which are shown on the right. The size and shape of the trunk and branches can also help to identify a tree, and scientists record the tree's girth by measuring the distance around the trunk at chest height. You can study trees in your backyard, a local park or the wood following the same checks. Choose an area of mixed woodland with many different trees. Always take an adult with you to keep you safe.

leaf from a plane tree

seedcase from a sycamore tree

hips and leaves from a cockspur thorn tree

a chestnut and its case from a horse chestnut tree

seeds from a lime tree

acorn and its cup from an oak tree

Identifying trees

1 Walk along a path in a park or in the woods. Try to identify the trees you find there from their general height and shape. Use a field guide on trees to help you.

2 Bark can help you identify some trees. Silver birch bark is smooth and white with dark cracks. Match the bark of different trees with pictures in your guide.

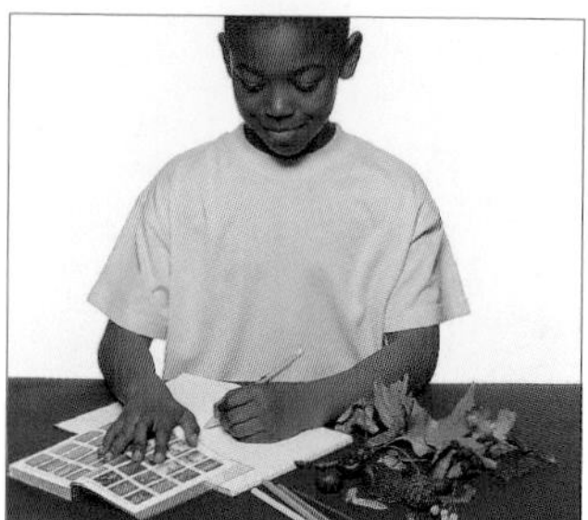

3 Study leaf tones and shapes, and the fruits and seeds of trees. Learn to identify trees with the help of the field guide, and make a record of them in a notebook.

Measuring a tree's height

YOU WILL NEED

Identifying trees: Field guide to local trees, notebook, pen, coloured pencils.

Measuring a tree's height: Long ruler, 1m/1yd-long stick, felt-tipped pen.

1 With the long ruler, measure 19m/19yd from the tree and push the stick into the ground. Measure another 1m/1yd from the stick and lie down straight on the ground.

2 Use one eye to line up the top of the tree with the stick. Get a friend to mark this point on the stick in the ground. The height of the tree is 20 times this distance.

Measuring a tree's girth

YOU WILL NEED

Adhesive tape, string, long ruler or tape measure, pen, notebook, coloured pencils, graph paper, field guide.

1 Stick a piece of adhesive tape on the end of a piece of string. Wrap the string around a tree trunk at chest height. Mark where it meets the tape with your finger.

2 Lay the string along the long ruler to find the length. This number is the girth of the tree. Measure another tree of the same species. Is its girth the same? Why might they differ?

3 Make a chart with drawings of the different trees that you have measured. The trees with the thickest trunks are usually older than those with slender trunks.

▲ **Rings of age**

You can clearly see the growth rings on the trunk of this old oak tree. Each year, the tree grows a new ring of wood just under the bark.

Looking at bark

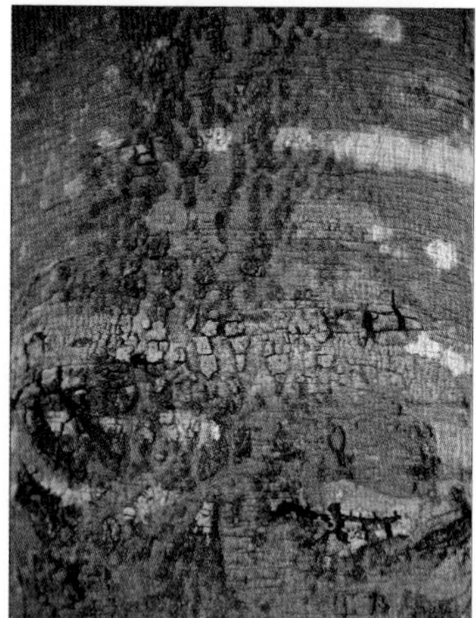

▲ **Close-up view**
If you look closely at the bark of a tree, you can discover many clues about its life. Plants and fungi may be clinging to the surface. There might also be insects and other tiny creatures hiding inside cracks...

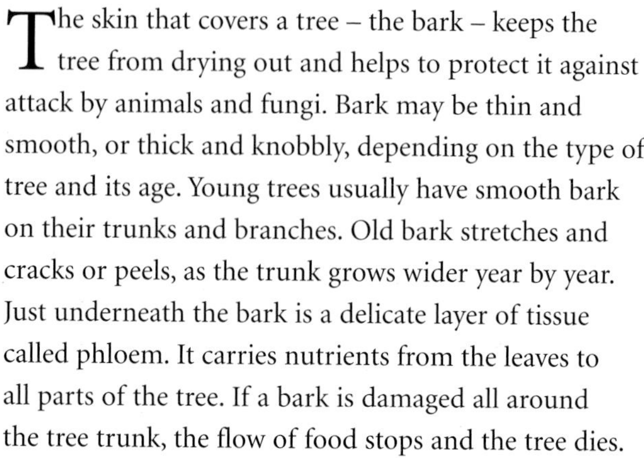

The skin that covers a tree – the bark – keeps the tree from drying out and helps to protect it against attack by animals and fungi. Bark may be thin and smooth, or thick and knobbly, depending on the type of tree and its age. Young trees usually have smooth bark on their trunks and branches. Old bark stretches and cracks or peels, as the trunk grows wider year by year. Just underneath the bark is a delicate layer of tissue called phloem. It carries nutrients from the leaves to all parts of the tree. If a bark is damaged all around the tree trunk, the flow of food stops and the tree dies.

The appearance of the bark can help you decide what species (type) a tree is. Different trees have different kinds of bark. A mature beech tree has smooth, thin bark that is about 1cm/½in deep. A redwood tree of the same size has hairy, fibrous bark that is up to 15cm/6in thick. Many conifers, such as pines and spruces, have bark that flakes off. Follow the first two projects and become a bark detective, by studying the bark up close and making a collection of your own bark rubbings. The third project will help you estimate the size of a tree.

YOU WILL NEED
Magnifying glass, field guide, notebook, pencil.

Become a bark detective

1 Bark does not stretch, but cracks and peels as a tree grows. Use a magnifying glass to search in the cracks during the spring and summer for tiny insects and other creatures.

2 The bark has fallen away from this dead tree, revealing the holes chewed by beetle grubs underneath. Some grubs live under the bark for several years.

3 Where the bark is damp, you will often find powdery green patches. These are millions of microscopic plants called algae, which live side by side on the bark's surface.

Bark rubbing book

YOU WILL NEED
Paper, wax crayons, pencil, thin green card, bradawl or hole puncher, ribbon, adhesive.

1 Ask a friend to hold a sheet of paper steady against the bark. Rub the side of a crayon over the paper with long, even strokes. Write the name of the tree beside each rubbing.

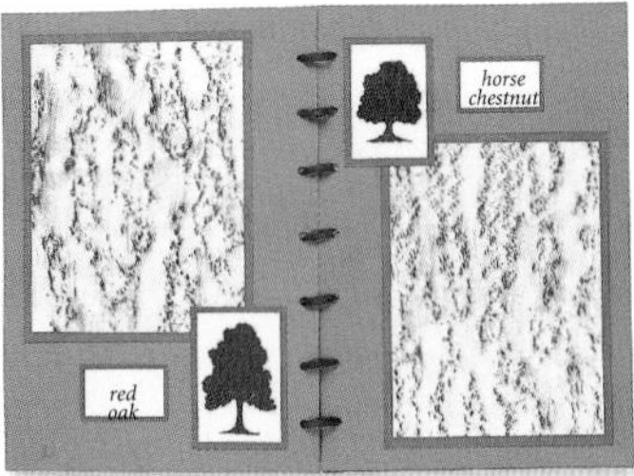

2 Punch holes into pieces of green card and bind them together with ribbon. Stick your rubbings on to each page. You could include a silhouette of each tree, too.

Measuring the crown

YOU WILL NEED
Compass, marker, long ruler, graph paper, ruler, coloured pencils.

1 Using the compass, walk away from the tree toward north. Ask a friend to call out when you reach the edge of the area covered by the leaves. Place a marker at this point.

2 Repeat for the other seven main compass directions (NE, E, SE, S, SW, W, NW). Measure the distances back to the trunk with a long ruler and note them down.

3 Plot your results on a piece of graph paper. Measure 1cm/½in on the paper for each metre/yard on the ground. Draw lines from the middle of the paper, for each compass direction.

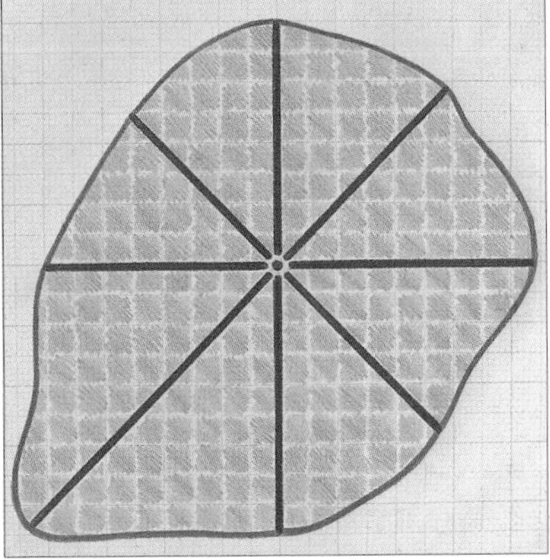

What you have sketched and filled in shows the shape of the area covered by trees leaves and branches (the crown). Count the squares and half squares to find the size of the area of the crown. Do not count part-squares if they are less than a half. Each 1cm/½in square represents 1m/1yd. Compare with other trees in the area. Generally, the older the tree, the more likely it will have a larger crown.

Specimen collection

Different kinds of trees grow naturally in different parts of the world. Where they grow depends mainly on climate. Look closely at trees in winter and you will see that even deciduous trees are not completely bare. Each twig has buds along its sides and at the tip. Buds have protective skins with tiny immature leaves and stems curled up inside. When spring sunshine warms the trees, buds begin to grow and swell. Finally, they burst open and small leaves emerge. Leaves contain pipes called veins. Water pumps into these veins, making the leaves stiffen and flatten as they grow to full size.

To learn about trees, you can make a collection of dead leaves, cones and bark from each one you study. Do not forget to look for things throughout the year – flowers and buds in spring, seeds and fruit in the fall. Label your collection.

YOU WILL NEED

Tree specimens (leaves, cones, bark chips), heavy books, kitchen paper, glue, notebook, field guide, magnifying glass, shoe box, pieces of thin card.

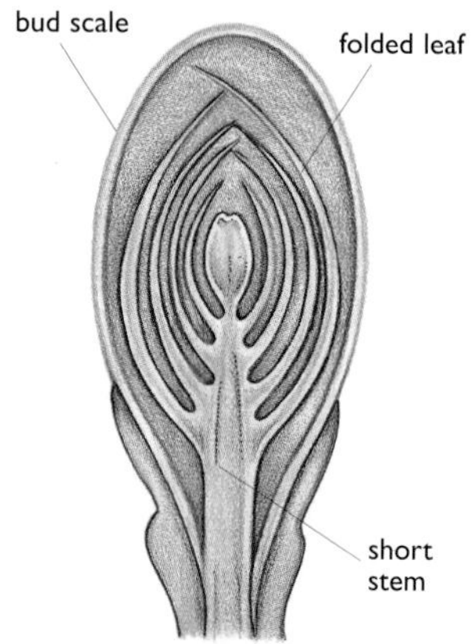

▲ Budding
Buds grow in the middle of a twig between two leaf stems. An unopened bud contains tiny leaves, and a shoot that will grow in spring and make the leaf stem longer. The illustration above shows what it looks like inside.

Tree zones

Evergreen conifer trees, such as pine and firs, usually grow where the climate is cold. Long, snowy winters are followed by short, cool summers, with moderate amounts of rain. Forests of conifers grow in a band across North America, Europe and Asia.

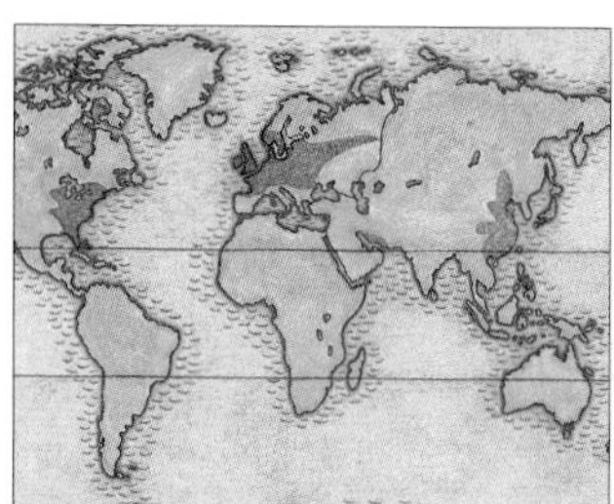

Broad-leaved deciduous trees, such as oak, ash, and maple, grow in temperate climates away from hot, dry tropics or the snowy poles. There are more kinds of trees than in a coniferous forest. Temperate forests are found in North America, Europe, Asia and New Zealand.

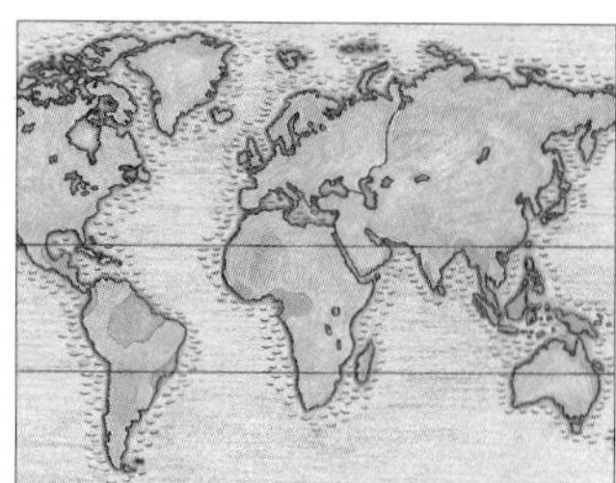

Tropical countries lie close to the Equator. The weather is hot, and daylight lasts for 12 hours a day for most of the year. Dense rainforests grow where heavy rain falls almost continuously, such as South America, Africa, Asia and Australasia.

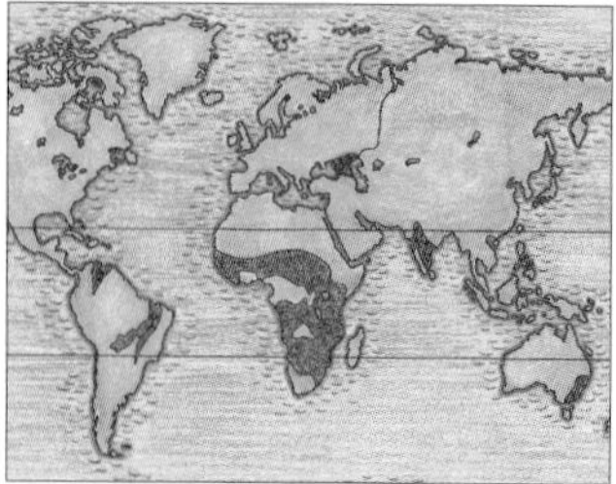

Savanna is a dry, tropical grassland, with some shrubs and bushes. Trees grow alone, or in widely spaced small groups. Forests cannot grow because the dry season lasts most of the year. Trees that do grow here are species that can survive for long periods without water.

Collecting specimens

1 How many different leaves and cones can you find? Make sure you note down the name of the tree that each specimen comes from. Start a collection with your friends.

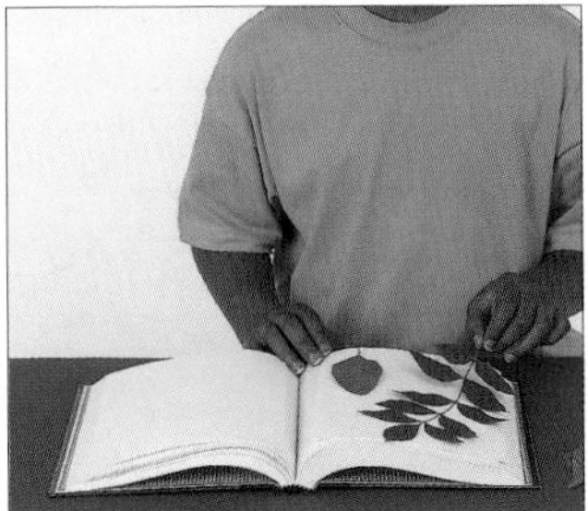

2 To dry and flatten your leaves, place sheets of kitchen paper between the pages of a large and heavy book. Lay your leaves out on the paper on one side only. Close the book.

3 Pile more books on top. Make sure the pile cannot topple over and will not get disturbed. The weight presses the leaves flat, and the kitchen paper absorbs moisture.

4 Wait for at least one month, until the leaves are flat and dry. Glue them into your notebook, or on to sheets of thick paper, and make them into a book. Use a field guide to identify each leaf.

5 For bark specimens, only collect bark from dead trees that have fallen over. You can make bark rubbings from living trees. See page 81 for instructions on how to make rubbings.

6 Springtime flowers soon wither and die. These young horse chestnuts will last much longer. It is better to take photographs of flowers, rather than pick them.

7 You can look at young cones and leaves from the lowest branches of evergreen pines, firs and cedars. Look under these trees for cones that have fallen.

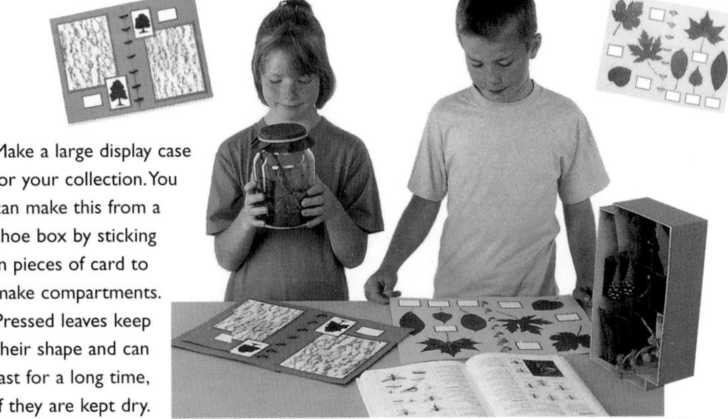

Make a large display case for your collection. You can make this from a shoe box by sticking in pieces of card to make compartments. Pressed leaves keep their shape and can last for a long time, if they are kept dry.

How plants grow

All plants need water to live. They do not take in food as animals do, but make their own using water from the ground, and carbon dioxide gas from the air. Water is absorbed through a plant's roots. It travels up through the stem or trunk into the leaves, shoots, and flowers. The water also carries the nutrients from the soil to all parts of the plant. In the leaves, nutrients and water are used for photosynthesis, the process of making energy from light. Excess water not needed by the plant evaporates back into the air in the form of water vapour in a process called transpiration. You can see how much water vapour is transpired by a plant in the first experiment.

When a seed begins to grow, we say that it has germinated. Germination occurs when conditions are warm and moist enough for the seed to swell and split its skin. A tiny root grows downward, and a thin shoot pushes upwards toward the light. The second project shows you how to germinate a seed and help it grow into a tree. Germinating a seed in this way takes about two months.

leaves absorb carbon dioxide and release oxygen though tiny holes on their undersides

energy is absorbed from the Sun on the top sides of the leaves

chlorophyll in leaves combines carbon dioxide gas and water to make glucose and oxygen

roots take in water and minerals

▲ Converting energy
Photosynthesis is the process through which plants use the water in the ground and the energy in sunlight to make their food. Leaves take in carbon dioxide and water to make oxygen and glucose (sugar). Glucose flows to all parts of the plant, supplying energy for growth. Oxygen gas escapes through the holes on the underside of the leaves. The oxygen is released back into the air. We need oxygen to breathe.

Survival in the wetlands ▸
Swamps are places where the ground is permanently waterlogged, such as in muddy river estuaries. Most trees cannot survive in swamps, because they need fresh water and air around their roots. Some types of mangroves have breathing roots that grow upwards, so that their tips are above the surface of the water. Mangrove swamps are home to kingfishers, giant water bugs, crabs, turtles, crocodiles and mudskippers, a type of fish that spends much of its time out of water.

Evaporation in action

YOU WILL NEED

Evaporation in action: House plant, watering can, clear plastic bag, adhesive tape, scissors.

Germinate an acorn: 10cm/4in (diameter) flower pot, soil mix, gloves, acorns or another tree's seeds, trowel, watering can.

1 Water the house plant well using a watering can. Water the plant at the base, so the roots can draw the water up. If you water the plant from the top, water just the soil, not the plant itself.

2 Place a large, transparent plastic bag over the plant, taking care not to damage the leaves. Tape the bag tightly around the pot. Leave the plant overnight.

◂ **Floating water**

Trees pass millions of litres/gallons of water vapour into the air each day. The vapour forms thick clouds of tiny water droplets over the forest.

3 Look at the plant the next day. Inside the bag, water vapour given off by the plant turns back into water. The air inside is warm and moist, like the air in a rainforest.

Germinate an acorn

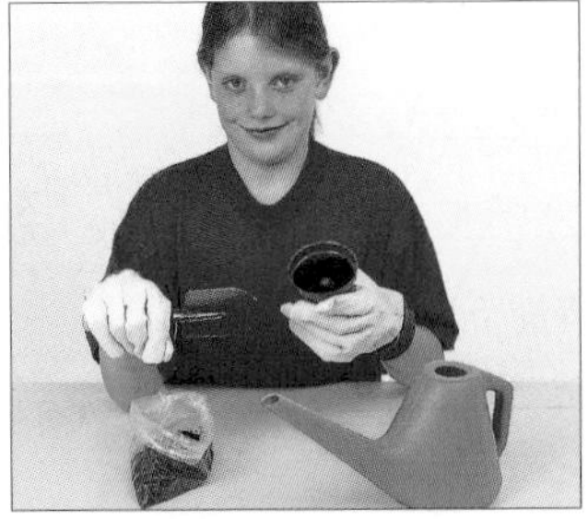

1 Fill the flower pot with soil mix and bury an acorn just beneath the surface. Put it in a warm place and keep the soil moist. Plant several acorns, since one may not germinate.

2 When a tiny tree starts to grow by itself, it is called a seedling. It needs light and regular watering to grow well. Do not soak the soil with water, or the roots will rot and die.

3 Your seedling should grow rapidly for a few weeks and then stop. During the winter, it will need little water. In the spring, you can take the seedling out of its pot and plant it outside.

Reaching for light

Look at a leaf and you will see that the top side is usually greener than the underside. This is because there is more chlorophyll, a green substance that traps energy from sunlight. Plants cannot move around to find food as animals do. Instead, they make their own. The green cells work like tiny solar panels, using sunlight to combine carbon dioxide gas from the air and water from the ground. The cells then produce a sugar (glucose) and oxygen gas. This process is called photosynthesis. Without light, plants cannot make their food.

Photosynthesis is the ultimate source of food on Earth, because animals eat plants or other animals that live on plants. Photosynthesis is also the source of all oxygen in our atmosphere. The projects show how plants try to reach the light. Epiphytes are special kinds of plants that do not need to grow in soil. They live on high branches in the rainforests to get closer to the light.

▲ **Catching the rays**
Trees spread their leaves widely to absorb as much energy as they can from sunlight. They use the energy to make a sugary substance called glucose. Liquids flow in and out of leaves through veins. Veins also act like ribs that help to stiffen the leaf and keep it flat.

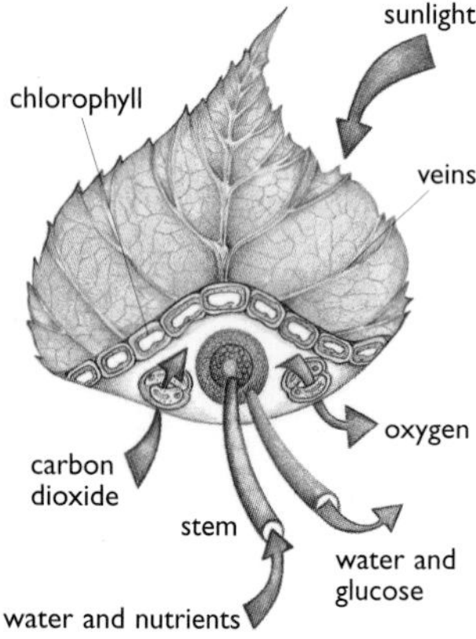

▲ **Making energy**
Photosynthesis happens near the top surface of a leaf, where sunlight has the strongest impact.

Grow your own epiphyte

1 Put on a pair of gloves to protect your hands. Wrap moss around one end of the branch or a piece of driftwood. Tie the moss securely in place with thread.

2 Pile some gravel into a sturdy plant pot, until the pot is almost full. It needs to be almost full to support the wood. You could use a trowel to help you transfer the gravel.

3 Now push the branch or driftwood down into the gravel, until it stands up in the pot without tipping it over. Use a water spray to spray the moss with water.

4 Arrange the epiphytes (available from garden stores) by pressing them gently into the moss. A drop of glue on the base of each plant will help to hold it in place.

5 Remember to spray the epiphytes from time to time with water. You could also add a few drops of liquid plant food, to help the epiphytes to grow.

Epiphytes grow well indoors and make an unusual display. They do not need soil to grow. Instead, they wrap their roots around a branch.

Searching for the light

YOU WILL NEED

Grow your own epiphyte: Garden gloves, sphagnum moss, branch or driftwood, thread, gravel, plant pot, trowel, water spray, epiphytes, glue, liquid plant food.

Searching for the light: Shoe box, scissors, cardboard, tape, black paint, paintbrush, garden gloves, runner (green) bean, plant pot, soil mix, water.

1 Watch a plant search for the light as it grows, by making a maze. Cut a hole in the end of a shoe box and stick eight flaps of cardboard inside with adhesive tape, as shown here.

2 Paint the inside of the box and lid black all over. The black paint will stop the light that enters through the hole from being reflected around inside the box.

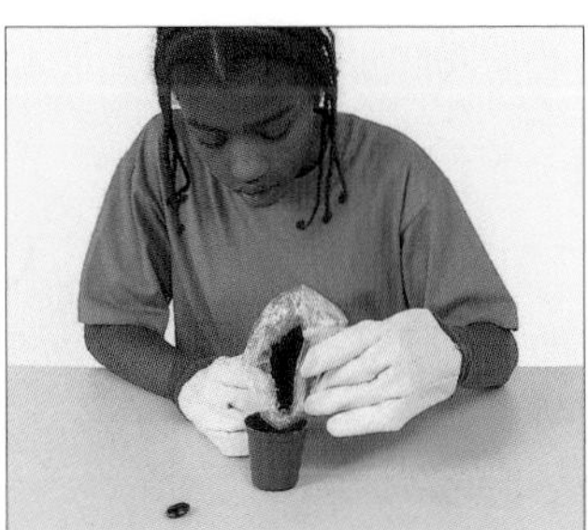

3 Wearing gloves, plant a runner bean in a small pot of soil mix. Water the soil each day to keep it moist, but not too wet. On some days, no water may be needed.

4 When the plant has a shoot, stand it at the bottom of your maze. Close the lid and place the maze in a sunny spot. Once a day, remove the lid to see if the seedling needs watering.

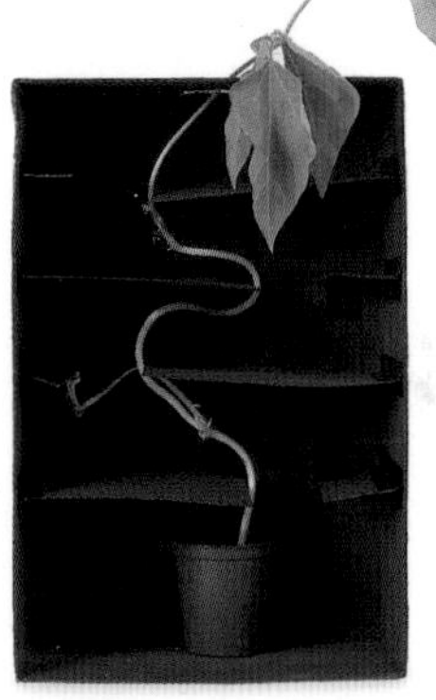

The plant will find its way through the maze as it steadily moves toward the light. Eventually, it will poke out through the hole at the top of the shoe box.

Natural water pumps

When you look at a tree, you only see a part of it. Unseen roots spread out underground as wide as the branches above. These roots anchor a tree in the ground and hold it up against the force of the wind. Roots also help the tree to grow, by taking up water and nutrients from the soil through the trunk to the leaves. Trees act like a natural pump – many trees over 50m/165ft tall pump hundreds of litres/gallons of water a day in order to grow. You can suck a drink up through a straw, but trees cannot do this. They use a method called osmosis to draw the water upwards. The first experiment shows how osmosis works. Water inside the roots (sap) has a higher concentration of sugar than the water outside. The process of osmosis draws water from the soil, where the concentration is low, to inside the root, where concentration is high.

The second experiment uses dyed water to show how water actually travels up a plant's root. All living things are made up of little units called cells. Water can travel through cell walls but sugars cannot. During osmosis, water always moves in a set direction – from the side where there is less sugar dissolved in it to the side where there is more.

▲ **Suck it and see**
To find out how difficult it is to suck up water, carefully tape together straws with adhesive tape. The longer the straw, the more difficult it is for you to suck up the drink. The best mechanical pumps can only manage 10m/30ft.

How osmosis works

YOU WILL NEED
Large potato, ruler, chopping board, peeler, knife, teaspoon, two shallow dishes, water, sugar.

1 You will need a large, smooth potato about 10cm/4in long and 6cm/2½in across. Carefully peel the potato on a chopping board to protect the work surface.

2 Cut the peeled potato in half, and then slice off the rounded ends. You will now have two round potato slices. Each slice should be about 3cm/1½in thick.

3 Use a teaspoon to scoop out a hollow in each potato slice. Place each slice in its own shallow dish and fill the dishes with water to about 1cm/1½in in depth.

4 Half fill both hollows with water. Add 2.5ml/½ tsp of sugar to one hollow. Cover and leave the potatoes for one day. (*Dye has been added to the water here to make it show up.*)

5 The level of liquid in the sugary hollow has risen. Osmosis has made more water move into this potato from the dish. The level in the other potato has not risen.

Osmosis in action

YOU WILL NEED

Water, two tall drinking glasses, water-soluble ink or food dye, white carnation, scissors, adhesive tape.

1 Pour some water into two tall drinking glasses. Add a few drops of ink or food dye to one of the glasses to give the water a strong, bright hue.

2 Use scissors to split the stem of the carnation lengthwise to about half way up the stem. Bind the stem with adhesive tape, so that it does not split any further.

3 Place the glasses side by side on a window sill, and stand one half of the stem in each glass. Lean the flower against the window if it will not stand up on its own.

4 After a few hours, check to see what has happened. One half of the flower will be tinted with the dye. The other half of the flower will have remained white.

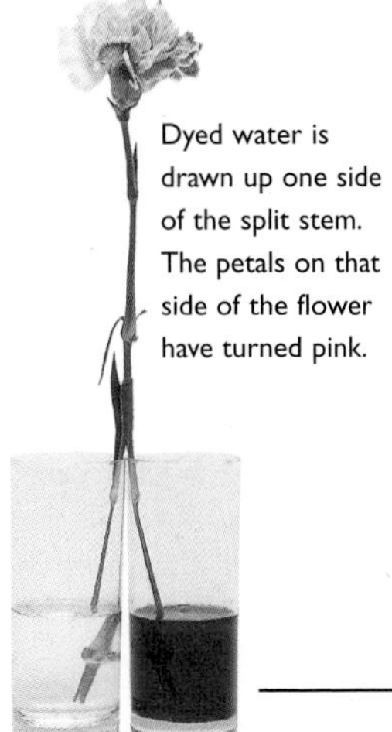

Dyed water is drawn up one side of the split stem. The petals on that side of the flower have turned pink.

Seeds and plant life

Most plants reproduce by making seeds, which sprout and grow into new plants. To produce seeds, plants must be fertilized by pollen, usually from another plant of the same species (kind). Many plants rely on insects, such as bees and butterflies, to spread pollen. Seeds are mostly spread by animals that eat the fruit produced by plants, and by the wind. In some plants, such as those in rainforests, seeds may also be carried by water. The plants in your local area disperse (spread) their seeds in these ways, too. In the company of an adult, you can survey the seeds and plants in the local woods.

YOU WILL NEED

Eight pegs, long ruler or tape measure, string, field guide, pen, notebook, coloured pencils and pens, graph paper.

Performing a plant survey

1 Choose a patch of ground to sample and put in a peg. Measure 1m/1yd with the ruler, and put in another peg. Stretch and tie a piece of string between the pegs.

2 Now measure the remaining sides, pushing in two more pegs and stretching and tying string between them to mark out one square metre/yard.

3 Measure and mark the midpoint of each piece of stretched string with pegs. Stretch more string between these pegs to divide the square into quarters.

4 Use your field guide to help you to identify the plant species growing in each quarter of the square. Do different plants, or the same ones, grow in each area?

5 Draw a chart on graph paper to record each plant's position. Use different colours for each plant type that you found. Add up the total number of each type of plant.

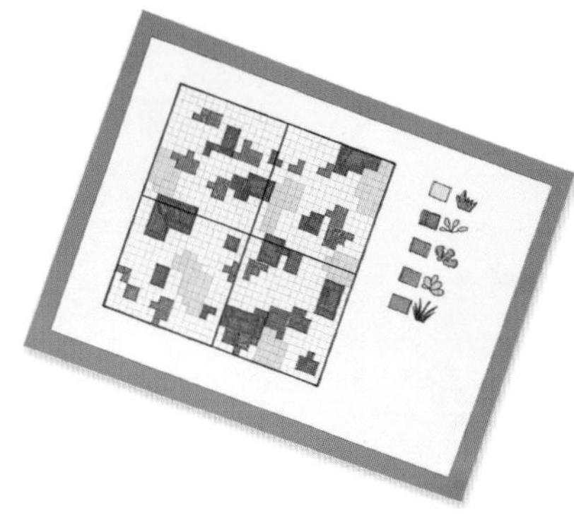

Looking at seed dispersal

YOU WILL NEED

Field guide, collecting pot, thin white fabric, rubber band, notebook, pencil, coloured pencils.

1 Look for nibbled nuts and acorns. These seeds provide food for many animals. Collect seeds in a pot, cover them with fabric and secure with a rubber band.

2 Visit your local pond or stream to find seeds, such as alders, that are dispersed by water. Use your field guide to identify any seeds you see floating on the water.

3 Maple and sycamore trees have light seeds with wings. As they fall, the wings spin the seed through the air, helping it to fly farther and germinate far from the parent tree.

4 Find a dandelion head. Plants such as dandelions have very light seeds, each with its own small parachute of fine threads. These are carried away by the wind.

5 Look for the seed capsules of poppies. They are like pepper shakers with hundreds of tiny seeds inside. As the wind shakes the capsule, the seeds pop out and scatter widely.

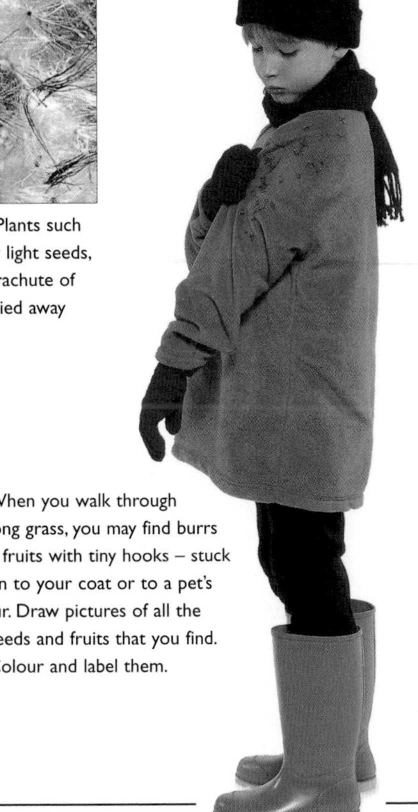

When you walk through long grass, you may find burrs – fruits with tiny hooks – stuck on to your coat or to a pet's fur. Draw pictures of all the seeds and fruits that you find. Colour and label them.

Growing from fruit

There are many kinds of fruits grown in the garden. Some fruits are soft, such as apples and oranges, and others are hard, such as acorns and walnuts. Even tough little hawthorn berries and sycamore wings are fruits. Fruits all have seeds protected inside a container. The container may be the soft flesh of a plum or the hard shell of a hazelnut. You can discover the seeds inside different fruits. Some examples are given here. If you want to try others, use fruits bought from your local grocery store, since some wild berries are poisonous.

YOU WILL NEED
Looking at apple seeds: Apple, chopping board, sharp knife, tweezers, magnifying glass.
Looking inside a nut: Hazelnuts, nutcracker, scissors, magnifying glass.
How a seed grows: Blotting paper or newspaper, jar, broad (fava) bean or runner (green) bean seed, water.
Tropical seeds: Avocado pit, three toothpicks, jar, water, gloves, pot, trowel, soil mix.

◂ Soft fruits
These fruits are soft, fleshy, and sweet. Like most fruits, they have grown from the reproductive ovaries inside female flowers. Open any fruit, and inside you will find seeds.

Looking at apple seeds

1 Cut open an apple with a sharp knife. Inside you will find several brown seeds in the middle. Use the tweezers to remove as many of the seeds as you want.

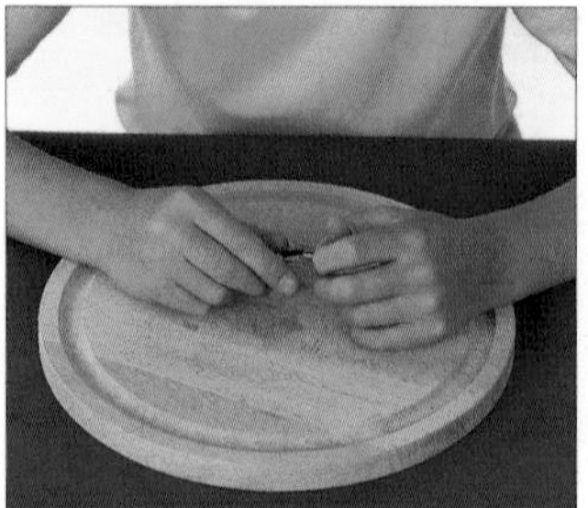

2 Use the tweezers to carefully remove the soft outer skin of a seed. Underneath the skin, you will find the slippery white seed. Treat it carefully – it is very delicate.

3 Look through a magnifying glass to see the embryo (at the tip). The rest of the seed is the cotyledon, which provides food so the embryo will grow into a new root and shoot.

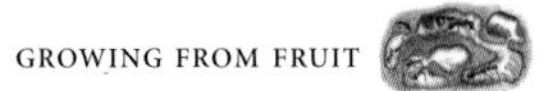

Looking inside a nut

1 Nuts are fruits that have their seeds inside a hard shell. Carefully crack open a hazelnut with a pair of nutcrackers, and look for the nut kernel (seed) inside.

2 Use scissors to scrape off the dark outer skin from the kernel. You should then be able to separate the white hazelnut into two halves. Look at these with a magnifying glass.

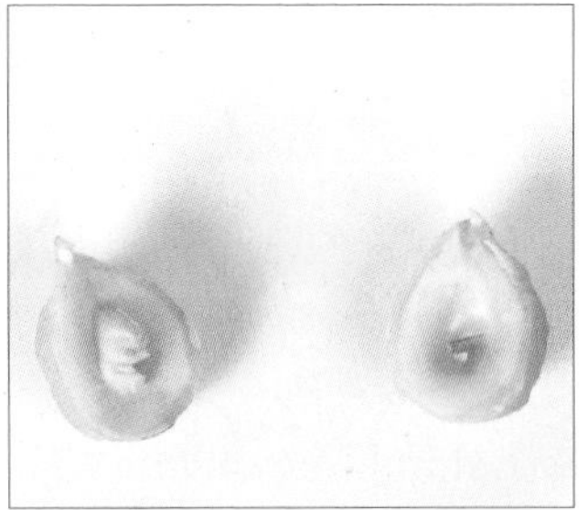

3 Inside the nut is a tiny embryo. This part grows into roots and a stem. The two larger parts are the cotyledons, which supply energy for the sprouting seed to grow.

How a seed grows

1 Curl blotting paper inside a jar. Push a bean seed halfway down between the paper and the glass. Add water to a depth of 2cm/¾in and stand the jar in a light, warm place.

2 When the seed germinates, you will see the root growing downwards. Turn the jar so that the root points to the right. What do you think will happen?

As the root continues to grow, it changes direction so that it is growing downwards again.

Tropical seeds

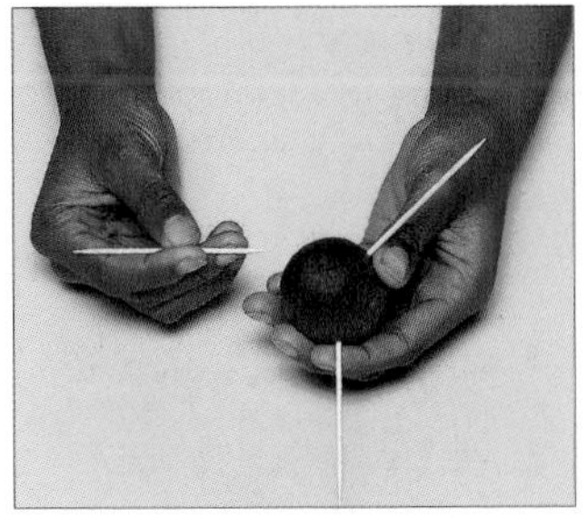

1 An avocado pit is the seed of the avocado plant. Clean off any flesh left on the pit, and then carefully push three toothpicks into the pit, as shown above.

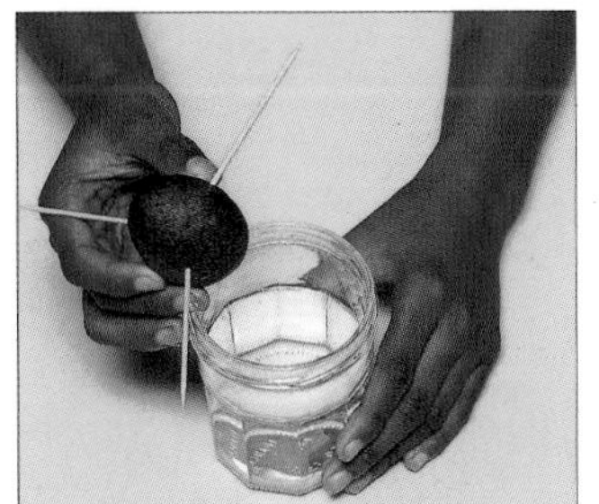

2 Fill a glass jar with water and suspend the pit, so that it just touches the waterline. Keep the jar in a warm, shady place, and top up the water regularly.

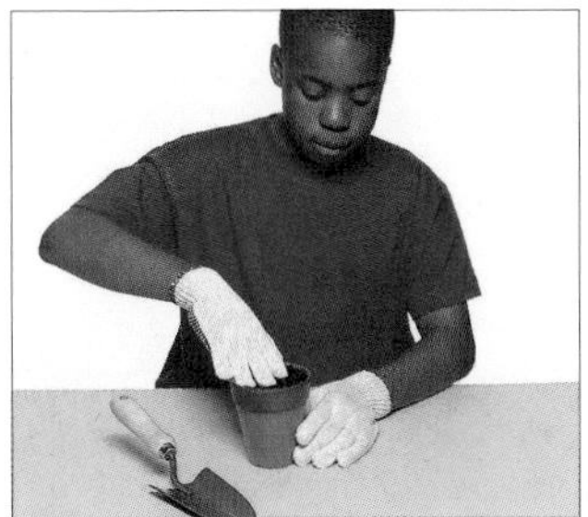

3 When roots begin to grow downwards, plant the pit in a pot filled with soil mix. Place the pot where the air is warm and humid, and wait for your seedling to grow.

Life in the forest

People who live in forests build their homes from materials found in the forest. In South America, the Yanomami tribe's large, round huts are made with trees bent into a dome shape, lashed with vines and thatched with palm leaves. The Yanomami sleep on the roof in hammocks made of woven grasses, slung from the rafters. Scientists who work in rainforests sometimes build temporary shelters with branches. You can build a shelter by following these instructions, but you may need the help of an adult. When looking for branches to make your shelter with, take an adult with you. Collect the branches from your backyard or a public area. Do not cut them from trees – always gather them from the ground, where they have fallen naturally.

YOU WILL NEED

Five sturdy branches, rope or thick string, a friend or adult to help, ropes or strings, eight pegs, tarpaulin, ground sheet, two poles.

▲ **Temperate forests**
Beech, ash and oak grow in this northern European forest. Birds and squirrels live in the trees. Bluebells and wood anemones grow on the forest floor. Worms, moles and badgers burrow underground. Larger animals include deer, wild pigs and bears.

▲ **Conifer forests**
Hemlocks, cypresses and giant redwoods grow in conifer forests in North America. Woodpeckers and chipmunks search for food in the trees. Ferns grow on the forest floor. Moose and beavers live near lakes, and black bears scavenge for food.

▲ **Trees in the savanna**
The African savanna is dotted with drought-resistant trees, such as baobabs (bottle trees) and acacias. Herds of zebra, antelope and gazelles feed on grass. Taller giraffes and elephants can reach up into the trees for fresh leaves.

▲ **Tropical rainforest**
Many trees and climbing plants live in tropical rainforests, such as the Amazon of South America. Monkeys and bright birds live high up in the trees, where there is light and food. Dense, rotting vegetation covers the ground.

Build a shelter

1 Lash the ends of two sturdy branches together with rope or string. Stand the branches upright to make an A-frame. You could tie the A-frame to a tree for extra support.

2 Lash two more branches together. Stand them upright about 2m/6¼ft from the first A-frame. Place a lighter branch on top to make a ridge pole and lash it in place.

3 Attach two ropes or strings to each of the A-frames and peg the ropes securely into the ground. Now throw a tarpaulin over the ridge pole to form the roof.

4 Attach some ropes or strings to the eyeholes in the corners of the tarpaulin, and peg them securely into the ground. Stretch the tarpaulin tight to make the roof.

5 Thread string through the eyeholes on opposite sides of the ground sheet, to make the sheet into a sort of tube. Push two poles inside the sheet, one on each side.

6 Pull the two poles apart to make a stretcher shape that will fit inside the shelter. This will form the hammock, so that you will be able to rest off the ground.

7 Wedge the stretcher inside your shelter, so that the poles rest on the outside of the upright A-frames. Make sure your hammock is secure and will not slip down the poles.

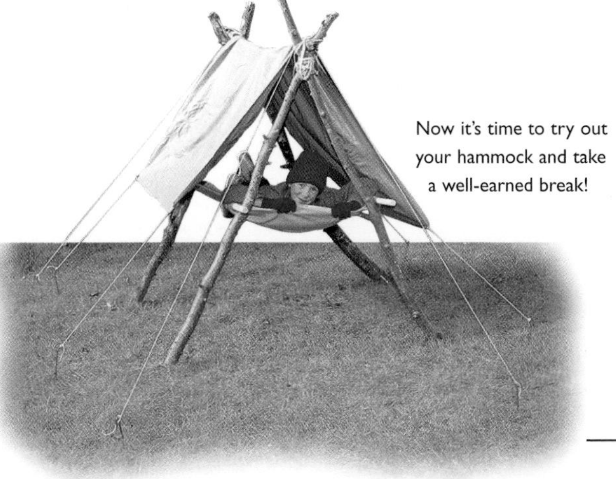

Now it's time to try out your hammock and take a well-earned break!

Soil erosion

All around the world, rainforests are being cut down at an alarming rate. At the beginning of the 1900s, tropical forests covered about twice the area they do today. Experts estimate that an area of rainforest about the size of England is lost each year. One of the main reasons for this is logging – the felling of trees for timber. Many rainforest trees are made of valuable hardwoods, such as teak and mahogany, which are used for building houses and making furniture. Trees are also cleared to create roads and new pasture for cattle.

The roots of trees and other plants help to hold forest soil together. When the trees are felled, the soil is left bare. During heavy rainfall, the earth is washed away, just as it is in the first project. However, when forests are left alone, they sustain themselves indefinitely, recycling water and nutrients from the soil. You can see how this works by growing a mini-jungle. The bottle or jar reproduces the warm, moist conditions and constant high temperatures of a rainforest. The plants recycle their own moisture, so they rarely need watering.

▲ Vanishing forests
This illustration shows the effects of deforestation. Tree roots help to hold the soil in place, and leaves absorb the force of falling rain. When forests are cut down, soil is washed away, and exposed earth dries up and hardens.

YOU WILL NEED
House plant, two plastic cups, plant pot, soil or soil mix, two watering cans.

Looking at soil erosion

1 Fit the house plant into the neck of one of the plastic cups. Fill the empty plant pot with soil or soil mix. Place the pot into the neck of the other plastic cup.

2 Pour water on to the house plant and into the pot of soil. What happens? You will find that water passes more quickly through the pot without the plant.

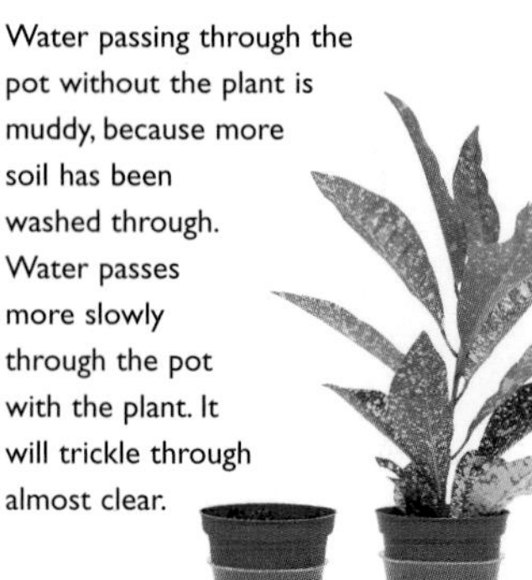

Water passing through the pot without the plant is muddy, because more soil has been washed through. Water passes more slowly through the pot with the plant. It will trickle through almost clear.

Plant a mini-jungle

YOU WILL NEED

Large plastic bottle or jar with a lid, gloves, gravel, charcoal, soil mix, spoon or trowel, small tropical plants, plant sprayer or watering can with sprinkler rose.

1 Wash your large plastic bottle or jar to make sure that it is clean. Place handfuls of gravel into the bottom of the bottle, to make the lowest layer of the mini-jungle.

2 Combine a little charcoal with the soil mix. Add a deep layer of the mixture on top of the gravel, and then smooth out the soil so that it is level.

3 Make some large holes for the plants in the soil with a spoon or trowel. Then gently lift the plants out of their pots and lower them into the holes you have made.

4 Tamp the soil down around the base of each plant. You can use a spoon or a trowel to do this, if you find it difficult to reach that far with your fingers.

5 Spray the plants and soil quite thoroughly with water from a plant sprayer, or using a watering can with a sprinkler attachment. This is your tropical rain!

6 Put the lid on the bottle or jar, and your mini-jungle is complete. The water you have sprayed is recycled inside the bottle or jar, so you will not need to water your jungle often. Moisture from the plants condenses on the sides of the bottle or jar. It will then drip down into the soil, to be reused.

The balance of life

Life on Earth is a vast jigsaw of plant and animal activity. The world can be split into vegetation regions according to the kind of plants that thrive there. Scientists often break down the vegetation regions into smaller units, such as tropical rainforests or freshwater lakes. They might go further to identify individual trees or a pond. Each unit, where the creatures living there interact with each other, is called an ecosystem.

An ecosystem is a community of living things, or organisms, that all depend on each other. An aquarium like the one in the project is a miniature freshwater ecosystem. All plants need particular conditions of soil and climate to survive. Animals also survive by adapting to, and interacting with, their surroundings and the local climate.

If a particular species from an ecosystem is removed, the existence of other living things is threatened. If the plants on which a certain caterpillar feeds are destroyed, the caterpillars die. Eventually, the birds that feed on the caterpillars, and the foxes that feed on the birds would starve.

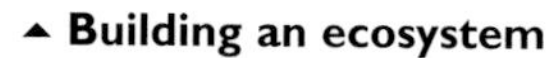

▲ Building an ecosystem
When there is enough warmth and moisture in an area of bare, rocky land, simple plants grow. The first to take hold are mosses and lichens. They are followed by tough grasses, which hold the soil together. As they die and rot, they add nutrients to the soil, preparing it for bigger plants to grow. Soon there is enough to support small shrubs and tough trees, such as pines, and eventually deciduous trees such as oaks. This process is called vegetation succession. It would take about 200 years for deciduous woodland to evolve from the moss and lichen stage.

Feeding habits ▸
Humans and animals depend on other living things for food. This picture shows how this food chain or web works. A grasshopper eats a leaf of grass, a thrush may eat the grasshopper, and a kestrel may eat the thrush. When the kestrel dies, bacteria break its body down and add nutrients to the soil, so that new plants can grow. Herbivorous animals eat plants only. Carnivores are meat eaters, and omnivores eat both animals and plants. Plants make their own food from sunlight, and so they are called autotrophs (self-feeders).

Make your own aquarium ecosystem

YOU WILL NEED

Gravel, net, plastic bowl, jug (pitcher), water, aquarium tank, rocks and pieces of wood, water plants, pondwater, water animals.

1 Put the gravel in a net. Rinse it in a plastic bowl of water, or run it under the cold water tap in the sink. This will discourage the formation of green algae.

2 Spread the gravel unevenly over base of the tank to a depth of about 3cm/1¼in. Add rocks and pieces of wood. These give surfaces for snails to feed on.

3 Fill the tank to about the halfway mark with tap water. Pour the water gently from a jug to avoid disturbing the landscape and churning up the gravel.

4 Add some water plants from an aquarium store. Keep some of them in their pots, but remove the others gently. Then root them in the gravel.

5 Now add a pitcherful of pondwater. This will contain organisms, such as *daphnia* (water fleas), which add to the life of your aquarium. You can buy pondwater in a garden store.

6 Add a few of the water animals you have collected from local ponds, such as tadpoles in frog spawn, or water snails. Take care not to overcrowd the aquarium.

7 Place the tank in bright light, but not in direct sunlight. You can watch the plants in the tank grow. Keep the water clean by removing dead matter from the gravel every few weeks.

Animal tracks and footprints

Wild creatures in the forest usually run away when humans approach. However, you can learn a lot about birds and other animals by looking at their tracks. You could go to a wood with an adult to hunt for animal tracks on soft or wet ground. The banks of streams and rivers are often criss-crossed by prints from animals who have gone there to drink.

Different groups of animals (mammals, birds, reptiles and amphibians) leave different tracks. The first project shows you how to look for these prints. Tracks give clues about the size and weight of the animal. They also show how animals move – whether they run, hop, slide or slither. Large, heavy birds for example, such as geese, waddle along – shifting their weight from side to side. Their prints show that they place one foot in front of the other and slightly to the side, rather like the way humans walk. Small birds, such as sparrows and finches, hop along on thin legs and feet. They leave tracks of tiny prints running side by side. Draw the prints or take a photograph, and record in a notebook the date and place, ground conditions and other observations. The second project shows you how to make casts of the most interesting footprints.

▲ **Out and about**
Study the tracks that you have found very carefully. What do they tell you about the way the animal that made them moved – did it hop, run or waddle? Use a field guide to animal tracks to help you identify the animals that left them.

YOU WILL NEED

Magnifying glass, camera, notebook, pencil, field guide.

Animal tracks

1 When you find a footprint, count the number of toes. Can you see any claws? A fox's paw is rounded, with four toes and claws. Take photos or make drawings of animal tracks you see.

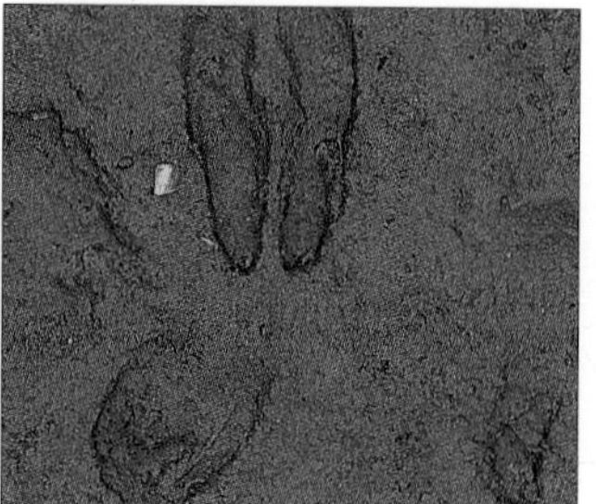

2 Deer have narrow, split hooves with just two toes. They leave deep tracks, because they walk with all their weight on their toes, rather than evenly spread throughout their feet.

3 Most birds have long, spindly feet, with either three or four toes. All ducks and some wading birds have webbed feet. The web shows up in the outline of the print.

Footprint cast

YOU WILL NEED
Protective gloves, field guide, thin card, paper clip, plaster of Paris, water, mixing bowl, spoon, trowel, scrubbing brush, paintbrush, paints or varnish, water pot.

1 Find a clear animal track, either in sand or dry mud. Remove any loose twigs or leaves around the print. (Remember to wear gloves if you are working in soil.)

2 Look for bird footprints in wet sand or mud. Tracks show the size of the bird that made it, and what group of birds it belongs to. Use a field guide to identify the bird that made the print.

3 Bend a strip of card into a ring large enough to fit around the print, and fasten the card ring with a paper clip. Place the ring over the print.

4 Mix the plaster of Paris with a little water in a bowl, according to the instructions on the packet. Stir the mixture until it is a thick and even paste with no lumps.

5 Carefully spoon enough plaster of Paris on to the print to cover it completely. After 15 minutes, the cast will be dry enough for you to pick it up.

6 Use a trowel to prize the cast loose. Carefully peel off the paper ring. Clean up the cast by brushing off any loose soil or sand with a scrubbing brush.

7 Allow the plaster cast to dry for 24 hours. After this, you could paint or varnish the cast. Try painting the raised footprint one colour and the background another colour.

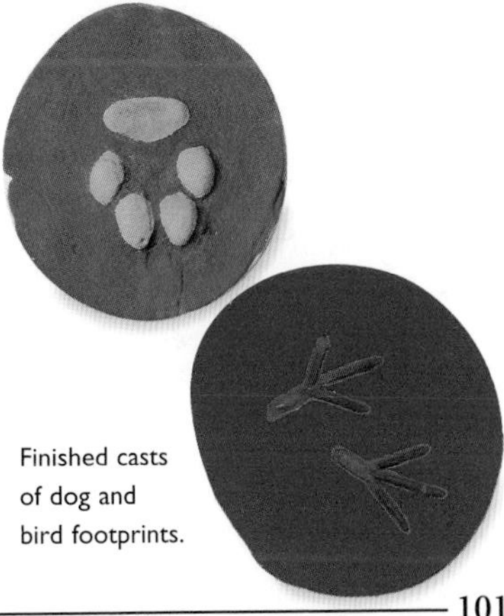

Finished casts of dog and bird footprints.

Searching for insects

▲ Feet tasters
The housefly has taste sensors on its feet. It sucks up its liquid through spongy mouthparts as soon as it lands.

Insects make up three-quarters of all animal species (kinds) on the Earth. Insects are everywhere, so they are easy to find. The best place to start is your backyard or a local park. If there is a good range of plants, up to 300 species of beetles can be found in a very small area, such as gardens. There may be up to 200 kinds of flies, 90 different bugs and many species of bees, ants, wasps, moths and butterflies.

To identify the species living in a particular area, scientists mark a square, and search all the places where creatures hide – under leaves, stones and logs, and in tiny crevices in trees. Scientists may leave pitfall traps in the ground or hang traps in the trees. You can find creatures locally using the type of trap demonstrated in the first project. The second project shows you how to make a simple pooter, which enables you to collect insects without harming them. Wear gloves when handling insects, because some may sting or bite. Always take an adult out with you.

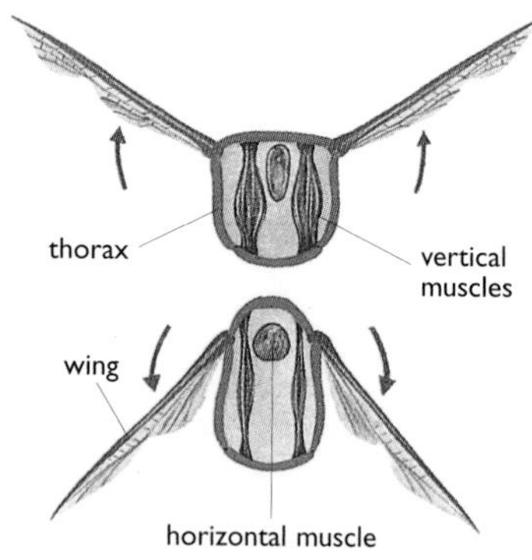

▲ How insects fly
Insects have no muscles in their wings. Instead the wings are hinged to the insect's thorax. They move up and down as the thorax changes shape. As the roof of the thorax is pulled down, the wings flick up. As the ends of the thorax are pulled in, the wings flick down.

Pitfall trap

1 If you have a backyard, ask an adult to show you a place where you can dig a small hole. Use a trowel to dig a hole in damp earth, which is large enough for the jar to fit in.

2 Place the jar in the hole. Firm the earth back around the sides of the jar with your hands. Put small, fresh leaves in the bottom of the jar for minibeast bait.

3 Place some small stones around the trap, and balance a large flat stone or tile on top, to prevent the minibeast trap from filling up with rain. Leave it overnight.

4 In the morning, remove the jar. Place a piece of thin white fabric over the top and secure it with a rubber band. Study any minibeasts you have caught using a magnifying glass.

5 Use a field guide to identify the minibeasts you have caught. When you have finished, remember to release the creatures near to where you found them.

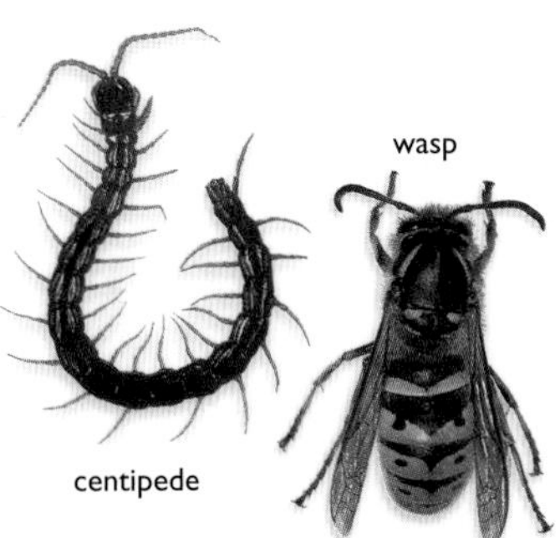

▲ **Show a leg**
Centipedes, like insects, are members of the arthropod group. They have many legs, one pair on each body segment. Adult insects, such as this queen wasp, have bodies in three main sections and six legs. Most also have wings.

Make a pooter

YOU WILL NEED

Pitfall trap: Garden gloves, trowel, glass jar, leaves, small stones, large flat stone or tile, thin white fabric, rubber band, magnifying glass, field guide.

Make a pooter: Small plastic bottle, scissors, non-hardening modelling material, wide bendable straws, thin white fabric, rubber band, sharp pencil.

1 Cut off the bottom of the plastic bottle. Roll out one large and one small ball of modelling material. Flatten out the large ball and shape it over the bottom of the bottle.

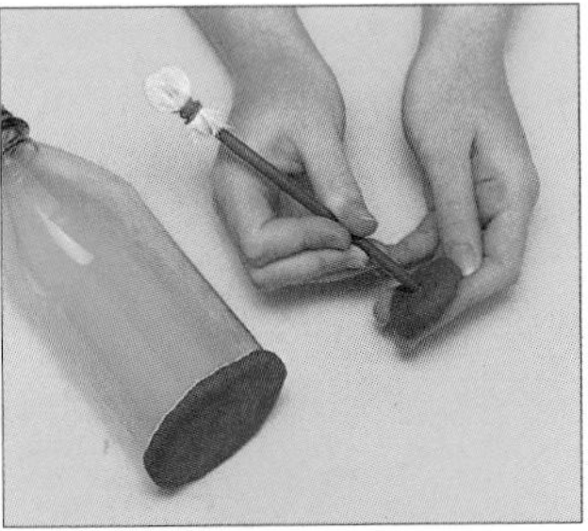

2 To make a filter, cut a short piece of straw. Secure a piece of fabric around the straw with a rubber band. Push the other end through the small lump of modelling material.

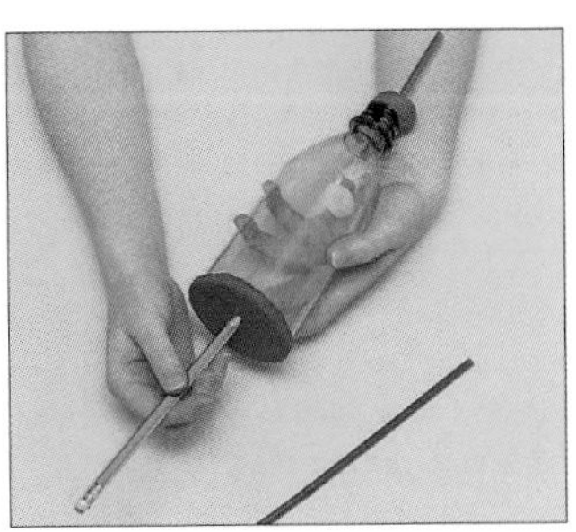

3 Fit the filter into the neck of the bottle by shaping the modelling material. Make a hole in the bottom flap with a sharp pencil. Push a long straw into the hole you have made.

4 Look for a small insect to study. (Big insects would get damaged.) Aim the end of the long straw over the insect. Suck on the short straw to draw the insect safely into the pooter.

5 When you have finished studying your insect, take it back to where you found it. To release the insect, carefully remove the bottom flap and gently shake the insect out.

What is an insect?

Birds, reptiles and mammals all have internal skeletons to provide a framework for their bodies. Insects are different – they have skeletons on the outside. Their soft body parts are protected by a hard case called an exoskeleton. This forms a waterproof barrier around the insect. It prevents the insect from drying out and air from passing through. Unlike birds and mammals, insects are cold-blooded animals. This means the temperature of an insect's body is about the same as its surroundings. To warm up, an insect basks in the sunshine. When it gets too hot, it moves into the shade.

Insects are fragile. It can be difficult to pick them up and examine them without harming them. When studying insects, use a notebook to record what you see. Write down the date, time, weather conditions and place where you found the insect. Use a field guide to help you make an identification. The projects here show you how to keep a record of the insects that you see. Look at the mouthparts and antennae. Think about the shape of the insect's body. Is it short or long? Does the insect have hard wing cases, or long legs?

YOU WILL NEED

Drawing insects: Magnifying glass, pencil, notebook, coloured pencils.

Insect survey: Gloves, four tent pegs, string, tape measure, glass jar, magnifying glass, pen, notebook, field guide, coloured pencils.

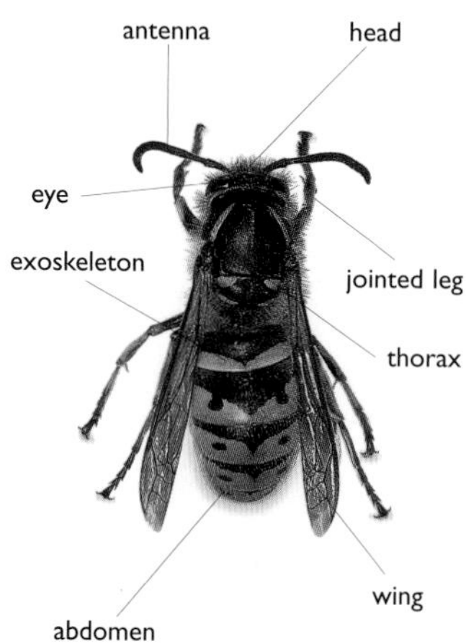

▲ Wasp sections

The bodies of adult insects have three sections – head, thorax and abdomen. Like this wasp, each section is made of small plates that fit together at flexible joints. The head carries the mouth parts, antennae and eyes. The legs and wings are attached to the thorax. The abdomen contains the reproductive organs and part of the digestive system.

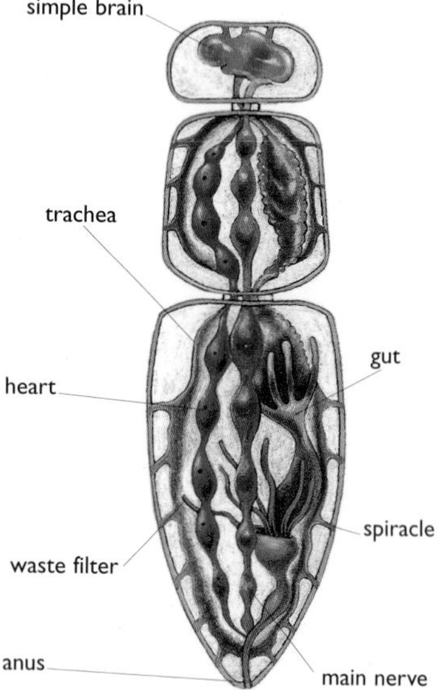

◀ Inside the insect

An insect's internal systems are protected by its hard exoskeleton. This diagram shows the main systems separated and tinted to make them clear. The nervous system (purple) sends messages from the senses to the brain. In the respiratory system (grey), air enters the body through tiny holes along each side of the insect's body, called spiracles. Pipes called tracheae carry the air to other parts of the body. In the circulatory system (red), several hearts, arranged in a row, pump blood around the body. The digestive system (green, orange) processes food.

Drawing insects

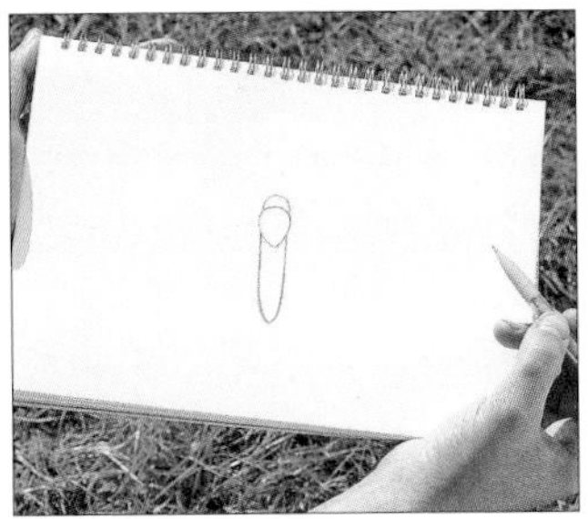

1 Find an insect and use the magnifying glass to study it closely. Start by drawing three ovals to show the head, the thorax and the abdomen of the insect.

2 Can you see the insect's legs? Copy them on your drawing. Now copy the size and shape of the insect's antennae. Draw the eyes and add the outline of the wings.

3 Now draw any markings that you notice on the insect's body and wings (if it has them). Finish your drawing by shading it in as accurately as you can.

Insect survey

1 Find an area of long grass. Wearing gloves to protect your hands, use the tent pegs, a measuring tape, and string to mark a square measuring 1m/1yd on each side.

2 What insects can you find inside the square? Use a collecting jar and a magnifying glass to study them. Write down what you have found in a notebook.

3 Now mark out a square yard in a different place. Try an area with flowers or a hedge. You may find aphids and greenfly on plant stems, and shieldbugs under leaves.

4 Move a fallen log to see what kinds of insects live underneath. Make sure you wear gloves to protect your hands. You may find beetles under logs, and woodlice and earwigs under bark.

5 Still wearing gloves, carefully look under some stones. What kinds of creatures prefer this dark, damp habitat? You may find worms, snails, ground beetles or an ants' nest.

Use your field guide to identify your discoveries. How many different species did you find in each area? Make a chart to record the results of your survey.

Studying insect life

▲ **Insect pollination**

This wasp is visiting a flower to feed on its sugary nectar. It sucks up the nectar with its tongue, to feed the larvae (young) in its nest. As the wasp reaches into the center of the flower, pollen from the flower rubs off on the insect's body. This is then carried by the wasp to the next flower.

Woods are great places to go insect watching. Trees offer food and shelter from the weather, so they are an ideal habitat for insects. The number of insects you find may depend on the season. In the spring, wild flowers bloom and attract insects. In the summer, the woods offer insects sunny clearings and cool shade. Choose a large tree and make a survey of all the insects you can find on a single branch. Make a tree trap to catch insects active at night.

Many insects depend on plants, but many plants depend on insects too. Insects help to pollinate plants by carrying pollen from the same plant to another of its species. Many plants have pink, red or orange flowers, because these are the tones that butterflies see well. Other flowers have special markings called nectar guides, leading from the base of the petals. Some show up only in ultraviolet light. Insects such as bees have eyes that are sensitive to this light, and they follow these guides to the middle of the flower.

Human vision

Insect vision

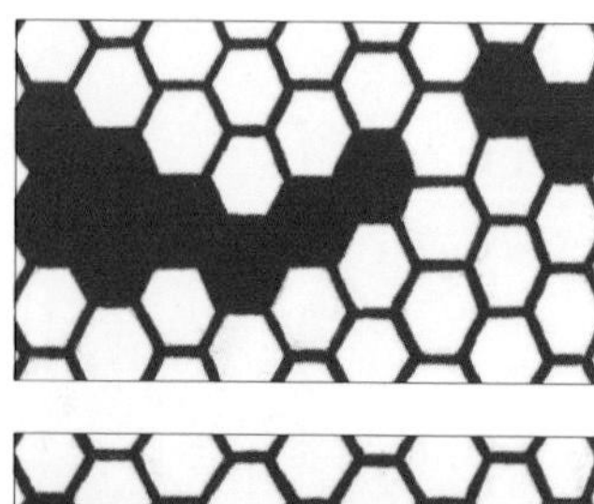

◂ **Seeing is believing**

Insect vision is very different from ours. Experts think each lens of an insect's compound eye sees a small part of a scene. This gives a mosaic-like view that is built up into a bigger picture. These diagrams compare how we see a moving insect, and what experts think an insect sees. An insect can sense tiny movements our eyes would hardly notice, because they have many more lenses that are affected.

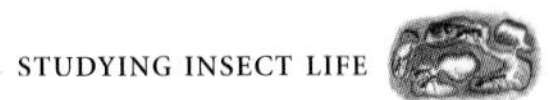

Make a tree trap

YOU WILL NEED

Make a tree trap: Scissors, small plastic bottle, strong adhesive tape, string, ham, magnifying glass, field guide, notebook, pen or pencil.

Life on a branch: Old white sheet, collecting jars, paintbrush, magnifying glass, field guide, notebook, pen or pencil, coloured pencils.

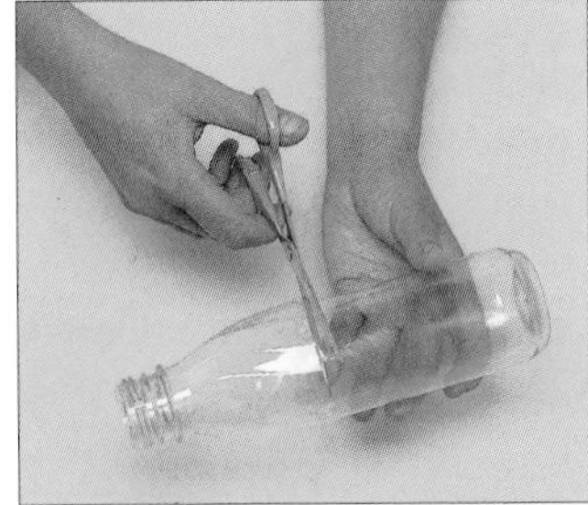

1 Using a pair of sharp scissors, carefully cut the plastic bottle in half widthways. Ask an adult to help you to do this, if you find it too difficult.

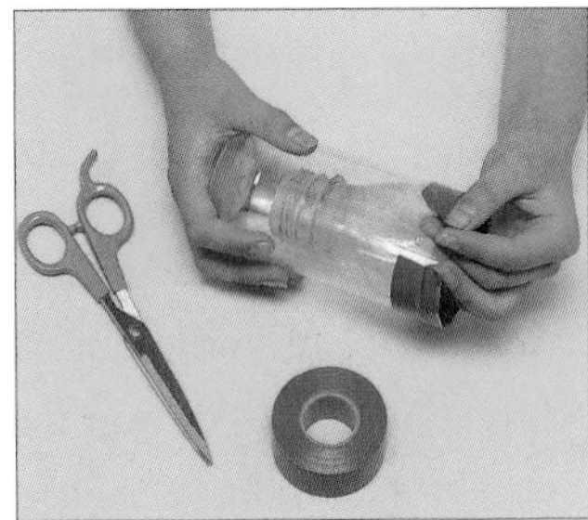

2 Turn the neck half of the bottle around and push it inside the bottom half. Now tape the two halves of the bottle together using strong adhesive tape.

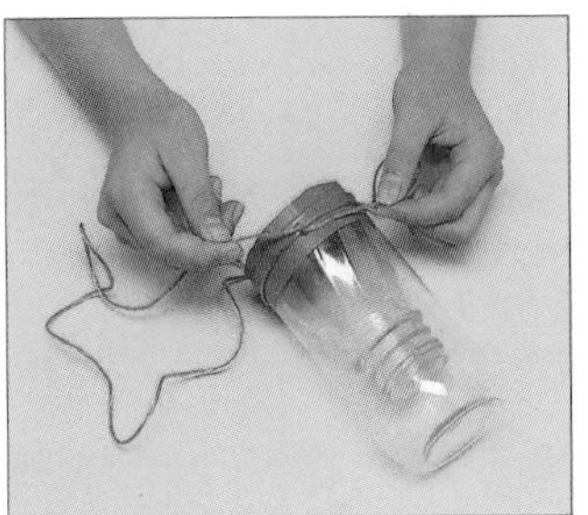

3 Cut a long piece of string. Loop the string around the open end of the trap and tie it into a knot. Place a small piece of ham inside the trap to act as insect bait.

4 Carefully tie the trap along the branch of a tree, or hang the trap down underneath the branch. Leave the trap out overnight. Go back the next morning to check it.

5 Use your field guide to identify the insects that you have caught. Record your findings in a notebook. Release the insects when you have identified them.

Life on a branch

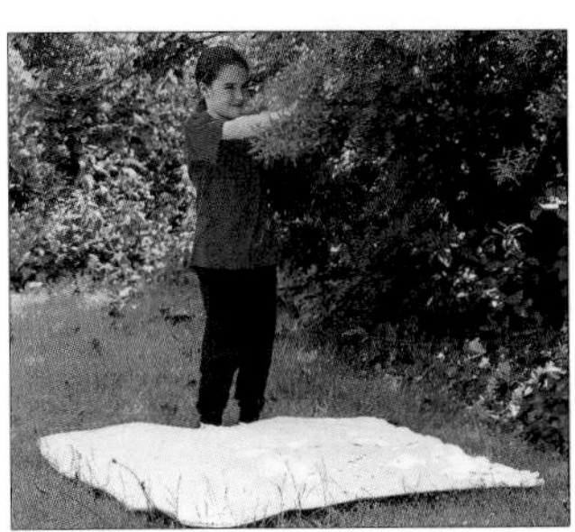

1 Spread out the white sheet below a branch. Shake the branch to dislodge the insects on to the sheet. If the branch is high, tap it with a stick. Be sure not to damage the tree.

2 Sweep the insects that drop on to the sheet into collecting jars for you to study. Use a paintbrush to carefully transfer the insects without harming them.

Use a field guide to identify the insects. Try surveying another type of tree. Make a chart, as above, to show the different species found on the various trees.

Insects in disguise

Most insects try to escape from predators by flying away. But it is even better not to be seen at all. Insects that hunt other creatures also need to be invisible to creep up unnoticed on their prey. Many insects have special tones and patterns on their bodies to help them look like leaves, seeds, twigs or stones. These natural disguises are called camouflage.

Stick insects change their body tone to match their surroundings, and so remain hidden almost anywhere. Their long slender bodies and stick-like legs make them hard to see among twigs and leaves. Stick insects are easy to take care of at home. You can buy them at some pet stores. Try the test opposite to find out more about camouflage.

You could look outside for ways in which insects disguise themselves. The last project shows you how to attract insects, such as butterflies and wasps, by planting flowers and herbs. Remember to ask permission from an adult before you start.

▲ **Hidden hunter**

Insects are attracted by the bright colours and sweet scents of flowers. The markings on this wasp are almost the same as the flower it is feeding on.

▲ **Prickles and bristles**

A pair of giant, prickly leaf insects with the green female (*right*) and the smaller male (*left*). The wings of the male are folded along its back. The safest way to pick up leaf or stick insects is by placing your fingers on each side of the body.

YOU WILL NEED

Camouflage test: Scissors, light and dark green paper, two cardboard boxes, tape, stick insects, paintbrush, privet or ivy leaves, kitchen paper, white fabric, non-hardening modelling material, notebook, coloured pencils.

Rearing stick insects: Earth, small tank or large jar, privet or ivy leaves, glass of water, sticks, stick insects, kitchen paper.

Plant a window box: Garden gloves, window box or large tub, earth, soil mix (optional), packet of wildflower seeds, watering can, notebook, pencil, field guide.

Camouflage test

1 Cut pieces of paper to line the insides of the cardboard boxes. Make one box light green, and the other dark green. Attach the paper with adhesive tape.

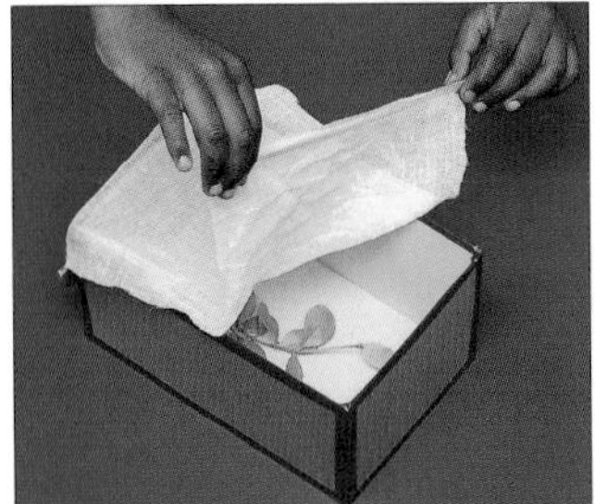

2 Transfer your stick insects with a paintbrush to the light green box. Add leaves and damp kitchen paper. Cover with white fabric weighted at the corners with modelling material.

3 Leave the box in a light place for a day. Record the insects' colour with coloured pencils. Put the insects in the darker box. After a day, check to see if they have changed.

Rearing stick insects

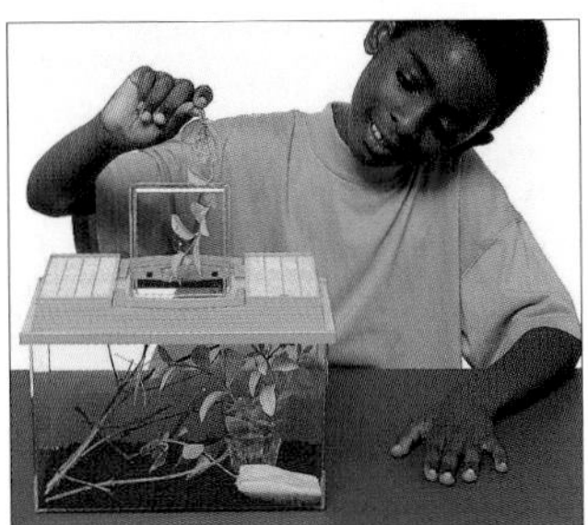

1 Put a layer of earth in the bottom of a tank or a large jar, with a tight-fitting lid with small air holes. Add privet or ivy leaves in a glass of water, some sticks and your stick insects.

2 Put some wet kitchen paper in a corner, so that the insects have enough moisture. Remember to replace the paper regularly. Ask the pet store if your insects need anything else.

Plant a window box

1 Wearing gloves, fill a window box or a large tub with earth. You could add some soil mix to the earth, and mix it in. The container should be about three-quarters full of earth.

2 Scatter wildflower seeds over the soil. You can buy seeds, such as daisy and bird's-foot trefoil, at a nursery. Do not dig up wild plants. Cover the seeds with more earth.

3 The seedlings will come up in a few weeks. Water the young plants regularly. As the plants grow, record in your notebook which insects visit and feed on them.

Insects to watch

As insects eat, they leave behind damaged plants and other signs of feeding. Sometimes these signs are easier to spot than the insects themselves. Look in a small area, such as a fallen log, a shrub or a bush. Hundreds of insects will be near, but most are small and wary. Discover the eating habits and preferences of different insects in the first project.

Look for freshwater insects, such as beetles and bugs in ponds and streams. Spring and summer are good times to look, because the young insects turn into adults at these times. You could even make a small pool for insects in your yard. Ask a responsible adult if you may dig the pond. To catch water insects, you will need a net, which you can make easily yourself. When you catch insects at the pond, take an adult with you for safety. Approach the water quietly, to disturb the wildlife as little as possible. Different insects live in various places in the pond or stream. Some live near the surface, while others swim near the bottom. Gently lift up stones and pebbles to find the creatures that lurk on the underside. Always replace them carefully, so that you disturb the habitat as little as possible.

▲ **Mmm, tasty...**
Most plant-eating insects prefer one particular food, and may eat only a part of that food plant. Some insects leave ragged holes in leaves. Aphids and other bugs leave brown and yellow lines on crops when they suck out the sap.

Food samples

YOU WILL NEED

Cardboard, pair of compasses and a pencil, scissors, four garden sticks, small samples of food (such as honey, meat, cheese and fruit), notebook, field guide.

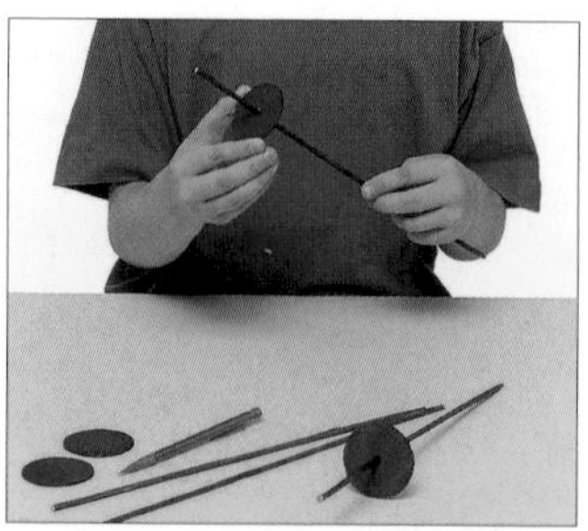

1 Draw four circles on the cardboard with the compasses. Cut them out. Use the point of a pencil to make holes in the middles of the circles. Push the sticks through the holes.

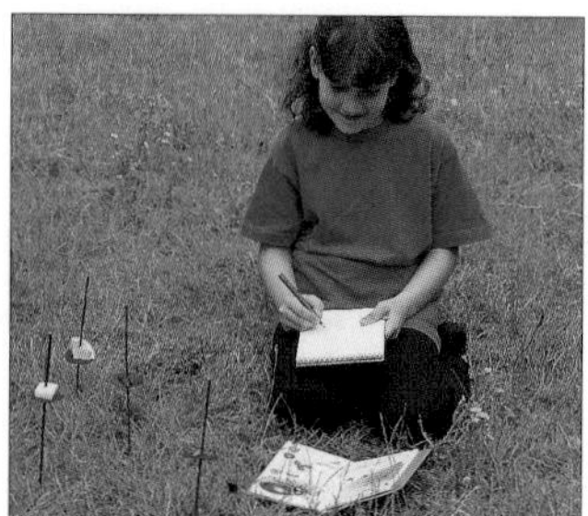

2 Plant the sticks in the ground. Push the food samples on the sticks, so they rest on the circles. Do insects prefer certain foods? Are there more insects around at different times of day?

Insect pool

1 Wear gloves when you are making your insect pool. Dig a hollow in the ground with the trowel. The hole should be big enough to fit an old plastic bowl inside.

2 Place the bowl in the hollow and press it down firmly. Spread gravel on the bottom and put in the water plants. Place stones arond the edge of the bowl and inside it.

3 Then fill the bowl with water, using a watering can. Your pool is now finished and ready for occupation. Insects and other animal life will soon be attracted to the pool.

YOU WILL NEED
Insect pool: Garden gloves, trowel, plastic bowl, gravel, water plants, large stones, watering can. **Make a pond net:** Wire, thin sock, pliers, long pole or broom handle, jubilee clip from a hardware store, screwdriver, jug (pitcher), empty plastic ice-cream container, magnifying glass, field guide.

Make a pond net

1 Begin your pond net by threading wire in and out through the top of a thin sock. You may need to use a pair of pliers to bend the wire into a circle.

2 Use the pair of pliers to twist the ends of the wire together, to make the net secure. Ask an adult to help if you need to. Now position the net at the end of a long pole.

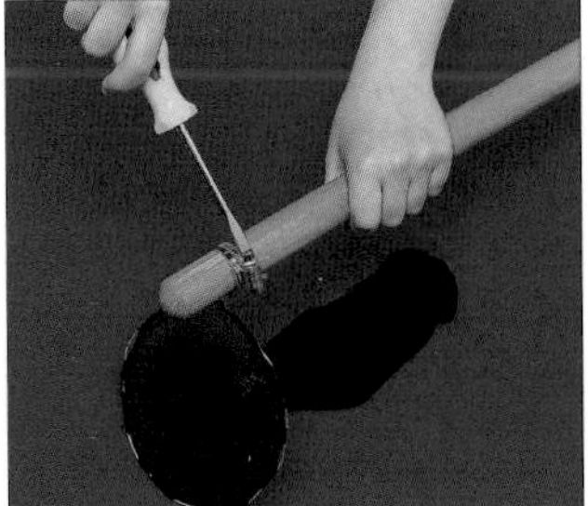

3 Carefully thread the jubilee clip over the pole, and push the twisted wires under the clip, as shown above. Tighten the clip using a screwdriver. Ask an adult to help you do this.

4 Down at the pond, capture insects by sweeping your net gently through the water. Lightly tap the stems of plants to knock other insects into your net.

5 Empty a jug of pond water into a container. Empty your net into it. Study the creatures you have caught. Tip the water and creatures back into the pond when you have finished.

Moths and butterflies

All butterflies and moths go through a metamorphosis (change). They start as caterpillars then, as pupae, encase themselves in a cocoon, where a remarkable change takes place, and they finally emerge as adults. Caterpillars feed on leafy plants, such as grasses and nettles. Adult moths and butterflies gather on plants with nectar-bearing flowers. As you will see from the projects here, bright lights and a mixture of fruit and sugar will bring moths fluttering.

Some butterflies have wings with warning markings. The markings tell predators that they are poisonous to eat. Other butterflies are harmless, but mimic (copy) poisonous species. Their markings fool predators into avoiding them, too. The best way to attract butterflies is to plant a butterfly garden. Choose plants that bloom at various times of the year.

▲ Beating around the bush
The sweet-smelling purple buddleja is a popular plant with butterflies, and so has gained the nickname butterfly bush. Butterflies attracted to buddleja include small tortoiseshells (*shown here*), peacocks, painted ladies, commas and red admirals.

▲ Antennae ID
You can tell a butterfly from a moth by looking at the antennae (feelers). Many butterflies have antennae with clubbed tips, like this swallowtail. Moths' antennae vary, but most are straight or feathered.

Torchlight attraction

1 Wearing gloves, dig a small hole in the garden with a trowel. Do this in the daylight, and remember to ask an adult's permission first before you start to dig.

2 Check that your torch fits inside the hole. At dusk turn on the torch and put it inside the hole. Fill any gaps with earth to hold the torch securely in position.

3 Step back and watch the moths flutter around the light. You could try taking flash photographs of the insects with a camera. How did your photos turn out?

Sweet moth feast

1 Begin by measuring out about 500g/1¼lb/scant 2 cups of soft light brown sugar with a spoon into your scales, or a measuring bowl. Pour the measured sugar into your mixing bowl.

2 Add the overripe fruit to the mixing bowl, and mash it with a fork. Keep mashing until the fruit has become a pulp. Add some warm water until the mixture becomes runny.

3 Paint the mixture on to a tree trunk or a fence post. Return when it is dark. Take a torch to help you see the moths feeding, and a field guide to help you to identify them.

Butterfly garden

YOU WILL NEED

Torchlight attraction: Garden gloves, trowel, torch (flashlight), camera.

Sweet moth feast: Soft light brown sugar, spoon, food scales, mixing bowl, ripe fruit, fork, warm water, paintbrush, torch (flashlight), field guide.

Butterfly garden: Seeds or young plants, gloves, trowel, rake, watering can, notebook, pencil, field guide.

1 First you need to grow some plants from seed – or buy young plants. Wearing a pair of gloves, dig up your chosen patch of earth with a trowel.

2 Break up any large clods of earth with a rake or trowel. Now start to rake over the top of your plot, so that the earth is evenly spread and crumbly.

3 Dig several small holes for your plants with the trowel. Place the plants in the holes, and press the earth down firmly with gloved hands around the base of each plant.

4 Water the plants well. They will need to be watered regularly through the spring and summer. Sunlight will scorch wet leaves during the day, so water your plants at dusk.

5 Record which butterflies you see visiting your flowers. A field guide will help you to identify them. Which species prefer which flowers? And which is the most popular plant?

Watching a caterpillar grow

These projects show you how to prepare a home for caterpillars. Look for caterpillars on plants where you see half-eaten leaves – they may be hiding on the undersides. Take some of these leaves with the caterpillars you find. Use a field guide to identify the species you have found, and which plants they prefer. Try not to touch caterpillars directly with your fingers, since some species may sting. Pick them up using a paintbrush, or encourage them to climb on to a leaf. Carry them in a jar. At home, keep the caterpillars out of direct sunlight, in a moist, cool place. Try not to disturb them. Clean the box regularly, and replace old leaves with fresh ones.

YOU WILL NEED

Scissors, cardboard box, adhesive tape, thin white fabric or netting, non-hardening modelling material, rubber gloves, fresh leaves, kitchen paper, collecting jar containing caterpillars, ruler, pencil, notebook, field guide, coloured pencils.

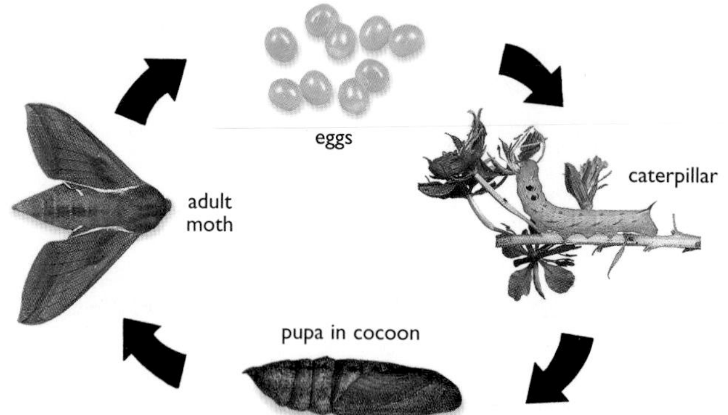

◂ Complete metamorphosis When butterflies, moths, ants and bees change during their lives, it is called complete metamorphosis. The life cycle of the elephant hawk moth (shown here) has four separate stages. The moth begins life as an egg. The egg hatches a caterpillar, which spends almost all of its time feeding. When the caterpillar is fully grown, it burrows into the ground and sheds its skin to reveal a pupa, a stage at which the larva changes into the adult insect when cocooned in a protective case. Finally, the case splits and the adult moth emerges.

Keeping caterpillars

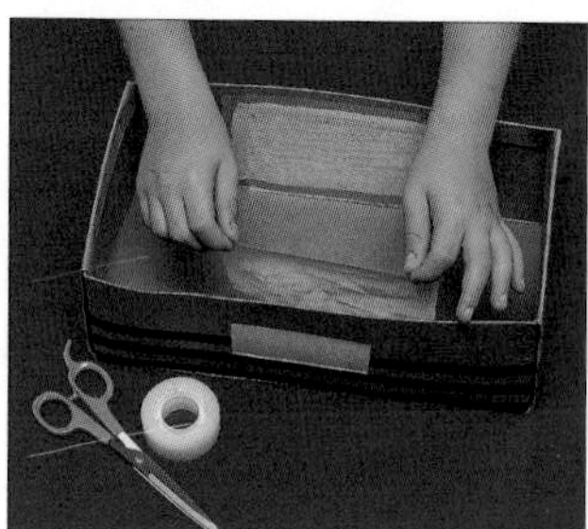

1 Cut holes in the sides of the box for windows. Using strong tape, cut out and stick pieces of fabric or netting over the windows to cover them securely.

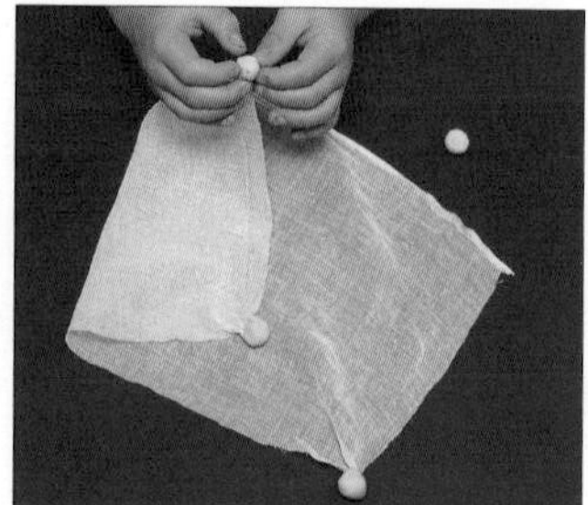

2 Now cut a large piece of thin white fabric to make the cage lid. Weight the corners of the fabric down with modelling material, to prevent the caterpillars from escaping.

3 Wearing a pair of gloves, put some fresh leaves inside the box. Make sure that they are from a plant your caterpillars eat. Be sure to provide fresh leaves daily.

4 Put some damp kitchen paper in a corner of the box to provide moisture. Carefully transfer your caterpillars from the collecting jar to the box. Cover with the lid.

5 Check your caterpillars every day, and replace the damp kitchen paper. Record how much they eat and how big they are. Remember to replace the leaves daily.

6 Watch how your caterpillars feed and move around on the leaves. Record the dates when you see them moulting (shedding skin). How many times did they shed their skins?

7 When it has finished growing, the caterpillar will change into a pupa, or chrysalis. It will attach itself to the stem of a food plant, and form a new skin. Make a note of the date.

8 Check your pupa every day, and write down the date when you see the case splitting. Compare your two dates. How long did the insect spend as a pupa?

9 You will see a butterfly or moth struggle out of the old skin. The insect rests and pumps blood into its crumpled wings to straighten them out before flying off.

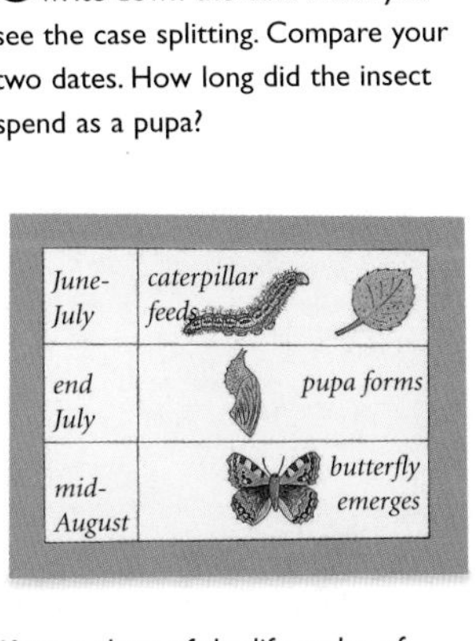

June-July	*caterpillar feeds*
end July	*pupa forms*
mid-August	*butterfly emerges*

Keep a chart of the life cycles of your insects.

When the caterpillars become adult moths or butterflies, it is time to let them go. Take the insects back to where you found them. Lift the lid off the box, and let them fly away.

Crawling colonies

Unlike most insects, ants live in colonies. They are known as social insects, as opposed to solitary insects. Ants are different to flying insects, such as butterflies and bees, yet they behave in a similar way. An ant colony is like an underground city with millions of insects, each with its own role to play. Queen ants (of which there may be several in one nest) lay eggs. Undeveloped females called workers perform the essential tasks of the colony. They scurry around, searching for food, and bring it to the nest.

The key to the smooth running of the colony is good communication. Ants cannot see well, so they communicate by touch and smell. When two ants meet, they touch antennae (feelers). When an ant finds a food source, it hurries back to the nest, pressing its body close to the ground as it runs. This leaves a trail of scent, which the other ants can follow to reach the food.

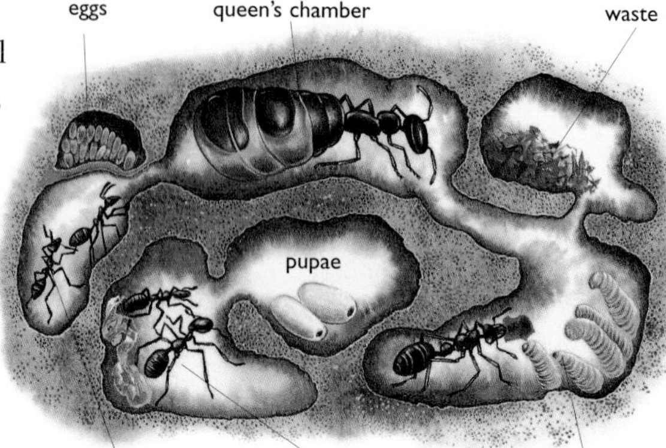

▲ **Inside an ants' nest**
Ants' nests are usually underground. A nest has many chambers, or rooms, and passages. Different chambers contain the eggs, larvae (young), pupae and the queen. Other chambers are used to store food and waste. Worker ants alter the temperature of the nest by opening or closing passages.

YOU WILL NEED
Garden gloves, peeled ripe fruit, piece of paper, magnifying glass.

Watching ant trails

1 Wearing gloves, find a trail of ants. Follow the trail to discover where the ants are going. Does the trail lead to food? Rub out part of the trail and see what happens.

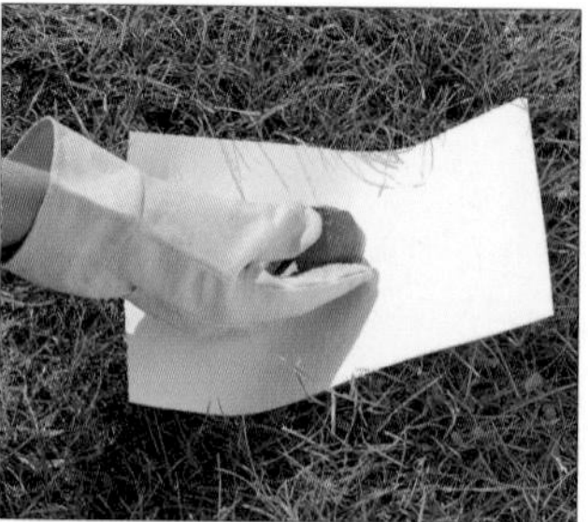

2 Now put fruit down on a piece of paper near the trail of ants. The paper will make it easier to see the ants. When the workers find the fruit, watch and see what happens.

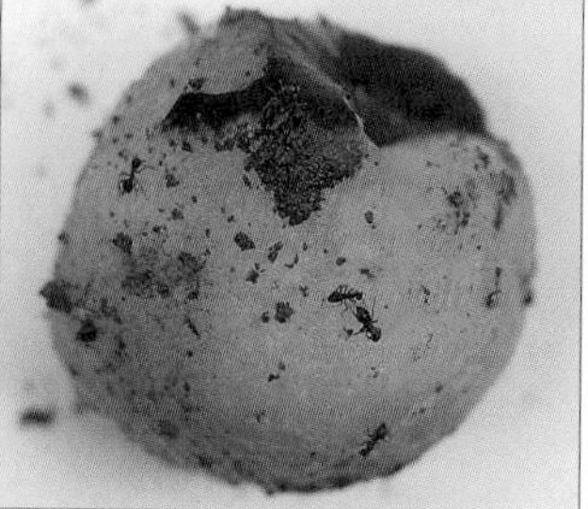

3 Once an ant has laid a scent trail to the fruit, others will follow. Move the fruit to another part of the paper. What happens next? Do the ants go straight to the new food site?

Make an ant home

YOU WILL NEED

Ruler, scissors, purple paper, large jar, adhesive tape, garden gloves, trowel, earth, fallen leaves, paintbrush, jar containing ants, ripe fruit or preserve, kitchen paper, thin white fabric.

1 Measure and carefully cut a piece of purple paper that is large enough to fit around the jar. Secure the paper in position around the jar with tape.

2 Wearing a pair of gloves, use the trowel to fill the jar with earth until the jar is almost full. Carefully place a few leaves on top of the earth.

3 Capture some garden ants using a paintbrush and collecting jar. Let the ants crawl on to the paintbrush. Then tap the jar, so that the ants fall in. Transfer the ants to their new home.

4 Feed your ants with a piece of ripe fruit or some preserve. Some damp kitchen paper will provide moisture. Feed your ants daily and refresh the leaves and moist paper regularly.

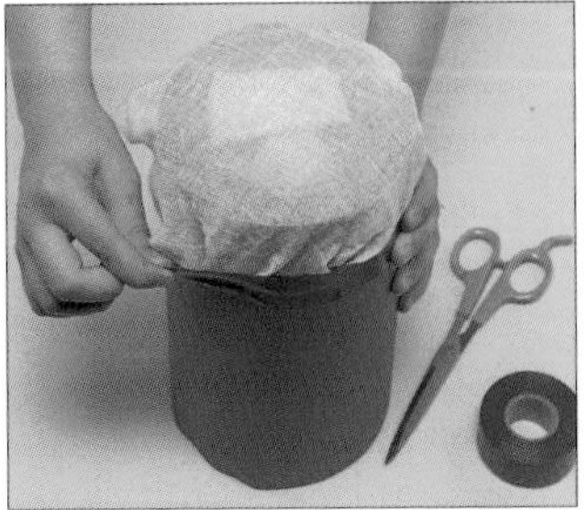

5 Cover the top of the jar with a piece of thin white fabric, so that the ants cannot escape. Secure the fabric with adhesive tape. Keep your ant home in a cool place.

6 After a few days, remove the tape and lift the paper to observe your ant home. There will now be winding tunnels, built by the ants, against the sides of the jar.

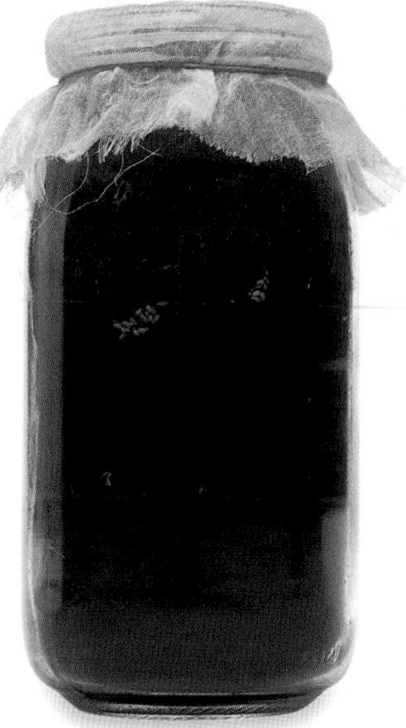

If you have caught a queen ant, you may see the workers tending the eggs or larvae in special chambers.

Discovering birds

There are birds living in all areas of the world. They inhabit icy polar regions, tropical wet rainforests and scorching hot deserts. Birds are also found in crowded cities, on high mountains and on remote islands.

Birds vary in size. The tiny hummingbird of Cuba is no larger than a bumblebee. The African ostrich, at the other extreme, stands 2.5m/8ft high. Birds are warm-blooded creatures like mammals, but they lay eggs, as reptiles and amphibians do. Unlike other animals, birds' bodies are covered with strong, lightweight feathers. These help birds to fly, although there are a few species that cannot fly.

There are more than 8,600 different species (kinds) of birds. Scientist divide all these birds into groups called orders. The 28 bird orders are divided into smaller groups, called families, and each family contains several species. Species in the same family tend to have a similar body shape, which makes them suited to a certain way of life. For example, ducks have wide bodies and webbed feet to help them move through water.

The largest bird species often live the longest. Giant albatrosses can live for 80 years. Small songbird species, such as blue tits and sparrows, may live for just one year.

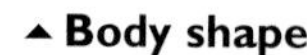

▲ **Body shape**
Birds have a basic body shape that varies in size and shape according to species. All birds have a beak, instead of jaws with teeth, and scaly legs and feet. Flying birds have a skeleton that is geared for efficient flight. Powerful wings and a feathered tail help with stability and steering. The wings and legs are arranged close to the middle of the body, to help with balance.

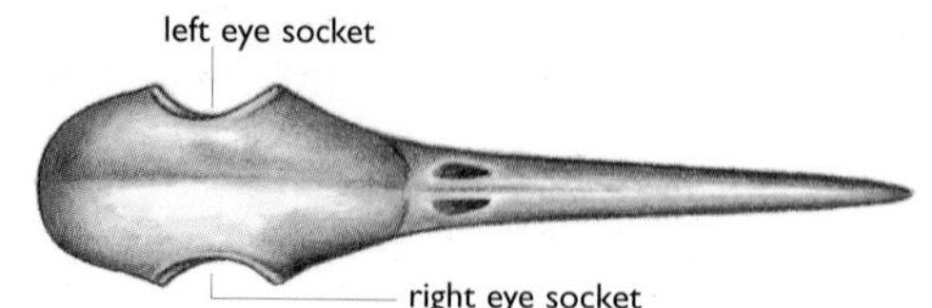

▲ **Field of vision for a woodcock**
A woodcock eats earthworms and insects. It does not need to spot prey like an owl does, but must look for enemies. Its eyes are on the side of its head. This enables it to see all around itself.

YOU WILL NEED

Looking at diving birds: Field guide, stopwatch or watch with a second hand, notebook, pen, drawing pad, coloured pencils.

Drawing birds: Drawing pad, pen and pencils, notebook.

Looking at diving birds

1 Choose a pond or a lake for bird-watching. See where different species feed. Notice where they dive and reappear. Use a field guide to help you to identify species.

2 Now find out how long the different birds spend under the water. Use your stopwatch to time their dives. Do they feed underwater, or bring food to the surface?

3 Record the times in your notebook. Which bird stays underwater for the longest time? Do you think that this is affected by the depth of the water?

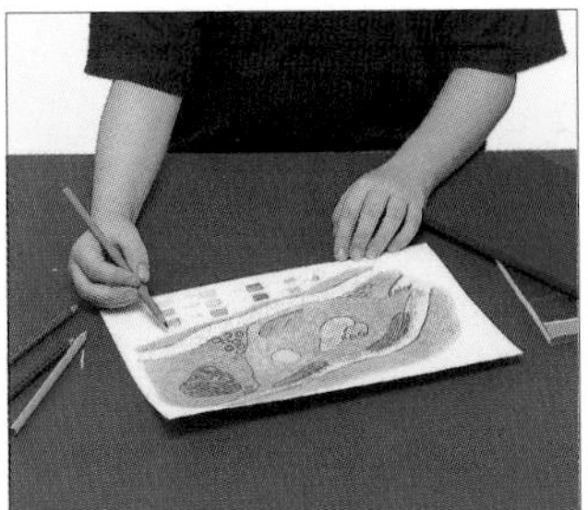

4 In your notebook, make a rough map of the pond or lake. When you get home, do a neater version and shade it in. Show vegetation such as grass or reeds.

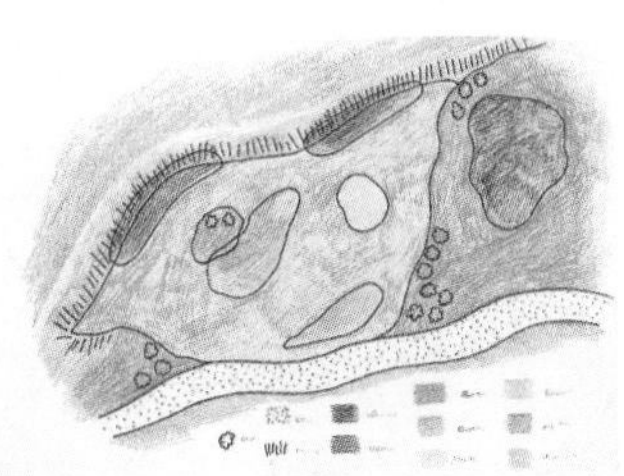

5 On your map, use different pencils to mark where various species of birds swim and feed. Remember to draw a key to explain which bird each shade represents.

Drawing birds

1 You do not have to be a great artist to draw birds. Study the shape of the bird. Notice how long the neck is. Start with simple ovals for the head and body.

2 Look at the shape of the bird's beak, and at its neck and tail. If you can see the legs, how long are they? Can you see the feet? Add these details to your drawing.

Now add a pair of wings and other details, such as the face and tail. Make notes about the bird's appearance, so that you can shade your drawing in later.

Bird-watching

Birds are among the easiest animals to spot and study from your home or school. To see a wider range of species (kinds), you could try bird-watching in a local park, pond or woodland area. Always take an adult with you. Birds are shy creatures with sharp eyesight and hearing. They are always on the lookout for enemies, so keep very quiet and still when bird-watching. If you make yourself a hide, like the one shown, bird-watching will be much easier.

YOU WILL NEED

Using binoculars: Binoculars.

Build a hide: Eight short canes or poles, six longer canes, string, scissors, canvas or tarpaulin, safety pins, four tent pegs, leaves and twigs, lightweight binoculars.

Using binoculars

1 Lightweight binoculars are very useful on bird-watching trips. Remove them from the case, and hang them around your neck so you are ready to use them.

2 When you see a bird, do not look down, or you may lose sight of it. Keep watching it, and slowly raise the binoculars to your eyes. Try to avoid making any sudden movements.

3 Now adjust the focusing wheel on your binoculars, to bring the bird into focus. You may find this difficult to do at first, but it will become easier with practice.

Build a hide

1 You will need a friend to help you. Lay four short canes on the ground in a square. Tie the ends with string. Make another square the same size, to form the roof.

2 Get your friend to stand inside the base. Your friend should hold the roof in position, while you tie four long canes to the base and roof to form the sides.

3 Now strengthen the structure of your hide. Add two long canes to make cross-pieces on opposite sides of the hide. Tie the canes in place with a piece of string.

4 Drape your hide with the canvas or tarpaulin. Add a smaller piece for the roof. Fasten the edges with safety pins. For extra security, fix the base to the ground with tent pegs.

5 Now cover the cloth with some leaves and twigs. These will camouflage your hide, so that it will blend in with the woods and will be less obvious to birds.

6 Once inside the hide, look out through the gaps in the seams, between the safety pins. Try using your binoculars. Keep still and quiet, and birds will soon approach.

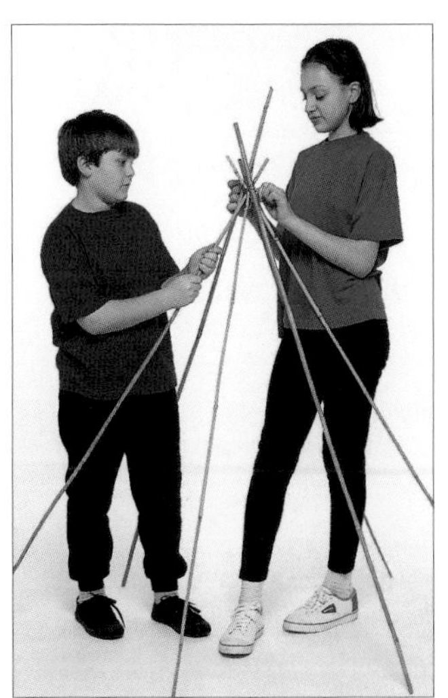

A tepee is another, simpler kind of hide. You will need four to six canes, string, a tarpaulin, safety pins and maybe tent pegs. Fan the canes to form a pyramid shape and tie the top ends with string. Drape the tarpaulin over this, and fasten it with safety pins.

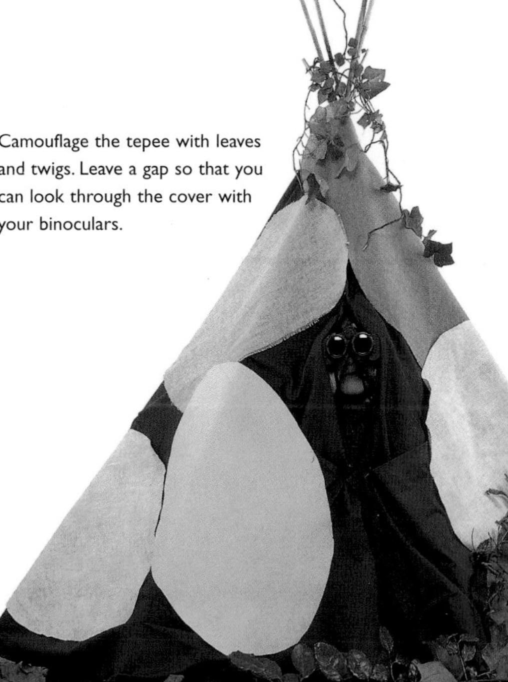

Camouflage the tepee with leaves and twigs. Leave a gap so that you can look through the cover with your binoculars.

Listening to birds

The voices of singing birds that seem beautiful to us often have many meanings. A bird's song identifies what species (kind) it is as well as each bird as an individual. Male birds sing to establish their own territories. A territory is a patch of ground where the birds intend to breed and feed. In Antarctica, a parent penguin finds its chick among thousands of other chicks by its cry. Birds also call to warn of danger and to attract a mate. Birds that flock together use contact calls to keep in a tight group.

You can make a birdbath for the birds who visit your garden in the first project. Listening to birdsong is a good way of identifying birds. The best times of the day to listen to birds are at dawn and dusk, when they sing the loudest. It is fun to make recordings of the different bird songs that you come across. Use a portable tape recorder with a long cord, so that you can position the microphone farther away. Tape the microphone to a stick, so that the sounds of your hands will not be recorded. Headphones will let you check what you are recording. To achieve even better results, make yourself a sound reflector, as shown in the third project.

▲ **Hooters of the night**
An owl's night-time hooting is a well-recognized sound. Owls have excellent eyesight. This makes them good hunters in the dark. Some have flat disc-shaped faces. These help direct sound into the ears at the side of the head.

YOU WILL NEED

Trowel, rubber gloves, large dish or old garbage bin lid, stones, bucket of water.

Build a birdbath

1 Use your trowel to dig a hollow in the earth. It should be big enough to fit your garbage bin lid or dish. Place the dish in the hollow, and press it down firmly, making sure it is flat.

2 Now place a few large stones in your garbage bin lid or dish. Birds who come to your garden will use these stones to stand on, to get in and out of your birdbath.

3 Pour water into the bath, to a depth of 10–15cm/4–6in. The tops of the stones should stick up above the water, so that birds can spot them and land on them easily.

Taping birdsong

YOU WILL NEED

Taping birdsong: Portable tape recorder, microphone and headphones, blank cassette tapes, notebook, pencil, camping mat, field guide.

Sound reflector: Old umbrella, foil, adhesive tape, tape recorder, microphone and headphones, blank cassette tape.

1 Become familiar with the songs of birds that live in your area by listening to recordings on CD or on the Internet. You can borrow CDs from your local library.

2 Outside, position yourself behind a tree or bush, if possible. Set up the microphone on a long cord by a bird table, or near a perch where you see a bird singing.

3 To record, press the record and pause buttons, releasing the pause button when you want to record. Listen with the headphones, and note down the time, place and weather.

When you get home, listen to the calls you have recorded very carefully. Most field guides give details of birdcalls and will be able to help you identify the songs.

Sound reflector

1 Cover the inside of an old umbrella with sheets of foil. Carefully bend the foil over the edges of the umbrella and tape it down securely. Overlap the sheets of foil as needed.

2 Fix the microphone to the stem of the umbrella, with the mike head pointing toward the shade. Try the mike in different positions – about 15–20cm/6–8in away from the shade.

3 Set up your reflector where birds are singing. The reflector will channel sounds and amplify them (make them louder). Give birds time to get to used to this strange object.

Birds' nests

Nests are warm, safe places where birds lay eggs, and where the nestlings (baby birds) develop after they have hatched. Birds do not sleep in their nests at night. Instead, they roost on perches in sheltered places, such as hedges and trees.

Constructing the nest is usually the female's job. The first step is to choose a good site. Then the materials are gathered. Twigs, leaves, feathers, moss, wool and mud are all used by various birds. The nest-building bird pushes the materials into place and hollows out the inside with her body. The finished nest may be lined with soft materials, such as feathers, to protect the eggs.

Nesting birds are fascinating to study. Attract birds into your garden, and help them to nest and raise their young by building a nesting box in the early spring. You may see birds fly by with nesting materials in their beaks, looking for a place to build. Many birds build their nests wedged in the forks of tree branches. Nest-building uses up a lot of time and energy. It may take between a week and a month, yet most nests last for just one breeding season, and are ruined by winter weather.

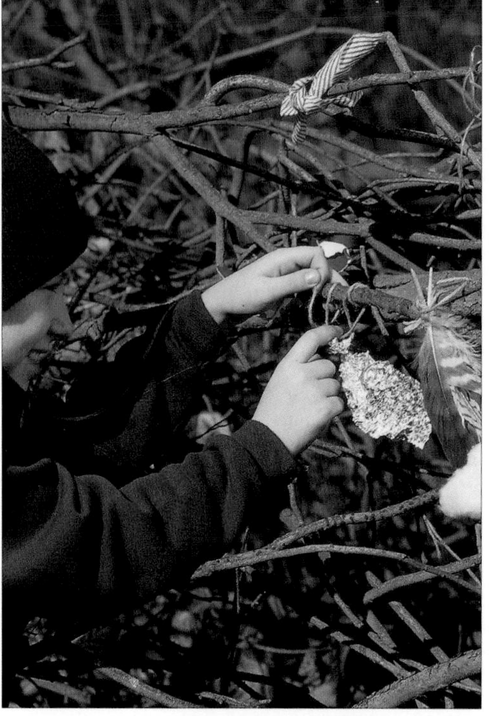

▲ Nesting materials
In the spring, try hanging nesting material from branches or a window sill. You can use wool, string, grass, moss and feathers. You could also try paper tissue, straw and animal hair. Different bird species like different materials. Try and find out which ones are chosen by various birds.

▼ Template

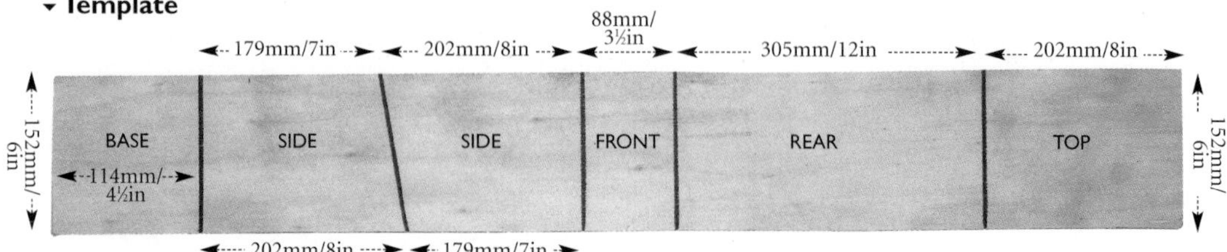

Use 15mm/⅝in thick pine or plywood. Ask an adult to cut pieces to the sizes and shapes shown above.

Build a nesting box

YOU WILL NEED

Wood (cut into pieces by an adult as shown), wood glue, hammer, nails or panel pins, pencil, strip of sacking or rubber (for the hinge), varnish, brush.

1 When all the pieces of wood have been cut by an adult, arrange them in position to make sure that they all fit properly. Glue the low front of the box to the base.

2 Now add one of the side pieces to the base of your nesting box. Glue it in place. Next, add the other side piece to the opposite edge of the base and glue that into position, too.

3 Nail all the pieces together. Take great care with the hammer. You could ask an adult to help. Place the box in the middle of the rear board, and draw around it in pencil.

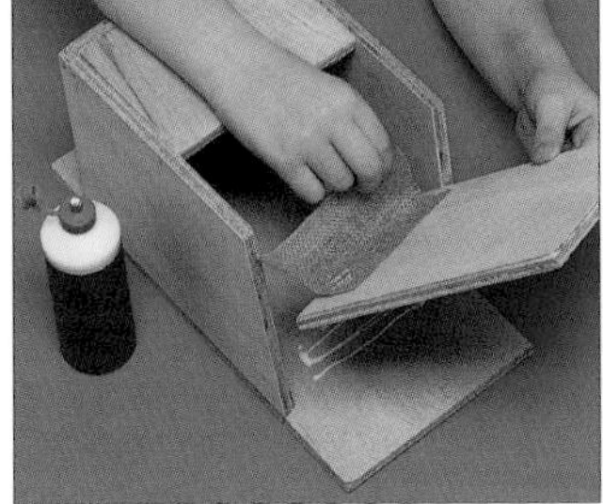

4 Using your pencil guidelines, nail the rear board to the box. Add the roof by gluing and nailing the sacking hinge. Now your nesting box is ready to use.

5 Your nesting box will last much longer if you give it a coat of varnish, inside and out, to protect it. Leave the box overnight to let the varnish dry completely.

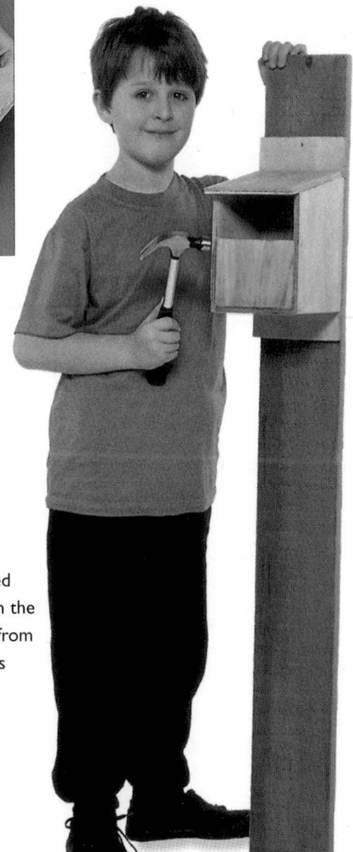

Nail your box to a tree, shed or post, about 2m/6½ft from the ground. Face the box away from any direct sunlight, since this may harm very young birds.

Feed the birds

Put bird food out in a safe place, and you will discover one of the best ways of studying birds close up. You can make your own bird cake, such as the one here, and put out kitchen scraps such as stale breadcrumbs, cheese, fruit, cooked rice, cooked pasta, uncooked pastry and bacon rind. Birds will really appreciate these tidbits, particularly in cold weather, when the ground is hard to peck at for worms and trees are bare of fruit and berries. Count how many different kinds of birds visit. Also, notice which species (kind) prefer each kind of food. Note down the date, time and weather when you first see a new species. Do the birds feed quietly together, or do they fight over the scraps?

▲ Winter feed
Fruit is an important food for many birds, particularly in winter. Garden species such as thrushes and blackbirds will peck at apples, leaving large, irregular holes.

◄ Shells and nuts
Look for nut shells gnawed by animals. Squirrels and mice leave neat holes and teethmarks. Birds leave peck-marks or jagged edges, or they crack nuts in half, such as the top two nuts here. Song thrushes feed on snails. They smash the shell against a stone. The stone is called the thrush's anvil. You may be lucky and find shell remains beside a stone.

Make a bird cake

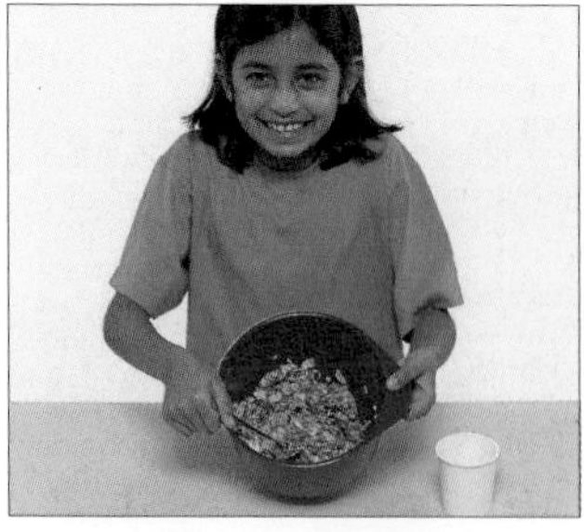

1 Soften the vegetable fat on a radiator or get an adult to help you melt it in a pan. Chop the nuts, then mix with the oatmeal and crumbs in a bowl. Add the melted fat and mix.

2 Cut a long piece of string. Tie a really big knot in one end. Put the string into the cup, so that the knotted end is at the bottom, and spoon the mixture into the cup.

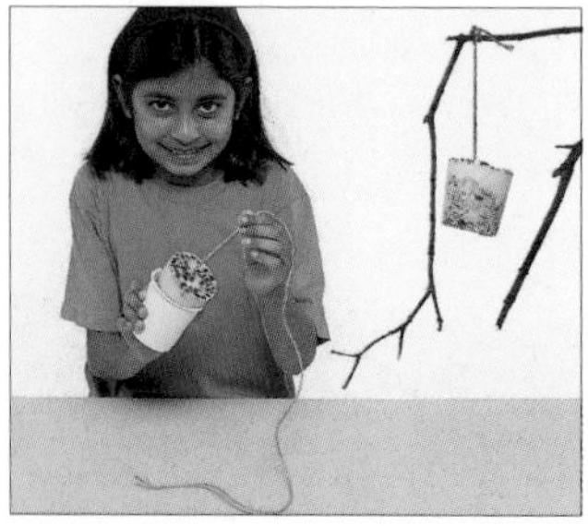

3 Ensure that the end of the string comes out through the middle of the mixture. When the mixture is set, pull the string to remove the cake. Hang it on a tree branch or window sill.

Build a bird table

YOU WILL NEED

Make a bird cake: Vegetable fat, nuts, oatmeal, crumbs, spoon, bowl, string, scissors, cup.

Build a bird table: 20 x 30cm/8 x 12in plywood board, two strips of wood 25cm/10in long and two 15cm/6in long, glue, hammer, nails or panel pins, brush, varnish, four eye-hooks, string, scissors.

1 Lay the wooden strips along the edges of your plywood board, as shown. Now glue the strips of wood into position, so that the ends fit neatly together.

2 When the glue is dry, turn the board over. Carefully hammer nails through it, into the strips. If you find using a hammer difficult, you could ask an adult to help you to do this.

3 Paint the top surface of your bird table with a coat of varnish, to make it waterproof. When this coat is dry, turn the table over, and coat the underside too.

4 Screw eye-hooks into the strips at the four corners of the table. Now cut two pieces of string about 30cm/12in long. Tie the ends of the strings to the hooks.

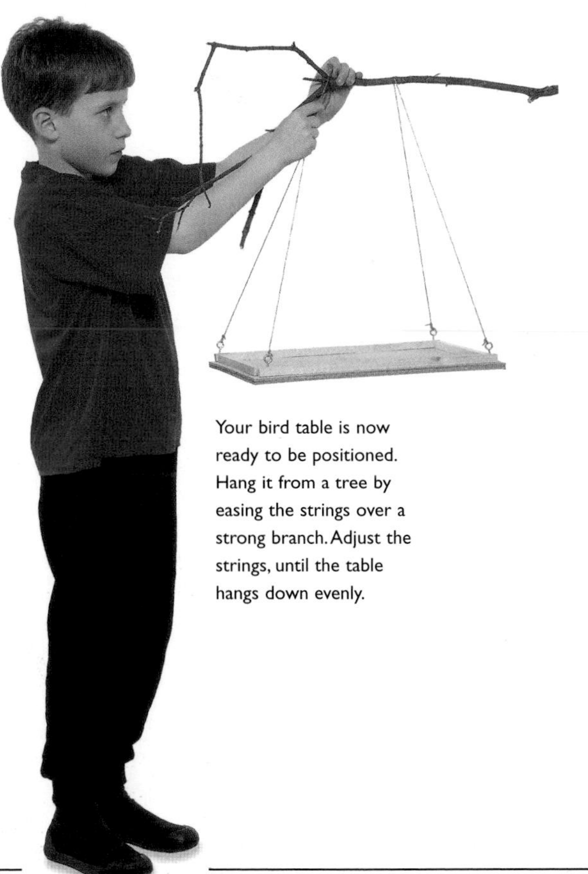

Your bird table is now ready to be positioned. Hang it from a tree by easing the strings over a strong branch. Adjust the strings, until the table hangs down evenly.

Tell-tale bird traces

In nature, birds peck at nuts, fruit and berries. Their beaks leave tell-tale marks. These signs can help you to identify the birds that made them. A good field guide will help you to find out whether food remains have been left by birds rather than small animals, such as mice and squirrels. Hunters, such as owls, leave special food remains behind. They swallow voles, mice and even small birds whole. Once or twice a day, the bird chokes up the remains that it cannot digest, in a tightly packed ball, or pellets. By examining a pellet closely, as in the second project, you can discover exactly what the hunting animal caught the previous day.

Bird feathers are made of a flexible substance, called keratin, that is also found in human hair and nails. They are amazingly strong, but weigh almost nothing. Feathers are windproof and most are waterproof. Feathers are used in flying and to help keep birds warm and dry. Some male birds use bright plumage (feathers) to attract a mate. The shade of plumage may also help to camouflage a bird from predators. Watch for dropped feathers around your bird table.

▲ Searching for pellets
Look around the base of trees for all kinds of interesting animal remains. Pellets left by hunting birds are found under trees with low branches, where the birds may perch.

▼ Mounting feathers
Cut slits in a page of a notebook and slide them in. This also makes the feathers easy to remove.

▲ Light as air
Down feathers are light and fluffy. They lie next to the bird's skin, and help keep the bird warm.

▲ Flying high
Flight feathers are found on the wings and tail, and are strong and stiff. Tail feathers help with steering.

◀ Flight aid
Body or contour feathers cover the bird's body and give it a streamlined shape, which helps it fly well.

Finding out about feathers

1 Study a bird's flight feather under a magnifying glass. Split the feather's barbs (individual strands). You can now observe the barbules (the fringed edges).

2 Repair the feather's surface, just as a bird does during preening. Smooth the barbs between your finger and thumb, so that they join back together properly.

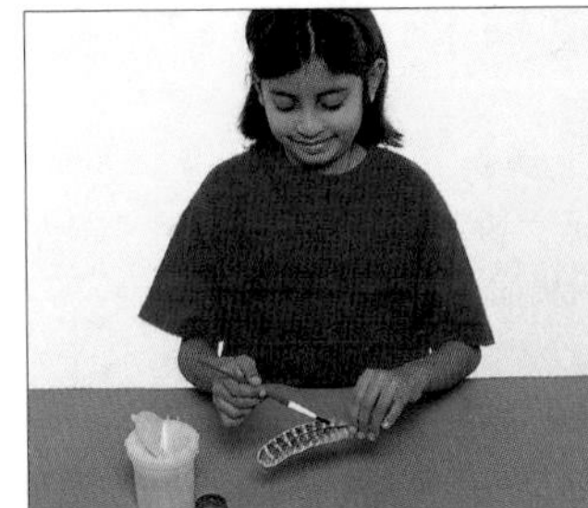

3 Now try another experiment. Add a little water to some paint, and brush it on your flight feather. What happens to the paint? Why do you think this is?

YOU WILL NEED

Finding out about feathers: Feathers, magnifying glass, water, paint, water pot, paintbrush.

Dissect an owl pellet: Rubber gloves, owl pellet, bowl, warm water, dishwashing detergent, tweezers, kitchen paper, small box, tissue paper.

Dissect an owl pellet

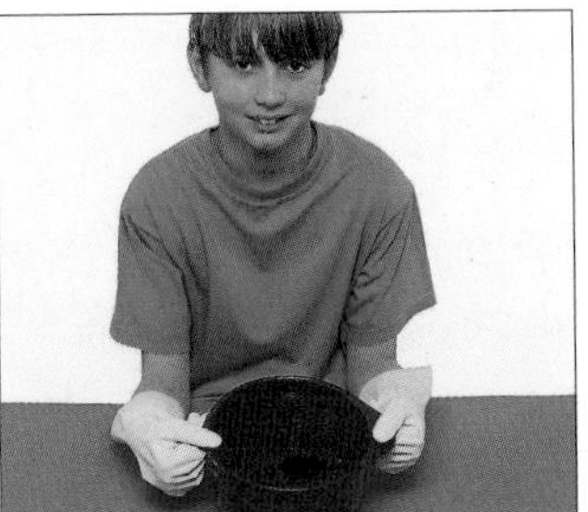

1 Wear rubber gloves for this project. First, soak the owl pellet in a bowl of warm water with a little dishwashing detergent added. Leave the pellet until it has softened.

2 Using a pair of tweezers, gently begin to pull the pellet apart. Inside, you will find the fur, teeth, skulls and other bones of small animals that the owl has eaten.

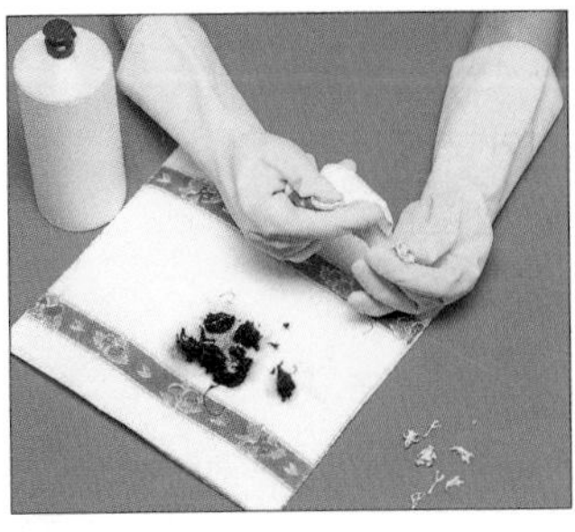

3 Use the tweezers to carefully separate the bones from the fur. Wash the bones in warm, soapy water, and pat them dry gently with a kitchen paper.

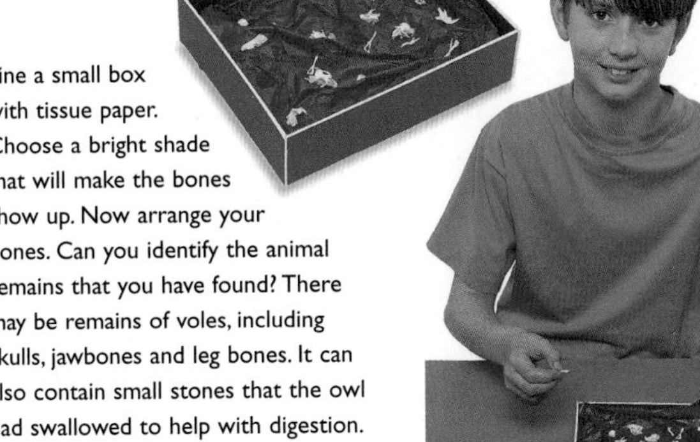

Line a small box with tissue paper. Choose a bright shade that will make the bones show up. Now arrange your bones. Can you identify the animal remains that you have found? There may be remains of voles, including skulls, jawbones and leg bones. It can also contain small stones that the owl had swallowed to help with digestion.

Bird travel and flight

Many birds travel vast distances each year. They may travel to escape the chill of winter, to find food or a safe nesting site. Departure is often triggered by the shortening daylight hours of the autumn (fall). In the spring, the birds travel back again. These journeys are called migrations. Many species (kinds) do not feed while they travel, so must fatten up before they leave. Migrating birds face many dangers. They may get lost in storms or be killed by predators. Thousands die of hunger, thirst and exhaustion.

Flying takes up a lot of energy, but has many advantages for birds. Hovering uses the most energy of all. However, birds are able to save their energy by gliding on air currents. Large birds soar upwards into air currents, with their wings outstretched to trap as much air as possible. Making an aerofoil (airfoil) in the project opposite shows how the shape of a wing produces lift. Then build a spiral model to see how birds circle in warm air currents without flapping their wings.

▲ Lift and flight
A bird's wing is slightly curved at the top, and flatter underneath. A shape like this, which is designed to provide uplift in flight, is called an aerofoil (airfoil). As the bird moves through the air, the curved shape makes the air travel faster over the wing than beneath it. This makes an area of low air pressure above the wing, which allows the bird to rise. Aircraft are able to fly, because their wings are a similar shape to a bird's wings.

Migration routes

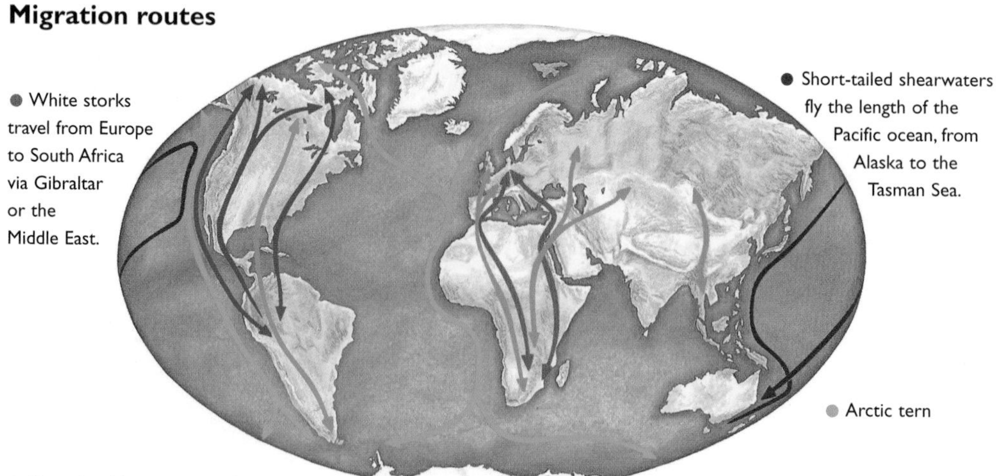

● White storks travel from Europe to South Africa via Gibraltar or the Middle East.

● Short-tailed shearwaters fly the length of the Pacific ocean, from Alaska to the Tasman Sea.

● Arctic tern

● Peregrine falcons migrate from Canada to Argentina. They are also found in Europe and Asia.

● American golden plover

● Swallows migrate from northern Europe and Asia, to South Africa and back again – nearly 20,000km/12,500 miles.

How a wing works

1 Cut a strip of paper about 30cm/12in long. Glue the ends together firmly. When the glue is dry, bend the paper into a wing shape, curved on top and flat underneath.

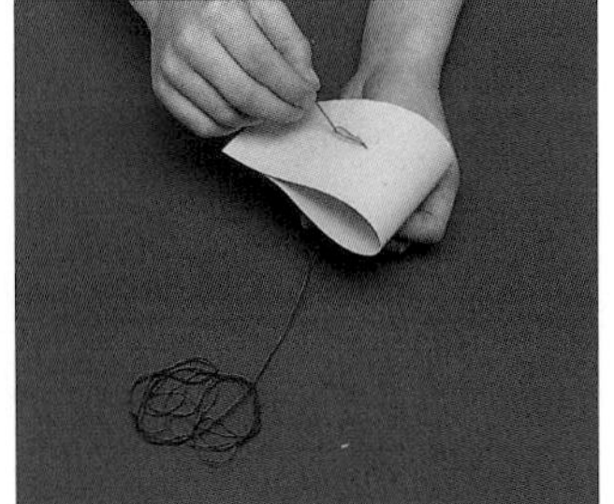

2 Mark the middle of the wing. Thread a long piece of thread on to a needle and push it through the middle of the wing. Gently pull the aerofoil (airfoil) down the thread.

3 Now get a friend to hold the thread taut. Blow hard against the curved edge of the aerofoil, and watch the wing rise up the thread – just as an airplane or a bird's wing lifts.

Soaring spiral

YOU WILL NEED

How a wing works: Paper, scissors, glue, pencil, needle, thread.

Soaring spiral: Thick paper, pair of compasses, pencil, coloured pencils/felt-tipped pens, scissors, pencil with eraser on end, reel of thread, pin, thimble.

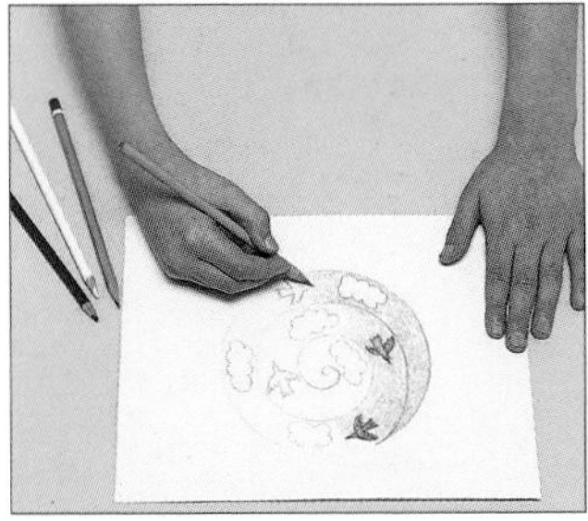

1 Use a pair of compasses and a pencil to draw a circle on a piece of paper. Now draw and shade in a spiral shape with buzzards (or other birds) flying around it.

2 Carefully cut out the decorated paper spiral. Use a pencil to make the hole left in the middle of the spiral by your compasses, big enough to fit over the thimble.

3 Fit the pencil point into the reel. Put the pin in the eraser. Push the thimble through the hole in the paper spiral, so that it sits over the thimble. Balance the thimble on the pin.

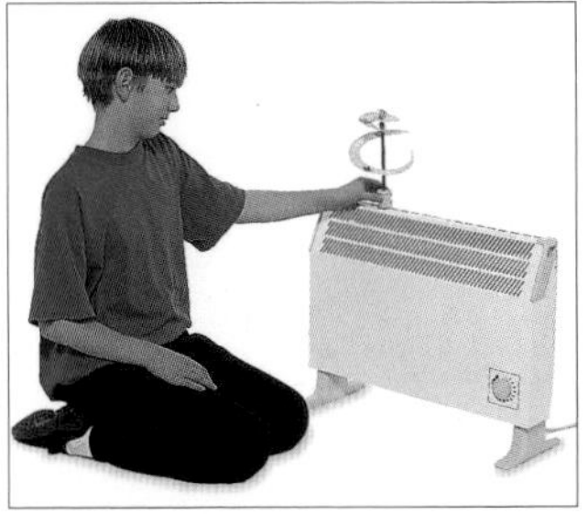

4 Stand your model on a radiator. Now watch the buzzards circling around in the warm air currents that rise from the radiator. Your model must be well balanced to work properly.

Physical and Material Marvels

We live in a world of engineering marvels – of soaring skyscrapers, wide-spanning bridges, and massive dams. We can communicate with almost everyone, anywhere on the Earth, and even in Space. This section shows the part that science and technology have played in setting the pace of change. Science accumulates knowledge about the world by observation, study and experiment. Technology puts the knowledge into practical use as inventions, to improve the quality of life.

Chemical change

Over the past 100 years, scientists have invented many substances, such as plastics, medicines and detergents, that we take for granted today. These substances are created by chemical reactions. In a chemical reaction, a new substance (called a product) is made as a result of other substances (called reactants) undergoing chemical change. Many chemical reactions happen naturally, such as oil (petrol) and gas, which form from the remains of animals and plants. They are called hydrocarbons, because they are mixtures of hydrogen and carbon.

The following experiments demonstrate the three main ways in which chemical reactions can happen – by passing electricity through substances, by heating them, or simply by mixing them together. In the first, electricity breaks down salty water to make chlorine (the disinfectant often used in swimming pools). In the second, heat turns sugar, which is made from carbon, hydrogen and oxygen, into pure carbon. Finally, you make the gas used in some fire extinguishers by mixing bicarbonate of soda (baking soda) and vinegar together.

WARNING!
Please take care when using electrical equipment. Always have an adult present.

▲ **Checking up**
A technician is ensuring all the bottles of chemicals are correctly labelled. Accuracy is very important in science.

YOU WILL NEED

Electrolysis: Battery (4–6 volts), bulb and holder, wires, wire strippers, screwdriver, paper clips, salt, jar, water.

Heat changes: Old pan, teaspoon, sugar, stove.

Getting a reaction: Teaspoon, bicarbonate of soda (baking soda), glass bowl, vinegar, matches.

How oil is formed

The story of oil begins in warm seas full of living things. As they die, they fall to the bottom of the sea floor to decay into thick, black mud.

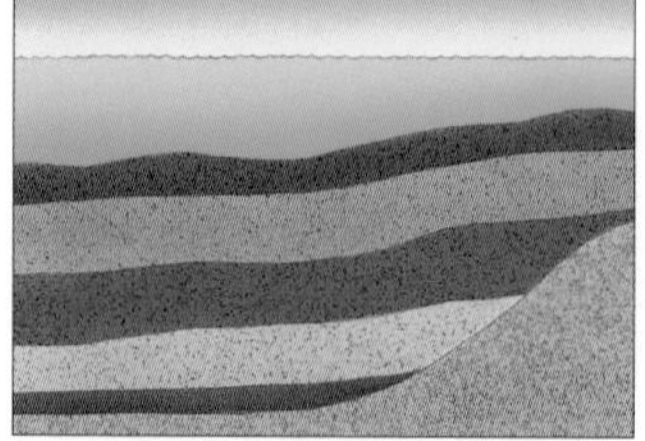

In time, mud is buried beneath many layers of sand, with clay in between. The sediments (deposits) sink deeper and deeper, and also become hotter.

After millions of years, the sediments fold under pressure. Oil from the black mud is forced into sandstones and trapped under the layers of clay.

Electrolysis

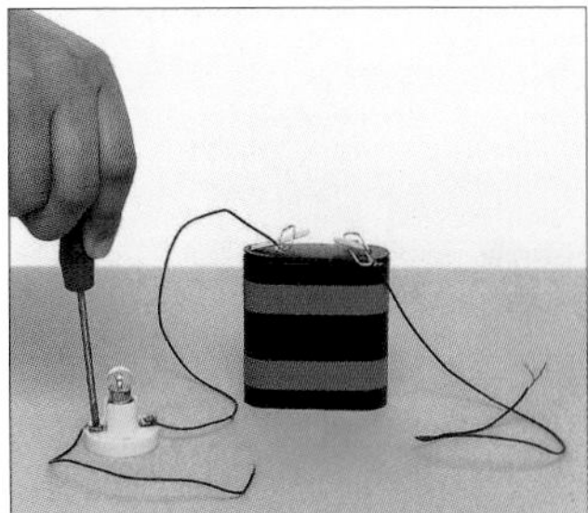

1 With adult help, connect the battery and bulb holder with wires, as shown. Remove 1cm/½in of insulation from each end of wire. Use the paper clips to attach the wires to the battery.

2 Stir salt into a jar of water until no more dissolves. Dip the two bare wire ends into the mixture and hold them about 1cm/½in apart. Look for bubbles forming around them.

3 The bulb should light to show that electricity is passing through. Carefully sniff the jar from 20cm/8in away. What does it smell like? The smell is like swimming pools!

Heat changes

1 Make sure the pan is completely dry. Spread one teaspoonful of sugar across the bottom of the pan. Aim for a thin layer – about 5mm/¼in thick.

2 With adult supervision, place the pan over a low heat. After a few minutes, the sugar will start to melt into a thick, brown liquid. You may begin to see a few wisps of steam.

3 The sugar starts to bubble as it breaks down and gives off steam. If you continue heating the sugar, the brown, sticky liquid will change to solid black carbon.

Getting a reaction

1 Place three heaped spoonfuls of bicarbonate of soda in the bowl. Cooks often add this white powder to vegetables, such as peas and carrots. It helps to keep their natural colour.

2 Carefully pour vinegar into the bowl. As the liquid mixes with the bicarbonate of soda, a chemical reaction happens. The mixture bubbles as a gas is given off.

The gas is called carbon dioxide. Ask an adult to lower a lighted match into the bowl. The flame goes out when it meets the gas.

Tests with yeast

For thousands of years, people all over the world have used yeast for brewing beer and baking bread. Yeast is a type of fungus that lives on the skins of many fruits. Just a spoonful of yeast contains millions of separate, single-celled (very simple) organisms. Each one works like a tiny chemical factory, taking in sugar, and giving out alcohol and carbon dioxide gas. While they feed, the yeast cells grow larger and then reproduce by splitting in half.

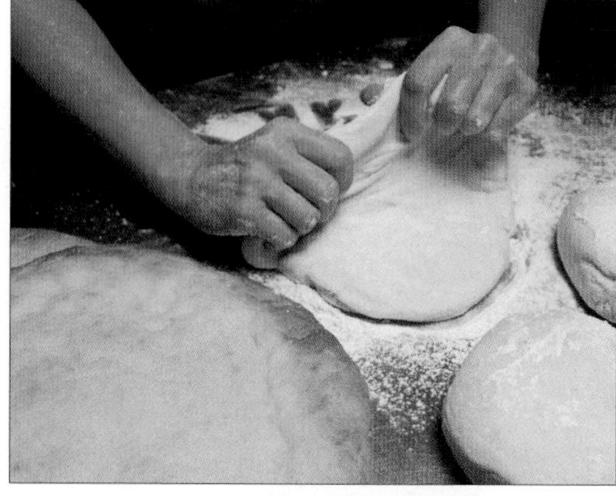

▲ **Kneading dough**
Bread is kneaded into a soft dough and then left in a warm place to rise. The dough is then kneaded again before it is baked. This process makes the yeast produce as many bubbles of gas as possible, so that the bread is light.

Yeast turns grape juice into alcoholic wine, and makes beer from mixtures of grain and water. When it is added to uncooked dough, yeast produces gas bubbles that make the bread light and soft. Brewing and baking are important modern industries that depend on yeast working quickly.

This project consists of four separate experiments. By comparing the results, you can discover the best conditions for yeast to grow. It needs a moist environment to be active. Lack of moisture makes the cells dry out and hibernate (sleep). Add water to dried, powdered yeast, and – even after many years – it will become active again.

Finding the best conditions

YOU WILL NEED

Measuring cup, water, kettle, adhesive labels, four small glass jars, teaspoon, dried yeast granules, sugar, scissors, transluscent food covering, three rubber bands, two heatproof bowls, ice cubes.

1 Half fill a kettle with water. Ask an adult to boil it for you, and then put it aside to cool. Boiling the water kills all living organisms that might stop the yeast from growing.

2 Label the glass jars, one to four. Put a level teaspoonful of dried yeast into each jar, as shown above. Then put the same amount of sugar into each jar.

3 Pour 150ml/¼ pint/⅔ cup of the cooled water into the first three jars. Stir to dissolve the sugar. Do not pour water into the fourth jar. Put this jar away in a warm place.

4 Cut out pieces of food covering about twice a jar's width. Stretch one across the neck of each remaining jar, and secure it with a rubber band. Put the first jar in a warm place.

5 Place the second jar in a glass bowl. Put some ice cubes and cold water into the bowl. This will keep the jar's temperature close to freezing.

6 Place the third jar in another glass bowl. Pour in some hot water that is almost too hot to touch. Be careful not to use boiling water, or the jar may crack.

high temperature

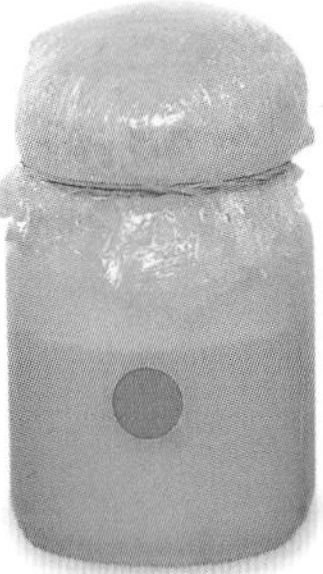

warm temperature

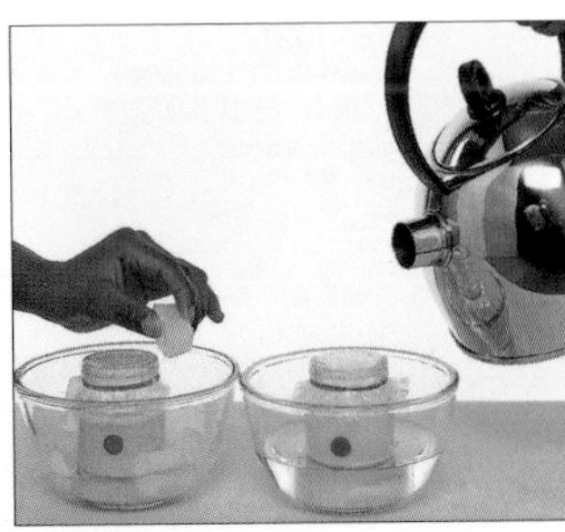

7 Regularly check all four jars over the next two hours. As the ice around the second jar melts, add more to keep the temperature low. Add more hot water to keep the third jar hot.

cold temperature

dry jar

In the jar that was kept hot, the yeast is a cloudy layer at the bottom, killed by the heat. The jar that was kept cold has only a little froth on the surface, because the cold has slowed down the yeast.

The yeast that was kept warm has fed on the water and sugar, and its gas is pushing up the food covering. In the dry jar there are no signs of activity, because the yeast is hibernating.

Preservation and decay

▲ **Protected by the gods**
Turning the body of a great Egyptian pharaoh into a mummy was a complicated process. In addition to the preserving process, a jackal-masked priest performed sacred rituals.

Decay is the breaking up of dead organic matter, such as animals and plants. It results when invisible creatures called bacteria, and tiny fungi called moulds, breed. The bodies of living plants and animals fight these agents of destruction, but as soon as the animals die, decay begins. Bacteria and moulds that cause decay need water to live, so decay happens best in damp conditions.

The process of preserving something aims to stop it from decaying. The ancient Egyptians were skilled at mummifying (preserving) their kings' bodies. They removed moist internal organs, such as the intestines, heart, liver and brain. Then they buried the body in natron, a kind of salt. This dried out all the fluids that speed up decay. The body was then wrapped in bandages. The bandages had been soaked in oily resins that killed bacteria and moulds in a similar way to modern antiseptic creams. You can practice slowing down and speeding up the process of decay in these two experiments.

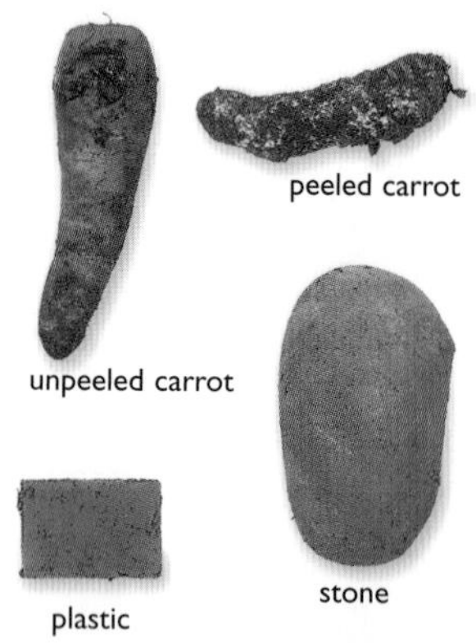

What decays?

1 Peel one of the apples and one of the carrots. Line the tray with some newspaper. Add a layer of compost and place all the items on top. Add more compost to cover the items.

2 Dig a shallow hole in a shady spot and put the tray in it. Cover it with soil so that you can just see its top edges. Buried like this, the items will stay damp. Dig the tray up after a week.

Examine the results. Fruit and vegetables are attacked quickly by bacteria and moulds, especially if they have no skins. Wood takes months to decay. Stone and plastic do not decay.

Preventing decay

YOU WILL NEED

What decays?: Rubber gloves, knife or peeler, two apples, two carrots, plastic tray with holes, newspaper, compost, stone, plastic object, piece of wood, spade.

Preventing decay: Three slices of bread, three plastic bags with ties, antiseptic cream, three tags, pen, knife, rubber gloves.

1 Put one slice of ordinary bread into a plastic bag, and seal it with a tie. Now toast another slice of bread until it is crispy and dry. Seal the toast in another plastic bag.

2 Spread some antiseptic cream, which is designed to kill germs, over one side of a third slice. Seal the antiseptic cream-coated third slice in another plastic bag.

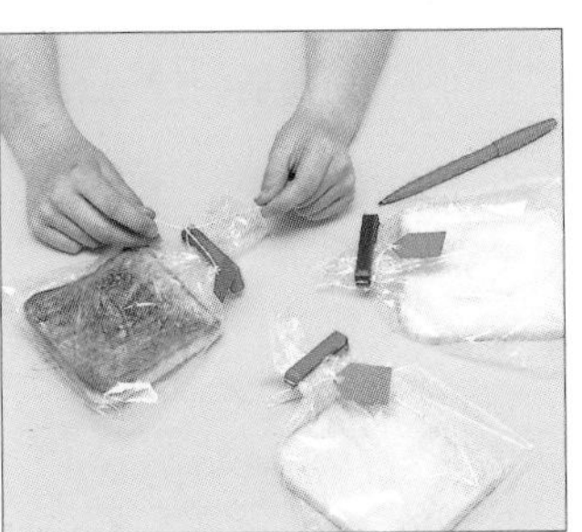

3 Label each plastic bag. Leave them in a warm place and check them once a day. Bacteria and moulds are everywhere. What will they do inside your plastic bags?

▲ **Dry toast**
Look at the slices. Mould and bacteria cannot grow on the dry toast, since there is no moisture.

Do not open the bags when you have finished looking at the results. Keep the moulds and bacteria wrapped inside their plastic bags, and drop the bags into a garbage bin.

▲ **Antiseptic cream**
The chemicals in the antiseptic cream have killed any germs on the cream-covered slice of bread.

▲ **Ordinary bread**
The ordinary slice of bread is very mouldy. Mould and bacteria have thrived in the moist conditions.

Stone and concrete

Buildings that are made of hard stone last much longer than those made of dried earth or bricks. The people who lived in early civilizations carved stone with simple hammers and chisels – the same as you will try to do in the first experiment. When the ancient Egyptians built the pyramids more than 4,000 years ago, they had to drive large wedges into cracks in the rock face to lever off blocks of stone.

Ancient peoples used stone that they found locally, and gradually learned to use different rocks for different jobs. The Inca people of South America built with granite, a hard, igneous (volcanic) rock. The ancient Egyptians also used granite, but limestone, a softer, more easily carved sedimentary rock, was common too. Certain rocks, such as marble, were selected for decorative effects, because of their beautiful patterns and tones. Many modern buildings are made of concrete, a mixture of ground-down rocks and minerals. You can test its strength in the second experiment.

Great Pyramid, Giza

Statue of Liberty

Nelson's Column

Sydney Opera House

▲ Ancient scale
The Great Pyramid in Egypt is the largest stone building in the world, even though it was built over 4,000 years ago. It is made up of over 2 million blocks of stone, each of which weighs an average of 2½ tons.

YOU WILL NEED
Blunt, round-ended knife, solid foam chunk used by flower-arrangers, foamed concrete (fairly soft) type of building brick.

Cutting and carving

1 Could you be a sculptor? Practice by marking out a simple shape on the flower-arranging foam. Use the knife to cut around it. How easy is it to use this material?

2 Now do the same with your building brick. This is much harder, but it is still softer than stone. Make sure that the knife blade is pointed away from you.

Now you know how hard it is to carve material that is much softer than stone. How long do you think it would take you to carve real stone with simple tools?

Mix your own concrete

YOU WILL NEED
Rubber gloves, measuring cup, sand, bucket, cement, gravel, water, stirring stick, old metal tray, small thin box, foil.

1 Place one cupful of sand in a bucket. Add two cups of cement and a handful of gravel. Take care not to touch the cement with your bare hands.

2 Add some water to the mixture, little by little. Keep stirring all the time, until the mixture has the consistency of oatmeal. Mix it well with the stick.

3 Pour the wet concrete on to a shallow metal tray and spread it out. Leave it to solidify for about half an hour. Wash all the other equipment you have used immediately.

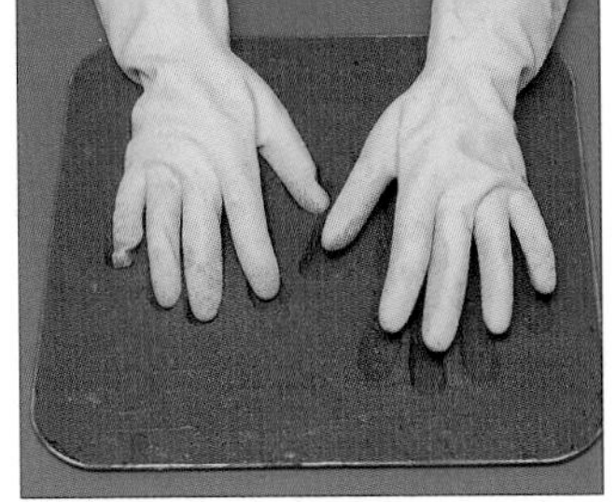

4 Now you can shape the concrete. Make impressions of your hands, or write with the stick. The marks will be permanent once the concrete has set. Do not use your bare hands.

hand prints in concrete

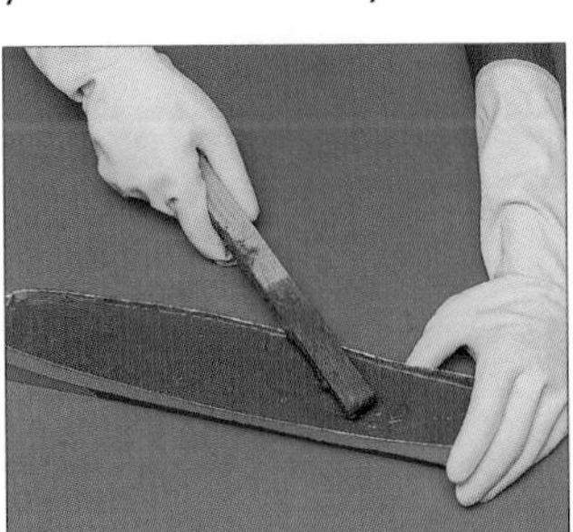

5 You could make a concrete brick like those used in the construction industry. Line a small, strong box with foil. Pour in the concrete and smooth the top with the stick.

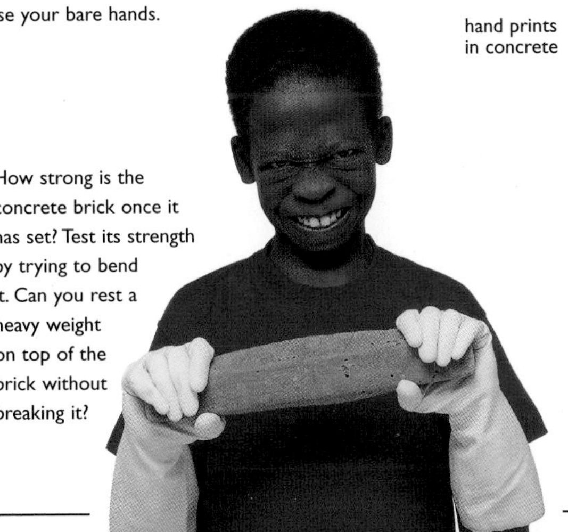

How strong is the concrete brick once it has set? Test its strength by trying to bend it. Can you rest a heavy weight on top of the brick without breaking it?

Building bridges

A platform bridge was a very early human invention, dating back tens of thousands of years. The simplest platform bridges were just a tree trunk or a single slab of stone, laid across a narrow river or steep gully, so that people could get across. Many modern platform bridges are hollow and made of steel. The model here shows how thin folded sheets make platform bridges stronger.

If you stand on a simple platform bridge, the downward force of your weight makes it sag in the middle. Too much weight can snap a flat wooden plank or crack a stone slab. As the second experiment shows, however, arch bridges do not sag when loaded. They curve up and over the gap that they span, and the forces acting on the arch squeeze it together. Weight from above is pushed outward, so that the load spreads to the side supports. The Romans were among the first to build arch bridges.

YOU WILL NEED

Make a platform: Scissors, thin card, ruler, pen, two boards 20 x 20cm/8 x 8in, non-hardening modelling material.

Make an arch: Newspaper, two house bricks, ruler, sand, six wooden toy building blocks, plaster, water, plastic spoon, foil tray, plastic knife.

Make a platform

1 Cut out four strips of card 40 x 10cm/16 x 4in. With a ruler and pen, draw lines 1cm/½in apart across each card. Fold each card back and forth across the lines, to form zigzag pleats.

2 Lay one board flat on the table. Stand a piece of pleated card upright along the board's edges. Repeat for the other three sides. Use modelling clay to secure each corner.

3 When all sides of the platform are in place, lay the second board on top. Push downward with your hand. Pleating the card has made the platform very strong. Your platform is stronger than a platform bridge, because it is supported on four sides. Without this support, it would sag in the middle.

Make an arch

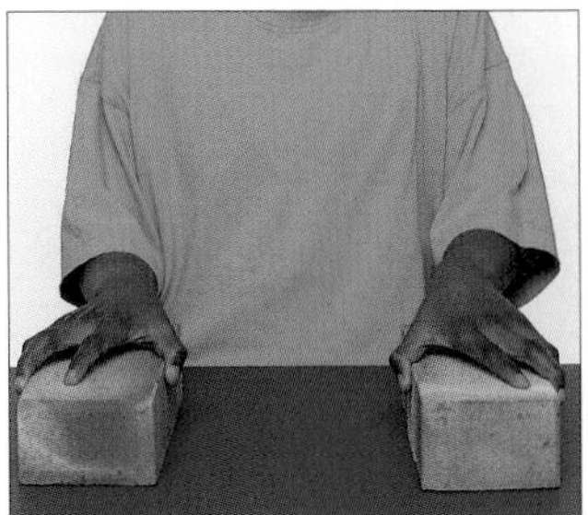

1 Although it is not shown in this picture, it would be a good idea to cover the surface with newspaper first. Place the two bricks on the work surface about 20cm/8in apart.

2 Pile sand between the bricks, and smooth it with your hands to make a curved mound. Place the wooden blocks side by side across the sand. They should touch the outer blocks.

3 The inner blocks touch each other but have V-shaped gaps between them. Mix the plaster with water until it forms a stiff paste. Use the knife to fill gaps between the blocks with paste.

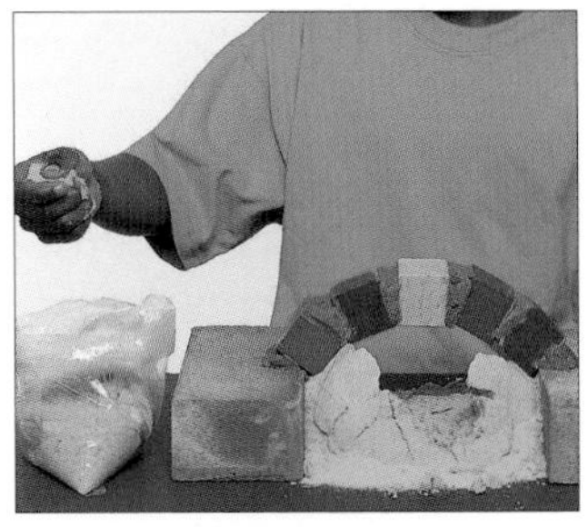

4 Make sure you have filled each space where the arch meets the bricks. Wait for the plaster to dry. Once it is dry, remove the sand from underneath the arch.

5 Push down on the arch and feel how firm it is. The weight that you are putting on the bridge is supported by the two bricks at the side. This bridge is stronger than a platform bridge, and does not sag in the middle. Like stone slabs in real bridges, the wooden toy blocks make a remarkably strong curve.

toy building blocks

Tunnel construction

A tunnel has to bear the weight of millions of tons of rocks and earth – or even water – above it. One way of doing this is to make lots of brick arches that together run the length of the tunnel. An arched roof is much stronger than a flat one, because weight from above is pushed out sideways, as the first experiment shows. In the second project, you place a wedge-shaped keystone at the peak of the arch. In real life, this keystone locks the whole structure together. It compresses (squeezes) the bricks on either side, to make the arch self-supporting and very strong.

Today, a long, trainlike machine is used to bore tunnels. A big drill carves out the hole, sending the waste backwards on a conveyor belt. Behind it, robotic cranes lift precast concrete sections of the tube-shaped tunnel into place.

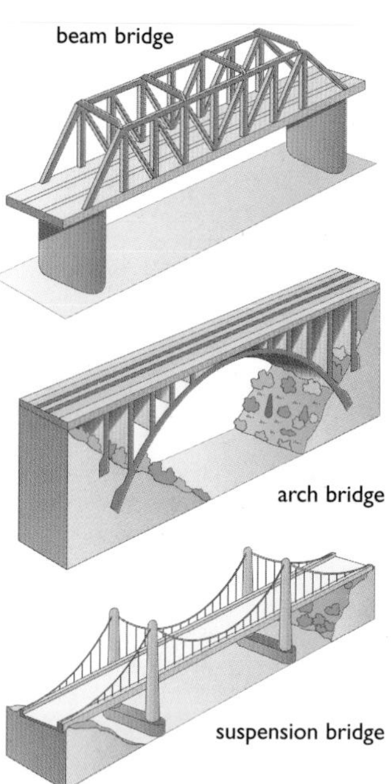

▲ Bridge types
The beam bridge (*top*) is made of horizontal platform supported on two or more piers (pillars). Arch bridges (*middle*) are built over steep valleys and rivers. Suspension bridges (*bottom*) support the longest bridges. The weight of the platform is carried by steel wires that hang from cables. The cables are held up by concrete towers and anchored firmly at the valley's sides.

▼ Templates

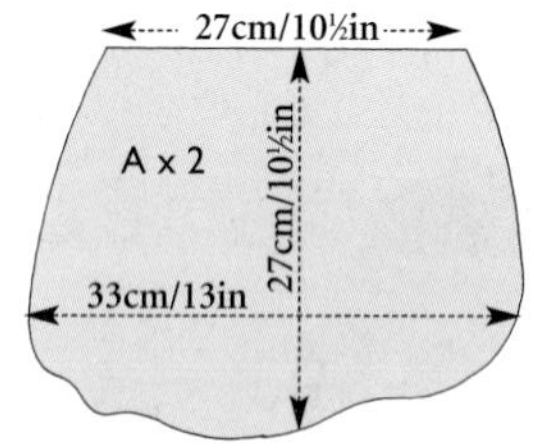

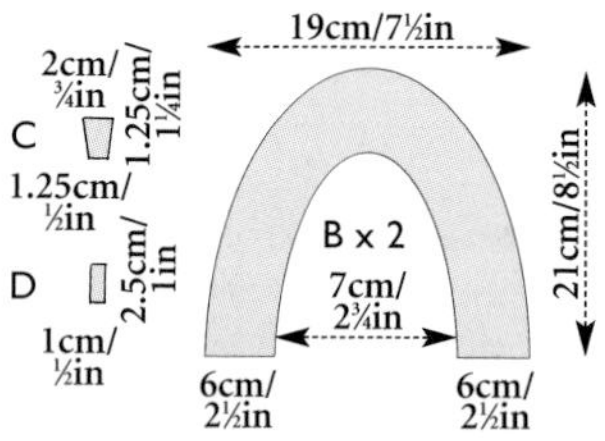

Strength test

YOU WILL NEED
Two pieces of cardboard (width roughly the same as the length of the blocks or bricks), two wooden building blocks or house bricks, a few heavy pebbles.

1 Place one of the pieces of cardboard on top of the building blocks. Place pebbles on top, as shown above. You will see that the tunnel roof sags under the weight.

2 Curve a second piece of cardboard under the flat roof, as shown. The roof supports the weight of the pebbles because the arch supports the flat section, making it stronger.

Tunnel in a landscape

YOU WILL NEED

Masking tape, two pieces of cardboard measuring 36 x 30cm/14½ x 12in and 46 x 27cm/18½ x 10½in, ruler, pencil, scissors, thin card measuring 44 x 40cm/17¾ x 16in, newspaper, cup of flour, ½ cup of water, acrylic paints, paintbrush, water pot, thin card (A4 size/8¼ x 11¾in), white glue, glue brush, old sponge.

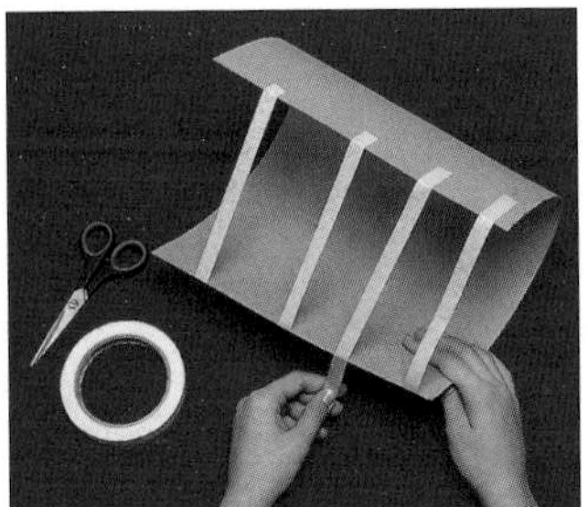

1 Tear off about four long strips of masking tape. Curve the 46 x 27cm/18½ x 10½in rectangle of cardboard lengthways. Use the tape to hold the curve in place.

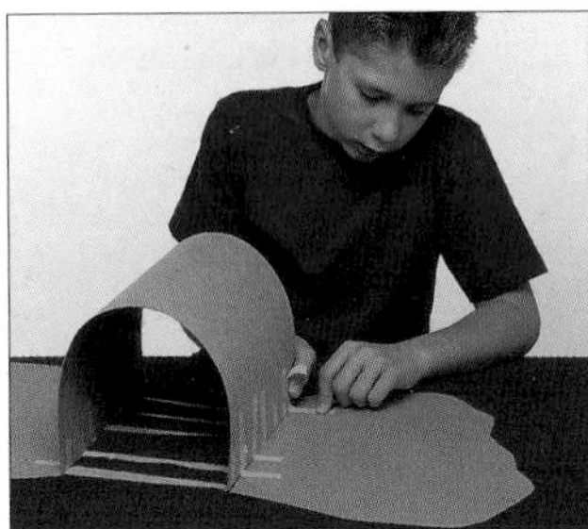

2 Copy the two templates A on to two 36 x 30cm/14½ x 12in pieces of cardboard. Cut out the shapes. Attach each one to the sides of the tunnel, and secure with tape, as shown above.

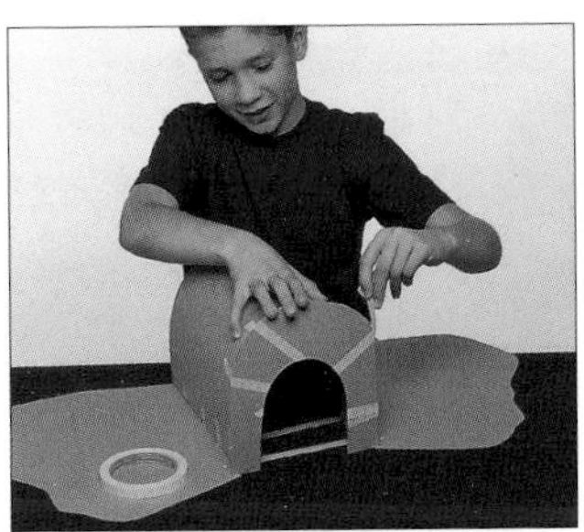

3 Fold the 44 x 40cm/17¾ x 16in thin card in half. Copy the arch template B on to the card. Cut out to make the two tunnel entrances. Stick these to the tunnel with masking tape, as shown.

4 Scrunch newspaper into balls, and tape to the tunnel and landscape. Mix the flour and water to make a thick paste. Dip newspaper strips in the paste. Lay them over the tunnel.

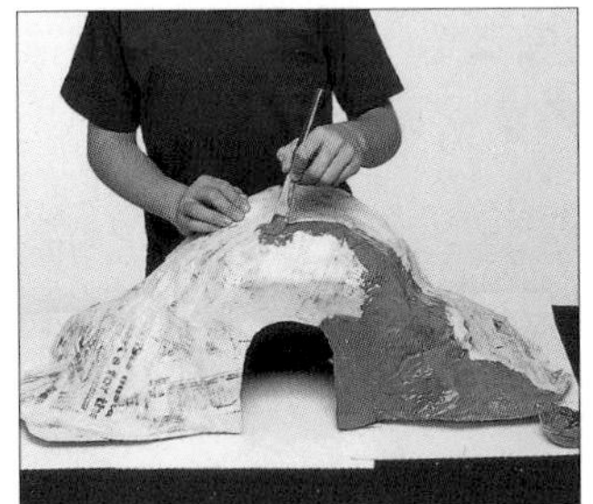

5 Leave to dry overnight. When completely dry and hard, paint the tunnel and landscape green. Apply up to three coats, letting each one dry before you apply the next.

6 Paint the thin card to look like brick. Draw and cut out templates C and D. Draw around them on to the brick card, to make the keystone and lots of bricks. Allow paint to dry.

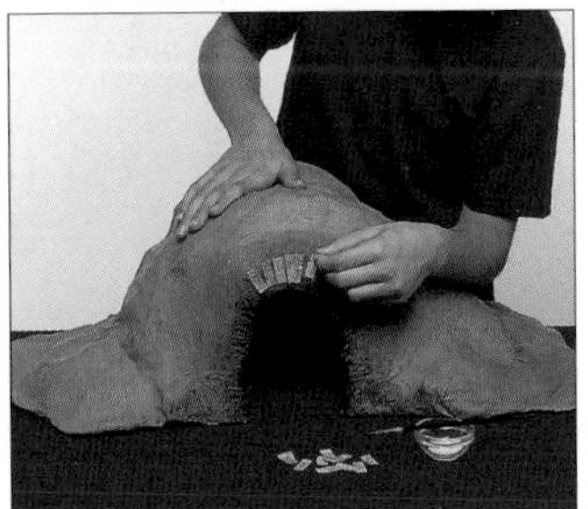

7 Glue the keystone at the top of the tunnel entrance. Then glue bricks around the arch at either side of the keystone. In real tunnels, there are keystones along the tunnel length.

8 Dip pieces of old sponge into green acrylic paint to make bushes. Leave to dry. Stick them on the landscape. Apply three coats of paint to the whole landscape.

The strength of a pyramid

Over a period of more than 4,500 years, people in different parts of the world built huge pyramids. The oldest Egyptian pyramids were started almost 4,600 years ago, while the youngest pyramids in Central America were finished about 600 years ago. Each one took a long time to build, sometimes over 50 years, and involved thousands of people.

Why did these civilizations opt for a pyramidal structure rather than a cube or a rectangle for their monuments? These experiments will help you to find out. In the first, by changing a cube into a pyramid, you end up with a structure that is three times taller than the original cube. A pyramid makes good use of material, by making the structure as high as possible. The second project shows that triangular shapes are more rigid than squares and do not collapse as easily. When an earthquake destroyed the Egyptian city of Cairo 700 years ago, the pyramids stood firm. Modern materials and technology make it possible to build tall, rectangular buildings that are strong and stable.

▲ **Steep challenge**
The Egyptians had no cranes to help them move the enormous slabs of stone used to build the pyramids. Workers built ramps of hard-packed earth. They hauled the slabs up these using plant-fibre ropes and wooden rollers. As the pyramid grew, the ramps became longer and steeper. When the pyramid was finished, the ramps were removed.

Bases and heights

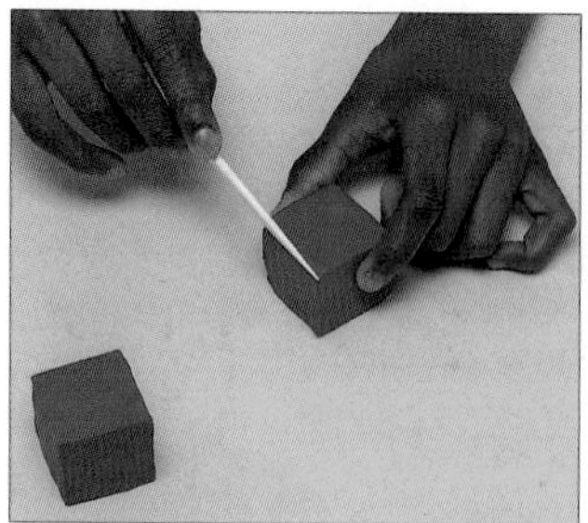

1 Make two cubes from modelling material. The faces should measure about 3–4cm/1–1½in, but they must all be the same. Use a ruler to check your measurements.

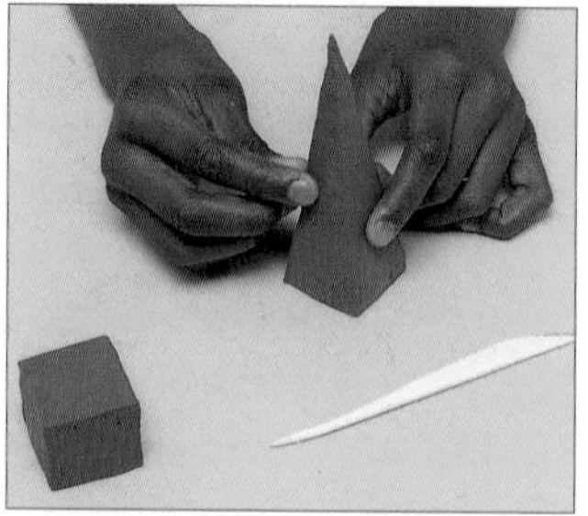

2 Reshape one of the cubes to form a tall, square-based pyramid. Its base must be the same size as the original cube. You now have a cube and a pyramid.

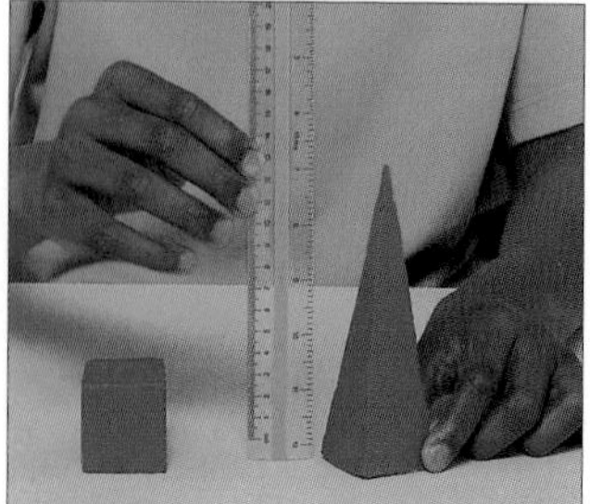

3 Now measure the cube and pyramid. They have the same volume and the same size base. The pyramid is three times taller, but is strong and more stable.

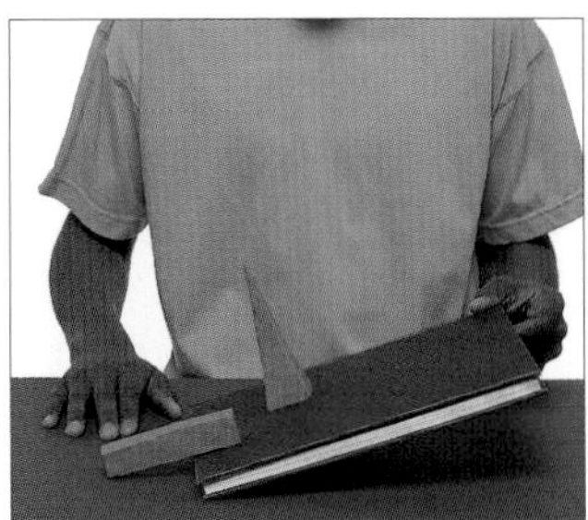

4 Make the cube into a long slabs. Place the slab and the pyramid on a book. Slowly tilt the book, to imitate the effect of an earthquake. The slab topples over before the pyramid does.

5 Make another smaller cube and pyramid from modelling material. Make sure that they are the same height. Their bases must also be the same size.

6 Do the same book test with the two smaller shapes. You should still find that the pyramid is the more stable of the two shapes. It is the second of the two shapes to fall over.

A question of strength

YOU WILL NEED

Bases and heights: Non-hardening modelling material, plastic modelling knife, ruler, book.

A question of strength: 20 large plastic drinking straws, reusable adhesive.

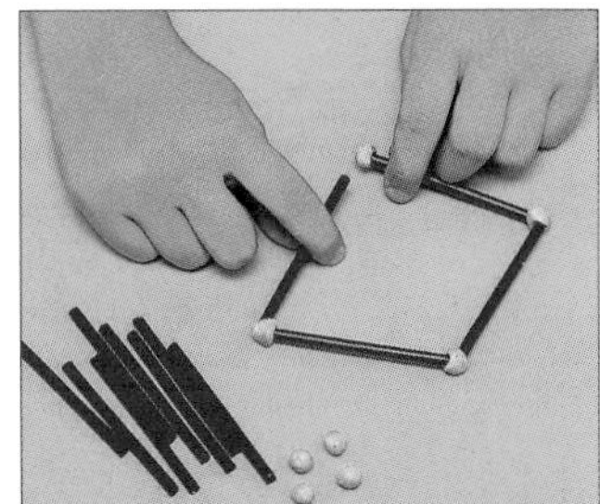

1 For this project, you will need two models – a cube and a square-based pyramid. Make them out of large plastic drinking straws and reusable adhesive. First, make the cube.

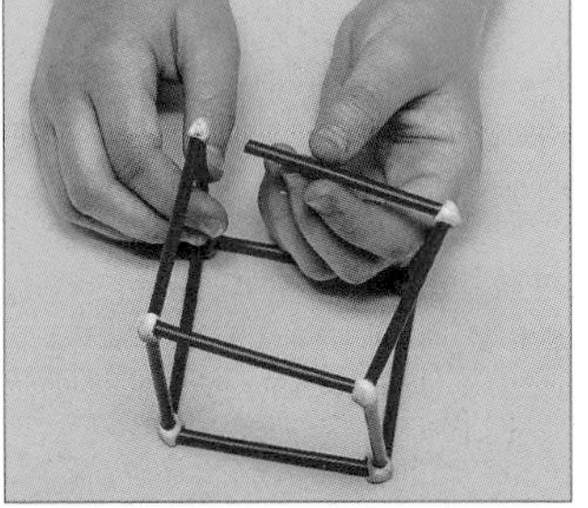

2 After fixing four straws to make the base of your cube, you need eight more to finish it. Make sure that your cube is even, with each face the same size.

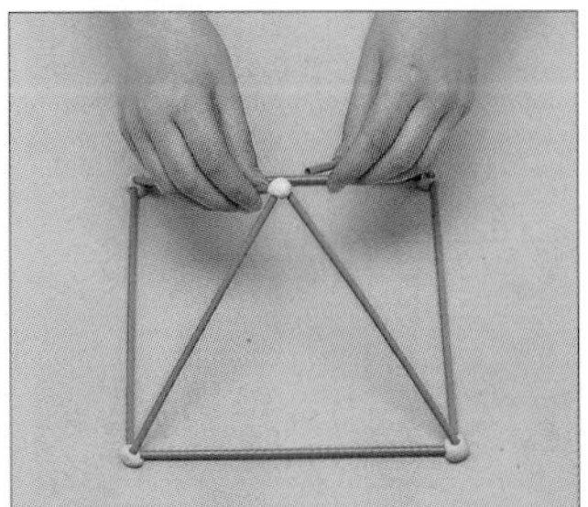

3 Now make a square-based pyramid. The base should be the same size as the base of your cube. Make the base, and just fix four more straws to it to complete your pyramid.

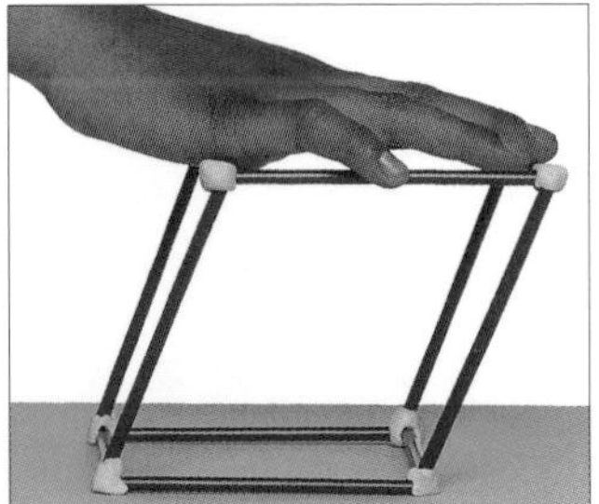

4 Push down gently with your hand over the middle of the cube. Move your hand slightly to one side as you push down, and you will feel the cube start to collapse.

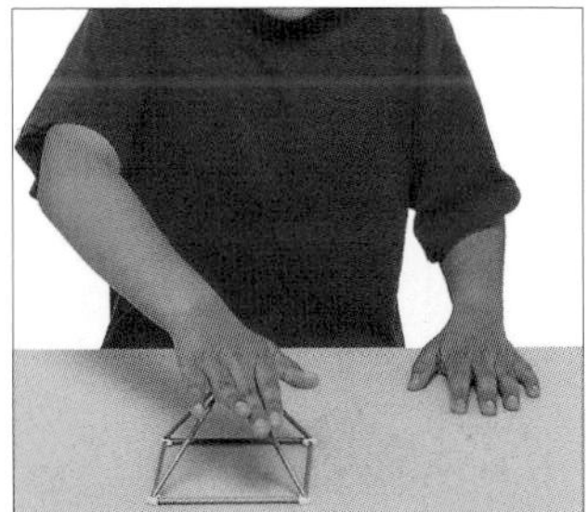

5 Repeat this with the pyramid. You can feel how much more rigid this shape is, and it does not collapse. This is because a pyramid has triangular-shaped faces that meet at a central point.

Surveying a site

Making precise measurements in order to put up a building is called surveying. Accurate building requires two things. There must be a level base to the building, and building slabs must be laid absolutely flat, with their sides perfectly vertical, at right angles to the ground. Builders use plumb lines to check that verticals are absolutely true. A plumb line is a weight on the end of a line, which holds the line straight. These experiments show how to use water levels or a plumb line to measure differences in heights on a site.

▲ **The lie of the land**
A modern surveyor makes a detailed examination of the land before building work can start.

Is it vertical?

1 Make your own plumb line by fixing a 3cm/1¼in ball of modelling material to a piece of string. Make a large knot in the string and shape the material around it.

2 Push your stick into the ground. Make it as vertical as possible (pointing straight upwards). Keep moving it slightly, until you are sure it is straight.

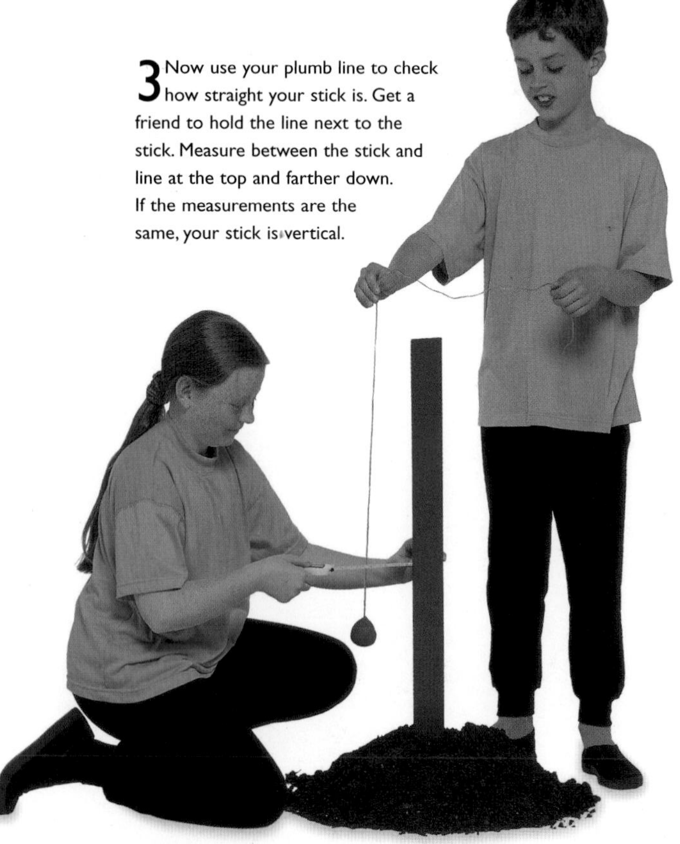

3 Now use your plumb line to check how straight your stick is. Get a friend to hold the line next to the stick. Measure between the stick and line at the top and farther down. If the measurements are the same, your stick is vertical.

Is your site level?

YOU WILL NEED

Is it vertical?: Non-hardening modelling material, string, a stick (about 1m/1yd long), tape measure.

Is your site level?: Wooden stick 1m/1yd long, plank of wood 40 x 10cm/16 x 4in, nails, hammer, screw-in hooks, clear plastic piping (1cm/½in diameter), jug (pitcher), water dyed with ink, funnel, tape measure, wooden pole 1m/1yd long, pen.

1 Here, you are making a simple version of a surveyor's level. With adult help, nail the short plank of wood to the top of the long wooden stick. Take care with the hammer.

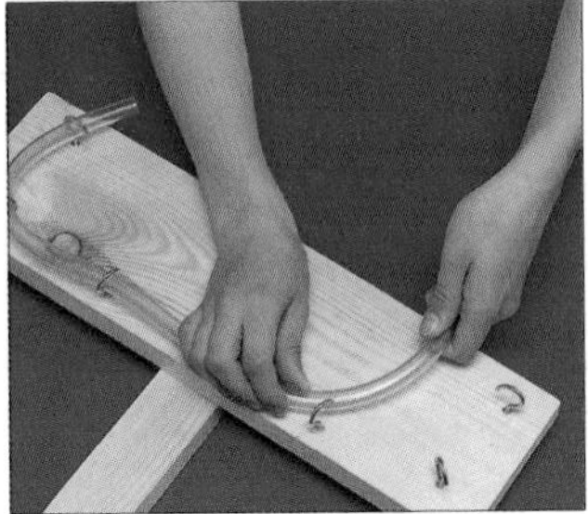

2 Now screw the hooks in along the bottom and up the sides of the plank. Thread the piping through the hooks. About 2cm/¾in of piping should stick up above the plank.

3 Get a friend to hold the device upright. Now, very carefully, pour the water into the pipe, using a funnel. The water level should come just above the piece of wood.

4 The friend holds the pole up 5m/5yd away. You look along the water levels so they line up, and also line up with the pole. The friend moves a finger up and down the pole. Shout when the friend's finger lines up with the water levels.

5 The friend marks this on the pole, then moves to another spot. Repeat step 4. The distance between the two marks on the pole shows the difference in level between the two places.

Powerful levers

One of the simplest and oldest gadgets in the world is the lever. Any rod or stick can act as a lever, helping to move heavy objects or prise things apart. Levers are also used for lifting, cutting and squashing. The action of a lever can make a push more forceful, or make it a smaller push. It can also change the direction of a push. The difference between the size of the push you make on a lever (the effort) and the push the lever itself makes (the load) is called mechanical advantage. A lever on a central pivot can also be used as a balance. The lever balances if the effect of the force (push) on one side of the pivot is the same as the effect of the force on the other. A seesaw is one sort of balancing lever. It is a plank balanced on a central post or pivot. A big person can balance someone small and light if they sit nearer to the central pivot of the seesaw.

▲ Using a simple lever

A spoon can be a lever. This girl is using the spoon as a simple lever to lift the lid off a can of paint. The lever arm pivots on the lip of the can. As the girl pushes down on the long end, the shorter end wedged under the lid lifts it up with greater force, making the stiff lid move.

▲ Cracking a nut

The strong crushing action of the nutcracker's jaws is produced by pressing the two lever arms together. A pair of nutcrackers, like a pair of scissors or a pair of pliers, has two lever arms joined at a pivot. The levers make the effort you use about four times bigger, allowing you to break the nut easily. Putting the pivot at the end of the nutcracker rather than toward the middle (as in a pair of scissors), means that the arms of the cracker can be shorter, but still create a force just as big.

lever arm

jaws

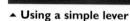

pivot

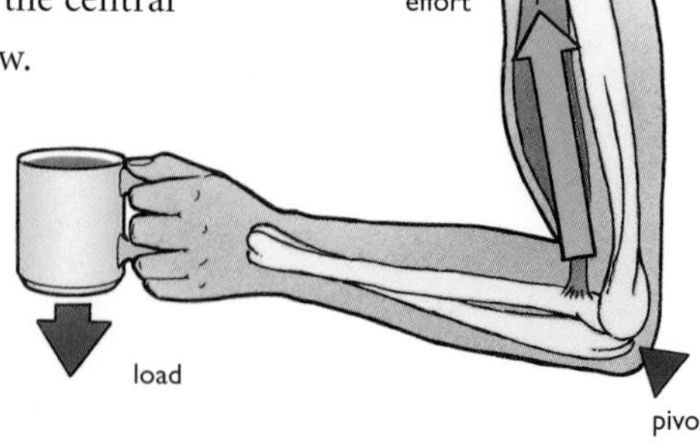

▲ Body levers

Did you know that some parts of your body are levers? Every time you brush your hair or get up from a chair, the bones in your arms and legs act as levers. As your arm lifts up an object, your elbow is the pivot. Effort from the upper arm is transferred to your lower arm, so that you can pick up the load in your hand.

Levers and lifting

YOU WILL NEED

Levers and lifting: Ruler, book, pivot (box).

Balancing a seesaw: Pivot, plank of wood (seesaw).

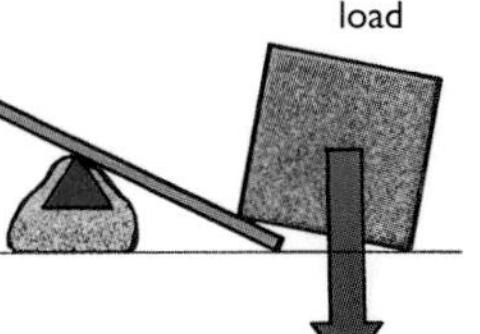

1 A ruler can be used as a lever to lift a book. With the pivot (the box) near the book, only a small effort is needed to lift the book up. The lever makes the push greater.

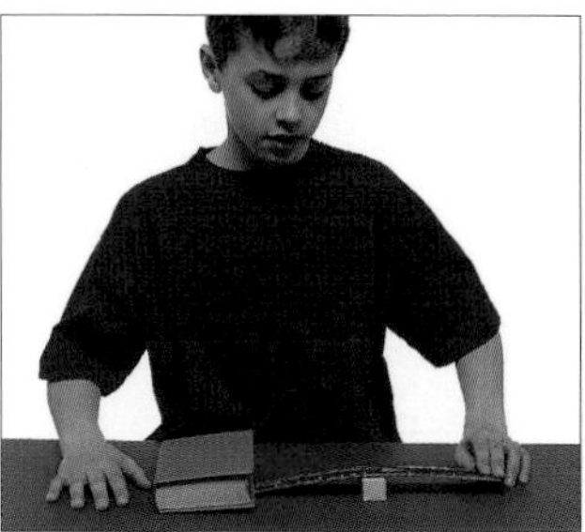

2 When the pivot is moved to the middle of the lever, the effort needed to lift the book up is equal to the book's weight. The effort and the load are the same.

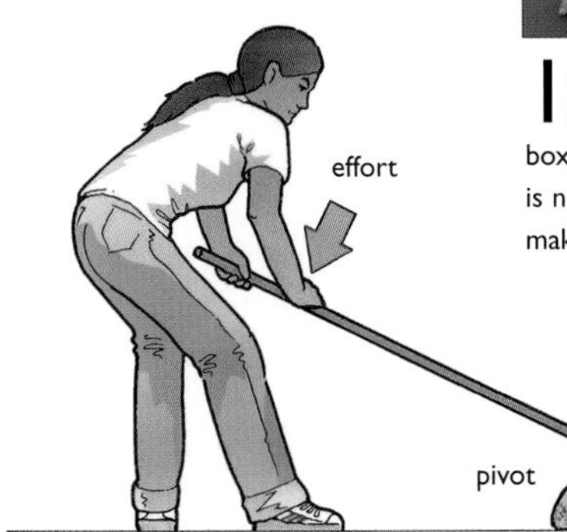

▲ **How a lever works**
A lever tilts on a pivot, which is nearer to the end of the lever with the load on it. The effort, or force, is the push you make on the long end of the lever to lift the weight of the load.

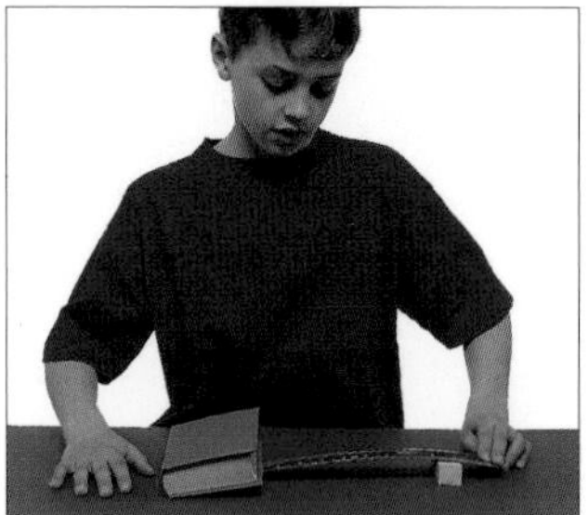

3 When the pivot is near where you are pressing, more effort is needed to lift the book. The force of the push needed to lift the book is now larger than the book's weight.

Balancing a seesaw

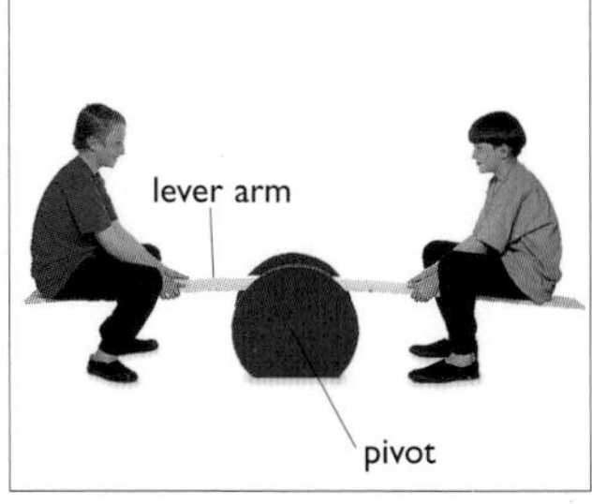

1 Ask a friend of equal weight to sit on one side of the seesaw, while you sit on the other side. If you sit the same distance from the pivot, you make the seesaw balance.

2 Ask another friend to join you on the seesaw. By adding another person, that side of the seesaw will overbalance. The pair's greater weight will easily lift the lighter person.

3 Get the pair to move nearer to the pivot of the seesaw. Their weight can be balanced by the lighter person moving farther away from the pivot. The seesaw will be equally balanced.

Levers at work

Find out how to make three different kinds of lever in these experiments. The first is a can crusher that uses a lever action to squash a can. The second is a gripper for picking up small objects, just like a pair of tweezers. It can also work as a nutcracker. In a pair of nutcrackers, the load (in this case a grape or a nut) is between the pivot (the pencil) and the effort (where you push). In a pair of tweezers, the effort is between the pivot and the load.

The third experiment is a balance scale. It is like the ones used by the Romans about 2,000 years ago. It works by balancing the weight of an object against a known weight, in this case a bag of coins. The coins are moved along the lever arm, until they balance the object being weighed. The farther away from the pivot the weighed bag is, the greater turning effect it has on the lever arm. The heavier the weight being measured, the farther away the bag must be moved to balance the arm. The weight is read against the scale along the arm.

YOU WILL NEED

Two short planks of wood about 40 x 10cm/16 x 4in and 1–2cm/½–¾in thick, hinge, screws, screwdriver, two coffee-jar lids, glue, empty can.

Can crusher

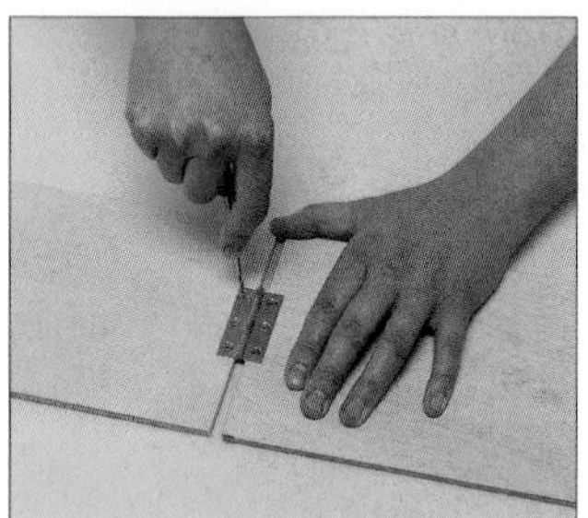

1 Lay the two planks of wood end to end. Ask an adult to help you screw them together with a hinge, using screws and a screwdriver. Make sure the hinge is secure.

2 Glue a jar lid to the inside edge of each plank of wood, with the top of the lid face down. The lids should be about halfway along each plank and the same distance from the hinge.

To crush a can, put the can in between the lids, so that it is held in place. Press down hard on the top piece of wood.

Gripper

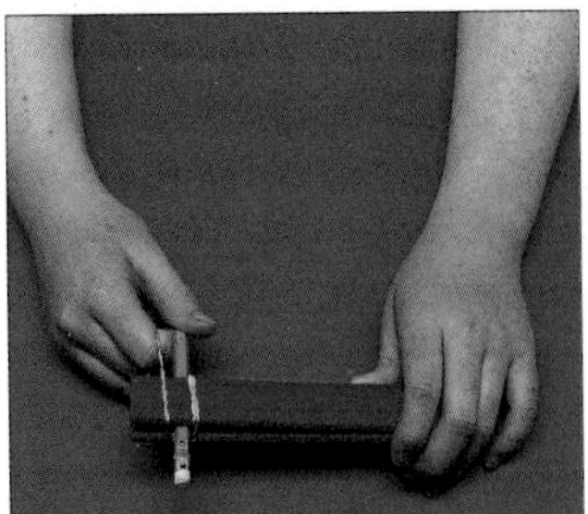

1 Put the pencil between the two pieces of wood, near one end. Wrap the rubber bands tightly around the pieces of wood to make a pivot. You have now made the gripper.

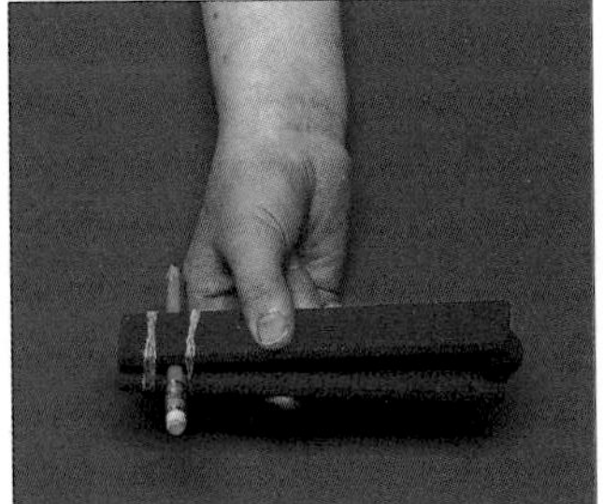

2 Hold the gripper near the pivot to make it act like a pair of tweezers. See if you can pick up a delicate object, such as a grape, without crushing the object.

3 Hold the gripper at the end farthest away from the pivot. Now your lever operates as a pair of nutcrackers. The effort at the point you push is increased.

Balance scale

YOU WILL NEED

Gripper: Short pencil, two pieces of wood each about 15cm/6in long, thick rubber bands, objects to pick up or squash, such as nuts.

Balance scale: Cardboard 50 x 8cm/20 x 3in, thin card, scissors, string, ruler, hole punch, 12cm/4½in circle of card, tape, 100g/4oz of coins, felt-tipped pen, objects to weigh.

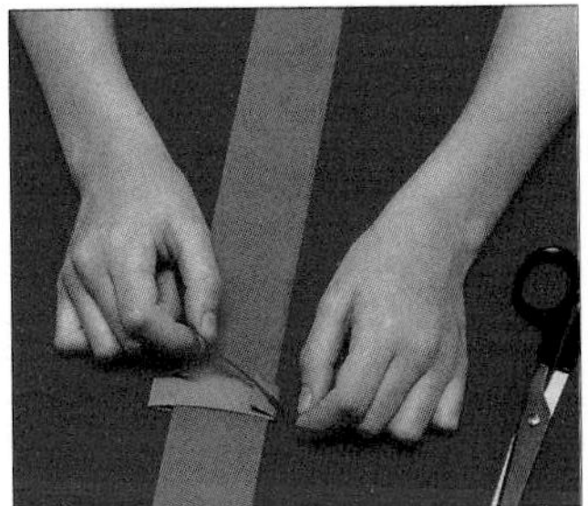

1 Make the arm by folding the cardboard in two. Make a loop of thin card and fold it loosely around the arm 11cm/4¼in from one end. Tie a piece of string to this support.

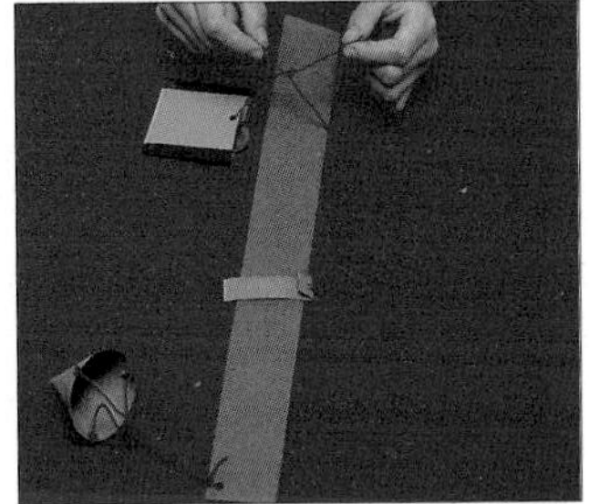

2 Make a hole 1cm/½in from the arm's end. Make the card circle into a cone. Tie it to the hole. Make an envelope from thin card, and tie it to a loop so that it hangs over the arm.

3 Put the coins in the envelope and seal it up. Starting from the middle of the support, make a mark every 5cm/2in along the arm. This scale will tell you the weight of an object.

To weigh an object, put it in the cone and slide the envelope of coins backwards and forwards along the arm, until the arm balances. Each mark along the scale equals 50g/2oz. In this picture, the object being weighed is about 75g/3oz.

The power of energy

Nothing can happen without energy. Energy is needed to do work, such as making things move. To make something move, a source of energy is needed. For example, an engine works by burning fuel – a storage of chemical energy. The two experiments here explore different ways in which energy can be captured to make something move.

The turbine experiment shows how the energy in flowing water makes a bottle spin. This energy is used in hydroelectric power stations to generate electricity. The second project shows how electrical energy from a battery spins a motor. Electric motors are used in many household appliances, such as vacuum cleaners and washing machines. The development of the steam engine and the electric motor in the 1800s provided new sources of energy that were able to power ships and railway engines, and later to light homes and streets.

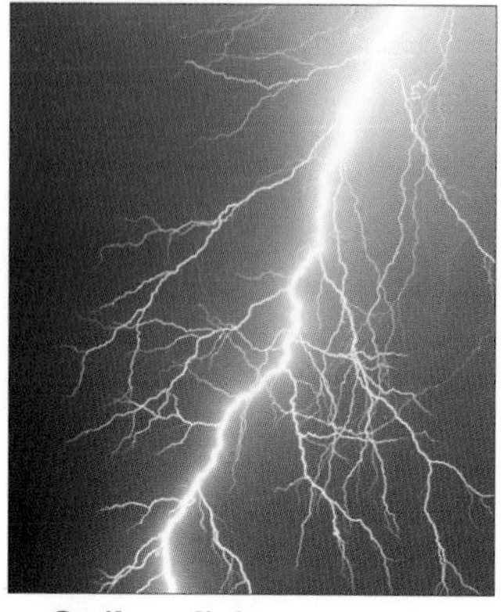

▲ **Strike a light**
Lightning is a massive discharge of energy from a thundercloud. The cloud gets overloaded with electrically charged particles of water and ice.

YOU WILL NEED
Scissors, plastic bottle, pencil, two wide drinking straws, plastic tape, thin string, tray, water.

Turbine

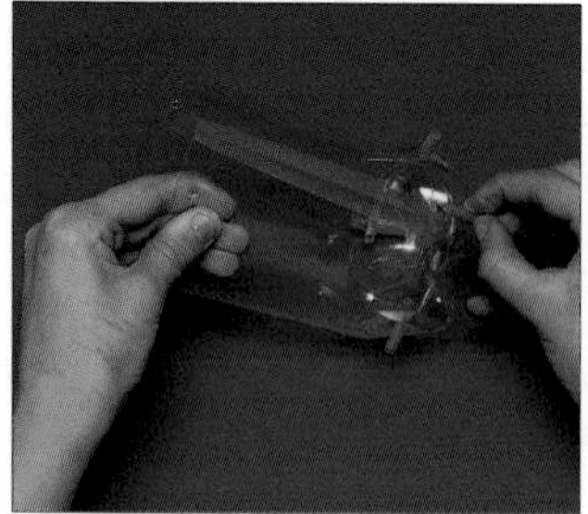

1 Cut off the bottle's top with adult help. Use the pencil to poke holes around its base. Cut the straws and push them through the holes. Use tape to hold the straws in place.

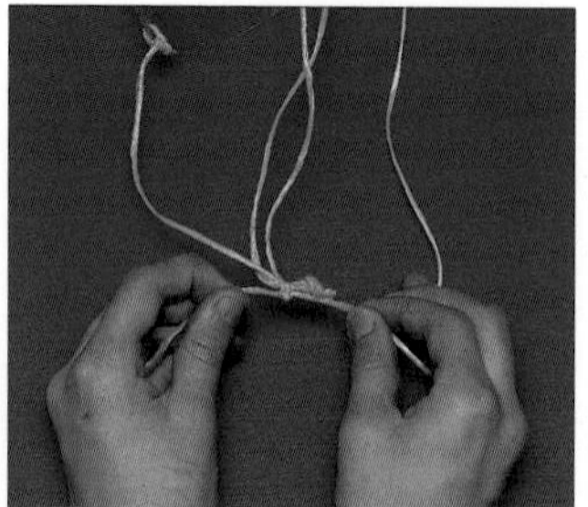

2 Poke three holes around the top of the bottle. Tie three equal pieces of string through the holes, and join them to one long piece of string.

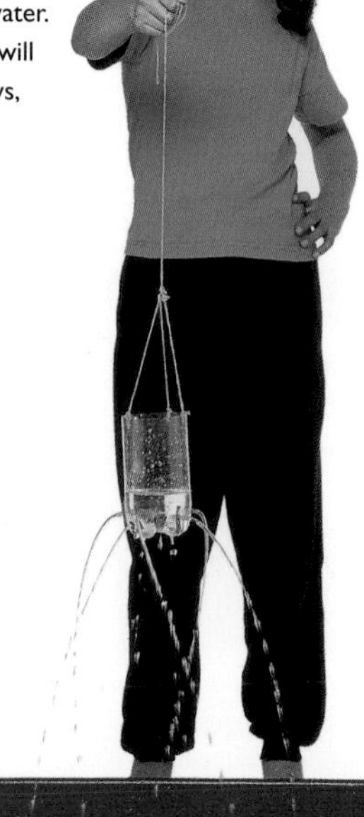

3 Hold your turbine over a tray, or outdoors, so that you will not make a mess with the water. Fill the bottle with water. It will squirt out through the straws, making the bottle spin.

Electric motor

YOU WILL NEED

Bradawl, two (red) end supports 5 x 5cm/2 x 2in, ruler, glue for plastic, (blue) plastic modelling board 15 x 10 x 0.5cm/6 x 4 x ¼in, scissors, drinking straw, two (yellow) coil supports 6 x 5cm/2½ x 2in, two (white) coil support spacers 4 x 1cm/1½ x 1in, wire strippers, insulated (plastic coated) copper wire, thread reel, foil, thin tape, knitting needle 15cm/6in long, two (green) magnet supports 3cm/1¼in high, two powerful bar magnets, four paper clips, two flexible connecting wires 20cm/8in long, thick plastic tape, 6-volt battery.

1 Use the bradawl to make a hole 1cm/½in from the top of each of the two end supports. Glue them to the base board, 1cm/½in inwards from the shorter edges.

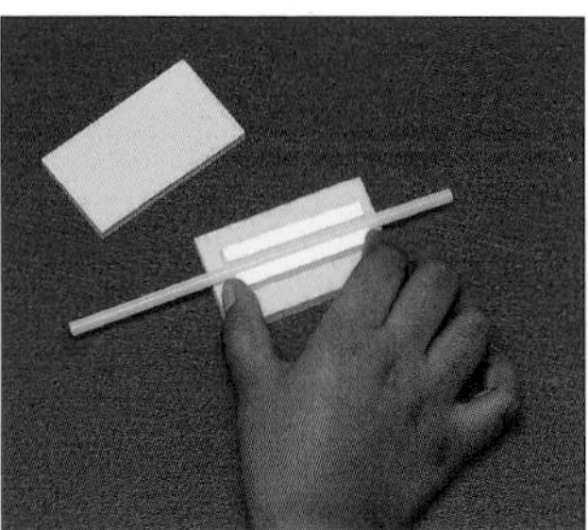

2 Cut a length of straw 12cm/4½in long. Glue the straw to one coil support. Glue the two coil support spacers to either side of the straw. Glue the second support over the top.

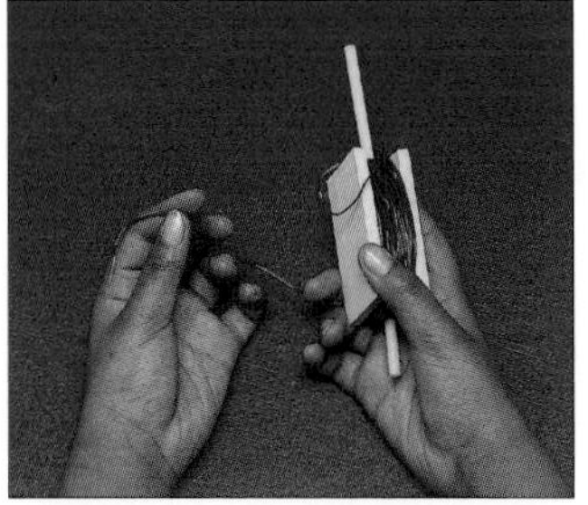

3 Strip 2cm/¾in of insulation from one end of the wire and 3cm/1¼in from the other, with adult help. Wind the wire between the coil supports. Slide the reel on to the straw.

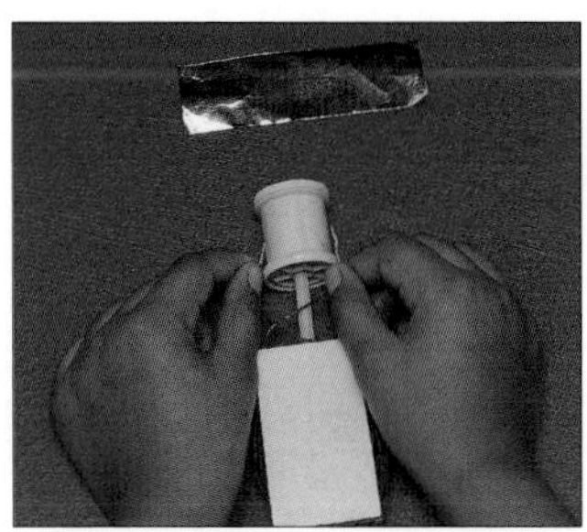

4 Cut a foil strip the width of the reel, to fit three-quarters of the way around the reel. Cut it in half. Put the wire ends against the reel. Tape foil over each wire so it is under the foil's middle.

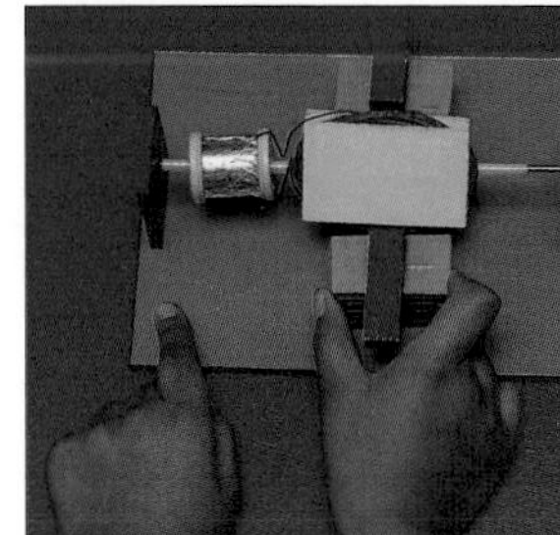

5 Stick the reel to the straw. Hold it between the end supports. Slide the knitting needle through the hole in each end support. Secure the coil support with green magnet supports.

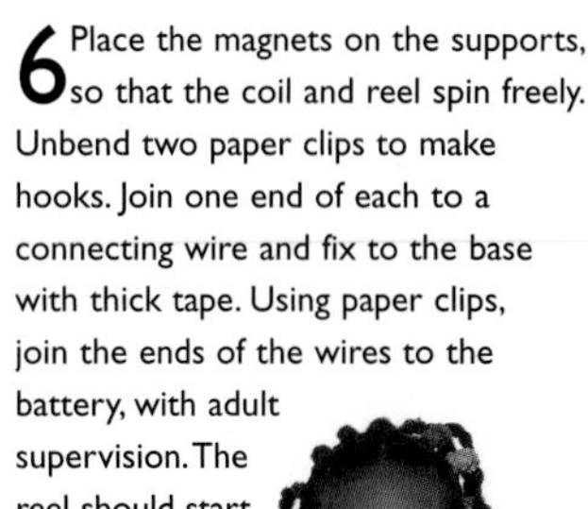

6 Place the magnets on the supports, so that the coil and reel spin freely. Unbend two paper clips to make hooks. Join one end of each to a connecting wire and fix to the base with thick tape. Using paper clips, join the ends of the wires to the battery, with adult supervision. The reel should start spinning around.

Wind and water power

Modern windmills called wind turbines are used to generate electricity. The most efficient wind turbines only have two or three blades, like the propeller of an aircraft. Sometimes just a couple of large turbines can generate enough electricity to meet all the power needs of a small community.

There are several shapes of wind turbine. One of the most efficient is the vertical-axis type. This has an axle like the dowel one in the first project. It is very efficient, because it works no matter which way the wind is blowing. The second experiment shows you how to make a water wheel that captures the energy of falling water to lift a small weight. Pour water from different heights to see if it makes a difference to the wheel's speed.

▲ **Wind for milling**
A windmill uses the power of the wind to turn heavy mill stones that grind grain to make flour. The whole building can be turned around, so that it faces into the wind. The speed of the mill is controlled by opening and closing slots in the sails. Inside a windmill is an arrangement of gear wheels, which transfers power from the sails to the grinding stones.

YOU WILL NEED
Plastic bottle, scissors, tape, ruler, thin dowel, drawing pins (thumb tacks).

Make a windmill

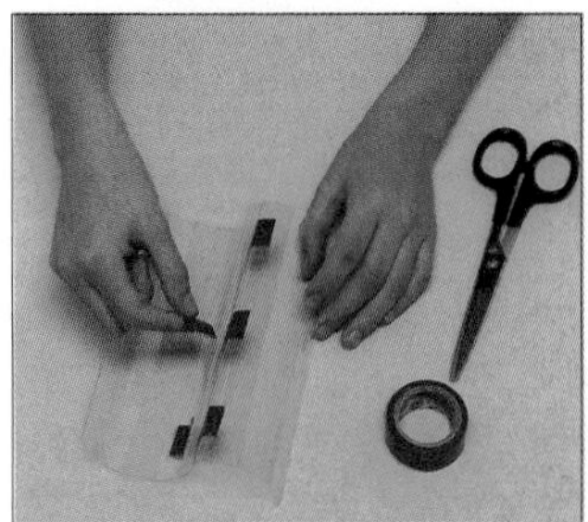

1 Cut the top and bottom off the bottle to leave a tube. Cut the tube in half lengthwise, then stick the two halves together in an S shape, so that the edges overlap by 2cm/¾in.

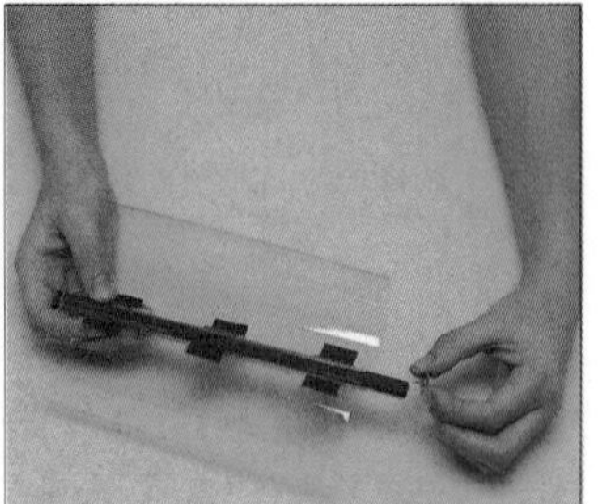

2 The piece of dowel should be about 4cm/1½in longer than the vanes. Slide it into the slot between the vanes. Press a drawing pin gently into each end of the dowel.

To make the windmill spin, hold it vertically with your fingers on the thumb tacks at each end of the dowel. Blow on the vanes. The windmill will spin easily.

Make a water wheel

YOU WILL NEED
Large plastic bottle, scissors, wire (ask an adult to cut the bottom out of a coat hanger), cork, knife, adhesive tape, string, small weight, jug (pitcher), water, large plate.

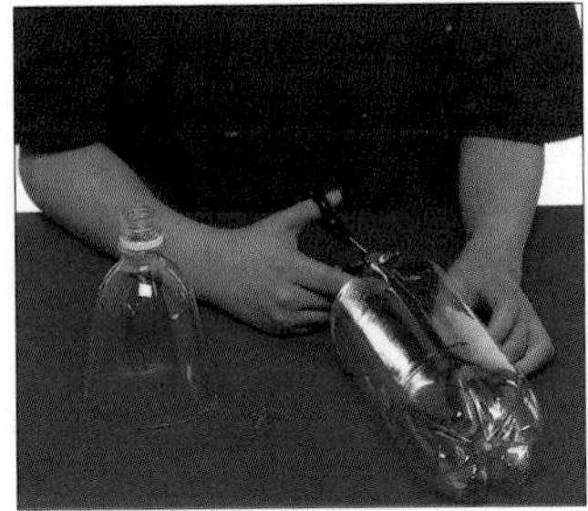

1 Cut the top third off the plastic bottle. Cut a small hole in the bottom piece near the base (this is to let the water out). Cut a V-shape on each side of the rim.

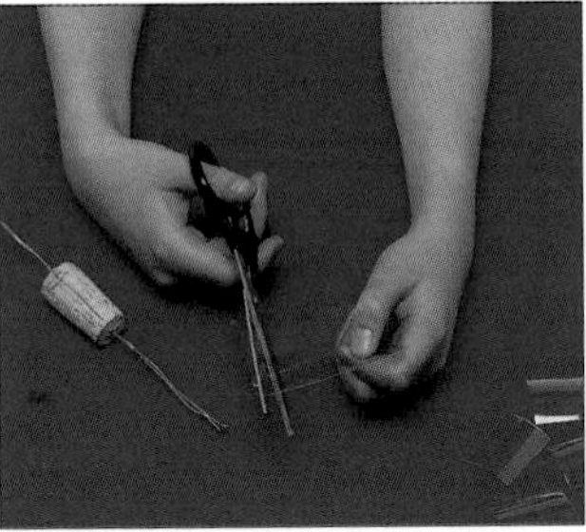

2 Ask an adult to push the wire through the middle of the cork to make an axle. From the top third of the plastic bottle, cut six small curved vanes (blades), as shown above.

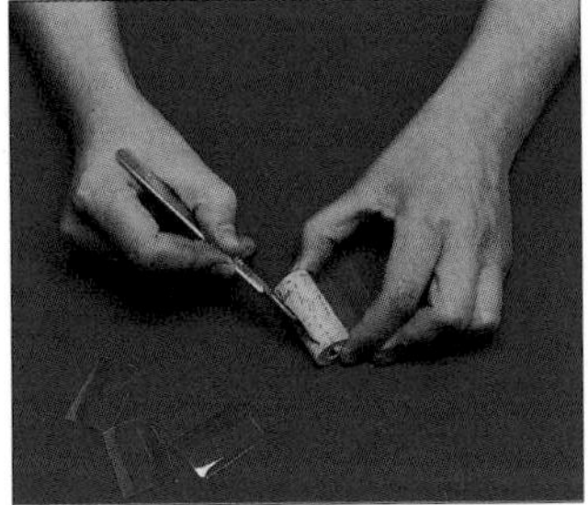

3 Ask an adult to cut six slots in the cork with a knife. (This might be easier without the wire.) Push the plastic vanes into the slots to make the water wheel.

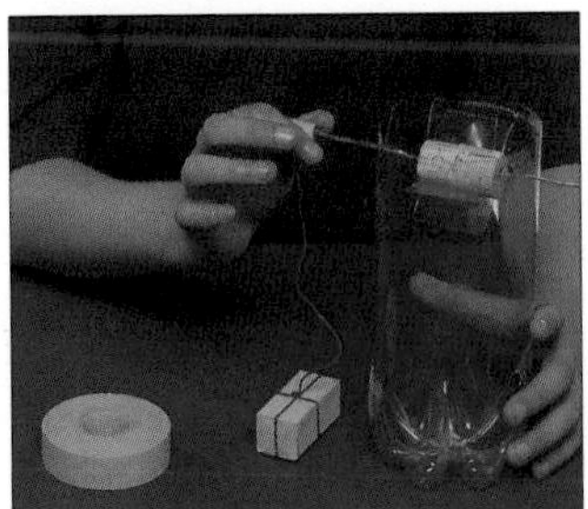

4 Rest the wheel's axle in the V-shaped slots. Tape a piece of string towards one end of the axle, and tie a small weight to the end of the string. Fill a jug with water.

5 Put the water wheel on a large plate or in the sink. Pour water on to the wheel, so that it hits the upward-curving vanes. As the wheel turns, the weight should be lifted up.

Energy from liquid and air

Hydraulic machines have parts that are moved by liquid. Pneumatic machines have parts that are moved by a gas such as air. A hydraulic system has a pipe filled with a liquid, such as oil, and a piston that moves to and fro within the pipe. Pushing liquid into the pipe forces the piston to move, transmitting power from one end of the pipe to the other. In a simple pneumatic system, compressed air forces a piston to move.

In the first experiment, you make a hydraulic machine powered by water pressure. Water is poured from a central reservoir (the jug/pitcher of water) into a pipe. The water fills up a plastic bag. The bag expands and forces up the piston (the lid), which in turn raises a heavy object. Many cranes and trucks use this principle to lift heavy loads. In the air pump project, you discover the basic principles of how vacuum cleaners work. Finally, you make a miniature vacuum cleaner. Air is sucked in one hole and pushed out of another. A valve stops it from being sucked in and pushed out of the wrong holes.

◂ Filling an empty space
Modern vacuum cleaners have an air pump operated by an electric motor. The pump creates a vacuum inside the cleaner. Dust rushes in from the outside to fill the vacuum.

YOU WILL NEED

Large plastic bottle, scissors, airtight plastic bag, plastic tube, adhesive tape, plastic funnel, spray can lid, heavy book, jug (pitcher) of water.

Make a hydraulic lifter

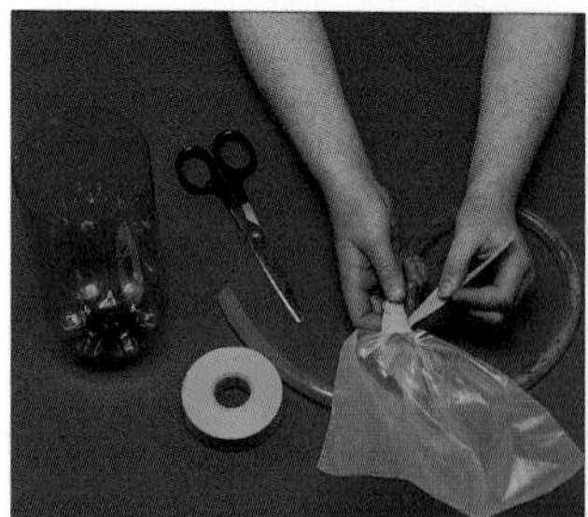

1 Cut the top off the large plastic bottle. Make sure the plastic bag is airtight, and wrap its neck over the end of a piece of plastic tube. Seal the bag to the tube with adhesive tape.

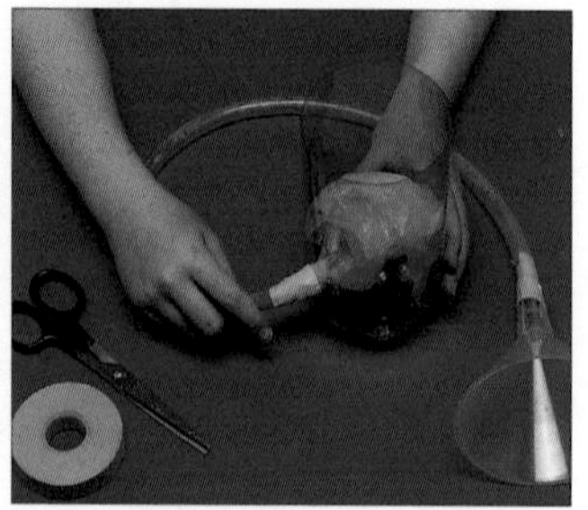

2 Fix a funnel to the other end of the tube. Make a hole at the base of the bottle, and feed the bag and tube through. The bag should sit in the bottom of the bottle.

3 Put the spray can lid on top of the bag, and rest a heavy book on top of the bottle. Lift the funnel end of the tube up, and slowly pour in water. What happens to the lid and the book?

Make an air pump

YOU WILL NEED
Make an air pump: Large plastic bottle, scissors, hammer, small nails, wooden stick or dowel, ruler, thin card, adhesive tape, ping-pong ball. **Make a vacuum cleaner:** String, tissue paper, glue.

1 Cut around the large plastic bottle, about one third up from the bottom. Cut a slit down the side of the bottom part of the bottle, so that it will slide inside the top part.

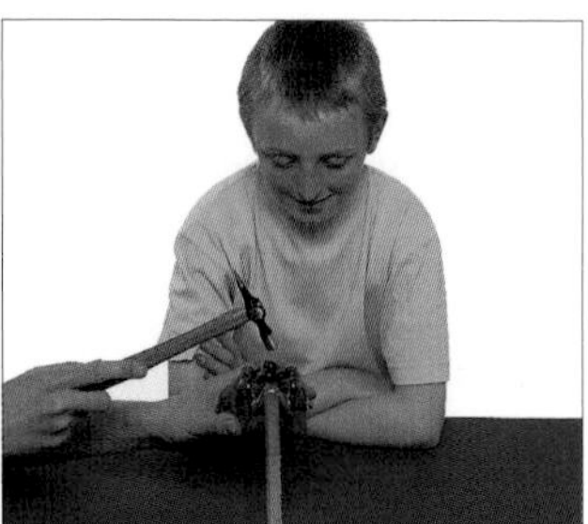

2 Ask an adult to help you nail the bottom of the bottle to the end of a wooden stick or a piece of dowel. You have now made a piston for your air pump.

3 Cut a hole about 1cm/½in across near the neck of the bottle. Cut a piece of card about 2 x 2cm/¾ x ¾in. Tape one edge of the card to the bottle to form a flap over the hole.

4 Drop a ping-pong ball into the top part of the bottle, so that it rests in the neck. Push the bottom part of the bottle (the piston) into the top part (the cylinder).

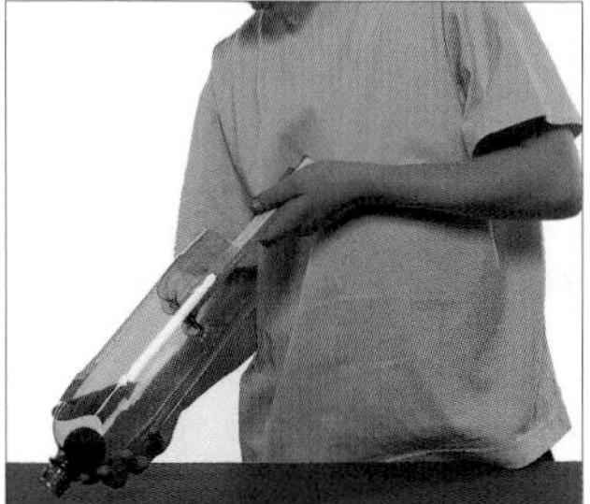

5 Move the piston in and out, to suck air into the bottle and out of the hole. Can you see how both the valves work? The flap should automatically close when you pull the piston out.

Make a vacuum cleaner

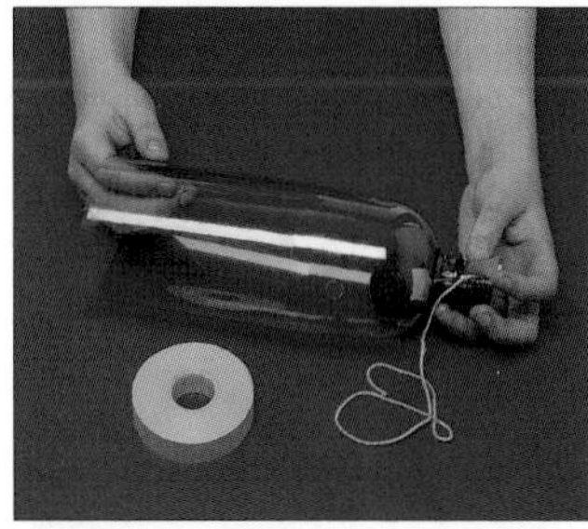

1 Make the air pump from the project above without the card flap. Tape string to the ball, feed it through the bottle's neck, and tape it down, so that the ball is held near the neck.

2 Make a tissue paper bag and glue it over the hole near the neck of the bottle. Air from the pump will go through the bag, and anything the vacuum picks up should be trapped.

3 Try picking up tiny bits of paper with the vacuum. Pull the piston out sharply to suck the bits of paper into the bottle. Push the piston back in gently to pump the paper into the bag.

How magnets work

Magnets are usually made of the metal iron, or another material that has lots of iron in it, such as steel. Magnets can be various shapes, but all of them have the ability to pull things toward themselves. This invisible force is called magnetism. Magnets only attract (pull) metals that are made of iron or that contain iron.

Magnetism is concentrated around the poles (ends) of a magnet. A magnet has two poles, called the north pole and the south pole. The two poles may look the same but they behave differently. Put one pole of a magnet near to a pole of another magnet, and watch what happens. You may feel an attraction (pulling) force as the two poles stick together. Alternatively, you may feel a repulsion (pushing) force, as the two poles push away from each other. In all magnets, identical poles will repel (push away) each other, while different poles will pull towards each other.

Is a big magnet more powerful than a small one? Not always. You cannot tell how powerful a magnet is just by looking at it. Compare the strength and power of different magnets in the projects opposite.

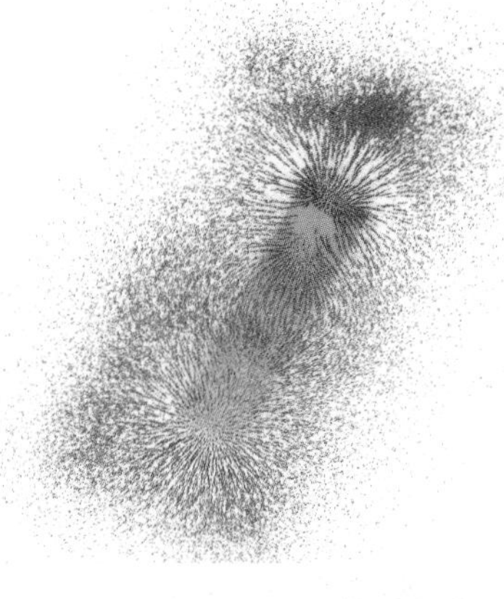

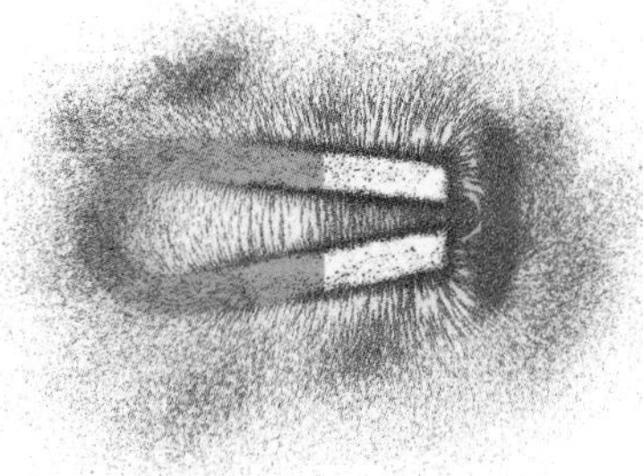

▲ Seeing magnetism
You cannot see the magnetic force around a magnet, but you can see the effects of its presence when an iron nail sticks to a magnet. You can see the shape of a magnetic field by using tiny, powderlike pieces of iron, called iron filings. Iron filings reveal that the lines and strength of the magnetic force are concentrated around and between the poles at the end of the horseshoe magnet. On a bar magnet, they line up to show how the magnetic force spreads out from the poles (ends).

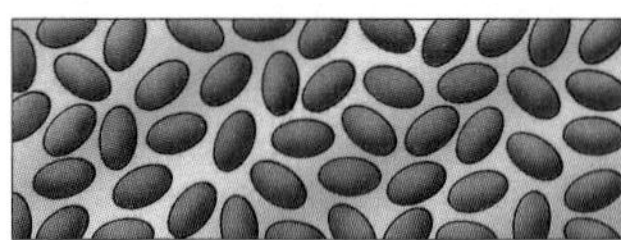

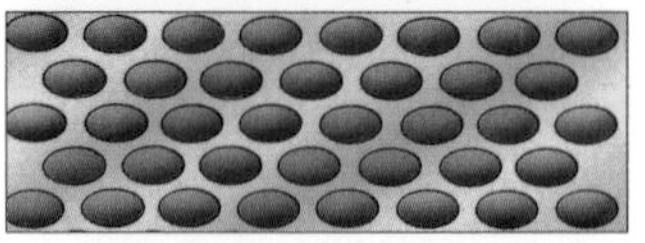

Tiny magnets ▸
Think of a bar of iron as having millions of micromagnets inside it. These are called domains. If they are all jumbled up, the bar is not a magnet. If the micromagnets in a bar are lined up and point the same way, it is a magnet.

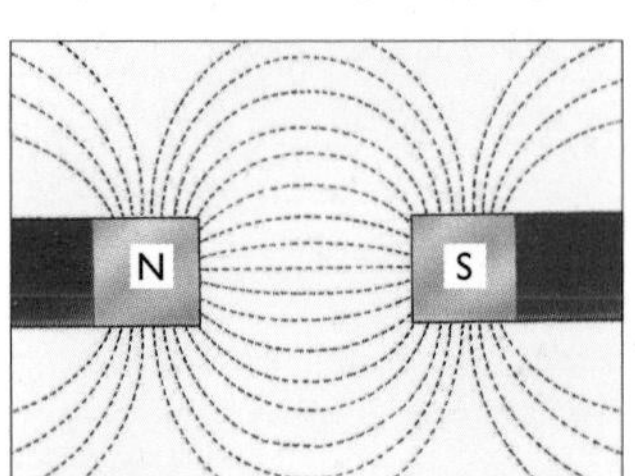

◂ Attraction and repulsion ▸
The poles of two magnets that are different or opposite will attract. Magnetic lines of force from north and south poles pull together and join. The poles of two magnets that are the same will repel or push each other apart.

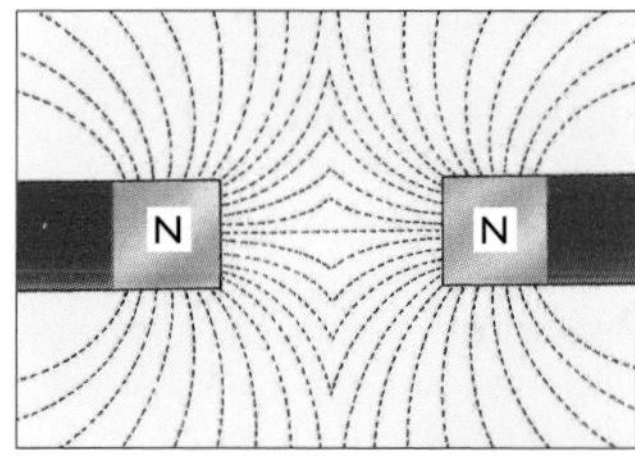

Strength of a magnet

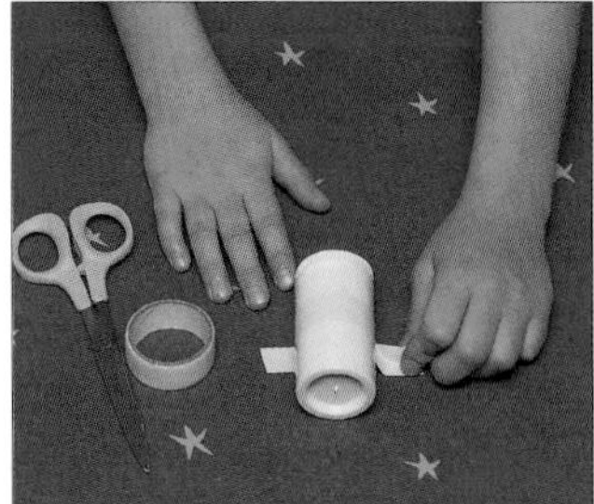

1 Cut off a piece of tape and use it to tape the round container firmly to the work surface. The round container will act as the pivot, or the balancer.

2 Attach a magnet to one end of the ruler with a rubber band and some washers to the other end of the ruler. Position the middle of the ruler on the balancer.

3 Hold another magnet above the first. Lower it until the ruler tips over. Measure its height above the table. The higher it is when the ruler tips over, the stronger the magnet.

YOU WILL NEED

Strength of a magnet: Scissors, adhesive tape, round plastic container, two magnets, ruler, rubber bands, steel washers.

Power of a magnet: Pencil, drawing pins (thumb tacks), strong thread, cardboard, ruler with holes at both ends and in the middle, scissors, adhesive tape, rubber bands, adhesive dots, pen, two small bar magnets.

Power of a magnet

1 Attach one end of the thread to a pin and the other to a pencil. Draw two quarter-circles on cardboard. Make the distance from the pin to the curved edge the same as the length of the ruler.

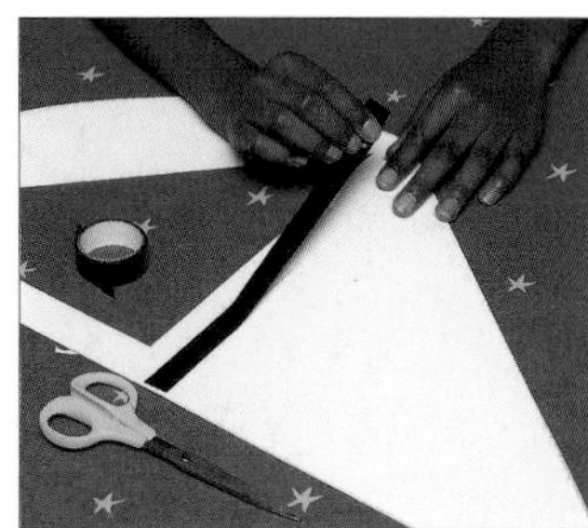

2 Draw a triangle in one quarter-circle and cut it out. Using the triangle as a template, cut out a triangle from the other quarter-circle. Tape them together.

3 Push a tack through the ruler's end hole, so that it pivots. Attach rubber bands from the ruler's middle hole to the quarter-circle's side. Add dots labelled N and S to each ruler end.

Stand the magnet measurer upright. Attach one magnet to the ruler's top end with a rubber band. Bring the unlike pole of another magnet near it. How far can it pull the ruler? Stronger magnets pull it farther.

Magnetic Earth

The Earth behaves as if there is a giant bar magnet running through its middle from pole to pole. This affects every magnetic material that comes within its reach. If you hold a magnet so that it can rotate freely, it always ends up with one end pointing to the Earth's North Pole and the other to the South Pole. This is how a compass works – the needle automatically swings to the North. The Earth's magnetism comes from its inner core of iron and nickel.

You can use the compass you make here to plot a magnetic field like the Earth's. The Earth's magnetic field is slightly tilted, so compasses do not swing exactly toward the North Pole, but to a point a little way off from northern Canada. This direction is known as magnetic north.

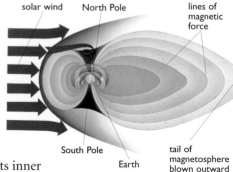

solar wind
North Pole
lines of magnetic force
South Pole
Earth
tail of magnetosphere blown outward by solar wind

▲ Magnetic protection
The effects of Earth's magnetism extend 60,000km/37,000 miles out into Space. In fact, there is a vast magnetic force field around the Earth called the magnetosphere. This traps electrically charged particles and so protects the Earth from the solar wind – the deadly stream of charged particles hurtling from the Sun.

Make a compass

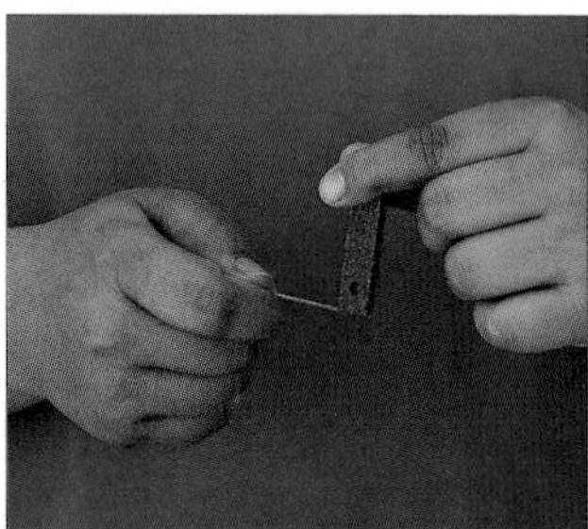

1 To turn the needle into a magnet, stroke the end of the magnet slowly along it. Repeat this in the same direction for about 45 seconds. This magnetizes the needle.

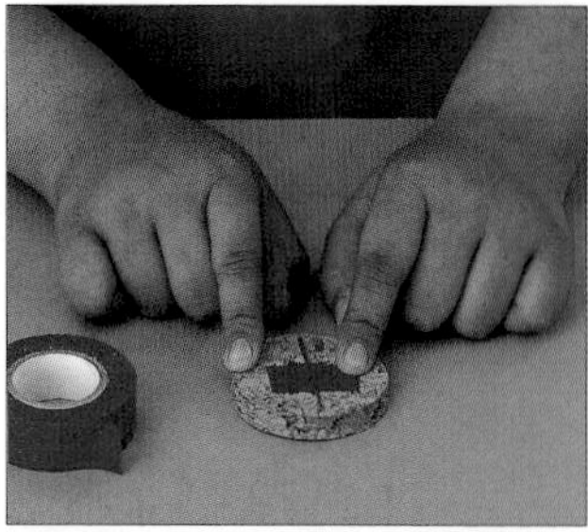

2 Place the magnetized needle on the slice of cork. Make sure that it is exactly in the middle, otherwise it will not spin evenly. Tape the needle into place.

3 Fill the bowl nearly to the brim with water, and float the cork in it. Make sure the cork is exactly in the middle and can turn without rubbing on the edges of the bowl.

The Earth's magnetic field should now swivel the needle on the cork. One end of the needle will always point to the north. That end is its north pole.

Magnetic field

YOU WILL NEED

Make a compass: Steel needle, bar magnet, slice of cork, adhesive tape, small bowl, water.

Magnetic field: Large sheet of paper, bar magnet, your needle compass from the first project, pencil.

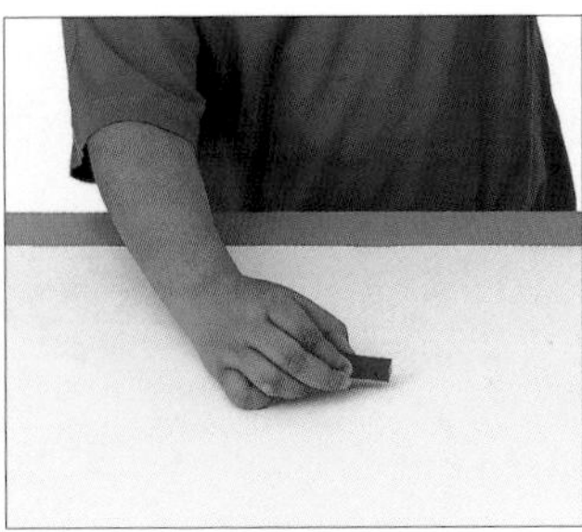

1 Lay a large sheet of paper on a table. Put the magnet in the middle of the paper. Set up your needle compass a few centimetres/an inch or two away from one end of the magnet.

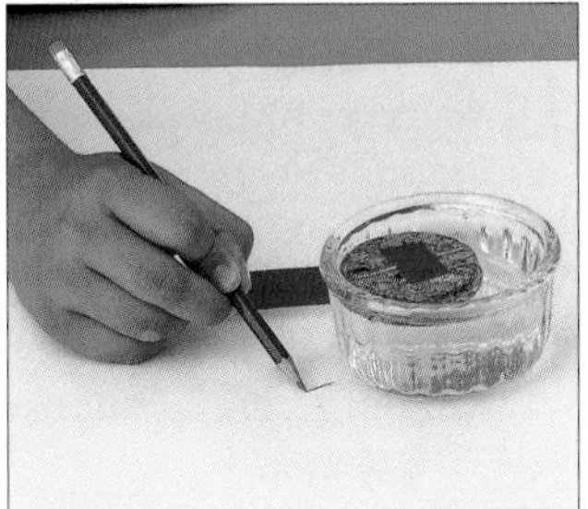

2 Wait as the compass needle settles in a particular direction as it is turned by the magnet. Make a pencil mark on the paper to show which way it is pointing.

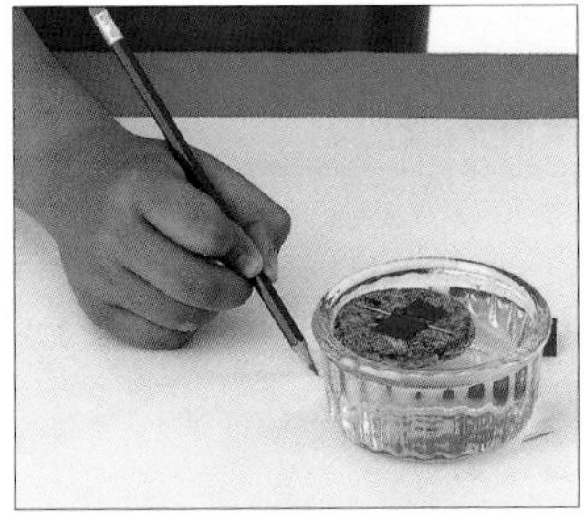

3 Move the compass a little way toward the other end of the magnet. Mark a line on the paper to show which way the needle is pointing now.

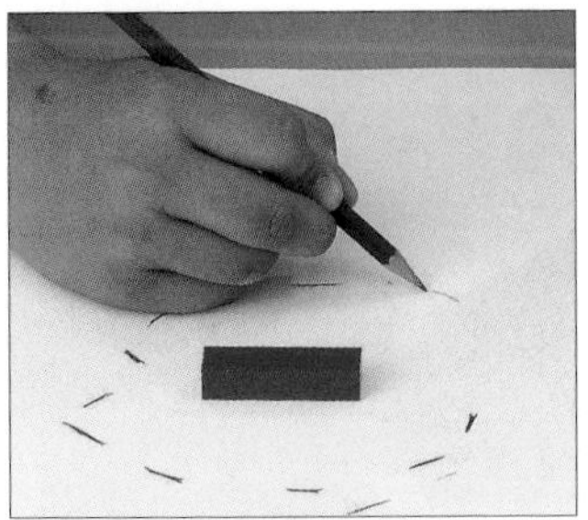

4 Repeat Step 3 for about 25 different positions around the magnet. Try the compass both near the magnet and farther away. You should now have a pattern of marks.

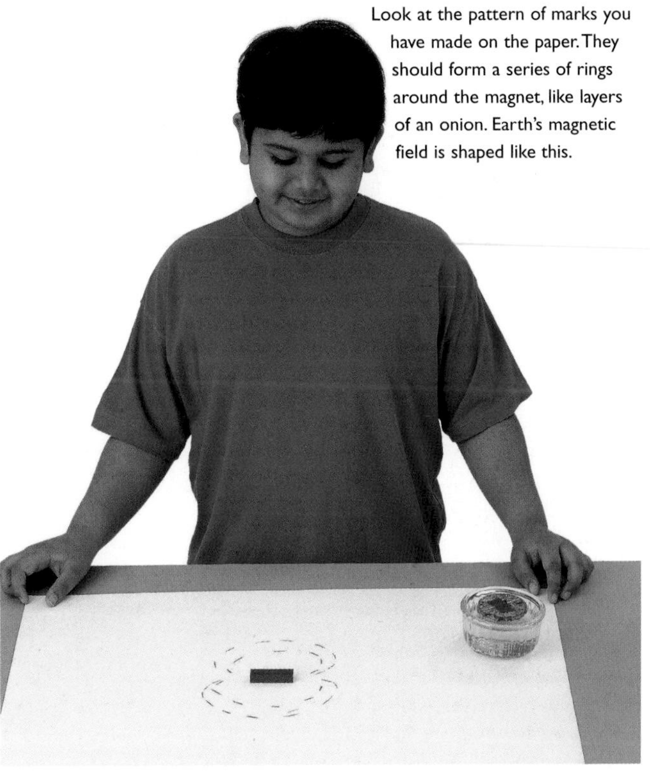

Look at the pattern of marks you have made on the paper. They should form a series of rings around the magnet, like layers of an onion. Earth's magnetic field is shaped like this.

Magnets and maps

Look at a map – which way up does it go? Maps are important. They let us know our location. Without magnets, we would not know how to use a map or find our way around an area. Compass needles are tiny magnets that rotate to point to the Earth's magnetic north. Look on a local map to find a diagram of the compass points, an arrow, or 'N' that indicates north. Then set a compass so that the needle points north. Turn the map so that its north faces the same way as the compass north. Now the map is lined up accurately in relation to the landscape. If you are on a hilltop with wide views, you can see how the map is a tiny plan of the countryside around.

▲ Magnetic migration
The yellow arrows show the migration routes of the Arctic tern. The routes follow the Earth's magnetic force. The tern flies from north to south and then, later in the year, from south to north. Birds may also use rivers, mountains, coastlines, the Sun, Moon and stars to help them find their way.

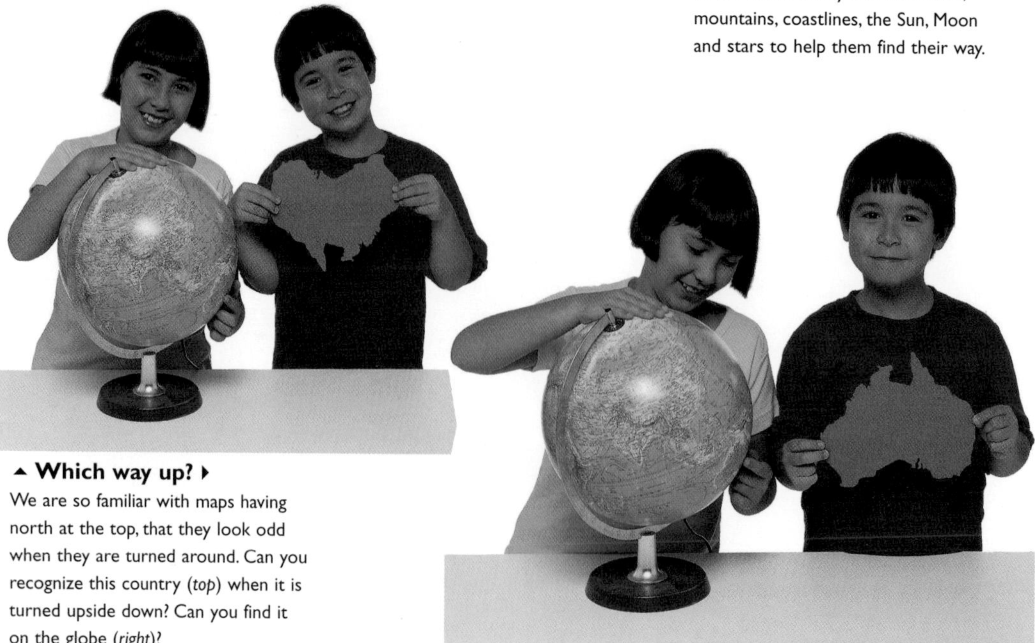

▲ Which way up? ▸
We are so familiar with maps having north at the top, that they look odd when they are turned around. Can you recognize this country (*top*) when it is turned upside down? Can you find it on the globe (*right*)?

Loop compass

1 Straighten out a paper clip. Magnetize it by stroking it with the strong magnet. Cut a circle of card, bend the wire into a large loop, and insert it into holes in the card.

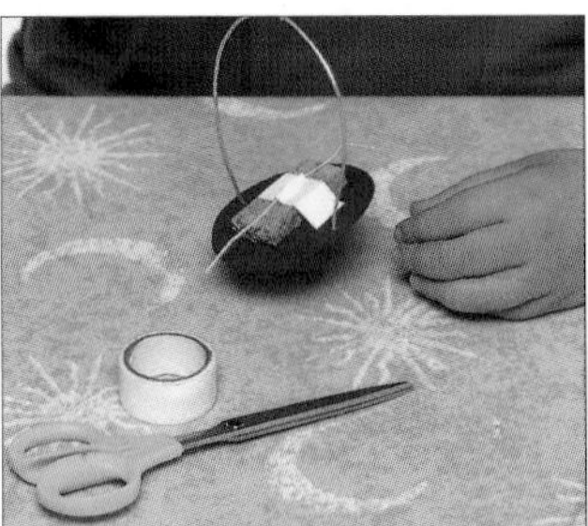

2 Tape the paper clip to the piece of cork and to the card circle. Tie the thread to the top of the wire loop. Let it hang and twirl around freely. It is now ready to test.

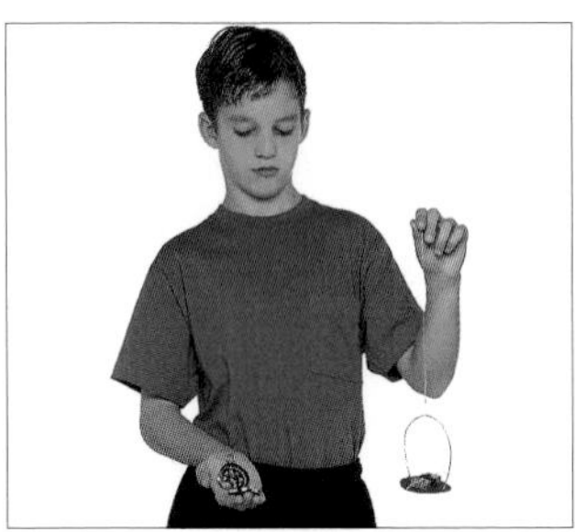

3 Does the paper clip magnet work as a compass needle and point north and south? Check it with the store-bought compass. What do you find happens?

Drawing a maze

YOU WILL NEED

Loop compass: Paper clip, strong magnet, thin card, scissors, thin wire, adhesive tape, cork tile, thread, store-bought compass.

Drawing a maze: Cardboard, coloured pens, compass.

1 Draw a maze on cardboard. Make it vibrant and fun. Put in some dead ends and false turns. Make sure one route leads all the way through from one end of the maze to another!

2 Record your course through the maze, using compass points for the direction. You can limit the information to north, south, east and west or include northeast, southwest and so on.

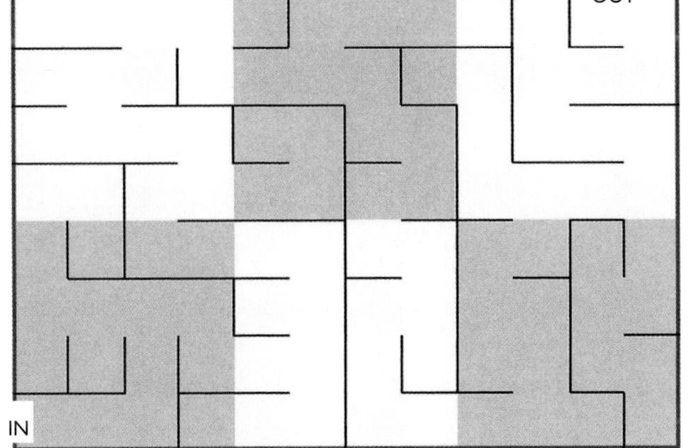

Can you find your way through this maze? When you have made it to the other side, try recording your route with compass points. At the beginning of the journey, you head east, turn north and then go east again. Can you complete these instructions for the entire journey?

Electric magnets

Some magnets, such as bar and horseshoe magnets, are permanent. They have what scientists call 'spontaneous permanent magnetism'. Their magnetism needs no outside force or energy to create it. A way of making magnetism is by using electricity. When electricity flows through a wire or another similar conducting (carrying) material, it produces a magnetic field around the wire. This is called electromagnetism or EM. In fact, magnetism and electricity are very closely linked. Each can be used to make the other. EM is used in many tools, machines and devices. Some electromagnetic machines use the electricity from batteries. Others need the much more powerful mains electricity from wall sockets.

The first practical electromagnets were made by the British bootmaker and spare-time scientist, William Sturgeon. He used them to amaze audiences at his science shows in the 1820s. The basic design has hardly changed since. You can make a similar electromagnet in the projects.

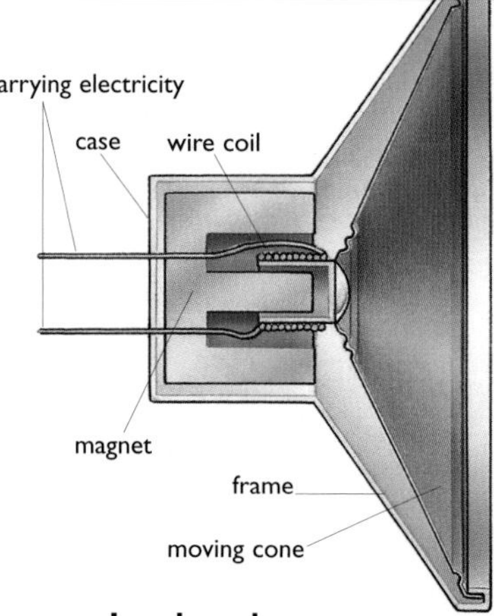

▲ Loudspeaker
Electrical signals are transferred to the loudspeaker along a connecting wire (speaker lead). Electricity flows through the wire coil, which is attached to the plastic speaker cone. The signals make the coil into an electromagnet that varies in strength. This magnetic field is itself inside the field of a strong permanent magnet. The two fields interact, with like poles repelling. This makes the coil move or vibrate, and the loudspeaker cone vibrates, too. This in turn sends out sound waves.

▸ Creating a magnetic field
As electricity flows through a wire, a magnetic field is created around it. The magnetic lines of force flow in circles around the wire. This is called an electromagnetic field. As soon as the electricity is switched off, the magnetism stops.

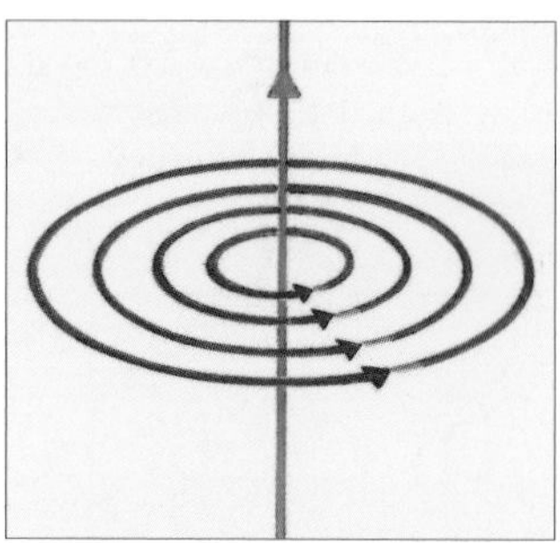

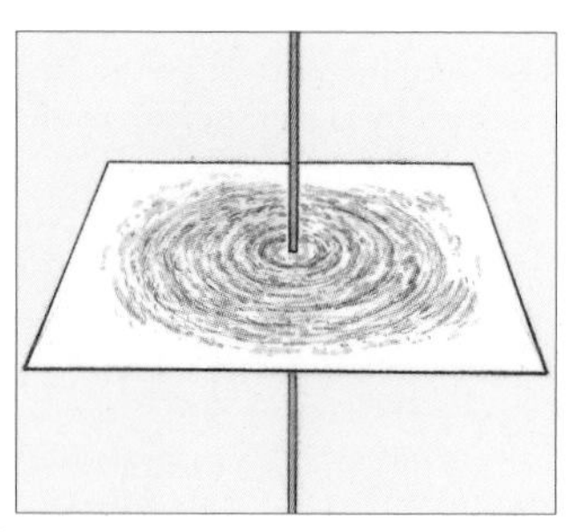

◂ Seeing electromagnetism
If iron filings are sprinkled on to a piece of cardboard that has an electricity-carrying wire through it, the filings are affected by the magnetic field. They arrange themselves in circles to show the lines of magnetic force, as they do with an ordinary magnet.

▾ Are you receiving me?
The earpiece of a telephone receives varying electrical signals from the mouthpiece of the telephone held at other end of the line. The earpiece works like a simple loudspeaker to recreate the sounds of the speaking person's voice.

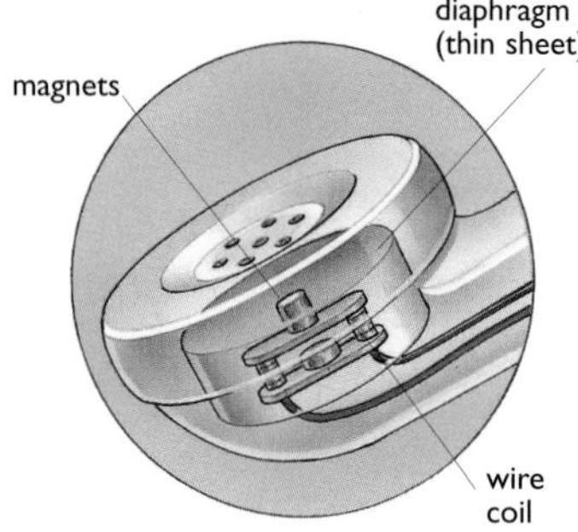

Electromagnet

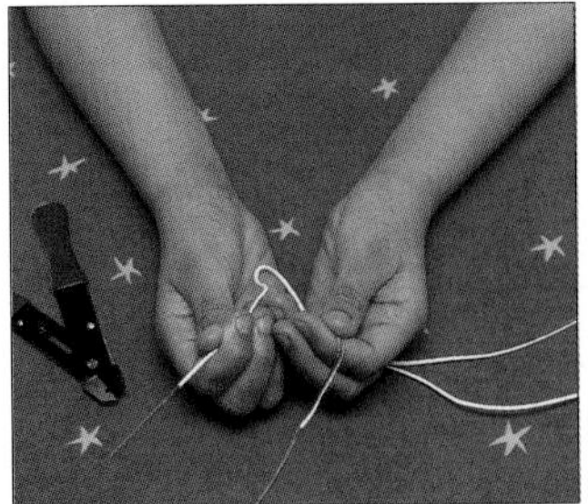

1 Using the wire strippers and with close adult supervision, carefully remove 2.5cm/1in plastic insulation from each end of the wire. These bare ends will connect to the battery.

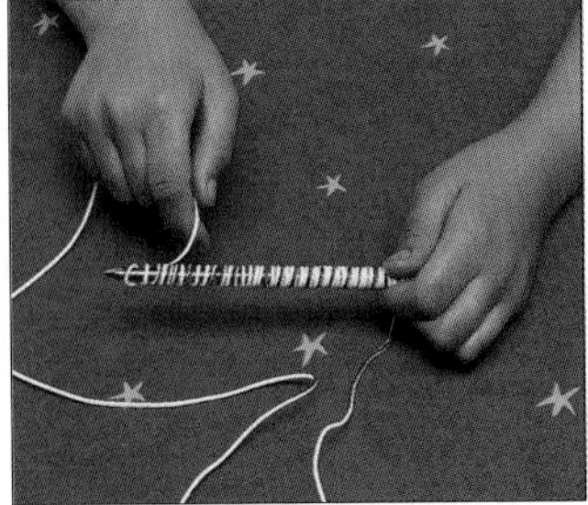

2 Carefully wrap the wire into a tight coil around the iron nail. The plastic insulation around the wire conducts the electricity around the iron nail.

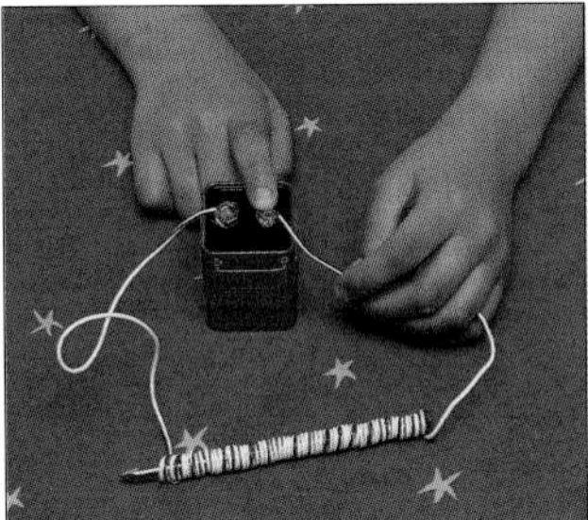

3 With close adult supervision, connect the wire's ends to the battery terminals. There may be a small spark, so take great care. Test the electromagnet by picking up paper clips.

YOU WILL NEED

Electromagnet: Wire strippers, 2m/2yd of wire (insulated, plastic-coated, multistrand copper), large iron nail, 9-volt battery, paper clips.

Adding a switch: Hole punch, piece of thin card, brass fasteners.

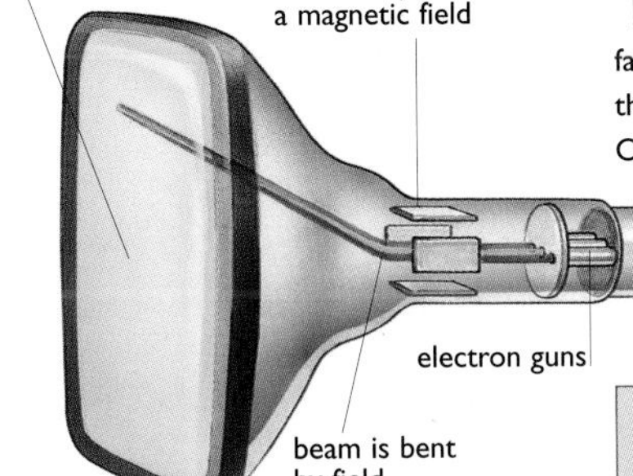

▲ Inside a television

Television sets, computer monitors and other similar screens have electromagnet-type devices inside. These are usually shaped like flat plates. They bend the beam that scans across the screen line by line, to build up the picture. This occurs many times every second.

Adding a switch

1 Make two equal holes in the piece of card. Push the brass fasteners into them. Push one of the fasteners through a paper clip first. Open out the legs of the fasteners.

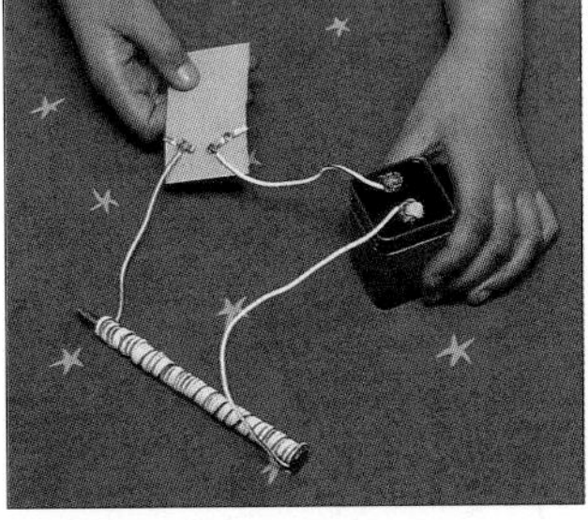

2 With adult supervision, connect one end of electromagnet wires to the fastener. Connect the other to a battery terminal. Attach the remaining fastener to the other terminal with short wire. Turn the card over.

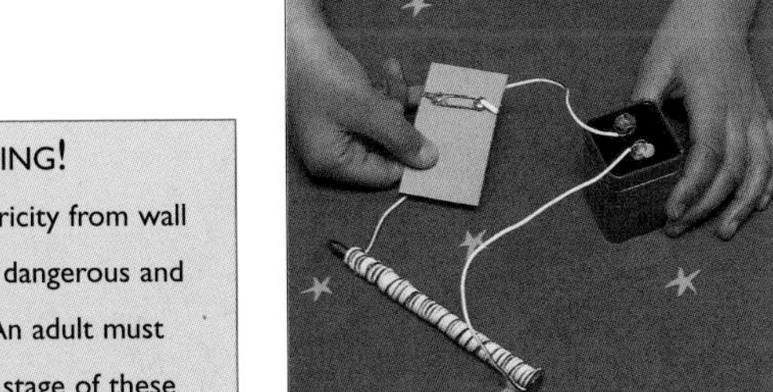

3 Push the paper clip attached to one fastener away from the other fastener. No electricity flows. Turn the clip to touch the fastener. Electricity flows, switching on the electromagnet.

WARNING!

NEVER use electricity from wall sockets. It is too dangerous and could kill you. An adult must supervise every stage of these projects and you must make sure you follow the instructions exactly and use the correct equipment. Do not use a more powerful battery.

Computer data storage

The hard drive of a computer consists of a number of flat, circular discs or plates. Each one of these discs is coated with tiny magnetic particles. The hard drive also contains a controlling mechanism called the read/write head. This is positioned slightly above the magnetic discs. Data (information) is sent to the magnetic discs as a series of electrical pulses. These are sent to the read/write head, which contains a tiny electromagnet. The head magnetizes the tiny magnetic particles on the surface of the discs. This pattern of particles on the discs represents the data. You can see how this happens in the project.

When reading information, the magnetized particles create a small current in the read/write head as the discs spin under it. This is then converted by circuits into binary code, a number system that computers use. The code is based on just two numbers (binary means two), 0 and 1. Different combinations represent the letters of the alphabet.

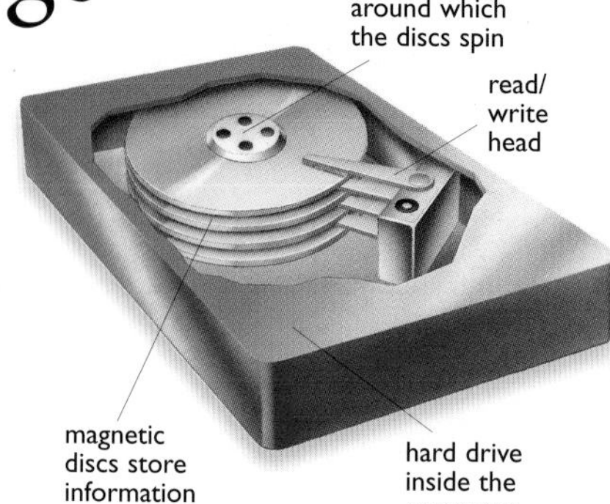

▲ **Inside the hard drive**
A typical computer hard drive consists of a stack of thin discs, called a platter. The upper surface of each disc is coated with tiny magnetic particles, and each disc has its own read/write head on a movable arm. When storing and reading information, the discs spin at very high speeds (up to 120 revolutions per second).

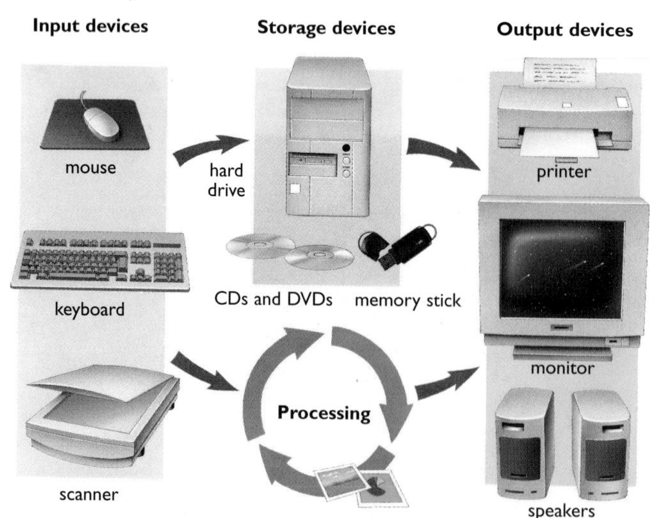

◀ **Using computers**
When people use a computer, they are doing four different things:

1. Inputting data (information) using an input device, such as a mouse, keyboard or scanner.

2. Storing the data on a hard drive, CDs, DVDs or a memory stick, so that it can be reused.

3. Working with the data they put in (often called processing).

4. Retrieving and looking at the data using an output device, such as a printer, monitor or speakers.

Storing data on disc

YOU WILL NEED

Pen or pencil, pair of compasses, thin white card, scissors, ruler, red marker pen, non-hardening modelling material, plastic drinking cup, drawing pin (thumb tack), paper clips, magnet.

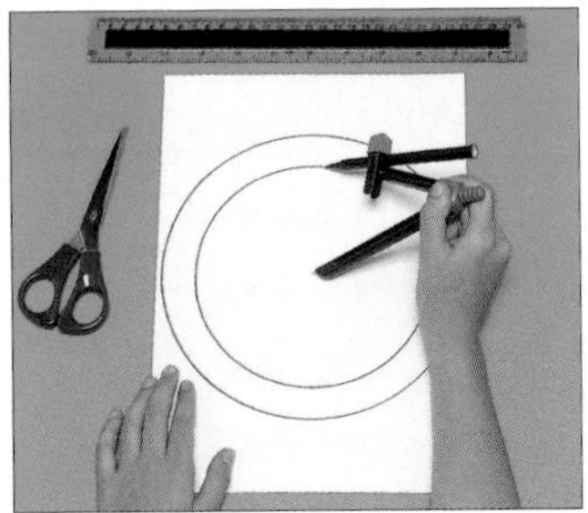

1 Draw a circle with a diameter of 20cm/8in on the piece of card. Draw three more circles inside, each with a diameter 2cm/¾in smaller than the one before. Cut out the largest circle.

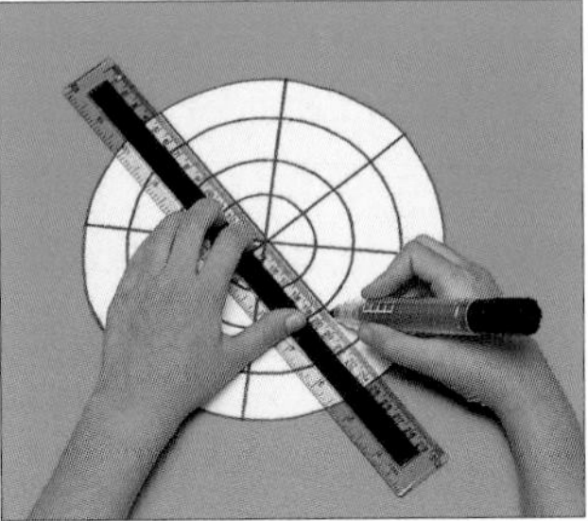

2 Position a ruler at the middle of the circle where the compass point has made a hole. Draw four lines through the middle to divide the circle into eight equal parts.

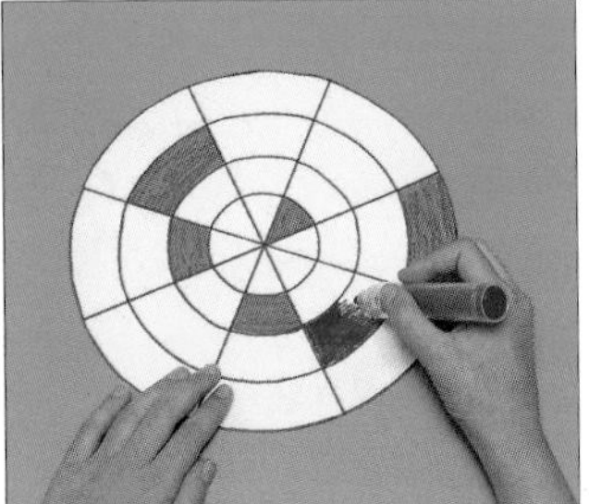

3 Use a red marker to shade in six or seven sections, as shown above. Leave the remaining section white. The white areas represent full disc space. Red areas are empty disc space.

4 Attach some modelling material to the rim of a plastic cup. Then turn it upside down on a smooth surface. Press it down gently to make sure it is secure. Place the circle on top.

5 Push the drawing pin through the middle of the circle into the cup. Make sure the circle can turn. Put paper clips on the surface. Hold the magnet under the circle. Move it around.

The paper clips will move around the surface of the circle, and all line up in one section of the circle. This is what happens to the magnetic particles on a hard disc when an electric current is passed through them by the read/write head. In a computer, the way the magnetic particles line up is a record of the data stored on the hard disc. Remove the paper clips from the circle. Spin it clockwise with one hand, and with a finger of the other hand, touch areas of the circle. If you stop the circle on a white part, you have found data. If you stop on a red section, you have found empty disc space.

Fun with magnets

Many tricks rely on the invisible power of magnets. For example, did you know that you can remove paper clips from water without getting your fingers wet? The first project shows you how to make a paper bat that hovers in mid-air.

Magnets are used to recover pieces of wrecked ships from awkward and dangerous places on the sea bed, where the water might be murky. The magnetic fishing game here demonstrates how magnets are used in this way.

▲ **Floating trick**
Put paper clips in a beaker of water, and slide the magnet up the side. The paper clips will follow, dragged along by the magnet, until they reach the rim.

YOU WILL NEED

Bat magnet: Black paper, white pencil, scissors, stiff paper, adhesive tape, stiff wire, string, paper clips, strong magnet.

Magnetic fishing: Different coloured plastic bags, felt-tipped pen, scissors, paper clips, magnets, string, wooden dowel, adhesive tape, deep plate or shallow bowl, water, jug (pitcher) or watering can.

Bat magnet

1 Draw a large bat shape on to a sheet of black paper with the white pencil. (You could fold the paper in half first to make sure that your bat is symmetrical.) Cut out the bat shape.

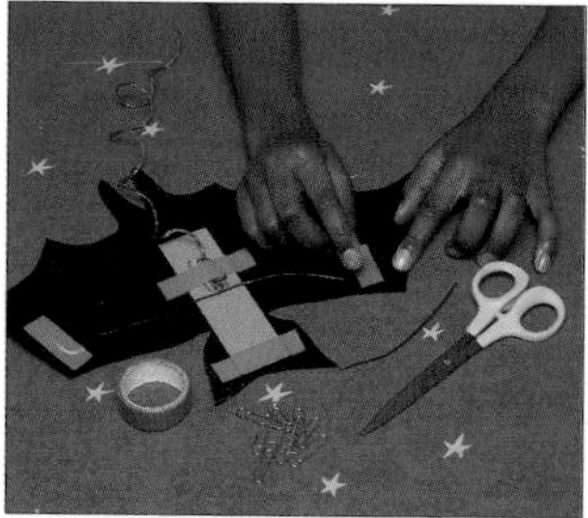

2 Tape pieces of stiff paper to the bat's underside, as shown. Then tape lengths of stiff wire across each of the wings. Secure the wire with a piece of string.

3 Place several paper clips on the pieces of paper that you have used to stiffen the bat. Cover each paper clip with a piece of tape to keep it secure.

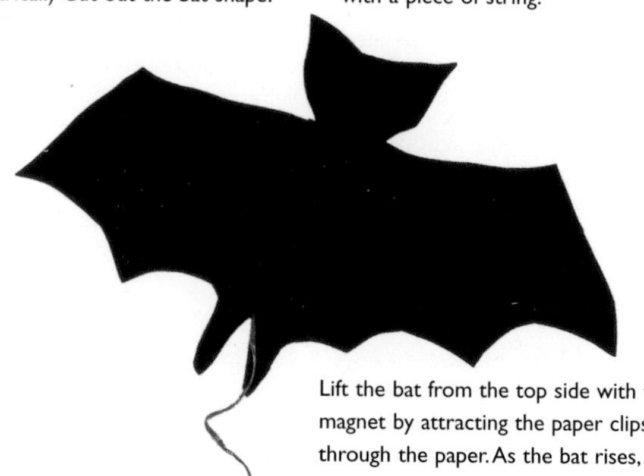

Lift the bat from the top side with the magnet by attracting the paper clips through the paper. As the bat rises, the string lengthens. Can you lift the magnet so that the bat hovers in mid-air?

Magnetic fishing

1 Draw some fish shapes on to the plastic bags with the felt-tipped pen. Keep the bags as still as possible while you do this. Cut out the shapes carefully with the scissors.

2 Decorate each of the fish with the pen. Draw scales and a face on one side of each fish, and write a different number on the other side of each fish.

3 Attach a steel paper clip to each fish. Make sure the paper clips are firmly attached. This will allow you to catch the fish with a magnetic rod.

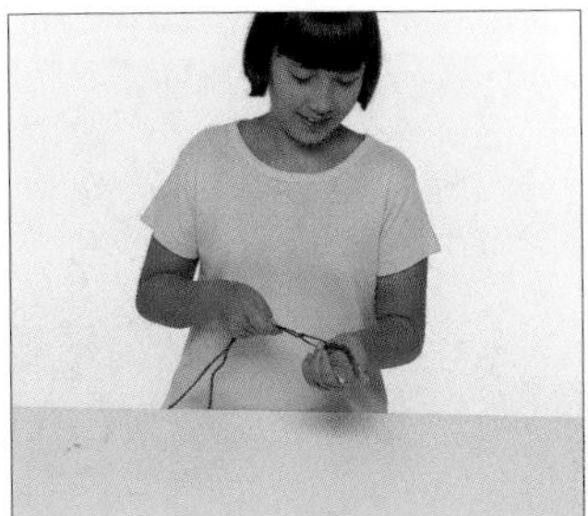

4 Tie a magnet to one end of a piece of string. If you tie the string around the middle of the magnet, it will be very secure and the magnet won't fall out.

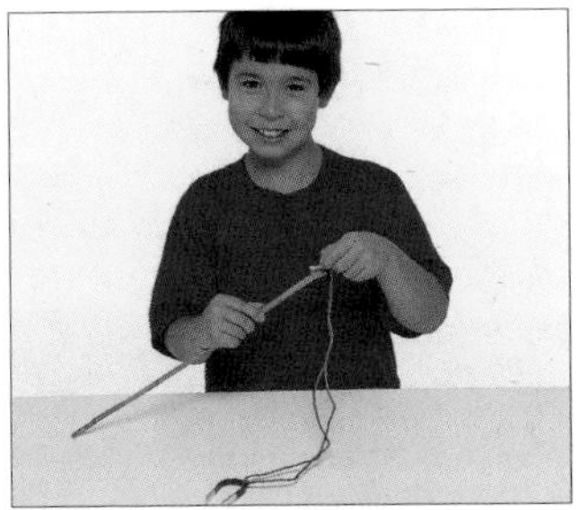

5 Tape the string that is attached to the magnet, to the end of some wooden dowel with tape. Make sure it is fixed on securely, or it may float off in the water.

6 Put all of your fish, scale side up, in a plate or bowl, and fill with water from a jug or watering can. You are now ready to start the fishing game.

WARNING!

Keep plastic bags away from small children, as they can be very dangerous.

Lower your fishing rods into the water to catch the fish. The paper clips will be attracted to the magnets on the ends of the rods. Lift your fish out of the pond. When there are no fish left, count up the points on the back of your fish, and the highest score wins.

Magnet sports

You can make your own table-top car race, using some magnets. Small, flat bar and ring magnets are best. The trick is to stay on the track and speed along, but not so fast that the magnet loses your car! If that happens, the race is over. The second project shows you how to create your own Olympic Games using an electromagnet. A washer represents a discus, a nut a shot put, and a nail a javelin. Use the electromagnet to throw each of them. When you switch off the electromagnet, it releases the iron or the steel object.

YOU WILL NEED

White glue, small ring or bar magnets, glue spreader, two 30cm/12in rulers or strips of wood, sheets of thin coloured card, pens, scissors, stick-on stars or similar shapes, steel paper clips, large sheet of cardboard, two books.

Magnetic racing

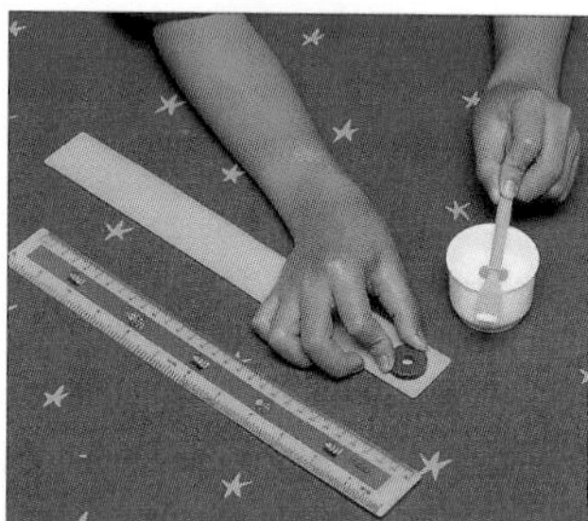

1 Carefully glue a magnet to the end of each ruler or strip of wood. Use 30cm/12in rulers if you can, or if these are unavailable, use similar-sized strips of wood.

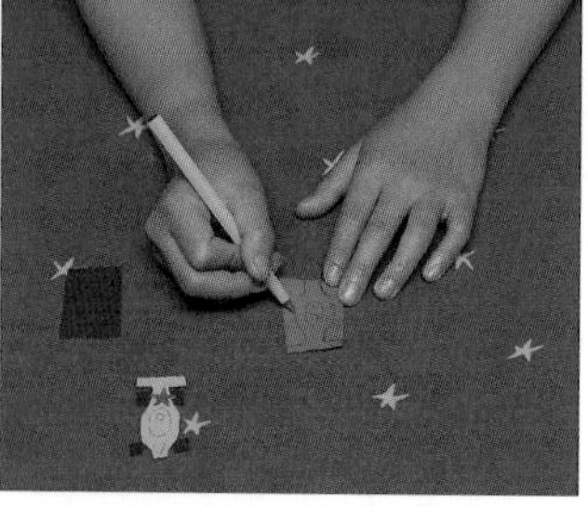

2 Draw the shapes of some racing cars on the card. You can make the wheels a different tone and maybe add stripes, too, so that each car looks different.

3 Carefully cut out the racing car shapes with scissors. Decorate the cars with stick-on shapes, such as stars, to make up your own racing team.

4 Glue a steel paper clip to the underside of each racing car. Let the glue dry thoroughly while you draw a racing track on a large sheet of cardboard.

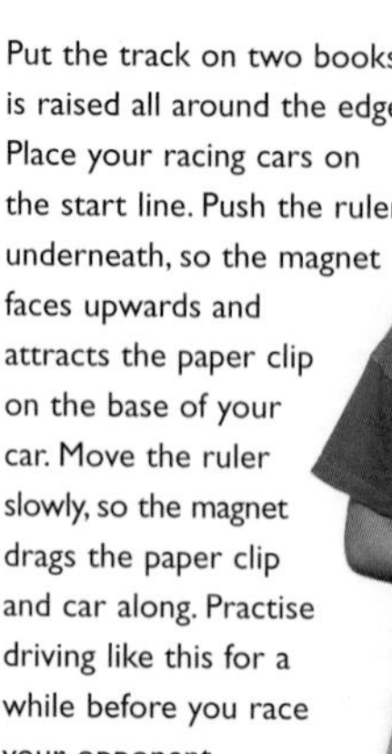

Put the track on two books, so it is raised all around the edges. Place your racing cars on the start line. Push the ruler underneath, so the magnet faces upwards and attracts the paper clip on the base of your car. Move the ruler slowly, so the magnet drags the paper clip and car along. Practise driving like this for a while before you race your opponent.

Electromagnetic Olympics

YOU WILL NEED

Sheets of thin card, scissors, white glue, glue spreader, adhesive tape, felt-tipped pen, decorative stick-on shapes, large iron nail, insulated (plastic-coated) copper wire, wire strippers, battery, paper clip, washer, small nails, nut.

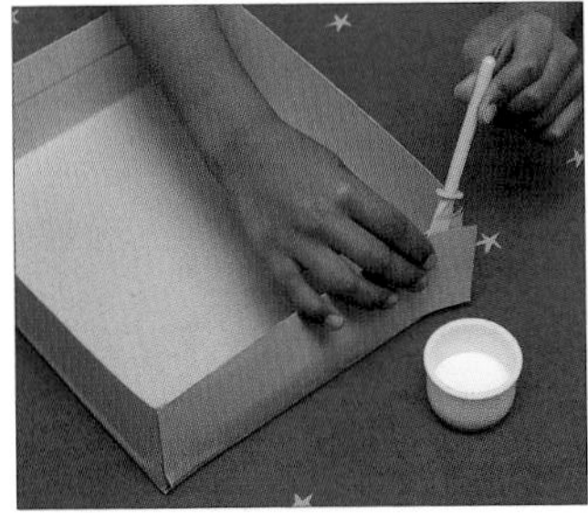

1 Cut a sheet of card into a base about 50 x 40cm/20 x 16in. Cut four strips the same length and 10–15cm/4–6in deep, for the sides. Glue the sides and base together.

2 Cut out squares of card for the scoreboard, and tape them together to make a sheet that will fit neatly into the box. Write numbers on them and decorate them.

3 Fit the scoreboard into the box. It is best not to glue it, since you may wish to take it out and change the scores, or make a new scoreboard as you become an expert at the games.

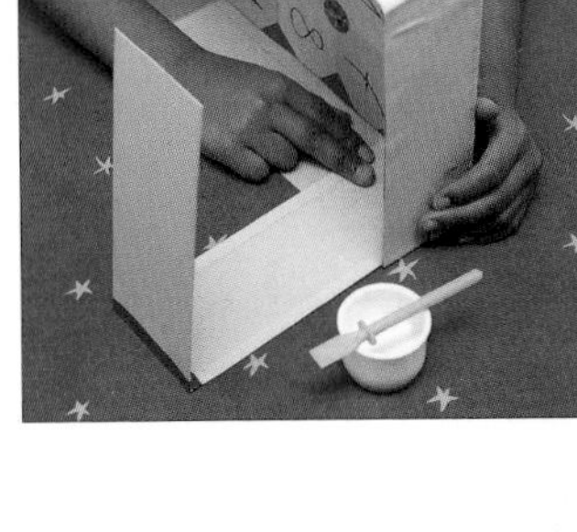

4 Cut two more card strips. Tape them together at each of their short edges. Glue the other short edges inside the box, on opposite sides. Position this 'arch' at one end of the box.

5 Make an electromagnet from the nail and wire. Tape it to the arch, so it hangs below by its wires. Connect the free ends of the wire to the battery. Use a paper clip as a battery switch.

Push the nail that hangs below the wires to test that it swings back and forth. Switch on the nail electromagnet using the paper clip switch. It should attract an iron or steel object, such as the nail, which is the javelin. Push the nail electromagnet so it swings back and forth. Turn off the switch, and the javelin will be released. Note where this lands on the scoreboard.

Images from light

The picture on a television screen is made up of thin lines of light. In the first project, you will see that a television picture is made up from rows of dots of coloured light. The picture consists of just three colours – red, green and blue. Viewed from a distance, these mix to produce a full range of colours – as the second experiment demonstrates. Plasma screens work in a similar way, although instead of using a cathode ray tube, the image is produced by passing a current across a gas (plasma) to produce ultraviolet photons. These are translated into visible red, green and blue light when they interact with a phosphor layer on a sheet of glass.

Scanners work in a similar way to television. When you insert a sheet of paper, a beam of light moves back and forth across it and sensors read the paper. This information is then changed into a code and sent to a computer. At the receiving end, the code is translated into dots, which are either printed to produce a facsimile (copy) of the original, or appear on a computer screen as an image.

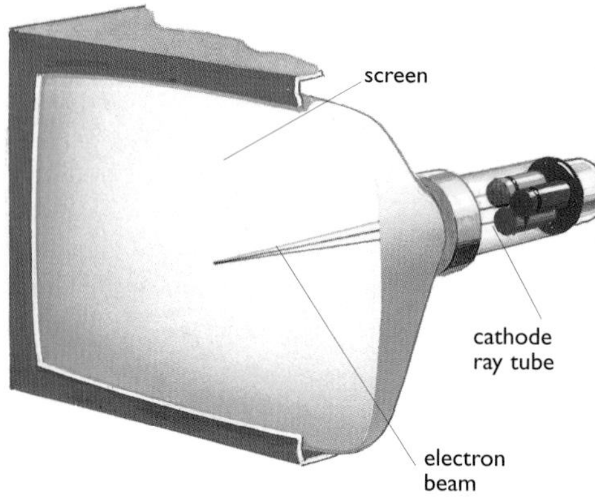

▲ Tube travel
The cathode ray tube is the heart of a television. Pictures are received in the form of electrical impulses. These impulses control a stream of electrons inside the cathode ray tube. The electron beam scans across the screen and creates the pictures as points of coloured light. This is the picture that the viewer sees.

YOU WILL NEED

TV screen: TV set, torch (flashlight), powerful magnifying glass.

Secondary colours: Red, green, and blue transparent plastic sheet, three powerful torches (flashlights), three rubber bands, thin black card.

Digital images: Ruler, pencil, tracing paper, photograph, black felt-tipped pen.

TV screen

1 Turn off the TV. Shine the torch close to the screen and look through the magnifying glass. You will see that the screen is covered in very fine lines.

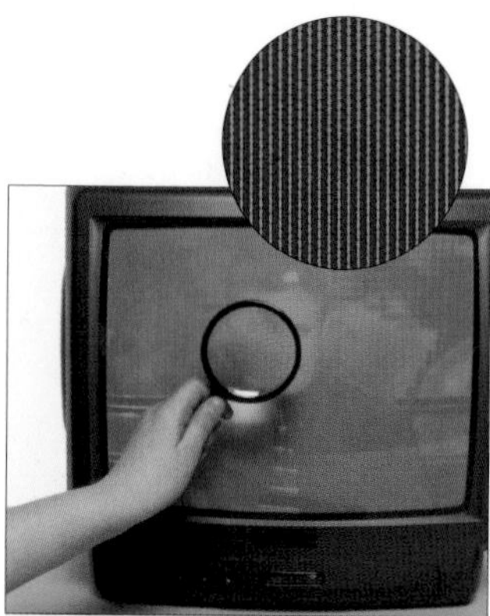

2 Turn on the TV and view the screen through the magnifying glass. The picture is made up of minute rectangles of light coloured red, green and blue.

Secondary colours

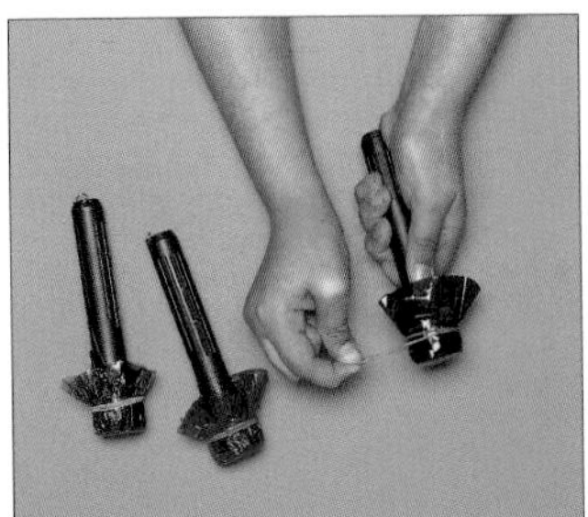

1 Attach a piece of coloured plastic over the end of each of your three torches. Stretch the plastic tightly, and use a rubber band to hold it firmly in place.

2 Turn on the torches on to the black card. You can see the three different primary colours of red, green and blue on the black card.

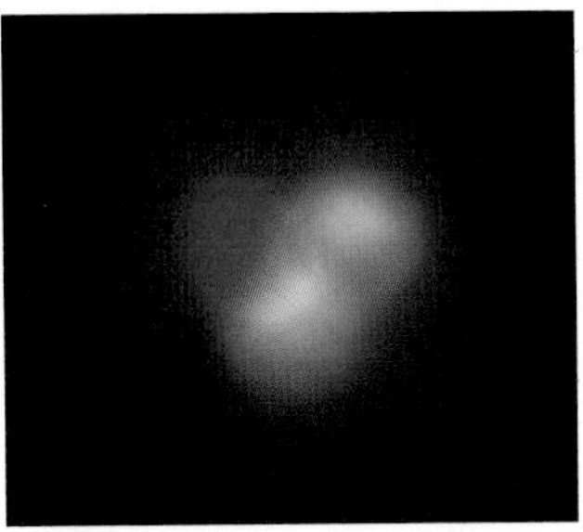

3 Position the torches so that the three circles of coloured light overlap in a clover-leaf pattern. Overlapping colours mix to give new, secondary colours.

Digital images

1 Draw lines 5mm/¼in apart to cover the tracing paper in squares. Put the paper over the photograph. Use the pen to fill each dark square. Leave each light square blank.

The picture is made from squares that are either black or white.

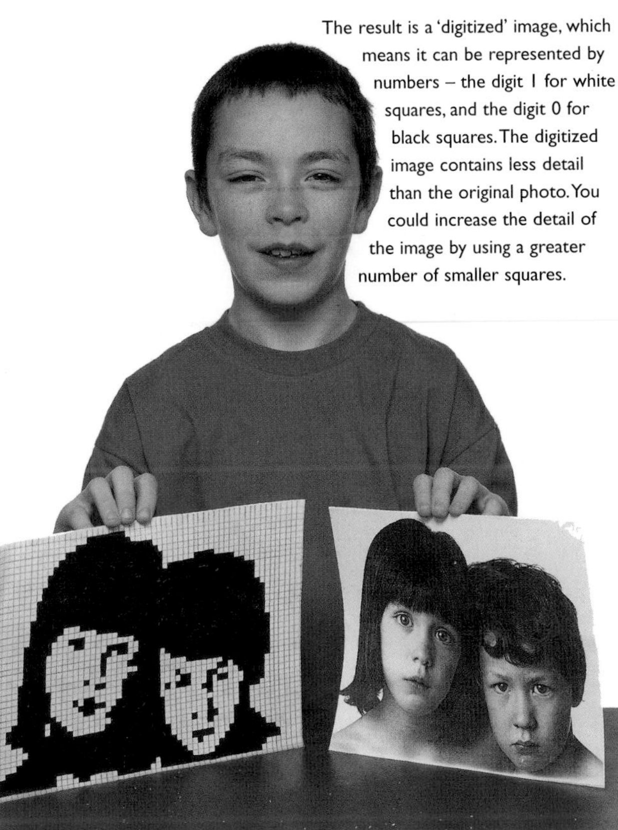

The result is a 'digitized' image, which means it can be represented by numbers – the digit 1 for white squares, and the digit 0 for black squares. The digitized image contains less detail than the original photo. You could increase the detail of the image by using a greater number of smaller squares.

Cameras and light

What is the vital piece of equipment you must not forget if you are going away on a trip or having a birthday party? Your camera! To most people, a camera is simply a device for taking snapshots of their friends, family and places. In fact, modern cameras are sophisticated light-recording machines that make use of the very latest breakthroughs in technology and computer science.

Cameras work in a similar way to your eyes, but they make a permanent record of a scene that you can share with other people. They record scenes either on film or digitally by collecting light from that scene and turning it into a picture. Although light appears to be white, it is actually made up of light of many colours like a rainbow. The first experiment shows you how to break the light spectrum into its component parts by shining light through water.

Cameras have three basic parts. The camera body holds the film or a silicon chip. The shutter opens to allow light to come through to the lens. The lens bends rays of light and directs them on to the film or silicon chip to make a picture. In the second experiment, you can collect light to make a picture, in the same way that a camera works.

YOU WILL NEED

Split light into a rainbow: Mirror, dish, reusable adhesive, jug (pitcher), water, torch (flashlight), thin white card.

Make your own viewer: Small cardboard box, scissors, ruler, thin card, sharp pencil, adhesive tape, tracing paper.

Split light into a rainbow

1 Lean the mirror against the inner side of the dish. Use two pieces of reusable adhesive to stick both sides of the mirror to the dish at an angle.

2 Pour water into the dish until it is about 4cm/1½in in depth. Notice that as you fill the dish, a wedge-shaped volume of water is created alongside the mirror.

3 Switch on the flashlight. Shine the beam from the flashlight on to the surface of the water in front of the mirror. This should produce a spectrum or 'rainbow'.

4 In dim light, hold up the piece of white card above the dish to look at your rainbow. You may need to alter the positions of the card and flashlight before you can see it properly.

Make your own viewer

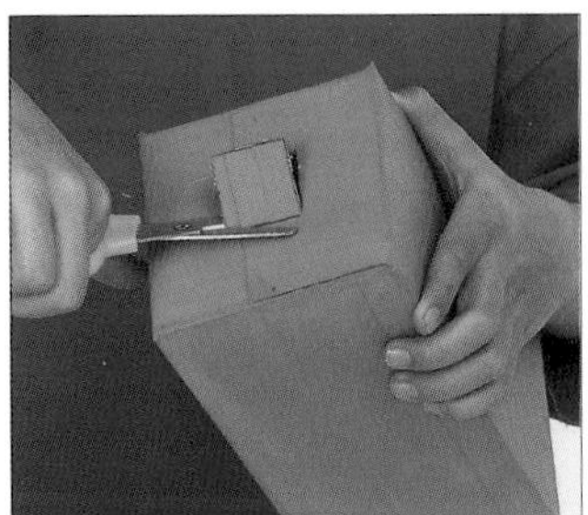

1 Use a pair of sharp scissors to cut a small square hole, about 1.5 x 1.5cm/¾ x ¾in, in one end of the cardboard box. You may need an adult's help to do this.

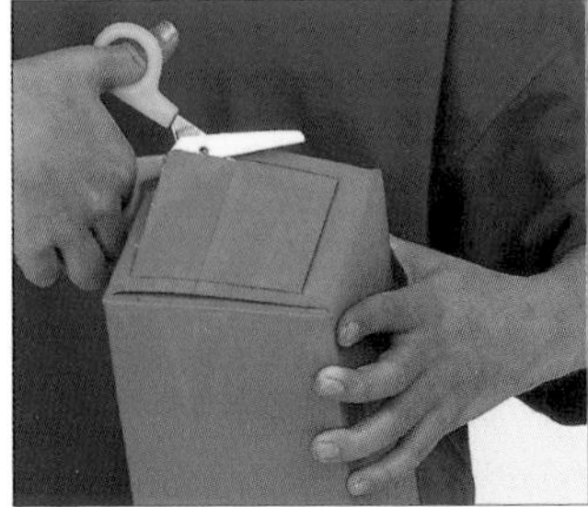

2 Now cut a much larger square hole in the other end of your cardboard box. Cut out most of the end of the box, as shown in the picture.

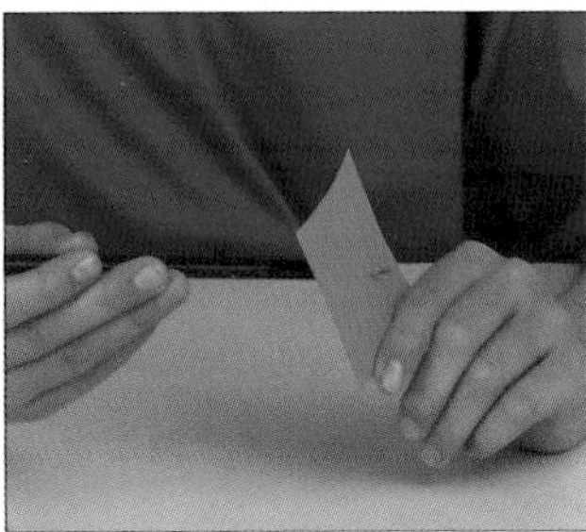

3 Cut a square of thin card about 4 x 4cm/1½ x 1½in. Find the middle of the card using a ruler. Use a sharp pencil to pierce a tiny hole in the middle of the card.

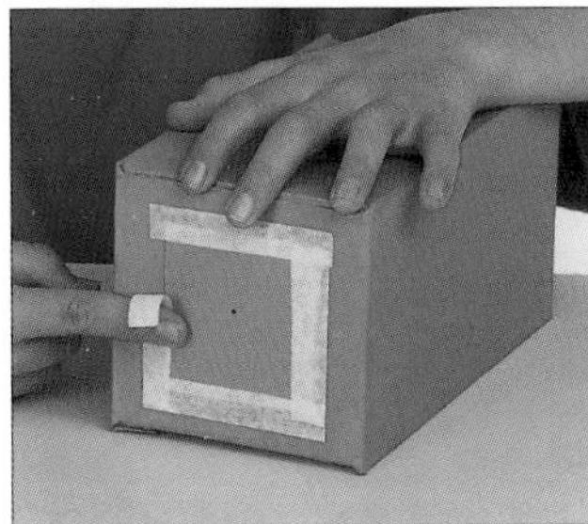

4 Place the piece of thin card over the outside of the smaller hole on the box. Make sure that the pencil hole is in the middle of the square hole. Now tape it into place.

5 Cut a square of tracing paper slightly bigger than the larger hole at the other end of the box. Stick it securely over that hole. Your viewer is now ready to use.

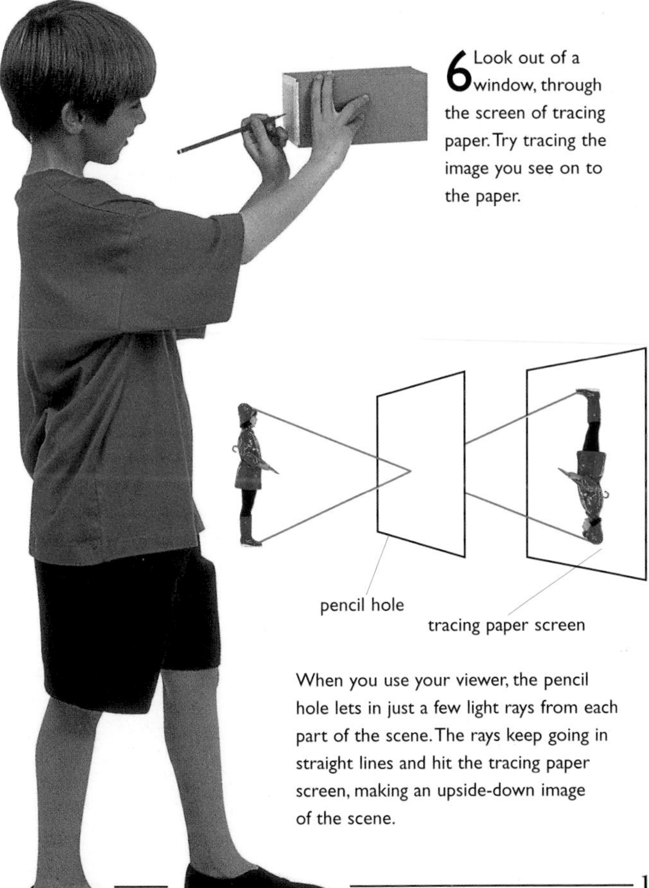

6 Look out of a window, through the screen of tracing paper. Try tracing the image you see on to the paper.

When you use your viewer, the pencil hole lets in just a few light rays from each part of the scene. The rays keep going in straight lines and hit the tracing paper screen, making an upside-down image of the scene.

A photographic image on film

Having created a focused image of a scene, a camera must have some way of recording the image. This is the job of the film or, in the case of digital cameras, the silicon chip that is covered in light-sensitive spots called photosites.

Film is coated with chemicals that are affected by light. When an image strikes the film, the coating records the patterns of light, dark and colour. Film has to be developed with chemicals before you can see the recorded pictures. Digital cameras, however, record the image electronically as binary code (0s and 1s), which needs to be translated into an image by a computer. So, for this project, film is a better way of showing how light can affect chemicals and produce a picture.

It does not matter if you do not have a film camera, as you do not need one to see how film works. In fact, you do not even need a film! You can use black and white photographic paper instead. Photographic paper is the paper that prints are made on. It works in the same way as film. Here, you can see how to make a picture called a photogram by covering some parts of a sheet of photographic paper with objects and then shining light on the sheet. When the paper is developed, the areas that were hit by the light turn black, leaving you an image of the objects.

YOU WILL NEED

Developer for paper (not film) and fixer (both from a photographic supplier), rubber gloves, protective glasses, plastic dishes, desk lamp, photographic paper, different-shaped objects, such as keys and scissors, plastic tongs.

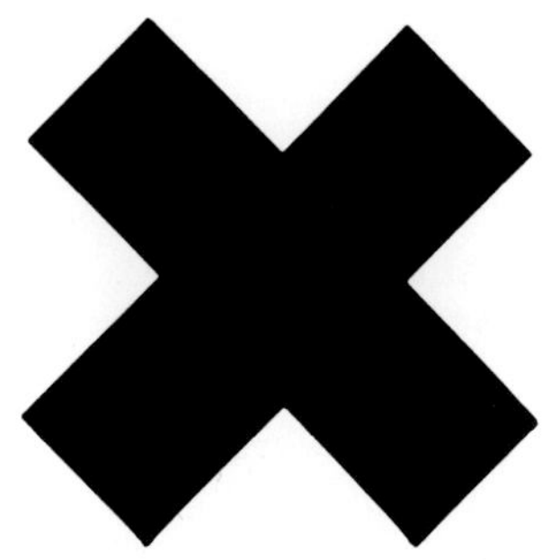

▲ Danger!
This symbol on photographic chemical bottles means that they can be dangerous if not used with care. Always wear protective gloves and goggles.

◄ Photographic paper
For black and white prints, you need a paper called monochrome paper. Buy the smallest size you can, and choose grade 2 if possible, with a gloss (shiny) finish. The paper comes in a light-proof envelope or box. Only open the envelope in complete darkness. The paper is in a second black polyurethene envelope. You will also need two photographic chemicals – developer for paper (not film) and fixer. Buy them from a photographic supplier, and ask an adult to help you use them safely.

Make your own photogram

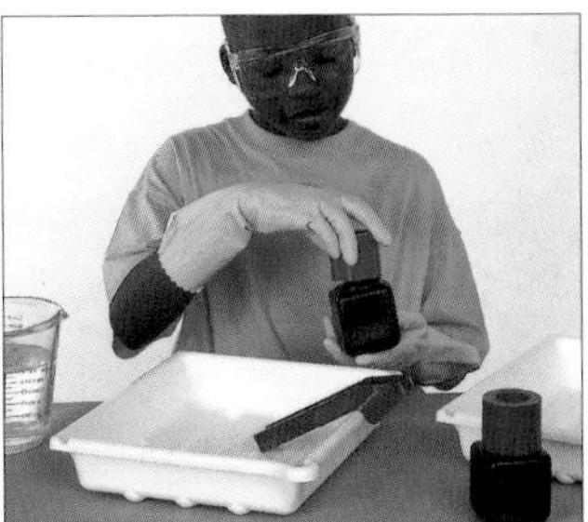

1 Ask an adult to help you follow the instructions to dilute the chemicals with water. Protect your eyes and hands when handling them. Store the diluted chemicals in plastic bottles.

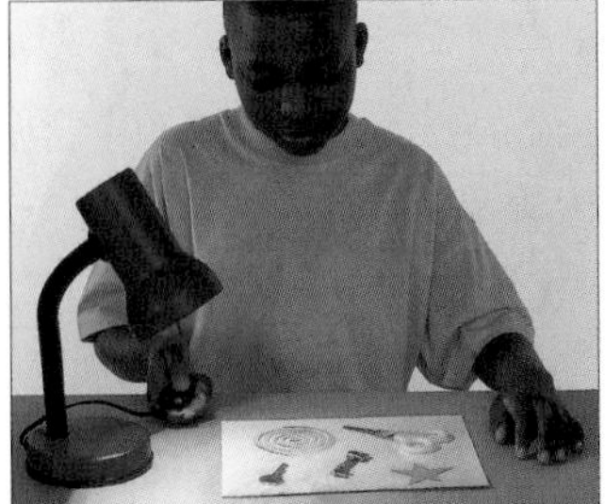

2 Turn off the lamp. Lay a sheet of photographic paper down, shiny side up. Put some objects on it. Then turn the lamp on again for a few seconds.

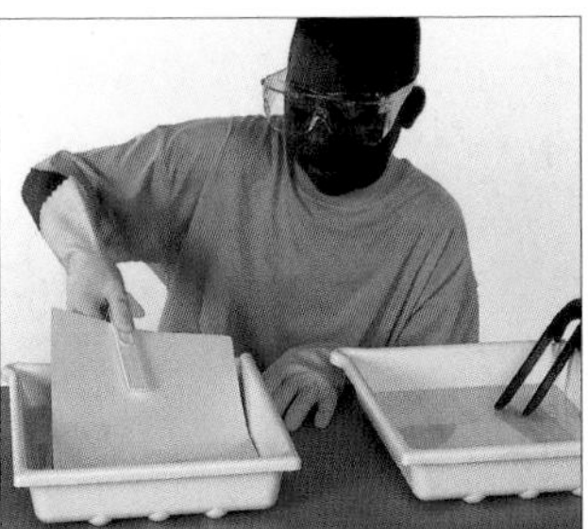

3 Pick up the paper with the tongs, and put it into the dish of developer. Push the paper down, so that it is completely underneath the liquid.

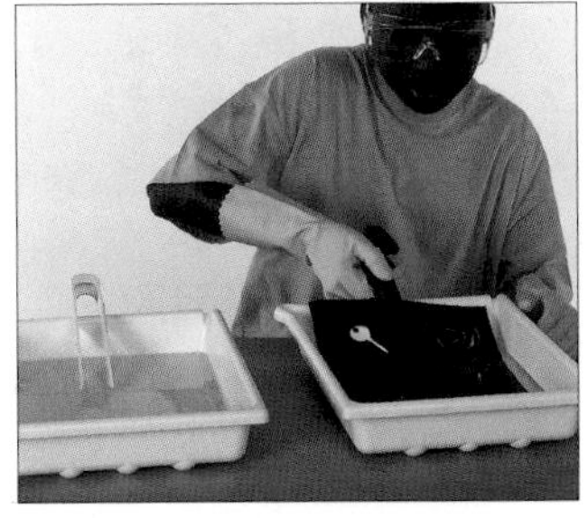

4 After a minute, use the tongs to move the paper into the fixer. Leave the paper right under the liquid for a minute, until the image is fixed.

images made on photographic paper

5 Now you can turn the light back on. Using the tongs, lift the paper out of the fixer and wash it with running water for a few minutes. Then lay the paper on a flat surface to dry. This technique is an excellent way of producing unique invitations and greetings cards quickly and effectively.

Getting in focus

Before taking a photograph, you need to make sure that your subject is in focus. When it is, all the rays of light that leave a point on the subject are bent by the lens, so that they hit the correct place on the film or silicon chip. This makes a clear, sharp image. Parts of the scene inside or behind the subject may not be in focus. On some cameras, you have to choose the part of the scene that you want to be in focus. Autofocus cameras focus the lens by automatically choosing the object at the middle of the image to be taken.

This experiment involves making a simple camera with just a few basic pieces of equipment. It uses photographic paper (paper with a light-sensitive coating on one side) instead of film, and a pinhole instead of a lens. When the paper is processed, you will have a negative. The 'Easy prints' project on the next page shows you how to develop it.

viewfinder
lens
pentaprism
light ray
mirror

▲ Focusing SLRs
With an SLR (single lens reflex) camera, you can see exactly what the image looks like through the viewfinder. On a manual-focus SLR, you turn a ring around the lens until your subject comes into focus. When the subject is in focus, the light rays meet on the film focal plane. This is the exposed part of the film that is held flat at the back of the camera by a pressure plate. You can see it if you open the back of your camera when it is empty.

YOU WILL NEED
Pinhole box viewer, foil, scissors, adhesive tape, pencil, black paper, thin card, ruler, heavy light-proof cloth or plastic sheet, photographic paper, rubber band.

◄ Get it sharp
In this photograph (*left*), the subject is in sharp focus. You can see all the fine detail. When the same shot is out of focus (*below*), it makes the subject look blurred. Autofocus cameras focus on the object in the middle of the viewfinder and do the job of focusing for you.

Making a pinhole camera

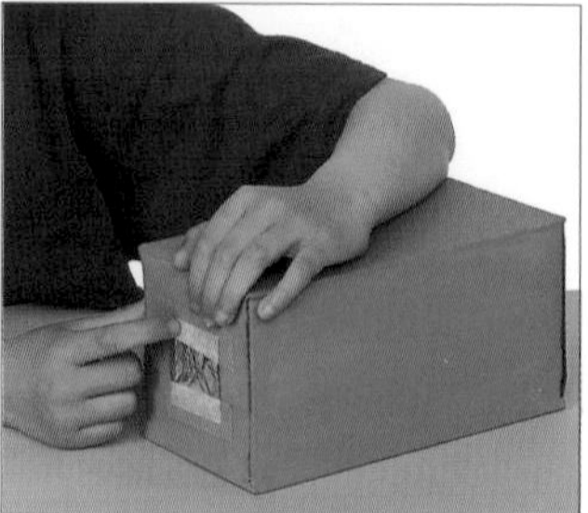

1 Make the pinhole viewer from the 'Make your own viewer' project, but remove the tracing-paper screen. Replace the 4cm/1½in card square with foil.

2 Pierce a hole, 2mm/$\frac{1}{16}$in across, in the middle of the foil using a sharp pencil. Open the back of the box. Roll up some black paper, and fit it through the large hole to line the inside.

3 Cut a square of card large enough to completely cover the foil. Tape just the top edge of the square of card to the box, so that it will act as a shutter.

4 Measure and cut a square of card to fit across the other end of the box. Tape it to one edge, so that it closes over the hole like a door or flap.

5 Lay the heavy light-proof cloth or light-proof plastic sheet on the working surface. Cut a piece of the cloth or sheet large enough to fold around the end of the box.

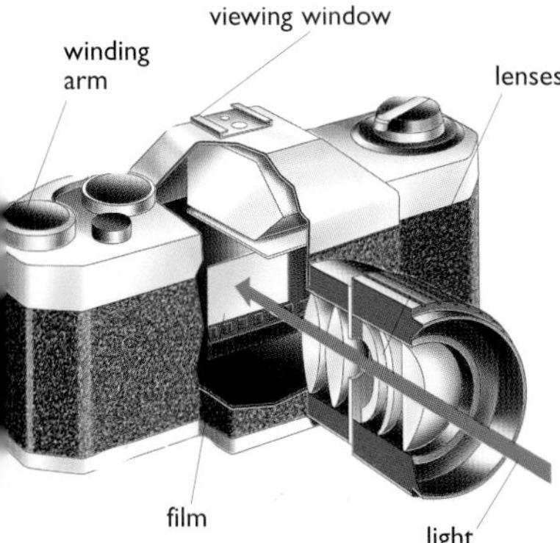

▲ **Reflex action**

In a single lens reflex camera, light enters through the lenses at the front and strikes the film at the back. Users can see clearly what they are photographing by means of a prism mounted in the camera.

6 In a completely dark room, and feeling with your fingers, put a piece of the photographic paper underneath the flap at the end of the box.

7 Close the flap, then, still feeling with your fingers, wrap the cloth or plastic sheet tightly over it. Next, put a rubber band tightly around the box to secure it.

8 Now you can turn the light on. Point the camera at a well-lit object and open the shutter. Leave the camera perfectly still for about five minutes, and then close the shutter.

Letting in the light

Exposure is the word for the amount of light that reaches the film or silicon chip in your camera. The aperture (opening) is a hole behind the lens that can be adjusted to let more or less light. Changing the aperture affects both the brightness of an image and the depth of field that is in focus. Your eyes work in the same way. If the light is bright, your pupils get smaller to protect your retinas. If the light is dim, then the pupils enlarge to let in more light. In the experiment opposite, you can investigate different apertures for yourself.

One of the first things photographers want to do is to get their films developed or view the image on the camera, so that they can see how the pictures have turned out. If you have just taken a photograph with the pinhole camera you made in an earlier project, you can find out how easy it is to turn it into a photographic print in the project below.

YOU WILL NEED

Easy prints: Photographic paper and chemicals, negative from pin-hole camera, torch (flashlight) or desk lamp, safety glasses, rubber gloves, plastic dishes, plastic tongs or tweezers.

Amazing apertures: Magnifying glass, cardboard tube, adhesive tape, scissors, thin card, tracing paper, desk lamp.

▲ **How does a shutter work?** Open the back of your camera (when there is no film inside). Place a small strip of tracing paper where your film usually goes. Aim the camera at a subject and press the shutter release button. You should see a brief flash of the image on your tracing paper.

Easy prints

1 In a totally dark room, lay a fresh sheet of photographic paper on a flat surface, shiny side up. Lay the negative from your pinhole camera face down on top.

2 Shine a torch or a desk lamp on the top of the two papers for a few seconds. Turn the light off, and remove your paper negative. Put on the safety glasses and gloves.

3 Put the fresh paper into a tray of developing fluid, then fix and wash the paper (see the project on 'Making your own photogram'). You should end up with a print of the original image.

Amazing apertures

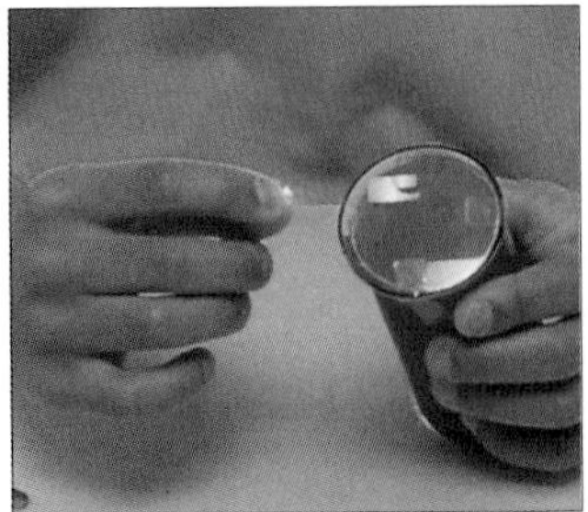

1 Make sure that your magnifying glass fits into your cardboard tube. Then carefully attach the magnifying glass to one end of the tube using small pieces of adhesive tape.

2 Roll a piece of thin card around the other end of the cardboard tube. Tape the top edge down so that it makes another tube that slides on and off the first one.

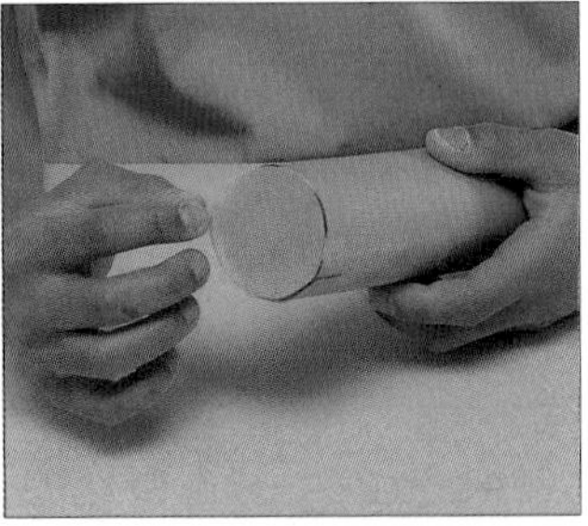

3 Cut out a circle of tracing paper with a diameter the same as the sliding card tube. Use tape to attach it across the end of the tube. This will form your viewing screen.

4 With the viewing screen facing toward you, aim your tube at a desk lamp that is turned on. Can you see an image of the bulb on the screen?

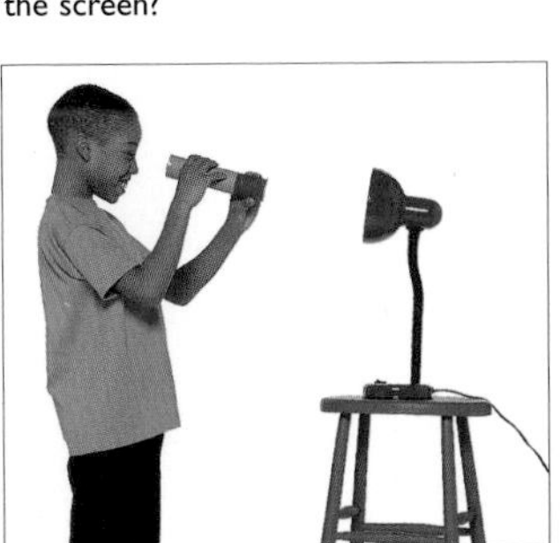

5 Slide the tubes slowly together, until the image of the bulb is clear and in focus. Now adjust the tubes again so that the image is slightly out of focus.

6 Cut a hole (about 5mm/¼in wide) in a piece of card, to make a small aperture. Look at the light bulb again and hold the card in front of the lens. The smaller aperture will bring the light bulb into focus. Is it clearer? Can you read the writing on the bulb?

How telescopes work

Optical telescopes use lenses or mirrors to make distant objects look bigger and brighter. Lens telescopes are also called refractors. Mirror telescopes are called reflectors. Most large astronomical telescopes for looking at stars are reflectors.

The first experiment shows you how to make a reflecting telescope, using a mirror. A reflecting telescope's main mirror is curved, so that light rays bounce off at an angle.

The refracting telescope in the second experiment uses lenses. There are difficulties involved in making big lenses, which is why most of the telescopes used in astronomy are reflectors. Our brains work out how big an object is by analyzing the angle of the light rays from it as the rays enter our eyes. Telescopes use lenses or mirrors to change this angle. Bending light rays from distant objects makes them seem larger than they would appear to the naked eye.

YOU WILL NEED
Desk lamp, thick purple paper, felt-tipped pen, scissors, adhesive tape, small mirror, non-hardening modelling material, magnifying glass.

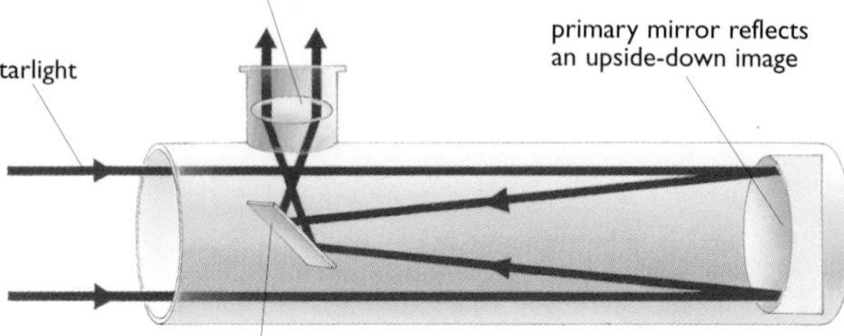

▲ **Reflecting telescope**
Light reflects off the primary mirror. The light rays bounce off a small secondary mirror, and are focused and magnified by an eyepiece lens. Astronomers use telescopes to help them study the stars and other planets. Telescopes are often built on top of mountains, for the clearest views. There, the air is thin and there are no lights from towns. The William Herschel Telescope (WHT) is located 2,400m/8,000ft above sea level on top of an extinct volcano on La Palma, in the Canary Islands.

Make a single-mirror reflecting telescope

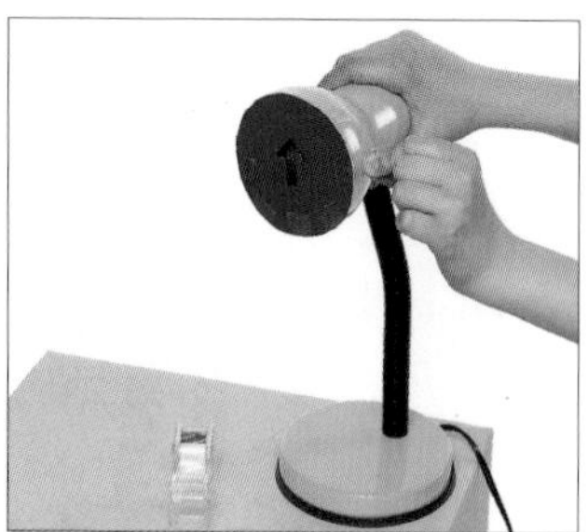

1 Draw a circle around the front of the desk lamp on a sheet of purple paper. Cut it out. Then cut out an arrow in the middle. Stick the circle on to the front of the lamp.

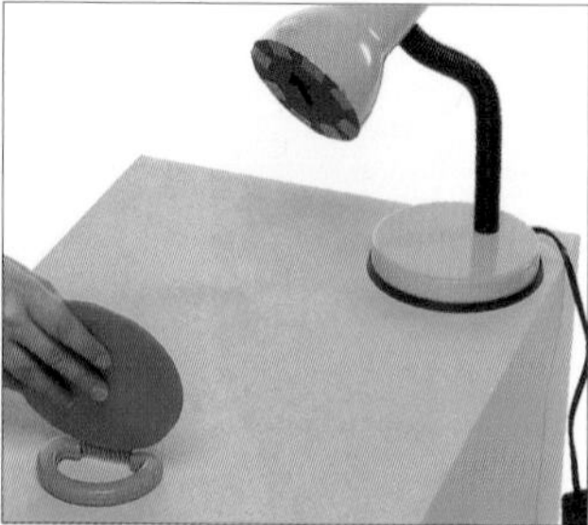

2 Set up the desk lamp and mirror so that the mirror reflects the light from the lamp on to a nearby wall. Use modelling material to help support the mirror, if necessary.

3 Set up the magnifying glass, so that light reflecting from the mirror passes through it. The lens magnifies and focuses the light, projecting an upside-down arrow.

Make a refracting telescope

YOU WILL NEED
Desk lamp, thick red paper, felt-tipped pen, scissors, adhesive tape, two magnifying glasses, non-hardening modelling material.

1 Draw around the front of the desk lamp on a sheet of red paper. Using scissors, cut out a star in the middle of the circle. Then cut out the circle, as shown above.

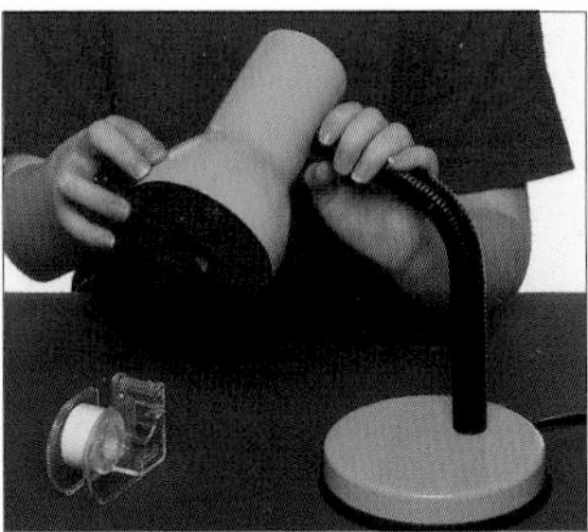

2 Using tape, fasten the circle of paper securely over the front of the desk lamp. Make sure that it does not touch the bulb, because this could cause the paper to burn.

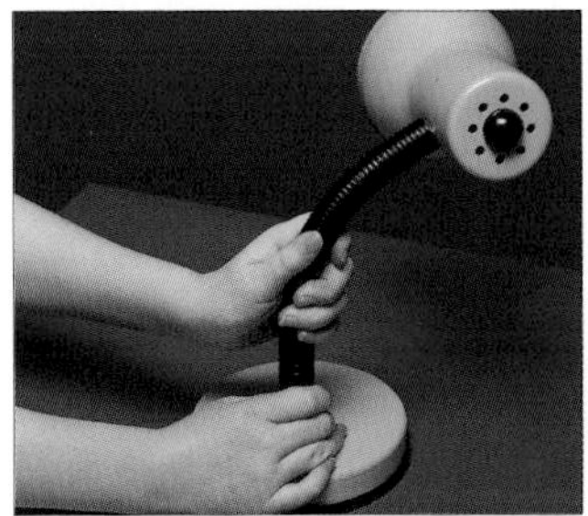

3 Position the desk lamp so that it shines on a nearby wall. Adjust the angle of the lamp if necessary. Make sure that the lamp's base is stable, to prevent it from tipping over.

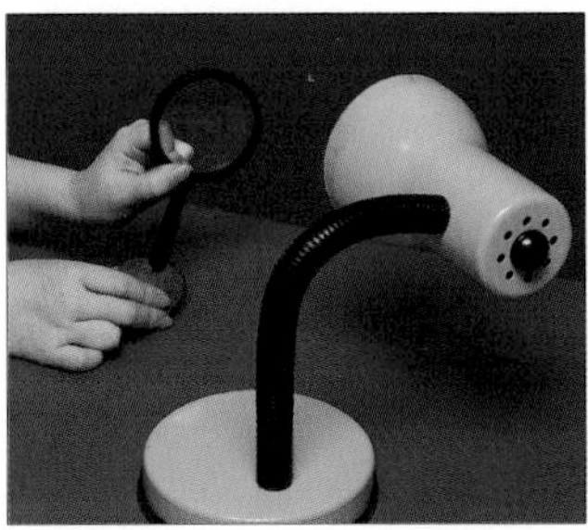

4 Position a magnifying glass between the lamp and the wall. To support the glass and fix it in place, take the handle and wedge it firmly in a lump of modelling material.

5 Turn on the lamp. Adjust the magnifying glass, so that the light passing through it appears as a blurred patch of light on the wall. The glass acts like a telescope's objective lens.

6 Position the second lens behind the first lens. This acts as an eyepiece lens. Adjust the eyepiece lens, until the light is focused to form the sharp image of the star.

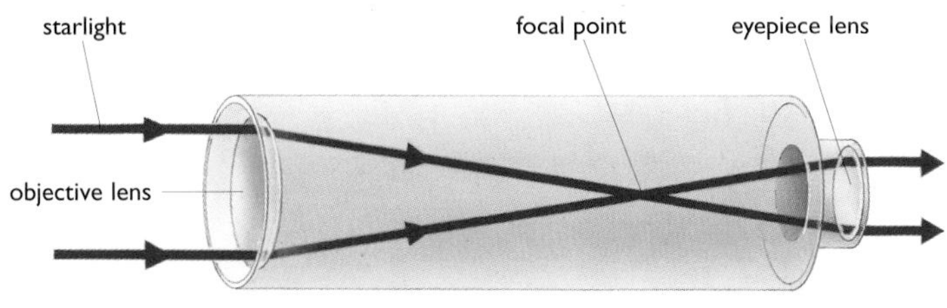

▲ **Refracting telescope**
Light from a distant star passes through the objective lens. The light rays from distant objects change direction as they enter the lens, and again as they leave it. A magnified, blurry image of the star appears. The image is brought into focus by the lens in the eyepiece.

Satellites and orbits

The movement of a satellite around the Earth is fixed in either a circular or an elliptical (oval) orbit. The satellite can be positioned in a polar orbit, circling the Earth from pole to pole, or placed in an equatorial orbit around the Equator, or in any orbit in between. It may cross the sky several times a day in a low Earth orbit (LEO), or it may hang in one place, in geostationary orbit. In the first project you can see for yourself how geostationary orbits work.

The type of orbit is chosen according to the job the satellite is there to do. Most communications and weather satellites are placed in geostationary orbit 36,000km/22,000 miles above the Equator. A satellite in this orbit keeps pace with the turning Earth, and appears to hang motionless over the same spot on the ground. Once a radio dish on the ground is aimed at the satellite, the dish need not be moved again. Other satellites have to be tracked using movable radio dishes that follow the satellite as it crosses the sky. The second project demonstrates the way in which satellites relay signals from one place to another.

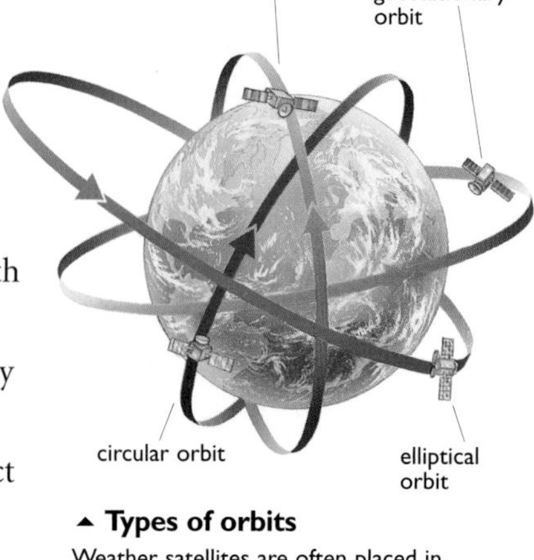

▲ **Types of orbits**
Weather satellites are often placed in geostationary orbits. They always face the same part of the Earth. Polar orbits are often chosen for scientific-survey satellites. As the satellite orbits from pole to pole, the Earth turns below it. In time, the satellite passes over every point on the Earth's surface.

YOU WILL NEED
15 strips of thin blue card, 30 strips of thin red card, rope, a friend.

Geostationary orbit

1 Use the card strips to mark a blue circle, with a larger red circle around it on the ground. Hold one end of the rope, and ask a friend to hold the other end.

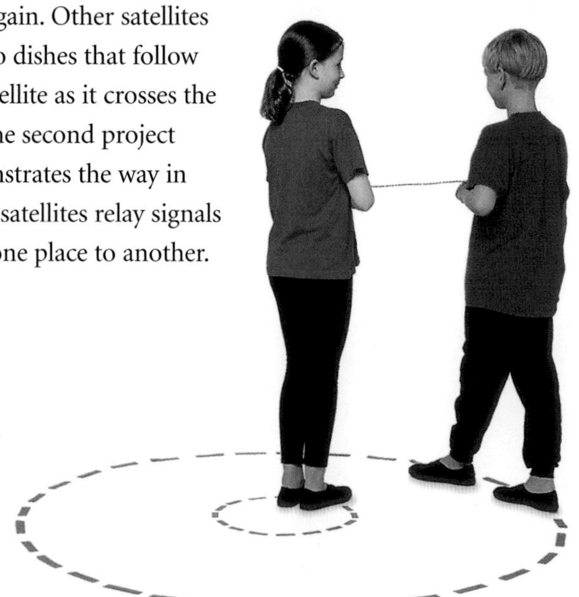

2 Walk around the inner circle, while your friend walks around the outer circle. The blue inner circle represents the Earth, and the outer circle represents the orbit of a satellite around the Earth. If your orbiting friend keeps pace with you as you walk, your human satellite is in a geostationary orbit.

Make a satellite relay

YOU WILL NEED

Scissors, blue paper, tin can, adhesive tape, long ruler, thin card, flat mirror, non-hardening modelling material, torch (flashlight).

1 Using the scissors, cut out a rectangle of blue paper just big enough to wrap around the tin can. Tape it in place. The tin can will act as a ground-based radio receiver.

2 Measure out a 10 x 10cm/4 x 4in piece of card with the ruler. Cut it out and stick it to one side of the tin can. This will act as an antenna on your tin-can receiver.

3 Place the tin can on the floor. Take the long ruler and lay it on the floor directly in front of the tin can. Place it on the opposite side to the antenna, as shown above.

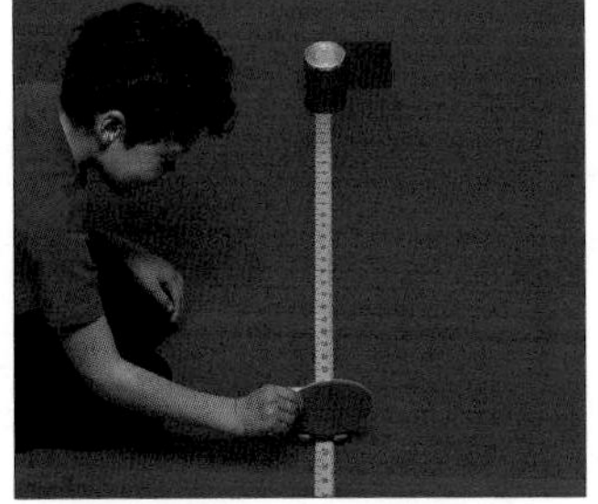

4 Place the mirror on the ruler about 75cm/2½ft from the tin can. The mirror will act like a satellite in geostationary orbit relaying signals. Fix in place with modelling material.

5 Darken the room. Place the torch beside the can, as shown. The torch will send out light beams in the same way that a ground-based transmitter sends out radio waves.

6 Switch on the torch. Move the mirror along the yardstick. Keep moving it, until the light beams are reflected off the mirror satellite and on to the antenna of the tin can.

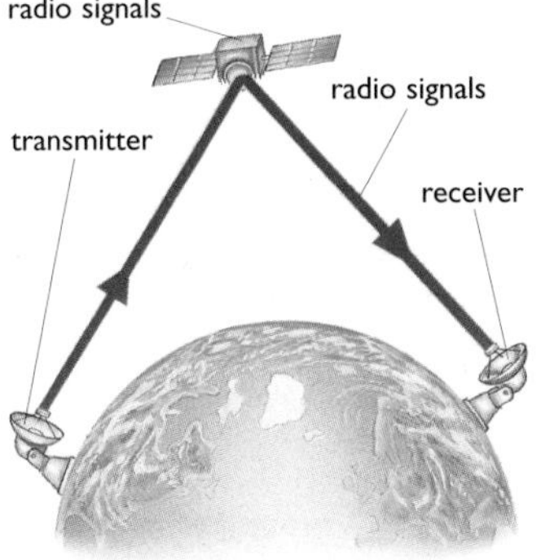

◂ Redirecting radio waves

Comsats (communication satellites) in geostationary orbit above the Equator allow radio transmissions to be sent to anywhere on the Earth's surface. Radio signals are transmitted from one side of the planet, and aimed at the orbiting satellite. The comsat then relays (redirects) the signal to a receiver on the opposite side of the Earth.

Power boost in Space

Some space probes, including *Pioneer 10* and *11*, used gravity boosts to help them travel through the Solar System. To get a boost, a probe passes by a planet and becomes attracted by its gravity. It is pulled by the planet on its orbit around the Sun. Some of the planet's orbital speed is transferred to the probe, which is then catapulted towards the next planet to be visited. This slingshot effect is vital, as robot spacecraft would not be able to carry enough fuel to change course from planet to planet. The first project shows how the slingshot effect works. Space probes send back information to Earth by radio signals. These are collected by large dish antennae on Earth. The second project shows why many of the radio antennae used are dish-shaped.

▾ Pioneering probes

Probes have landed on or flown past almost every planet in the Solar System. The most widely travelled Deep Space probes are *Pioneer 10* and *11*, and *Voyager 1* and 2, which have toured most of the Solar System's outer planets. They used the pull of gravity from each planet they passed to change their course and send them to the next planet. *Pioneer 10* flew past Jupiter, and the flight path of the *Pioneer 11* probe took it past Jupiter and then to Saturn.

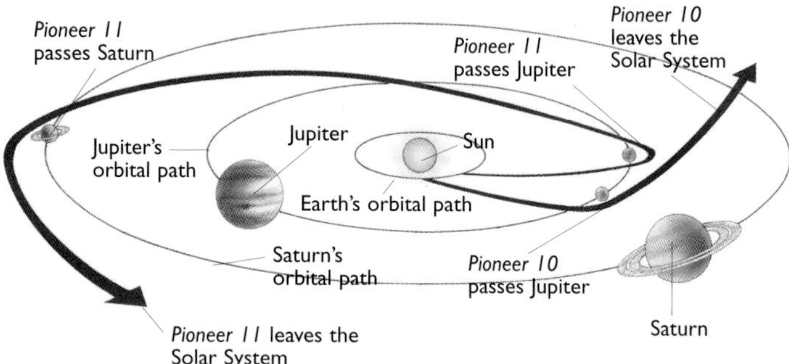

YOU WILL NEED
Two thick books (of equal thickness), 60 x 30cm/24 x 12in piece of cardboard, marble-sized steel ball, strong magnet, adhesive tape, two 30cm/12in lengths of wooden dowel.

Gravity boost

1 Place the books flat on a table about 15cm/6in apart. Lay the piece of cardboard on top of the books, then roll the steel-ball space probe across it. It moves smoothly across the surface.

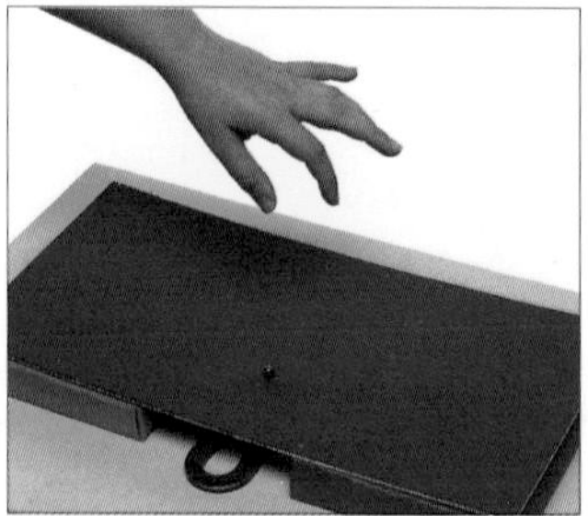

2 Place the magnet under the cardboard. Roll the steel-ball probe across the cardboard. It is drawn toward the magnet planet by the gravity-like pull of its magnetic field.

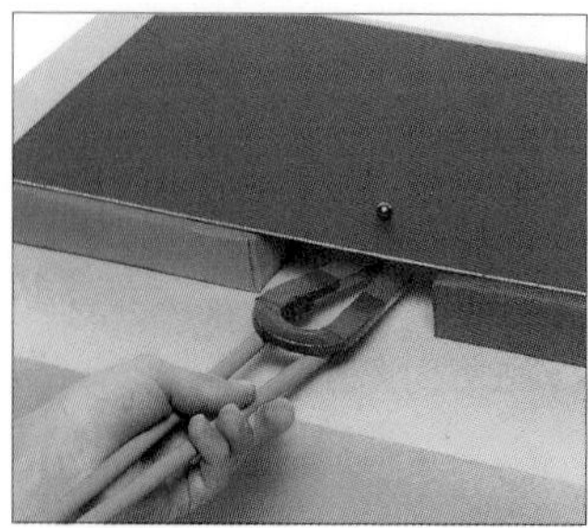

3 Tape the magnet to the dowel. Roll the ball and then pull the magnet away. The ball speeds up and is pulled along by the magnet planet, like a probe getting a gravity boost.

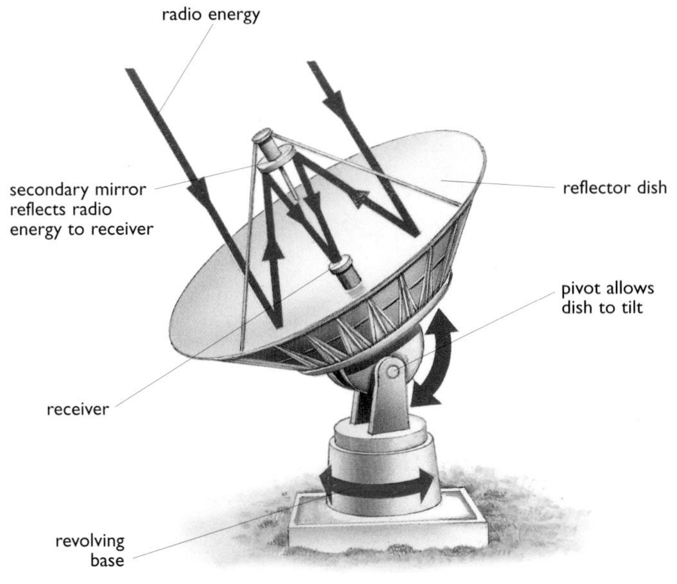

◂ Beaming waves

Dish antennae reflect their collected radio energy back to the receiver. Space probes use their antennae to receive radio signals from mission control on Earth. The receiver can also act as a transmitter, allowing the probe to send back its findings to Earth.

YOU WILL NEED

Plain postcard, pencil, ruler, scissors, 60 x 100cm/2 x 3ft piece of cardboard, non-hardening modelling material, 20 x 50cm/8 x 20in strip of mirror board, torch (flashlight).

Make a dish antenna

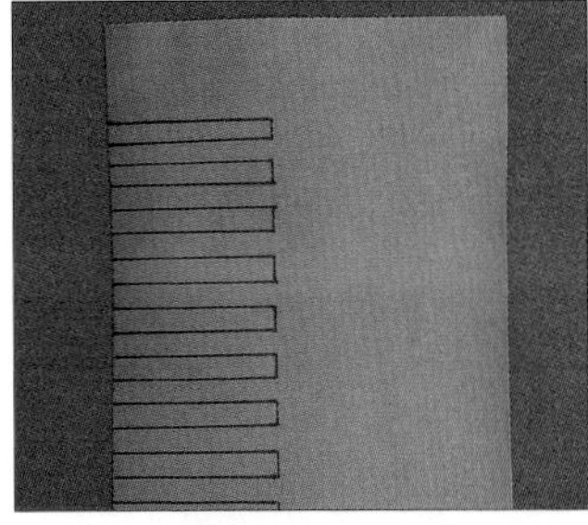

1 Draw nine thin slits on the postcard using the pencil and ruler. Each slit should measure 2.5cm x 0.5mm/1 x ¼in. They should be equally spaced out from each other, 5mm/¼in apart.

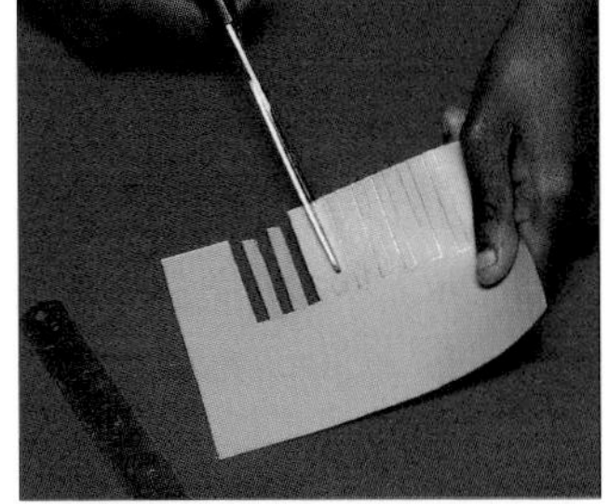

2 Using the scissors, carefully cut out the slits in the postcard. The slits in the card will filter light, splitting it up into thin rays that will reflect off the curve of the antenna.

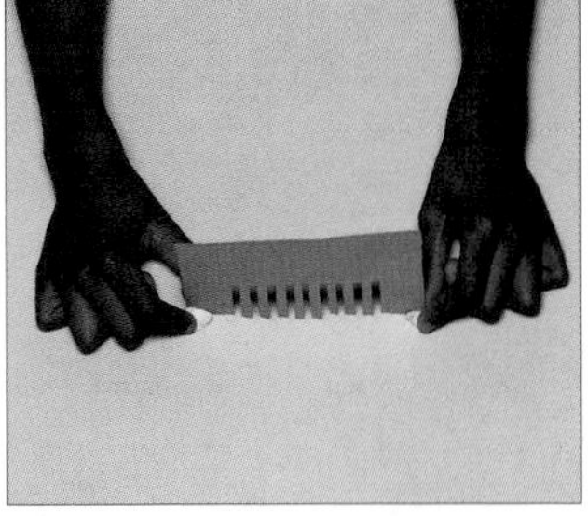

3 Place the large piece of thick cardboard on a table. Stand the postcard 40cm/16in from one end of the card, with the slits facing down. Fix it in position with modelling material.

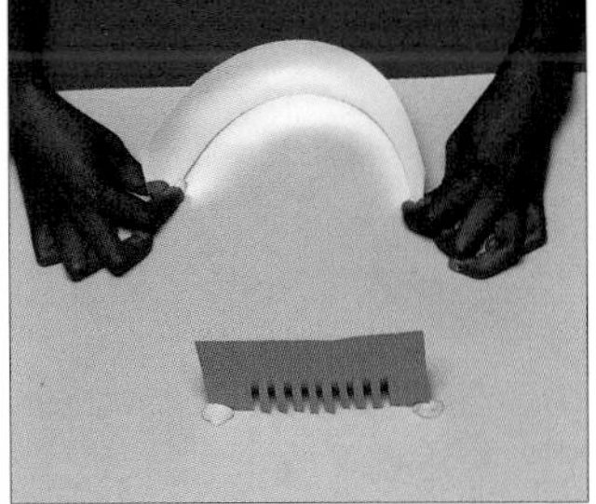

4 Bend the reflective mirror board to form a semicircular antenna, as shown. Stand it at one end of the thick cardboard base. Then fix it firmly in position using modelling material.

5 Switch on the torch. Direct the light beam, so that it shines through the slits in the postcard. The light is split into thin rays, which reflect off the mirror board.

6 Darken the room. Move the torch until the light rays reflecting off the curved mirror are brought together at one spot, like radio waves on a dish antenna.

Listen to this

Sound is energy that moves back and forth through the air in the form of vibrations. These vibrations spread outward as waves, like the ripples caused by a stone when it is dropped into rather still water.

The first experiment demonstrates the existence and energy of sound waves. Channelling the sound inside a tube concentrates the waves in the direction of the tube. By channelling sound toward a candle, you can use the energy to blow out the flame.

The second experiment is all about the strength of sound waves. It shows that sounds get quieter if their waves are allowed to spread out. Scientists say that loud sounds have large amplitudes (variations of range).

In the final project, you can investigate pitch, or the range of sounds, by making a set of panpipes. Low sounds consist of a small number of vibrations every second. Musicians describe these sounds as having 'low pitch', but scientists report the sounds as 'low frequency'. The panpipes show that pitch depends on the length of each pipe.

▲ **Play it again, Sam!**
You can play deep, low notes on a bass guitar. The sound waves vibrate slowly with a frequency as low as 50 times each second. High notes vibrate much more rapidly.

How sound travels

1 Stretch the food covering tightly over the end of the tube. Use the band to fasten it in place. You could also use a flat piece of rubber cut from a balloon instead of the food covering.

2 Ask an adult to light the candle. Point the tube at the candle, with the open end 10cm/4in from the flame. Give the food covering a sharp tap with the flat of your hand.

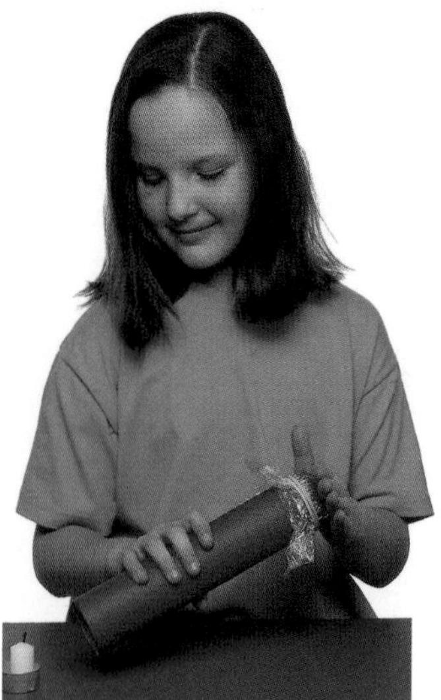

You will hear the sound coming out of the tube. It consists of pressure waves in the air. The tube concentrates the sound waves toward the candle flame and puts it out.

Sound waves

YOU WILL NEED

How sound travels: Transluscent food covering, tube of cardboard, rubber band, candle, matches.

Sound waves: Ticking watch, tube 5cm x 1m/2 x 36in long.

How to make panpipes: Scissors, wide drinking straws, non-hardening modelling material, cardboard, adhesive tape.

1 Place the watch close to your ear. You can hear a ticking sound coming from it. The sound becomes fainter when you move the watch away from your ear.

2 Place one end of the tube over a friend's ear, and hold the watch at the other end. The tube concentrates the sound and does not let it spread out. She can hear the watch clearly.

How to make panpipes

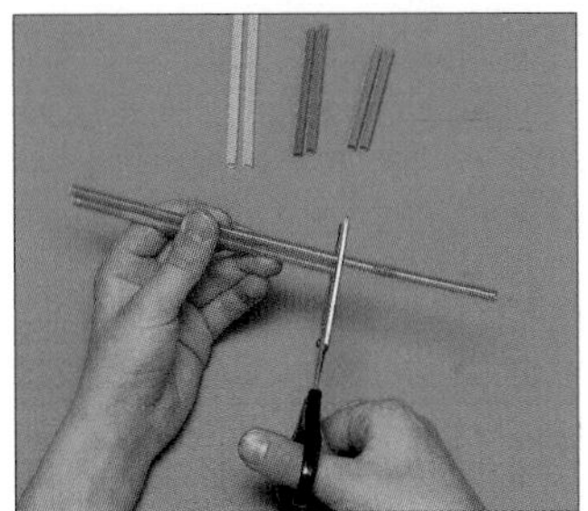

1 Cut the drinking straws so that you have four pairs that are 9cm/3½in, 8cm/3in, 7cm/2½in and 6cm/2in long. Block up one end of each straw with a small piece of modelling material.

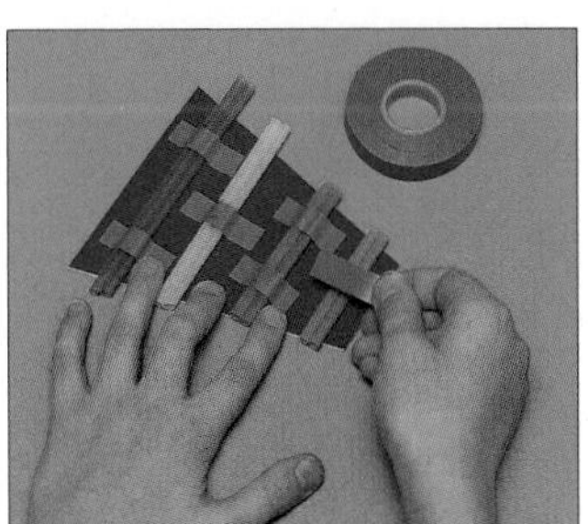

2 Carefully cut out the card to the same shape as the blue piece shown above. Fix the straws into place with the tape from long to short, to align with card, as shown.

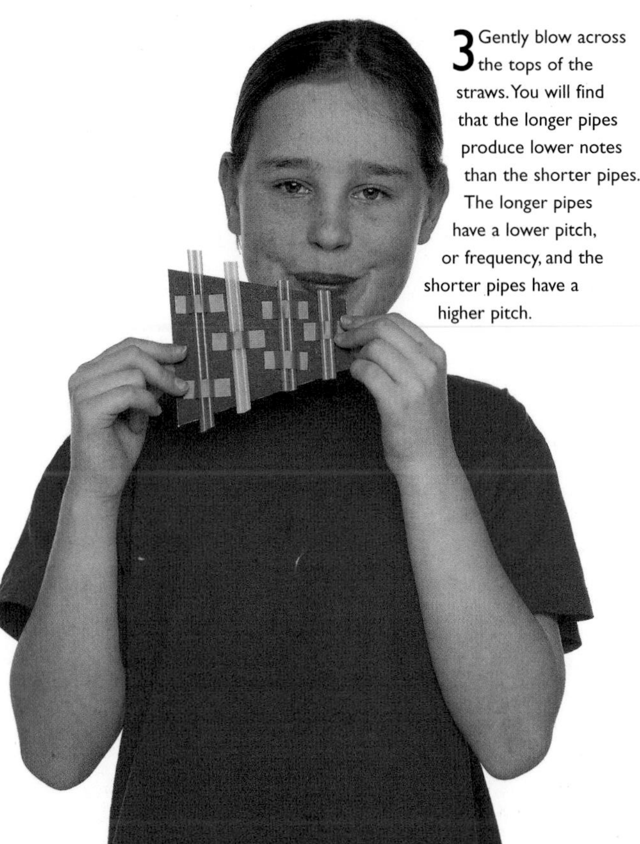

3 Gently blow across the tops of the straws. You will find that the longer pipes produce lower notes than the shorter pipes. The longer pipes have a lower pitch, or frequency, and the shorter pipes have a higher pitch.

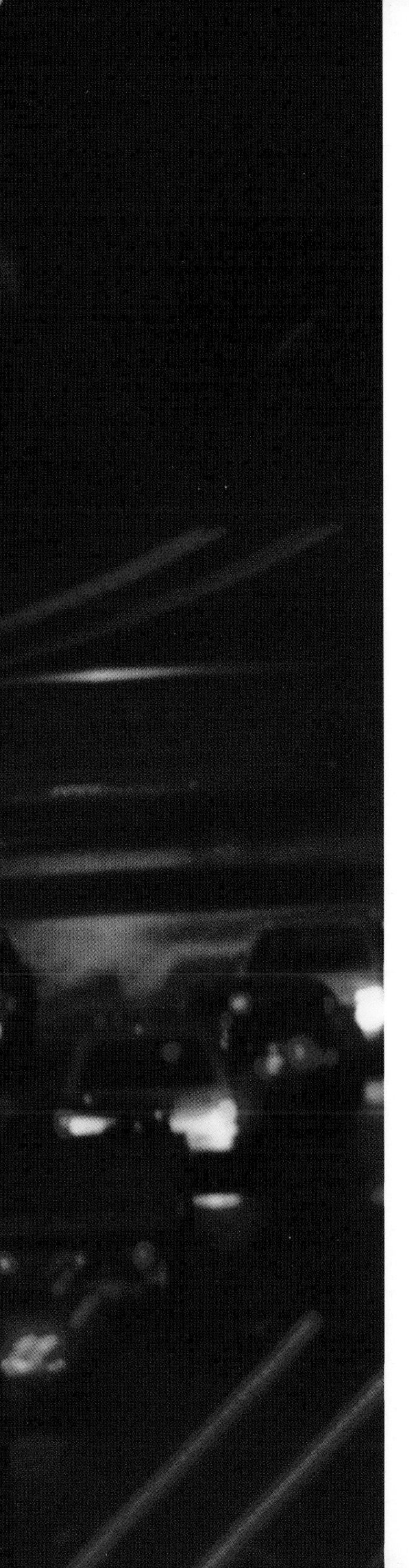

Travel and Transportation

The most powerful, luxurious and specialized forms of transportation today all evolved from simple scientific principles. The trick of keeping a luxury passenger liner or a massive oil tanker afloat is basically the same as it was for early humans with their canoes and coracles. Many of the secrets of superpowered vehicles are the result of learning to make use of simple forces such as jet propulsion, thrust and lift, and combining them with other inventions and new materials. On the following pages, you will discover how boats, trains, cars, planes and spacecraft work by experimenting with the forces that make them go.

Simple boats

Some of the earliest and simplest types of boat are still made today. Small reed boats are still built in southern Iraq and on Lake Titicaca in South America in a similar way to the one in the project below. Reed boats are made by tying thousands of river reeds together into huge bundles. The bundles are then tied together to make hull shapes. In ancient Egypt, large boats were made like this, from papyrus reeds. Some historians believe that Egyptians may have made long ocean crossings in papyrus craft.

YOU WILL NEED

Make a reed craft: Large bunch of raffia, scissors, ruler, tank of water.

Make a coracle: Scissors, craft cane, string, dark cotton cloth, white glue and glue brush, tank of water.

The model in the second project is of a coracle. This is a round boat made by covering a light wooden frame with animal hides. Coracles are also still made, but are now covered with canvas treated with tar instead of animal hide. Coracles were small enough for one person to paddle along a river and were used for fishing. When you are out near a river or lake, take photographs or make drawings of other simple craft, such as canoes and punts. See if you can make working models of them, too.

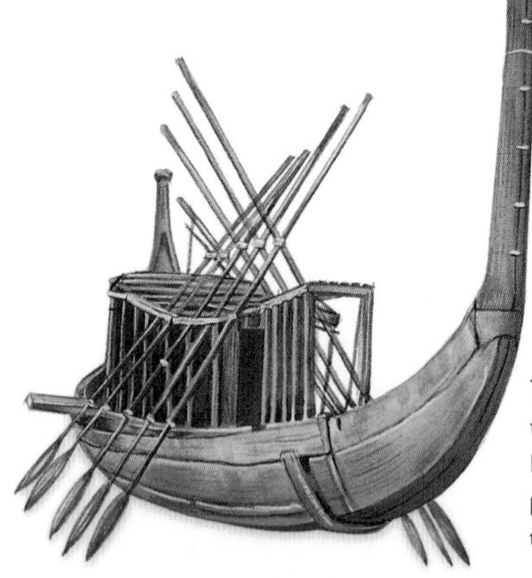

◂ Afterlife evidence
This boat was found in a pit alongside the Great Pyramid of Egypt in 1954. It is believed to have been used as a pharaoh's funeral boat, which ferried the dead pharaoh to the afterlife.

Make a reed craft

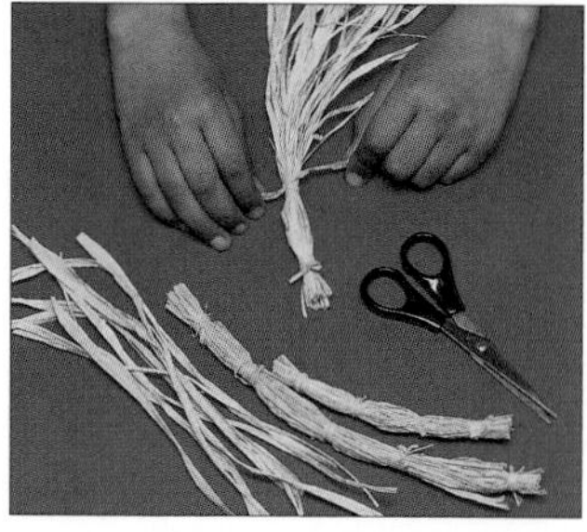

1 Make bundles of raffia by tying a few dozen strands together with a short piece of raffia. You will need two bundles about 20cm/8in long and two more about 25cm/10in long.

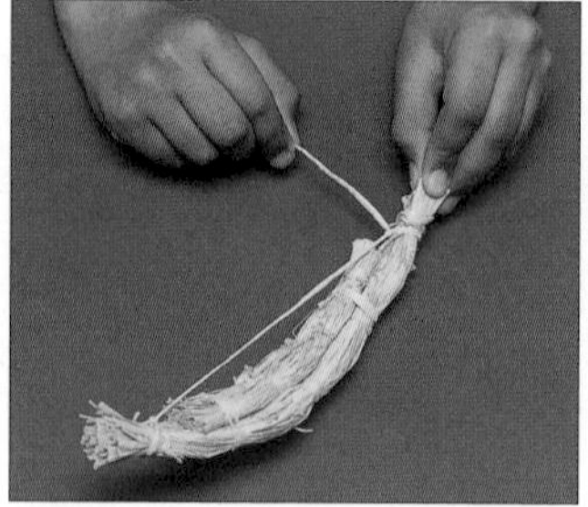

2 Tie the two long bundles and the two short bundles together. Tie the short bundles on top of the long ones. Fix a strand between each end, to make the ends bend up.

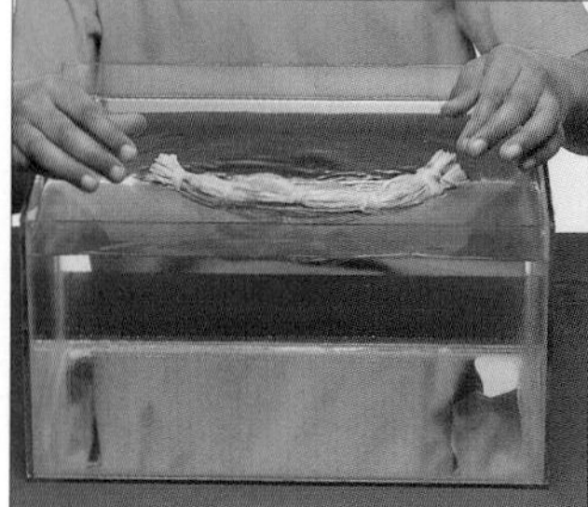

3 Gently lower the reed boat on to the surface of a tank of water. How well does it float? Does it stay upright? Try leaving it in the water to see if it becomes waterlogged.

Make a coracle

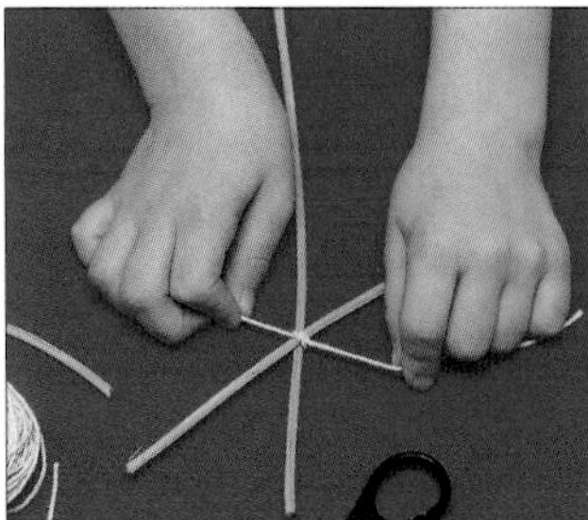

1 Cut one long piece of cane and three short pieces. Using short pieces of string, tie all three of the short pieces of cane to the long piece to make a triple-armed cross.

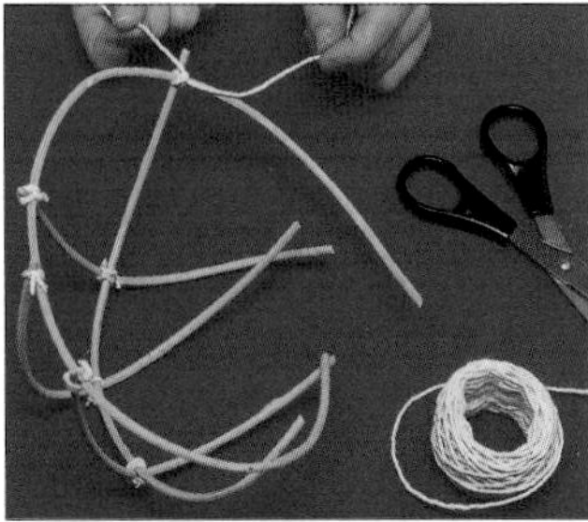

2 Cut a much longer piece of cane. Form it into a loop, and tie it to all the ends of the triple cross shape. Bend the ends of the cross up as you tie them to form a dish shape.

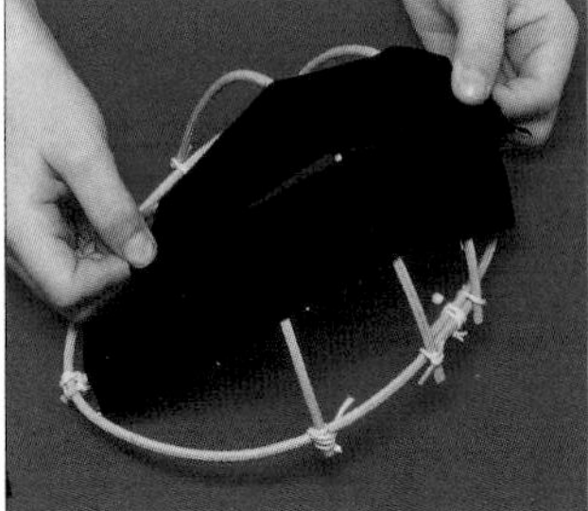

3 Cut pieces of cotton cloth about 15 x 5cm/6 x 2in. Apply glue to the outside of the frame, and place the pieces over it. Glue the pieces to each other where they overlap.

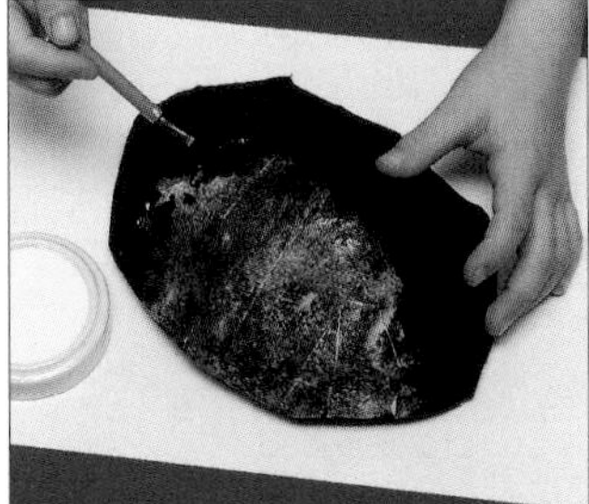

4 Glue down the cloth where it folds over the top of the frame. Put two coats of glue on the outside of the cloth to waterproof it. Leave the glue to dry completely.

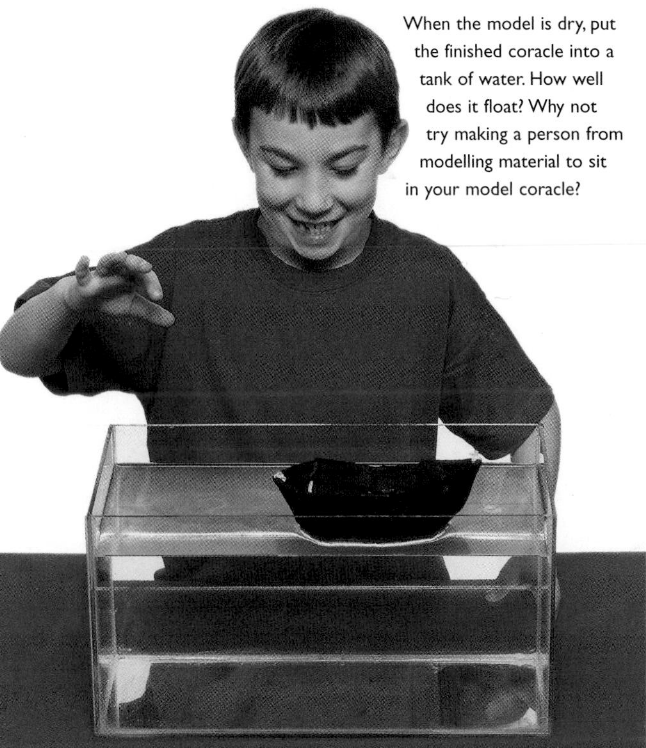

When the model is dry, put the finished coracle into a tank of water. How well does it float? Why not try making a person from modelling material to sit in your model coracle?

Early Britons used coracles 9,000 years ago. Coracles are light to carry, easy to use, and stable enough to fish from.

Sail power

When you launch your model sailing boat, you can get an idea of how it is propelled by the wind. To sail in the direction they want to go, sailors must be aware of wind direction, so that they can adjust the position of the sails to make best use of it. If sailing boats face straight into the wind, the sails flap uselessly, and the boat is in a 'no-go zone'. They can, however, sail into oncoming wind by taking a zigzag course. This is called tacking. The wind blows against one side of the sail to propel the boat diagonally upwind. When the boat changes tack, the wind blows against the other side of the sail, and the boat goes forwards on the opposite diagonal. If the wind is blowing from behind the boat, the sail is set at right angles to the boat like an open wing, so that it is filled by the wind.

mainsail
mainmast
batten (sail stiffener)
jib
tiller
boom
hull
rudder
centreboard

▲ **Parts of a sailboat**
Sailboats usually have a crew of two people. A helmsman operates the tiller and the mainsail, and a crew who works the jib and centreboard (which stops the boat from drifting sideways).

YOU WILL NEED
Pencil, ruler, cardboard, scissors, adhesive tape, plastic sheet, stapler, bradawl, non-hardening modelling material, thin garden canes, coloured paper, plastic straw, small plastic bottle, string, paper clip, sheet of paper.

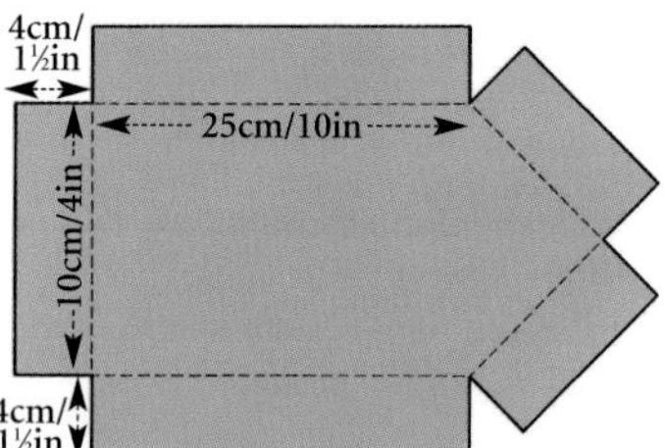

Template ▸

Make a sailboat

1 Cut out your hull shape from thick cardboard, using the template above as a guide. Score along the dotted lines with the scissors. Use adhesive tape to fasten the sides together.

2 Lay the hull on a plastic sheet. Cut the plastic around the hull, allowing enough to cover the sides and overlap at the top by 5cm/2in. Fold the sheet over the hull and staple it in place.

3 Make a hole in the middle of a strip of cardboard a little wider than the hull. Staple in place. Put modelling material under the hole, and push a 30cm/12in cane through the hole into it.

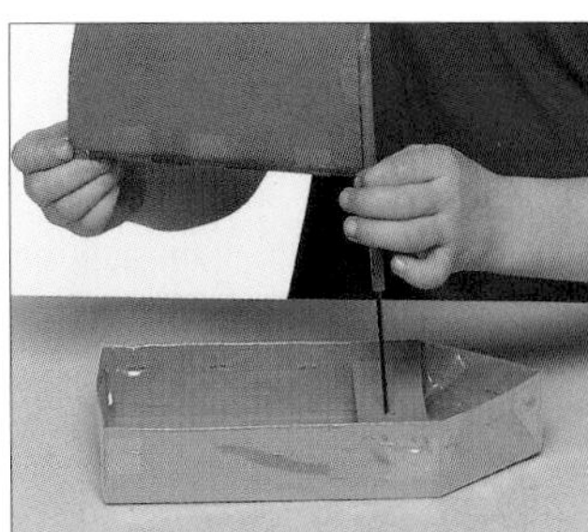

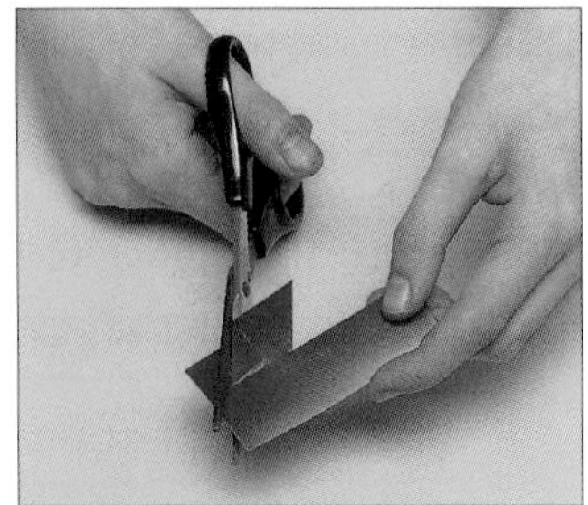

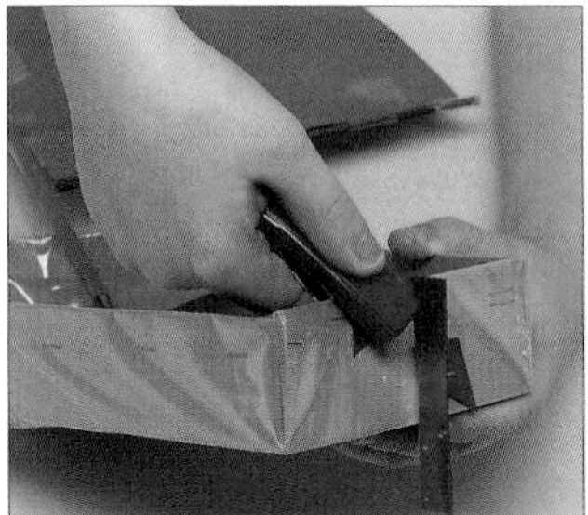

4 Cut a sail from coloured paper with a base of about 20cm/8in. Attach the straw along the side and a garden cane along the bottom with tape. Slip the straw over the mast.

5 Cut an L-shape (about 8cm/3in long, 4cm/1½in wide at the base and 2cm/¾in wide at the top) from the small plastic bottle. Cut the base of the L in half to make two slanted tabs.

6 Fold back the two tabs of the L-shaped plastic in opposite directions, as shown, and staple them to the stern (back) of the boat. This is the boat's rudder.

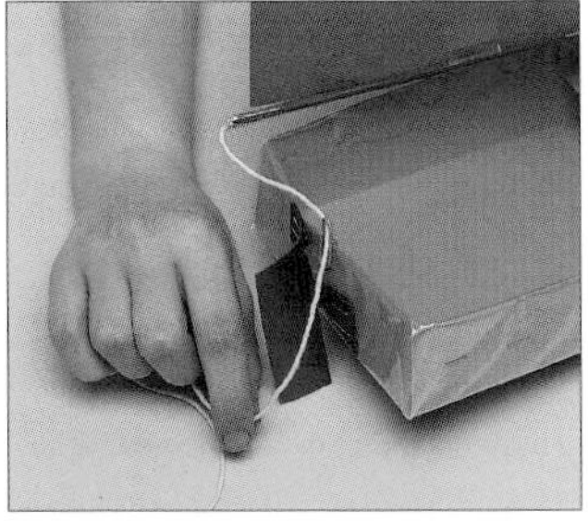

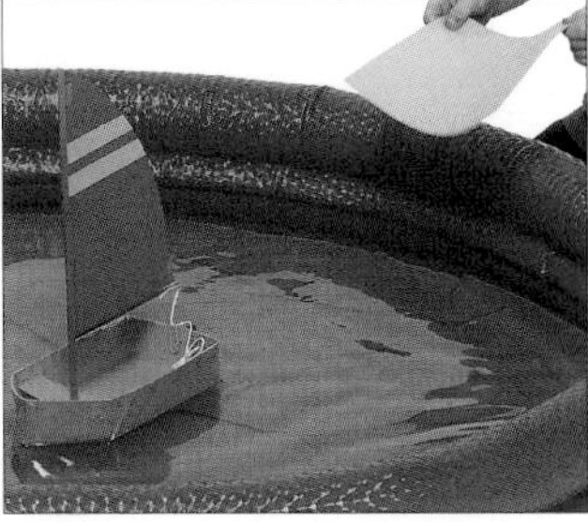

7 Cut a piece of string about 20cm/8in long. Tape one end to the back of the boom (the cane), and feed the other end through a paper clip attached to the back of the boat.

8 To test out how your sail boat works, make a breeze by waving a large sheet of paper near to the boat. Adjust the string to move the sail into the right position.

When you have finished your boat, you could try making and adding a centreboard. Attach a cardboard oblong at right angles to the bottom of the boat. It will stop your boat from drifting sideways in the wind.

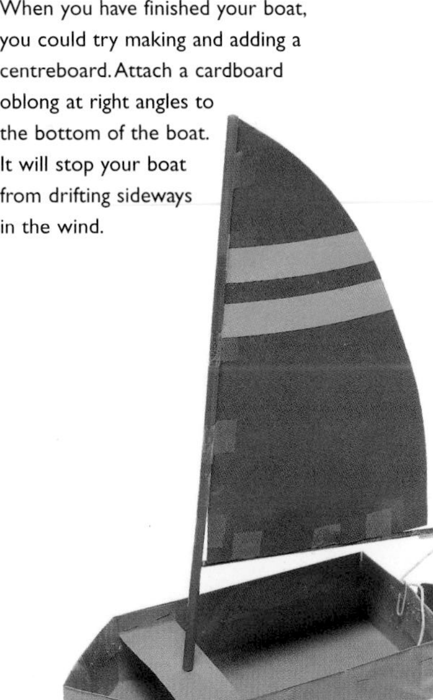

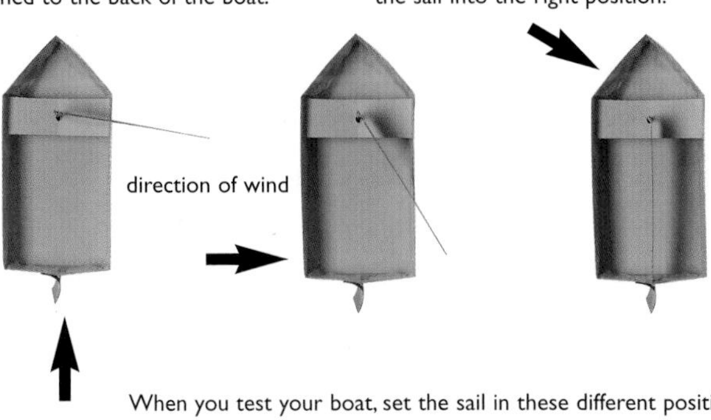

When you test your boat, set the sail in these different positions. Alter the position of the sail by using the string taped to the boom (cane). Follow the arrows shown here to see which way the wind should be blowing from in each case. Try blowing from other directions to see if this makes a difference to your boat.

How ships float

The simplest boats, such as rafts, float because the material they are made of is less dense (lighter) than water. Heavy ships can float, because the water they are floating in pushes upwards against them. This pushing force is called upthrust. The first experiment shows that an object will float if the upthrust of the water is great enough to overcome the downward push of the object's weight. The size of the upthrust depends on how much water the object pushes out of the way. When you put an object in water and let it go, it settles into the water, pushing liquid out of the way. The farther it goes in, the more water it pushes away and the more upthrust acts on it. When the upthrust becomes the same as the object's weight, the object floats.

The second project shows you a hollow hull. If you push a light, hollow ball under water, it will spring back up. Upthrust from the water makes a hollow hull float in the same way. The higher the density of water, the greater the upthrust. This means that ships float slightly higher in salt water, since this is more dense than fresh water.

▲ **Measuring density**
The density of water is measured with a hydrometer. You can make one by putting a lump of modelling material on the end of a straw. Put it in a glass of water, and mark the water level with tape. Now put the straw in an equal amount of salty water. What happens?

Testing upthrust

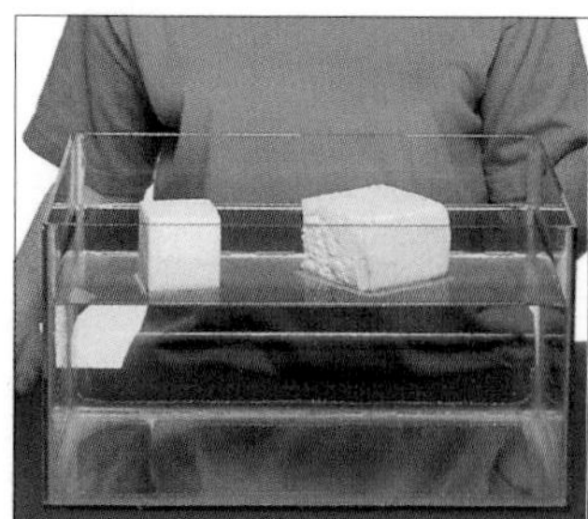

1 Put the two styrofoam chunks into a large tank of water. They will float well, because their material is so light. Only a small amount of upthrust is needed.

2 Try pushing the chunks under the water. Now you are pushing lots of water aside. Can you feel upthrust pushing back? The bigger chunk will experience more upthrust.

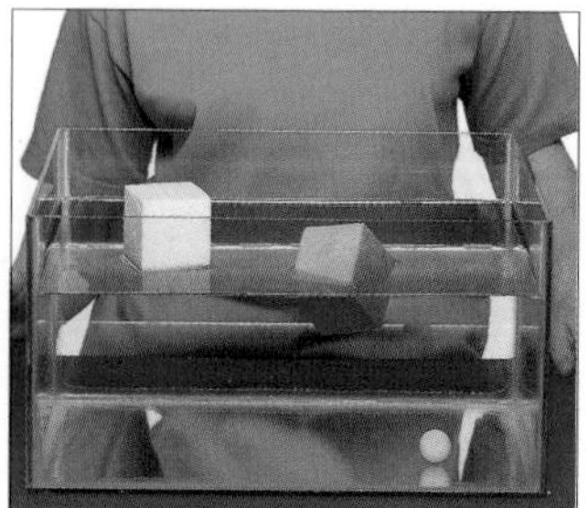

3 A wooden block floats deeper in the water, because wood is more dense (heavier) than styrofoam. A marble sinks because the upthrust on it is not as great as its weight.

Hollow hulls

YOU WILL NEED

Testing upthrust: Two chunks of styrofoam (one twice the size of the other), tank of water, wooden block, marble.

Hollow hulls: Scissors, foil, ruler, tank of water, paper towel, marbles.

1 Put a piece of foil about 20 x 15cm/ 8 x 6in into a tank of water. With just the slightest push, it will sink. This is because it does not displace much water, so there is very little upthrust.

2 Lift the sheet of foil out of the water, and dry it carefully with a paper towel. Now form it into a simple boat shape with your fingers. Take care not to tear the foil.

3 Put your foil boat into the water. It should now float. It will not sink so easily. Its shape pushes aside much more water than it did when it was flat, so the upthrust is greater.

This simple foil boat works like a real ship's hull. Even though it is made of metal, it is filled with air. This gives the hull shape a much lower overall density.

Try filling your foil boat with small objects, such as marbles, for cargo. As you put more marbles in, it will float lower and lower. How many marbles can your boat hold before it sinks?

What's in a hull?

Whenever an object such as a ship moves through the water, the water slows it down. The push made by the water is called water resistance, or drag. The faster the object moves, the greater the water resistance becomes.

If you look around a busy port, you will see dozens of different hull designs. Sleek, narrow hulls with sharp bows cause less resistance than wide hulls with square bows, so they can move through the water faster.

You can test how the shape of a bow affects the speed of a ship in this experiment. The deeper a hull sits in the water, the more resistance there is. Some hulls are designed to sit just on top of the water. For example, a small speedboat has a flaring, shallow V-shaped hull designed to skim across the surface. A cargo ship has a square hull that sits lower in the water. Speed is not as important for the cargo ship as it is for the speedboat. Instead, the cargo ship is designed for stability, and to carry as much as possible.

▲ Templates
Use these three templates to help you cut out and make the three boat shapes in this project.

YOU WILL NEED

Ruler, pen or pencil, coloured cardboard, scissors, adhesive tape, foil, three paper clips, non-hardening modelling material, food scale, string, large plastic bowl, watering can, three equal-sized wooden bricks.

Testing hull shapes

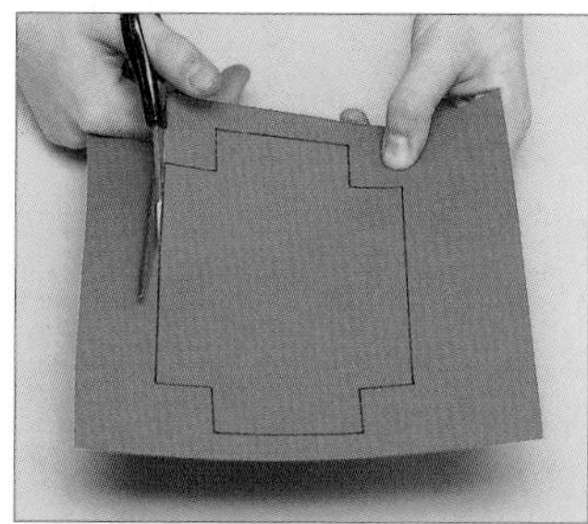

1 Use a ruler to draw the three templates shown left on sheets of stiff cardboard. Make sure the corners are square and the edges straight. Carefully cut out the shapes.

2 Using scissors, score along the lines inside the base of the square boat (shown as dotted lines left). Bend up the sides, and use adhesive tape to fix the corners together.

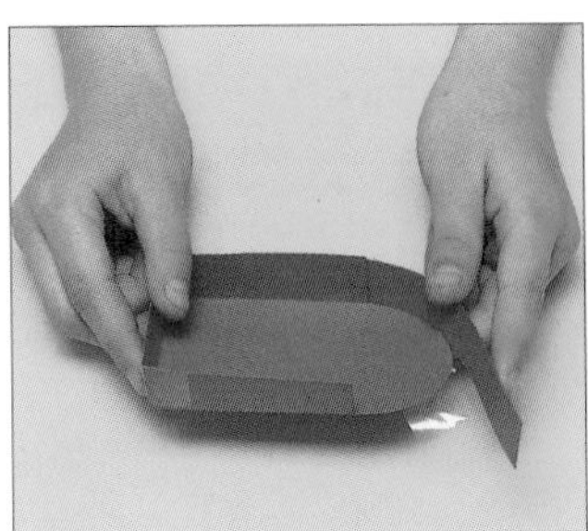

3 Make the round-ended and pointed boats in the same way as the first boat. Use a separate piece of cardboard to make the round bow, and tape it to the base in several places.

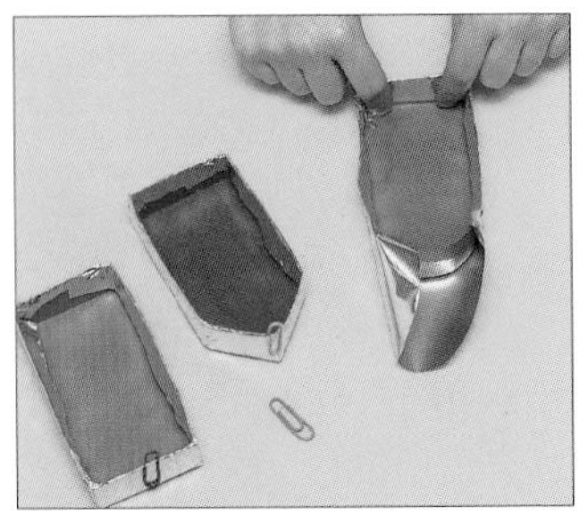

4 Now cover the outside of each shape with foil, neatly folding the foil over the sides. This will make the shapes more waterproof. Fix a paper clip to the bow (front) of each boat.

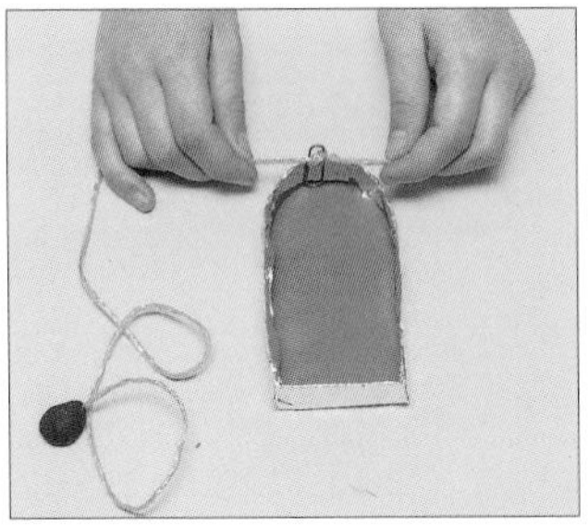

5 Roll out three balls of modelling material about the size of a walnut. Weigh the balls to make sure they are the same weight. Attach a ball to the bow of each boat with string.

6 Put a large plastic bowl on a table or a strong box. Use a watering can to pour water into the trough. The water should be about 1cm/½in from the top of the bowl.

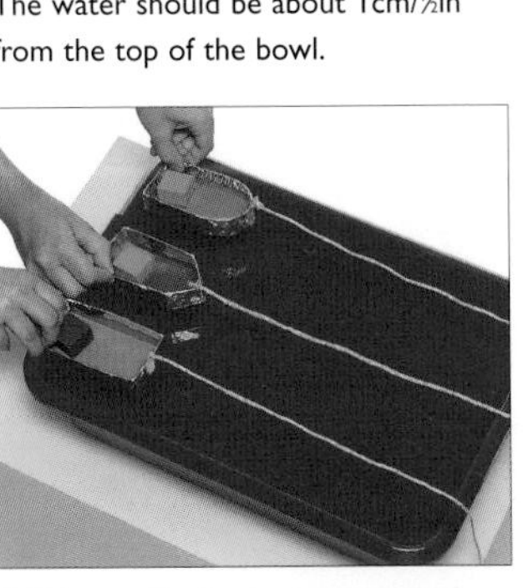

7 Line up the boats at one end of the bowl. Hang the strings and modelling material balls down over the other end. Put a small wooden brick inside each boat.

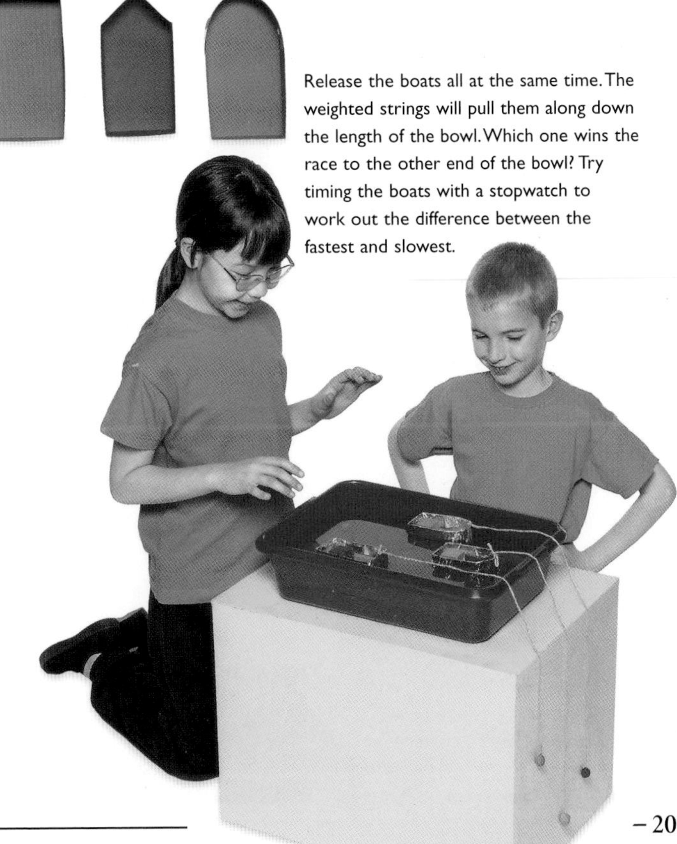

Release the boats all at the same time. The weighted strings will pull them along down the length of the bowl. Which one wins the race to the other end of the bowl? Try timing the boats with a stopwatch to work out the difference between the fastest and slowest.

Ship stability

Many ships look as though they are top heavy, so how do they manage to stay upright and not capsize? These projects will help you understand why. When a ship tips over, the hull on that side sinks into the water. On the other side it rises up out of the water. The water creates more upthrust on the side that sinks in, pushing the ship upright again. The more one side of the hull sinks in, the greater the resistance, and the harder it is for the hull to tip over further. A catamaran like the one in the project is extra-stable because it has double hulls against which the water can push.

The position of the cargo in the hull of the ship is important. Heavy cargo high up on deck makes the ship top-heavy and more likely to tip over. Heavy cargo low down in the hull gives the ship stability. Cargo that can move is dangerous, because it could slip to one side of the ship, causing it to tip suddenly. You will be able to test the effects of different weights in square and rounded hulls in the second experiment.

YOU WILL NEED

Make a catamaran: Small plastic bottle, scissors, garden cane, rubber bands, tank or bowl of water, cargo.

Loading cargo: Plastic bottle and square tub of similar size, scissors, tank or bowl of water, wooden bricks, non-hardening modelling material.

Make a catamaran

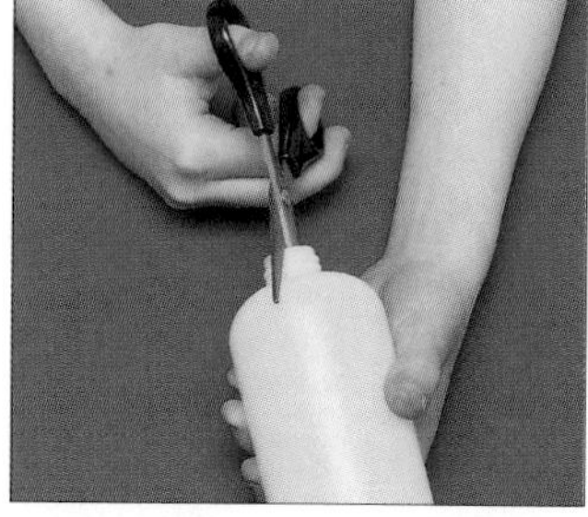

1 Remove the top from a small plastic bottle, and carefully cut the bottle in half lengthways. This will leave you with two identical shapes to form the catamaran hulls.

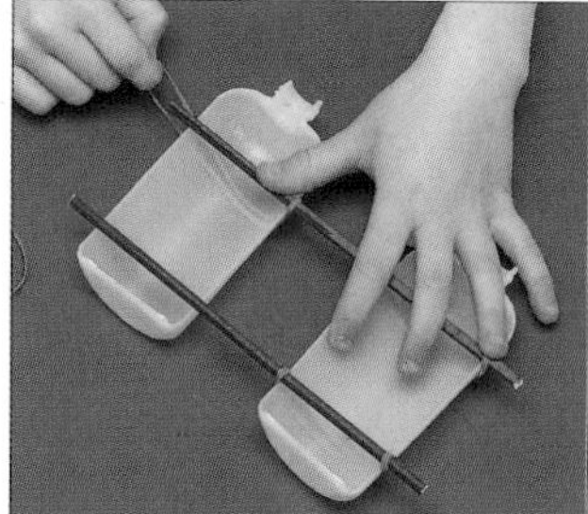

2 Place the two halves of the bottle side by side. Lay two medium-length pieces of garden cane on top. Securely fasten the canes to the bottle halves using rubber bands.

Put your completed catamaran into a tank or bowl of water. Load the hulls with cargo such as wooden bricks. Can you make your boat capsize?

Loading cargo

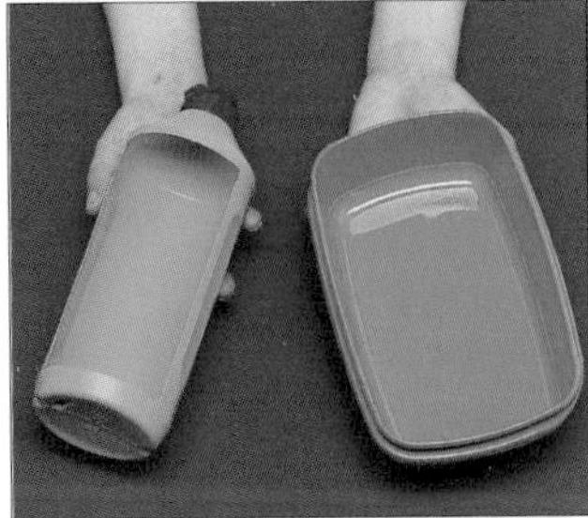

1 For this project, you need one container with a round hull shape and another about the same size with a square hull shape. Cut a strip from the round container to make a hold.

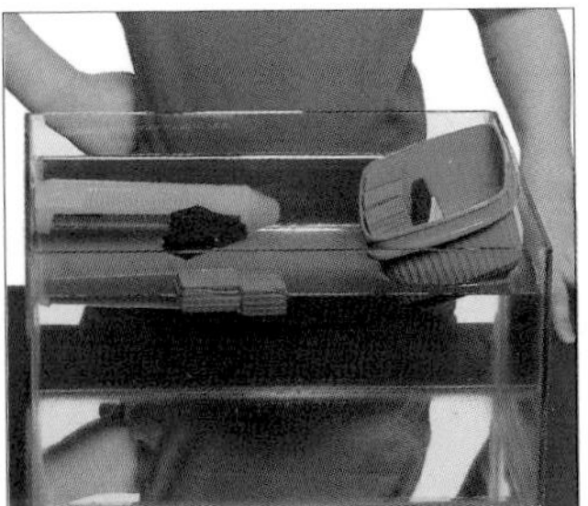

2 Put both containers in a tank or bowl of water. Gradually load one side of each hull with wooden bricks. Which hull capsizes first? Which hull is more stable?

3 Now load the square hull evenly with wooden bricks. You should be able to get a lot more in. Press down on one side of the hull. Can you feel the hull trying to stabilize itself?

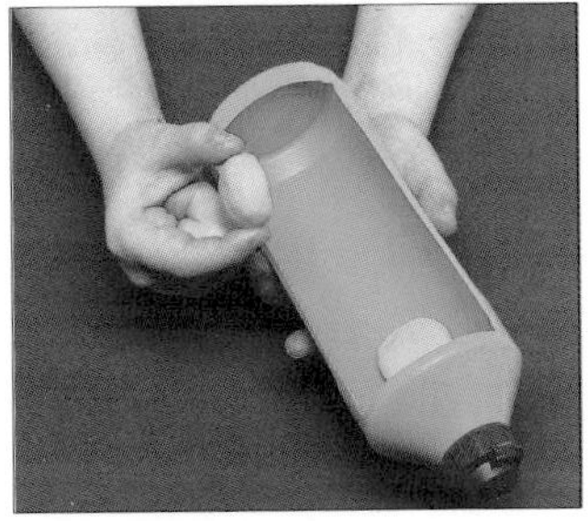

4 To stabilize the round hull, press some lumps of modelling material into the bottom of the hull. This adds weight, known as ballast, to the bottom of the hull.

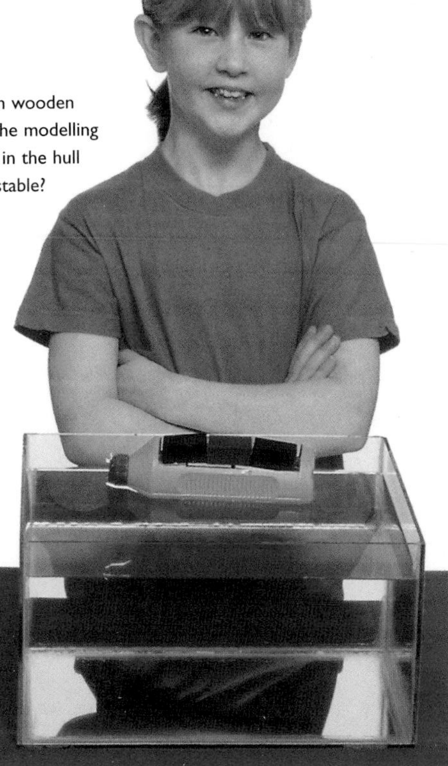

Reload the round hull with wooden bricks. Can you see how the modelling material ballast low down in the hull has made the craft more stable?

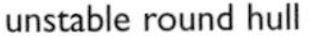

unstable round hull

stable square hull

When a round hull tips to one side, there is little change to the amount of hull underwater. This makes the shape unstable. When a square hull tips to one side, there is a great change in the amount of hull underwater on that side. This makes it stable.

Power and steering afloat

The model boat in this project is fitted with two basic devices for controlling water craft. Both operate underwater. The propeller is driven by the engine of a motor- or steam-powered boat. It rotates very fast and pushes the craft through the water. In the project, the engine power comes from the energy stored in a wound-up rubber band. As in real-life propellers, the blades are set at different angles, and push the water backwards, so thrusting the vessel forwards, as it spins. You could try making different propeller designs – with more blades set at different angles, for example – and testing them to see which works best.

A rudder is used to steer both sail- and motor-powered boats. It is controlled by a handle called a tiller, or a wheel, on the boat. As in your model boat, the rudder can be moved to different positions to make the boat turn left or right, but will only work when the boat is actually moving. In addition to making the boat turn left and right, the rudder also keeps the boat going in a straight line when it is set straight.

▲ Making a connection
In a large cruise yacht, the rudder is moved by wires linked to the wheel in the cockpit. The wheel drives the sprocket, which moves a chain. Wires attached to the chain move the rudder via pulleys. The yacht is also equipped with a diesel engine that is connected to a single propeller via a driveshaft.

YOU WILL NEED
Cork, bradawl, scissors, small plastic bottle, large plastic bottle, large paper clip, pliers (optional), ruler, bead, long rubber bands, small pencil, pool, thin garden cane.

Make a powered boat

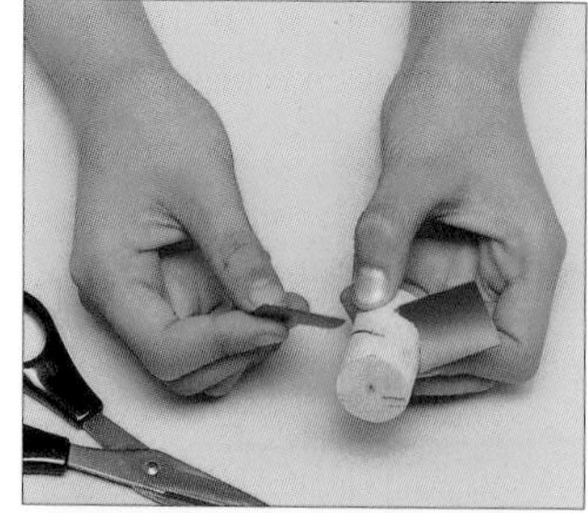

1 Make a hole through the middle of the cork using a bradawl. Cut a diagonal slot in either side of the cork. Push two strips of plastic cut from a small bottle into the slots.

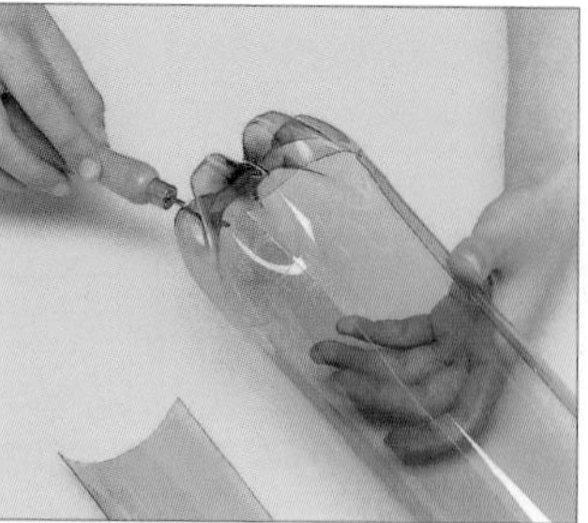

2 Cut an oblong strip from one side of the large plastic bottle. This slot is the top of your boat. With the bradawl, make a small hole at the back of your bottle in the bottom.

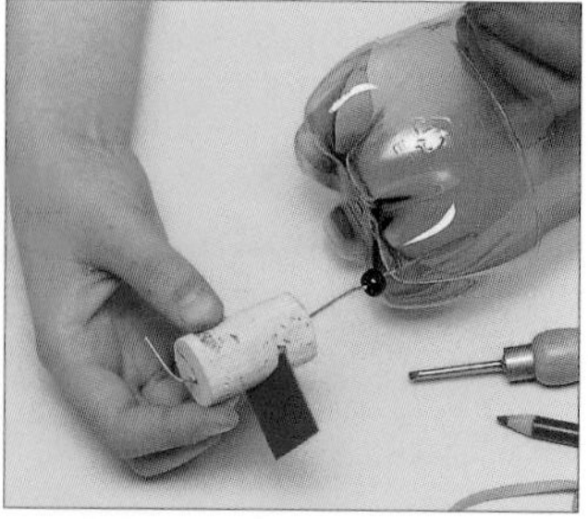

3 Straighten a large paper clip (you may need pliers). Bend the last 1.5cm/½in of wire at right angles. Push the wire through the cork, and thread it through the bead and small hole.

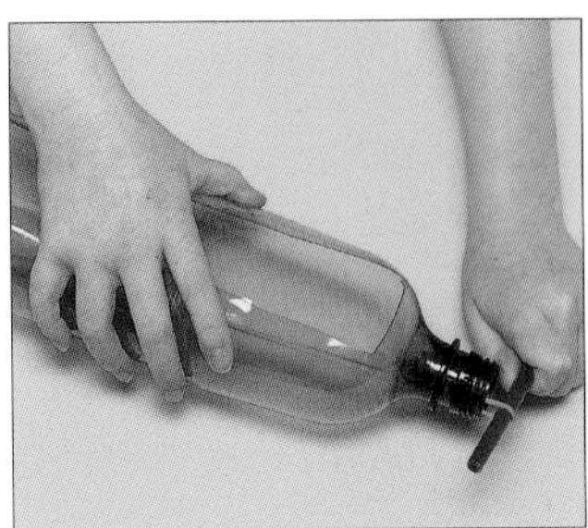

4 Bend the end of the wire inside the bottle. Hook a rubber band over the wire, and stretch it up through the neck of the bottle. Secure it in place with a pencil.

5 To wind up the band, turn the pencil as you hold on to the propeller. Keep holding the propeller until you put the boat into the water and release it. What happens?

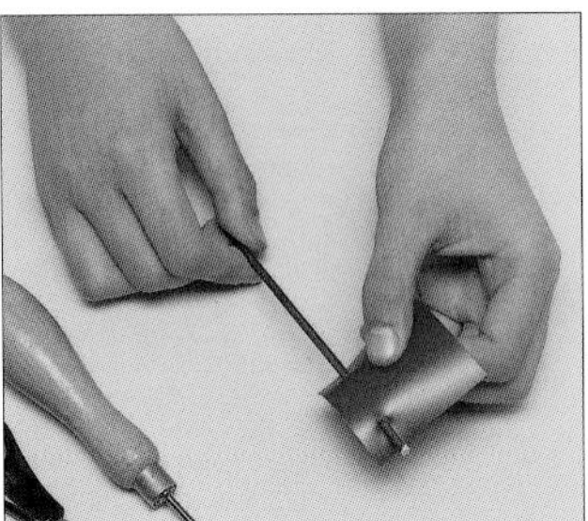

6 Now make a rudder for your boat. Cut a piece of plastic about 4 x 4cm/1½ x 1½in and pierce two holes near one edge. Push a piece of thin cane through the two holes.

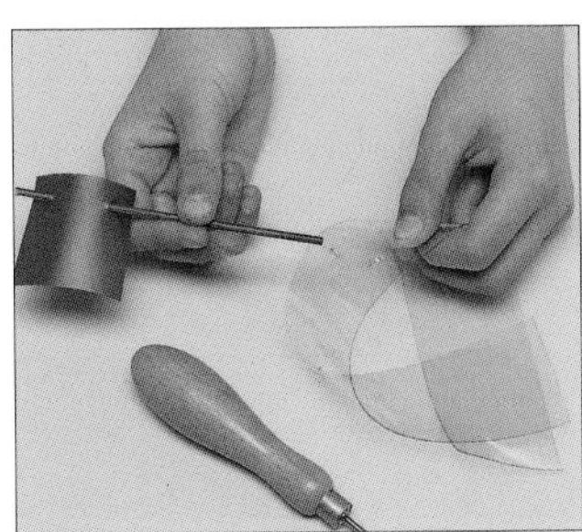

7 Use the strip of plastic cut from the large bottle to support your rudder. Pierce two holes about 2cm/¾in apart in the middle of the strip, and push the cane through them.

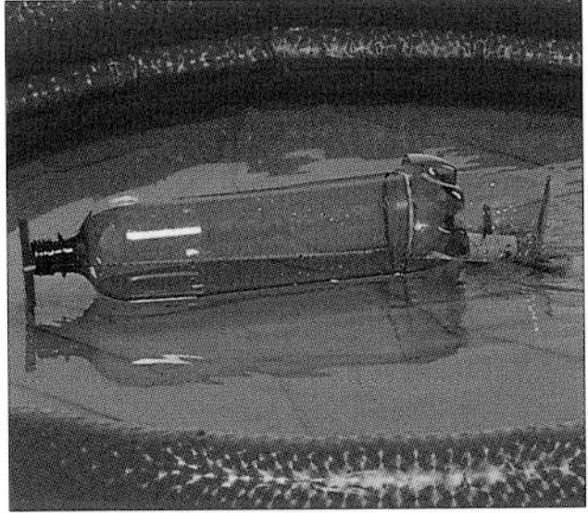

8 Fix the rudder support to the bottle with a rubber band, so that the rudder is clear of the propeller. Wind up the pencil, and put your boat back in the water.

Like a real boat builder, you will want to test the controls of your boat. To do this, start with the rudder in the middle to make the boat go straight. Next, try turning the rudder from side to side. What happens? How tight a circle can you make your boat turn in?

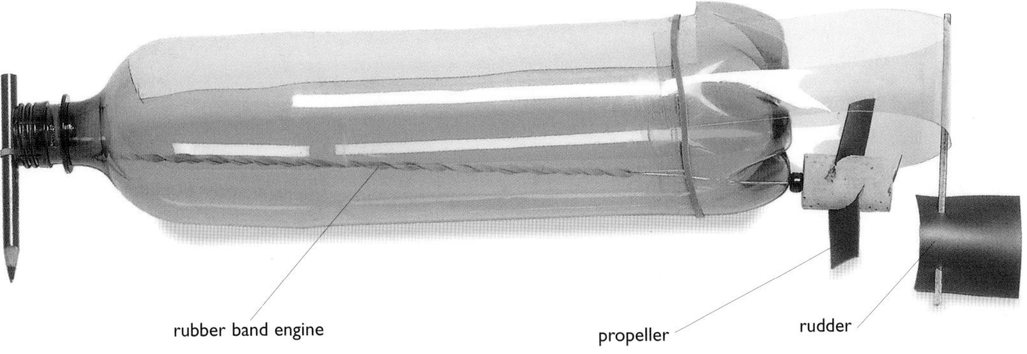

Safety at sea

There are various ways in which ships can be designed to keep afloat. All ships have bilge pumps that pump out water that has collected in the bottom of the hull and expel it into the sea or river. Many sailboats and canoes are fitted with bags of air or styrofoam bricks inside to keep them buoyant (afloat). Most lifeboats are self-righting, which means that they bob back upright if they capsize, like the model in the first project. Self-righting lifeboats are completely watertight – even the air inlets in inflatable lifeboats have seals to keep out water. Heavy engines are set low down and the hull and high cabins are full of air. This arrangement makes the lifeboat flip upright automatically.

The second and third projects show how hydrofoils and hovercrafts work.These are fast boats, designed for short sea crossings. A hydrofoil is the fastest type of ferry. Under the hull, there are winglike foils. Water flows faster over the foil's curved upper surface than it does over the flat lower surface, creating lift. When going at high speed, the foils lift the hull clear of the water.

Try the third project to see how hovercrafts skim across the water supported on cushions of air. Buoyancy tanks stop the hovercraft from sinking if the air cushion fails.

YOU WILL NEED

Pencil, ruler, strofoam tile, scissors, non-hardening modelling material, rubber bands, tank or bowl of water, small plastic tub.

Self-righting boat

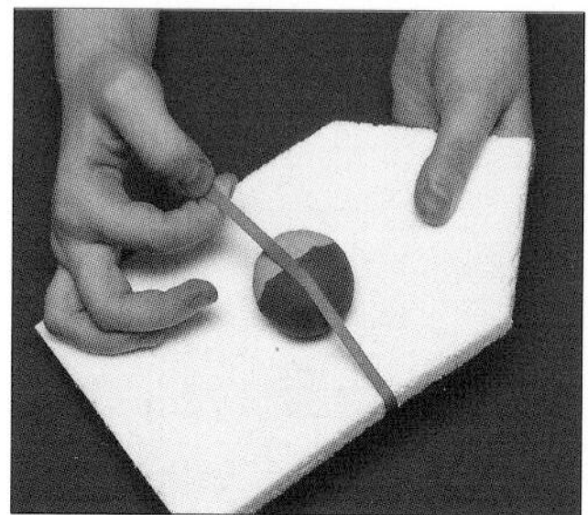

1 Cut a boat shape about 15 x 10cm/6 x 4in from styrofoam. Attach a golf-ball sized lump of modelling material to one side of your boat shape with a rubber band.

2 Put your boat into a tank or bowl of water. Have the modelling material, which represents the crew and equipment, on top. If you capsize the boat, it will stay capsized.

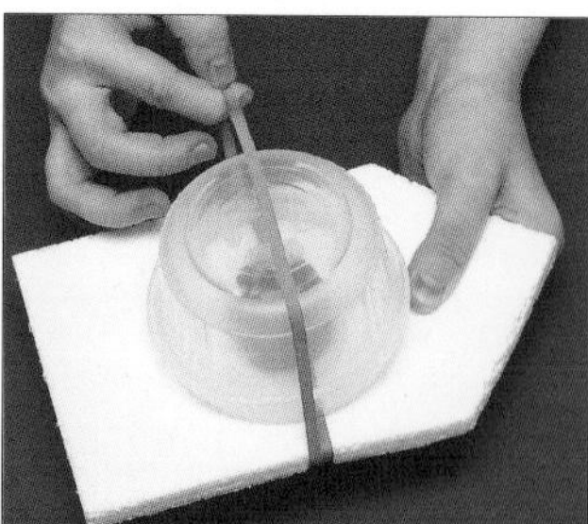

3 Add another lump of modelling material underneath the boat, to represent heavy engines or ballast. Add an upturned plastic tub on top to represent a watertight cabin.

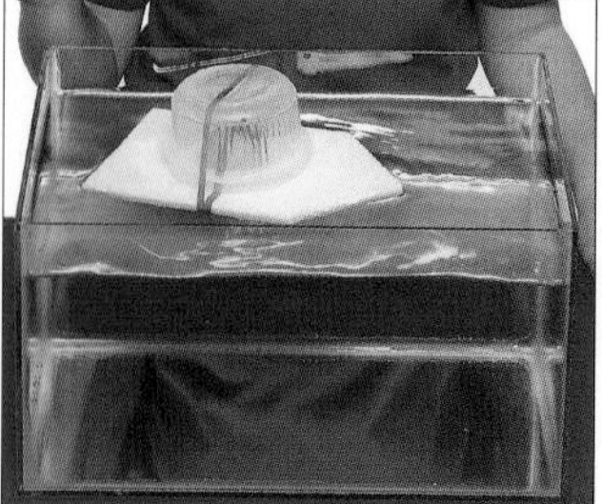

4 Now try to capsize it again, and it will flip back upright. This is because the air, trapped underwater by the tub and a heavy weight on top, forces the boat upright again.

How a hydrofoil works

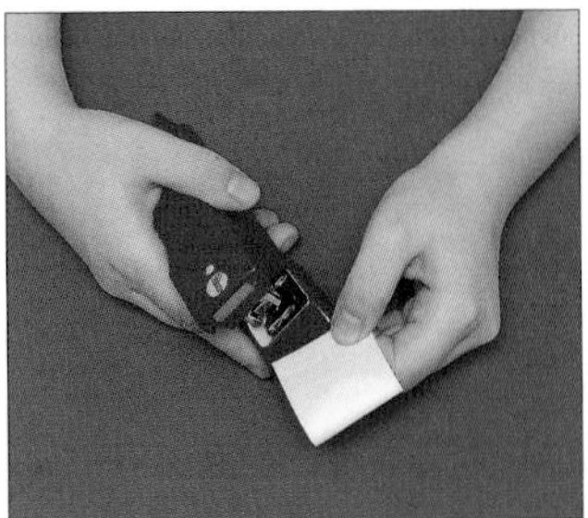

1 Cut a rectangle of plastic, about 5 x 10cm/2 x 4in, from the lid of the margarine container. Fold it in half. Staple the ends together 1cm/½in in from the back edge.

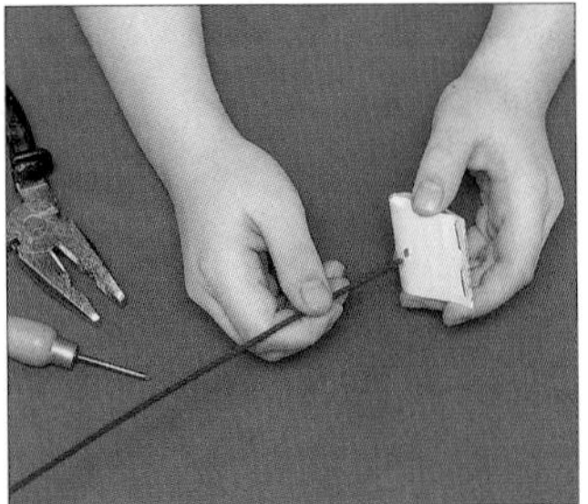

2 Use a bradawl to make a hole in the front of the hydrofoil 1cm/½in away from the folded edge. Use pliers to bend 1.5cm/¾in of one end of the wire. Slide the hydrofoil on to the wire.

3 Make sure the hydrofoil moves freely on the wire. Move your hydrofoil in air – it will not lift up, because air is far less dense than water. Pull it through water, and it will rise up the wire.

YOU WILL NEED

How a hydrofoil works:

Margarine tub lid, ruler, scissors, stapler, bradawl, pliers, coat hanger wire (ask an adult to cut it), tank or bowl of water.

How a hovercraft works: Ruler, styrofoam tray, pencil, balloon, balloon pump, button.

How a hovercraft works

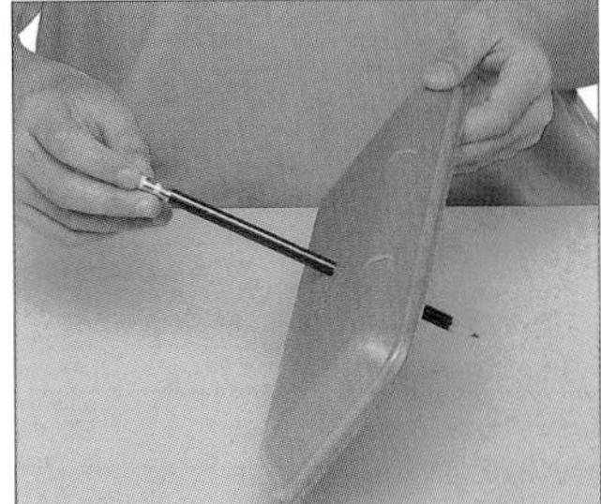

1 Use a ruler to find the middle of the styrofoam tray. Poke a hole through the middle with the pointed end of a pencil. The hole should be about 1cm/½in across.

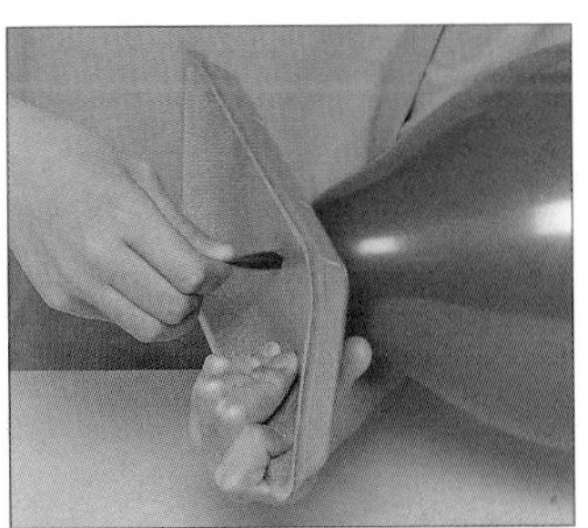

2 Blow up the balloon with the pump, and carefully push its neck through the hole. Keep pinching the neck of the balloon to stop the air from escaping.

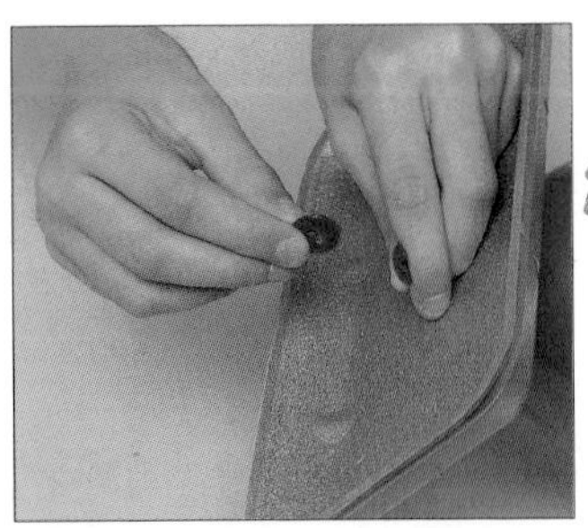

3 Keep pinching the neck of the balloon with one hand, using the other hand to slip the button into the neck. The button will control how fast the air escapes.

4 Place the tray on a table. Air escapes steadily from under the tray's edges, lifting it up a tiny bit. Give the tray a gentle push, and it will skate over the surface.

Submarine action

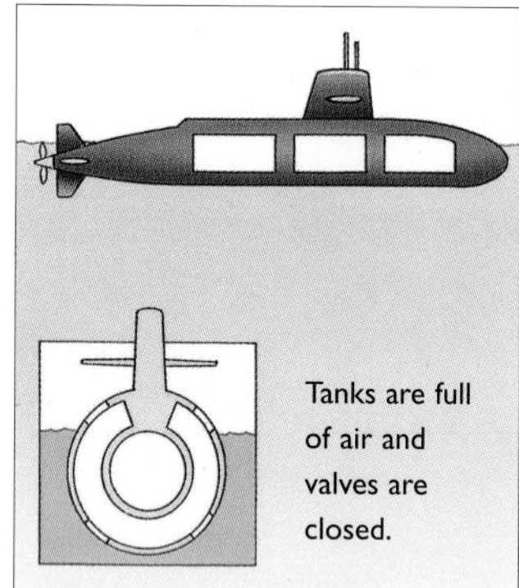

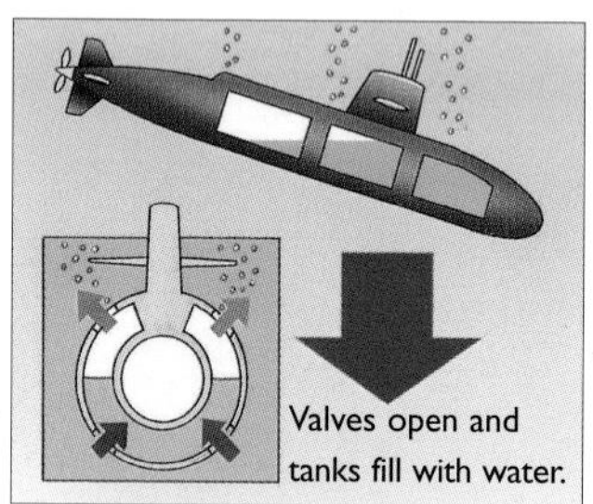

of air and
valves are

Valves open and
tanks fill with water.

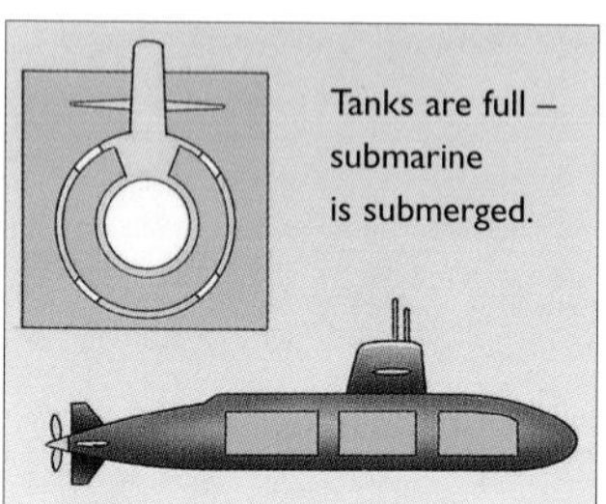

is submerged.

Air is forced
in, so water is
forced out.

A submarine dives by making itself heavier so that it sinks. It surfaces again by making itself lighter. Submarines use large tanks called buoyancy tanks. When the submarine is on the surface, these tanks are full of air. To make the submarine dive, the tanks are flooded with seawater, making the submarine heavy enough to sink. To make the submarine surface again, compressed air is pumped into the tanks, forcing the water out. This makes the submarine lighter, and it floats to the surface. When submarines are underwater, they move up and down using tiny wings called hydroplanes. These work like rudders to control the submarine's direction. Submarines need very strong hulls to prevent them from being crushed by the huge pressure under the water. As submarines dive, the weight of the water pressing down on them becomes greater and greater. You can see how this works by making this model.

YOU WILL NEED

Large plastic bottle, sand, plastic funnel, tank of water, two small plastic bottles, bradawl, scissors, ruler, two plastic drinking straws, rubber bands, non-hardening modelling material, two bulldog clips.

Make a submarine

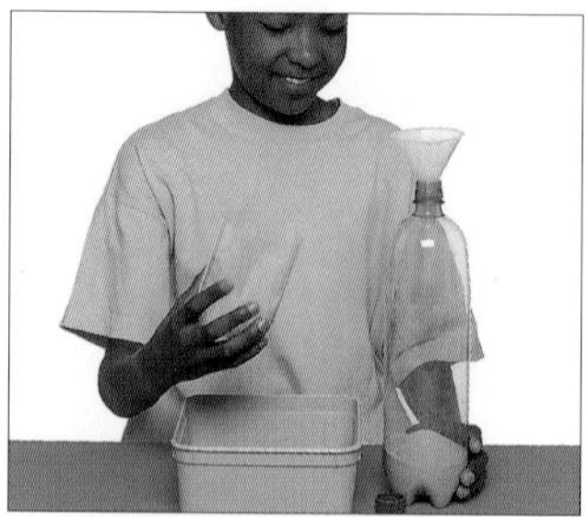

1 Fill the large plastic bottle with sand using a funnel. Fill it until it just sinks in a tank of water. Test the bottle (cap firmly screwed on) to find the right amount of sand.

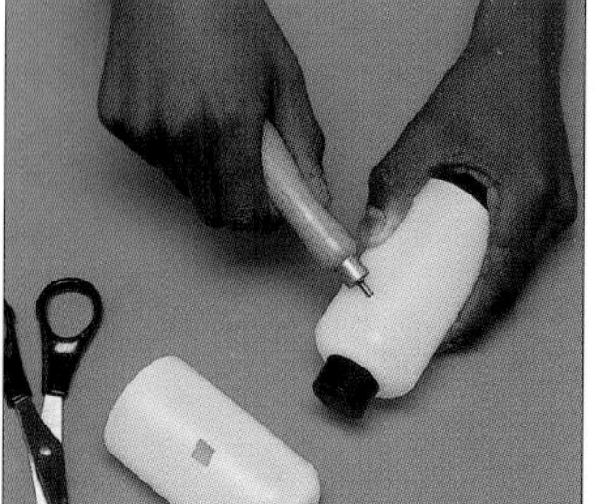

2 With adult help, make a large hole (about 1cm/½in across) in one side of two small plastic bottles. On the other side make a small hole, big enough for a plastic straw to fit into.

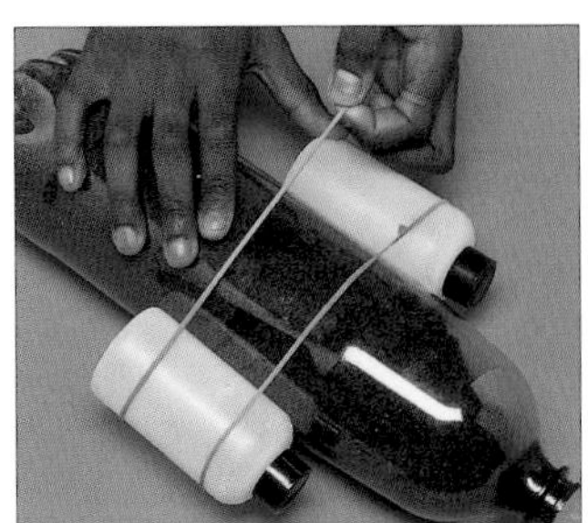

3 Attach the two small bottles to both sides of the large bottle using rubber bands. Twist the small bottles so that the small hole on each one points upwards.

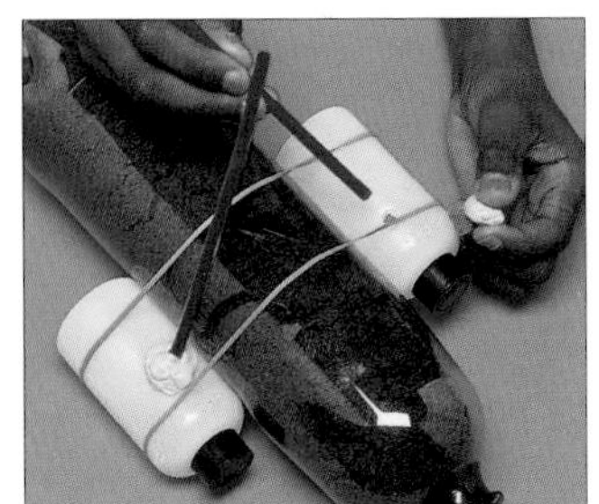

4 Push a plastic straw into each small hole, so that a bit pokes through. Seal around the base of the straws with modelling material to make a watertight joint.

5 Put a small bulldog clip about halfway down each straw. The clips need to be strong enough to squash the straw and stop air from being forced out by the water.

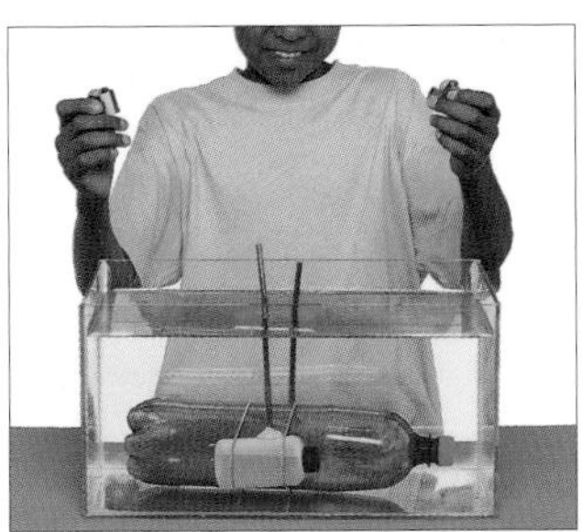

6 Put your model submarine in a tank of water. With the clips on, it should float. Remove the clips and water will flood the buoyancy tanks. The submarine will sink.

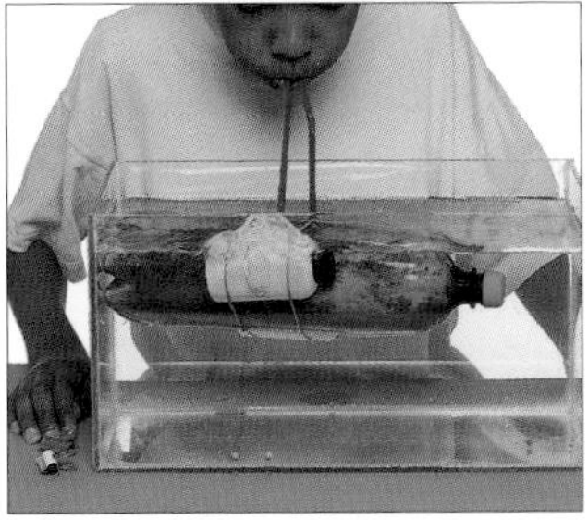

7 To make the submarine surface again, blow slowly into both straws at once. The air will force the water out of the buoyancy tanks, and the submarine will rise to the surface.

This is the finished model submarine. You might find that your model sinks bow (front) first, or stern (back) first. If this is the case, level it by shaking the sand evenly inside the bottle.

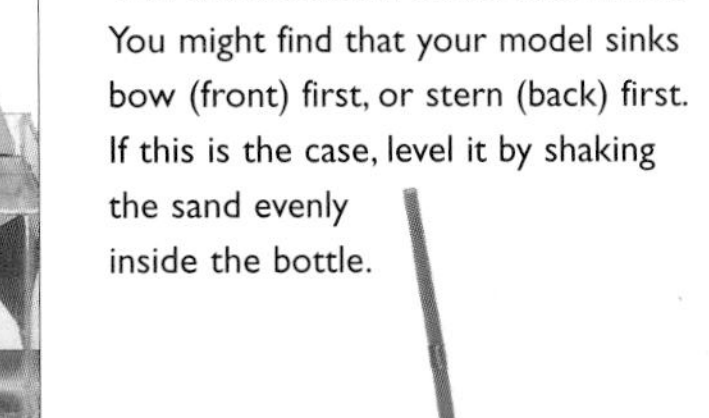

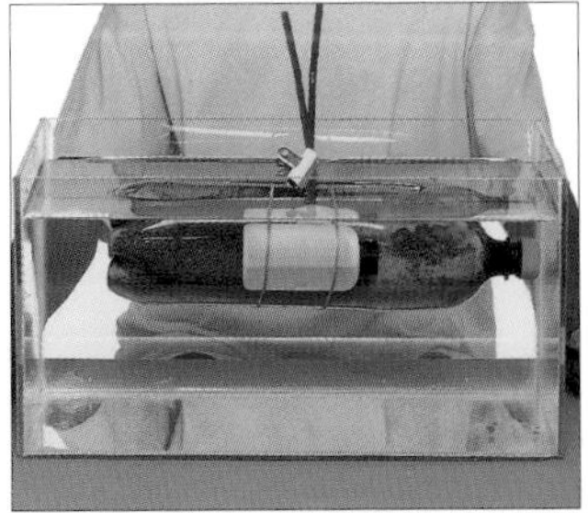

8 When your model submarine has resurfaced, keep blowing slowly into the tanks. Replace each bulldog clip and your model submarine will remain floating on the surface.

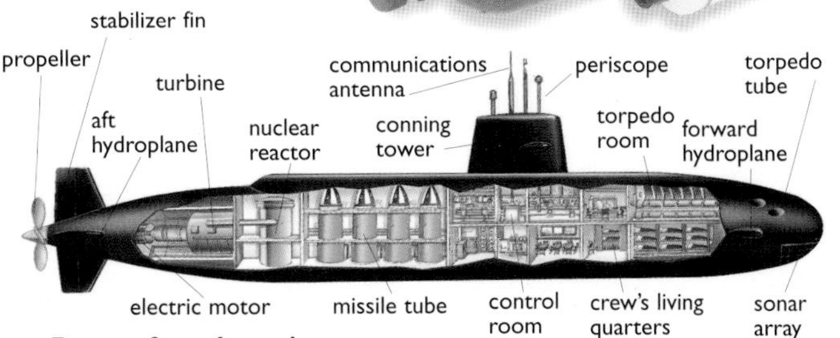

▲ **Parts of a submarine**

A modern submarine, such as this nuclear ballistic missile submarine, is almost as long as a football field – 91m/100yd. It has an engine and propeller at the stern, and is operated by a crew of 140. Steam drives the turbines that turn the propeller. A submarine's hull is strong, but few submarines can go below 500m/1,600ft.

Making rails

A full freight or passenger train is heavy, so the track it runs on has to be tough. Nowadays, rails are made from steel, which is a much stronger material than the cast iron used for the first railways. The shape of the rail also helps to make it strong. If you sliced through a rail from top to bottom, you would see it has an 'I'-shaped cross section. The broad, flat bottom narrows into the 'waist' of the I, and widens again into a curved head. Most countries use a rail shaped like this.

Tracks are made up of pieces of rail, which are laid on wooden or concrete crossbeams called sleepers. Train wheels are a set distance apart, so rails must be a set distance apart, too. The distance between rails is called the gauge. This project will show you how to make sets of railway tracks for the models on the following pages. Make at least two sets of tracks – the more tracks you make, the farther your train can travel.

YOU WILL NEED

Two sheets of cardboard measuring 26 x 11cm/10¼ x 4¼in, pencil, ruler, scissors, white glue and glue brush, silver and brown paint, paintbrush, water pot, one sheet of foam board measuring 13 x 20cm/5 x 8in, one sheet of paper, masking tape, one sheet of thin card measuring 10 x 5cm/4 x 2in.

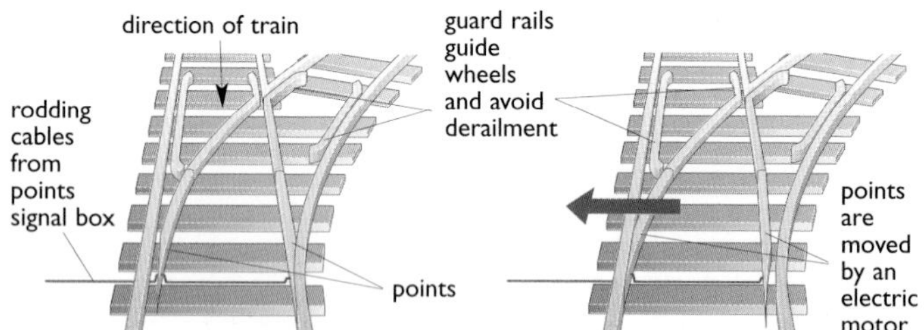

◂ Points system

Trains are switched from one track to another using points. Part of the track (the blade) moves to guide the wheels smoothly from one route to another. A signaller moves the blades by pulling a lever in the signal box. The blade and the lever are connected by metal rods. The lever cannot be pulled unless the signal is clear.

Making tracks

1 Place one 26 x 11cm/10¼in x 4¼in piece of card lengthways. Draw a line 1cm/½in in from each of the outside edges. Draw two more lines, 3.5cm/2¼in in from the outside edges. This is side A.

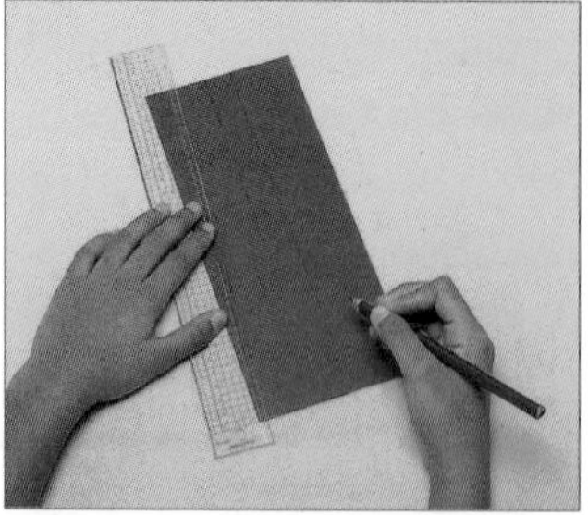

2 Turn the cardboard over (side B) and place it lengthways. Draw lines 4cm/1½in and 4.75cm/1¾in in from each edge. Repeat Steps 1 and 2 with the second piece of 26 x 11cm/10¼in x 4¼in card.

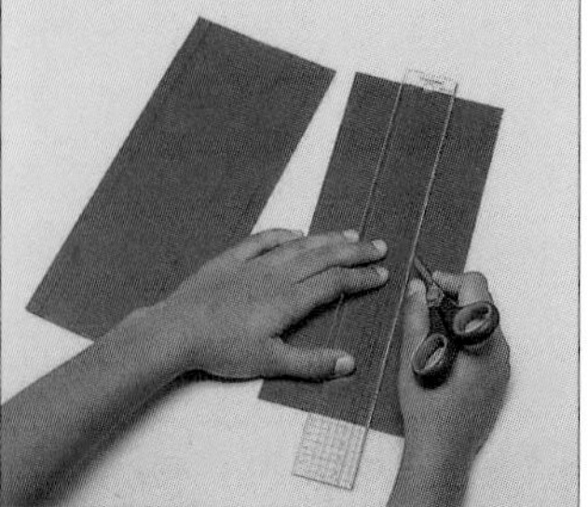

3 Hold the ruler firmly against one of the lines you have drawn. Use the tip of a pair of scissors to score along the line. Repeat for all lines on both sides of both pieces of cardboard.

4 Place the cards A side up. For each piece in turn, fold firmly along the two lines. Fold up from the scored side. Turn the card over. Repeat for the lines on side B.

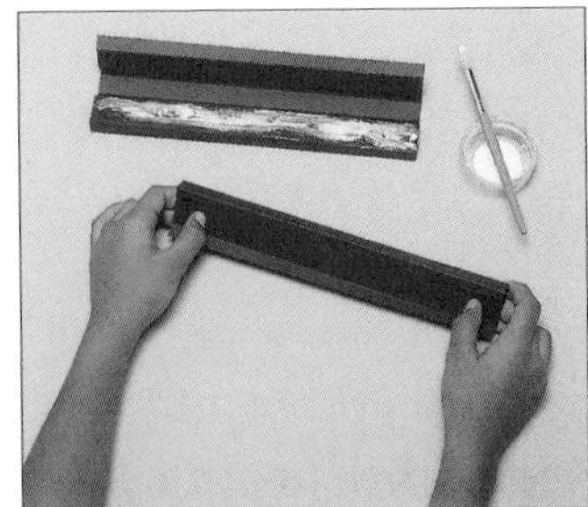

5 With the A side up, press the folds into the I-shape of the rail. Open out again. Glue the B side of the 2cm/¾in wide middle section, as shown. Repeat for the second rail.

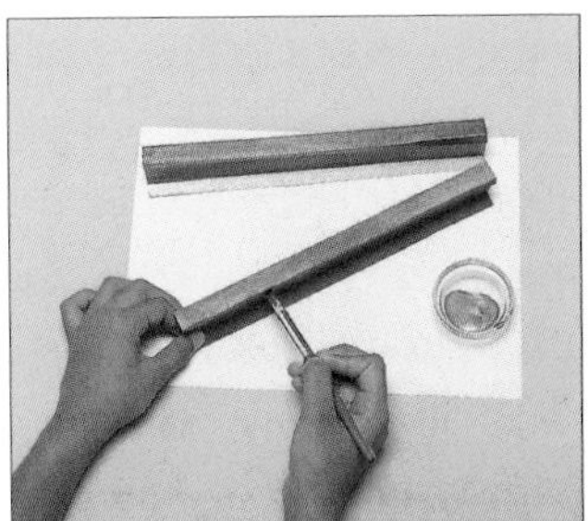

6 Give your two rails a metallic look by painting the upper (A) sides silver. Leave the paint to dry, and then apply a second coat. Leave the second coat to dry.

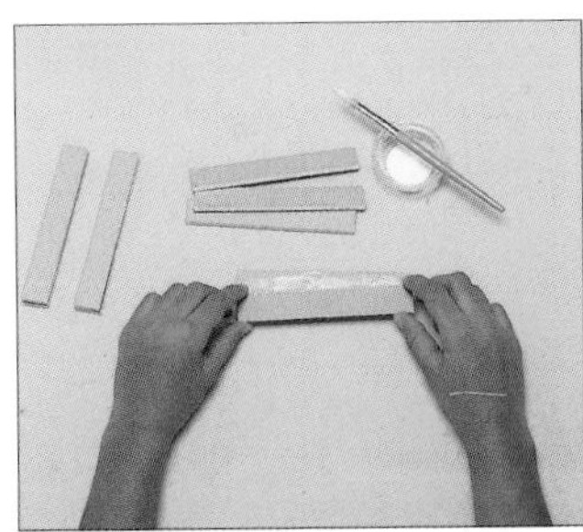

7 Use a pencil and ruler to mark ten 13 x 2cm/5 x ¾in strips on the foam board. Cut them out. Glue two strips together to make five thick railway sleepers. Leave them to dry.

8 Paint the sleepers brown on their tops and sides, to make them look like wood. Leave them to dry, then apply a second coat of paint. Leave the second coat to dry, too.

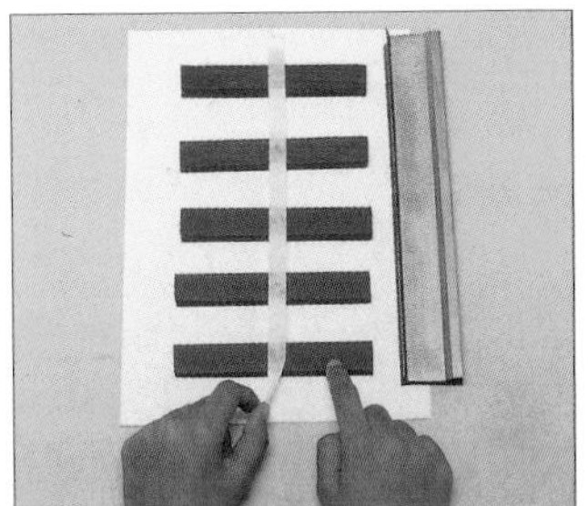

9 Lay the sleepers on the piece of paper, 3cm/1¼in apart. Make sure that they are exactly parallel to each other. Run a strip of masking tape down the middle to hold them in place.

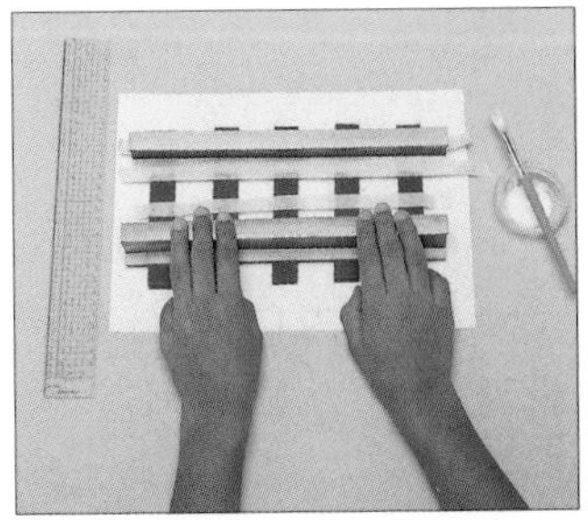

10 Glue the base of a rail, and press into place with the outside edge of the rail 1.5cm/¾in in from the edge of the sleeper. Repeat with the other track. Secure with masking tape until it is dry.

Make several sets of rails. To join the rails together, roll up the thin card. Insert one end into the top of the I-shape. Push the second rail into the other end.

Rolling stock

The vehicle and machinery that is carried by a modern locomotive's underframe and wheels may weigh up to 100 tons. As bigger and more powerful locomotives were built, more wheels were added to carry the extra weight. Early steam locomotives had only two pairs of wheels. Later steam locomotives had two, three or four pairs of driving wheels, one pair of which was directly driven from the cylinders. The cylinders house the pistons, whose movement pushes the driving wheels around via a connecting rod.

The other wheels are connected to the driving wheel by a coupling rod, so that they turn at the same time. The small wheels in front of the driving wheels are called leading wheels. The ones behind are the trailing wheels. Locomotives are defined by the total number of wheels they have. For example, a 4-4-0 type locomotive has four leading, four driving and no trailing wheels. This project shows you how to make an underframe for a 4-4-0 type locomotive, which will run on the tracks described on the previous page. The following page shows how to make a locomotive to sit on the underframe.

YOU WILL NEED

Large sheet of cardboard, pencil, ruler, pair of compasses, scissors, white glue and glue brush, masking tape, four 10cm/4in lengths of 0.5cm/¼in diameter dowel, four pieces of 5 x 5cm/2 x 2in thin card, silver and black paint, paintbrush, water pot, four map pins.

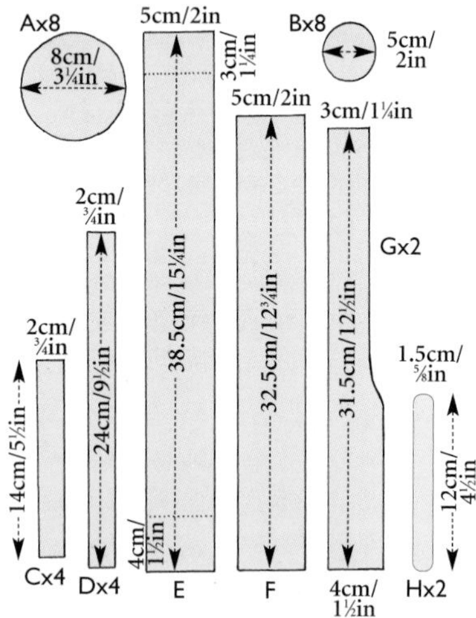

▲ **Templates**
Draw and cut out the templates from the cardboard. Use a pair of compasses to draw the wheel templates A and B.

Make an underframe

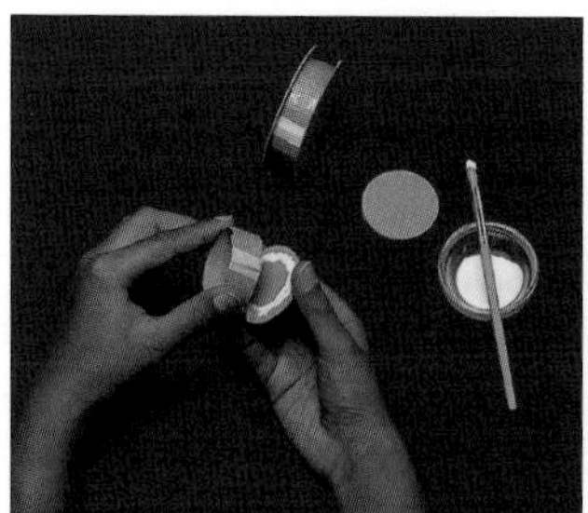

1 Roll the rim templates C and D into rings. Glue and tape to hold. Glue each small wheel circle to each side of a small ring, as shown. Repeat for the big wheels. Leave to dry.

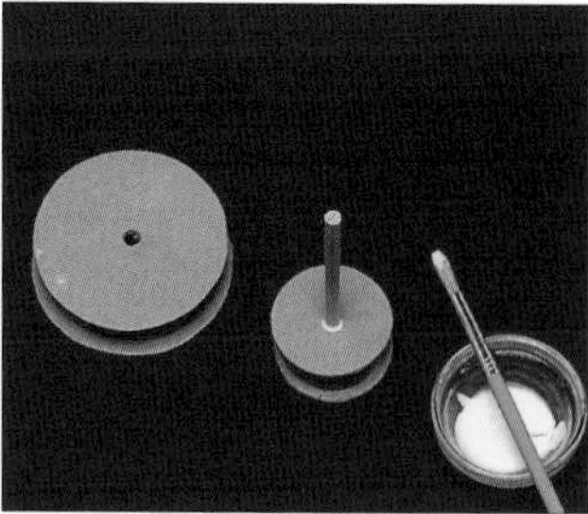

2 Use a pencil to enlarge the compass hole on one side of each wheel. Glue one end of each piece of dowel. Push them into the holes of two big and two small wheels.

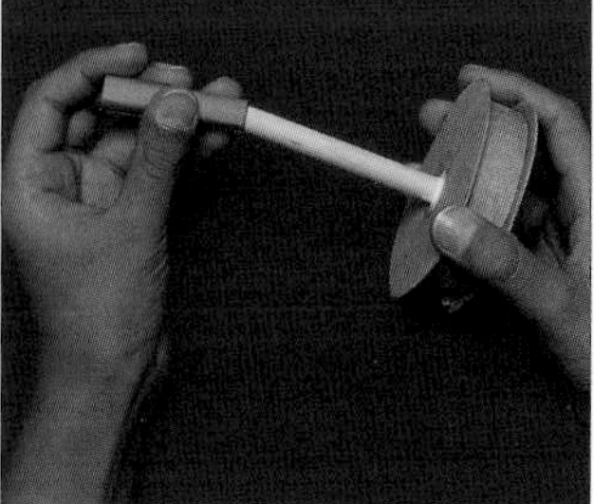

3 Roll the 5 x 5cm/2 x 2in card into sleeves to fit loosely over each piece of dowel. Tape to hold. Make wheel pairs by fixing the remaining wheels to the dowel as described in Step 2.

4 When the glue is dry, paint all four pairs of wheels silver. You do not need to paint the dowel axles. Paint two coats, letting the first dry before you apply the second.

5 Use a ruler and pencil to mark eight equal segments on the outside of each wheel. Paint a small circle over the compass hole, and the middle of each segment black.

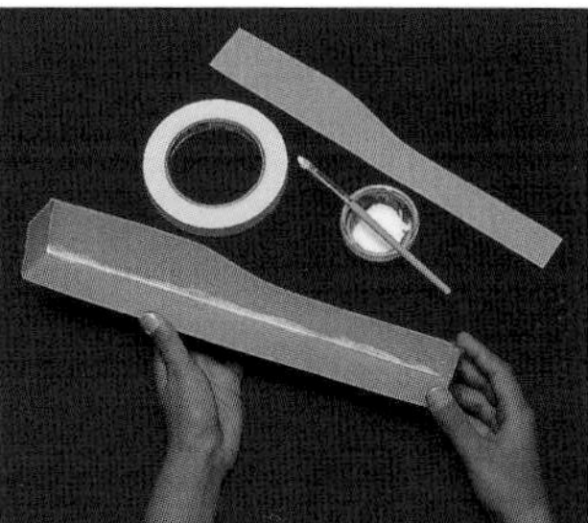

6 Fold along the dotted lines on E. Glue all three straight edges of template G and stick to template E. Repeat this for the other side. Secure all joints with masking tape.

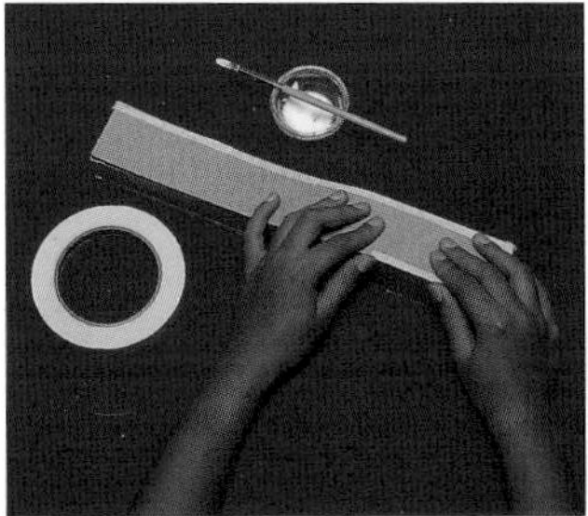

7 Glue the open edges of the underframe. Fit template F on top and hold until firm. Tape over the joints. Give the underframe two coats of black paint. Leave to dry.

8 Glue the card sleeves to the base of the underframe. Small wheel axles go 3cm/1¼in and 7cm/2¾in from the front; big wheels go 3.5cm/1¼in and 13cm/5in from the back. Tape to secure.

9 Paint the coupling rods (H) with a coat of silver paint. Allow the paint to dry thoroughly. Then give the coupling rods a second coat of paint, and leave them to dry.

10 Press a map pin through each end of the coupling rods, about 0.5cm/¼in from the edge. Carefully press the pin into each big wheel about 1.5cm/⅝in beneath the middle.

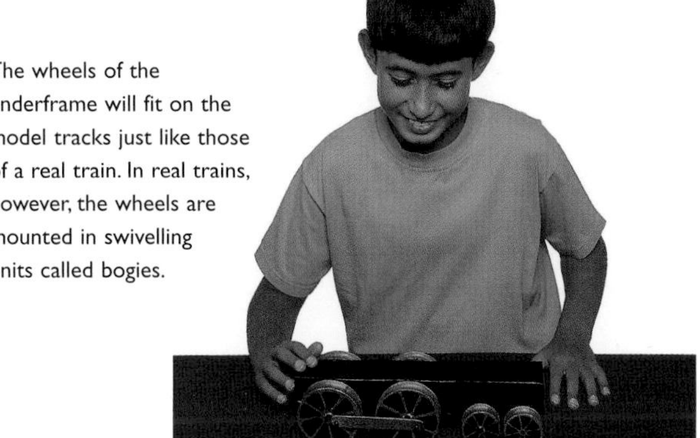

The wheels of the underframe will fit on the model tracks just like those of a real train. In real trains, however, the wheels are mounted in swivelling units called bogies.

Locomotive

Toy trains started to go on sale during the mid-1800s. Early models were made of brightly painted wood, and often had a wooden track to run along. Soon, metal trains went on sale, many of them made from tinplate (thin sheets of iron or steel coated with tin). Some of these metal toy trains had wind-up, clockwork motors. Clockwork toy trains were first sold in the USA during the 1880s. The most sophisticated model trains were steam-powered, with tiny engines fired by methyl alcohol burners. Later models were powered by electric motors.

Railroad companies often devised special colour schemes, called liveries, for their locomotives and carriages. Steam locomotives had brass and copper decoration, and some also carried the company's logo or badge. Many toy trains are also painted in the livery of a real railroad company. The shape of the locomotive you can make in this project has an engine house that is typical of the real locomotives made in the 1930s. The driver and fireman would have shared the cabin of the locomotive. The driver controlled the speed of the train, and the fireman made sure there was a good supply of steam.

YOU WILL NEED
26 x 26cm/10¼ x 10¼in cardboard, ruler, masking tape, scissors, 10 x 10cm/ 4 x 4in card, pencil, white glue and glue brush, cardboard for templates, paints, paintbrush, water pot, underframe, two drawing pins (thumb tacks), 11 x 1cm/ 4¼ x ½in thin red card, split pin.

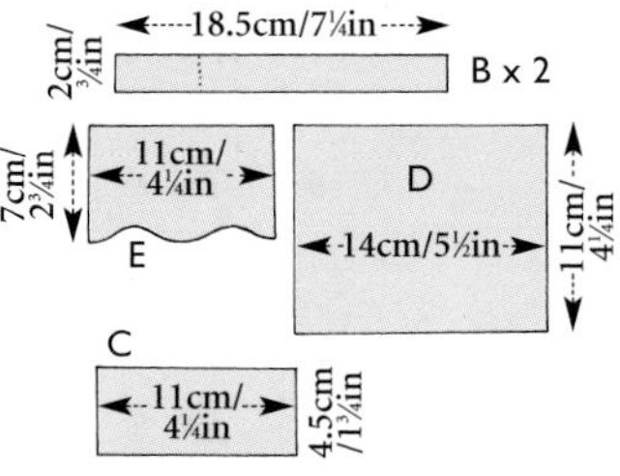

▲ **Templates**
Draw and cut out the templates from the cardboard.

Make a toy train

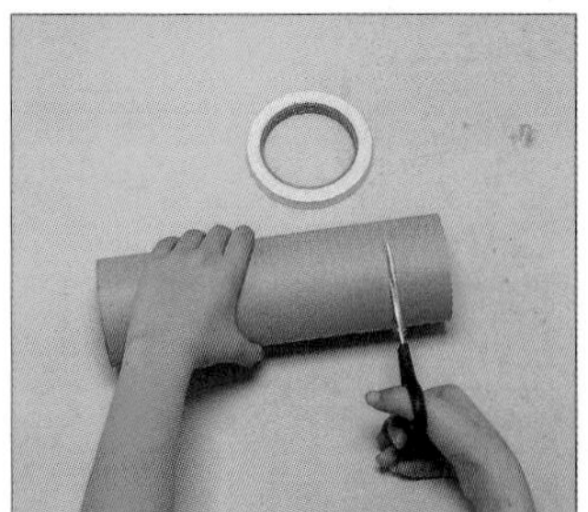

1 Roll the 26 x 26cm/10¼ x 10¼in cardboard into an 8cm/3¼in-diameter tube. Secure it with tape. Using the scissors, cut a 6cm/2½in slit, 21cm/8½in from one end of the tube.

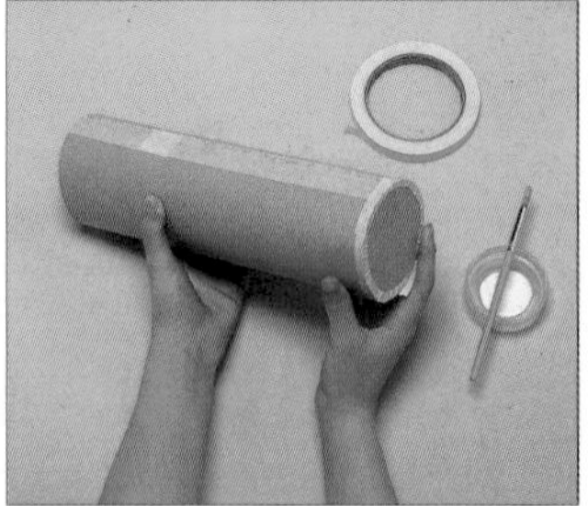

2 Hold the tube upright on the 10 x 10cm/4 x 4in piece of cardboard. Draw around it. Cut this circle out. Glue the circle to the tube end farthest away from the slit. Tape to secure.

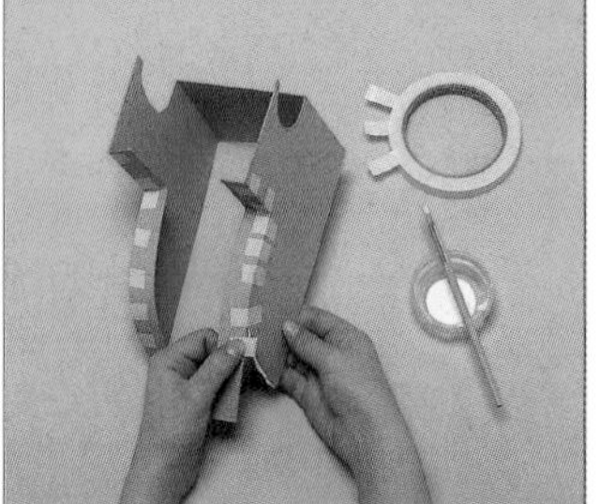

3 Copy and cut out the templates. Fold template A along the dotted lines. Fold templates B upward along the dotted line. Glue both strips to the cabin, as shown, and secure with tape.

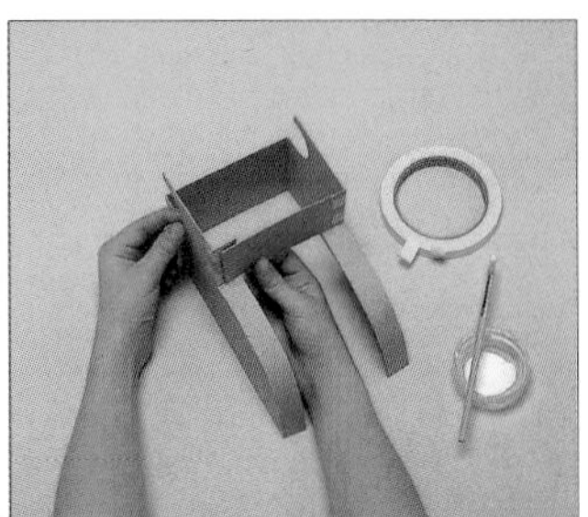

4 When the glue is dry, gently peel off the masking tape. Now glue on template C, as shown above. Hold it in place with masking tape until the glue dries, then remove the tape.

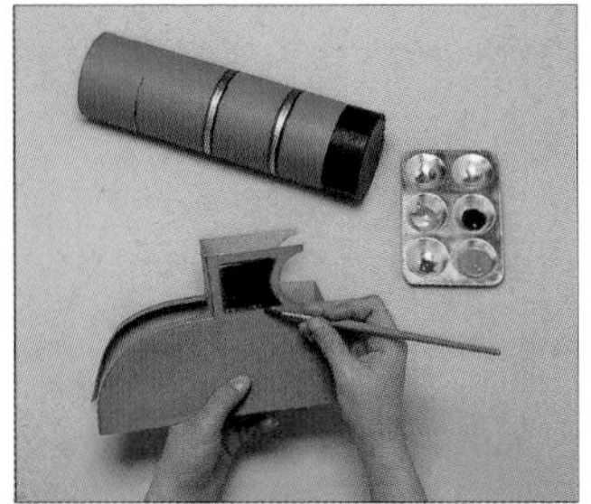

5 Apply two coats of green paint to the outside of the locomotive. Let the first coat dry before applying the second. Then paint the black parts. Add the red and gold last.

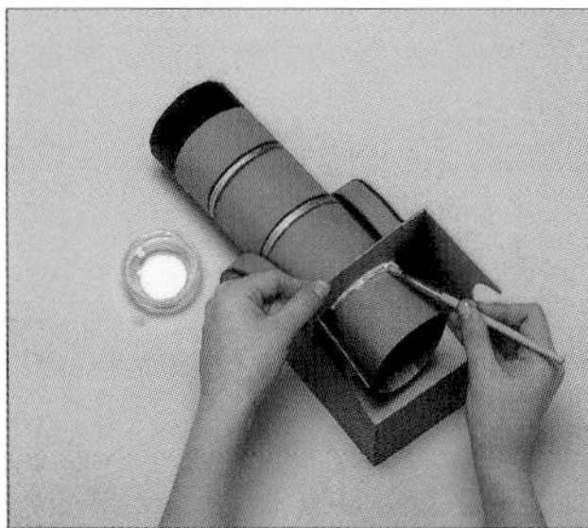

6 Glue around the bottom edge of the cabin front C. Put a little glue over the slit in the tube. Fit the front of the cabin into the slit. Leave the locomotive to one side to dry.

7 Give roof template D two coats of black paint. Let the paint dry between coats. Glue the top edges of the cabin, and place the black roof on top. Leave until dry and firm.

8 Glue the bottom of the cylindrical part of the train to the underframe you made in the 'Underframe' project. Press drawing pins into the back of the cabin and underframe.

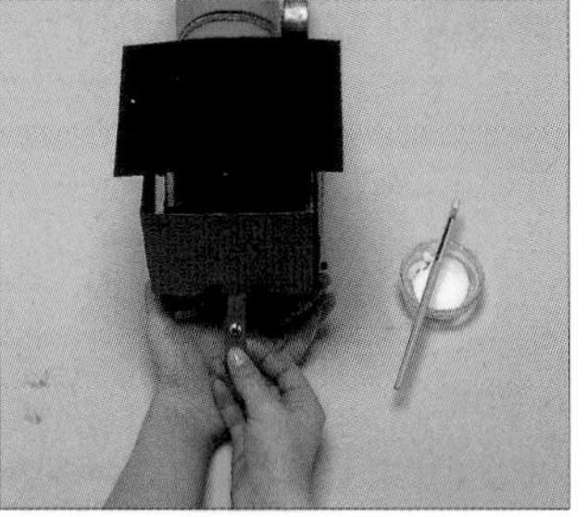

9 Glue both sides of one end of the red strip. Slot this between the underframe and the cabin, between the drawing pins. When it is firm, fold the strip and insert the split pin.

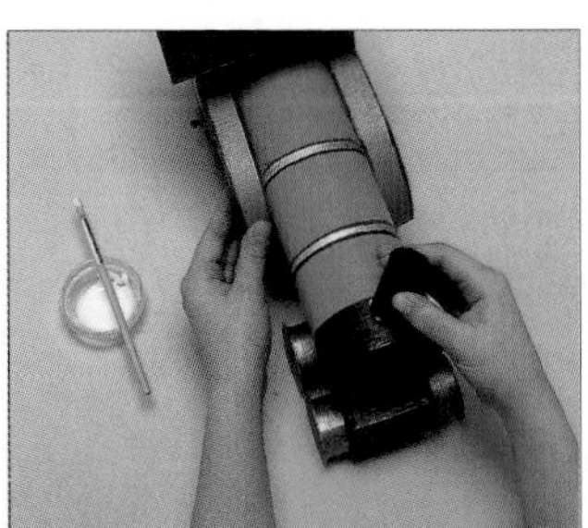

10 Paint one side of template E black. When it is dry, roll it into a tube and secure with masking tape. Glue the wavy edge and secure it to the front of the locomotive, as shown.

Just like a real locomotive, your model train has been painted with a scheme, in this case red, black and gold decoration. The locomotive is now ready to run on the railway line you made in the 'Making tracks' project on p210.

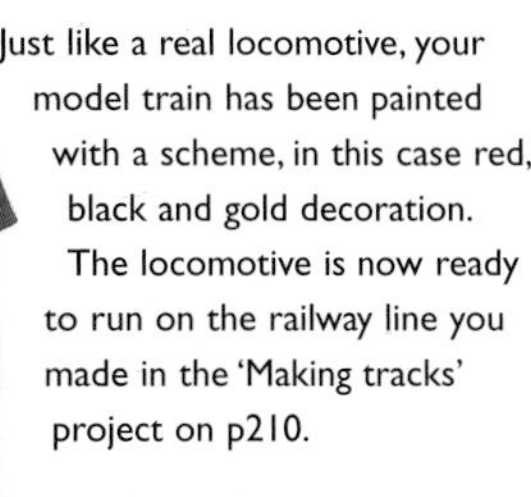

Brake van

Few early steam locomotives had brakes. If the driver needed to stop quickly, he had to throw the engine into reverse. By the early 1860s, braking systems for steam locomotives had been invented. Some passenger carriages also had their own handbrakes which were operated by the carriage guards. A brake van was added to the back of trains, too, but its brakes were operated by a guard riding inside. Old-style brake vans, like the one in this project, sat at the end of the train, so that the guard could make sure that all the carriages stayed coupled.

The problem was that the train driver had no control over the rest of the train. When he wanted to stop, he had to blow the engine whistle to warn each of the carriage guards to apply their brakes. The brakes on a locomotive and its carriages or wagons needed to be linked. This was made possible by the invention of an air-braking system in 1869. When the driver applies the brakes, compressed air travels along pipes that link all the train, and presses brake shoes. Air brakes are now used on nearly all the world's railroads.

YOU WILL NEED

Large piece of cardboard, small piece of thin red card for template J, ruler, pencil, scissors, white glue and brush, masking tape, four 10cm/4in lengths of 5mm/¼in-diameter dowel, acrylic paints, brush, pot, two 3cm/1¼in lengths of 5mm/¼in-diameter dowel, pair of compasses.

Templates

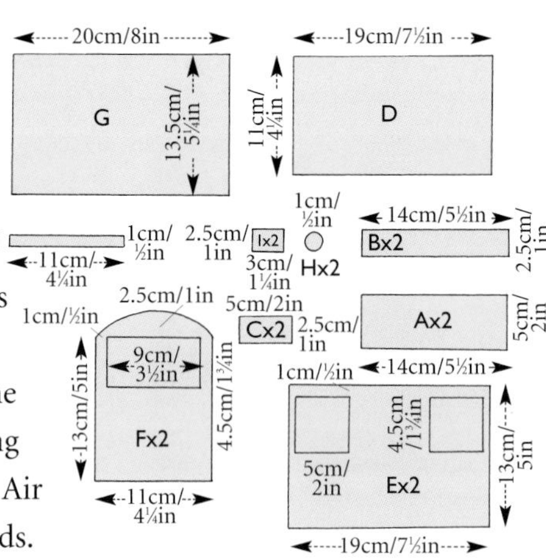

Make a brake van

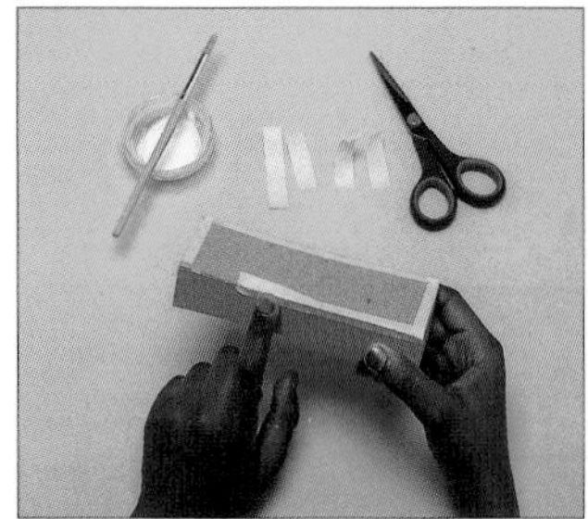

1 Copy the templates on to cardboard and cut them out. Glue templates A, B, and C together to make the underframe as shown. Tape over the joints to secure them.

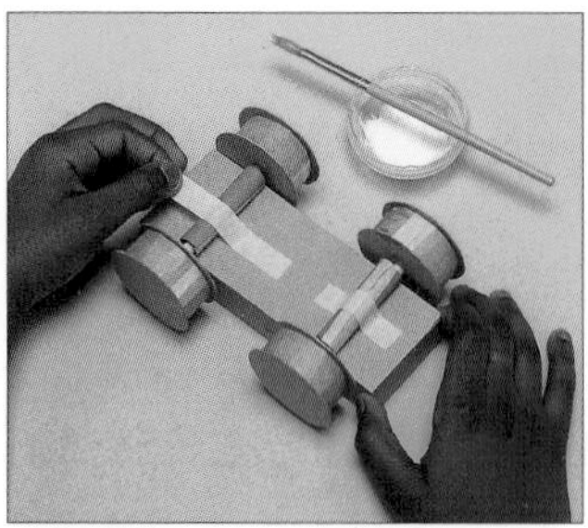

2 Make and paint two pairs of small wheels (5cm/2in diameter) following Steps 1 through 3 in the 'Underframe' project on p212. Glue and tape the wheel pairs to the underframe.

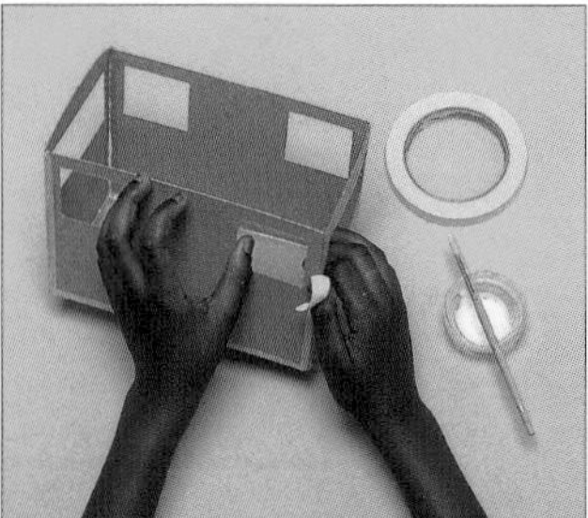

3 Glue the bottom edges of the van sides (E) to the van base (D). Then glue on the van ends (F). Secure the joints with masking tape until the glue is dry.

4 Paint the brake van brown with black details, and the wheels and underframe black and silver. Apply two coats of paint, letting each one dry between coats.

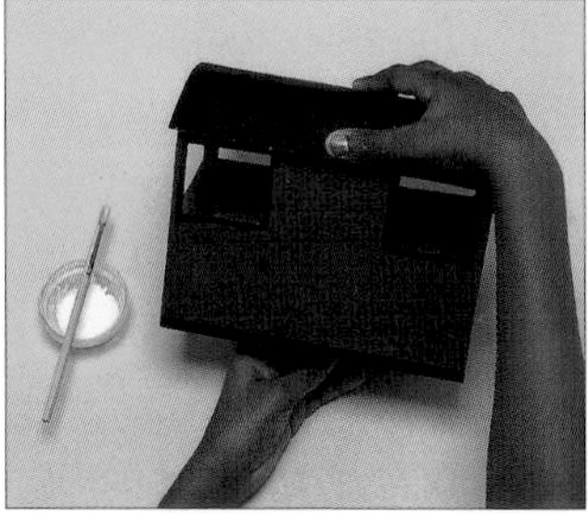

5 Paint one side of template G black. Let the paint dry before applying a second coat. Glue the top edges of the van. Bend the roof to fit on the top of the van, as shown above.

6 Apply glue to the top surface of the underframe. Stick the brake van centrally on top. Press it together until the glue holds firm. Leave the model to dry completely.

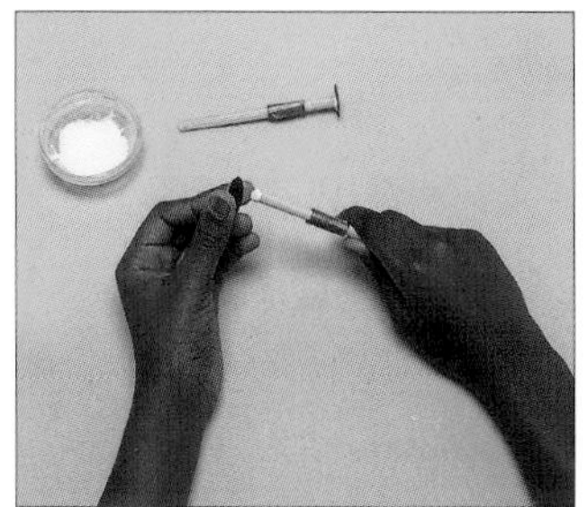

7 Roll up templates I into two 2cm/¾in tubes to fit loosely over the 3cm/1¼in pieces of dowel. Tape to hold. Paint them silver. Paint the buffer templates H black and stick on each dowel.

8 Use compasses to pierce two holes 2.5cm/1in from each side of the van and 1.5cm/⅝in up. Enlarge with a pencil. Glue the end of each dowel buffer. Slot it into the hole. Leave to dry.

9 Cut a 2cm/¾in slot between the buffers. Fold the red card template J in half. Glue each open end of the loop, and push them through the slot. Press down to hold firm.

The brake van will also run on the tracks you made in the 'Making tracks' project on p210. You can also join the red-card coupling to join the brake van to the model locomotive you made in the 'Toy train' project on p214. On old-style railways, the brake van had one of two brake systems. One had hand-operated brakes that worked on the tread of the brake van's wheels. The other had a valve that allowed the guard to apply air brakes to all of the vehicles in the train.

Monorail

The first trains to run on a single rail rather than a twin track date back to the 1820s. As with early trains, these early monorails were pulled by horses and carried heavy materials, such as building bricks, rather than passengers. About 60 years later, engineers designed steam locomotives that hauled carriages along an A-shaped rail. However, neither the trains nor the carriages were very stable. Loads had to be carefully balanced on either side of the A-frame to stop them tipping over.

Today's monorails are completely stable, with several sets of rubber wheels to give a smooth ride. They are powered by electricity, and many are driverless. Driverless monorail trains are controlled by computers that tell them when to stop, start, speed up or slow down. This project shows you how to make a train that runs on the 'straddle' system monorail. The body of the train straddles over the rail.

Monorails are not widely used today, because they are more expensive to run than two-track railroads. The special track costs more to build than twin rails, and the cars cannot be switched from one track to another.

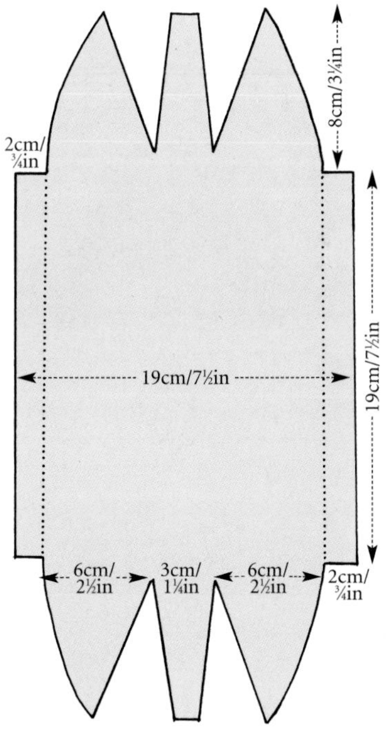

▲ **Template**
Draw and cut out the template from the cardboard.

Make a monorail

YOU WILL NEED

Protective paper, 72cm/28in piece of wood (4 x 4cm/1½ x 1½in), acrylic paints, paintbrush, water pot, 67cm/26in length of plastic curtain rail (with screws, end fittings and four plastic runners), saw, screwdriver, sheet of red cardboard, pencil, ruler, scissors, double-sided tape, 18cm/7in piece of 2.5cm/1in-thick foam board, white glue and brush, black felt-tipped pen.

1 Cover the work surface with paper to protect it. Then paint the piece of wood yellow. Let the first coat dry thoroughly before applying a second coat of paint.

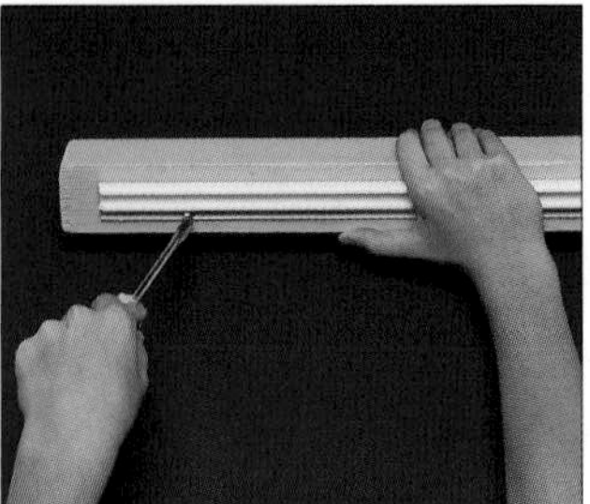

2 Ask an adult to saw the curtain rail to size if necessary. Place the track in the middle of the wood, and screw it into place. Screw in the end fittings at one end of the rail.

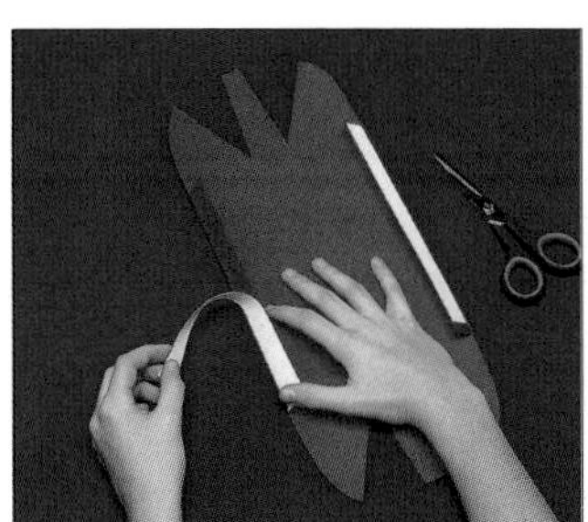

3 Copy the template onto the red card and cut it out. Score along the dotted lines and fold it inward. Stick double-sided tape along the outside of each folded section.

4 Remove the backing from the tape. Stick one side of the foam on to it. Fold the card over and press the other piece of double-sided tape to the opposite side of the foam.

5 Overlap the pointed ends at the back and front of the train and glue. Then glue the inside end of the top flaps, back and front. Fold them over and press firmly to secure.

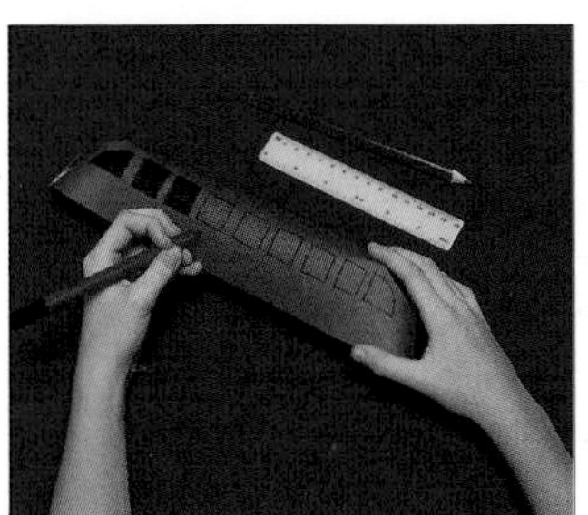

6 Pencil in windows along both sides of the train. Fill them in with a black felt-tipped pen. Paint decorative yellow and black stripes along the bottom of the windows.

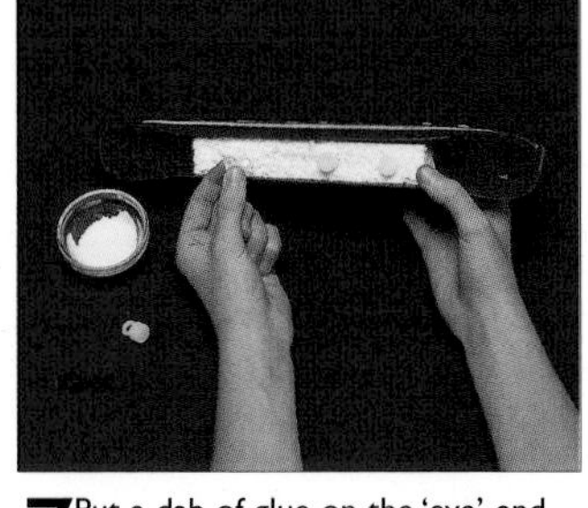

7 Put a dab of glue on the 'eye' end of each plastic runner. Hold the train, foam bottom toward you. Push each runner into the foam at roughly equal intervals.

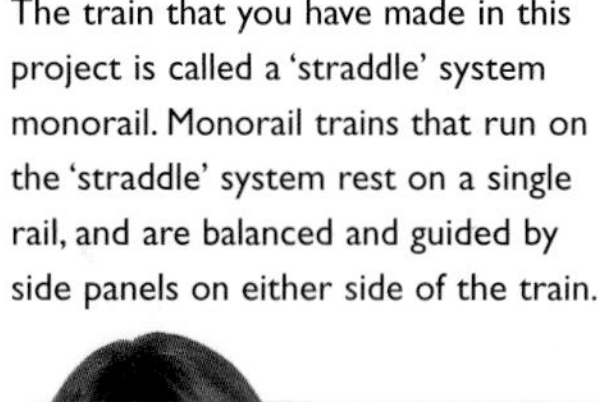

The train that you have made in this project is called a 'straddle' system monorail. Monorail trains that run on the 'straddle' system rest on a single rail, and are balanced and guided by side panels on either side of the train.

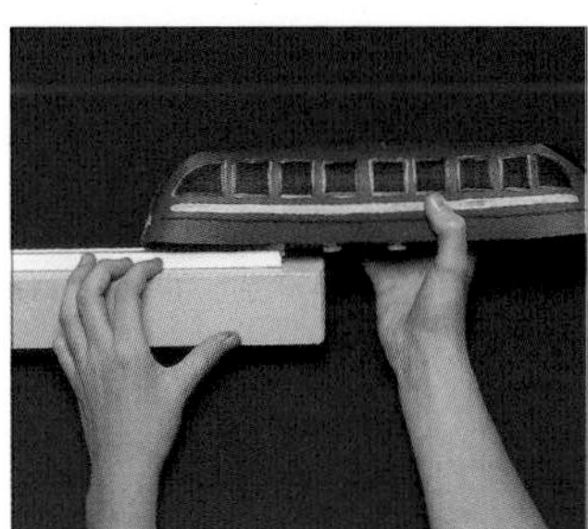

8 Stand the track on a flat surface. At the end of the track without an end stop, feed each plastic runner into the track. Run the train back and forth along the track.

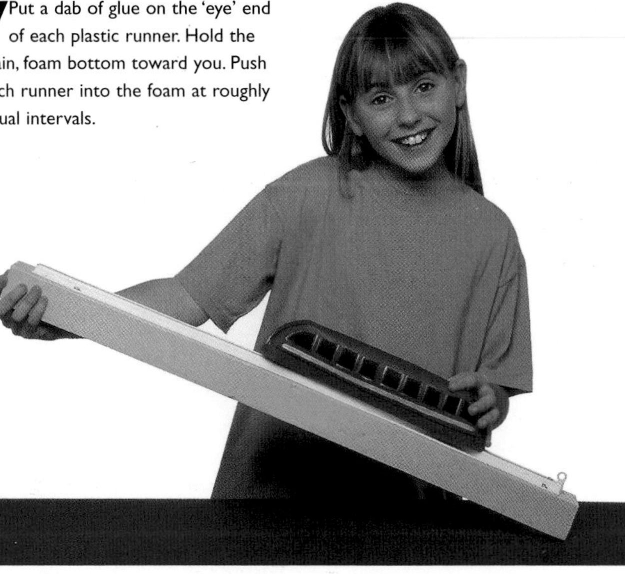

Making car wheels turn

cylinder head
spark plug
cylinder
piston
con (connecting) rod
crankshaft

▲ **Working together**
Most car engines have four cylinders arranged like this. You can see the pistons and cylinders. Four rods, one from each piston, turn metal joints attached to the crankshaft. As the rods turn the joints, the crankshaft moves around. This movement is transmitted to the wheels, via the gearbox, which controls how fast the wheels turn relative to the engine.

This experiment shows how one kind of movement – that goes around and around – can be converted into an up-and-down movement. This idea is applied to cars to make the wheels go around, but it happens the other way around. The up-and-down movement of the pistons is changed into the circular motion of the crankshaft and wheels.

When a car engine is switched on, fuel ignites and hot gases are produced in the cylinders. The gases force close-fitting pistons down the cylinders in which they are housed. The pistons are connected to the crankshaft (a rod that connects eventually to the wheels), so that as they move up and down, the crankshaft rotates. This, in turn, makes the wheels go around. One up-and-down movement of a piston results in one turn of the crankshaft. The wheels rotate once for about every three to six turns of the crankshaft.

YOU WILL NEED
Shoe box, thin metal rod about 2mm/ $\frac{1}{16}$in in diameter, pliers, jar lid, adhesive tape, scissors, thick plastic straw, ruler, pencil, stiff paper, at least four different felt-tipped pens, thin plastic straw.

Changing motion

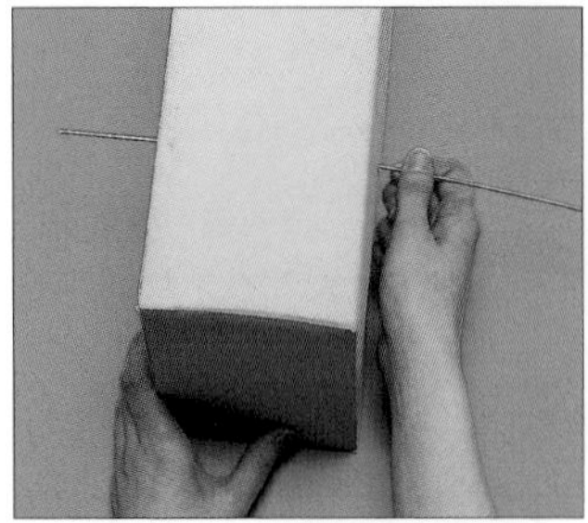

1 Place the shoe box narrow-side-down on a flat surface. With one hand, push the metal rod through the middle, making sure that your other hand will not get jabbed by the rod.

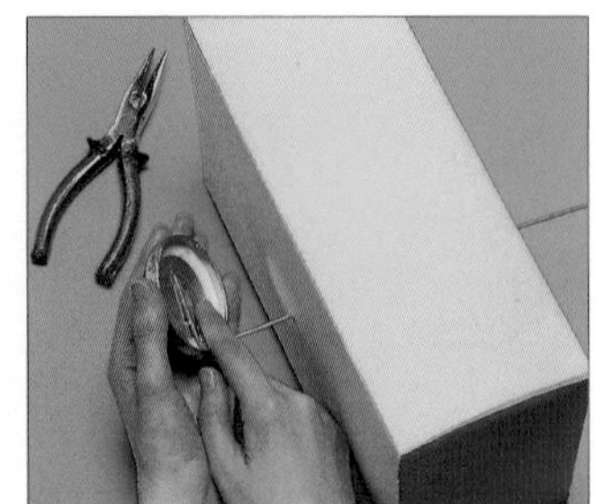

2 Using the pliers, bend the rod at right angles where it comes out of the box. Attach the jar lid to it with tape. Push the lid until it rests against the side of the box.

3 Carefully use the pliers to bend the piece of rod sticking out of the other side of the box. This will make a handle for the piston, so that you will be able to turn it easily.

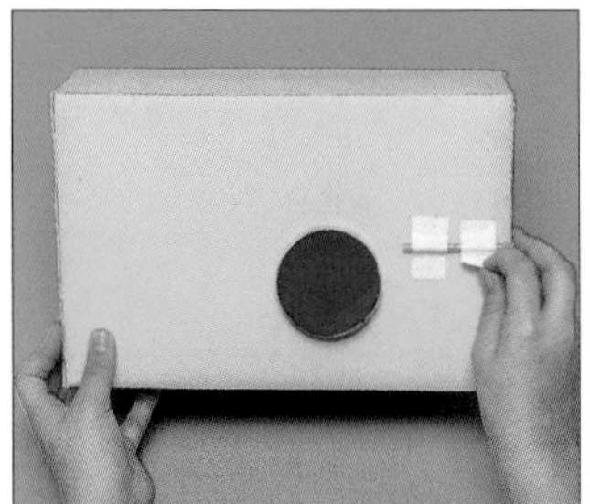

4 Cut a piece of thick plastic straw about 5cm/2in long, and tape it to the side of the box close to the jar lid. Make sure that it just sticks up beyond the edge of the box.

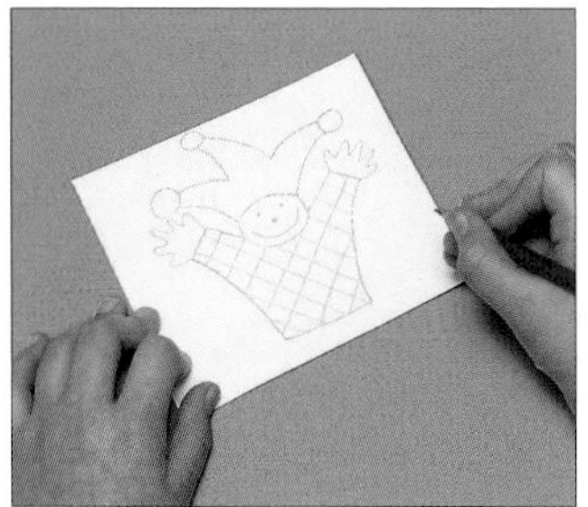

5 Draw a design in pencil on a piece of stiff paper. Copy the jester shown in this project, or draw a simple clown. Choose something that looks good when it moves.

6 Using the felt-tipped pens, shade the design until it looks the way you want it to. The more vivid the figure is, the nicer it will look on the top of the piston.

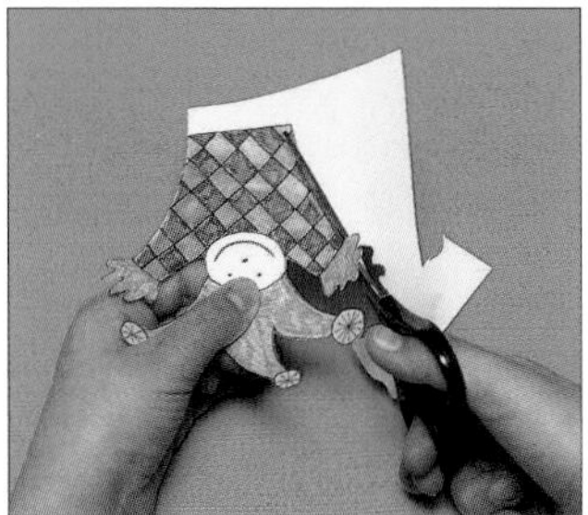

7 Carefully cut the finished drawing out of the paper. Make sure that you have a clean-edged design. Try not to smudge the felt-tipped pen with your fingers.

8 Turn the drawing over. Use the tape to attach the thin plastic straw to the bottom of the drawing. About 2cm/¾in of straw should be attached.

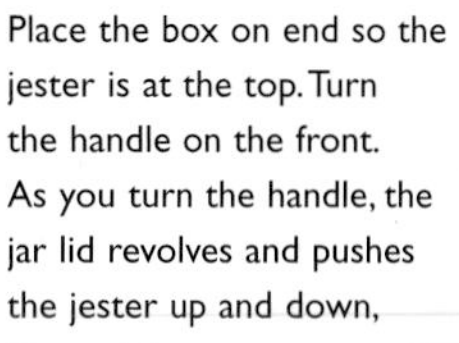

Place the box on end so the jester is at the top. Turn the handle on the front. As you turn the handle, the jar lid revolves and pushes the jester up and down, like a piston.

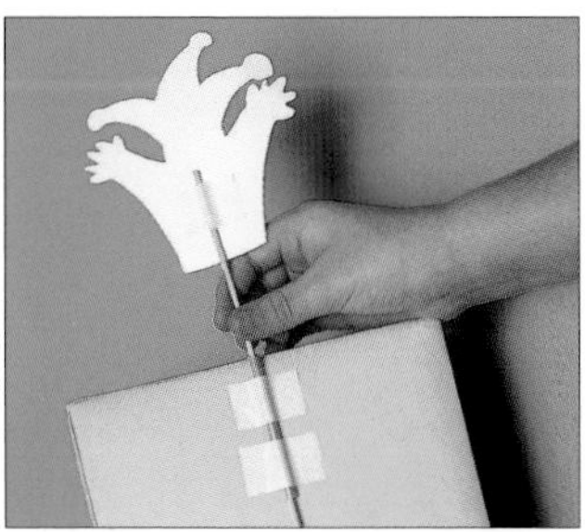

9 Slide the straw attached to the drawing into the straw taped to the box. It will come out of the other end. Push down so that the straw touches the edge of the jar lid.

Changing gear

Gears in a car help transfer movement in the most efficient way. They do this by transmitting movement from the crankshaft (which links engine and wheels) to another shaft called the propeller shaft. The propeller shaft rotates more slowly than the crankshaft and adapts the movement, so that the car can cope better with different speeds and efforts, such as starting and going uphill. The change in speed of rotation between the two shafts is controlled from the car's gearbox. As a driver changes gear, toothed wheels that are connected to the crankshaft engage with other toothed wheels joined to the propeller shaft. The difference in the number of teeth on each wheel determines the number of times the wheels turn, as the first project demonstrates. The second experiment shows how gear wheels work in a car. The larger corrugated cardboard wheel has more teeth than the two smaller wheels.

▲ Wheels within wheels
The car's engine turns the crankshaft with different-sized gears (toothed wheels) on it. High gears are used for more speed, because the big wheel turns the small wheel faster. The gear system is called the transmission – it transmits (moves) the engine's power to the car's wheels. Most cars have five gears. The biggest is needed for slow speeds, and the smallest for high speeds.

YOU WILL NEED

Pair of compasses, ruler, pencil, sheet of white paper, black pen, scissors, sheet of thin card, two strips of corrugated cardboard, adhesive tape, three different felt-tipped pens.

Drawing the gears

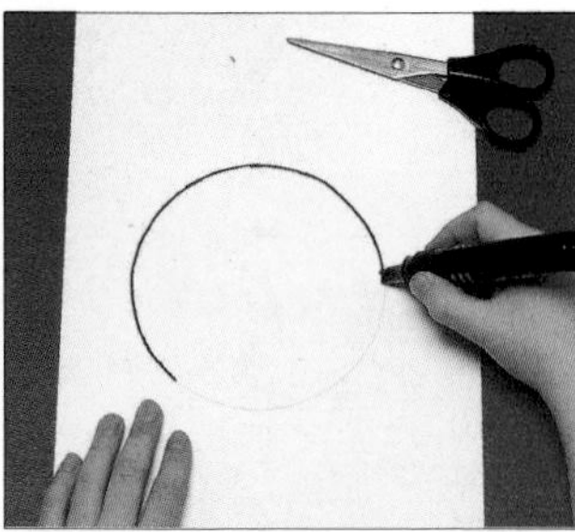

1 Using the compasses, trace a 14cm/5½in-diameter circle on the paper. Draw over it with the pen and cut it out. On the card, trace, draw and cut out an 11cm/4¼in-diameter circle.

2 Tape corrugated card around the circles. Make a hole in the small circle wide enough for the tip of a felt-tipped pen. Turn the small wheel inside the larger. Trace the path in felt-tipped pen.

3 Make a second hole in the small wheel. Turn the small gear inside the larger using another felt-tipped pen. Make a third hole in the small wheel and use a third felt-tipped pen.

Three-gear machine

YOU WILL NEED

Pair of compasses, ruler, pencil, sheet of cardboard, pen, scissors, three strips of corrugated cardboard, adhesive tape, piece of fibreboard, white glue, 6cm/2½in piece of 12m/⅝in-diameter wood dowel, three map pins.

1 Use the compasses to trace one 14cm/5½in-diameter and two 11cm/4¼in-diameter circles on the cardboard. Draw around the edges with the pen, and cut the circles out.

2 Carefully wrap the strips of corrugated cardboard around the circles, using one strip per circle, corrugated side out. Tape each strip to the bottom of the circles.

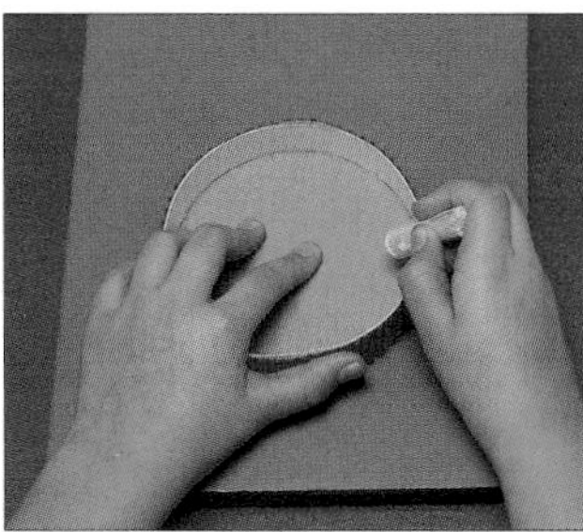

3 Place the largest gear wheel on the piece of fibreboard. Hold the gear down and glue the dowel on to the side of the gear base at the edge of the wheel. Leave it until it is dry.

4 Position all three gears on the fibreboard, with the edges just touching each other. Pin each of them firmly to the fibreboard with a map pin, but allow them to turn.

5 Gently turn the dowel on the largest gear. As that gear turns, the two others that are linked together by the corrugated card will turn against it.

As you turn the gears, notice how they move in opposite directions to each other. Now you have a three-gear machine, where the energy from each gear is being transferred to the others, just like the gears in a car.

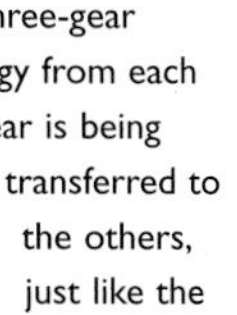

Car control

Cars have two kinds of brakes. Parking brakes lock the rear wheels when the car is standing still. Disc brakes slow down the car when it is moving, in the same way that the sandpaper slows the model wheel in the first experiment.

The second project shows how a device called the camshaft controls the flow of fuel into the cylinders. The camshaft is designed so as to have a regular action that opens one valve and closes another at the same time. Inlet valves let fuel and air into the engine, and burned waste gases are removed via the outlet valves. The camshaft controls make the engine run smoothly.

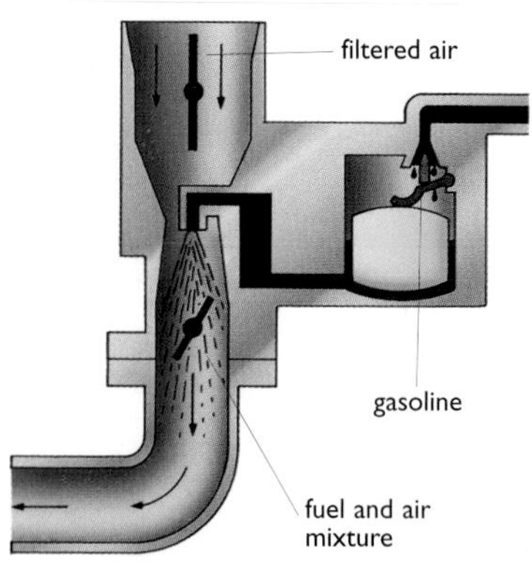

▲ The carburettor

Fuel and air enter the carburettor in just the right quantities for the car to run smoothly. The mixture is then fed into the cylinders. Pressing the accelerator pedal in a car allows more air and fuel into the engine to make it run faster, so speeding up the car.

YOU WILL NEED
Disc brakes: Scissors, 40cm/16in piece of fabric, circular cardboard box with lid, tape, pencil, 20cm/8in piece of 12mm/⅝in-diameter wood dowel, white glue, glue brush, 7 x 11cm/2¾ x 4¼in medium sandpaper, 6 x 10cm/2½ x 4in block, two plastic cups, insulation tape. **How valves work:** Scissors, 12cm/4½in square of cardboard, masking tape, cardboard tube with plastic lid, pencil.

Stopping ▶

When a driver presses the brake pedal, a piston presses together two pads, one on either side of the disc to which the wheel is attached. This strong grip stops the disc from turning, and as the disc slows, so do the wheels.

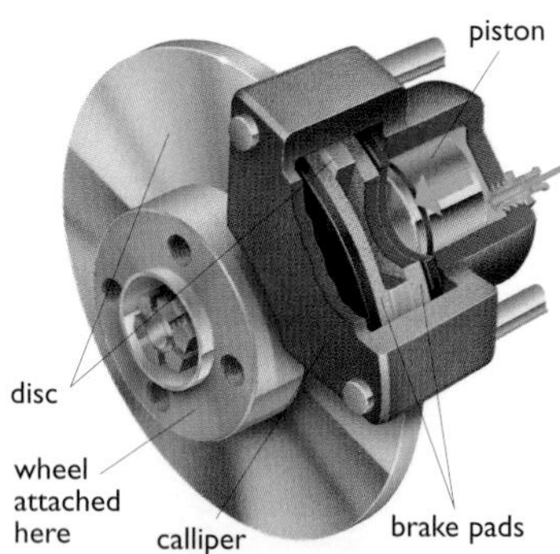

Disc brakes

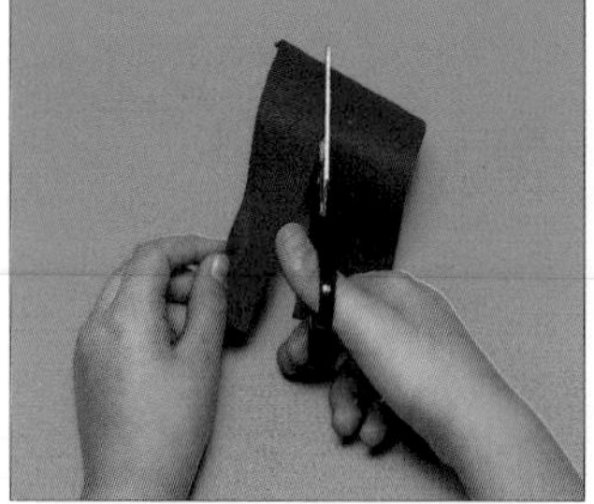

1 Use the scissors to cut a narrow 40cm/16in strip from the fabric. You may have to use special fabric-cutting scissors if your ordinary scissors are not sharp enough.

2 Take the strip of fabric you have cut out and wrap it around the rim of the circular cardboard box. Secure it firmly in place with small pieces of tape.

3 Make a hole in the middle of the box's lid with a pencil. Twist the pencil until it comes through the base of the box. Now gently push the wood dowel through both holes.

4 Spread lots of glue on to the sandpaper's smooth side. Wrap the sandpaper carefully over the top of the wood block. Pressing firmly, stick it together. Leave it to dry.

5 Stand two plastic cups upside down. Rest either end of the dowel on each cup. Cut two small pieces of insulation tape. Use them to fix each end of the dowel to the cup bases.

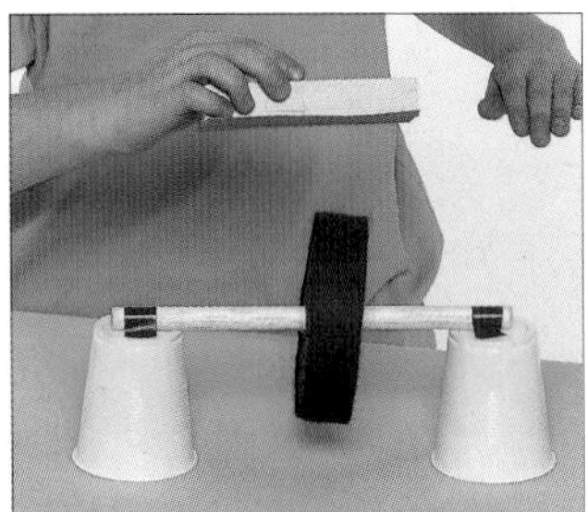

6 Spin the lid fast on the dowel. As it spins, bring the sandpaper into contact with the edge of the lid. Test the brake disc to see how quickly you can stop the lid.

How valves work

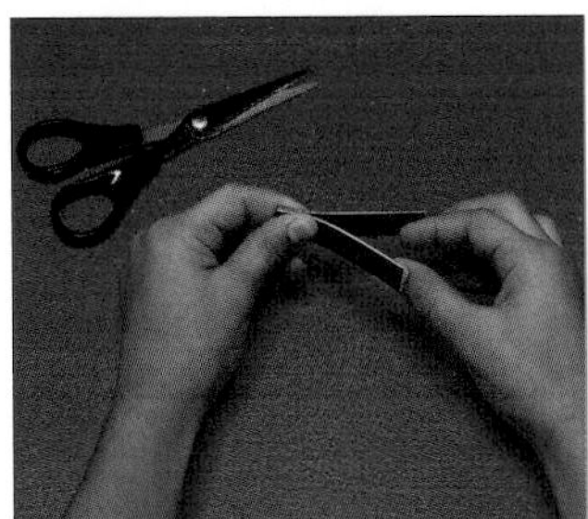

1 Use scissors to cut a 1 x 12cm/ ½ x 4½in strip from the cardboard. Double it over in the middle. Hold it with your fingertips. Bend the two ends of the card away from one another.

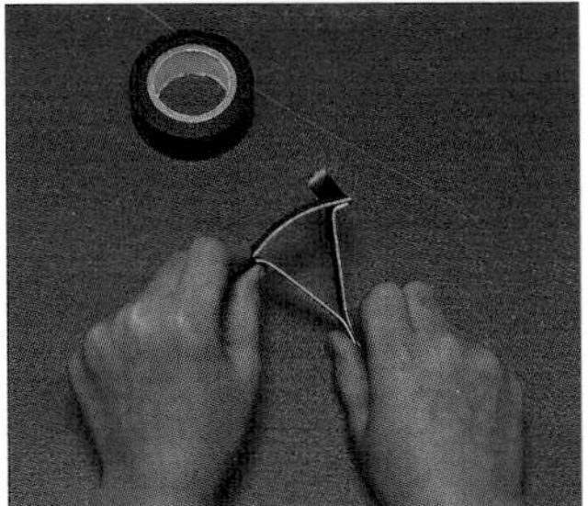

2 Cut a 1 x 4cm/½ x 1½in strip from the original piece of card. Use masking tape to fix the card strip to the bent bottom ends of the first piece. This makes a triangle shape.

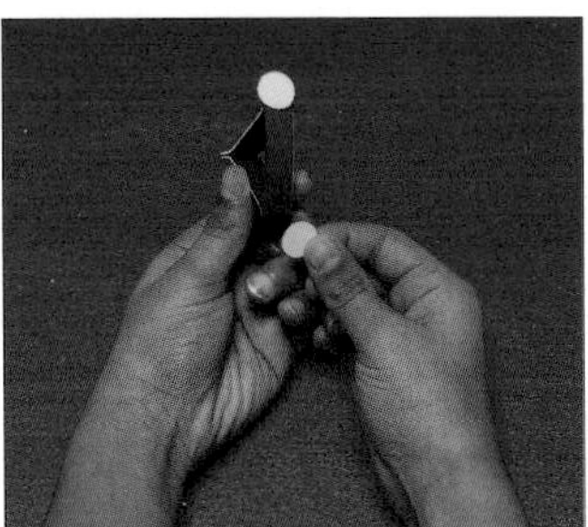

3 Use the scissors to cut out two small circle shapes from the original piece of card. Use masking tape to secure them to the bottom piece of the triangle you have made.

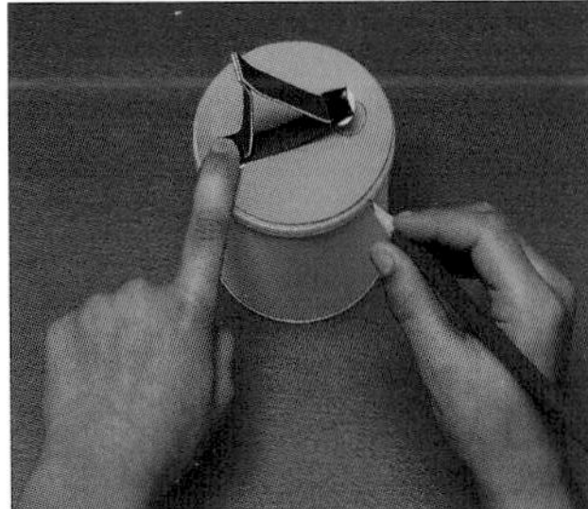

4 Put the cardboard triangle on top of the cardboard tube. The circles should touch the plastic lid. With a pencil, mark the position where the circles sit on the lid.

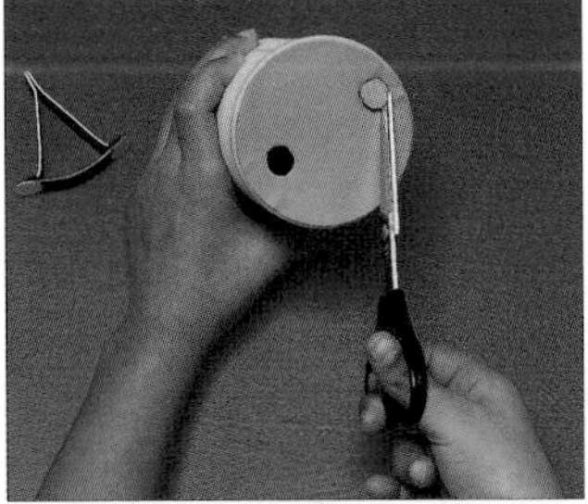

5 Using the scissors, carefully cut around the pencil marks you have made in the plastic lid of the tube. These form an inlet and an outlet. As one valve opens, the other will close.

6 Now you can rock the triangle back and forth, to cover and uncover the two holes. This is just how a camshaft opens and shuts the inlet and outlet valves in a car's cylinder.

Keeping cool

▲ **Mass production**
All the separate parts of a car are mass-produced and then assembled (put together) on a production line to make the finished vehicle. Almost all cars are assembled on production lines today. Robots do much of the work.

The explosion of fuel and air that fires a car's engine generates a great deal of heat. Friction (rubbing together of two surfaces), as the engine parts move together at speed, also creates heat. If the heat level is not kept down, the engine stops working. Metal parts expand, seize up and stop. To cool the engine, water from the car's radiator is pumped around the hottest parts of the engine – the combustion chambers, where the fuel ignites, and the cylinders. The moving water carries heat away from the hottest parts of the engine. The radiator cools the hot water from the engine by using a fan. The fan is driven by a belt connected to the engine. This project shows how a belt transfers turning movement from one shaft to another. This is how a car's engine turns the fan belt.

YOU WILL NEED

Ruler, 16cm/6¼in square of thin cloth, scissors, five reels of thread, glue stick, wooden board, pencil, five flat-headed nails 4cm/1½in long, hammer, 1m x 2.5cm/1yd x 1in velvet ribbon, adhesive tape, pair of compasses, five pieces of 10cm/4in-square card, five wooden skewers.

Fan belt

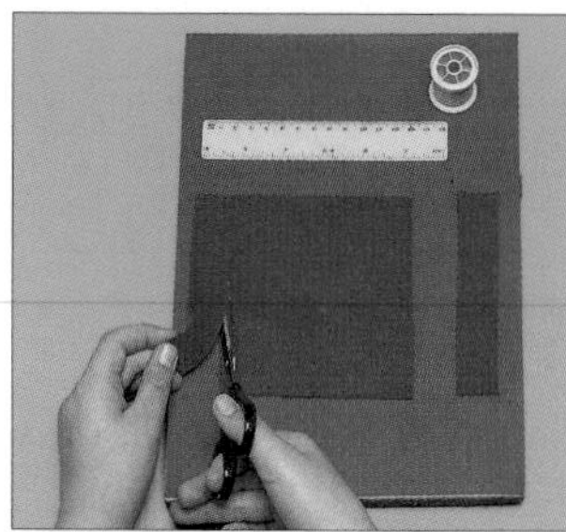

1 Using the ruler, measure five 2.5cm/1in-wide strips on the thin cloth. The height of the reels of thread should be more than 2.5cm/1in. Use the scissors to cut out each strip.

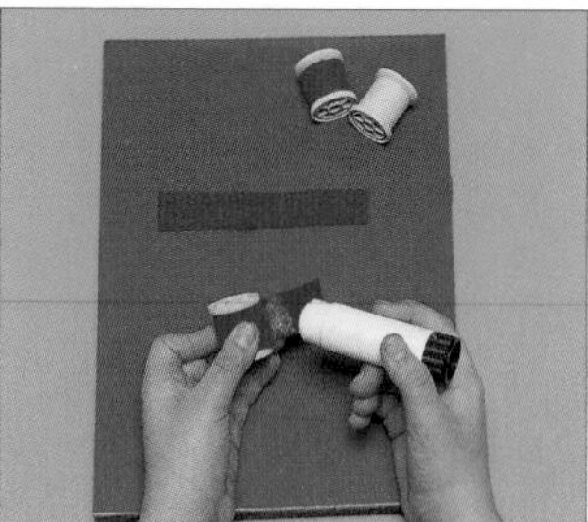

2 Wrap one of the fabric strips around each of the five reels of thread. Glue each strip at the end, so that it sits firmly around the reel and will not come loose.

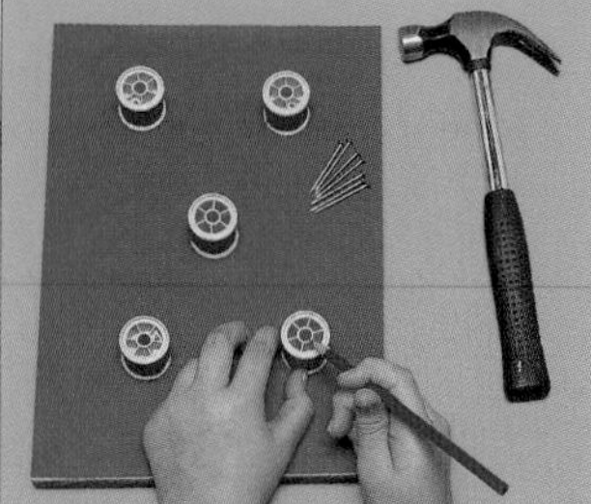

3 Place the reels on the wooden board, as shown above. Trace the outlines with a pencil. Put the nails through the middle of the reels and carefully hammer them into the board.

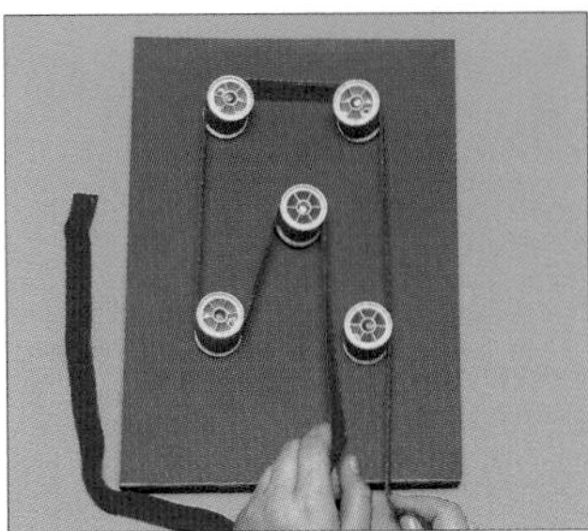

4 Wind the ribbon around the reels, with the velvet side against four of the reels. Cut the ribbon at the point where you can join both ends around the fifth reel.

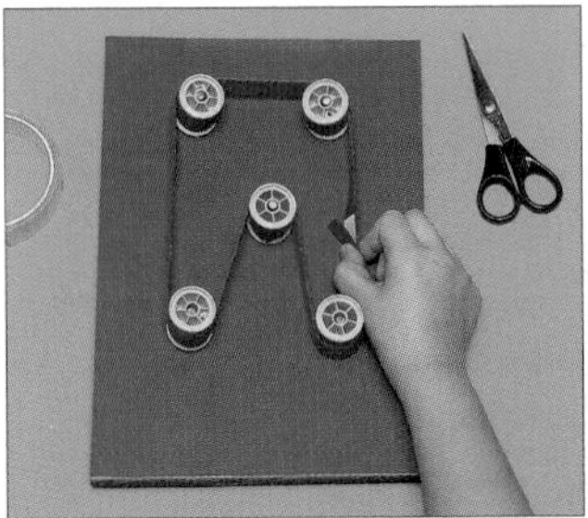

5 Tape the two ends of the ribbon together. Make sure that the ribbon wraps firmly around all of the five reels, but not so tightly that it can't move.

6 Use the compasses to draw circles about 7cm/1¾in in diameter on to the five pieces of card. Then carefully draw freehand spiral shapes inside each circle.

7 Use the scissors to cut each spiral out of each of the pieces of card. Start from the outside edge, and gradually work your way in along the lines of the spiral.

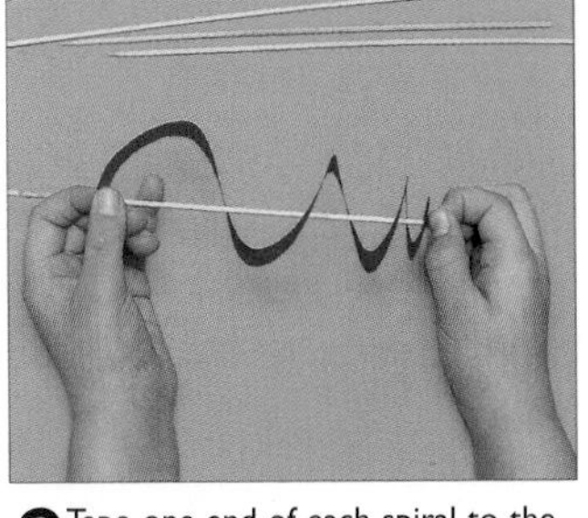

8 Tape one end of each spiral to the end of a skewer. Wind the other end of the spiral around the skewer stick a few times. Tape it close to the opposite end of the skewer.

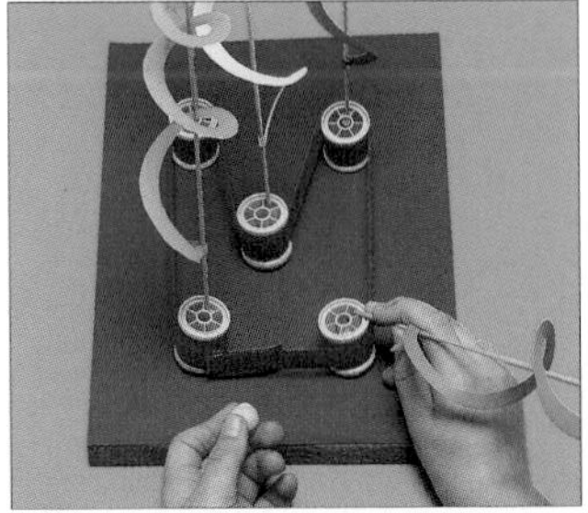

9 Put a small amount of tape on to the end of each wooden skewer. Then place each skewer into one of the empty holes in the top of each reel of thread.

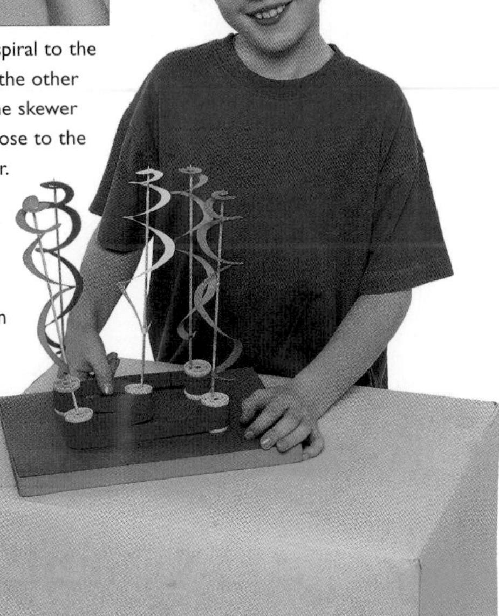

Now you are ready to turn the belt. Like a fan belt in a car, it turns the fans around. This is a five-fan machine. You can add more fans if you like.

Prototype car

When you make your model car, choose the paint carefully. Do you want bright tones that will be noticed, or cool, fashionable shades? Car manufacturers call in teams of people to help them decide what a car should look like. Stylists and design and production engineers join forces with the sales team to develop cars they hope people will buy. They think about the paint, how much people are prepared to pay, and what features they want, from air-conditioning to special car seats.

Before a new car is launched to the public, detailed models are made and tested to investigate the car's aerodynamics (how air flows over its shape). Finally, a prototype (early version) of the car is built and tested for road handling, engine quality and comfort.

YOU WILL NEED

Model car: Two sheets of cardboard, pair of compasses, ruler, pencil, scissors, white glue, glue brush, bradawl, 15cm/6in square of thin coloured card, pliers, four paper clips, two 10cm/4in lengths of 12mm/⅝in-diameter wood dowel, tape.

Decorate your car: Two shades of acrylic paint, medium paintbrushes, pencil, two pieces of card, a piece of thin white card, two shades of felt-tipped pens, scissors, white glue.

Wire basket ▸
Car designers today make use of CAD (computer-aided design) software to help them create a three-dimensional image of a new car design. Wire-frame (see-through) computer images show the car from any angle. They also show how all the parts of the car fit together.

Model car

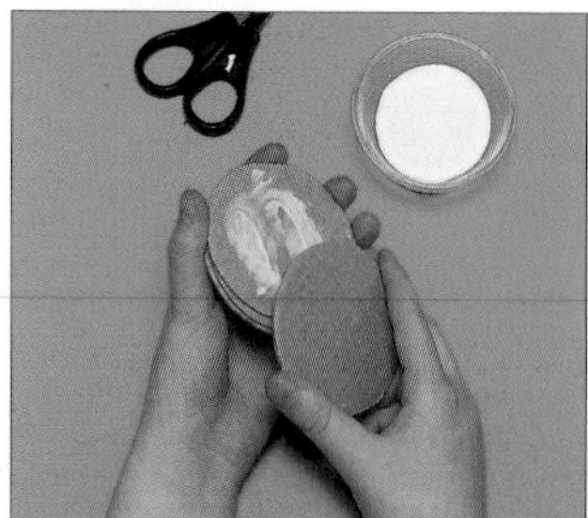

1 Draw and cut out four 2.5cm/1in and eight 6cm/2½in diameter cardboard circles. Glue the 6cm/2½in circles to make four wheels. Glue a 2.5cm/1in circle to the middle of each wheel.

2 Use the bradawl to make a hole in the middle of each wheel. Cut four 4mm/⅛in strips of coloured card. Wrap one each around the wheel rims. Glue the overlapping ends.

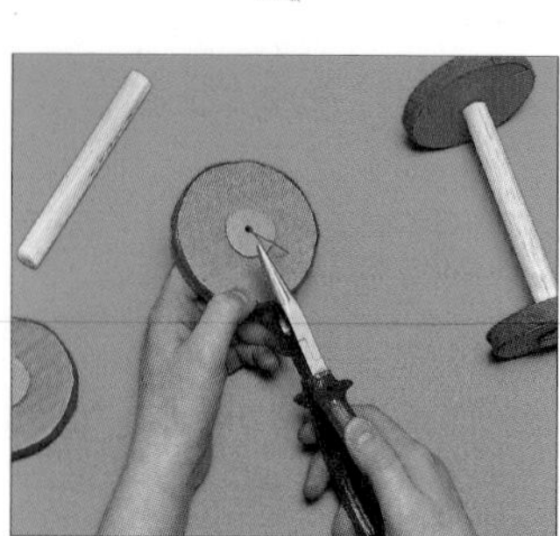

3 Push straightened paper clips into the holes and bend the outer ends with pliers. Fix the wheels to the two pieces of dowel by pushing the paper clips into the ends.

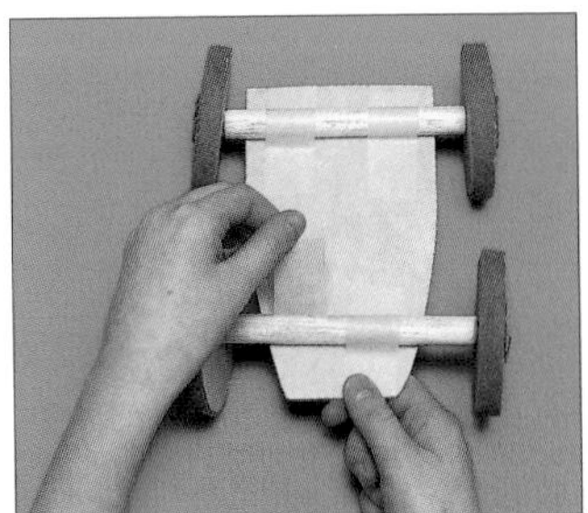

4 Cut a piece of 8 x 15cm/2¾ x 6in cardboard. Trim one end to make it 6cm/2½in wide. Tape the axles to the card, one at each end. Make sure they are long enough for the wheels to rotate freely.

5 Cut a piece of cardboard 8 x 35cm/3¼ x 14in. Double it over and bend it into a British cab shape. Tape the two loose ends together. Stick the base of the cab shape to the car base.

6 Cut two cardboard shapes 15cm/6in long and 10cm/4in high. Trim them with the scissors to the same shape as the side of your car cab. Attach the sides to the cab with tape.

Decorate your car

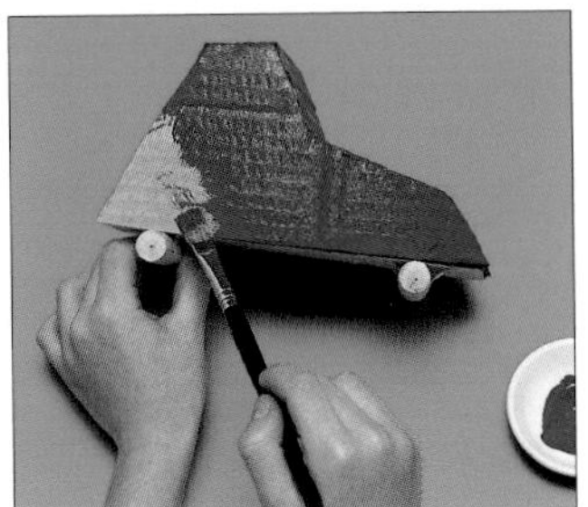

1 Remove the wheels from your car. Paint the sides and top of the cab with one of the two shades of paint. Leave it to dry. Then paint it with the same shade again, and leave it to dry.

2 Draw exciting designs for the sides of the car and a driver to go behind the windscreen. Draw some head lamps and some exhaust fumes. Add patterns with the felt-tipped pens.

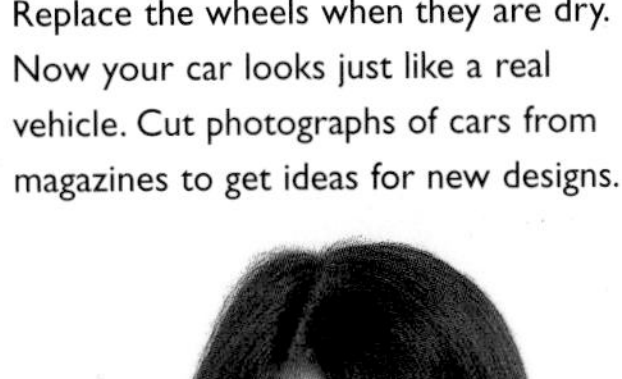

Replace the wheels when they are dry. Now your car looks just like a real vehicle. Cut photographs of cars from magazines to get ideas for new designs.

3 Let the paint dry for a couple of hours. Cut the designs out of the card. Glue them to the sides and back of the car. Paint the wheels with the shade of paint you haven't used.

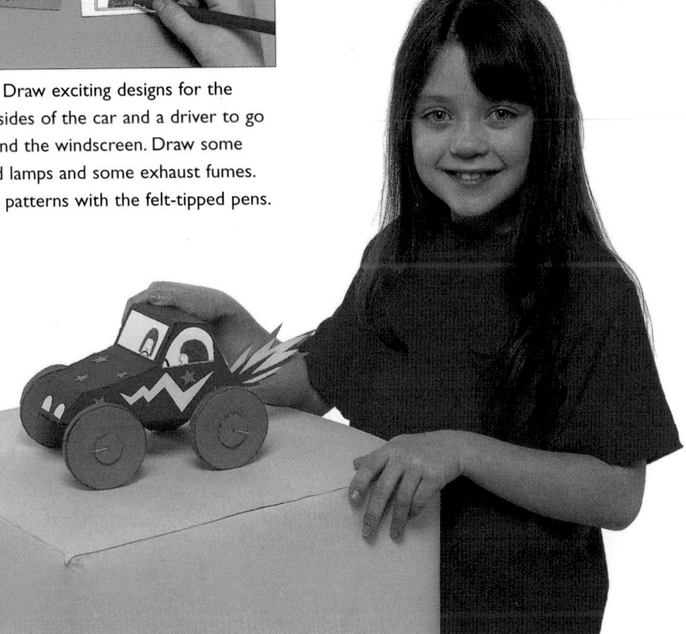

Parachutes and balloons

Parachutes fall slowly because air is trapped beneath them. They are deliberately designed to have very high drag. Drag is the force that works against the direction of anything that flies through the air. The amount of drag depends on the shape. A fat, lumpy shape, such as the parachute in the first project, has lots of drag and falls slowly.

Hot air balloons rise into the air, because the hot air inside them is lighter than the air outside. Real balloons use gas burners, but the project here uses a hair dryer to make the balloon rise.

YOU WILL NEED

Felt-tipped pen, a large plate, thin fabric, scissors, needle, thread, adhesive tape, plastic thread reel.

Mini-parachute jump

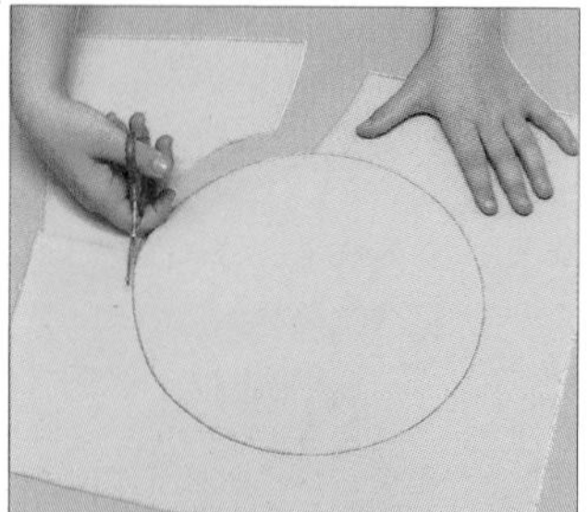

1 Use the felt-tipped pen to draw around the plate on the fabric. Using the scissors, carefully cut out the circle to make what will be the parachute's canopy.

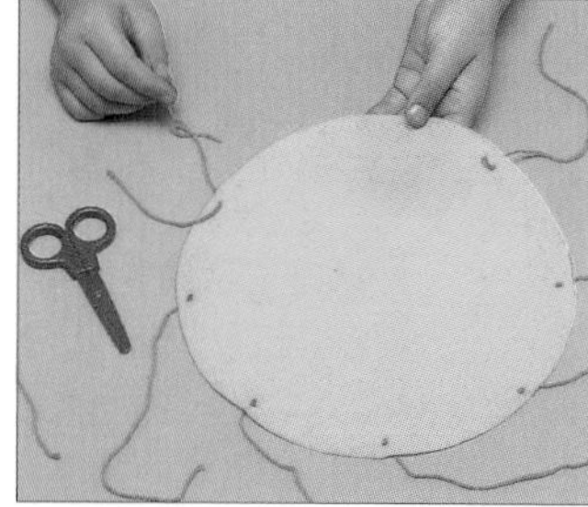

2 Make about eight equally spaced marks around the edge of the circle. Use a needle to sew on one 30cm/12in long piece of thread to each point you have marked.

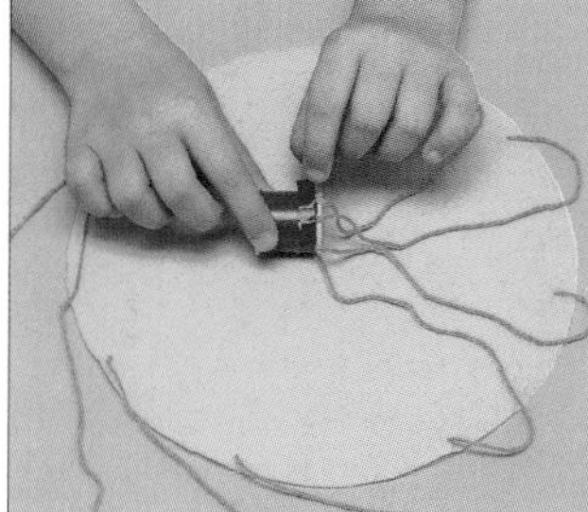

3 Use tape to secure the free end of each thread to a reel. Use a plastic reel, because a wooden one will be too heavy for your parachute.

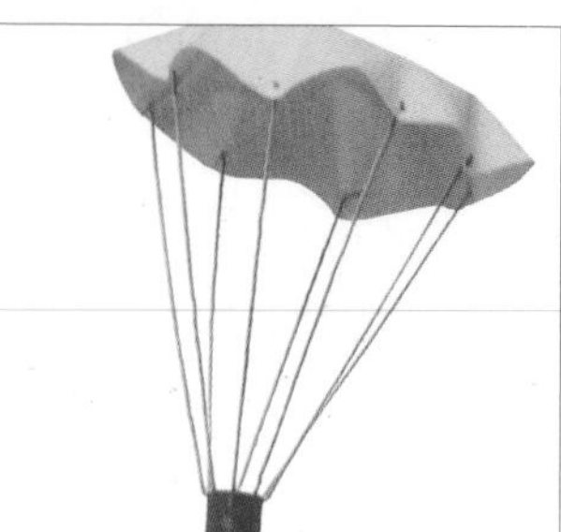

4 Hold the parachute so that the canopy is open and the thread reel dangles down. Stand by an upstairs window, or use a step-ladder to get as high as you can – but be very careful!

Let your parachute go from as high up as possible. As it falls, the canopy will open and fill with air. The larger the canopy, the slower the parachute will fall.

Ballooning around

YOU WILL NEED
Pencil, cardboard, ruler, scissors, sheets of tissue paper, glue stick, hair dryer.

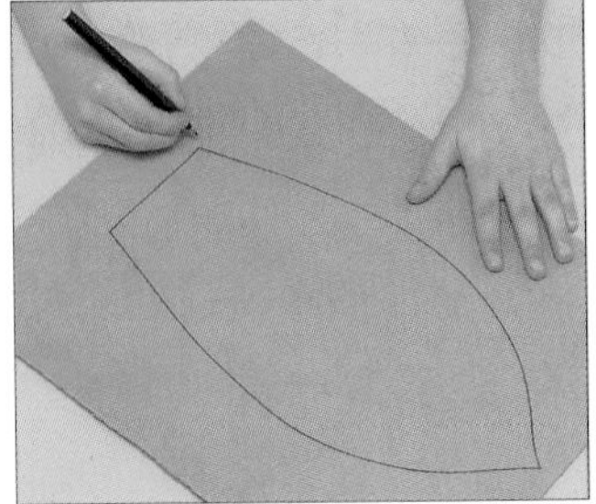

1 To make a template, draw a petal shape on cardboard and carefully cut it out. The shape should be 30cm/12in long and 12cm/4½in across with a flat bottom edge.

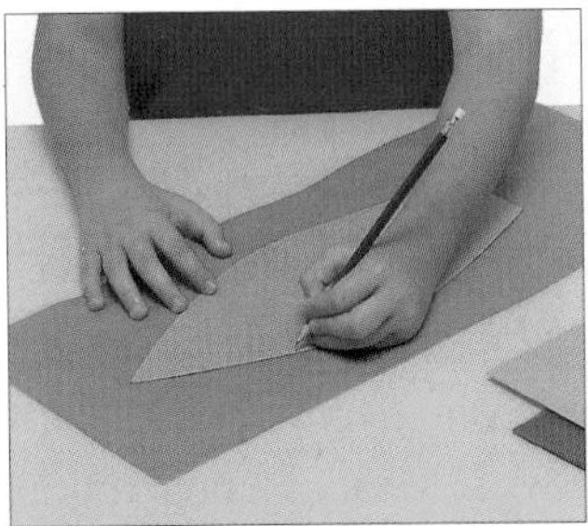

2 Draw around your template on seven pieces of coloured tissue paper. Be very careful not to rip the tissue paper with the tip of your pencil.

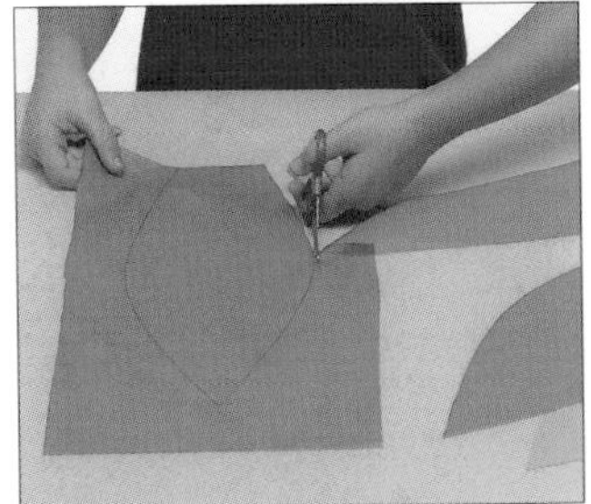

3 Use the pair of scissors to carefully cut out the shapes you have drawn. You should now have seven petals that are all the same size and shape.

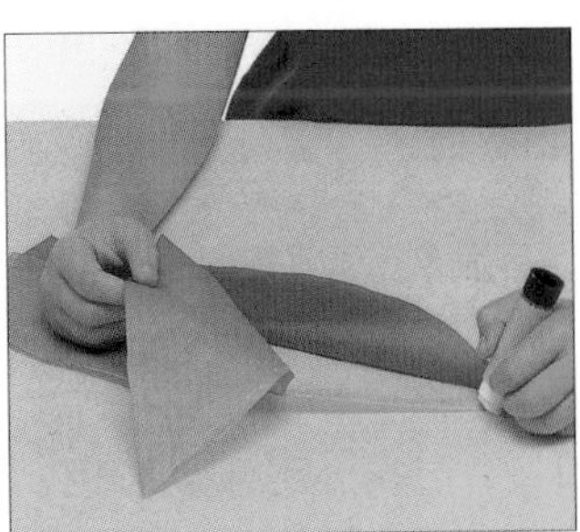

4 Glue along one edge of a petal. Lay another petal on top, and press it down. Open it out and stick on another petal in the same way. Keep going until the balloon is complete.

To fly your balloon, hold its neck open and fill the inside with hot air from a hair dryer. After ten seconds, switch off the hair dryer and let go of your balloon to launch it into the air.

Streamlined design

Think of a sleek canoe moving through the water. Its streamlined shape hardly makes any ripples as it passes. Streamlined shapes also move easily through the air. They have low drag (air resistance). Angular shapes have more drag than rounded ones. The shape of a fast-moving fish has to be very streamlined. A fish such as a tuna has a blunt front end, is broadest about a third of the way along, then tapers towards the tail. This creates less drag as it moves through water than a shape with a pointed front end that broadens at the back. Water flows along each side of the tuna to rejoin without creating turbulence. The 'Shape race' gives you a chance to design and test your own streamlined shapes.

Just as things that are moving in the air experience drag, so do stationary objects in the wind. Kites, such as the one here, are held up in the air by drag from the wind. For more than 3,000 years, people have been making and flying kites. The essential, but simple, secret is that it must be as light as possible for its size, so that it catches as much wind as possible. The kite design shown in this project has been used for many hundreds of years. Try flying it first of all in a steady wind, and experiment with the position of the bridle and the length of the tail.

YOU WILL NEED

Pen, ruler, two bamboo canes (one about two-thirds as long as the other), string, scissors, adhesive tape, sheet of thin fabric or plastic, fabric glue, coloured paper.

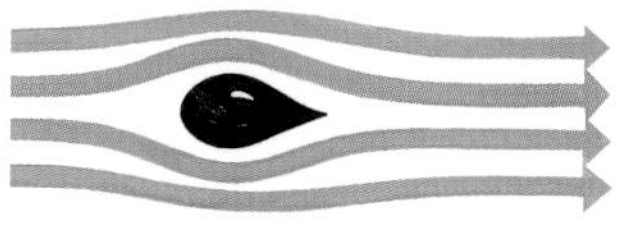

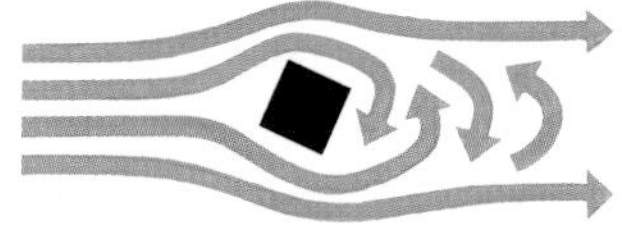

▲ How air flows work
Air flows in gentle curves around the streamlined shape (*top*). Angles and sharp curves break up the flow and increase drag (*bottom*).

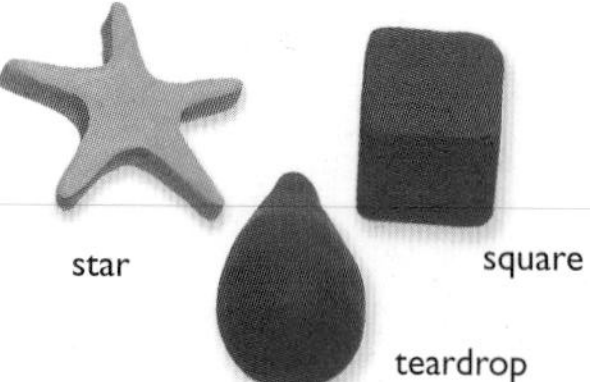

▲ Shape race
Make different shapes (as shown above) from balls of modelling material that are exactly the same size. Race your shapes in water – the most streamlined shape should reach the bottom first.

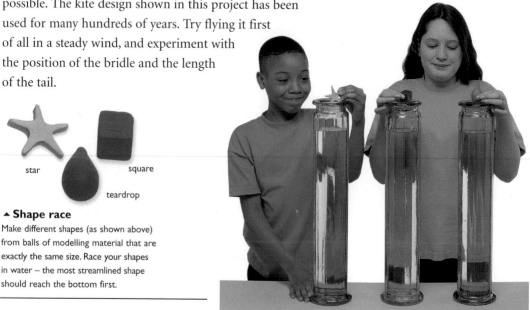

Make a kite

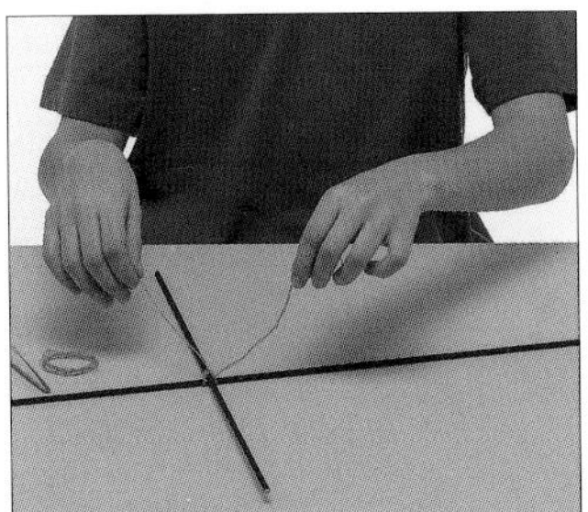

1 To make the frame, mark the middle of the short cane and mark one-third of the way up the long cane. Tie the canes together crosswise at the marks with string.

2 Tape string around the ends of the canes and secure it at the top. This will stop the canes from moving, and it will also support the edges of your finished kite.

3 Lay the frame on top of the sheet of fabric or plastic. Cut around it, 2cm/¾in away from the kite's edge. This will give you enough to fold over the string outline.

4 Fold each edge of the material over the frame, and stick the edges down firmly with fabric glue (or adhesive tape if you are making the kite from plastic). Let the glue dry.

5 Tie a piece of string to the long cane, as shown – this is called the bridle. Tie the end of the ball of string to the middle of the bridle to make the tether.

6 Fold sheets of paper in zigzags. Tie them at about 25cm/10in intervals along a piece of string that is about twice as long as the kite. Glue or tie the tail to the bottom tip of the kite.

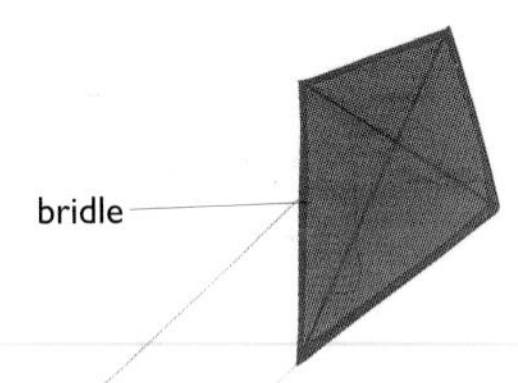

Now your kite is ready to fly! With the wind blowing on your back, reel out about 10m/10yd of tether. Ask an adult to gently launch the kite into the air. If it is not very windy, run into the breeze, pulling the kite to get it airborne. Now that you have built this kite, try experimenting with other materials and shapes, to find out which ones work well.

Curve and lift

Birds, gliders and airplanes all have wings. Their wings can be all sorts of different shapes and sizes, but they all have the same aerofoil (airfoil) design. This means that the top side of the wing is more curved than the underside. The aerofoil shape provides lift when air moves over it. Air flows faster over the curved upper surface than over the flatter lower surface. This reduces the air pressure above the wing, and lets the higher air pressure underneath lift it up.

You can make and test a model aerofoil by following the instructions in these projects. In the frisbee project, the shape of the frisbee allows the air to move smoothly over and under it. The frisbee spins as it flies. The spinning motion helps to steady it. The second project shows you how moving air, in this case, from an electric fan or hair dryer, can lift the wings with an aerofoil shape upwards.

YOU WILL NEED

Fly a frisbee: Large plate, cardboard, pencil, scissors, ruler, adhesive tape.

Aerofoil antics: Paper, pencil, ruler, scissors, adhesive tape, glue stick, plastic drinking straw, thick thread, fan or hair dryer.

Fly a frisbee

1 Place the plate face down on the cardboard, and draw around it with a pencil. Cut out the circle of cardboard. Draw slots 1.5cm/¾ in deep around the edge and cut these, as shown.

2 The cut slots around the edge will make tabs. Bend the tabs down slightly. Overlap them a little and stick them together with small pieces of adhesive tape.

Fly your frisbee outside, away from people. Hold it at the front and spin it away from you and up. It should glide through the air smoothly as the air pressure above it is reduced. Play toss-and-catch games with your friends. You could even have your own championship match! Commercial frisbees were introduced into the USA in the 1950s.

Aerofoil (airfoil) antics

1 Use a ruler to measure a rectangle of paper about 15cm/6in wide and 20cm/8in long. Use scissors to carefully cut out the shape. This will be your wing.

2 Fold the paper over, approximately in half. Use tape to fix the top edge 1cm/½in away from the bottom edge. Take care not to crease the paper as you do this.

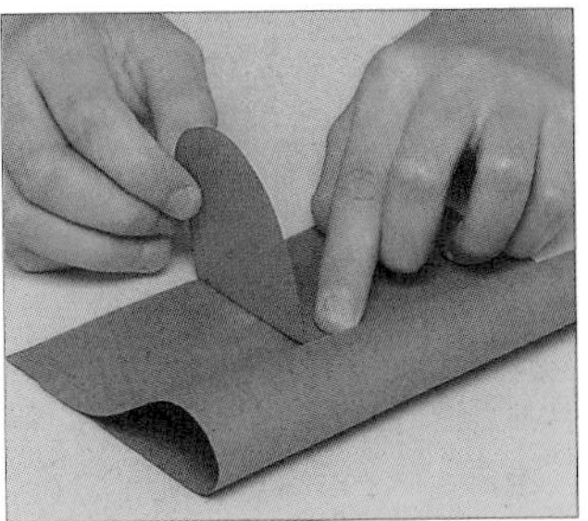

3 Cut out and stick on a small paper fin near the rear edge of your wing, as shown above. This will keep the wing facing into the airflow when you test it.

4 With a sharp pencil, carefully poke a hole through the top and bottom of your wing, near the front edge. Push a straw through the holes and glue it in place in the middle.

5 Cut a 1m/1yd-long piece of thick thread and thread it through the straw. Make sure that the thread can slide easily through the straw and does not catch.

Hold the thread tight, and ask a friend to blow air from a fan or hair dryer over the wing. Watch it take off! This happens because the shape decreases the air pressure above the wing.

Jet propulsion

A jet engine produces thrust from a roaring jet of super-hot gas. Its construction looks complicated, but the way it works is very simple. A powerful jet of gas moving in one direction produces thrust in the other direction. Imagine you are standing on a skateboard and squirting a powerful hose forwards. Jet propulsion will push you backwards. This reaction has been known for nearly 2,000 years, but it was not until the 1930s that it was applied to an engine.

In the first experiment, you can make a jet zoom along a string. The jet engine is like a balloon that produces thrust from escaping air. The second project demonstrates how a turbine works. Hot air produced by the gas jet turns the blades of the turbine. The turbine drives the fan at the front of the jet engine. These projects may seem simple, but they use the same scientific principles that propel all jet airplanes through the air.

YOU WILL NEED

Balloon jet: Long, thin balloon, scissors, adhesive tape, drinking straw, string.

Turbine lights: Foil pie pan, scissors, pair of compasses, protractor, ruler, pin, 7.5cm/3in length of 3mm/⅛in dowel, adhesive tape, bead, thread reel, non-hardening modelling material, plate, four night light candles, matches.

Balloon jet

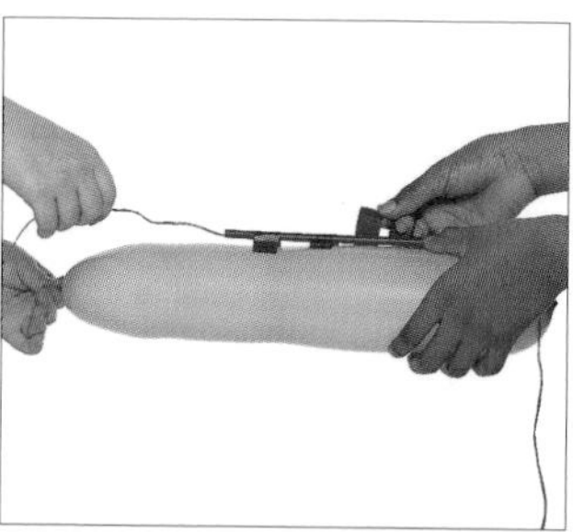

1 Blow up the balloon and, while a friend holds the neck, tape the straw to its top. Thread the string through the straw and, holding it level, tie it to something to keep it in place.

▲ **Practical plane**
This passenger plane has four engines, two on each wing. Jet engines have revolutionized international travel. These planes carry millions of passengers around the world every year.

2 Let go of the neck of the balloon. A stream of air jets backwards and produces thrust. This propels the balloon forwards along the string at high speed.

Turbine lights

1 Using scissors, cut out the bottom of a large foil pie pan as evenly as possible. Make a small hole in the middle of the pan with the point of the compass.

2 Mark a smaller circle in the middle. Use a protractor to mark 16 equal sections of 22.5 degrees, and cut along each one to the inner circle. Use one scissor to cut along each line, if possible.

3 Angle the blades by holding the inner tip and twisting the outer edges 20 to 30 degrees. The middle of the inner tip should be flat, in line with the middle of the disc.

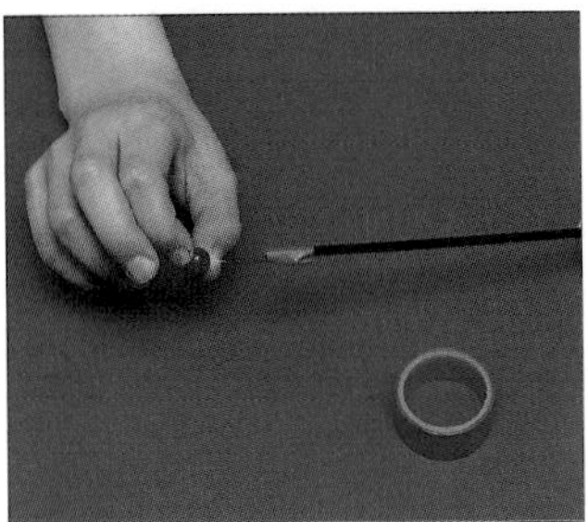

4 Tape the blunt end of the pin to one end of the dowel. Finish it off neatly and trim if necessary. Place the bead on the pin. This will allow the finished turbine to spin freely.

◂ Jet engine

The huge blades at the front of a jet engine suck in air and compress it. Fuel burns in the air to produce jets of hot air that blast from the rear of the engine, producing thrust.

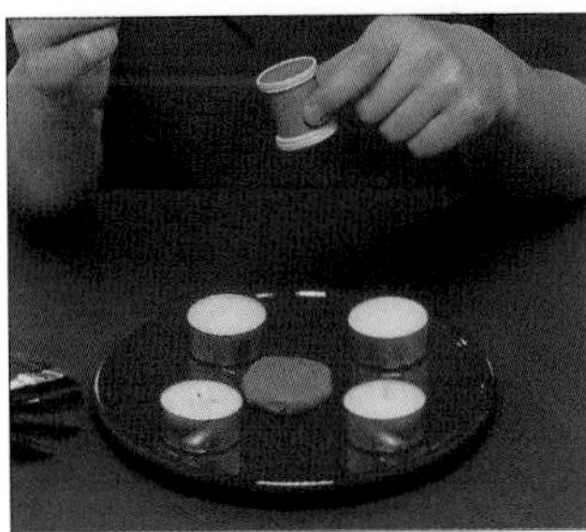

5 Put the dowel in the reel and press the reel into the modelling material in the middle of the plate. Place the candles on the plate around the reel.

Place the hole in the middle of the turbine over the pin. Ask an adult to light the candles. Hot air will spin the blades.

Propeller flight

Propellers work in two different ways. When a propeller spins, it makes air move past it. Propeller-driven aircraft use this effect to produce thrust. Moving air also causes the propeller to spin. The projects here look at propellers working in these two ways. In the first one, you can make a simple paper propeller called a spinner. As the spinner falls, moving air rushes past the blades, making it revolve. This acts just like the fruits and seeds of maple and sycamore trees, which have twin propeller blades. As they drop from the tree, they spin and catch the wind, and are carried far away.

In the second project, you can make a spinning propeller fly upwards through the air. The propeller-like blades are set at an angle, like the blades of a fan. They whirl around and make air move. The moving air produces thrust and lifts the propeller upwards. Children first flew propellers like these 600 years ago in China.

▲ **Lift off**
An aerofoil's (airfoil's) curved shape causes the air to flow faster over its upper surface than its lower surface. This reduces pressure from above and causes lift.

In a spin

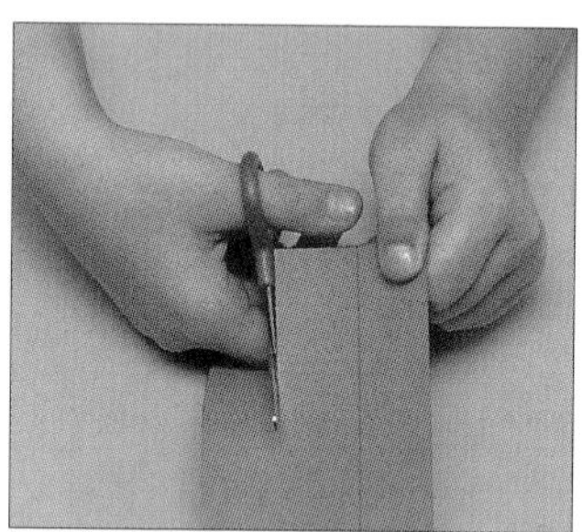

1 Take a piece of paper, 15 x 9cm/ 6 x 3¾in, and draw a T-shape on it, as shown in the picture above. With a pair of scissors, cut along the two long lines of the T.

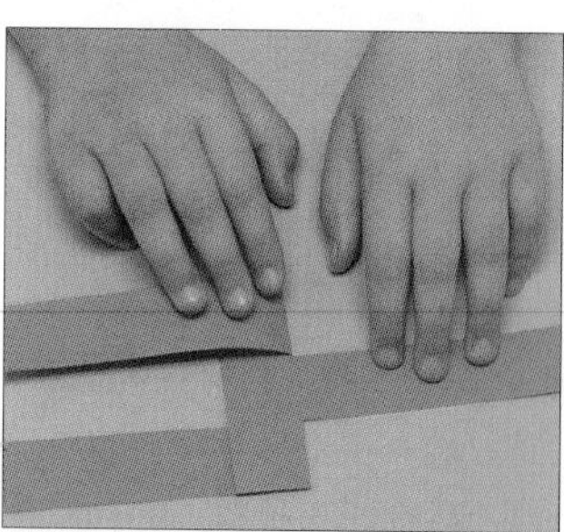

2 Fold one side strip forwards and one backwards, as shown above, making two blades and a stalk. Attach a paper clip to the bottom. Open the blades flat.

3 Drop the spinner and watch what happens. Before dropping it again, try giving each blade a twist to make your spinner spin around even faster.

Let's twist

YOU WILL NEED

In a spin: Paper, ruler, pencil, scissors, paper clip.

Let's twist: Thin card, ruler, pair of compasses, protractor, pen, scissors, 1cm/½in slice of cork, bradawl, 7.5cm/3in length of 3mm/⅛in-diameter dowel, model glue, string, thread reel.

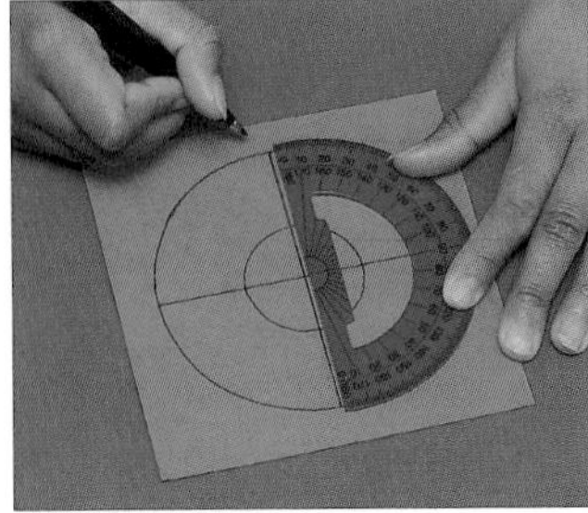

1 With the compasses, draw a circle 10cm/4in across on the card. Draw a circle 4cm/1½in across in the middle. With the protractor, draw lines dividing the circle into 16 equal sections.

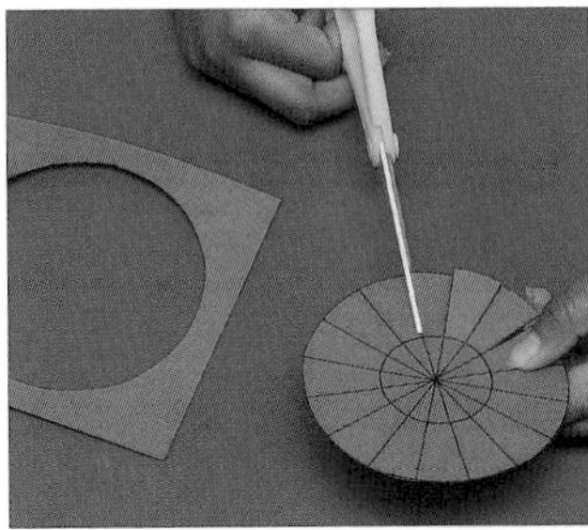

2 Carefully cut out the circle and along the lines to the smaller circle. Twist the blades sideways a little. Try to give each blade the same amount of twist, about 20 or 30 degrees.

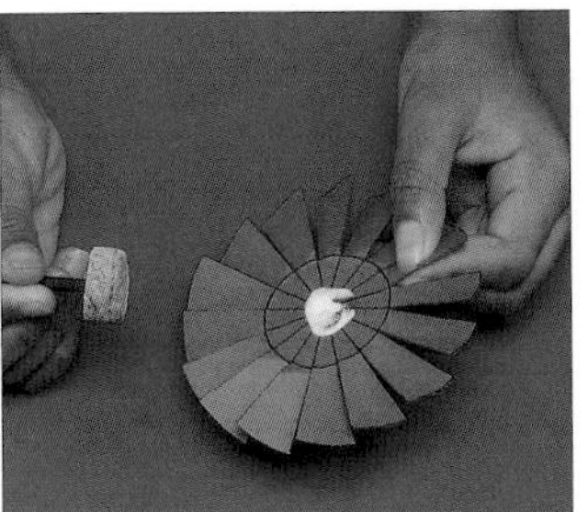

3 Make a hole in the middle of the cork slice with a bradawl. Put glue on the end of the dowel, and push it into the hole. Glue the cork to the middle of the propeller.

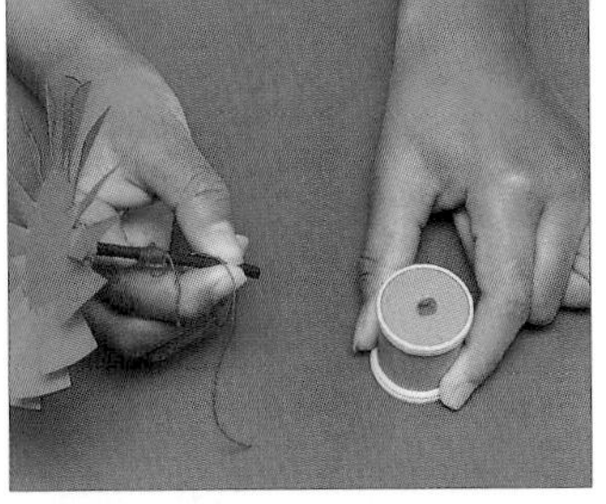

4 When the glue has dried, wind a long piece of string around the dowel. Drop the dowel into the thread reel launcher. You are now ready for a test flight.

Pull steadily on the string to move the propeller around. As the end of the string comes off, the blades produce enough thrust to lift the spinning propeller out of the launcher and into the air.

Model planes

Although a model is much smaller than a real full-size aircraft, it flies in exactly the same way. The control surfaces on the wings and the tail of a model plane or real aircraft work by changing the way in which air flows over the aircraft. This allows the pilot to steer the aircraft in different directions. Working together, the rudder and movable flaps called ailerons on the rear edge of each wing make the plane turn to the left or right. Moving flaps called elevators on the tail make the nose of the plane go up or down.

The scientific rules of flying are the same for any aircraft, from an airliner weighing 350 tons to this model made from paper, adhesive tape and a drinking straw. Making this model plane allows you to see how control surfaces, such as the aileron, rudder and elevators, work. The flight of any plane is very sensitive to the angle of the controls. They need to be only a slight angle from their flat position to make the plane turn. Too big an angle will make the model unstable.

ailerons

roll

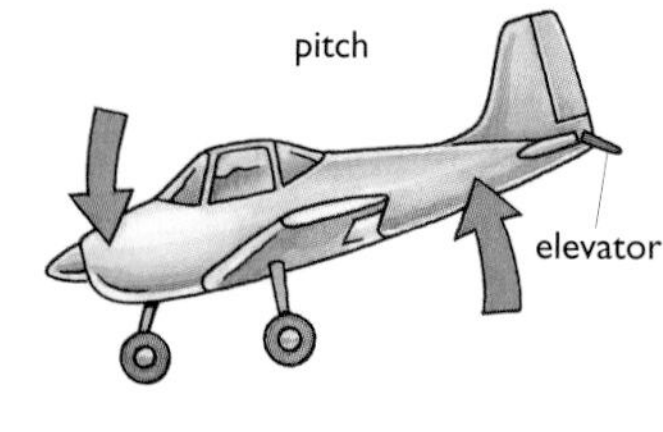

rudder

yaw

▲ How to fly a plane
To turn the aircraft (yaw), the pilot turns the rudder to one side. To make the aircraft descend or climb (pitch), the pilot adjusts the elevators on the tailplane. To roll (tilt or bank) the aircraft to the left or right, the ailerons are raised on one wing and lowered on the other.

Glide along

YOU WILL NEED

Pencil, set square, ruler, paper, scissors, glue stick, adhesive tape, drinking straw, paper clips or non-hardening modelling material.

1 Draw two rectangles, 22 x 10cm/8¾ x 4in and 20 x 3.5cm/8 x 1¼in. Mark ailerons 6 x 1cm/2½ x ½in on two corners of the larger one. Cut out two elevators 3.5 x 1cm/1½ x ½in on the other.

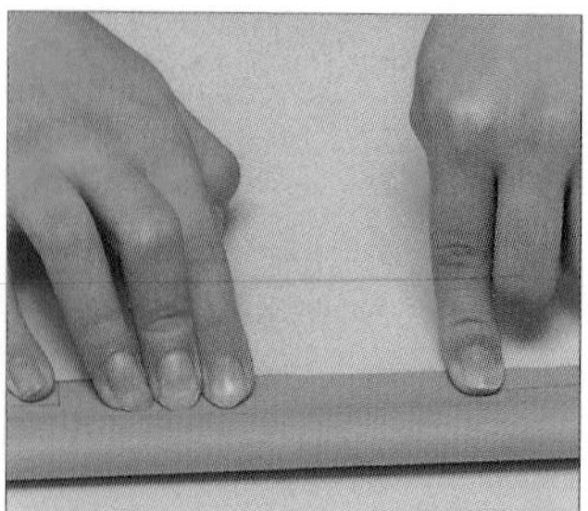

2 To make the wings, wrap the larger rectangle over a pencil and glue along the edges. Remove the pencil and make cuts along the 1cm/½in lines to allow the ailerons to move.

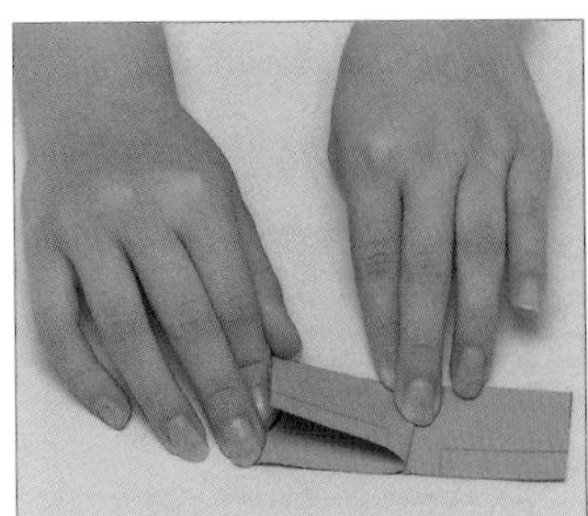

3 To make the tail, fold the smaller rectangle in half twice to form a W. Glue its middle to make the fin. Cut along the two 1cm/½in lines. Make a 1cm/½in cut on the fin to make a rudder.

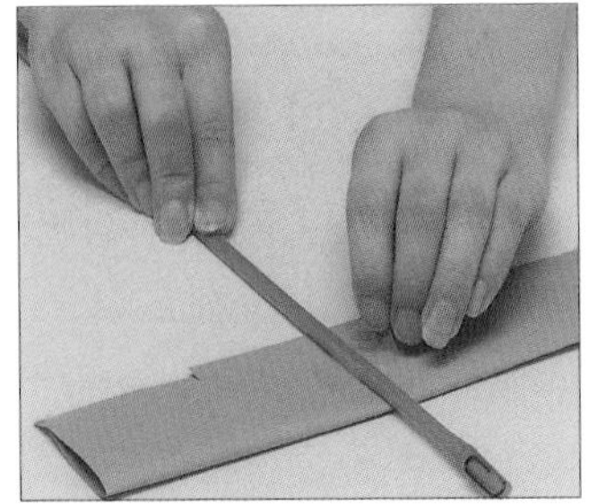

4 Use adhesive tape to fix the wings and tail to the drinking straw (the plane's fuselage, or body). Position the wings about one quarter of the way along the straw.

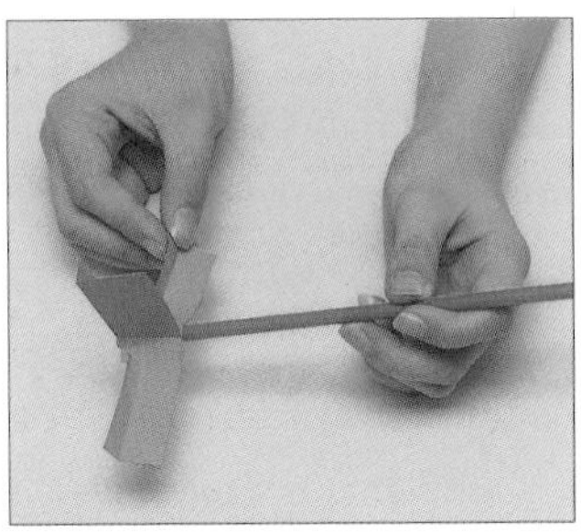

5 Try adjusting the control surfaces. Bend the elevators on the tail slightly up. This will make the plane climb as it flies. Bend the elevators down to make it dive.

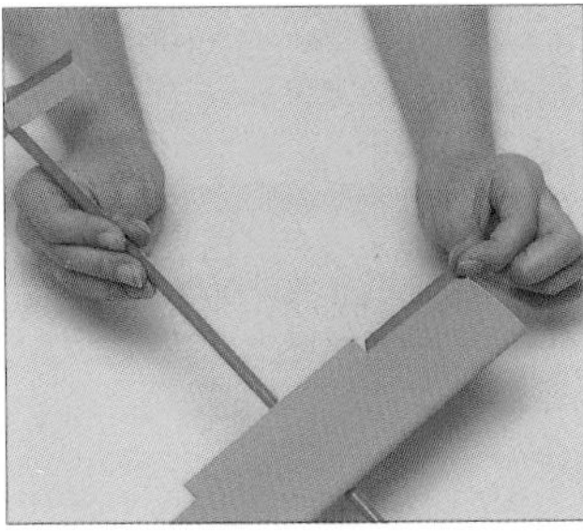

6 Bend the left-hand aileron up and the right-hand aileron down the same amount. Bend the rudder to the left. This will make the plane turn to the left as it flies.

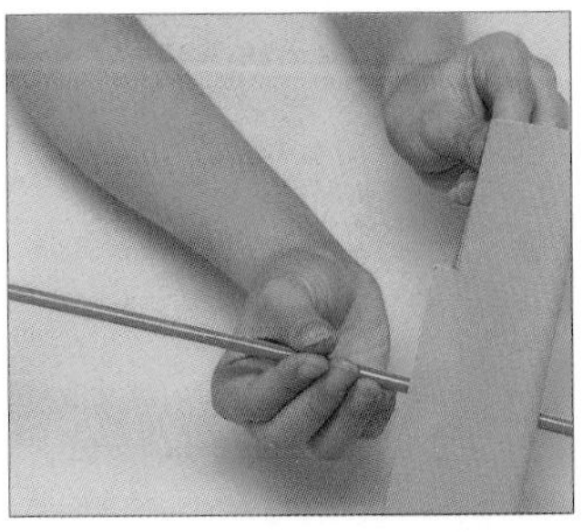

7 Bend the right-hand aileron up and the left-hand aileron down. Bend the rudder to the right slightly and the plane will turn to the right. Can you make it fly in a circle?

Launch your plane by throwing it steadily straight ahead. To make it fly even farther, use paper clips or modelling material to weight the nose.

Escaping from Earth

The function of a space rocket is to carry a satellite or astronauts into Space. To do this, it has to overcome gravity (the force that pulls everything down to Earth). If a rocket's engines are not powerful enough, gravity will win and pull the rocket back to Earth. With more powerful engines, the rocket's attempt to fly into Space is exactly equalled by the pull of gravity. With these two forces in perfect balance, a spacecraft will continue to circle the Earth. If the rocket is even more powerful, it can fly fast enough to escape from Earth's gravity altogether and head toward the Moon and the planets. The speed that it needs to reach to do this is called escape velocity. You can see this in action by trying an experiment using a magnet and ball-bearings. You can also try launching your own cork model rocket from a plastic bottle.

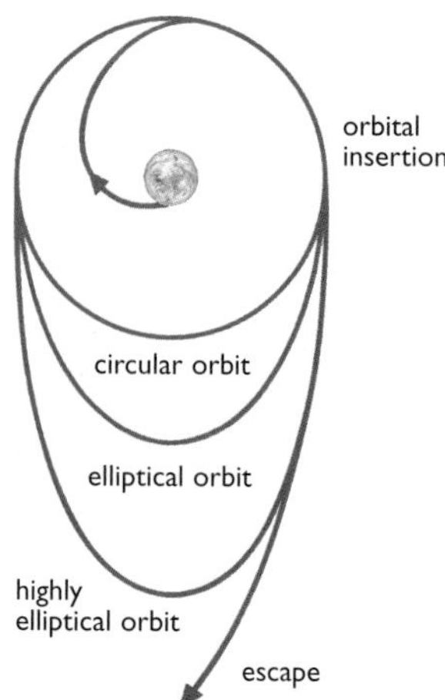

▲ Escape velocity
To go into orbit around the Earth, a spacecraft must reach a velocity of at least 28,500km/h/17,500mph. Depending on how fast it is travelling, the spacecraft may go into a circular, elliptical, or highly elliptical orbit. If it reaches a velocity of 40,200km/h/25,000mph, the spacecraft escapes from the Earth's gravity.

Launch a rocket

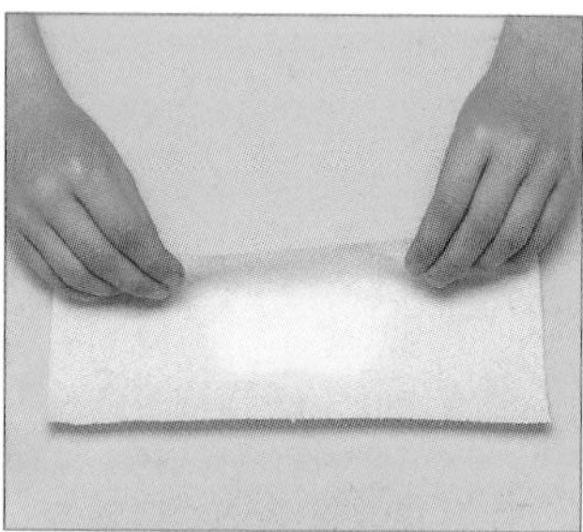

1 Place a teaspoon of bicarbonate of soda directly in the middle of a 10 x 20cm/4 x 8in piece of kitchen paper. Roll up the paper and twist the ends to keep the soda fuel inside.

2 Pour half a cup of water and the same of vinegar into the bottle. Fix paper streamers or a ribbon to the the cork with a pin. Drop the kitchen paper inside the bottle.

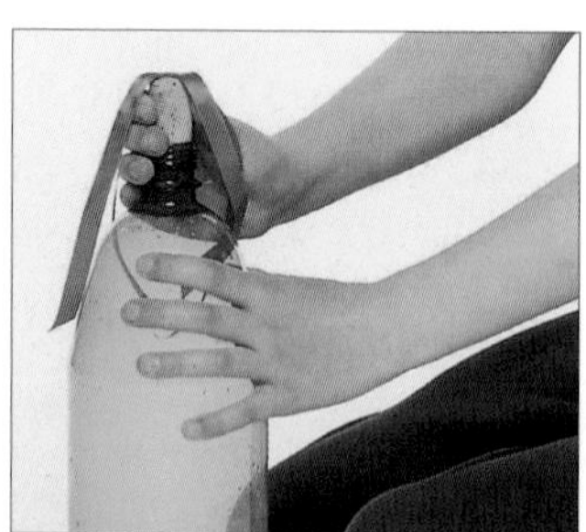

3 Push the cork in immediately so that it is a snug fit, but not too tight. Quickly take the bottle outside. Then move at least 3m/3yd away from it and watch what happens.

A chemical reaction between the vinegar (representing liquid oxygen) and bicarbonate of soda (baking soda) (representing fuel) produces carbon dioxide gas. The gas pressure inside the bottle pushes against the cork. The cork is blasted into the air like a rocket lifting off. However, in a real rocket, the gas is jetted out of the actual spacecraft, propelling it forwards.

YOU WILL NEED

Launch a rocket: Bicarbonate of soda (baking soda), kitchen paper, water, vinegar, 2-litre/½ gallon plastic bottle, paper streamers or ribbon, cork, pin.

Escaping from gravity: Thin card, ruler, pencil, scissors, magnetic strip, white glue, glue brush, 10 x 5cm/ 4 x 2in piece of plastic, baking tray, non-hardening modelling material, adhesive tape, ball-bearings.

Escaping from gravity

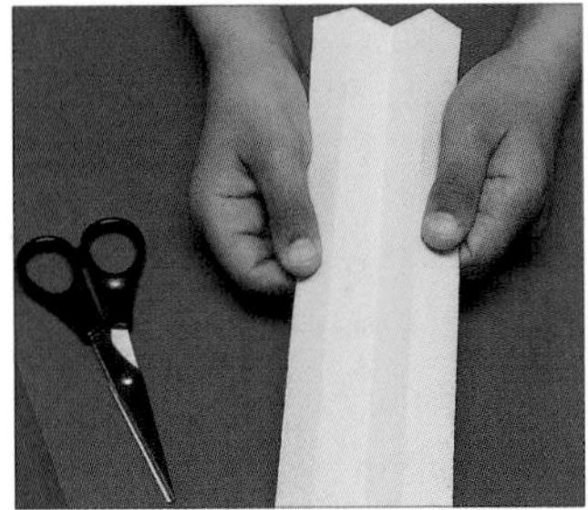

1 Measure out a 30 x 10cm/12 x 4in strip of thin card using a ruler. Cut it out with the scissors. Fold it lengthwise into four sections to form an M-shaped trough.

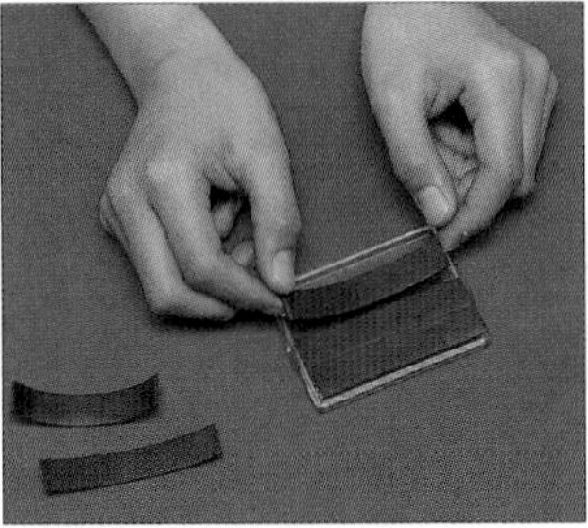

2 Cut the magnetic strip into five short pieces. Glue these short strips to the plastic base, so that they form a large, square bar magnet, as shown above.

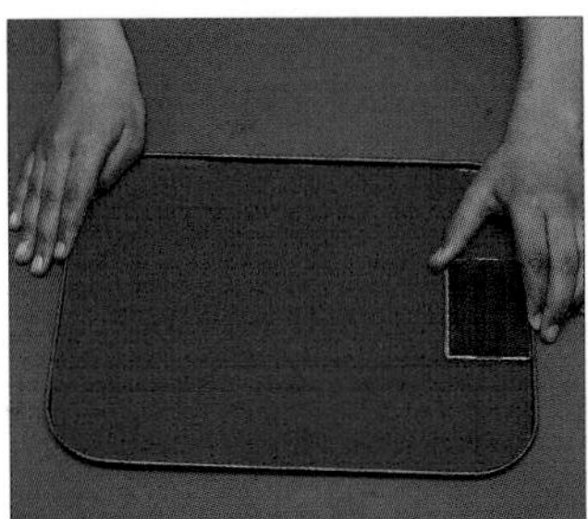

3 Fix the magnet firmly to one end of the tray with some of the modelling material. Position it roughly in the middle. The magnet simulates the pull of the Earth's gravity.

4 Position one end of the trough over the edge of the magnet. Attach it to the magnet with tape. The trough represents the path of a rocket as it ascends into orbit.

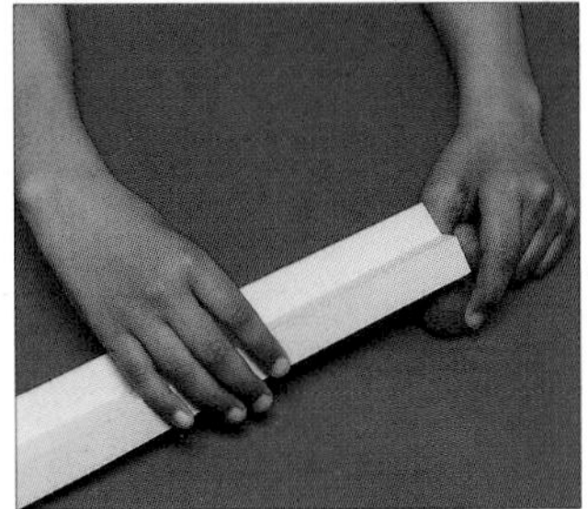

5 Roll the remaining modelling material into a round ball. Position the ball underneath the other end of the M-shaped trough. This raises the trough at a slight angle.

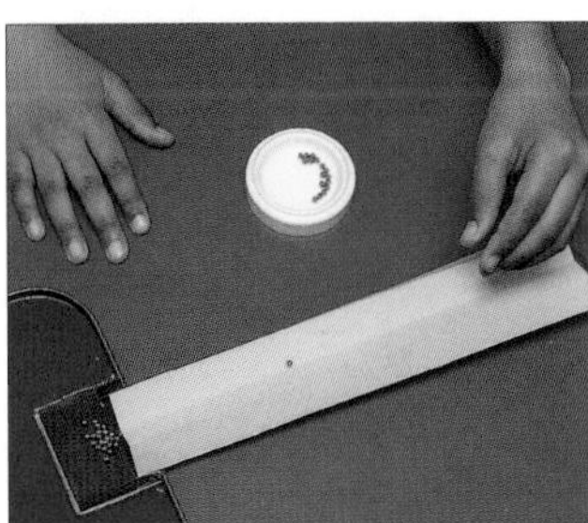

6 At the end of the trough, place a ball-bearing and let it roll down. It sticks to the magnet. The ball-bearing's velocity along the trough isn't fast enough to escape the magnet's pull.

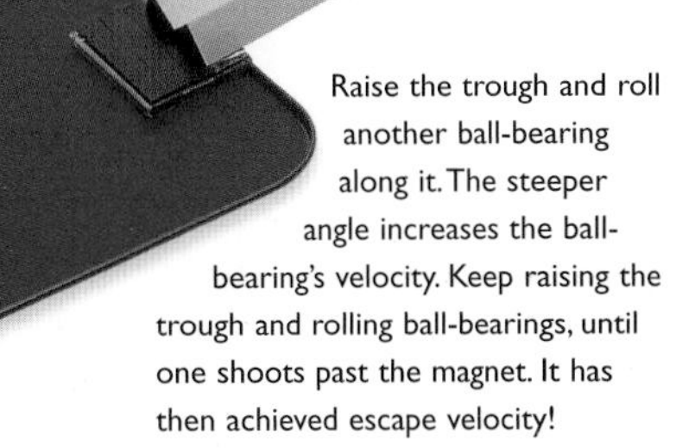

Raise the trough and roll another ball-bearing along it. The steeper angle increases the ball-bearing's velocity. Keep raising the trough and rolling ball-bearings, until one shoots past the magnet. It has then achieved escape velocity!

Rocket launch

Space rockets rely on jet propulsion to fly. When the rocket burns its fuel, a stream of hot gases roars out from the tail end and the rocket surges forwards. Jets flying lower than 25,000m/82,000ft can burn their fuel using oxygen from the air. Space rockets need to carry oxygen with them, because above 25,000m/82,000ft, the air thins and there is not enough oxygen.

Deep in the sea, octopuses also rely on jet propulsion to escape from their enemies. They squirt out a jet of water and shoot off in the opposite direction.

This experiment shows you how to make and fly a rocket that uses jet propulsion. The thrust of a rocket depends on the mass of propellant that it shoots out every second. Water is a much better propellant than hot gas, because it is so much heavier.

Follow these instructions carefully and your rocket could fly about 25m/80ft above the ground. You may need adult to help make some parts of this rocket and to launch it. When you are ready for a test flight, set your rocket up in an open space, well away from trees and buildings. This rocket is very powerful – you must not stand over it while it is being launched. Wear clothes that you do not mind getting very wet!

▲ Inside a rocket
This is a liquid-powered rocket. It carries liquid oxygen to burn its fuel (liquid hydrogen). The hydrogen and oxygen are pumped into the combustion chamber. The hydrogen burns furiously in the oxygen. The exhaust produces immense thrust.

Make a rocket

YOU WILL NEED
Thin white card, pen, ruler, thin coloured card, scissors, plastic bottle, strong adhesive tape, funnel, jug (pitcher) of water, cork, bradawl, air valve, plastic tube, bicycle pump.

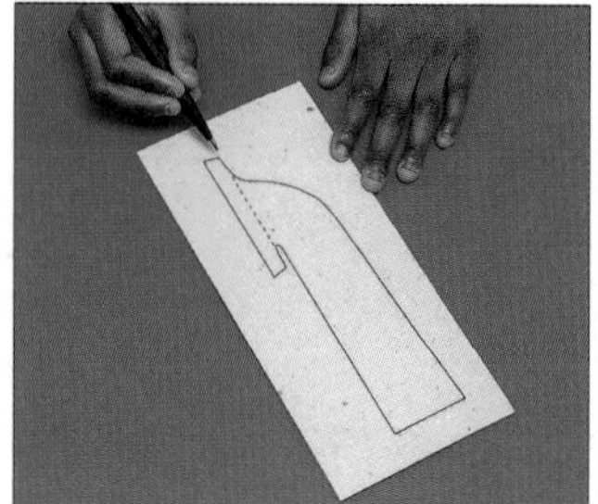

1 Rockets have fins to make them fly straight. Draw out this fin template (it is about 20cm/8in long) on plain card and use it to cut out four fins from coloured card.

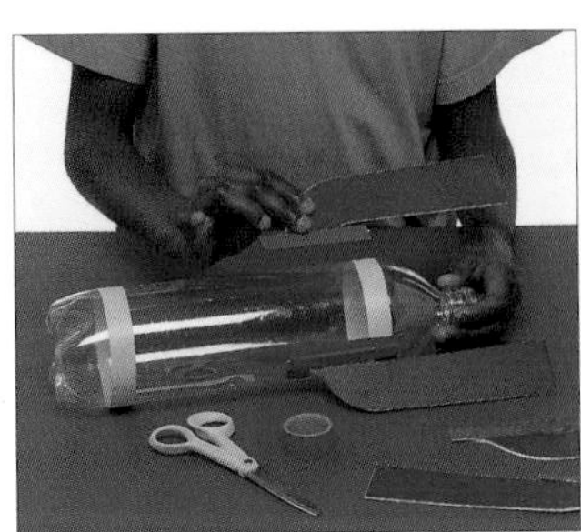

2 Decorate your bottle to look like a rocket. Fold the tab at the top of each fin. Use long pieces of strong tape to attach the fins to the bottle firmly.

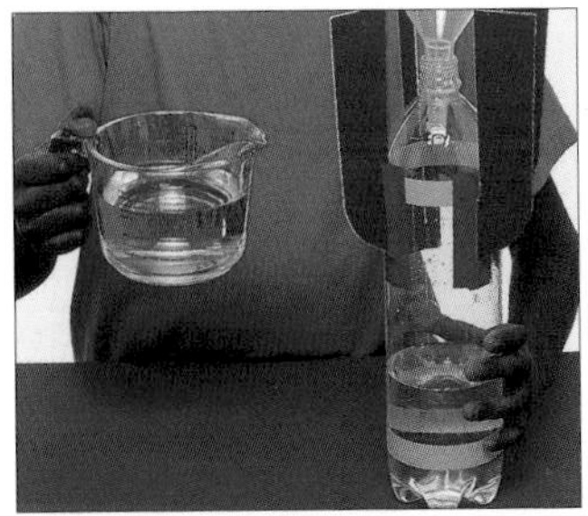

3 Use the jug and funnel to half-fill the bottle with water. (The water is the propellant. Compressed air above the water will provide the energy that makes the thrust.)

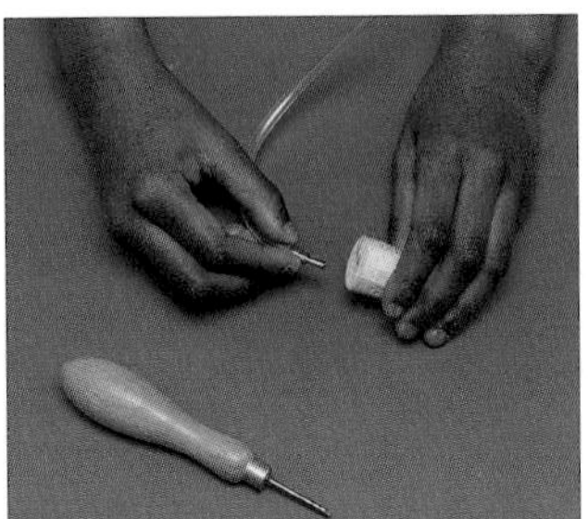

4 Use the bradawl to drill a hole carefully through the cork. Push the wide end of the air valve into the plastic tube. Push the valve through the hole in the cork.

5 Hold the bottle with one hand, and push the cork and the valve into the neck of the bottle using the other hand. Push it in firmly so that the cork does not slide out too easily.

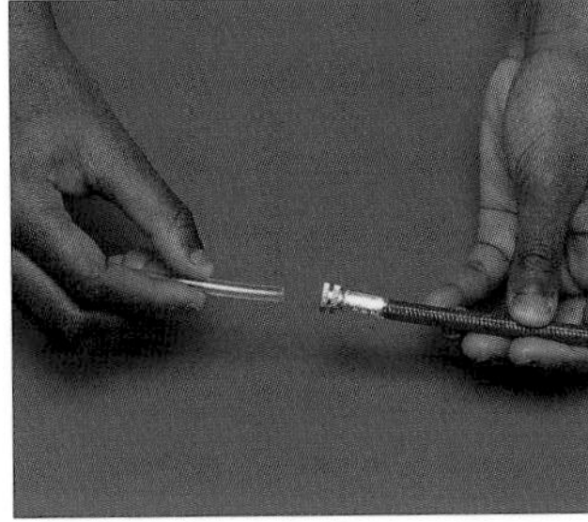

6 Attach the other end of the plastic tube to the bicycle pump. Turn your rocket the right way up – you are now ready to launch your rocket outside.

Look for a launch site far away from trees and buildings. Stand the rocket on its tail fins, and tell everyone to stand well back. Start pumping. Bubbles of air will rise up through the water. When the pressure in the bottle gets high enough, the cork and the water will be forced out and the rocket will fly upwards. Be careful not to stand over the bottle!

Going to the Moon

Plotting a course through Space is more complicated than travelling over land. Pilots follow natural features, such as hills, valleys and rivers; at high altitudes, they use radio beacons on the ground or satellite signals. The problem with journeying from the Earth to the Moon is that both are moving, as the first project illustrates. The second project shows how a heavy craft gets to the Moon. Staged rockets release their sections as they progress into Space, so reducing the weight of the rocket.

If a spacecraft was aimed straight at the Moon when it set off from Earth, the Moon would have moved on around its orbit by the time the craft arrived. If the spacecraft corrected its direction to follow the Moon's orbit, it would use too much fuel. Spacecraft are therefore aimed at the position the Moon will be in by the time the craft arrives. They navigate by the stars.

YOU WILL NEED

Moving target: String, ruler, scissors, masking tape, metal washer, book, small balls of paper.

Two-stage rocket: Two paper or plastic cups, scissors, long balloon and pump, adhesive tape, round balloon.

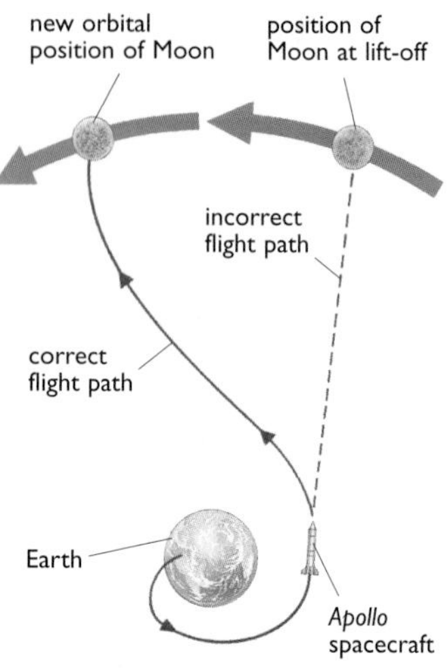

▲ **Flight paths to the Moon**
This diagram shows two possible flight paths for an *Apollo* spacecraft. Aiming directly at the Moon does not allow for its movement as it orbits the Earth. The correct, efficient route compensates for the Moon's orbital movements by aiming ahead of its position at lift-off.

Moving target

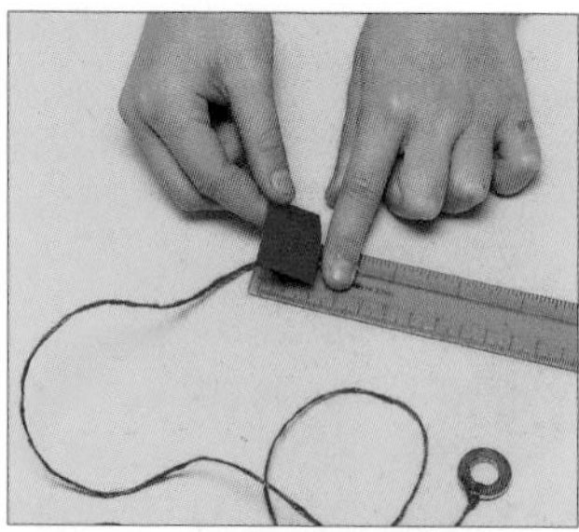

1 Measure 2m/2ft of string with the ruler. Cut it off with scissors. Tape one end of the string to one end of the ruler. Tie a washer to the other end of the string.

2 Place the ruler on a table or box, with the string hanging over the edge. Weight it down with a heavy book. Try hitting the washer by throwing small balls of paper at it.

3 Start the washer swinging, and try to hit it again with the paper balls. See how much more difficult it is to hit a moving target, like a spacecraft aiming at the moving Moon.

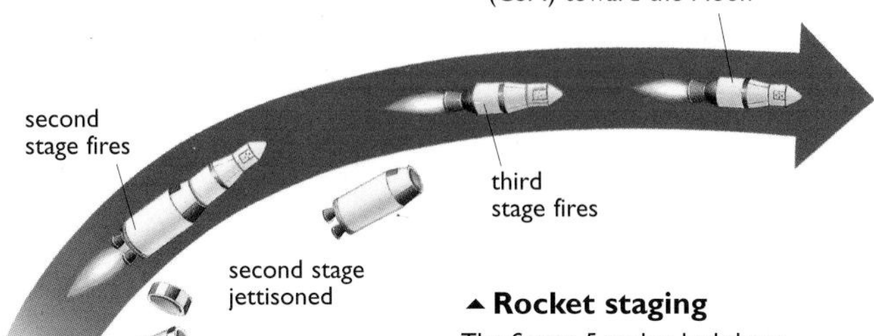

▲ Rocket staging

The *Saturn 5* rocket had three stages. The first two powered the spacecraft up through the atmosphere. The third stage propelled it into orbit, and then gave an extra push to send the craft on its way to the Moon.

Two-stage rocket

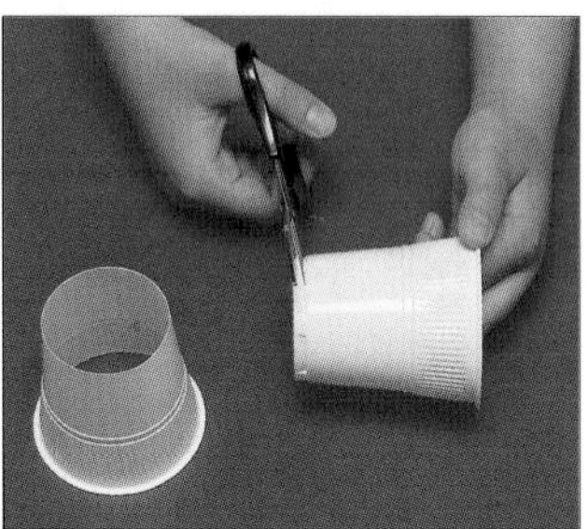

1 Using scissors, carefully cut the bottoms out of the paper or plastic cups. These will serve as the linking collar between the two stages of the balloon rocket.

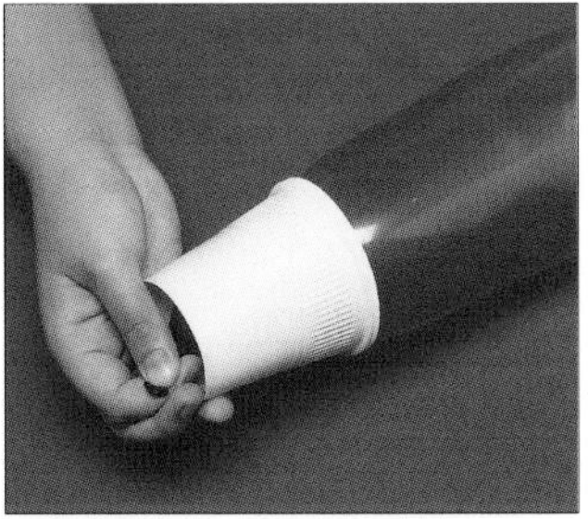

2 Partly blow up the long balloon with the pump. Pull the neck of the balloon through the paper or plastic cups. This balloon will be your two-stage rocket's second stage.

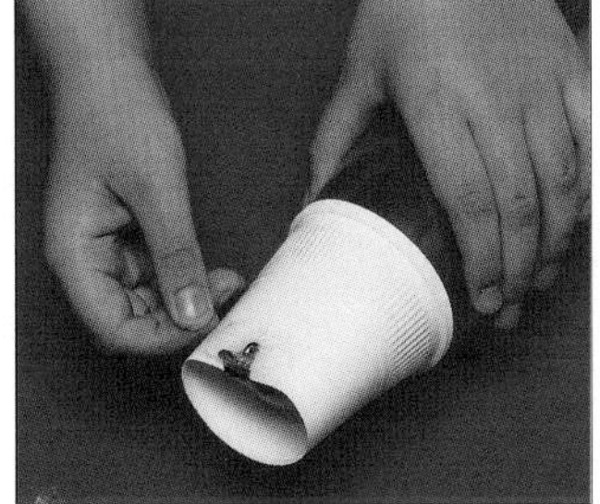

3 Fold the neck of the long balloon over the side of the cups. Tape the end of the neck of the balloon to the cups to stop the air from escaping, as shown.

4 Carefully push the round balloon into the open end of the paper or plastic cups, as shown. This balloon will form the first stage of your two-stage balloon rocket.

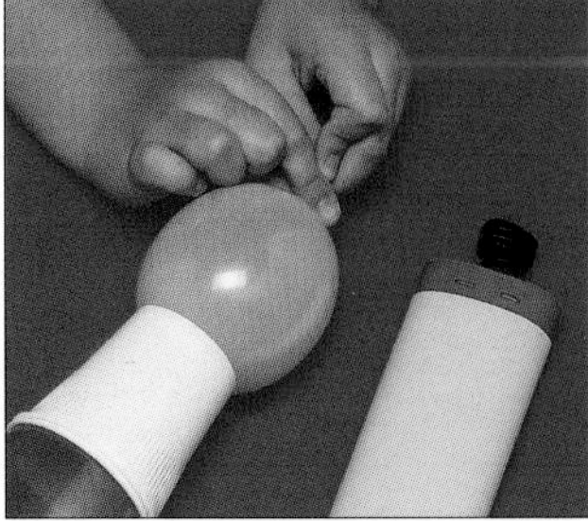

5 Blow up the round balloon, so that it wedges the neck of the long balloon in place inside the cups. Hold the neck of the round balloon to keep the air inside it.

Peel the tape off the neck of the long balloon. Hold the rocket as shown. Let go of the round balloon's neck. Air rushes out, launching the first stage of the rocket. It then falls away, launching the second-stage balloon.

Artificial gravity

Space voyagers in orbit far away from Earth do not feel the pull of gravity. They feel weightless, as if they are forever falling. In a state of weightlessness, there is no up or down, because up and down are created by the force known as gravity. Even experienced pilots and astronauts sometimes feel uncomfortable and ill until they get used to being weightless. Weightlessness also has damaging effects on the human body. Future Space Stations and spacecraft designed for very long spaceflights may create artificial gravity to protect their occupants from the effects of weightlessness.

In this project, you can explore a theoretical method of creating artificial gravity that uses rotation by making a centrifuge. Moving objects tend to travel in straight lines. When you whirl around a ball attached to the end of a piece of string, it tries to fly off in a straight line, stopped only by the string. Inside a rotating spacecraft, the solid outer walls would stop astronauts flying off in straight lines. This would feel like the astronauts were being pushed down to the ground, just like the effect of gravity on Earth.

YOU WILL NEED

Four cardboard triangles (30 x 10 x 22.5cm/12 x 4 x 8¾in), dishwashing detergent bottle, adhesive tape, bradawl, wooden skewer, long rubber band, masking tape, three paper clips, pliers, cardboard strip (50 x 5cm/20 x 2in), small bead, scissors, drinking straw, two small plastic cups, non-hardening modelling material, water, food dye.

Make a centrifuge

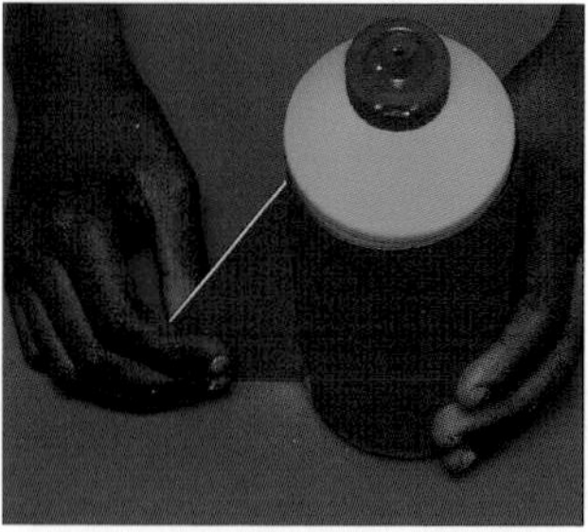

1 Take the four cardboard triangles and tape them to the sides of the bottle, as shown. These will provide the dishwashing detergent centrifuge with a broad, stable base to stand on.

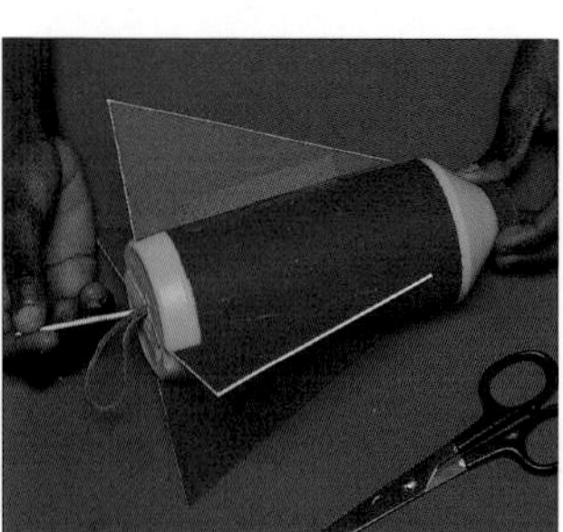

2 Using the bradawl, make a hole in the bottom of the detergent bottle. Push one end of the rubber band almost all the way into the hole using a wooden skewer.

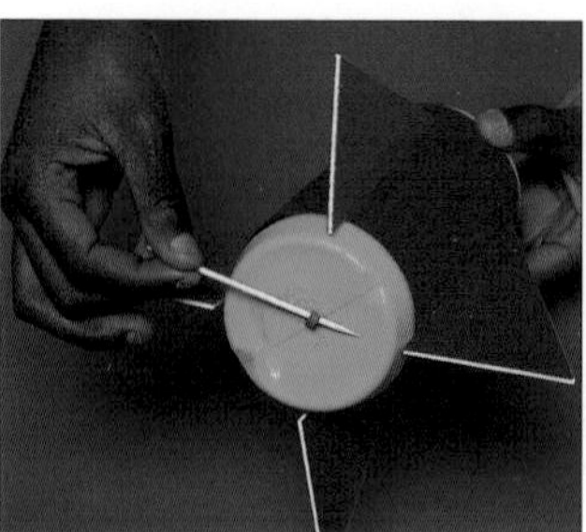

3 Pass the wooden skewer through the small loop of rubber band projecting from the hole, as shown. Leave an equal amount of skewer on either side of the bottle.

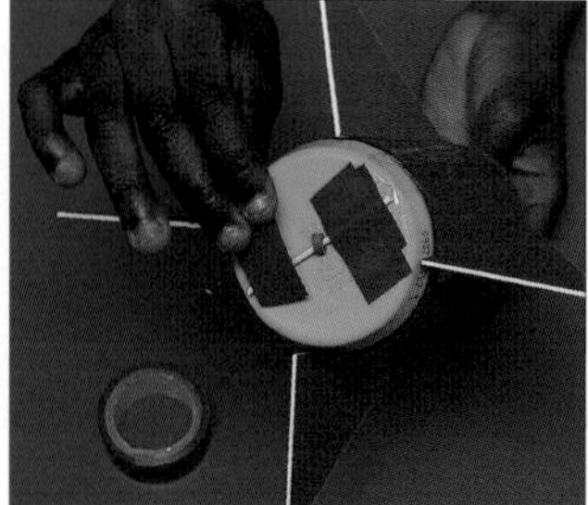

4 Take the masking tape and firmly secure the wooden skewer to the base of the detergent bottle. Make sure that the skewer is fixed so tightly that it cannot move.

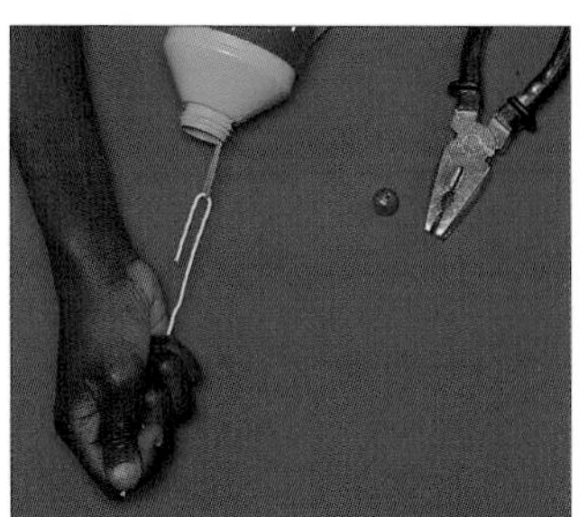

5 Straighten out one end of a paper clip with pliers. Dip the hooked end of the clip into the neck of the bottle. Catch the rubber band with the hook and pull it out.

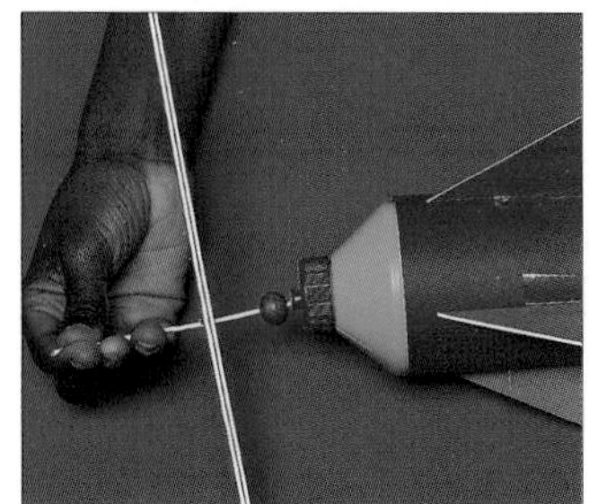

6 Using the bradawl, make a hole in the middle of the cardboard strip. Thread the end of the hooked paper clip through the bead. Then thread it through the hole in the cardboard.

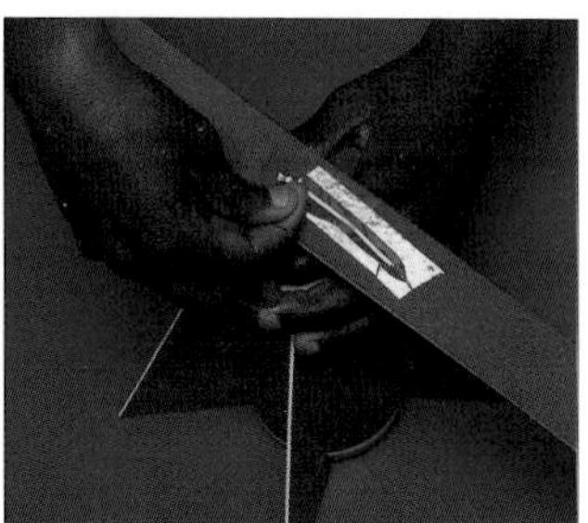

7 Carefully bend the end of the paper clip down on to the cardboard strip. Using the adhesive tape, fix the end of the clip securely into place, as shown above.

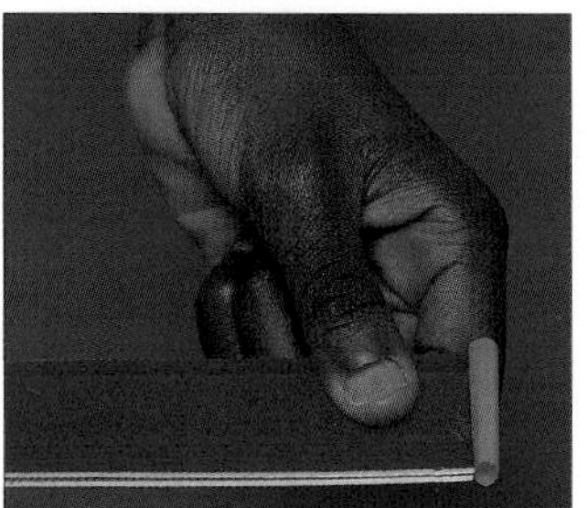

8 Use the scissors to cut two short pieces of drinking straw. Each piece should measure 5cm/2in in length. Fix one piece to each end of the cardboard strip with the tape.

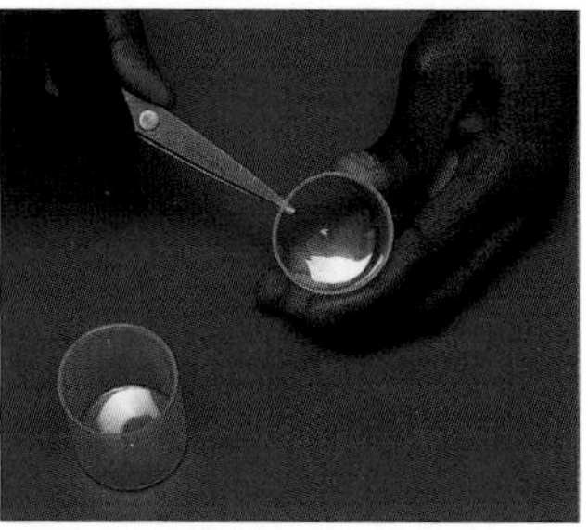

9 Take one of the small plastic cups. Carefully make a hole with the scissors on both sides of the cup near the top. Now make holes in the second cup in the same way.

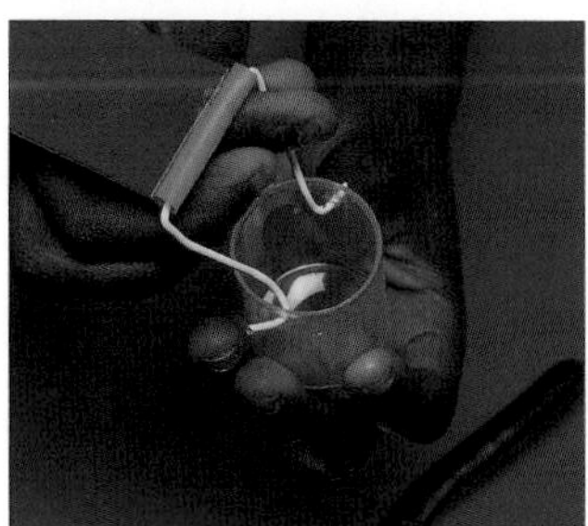

10 Straighten two paper clips with pliers. Thread a clip through each straw. Bend the ends of the clips into hooks using pliers. Thread the ends of the clips through the holes in the cups.

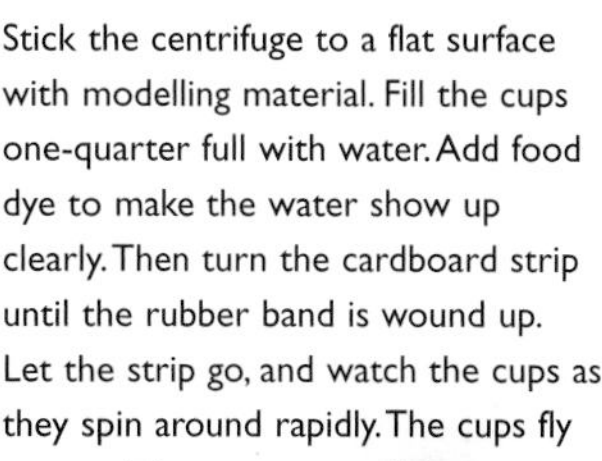

Stick the centrifuge to a flat surface with modelling material. Fill the cups one-quarter full with water. Add food dye to make the water show up clearly. Then turn the cardboard strip until the rubber band is wound up. Let the strip go, and watch the cups as they spin around rapidly. The cups fly outward, but the water is held in place by bases of the cups.

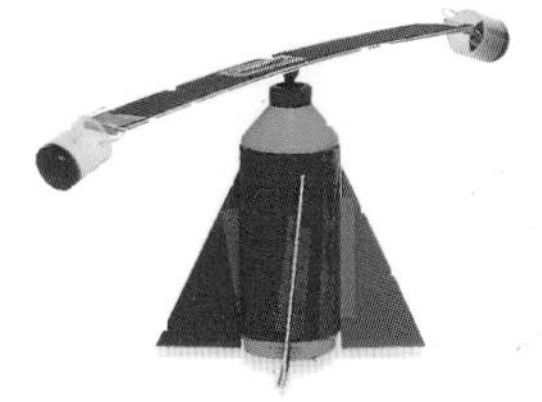

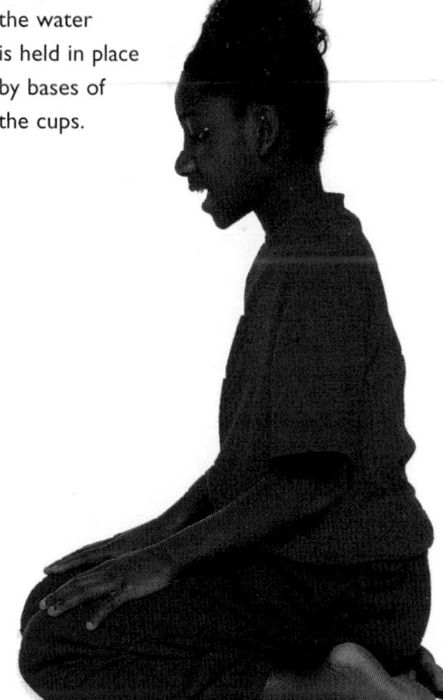

Working in Space

▲ **Working in a spacesuit**
Bulky spacesuits make working in Space difficult. Spacesuit designers are always trying to improve them. The more flexible a suit is, the less tiring it is to work in. This means that an astronaut can work outside for longer periods, which is a great help when they are making repairs.

There is no gravity outside the pressurized crew compartment of a shuttle in Space. This makes work more difficult than on Earth. On Earth, gravity pulls us down to the ground. We can then use friction against the ground in order to move around. If a weightless astronaut pushes a handle in zero gravity, he or she would fly away in the opposite direction! This means that astronauts have to be anchored to something solid before doing any work. A spacesuit makes it even more difficult to move. The astronaut has to push against the suit to close a hand, or bend an arm or leg.

Spacesuit gloves have thin rubber fingerpacks, so that astronauts can feel things through them, but their sense of touch is still very limited. The first project simulates the experience of working in a spacesuit by using rubber gloves, a bowl of water and some nuts and bolts. Then make a robot arm like the shuttle's remote manipulator system (RMS), which is used to launch and retrieve satellites.

Nuts and bolts

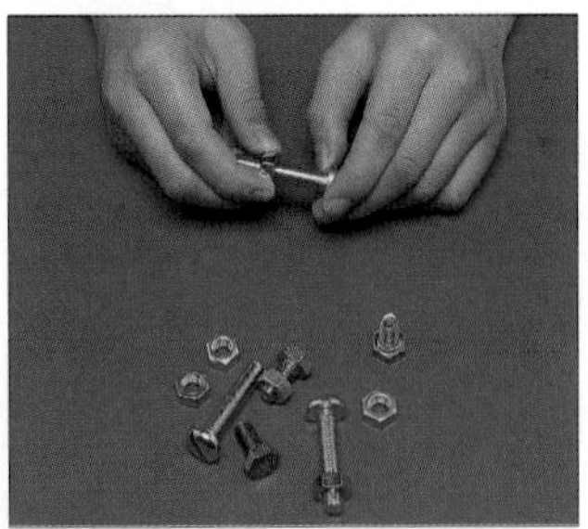

1 Take the nuts and bolts, and place them on a table. Now try picking them up and screwing them together. You should find this a very easy task to achieve!

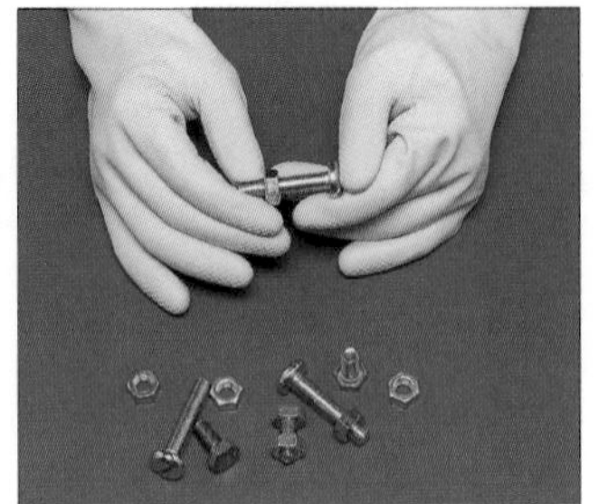

2 Now try screwing the nuts and bolts together with the gloves on. This is more difficult, like trying to perform a delicate task on Earth wearing bulky spacesuit gloves.

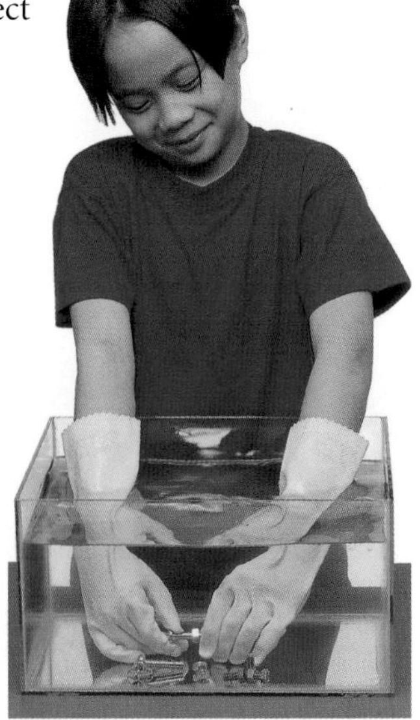

3 Fill the bowl with water. Add the nuts and bolts. Try screwing them together with the gloves on. This is very difficult, like working in a spacesuit outside a spacecraft.

Make a robot arm

YOU WILL NEED

Working in Space: Nuts and bolts, rubber gloves, bowl, water.

Make a robot arm: Cardboard, ruler, scissors, bradawl, two split pins, dowel, picture hook, two paper clips, ball of non-hardening modelling material.

1 Use the ruler to measure three 28 x 5cm/11 x 2in cardboard strips. Cut them out. Use a bradawl to make a hole 2.5cm/1in from the ends of each strip. Join the strips with split pins.

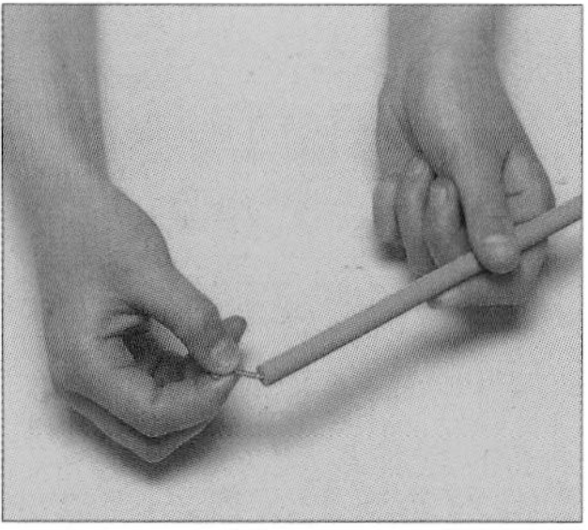

2 Take the hook and screw it into the end of the dowel. The dowel will be used to control the robot arm remotely, just as shuttle astronauts remotely operate the RMS.

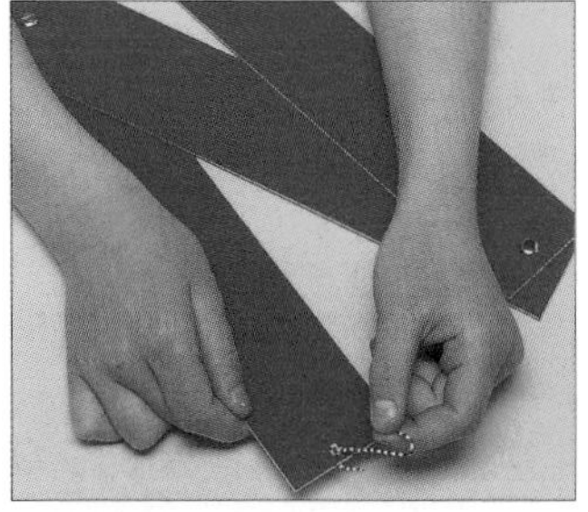

3 Now carefully bend one of the paper clips into the shape of the letter S. To attach the paper clip, pass it through the hole in the end of the cardboard arm, as shown.

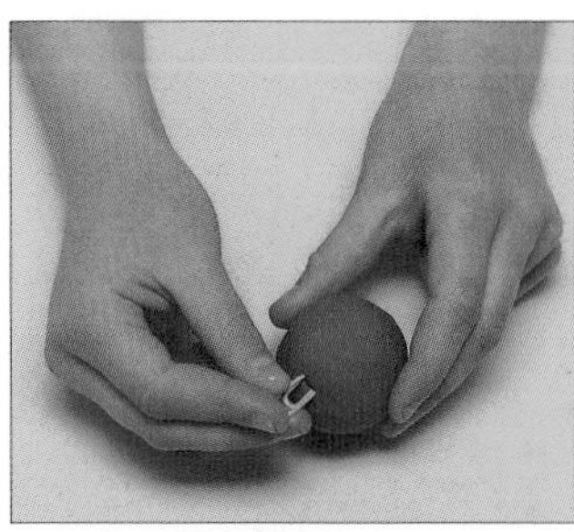

4 Take the modelling material and roll it into a ball about the size of a walnut. Then take the second paper clip and push it firmly into the ball, as shown.

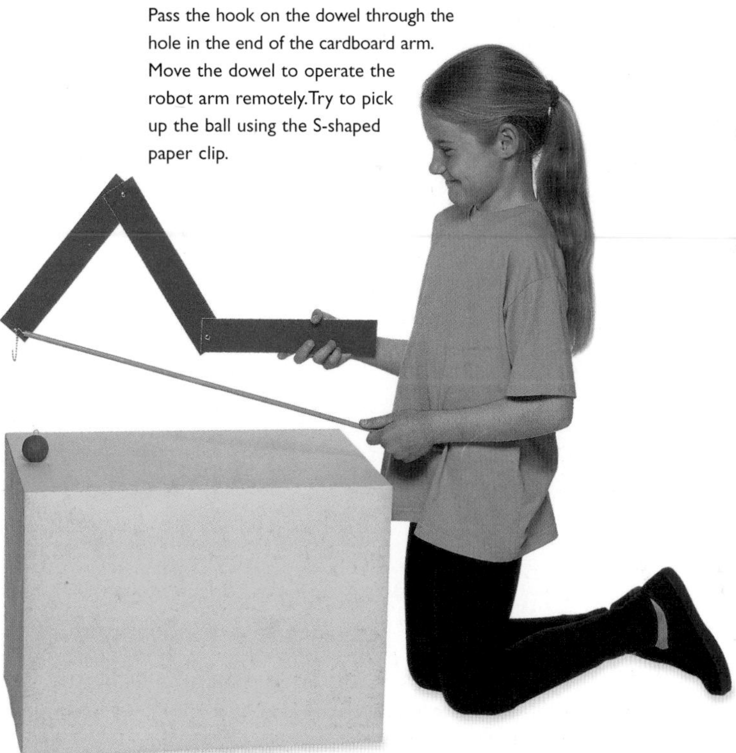

Pass the hook on the dowel through the hole in the end of the cardboard arm. Move the dowel to operate the robot arm remotely. Try to pick up the ball using the S-shaped paper clip.

Great History Projects

History at Home

History is the study of the past. It looks at the important events that have happened in the last 10,000 years, such as wars, revolutions and the lives of kings, queens and emperors. It is also about how everyday people, such as hunters, farmers, traders, soldiers and children, have lived since humans first evolved more than 2.5 million years ago. It looks at their homes, their food, their customs and how they entertained themselves.

Changing lives

Early people led very simple lives. They moved from place to place, hunting for food. Lifestyles began to change when people began to grow their own food. They settled in one place, and villages, towns and cities grew. It was then that people began to do specialized jobs, such as farming, making tools, clothes or cooking pots, and they began to buy and sell things. They formed armies to defend themselves against hostile invaders. Most people lived in one place all their lives, and they knew very little about the rest of the world, where customs and entertainment were developing in very different ways. For millions of us, life changed a great deal in the last century with the rise of transport and communications, but in many parts of the world people still live as they have for hundreds of years. The events of history have affected the way we all live today, and one day our lives will become a part of history too.

The point of projects

Doing the projects in this section will show you how people in the past made a whole range of different things, from giant castles to tiny snacks. The projects will also show you the way that many historical objects from around the world were used. You will see how craftspeople worked with the materials they found around them, such as wood, mud, feathers and shells, before modern materials such as plastics were invented.

Finding your way around this part of the book

This half of the book is divided into four sections of projects, each exploring a different aspect of life in historical times.

Houses and Homes looks at life at home through history. You will see different traditional designs of homes from around the world, how homes were decorated, and examples of food that people ate.

Fashion and Accessories explores what people used to wear. You will see how people made cloth from animal hairs and plant fibres, clothes for keeping warm and for special occasions, and what jewellery and other fashion accessories they made.

Science and Technology looks at examples of discoveries and inventions through history. You will see how people developed simple machines, writing, simple boats and wheeled vehicles for travelling and carrying cargo, and weapons and armour for use on battlefields in ancient times.

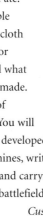

Customs, Arts and Entertainment explores ancient pastimes and customs. You will see how people made art, objects for celebrations and festivals, musical instruments, theatre costumes, toys and games.

PROJECT HINTS

- Before you start, tell an adult what you are going to do. Show him or her the experiment and explain where and how you intend to do it.
- Make sure you have all the necessary items required for the project and that the materials and equipment are clean. You should be able to find everything you need either in your home or from a local store.
- Read the whole project first. Then read each step and make sure you understand it before you begin. All the projects are safe as long as you follow the instructions exactly, and ask for adult help when advised to do so.
- When you have finished a project, clear everything away safely, and remember to wash your hands!
- If you are using any food, make sure you have permission to use it and throw it away after you have finished. If a project advises using gloves, be sure to do so.
- Do not worry if a project doesn't work or you miss what happens. Try to work out why it has gone wrong and do the project again. It's all part of the fun!

Early farmers in northern Europe, c. 5000BC

Houses and Homes

Homes provide shelter from the elements first and foremost, but they can be much more than simply a resting place. They can give clues as to what materials were locally available at the time of their construction, and reflect the owner's status and taste. This section investigates a whole host of homes from a variety of different cultures. It takes a look inside to examine some typical features, and recreates some popular dishes of the past.

Different Homes

People have always needed to shelter from the weather, and somewhere warm and comfortable to sleep at night. The design of most homes throughout the world depends on the climate. People living in hot countries need their homes to be as cool and airy as possible, while people in cold countries need their homes to be snug and warm. The materials that people use to build their homes usually depend on what they can find around them. Stone, mud, straw and wood are all natural materials that have been used to build homes for thousands of years. By contrast, many modern homes are built from artificial materials such as concrete, steel and glass.

▲ Cool currents
The ancient Greeks built their houses from sun-dried mud bricks laid on stone foundations. The roofs were covered with pottery tiles. Rooms were arranged around an open courtyard so that cool air could build up and circulate through the rooms during the heat of the day.

King of the castle ▶
During the Middle Ages, between 1000 and 1500, castles were built all over Europe, in Scandinavia, Britain, France and Germany, and south to the Mediterranean Sea. They were also built in the Middle East during the Crusades. Castles were built by important people such as kings or queens. They were not only splendid homes that the owners could show off to their friends, but military bases from which the surrounding lands were defended.

◂ Outdoor rooms

The Incas lived in the Andes Mountains in what is now Peru. They built their homes from large blocks of granite, which they quarried from the nearby mountains. The blocks fitted together without mortar. The resulting thick walls provided insulation against the bitter winter cold. A courtyard acted as a large outside room and was used just as much as the inside of the house for everyday living.

Etruscan palace ▸

The Etruscans lived between the Arno and Tiber rivers in western Italy around 2,500 years ago. Wealthy Etruscan families built luxurious palaces decorated with beautiful figurines, bronze statues and engraved mirrors. The Etruscans grew rich by mining copper, tin and iron and trading with the neighbouring Greeks and Phoenicians.

◂ Wood and bark

The Iroquois people lived in a densely wooded region of North America. They built their longhouses using a wooden framework covered with sheets of thick bark. The barrel-shaped roofs allowed the rain to run off. These houses were huge because several families lived in each one.

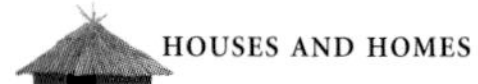

Hunter's home

People have always needed protection from the weather. For most of human history, the Earth's climate has been much colder than it is today. Early humans lived in huts out in the open during summer, but moved into caves when the harsh winter weather came. They built stone windbreaks across the entrances. Inside, there were inner huts made of branches and animal bones to provide further protection from the cold. Hunters following herds of game built temporary shelters of branches and leaves in the summer. Families lived in camps of huts made of branches and animal skins. Farther north, where there were no caves and few trees, people built huts from mammoths' leg bones and tusks. Wherever they settled, however, it was very important to be near a supply of fresh water.

▲ A place to shelter
At Terra Almata, southern France, hominids (early humans) lived in groups. They established camps made up of several simple shelters, to which they returned year after year. The huts were made of tree branches and weighted down with stones.

YOU WILL NEED

Self-hardening clay, cutting board, modelling tool, twigs, ruler, scissors, card, brown and green acrylic paint, water pot, paintbrushes, white glue and glue brush, fake grass or green fabric.

◄ Skin huts
Huts at Monte Verde, Chile, were made of wood covered with animal skins. They are the earliest evidence for human-made shelters in the Americas. The remains were preserved in peaty soil, along with other items, such as a wooden bowl and digging sticks.

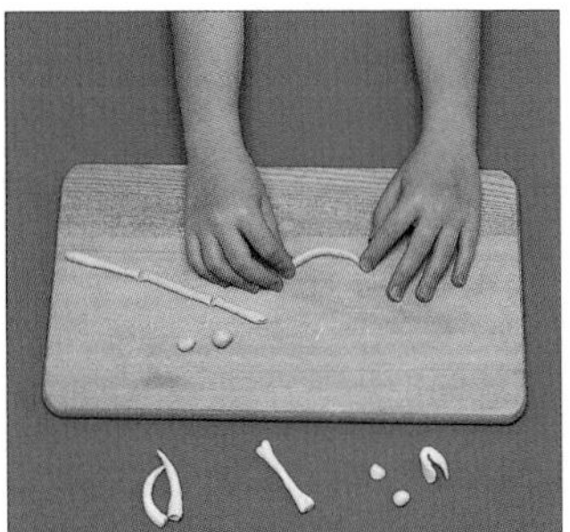

1 Roll out lengths of self-hardening clay, and shape them to look like long and short mammoth bones and tusks. Then make some small clay stones in different sizes.

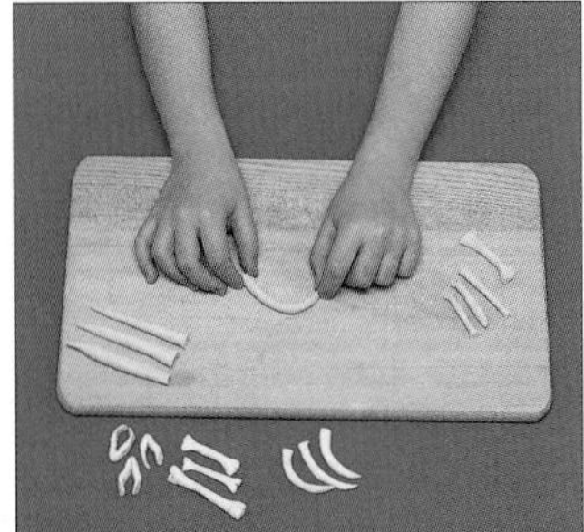

2 Use the modelling tool to shape the ends of the bones. Then use it to make the stones look uneven. Lay the bones and stones on the cutting board to dry.

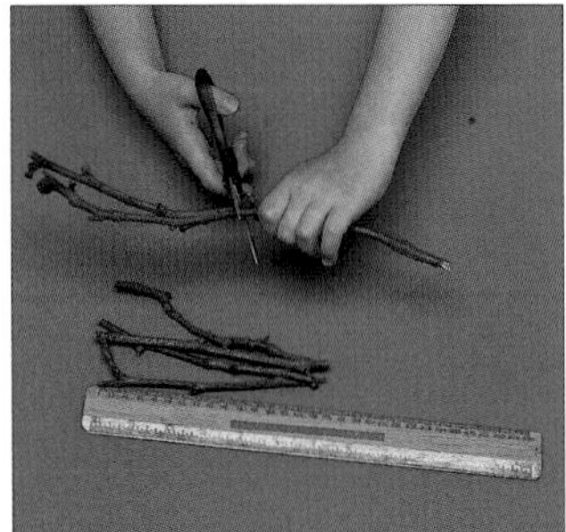

3 Lay the twigs next to a ruler. Then use a pair of scissors to cut the twigs so that they are about 15cm/6in long. You will need about eight evenly sized twigs in all.

4 Roll out some more clay and spread it unevenly over a piece of card. Paint the clay a brown-green colour to look like soil and grass. Do not leave the base to dry.

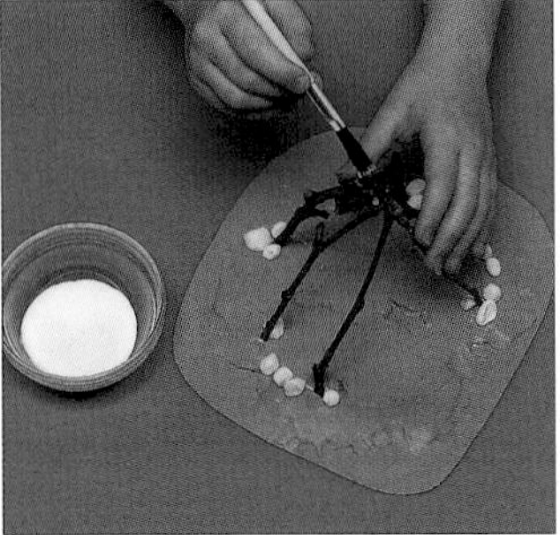

5 Push the twigs into the clay base, and arch them over to form a cone-shaped frame. Glue a few stones on to the clay at the base of each of the twigs.

6 Cover the twigs with pieces of fake grass or green fabric. Leave a gap at one side for the entrance. Glue the pieces in place. Take care not to cover up the stones around the base.

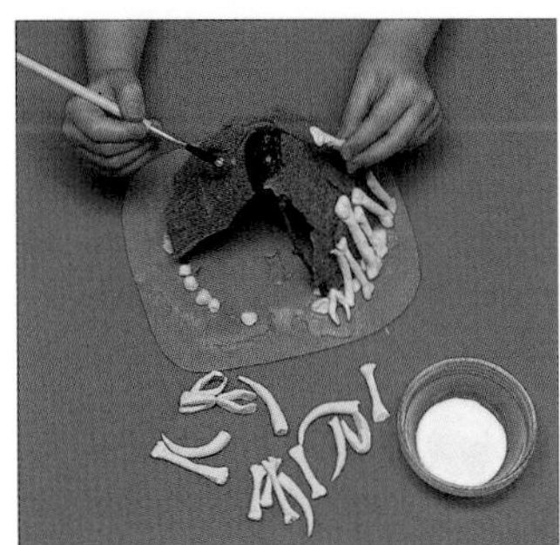

7 Neatly glue the long mammoth bones and tusks all over the outside of the hunter's shelter. Fill in any gaps with smaller bones. Leave the hunter's home to dry.

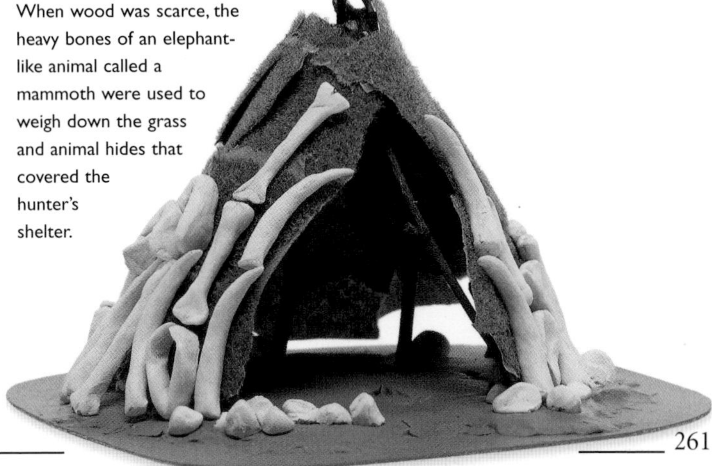

When wood was scarce, the heavy bones of an elephant-like animal called a mammoth were used to weigh down the grass and animal hides that covered the hunter's shelter.

Mud-brick house

The great cities of ancient Egypt were built along the banks of the River Nile. Small towns grew up haphazardly around them. Special workers' towns, such as Deir el-Medina, were also set up around major burial sites and temples to be close to the building work.

Mud brick was used for most buildings, from royal palaces to workers' dwellings. Only temples and pyramids were built to last – they were made from stone. Most homes had roofs supported with palm logs and floors of packed earth. In the evenings, people would sit on the flat roofs or walk in the cool, shady gardens.

▲ Tomb workers
The village of Deir el-Medina housed the skilled workers who built the royal tombs in the Valley of the Kings. The men were required to work for eight days out of ten.

▲ Mud brick
The Egyptians dried bricks in the Sun using the thick clay soil left behind by the Nile floods. The clay was taken to a brick yard and mixed with water, pebbles and chopped straw.

▾ Templates

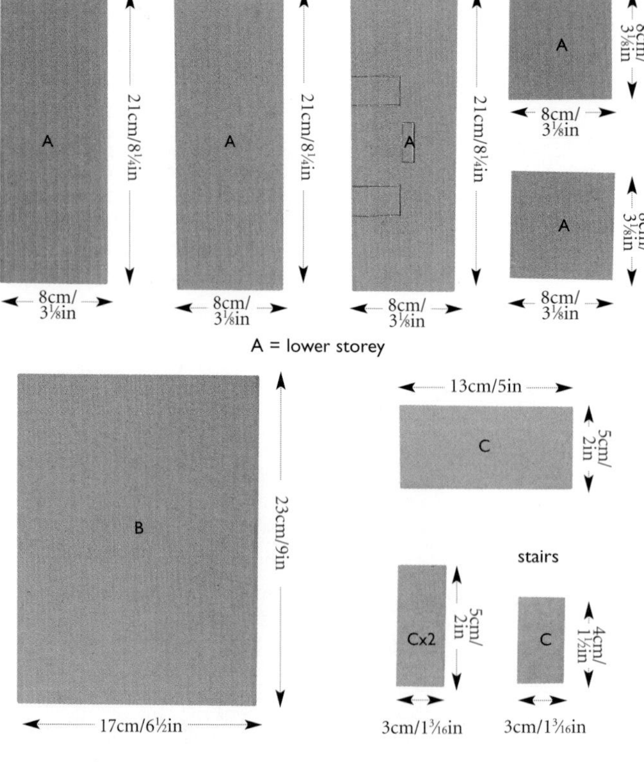

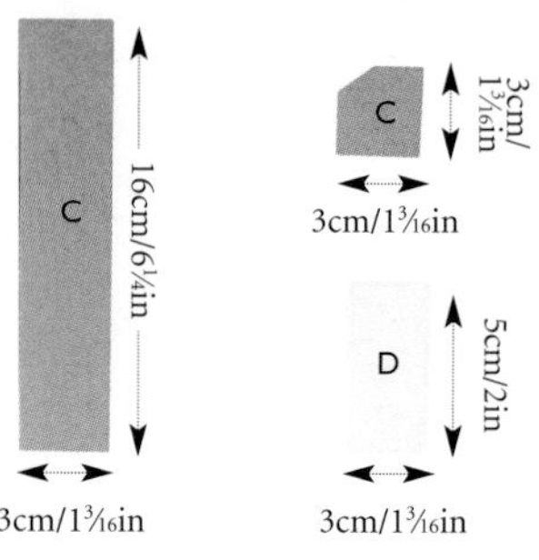

B = base C = upper storey D = sunshade roof

YOU WILL NEED

Thick card, 4 x 3cm/1⅝ x 1³⁄₁₆in thin card (for stairs), pencil, ruler, scissors, white glue and glue brush, masking tape, balsa wood, plaster of Paris, water pot and brush, acrylic paint (green, white, yellow and red), paintbrush, sandpaper, straw.

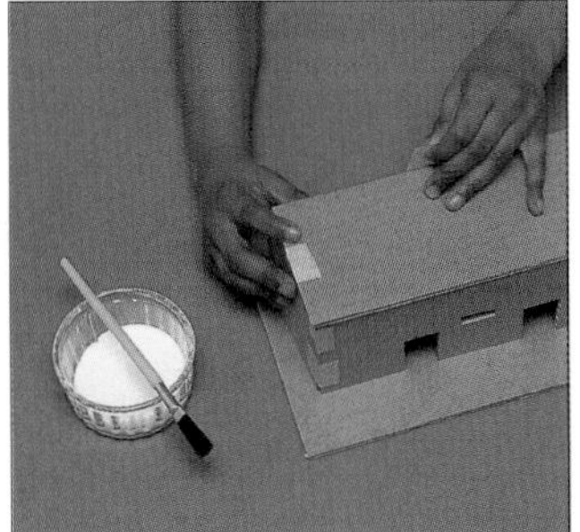

1 Use the templates to measure and cut out the pieces for the house. Glue together the base board, walls and ceiling of the lower storey. Reinforce the joints with masking tape.

2 Glue together the roof and walls of the top storey. Fold the thin card as shown for the stairs, and glue into place. Tape joints to reinforce. Glue the top storey to the lower storey.

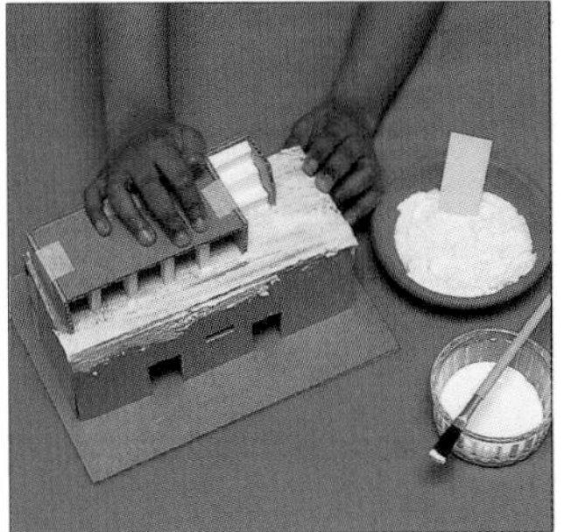

3 Glue balsa pillars into the front of the top storey. When the house is dry, cover it in a wet paste of plaster of Paris. Paint the pillars red or another colour of your choice.

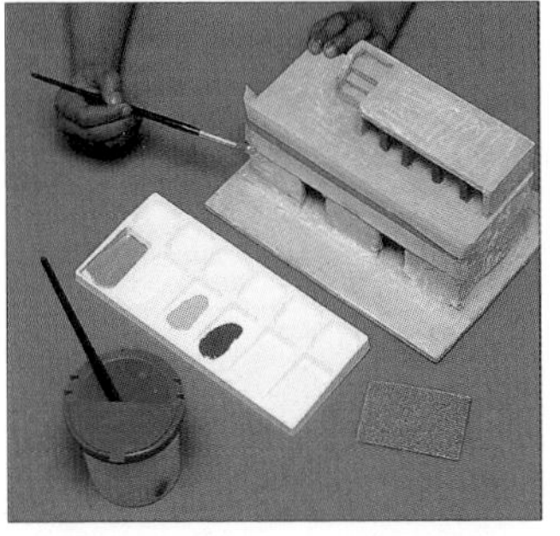

4 Paint your model the same colour as dried mud. Next paint a green strip along the wall. Use the masking tape to ensure the edges are straight. Sand any rough edges.

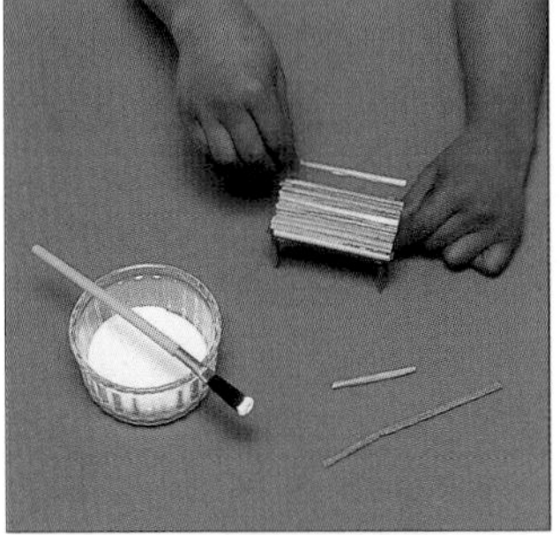

5 Now make a shelter for the rooftop. Use four balsa struts as supports. Glue the piece of card (D) and cover it with pieces of straw. Glue the shelter into place.

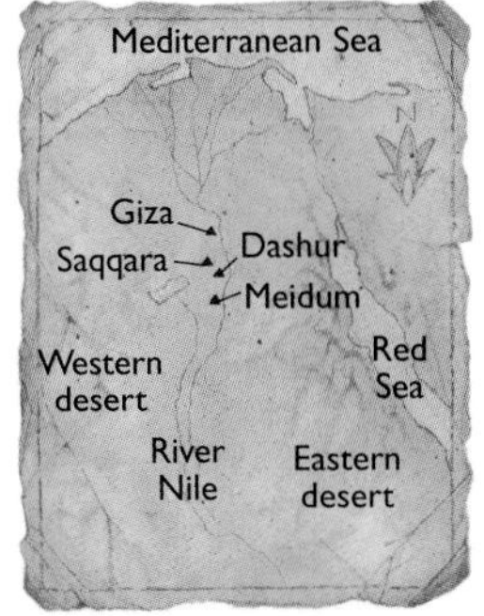

▲ Living by the river
Egyptians built their homes along the banks of the River Nile. Many pyramids, such as those at Giza, are found here, too.

Egyptian houses had a large main room that opened directly into the street. In many homes, stairs led up to the roof. People slept there during hot weather.

Roman house

Only the wealthiest Romans could afford to live in a private house. The front door opened on to a short passage leading to the *atrium*, a central court or entrance hall. Front rooms on either side of the passage were usually bedrooms. Sometimes, though, they were used as workshops or shops and had shutters that opened out to the street.

The centre of the atrium was open to the sky. Below this opening was a small pool to collect rainwater. If you were a guest or had business, you would be shown into the office, or *tablinium*. The dining room, or *triclinium*, was often the grandest room of all. Extremely wealthy Romans also had a summer dining room, which looked out on to the garden.

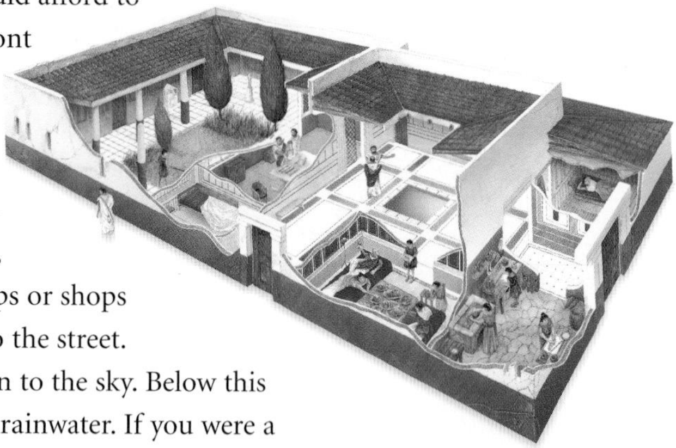

▲ House and garden
The outside of a Roman town house was usually very plain, but inside it was decorated with colourful wall paintings and intricate mosaics.

▼ Templates

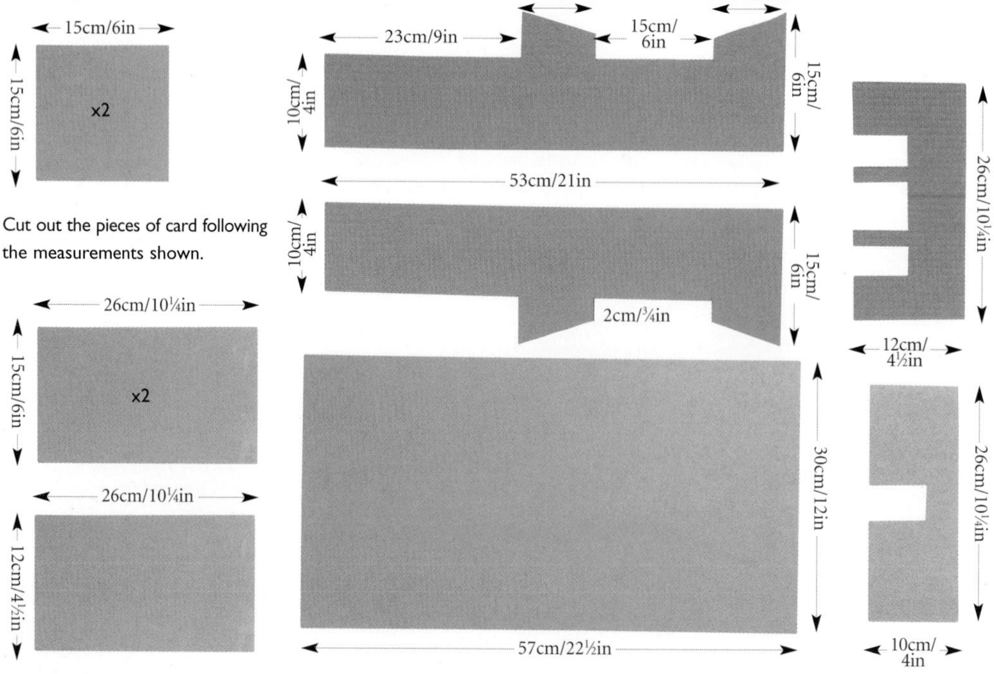

Cut out the pieces of card following the measurements shown.

15cm/6in
15cm/6in
x2
26cm/10¼in
15cm/6in
x2
26cm/10¼in
12cm/4½in
7.5cm/3in
7.5cm/3in
23cm/9in
15cm/6in
10cm/4in
15cm/6in
53cm/21in
10cm/4in
15cm/6in
2cm/¾in
30cm/12in
57cm/22½in
26cm/10¼in
12cm/4½in
26cm/10¼in
10cm/4in

YOU WILL NEED

Pencil, ruler, thick card, scissors, white glue and glue brush, masking tape, corrugated card, acrylic paints, paintbrushes, water pot, thin card.

▲ Garden delights
Trailing ivy and sweet-smelling roses often grew in the beautiful walled gardens of a Roman house.

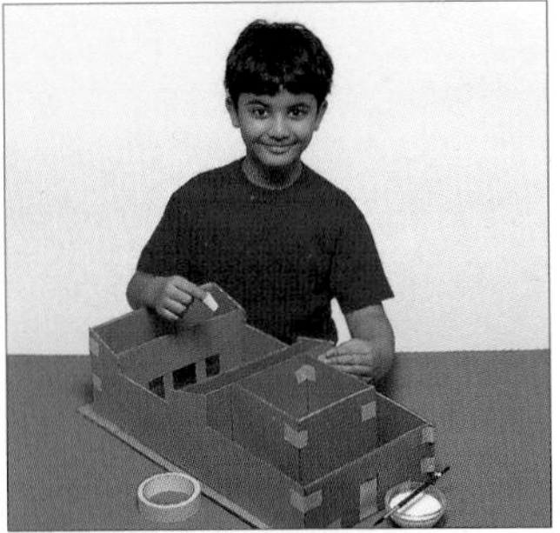

1 When you have cut out all the templates, edge each piece with glue. Press the templates together and reinforce with masking tape, as shown. These form the walls of your house.

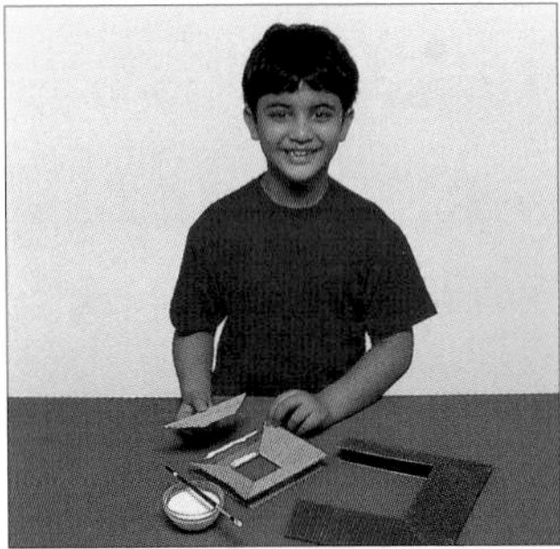

2 Measure your model and cut out pieces of corrugated card for the roof sections. Stick them together with glue, as shown above. Paint all of the roofs with red paint.

3 Rain water running down the roof above the atrium was directed into a pool by gutters and water spouts. Make gutters from strips of thin card and pierce holes for the spouts.

4 Paint the walls of the house, using masking tape to get a straight line. Glue on the roof sections. You could then cover the walls of the house with some authentic Roman graffiti.

Roman houses had high, windowless walls to keep out the Sun, making it cool and shady inside. High ceilings and wide doors made the most of the light from the open atrium and garden. Houses were made from whatever building materials were available, and included stone, mud bricks, cement and timber. Clay tiles usually covered the roof.

Celtic roundhouse

It was dark and smoky inside a Celtic roundhouse, but quite cosy and comfortable. A thatched roof kept the house warm in the winter and cool in the summer. Houses were heated by a wood or peat fire burning in a pit in the centre of the room. The hearth was the heart of the home, and the fire was kept burning day and night, all year round. Smoke from the fire escaped through the thatch.

straw

YOU WILL NEED

String, ruler, felt-tipped pen, brown card, scissors, two pieces of stiff white card (78 x 12cm/30¾in x 4½in), white glue and glue brush, masking tape, non-hardening modelling material, rolling pin, straw, corrugated card, seven pieces of 45cm/18in-long dowel, bradawl.

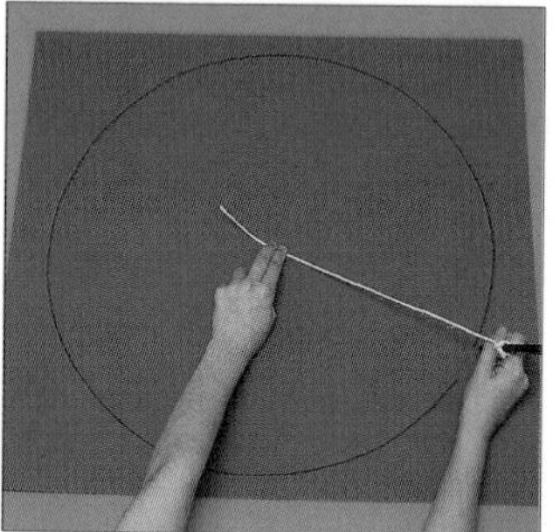

1 Use the piece of string, a ruler and a felt-tipped pen to draw a circle with a radius of 25cm/10in on the brown card. Carefully cut out the circle using a pair of scissors.

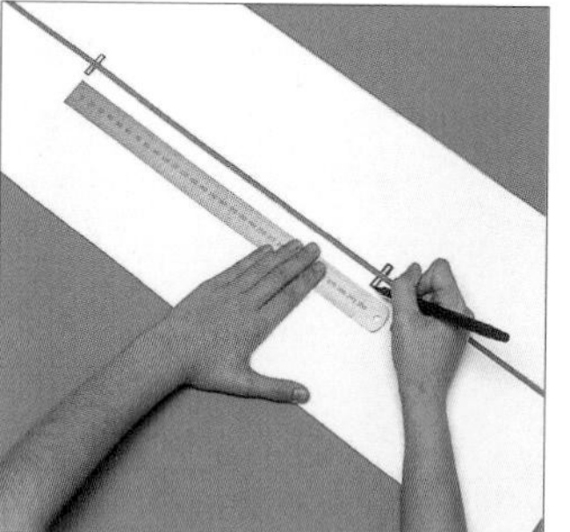

2 Draw a mark every 30cm/12in along the edges of the two pieces of white card. Cut into each mark to make a notch. Glue the two pieces of card together at one end.

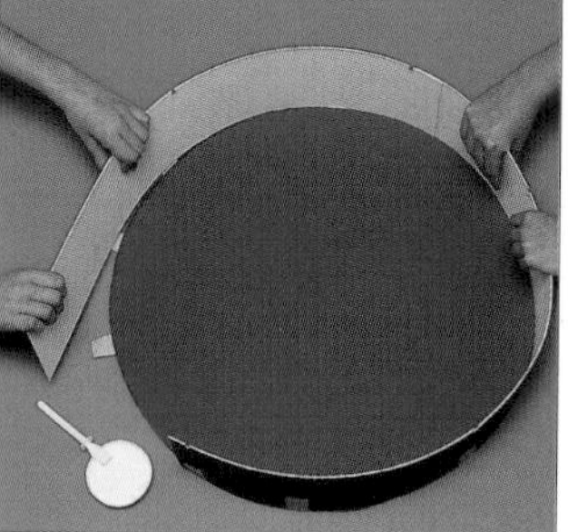

3 Fit the card wall to the base of your house, making sure that the notches are along the top. Glue the wall in place and secure it with masking tape.

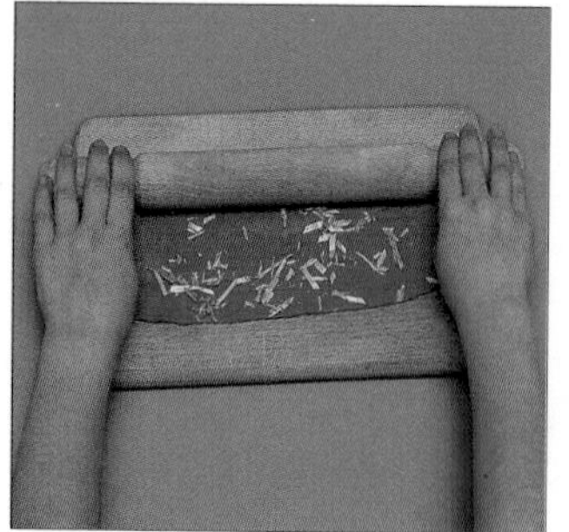

4 Roll out the modelling material into sections 13cm/5in wide. Sprinkle straw on to the modelling material and roll it into the surface. Make enough sections to cover the card wall.

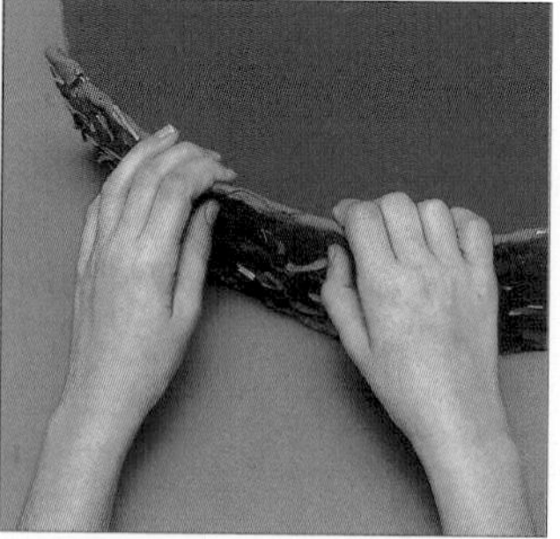

5 Firmly press each modelling material section on to the card wall until the whole wall is covered. Remember to leave a space where the notches are at the top of the wall.

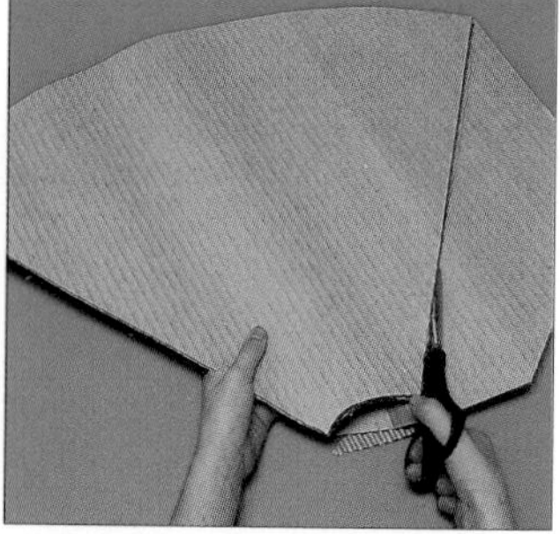

6 Cut a large circle with a diameter of 91cm/3ft from the corrugated card. Cut a small circle in the centre. Cut the large circle into sections 56cm/22in wide along the edge.

7 Glue pieces of straw on to each piece of card. These will form the roof sections. Start on the outside edge and work your way in towards the centre. Use three layers of straw.

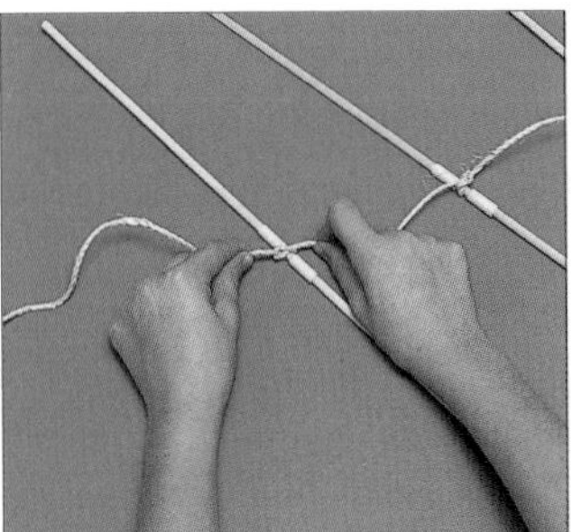

8 Wrap two pieces of masking tape 1cm/½in apart around the middle of six lengths of dowel. Tie string between the tape pieces. Allow a 13cm/5in length of string between each stick.

9 Place one length of dowel in the middle of the base. Secure it with modelling material. Place the tied sticks over the base, as shown above. Lodge the sticks into the wall notches.

10 Fix the sticks in place in the wall notches using modelling material. Cover with an extra piece. Tie the top of the sticks to the upright stick using more string.

11 Tie together the ends of the string between the last two sticks that make up the roof section. Remember to keep the string taut to stop the roof from collapsing.

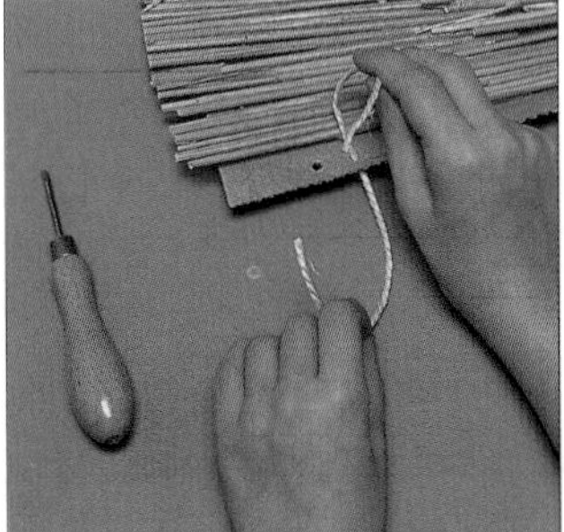

12 Use the bradawl to pierce two holes on both edges at the top and bottom of each straw roof section. Carefully thread a piece of string through each hole.

13 Use the ends of the string to tie the straw roof sections firmly on to the roof structure. Carry on adding the straw sections until the roof is completely covered.

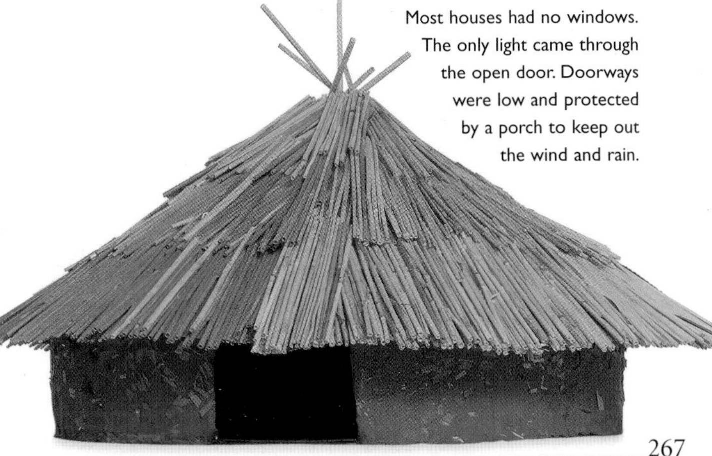

Most houses had no windows. The only light came through the open door. Doorways were low and protected by a porch to keep out the wind and rain.

Native American tepee

Many Native American tribes, such as the Cheyenne of the Great Plains, were nomadic. Their life was dependent on the movement of buffalo. The animals supplied the tribe with food, clothing and shelter. Many tribes lived in tepees, which were easy to build and also easy to pack up when it was time to move on.

Your tepee is a simple version of a Plains tepee. These were large, heavy shelters made from stretched and tanned buffalo skin.

YOU WILL NEED

Old double sheet (measuring around 250 x 78cm/98½ x 30¾in) cut into a semicircle with a diameter of 152cm/59⅞in, scissors, pencil, tape measure, large and small paintbrushes, acrylic paints, water pot, string, 12 bamboo sticks, three small sticks, large stones.

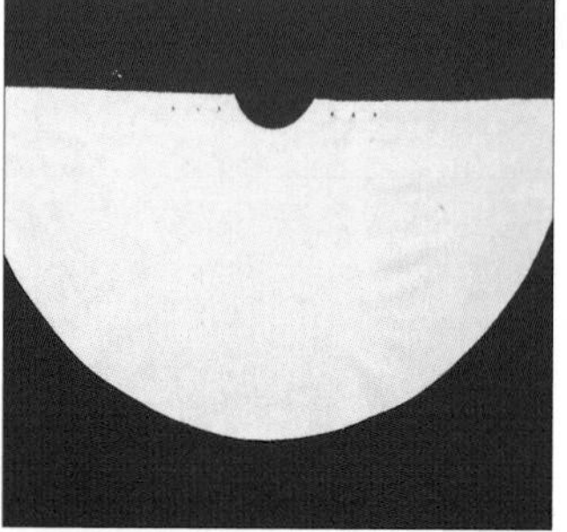

1 Cut out a smaller semicircle 46cm/18⅛in across and 20cm/8in deep. Make three holes either side of this semicircle. Start 6cm/2½in from the centre and 3cm/$1\frac{3}{16}$in from the flat edge.

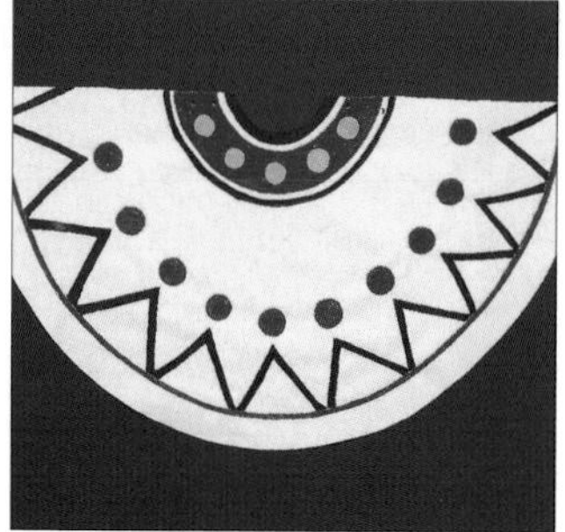

2 Using a pencil and tape measure, draw out a pattern of triangles, lines and circles on the sheet. Make the pattern bold and simple, similar to the one shown. Paint it and leave it to dry.

3 Tie three bamboo sticks together at one end and arrange them on the ground to form a tripod. Lean the remaining bamboo sticks against the tripod. Leave a gap for the entrance.

4 Now take the painted sheet (your tepee cover) and wrap it over the bamboo frame. Overlap the two sides at the top of the frame so that the holes you made earlier join up.

5 Insert a small stick through the two top holes to join them. Do this for each of the other holes. You can place stones around the bottom of the sheet to secure your tepee.

Arctic igloo

In the Inuit language, the word *iglu* was actually used to describe any type of house. A shelter such as the one you can build below was called an *igluigaq*. Most Inuit igloos were simple dome-like structures, which were used as shelters during the winter hunting trips. A small entrance tunnel prevented cold winds from entering the igloo and trapped warm air inside. Outside, the temperature could be as low as –70°C/–158°F. Inside, heat from the stove, candles and the warmth of the hunter's body kept the air at around 5°C/41°F.

YOU WILL NEED

Self-hardening clay, cutting board, rolling pin, ruler, modelling tool, scissors, thick card (20 x 20cm/8 x 8in), pair of compasses, pencil, water pot, white paint, paintbrush.

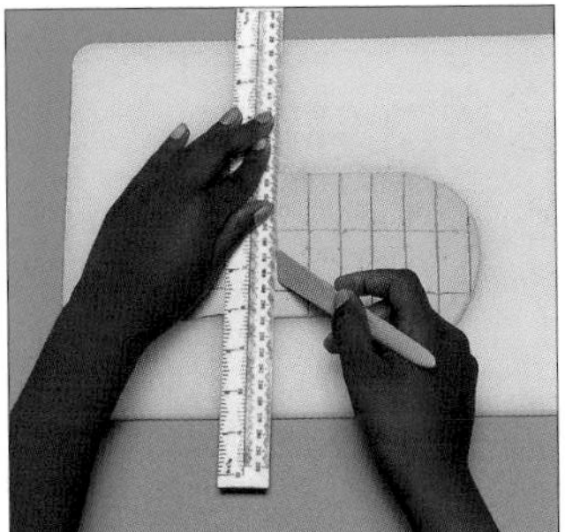

1 Roll out the clay. It should be 8mm/5/16in thick. Cut out 30 blocks of clay. Twenty-four of the blocks must be 4 x 2cm/1½ x ¾in and the other six blocks must be 2 x 1cm/¾ x ½in.

2 Cut out some card to make an irregular base shape. Roll out more clay (8mm/5/16in thick). Put the template on the clay and cut around it to make the base of the igloo.

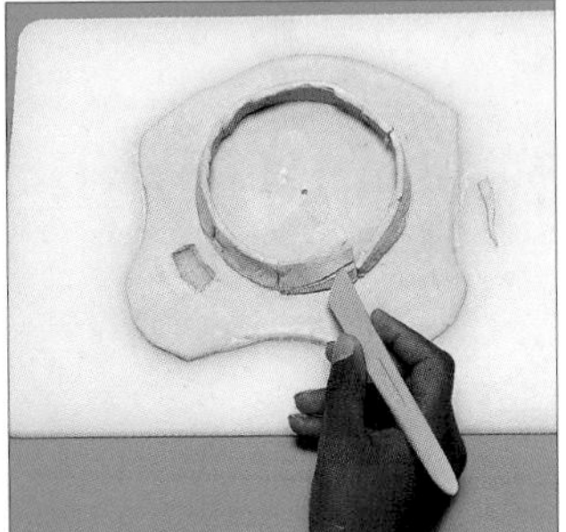

3 Mark a circle (diameter 12cm/4½in) on the base. Cut out a rectangle on the edge of the circle (2 x 4cm/¾ x 1½in). Stick nine blocks around the circle using water. Cut across two blocks, as shown.

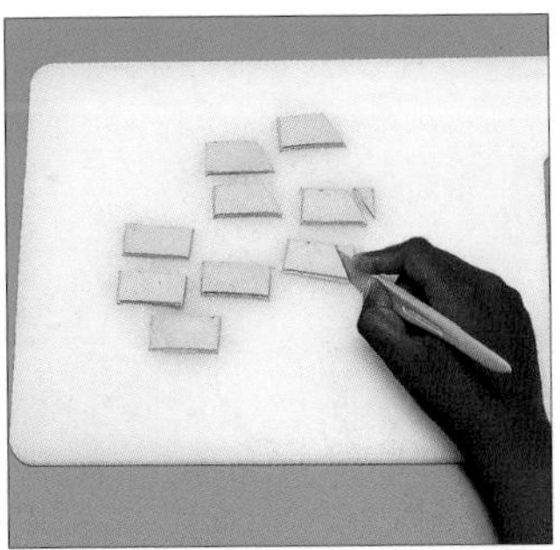

4 Using your modelling tool, carefully cut a small piece of clay from the corner of each of the remaining blocks of clay, as shown above. Discard the pieces of cut clay.

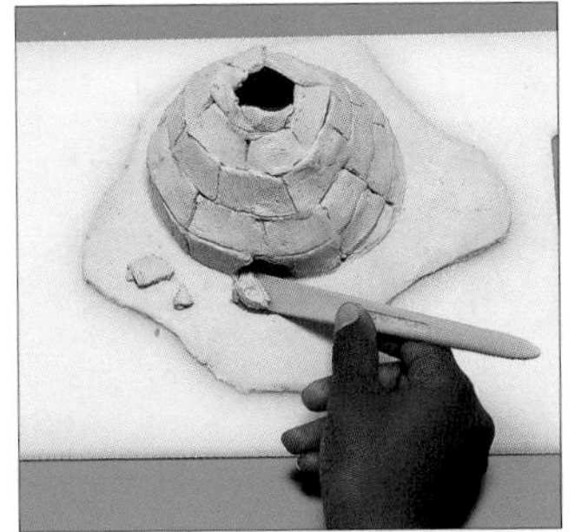

5 Build up the igloo dome, slanting each block in as you go. Use the six small blocks at the top and leave a gap. Form an entrance behind the rectangle cut into the base. Then paint it white.

Inuit hunters made temporary shelters by fitting ice blocks together to form a spiralling, dome-shaped igloo. Only firmly packed snow was used to make the ice blocks.

Medieval castle

In the Middle Ages, castles were built as fortified homes for wealthy lords. The castle needed to be big enough for the lord's family, servants and private army, and strong enough to withstand attack. The outer walls were very high to prevent attackers from climbing over them.

Building a castle ▸

Hundreds of workers were needed to build a castle. Raw materials such as stone, timber and iron had to be transported to the site, often over great distances.

▾ Templates

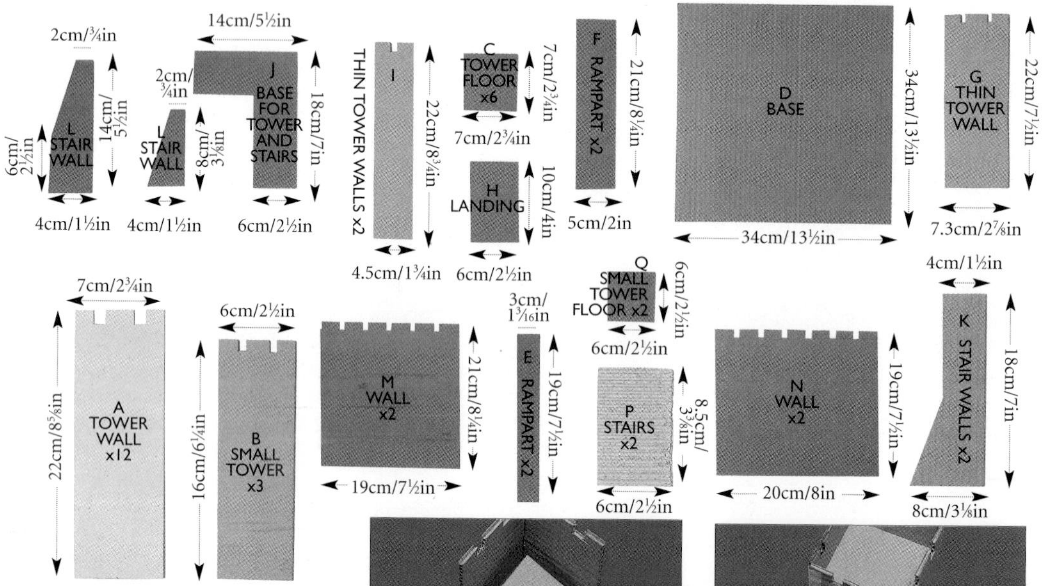

L STAIR WALL – 2cm/¾in, 14cm/5½in, 6cm/2½in, 4cm/1½in

L STAIR WALL – 2cm/¾in, 8cm/3⅛in, 4cm/1½in

J BASE FOR TOWER AND STAIRS – 14cm/5½in, 18cm/7in, 6cm/2½in

I THIN TOWER WALLS x2 – 22cm/8¾in, 4.5cm/1¾in

C TOWER FLOOR x6 – 7cm/2¾in, 7cm/2¾in

H LANDING – 10cm/4in, 6cm/2½in

F RAMPART x2 – 21cm/8¼in, 5cm/2in

D BASE – 34cm/13½in, 34cm/13½in

G THIN TOWER WALL – 22cm/7½in, 7.3cm/2⅞in

A TOWER WALL x12 – 7cm/2¾in, 22cm/8⅝in

B SMALL TOWER x3 – 6cm/2½in, 16cm/6¼in

M WALL x2 – 21cm/8¼in, 19cm/7½in

E RAMPART x2 – 3cm/1³⁄₁₆in, 19cm/7½in

Q SMALL TOWER FLOOR x2 – 6cm/2½in, 6cm/2½in

P STAIRS x2 – 8.5cm/3⅜in, 6cm/2½in

N WALL x2 – 19cm/7½in, 20cm/8in

K STAIR WALLS x2 – 4cm/1½in, 18cm/7in, 8cm/3⅛in

YOU WILL NEED

Ruler, pencil, scissors, four 50 x 76cm/20 x 30in sheets of thick card, 19 x 7cm/7½ x 2¾in sheet of thin card, 50 x 15cm/20 x 6in sheet of corrugated card, white glue and glue brush, masking tape, pair of compasses, acrylic paints, paintbrush, water pot.

1 Cut the stairs from the corrugated card, thin tower wall (G) from thin card and the rest from thick card. Glue two walls A on to tower floor C. Glue upper floor C in place.

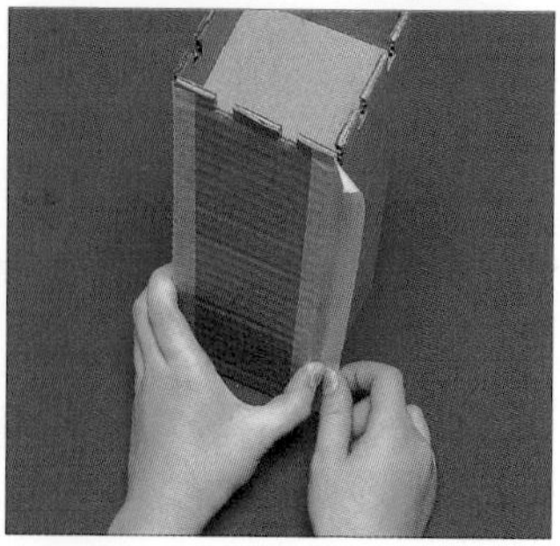

2 Glue the open edges of the floor, tower base and standing wall and stick the other two walls in place. Tape strips of masking tape over all the outside corners of the tower walls.

3 Draw a 9.5cm/3¾in-diameter circle on thick card. Mark it into quarters. Cut out two quarters for the thin tower floors. Glue the two right-angled walls I and the floors into position.

4 Glue the edges of the thin tower walls I. Curve thin card wall section G and stick it on to the right-angled walls. Strengthen the joins with masking tape. Glue tower on base D.

5 Glue the other towers at each corner of the castle base. Glue the bottom and side edges of the walls M and N and stick them between the towers. Glue ramparts E and F to the walls, as shown.

6 Make the small tower B in just the same way as you have made all the other towers. Put two of the walls in place, then the floors and finally the third wall.

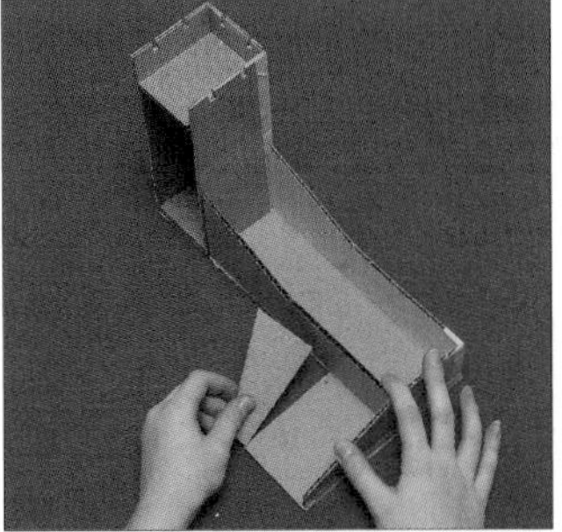

7 Glue the small tower at the end of the longer arm of the castle's stair base section J. Glue the two long stair walls K and each stair wall L into place, as shown above.

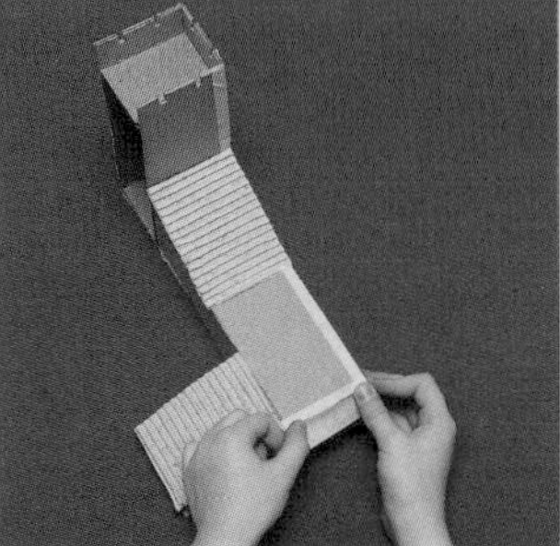

8 Glue landing H on to the straight edges of the stair walls. Stick stairs P on to the sloped edges. Secure with tape. Then stick the whole structure to one side wall of the castle.

9 Cut out some pieces of thick card and glue them to the walls of your castle and stair-tower. When you have finished, paint the castle to look like stone and paint in some windows.

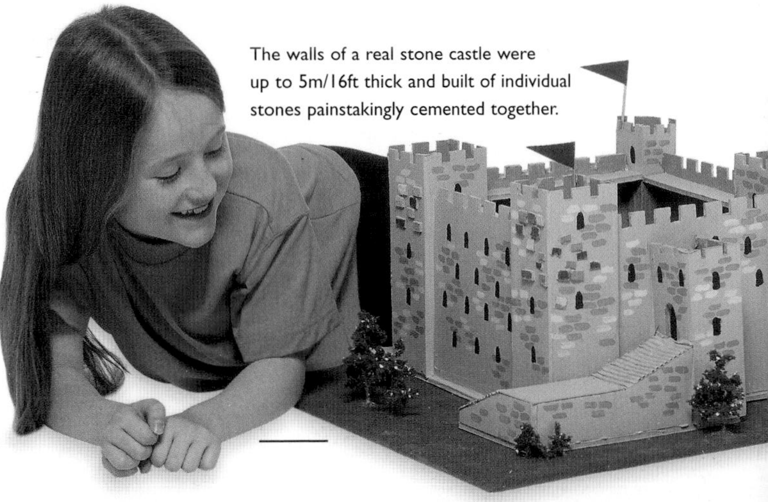

The walls of a real stone castle were up to 5m/16ft thick and built of individual stones painstakingly cemented together.

Inside the Home

Unless they happened to be very rich, most people throughout history have lived in simple but extremely functional homes. Most families had few pieces of furniture or other household items. Their homes consisted of one large room, which was used for a number of different activities, such as cooking, eating and sleeping. By contrast, modern homes are arranged so that separate rooms are used for specific activities, and each room is furnished for that purpose.

▲ Elaborate patterns
The Native American tribes of southwestern North America were renowned for their beautiful pottery. Each tribe used geometric designs and bright colours to decorate household objects, such as this striking tankard.

▲ Spacious layout
The rooms of a Chinese house from the Han Dynasty (206BC–AD220) were built around a courtyard and small garden. Family rooms were separate from the main reception area, which was used for entertaining.

▲ Greek vase
This Greek vase is in the Geometric Style, dating from between 1000BC and 700BC. The detailed pattern took a long time to create, so it was very expensive to buy. The vase would have been used only for special occasions.

Lasting tradition ▸
Many modern lifestyles have not changed much over the centuries. The Japanese have long favoured simple interior spaces divided by light partitions instead of solid walls. Traditional paper windows have been replaced by glass, which captures the effect of paper.

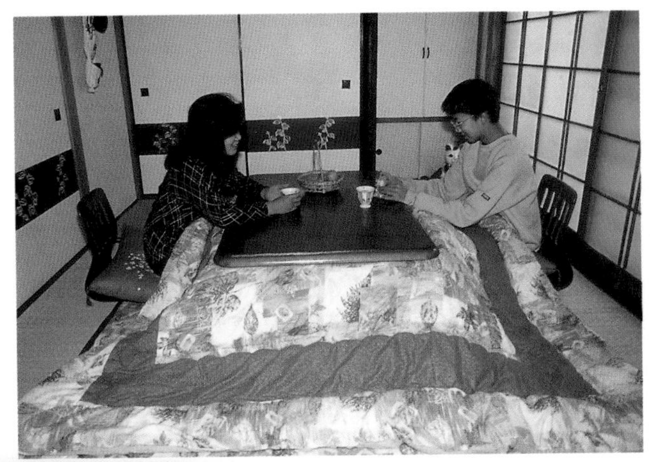

◂ All in one
Huts made from stone, turf and animal bones were built by the Thule people of the Arctic. The main feature of the inside of the hut was a fire. Animal skins were draped on the walls and floor to give insulation against the bitter cold.

House and garden ▸
Wealthy Japanese nobles lived in huge *shinden* (single-storey homes) with many different rooms. The various members of the noble family, and their servants, lived in different parts of the *shinden*. Streams flowed from the garden through the rooms of the house.

Egyptian tiles

The ancient Egyptians loved to decorate their surroundings. Wealthy citizens had the walls of their homes plastered and painted in bright colours. The rooms of their houses included bedrooms, living rooms, kitchens in thatched courtyards and workshops. Homes were furnished with beds, chairs, stools and benches. Many beautiful tiles have been found in the tombs of the pharaohs, and it is thought that they were used to decorate the furniture and floors of their magnificent palaces.

YOU WILL NEED

Two sheets of card, pencil, ruler, scissors, self-hardening clay, cutting board, rolling pin, modelling tool, sandpaper, acrylic paint (blue, gold, green and yellow ochre), paintbrush, water pot.

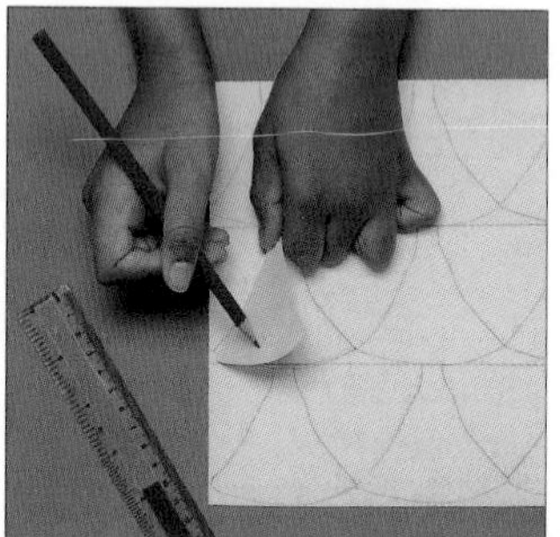

1 Copy the two tile shapes, about 5cm/2in deep, on one sheet of card. Cut them out. Draw around them on the other sheet to make the whole pattern. Trim the edge as in Step 2.

2 Roll out the clay on to a cutting board with a rolling pin. Place the overall outline over the clay and carefully trim the edges using the modelling tool. Discard the extra clay.

3 Mark the individual tile patterns on to the clay. Cut through the lines but do not separate them fully. Score patterns of leaves and flowers on to the surface of the clay. Separate each tile.

4 When one side of each tile has dried, turn the tile over and leave the other side to dry. When the tiles are fully dry, use a piece of sandpaper to smooth off the edges.

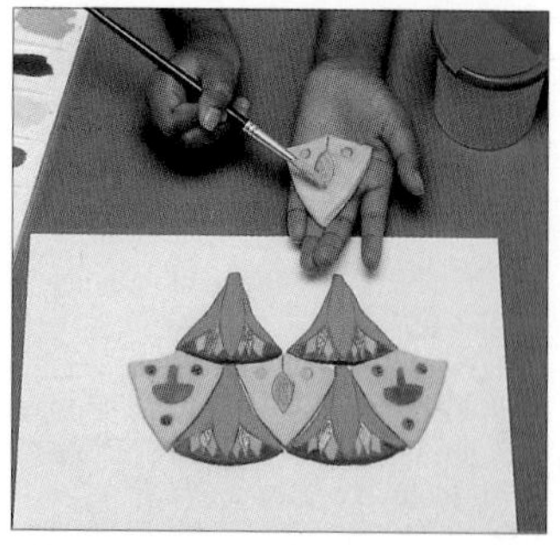

5 The tiles are now ready to paint. Use bright colours to paint over the patterns you made earlier. When you have finished, leave the tiles to dry in a warm place.

The tiles you have made are similar to ones found at a royal palace in Thebes, the capital city of ancient Egypt. The design looks rather like a lotus, the sacred flower of ancient Egypt.

Greek dolphin fresco

Frescoes – paintings on plaster – were a popular way of decorating the walls of palaces on the Greek island of Crete. To make the frescoes last as long as possible, they were painted directly on to wet plaster. Most Greek frescoes show scenes from palace life and the natural world. The paintings are a vital source of information for modern historians. A large fresco decorated the walls of the queen's apartments in a magnificent palace at Knossos. The fresco shows lively dolphins and fish swimming underwater.

YOU WILL NEED

Pencil, sheet of white paper (21 x 19cm/8¼ x 7½in), rolling pin, self-hardening clay, cutting board, rolling pin, modelling tool, ruler, pin, sandpaper, acrylic paints, paintbrush, water pot.

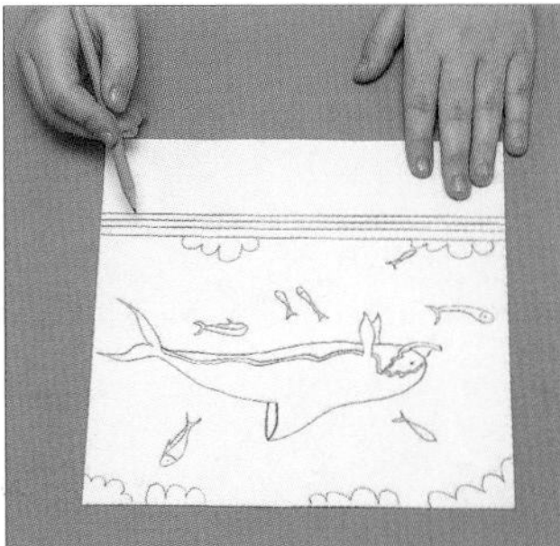

1 Draw a picture of a dolphin on to the sheet of white paper. Add some smaller fish and some seaweed for decoration. Refer to the final picture as a guide for your drawing.

2 Roll out some clay. Tidy up the edges using the modelling tool and ruler. Place your picture over the clay and use a pin to prick holes through the outline on to the clay below.

3 Peel the paper off to reveal your picture marked out in dots. Leave the base to dry completely. Then sand it down with fine sandpaper for a smooth finish.

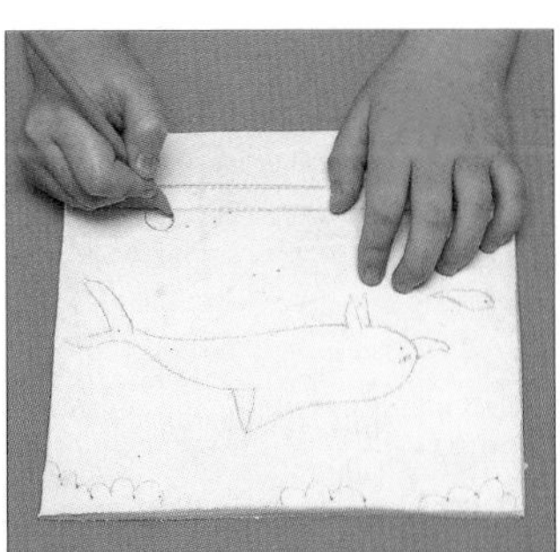

4 Use your pencil to join up the dots on the surface of the clay. Do not press too hard on the clay. When you have finished, you will have a replica of your original drawing.

5 You can then begin to paint the picture. When you have finished, paint in two stripes at the bottom of the picture. These indicate where the fresco would have ended on the wall.

Today, the frescoes at Knossos are copies based on fragments of the original pictures. They are a valuable source of information about Minoan customs.

Roman mosaic

The Romans loved to decorate their homes, and the floors of some wealthy houses were covered with mosaic pictures. These pictures might show hunting scenes, the harvest or Roman gods. They were made by using *tesserae* – cubes of stone, pottery or glass – which were pressed into soft cement. Making a mosaic was rather like doing a jigsaw puzzle.

tesserae

Tiny tiles ▲
The floor of a room in an average Roman town house may have been made up of over 100,000 tesserae.

YOU WILL NEED

Paper, pencil, ruler, scissors, large sheet of card, self-hardening clay, rolling pin, cutting board, modelling tool, acrylic paints, paintbrush, water pot, clear varnish and brush (optional), plaster paste, spreader, muslin rag.

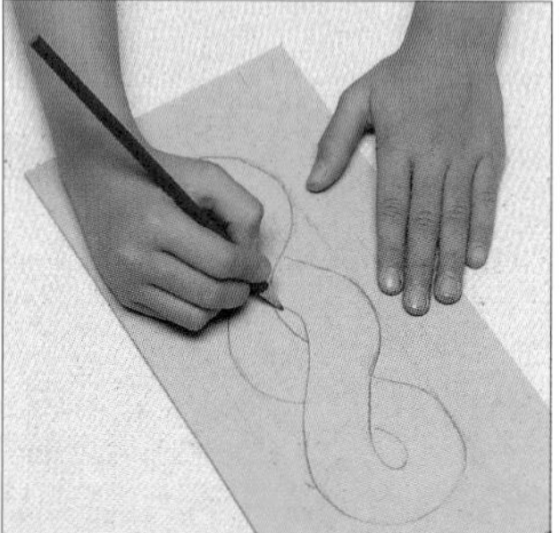

1 Sketch your design on to a rough sheet of paper. A simple design is always easier to work with. Cut the sheet of card to measure 25 x 10cm/10 x 4in. Copy your design on to it.

2 Roll out the clay on the cutting board. Use a ruler to measure out small squares (your tiles) on the clay. Cut out the tiles using the modelling tool and then leave them to dry.

3 Paint the dry tiles different colours, as shown above. When the paint is dry, you can give the tiles a coat of varnish for extra strength and shine. Leave the tiles to dry completely.

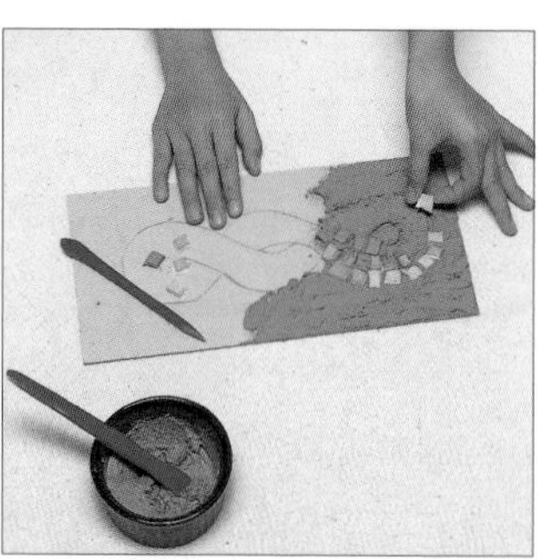

4 Spread plaster paste on to the sheet of card, a small part at a time. While the paste is still wet, press in your tiles, following your design. Use the rough sketch as an extra guide.

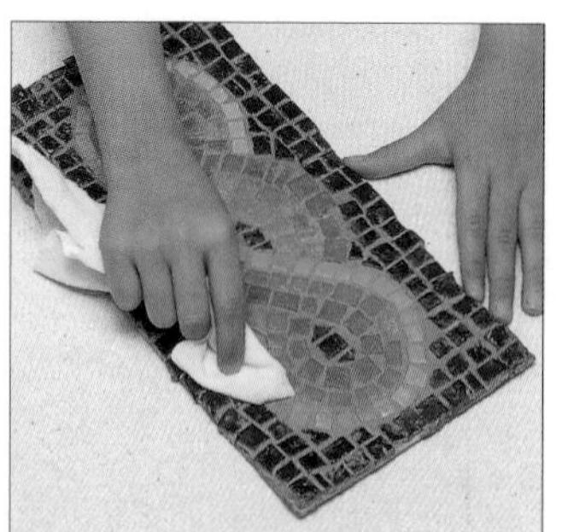

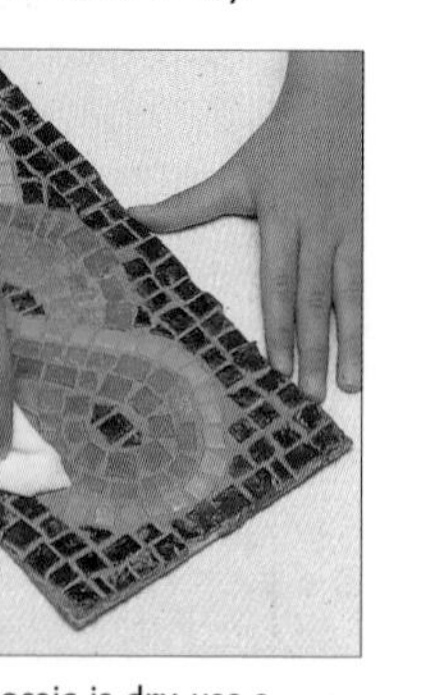

5 When the mosaic is dry, use a muslin rag to polish the surface of the tiles. Any other soft, dry rag will do. When you have finished, you can display your mosaic in your house.

Mosaics were displayed in dining rooms and courtyards where visitors would see them.

Roman kitchen

The kitchens of wealthy Romans were equipped with all kinds of bronze pots, pans, strainers and ladles. Pottery storage jars held wine, olive oil and sauces. Herbs, vegetables and joints of meat hung from hooks in the roof. There were no cans, and no fridges or freezers to keep the food fresh. Instead, food had to be preserved in oil or by drying, smoking, salting or pickling. Food was boiled, fried, grilled (broiled) and stewed. Larger kitchens might include stone ovens for baking bread or spits for roasting meat.

YOU WILL NEED

Ruler, pencil, thick card, scissors, white glue and glue brush, masking tape, acrylic paints, paintbrush, water pot, red felt-tipped pen, plaster paste, sandpaper, balsa wood, self-hardening clay, cutting board, modelling tool.

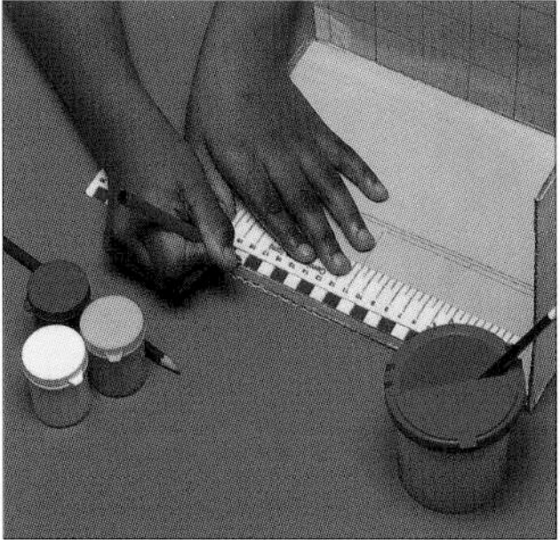

1 Glue pieces of card to make the walls and floor. Secure with masking tape. Paint the floor grey and pencil in stone tiles. Paint the walls yellow and blue. Draw on stripes with the red pen.

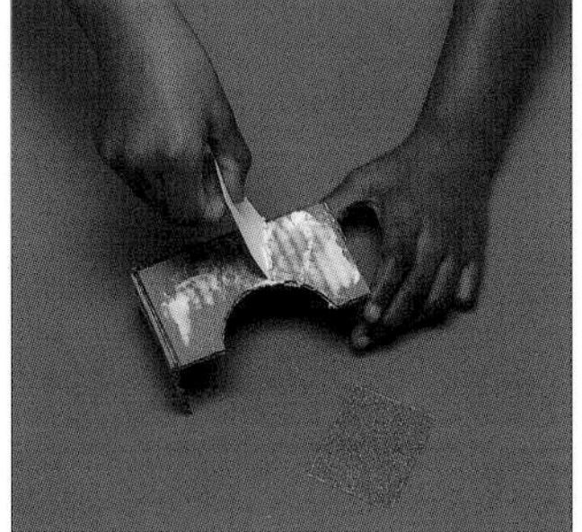

2 Use some card to make a stove and coat it with plaster paste. When it is dry, rub it smooth with sandpaper. Make a grate from two strips of card and four bits of balsa wood, glued together.

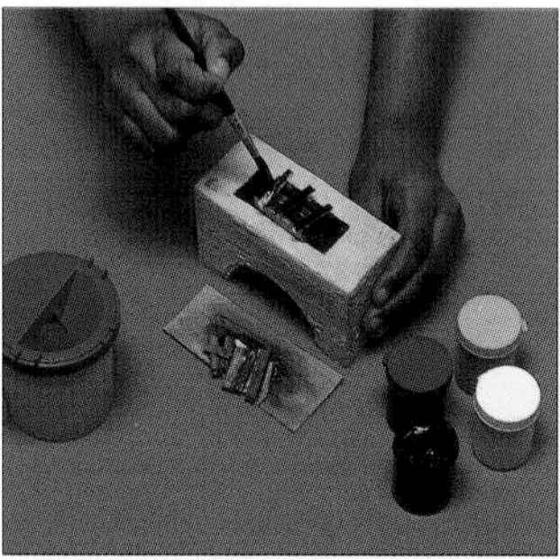

3 Use some acrylic paints to colour the stove, as shown above. Use small pieces of balsa wood to make a pile of wood fuel to store underneath the stove.

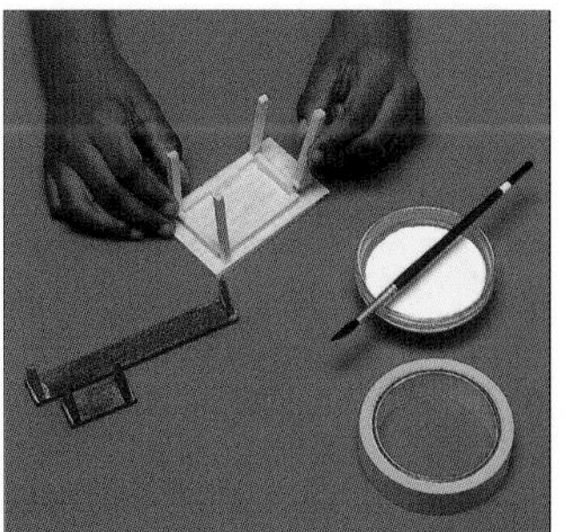

4 Make a table and shelves from pieces of balsa wood, as shown above. Glue them together and secure the joins with masking tape. Leave them to dry before painting them brown.

5 Use a piece of clay to model pots, pans, bowls, storage jars, perhaps even a frying pan or an egg poacher. Leave the utensils to dry before painting them a suitable colour.

Foods in a Roman kitchen were stored in baskets, bowls or sacks. Wine, oil and sauces were stored in pottery jars called *amphorae*.

Chinese lantern

Festivals in China are linked to agricultural seasons. These festivals include celebrations of sowing and harvest, dances, horse racing and the eating of specially prepared foods. The Chinese festival best known around the world today is the New Year or Spring Festival. Its date falls on the first full moon between January 21 and February 19. At the end of the Chinese New Year, dumplings made of rice flour are prepared for the Lantern Festival. This festival began during the Tang Dynasty or 'Golden Age' (AD618–906) – a time when the arts prospered, new trade routes opened in foreign lands, and boundaries expanded as a result of successful military campaigns.

▲ **Bright lights**

During the Lantern Festival, lanterns are hung outside the house to represent the first full moon of the Chinese New Year. Lanterns were once made from silk or glass, and decorated with ornate images or calligraphy (handwriting).

Templates

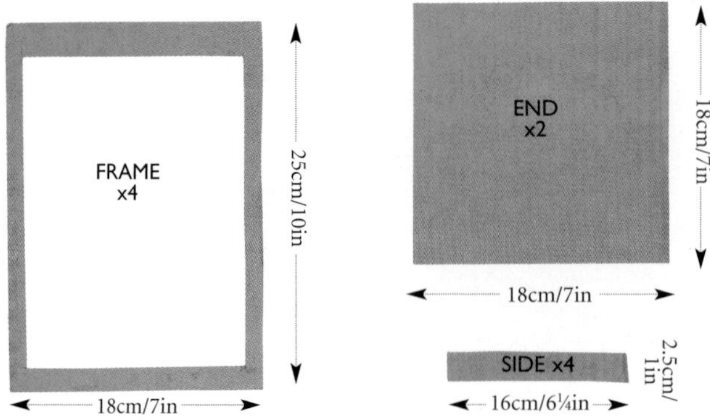

Using the measurements above, draw the ten templates on to thick card (the templates are not drawn to scale). Cut them out carefully using a pair of scissors.

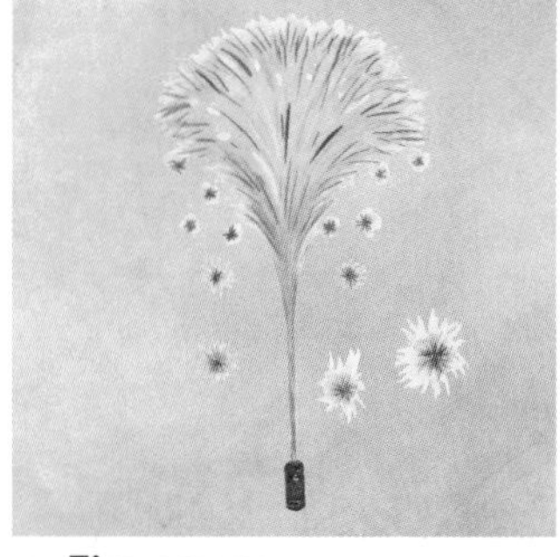

▲ **Fire power**

You could decorate your lantern with a firework display. The Chinese invented gunpowder in the AD700s. It was first used to make fireworks in the 900s.

YOU WILL NEED

Thick card, pencil, ruler, scissors, pair of compasses, white glue and glue brush, red tissue paper, blue acrylic paint, paintbrush, water pot, thin blue and yellow card, wire, masking tape, bamboo stick, small torch (flashlight), fringing fabric.

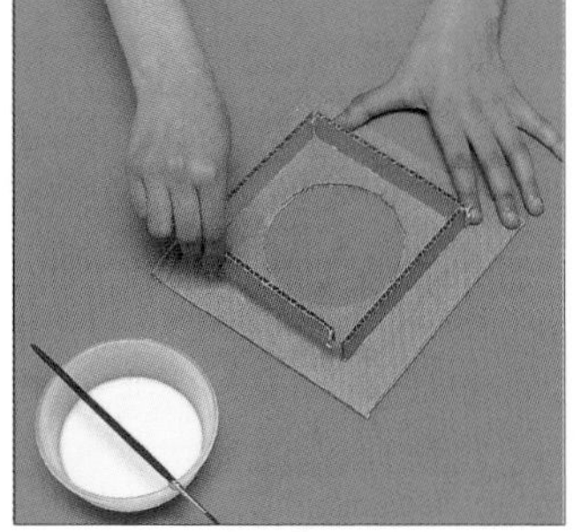

1 Using a pair of compasses, draw an 8cm/3⅛in-diameter circle in the middle of one of the end pieces. Cut out the circle using the scissors. Glue on the four sides.

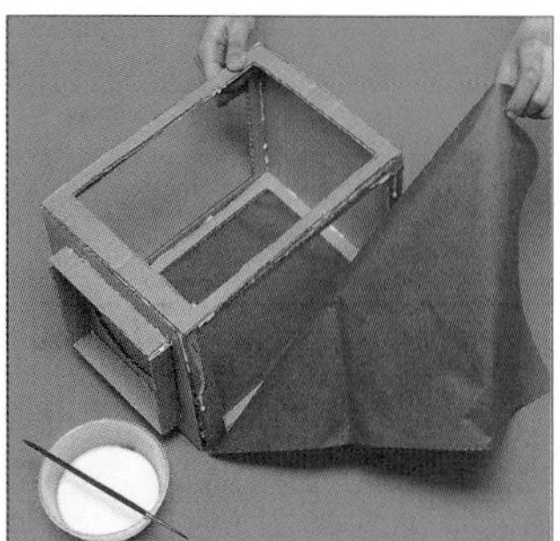

2 Glue together the four frame pieces. Then glue both end pieces on to the frame. When it is dry, cover the frame with red tissue paper. Glue one side at a time.

3 Paint the top of the lantern blue. Cut the borders out of blue card. Glue to the top and bottom of the frame. Stick a thin strip of yellow card to the bottom to make a border.

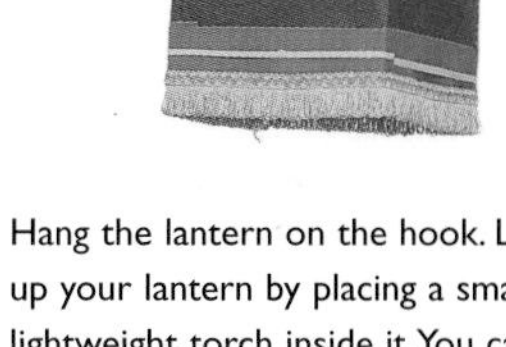

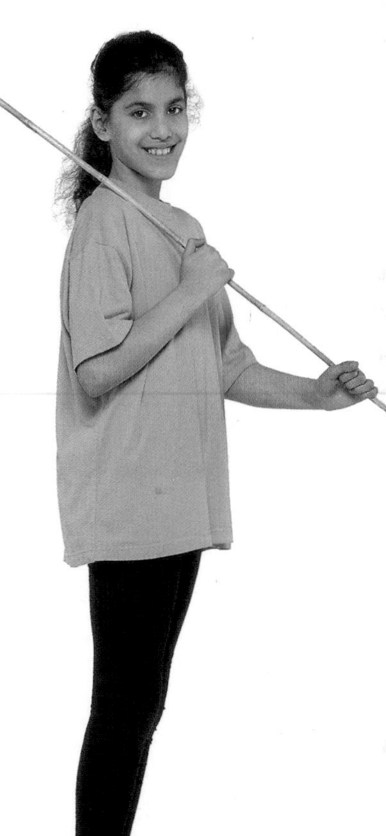

Hang the lantern on the hook. Light up your lantern by placing a small, lightweight torch inside it. You can decorate the bottom of the lantern with some fringing fabric.

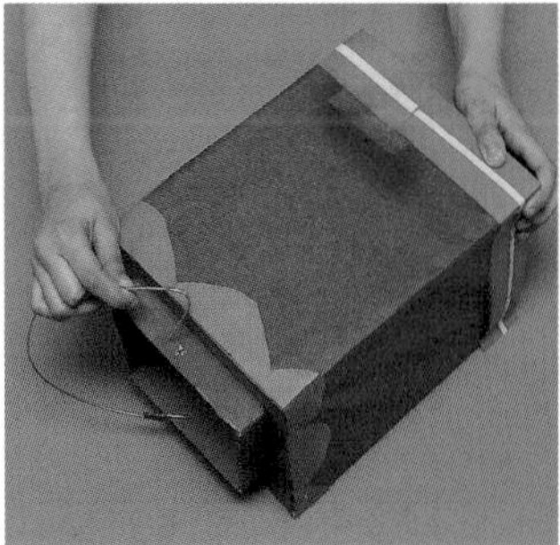

4 Make two small holes opposite each other at the top of the lantern, as shown above. Pass the ends of a loop of wire through the holes. Tape the ends to secure the wire.

5 Make a hook from thick card. Split the ends opposite the hook, as shown above. Wrap the ends around the bamboo stick and glue them together, securing with masking tape.

Japanese paper screen

Builders faced many challenges when they designed homes in ancient Japan. Not only did buildings have to provide shelter against extremes of climate, they also had to withstand earthquakes. Lightweight, single-storey houses were made of straw, paper and wood. These would bend and sway in an earthquake. If they did collapse, or were swept away by floods, they would be less likely than a stone building to injure the people inside.

Japanese buildings were designed as a series of box-like rooms. A one-room hut was sufficient for a farming family. Dividing screens and partitions could be moved around to suit people's needs. Many houses had verandas (open platforms) beneath overhanging eaves. People could sit here taking in the fresh air, keeping lookout or enjoying the view.

▲ Screened off
Wood and paper were used to make screens for both the outer and inner walls of many Japanese homes. The screens were pushed back to provide peaceful garden views and welcome cool breezes during the hot summer.

▲ Fine work
Folding screens became decorative items as well as providing privacy and protection from draughts. This panel was made during the Edo period (1603–1868), when crafts flourished.

Simple living ▸
Modern rural Japanese homes are built in the same way and using similar materials to those of ancient Japan. Screens and sliding walls can be moved to block draughts and for privacy. Straw and rush mats, called *tatami,* cover the floor.

YOU WILL NEED

Gold paper (48 x 44cm/ 19 x 17½in), pencil, ruler, scissors, thick card (48 x 22cm/19 x 8¾in), craft knife, cutting board, white glue and glue brush, fabric paints, paintbrush, water pot, fabric tape.

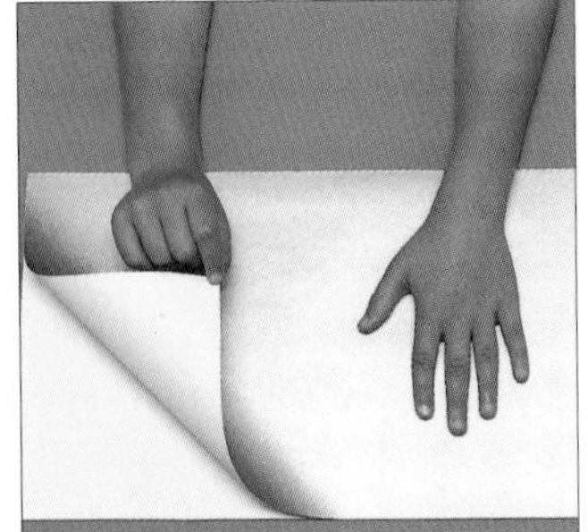

1 Cut two pieces of gold paper to measure 48 x 22cm/19 x 8¾in. Use a craft knife to cut out a piece of card the same size. Stick the gold paper to each side of the card.

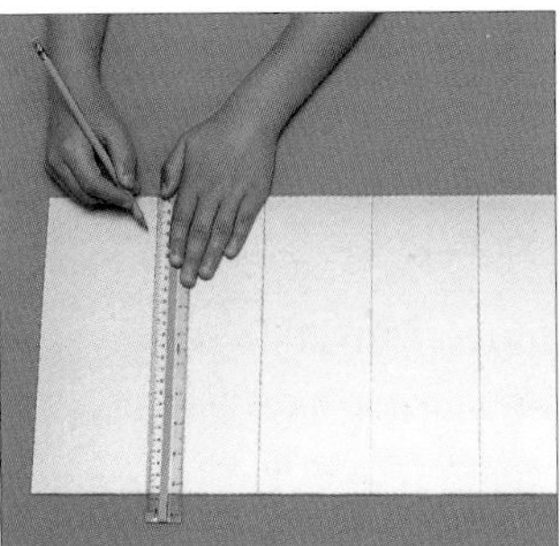

2 When the glue has dried, use a ruler and pencil to mark out six panels of equal size on one side of the gold-covered card. Each panel should measure 22 x 8cm/8¾ x 3⅛in.

3 Now turn the card over. Paint a traditional picture of Japanese irises in shades of blue and green fabric paint, as shown above. Leave the paint to dry.

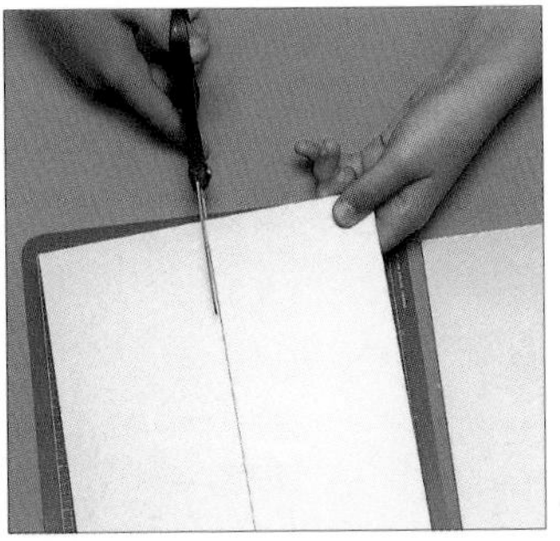

4 Turn the screen over so the plain, unpainted side is facing you. Using scissors or a craft knife, carefully cut out each panel along the lines that you marked earlier.

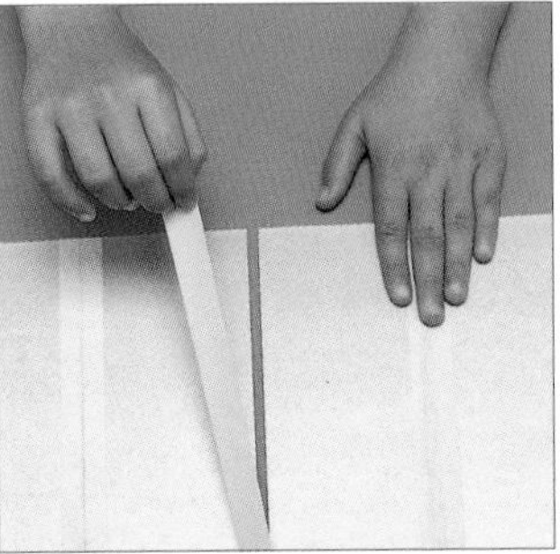

5 Now use fabric tape to join each of your panels together, leaving a small gap between each panel. The tape will act as a hinge for each section of your Japanese screen.

Irises are a popular image in Japanese homes. The pretty blue flowers are a symbol of absent friends.

Native American tankard

The Native Americans were highly skilled craftspeople. Most tribes wove baskets and blankets from plant fibres. Some baskets were coiled so tightly that they could hold water. The tribes of the Southwest were renowned for their pottery. The Apache tribe made black and white bowls that became known as burial pots. This was because they were broken when their owner died and buried with the body. Archaeologists have also found beautiful pots dating back to around 1000BC.

YOU WILL NEED

Self-hardening clay, cutting board, rolling board, water pot, pencil, selection of acrylic or poster paints, selection of paintbrushes, non-toxic varnish.

1 Roll out a slab of clay into a flat circle 10cm/4in across. Roll two sausage shapes. Dampen the perimeter of the circle and then stick one end of the sausage to it, as shown above.

2 Coil the sausage around. When the first sausage runs out, use the other clay sausage. Use your damp fingers to smooth the coils into a tankard shape and smooth the outside.

3 Roll out another small sausage shape of clay to make the handle of the tankard. Dampen the ends and press it on to the clay pot to make a handle shape. Leave it to dry.

4 Using a sharp pencil, mark out a striking design on your tankard. You can follow the traditional Indian design shown here, or you could make up one of your own.

5 Using poster paints or acrylic paints, colour in the pattern. Use a fine brush for tiny checked patterns and thin lines. When it is dry, coat the mug with one or two layers of varnish.

Each tribe had its unique designs and used certain colours. The geometric patterns on the tankard above were common to tribes of the Southwest.

Viking drinking horn

The Viking sagas (long stories) tell of many drunken celebrations. They helped relieve the strain of the long dark winters. Warriors would have toasted each other with beer or mead (an alcoholic drink made by fermenting honey). They drank from drinking horns made from the horns of cattle. Unless a drinking horn was being passed around a number of people, it could not be put down and the contents had to be consumed in one go. Drink was ladled out from giant barrels and tubs.

YOU WILL NEED

Thick paper, pencil, ruler, scissors, mug, masking tape, brown paper, self-hardening clay, newspaper, water pot, acrylic paints, paintbrush, silver paper, white glue and glue brush.

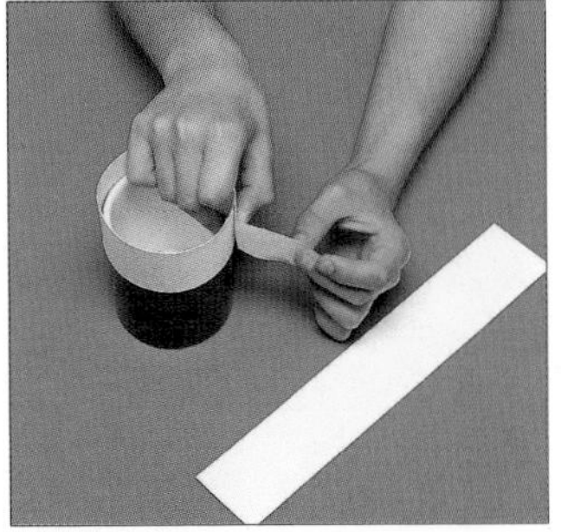

1 Cut the thick paper into 28cm/11in-long strips all with different widths. Roll the widest strip into a ring using the rim of a mug as a guide. Secure the paper ring with masking tape.

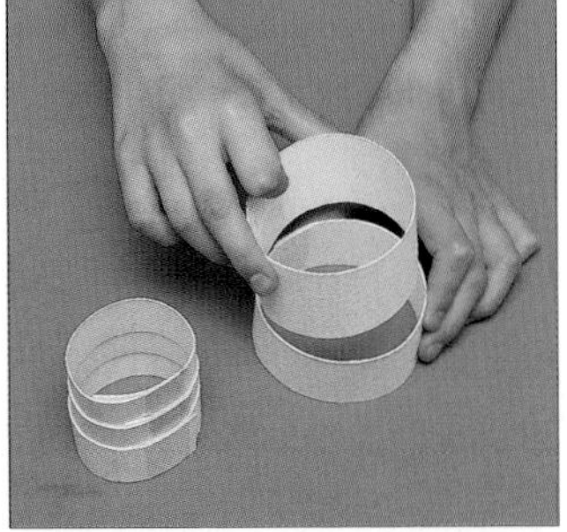

2 Roll up the next widest strip, and secure it with masking tape. Place the small ring inside the large ring and fix with tape. Make more rings, each one a bit smaller than the one before.

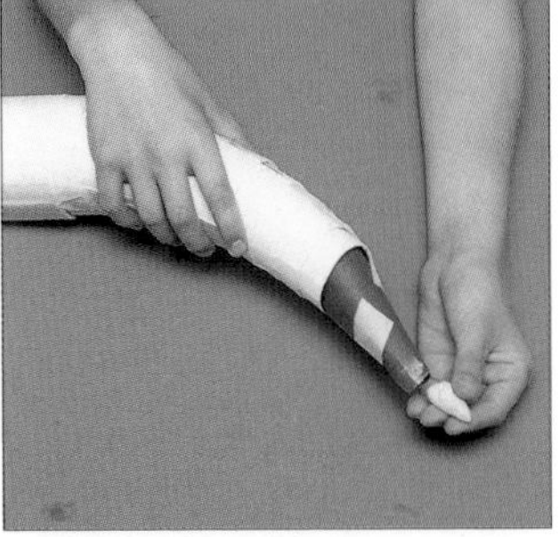

3 Place each small ring into the next largest, binding with tape to make a tapered horn. Roll brown paper into a cone to make a point and bind it in position. Round off the end with clay.

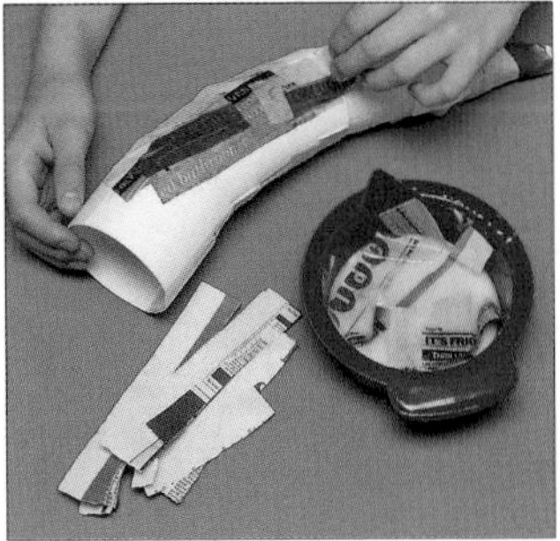

4 Cover the horn with papier mâché. Cut strips of newspaper, soak them in water and glue them to the horn. Leave to dry and then add more layers of papier mâché. Leave to dry again.

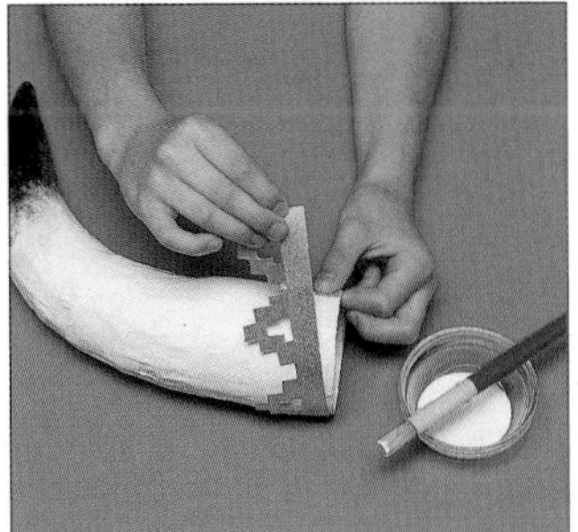

5 When dry, paint the horn white, giving it a black or brown tip. Cut the silver paper into a pattern and glue it to the rim of the horn. Viking horns were often decorated with silver.

Drinking horns were used on special occasions such as festivals and victory celebrations.

Arctic oil lamp

The Arctic is one of the wildest, harshest, environments on Earth. Arctic winters are long, dark and bitterly cold. A thick layer of snow and ice blankets the region for much of the year. A fire was the main feature of an Arctic home. In Inuit shelters, seal or whale blubber were burned in stone lamps to provide light and additional heat. With fires and lamps burning, the shelters could be surprisingly warm and bright.

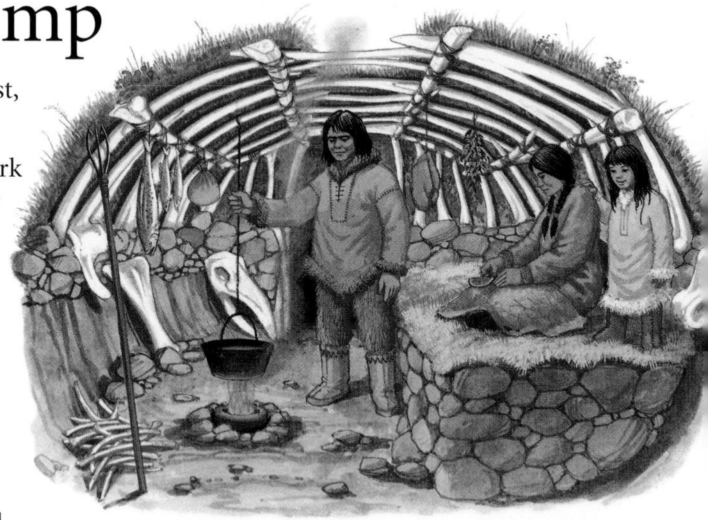

▲ Underground houses

Ancient Arctic peoples built their houses under the ground to protect them from the freezing conditions above. Often, the walls and floor were lined with animal skins to provide extra insulation against the cold.

▲ Colony in the cold

When Viking warrior Erik the Red landed in Greenland in AD983, he and his men built houses of turf and stone. These shelters provided excellent insulation against the cold.

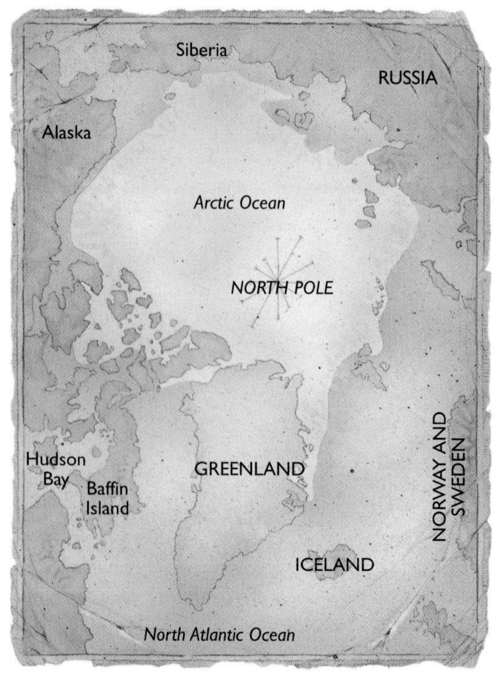

A harsh climate ▶

The Arctic lies at the far north of our planet within the Arctic Circle. Much of the Arctic is a vast, frozen ocean, surrounded by the northernmost parts of Asia, Europe, North America and Greenland. The Arctic is characterized by low temperatures, often as low as –70°C/–158°F in the winter. For anyone living in the region, it is vital to keep as warm as possible. Homes may be buried underground, with an entrance through the roof.

YOU WILL NEED

Self-hardening clay, rolling pin, cutting board, ruler, pair of compasses, sharp pencil, modelling tool, water pot, dark grey and light grey paint, small paintbrush.

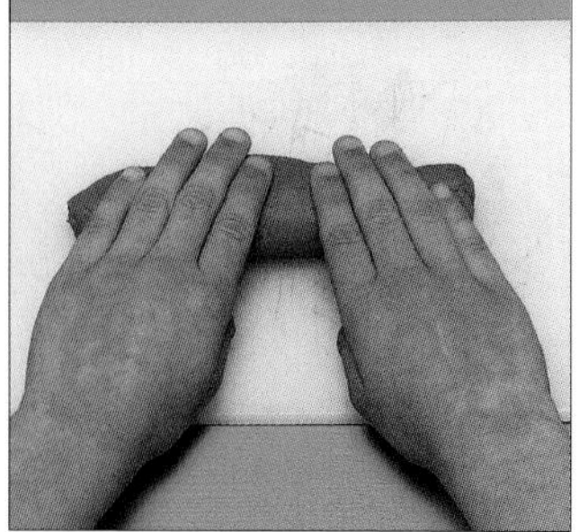

1 Roll out a piece of clay. Draw out a circle with a radius of 5cm/2in, and cut the circle out using the modelling tool. Roll more clay out into a sausage shape 30cm/1ft long and 2cm/¾in thick.

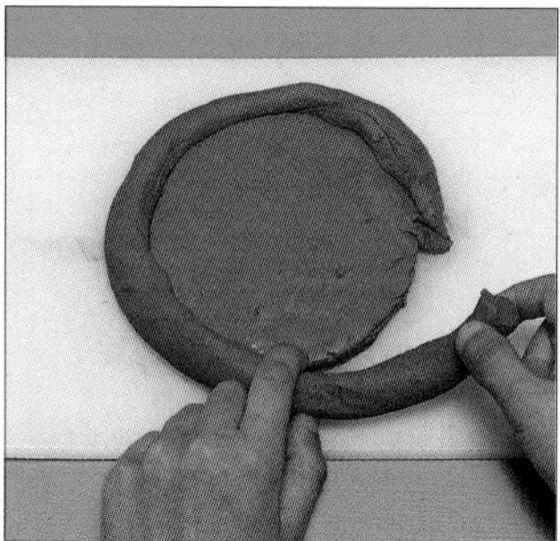

2 Wet the edge of the clay circle and stick the sausage shape around it. Use the rounded end of the modelling tool to blend the edges firmly into the base.

3 Use your modelling tool to cut a small triangular notch at the edge of the circle. This will make a small lip for the front of your oil lamp.

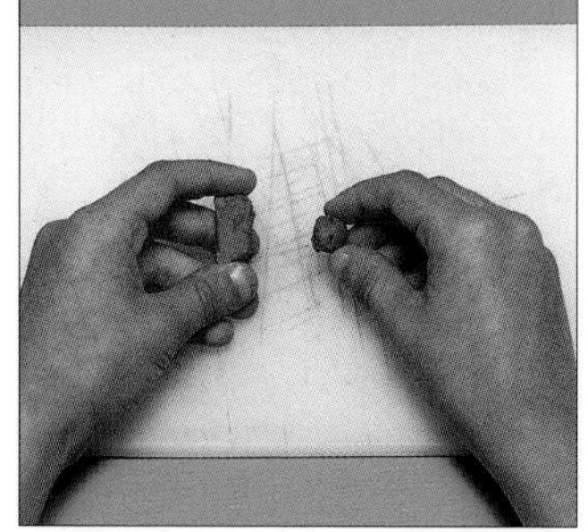

4 Shape a piece of clay into a small head. Use another piece to shape some shoulders. Stick the head to the shoulders by wetting the clay and holding the pieces firmly together.

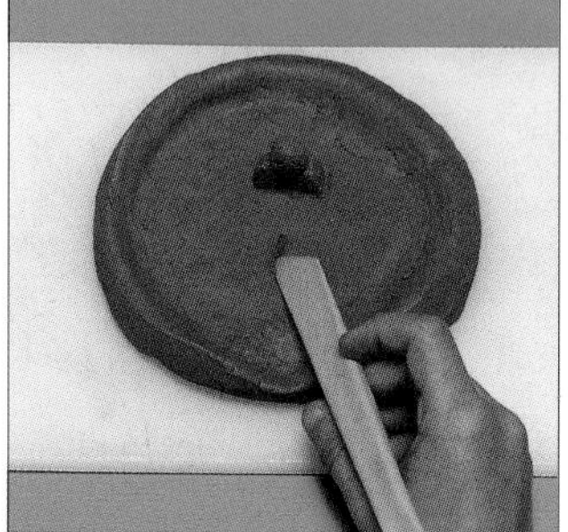

5 Stick the small figure just off centre on the base of the oil lamp. Then use the modelling tool to make a small groove on the base. This is for holding the oil.

6 Decorate the edge of the lamp with extra pieces of clay. Once dry, paint the lamp using dark grey and light grey paint. Safety note: *Do not attempt to burn anything in your lamp.*

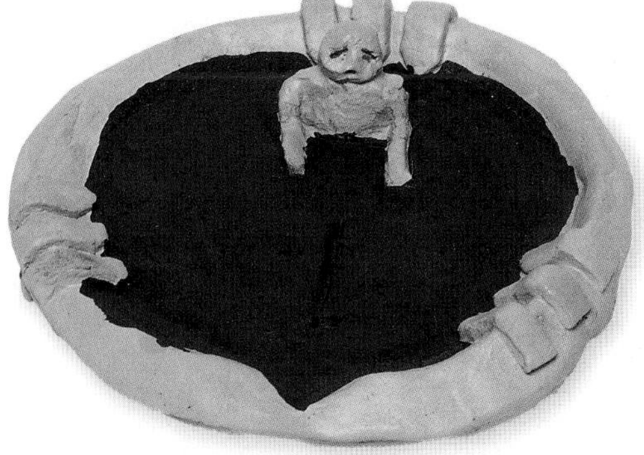

Stone lamps burning seal or whale blubber (fat) cast a warm glow in homes throughout the Arctic region. A lighted wick of moss or animal fur was placed in a bowl filled with fat, and the lamp was left to burn slowly.

Food and Feasts

barley wheat

corn

squashes

▲ Fruits of the soil

The first plants to be cultivated already grew in the wild. For example, wheat and barley were grown from wild plants in the Middle East. Corn, squashes and beans were the first to be grown in Central America.

A great change in human history took place around 10,000BC. Instead of gathering the seeds of wild plants, people began to grow their own food. They selected and sowed seeds from the healthiest plants to produce crops to harvest for food. People also began to breed cattle, goats and sheep for meat and milk. Different traditions surrounding the preparation, cooking and eating of food developed. Food was a way of showing hospitality to family and strangers. Some foods were given a religious meaning and came to be used for special festivals.

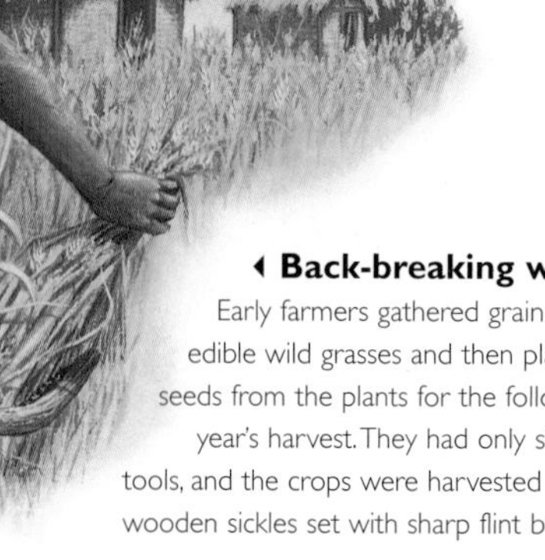

◀ Back-breaking work

Early farmers gathered grain from edible wild grasses and then planted seeds from the plants for the following year's harvest. They had only simple tools, and the crops were harvested using wooden sickles set with sharp flint blades.

▲ Jobs for the family

Farmers on this settlement in Germany are thatching the roof of a longhouse. The women are grinding grain between stones to make bread. They will add water to the flour and shape the dough into flat loaves, which will be baked in a clay oven.

cattle

▲ A farming village

The farmers of this village in southern England have built round, thatched houses next to their wheat fields. They also keep domesticated cattle for milk, meat and skins. Every morning the cattle were led from the village to pastures outside.

Domestication ▸

When people changed from hunting to farming, they caught very young animals to raise by hand. Larger, more aggressive animals were killed. Gradually, new domesticated strains evolved from the smaller, more docile animals. Domestic cattle were bred from large, wild animals called aurochs in this way.

auroch

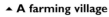

Stone Age food

The hunter-gatherers of the Stone Age had a varied diet. Gradually, they learned that they could eat certain plants and got to know where and when they could find them. From spring to autumn, women and children foraged for berries, nuts, eggs, and the roots, shoots and leaves of vegetables. In summer, fruits and plant seeds were picked and stored to eat or sow later.

dandelion leaves

woodland fungus

◂ Foraging for food

The food that prehistoric people ate came mostly from plants. Woodlands in autumn were a rich source of food, with plenty of fruits, fungi and nuts.

YOU WILL NEED

Pan, 500g/1¼lb blueberries, 500g/1¼lb blackberries, wooden spoon, 200g/7oz whole hazelnuts, honeycomb, tablespoon, ladle, serving bowl.

1 Choose fruit that is fresh and firm. Wash your hands before you start, and ask an adult to help you cook. Wash the blueberries and pour them into a large pan.

2 Next wash the blackberries and pour them into the pan with the blueberries. Use a wooden spoon to stir the fruits gently without crushing them.

3 Take the whole hazlenuts and pour them into the pan with the blueberries and blackberries. Carefully stir the contents until the fruits and nuts are thoroughly mixed.

4 Add six tablespoons of honey from the honeycomb. (You could use honey from a jar instead.) Then ask an adult to help you cook the mixture, gradually bringing it to the boil.

5 Simmer the fruit and nut mixture for about 20 minutes. Take the pan off the stove and leave it to cool. Use a ladle to transfer your dessert into a serving bowl.

In prehistoric times, people cooked fruit in this way to preserve it as jam. Clay pots were used for cooking and storing the jam.

Egyptian pastries

People in ancient Egypt were often given food as payment for their work. Foods such as bread, onions and salted fish were washed down with sweet, grainy beer. Flour was often gritty, and the teeth of many mummified bodies show signs of severe wear and tear. An Egyptian meal could be finished off with nuts, such as almonds, or sweet fruits, such as figs and dates.

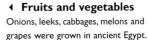

onions

◂ Fruits and vegetables
Onions, leeks, cabbages, melons and grapes were grown in ancient Egypt.

YOU WILL NEED
Mxing bowl, wooden spoon, 200g/7oz stoneground flour, ½ tsp salt, 1tsp baking powder, 75g/3oz chopped butter, 60g/2¼oz honey, 3 tbsp milk, floured surface, caraway seeds, baking tray.

1 Mix the flour, salt and baking powder in the bowl. Add the chopped butter. Using your fingers, rub the butter into the mixture until it resembles fine breadcrumbs.

2 Add 40g/1½oz of honey and combine it with the mixture. Stir in the milk to form a stiff dough. Shape the dough into a ball and place it on a floured board or work surface.

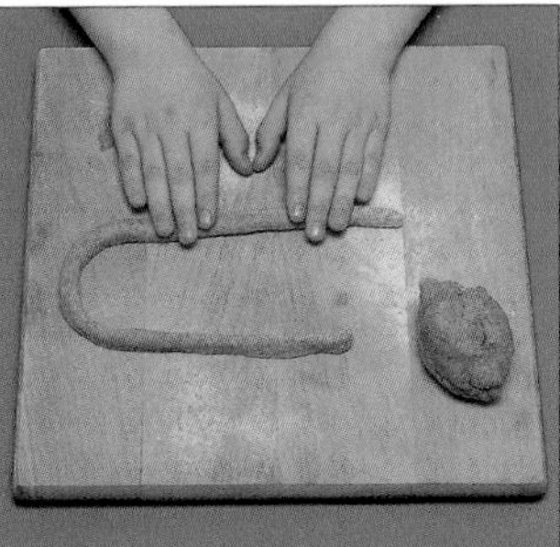

3 Divide the dough into three. Roll each piece into long strips, as shown above. Take each strip and coil it into a spiral to make a cake. Make two other cakes in the same way.

4 Now sprinkle each spiral cake with caraway seeds, and place them on to a greased baking tray. Finish off by glazing the cakes with the remainder of the honey.

5 Ask an adult to bake the cakes in an oven at 180°C/350°F/Gas Mark 4 for approximately 20 minutes. When they are ready, take the cakes out and leave them to cool.

Egyptian pastries were often shaped in spirals. Other popular shapes were rings like doughnuts. The Egyptians did not have sugar, so their cakes were sweetened with honey.

Greek pancakes

Meals in ancient Greece were based around fish, home-baked bread and vegetables such as onions, beans, lentils, leeks and radishes. Chickens and pigeons were kept for their eggs and meat, and a cow or a few goats or sheep for milk and cheese. Pancakes like the ones in this project made handy snacks.

◂ **Drying fruits**
Raisins (dried grapes), apricots and olives were plentiful in the Mediterranean, and were used for cooking.

YOU WILL NEED

8 tbsp clear honey, spoon, small bowl, 100g/$3\frac{1}{2}$oz flour, sieve, mixing bowl, fork, 200ml/7fl oz/$\frac{7}{8}$ cup water, frying pan, sesame seeds, 1tbsp olive oil, spatula, serving plate.

1 First measure the honey into a small bowl. Then make the pancake mix. Sift the flour into a mixing bowl. Then, using a fork, stir the water into the flour. Mix into a runny paste.

2 Spoon the honey into the pancake mixture a little at a time. Mix it with a fork, making sure that the mixture is nice and smooth, and that there are no lumps.

3 Ask an adult to help you with the next two steps. Heat the frying pan. Sprinkle in the sesame seeds and cook them until they are brown. Set the seeds aside to cool.

4 Heat a tablespoon of olive oil in a frying pan. Pour a quarter of the pancake mixture into the frying pan. Cook on both sides for about four minutes until golden brown.

5 Serve the pancake on a plate. Sprinkle on a handful of sesame seeds and pour extra honey over the top. Cook the rest of the pancake mixture in the same way.

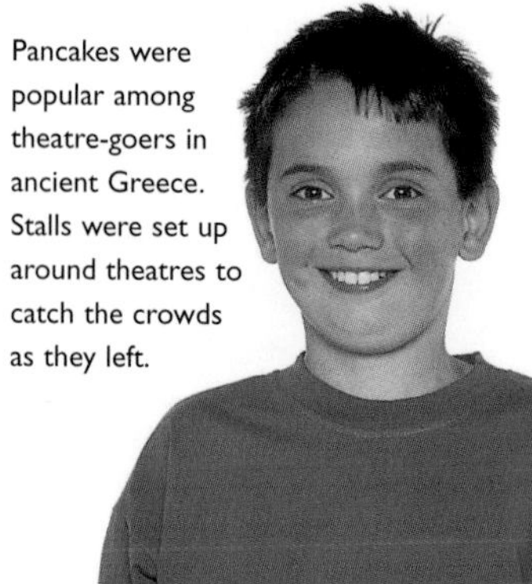

Pancakes were popular among theatre-goers in ancient Greece. Stalls were set up around theatres to catch the crowds as they left.

Roman honeyed dates

Many Roman town-dwellers lived in homes without kitchens. They ate takeaway meals brought from the many food stalls and bars in town. Breakfast may only have been a quick snack of bread, honey and olives. Lunch, too, was a light meal, perhaps of eggs, or cold meats and fruit. The main meal of the day was *cena* (dinner). This might start with shellfish or a salad, followed by a main meal of roast pork, veal, chicken or goose with vegetables. *Cena* finished with a sweet course of fruit or honey cakes.

YOU WILL NEED

Chopping board, sharp knife, dates, hazlenuts, walnuts, pecan nuts, almonds, pestle and mortar, salt, 175ml/6fl oz/¾ cup honey, frying pan, wooden spoon, serving dish, a few fresh mint leaves.

1 Slit open the dates with the knife on the chopping board. Remove the stone (pit) inside. Be sure not to cut the dates completely in half, and use the knife carefully.

2 Set aside the hazelnuts. Chop up the rest of the nuts. Use a pestle and mortar to grind them into smaller pieces. Stuff a small amount into the middle of each date.

3 Pour some salt on to the chopping board and lightly roll each of the stuffed dates in it. Make sure the dates are coated all over, but do not use too much salt.

4 Slowly melt the honey in a frying pan on a slow heat. Lightly fry the dates for about five minutes, turning them with a wooden spoon. Ask an adult to help you use the stove.

5 Arrange the stuffed dates in a shallow serving dish. Sprinkle over the whole hazelnuts, some of the chopped nuts and a few fresh mint leaves. The dates are now ready to eat!

The Romans loved sweet dishes made from nuts and dates imported from North Africa. They also used dates to make sauces for savoury fish dishes.

Indian chickpea curry

The diet of most people in ancient India depended on what plants were grown around them. In the areas of high rainfall, rice was the main food. In drier areas, people grew wheat and made it into bread.

Religion affected diet, too. Buddhists did not agree with killing animals, so they were vegetarians. Most Hindus became vegetarian, too. Hindus believed the cow was holy, so eating beef was forbidden. Muslims were forbidden to eat pork, although they did eat other meats. Chickpeas, peas, lentils and cheese provided healthy alternatives to meat.

The Indians used many spices in cooking to add flavour, to sharpen the appetite or aid digestion. Ginger, turmeric, cinnamon and cumin have been used from early times. Chilli was introduced from the Americas after the 1500s.

▲ Staple food
Rice cultivation has been the dominant agricultural activity in most parts of India since ancient times. The starchy, grain-like seeds form the main part of most Indian dishes. A rice plant's roots must be submerged in water, so a reliable irrigation system was essential if farmers were to obtain a good yield.

YOU WILL NEED

Knife, chopping board, small onion, 2 tbsp vegetable oil, wok, wooden spoon, 4cm/1½in cube of fresh ginger root, two cloves of garlic, ¼ tsp turmeric, 450g/1lb tomatoes, 225g/8oz cooked chickpeas, salt and pepper, 2 tbsp chopped fresh coriander (cilantro), 2 tsp garum masala, coriander (cilantro) leaves for garnish, a lime.

1 Ask an adult to help you cook. Finely chop the onion. Heat the oil in a wok or frying pan. Fry the onion in the oil for 2–3 minutes until it is soft.

2 Finely chop the ginger and add it to the wok. Chop the garlic cloves and add them to the wok, too, along with the turmeric. Cook gently for another minute.

3 Peel the tomatoes, cut them in half and remove all the seeds. Roughly chop the tomatoes up and add them to the onion, garlic and spice mixture in the wok.

4 Add the cooked chickpeas to the pan. Gently bring the mixture to the boil, then simmer gently for around 10–15 minutes until the sauce has reduced to a thick paste.

turmeric

cardamom pods

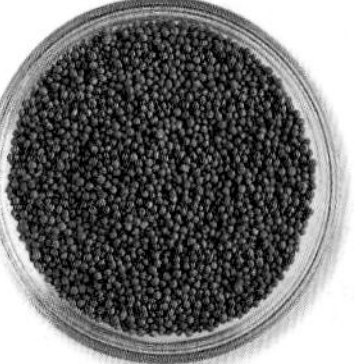

black mustard seeds

▲ Essential spices

Turmeric is ground from the root of a plant to give food an earthy flavour and yellow colour. Black mustard seed has a smoky, bitter taste. Cardamom gives a musky, sugary flavour suitable for both sweet and savoury dishes.

5 Taste the curry and add salt and pepper as seasoning if required. The curry should taste spicy but not so hot that it burns your mouth – or those of your guests!

6 Add the chopped fresh coriander to the curry, along with the garum masala. Garnish with a scattering of fresh coriander leaves and serve with a slice of lime.

mango leaves

limes

rice flour

▲ Good-luck food

Various foods and plants were placed at the entrance of an Indian home for good luck. Rice-flour pictures were drawn on the step, and mango leaves and limes were hung above the door.

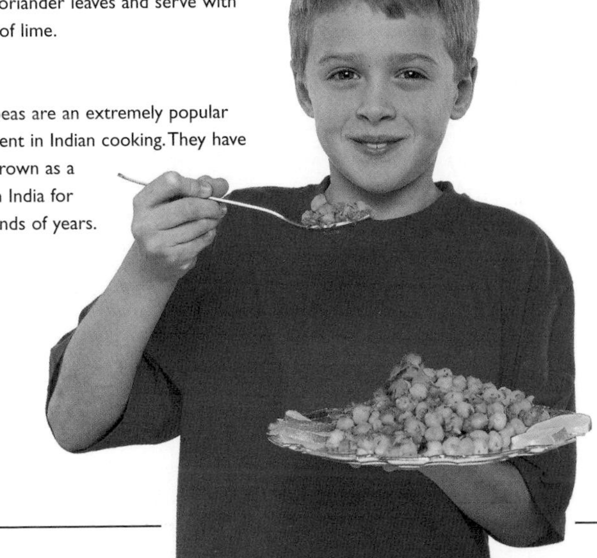

Chickpeas are an extremely popular ingredient in Indian cooking. They have been grown as a crop in India for thousands of years.

Chinese bean soup

Rice was the basis of most meals in ancient China, especially in the south where it was grown. It was often added to soup. People from the north made noodles and buns from wheat flour instead. They also made pancakes and dumplings, as well as lamb and duck dishes. For most people, however, meat was a luxury.

millet

rice

mung beans

sesame seeds

◂ Cooking in China
Mung beans, rice, millet and sesame seeds are all important additions to Chinese dishes and sauces.

YOU WILL NEED
Measuring jug (pitcher), bowl, water, scales, 225g/8oz aduki beans, 3 tsp ground nuts, 4 tsp short-grain rice, tangerine, pan, wooden spoon, 175g/6oz sugar, liquidizer, sieve, serving bowls.

1 Measure 1 litre/1¾ pints of water in the jug. Weigh, wash and drain the beans, nuts and rice and put them in a bowl. Add water and leave overnight to soak. Do not drain off the water.

2 Wash and dry the tangerine. Then carefully use your fingers to ease off the peel in one long, continuous strip. Leave the peel overnight to become hard and dry.

3 Put beans, rice and liquid into a pan. Add the peel and 500ml/17fl oz/2¼ cups water. Ask an adult to help you bring the mixture to the boil. Cover the pan and simmer for 2 hours.

4 Use the scales to weigh out the sugar. When the water has boiled off and is just covering the beans, add the sugar. Simmer until the sugar has completely dissolved.

5 Remove and discard the tangerine peel. Leave the soup to cool. Then liquidize the mixture. Strain any lumps with a sieve. Pour the soup into bowls and serve.

Most peasant farmers lived on a simple diet. Red bean soup with rice was a typical meal.

Japanese rice balls

Food in Japan has always been simple and healthy. The diet is based on rice, millet, wheat or barley, which is boiled, steamed or made into noodles. Many foods are flavoured with soy sauce, made from fermented soya beans. Another nutritious soya product, tofu (beancurd), is made from soya beans softened and pulped in water. The pulp is formed into blocks and left to set.

seaweed

mussels

◂ Treasures from the sea

Japan is an island, so seafood, such as mussels and seaweed, is an important part of the Japanese diet.

YOU WILL NEED
7 cups Japanese rice, pan, sieve, wooden spoon, mixing bowls, 1 tbsp salt, chopping board, 1 tbsp black sesame seeds, ½ sheet yaki nori seaweed, knife, cucumber, serving dish.

1 Ask an adult to help you boil the rice. When the rice is cooked, drain it in the sieve but do not rinse it. The rice should remain sticky. Place the rice in one mixing bowl and salt in another.

2 Wash your hands thoroughly. Then wet the palms of both hands with cold water. Next, put a finger into the bowl of salt and rub a little on to your palms.

3 Place about one eighth of the rice on one hand. Use both your hands to shape the rice into a triangular shape. You should press firmly but not too hard.

4 Make seven more rice balls in the same way. When you have made them all, sprinkle some of the sesame seeds over each one to add some flavour to the rice balls.

5 Cut a strip of yaki nori seaweed into four pieces and wrap some of your rice balls in it. Put the *onigiri* on a serving dish and garnish them with sliced cucumber.

Rice was introduced from China in AD100, and remains the staple food of Japan.

Celtic cakes

In Celtic times, you would have had to watch how many oatcakes you ate. The Celts did not approve of people getting too fat. Roman writers reported that Celtic warriors were told not to let out their belts, but to lose weight when clothes around their waists became too tight. The Celts produced most of their own food on their farms. All they needed to buy were products such as salt.

apples

◂ **Home-grown fruits**
In Celtic times, many fruits were available that are familiar to us today.

YOU WILL NEED

225g/8oz oatmeal, bowl, 75g3oz plain (all-purpose) flour, sieve, salt, wooden spoon, baking soda, 50g/2oz butter, pan, water, heat-resistant glass, chopping board, rolling pin, glass, baking tray, wire tray.

1 Under adult supervision, preheat an oven to 220°C/425°F/Gas Mark 7. Put the oatmeal into the bowl. Sift the flour into the bowl and add the salt. Mix the ingredients with a wooden spoon.

2 Add the baking soda. Mix it in well, and then put the bowl to one side. Melt the butter in a small pan over a low heat. Add it to the oat and flour mixture.

3 Boil some water and gradually add it to the oatmeal and flour mixture, straight from the kettle or in a heat-resistant glass. Stir well until you have a firm dough.

4 Turn the dough out on to a board sprinkled with a little oatmeal and flour. Roll the dough until it is about 1cm/⅜in thick. Use a glass to cut the dough into about 24 circles.

5 Place the circles of dough on a greased baking tray. Bake in an oven for about 15 minutes. Allow the oatcakes to cool on a wire tray before serving them.

Enjoy your oatcakes plain, or eat them with butter, honey or cheese.

Viking bread

A typical Viking family ate twice a day. The food was usually prepared on a central hearth, although some large farmhouses had separate kitchens. Oats, barley and rye were made into bread and porridge. The hand-ground flour was often coarse and gritty. Poor people added split peas and bark to make it go further, and their teeth became worn down. Dough was mixed in large wooden troughs and baked in ovens or on stone griddles. Goat, beef and horse meat were roasted or stewed in cauldrons over a fire.

YOU WILL NEED

2 cups white bread flour, 3 cups wholemeal flour, sieve, mixing bowl, 1 tsp baking powder, 1 tsp salt, 1 cup edible seeds, 2 cups warm water, wooden spoon or spatula, baking tray.

1 Sift the flours into a bowl. Add the baking powder and salt. Stir half of the seeds into the bowl. Sunflower seeds give a crunchy texture, but you could use any other edible seeds.

2 Add 2 cups of warm water and stir the mixture with a wooden spoon or spatula. At this stage, the mixture should become quite stiff and difficult to stir.

3 Use your hands to knead the mixture into a stiff dough. Before you start, dust your hands with some of the flour to stop the mixture sticking to them.

4 When the dough is well kneaded and no longer sticks to your hands, put it on a greased baking tray. Sprinkle the rest of your seeds over the top of the loaf.

5 Put the baking tray in a cold oven. Ask an adult to turn the oven to 190°C/375°F/Gas Mark 5. Cook the bread for 1 hour. Cooking the bread from cold will help the loaf to rise.

The Vikings put split peas in bread to add flavour and bulk, but sunflower seeds are just as tasty! Bread made from barley was most common, but wealthy Vikings ate loaves made from finer wheat flour.

Native American corn cakes

Tribes of North America have hunted, fished and gathered their own food from the earliest days. The Inuit fished from kayaks or through holes in the ice. Calusa tribes of the Southeast farmed the sea, sectioning off areas for shellfish. Tribes of the Northwest coast also harvested the sea. They therefore had little reason to develop farming, although they did cultivate tobacco.

For many peoples, however, farming was an important way of life. The Pueblos of the Southwest cultivated corn and made a thin bread, rather like your tortilla. Tribes on the fertile east coast, such as the Secotan, set fire to land to clear it for farming, and then planted thriving vegetable gardens. As well as the staple corn, squash and beans, they grew berries, tomatoes, vanilla pods and asparagus. Archaeologists have found evidence of a type of popcorn dating from 4000BC.

▲ Offerings to the dead
The Shawnee Feast of the Dead was held each year to honour the spirits of the dead tribal members. People would place luxurious fruits and food, such as artichokes and plums, on the graves and light candles all round.

▲ Harvesting the land
The area and environment tribes lived in determined what they ate. Tribes of the Northwest who lived on the coast took their food from the sea. For many tribes on the fertile eastern coast, farming was an important way of life.

▲ Vegetable crops
Corn was the staple food for most Native American tribes. Two other important vegetable crops were squashes and beans.

YOU WILL NEED

200g/7oz corn tortilla flour or plain (all-purpose) flour, measuring scales, sieve, mixing bowl, jug (pitcher), cold water, metal spoon, chopping board, rolling pin, frying pan, a little vegetable oil for cooking, honey.

1 Measure out the corn tortilla flour or plain flour using the measuring scales. Carefully sift the flour into the mixing bowl. Fill the jug with cold water.

2 Slowly add the water to the flour in the mixing bowl. Add a little water at a time, stirring all the time as you pour, until the mixture forms a stiff dough.

3 Using your hands, gently knead the mixture. Keep kneading the dough until it is not too sticky to touch. You may need to add a little more flour to get the consistency right.

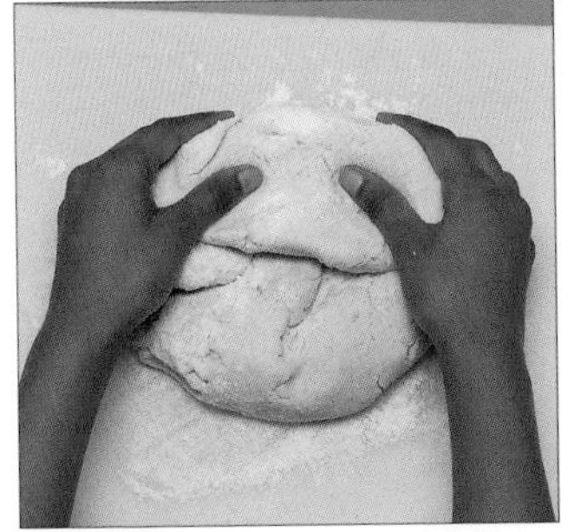

4 Sprinkle flour over the board. Take the dough from the bowl and knead it on the floured chopping board for about 10 minutes. Leave the dough to stand for 30 minutes.

5 Pull off a small lump of dough. Roll it between your hands to form a flattened ball. Repeat this process until you have made all the dough into flattened balls.

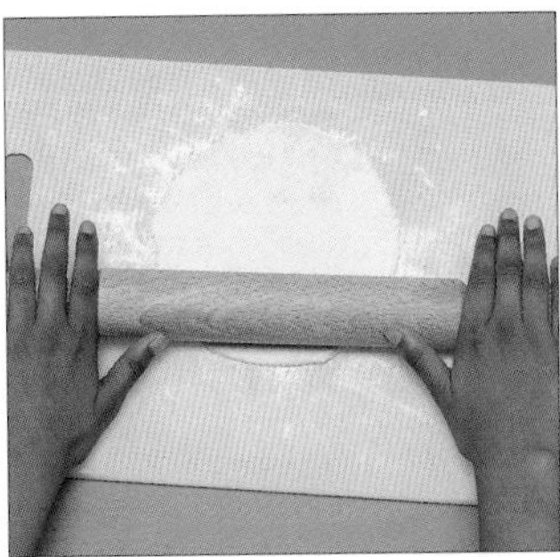

6 Keep kneading the dough balls until they form flat, round shapes. Finish them off by using the rolling pin to roll them into flat, thin cakes called tortillas.

7 Ask an adult to help you cook the tortillas. Heat a heavy frying pan or griddle. Gently cook the cakes in a little oil one by one until they are lightly browned on both sides.

Tortillas were usually eaten with savoury food, but they also taste delicious with honey.

Aztec tortillas

Mesoamerican people usually ate their main meal around noon, and had a smaller snack in the evening. Ordinary people's food was plain – but very healthy – as long as there was enough of it. Everyday meals were based on corn (which was ground down for tortillas), beans, vegetables and fruit. (Bell) peppers, tomatoes, pumpkins and avocados were popular, and the Aztecs also ate boiled cactus leaves. Soup made from wild herbs or seeds boiled in water was also a favourite. Meat and fish were luxuries. Deer, rabbit, turkey and dog were cooked for feasts, as well as frogs, lizards and turtles. The Aztecs also ate fish eggs and algae from the lakes.

tomato

avocado

▲ New food
Today, many Central American meals still include tomatoes, (bell) peppers, chilli peppers and avocados. These fruits and vegetables were first introduced to Europe and Asia in the years after the conquest of Mesoamerica.

mixed beans

prickly pear

▲ Vegetarian diet
Beans were an important part of the Mesoamerican diet, and so was the fruit of the prickly pear cactus. The fine spines had to be carefully removed first!

◀ Floating gardens
Chinampas were very productive floating gardens. Layers of twigs and branches were sunk beneath the surface of a lake and weighted with stones. The government passed laws telling farmers when to sow seeds to ensure there would be a steady supply of vegetables for sale in the market.

YOU WILL NEED

Measuring scales, 225g/8oz plain (all-purpose) flour, 1 tsp salt, mixing bowl, 1 tbsp butter, water jug (pitcher), 120ml/1½ cups cold water, teaspoon, rolling pin, chopping board, a little vegetable oil for frying, non-stick frying pan.

1 Weigh out all the ingredients. Mix the flour and salt together in a bowl. Rub the butter into the mixture until it looks like breadcrumbs. Then pour in the water a teaspoon at a time.

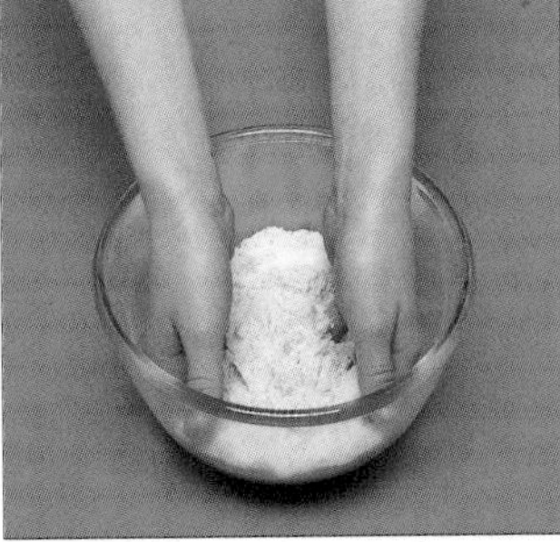

2 Use your hands to mix everything together until you have a loose mixture of dough. Do not worry if there is still some dry mixture around the sides of the bowl.

3 Knead the dough for at least 10 minutes until it is smooth. If the dough on your hands gets too sticky, you could add a little plain flour to the bowl.

4 Tip the dough out of the bowl on to a floured chopping board. Divide it into egg-sized balls using your hands or a knife. You should have enough for about 12 balls.

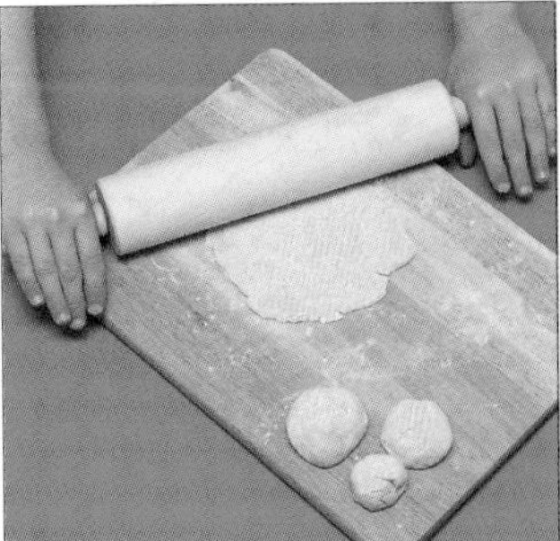

5 Sprinkle the board and the rolling pin with a little plain flour to stop the dough from sticking. Then roll each ball of dough into a thin pancake shape called a tortilla.

6 Ask an adult to help you fry the tortillas using a non-stick frying pan. Fry each tortilla for 1 minute on each side. You can use a little oil in the pan if you want to.

You could eat your tortillas with a spicy bean stew or juicy tomatoes and avocados. In Aztec times, tortillas were cooked on a hot baking-stone.

Inca bean stew

The wealthiest members of Inca society entertained their visitors with banquets of venison, duck, fresh fish and tropical fruits, such as bananas and guavas. Honey was used as a sweetener. Peasants ate squash and other vegetables in a stew or soup like the one in the project, and added fish if it was available. Families kept guinea pigs for meat, but most of their food was based on a vegetarian diet. The bulk of any meal was made up of starchy foods. These were prepared from grains such as corn or quinoa, or from root crops such as potatoes, cassava or a highland plant called *oca*. A strong beer called *chicha* was made from corn.

▲ Common crops
Many of the world's common crops were first grown and then cultivated in the Americas. These include cassava and sweet potatoes.

▲ Tropical taste
Chilli peppers and peanuts are just two of a number of tropical crops that grow in the Americas.

◀ A fertile land
Corn was common across Central and South America. Potatoes and quinoa were grown in the area occupied by present-day Chile, Peru and Ecuador. Squashes and beans were cultivated mainly in Central America.

YOU WILL NEED

250g/9oz dried haricot (navy) beans, bowl, cold water, sieve, large and medium pans, 4 tomatoes, knife, chopping board, 500g/1¼lb pumpkin, 2 tbsp paprika, mixed herbs, salt, black pepper, 100g/3¾oz corn.

1 Wash and then soak the beans in water for 4 hours. Drain and then put them into a large pan. Cover with water. Ask an adult to help you boil the beans. Simmer for 2 hours.

2 While the beans are cooking, chop up the tomatoes into fine pieces. Peel the pumpkin and remove and discard the seeds. Cut the fleshy part of the pumpkin into 2cm/¾in cubes.

3 Ask an adult to help you heat 100ml/3½fl oz of water in a medium pan. Stir in the paprika and bring to the boil. Add the tomatoes and a pinch of mixed herbs. Season with salt and pepper.

4 Simmer for 15 minutes until the mixture is thick and well blended. Drain the beans and add them to the tomato mixture. Add the pumpkin and then simmer for 15 minutes.

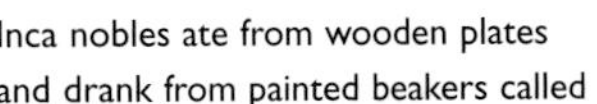

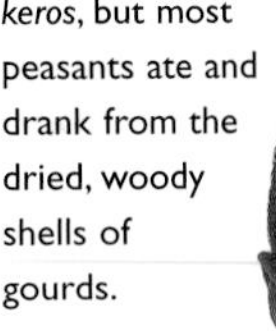

Inca nobles ate from wooden plates and drank from painted beakers called *keros*, but most peasants ate and drank from the dried, woody shells of gourds.

5 Add the corn and simmer the tomato mixture for an additional 5 minutes until the pumpkin has almost disintegrated and the stew is nice and thick.

6 Carefully taste the tomato and bean stew, and add more salt and pepper if you think it is necessary. Serve in bowls. Cornbread or tortillas would be an ideal accompaniment.

Medieval flan

It was quite usual to have a mixture of sweet and savoury dishes in one course at a medieval castle feast. The flan you can make here mixes savoury cheese with sugar and spice, all in one dish. Other sweet pies might have been made with cream, eggs, dates and prunes. In medieval times, food was often coloured with vegetable dyes such as saffron, sandalwood or sometimes even gold. The pinch of saffron in the cream cheese mixture of this dish gives the flan a rich yellow colour. Saffron is expensive because it comes only from the flowers of a type of Mediterranean crocus, and is difficult to get hold of. For hundreds of years, it has been seen as a sign of wealth and status.

Remember to wash and clear up your mess when you have finished cooking. Before the days of cleaning products and dishwashers, dirty pots and pans were scoured clean using sand and soapy herbs.

▲ **Tasty bites**
It was not considered to be good manners to feed the castle dogs and cats from the table, but leftover bones and scraps of food were usually tossed on the floor. People also spat on the floor (this was considered to be polite), which quickly became dirty and was not cleaned very often. Straw covered the floor and would be changed for new straw periodically.

YOU WILL NEED

Measuring scales, two mixing bowls, four small bowls, plate, egg cup, tea strainer, fork, whisk, spoon, chopping board, rolling pin, greased paper, 15cm/6in-diameter flan tin, knife, two large eggs, pinch of saffron, hot water, 170g/5¾oz cream cheese, 1 tbsp sugar, 1 tsp powdered ginger, salt, 250g/9oz pack of ready-made shortcrust pastry, flour.

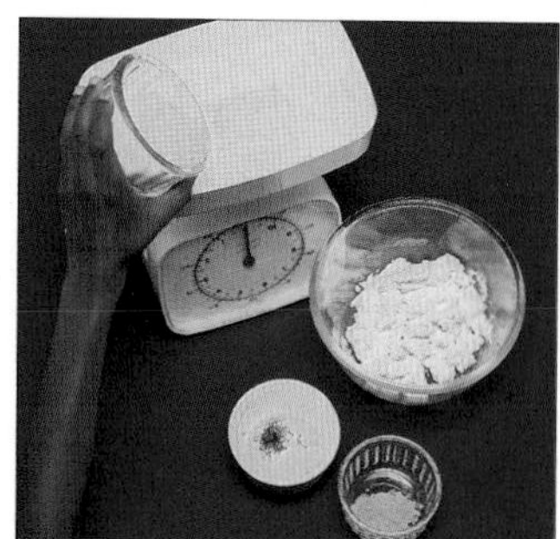

1 Have all your bowls and utensils laid out and ready to use. Weigh out all the ingredients carefully using the scales. Place them in separate bowls on the work surface.

2 Break each egg in turn on to a plate. Place an egg cup over the yolk. Tip the plate over a bowl and discard the egg whites. Transfer the yolks into a bowl.

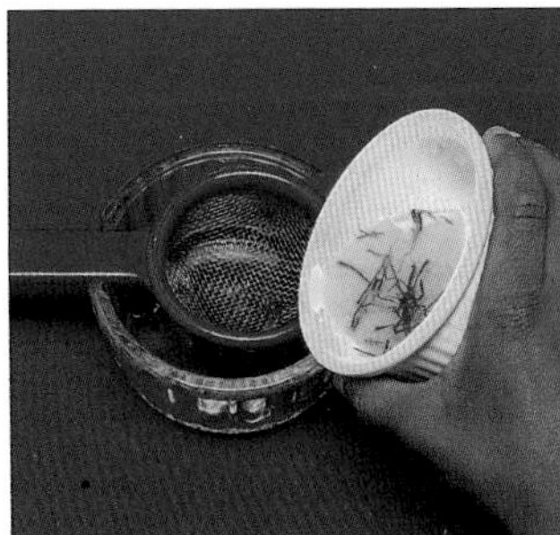

3 Put the saffron in a bowl. Heat some water and pour a little of it over the saffron. Leave until the water turns golden and then strain the liquid into another bowl.

4 Use a metal fork to mash up the cream cheese in a mixing bowl. Carry on blending until there are no lumps, and the cream cheese is of a soft and creamy consistency.

5 Add the tablespoon of sugar to the egg yolks. Use a whisk to beat the egg and sugar together. Continue until the mixture has thickened a little.

6 Gradually add the cream cheese to the egg and sugar mixture. Use the whisk to gently beat in the cream cheese until it has completely blended with the egg and sugar.

7 Add the powdered ginger, salt and saffron water to the cream cheese and egg mixture. Stir all the ingredients thoroughly. Ask an adult to preheat the oven to 200°C/400°F/Gas Mark 6.

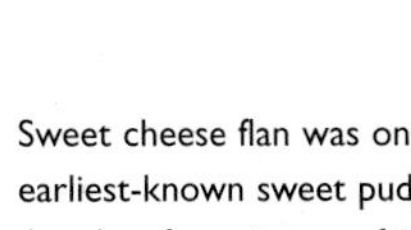

Sweet cheese flan was one of the earliest-known sweet puddings. Another favourite was fried bread flavoured with sugar and sherry.

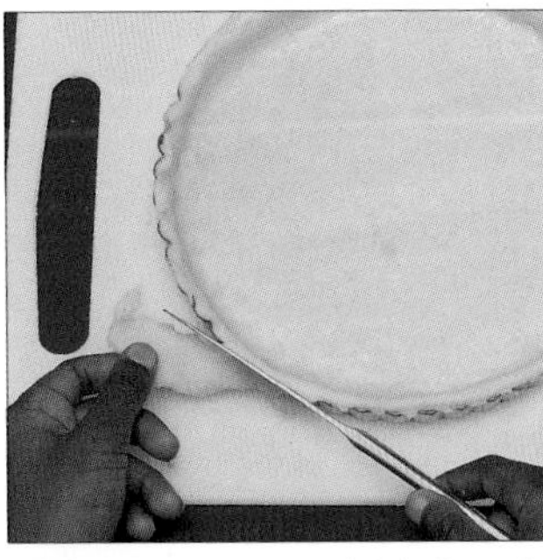

8 Roll the pastry on a lightly floured board. Smear greased paper over the flan tin and cover with the pastry. Press the pastry into the edges of the tin and trim the excess pastry.

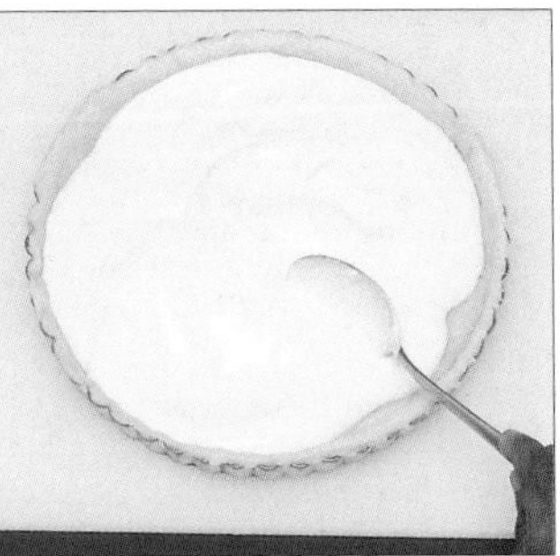

9 Spoon the cream cheese mixture over the pastry base and smooth it out to lay flat. Ask an adult to place the flan in the centre of the preheated oven, and bake for 20–30 minutes.

Halloween feast

Cook some scary food for a Halloween party on October 31. Then, the Sun was said to be so low that the gates of the underworld were opened to let in the light. As the gates opened, demons and spectres escaped on to Earth.

YOU WILL NEED

Cookies: Thick card, pencil, scissors, 115g/4oz butter, bowl, 90g/3½oz sugar, wooden spoon, one egg, 270g/9½oz plain (all-purpose) flour, black food colouring, chopping board, rolling pin, knife, baking tray, wire tray, red and green icing.

Scary face: One large baking potato, chopping board, knife, spoon, bowl, green food colouring, 50g/2oz butter, 50g/2oz grated cheese, salt, pepper, fork, one carrot, one red (bell) pepper, salad onions, one cooked sausage, grated orange cheese.

Ghoulish drink: Coloured plastic straws, white glue and glue brush, toy spiders, drinking glass, plate, ice cream, fizzy drink, chocolate flakes.

Cat and bat cookies

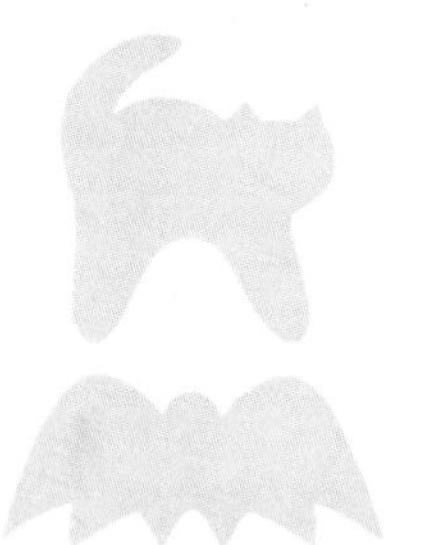

1 Scale up the bat and cat templates. Draw them on to the thick card, and then cut them out. You could make other shapes such as jack-o'-lanterns, pumpkins, witches' hats and ghosts.

2 Put the butter into a mixing bowl. (Take it out of the fridge in advance to soften it.) Add the sugar and stir with a wooden spoon until mixture is fluffy and creamy.

3 Add one beaten egg, the plain flour and a few drops of black food colouring to the bowl. Stir the mixture until it forms a stiff dough. Make sure the food colouring blends in well.

4 Roll the dough out on to a chopping board until it is about 1cm/⅜in thick. Place the cat and bat templates on to the dough and cut around them with a blunt knife.

5 Roll out the leftover dough and cut out more bat and cat shapes. Place them on to a non-stick baking tray. Ask an adult to bake the animal cookies for 20 minutes at 190°C/374°F/Gas Mark 5.

6 When they are done, remove the cookies from the oven and place them on a wire tray. When cool, use red and green icing to add features such as eyes and noses.

Scary potato face

1 Ask an adult to bake a large baking potato. When it has cooled, use a knife to cut off the top. Then spoon out the insides into a mixing bowl. Add green food colouring and mix well.

2 Add the butter and grated cheese and season the potato mixture with salt and pepper. Mix thoroughly with a fork. Spoon the potato mixture back into the potato skin and keep it warm.

3 Use a knife to slice the carrot, red pepper and onion ends into strips for hair, mouth and eyebrows, as shown above. Slice the sausage to make eyes. Sprinkle with grated orange cheese.

Ghoulish drink

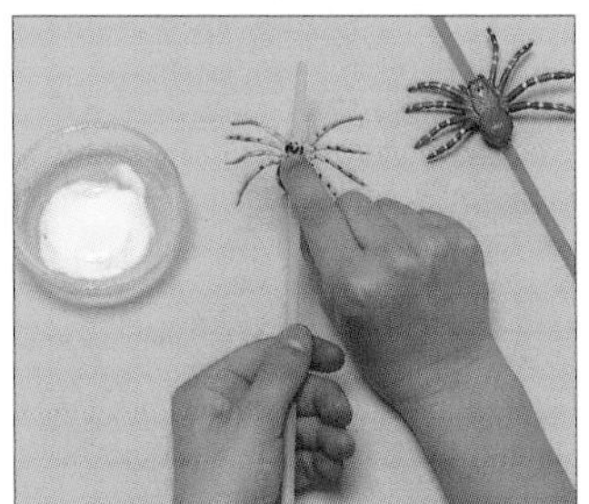

1 You need one plastic straw for each drink you make. Use a glue brush to dab glue near one end of the straw. Fix a toy spider firmly in place. Leave to dry completely.

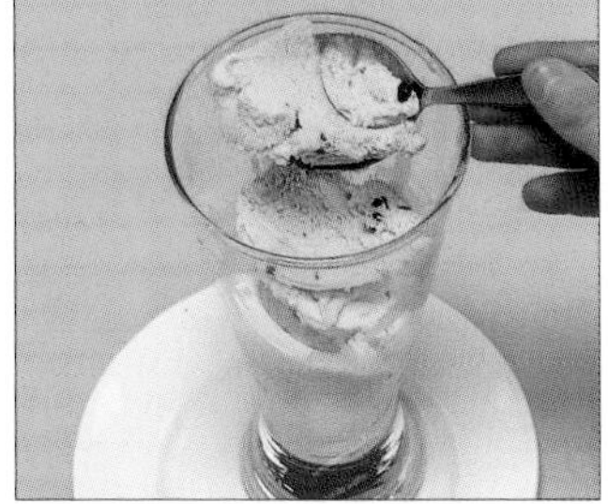

2 Put the glass on to a small plate. Put three of four tablespoons of ice cream in the glass. Mint chocolate chip looks good, because it is a ghoulish green colour.

3 Pour a fizzy drink over the ice cream. A lime drink works well because it is a ghastly green colour like the ice cream. Pour in enough so that the ice cream really froths up.

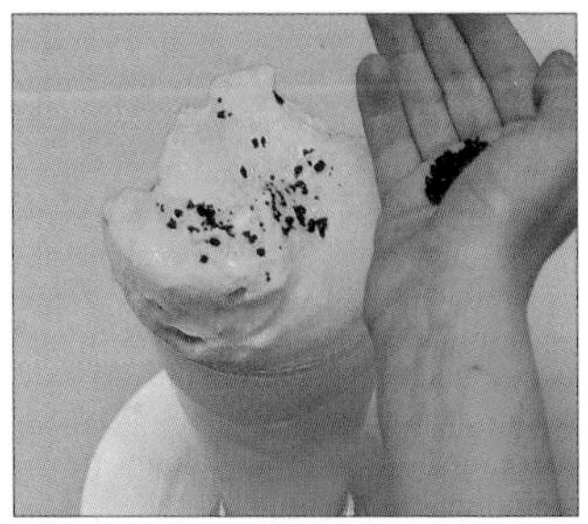

4 Sprinkle little flakes of chocolate over the top. You could add mini marshmallows or hundreds and thousands instead. Stick a decorative straw into each drink you make.

With these tasty treats, your party is bound to be a scream! Be sure to make enough food and drink for everyone you have invited.

Cowboy cookout

People were constantly on the move in the West. Native Americans followed herds of buffalo, settlers travelled in wagon trains and cowboys drove cattle. Everyone had to carry food with them and hunt animals for fresh meat.

Whatever food the cowboys carried with them was stored in their rolling kitchen, which was called the chuck wagon. One man had the job of cooking for all the others. This project shows you how to make the kind of meal a group of cowboys would have eaten on the trail.

▲ **Hung out to dry**
Native Americans hung strips of buffalo meat over poles in the open air. The Sun's heat dried and preserved the meat.

YOU WILL NEED

Two frying pans, cooking oil, garlic, wooden spoon, can of tomatoes, mild chilli powder, teaspoon, sieve, canned beans, stock cube, mixing bowl, 250g/9oz plain (all-purpose) flour, 50g/2oz cornmeal, salt, knife, warm water, chopping board, rolling pin, spatula.

1 Ask an adult to help you with your cowboy cookout. Heat a little oil in a frying pan. Crush two cloves of garlic and fry gently until soft and a light golden brown colour.

2 Open the can of tomatoes and add the contents to the garlic in the frying pan. Heat the tomatoes for a few moments, until they are warmed through.

3 Stir 1 teaspoon of mild chilli powder into the tomato sauce. Taste it to see if it is spicy enough. If not, add a little more chilli powder, but make sure not to add too much.

4 Drain the liquid from the different cans of beans. Kidney beans, butter beans and pinto beans are a delicious combination. Stir the sauce and warm it through for a few minutes.

5 Crumble a stock cube into the tomato and chilli bean sauce, and stir it in well. If the mixture becomes too dry, you may need to add a little hot water from a kettle.

6 Cook the bean sauce over a low heat for about 10 minutes. Remove it from the stove, and leave it to one side. You can now make the tortillas for your cowboy feast.

7 Add the flour, cornmeal and a pinch of salt into the bowl and pour in a little warm water. Gradually add more and more water, until the mixture forms a stiff dough.

8 Sprinkle some flour over a chopping board and vigorously knead the dough until it feels stretchy and elastic. If the dough is too dry, try adding some more water to it.

9 Divide the dough mixture into six equal portions. Use your hands to shape each one into a ball. Then coat the outside of each ball lightly with a little flour.

10 Dust the chopping board with more flour. Using a rolling pin dusted with flour, roll out each ball into a flat circle. You should try to roll each one as thinly as you possibly can.

11 Heat some oil in the second frying pan. Place one dough circle, called a tortilla, into the pan. When the edges curl, use a spatula to flip it over to cook on the other side.

12 When each tortilla is cooked, put it on a plate. Reheat the tomato and chilli bean sauce. Spoon some over half the tortilla. Fold over the other half. Serve immediately.

You might like to invite a few friends over for this delicious cowboy feast. Serve your tortillas on tin plates, just like the ones used by real cowboys.

Mesoamerican workers making accessories with feathers

Fashion and Accessories

Some clothes are made for work and comfort, while others are designed to show how important the wearer is. Jewellery and other accessories, such as headwear, are often a sign of the wearer's wealth. This section looks at the practical clothes worn by people through the ages. It also examines the distinctive styles, fashions and materials adopted by different cultures throughout the world.

Fashion and Clothing

Unlike animals and birds, humans do not have fur and feathers to keep them warm. One of the main reasons we wear clothes is to protect ourselves from the weather – the Sun as well as the cold. However, clothes are much more than just a form of protection. They have long been used as statements about the people who wear them. Special clothes worn by different groups of people indicated their position in society, their religious beliefs or the sort of work they did. From the very earliest times, people also cared about how they looked. So they decorated their clothes with shells and beads, and coloured threads were woven together to produce brightly patterned materials.

▲ The first clothing
Animals were hunted by early people, not only for their meat but also for their skins. These were scraped clean and shaped with sharp stone tools. Later, methods of treating the skins made them soft and supple, and therefore comfortable to wear.

◂ Cool, crisp linen
The clothes worn by the ancient Greeks were simple and elegant. The most common piece of clothing was a loose linen tunic. This was cool and comfortable to wear during the hot summer months.

◂ Wedding clothes

The Aztec people of Mexico wore clothes made of cotton. Here a man and woman are shown in their wedding outfits. Their cloaks have been tied together to show that the couple are now bound in marriage.

◂ A warrior's clothes

The samurai were an elite warrior class of old Japan. The formal clothes of a samurai were called *kami-shimo*. They showed his high status. The outfit consisted of a winged jacket, known as a *kataginu,* with matching trousers, called *hakama,* worn over a long tunic called a *kimono.*

▾ Rich embroidery

This picture shows the Hindu god Brahma wearing red pantaloons and a gold hat. The woman to the left is wearing a traditional Indian form of dress called a sari. The clothes are very simple, but they are made from beautifully embroidered silk, which indicates the importance of the people wearing them.

Stone Age dyed cloth

The hunters of the last Ice Age were the first people to wear clothes to protect them from the cold. They sewed animal hides together with strips of leather. The first clothes included simple trousers, tunics and cloaks, decorated with beads of coloured stones, teeth and shells. Fur boots were stitched together with leather laces.

Furs were prepared by stretching out the hides and scraping them clean. The clothes were cut out and holes were made around the edges of the pieces with a sharp, pointed stone called an awl. This made it easier to pass a bone needle through the hide. Cleaned hides were also used to make tents, bags and bedding. After sheep were domesticated in the Near East, wool was used to weave cloth. Plant fibres, such as flax, cotton, bark and cactus, were used elsewhere. The cloth was coloured and decorated with plant dyes.

oak bark

dyer's broom

birch bark

▲ Nature's colours
Stone Age people used the flowers, stems, bark and leaves of many plants to make brightly coloured dyes.

▼ Mammoth shelter
During most of the last 100,000 years, the Earth's climate has been much colder than it is today. Stone Age people dressed warmly. Their clothes kept out the cold and the rain.

YOU WILL NEED

Natural dyes (such as walnuts, elderberries and safflower), tablespoon, pan, pestle and mortar, water, sieve, bowl, old white cloth or chamois leather, rubber gloves (optional), white card, white T-shirt, wooden spoon. (Many natural dyes can be found in good health food stores.)

1 Choose your first dye and put between 8 and 12 tablespoons of the dye into an old pan. You may need to crush or shred the dye with a pestle and mortar.

2 Cover the dye with water, ask an adult to bring it to the boil, and then simmer for 1 hour. Leave it to cool. Pour the dye through a sieve into a bowl to remove the lumps.

3 Test the dye using a piece of cloth or chamois leather. Dip the cloth into the dye for a few minutes. You could wear rubber gloves to stop any dye getting on to your hands.

4 Lay the cloth or chamois leather patch on to a piece of white card and leave it to dry. Be careful not to drip the dye over clothes or upholstery while you work.

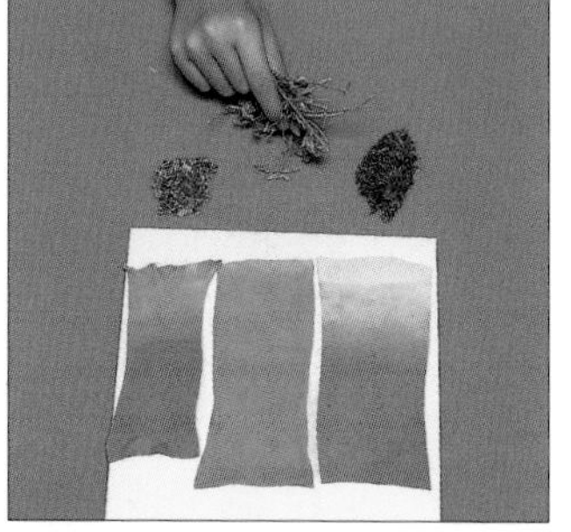

5 Make up the two other dyes and test them out in the same way. When all three pieces of cloth or leather are dry, compare the patches and choose your favourite colour.

6 Dye a white T-shirt by preparing it in your chosen dye. Try to make sure that the T-shirt is dyed evenly all over. Make sure it is completely dry before you try it on.

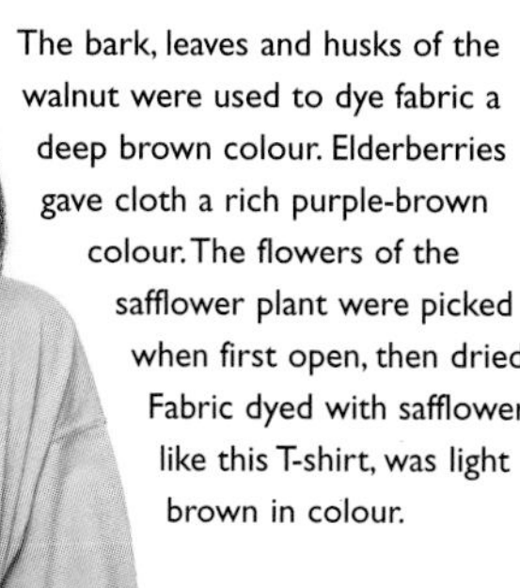

The bark, leaves and husks of the walnut were used to dye fabric a deep brown colour. Elderberries gave cloth a rich purple-brown colour. The flowers of the safflower plant were picked when first open, then dried. Fabric dyed with safflower, like this T-shirt, was light brown in colour.

Greek chiton

Clothes were styled simply in ancient Greece. Both men and women wore long tunics. These draped loosely for comfort, and were held in place with pins or brooches. Heavy cloaks were worn for travelling or in bad weather. Clothes were made of home-spun wool and linen. Fabrics were coloured with dyes made from plants, insects and shellfish.

cotton

linen

◂ Style at a price
Only the wealthiest Greeks wore clothes made from cotton or linen. Poorer citizens wore clothes made from home-spun wool.

YOU WILL NEED

Tape measure, rectangle of cloth – the width should measure the same as the height of your shoulder, scissors, pins, chalk, needle, thread, 12 metal buttons (with loops), cord.

1 Measure your arm span from wrist to wrist and double the figure. Measure your length from shoulder to ankle. Cut your cloth to these figures. Fold the fabric in half widthways.

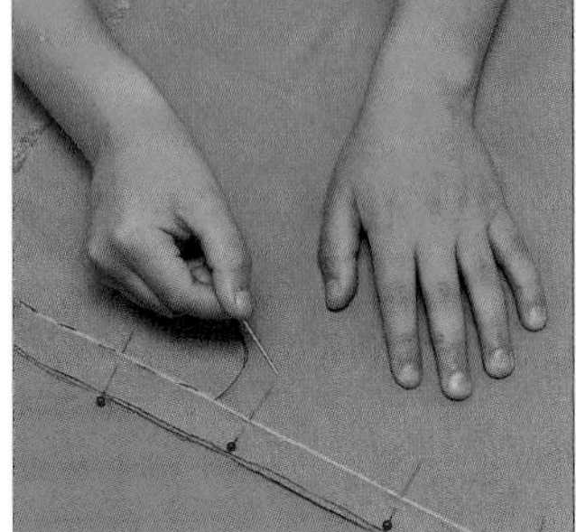

2 Pin the two sides together. Draw a chalk line across the fabric, 2cm/¾in in from the edge. Sew along the line, turn the material inside out and re-fold the fabric so the seam is at the back.

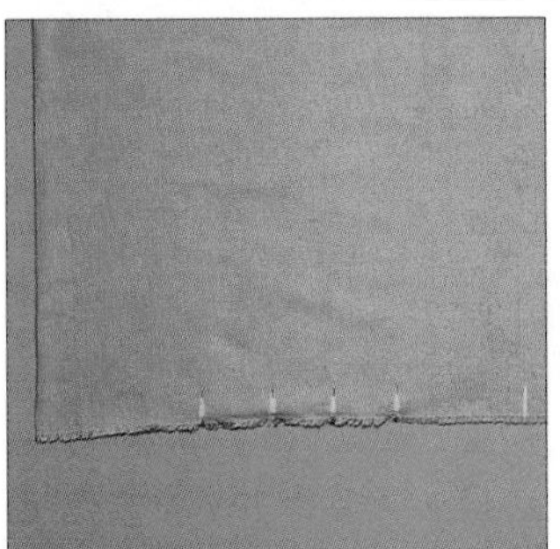

3 At one of the open ends of the fabric, mark a central gap for your head. Pin the fabric together there. From the head gap, mark a point every 5cm/2in to the end of the fabric.

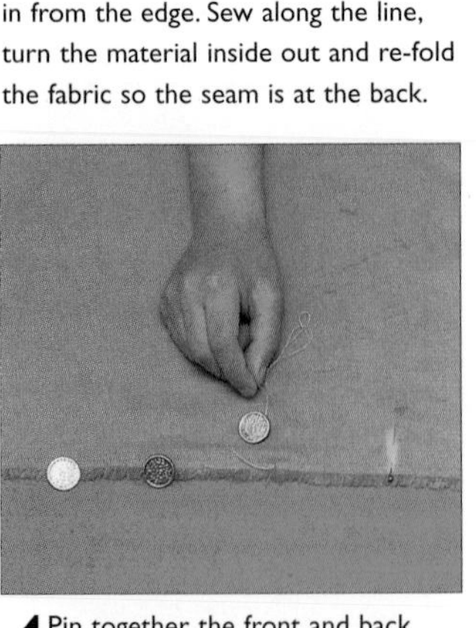

4 Pin together the front and back along these points. At each pin, sew on a button to hold the two sides of fabric together. To secure the button, sew through the loop several times.

Tie the cord around your waist. If it is too long, cut it to the right length, but leave enough cord to tie. Bunch the chiton material up, over the cord.

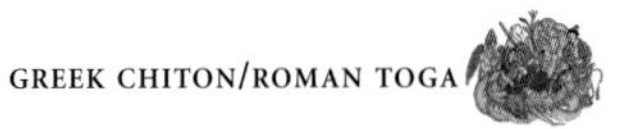

Roman toga

Most Roman clothes were made of wool that had been spun and woven by hand at home or in a workshop. The most common style of clothing was the tunic, which was practical for active people such as workers and slaves. Important men also wore a garment called a toga. This was a 6m/19½ft length of cloth with a curved edge, wrapped around the body and draped over the shoulder.

◂ A change in colour
Roman women wore a long dress called a stola over an under-tunic. Only married women wore dresses dyed in bright colours. Girls dressed in white.

YOU WILL NEED

Double-sided adhesive tape, purple ribbon, old white sheet, scissors, long T-shirt, cord.

1 Use double-sided adhesive tape to stick the ribbon along the long edge of the sheet. Cut one corner off, as shown. Put on a long white T-shirt tied at the waist with a cord.

2 Get a friend to hold the long edge of the fabric behind you. The cut corner should be on your left-hand side. Drape about a quarter of the toga over your left arm and shoulder.

3 Bring the rest of the toga round to the front, passing it under your right arm. Hook the toga up by tucking a few folds of the material securely into the cord around your waist.

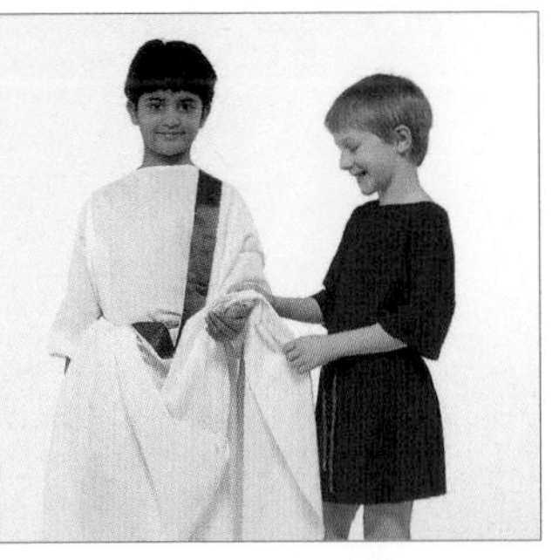

4 Now your friend can help you fold the rest of the toga neatly over your left arm, as shown above. If you prefer, you could drape it over your left shoulder.

Boys from wealthy families wore togas edged with a thin purple stripe until they reached the age of 16. After that time, they wore plain togas.

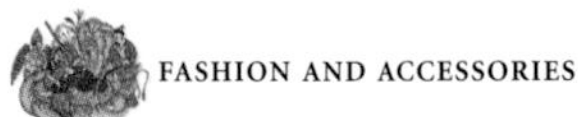

Indian sari

Clothing has always been very simple in India. Noble people, both men and women, usually wore a single piece of fabric that was draped around the hips, drawn up between the legs and then fastened securely again at the waist. Women wore bodices above the waist, but men were often bare-chested. Although their clothes were simple, people had elaborate hairstyles with flowers and other decorations. Men and women also wore a lot of jewellery, such as earrings, armbands, breastplates, nose rings and anklets. The Hindu male garment was called the dhoti, and the female garment gradually evolved into the sari – a single large cloth draped around the body, with a bodice worn underneath.

▲ A guide for the gods
A Brahmin (priest) looks after the temple and is a go-between for the worshipper and a god. He wears a sacred cotton cord across his chest to symbolize his position.

◀ Noble warriors
Society in ancient India was divided into three castes (classes). The noble warrior class (Kshatriya) was the next highest class after the Brahmin. Noble warriors wore expensive jewellery and used weapons such as bows and arrows, daggers, spears and swords.

▼ Holy water
Hindus have bathed in the sacred River Ganges for centuries. The religion states that bathing in its waters washes away sin. People wear their dhotis or saris when they bathe.

YOU WILL NEED

Silky or cotton fabric measuring 4 x 1m/4⅓ x 1yd, one large safety pin. Dip a cork into gold paint and press it along one long edge of the fabric to add decoration to the sari. Leave to dry before trying it on.

1 Hold one corner of the fabric to your stomach with the decorated border on the outside. Wrap the long side of the fabric once tightly around your waist.

2 Make a number of pleats where the fabric comes back around to the front of your body. Make them as even as you can. The pleats act as the underskirt of your sari.

3 Tuck the pleated section of the sari into the waist of the underskirt. You could use a safety pin to hold the pleats in place, while you practise tying the sari.

4 Take the excess length of fabric in your left hand and pass it all the way around your back. Take extra care that the pleats do not come out.

5 Now take the rest of the sari fabric in your right hand and lift it up so that it is level with your shoulders. Do this in front of a mirror, if possible, so that you can see what you are doing.

6 Swing the fabric over your left shoulder. The fabric should fall in gentle folds from your shoulder, across your body to the level of your waist. You may need to practise doing this.

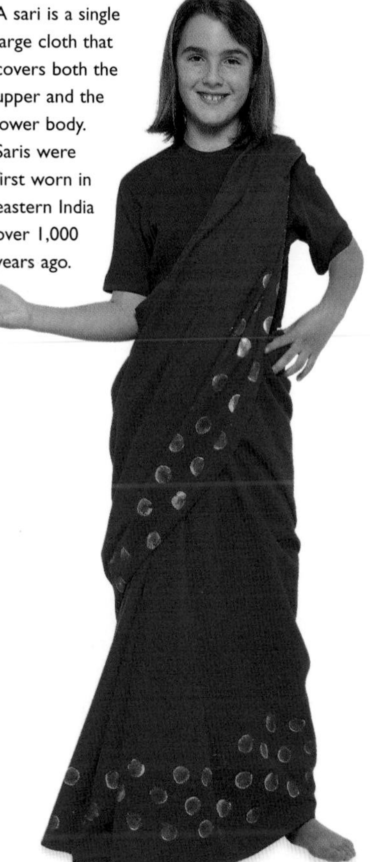

A sari is a single large cloth that covers both the upper and the lower body. Saris were first worn in eastern India over 1,000 years ago.

Native American robe

The clothes of most Native Americans were made from the skins of buffalo. Hunters performed elaborate dances before a hunt, and then headed off in search of animal tracks. Early hunters stalked the animals on foot, often disguised as other animals. Later, horses made the job a lot easier. Once the buffalo was killed, women and elder children usually processed the carcass. The skin was taken off in one piece and used to make clothes and covers. Meat was prepared for a feast to celebrate the successful hunt.

YOU WILL NEED

Three pieces of old bed sheet (one measuring 140 x 60cm/55 x 23½in and the other two measuring 40 x 34cm/16 x 13½in), pencil, tape measure, scissors, large needle, brown thread, felt (red, yellow, dark blue and light blue are the best colours to use), white glue and glue brush, black embroidery thread, red thread.

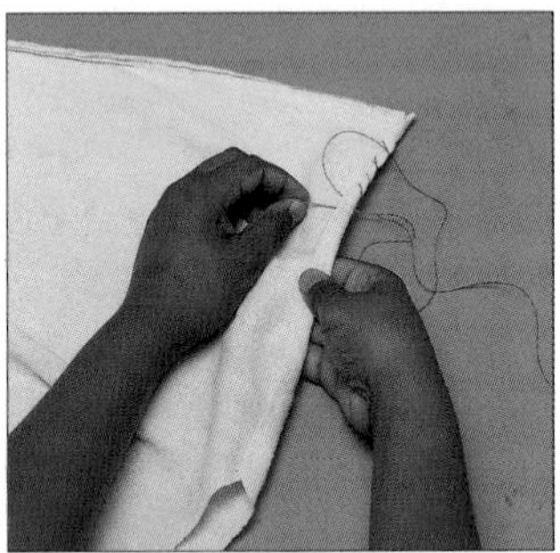

1 Fold the larger piece of fabric in half for the body. Draw and cut a curved neckline 22 x 6cm/8⅝ x 2½in on the fold. Roll the fabric over at the shoulders and stitch it down with brown thread.

2 Open the body fabric out flat and line up the two smaller fabric rectangles for the arm pieces with the centre of the stitched ridge. Stitch the top edge of the pieces on to the body.

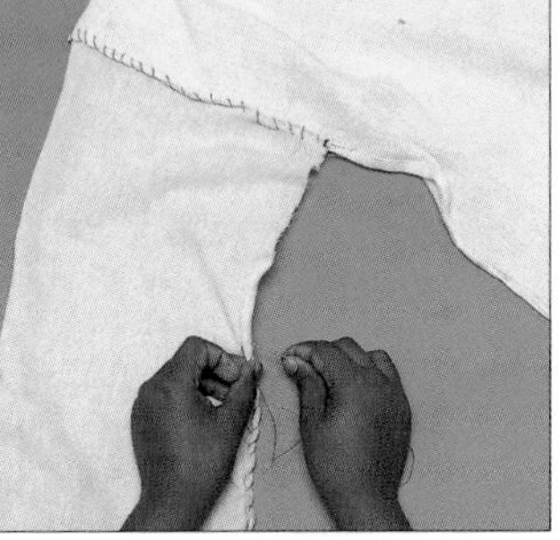

3 Fold the fabric in half again to see the shirt's shape. Now stitch up the undersides of the sleeves. (Native Americans did not usually sew the sides of skin robes together.)

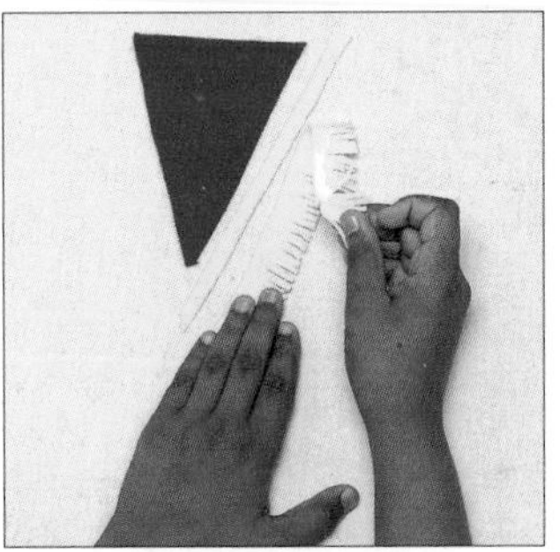

4 Your shirt is ready to decorate. Cut out strips and triangles of coloured felt and glue them on to the shirt. Make decorative fringes by cutting into one side of strips of felt.

5 Make fake hair strips by cutting 8cm/3⅛in lengths of black embroidery thread and tying them in bunches. Tie red thread tightly around the top, and then glue the fake hair on to your shirt.

Native Americans made their clothes from young buffaloes, and the resulting animal hide was called buckskin.

Inca tunic

The standard of Inca weaving was very high. The Inca people had to weave cloth for the state as a form of tax, and woven cloth was often used to pay officials. Inca men wore a loincloth around the waist, secured by a belt. Over this was a knee-length tunic, often made of alpaca – a fine, silky wool. Women wrapped themselves in a large rectangular piece of alpaca.

◂ Fighting force
Inca warriors decorated their war dress with brightly coloured feathers.

YOU WILL NEED

40cm/16in square of red felt, 160 x 65cm/63 x 25½in rectangle of blue felt, white glue and glue brush, tape measure, scissors, needle and thread, pencil, ruler, cream calico fabric, fabric paints, paintbrush, water pot.

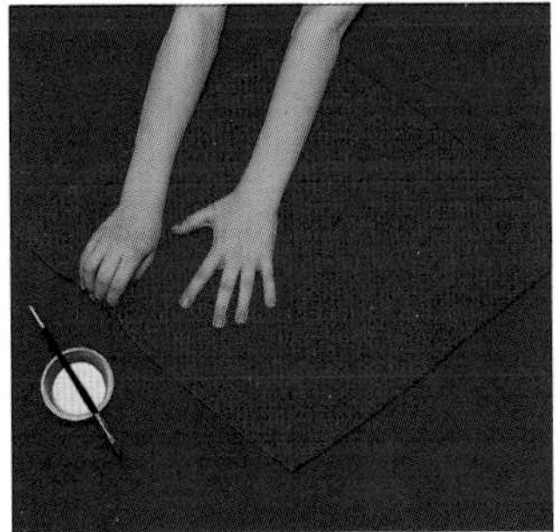

1 Place the blue felt flat on the table with the long side facing towards you. Position the red felt in the centre of the blue felt to form a diamond. Glue the red felt in place here.

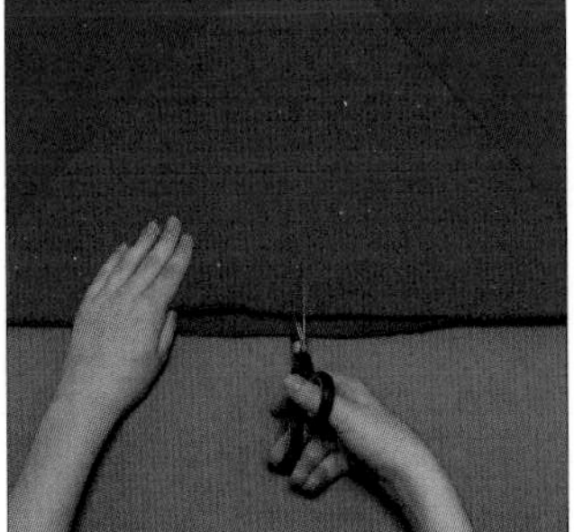

2 Cut a 22cm/8⅝in-long slit through the centre of both felt layers. Fold the fabric along the slit. Cut a 12cm/4½in-long slit through one double layer of fabric at right angles to the first slit, as shown.

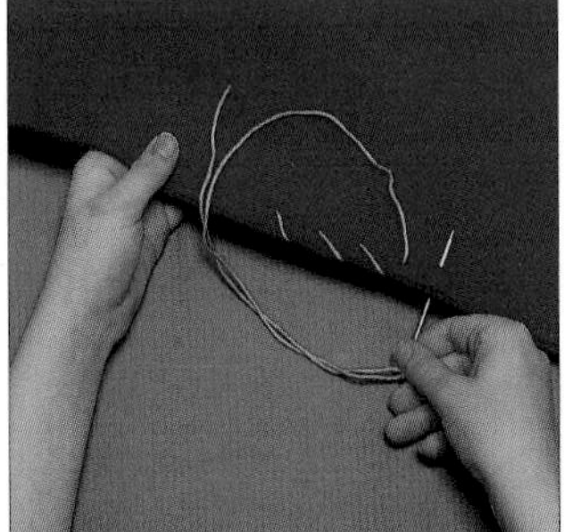

3 Use the needle and thread to sew together the sides of the tunic. Make the stitches as large as possible, and be sure to leave enough space for armholes at the top.

4 Draw lots of 5cm/2in squares in pencil on the cream calico fabric. Paint on colourful designs, as shown, and leave them to dry. Cut out the squares and glue them to your tunic.

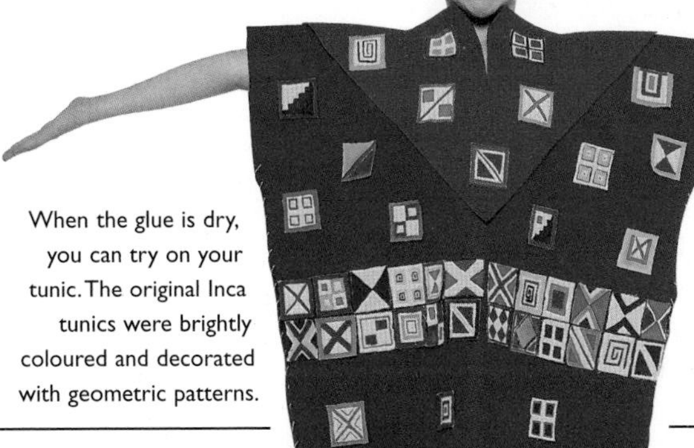

When the glue is dry, you can try on your tunic. The original Inca tunics were brightly coloured and decorated with geometric patterns.

Medieval witch

The familiar image of a witch – dressed in ragged clothes with a broomstick and a warty face – evolved from a much-feared folklore figure called the hag. Myths from ancient Egypt through to pre-Christian Europe tell of ugly old women who used supernatural powers to bring misfortune to those around them. During medieval times, many innocent old women who looked like hags became the victims of witch hunts. They were tried and usually found guilty, then sentenced to burn alive at the stake.

YOU WILL NEED

Black cotton fabric (200 x 110cm/79 x 43¼in), ruler, white pencil, scissors, needle, black thread, newspaper, stiff paintbrush, silver paint, two sheets of thin black card (42 x 59cm/16½ x 23¼in and 32 x 32cm/12½ x 12½in), adhesive tape, small piece of silver card, white glue and glue brush, green and black tissue paper.

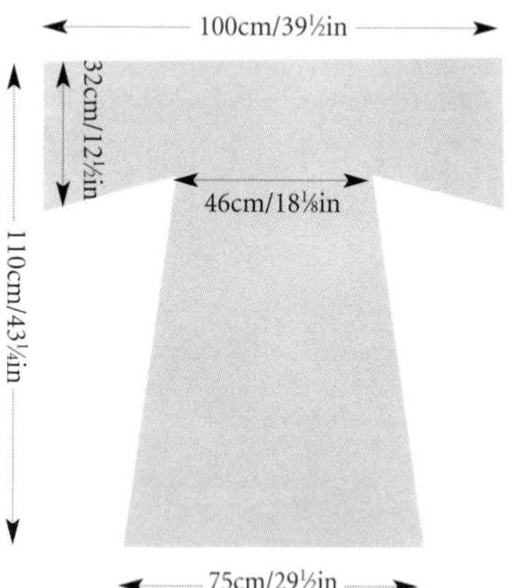

▲ **Template**

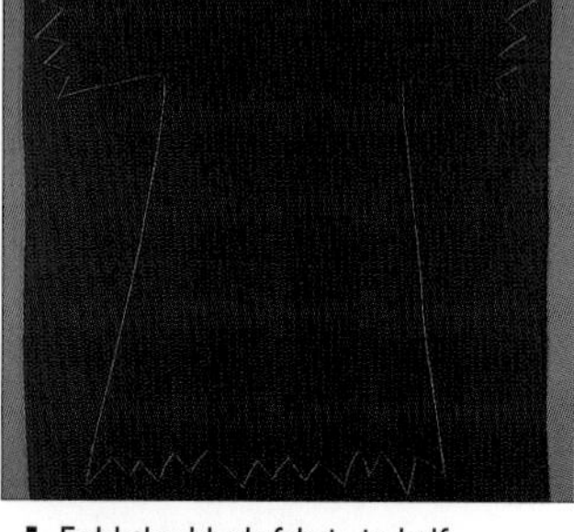

1 Fold the black fabric in half widthways. Lay it out on a flat surface. Then use the template to draw the witch's dress shape on to the fabric with a white pencil.

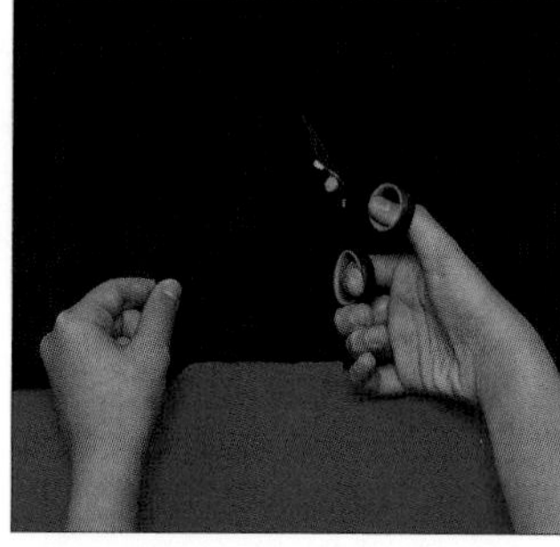

2 Cut out the dress shape. Cut a slit 24cm/9½in across in the middle of the folded edge for your neck. Then cut a second line 12cm/4½in long down the back of the fabric.

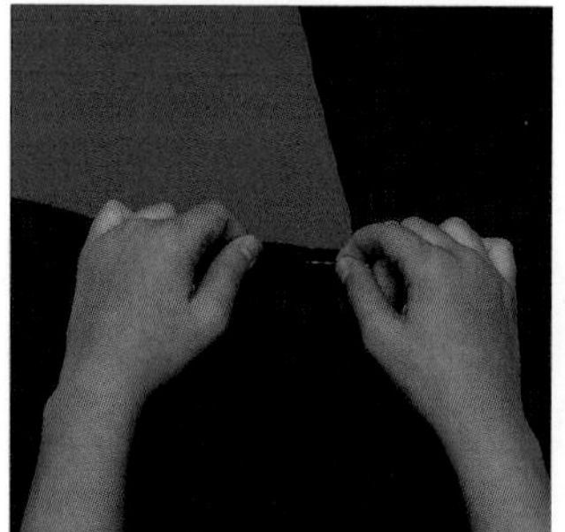

3 Turn the fabric inside out. Use a needle and some thread to sew a simple running stitch up each side of the witch's dress. Then sew under the arms of the dress.

4 Cut a jagged edge along the cuffs of each sleeve and along the bottom of the dress. Turn the dress inside out so that the fabric is right side out, and the stitches are hidden.

5 Lay the dress on a sheet of old newspaper. Dip a stiff brush in silver paint. Pull the bristles back towards you, and spray paint on to the fabric. When dry, spray the other side.

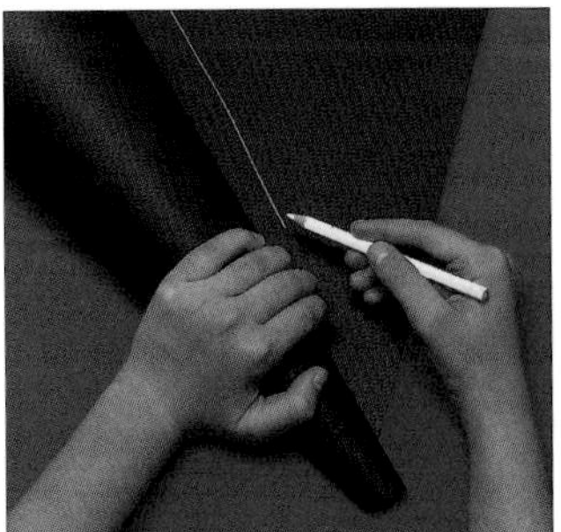

6 Roll the rectangle of thin, black card into the shape of a cone. Use a white pencil to draw a shape on the card to show where it overlaps and should be taped.

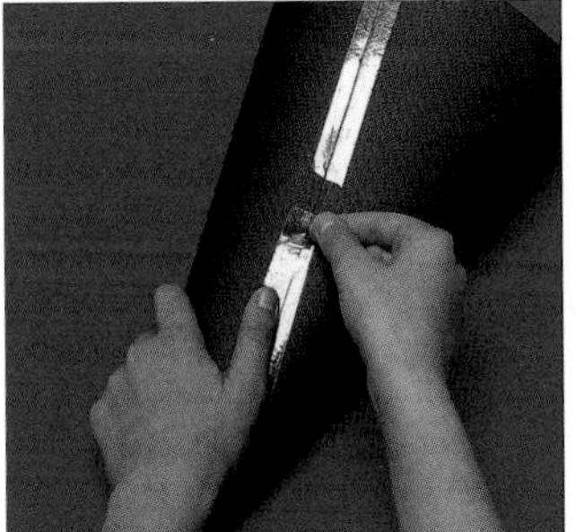

7 Cut away the excess card and roll the card back into a cone shape. Then secure it with adhesive tape. Trim the bottom edge of the cone to fit the size of your head.

8 Place the hat on the square black card. Use the white pencil to draw a rough circle around the rim about 5cm/2in away from it. Draw a second circle to fit exactly around the rim of the hat.

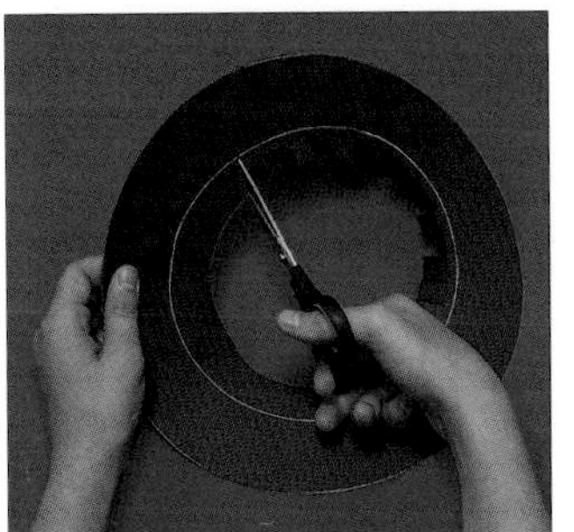

9 Cut around the outside ring. Then cut out the centre, making sure to leave an extra 3cm/$1\frac{3}{16}$in inside the white line ring. Make snips into the ring as far as the line to make small tabs.

10 Fit the rim of the hat on to the bottom of the cone-shaped section. Fold the tabs up inside the hat, and use small pieces of adhesive tape to fix the rim to the hat.

11 Draw a rectangular shape on to the silver card to make a hat buckle. Draw a second rectangle inside the first one. Cut out the buckle and glue it on to the front of the hat.

12 Cut sheets of green and black tissue into long strips to make witch's hair. Glue the strips all the way around the inside of the witch's hat, leaving a gap at the front by the buckle.

Complete the witch's look by using face paints. Paint dark lines under your eyes and around your mouth to make you look as if you have wrinkles. Black out one of your teeth. You will also need a broom, which you can make by tying twigs to an old broom handle.

Cowboy gear

The clothes of a typical cowboy had to be tough, because he spent a long time in the saddle. Overtrousers called chaps protected his legs from the cattle's horns, as well as from burn marks from throwing his lassos. High-heeled leather boots helped to keep the rider's feet in the stirrups on the saddle. The cowboy's hat was usually made from a type of hard-wearing wool called felt. A wide brim shielded his face from the Sun. Hats could also double up as water carriers for horses to drink from.

YOU WILL NEED

Leg chaps: Tape measure, pencil, paper, scissors, brown material (150 x 150cm/5 x 5ft), pins, needle, brown embroidery thread.

Felt hat: Tape measure, pencil, paper, scissors, brown felt (70 x 70cm/28 x 28in), stiffened fabric, pins, needle, brown embroidery thread, 3m/10ft thick wool in three different colours, adhesive tape.

Template

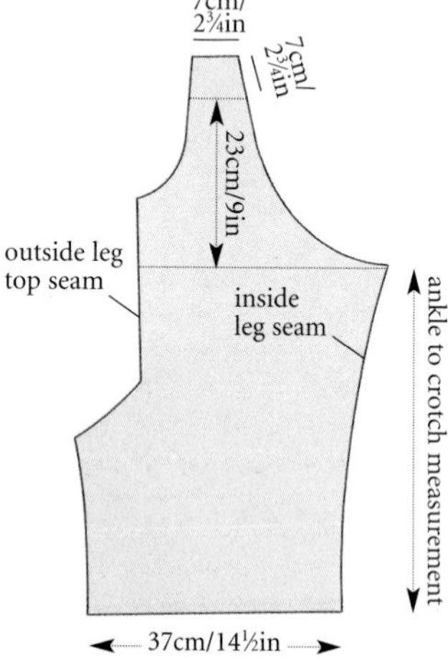

Leg chaps

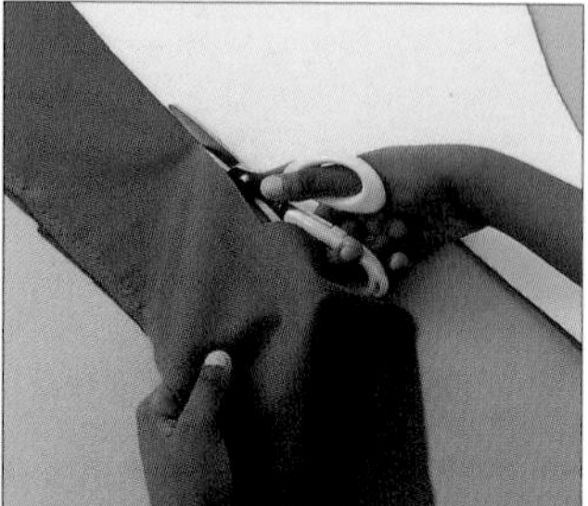

1 Cut two templates from paper. Fold the fabric in half to make a long thin piece with the right sides together. Pin the templates to the material. Cut around the fabric to make four pieces.

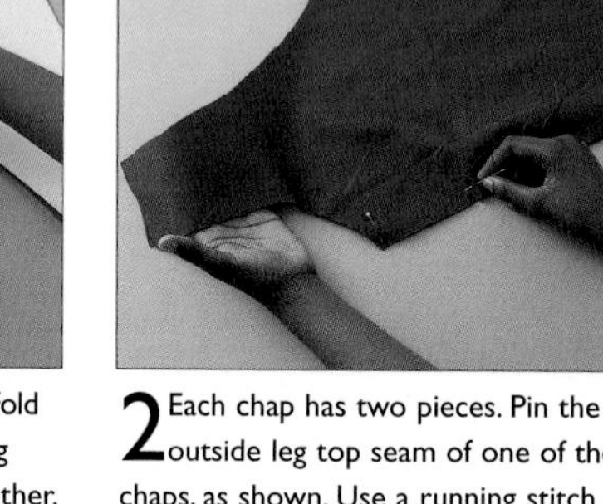

2 Each chap has two pieces. Pin the outside leg top seam of one of the chaps, as shown. Use a running stitch to sew 1.5cm/⅝in in from the cut edge. Pin and sew the inside leg seam.

3 Turn the leg the right way out. Following the top dotted line on the template, fold over the belt loops. Pin them along the bottom edge and then carefully stitch them.

4 Pin and then sew the outside part of the outside leg bottom seam 10cm/4in in from the cut edge. Make your stitches as neat as possible, as they will be visible when you wear the chaps.

5 Cut strips into the wide flap down the outside leg to make a fringe. Try not to cut into the seam. Repeat Steps 2 to 5 to make the second leg for your chaps.

Template

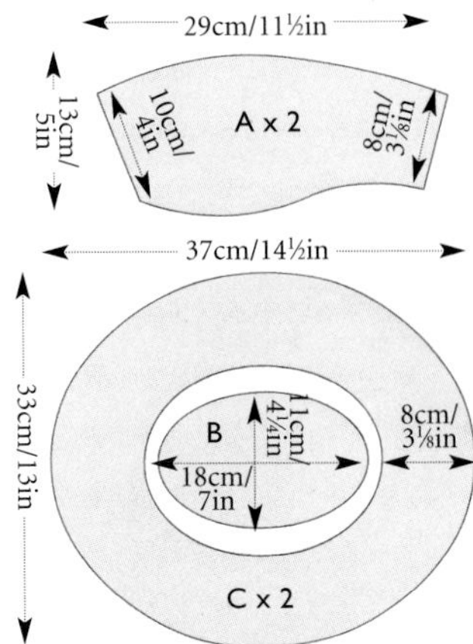

Felt hat

1 Make the templates from paper and pin them to the felt. Cut out. Pin and sew the two short sides of the hat (template A). Pin and sew the crown (template B) to the top of the sides.

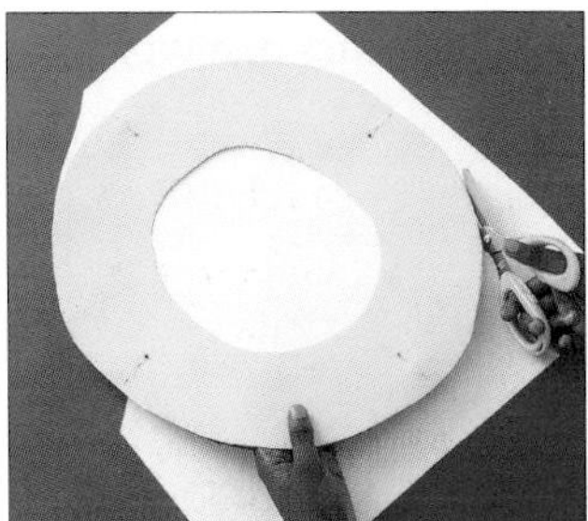

2 Take template C and pin it on to the piece of stiffened fabric. Cut around it, and then cut out the hole in the centre. The result will be used to make the brim of your cowboy hat.

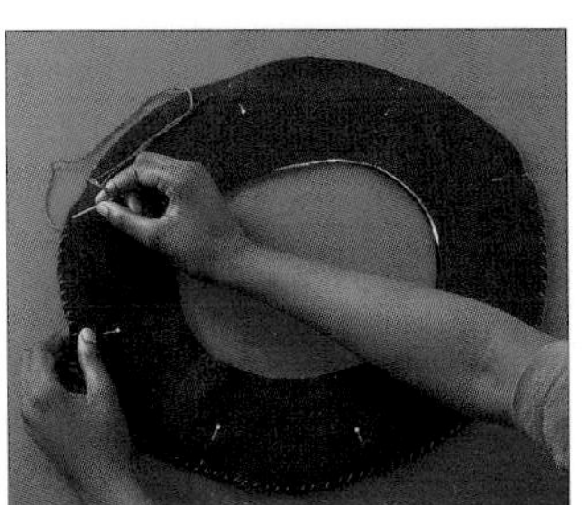

3 Sandwich the stiffened fabric between the two felt brims cut using template C and pin the two sides of the brim together. Sew the outside edge of all three pieces, as shown.

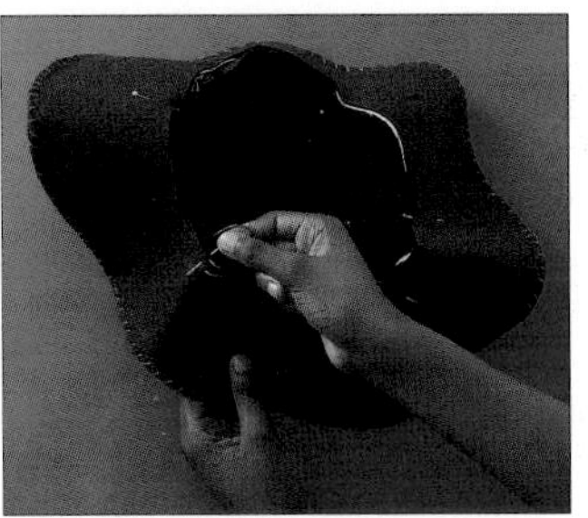

4 Turn the hat brim upside down and carefully pin it to the hat crown you have just made. This way, the seam will end up inside the hat. Sew the pieces together, as shown above.

To put on your chaps, pull each leg over your jeans. Then get someone to help you thread a thick leather belt through the loops front and back. Don't forget your hat and 'kerchief!

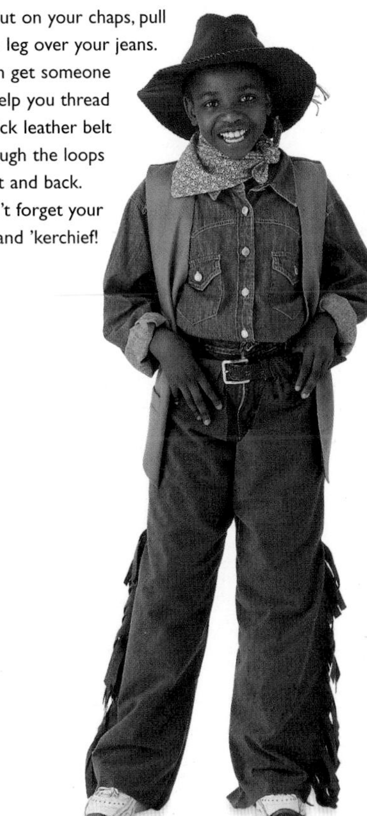

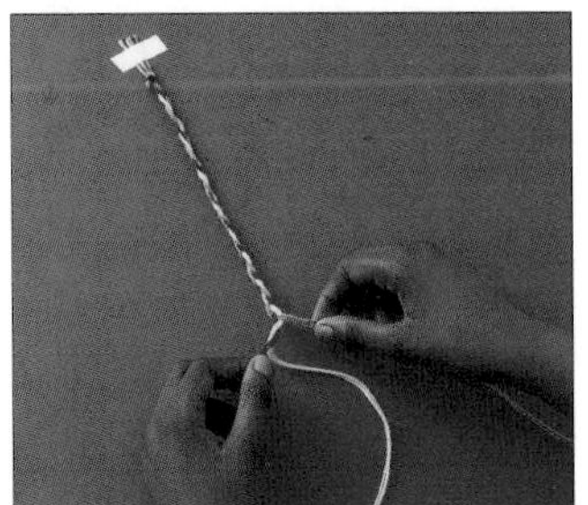

5 Cut 1m/39⅜in lengths from each of the three balls of coloured wool. Fold each strand of wool in half. Knot them at the top and tape them to a work surface. Then braid the wool together.

6 Finish the braid by tying a knot at each end. The braid will become the decorative band for your hat when you wrap it around the base of the crown and knot it tightly around the rim.

Hats and Headwear

Hats and headwear have been worn by men and women all over the world for thousands of years. Their original purpose was to protect the head from extremes of weather, but hats also became signs of status or official position. A crown came to indicate the authority of a king or queen, while religious and military leaders wore headgear that readily identified them and the position they held. As fashion accessories, hats and headwear have been made in bright colours, beautiful materials and all sorts of shapes. They have been decorated with feathers, beads, jewels and bows.

▲ **Sun worshipper**
Pharaoh Akhenaten of Egypt, shown worshipping the Sun god Aten, wore a number of different crowns to indicate his many different roles as ruler of Egypt. Here, Akhenaten is wearing a special type of hat to show his position as high priest.

◀ **A band of gold**
Boudicca, queen of the Iceni tribe in Celtic Britain, is shown wearing a gold band around her head. This band is called a diadem, and indicates her important position as a ruler. Rare and precious gold was considered to be the metal of royalty.

Imperial silk ▲

Puyi, the last emperor of China, ascended to the throne as a small boy. He is shown wearing richly embroidered silk robes and a small silk skullcap decorated with coloured embroidery.

▲ Mayan splendour

A mural showing two warriors from Central America standing over a captive. They are wearing the magnificent clothes of the Mayan nobility. The headdresses, decorated with feathers and even an animal head, indicate the importance of the two warriors.

◂ European adventurer

A Portuguese naval officer from the early 1600s wearing the typical clothes of his high social position. On his head he is wearing a small, neat hat called a copotain, which has a narrow brim and is made of fur or felt.

▲ Practical headwear

A Saami boy from Lapland wears a traditional pom-pom hat. It is a cheerful and very practical design for the Arctic climate.

Egyptian crown

The pharaohs of ancient Egypt wore many accessories to show that they were important. Pictures and statues showed them with special badges of royalty, such as crowns, headcloths, false beards, sceptres and a crook and flail held in each hand.

The word pharaoh comes from the Egyptian *per-aa* (great house or palace). Later, the word came to mean the person, or ruler, who lived in the palace. The pharaoh was the most important person in Egypt, and the link between the people and their gods. The Egyptians believed that on his death, the pharaoh became a god in his own right.

The pharaoh led a busy life. He was the high priest, the chief law-maker, the commander of the army, and in charge of the country's wealth. He had to be a clever politician, too. Generally, pharaohs were men, but queens could rule if a male successor was too young. A pharaoh could take several wives. In a royal family, it was common for fathers to marry daughters and for brothers to marry sisters. Sometimes, however, pharaohs married foreign princesses to make an alliance with another country.

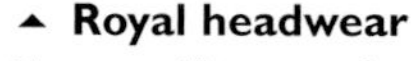

▲ Royal headwear
Thutmose III is remembered as a brave warrior king. This picture shows him wearing the headcloth that is one of the special symbols of royalty.

▲ Crowning glory
Rameses III was the last great warrior pharaoh. Here, Rameses is shown wearing an elaborate crown that is another special badge of royalty.

▼ Templates

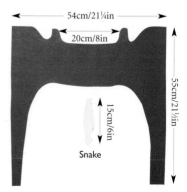

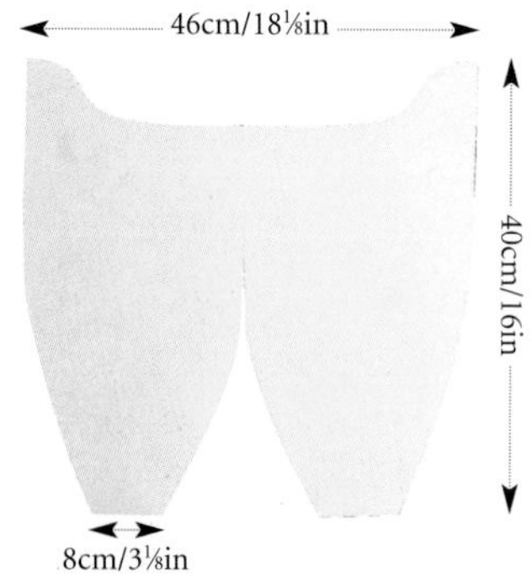

White crown of Upper Egypt

54cm/21¼in
20cm/8in
55cm/21½in
15cm/6in
Snake

Red crown of Lower Egypt

YOU WILL NEED

Two large sheets of card (red and white), pencil, ruler, scissors, masking tape, cardboard roll, bandage, tennis ball, white glue and glue brush, white and gold acrylic paints, water pot, paintbrush, beads, skewer.

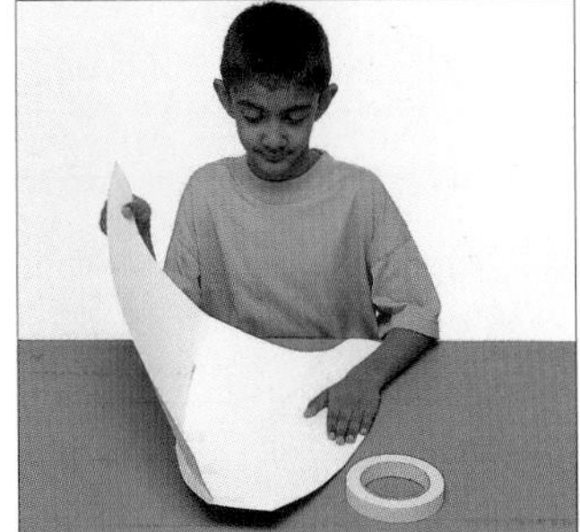

1 Make each section of the crown using the templates. Bend the white crown section into a cylinder. Use lengths of masking tape to join the two edges of the cylinder together.

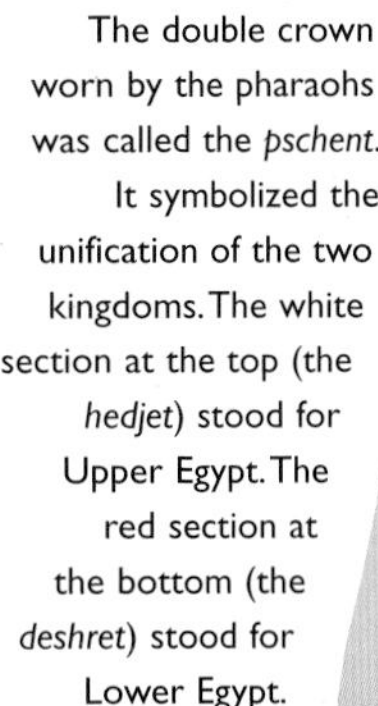

The double crown worn by the pharaohs was called the *pschent*. It symbolized the unification of the two kingdoms. The white section at the top (the *hedjet*) stood for Upper Egypt. The red section at the bottom (the *deshret*) stood for Lower Egypt.

2 Tape the cardboard roll into the hole at the top of your pharaoh's crown. Plug the end of the crown with bandages or a tennis ball wedged in position and glue down the edges.

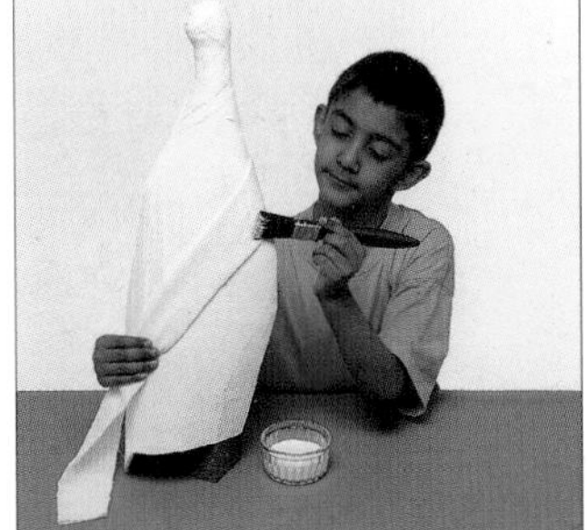

3 Wrap the white section of the crown with lengths of bandage. Paint over these with an equal mixture of white paint and glue. Leave the crown in a warm place to dry.

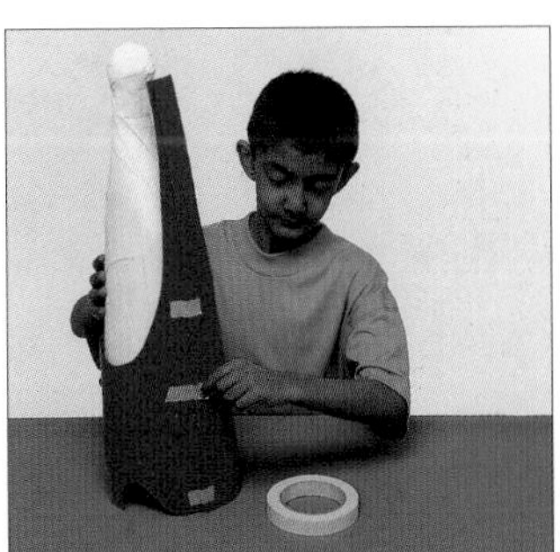

4 Now take the red crown section. Wrap it tightly around the white crown section, as shown above. Hold the two sections together using strips of masking tape.

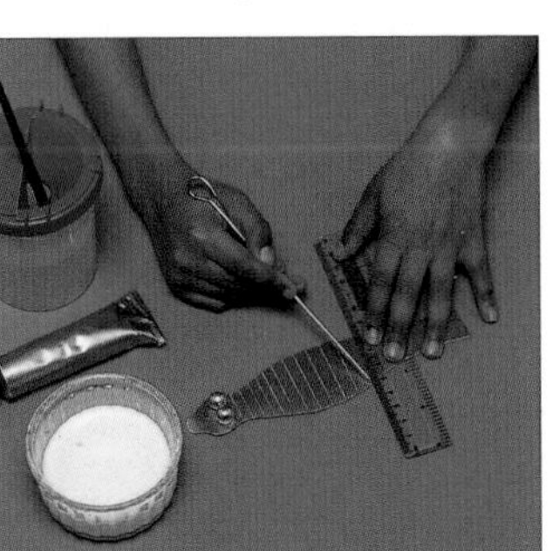

5 Paint the snake shape with gold acrylic paint and stick on beads for its eyes. When dry, score lines across its body with a skewer. Bend the body and glue it to the front of the crown.

Tribal headdress

One of the most popular images of a Native American is that of a warrior dressed in fringed buckskin and a war bonnet, and decorated with body paint and beads. That was just one style of dress, mainly used by the Plains tribes. A warrior had to earn the right to wear a headdress like the one you can make in this project. Each act of bravery during conflict earned the warrior the right to tie another feather to his headdress. Plains warriors also tied locks of their victims' hair to the front of their shirts.

YOU WILL NEED

1m x 1cm/1yd x ½in red ribbon, red upholstery tape (75 x 6cm/2½ft x 2in), ruler, masking tape, needle and thread, white paper, scissors, black paint, paintbrush, water pot, 3.7m/12ft balsa dowel, white glue and glue brush, six feathers, five pieces of different coloured felt, beads or sequins, pair of compasses, red paper, coloured ribbons.

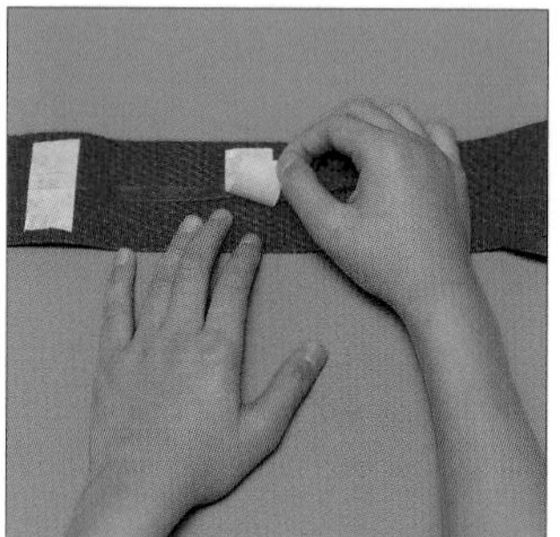

1 Lay the 1m/39⅜in-long red ribbon along the middle of the upholstery tape. Leave 12.5cm/4⅞in lengths at each end. Tape the ribbon on to the upholstery tape and sew it on.

2 Cut 26 feather shapes from the white paper, each 18cm/7in long and 4cm/1½in wide. Paint the tips black. When the paint is dry, make tiny cuts around the edges of the paper feathers.

3 Cut the balsa dowel into 26 lengths, each 14cm/5½in long. Carefully glue the dowel to the centre of the back of each feather, starting just below the painted black tip.

4 Take the six real bird feathers and tie them with cotton thread on to the bottom of six of the feathers you made earlier. These will be at the front of the headdress.

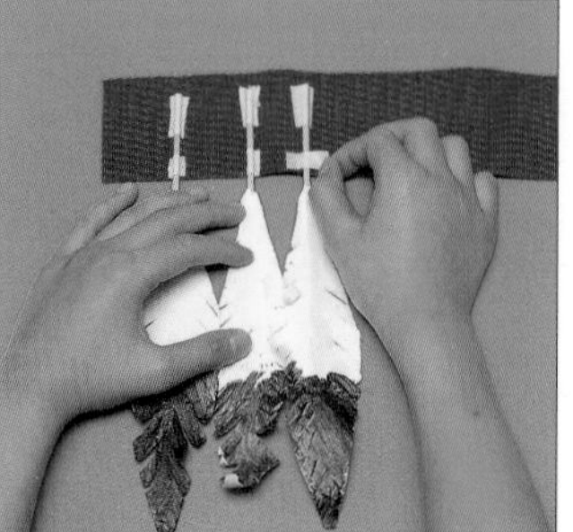

5 Glue and tape all the feathers on to the front of the red band, overlapping the feathers slightly as you go. Position them so that the six real feathers are in the centre.

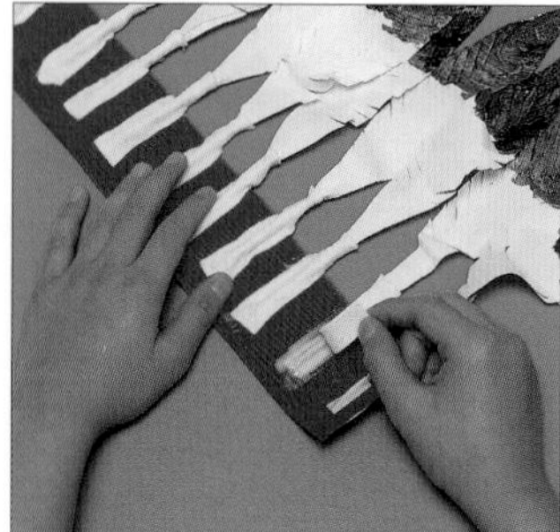

6 Measure and cut 26 lengths of white felt. Each piece of felt should be 6 x 1cm/2½ x ½in. Glue the felt strips over each piece of balsa dowel, so that the sticks are hidden.

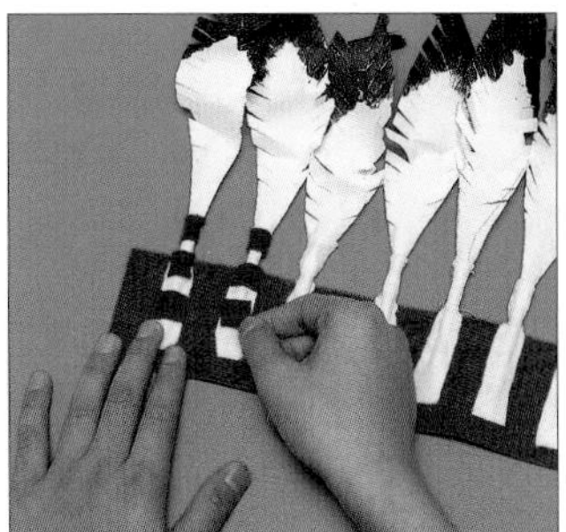

7 Cut out red felt pieces measuring 1.5 x 1cm/⅝ x ½in. Cut three pieces for five feathers at each end, and two pieces for the rest. Glue the red felt on to the white felt to make stripes.

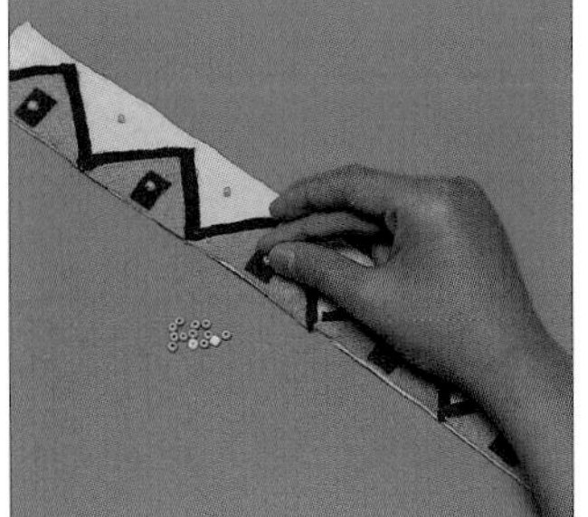

8 Cut out a 40 x 4cm/16 x 1½in band from yellow felt. Glue on triangles of dark blue and light blue felt and small squares of red felt, as shown. You can also decorate it with beads or sequins.

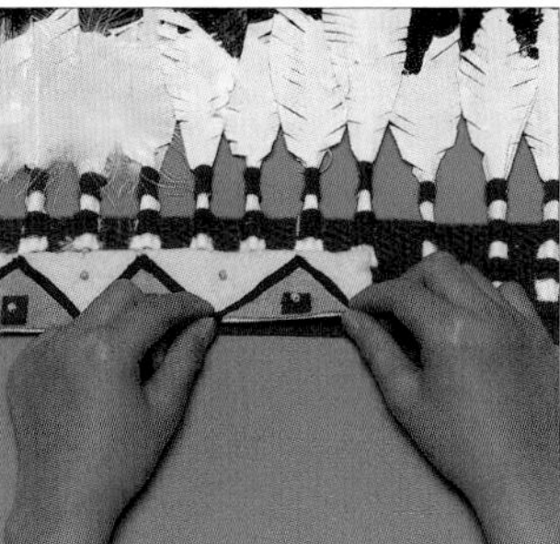

9 Carefully glue the decorative band on to the red band using a ruler to help you place it in the middle. Some feathers will show on either side of the band.

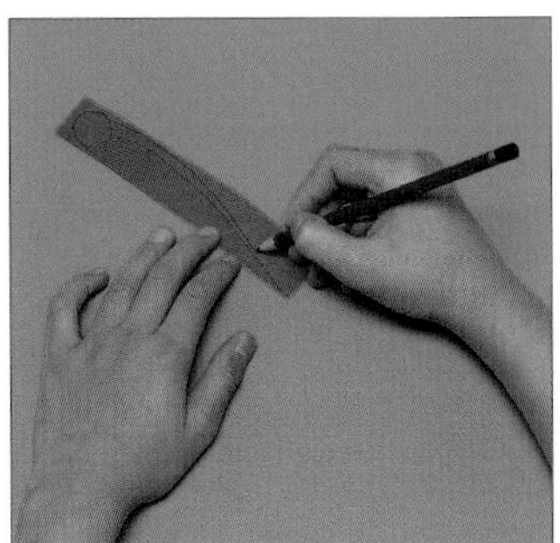

10 Draw a circle on to the red paper, 3cm/1³⁄₁₆in in diameter. Then draw a 15cm/6in-long tail feather starting at the circle. It should measure 1cm/⅜in across and taper to a point.

11 Draw seven more of these tail feathers and cut them out. Glue them on to the ends of the feathers on the middle of the band, so that the points stick into the air.

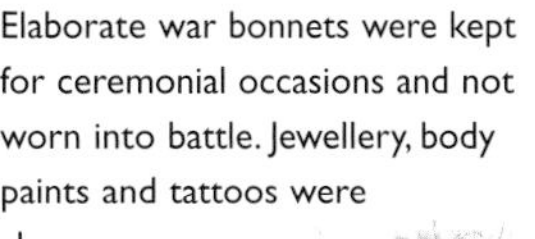

Elaborate war bonnets were kept for ceremonial occasions and not worn into battle. Jewellery, body paints and tattoos were also common.

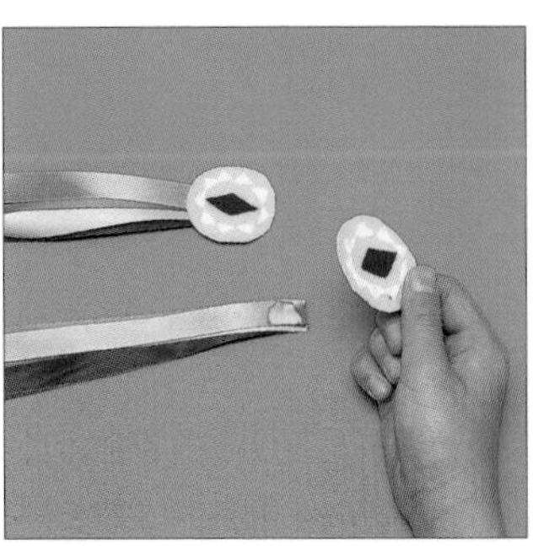

12 Cut out two circles of yellow felt, 5cm/2in in diameter. Decorate the felt circles with red and white felt shapes. Glue coloured ribbons to the backs of the circles.

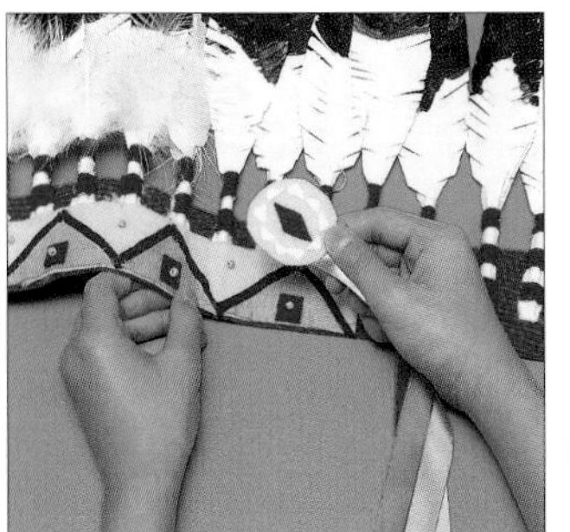

13 Finally, stick the felt circles on to the headdress on top of the decorative band. The circles should be placed so that the ribbons hang down either side by your ears.

Arctic Saami hat

Clothes in the Arctic were often beautiful as well as practical. Strips or patches of different furs were used to form designs and geometric patterns on outer clothes. Fur trimmings, toggles and other decorative fastenings added final touches to many clothes. Jewellery included pendants, bracelets, necklaces and brooches. Ornaments such as these were traditionally made of natural materials, such as bone and walrus ivory.

Inuit women from North America decorated clothes with birds' beaks, tiny feathers or porcupine quills. In Greenland, lace and glass beads were popular decorations. The clothes of the Saami from Scandinavia were the most colourful. Saami men, women and children wore blue outfits with a red and yellow trim. Men's costumes included tall hats and flared tunics. Women's clothes included flared skirts with embroidered hems and colourful hats, shawls and scarves.

▲ Animal insulation
In the bitter Arctic cold, people wore warm, waterproof clothing made from the skins of animals such as seals.

▲ Colourful costumes
A Saami herdsman in traditional dress holds aloft a reindeer calf born at the end of the spring migration.

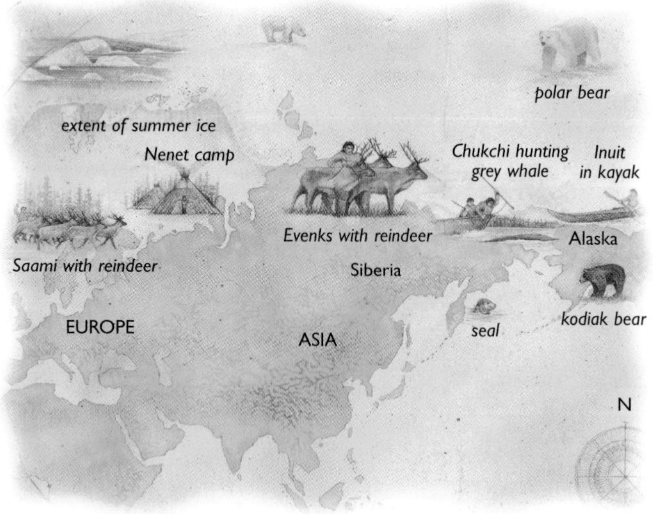

▲ Arctic inhabitants
This map shows some of the main groups of people who still live in the Arctic region. Many Arctic peoples, such as the Saami and Evenks, have long depended on reindeer for food and to make clothes, shelter and tools.

YOU WILL NEED

Red felt measuring 58 x 30cm/23 x 12in, ruler, pencil, black ribbon measuring 58 x 2cm/23 x ¾in, white glue and glue brush, coloured ribbon measuring 58cm/23in, white felt measuring 58cm/23in, pair of compasses, red card, scissors, ribbon strips (red, green and white) measuring 44 x 4cm/17½ x 1½in, red ribbon measuring 58 x 4cm/23 x 1½in.

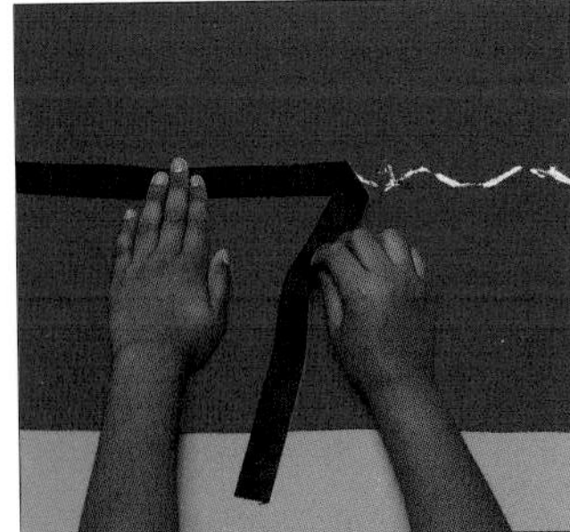

1 Use a ruler and pencil to mark out the centre of the piece of red felt along its length. Carefully glue the length of black ribbon along the centre line, as shown above.

2 Continue to decorate the red felt section with pieces of coloured ribbon. You can add some strips of white felt to add to your striking Saami hat design.

3 Cut out a circle of red card with a diameter of 18cm/7in. Draw a circle inside with a diameter of 15cm/6in. Cut into the larger circle as far as the 15cm/6in line to make a series of tabs.

4 Glue the ends of the decorated red felt section together, as shown above. You will need to wrap this felt section around your head and measure it to ensure the hat fits properly.

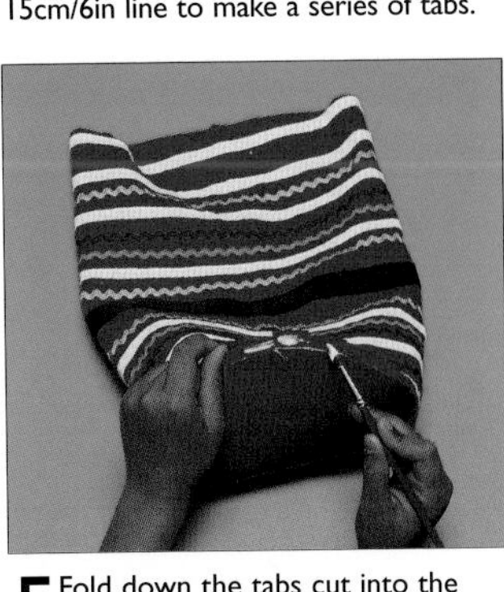

5 Fold down the tabs cut into the circle of red card. Dab them with glue, tuck them inside one end of the red felt section, and then stick them firmly to make the top of the hat.

6 While the hat is drying, glue the coloured ribbon strips together. Glue these strips 15cm/6in from the end of the 58cm/23in-long band of red ribbon. Glue this to the base of the hat.

The style of Saami hats varied from one place to another. In southern Norway, men's hats were tall and rounded. Further north, their hats had four points.

Medieval headpiece

In the Middle Ages, noble ladies hid their hair beneath a fancy headdress. The ring-shaped chaplet you can make in this project is one of the simpler headdress styles worn in medieval times. The more wealthy, fashionable and important a lady was, the more elaborate her clothes were. Some robes were embroidered and trimmed with fur – they were extremely expensive, and expected to last a lifetime. Traders came to the castle to present a choice of materials and designs. When the lady had chosen, tailors made the clothes.

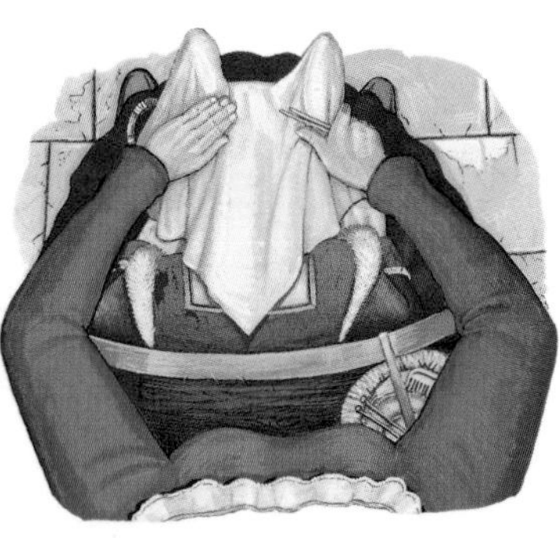

▲ **Dressed to impress**
A lady needs help from a maid to put on her complicated headpiece.

YOU WILL NEED

Pencil, ruler, corrugated card, scissors, masking tape, 2m/6½ft fine fabric, two sponges, 3–4m/10–13ft netting, string, acrylic paints, paintbrush, water pot, nylon stocking, cotton wool, ribbon, needle and thread, 1m/1yd gold braid, white glue and glue brush, 2 x 2cm/¾ x ¾in silver card, three 7cm/2¾in lengths of thin wire, beads.

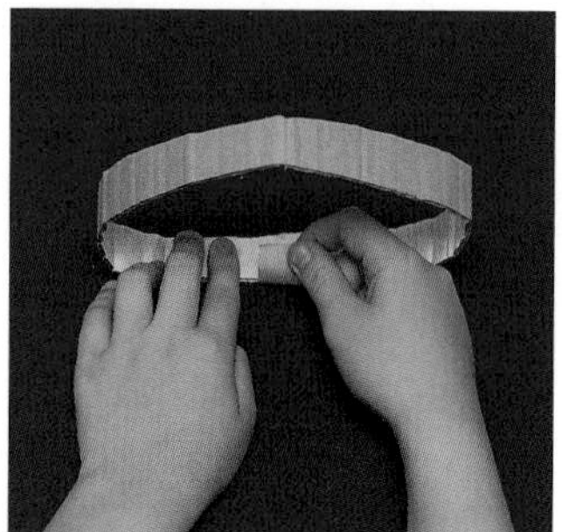

1 Cut a 4cm/1½in strip of corrugated card to fit around your head exactly, about 30cm/1ft in length. Overlap the ends of the strip and firmly secure them with masking tape.

2 Cut two squares of the fine fabric, each one big enough to wrap around the sponge. Then cut two squares of netting slightly larger than the fabric squares.

3 Lay the fabric squares over the net squares. Place a sponge in the middle of each fabric square. Gather the netting and fabric over the sponges and tie them with string.

4 Paint the card circle for your head. Thread two lengths of string through each sponge and net ball. Use the string to hang one ball on each side of the card circlet.

5 Cut the bottom half leg off a coloured nylon stocking. Pack the inside tightly with cotton wool to make a firm, full sausage shape. Knot the open end to close it.

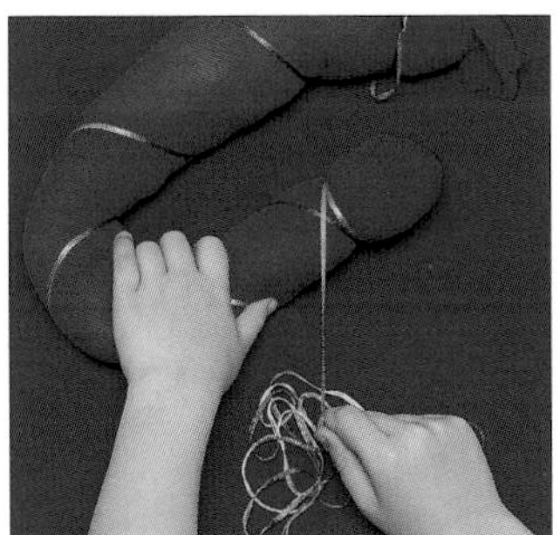

6 Tie the ribbon around one end of the sausage. Wind it diagonally along the sausage and then wind it back again to cross diagonally over the first row.

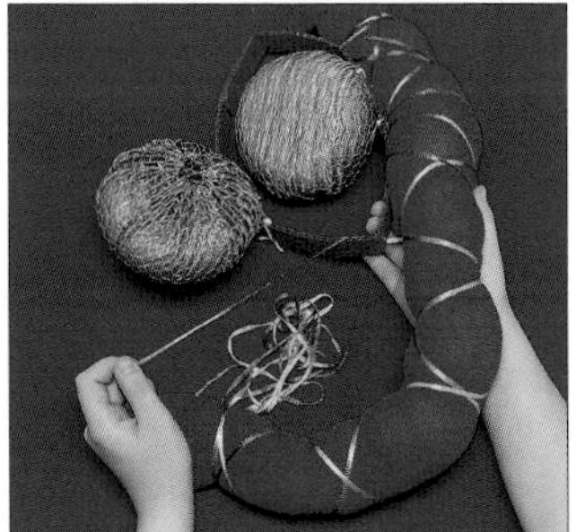

7 Thread more ribbon through the ribbon crossovers on the sausage. Then take the ribbon over and around the head circlet to join the sausage and band together.

8 Sew the two ends of the sausage shape together. Sew one end of the gold braid to cover the join. Then glue the braid around the sausage, as shown.

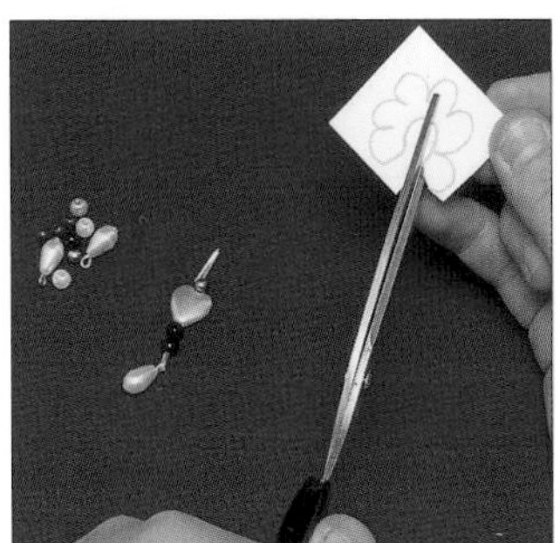

9 Cut out a flower shape from the 2 x 2cm/¾ x ¾in silver card, as shown. Bend one end of the wire into a hook. Thread some beads on to the other end. Then bend the wire over.

10 Glue the flower shape on to the front of the headdress. Hook the wire beads in the middle. Glue more beads and braid around the headdress.

11 Make a double pleat in the remaining length of fabric to make the veil. Secure the veil to the inside back half of the headdress with masking tape.

A real medieval hat was called a chaplet. It was made of silk or satin fabric and held in place by a hair net. The ring-shaped chaplet fitted on top of a veil, and the veil hung down at the back of the head. Ladies often shaved the hair at the front of their heads to make their foreheads look high. For an authentic medieval look, tuck your hair out of sight under the hat.

Weaving and Sewing

The very first clothes that people wore were made from tied grasses or tree bark, or the skins of animals. The invention of the sewing needle enabled people to join different pieces of material together. Clothes became more varied, and also fitted more comfortably. The weaving loom completely transformed the clothes people wore. Long lengths of cloth could be made into tents, mats and wall hangings, or cut and shaped into clothes. The weaving loom was one of the first pieces of industrial equipment to be used. The earliest known cloth was woven at least 7,000 years ago in what is now Palestine.

▲ Easy weaving
Backstrap looms were first used by the Incas around 2500BC, and continue to be used in Central and South America. The upright, or warp, threads are tensioned between an upright post and a beam attached to the weaver's waist. The cross, or weft, threads are passed in between.

woad

madder

◀ Colours for cloth
Vikings used the leaves, roots, bark and flowers of many plants to dye woollen cloth fabric. For example, a wild flower called weld, or dyer's rocket, produced yellow dye. The roots of the madder plant made a dark red dye. The leaves of woad plants produced a blue dye.

◀ Silken threads

A Japanese craftworker embroiders an intricate design into woven silk using a traditional-style loom. Luxurious and highly decorated textiles were made for the robes of the wealthy. Ordinary people wore plainer clothes of dyed cottons and, occasionally, silk.

porcupine quills

glass beads

▲ Quills and beads

Native Americans have used beads to decorate anything from moccasins to shirts, and to make jewellery. Glass beads brought by traders from the 1500s replaced bone beads and porcupine quills. Quills were usually boiled, dyed and flattened, then woven together to form patterned strips.

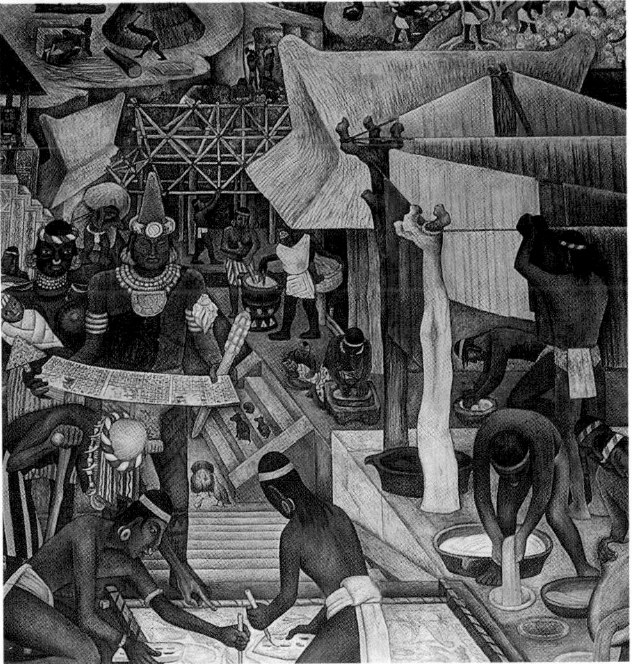

◀ Glowing colours

This painting by Diego Rivera shows craftworkers from the region of Tarascan, Central America, dyeing the hanks of yarn before they are woven into cloth. Mesoamerican dyes were made from fruits, flowers, shellfish and the cochineal beetles that lived on cactus plants.

Mesoamerican backstrap loom

In South and Central America, homes were not just places to eat and sleep. They were workplaces, too. Weaving was a skill learned by all women in Mesoamerica and in the Andean region, and they spent long hours spinning thread and weaving it into cloth. As well as making tunics, cloaks and other items of clothing for the family, they had to give some to the State as a form of tax payment.

Cotton was spun and woven into textiles for the wealthiest citizens of Mesoamerica. Peasants wore clothes made from the woven fibres of local plants such as the yucca and maguey. Yarn was dyed before it was woven. Most dyes originated from the flowers, fruits and leaves of plants, but some were extracted from shellfish and insects such as the cochineal beetle – a tiny insect that lives on cactus plants.

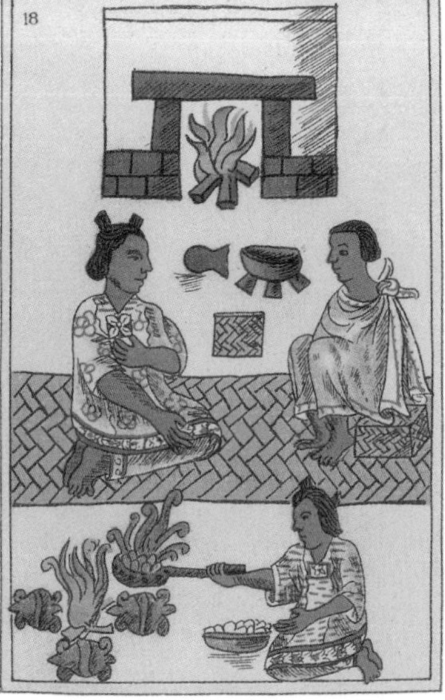

▲ **Skirts, tunics and cloaks**
A wealthy Aztec couple sit by the fire, while their hostess cooks a meal. Both of the women are wearing long skirts. The bright embroidery on their tunics is a sign of high rank.

▲ **Weaving fibres**
Threads spun from plant fibres were woven into cloth on backstrap looms such as this one. Rough fibres from the yucca and cactus plants made coarse cloth. The wealthy had silky textiles.

Down Mexico way ▶
These Mexican women are wearing warm woollen ponchos in bright colours that would also have appealed to their ancestors.

YOU WILL NEED

Two pieces of thick dowel about 70cm/27½in long, brown water-based paint, paintbrush, water pot, string, scissors, thick card, pencil, ruler, masking tape, yellow and red wool, needle.

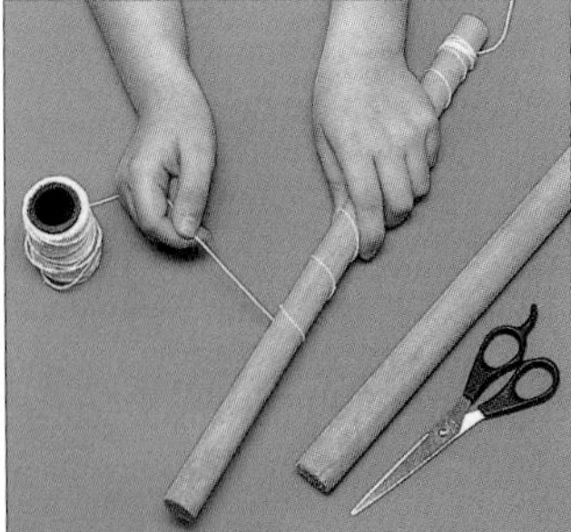

1 Paint the pieces of dowel brown. Leave them to dry. Tie a length of string to each length of dowel and wind it around. Leave a length of string loose at each end.

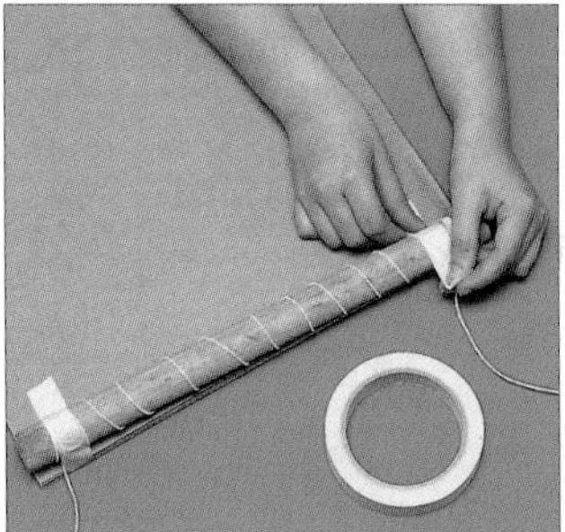

2 Cut a piece of thick card about 100 x 70cm/39½ x 27½in. This is a temporary base. Lightly fix the stringed dowel at the 70cm/27½in sides of the base using masking tape.

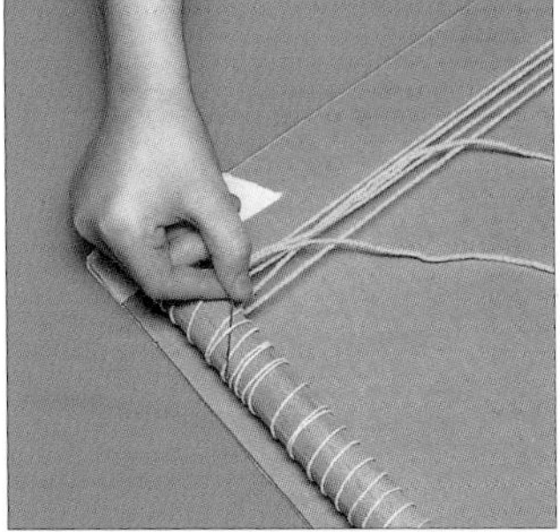

3 Now take your yellow wool. Thread the wool through the string loops using the needle and pull them through to the other end, as shown above. Try to keep the yellow wool taut.

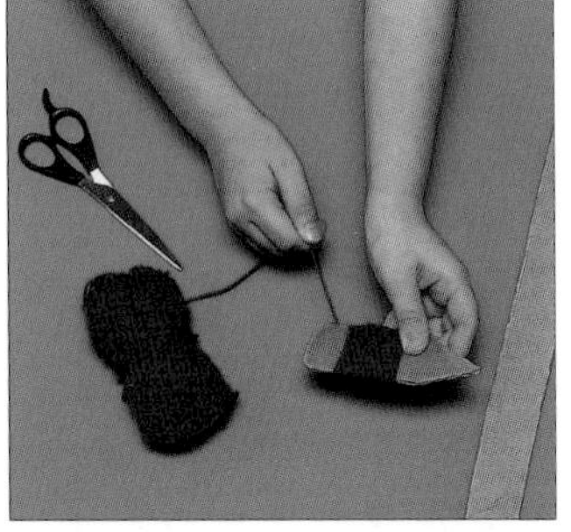

4 Cut a 30 x 3.5cm/12 x 1⅜in piece of thick card. Now cut a smaller rectangle of card with one pointed end, as shown above. Wind the red wool tightly around it.

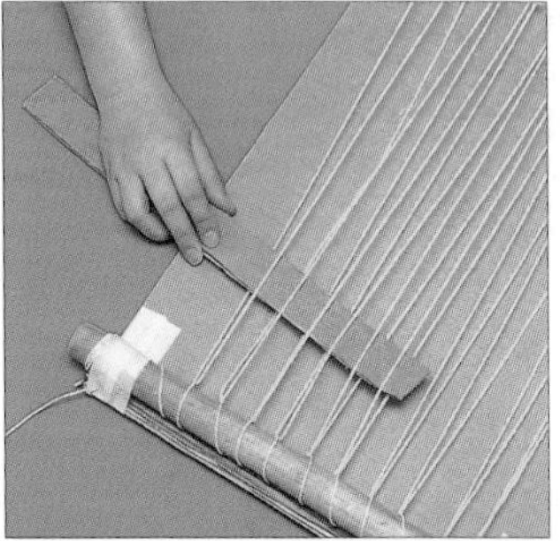

5 Slide the long card rectangle through every second thread. This device, called a shed rod, is turned on its side to lift the threads. Then tie one end of the red wool to the yellow wool.

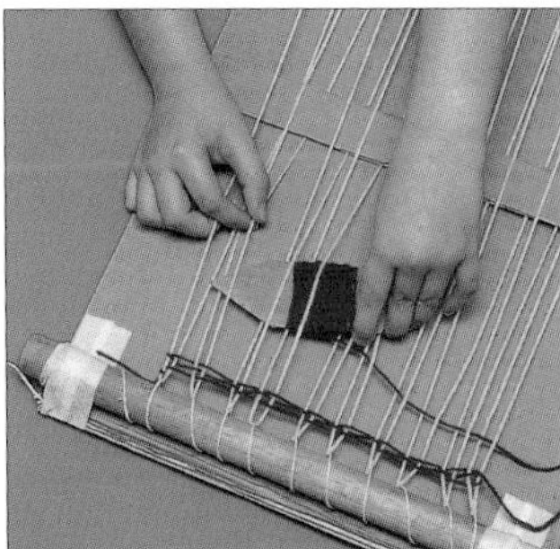

6 Turn the shed rod on its side to lift the threads and feed the red wool through the loom. Then with the shed rod flat, thread the red wool back through alternate yellow threads.

To continue weaving, take the loom off the cardboard base. Tie the loose string around your waist. Attach the other end of the loom to a post or tree with the string. Lean back to keep the long warp threads evenly taut.

Medieval needlework

In medieval Europe, most women were taught to spin and sew. Making small items, such as this medieval-style tapestry design, was a popular pastime. Before any needlework could begin, the canvas background had to be woven, and the yarns spun and dyed. Wool for spinning needlepoint yarn or weaving into cloth came from the sheep on the lord's estate. Linen for fine embroidery and cloth came from flax plants grown in the fields.

YOU WILL NEED

Large-eyed needle, double-stranded embroidery threads (red, orange, green and blue), scissors, old fabric, black pen, 9 x 8cm/3½ x 3⅛in tracing paper, soft-leaded pencil, adhesive tape, 15 x 15cm/6 x 6in white linen fabric, ruler.

Stem stitching

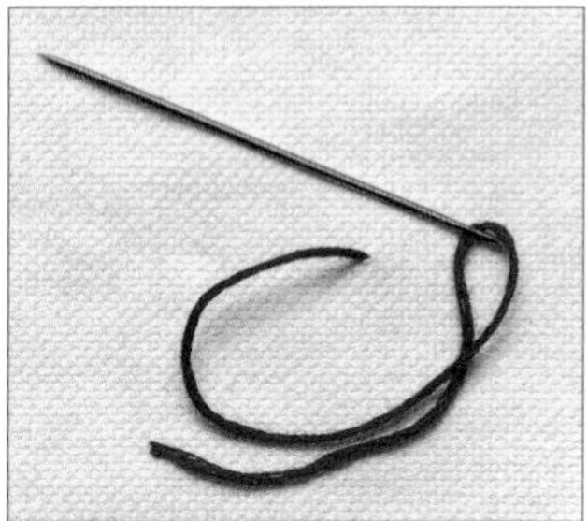

1 Practise the stem stitch on a scrap of old fabric. Push the needle and thread through from the back to the front of the fabric. Hold the end of the thread at the back of the fabric.

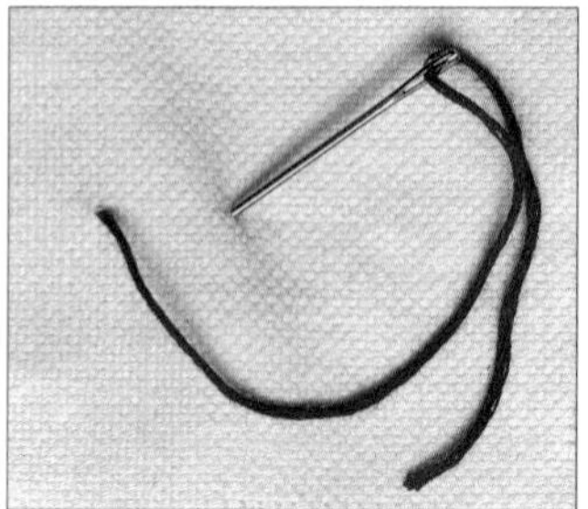

2 Tie a double knot in the thread at the back of the fabric. Then push the needle and thread into the fabric about 5mm/¼in along from your first insertion point.

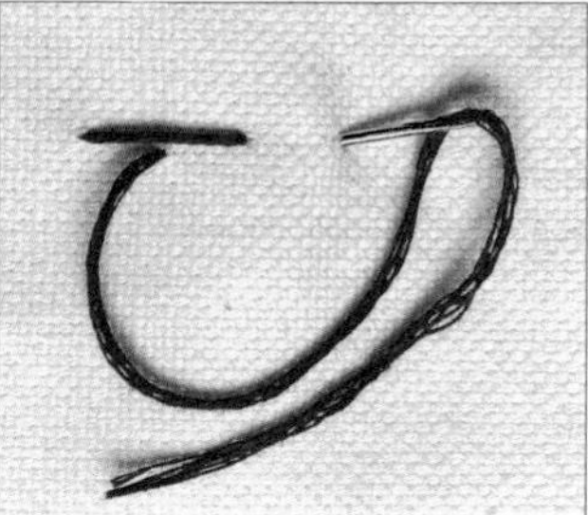

3 Pull the first stitch taut. Bring the needle up just beside the middle of the first stitch. Make a second 5mm/¼in stitch. Continue in the same way to make a line.

Medieval needlework

1 Use a black pen to copy the design from Step 9 on to the tracing paper. Turn the tracing paper over. Trace over the outline you have drawn with the soft-leaded pencil.

2 Tape the tracing paper (pencilled side down) on to the square of fabric. Trace over the motif once again, so that the pencilled image transfers on to the fabric.

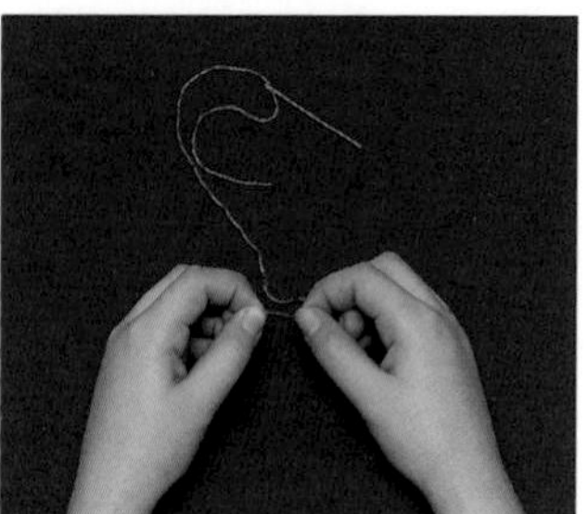

3 Cut a long piece of the orange double-stranded embroidery thread and thread the large-eyed needle. Tie a double knot at one end of the orange thread.

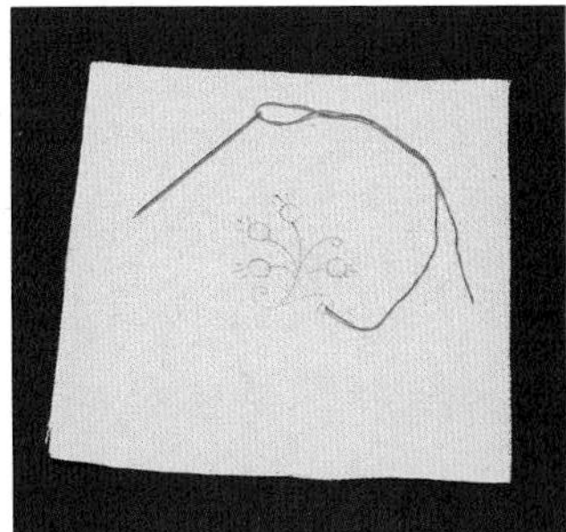

4 Start your embroidery with the scroll shape at the bottom of the design. Push the needle from the back of the fabric to the front. Pull the thread through.

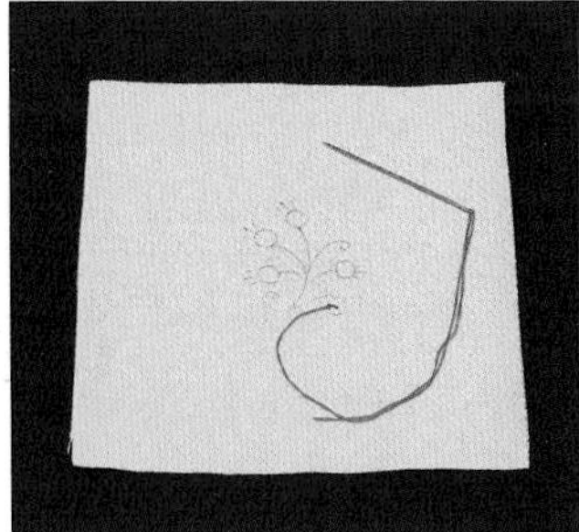

5 Push the thread through the fabric about 2mm/1⁄16in along the line of the scroll. Pull the thread through half way along the first stitch. (See 'Stem stitching' on the opposite page.)

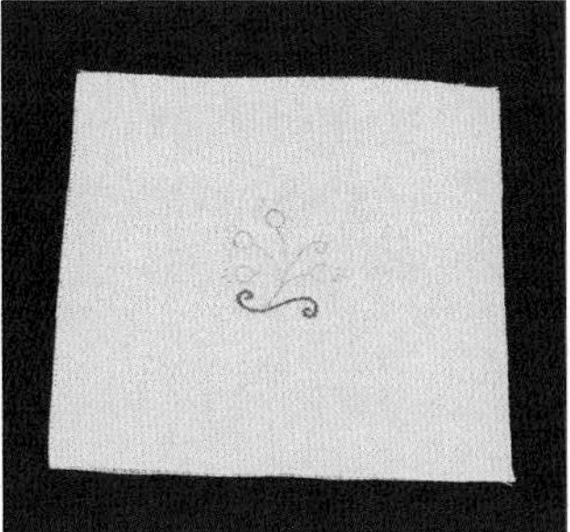

6 Carefully continue your stem stitches all the way along the scroll. The stitches should overlap so that they make a continuous and even, curved line.

7 Thread the needle with a length of green double-stranded embroidery thread. Start at the orange base of the stems and sew along each of the stems in the same way.

8 To sew the flower heads, thread the needle with a length of red embroidery thread. Sew the stem stitch in a circle. Sew a flower head at the end of every stem except one.

9 Thread the needle with the blue embroidery thread. Sew a single stitch for the short details on the flowers and two stitches for the longer, middle ones.

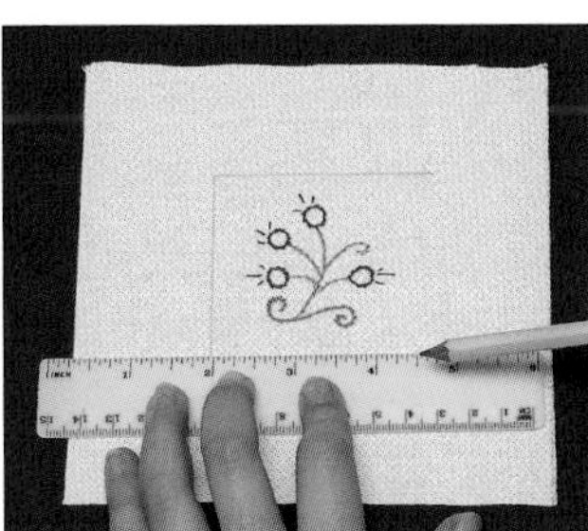

10 Mark a border in pencil 1cm/½in from the edge of the motif. Using a long length of red embroidery thread, follow the pencil lines as a guide for your border stitches.

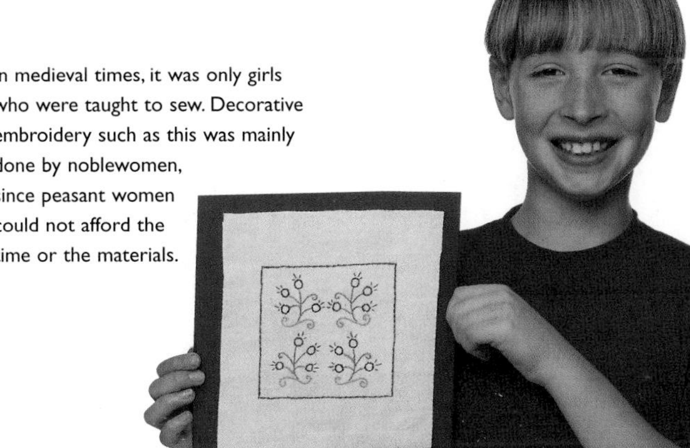

In medieval times, it was only girls who were taught to sew. Decorative embroidery such as this was mainly done by noblewomen, since peasant women could not afford the time or the materials.

American patchwork

The earliest settlers in the USA had to be self-sufficient, because they had little money and the nearest shops were usually in towns far away. They recycled old scraps of material into patchwork designs. Large designs were often stitched on to a linen or cotton backing, with padding in between, to make a quilt. Worn out scraps were transformed into decorative, cosy and long-lasting covers. The women sometimes met at each other's houses to make quilts. These gatherings were called quilting bees.

YOU WILL NEED

Stiff card measuring 15 x 10cm/6 x 4in, pencil, ruler, scissors, piece of paper measuring 30 x 30cm/12 x 12in, six pieces of patterned cotton fabric each measuring 15 x 10cm/6 x 4in, felt-tipped pen, pins, cotton thread, needle, blue cushion cover, cushion pad.

▾ Template

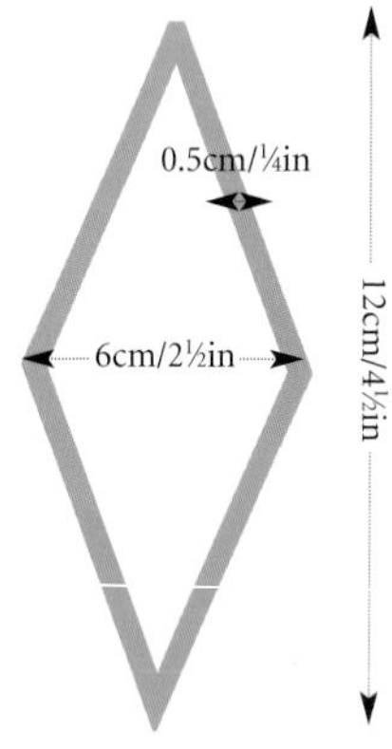

1 Copy the diamond-shaped template on to card and cut it out. Draw around the outside edge of the template on to paper. Contine another seven times to form the design shown above.

2 Choose six different patterned fabrics of the same thickness. On the back of one of the pieces of fabric, use a felt-tipped pen to draw round the inner and outer edges of the template.

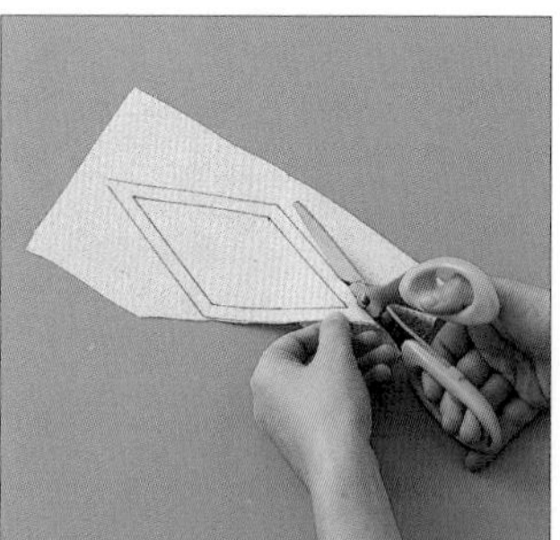

3 Mark out further diamonds on the other pieces of fabric until you have eight altogether. Then cut around the outside edges. The inner line is the edge of the seam – do not cut along it.

4 Arrange the fabric diamonds on the paper design in the way you want them to appear in the final patchwork design. Make sure you are happy with the design before you start to sew.

5 Take two of the diamonds that you want to go next to each other. Place one on top of the other with the patterned sides facing each other. Pin the diamonds together along one edge.

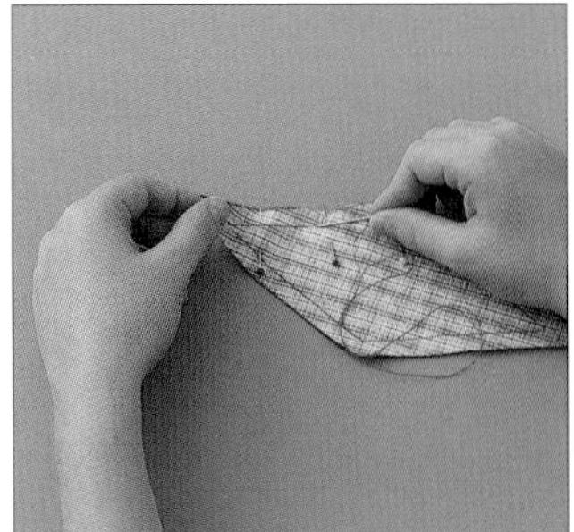

6 Sew the pinned edge of the diamond using a running stitch. Use the inner line that you drew on to the fabric with the template as a guide for the seam.

7 Repeat Steps 5 and 6 to pin and sew all the diamond fabric pieces together along one of their edges. When you have finished, the fabric pieces will form a star shape.

8 Fold the free edges of the fabric diamonds in along the felt-tipped lines and pin them together. You will be left with a loose corner of fabric at each point of the star.

9 Now use a running stitch to sew down the pinned edges of the fabric diamonds. Try to make the edges as flat and the stitches as small and neat as you can.

10 Turn the star shape over and trim off the loose corners at each point. You should now have a perfect piece of star-shaped patchwork.

11 Pin the star shape carefully in the middle of the blue cushion cover. Then sew it on using small, neat stitches. When you have finished, put a pad in the cushion cover.

Many patchwork designs created by the early settlers became part of the American craft tradition. Patchwork patterns are often given names such as log cabin or nine patch. This one is called eight-pointed star.

Accessories

Jewellery and other decorative accessories have been worn by men and women for thousands of years. Necklaces, earrings, rings, bracelets and ankle rings were made from materials such as shells, feathers, bones, glass beads, gold and precious stones. Accessories can give a clue to the status of the person wearing them. Wealthy people could afford finely crafted ornaments made from rare and expensive materials. Monarchs, priests, warriors and officials often wore badges and other accessories that identified their rank.

▲ Shell necklaces
In ancient times, people wore necklaces made of shells and animal teeth. At this time, jewellery may have been a sign that the wearer was an important person. Necklaces like this one have been found in Asia, as well as Australia. This indicates that the two continents were once linked by a common culture.

pumice stone

ash face pack

kohl

henna

Cosmetics ▲
In ancient Egypt, black eye kohl was made from galena, a type of poisonous lead. Later on, soot was used. Henna was painted on the nails and the soles of the feet to make them red. Popular beauty treatments included pumice stone to smooth rough skin and ash face packs.

Bead necklaces ▶
Mesopotamian necklaces sometimes had thousands of different beads on several separate strings. The large one here, found at a farming site called Choga Mami, has around 2,200 beads roughly shaped from clay.

Chinese costume ▸
Wealthy Chinese people often wore expensive and well-crafted jewellery, such as gilded pendants made from precious metals and inset with beautiful gemstones. Belt hooks and buckles became an essential part of a Chinese nobleman's clothing from about 300BC. They were highly decorated, and made from bronze.

◂ Spiritual headdress
Spiritual leaders called lamas educate people in Buddhism. In Tibet, lamas sometimes wear headdresses for religious services. The one pictured here depicts the five buddhas (enlightened ones) of meditation.

Enamelled brooch ▸
Many of the barbarian invaders of ancient Rome, such as the Visigoths, Vandals and Franks, were skilled craftworkers, as can be seen from this brooch.

◂ Precious amber
Its beautiful shades of gold, yellow and brown made amber extremely popular with Viking jewellers. They also used plain and coloured glass for making fine bead necklaces.

Tribal necklace

Stone Age necklaces were made from all sorts of natural objects, including pebbles, shells, fish bones, animal teeth and claws, nuts and seeds. Later, amber, jade, jet (fossilized coal) and hand-made clay beads were threaded on to thin strips of leather or twine made from plant fibres. Other jewellery included bracelets made of slices of mammoth tusk. People probably decorated their bodies and outlined their eyes with pigments such as red ochre. They may have tattooed and pierced their bodies, too.

YOU WILL NEED

Self-hardening clay, rolling pin, cutting board, modelling tool, sandpaper, ivory and black acrylic paint, paintbrush, water pot, ruler, pencil, 12 x 9cm/4½ x 3½in chamois leather, scissors, card, double-sided adhesive tape, white glue and glue brush, leather laces.

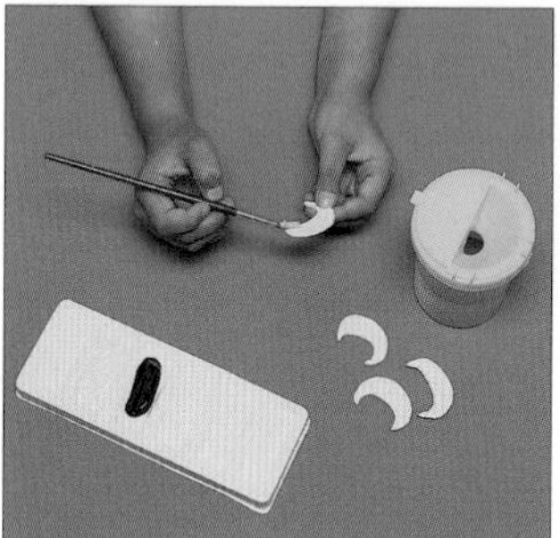

1 Roll out the clay on to a board. Cut out three crescent shapes with the modelling tool. Leave to dry. Rub the crescents gently with sandpaper and paint them an ivory colour.

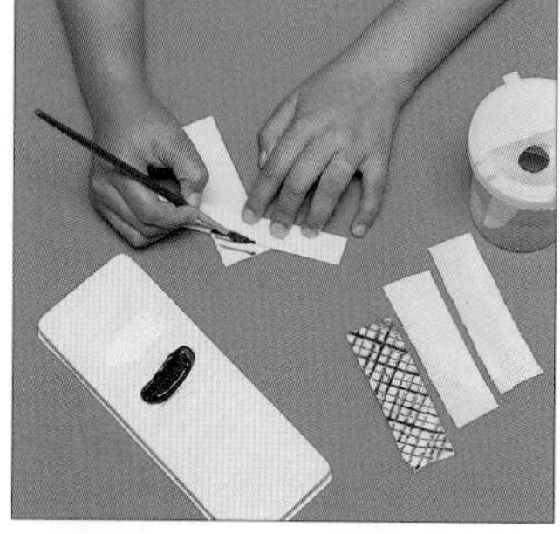

2 Cut four strips of leather to measure 9 x 3cm/3½ x 1³⁄₁₆in. Use the edge of a piece of card as a guide for your brush and make a criss-cross pattern on the strips of leather, as shown.

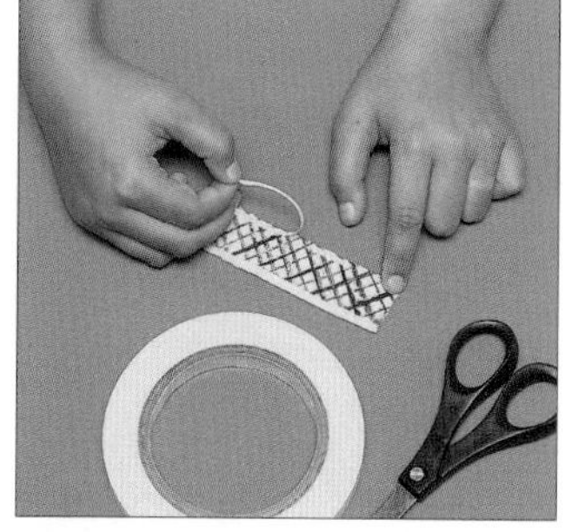

3 When the strips of leather are completely dry, fold the side edges of each strip in. Stick them securely in place with a piece of double-sided adhesive tape.

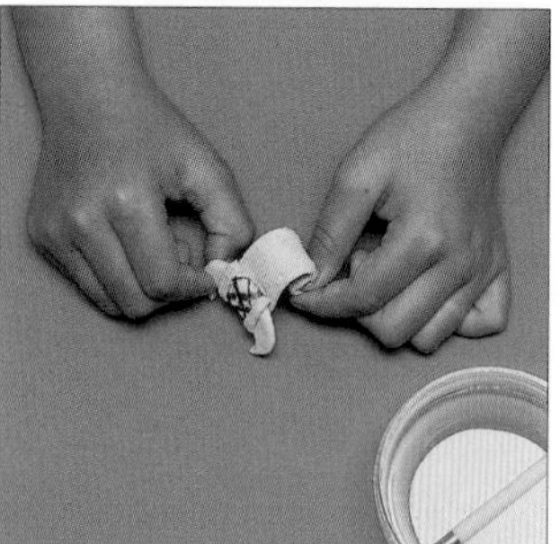

4 Brush glue on the middle of each clay crescent. Wrap a strip of leather around a crescent, leaving enough to form a loop at the top. Glue the loops in place. Paint three lines on each loop.

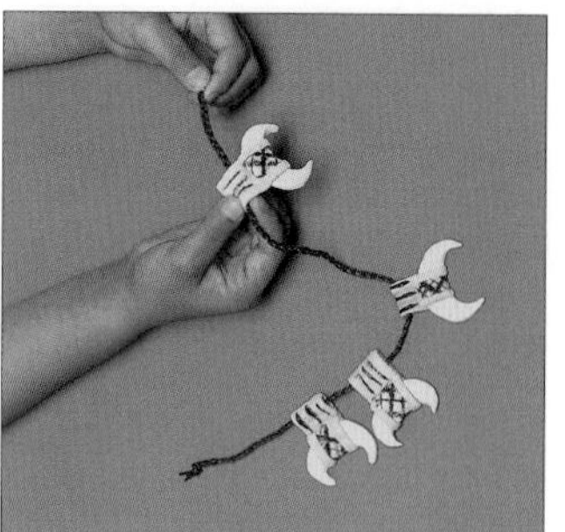

5 Plait three leather laces to make a thong to fit around your neck. Thread on the leopard's claws. Arrange the claws so that there are small spaces between them.

Stone Age people believed that wearing a leopard claw necklace gave them magical powers.

Egyptian mirror

The ancient Egyptians were fond of cosmetics. Cleopatra, who ruled Egypt in 51BC, used one of the first moisturizers to protect her skin from the effects of the desert sand. Both men and women wore green eyeshadow made from a mineral called malachite and black eyeliner made from a type of lead called galena. Mirrors were used by wealthy Egyptians for checking hairstyles, applying make-up or simply admiring their looks. The mirrors were made of polished copper or bronze, with handles of wood or ivory.

YOU WILL NEED

Self-hardening clay, modelling tool, cutting board, small piece of card or sandpaper, wire baking tray, small plate, mirror card, pencil, scissors, gold paint, paintbrush, water pot, white glue and glue brush.

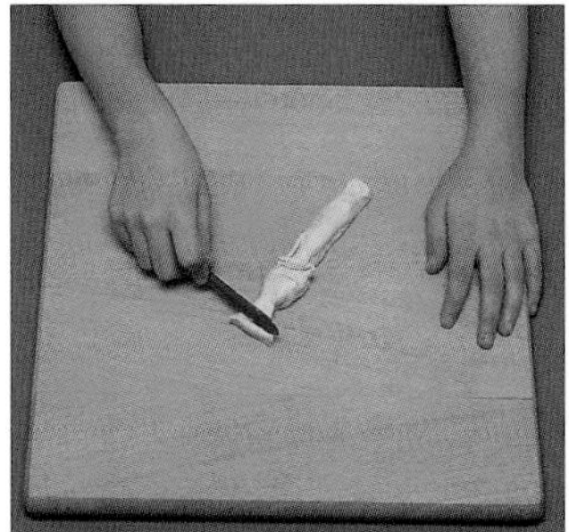

1 Roll a piece of self-hardening clay into a tube. Mould the tube into a handle shape. Use the modelling tool to decorate the handle in the shape of a god or with a flower design.

2 Make a slot in the handle with a piece of card or sandpaper. Place the handle on a wire baking tray and leave it in a warm place to dry. Turn the handle over after 2 hours.

3 Draw round a small plate on to the mirror card. Add a pointed bit to fit in the slot in the handle. Cut the mirror shape out. When the handle is dry, insert the mirror in the slot.

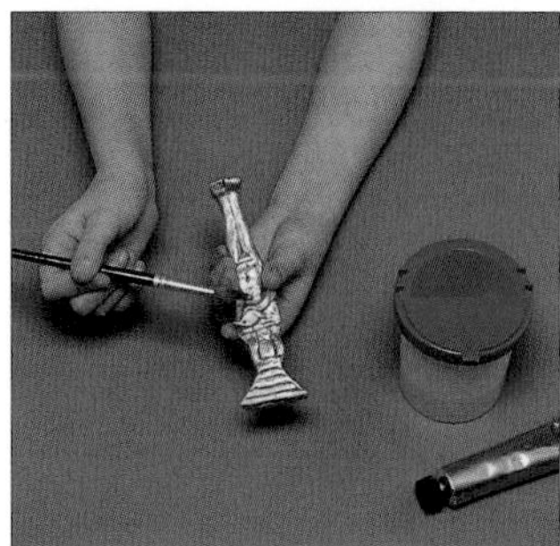

4 It is now time to paint the handle. Paint one side carefully with gold paint and leave it to dry. When it has dried, turn the handle over and paint the other side.

5 Finally, you can assemble your mirror. Cover the base of the mirror card in glue and insert it into the handle slot. Now your mirror is ready to use.

The shiny surfaces and shapes of mirrors reminded Egyptians of the Sun's disc, so they became religious symbols.

Egyptian pectoral

Archaeologists know that the Egyptians loved jewellery, because so much has been unearthed in their tombs. Some are beautifully made from precious stones and costly metals. Other pieces are much simpler and are made from materials such as pottery and bone. The Egyptian original of this pectoral (necklace) was made by a technique called *cloisonné*. Gold wire was worked into a framework with lots of little compartments or *cloisons*. These were filled with coloured enamel (glass) paste. Then the piece was fired.

YOU WILL NEED

Plain paper, pen, ruler, tracing paper, masking tape, scissors, rolling pin, self-hardening clay, cutting board, modelling tools, cocktail stick, medium paintbrush, acrylic paints, water pot, wood varnish, white spirit, white glue and glue brush, 90cm/3ft string.

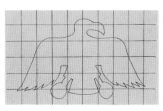

1 Take a sheet of paper and draw vertical lines 2cm/¾in apart and horizontal lines 2cm/¾in apart to make a grid, as shown. Copy the design above on to the grid, one square at a time.

2 Place the tracing paper over the design. Use masking tape to secure it. Use a pen and ruler to trace your design and the grid on to the tracing paper. Cut out the falcon shape.

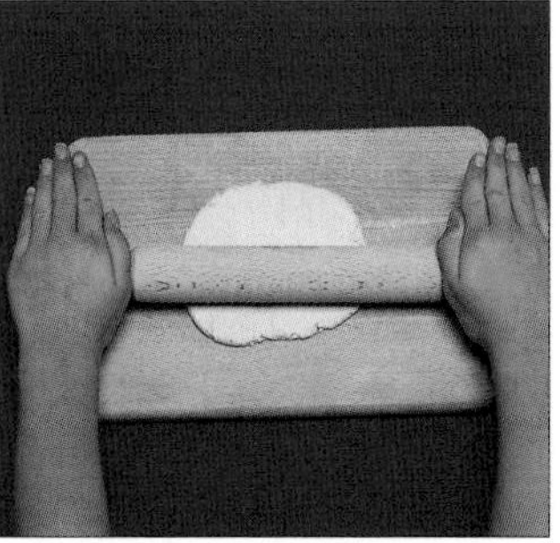

3 Place the self-hardening clay on to a cutting board. Use a rolling pin to flatten it out. Roll out the clay to measure 21 x 15cm/8¼ x 6in in size, with a thickness of 5cm/2in.

4 Use masking tape to fix the tracing paper to the clay. Trace the design and then use the modelling tool to cut around the outline of the falcon. Make sure you cut right through the clay.

5 Remove the tracing paper. Use a fine modelling tool to mould the detail. Use a cocktail stick to make a 3mm/⅛in hole on each wing, 2cm/¾in away from the top edge of the wing.

6 Leave the clay falcon to dry in a warm room. Use a medium-sized paintbrush and blue acrylic paint to colour body and wings of the falcon. Leave it to dry completely.

7 Use red, blue, green and gold acrylic paints to add decorative touches to the falcon, as shown above. Try to make the design look as if it is really made of precious gems and gold.

8 Clean the paintbrush in water and leave the falcon to dry. Use the clean brush to apply a thin coat of wood varnish over the model. Then clean the paintbrush with white spirit.

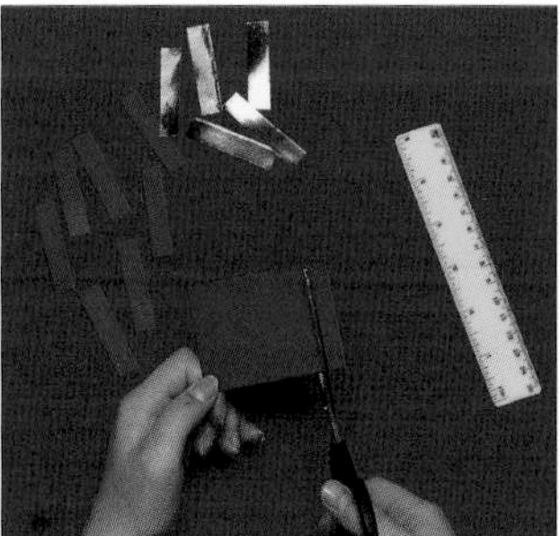

9 Paint five 5cm/2in square pieces of plain paper blue and five pieces gold. Cut each square into strips, each 1cm/½in wide. You will need 25 strips of each colour in total.

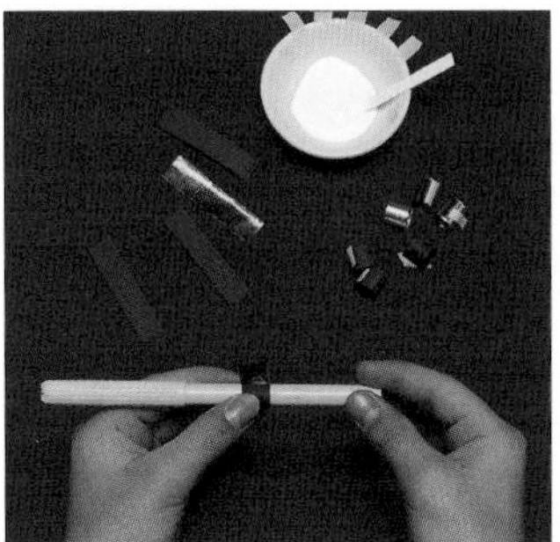

10 When the strips are dry, roll each one around a pen. Dab white glue on to the ends of the paper to stick them. Use masking tape to secure the ends of the paper until dry.

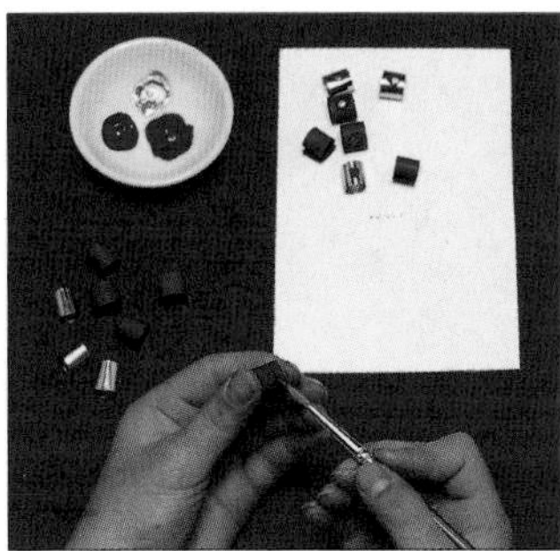

11 When the glue is dry, remove the tape and paint the paper tubes with red, blue and gold dots, as shown above. You now have 50 beads to make a necklace.

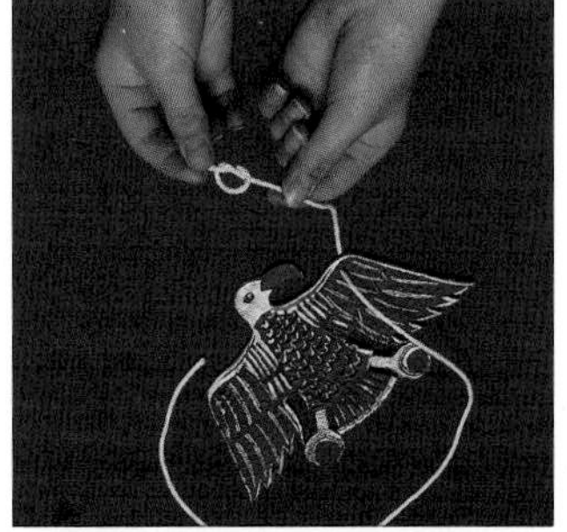

12 Cut two lengths of string, each 45cm/18in long. Thread one end of each piece of string through the holes in the falcon's wings. Tie a knot in the strings.

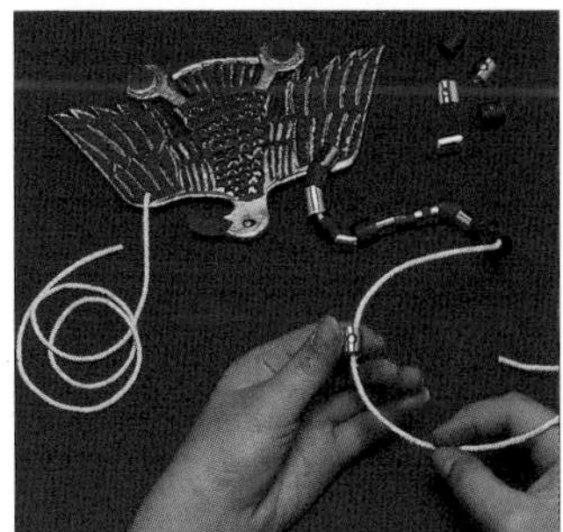

13 Thread the beads on to the pieces of string. Alternate the blue and gold beads. You should thread 25 beads on to each string to make the decorative necklace.

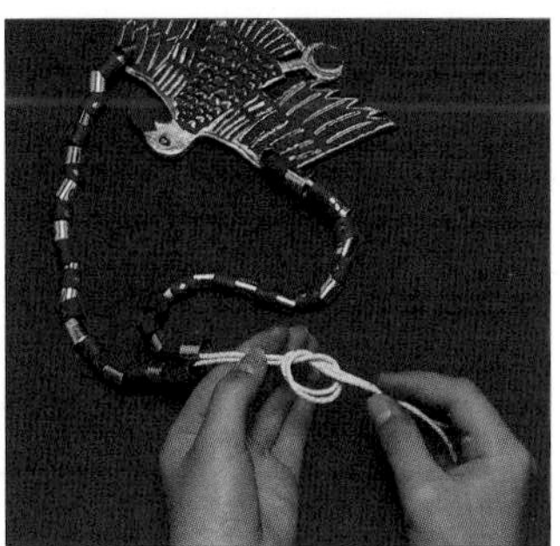

14 Finish threading all the beads on to the string. Tie the ends of the two pieces of string with a secure knot. Trim off excess string to finish off your necklace.

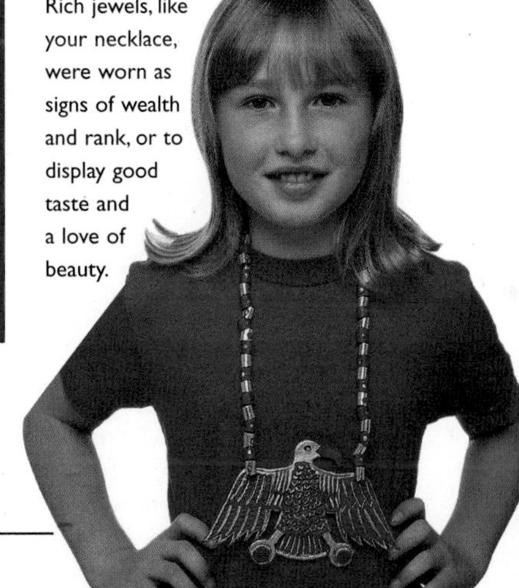

Rich jewels, like your necklace, were worn as signs of wealth and rank, or to display good taste and a love of beauty.

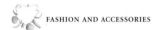

Chinese fan

Court dress in China varied greatly over the ages. Foreign invasions brought new fashions and dress codes. Government officials wore elegant robes that reflected their rank and social status. Beautiful silk robes patterned with *lung pao* (dragons) were worn by court ladies, officials and the emperor himself. Many people, both men and women, might carry a fan as a symbol of good upbringing, as well as to provide a cool breeze in the sweltering summer heat.

fan

YOU WILL NEED

Red tissue paper, thick card base (40 x 20cm/16 x 8in), masking tape, pair of compasses, ruler, pencil, acrylic paints (pink, light blue, cream, light green), paintbrush, water pot, scissors, 16 x 1cm/6¼ x ½in balsa strips (x15), barbecue stick, white glue and glue brush, thin card.

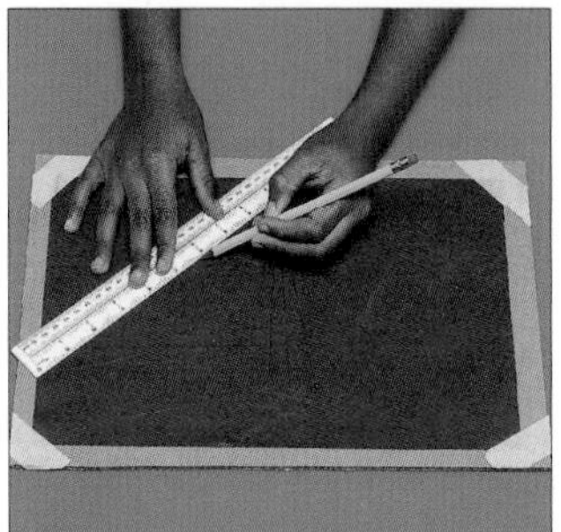

1 Tape tissue paper on to the base. Draw two semicircles (16cm/6¼in radius and 7cm/2¾in radius) from one side of the base. Draw even lines 1cm/⅜in apart between the two semicircles.

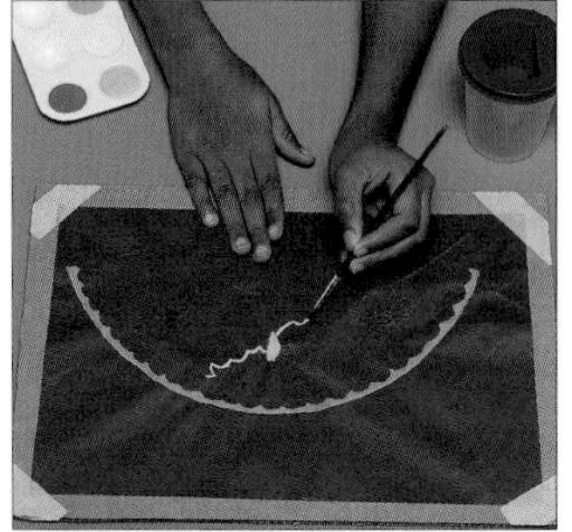

2 Draw a design on to the tissue paper. Paint in the details and leave the paint to dry. Then remove the paper from the base and cut out the fan along edges of the semicircles.

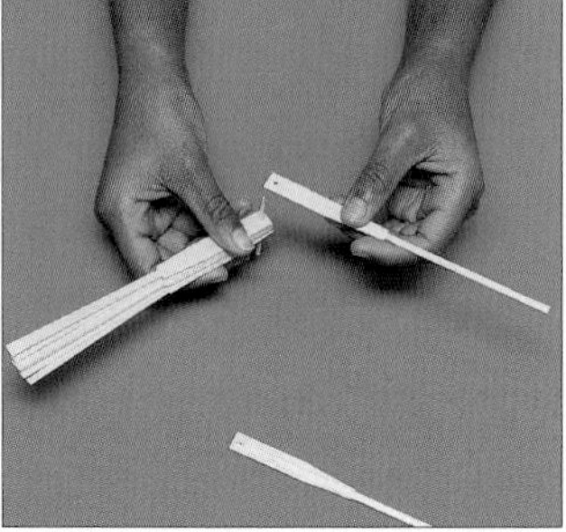

3 Use scissors to cut a sliver off each side of each balsa strip for half its length. Pierce a compass hole at the wide base of the strip. Thread the strips on to a barbecue stick.

4 Fold the decorated tissue paper backwards and forwards to form a concertina. Glue each alternate fold of the paper to the narrow ends of the balsa strips, as shown above.

5 Paint the outer strips of the fan pink and let the paint dry. Cut out two small card discs. Glue them over the ends of the barbecue stick to secure the strips, as shown above.

The earliest Chinese fans were made of feathers or of silk stretched over a flat frame. The folding fan came later.

Japanese fan

Until 1500, Japanese court fashions were based on traditional Chinese styles. Men and women wore long, flowing robes made of many layers of fine, glossy silk, held in place by a sash and cords. Flat fans, or *uchiwa,* like the one in this project, could be tucked into the sash when not in use. In the 1500s, *kimonos* (long, loose robes) became popular among wealthy artists, actors and craftworkers. Women wore wide silk sashes called *obis* on top of their kimonos. Men fastened their kimonos with narrow sashes.

YOU WILL NEED

Thick card measuring 38 x 26cm/15 x 10¼in, pencil, ruler, pair of compasses, protractor, blue felt-tipped pen, red paper measuring 30 x 26cm/12 x 10¼in, scissors, acrylic paints, paintbrush, water pot, glue stick.

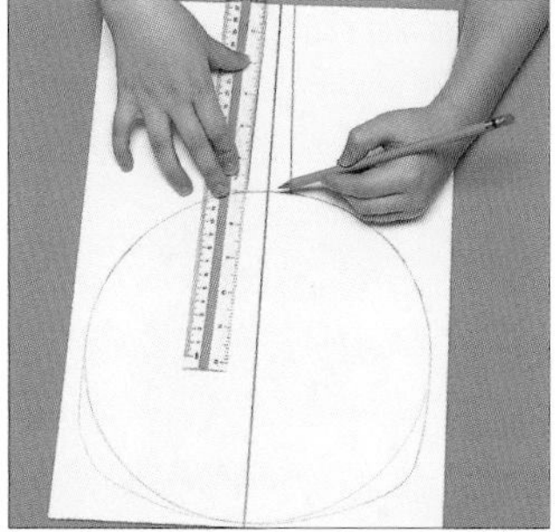

1 Draw a line down the centre of the thick card. Draw a circle 23cm/9in wide two-thirds of the way up. Add squared-off edges at the top of the circle. Draw a 15cm/6in-long handle.

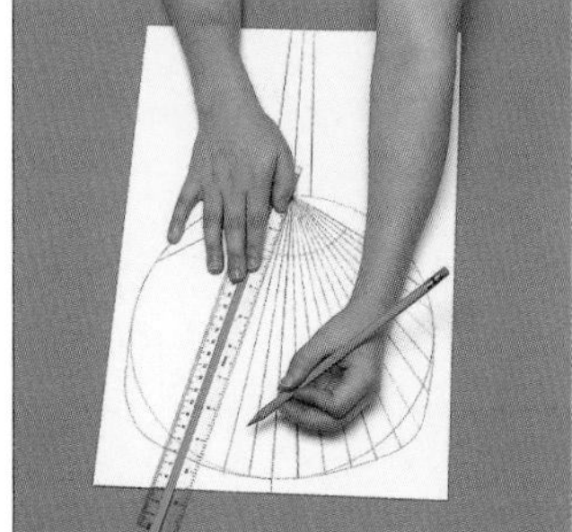

2 Place a protractor at the top of the handle and draw a semicircle around it. Now mark lines every 2.5 degrees. Draw pencil lines through these marks to the edge of the circle.

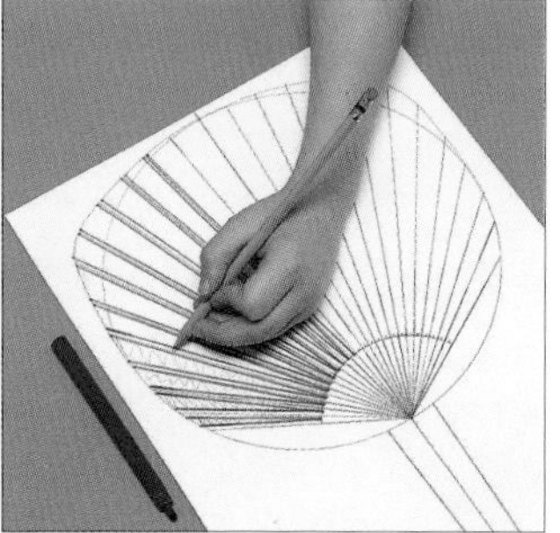

3 Draw a blue line 1cm/½in to the left of each pencil mark. Then draw a blue line 2mm/1/16in to the right of each of the pencil marks. Pencil in a rough squiggle in between the blue sections.

4 Cut out the fan. Draw around the fan shape on the red paper. Cut it out. Leave to one side. Then cut out the sections marked with squiggles on the white fan. Paint the white fan brown.

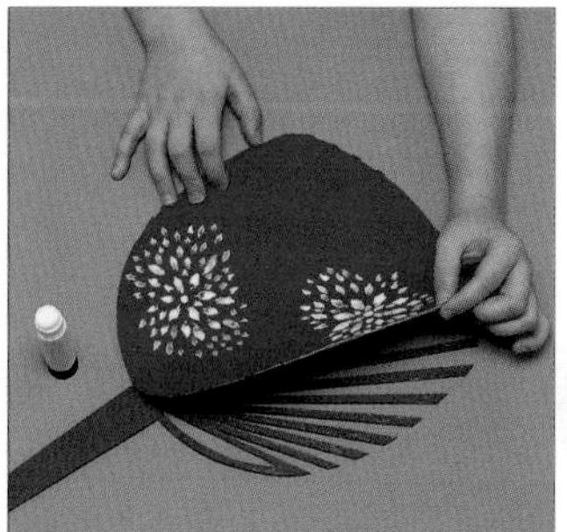

5 Leave the fan to dry. Paint the red paper with white flowers and leave to dry. Paste glue on to one side of the card fan. Stick the undecorated side of the red card to the fan.

Japanese noble ladies hid their faces in court. They used decorated fans such as this one as a screen.

Japanese netsuke fox

There is a long tradition among Japanese craftworkers of making everyday things as beautiful as possible. Craftworkers also created exquisite items for the wealthiest and most knowledgeable collectors. They used a wide variety of materials, including pottery, metal, lacquer, cloth, paper and bamboo. Ceramics ranged from plain, simple earthenware to delicate porcelain painted with brilliantly coloured glazes. Japanese metalworkers produced alloys (mixtures of metals) that were unknown elsewhere in the ancient world. Cloth was woven from many fibres in elaborate designs. Bamboo and other grasses were woven into elegant *tatami* (floor mats) and containers of all different shapes and sizes. Japanese craftworkers also made beautiful *inro*. These are little boxes, used like purses, that dangled from men's kimono sashes using a *netsuke* (carved toggle).

▲ **Keeping it safe**
Carved ivory or wooden toggles, called *netsuke*, were used to hold the inro in the waist sash of a kimono. Netsuke were shaped into representations of gods, dragons or living animals.

▲ **Boxes for belts**
These small boxes were originally designed for storing medicines. The first inro were plain and simple, but after about 1700 they were often decorated with exquisite designs. These inro have been lacquered (coated with a shiny substance made from the sap of the lacquer tree). Inside, they contain several compartments stacked on top of each other.

YOU WILL NEED

Paper, pencil, ruler, rolling pin, self-hardening clay, cutting board, modelling tool, balsa wood, fine sandpaper, acrylic paint, paintbrush, water pot, darning needle, cord, small box (for an inro), scissors, toggle, wide belt.

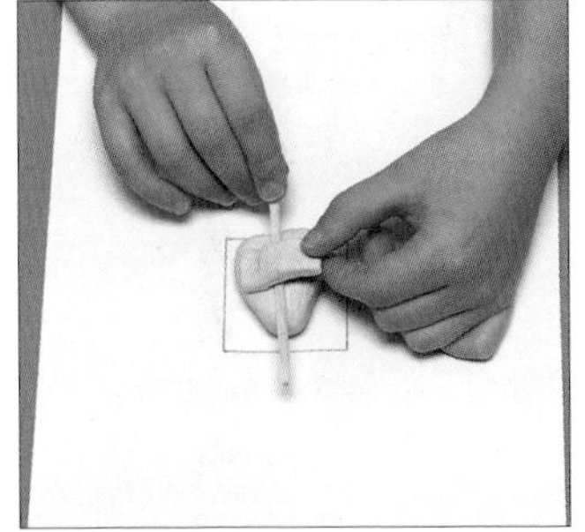

1 Draw a 5 x 5cm/2 x 2in square on to the paper. Roll out some clay to the size of the square. Shape a point at one end. Lay a length of balsa along the back. Secure it with a thin strip of clay.

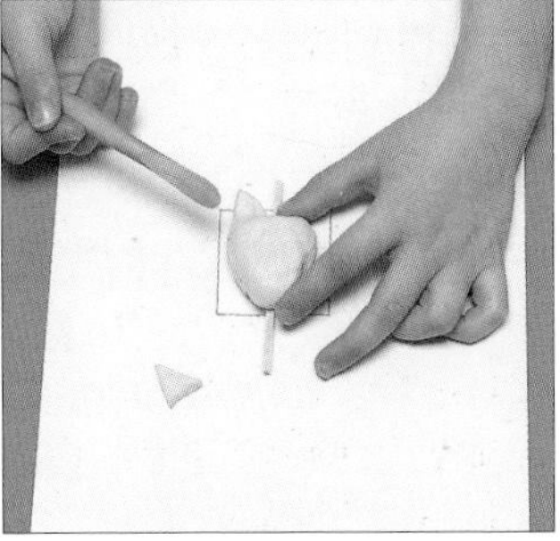

2 Turn the clay back on its right side. Cut out two triangles of clay for the ears. Join them to the head using a modelling tool. Make indentations to shape them into the ears of a fox.

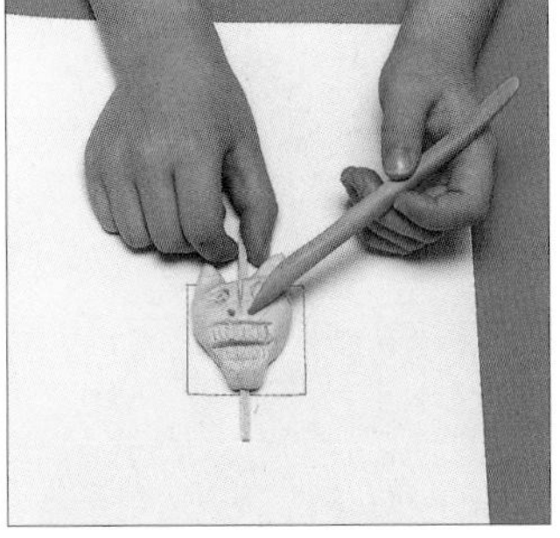

3 Use the handle of your modelling tool to make the fox's mouth. Carve eyes, nostrils, teeth and a frown line. Use the blunt end of the pencil to make holes for the fox's eyes.

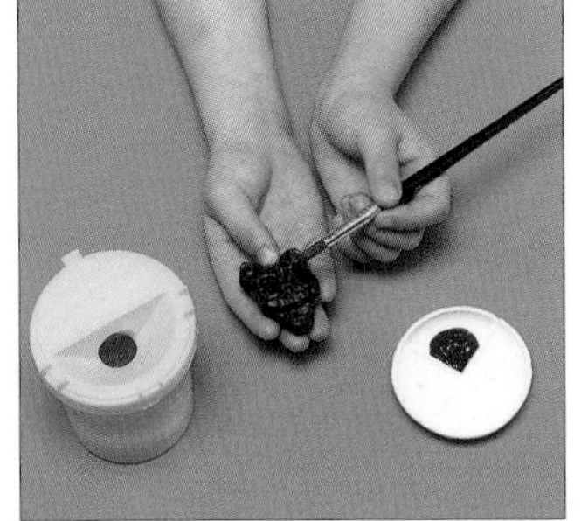

4 Leave the netsuke fox to dry. Then gently sand the netsuke and remove the balsa wood stick. Paint the netsuke with several layers of acrylic paint. Leave it in a warm place to dry.

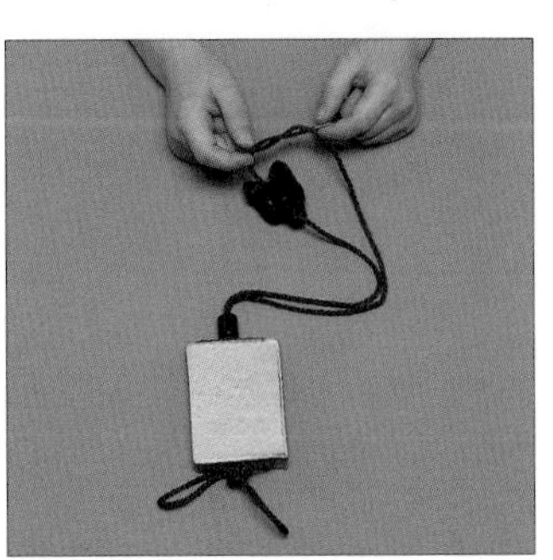

5 Thread some cord through four corners of a small box with a darning needle. Then thread the cord through the toggle and the hole on the netsuke left by the balsa wood.

6 Put a wide belt round your waist. Thread the netsuke under the belt. It should rest on the top of the belt, as shown above. The inro (box) should hang down.

Wear your inro dangling from your belt. In ancient Japan, inro were usually worn by men. They were held in place by carved toggles called netsuke.

Native American anklets

Most of the wars between different Native American tribes were fought over land or hunting territory, and later over horses. As European settlers began to occupy more land, many tribes fought to stop them. Before going into battle, Native American warriors performed a war dance to ask for spiritual guidance and protection during the conflict. Ceremonial dress and body painting was a feature of these occasions. The anklets in this project are similar to the ones worn by many tribes during their war dances.

YOU WILL NEED

Two strips of white felt (75 x 5cm/2½ft x 2in), ruler, felt-tipped pen, scissors, needle and strong thread, 16 small bells – eight for each anklet.

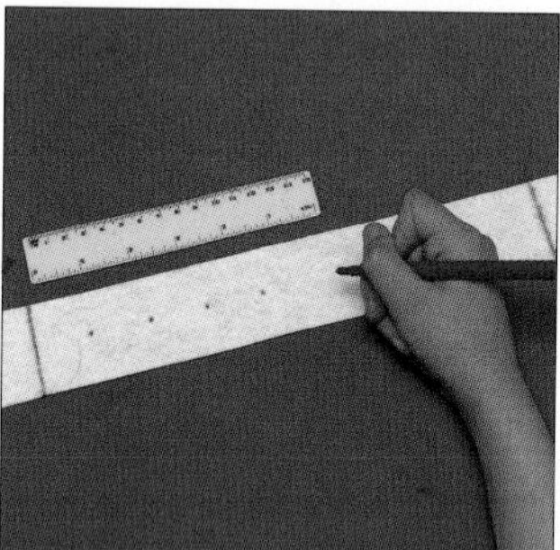

1 Mark two lines across the felt strips, 24cm/9½in in from each end. Make a series of marks in between these lines. Start 3cm/1 3/16in away from the line, then mark at 3cm/1 3/16in intervals.

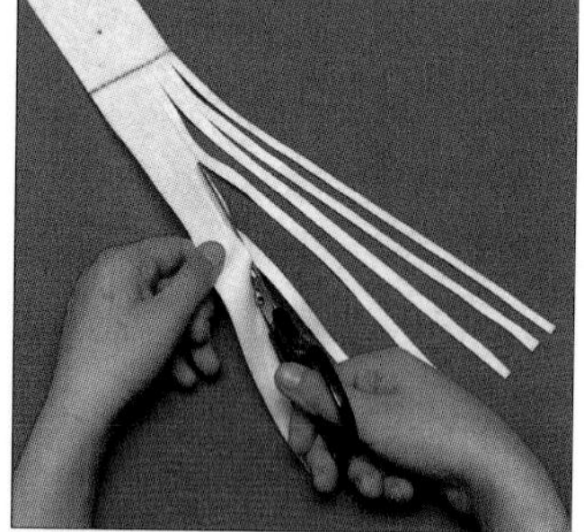

2 Create the fringing at each end of the anklet. Do this by cutting into both ends of the band up to the marked lines. Repeat the process for the other anklet.

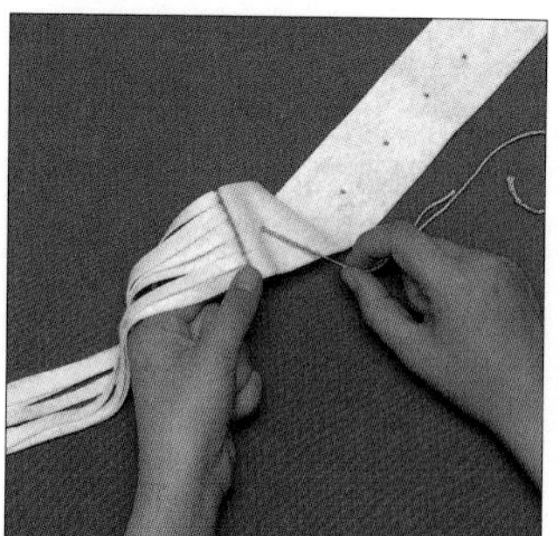

3 Thread a large needle with strong, doubled and knotted thread. Insert the needle into the fabric, and pull through until the knot hits the fabric.

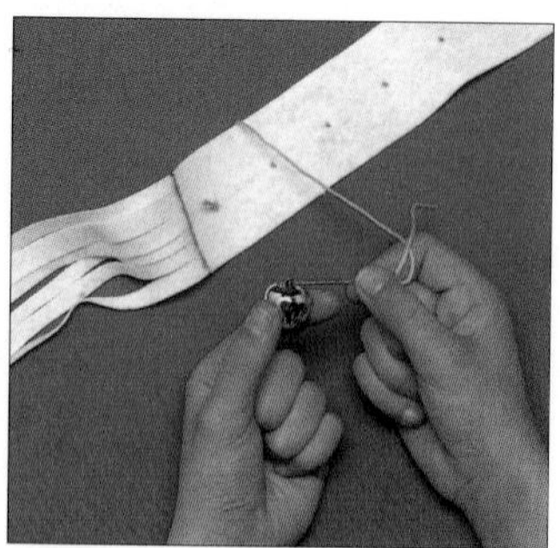

4 Thread a bell over the needle and up to the felt. Push the needle back through the felt. Knot the end on the opposite side to the bell. Trim excess thread. Repeat for the other seven bells.

Tie the anklets round your ankles. The bells of the North American Indians were sewn on to strips of animal hide. They were tied around the ankles and just under the knees, and worn for ceremonial dances.

Native American necklace

Tribes in North America took pride in their appearance. As well as wearing decorative necklaces, headdresses and other jewellery, many tribes wore tattoos as a sign of status or to gain protection from spirits. Hairstyles were important, too, and could indicate that a young man was unmarried or belonged to a warrior class. Woodlands men had a distinctive hairstyle. They braided their hair at the front and decorated it with turkey feathers. Some Plains warriors shaved their heads completely, leaving a long tuft on top.

YOU WILL NEED

Thin white paper strips, white glue and glue brush, acrylic paints (blue, turquoise and red), paintbrush, water pot, scissors, self-hardening clay, skewer, string.

1 Roll up the strips of thin white paper into 5mm/¼in tubes. Glue down the outer edge to seal the tubes and leave them to dry. Make three of these paper tubes.

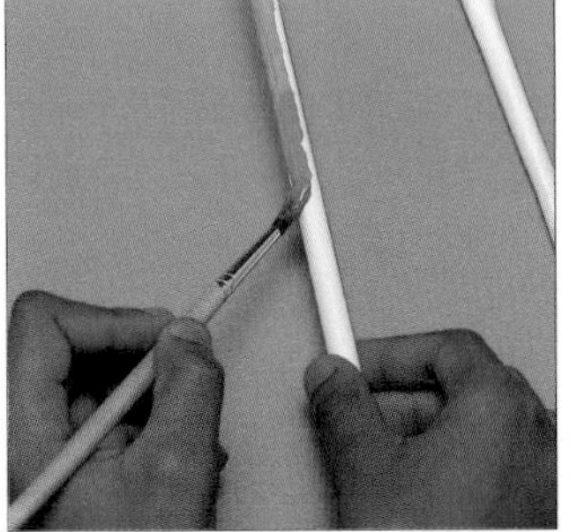

2 When the glue has dried, paint the rolls of paper. Paint one roll blue, one roll red and one roll turquoise, making sure that you cover all the white areas. Leave them to dry.

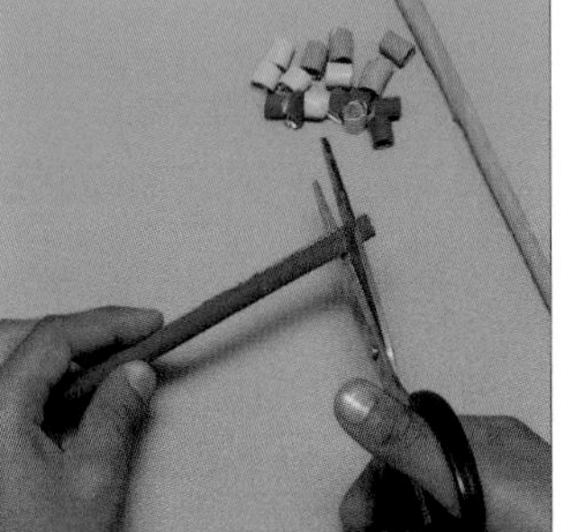

3 When they have dried, the painted paper tubes will have hardened slightly. Carefully cut the tubes to separate them into 1cm/½in pieces. These will be the beads of your necklace.

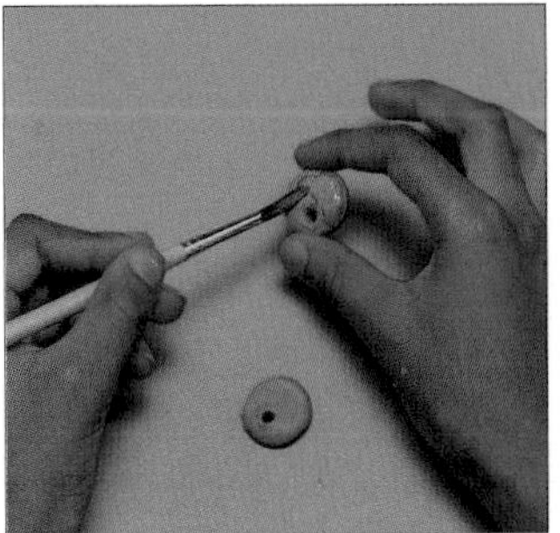

4 Roll the clay into two large clay beads. Pierce the centres with a skewer. Leave the beads to dry and harden. When they are ready, paint both of the beads blue. Leave to dry.

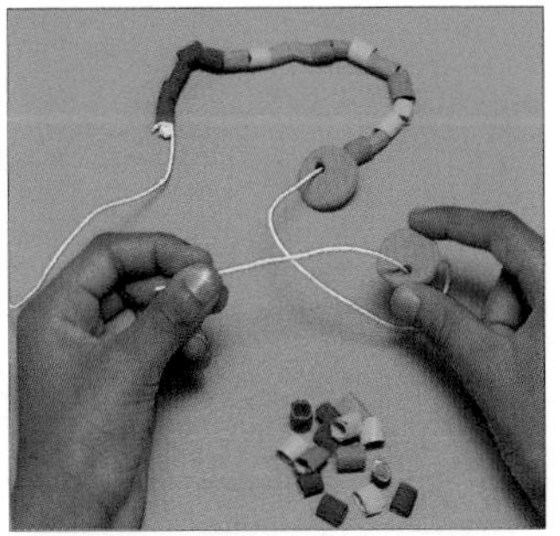

5 Thread the beads on to the string. Start with the clay beads which will hang in the centre. Then add blue either side, then turquoise, then red. Knot the ends together when you have finished.

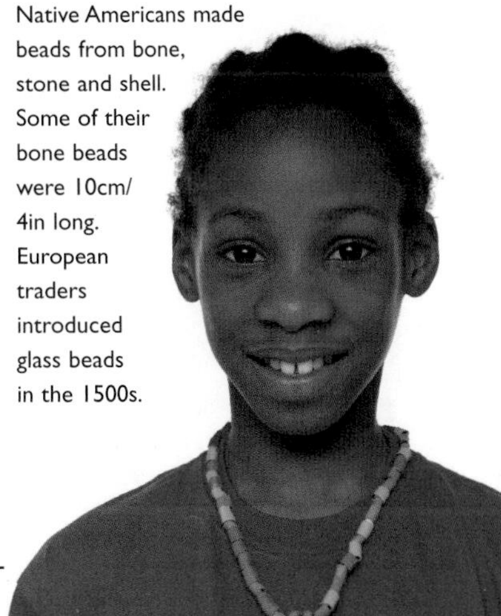

Native Americans made beads from bone, stone and shell. Some of their bone beads were 10cm/4in long. European traders introduced glass beads in the 1500s.

Glass bead jewellery

Native Americans were not only hunters and warriors, they were also artists and craftworkers. Tribespeople made everything they needed for themselves, from clothes and blankets to tools and weapons. The first settlers from Europe took coloured glass beads with them to the USA. Many Native American tribes bargained with traders for the beads. They developed great skill in using them to make brilliant, richly coloured patterns on dresses, trousers, shoes and many other possessions.

YOU WILL NEED

70cm/2½ft piece of narrow leather thong, ruler, scissors, 165cm/5½ft strong waxed thread, selection of glass and silver beads in different sizes, four brightly coloured dyed feathers, two glass and two silver beads with holes big enough to cover the knotted leather thong.

1 To make a Native American glass bead necklace, cut two strips of leather thong, each 15cm/6in long. You will use these strips to tie the finished necklace around your neck.

2 Next, take the waxed thread and carefully cut off one long piece about 25cm/10in long using the scissors. Then cut four smaller pieces of waxed thread, each 10cm/4in long.

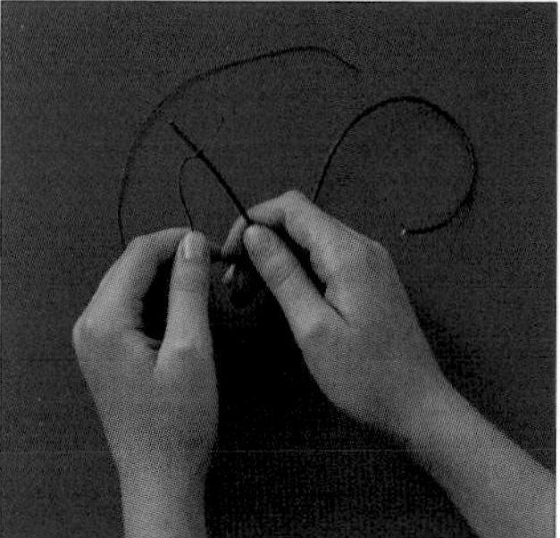

3 Knot one end of one leather strip to one end of the 25cm/10in-long waxed thread. Thread on one of the glass or silver beads with a hole that will cover the knot you have made.

4 Thread different beads on to the long piece of waxed thread until there is about a 10cm/4in gap left at the end. Thread the beads in a repeating pattern, or randomly, as you prefer.

5 Now make the four dangling pieces of the necklace. For each one, tie one end of the 10cm/4in-long piece of waxed thread around the quill of a brightly coloured feather.

6 Thread on some smaller beads, covering only half of each piece of waxed thread. Tie a knot to secure the beads. Again, you can thread them in a pattern, if you like.

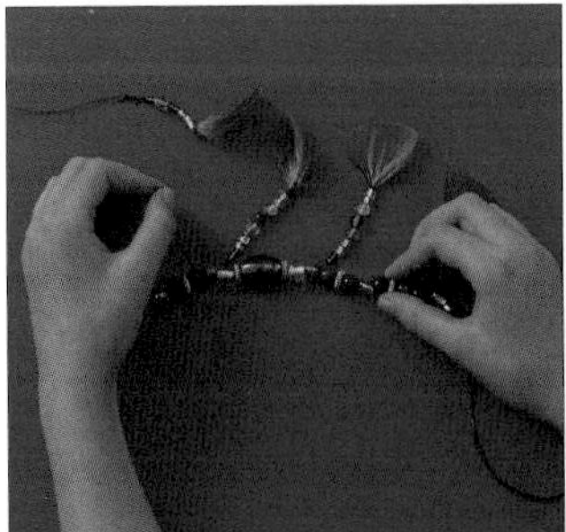

7 Tie each feathery piece on to the main necklace. Then tie on the second 15cm/6in-long leather thong at the free end. Cover the knot with one of the glass or silver beads with a big hole.

8 To make a bracelet to match your necklace, cut two 20cm/8in-long strips of leather thong. When the bracelet is finished, you will use these to tie it around your wrist.

9 Next, cut five lengths of waxed thread, each measuring about 20cm/8in in length. These threads are going to form the main part of your beaded bracelet.

10 Take the five lengths of waxed thread, and tie a big knot at one end to join them all together. Try to make the knot as small and as neat as possible.

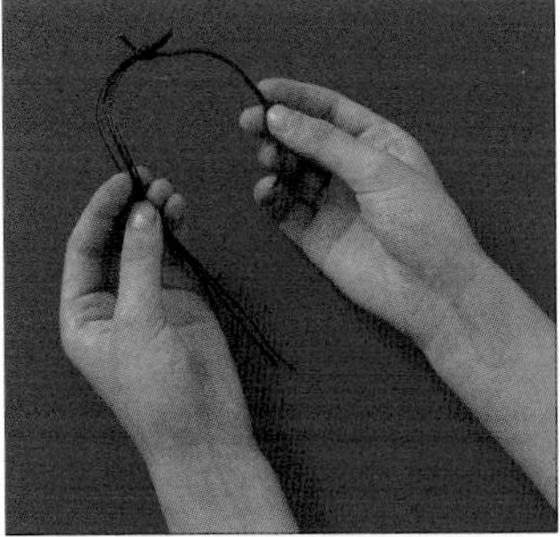

11 Take the knotted end of the waxed threads and carefully tie on one of the leather strips. Cover the knot with one of the glass or silver beads with a big hole.

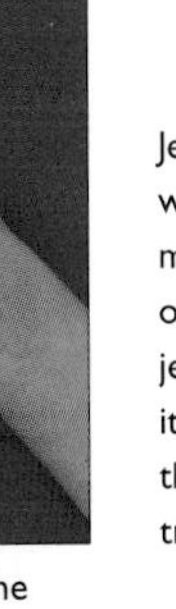

12 Thread some beads on to one of the waxed threads, keeping some thread spare. You can make a pattern or not, as you prefer. Then tie a knot to keep the beads in place.

13 Bead and knot all five waxed threads and then tie them all together. Tie on the last leather strip and cover the knot with a large bead. Now your bracelet is ready to wear.

Jewellery like this is still sold in the western USA. Today, Native Americans make all sorts of different jewellery items for the tourist trade.

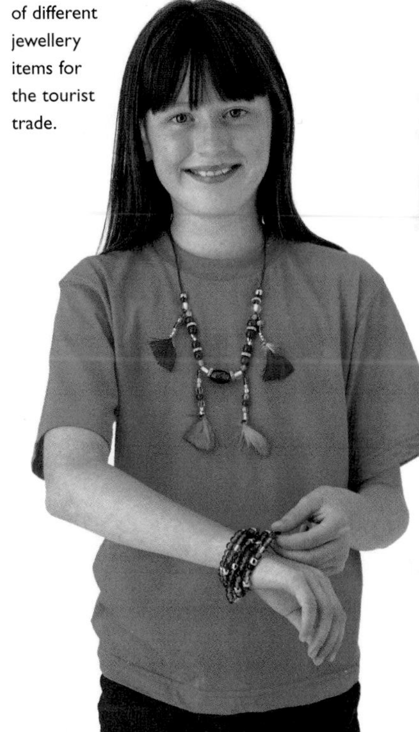

Arctic purse

Surviving in the Arctic was hard. Men and women had to work long hours to keep everyone warm, clothed and fed. Women looked after the domestic chores. Their work included tending the fire, cooking, preparing animal hides and looking after their children. Arctic women were also skilled at craftwork, and sewing was an extremely important job. They had to find time to make and repair all the family's clothes and bedding, as well as make items such as bags, purses and other useful containers.

YOU WILL NEED

Chamois leather (21 x 35cm/8½ x 14in), white glue and glue brush, pencil, ruler, scissors, shoelace (50cm/20in long), pieces of decorative felt (red, dark blue and light blue), two blue beads.

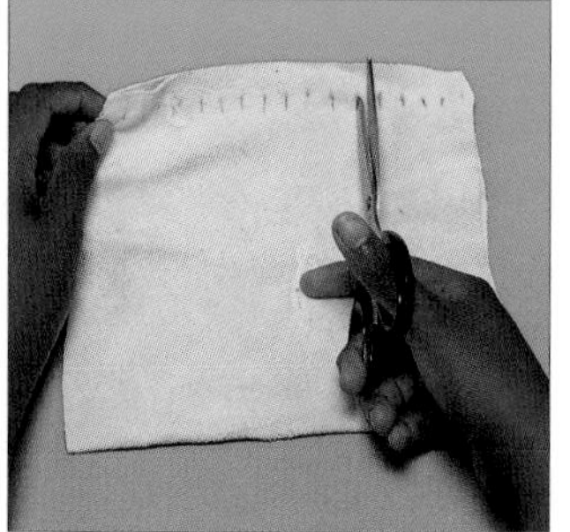

1 Fold the chamois leather in half. Glue down two sides, leaving one end open. Pencil in marks 1cm/½in apart on either side of the open end. Make small holes at these points with the scissors.

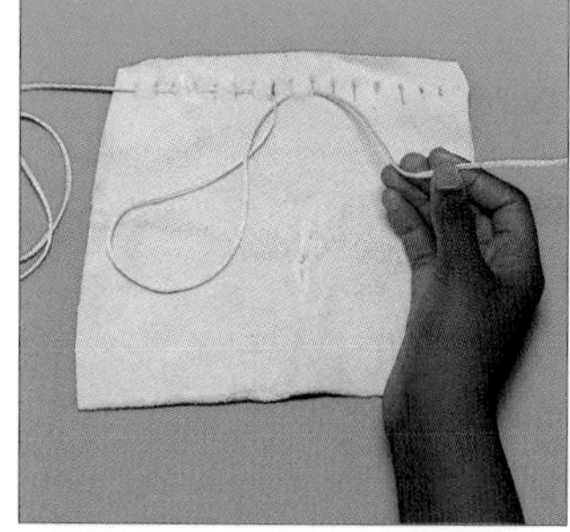

2 Thread a shoelace through the holes on both sides, as shown above. Tie the ends of the shoelace together, and leave an excess piece of lace hanging.

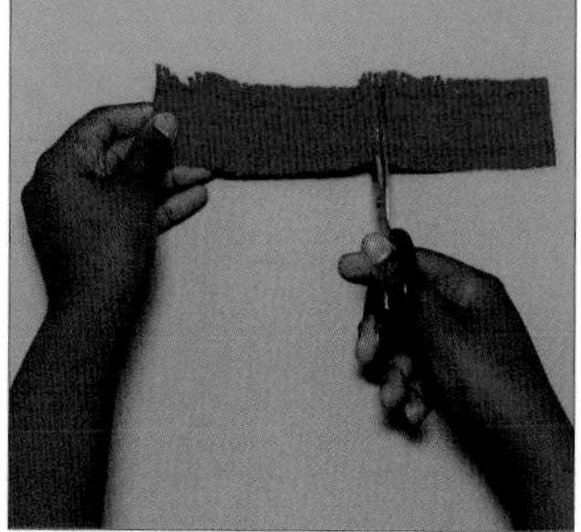

3 Cut two strips of red felt 21cm/8¼in long and 5cm/2in wide. Then mark and cut a narrow fringe about 1cm/½in deep along both edges of each red felt piece, as shown.

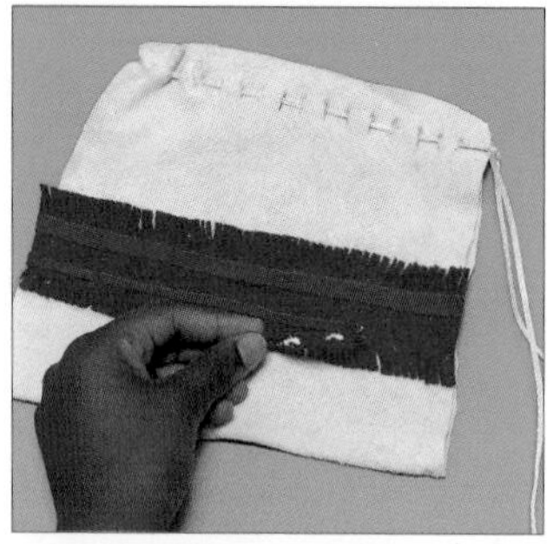

4 Glue strips of red fringing felt to either side of the purse. Add extra decoration by sticking 1cm/½in strips of dark blue and light blue felt on top of the red fringing felt and the purse.

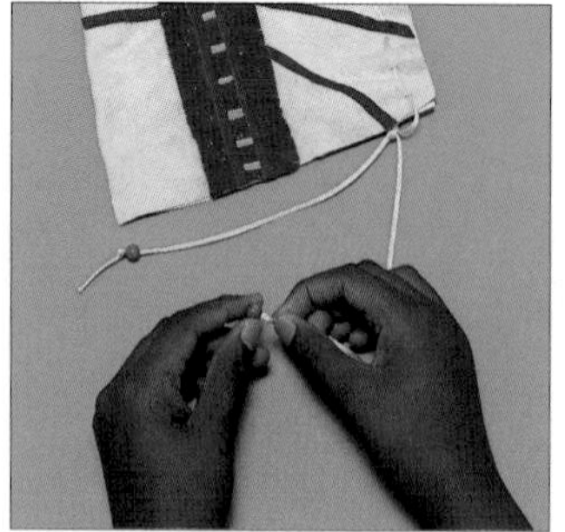

5 Tie the two blue beads securely to each of the excess shoelace. Close the purse by pulling the shoelace and tying a knot in it. Your Arctic purse is ready to use.

Drawstring purses such as this one were often made of soft deer hide called buckskin.

Celtic mirror

Metalworkers made many valuable Celtic items, from iron swords to the beautiful bronze handles of their mirrors. Patterns and techniques invented in one part of the Celtic world quickly spread to others. Metalworkers excelled in several different techniques. Heavy objects were cast from solid bronze using a clay mould. Thin sheets of silver and bronze were decorated with *repoussé* (pushed-out) designs. The designs were sketched on to the back of the metal, then gently hammered to create raised patterns.

YOU WILL NEED

Pair of compasses, pencil, ruler, stiff gold mirror card, scissors, tracing paper, pen, self-hardening clay, cutting board, gold paint, paintbrush, water pot, white glue and glue brush.

1 Use the compasses to draw a circle with a diameter of 22cm/8¾in on to the gold card. Cut the gold circle out. Use this circle as a template to draw a second circle on to gold card.

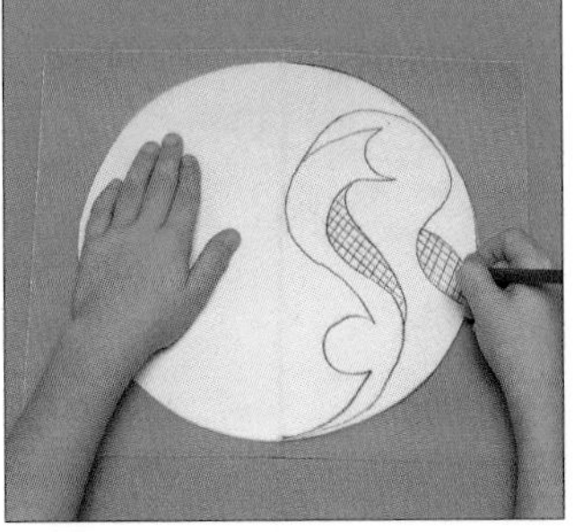

2 Cut out the second gold circle. Draw another circle on to some tracing paper. Fold the piece of tracing paper in half and draw on a Celtic pattern, like the one shown above.

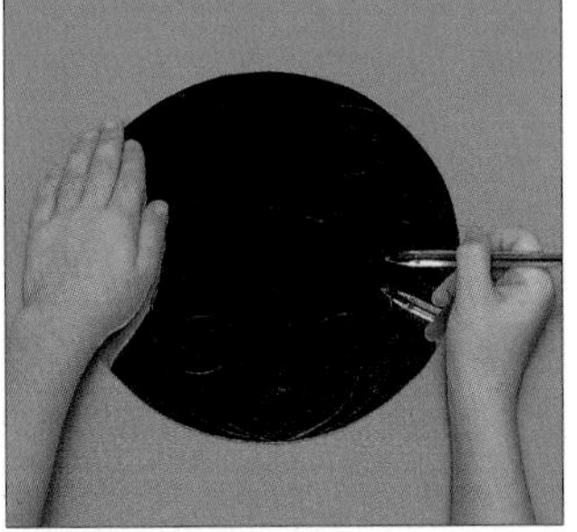

3 Lay the tracing paper on to one of the circles. Trace the pattern on to half of the gold circle, then turn the paper over and repeat the tracing. Go over the pattern with a pen.

4 Roll out several pieces of clay and sculpt them into a handle 15cm/6in long and 9cm/3½in wide. Leave to dry. Paint one side with gold paint. Leave to dry. Turn over and paint the other side.

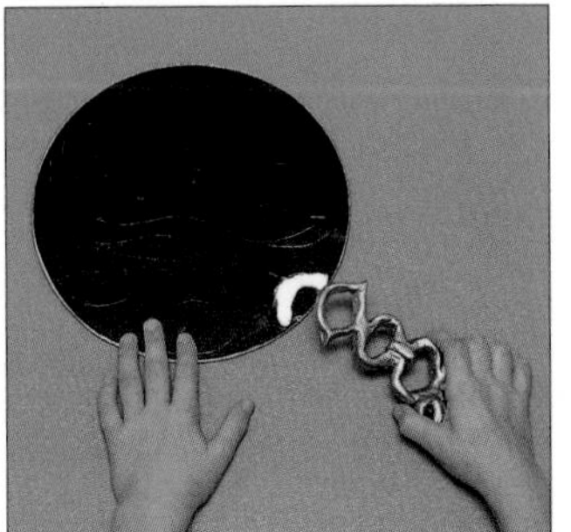

5 Stick the two pieces of mirror card together, white side to white side, with the gold sides facing out, as shown above. Glue the handle on to the side of the mirror when the paint has dried.

The bronze on a Celtic mirror would have been polished so that the owner could see his or her reflection on it.

Celtic torc

The Celts were skilled at many different crafts, including glass, jewellery, enamel and metalwork. Only wealthy people could afford items made from gold. Celtic chiefs often rewarded their best warriors with rich gifts of fine gold armbands. Heavy necklaces called torcs were also highly prized. The Celts believed that torcs had the power to protect people from evil spirits. For the same reason, the Celts often painted or tattooed their bodies with a dark blue dye taken from a plant called woad.

YOU WILL NEED

Self-hardening clay, cutting board, ruler, string, scissors, white glue and glue brush, gold or bronze paint, paintbrush, water pot.

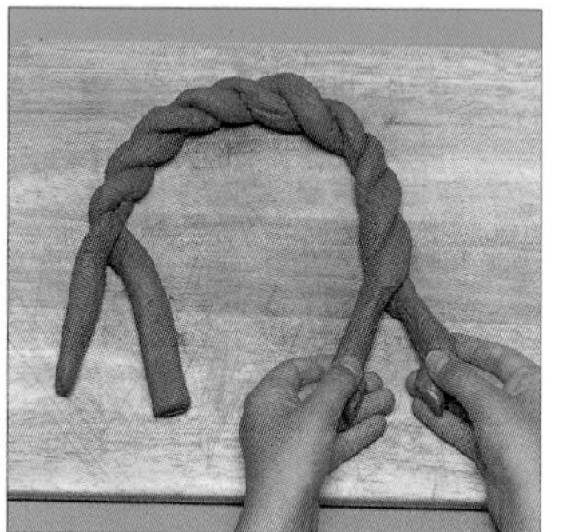

1 Roll out two lengths of clay about 60cm/2ft long and about 1cm/½in thick on the cutting board. Twist the rolls together, leaving about 5cm/2in of untwisted clay at either end.

2 Make loops out of the untwisted ends of the clay torc by joining them together, as shown above. Dampen the ends with a little water to help join the clay, if necessary.

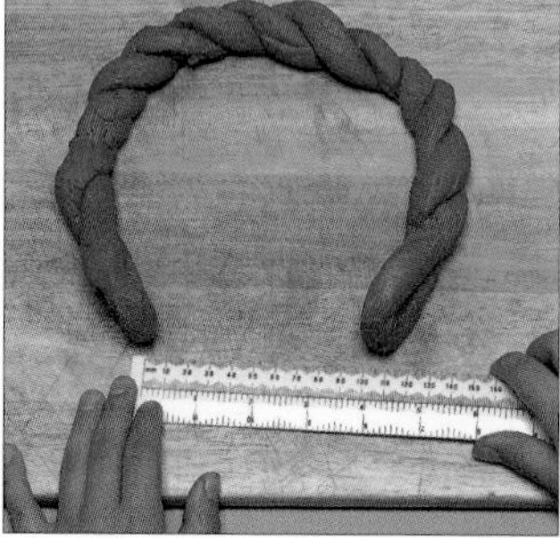

3 Use a ruler to measure an opening between the two looped ends. The ends should be about 9cm/3½in apart, so that the torc will fit easily around your neck. Let the torc begin to dry.

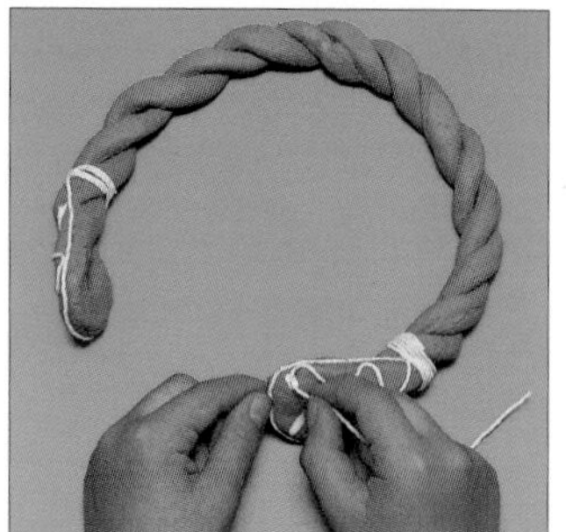

4 When the torc is partially dry, cut two pieces of string about 8cm/3⅛in in length. Use the string to decorate the looped ends of the torc. Glue the string securely in place.

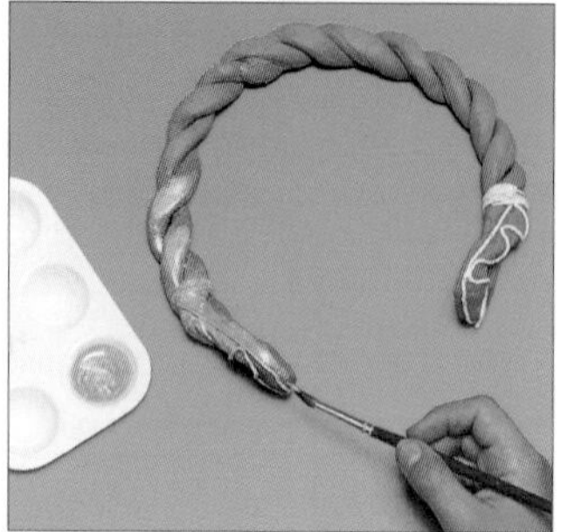

5 Allow the clay torc to dry out completely. When it is hard, cover the torc and decorative string with gold or bronze paint. Leave to dry again before you wear your torc.

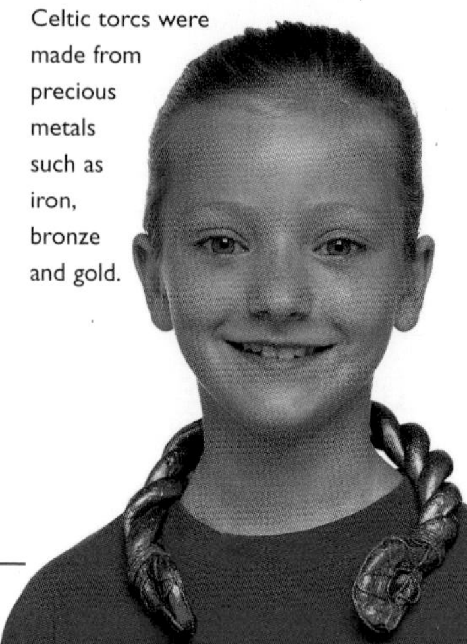

Celtic torcs were made from precious metals such as iron, bronze and gold.

Celtic brooch

Looking good was important to Celtic men and women, because it made people admire them. Ancient Roman reports suggest that different groups of men within Celtic society cut their hair and shaved their faces in different styles to show their status. Legends told that warriors who did not have naturally blonde hair (preferred by the Celts) bleached it with a mixture of urine and wood-ash. Jewellery was extremely important to the Celts. Bracelets, brooches and torcs were worn by all members of Celtic society.

YOU WILL NEED

Self-hardening clay, rolling pin, cutting board, modelling tool, sharp pencil, sandpaper, acrylic paints (light blue, dark blue and white), paintbrush, water pot, large safety pin, adhesive tape.

1 Roll out a 15 x 15cm/6 x 6in square of clay on to the cutting board. It should be about 5mm/¼in thick. Copy a dragon shape on to the clay, using the finished brooch as a guide.

2 Cut out the dragon shape. Then use the modelling tool to draw some of the features of the dragon into the centre of your brooch, as shown above.

3 Cut the centre hole out of the brooch. Add the dragon's two faces and more patterns using a modelling tool. Finish the patterns with the sharp end of a pencil. Let the brooch dry.

4 When the brooch has dried, gently hold it in one hand. With your other hand, sand the edges with a piece of smooth sandpaper until they are completely smooth.

5 Paint the brooch light blue. Add dark blue and white decoration, as shown above. Let the brooch dry. Stick a large safety pin on the back of the brooch with adhesive tape.

The brooch that inspired this design was called a dragon brooch. It was made in Britain in around AD 100.

Viking brooches

The Vikings loved showy jewellery – especially armbands, rings and gold and silver necklaces. These were often decorated with ornate designs. Jewellery was a sign of wealth and could be used instead of money to buy other goods.

Brooches were worn by Viking women. Typical dress for Viking women and girls was a long plain shift. This was made of wool or linen. Over this they wore a woollen tunic, with shoulder straps secured by ornate brooches. Between the brooches there was often a chain or a string of beads.

YOU WILL NEED

Self-hardening clay, rolling board, ruler, string, scissors, white glue and brush, bronze paint, sheet of white paper, water pot, paintbrush, pair of compasses, pencil, tracing paper, gold foil, card, safety pin.

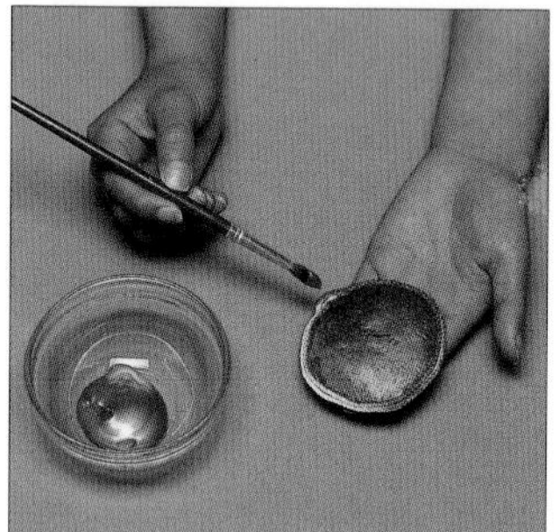

1 Roll two balls of clay into slightly domed disc shapes 2–3cm/¾–1 3/16in across. Let them dry. Glue string borders around them. Paint them with bronze paint. Leave them to dry.

2 Use compasses to draw two circles on a sheet of white paper. Make them the same size as your brooch shapes. Draw a Viking pattern in your circle or copy the one shown above.

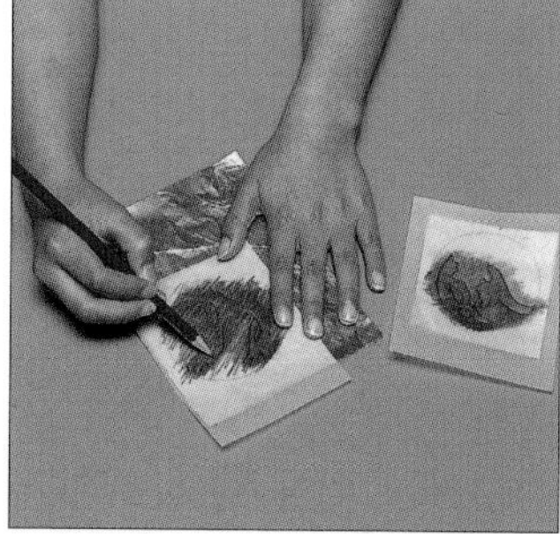

3 Use tracing paper to trace each pattern on to a piece of gold foil. Cut the patterns out in small pieces that will interlink. Take care not to tear the foil.

4 Glue each piece of the foil pattern on to the outside of one of the clay brooches. Leave the brooch to dry. Then glue the foil pattern on to the other clay brooch.

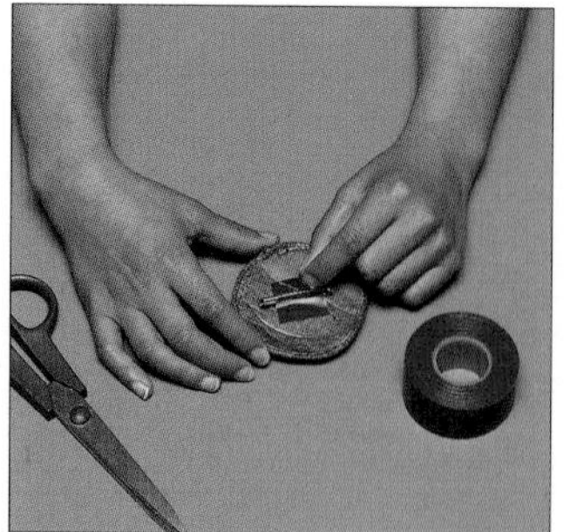

5 Cut and stick a circle of painted gold card on to the back of each brooch. Fix a safety pin on to the back of each brooch with masking tape. Your brooches are now ready to wear.

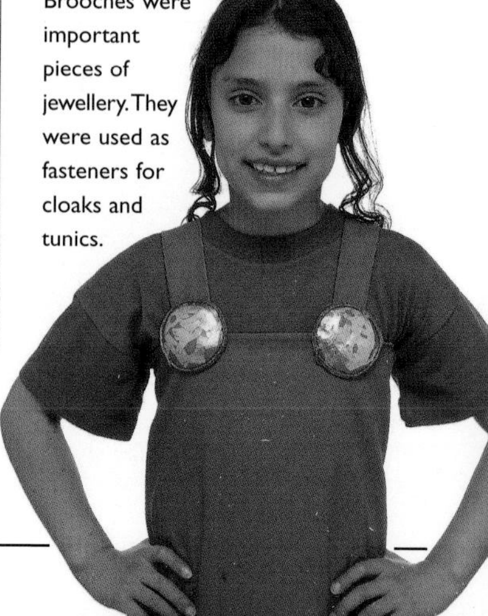

Brooches were important pieces of jewellery. They were used as fasteners for cloaks and tunics.

Viking bracelet

All Vikings turned their hand to craftwork. The men carved ivory and wood during the long winter evenings, and the women made woollen cloth. Professional craftworkers worked gold, silver and bronze and made fine jewellery from gemstones, amber and jet. Other beautiful objects were carved from antlers or walrus tusks. Homes and churches had beautiful wood carvings. Patterns included swirling loops and knots, and birds and animals interlaced with writhing snakes and strange monsters.

YOU WILL NEED

Tape measure, self-hardening clay, cutting board, white cord or string, scissors, modelling tool, silver paint, paintbrush, water pot.

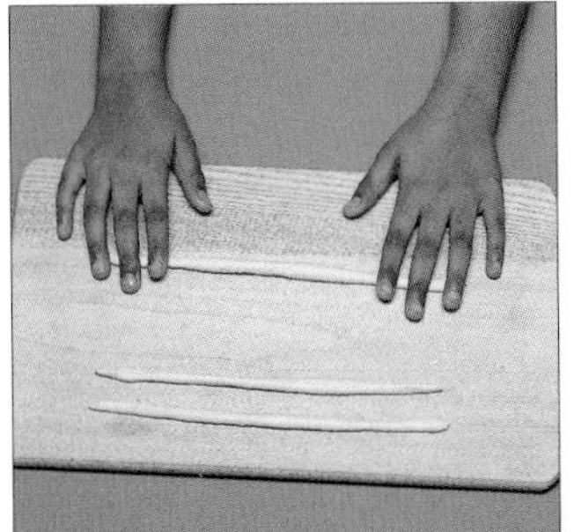

1 Measure your wrist with a tape measure. Roll three clay snakes just longer than the size of your wrist. This will ensure that the bracelet will pass over your hand but not fall off.

2 Lay out the clay snakes in a fan shape. Then cut two lengths of white cord a bit longer than the snakes, and braid the clay snakes and the two cords together, as shown above.

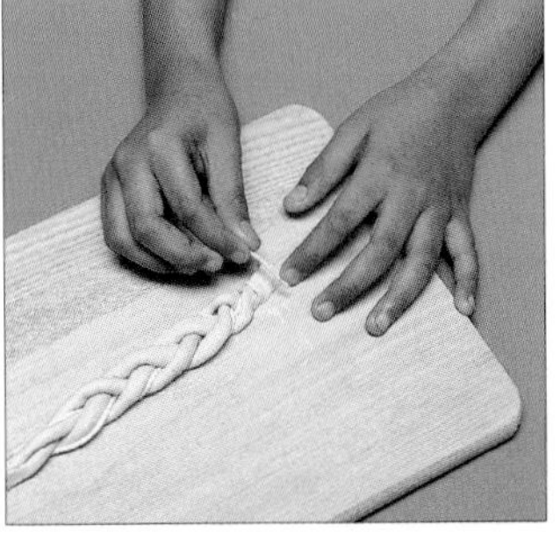

3 Trim each end of the clay and cord braid with a modelling tool. At each end, press the strands firmly together and secure them with a small roll of clay, as shown above.

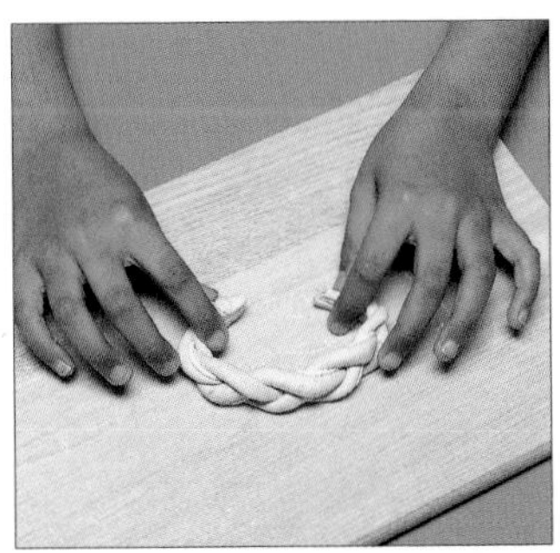

4 Carefully curl the bracelet round so it will fit neatly around your wrist. Make sure you leave the ends open. Leave the bracelet in a safe place to dry thoroughly.

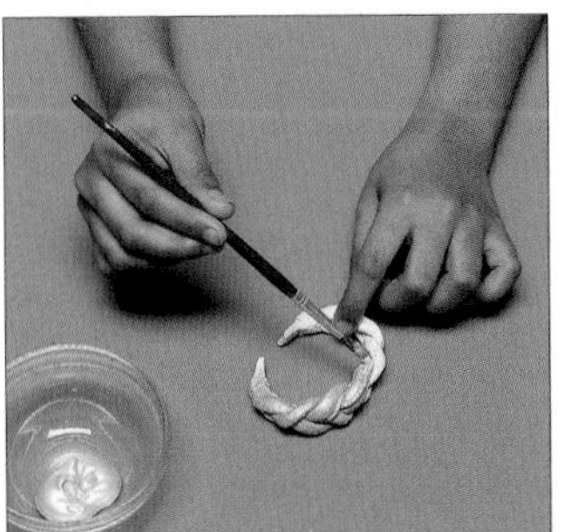

5 When the bracelet is completely dry, paint it with silver paint. Give it a second coat, if necessary. Leave the bracelet to dry again. When it is completely dry, you can try it on.

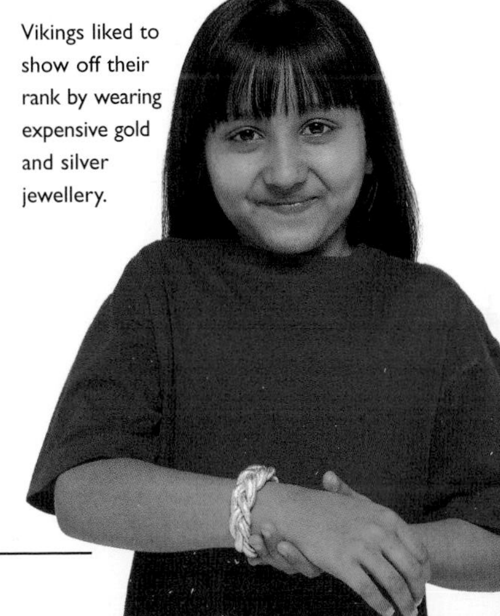

Vikings liked to show off their rank by wearing expensive gold and silver jewellery.

Aztec feather fan

Countless tropical birds live in Central America. Their brightly coloured feathers became an important item of trade in the Aztec world. Birds were hunted and raised in captivity for their feathers, which were arranged into elaborate patterns and designs. Skilled Aztec featherworkers wove beautiful garments, such as decorative headdresses, feather *ponchos* (shirts) and fans. Jewellery was popular, too, but it could only be worn by the ruler and the nobility. Earrings, necklaces, labrets (lip-plugs) and bracelets made of gold and precious stones were all popular items. As well as wearing jewellery, tattooing was a widespread practice in Mesoamerica.

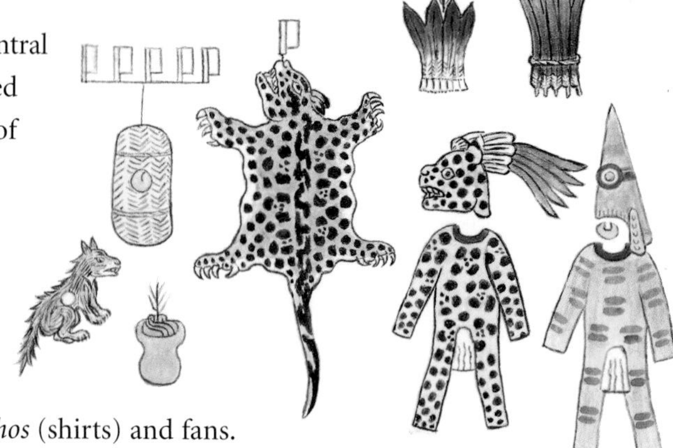

▲ **Tax collection**
The Aztecs loved feather decoration. These pictures show items that were collected as a form of tax payment from the lands they conquered.

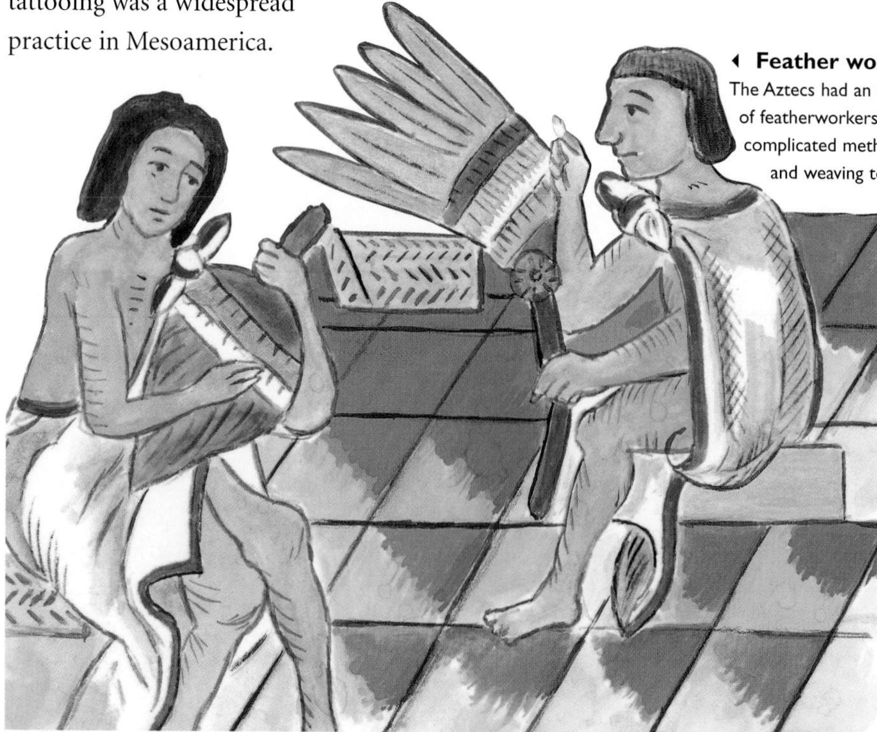

◀ **Feather work**
The Aztecs had an expert guild of featherworkers who used complicated methods of gluing and weaving to make items such as headdresses and fans.

YOU WILL NEED

Pair of compasses, pencil, ruler, thick card (90 x 45cm/3 x 1½ft), scissors, thin red card, green paper, double-sided adhesive tape, feathers (real or paper), roll of masking tape, acrylic paints, paintbrushes, water pot, coloured felt, white glue and glue brush, single-sided adhesive tape, coloured wool, bamboo cane.

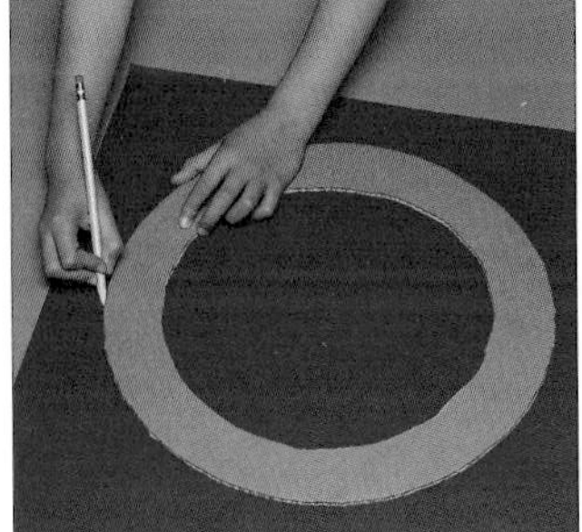

1 Use the compasses to draw two rings 45cm/18in in diameter and 8cm/3⅛in wide on thick card. Cut them out. Use a thick card ring to make another ring from the thin red card, as shown above.

2 Cut lots of leaf shapes from green paper. Stick them around the edge of one thick card ring using double-sided adhesive tape. Add some real feathers or ones made from paper.

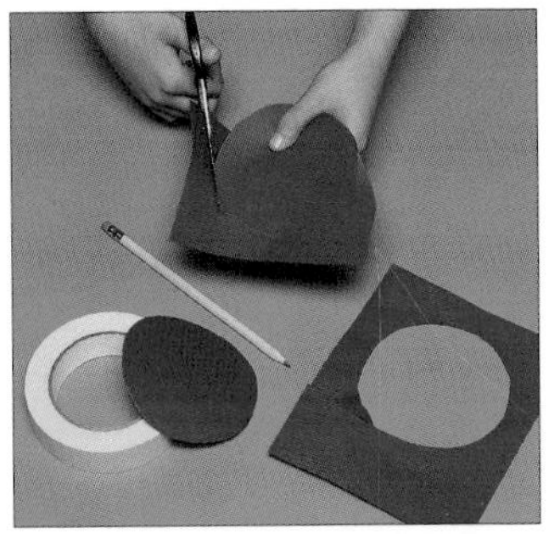

3 Cut two circles about 12cm/4½in in diameter from thin red card. Draw around something the right size, such as a roll of masking tape. These circles will be the centre of your feather fan.

4 Paint a flower on to one of the two smaller red circles, and a butterfly on the other. Cut lots of V-shapes from the felt and glue them to the large red ring.

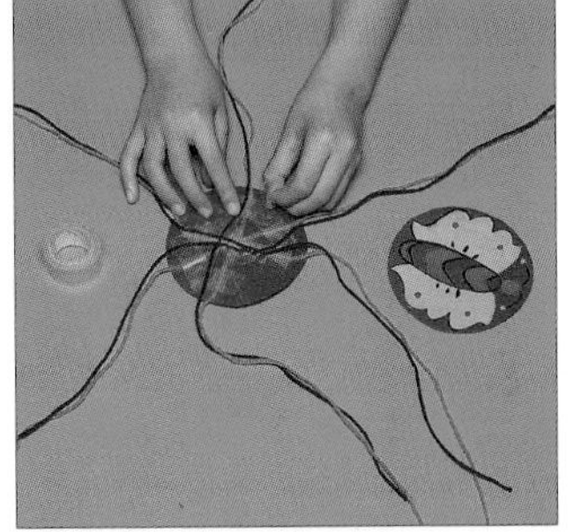

5 Using single-sided adhesive tape, fix lengths of coloured wool to the back of one of the red circles, as shown above. Place this red circle in the centre of the leafy ring.

6 Tape the wool to the outer ring. Glue the second card ring on top. Insert the cane in between. Stick the second red circle face up in the centre. Glue the larger outer ring on top.

Aztec nobles and rulers were cooled with beautiful feather fans such as the one you have made.

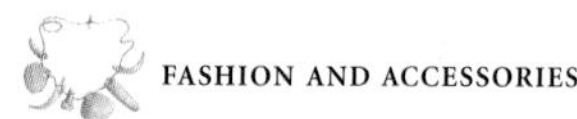

Buckles and badges

In the Wild West, lawmen wore a metal star pinned on the front of their jackets to identify themselves. It was their job to keep law and order. The first project here shows you how to make your own sheriff's badge.

Every belt needs a buckle, and one way a cowboy could get a new one was to win it as a prize at a special contest called a rodeo. Wearing this would show his friends how skilful he was as a cowboy. The second part of this project shows you how to make a prize belt buckle of your own.

▲ Tools of the trade
Cowboys had tough lives, and wore tough, practical clothes. This cowboy wears a gun at his belt and carries a rope lasso, or lariat, for roping cattle.

YOU WILL NEED

Self-hardening clay, rolling pin, cutting board, ruler, star-shaped pastry cutter, white glue and glue brush, kebab stick or sharpened pencil, water, flowerpot, modelling tool, large safety pin with flat plate, two strips of bias binding tape, 8cm/3⅛in-long needle and thread, silver poster paint, paintbrush, water pot, permanent black marker.

1 Roll a handful of clay out into two circles, each 5mm/¼in thick. With the star-shaped pastry cutter, press out a star from one of the clay circles. Lift the star from the surrounding clay.

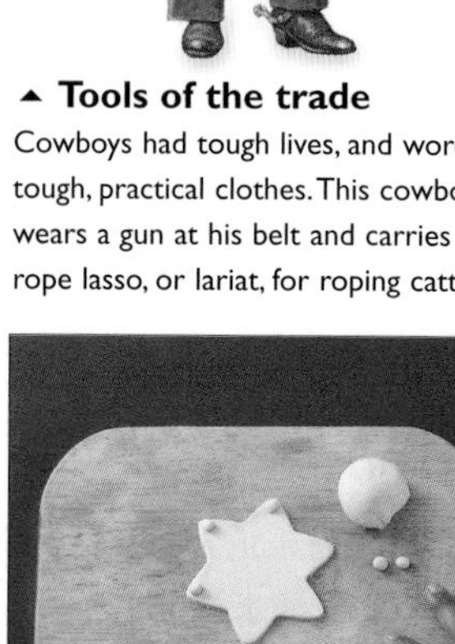

2 Roll out some of the excess clay to make six tiny balls. Each one should be about half the size of your fingernail. Glue each ball on a point of the star shape.

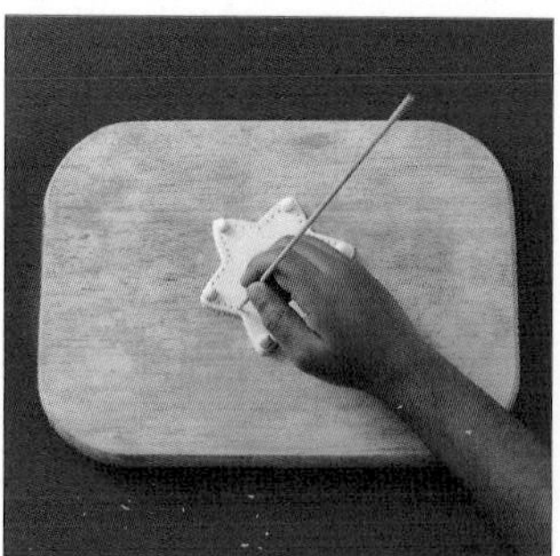

3 Use the pointed end of a kebab stick or a sharpened pencil to make a line of tiny dots around the edge of the star shape. Try to be as neat as you possibly can.

4 To give the star a curved shape, lightly brush the back of the star with water and press it on to the side of a flowerpot. Peel the star away gently. Leave it to dry overnight.

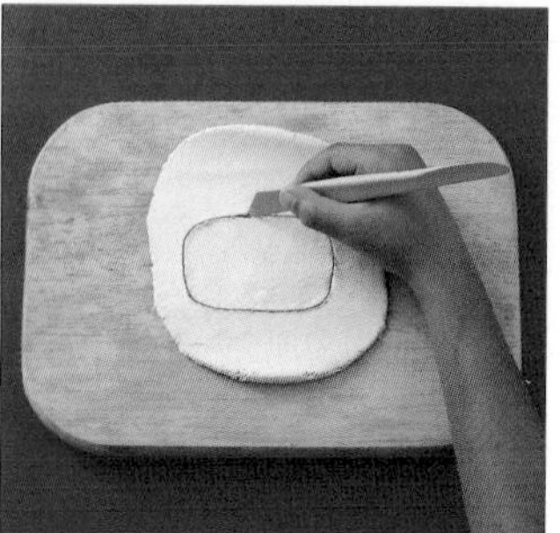

5 Roll out the second ball of clay. Use a modelling tool to cut a rectangular shape with rounded corners, as shown above. The rectangle should measure about 8 x 5cm/3⅛ x 2in.

6 Follow Step 2 again to make 12 more tiny modelling clay balls with excess clay. Then carefully glue the balls around the edge of the clay buckle.

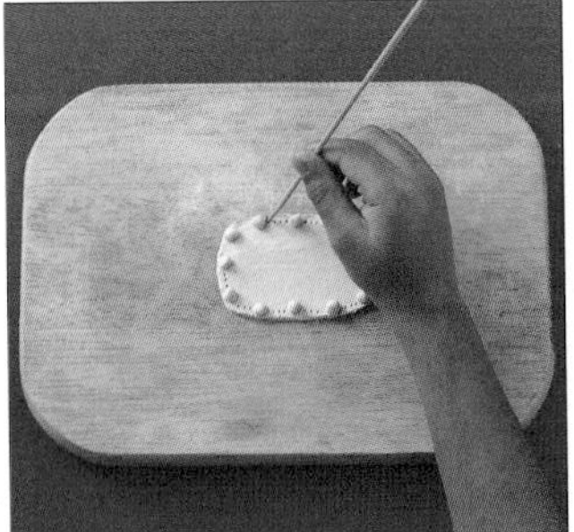

7 Once again, use the pointed end of a kebab stick or a sharpened pencil to add some decorative touches to the parts of the buckle between the balls, such as dots and swirls.

8 Follow Step 4 again to give the buckle a curved shape. When you are happy with the shape of the buckle, peel it off gently. Then leave it to dry overnight.

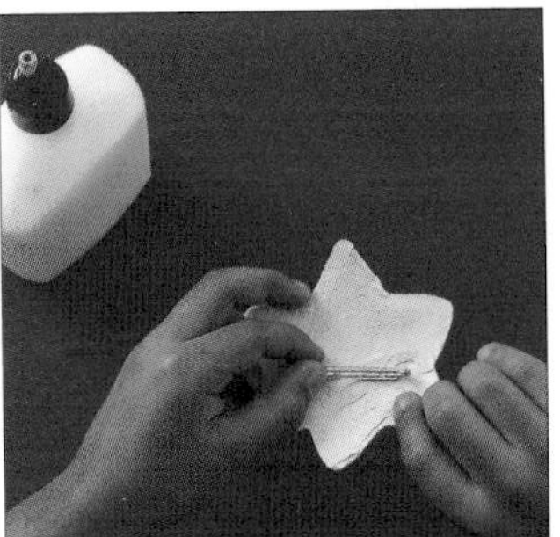

9 After 24 hours, when the clay star badge is dry, glue the plate of the safety pin to the back of the star. Carefully attach the pin to the flat space in the middle of the badge.

10 When the buckle is completely dry, glue two strips of bias binding tape across the back of the buckle. Use a running stitch to sew the ends together to make two loops.

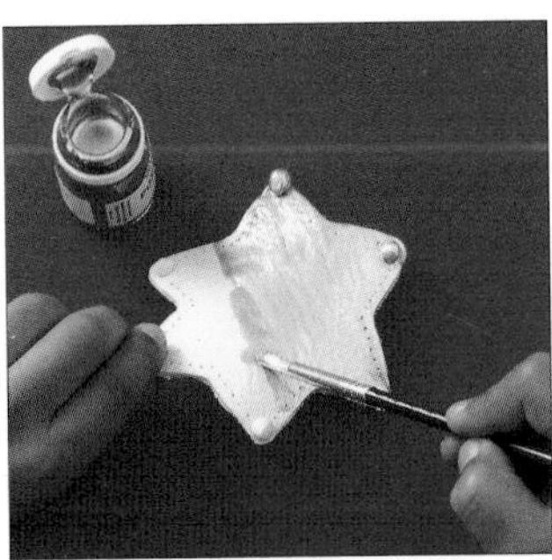

11 When the glue on the badge and buckle is completely dry, you can paint them both with silver paint to give them an authentic metallic sheen.

12 When the paint has dried, you can add the finishing touches using a permanent black marker. Try drawing a star shape in the middle of the badge and the buckle.

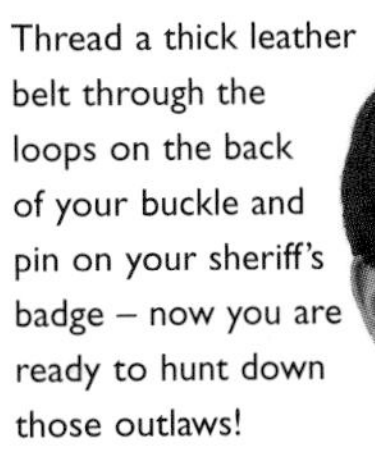

Thread a thick leather belt through the loops on the back of your buckle and pin on your sheriff's badge – now you are ready to hunt down those outlaws!

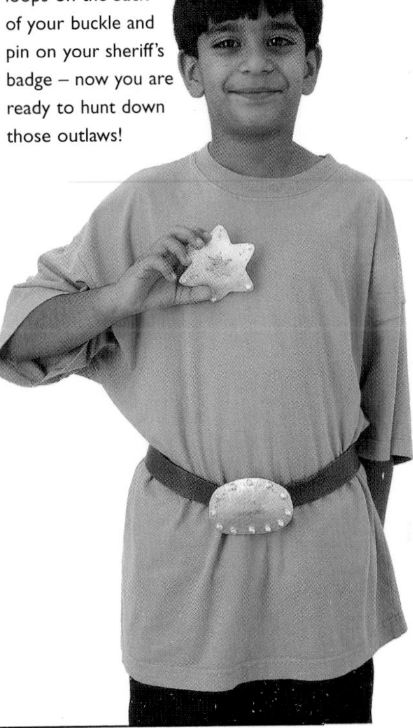

Ancient Egyptian agriculture on the bank of the River Nile

Science and Technology

Discovery, invention and progress went hand-in-hand with civilization. Systems of writing, weights and measures, currency and communication were vital to running a successful empire. Transport and travel were the key to trade and expansion of territory. The projects in this section provide an insight into the developing technologies, such as transport and warfare, that gave people the edge over their neighbours.

Inventions and Learning

Humans have striven to understand the world around them ever since they first walked on the Earth some 30,000 years ago. The earliest people lived by hunting animals and gathering fruit. Their inventions were simple tools and weapons. Farming and permanent settlements, and the subsequent development of towns and cities, made life much more complicated. This, together with increased wealth, prompted some remarkable scientific and technological breakthroughs. The world was changed dramatically by new inventions that made life ever easier and more efficient.

▲ Geometric calculations
The ancient Egyptians were skilled mathematicians, and made many new discoveries in geometry. For example, they knew how to calculate the height of a pyramid by measuring the length of its shadow on the ground.

◀ A Greek philosopher
Pythagoras of Samos (560–480BC) became one of the most highly respected Greek philosophers and teachers. Pythagoras believed that numbers were the perfect basis of life. He is most famous for his theory about right-angled triangles. This showed that if you square the two sides next to the right angle, the two add up to the square of the third side. (Squaring means multiplying a number by itself.)

◂ Arabian astrolabe
Scientists from the Arabian Peninsula developed the astrolabe between 1200 and 1300. The device consisted of a flat disc with a rod that could be pointed to the stars. The astrolabe helped Arab sailors find their way at sea.

▴ The first wheelbarrow
The ancient Chinese were highly inventive. During the Han Dynasty (from 207BC to AD220), technological developments included the invention of the wheelbarrow, some 1000 years before people in the West.

◂ Remarkable roads
The Romans were some of the greatest builders and engineers of the ancient world. Their road-building methods were unsurpassed for centuries. They began building roads in 334BC. By the time the Roman Empire was at its peak, at around AD117, they had laid down more than 85,000km/53,000 miles of roads.

Stone Age bow drill

Our ancestor, *Homo erectus*, learned to use fire at least 700,000 years ago. Early humans ate cooked food and had warmth and light at night. Fire was a useful way of keeping wild animals at bay, and was also used to harden the tips of wooden spears. Hunters waving flaming branches could scare large animals into ambushes. Most archaeologists believe that *Homo erectus* did not know how to make fire, but found smouldering logs after natural forest fires. Campfires were carefully kept alight, and hot ashes may have been carried to each new camp. Eventually, people learned that they could make fire by rubbing two dry sticks together. Then they found that striking a stone against pyrite (a type of rock) created a spark. By 4000BC, the bow drill had been invented. This made lighting a fire much easier.

YOU WILL NEED

Thick piece of dowel (25cm/10in long), craft knife, sandpaper, wood stain, paintbrush, water pot, balsa wood (8 x 8cm/3⅛ x 3⅛in), modelling tool, self-hardening clay, rolling pin, cutting board, scissors, chamois leather, raffia or straw.

▾ The first match
One way early people made fire was to put dry grass on a stick called a hearth. Then they rubbed another stick against the hearth to make a spark and set the grass alight.

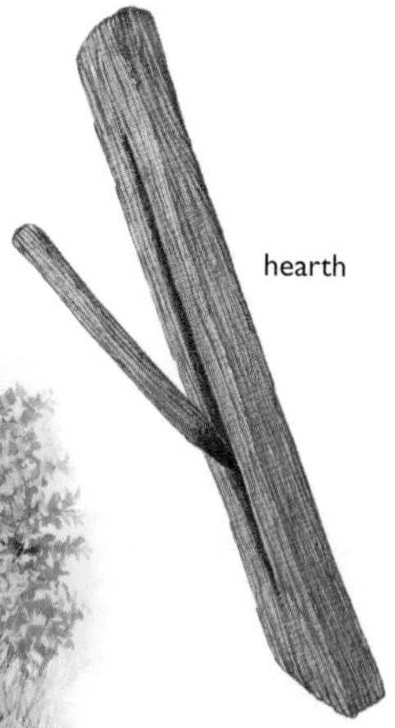

hearth

◂ Making dinner
Cave-dwelling *Homo erectus* people prepare to cook a meal in front of their cave. One member of the group makes stone tools, perhaps to cut up the dead animal. Another tends to the fire, and two children help an adult to dismember the carcass before it is cooked.

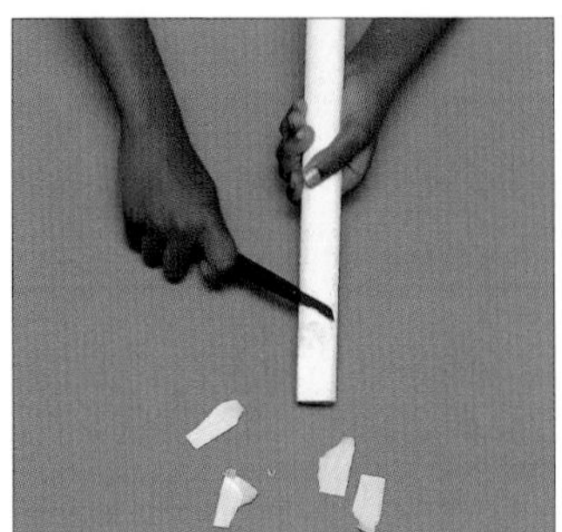

1 Shape one end of the piece of thick dowel into a point with a craft knife. The blade of the knife should always angle away from your body when you cut the wood.

2 Sand down the stick and apply a coat of wood stain. Cut out the balsa wood base into a shape roughly like the one shown above. Paint the base with wood stain. Leave it to dry.

3 Use a modelling tool to gouge a small hole in the centre of the balsa wood base. The sharpened end of the piece of dowel should fit into this hole.

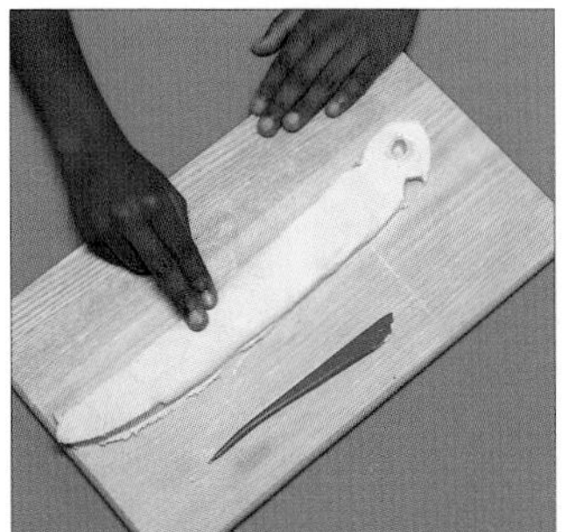

4 Roll out a piece of clay. Cut out a bone shape with a rounded end, as shown above. Make a hole in each end of the bone and smooth the sides with your fingers. Let the bone shape dry.

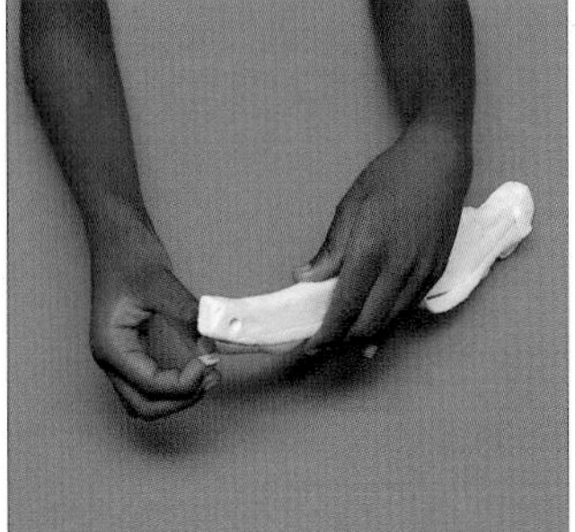

5 Use a pair of scissors to cut a thin strip of chamois leather twice as long as the bone. This will be the thong used to twist the bow drill. Tie the strip to one end of the bone.

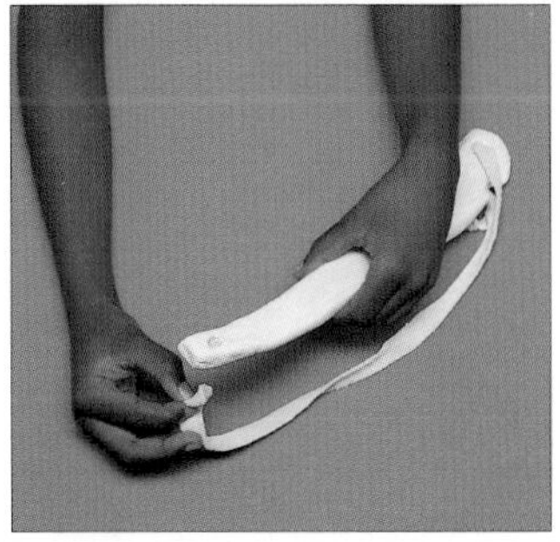

6 Thread the strip of chamois leather through the other hole. Tie a knot at the end to secure it. Now the bow piece is ready to be used with the drill you have already made.

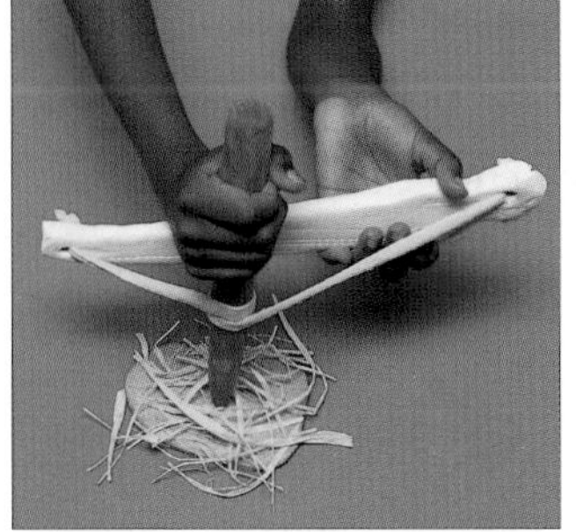

7 Scatter raffia or straw around the balsa wood base. Wrap the leather thong around the drill piece and place the pointed end of the drill in the hole on the base.

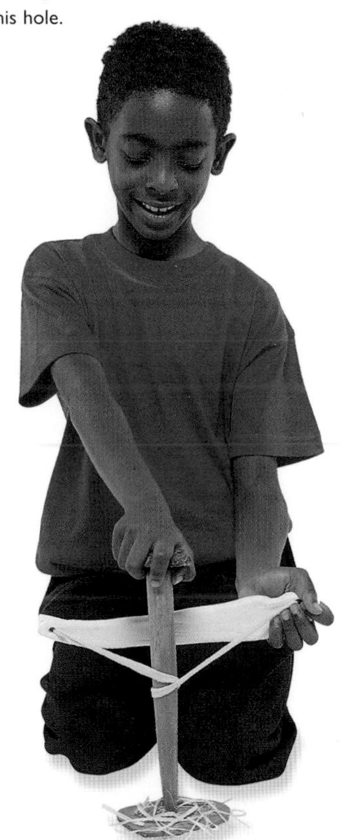

If you like, add a wood handle to the base to help you hold it. The bow drill you have made will not light real fires, but shows you how Stone Age people spun a drill to make fire.

Egyptian shaduf

The ancient Egyptians called the banks of the River Nile the Black Land. This was because the river flooded each year in June, depositing a rich, fertile, black mud. The land remained under water until autumn. During dry periods of the year, farmers dug channels and canals to carry water to irrigate their land. A lifting system called a shaduf was introduced to raise water from the river. The success of this farming cycle was vital. Years of low floodwaters or drought could spell disaster. If the crops failed, people went hungry.

▲ Home on the Nile
Most ancient Egyptians lived close to the River Nile. The river was the main means of transport, and provided water for their crops and their homes.

▼ Templates
Cut out the pieces of card, following the measurements shown.

A = irrigation channel and riverbank
B = river
C = water tank

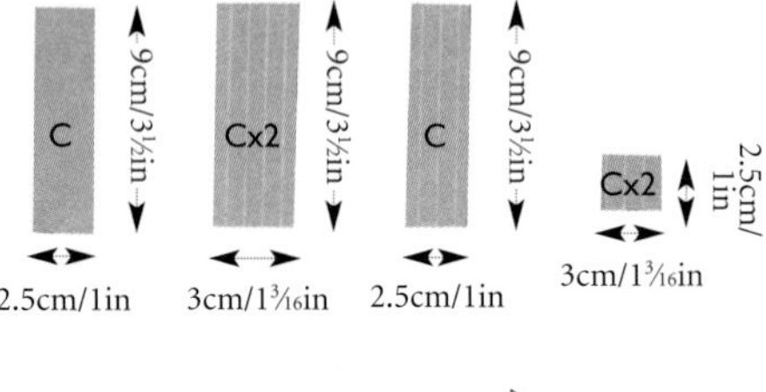

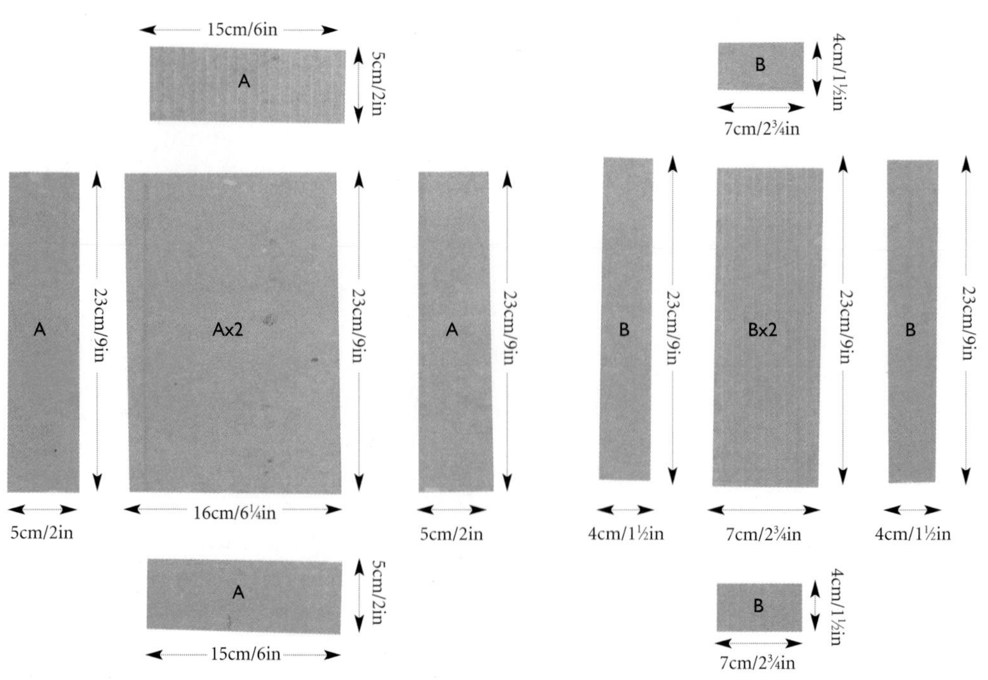

YOU WILL NEED

Card, pencil, ruler, scissors, white glue and glue brush, masking tape, acrylic paints (blue, green and brown), paintbrush, water pot, four balsa wood strips (two measuring 8cm/3⅛in and two 4cm/1½in), small stones, twig, self-hardening clay, hessian, string. Note: mix green paint with dried herbs for the grass mixture.

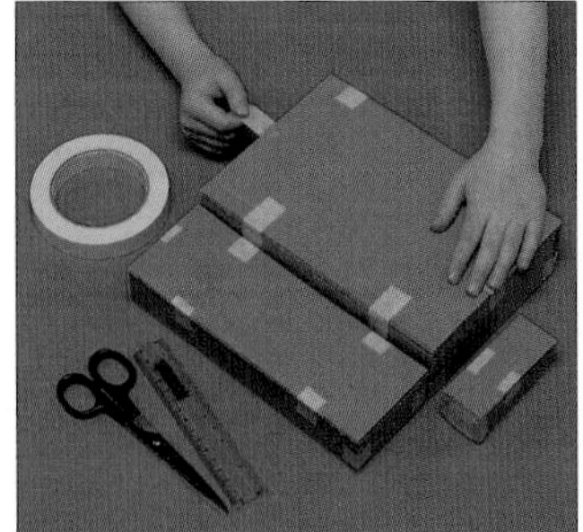

1 Glue the edges of boxes A, B and C, as shown above. Secure them with masking tape until they are dry. Then paint the river section B and the water tank C blue, and leave to dry.

2 Paint the box A with the green grass mixture on top, brown on the sides and the irrigation channel blue, as shown. Next, get the balsa strips to make the frame of the shaduf.

3 Glue the four balsa wood strips to make a frame. Support them with masking tape on a piece of card. When dry, paint the frame brown. Then glue the stones around the water tank.

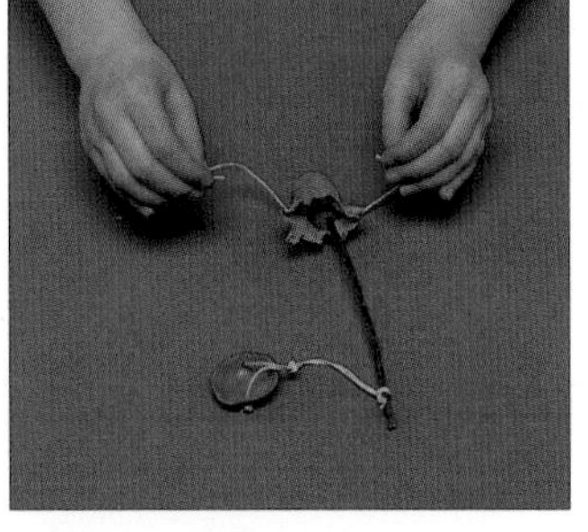

4 Use a twig for the pole of the shaduf. Make a weight from clay and wrap it in hessian. Tie it to one end of the pole. Make a bucket from clay, leaving two holes for the string.

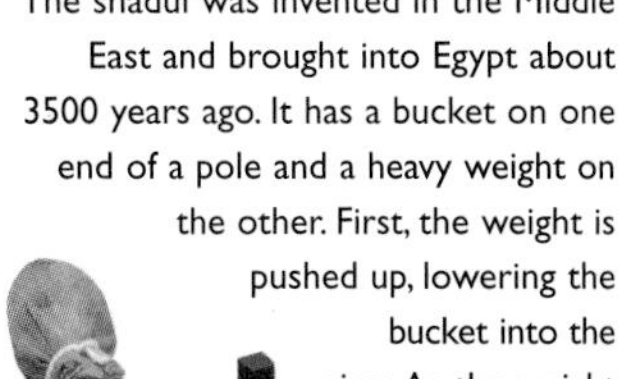

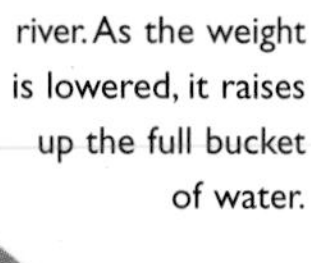

The shaduf was invented in the Middle East and brought into Egypt about 3500 years ago. It has a bucket on one end of a pole and a heavy weight on the other. First, the weight is pushed up, lowering the bucket into the river. As the weight is lowered, it raises up the full bucket of water.

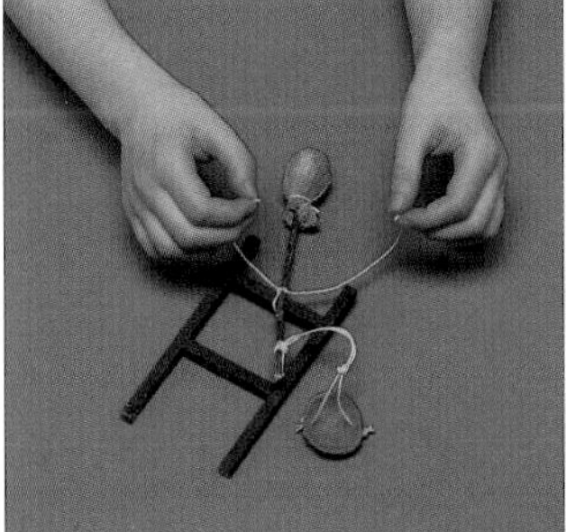

5 Using string, tie the bucket to the pole. Tie the pole, with its weight and bucket, to the frame of the shaduf. Glue the frame to the water tank, and then glue the tank to the riverbank section.

Archimedes' screw

The Greeks could afford to devote time to studying and thinking because their civilization was both wealthy and secure. They learned astrology from the Babylonians, and mathematics from the Egyptians. They used their knowledge to develop many practical inventions, including water clocks, cogwheels, gearing systems, slot machines and steam engines. However, these devices were not widely used, because there were many slaves to do the work instead.

Archimedes was the world's first great scientist. He developed theories that could be proved or disproved by practical experiment or mathematical calculation. One of his most famous inventions, the screw pump, is still used in some places in the Middle East almost 2,000 years after this scientific breakthrough. The device is used to lift water from irrigation canals and rivers on to dry fields.

▲ Great inventor
Archimedes of Syracuse in Sicily was born around 285BC, and spent most of his life in the city studying mathematics. He was killed when the Romans invaded Syracuse in 211BC.

weight

weight balanced by upthrust of water

◄ Variable weight
One of Archimedes' great breakthroughs was the discovery that an object weighs less in water than in air. This is why you can lift a heavy person in a swimming pool. The reason for this buoyancy is the natural upward push, or upthrust, of the water.

◄ Pump it up
Archimedes' screw is a very simple but effective pump. Inside a tube is a spiral, which scoops up the water as someone turns the handle at the top.

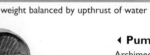

YOU WILL NEED

Clean plastic bottle, scissors, self-hardening clay, strong tape, length of clear plastic tubing, bowl of water, blue food colouring, empty glass bowl.

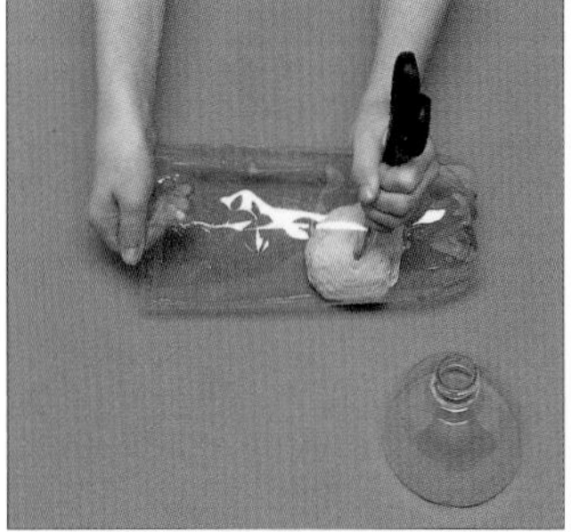

1 Cut off the top of the bottle. Put a lump of clay on the outside of the bottle, about 5cm/2in from the end, as shown. Punch a hole here with scissors, and cut off the bottom of the bottle.

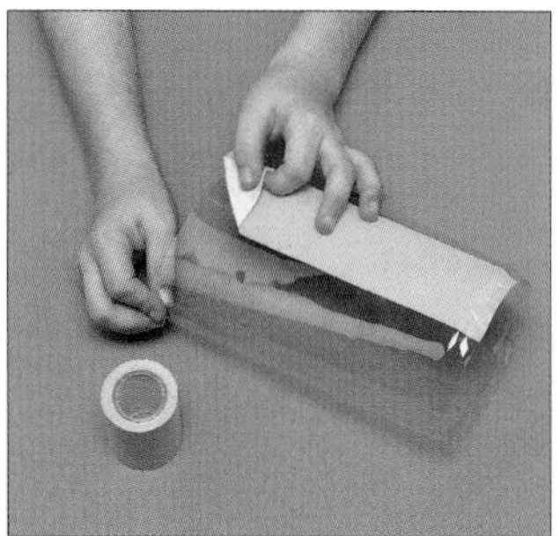

2 Cut a strip of strong tape about the same length as the bottle. Tape along the length of the cut bottle, as shown above. The tape will give the plastic tubing extra grip later on.

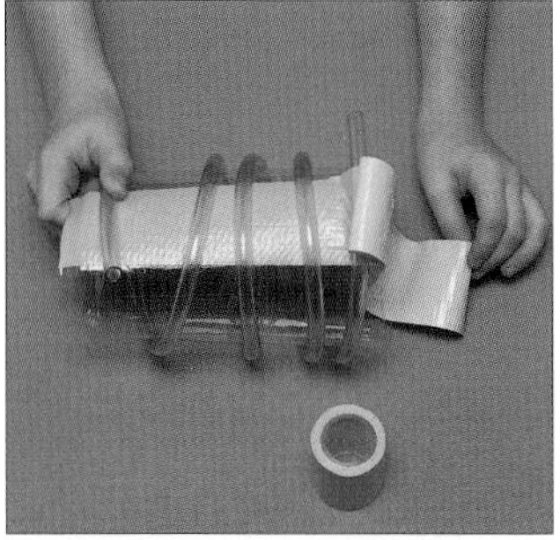

3 Twist the length of plastic tubing around the bottle from one end to the other, as shown above. Secure the length of tubing in place with another piece of tape.

4 Place a few drops of blue food colouring into a bowl of water. Add the food colouring slowly, and stir thoroughly so that the colour mixes evenly with the water.

The invention of the Archimedes' screw made it possible for farmers to water their fields from irrigation channels. It saved them from having to walk back and forth between the river and fields with their buckets.

5 Place one end of the bottle and tubing construction into the bowl of coloured water. Make sure that the tube at the opposite end is pointing towards an empty bowl.

6 Twist the bottle around in the bowl of blue water. As you do so, you will see the water start to travel up the tube and gradually fill up the empty bowl.

Roman groma

The Romans were great builders and engineers. As the legions conquered foreign lands, they built new roads to carry their supplies and messengers. The roads were very straight, stretching across great distances. Romans used a groma to measure right angles and to make sure roads were straight. The roads were built with a slight hump in the middle, so that rainwater drained off to the sides. Some were paved with stone. Others were covered with gravel or stone chips.

Roman engineers also used their skills to carry water supplies to their cities by building aqueducts. They built great domes, arched bridges and grand public buildings all across the Roman Empire, making use of whatever local materials were available. The Romans were also the first to develop concrete, which was cheaper and stronger than stone.

▲ ▼ Travel in the Empire
The Romans built strong stone bridges to carry roads high above rivers. Where ground was liable to flooding, they built embankments called aggers. Roman legions could move around the Roman Empire with astonishing speed, thanks to the road system.

◀ Building a road
The Romans laid a deep solid foundation of large stones for their roads. They covered this with a smooth surface of flat stones, with a raised centre, or crown, so that rainwater could drain off at either side. They also dug ditches along the sides of the road to carry the water away.

YOU WILL NEED

Large piece of strong corrugated card, ruler, pencil, scissors, balsa wood pole, masking tape, card square, white glue and glue brush, non-hardening modelling material, foil, string, large sewing needle, broom handle, acrylic paints, paintbrush, water pot.

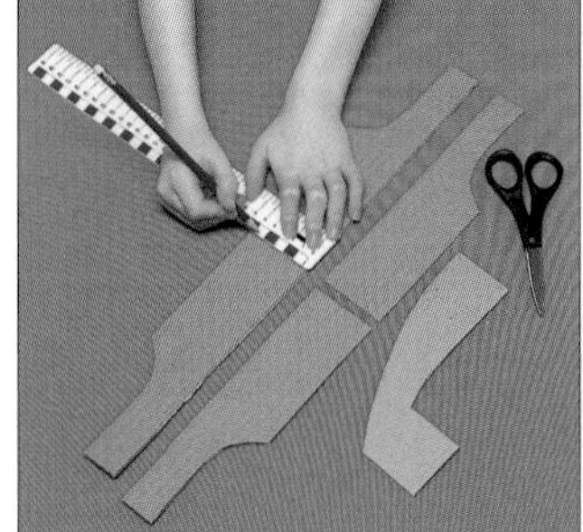

1 Cut three pieces of card: two 20 x 6cm/8 x 2½in, and one 40 x 6cm/16 x 2½in. Cut another piece 15 x 12cm/6 x 4½in for the handle of the groma. Cut them into the shapes shown above.

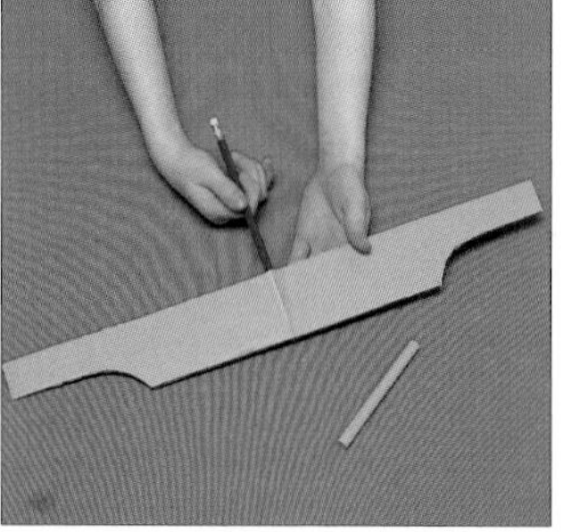

2 Measure to the centre of the long piece of card, and use a pencil to make a slot here between the corrugated layers. The slot is for the balsa wood pole.

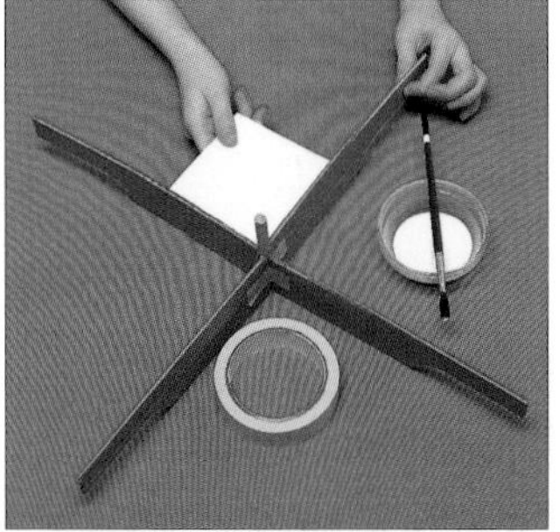

3 Slide the balsa wood pole into the slot, and tape the card pieces in a cross. Use the card square to ensure the four arms of the groma are at right angles. Glue and secure with tape.

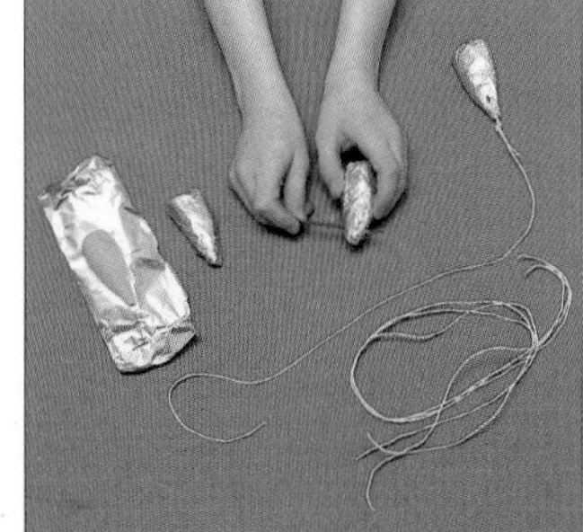

4 Roll lumps of modelling material into four small cones and cover each of them with foil. Then thread string through the tops of the cones to complete the plumblines.

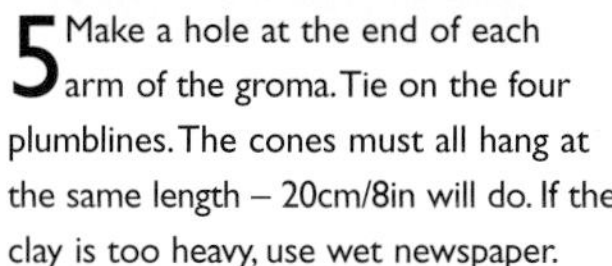

5 Make a hole at the end of each arm of the groma. Tie on the four plumblines. The cones must all hang at the same length – 20cm/8in will do. If the clay is too heavy, use wet newspaper.

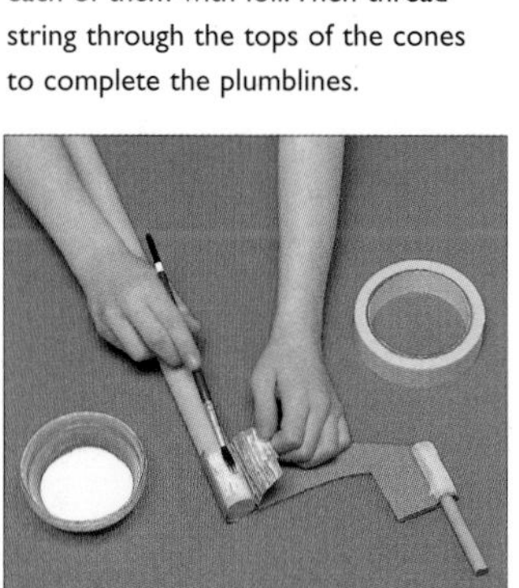

6 Split the top of the corrugated card handle piece. Wrap it around the balsa wood pole and glue it in place, as shown. Split and glue the other end to the broom handle. Now paint the groma.

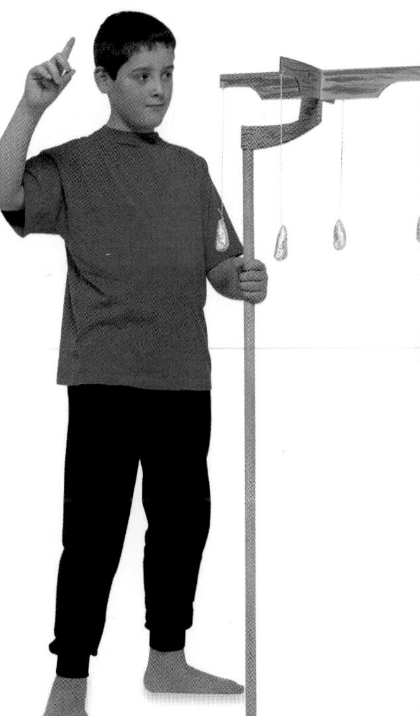

Slot the arms on to the balsa wood pole. Use the plumblines as a guide to make sure the pole is vertical. The arms can be used to line up objects in the distance.

Viking coin and die

The Vikings were successful merchants. Their home trade was based in towns such as Hedeby in Denmark, Birka in Sweden, and Kaupang in Norway. As they settled new lands, their trading routes began to spread far and wide. In about AD860, Swedish Vikings opened up new routes eastwards through the lands of the Slavs. Merchants crossed the Black Sea and the Caspian Sea, and travelled to Constantinople (Istanbul), capital of the Byzantine Empire, and to the great Arab city of Baghdad. Viking warehouses were full of casks of wine from Germany and bales of woollen cloth from England. There were furs and walrus ivory from the Arctic, and timber and iron from Scandinavia. Vikings also traded in wheat from the British Isles, and rye from Russia.

▲ **Trade exchange**
The Vikings used coins for buying and selling goods at home, but they bartered items with their trading partners. In the East, the Vikings supplied furs, beeswax and slaves in exchange for silk, jewellery and spices.

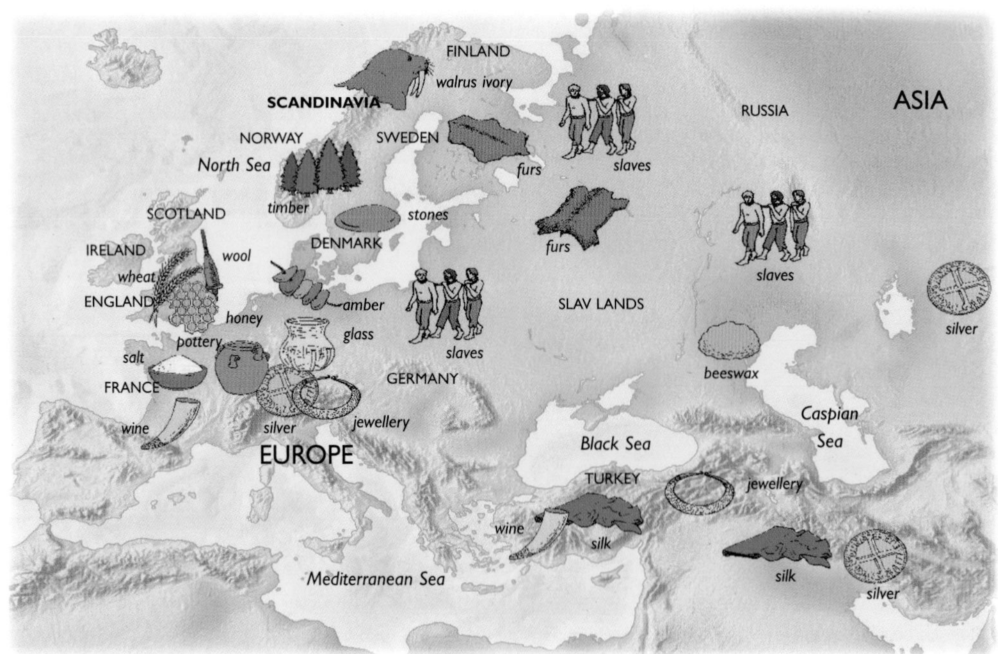

▲ **Trading nations**
The routes taken by the Viking traders fanned out south and east from Scandinavia. Trade networks with the East linked up with older routes, such as the Silk Road to China. Everyday items, such as pottery and wool, were brought back from western Europe.

YOU WILL NEED

Self-hardening clay, cutting board, rolling pin, pencil, thin card, pair of compasses, scissors, white glue and glue brush, bronze and silver paint, paintbrush, water pot, modelling tool.

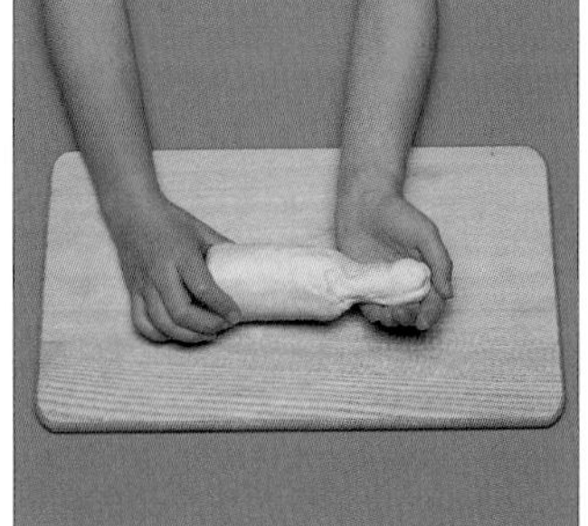

1 Roll out a large cylinder of clay on to a cutting board, and model a short, thick handle at one end. This will be the die. Leave the die to dry and harden in a warm place.

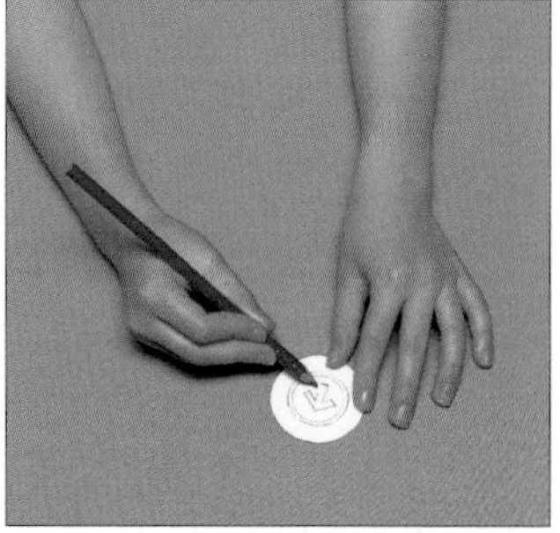

2 Draw a circle on a piece of thin card and cut it out. It should be about the same size as the flat end of the die. Use a pencil to draw a simple shape on the card circle.

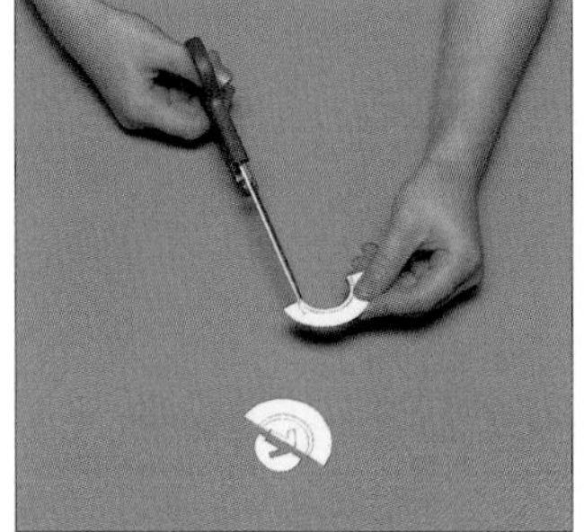

3 Cut the card circle in half and then cut out the shape, as shown above. If you find it hard to cut out your coin design, you could ask an adult to help you.

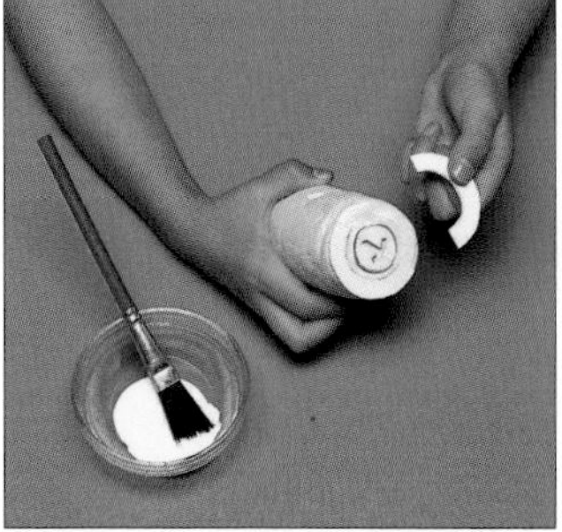

4 Glue the paper pieces on to the end of the die with white glue, as shown above. You may need to trim the pieces if they are too big to fit on to the end.

5 Viking dies would have been made of bronze or some other metal. Paint your die a bronze colour to look like metal. Make sure you give the die an even coat of paint. Leave to dry.

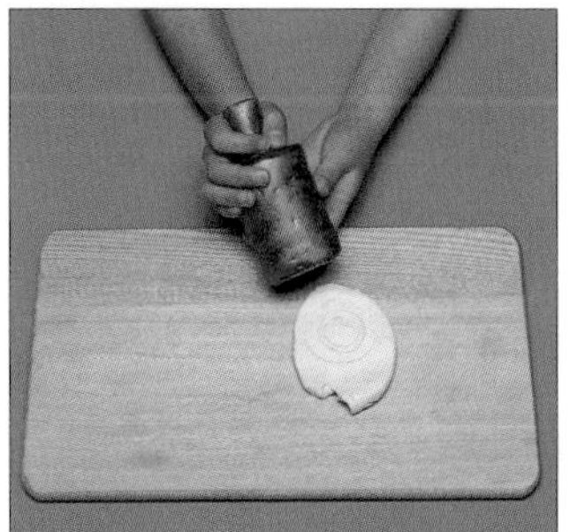

6 Roll out some more clay. Use the die to stamp an impression on to the clay. Use a modelling tool to cut around the edge of the circle, let the coin dry, and then paint it silver.

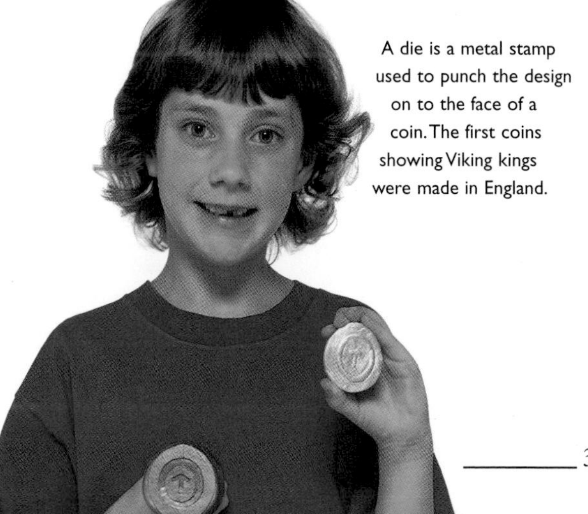

A die is a metal stamp used to punch the design on to the face of a coin. The first coins showing Viking kings were made in England.

Mayan codex

The Maya were the first, and only, Native American people to invent a complete system of writing. They wrote their symbols in folding books called codices. These symbols were also carved on buildings, painted on pottery and inscribed on precious stones. Maya writing used glyphs (pictures standing for words) and also picture-signs that represented sounds. The sound-signs could be joined together – similar to the letters of our alphabet – to spell out words and to make complete sentences.

▾ Names of days
These symbols represent some of the names of the 20 days from the farmers' calendar. The 20 days made 1 month, and there were 13 months in a year. These symbols were combined with a number from 1 to 13 to give the date, such as 'Three Vulture'. Days were named after familiar creatures or everyday things, such as a lizard or water. Each day also had its own god. Children were often named after the day on which they were born.

eagle

motion

rain

dog

serpent

monkey

reed

deer

grass

jaguar

vulture

rabbit

house

lizard

death's head

water

YOU WILL NEED

Thin card, ruler, pencil, scissors, white acrylic paint, large paintbrush, water pot, eraser, tracing paper (optional), acrylic paints, palette, selection of paintbrushes.

1 Draw a rectangle measuring 100 x 25cm/39½ x 10in on to the piece of thin card and cut it out. Cover the rectangle with an even coat of white acrylic paint. Leave it to dry.

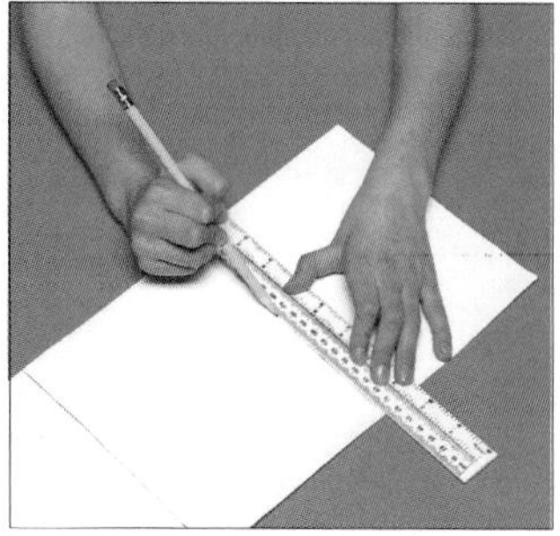

2 Using a pencil and ruler lightly draw in four fold lines, 20cm/8in apart on the painted card, as shown above. This will divide the card into five equal sections.

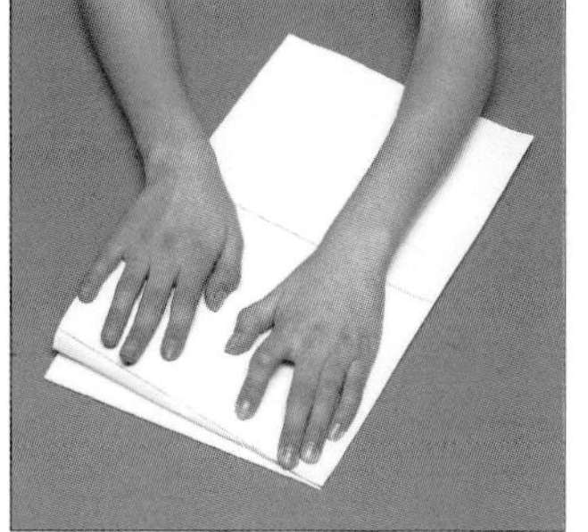

3 Carefully fold along the pencil lines to make a zig-zag book, as shown in the picture above. Unfold the card and rub out the pencil lines with an eraser.

4 To decorate your codex, you could trace or copy some of the Maya codex drawings from these pages. Alternatively, you could make up your own Mesoamerican symbols.

5 Paint your tracings or drawings using bright acrylic paints. Using the Maya numbers on this page as a guide, you could add some numbers to your codex, too.

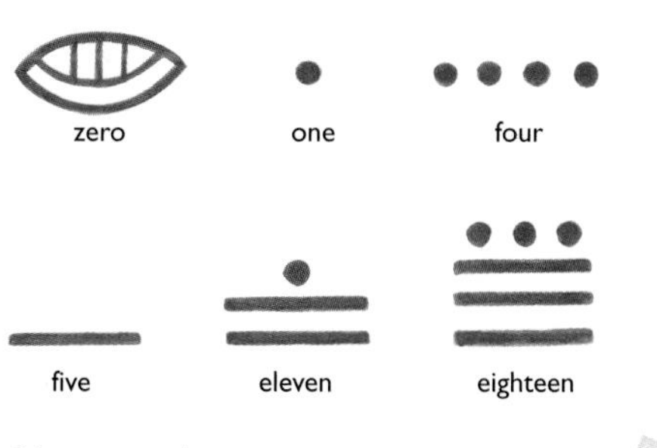

▲ **Maya numbers**
The Maya number system used only three signs – a dot for one, a bar for five, and the shell symbol for zero. Other numbers were made using a combination of these symbols.

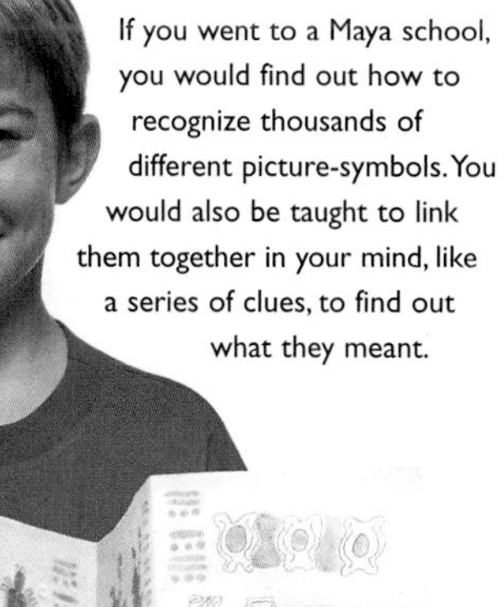

If you went to a Maya school, you would find out how to recognize thousands of different picture-symbols. You would also be taught to link them together in your mind, like a series of clues, to find out what they meant.

Inca quipu

Inca mathematicians used a decimal system (counting in tens). One way of recording numbers and other information was on a quipu. Knots on strings may have represented units, tens, hundreds, thousands, or even tens of thousands. To help with their arithmetic, people also placed pebbles or grains of maize in counting frames.

The Incas worked out calendars of twelve months by observing the Sun, Moon and stars as they moved across the sky. They knew that these movements marked regular changes in the seasons. Inca farmers used the calendar to tell them when to plant crops. Inca priests set up stone pillars outside the city of Cuzco to measure the movements of the Sun.

As in Europe at that time, astronomy, which is the study of the stars, was linked with astrology, which is the belief that the stars and planets influence human lives. Incas saw the night sky as being lit up by mythical characters. On dark nights, Inca priests looked for the band of stars that we call the Milky Way. They called it Mayu (Heavenly River), and thought its shape mirrored that of the Inca Empire.

▲ Star gazer
An Inca astrologer observes the position of the Sun. He is using a quipu. The Incas believed that careful watching of the stars and planets revealed their influence on our lives. They named one constellation (star pattern) the Llama. It was believed that it influenced llamas and those who herded them.

YOU WILL NEED

Waste paper, rope and string of various thicknesses, long ruler or tape measure, scissors, acrylic paints, paintbrush, water pot, 90cm/3ft length of thick rope.

1 Cut the rope and string into 15 lengths, each measuring between 15cm/6in and 80cm/31½in. Paint them in bright colours, such as red, yellow and green. Leave them to dry.

2 To make the top part of the quipu, take another piece of thick rope, measuring about 90cm/3ft in length. Tie a firm knot at each end of the rope, as shown above.

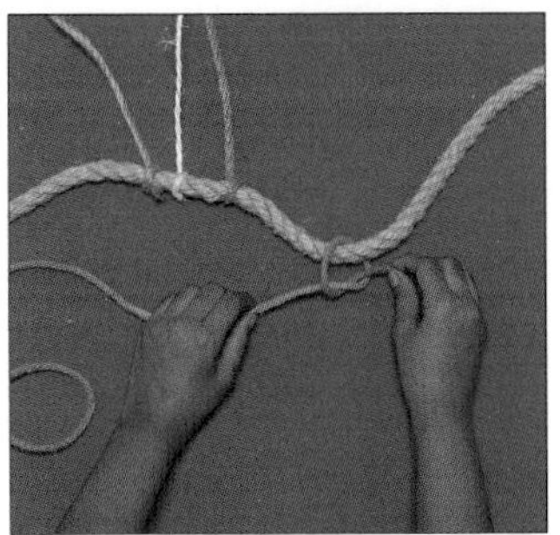

3 Next, take some thinner pieces of rope or string of various lengths and colours. Tie each one along the thicker piece of rope, so that they hang down on the same side.

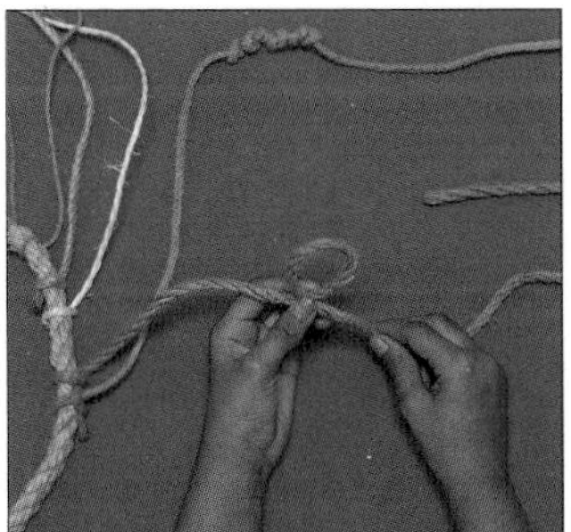

4 Tie knots in the thinner pieces of rope or string. One kind of knot that you might like to try begins by making a loop of rope, as shown in the picture above.

5 Pass one end of the rope through the loop. Pull the rope taut, but do not let go of the loop. Repeat this step until you have made a long knot. Pull the knot tight.

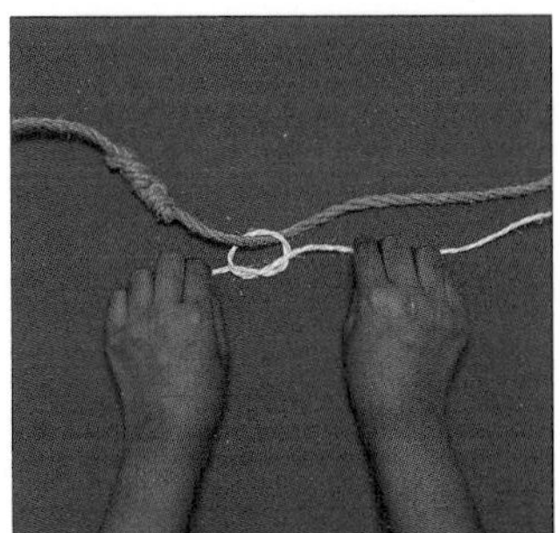

6 Make different sizes of knots on all the ropes and strings. Each knot could represent a family member, school lesson or other important detail of your life.

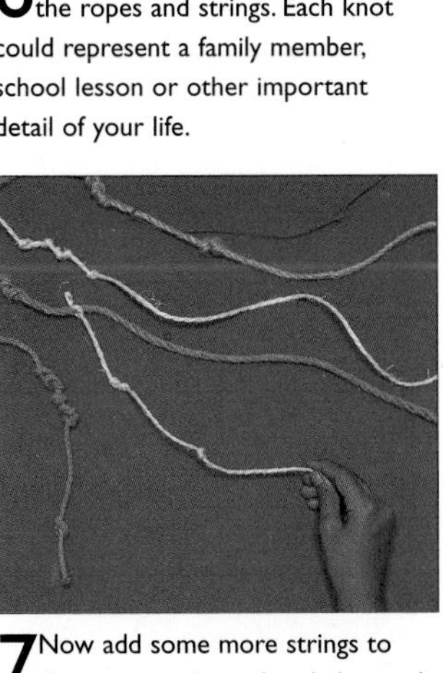

7 Now add some more strings to the ones you have already knotted. Your quipu may be seen by a lot of people, but only you will know what the ropes, strings and knots mean.

Vast amounts of information could be stored on a quipu. The quipu was rather like an Inca version of the computer. Learning how to use the quipu and distinguish the code of colours, knots and major and minor strings took many years.

Illuminating letters

Before a way of printing words was invented in the late 1400s, the only way to have more than one copy of a book was to write it out again by hand. This was a time-consuming process, and made books very valuable and rare. The pages were often beautifully illustrated with decorated letters like the one in this project. In Christian countries, many noble households had only one book – the Bible. Most books were kept in monastery libraries. In the 1500s, the only people who could read and write well were usually monks, priests or nuns. Kings and queens were also well educated.

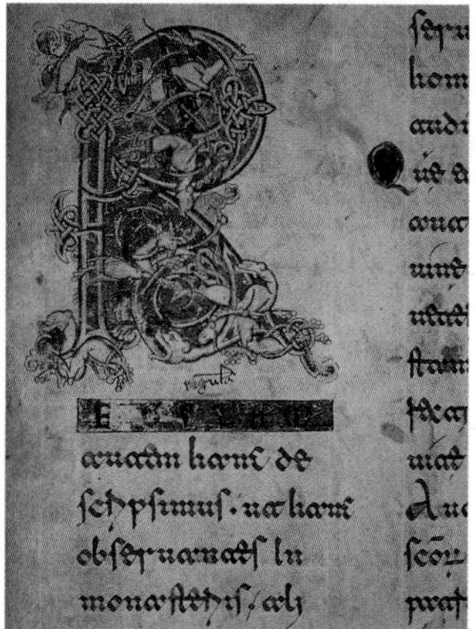

▲ **Lasting letters**
Many books were written on parchment, which lasted longer than paper.

YOU WILL NEED

Pair of compasses, pencil, ruler, 16 x 16cm/6¼ x 6¼in white art paper, eraser, acrylic paints, fine-tipped artist's paintbrushes, water pot, scissors, gold paint, white glue and glue brush, 26 x 26cm/10¼ x 10¼in richly coloured mounting card.

1 Set your compasses to a radius of 6cm/2½in. Place the point at the centre of the white art paper, and carefully draw a 12cm/4½in-diameter circle, as shown above.

2 Keep the compasses at the same radius. Place the point 2cm/¾in away from the centre of the first circle. Then draw a second circle, so that it overlaps with the first.

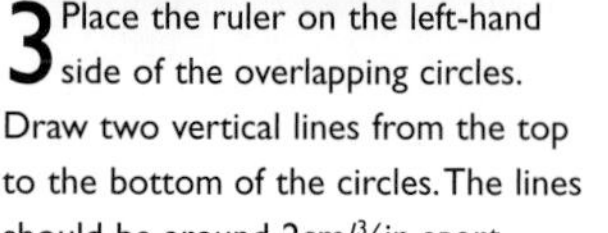

3 Place the ruler on the left-hand side of the overlapping circles. Draw two vertical lines from the top to the bottom of the circles. The lines should be around 2cm/¾in apart.

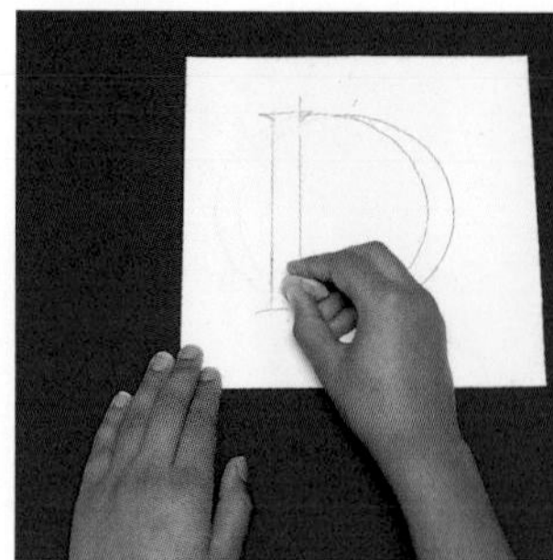

4 Rub out the lines of the circles to the left of the ruled lines. Use the ruler to draw two short lines to cap the top and the bottom of the vertical stem of the letter 'D'.

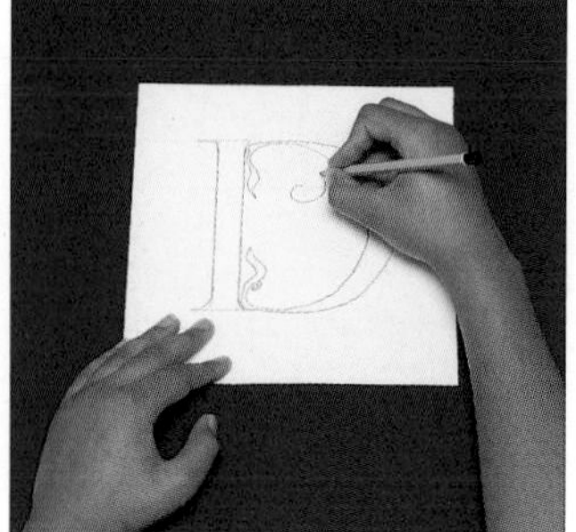

5 Extend the inner curve of the D into two squiggles at the top and bottom of the stem. Draw two simple spirals in the centre of the D, as shown in the picture above.

6 Use the spirals to help you to fill in the rest of your letter design. Double the curving lines to make stems and leaves, and add petals. Look at the picture above as a guide.

7 Draw two lines to the left of the vertical stem of the letter 'D'. Add a squiggle and leaves at the top and bottom, and also some decorative kinks, as shown above.

8 Use a pencil and ruler to draw a border around the letter about 1.5cm/⅝in wide. Leave the right-hand side until last. See how the curve of the D tips out of the border.

9 First paint the border using a bright colour. Carefully fill in the whole design using other colours. Make sure that each colour is dry before you fill in the next one.

10 When the paint is dry, use a ruler and scissors to trim the whole artwork to a 15cm/6in square. Then colour in the gold background. Leave it to dry on a flat surface.

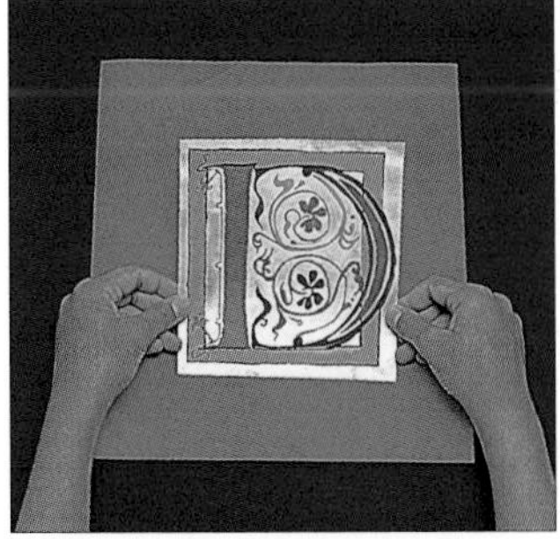

11 Spread white glue over the back surface of the artwork. Then carefully place it squarely in the centre of the mounting card, to add a richly coloured border to the letter.

In days gone by, there was lots to do before work could start. Animal skins were soaked, scraped and dried to make parchment. Feathers were sharpened into quills, and inks were mixed. Take time to draw and paint your illuminated letter. Monks and scribes were fast workers, but they still only managed to do two or three drawings a day. A mistake meant that the scribe would have to start again.

Pirate map

The area chosen for this map is the Spanish Main, which was a hotbed of pirates from the 1620s to the 1720s. When the Spanish first explored the Americas in the late 1400s, much of the surface of the Earth was unmapped territory. Consequently, many countries sent out naval expeditions to draw up detailed charts of distant waters for use by their trading ships. Most pirates had to make do with jotting down the details of the islands, coral reefs, coastlines and river mouths as they sailed by. Sometimes the pirates were lucky enough to capture a ship with up-to-date charts. Bound volumes of detailed nautical charts, known as waggoners, were a valuable prize for any pirate captain. When sailing into an unknown harbour, ships had to take a local guide or pilot on board – at the point of a sword, if necessary.

YOU WILL NEED

Thick art paper, ruler, pencil, scissors, strong black tea left to cool, paintbrush, fine black felt-tipped pen, eraser, colouring pencils, large and small bottle tops.

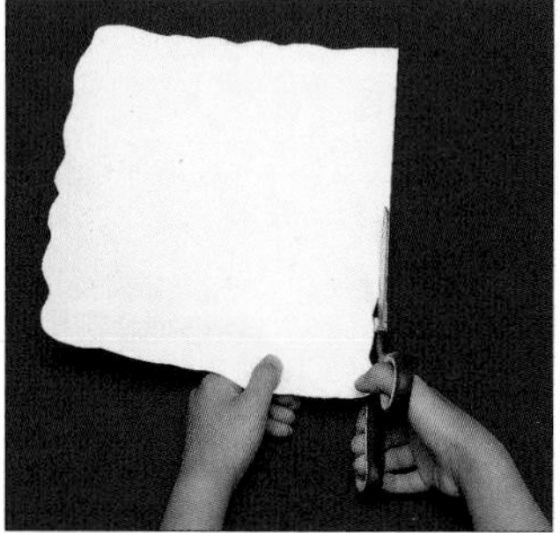

1 Measure a rectangle on the paper, 35 x 27cm/14 x 10½in. Cut it out, making the edges of the rectangle wavy and uneven to give the map an authentic aged and worn appearance.

2 Scrunch up the paper rectangle tightly into a ball. Then open and smooth it out on a flat surface. The creases will remain in the paper, giving the final map a used look.

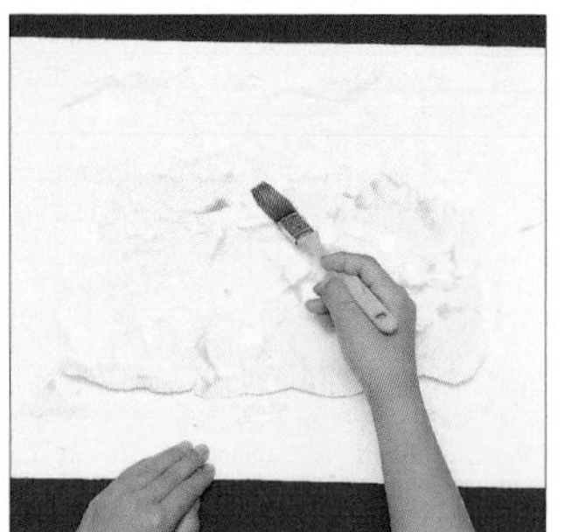

3 Paint cold, strong tea on to the scrunched-up paper. The tea will stain the paper brown to look like old, worn parchment. Then leave the paper until it is completely dry.

4 Smooth out the paper again. Stain the edges darker by brushing on more tea all the way around, from the outside inwards. Leave the paper to dry completely.

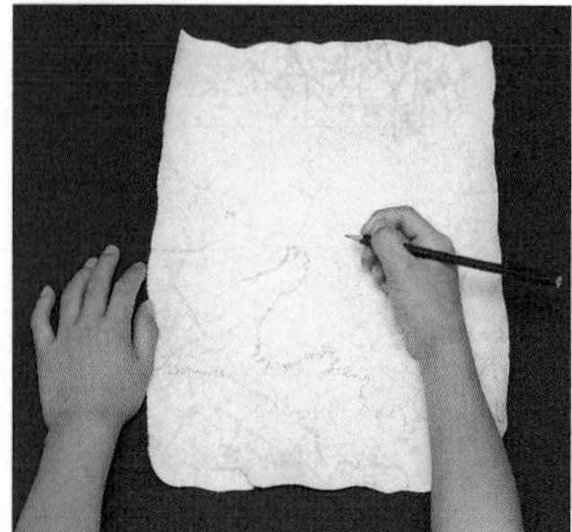

5 Copy the coastline from the finished map in Step 12, using your pencil. If you prefer, you could make up your own map, or trace a map from another book and use that instead.

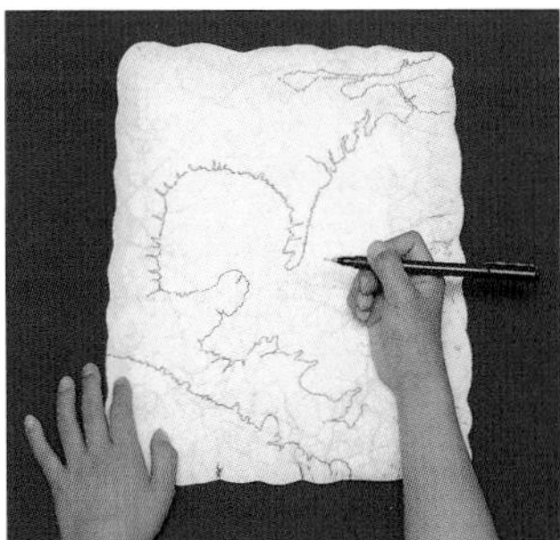

6 Carefully draw over the coastline with your fine black felt-tipped pen. Make sure that you do not smudge the ink with your hand. Rub out the pencil lines with an eraser.

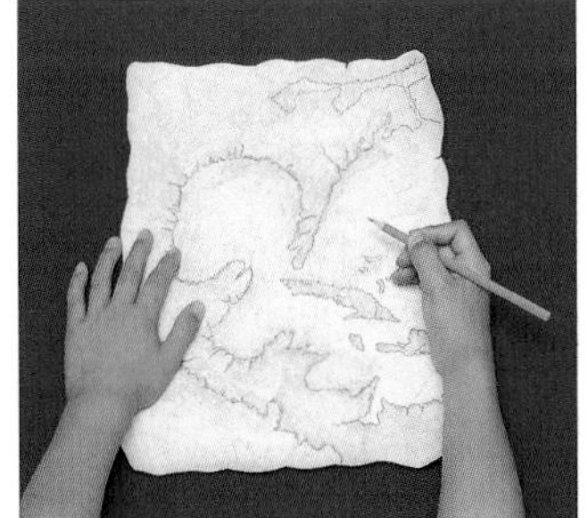

7 Colour the land green and the sea blue with your pencils. Graduate the colours, making them a little darker along the coastline, and then fading inland or out to sea.

8 Choose three landmarks, such as bays or headlands. Use the pencil and ruler to draw lines from the landmarks to a spot in the sea. This will mark your ship's position.

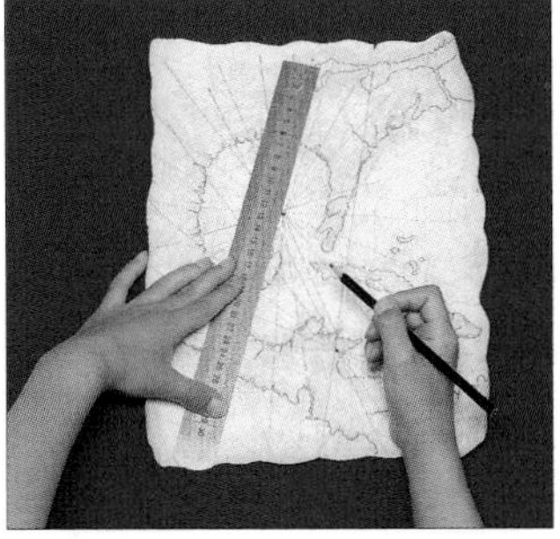

9 Use the ruler and a black pencil to draw straight lines across this position, or co-ordinate, as shown above. The resulting lines will look like the spokes of a wheel.

10 Draw around the large bottle top to make a circle on part of the map. Then draw an inner circle with the small bottle top to make a compass shape, as shown above.

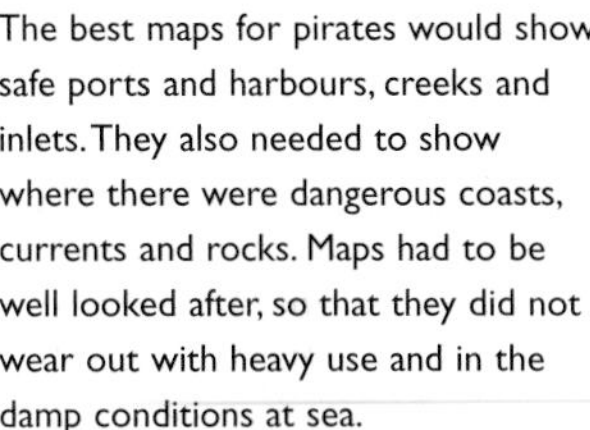

The best maps for pirates would show safe ports and harbours, creeks and inlets. They also needed to show where there were dangerous coasts, currents and rocks. Maps had to be well looked after, so that they did not wear out with heavy use and in the damp conditions at sea.

11 Draw small, elongated triangles pointing outwards from the inner circle along the co-ordinate lines. Use bright colouring pencils to fill in the triangles on the compass.

12 You can add more decorative details, such as arrow points on the compass, dolphins in the sea and treasure chests on the land. Your pirate map will then be complete.

Transport

People have often had to travel long distances for basic needs such as building materials, food and water. At first, everything had to be carried on foot, but the task was made much easier with the domestication of animals such as oxen and horses. These animals could be used to transport people and their goods. The invention of the wheel and boats also revolutionized transport. Early vehicles, such as carts and sailing boats, enabled people to travel much greater distances across land and by sea. Heavy loads could be transported much more quickly, too.

▲ Speed boat
An Arctic hunter paddles his kayak. Sea kayaks were used to hunt sea mammals such as seals and walruses. These sleek, light one-person vessels were powered and steered by a double-bladed paddle. The design was so successful that kayaks are still used today.

▲ Riding without stirrups
Celtic leader Vercingetorix, seen here mounted on his horse. Big, strong horses were introduced into western Europe from the lands east of the Black Sea. These mounts gave Celtic hunters and warriors a great advantage over their enemies.

◂ Camel caravan
Arab merchants blazed new trails across the deserts. They traded in luxuries such as precious metals, gemstones and incense. The trading group, with its processions of camels, is known as a caravan. Camels are well suited to life in the desert. They have enlarged, flexible foot pads, which help to spread their weight across the soft desert sand. Camels also have one or two humps on their backs, which contain fat and act as a food reserve.

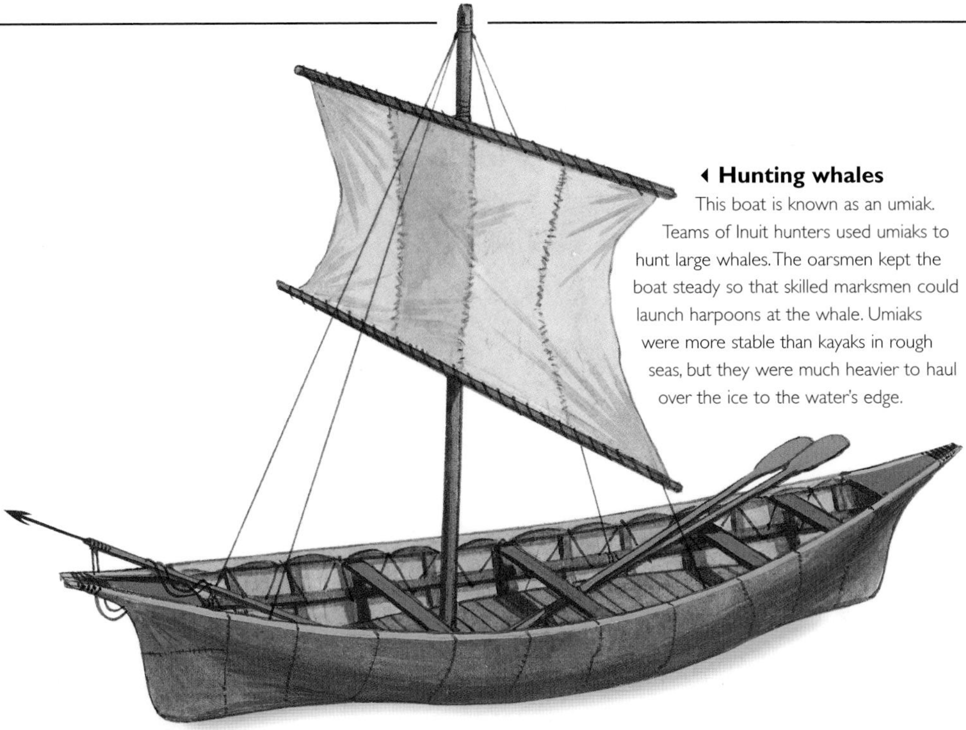

◂ Hunting whales

This boat is known as an umiak. Teams of Inuit hunters used umiaks to hunt large whales. The oarsmen kept the boat steady so that skilled marksmen could launch harpoons at the whale. Umiaks were more stable than kayaks in rough seas, but they were much heavier to haul over the ice to the water's edge.

▾ Icemobile

A modern-day Inuit of the Arctic drives his scooter across the ice and snow. Scooters have largely replaced the traditional sledges pulled by dogs. For most present-day Arctic people, life is a mix of ancient and modern ways. Many Arctic groups use the new technologies of the developed world while holding on to the traditions and culture of their ancestors.

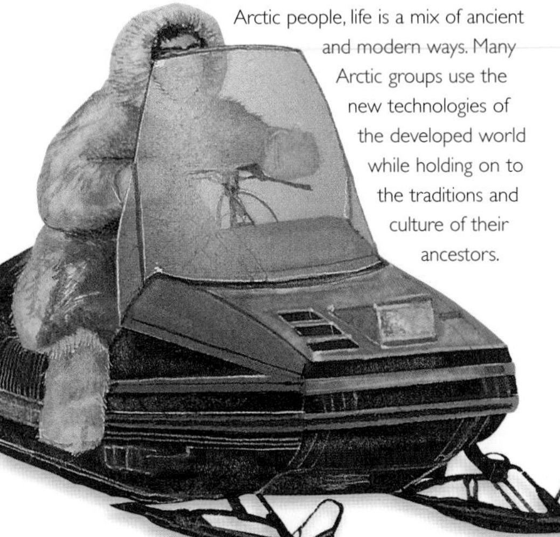

▴ High and mighty

A Mayan nobleman is carried in a portable bed known as a litter. This one is made from the hide of a wildcat called the jaguar. Spanish travellers reported that the Aztec emperor was carried in a litter, too. Blankets were also spread in front of the emperor as he walked, to stop his feet touching the ground.

Sumerian coracle

The ancient region of Mesopotamia was situated on the Tigris and Euphrates rivers and their tributaries. The rivers formed a vital transport and communications network around the country. The Sumerians lived in the south of Mesopotamia around 6,000 years ago. Later on, the land in north Mesopotamia became known as Assyria. The boat in this project is modelled on a Sumerian coracle. These boats were made from leather stretched over a wooden frame.

YOU WILL NEED

Self-hardening clay, wooden board, ruler, toothpick, paper, acrylic paints, paintbrush, water pot, piece of dowel measuring about 20cm/8in long, white glue and glue brush, water-based varnish and brush, string, scissors.

◂ Rowing the boat
The Phoenicians lived by the Mediterranean Sea to the west of Mesopotamia. They were the great sailors and shipbuilders of the time. Their ships were large and many-oared, and the sailors worked out how to navigate using the stars.

▴ Built on the banks
The ancient city of Nimrud, on the banks of the River Tigris, was part of the Assyrian Empire. Archaeologists have found the remains of several palaces and temples here.

1 Make a dish shape using the self-hardening clay. It should be about 14cm/5½in long, 11cm/4¼in wide and 4cm/1½in deep. Make a mast hole for the dowel mast. Attach it to the base.

2 Trim the excess clay around the top of the boat to smooth it out. Use a toothpick to make four small holes through the sides of the boat. Let the clay dry out completely.

3 When it is dry, paint the boat a light brown base colour. Cover the work surface with paper. Then use a brush and your fingers to flick contrast colours and create a mottled effect.

4 Put a drop of glue inside the mast hole. Put more glue around the end of the dowel mast, and then push it into the hole. The mast should stand upright in the centre of the clay boat.

5 Wait until the glue has dried and the mast stands firm. Then paint a layer of water-based varnish all over your boat. Let the first layer dry, and then paint another layer over it.

6 Take two lengths of string about 60cm/24in long. Tie the end of one piece through one of the holes you made earlier, around the top of the mast and into the opposite hole.

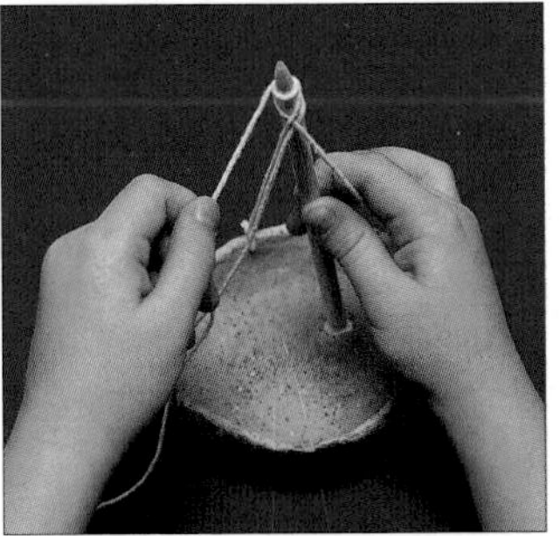

7 Complete the rigging of the boat by tying the other piece of string through the empty holes and around the top of the mast as before. Trim off the excess string.

Coracles, such as the one you have made, had a mast for a light sail. It was probably steered using oars or a punt pole. Small boats such as these are still used today on the River Euphrates.

Assyrian chariot

The wooden wheel was first used as a means of transport around 5,500 years ago in what is now the Middle East, and the news spread fast in neighbouring regions. In Sumerian times (3000–2000BC), wild asses hauled chariots, while oxen and mules were used for heavy loads. By about 900BC, the time of the Assyrian Empire, spoked wheels had replaced the earlier wheels made from a single piece of solid wood.

Roads varied in quality through the Assyrian Empire. Local paths were little more than tracks, but there were good roads between the main towns. These were well maintained so that messengers and state officials could reach their destination quickly. The Assyrians also perfected the art of chariot warfare, which gave them a big advantage over enemies who were fighting on foot. They could attack their enemies from above, and were able to move around the battlefield quickly.

▲ Unstoppable warriors
Chariots were mainly used by Assyrian kings and their courtiers when hunting and in battle. At rivers, the chariots were dismantled and carried across on boats, and people swam across using inflated animal skins as life belts.

▲ Wheeled procession
This artist's impression of a Sumerian funeral procession shows the solid wood wheel design of the early chariots in Mesopotamia. Rituals involving death and burial were an important part of Sumerian life.

▲ Education of a prince
Learning to drive a chariot and fight in battle were part of King Ashurbanipal's education as crown prince of Assyria. He was also taught foreign languages, and how to ride a horse and hunt.

YOU WILL NEED

Thick card, pair of compasses, ruler, pencil, scissors, pen, masking tape, newspaper, two card tubes, flour and water (for papier mâché), cream and brown acrylic paints, paintbrush, water pot, two pieces of dowel measuring 16cm/6¼in long, needle, four toothpicks.

1 Measure and cut out four card circles, each one 7cm/2¾in in diameter. Carefully use the scissors to make a hole in the centre of each circle. Enlarge the holes with a pen.

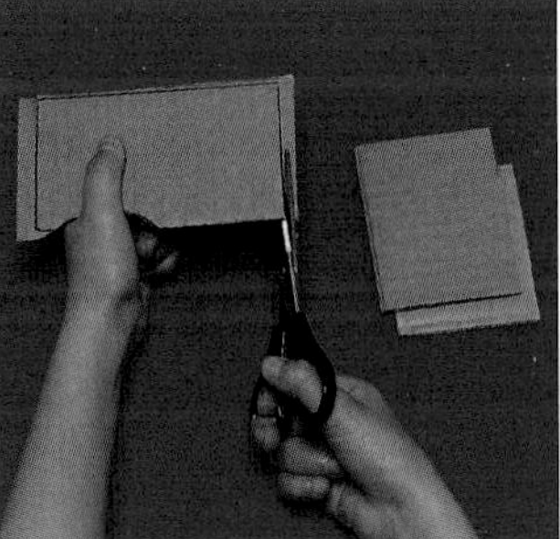

2 Cut out two sides, 12cm/4½in long and 7.5cm/3in wide, as shown, one back 9 x 7.5cm/3½ x 3in, one front 15 x 9cm/6 x 3½in, one top 9 x 7cm/3½ x 2¾in and one base 12 x 9cm/4½ x 3½in.

3 Trim the top of the front to two curves, as shown above. Stick the side pieces to the front and back using masking tape. Then stick on the base and the top of the chariot.

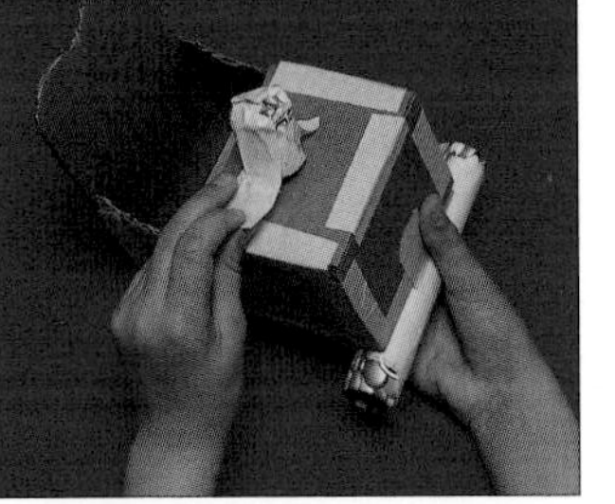

4 Roll up a piece of old newspaper to make a cylinder shape about 2.5cm/1in long and tape it to the chariot, as shown above. Attach the card tubes to the bottom of the chariot.

5 Mix a paste of flour and water. Dip newspaper strips into the paste to make papier mâché. Cover the chariot with layers of papier mâché until the card underneath is hidden. Let it all dry.

6 Paint the chariot. Use a needle to make a hole at each end of a piece of dowel. Insert a toothpick, add a wheel and insert into the tube. Secure another wheel at the other end. Repeat.

The solid-wheeled chariot you have made is based on a very early chariot design made in northern Mesopotamia around 4,000 years ago. When the spoked wheel replaced the solid wheel, chariots became lighter, faster and easier to steer.

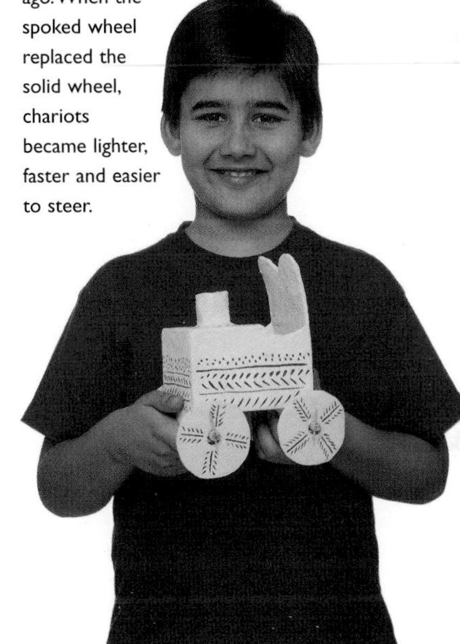

Chinese sampan

From early in China's history, its rivers, lakes and canals were its main highways. Fisherfolk propelled small wooden boats across the water with a single oar or pole at the stern. These were often roofed with mats, like the sampans still seen today. Large wooden sailing ships, which we call junks, sailed the open ocean. They were either keeled or flat-bottomed, with a high stern and square bows. Their sails were made of matting stiffened with strips of bamboo.

▲ Trading places

The map shows the extent of the Chinese Empire during the Ming Dynasty (1368–1644). Merchants transported luxury Chinese goods along the Silk Road, from Chang'an (Xian) to the Mediterranean Sea. Chinese traders also sailed across the South China Sea to Vietnam, Korea and Japan.

▼ Templates

Cut templates B, C, D and G from thick card. Cut templates A, E and F from thin card.

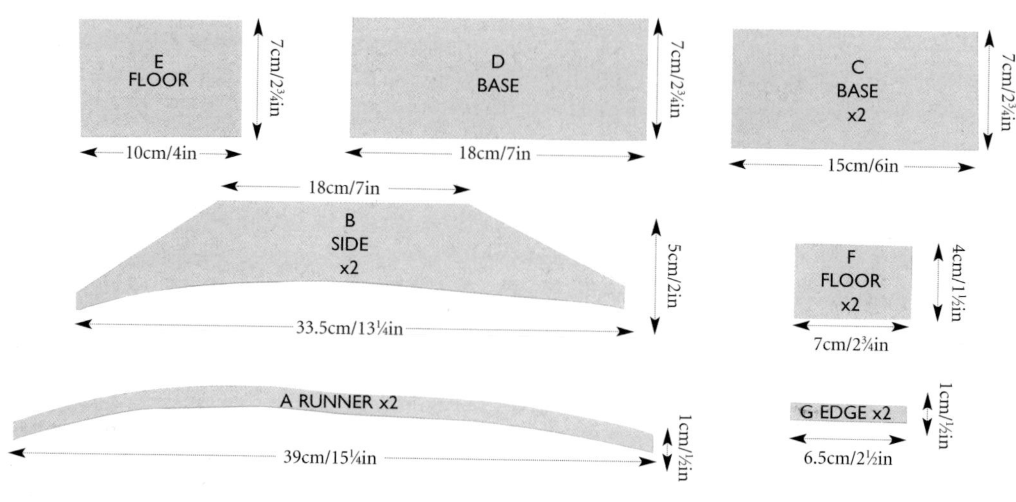

YOU WILL NEED
Thick card, thin card, ruler, pencil, scissors, white glue and glue brush, masking tape, seven wooden barbecue sticks, string, thin yellow paper, acrylic paints (black and dark brown), paintbrush and water pot.

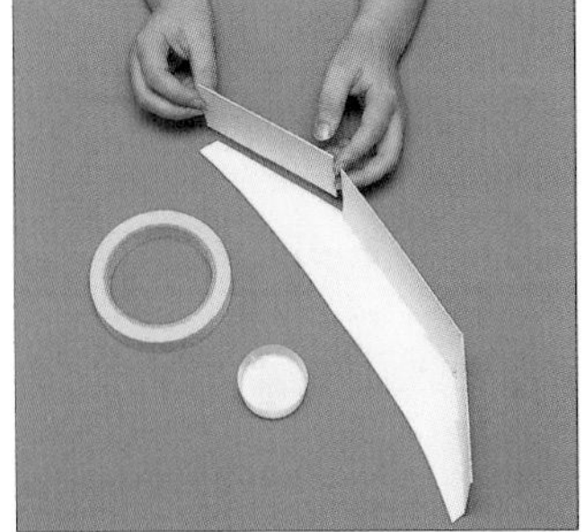

1 Glue base templates C and D to side template B, as shown. Hold the pieces together with strips of masking tape while the glue dries. When dry, remove the masking tape.

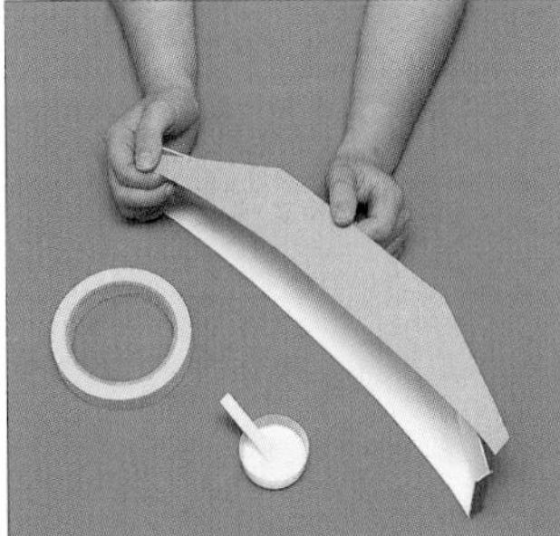

2 Glue the remaining side B to the boat. Stick the runner A pieces to the top of the sides and secure with masking tape. Make sure the ends jut out at the front and back of the boat.

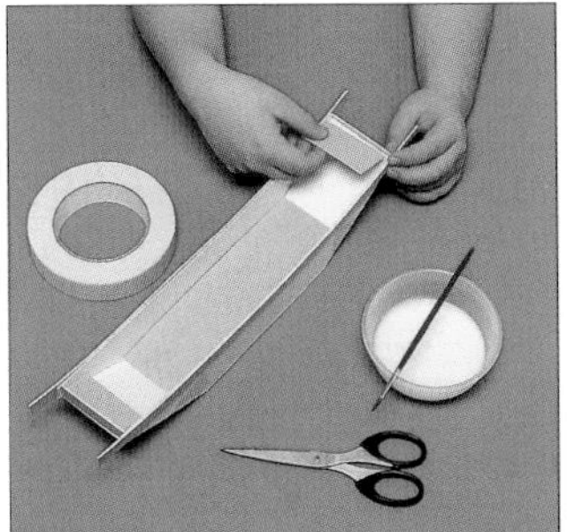

3 Glue floor E to the centre of the base. Add the floor F templates to the ends of the base. Stick the edge G templates in between the edge of the runners, and leave to dry.

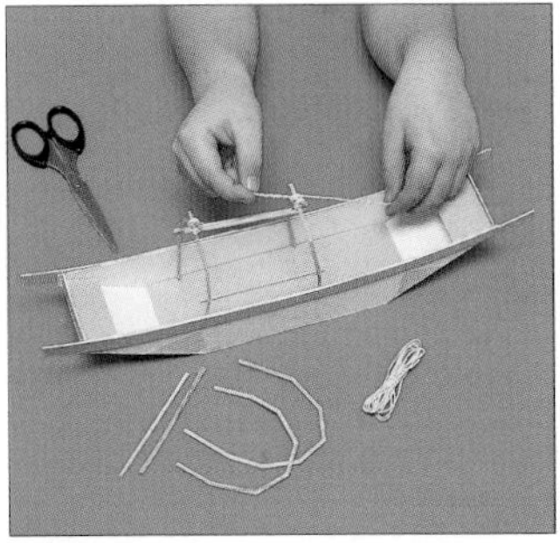

4 Bend two barbecue sticks into arches. Cut two sticks into struts. Tie struts to the sides and top of the arches. Make a second roof by bending three barbecue sticks into arches.

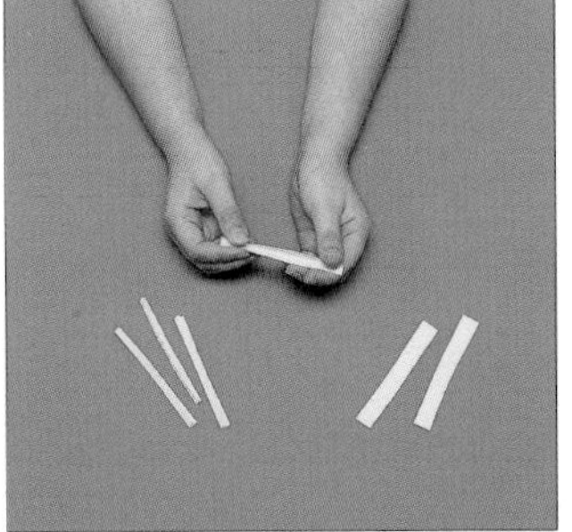

5 Cut the thin yellow paper into strips, each measuring 10 x 1cm/ 4 x ½in. Fold the strips in half, as shown. The strips will make the matting for the two boat roofs.

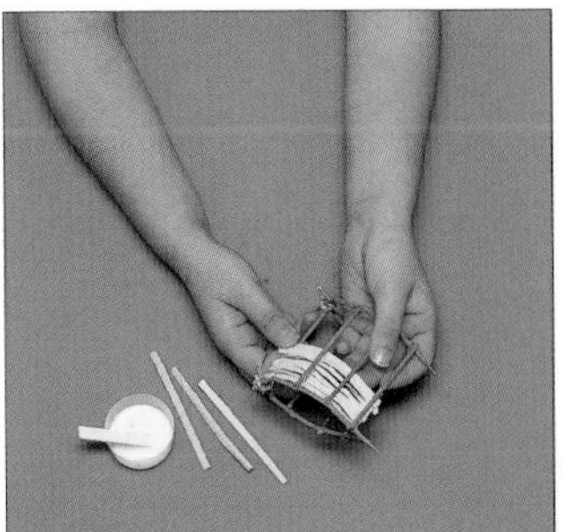

6 Paint the boat and the roof sections and allow them to dry. Glue the roof matting strips to the inside of the roofs. When the glue is dry, place the roofs inside the boat.

To add the finishing touch to your sampan, make a boatman with an oar and rowlock to propel the vessel.

Native American canoe

Many tribes native to North America were nomadic. At first, walking was their only form of transport across the land. Hunting and trade were the main reasons for travelling. Infants were carried in cradleboards, while Inuit babies in the Arctic were put into the hoods of their mothers' parkas. Carrying frames called travois were popular among those living on the Plains. Dogs dragged these frames at first, but horses replaced them in the late 1600s. Tribes could then travel greater distances to fresh hunting grounds.

Much of North America is covered with rivers, streams and lakes, so tribespeople were skilled boatbuilders. They used bark canoes in the woodlands, large cedar canoes on the Northwest Coast, and kayaks in the Arctic.

Arctic Ocean
N
Siberia
Bering Strait
Bering Sea
Alaska
Pacific Ocean
Northwest Coast

▲ **Into America**
The first Native Americans probably came from Siberia. They crossed land bridges at the Bering Strait around 13,000BC.

▼ **Templates**

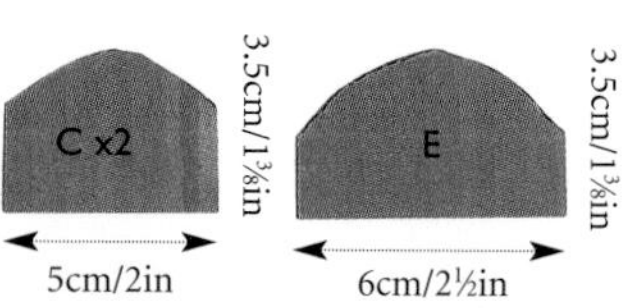

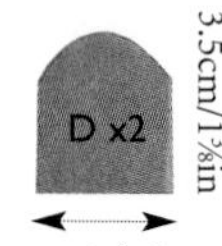

Cut two 42 x 1cm/16½ x ⅜in strips with angled ends and two 45 x 1cm/18 x ⅜in strips.

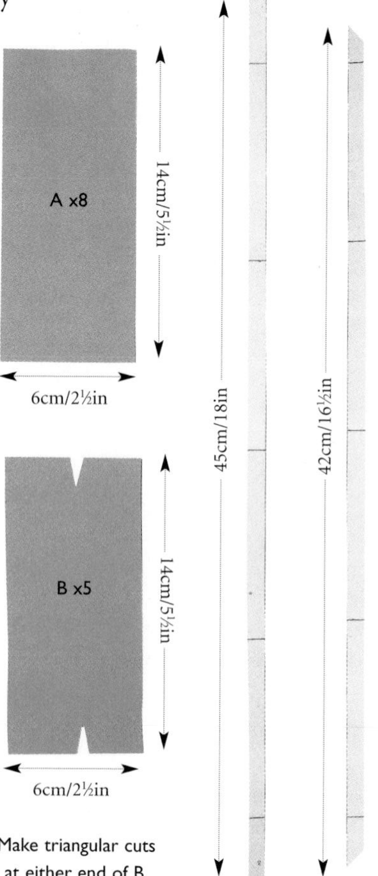

Make triangular cuts at either end of B.

YOU WILL NEED

Thick card (templates C, D and E), brown paper (templates A and B), cream paper (strips), pencil, ruler, scissors, white glue and glue brush, needle and thread, brown acrylic paints, paintbrush, water pot.

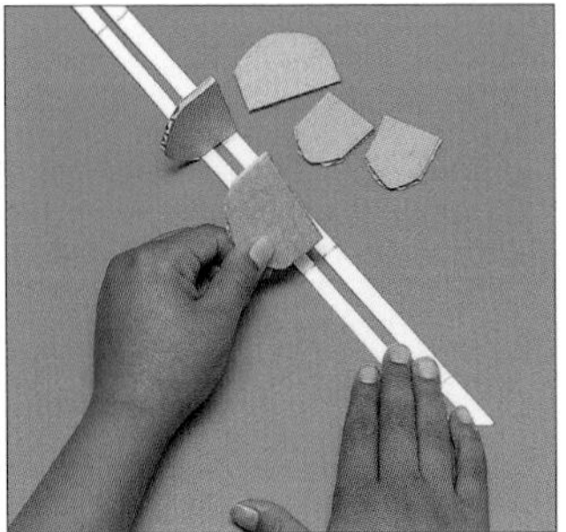

1 Cut out the templates. Starting at the centre, mark five evenly spaced lines on one 45cm/18in strip and one 42cm/16½in strip. Glue the side of the E template across the centres of the strips.

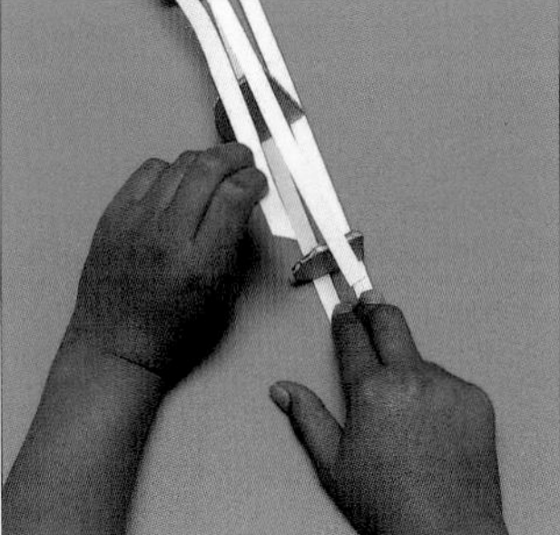

2 Glue the C template either side of the E template, and the D templates either side of those. Line up the other two strips, and glue those to the other sides of the C, D and E templates.

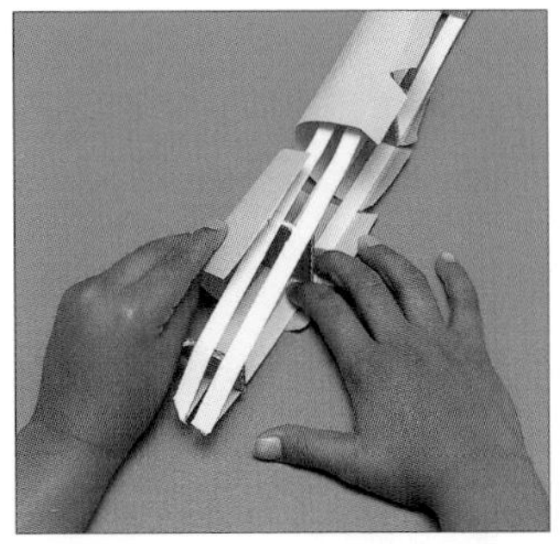

3 Glue the two 45cm/18in strips and the two 42cm/16½in strips at both ends. Glue templates B to the frame, making sure the cuts at either end fit over the C, D and E templates, as shown.

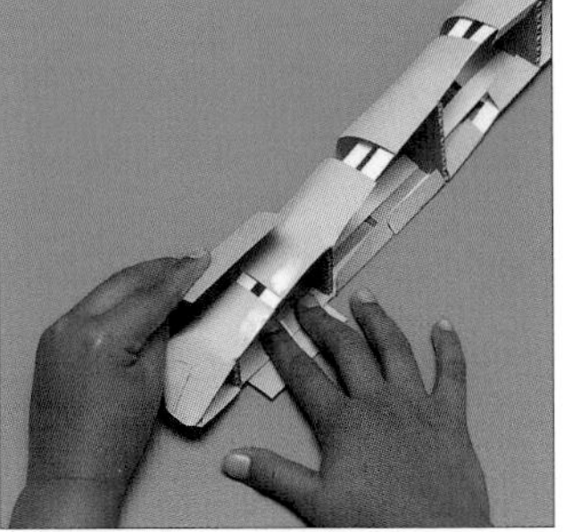

4 Tidy up the ends by gluing the excess paper around the frame of the canoe. Place four A templates over the gaps, and glue them to the top of the frame, as shown above.

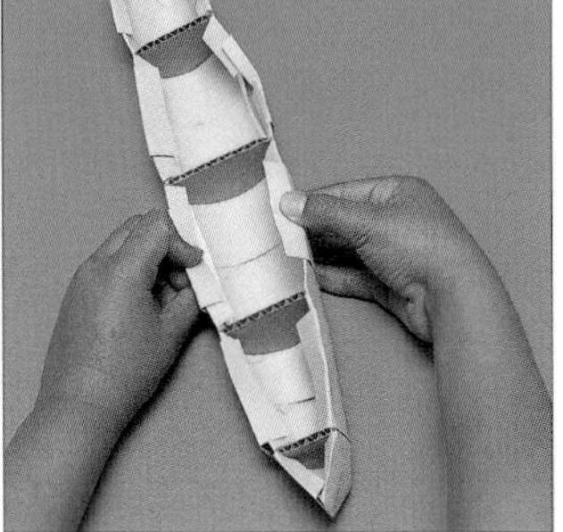

5 Stick the remaining A templates over the inside of the boat, until the entire frame is covered. Carefully fold over and glue the tops of the paper around the top edge of the boat.

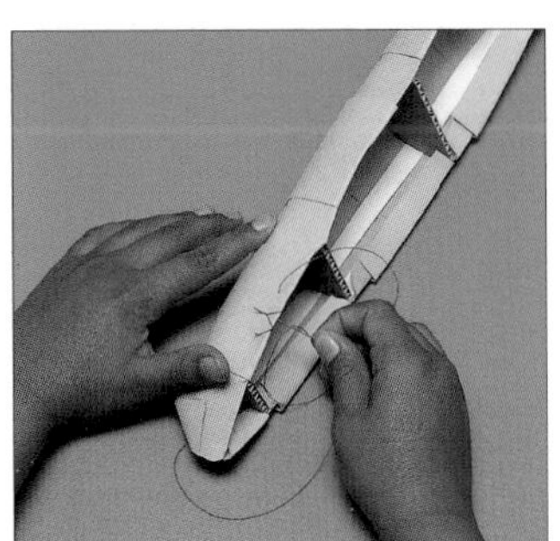

6 Thread the needle. Sew around the top edge of the boat to secure the flaps. Paint your boat brown and add detail. Make two paddles from thick card, and paint them dark brown.

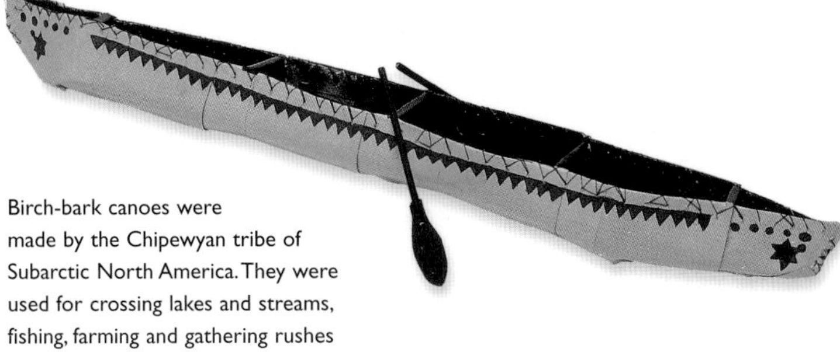

Birch-bark canoes were made by the Chipewyan tribe of Subarctic North America. They were used for crossing lakes and streams, fishing, farming and gathering rushes and wild rice.

Viking longship

The Vikings were excellent seafarers, and were among the most skilful shipbuilders the world has ever seen. One of the most famous Viking vessels was the longship. It could be up to 23m/75ft in length. This long sailing ship was used for ocean voyages and warfare, and it was shallow enough to row up a river. The longship had an open deck without cabins or benches. The rowers sat on hide-covered sea chests that contained their possessions, weapons and food rations.

YOU WILL NEED

Thick card, balsa wood strips and pole, pale and dark brown paper, plain paper, pencil, ruler, scissors, craft knife, acrylic paints (black, brown and red), paintbrush, water pot, white glue and glue brush, masking tape, string.

Templates

Ask an adult to cut out the card and balsa wood templates, following the measurements shown.

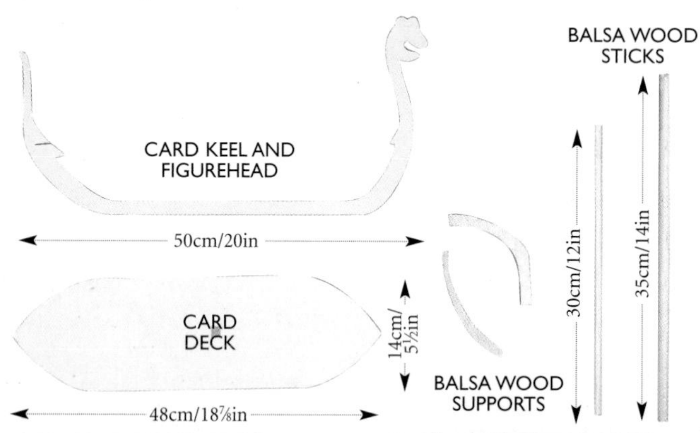

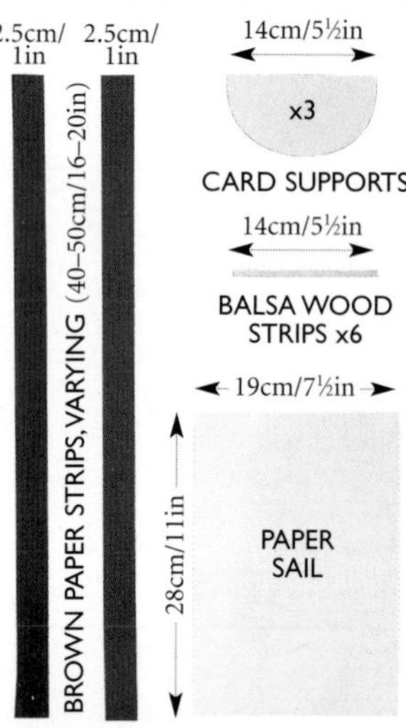

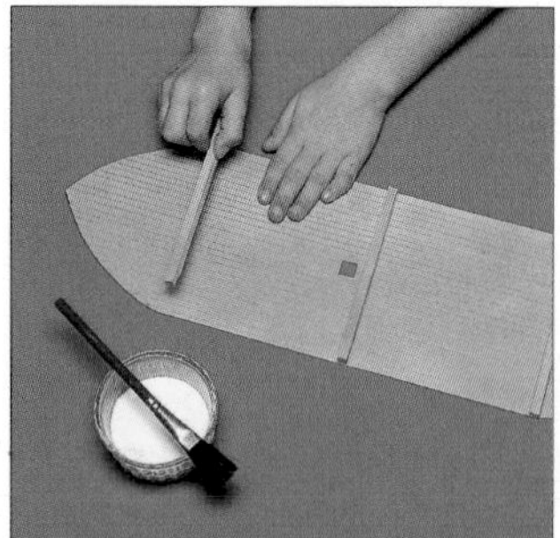

1 Paint the deck black on one side and brown on the other. Use a pencil to mark planks 5mm/¼in apart on the brown deck. Pierce a hole for the mast. Glue on three of the 14cm/5½in balsa strips.

2 Glue three 14cm/5½in balsa wood strips to the other side of the deck as in Step 1, matching them with the planks on the other side. Then glue on the three card supports as crossbeams.

3 Carefully paint one side of the keel and figurehead template, using bright red acrylic paint. Leave it to dry, turn it over and paint the other side of the card using the same colour.

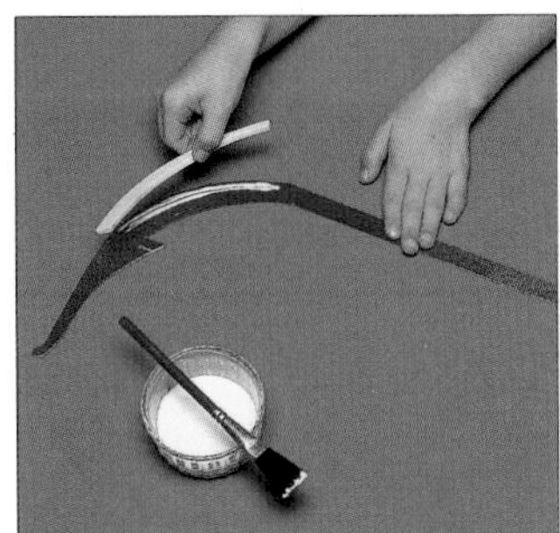

4 When the paint is completely dry, glue the two balsa wood supports either side of the curved parts of the keel, as shown. These will strengthen the keel and figurehead section.

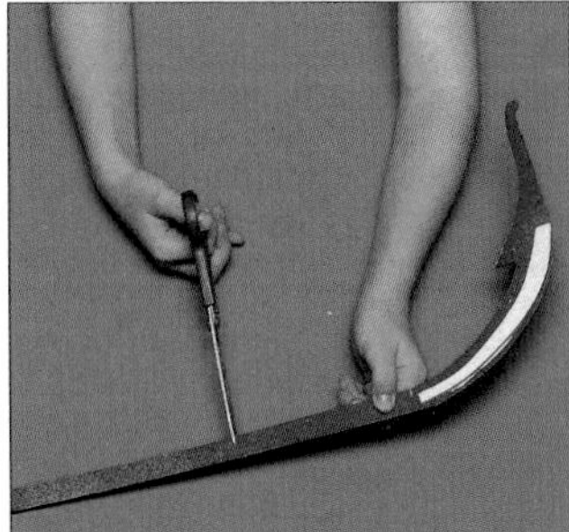

5 When the glue is dry, make three marks along the length of the keel, each one at a point that matches up to the crossbeams of the deck section. Use scissors to cut slots, as shown.

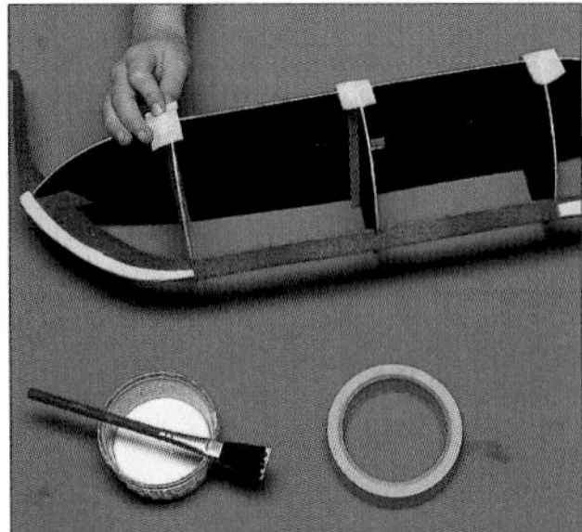

6 Slide the deck crossbeams into position on the keel slots, and glue them in place. Use masking tape to make sure the joins are firm while the glue is drying.

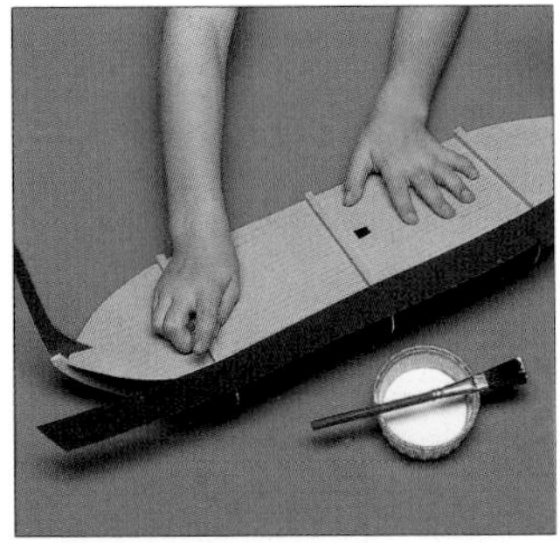

7 Use varying lengths of pale and dark brown paper strips for the planks, or 'strakes', along each side of the keel. Carefully glue each strip into position along each side.

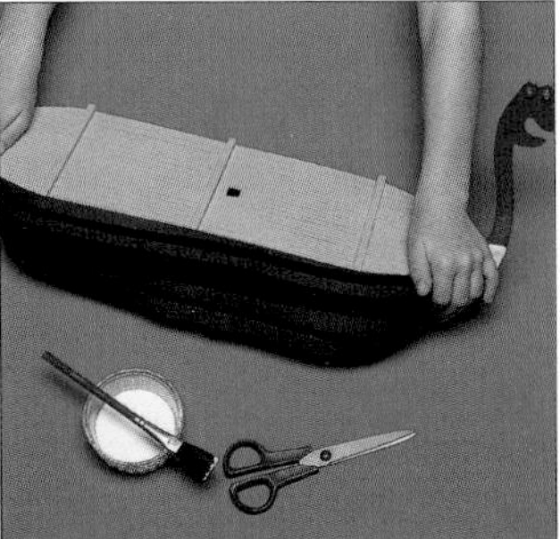

8 Continue gluing the strips into place. Alternate pale and dark brown strips to finish. Trim the excess off each strip as they get lower, so that they form a curve.

9 Make a mast using the 30cm/12in-long balsa wood and the 35cm/14in-long stick. Glue the two pieces firmly together and bind them with string, as shown above.

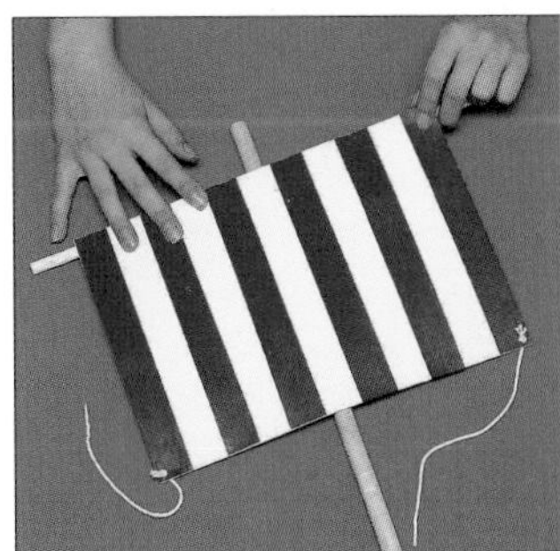

10 Paint the sail with red and white stripes. Glue the sail to the 30cm/12in cross beam. Attach string as rigging at the bottom of the sail. Add card eyes to the dragon on the figurehead.

A longship put to sea with a crew of around 30 fighting men. Each one knew how to fight, as well as how to man the oars. The round shields of the warriors were slotted along the side of the ship. An awning of sailcloth could be erected to keep off the Sun or rain.

Celtic wagon

After around 200BC, the Celts began to build fortified settlements as centres of government, craftwork and trade. Some grew up around existing hill forts or villages; others occupied fresh sites. The Romans called them *oppida* (towns). Some of the oppida were very large. For example, Manching, in southern Germany, covered about 380ha/ 940 acres, and its protective walls were over 7km/4 miles long.

Travel between the settlements was slow and difficult compared with today. There were no paved roads, although the Celts did build causeways of wood across marshy ground. Overland journeys were on foot or horseback, and only the wealthiest chieftains could afford to drive a chariot. The Celts used wooden carts pulled by oxen to transport heavy loads of farm produce, timber or salt. Oxen were very valuable and were the main source of wealth for many farmers.

YOU WILL NEED
White card, pencil, ruler, scissors, felt-tipped pen, white glue and glue brush, balsa wood, masking tape, sandpaper, pair of compasses, drawing pins (thumb tacks), leather thong, silver paint, paintbrush, water pot.

▾ Linking up
European trade routes followed great river valleys or connected small ports along the coast, from Ireland to Portugal. The Celts spread far and wide and, by 200BC, had even attacked and defeated the Romans in various parts of Europe, and had attacked Greece's holy temple of Apollo at Delphi.

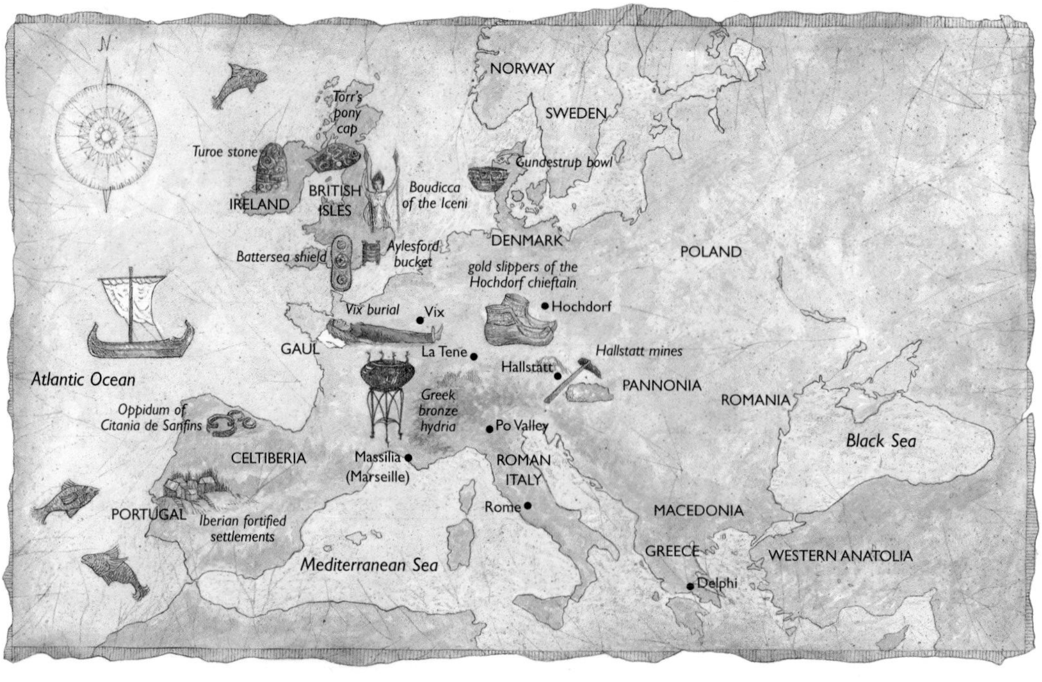

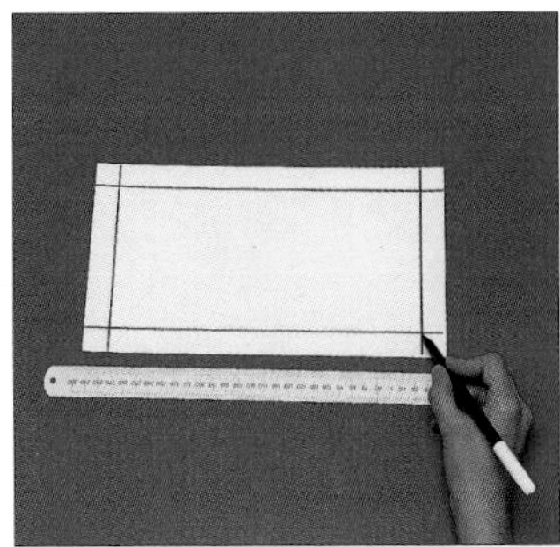

1 Measure and cut out a piece of white card to 29 x 16cm/11½ x 6¼in. Using a ruler and felt-tipped pen, draw lines to make a border 2cm/¾in in from the edges of the card, as shown above.

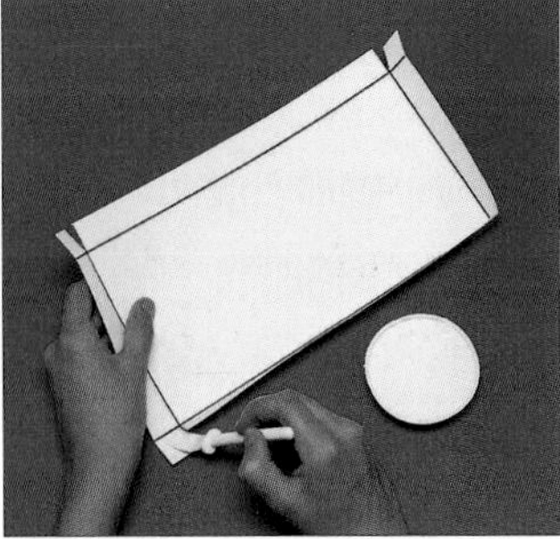

2 Make cuts in the corners of the card, as shown above. Score along each line and then fold the edges up to make a box shape. This will be the body of the wagon.

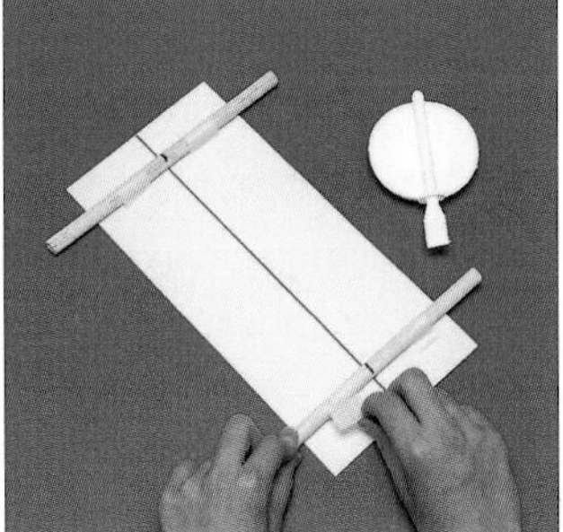

3 Measure and cut out another piece of card to 27 x 12cm/10½ x 4½in. Take two lengths of balsa wood, each 20cm/8in. Glue and tape the balsa across the card 4cm/1½in in from the two ends.

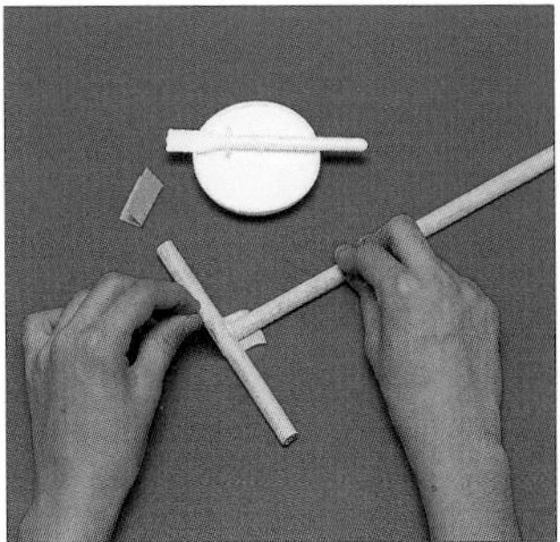

4 Take two sticks of balsa, one 26cm/10¼in long and the other 11cm/4¼in. Sand the end of the long stick to fit against the shorter piece. Glue the pieces together. Secure with tape until dry.

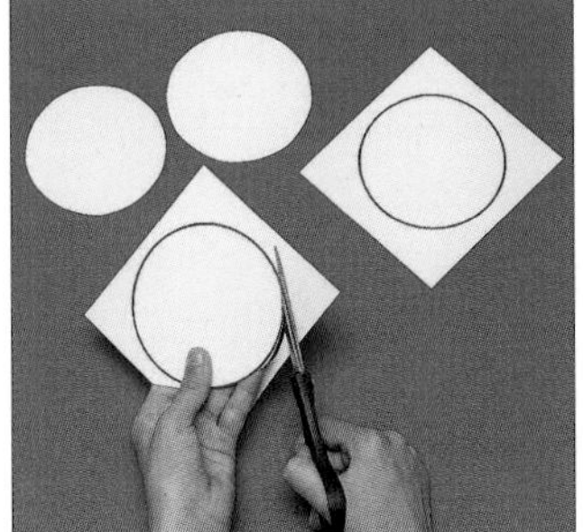

5 Use the compasses to draw four circles on four pieces of card, each measuring 10cm/4in in diameter. Then carefully cut the circles out, as shown above.

6 Glue the wagon body on to the card with balsa attached. Fix the wheels to the balsa wood shafts by pressing a drawing pin through the centre of each wheel.

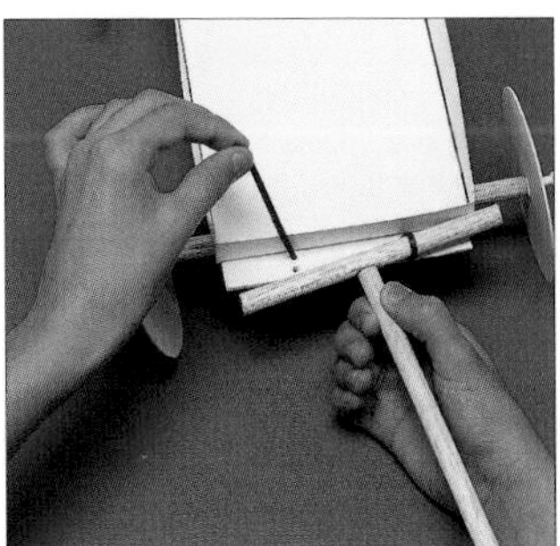

7 Pierce two holes in the front of the wagon. Thread the leather thong through the holes and tie it to the T-shaped steering pole you made in Step 4. Paint the wagon silver.

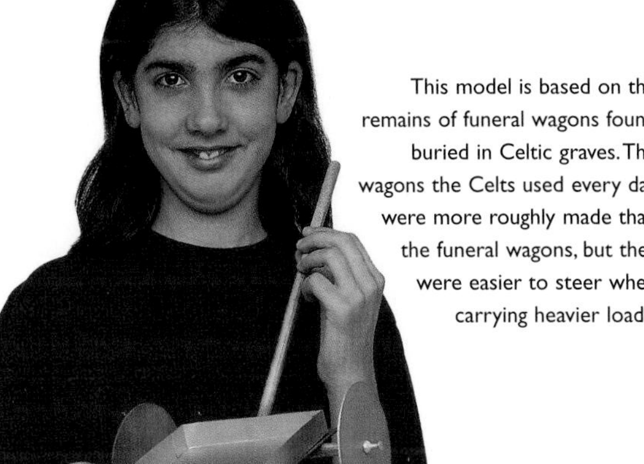

This model is based on the remains of funeral wagons found buried in Celtic graves. The wagons the Celts used every day were more roughly made than the funeral wagons, but they were easier to steer when carrying heavier loads.

Arctic sledge

The surface of the Arctic Ocean is partially frozen throughout the year, and in winter snow covers the land. In the past, sledges were the most common way of travelling over ice and snow. They were made from bone or timber, and lashed together with strips of animal hide or whale sinew. They glided over the snow on runners made from walrus tusks or wood. Arctic sledges had to be light enough to be pulled by animals, yet strong enough to carry an entire family and its belongings. In North America, the Inuit used huskies to pull their sledges. In Siberia and Scandinavia, however, reindeer were used to pull sledges. In ancient times, Arctic peoples often used skis to get around. They were made of wood, and the undersides were covered with strips of reindeer skin. The hairs on the skin pointed backwards, allowing the skier to climb up hills.

▲ Getting around
Today, petrol/gas-driven snowmobiles make for quick and easy travel across the Arctic ice. In the past, Arctic people relied on animals to pull sledges across the frozen landscape.

YOU WILL NEED
Thick card, balsa wood, ruler, pencil, scissors, craft knife, white glue and glue brush, masking tape, pair of compasses, barbecue stick, brown acrylic paint, paintbrush, water pot, string, chamois leather, card box.

▼ Travelling companions
Huskies are well adapted to life in the harsh Arctic cold. Their thick coats keep the animals warm in bitterly cold temperatures as low as –50°C/–122°F, and they can sleep peacefully in the fiercest of blizzards. The snow builds up against their fur and insulates them.

Templates

6.5cm/2⁹⁄₁₆in
A RUNNERS x4
54cm/21¼in

Draw the shapes on card (use balsa wood for template C), and cut them out. Glue two A templates together. Repeat this for the other two A templates. Do the same for all four B templates. Cover all the edges with masking tape.

4cm/1½in
C BASE SLATS x8
18cm/7in

3cm/1³⁄₁₆in
E BACK x1
18cm/7in

18cm/7in
8cm/3⅛in
D BACK SLAT x1

21cm/8½in
8cm/3⅛in
B SIDE x4

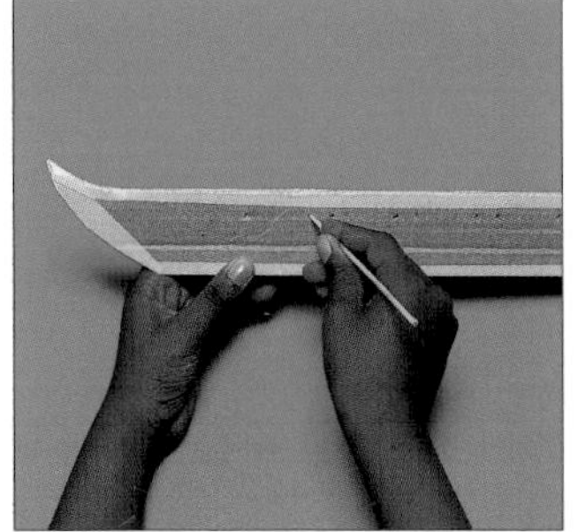

1 Using a small pair of compasses, make small holes along the top edge of the glued A templates. Use the end of a barbecue stick to make the holes a little larger.

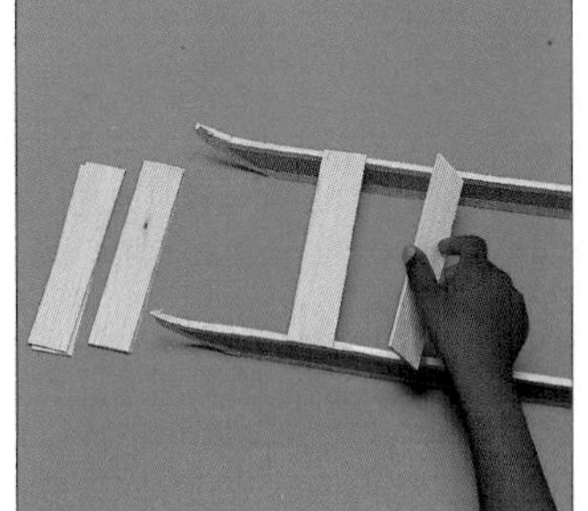

2 Glue the balsa wood slats C in position over the holes along the A templates, as shown above. You will need to use all eight balsa wood slats. Glue back slat D in position.

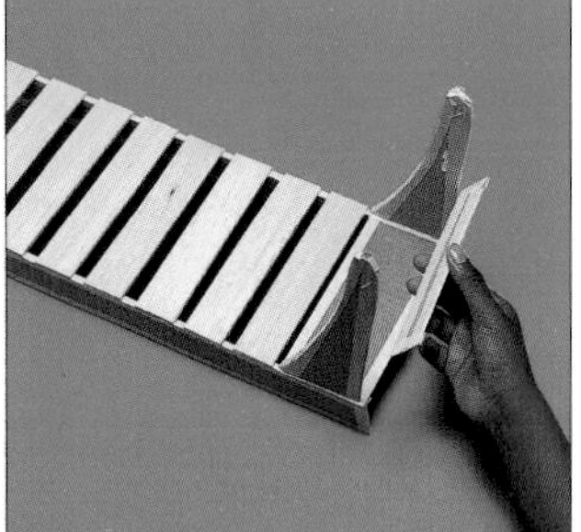

3 Carefully glue the B templates and the E template to the edge of the sledge, as shown above. Allow the glue to dry completely before painting the model sledge.

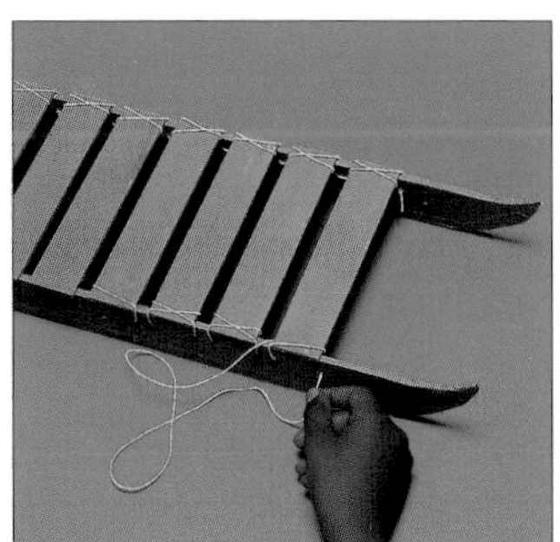

4 Thread lengths of string through the holes to secure the slats on each side. Decorate the sledge with a chamois-covered card box, and secure it to the sledge.

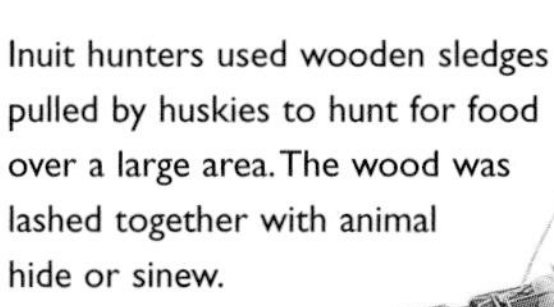

Inuit hunters used wooden sledges pulled by huskies to hunt for food over a large area. The wood was lashed together with animal hide or sinew.

Military Technology

People have always needed to defend themselves or fight for more land. The development of weaponry runs alongside the growth of the earliest civilizations. Weapons were needed, not just for hunting, but for defence and attack. From the very beginning, there were two distinct types of weapon – missiles such as the spear, which could be thrown from a distance, and strike weapons such as the club, which could be used at close quarters. Stone Age people used sharpened flints for daggers and spears. As time passed, these early weapons were eventually replaced by steel swords, heavy artillery and pistols.

▲ War chariot

The Hittites controlled much of Anatolia (modern-day Turkey) and parts of Mesopotamia and Syria. Much of their military success came from their skill as charioteers. Hittite chariots held up to three people – one to drive the horses and two to fight. Hittite charioteers were feared by their enemies.

◂ Light cavalry

The horse of this Persian warrior is not protected by armour, so it needs to be fast and nimble. The warrior carries only a short spear so that he can make a quick strike against the enemy and then retreat.

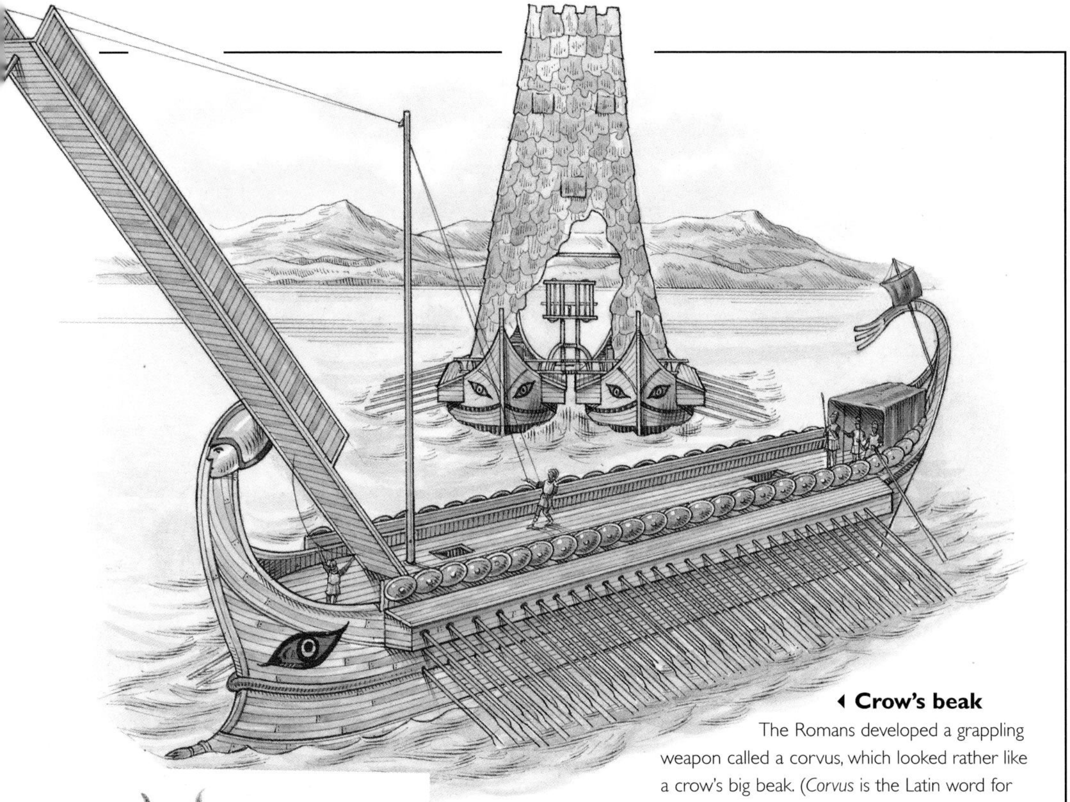

◂ Crow's beak

The Romans developed a grappling weapon called a corvus, which looked rather like a crow's big beak. (*Corvus* is the Latin word for crow.) It was a hinged gangplank with a spike that sank into the enemy ship's deck. Twin-hulled siege vessels carried fighting towers to the enemy.

◂ Warriors of Japan

Japanese warriors were called samurai. They fought with deadly two-handed swords, and were dressed in padded armour and helmets. The armour consisted of bamboo plates sewn on to a padded jacket. Mythical motifs decorated the helmet.

Top-heavy ▸

This Asian soldier carries an array of different weapons – a sword, a dagger, bow and arrows, an axe and a shield. The sword was heavier at the tip, which gave it greater weight when he swung it down on his enemy.

Greek sword and shield

When the Greeks went to war, it was usually to engage in raids and sieges of rival city states. Major battles with foreign powers were rare, but the results could be devastating. Army commanders chose their ground with care, and relied heavily on the discipline and training of their troops. The core of a Greek army consisted of foot soldiers called hoplites. Their strength as a fighting force lay in their bristling spears, singled-edged swords, overlapping shields and sheer weight of numbers.

YOU WILL NEED

String, pencil, pair of compasses, ruler, thick card, scissors, white glue and glue brush, gold paper, silver paper, masking tape, black acrylic paint, paintbrush, water pot, foil.

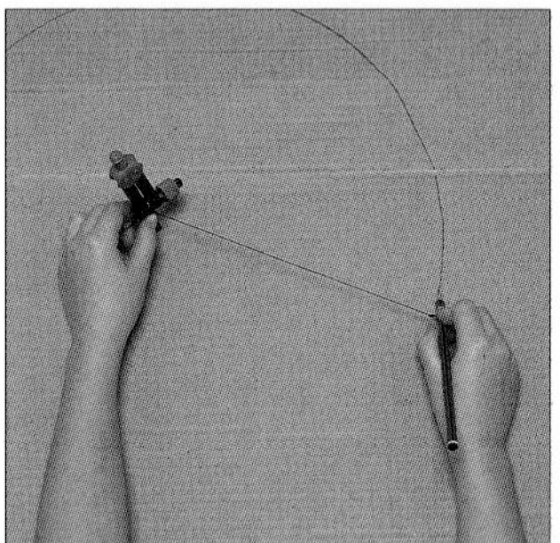

1 Tie a 22cm/8¾in length of string to a pencil and compasses. Draw a circle on to the card, as shown above. Carefully cut around the edge of the circle, using your scissors.

2 Make a cut into the centre of the circle, as shown. Line the edges of the cut with glue. Overlap the edges by 2cm/¾in, and stick them together so that your shield is slightly curved.

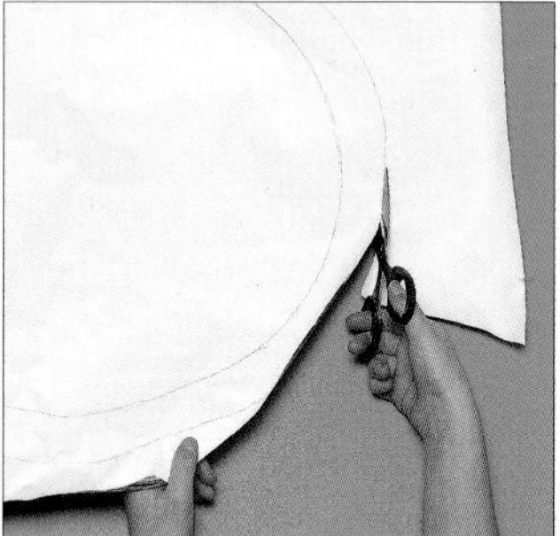

3 Place the card circle on to a piece of gold paper and draw around it. Draw another circle 2cm/¾in larger than the first. Cut out the larger gold circle, as shown above.

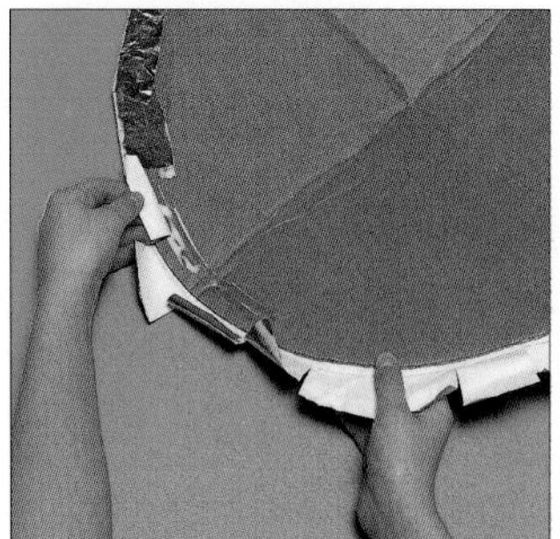

4 Glue the gold circle on to your card circle. Make small cuts along the edges of the gold paper. Fold the edges over the circle, and glue them to the back of the card circle.

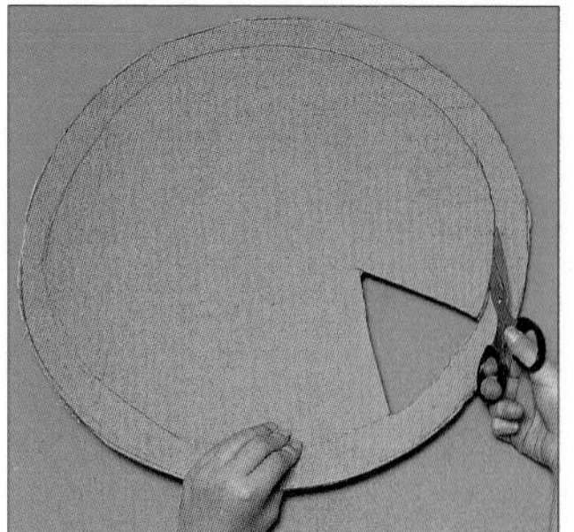

5 Use the string and compasses to draw another 22cm/8¾in circle on to a piece of card. Draw another circle 2cm/¾in smaller than the first. Cut out the inner circle in stages with scissors.

6 Cut through the ring of card in one place, as shown above. Cover the ring with silver paper. Wrap the silver paper around the card, and glue it down securely.

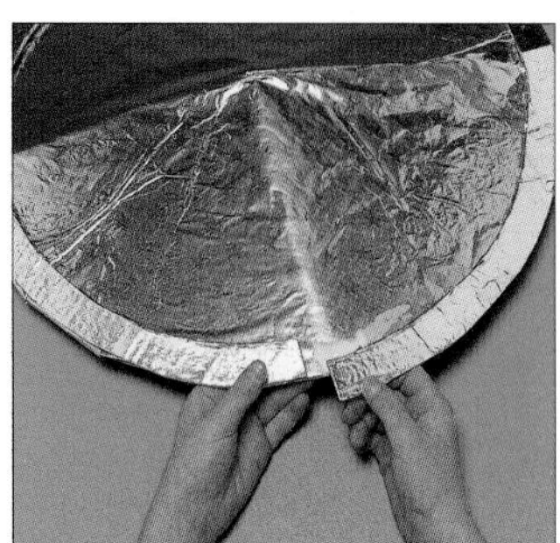

7 Glue the silver ring around the edge of the gold shield, as shown above. You will have to overlap the ends of the silver disc to fit it neatly around the shield.

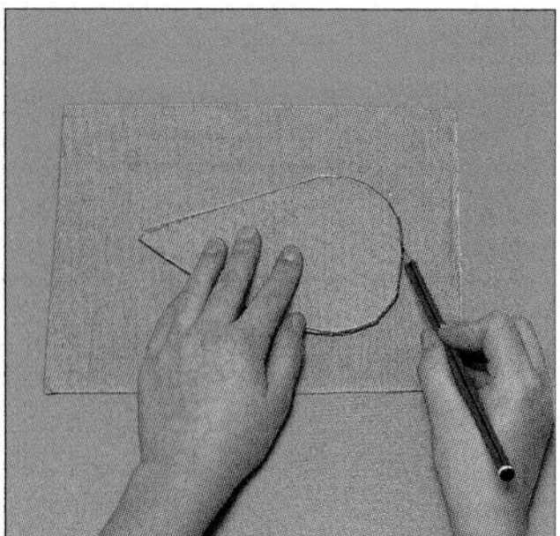

8 Draw a teardrop shape measuring about 12 x 8cm/4½ x 3⅛in on to a piece of thick card. Cut the teardrop shape out. Make four more teardrops, using the first one as a template.

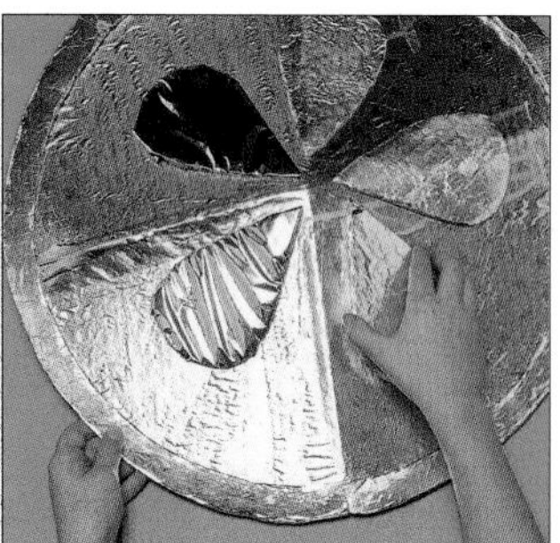

9 Cover and glue silver paper to three teardrops, and gold paper to two teardrops. Then glue the teardrops on to the gold shield, keeping them evenly spaced, as shown above.

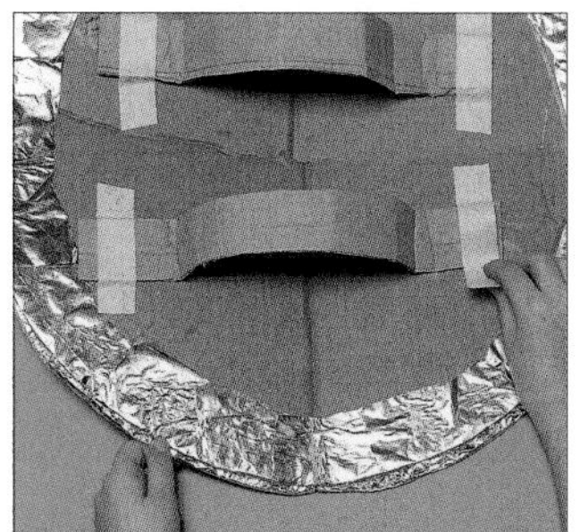

10 Cut out two strips of card 25 x 3cm/10 x 1 3/16in. Curve the strips. Glue them to the back of the shield to make handles big enough for your arm to fit through. Secure with masking tape.

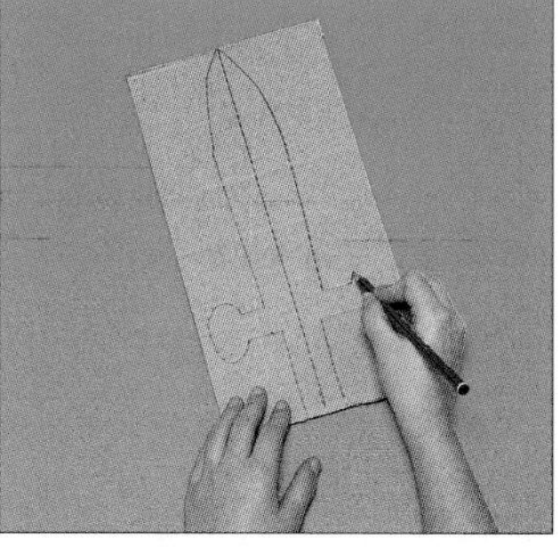

11 Cut out a rectangle of thick card measuring 30 x 15cm/ 12 x 6in. Draw a line down the centre of the card as a guide. Draw a sword shape on to the card.

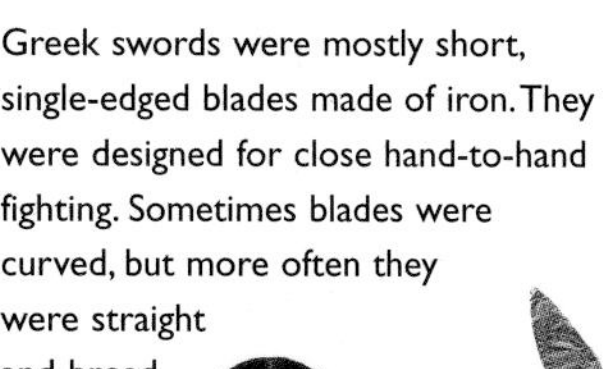

Greek swords were mostly short, single-edged blades made of iron. They were designed for close hand-to-hand fighting. Sometimes blades were curved, but more often they were straight and broad.

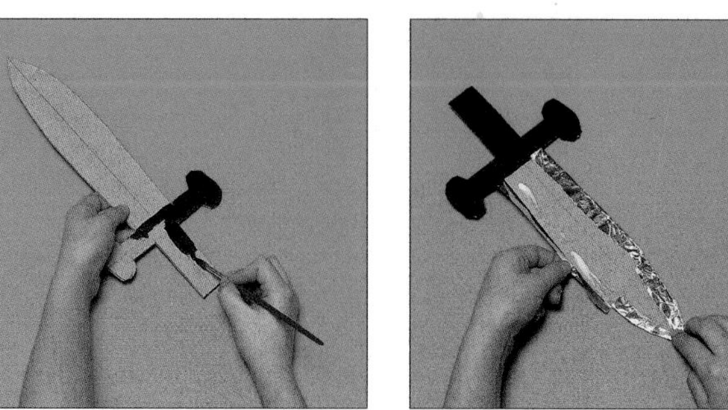

12 Cut out the sword shape from the card. Paint one side of the handle with black paint. When the paint is dry, turn the sword over and paint the other side of the handle.

13 Finally, cover both sides of the blade of the sword with foil, and neatly glue it down. The foil will give the blade of your sword a shiny surface.

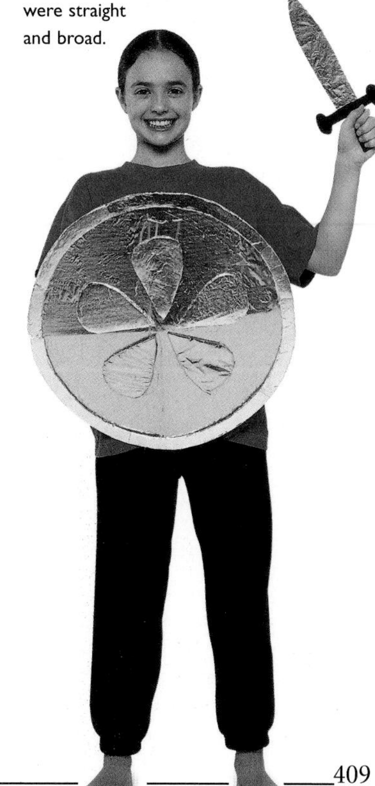

Greek warrior greaves

Greek men of fighting age were expected to swear allegiance to the army of the city in which they lived. In Sparta, the army was on duty all year round. In other parts of Greece, men gave up fighting in autumn to bring in the harvest and make wine. The only full-time soldiers in these states were the personal bodyguards of a ruler, or mercenaries who fought for anyone who paid them.

Armies consisted mainly of hoplites (foot soldiers) and cavalry (soldiers on horseback). The cavalry was less effective in war because the riders had no stirrups. The cavalry was mainly used for scouting, harassing a beaten enemy and carrying messages. The hoplites, who engaged in hand-to-hand combat, were the most important fighting force. The hoplites' armour consisted of a shield, helmet, spear, sword and metal shin protectors called greaves.

▲ Raw materials
Tin and copper were smelted to make bronze, the main material for Greek weaponry and armour. Bronze is harder than pure copper and, unlike iron, does not rust. As there was no tin in Greece, it was imported.

◀ Show of strength
The fighting force known as the hoplites was made up of middle-class men who could afford the weapons. The body of a hoplite soldier was protected by a bronze cuirass (a one-piece breastplate and backplate). The cuirass was worn over a leather tunic. Their bronze helmets were often crested with horsehair. Shields were usually round and decorated with a symbol.

YOU WILL NEED
Clear film (plastic wrap), plaster bandages, bowl of water, sheet of paper, kitchen paper (paper towels), scissors, cord, gold paint, paintbrush, water pot.

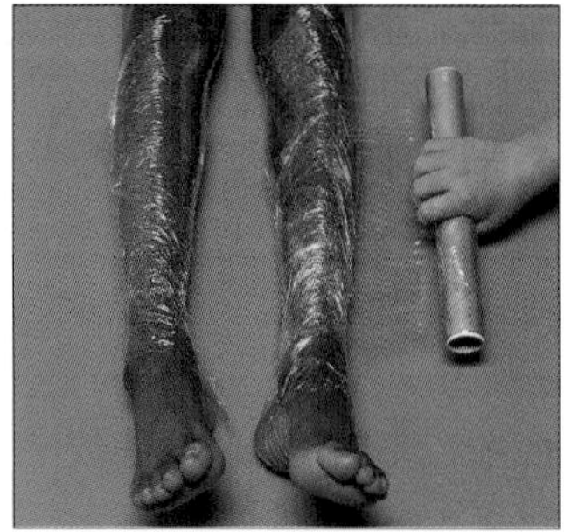

1 Ask a friend to help you with the first three steps. Loosely cover both of your legs (from your ankle to the top of your knee) in clear film, as shown above.

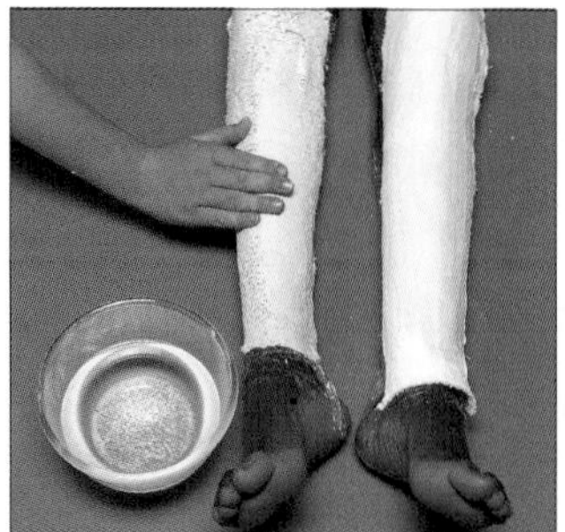

2 Soak each plaster bandage in water. Working from one side of your leg to another, smooth the bandage over the front of your leg. You will need to use several layers of plaster bandage.

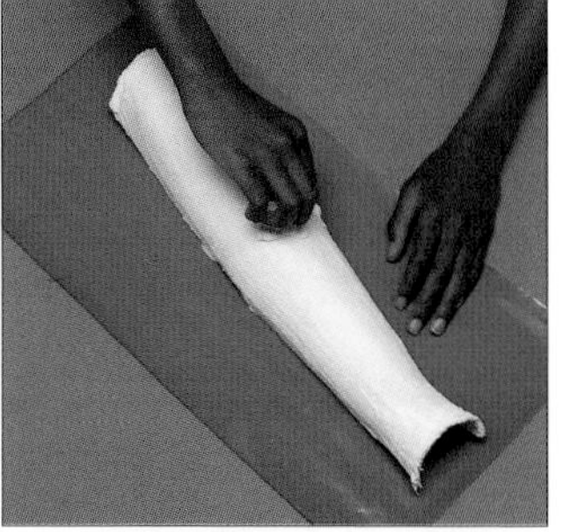

3 When you have finished, carefully remove each greave. Set them out on a sheet of paper. Dampen some kitchen paper and use it to smooth the greaves down. Let them dry.

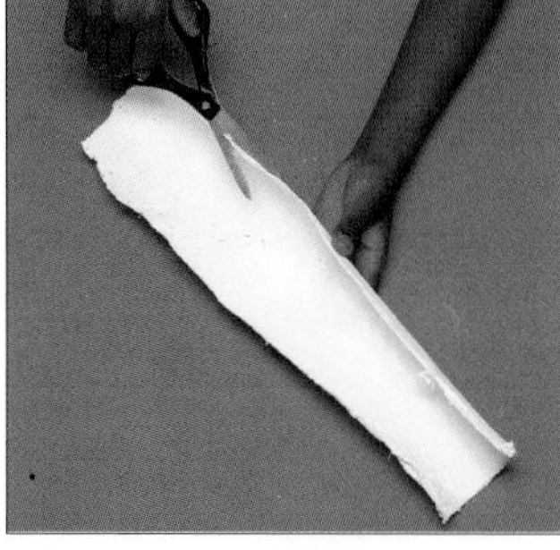

4 Trim the edges of the greaves with scissors to make them look neat. Measure four lengths of cord to fit around your legs – one below each knee and one above each ankle.

5 Lay the first cord in place on the back of the greaves where you want to tie them to your legs. Fix the cord in place with more wet plaster bandages. Repeat with the other three cords.

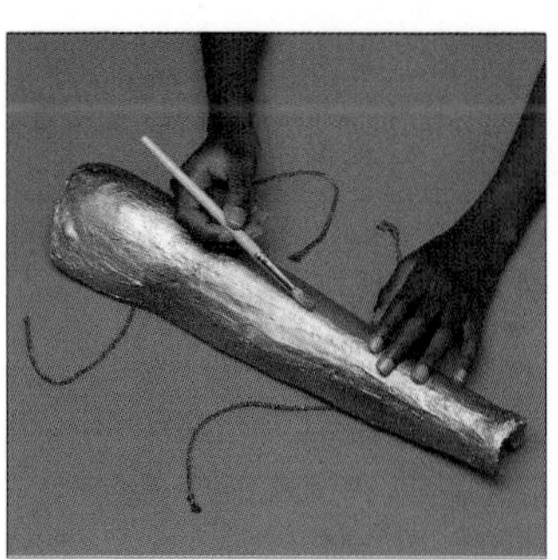

6 Let the plaster bandages dry with the cord in place. Now paint each greave with a layer of gold paint. Once they are dry, tie the greaves around your legs.

Greaves were attached to the lower legs to protect them in battle. Real greaves were made of bronze, and would have been very heavy.

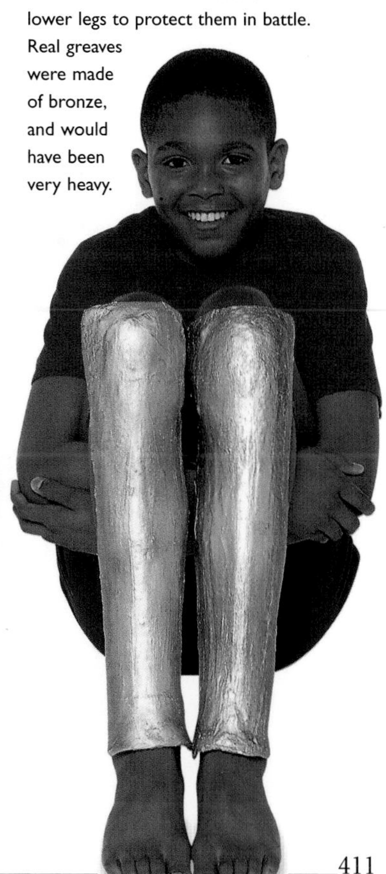

Roman armour

Soldiers in the Roman Empire were well equipped for fighting. A legionary was armed with a *pugio* (dagger) and a *gladius* (short iron sword) for stabbing and slashing. He also carried a *pilum* (javelin) of iron and wood. In the early days, a foot soldier's armour was a mail shirt, worn over a short, thick tunic. Officers wore a cuirass – a bronze casing that protected the chest and back. By about AD35, plate armour replaced the mail shirt. The iron plates (sections) were joined by hooks or leather straps. Early shields were oval, and later ones were oblong with curved edges. They were made of layers of wood glued together, covered in leather and linen. A metal boss over the central handle could be used to hit an enemy who got too close.

▲ Overseas duty
Roman soldiers were recruited from all parts of the enormous empire, including Africa. They were often sent on duty far away from their home. This was to make sure they did not desert.

▲ Highlight of the games
The chariot was not used a great deal by the Roman army. However, it was a popular sight at the public games held in Rome and other major cities. Most chariots held two people. If there was only one rider, he would tie the reins around his waist. This kept his hands free so he could use his weapons.

YOU WILL NEED

Tape measure, A1/34 x 22in sheets of metal-coloured card (one or two, depending on how big you are), pencil, scissors, white glue and glue brush, 2m/6½ft length of cord, pair of compasses.

1 Measure the size of your chest. Cut out three strips of card, 5cm/2in wide and long enough to fit around your chest. Cut out some thinner strips to stick the three main ones together.

2 Lay the wide strips flat and glue them together with the thin strips you cut. Let the glue dry. The Romans would have used leather straps to hold the wide metal pieces together.

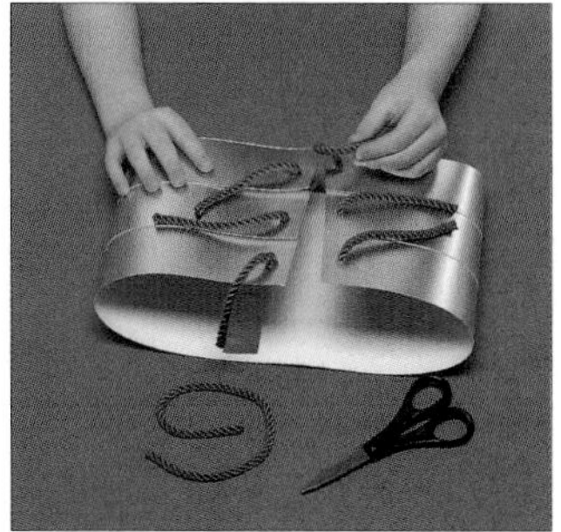

3 Bend the ends together, silver side out. Pierce a hole in the end of each strip using scissors. Cut 6 pieces of cord and pull through, knotting the cord at the back.

4 Cut a square of card as wide as your shoulders. Use the compasses to draw a 12cm/4½in-diameter circle in the centre. Cut the square in half, and cut away the half circles.

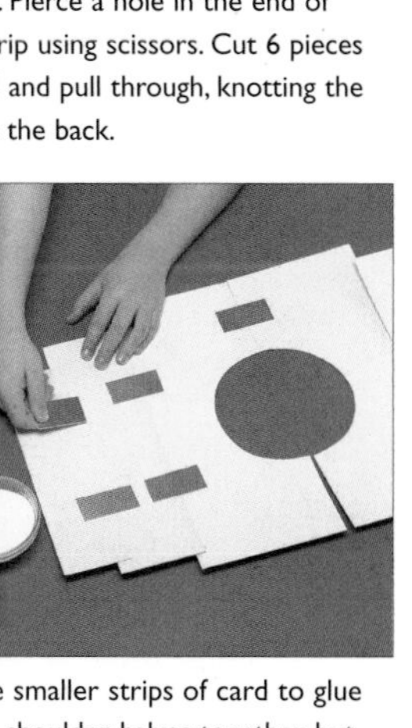

5 Use smaller strips of card to glue the shoulder halves together but leaving a neck hole. Cut out four more strips, two a little shorter than the others. Attach them in the same way.

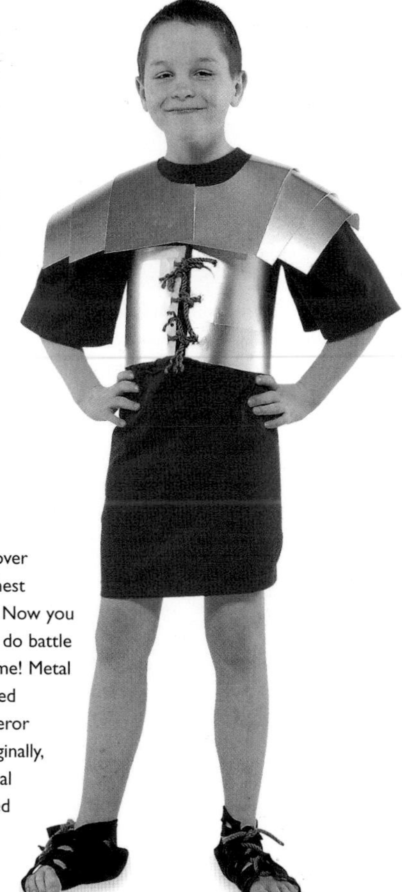

Put the shoulder piece over your head and tie the chest section around yourself. Now you are a legionary ready to do battle with the enemies of Rome! Metal strip armour was invented during the reign of Emperor Tiberius (AD 14–37). Originally, the various parts of metal strip armour were hinged and joined together either by hooks or by buckles and straps.

Japanese samurai helmet

During the Japanese civil wars, between 1185 and 1600, emperors, shoguns (governors) and daimyo (nobles) all relied on armies of samurai (warriors) to fight their battles. Samurai were skilled fighters. Members of each army were bound together by a solemn oath, sworn to their lord, who gave them rich rewards. The civil wars ended around 1600, when the Tokugawa Dynasty of shoguns came to power. After this time, samurai spent less time fighting, and served their lords as officials and business managers.

YOU WILL NEED

Thick card, pin, string, ruler, felt-tipped pen, scissors, tape measure, balloon, petroleum jelly, white glue, water, bowl, newspaper, pencil, self-hardening clay, bradawl, plain paper, gold card, acrylic paints, paintbrush, water pot, glue brush, masking tape, split pins, two 20cm/8in lengths of cord.

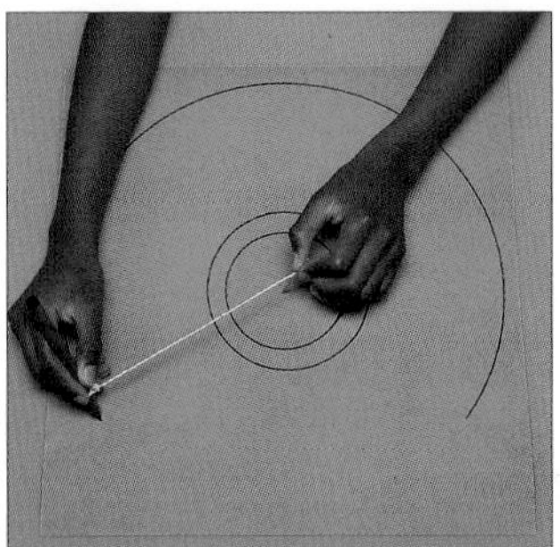

1 Draw an 18cm/7in-diameter circle on to a piece of thick card, using the pin, string and felt-tipped pen. Draw two larger circles 20cm/8in and 50cm/20in in diameter, as shown above.

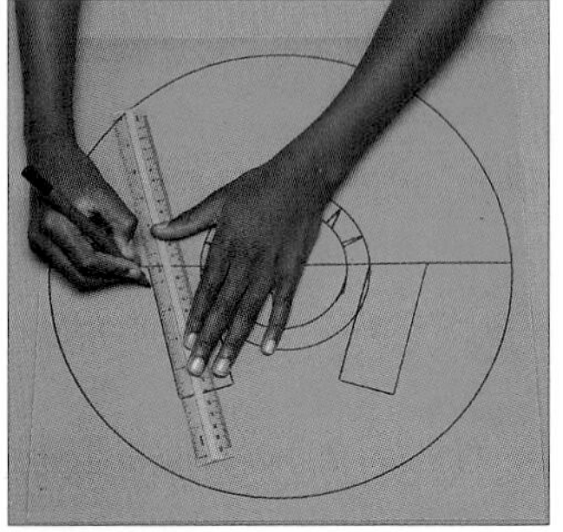

2 Draw a line across the centre of the three circles, using a ruler and felt-tipped pen. Draw lines for tabs in the middle semicircle. Add two flaps either side, as shown above.

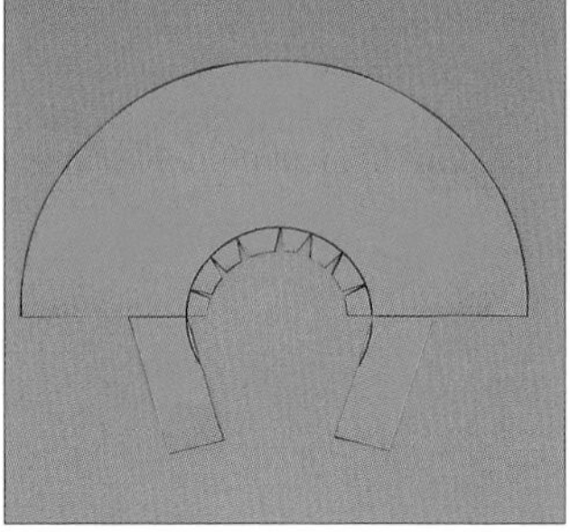

3 Cut out the neck protector piece completely, to make the shape shown above. Make sure that you cut carefully around the flaps and along the lines between the tabs.

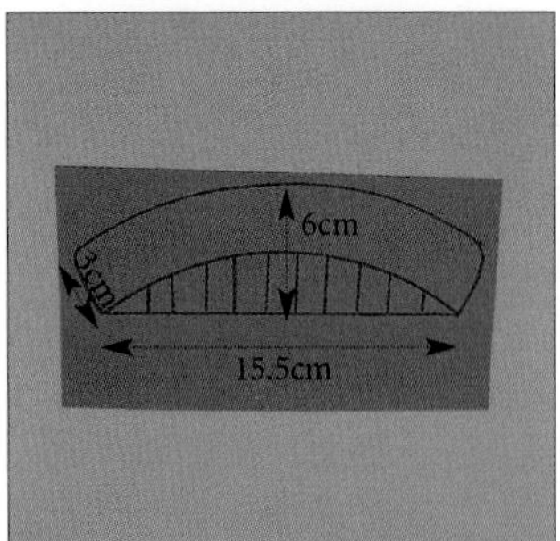

4 Draw the peak of the helmet on to another piece of card, using the measurements on the template above. Cut out the peak. Then blow up a balloon to the size of your head.

5 Cover the balloon with petroleum jelly. Tear newspaper into strips and add three layers of papier mâché (with two parts white glue to one part water) on the top and sides of the balloon.

6 When the papier mâché is dry, pop the balloon and trim the edges of the papier mâché cast. Ask a friend to make a mark with a pencil on either side of the helmet by your head.

7 Place a piece of self-hardening clay under the pencil marks. Make two holes – one above and one below each pencil mark – with a bradawl. Repeat on the other side of the helmet.

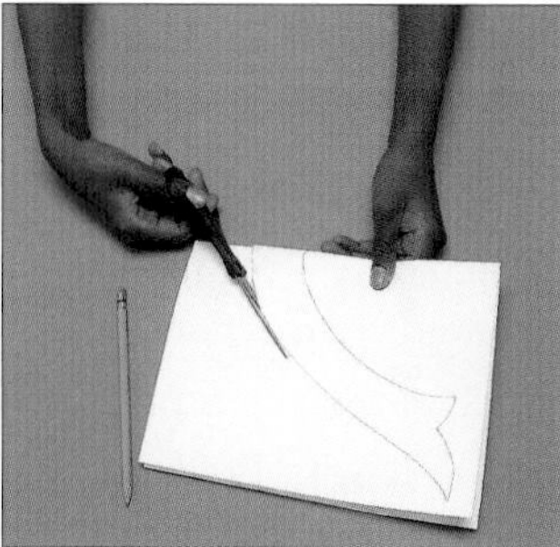

8 Fold a piece of A4/8½ x 12in paper in half, and draw a horn shape on to it, using the design shown above as a guide. Cut out the shape so that you have an identical pair of horns.

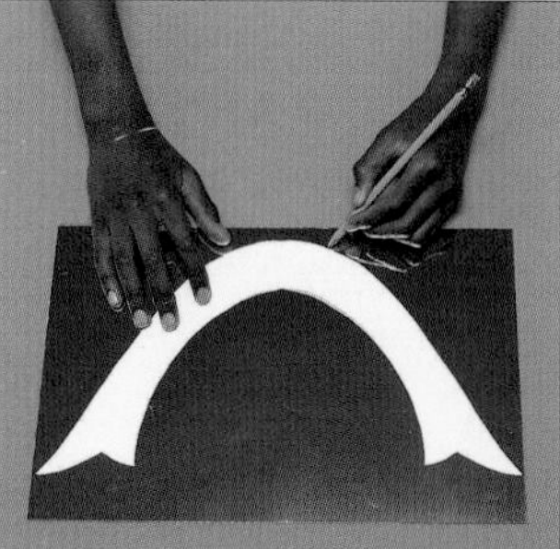

9 Take a piece of A4/8½ x 12in gold card. Using the paper horns you have drawn as a template, draw the shape on to the gold card. Carefully cut the horns out of the card.

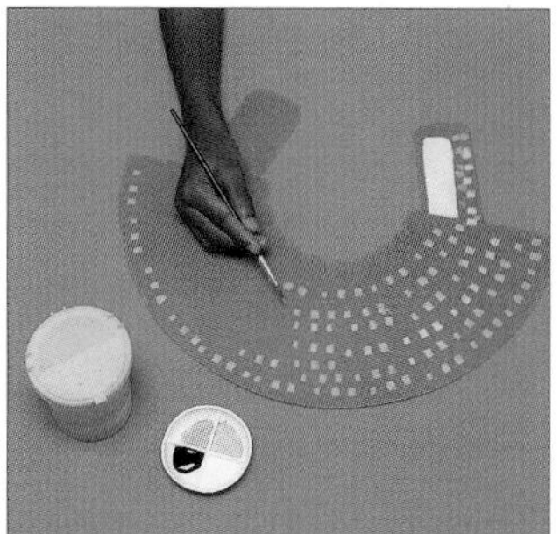

10 Paint a weave design on both sides of the neck protector and a cream block on each flap, as shown above. Paint your papier mâché helmet brown. Leave the paint to dry.

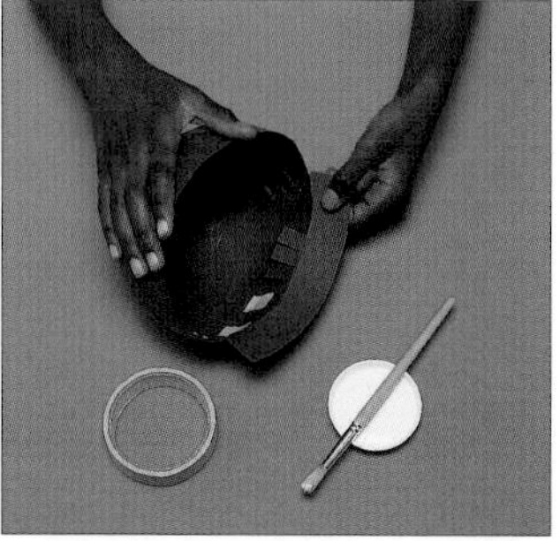

11 Cut and bend back the tabs on the peak of the helmet. Making sure the peak is at the front, glue the tabs to the inside, as shown above. Secure the tabs with masking tape.

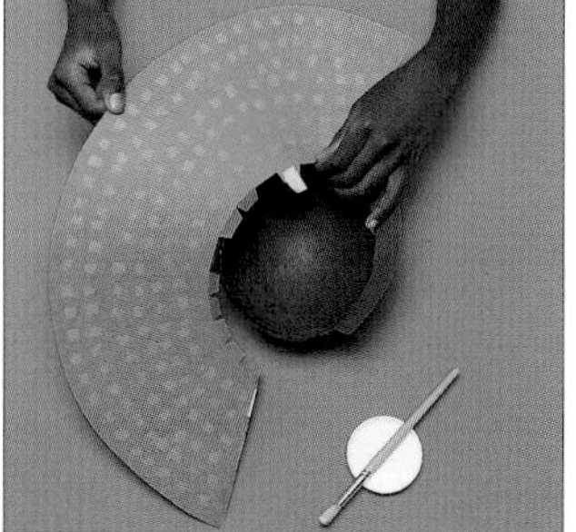

12 Now bend back the front flaps and the tabs of the neck protector and glue them to the helmet, as shown above. Leave the helmet to dry completely.

13 Glue the gold card horns to the front of the helmet, as shown above. Secure the horns with split pins. Use more split pins to decorate the ear flaps.

14 To wear your helmet, thread a piece of cord through one of the holes in the side of the helmet and tie a knot in the end. Thread the other end of the cord through the second hole. Repeat on the other side. Samurai helmets were often decorated with lacquered wood or metal crests mounted on the top of the helmet.

Viking shield

Norse warriors wore their own clothes and brought their own equipment to battle. Most wore caps of tough leather. Where metal helmets were worn, these were usually conical, and they sometimes had a bar to protect the nose. Viking raiders wore their everyday tunics and breeches and cloaks to keep out the cold. A rich Viking jarl (chieftain) might have a *brynja,* which was a shirt made up of interlinking rings of iron. Vikings also carried spears of various weights, longbows, deadly arrows and long-shafted battle axes on board the longship. The most prized weapon of all was the Viking sword. The blades of the swords were either made by Scandinavian blacksmiths or imported from Germany. A heavy shield, about 1m/1yd across, was made of wooden planks. It had an iron boss (central knob) and a rim of iron or leather.

YOU WILL NEED

Pair of compasses, pencil, card, string, scissors, red and gold paints, paintbrush, water pot, paper party bowl, newspaper, masking tape, white glue and glue brush, foil, brass split pins, craft knife, strip of wood, bias binding.

Mass attack
Viking raiders disembarking from their longships and racing into action, armed with their single-headed war axes. The Vikings used various axes for hacking the enemy at close range, or for throwing from a distance. These iron-bladed weapons were often elaborately decorated.

1 Use the compasses to draw a small circle in the centre of a large piece of card. Then use a length of string tied to a pencil to draw a big circle for the shield, as shown above.

2 Cut out the large circle. Then draw on a big, bold design, such as the one shown in this project. Paint the shield with red and gold paint. Let the paint dry completely.

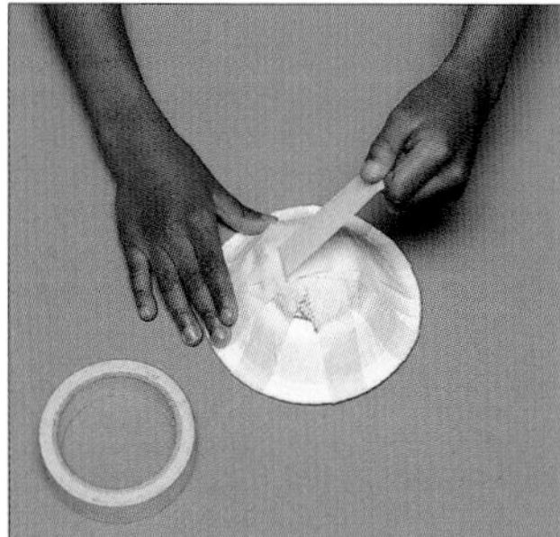

3 Use an upside down paper party bowl for the shield's central boss, or knob. Scrunch up some newspaper into a flattened ball and use masking tape to fix it to the top of the bowl.

4 Spread white glue over the bowl, and then cover it with foil. In Viking times, an iron boss would have strengthened the shield and protected the warrior's hand.

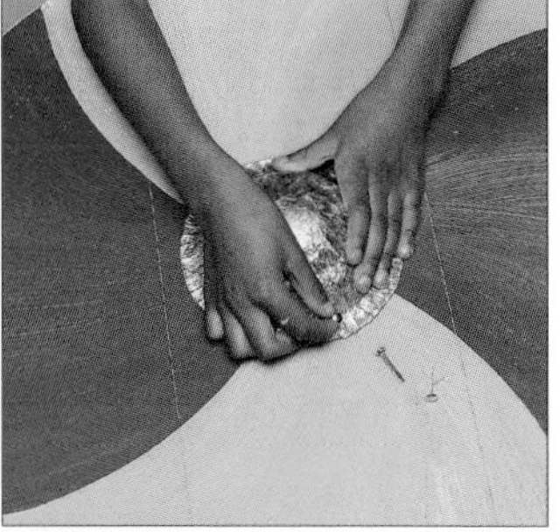

5 Glue the boss to the centre of your shield. Secure the boss with brass split pins punched through its edge and through the card of the shield.

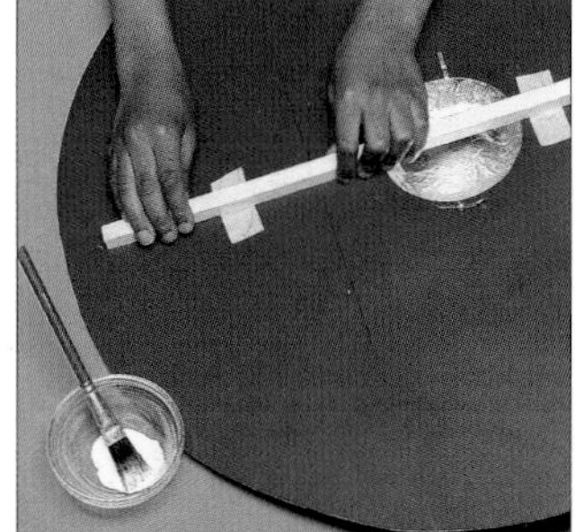

6 Ask an adult to cut a hole in the back of the shield where the boss is. Glue the strip of wood to the back of the shield and secure with strips of tape, as shown above.

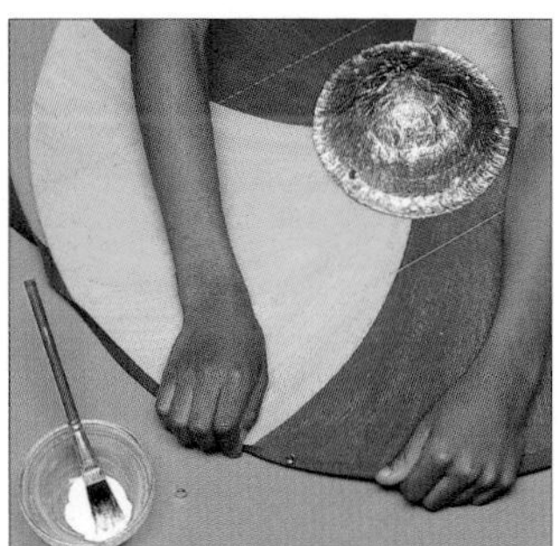

7 Attach the bias binding all the way around the rim of the shield, using some brass split pins or small dabs of glue. Your shield is now ready for use in a Viking battle!

Give your shield its own Viking-style name, such as 'Fist of Thor' or 'Swordbreaker'.

Knight's helmet

A helmet protected the eyes and head of a soldier in battle. A flat-topped helmet was introduced in the 1100s, but it did not deflect blows as well as a rounded helmet. The basinet helmet of the 1300s had a moveable visor over the face. The introduction of hinges and pivots in the 1400s meant that a shaped helmet could be put on over the head, and then closed to fit securely. From the 1500s, lighter, open helmets were worn. These were more comfortable, and soldiers could move around freely in battle.

YOU WILL NEED

Pencil, ruler, two large sheets of silver card, craft knife, cutting board, one large sheet of gold card, scissors, stapler and staples, white glue and glue brush, masking tape, pair of compasses, brass split pins.

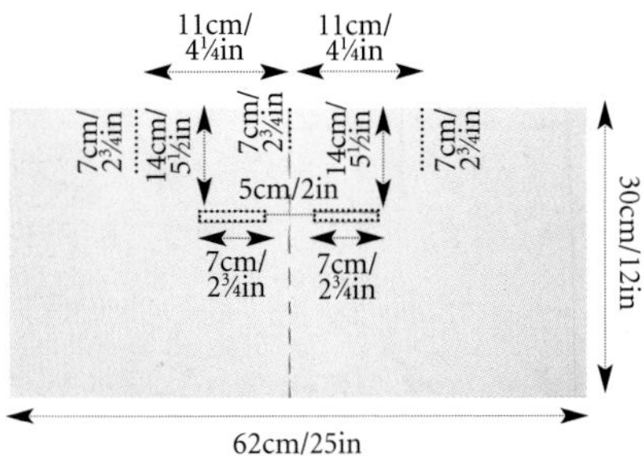

▲ Template
Using a pencil, draw the template for your knight's helmet on to one large sheet of silver card. Measure and mark all the dotted lines as shown.

1 Use a craft knife, ruler and cutting board to cut out the eye slits. Cut a 62 x 4cm/25 x 1½in strip of gold card. Place it beneath the slits and draw the slits on the gold card. Cut them out.

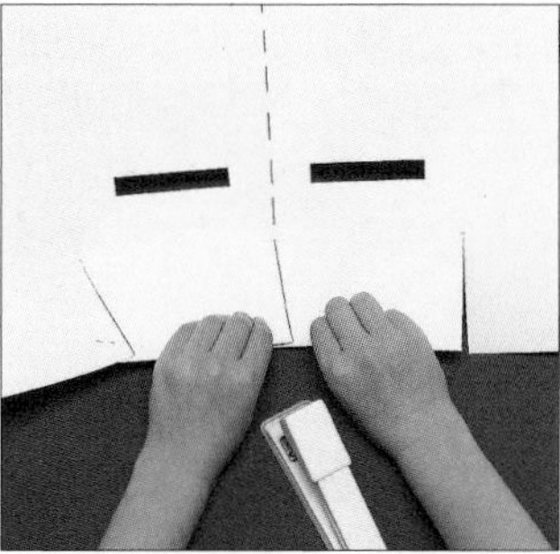

2 Cut along the three 7cm/2¾in dotted lines on the silver card template. Fold the card inwards, as shown above, to make the helmet curve. Staple the top of each overlapping section.

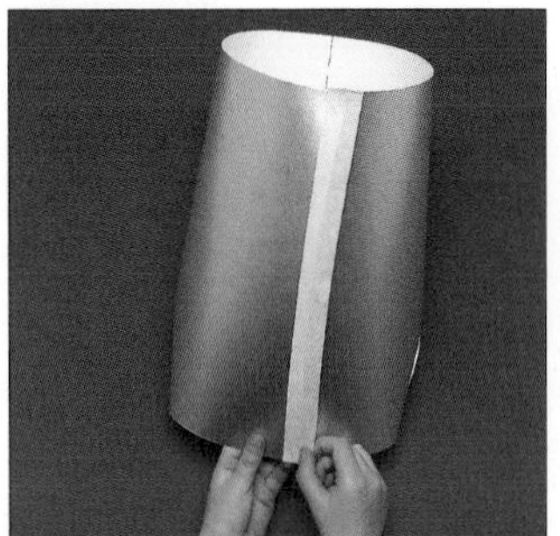

3 Curve the helmet into a long tube shape, as shown. Glue and staple the tube together at the top and bottom. Secure the join with masking tape until the glue dries.

4 Set the compasses to 10cm/4in and draw a circle (diameter 20cm/8in) on the remaining silver card. Then set the compasses to 9cm/3½in and draw an inner circle with a diameter of 18cm/7in.

5 Cut around the larger circle. Make cuts at 4cm/1½in intervals to the line of the inner circle. Bend them inwards, and overlap. Fix tape on the back of the silver card to hold them in place.

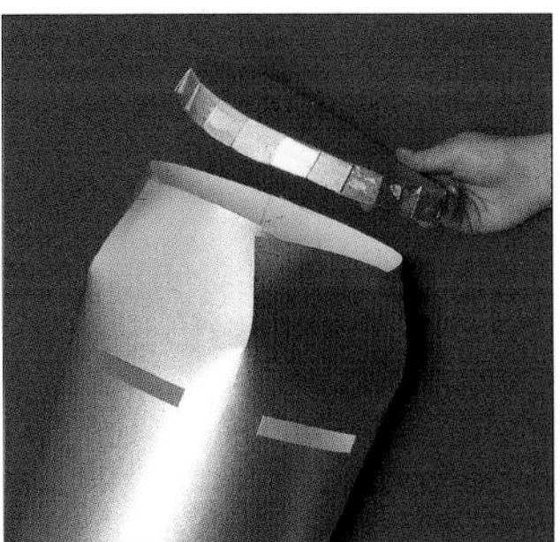

6 Put spots of glue on the outside top rim of the helmet. Hold the body of the helmet with one hand, and carefully glue the top of the helmet on to the body with the other.

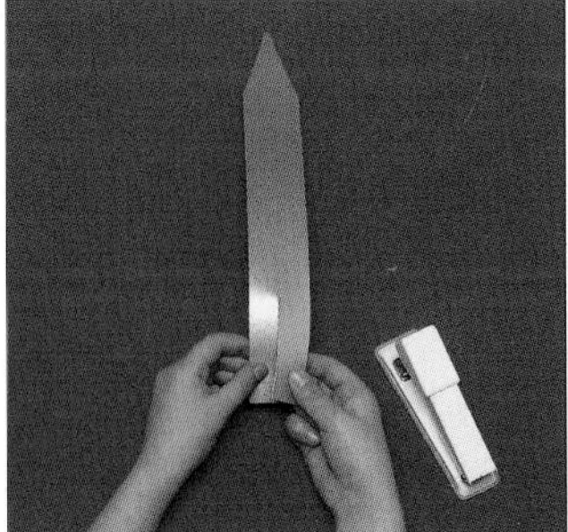

7 Cut a 30 x 4cm/12 x 1½in strip of gold card. Cut a point on one end of the strip. Cut a 7cm/2¾in slit down the middle of the other end. Overlap the two flaps by 1cm/½in, and staple.

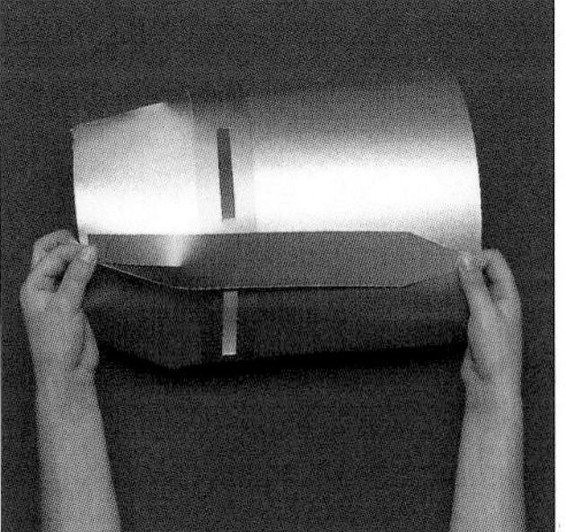

8 Staple the gold eye-slit strip into a circular band. Slip this over the helmet so that the eye slits match up. Glue it into position. Staple the nose piece in place between the eye slits.

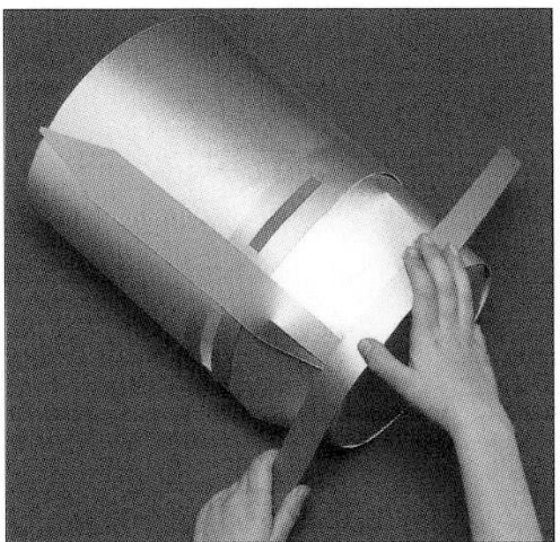

9 Cut a 62 x 2cm/25 x ¾in strip of gold card. Put spots of glue at intervals along the back of the card strip. Carefully stick the gold band around the top of the helmet.

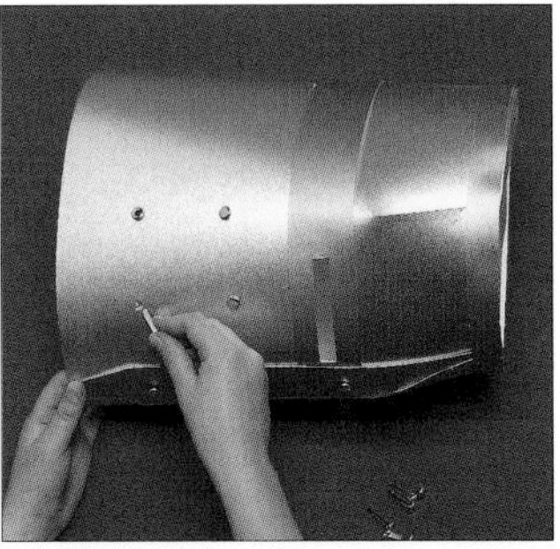

10 Use the pointed end of the compasses to pierce four holes on each 'cheek' of the helmet. Then make three holes along the nose piece. Push a brass split pin into each hole.

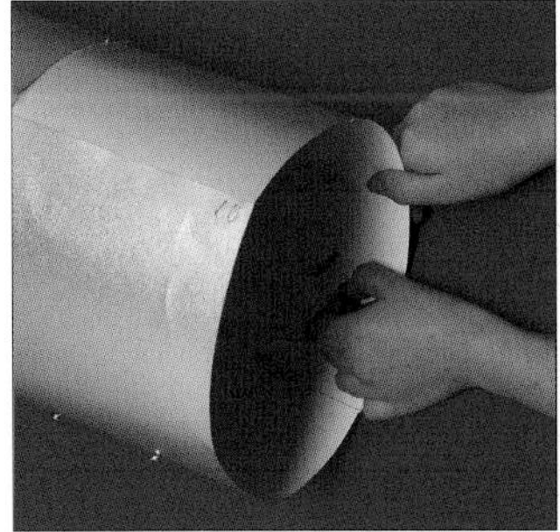

11 Split the pins, and then cover the back of each one with strips of masking tape so that they do not scratch your face when you wear the helmet.

The Christian knights who fought in the Crusades wore helmets rather like the one you have made. Between 1095 and 1272, European knights fought Muslim countries for control of the Holy Land. The Crusaders wore a chainmail shirt, called a hauberk, with a cloth surcoat over the top. European armourers picked up some design ideas from their Muslim enemies, who were well known for their skills in forging steel.

Medieval trebuchet

It took careful planning to mount a siege attack. Giant catapults played a vital role at the beginning of a siege. Their job was to weaken the castle defences before the foot soldiers moved in close. A deadly fire of boulders and flaming ammunition killed and maimed the fighters inside the castle walls. In the 1100s, powerful siege machines called trebuchets were developed to launch larger rocks over the castle walls. Decaying animals were also thrown over, in the hope of spreading disease among the people inside.

YOU WILL NEED

Card, pencil, ruler, craft knife, cutting board, two 28cm/11in and two 16cm/6¼in strips of balsa, wood glue, pair of compasses, 32cm/12½in and 22cm/8¾in length balsa dowel, two 20 x 3.5 x 0.5cm/8 x 1⅜ x ¼in pieces of balsa, scissors, four 25cm/10in lengths square balsa dowel, string, self-hardening clay, matchbox, acrylic paints, paintbrush, water pot.

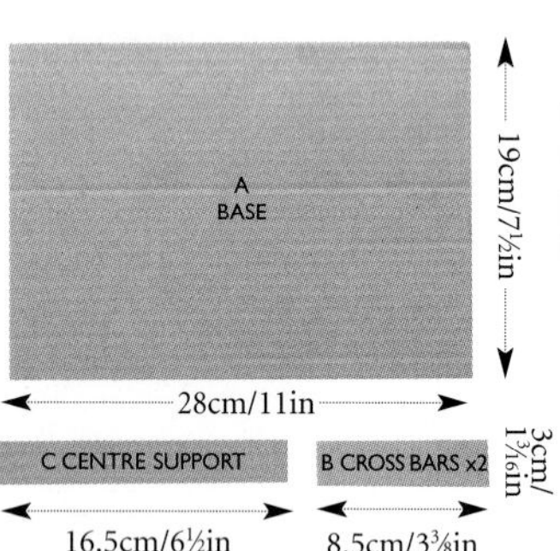

▲ Templates
Copy the templates on to a piece of thick card. Use a craft knife, cutting board and ruler to cut the pieces out.

1 Lay the base template A on to the work surface. Use wood glue to stick the two 28cm/11in lengths and two 16cm/6¼in lengths of balsa wood along each edge of the base section.

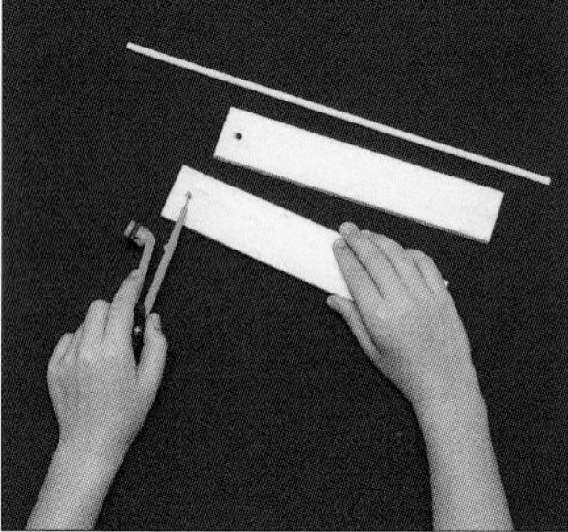

2 Use a sharp compass point to pierce a hole through the end of each of the 20cm/8in lengths of balsa wood for side supports, as shown in the picture above.

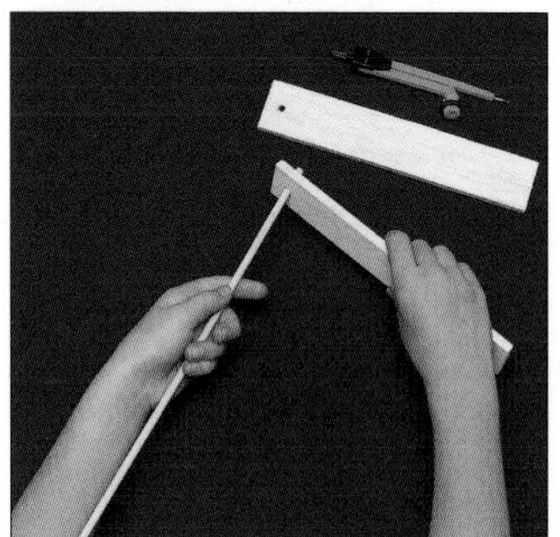

3 Use the sharp end of a pencil to make the hole a little bigger. Then push one of the pieces of balsa dowel through each of the holes to make them the same diameter.

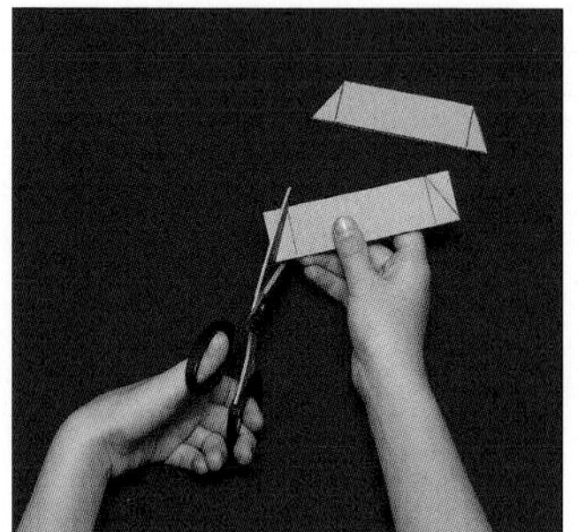

4 Use a pencil and ruler to draw two lines, 1cm/½in from each end of the two crossbar sections B. Make a diagonal cut from the corners to the lines, to make slanting edges.

5 Lay the 20cm/8in balsa wood side supports on to the work surface. Glue the crossbars into position below the holes, about 3.5cm/1⅜in below the top of the side supports, as shown.

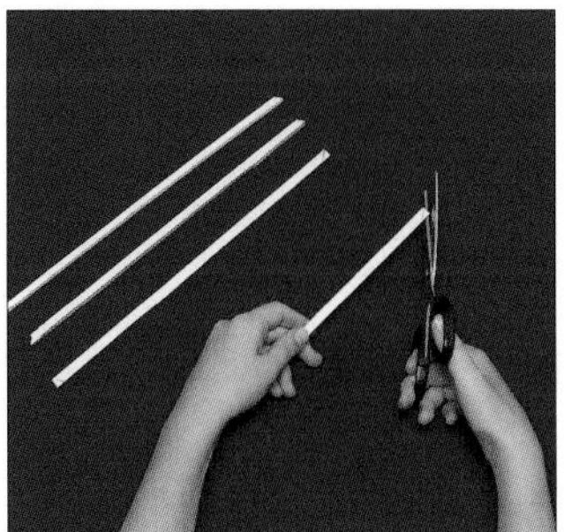

6 Place the four 25cm/10in lengths of balsa wood dowel on to the work surface. Ask an adult to help you cut both ends of the dowel diagonally at an angle of 45 degrees.

7 Glue the supports mid-way along each long side of the base section. Glue the 25cm/10in long balsa strips 2.5cm/1in from the corners to form a triangle over the top of the support.

8 Glue along the ends on one side of the 16.5cm/6½in-long centre support section. Stick it into place on the side supports, about 9cm/3½in from the base, as shown above.

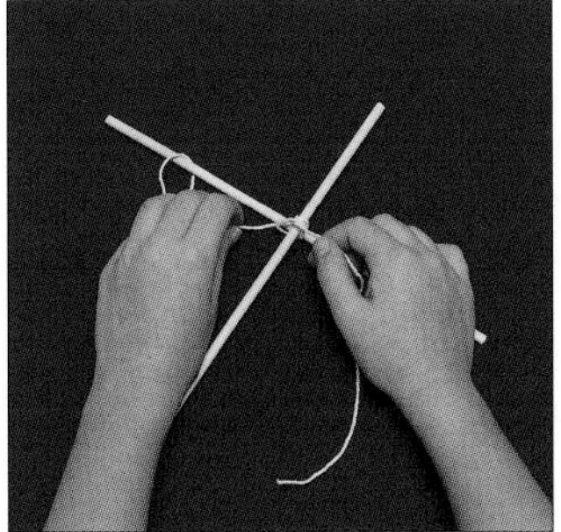

9 Make a 'T' shape with the 32cm/12½in and 22cm/8¾in lengths of round dowel, with the shorter cross piece 9cm/3½in from the top. Bind the pieces together tightly with string.

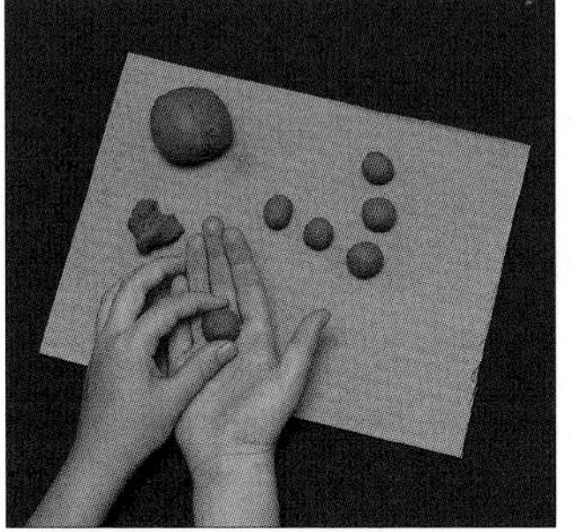

10 Roll some small pieces of clay in the palm of your hands. Mould one big ball about 5cm/2in in diameter, and some smaller balls. Leave the clay balls to one side to dry.

11 Glue the back of the inside of a matchbox. Stick this to the bottom of the long arm of the cross piece. Stick the big clay ball on to the other end.

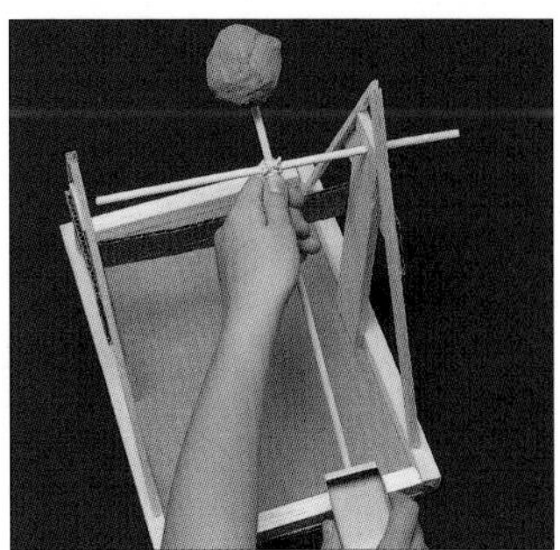

12 Fit the arms of the cross piece into the holes in the balsa wood side supports so that the matchbox is at the bottom. Finally, paint the model with acrylic paints.

Put some clay balls into the matchbox and raise the big ball. Drop it to let the missiles fly! The clay missiles fired from your trebuchet are unlikely to do much damage. However, with its long weighted arm and open support frame, the model trebuchet operates in much the same way as the real thing. The word *trebuchet* comes from a French word for a similar device that was used for shooting birds.

Cut-throat cutlass

The swords carried by pirates have varied greatly over the ages. Ancient Greek pirates fought with a 60cm/24in-long leaf-shaped blade, or with a curved cut-and-thrust blade called a kopis. Their Roman enemies fought with a short sword called a gladius. Viking swords were long and double-edged for heavy slashing. The rapier, introduced in the 1500s, was a light sword with a deadly, pointed blade, but it was too long and delicate for close-range fighting on board ship. The cutlass was the ideal weapon for that.

▲ **Pirate sword**
The most common and useful pirate weapon was probably the cutlass, used from the 1600s onwards.

YOU WILL NEED

Two pieces of stiff card measuring 45 x 5cm/18 x 2in, pencil, scissors, white glue and glue brush, newspaper, masking tape, one piece of stiff card (30 x 10cm/12 x 4in), one cup of flour, half a cup of water, mixing bowl, spoon, sandpaper, brown and silver acrylic paint, two paintbrushes, water pot, black felt-tipped pen, ruler, wood varnish.

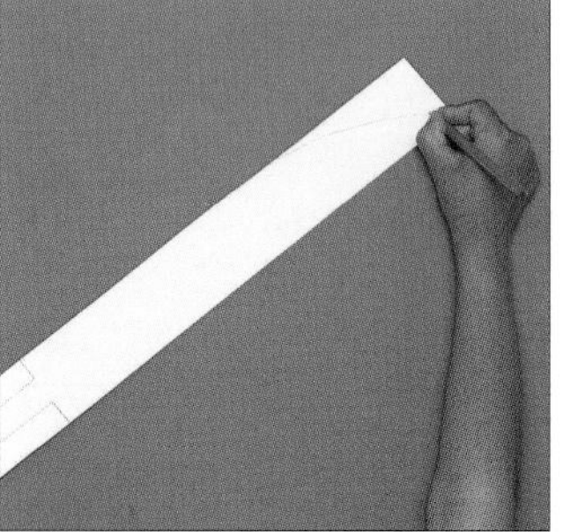

1 Take one piece of the stiff card measuring 45 x 5cm/18 x 2in. Carefully pencil in an outline of a cutlass blade and hilt on to the piece of card, as shown above.

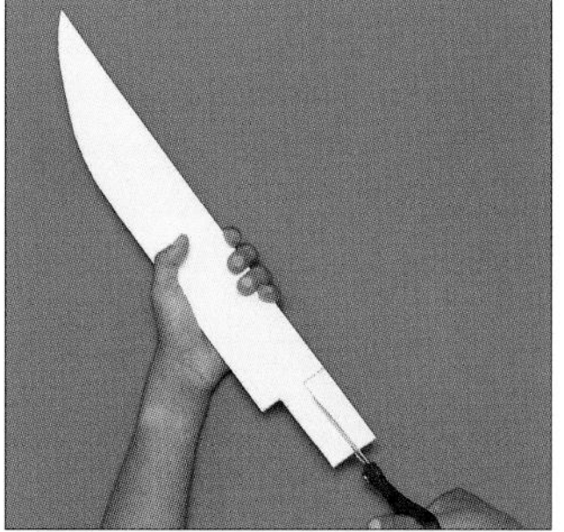

2 Use a pair of scissors to cut the shape out. Use this as a template to lay on the second piece of card. Draw around the template and then cut out a second cutlass shape.

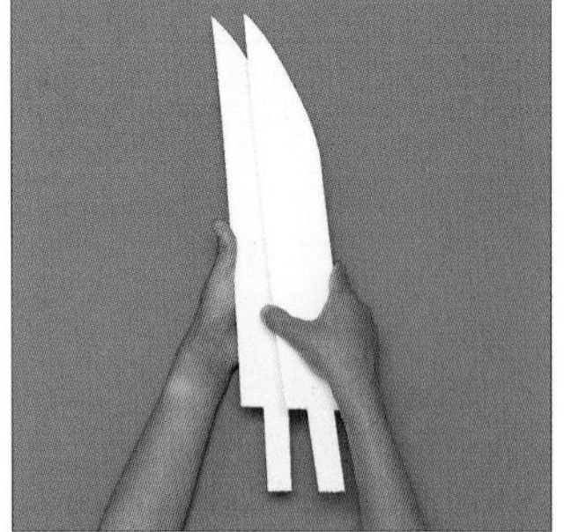

3 Lay the two matching sections of the cutlass on top of each other, as shown above. Glue them together. The double thickness gives the finished cutlass extra strength.

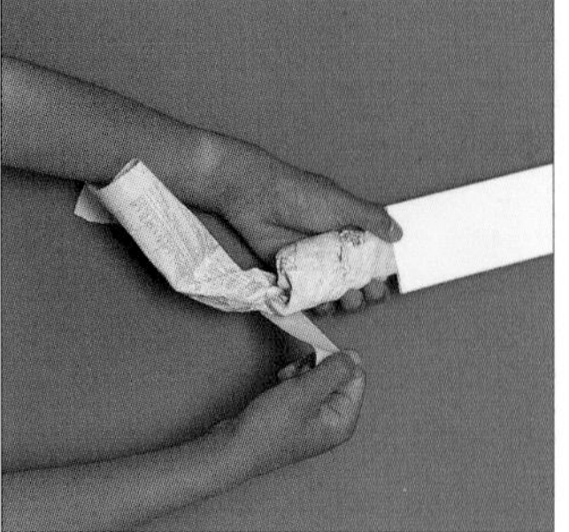

4 Twist a piece of newspaper into thick strips to wind around the hilt. The newspaper should be thick enough to make a comfortable handgrip. Bind the newspaper with masking tape.

5 Draw the shape of a cutlass handle on to the stiff piece of 30 x 10cm/12 x 4in card and cut it out. Make a cut down the middle of the wide end to about 2.5cm/1in short of the stem.

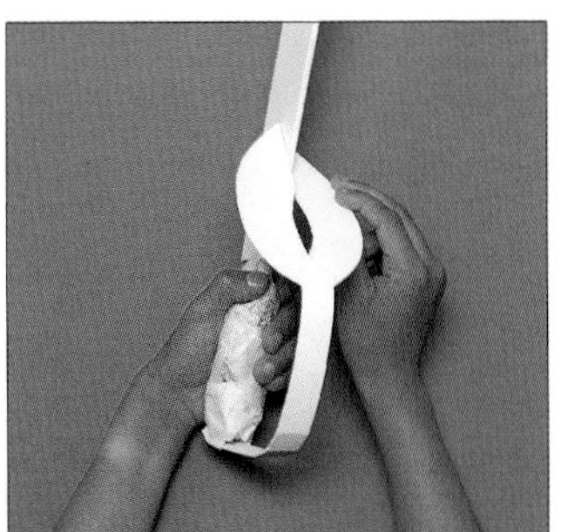

6 Tape the narrow stem of the handle to the end of the cutlass hilt. Bend the rest of the handle around to slot over the curved edge of the blade, as shown above.

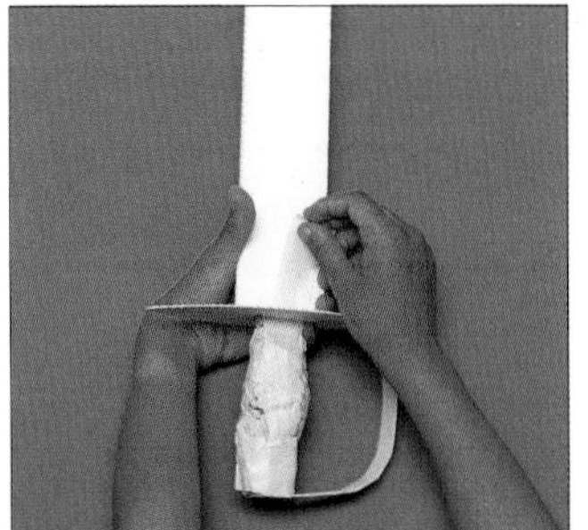

7 Make sure the oval lies flat against the hilt of the cutlass to form the hand guard. Use masking tape to seal the slit and to secure the handle of the cutlass to the blade.

8 Pour the flour into a mixing bowl and slowly add the water, a spoon at a time, mixing as you go. The mixture should form a smooth, thick paste similar to pancake batter.

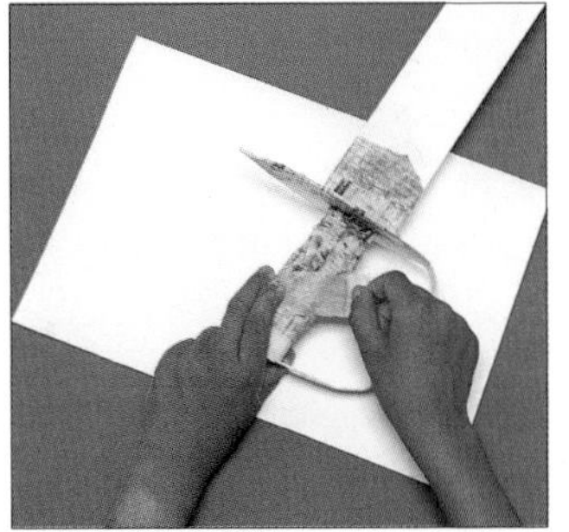

9 Tear newspaper into short strips and coat these with the paste. Cover the cutlass with three layers of papier mâché. Leave the cutlass in a warm place for several hours.

10 When the cutlass is dry, smooth it down using sandpaper. Paint the cutlass with acrylic paint, as shown. Allow the first coat to dry thoroughly, and then apply another coat of paint.

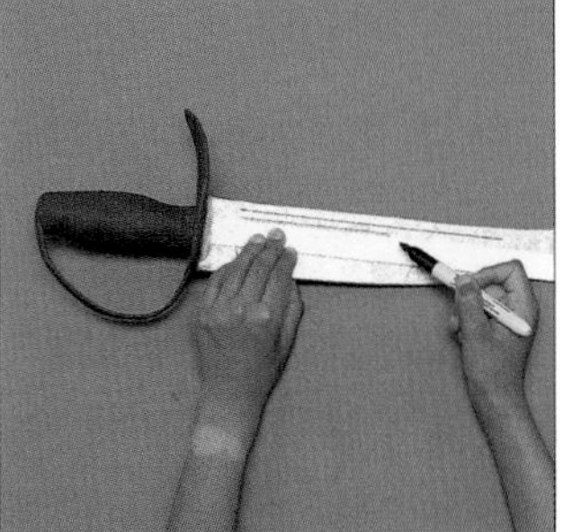

11 When the second coat of paint is completely dry, use a black felt-tipped pen and ruler to add fine details on the blade of the cutlass, as shown above.

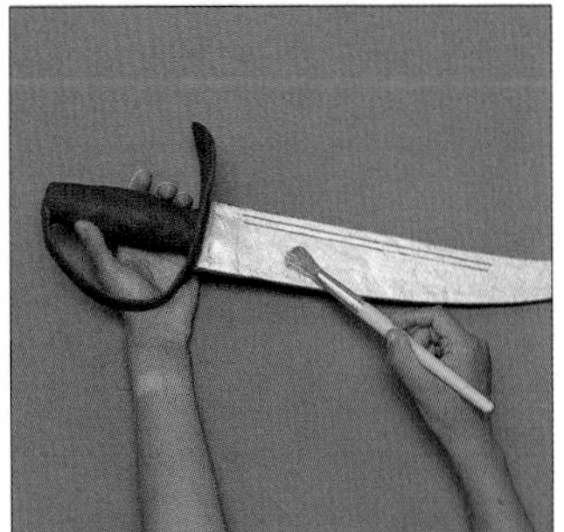

12 Finally, use a clean paintbrush to apply a coat of wood varnish to the blade and hilt. This will toughen the cutlass, as well as giving it a menacing glint.

The true cutlasses used by pirates and sailors from the 1600s onwards had a steel blade and a brass or iron hilt (handle). To stop their cutlass from rusting, pirates rubbed grease on to the blade.

An Inca funeral procession

Customs, Arts and Entertainment

Once the necessities of survival were mastered, people could turn their attention to spiritual and creative matters. In this section you will discover that many artefacts and customs were inspired by religious beliefs and rituals. You will also find early versions of sports, games, toys and entertainment that are still enjoyed by people today.

Arts and Crafts

No other species on the Earth has shown the ability to express itself in the same artistic way as humans. Archaeological evidence has shown that, over 50,000 years ago, the earliest humans decorated their bodies, tools and shelters with simple patterns and symbols. People then began to portray the world around them by painting images on the walls of caves. As society evolved, so did the art and culture. This is charted in history – from the early treasures of the Egyptian tombs, through the Golden Age of Greek art and Roman architecture, to the Renaissance – the revival of art and culture that formed the transition from the Middle Ages to our modern world.

▲ Cave paintings
Paintings of animals made more than 17,000 years ago have been found on the walls deep inside caves in Europe. They often show animals that were hunted at that time.

▲ Horse of stone
An early Egyptian stone carving of a horse's head, dating from around 1500BC. In Egyptian society, skilled artists and craftworkers formed a middle class between the poor labourers and rich officials and nobles.

◄ Skilled ironworkers
Metalworkers were some of the most important members of Celtic society. They made many of the items that Celtic people valued most, such as this magnificent iron axe head. It took many years for a metalworker to learn all the necessary skills, first to produce the metal from nuggets or lumps of ore, and then to shape it.

▲ Buried treasures

This Greek wine serving bowl, or krater, was found in a wood-lined burial chamber at Vix in eastern France. The tomb belonged to a Celtic princess, who was buried around 520BC. The princess was wearing a torc, or necklace, made of almost half a kilogram/a pound of pure gold.

Monster watch ▶

The entrance to an Assyrian palace in Mesopotamia was guarded by statues of huge monsters called lamassus. Lamassus were strange creatures with the bodies of lions or bulls, the wings of mighty birds, human heads and caps to show they had divine powers. Lamassus had five legs; the extra limb was so that they appeared to be standing still when viewed from the front.

◀ Tomb horse

By the 3rd century AD, Japan was governed by a culture known as the Yamato. When a Yamato emperor died, his huge burial tomb was filled with armour, jewellery and weapons to indicate his great power and wealth. People surrounded his burial site with thousands of pottery objects, such as this horse. These were meant to protect the tomb and its contents.

Stone warrior ▶

This statue of a proud warrior stood at Tula, the ancient capital city of the Toltec people. The Toltecs were rulers of northern Mexico from about AD950 to 1160. The warrior wears a butterfly-shaped breastplate. Butterflies have short but brilliant lives. For the Toltecs, they were a symbol of brave warriors and early death.

Stone Age hand art

From about 37,000BC, early humans began to carve marks on bones and use pebbles to count. Days may have been counted on calendar sticks. Experts have noticed dots and symbols in some cave paintings, which may be counting tallies or the very beginnings of a writing system. By 7000BC, tokens with symbols to represent numbers and objects were being used by traders in the Near East. Such tokens may have led to the first written script. This developed in about 3100BC, and was a form of picture-writing called cuneiform.

YOU WILL NEED

Self-hardening clay, rolling pin, cutting board, modelling tool, fine sandpaper, red and yellow acrylic paints, water, two spray bottles.

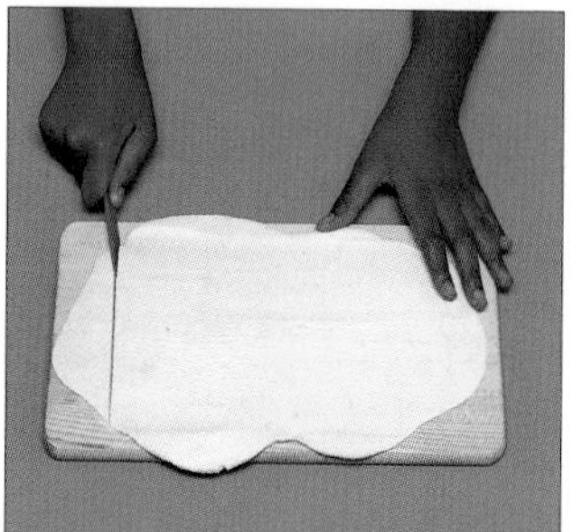

1 Roll out a piece of clay. Make sure it has an uneven surface similar to a cave wall. Use a modelling tool to trim the edges into a rough rectangle to look like a stone tablet.

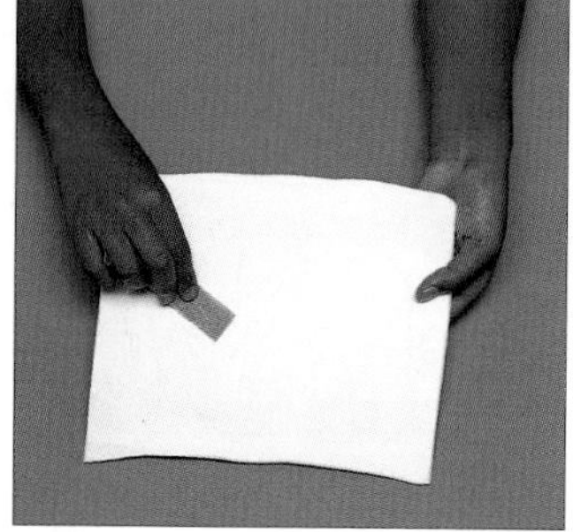

2 Leave the clay to dry. When the tablet is completely hard, rub it with fine sandpaper to get rid of any sharp edges, and to make a smooth surface for your cave painting.

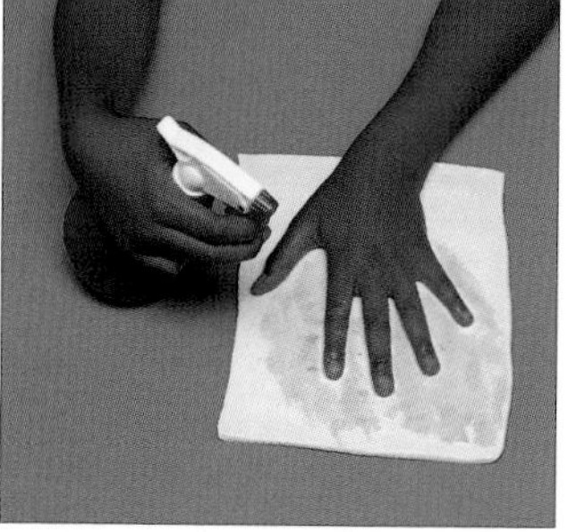

3 Mix the yellow paint with some water and fill a spray bottle. Mix the red paint in the same way. Put one hand on top of the clay tablet and spray plenty of yellow paint around it.

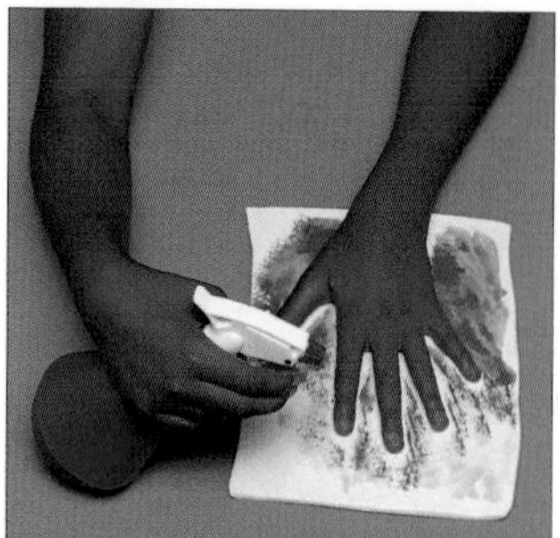

4 Keeping your hand in exactly the same position, spray on the red paint from the other bottle. Make sure you spray enough paint to leave a clear, sharp background.

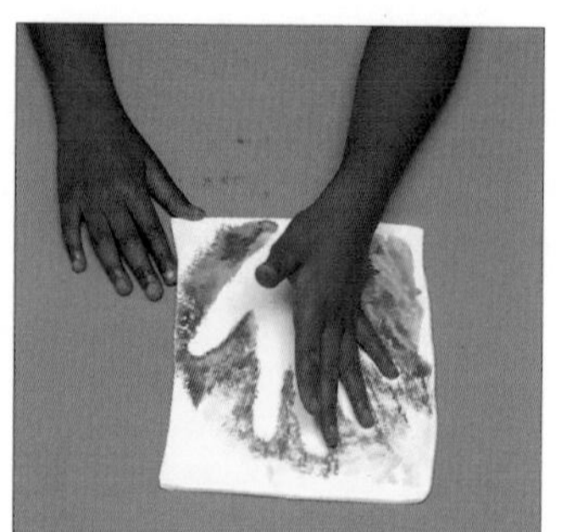

5 When you have finished your spray painting, carefully remove your hand. Take care not to smudge the paint, and then leave the tablet to dry. Wash your hands thoroughly.

This project is based on a Stone Age painting found in a cave in Argentina. The original artist blew paint through a reed, or even spat paint on to the wall.

Stone Age cave painting

The earliest Stone Age cave paintings date from around 40,000BC, and were etched on rocks in Australia. In Europe, the oldest works of art are cave paintings from about 28,000BC. Some caves in southwestern France and northern Spain are covered with paintings and engravings of animals, but show very few human figures. They were probably part of religious rituals. Stone Age artists also carved female figures, called Venus figurines, and decorated their tools and weapons with carved patterns and animal forms.

YOU WILL NEED

Self-hardening clay, rolling pin, cutting board, modelling tool, fine sandpaper, acrylic paints, paintbrush, water pot.

1 Roll out a piece of clay. Make sure it has an uneven surface similar to a cave wall. Then use a modelling tool to trim the edges into a neat rectangle shape.

2 Leave the clay to dry. When it is completely hard, rub it with fine sandpaper to get rid of any sharp edges, and to make a smooth surface for your painting.

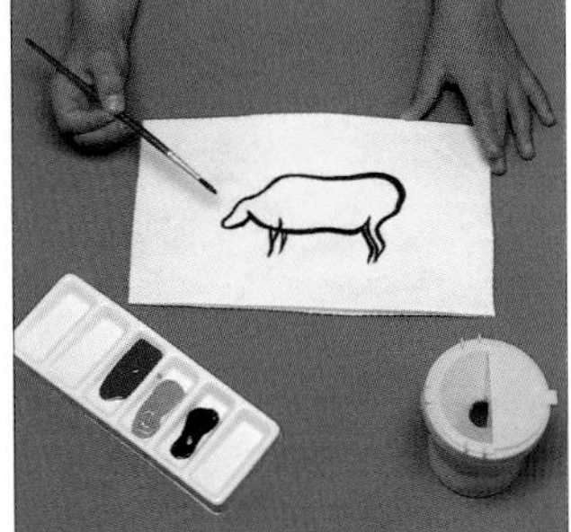

3 Paint the outline of an animal, such as this reindeer, using black acrylic paint. Exaggerate the size of the most obvious features, such as the muscular body and antlers.

4 When the outline is dry, mix black, red and yellow acrylic paints to make a warm, earthy colour. Use the colour you have mixed to fill in the outline of your chosen animal.

5 Finish your painting by highlighting some parts of the animal's body with reddish brown paint mixed to resemble red ochre. This is how Stone Age artists finished their paintings.

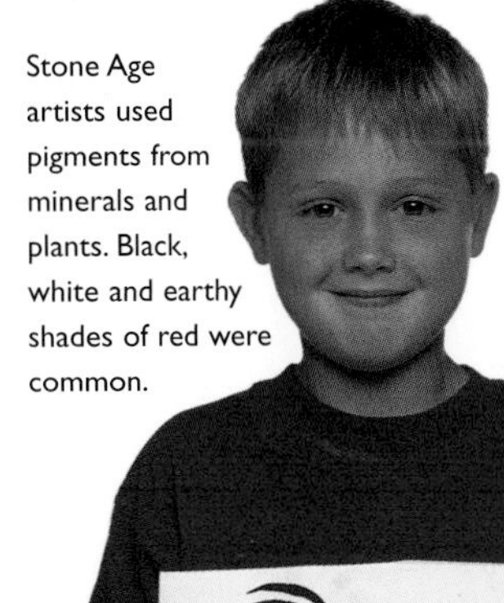

Stone Age artists used pigments from minerals and plants. Black, white and earthy shades of red were common.

Egyptian wall painting

The walls of many Egyptian tombs were covered with colourful pictures, which were very carefully made. First, the wall was coated several times with plaster. Then it was marked out in a grid pattern to make sure that each part of the design fitted neatly into the available space. Junior artists sketched the picture in red paint. Senior artists made corrections and went over the outlines in black ink. Finally, the outlines were filled in with paint. The step-by-step panel below shows you how to draw figures the Egyptian way.

YOU WILL NEED

Paper, pencil, black pen, ruler, red pen, piece of card, mixing bowl, plaster of Paris, water, wooden spoon, petroleum jelly, coarse sandpaper, acrylic paints, paint-brushes, water pot, 25cm/10in length of string, scissors, white fabric, white glue and glue brush.

To draw figures without a grid, start with simple lines and circles. Then add simple lines for limbs, and draw a tray on the shoulder. Round off the lines for the arms and legs.

Step 4

Complete the final design by drawing some features on the face, and food on the tray. It is easier to build up your picture this way.

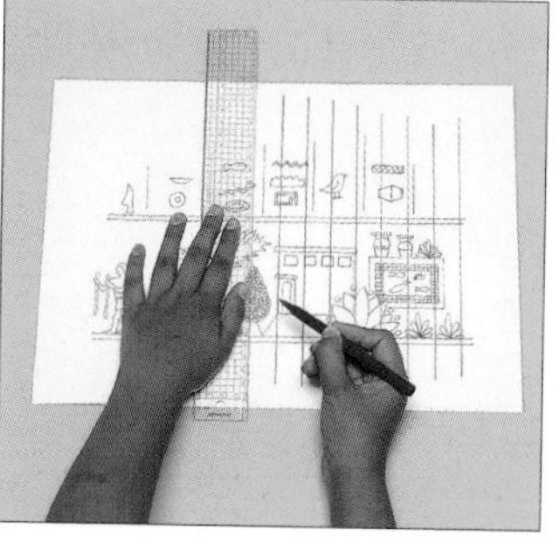

1 Draw a pencil design similar to the one shown in the final picture. Go over it with a black pen. Use a red pen and ruler to draw vertical and horizontal lines in a 2cm/¾in-square grid.

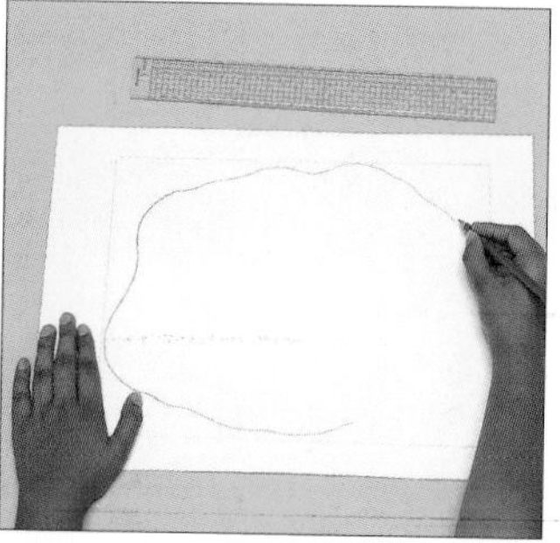

2 Measure the maximum length and maximum width of your design. Draw a rectangular box of the same size on a piece of card, then draw a wavy shape inside the box.

3 Mix the plaster of Paris and water in a bowl using a wooden spoon. The plaster of Paris should have a firm consistency, and the mixture should drop from the spoon in thick dollops.

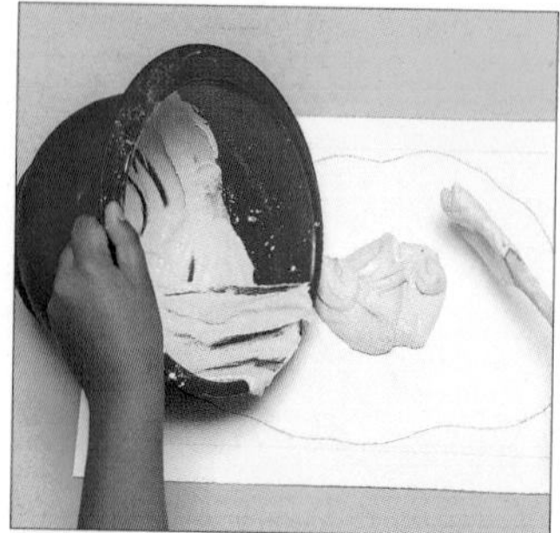

4 Smear a little petroleum jelly over the piece of card. This stops the plaster from sticking to the card. Then pour the plaster of Paris to cover the wavy shape you drew earlier.

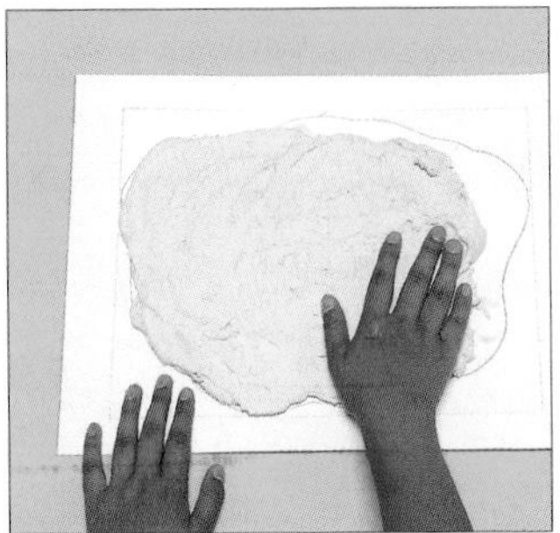

5 Spread the plaster mixture to a depth of about 8mm/⅜in. Then smooth the surface with your hand. Leave this shape to dry in a warm room for at least 2 hours.

6 When it is dry, gently rub the plaster with coarse sandpaper. Smooth the sandpaper over the rough edges, and all over the surface and sides of your slab of plaster.

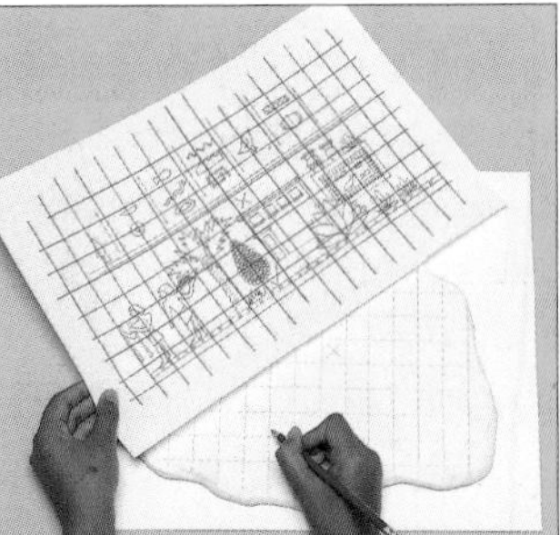

7 Use the ruler and pencil to draw another 2cm/¾in-square grid on the surface of the plaster. Carefully remove the piece of plaster from the card by lifting one edge at a time.

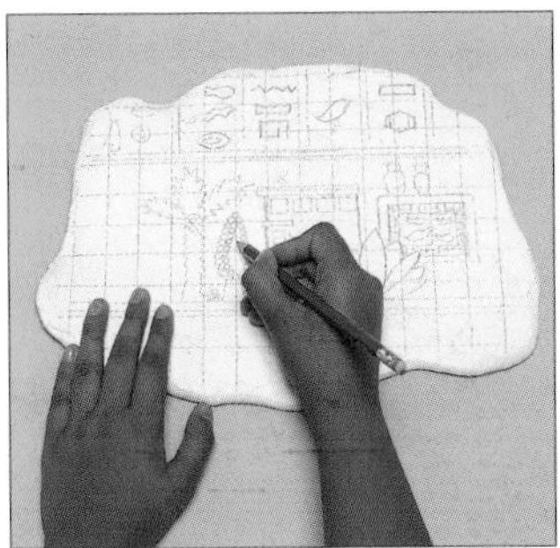

8 Transfer the design on the paper grid on to the plaster grid. Begin at the centre square and work outwards, copying one square at a time.

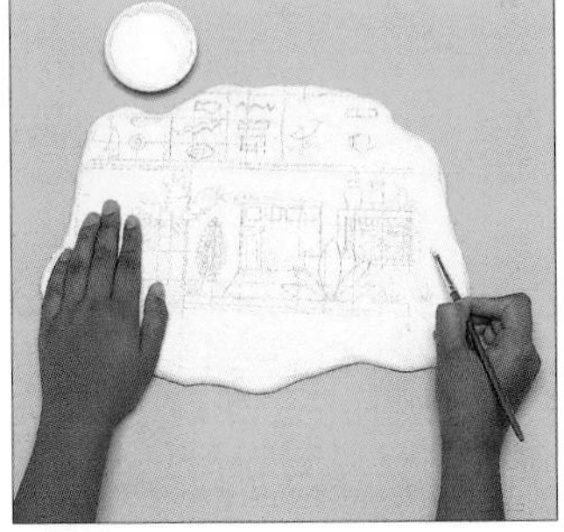

9 Use a fine paintbrush to paint the background of the plaster a cream colour. Then paint around the design itself. Leave the paint to dry for at least 1 hour before adding other colours.

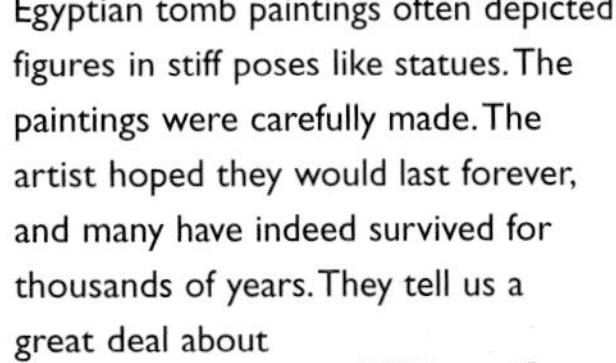

Egyptian tomb paintings often depicted figures in stiff poses like statues. The paintings were carefully made. The artist hoped they would last forever, and many have indeed survived for thousands of years. They tell us a great deal about how ancient Egyptians lived.

10 When the background is dry, add the details of the Egyptian painting, using a fine paintbrush. Paint the border using red, blue, yellow, black, white and gold acrylic paints.

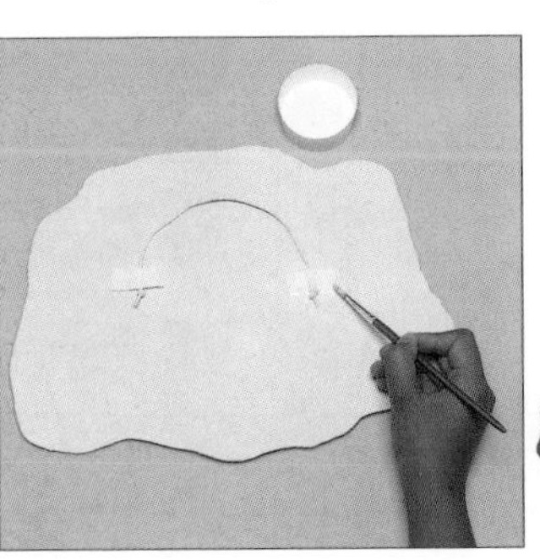

11 Tie a knot at each end of the piece of string. Cut two small pieces of fabric and glue them over the string, as shown above. When the glue is dry, you can hang your painting.

Greek vase

The artists and craftworkers of ancient Greece were admired for the quality of their work. They used a range of materials, such as metals, stone, wood, leather, bone, horn and glass. Most goods were made on a small scale in workshops surrounding the *agora* (marketplace). A craftsman might work on his own, or with the help of his family and a slave or two. In larger workshops, slaves laboured to produce bulk orders of popular goods. These might include shields, pottery and metalwork, all of which were traded around the Mediterranean Sea for a large profit.

YOU WILL NEED

Balloon, white glue, water, mixing bowl, newspaper, two rolls of masking tape, black pen, scissors, sheet of paper measuring 42 x 30cm/16½ x 12in, thick card, pencil, cream and black acrylic paints, paintbrush, water pot.

▲ Work of art
A good vase painter was a highly respected artist, and many signed their works. The export of vases was a major source of income for Athens.

▶ Storage space
Huge storage jars were used by the ancient Greeks to store food and drink. One jar could contain hundreds of litres/gallons of wine, olive oil or cereal. Handmade from clay, they kept food and drink cool in the hot Mediterranean climate.

1 Blow up a balloon. Soak strips of newspaper in one part white glue to two parts water to make papier mâché. Cover the balloon with two layers of papier mâché. Leave it to dry.

2 Using a roll of masking tape as a guide, draw and cut out two holes at the top and bottom of the papier mâché balloon. Discard the burst balloon.

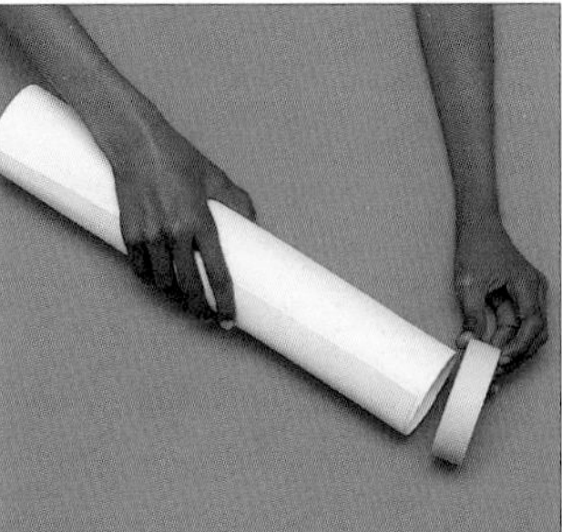

3 Roll the 42 x 30cm/16½ x 12in sheet of paper into a tube. Make sure it will fit through the middle of the roll of masking tape. Glue the paper tube in place, and secure with masking tape.

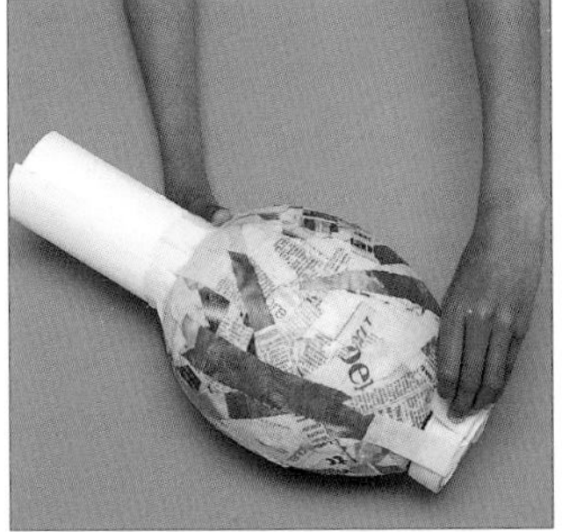

4 Push the tube through the middle of the papier mâché shape. Tape the tube into place. Push a roll of masking tape over the bottom of the paper tube, and tape, as shown above.

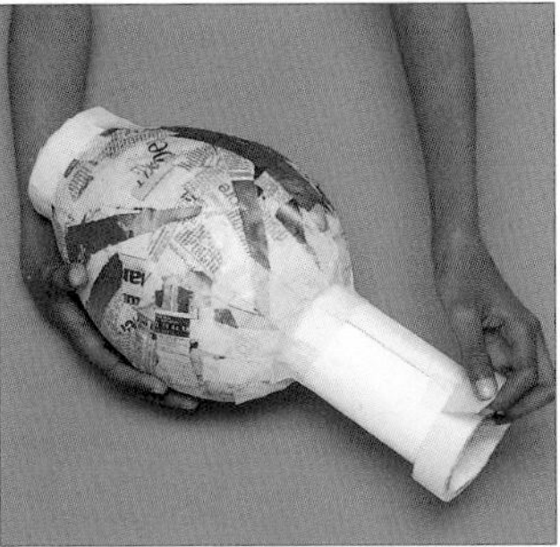

5 Attach the second roll of masking tape to the top of the paper tube. Make sure that both rolls of tape are securely fixed at either end of the paper tube.

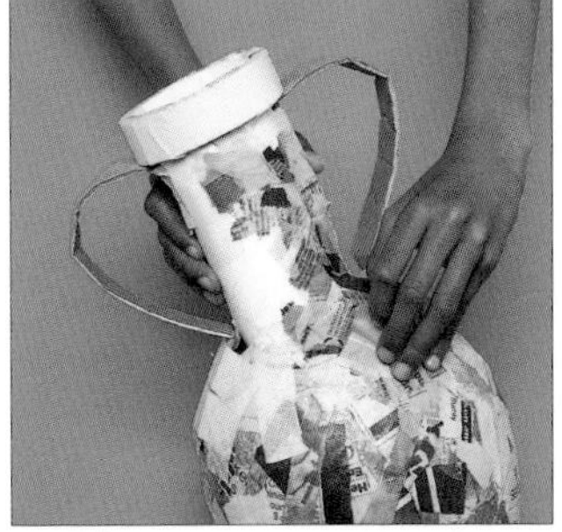

6 Cut two 15cm/6in strips of card. Fix them to either side of the vase for handles, as shown above. Cover the entire vase with more papier mâché, and leave to dry. Paint the vase cream.

7 When dry, use a pencil to copy the pattern above, or design a simple geometric pattern like the pots on the left. Paint over the design in black acrylic paint. Leave the vase to dry.

Greek vases such as the one you have made were called amphorae. They were given out as prizes at the Panathenaic games, and were decorated with sporting images.

Chinese silhouettes

Paper fine enough to write on, or to make cut-out patterns, such as the one in this project, was invented in China about AD105. Arts flourished as the Empire became more stable during the Seng Dynasty (AD960–1279) and the Ming Dynasty (1368–1644). Paintings appeared on walls, screens, fans and scrolls of silk and paper. Sometimes just a few brush strokes could capture the spirit of a subject. Chinese artists also produced beautiful woodcuts (prints made from a carved wooden block).

YOU WILL NEED

Thick coloured paper, pencil, small sharp scissors.

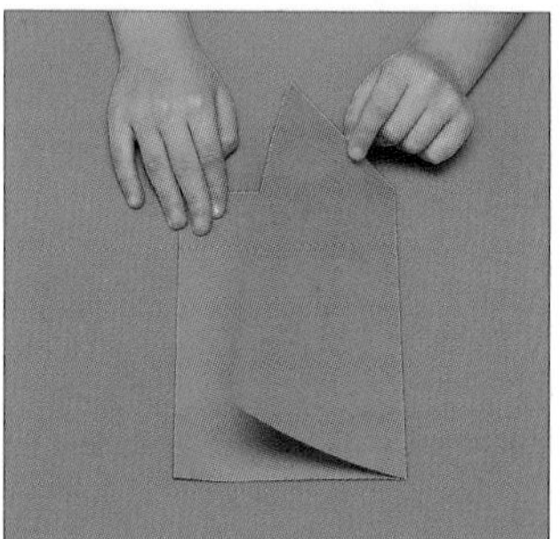

1 Take a piece of brightly coloured paper and lay it flat out on a hard work surface. Fold it in half widthways and make a firm crease along the fold, as shown above.

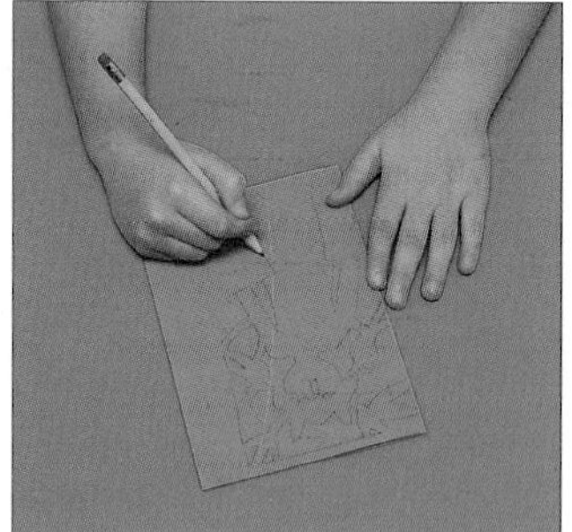

2 Use a pencil to draw a Chinese-style design on to the paper. Make a solid border around the non-folded edges. All the shapes in the design should touch the border or the fold.

3 Keeping the paper folded, cut out the shapes you have drawn. Make sure not to cut along the edges of the shapes on the fold. Cut away areas you want to discard in between the shapes.

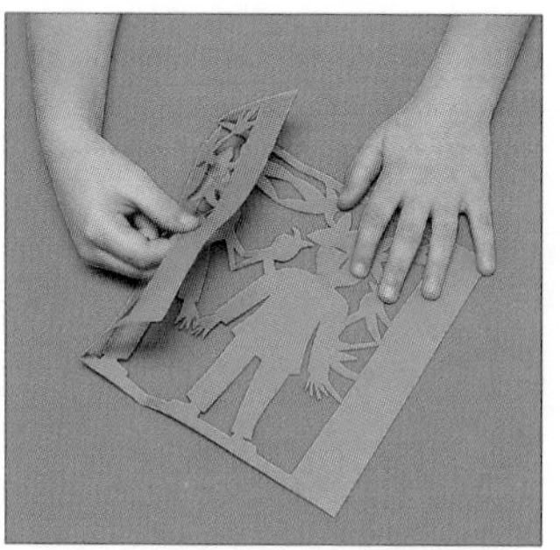

4 Open up the paper, taking care not to tear it. To add details to the cut-out figures, fold each figure in half separately. Pencil in the details to be cut along the crease.

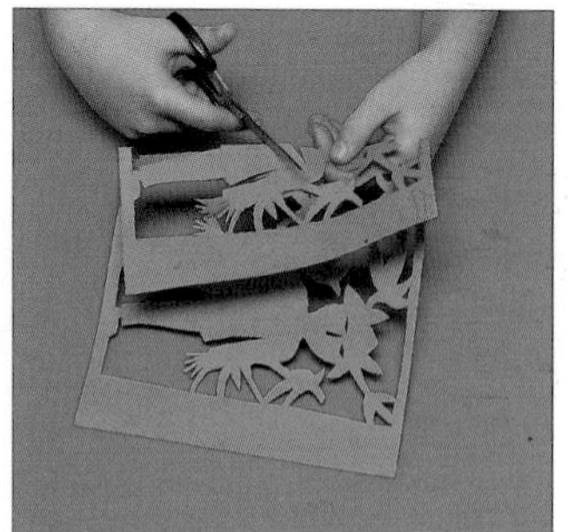

5 Carefully cut out the details you have marked along the crease. The cut-out details will be matched perfectly on the other side of the figure when you open the paper.

Display the design by sticking it to a window so that light shines through. In China, paper cut-outs are believed to bring luck and good fortune.

Japanese paper

The Japanese picked up paper-making skills from China around AD610, and improved on them. Mulberry and hemp were planted throughout the country, and were used to make paper as well as textiles. Japanese paper was stronger and finer-textured than Chinese paper. Soon there were many different colours and textures. Making paper was a work of art in itself. Calligraphy, the art of elegant writing, developed at the same time. Letter writers were judged on the paper they chose and their handwriting, as well as their words.

YOU WILL NEED

Eight pieces of wood (four at 33 x 2 x 1cm/13 x ¾ x ½in and four at 28 x 2 x 1cm/11 x ¾ x ½in), nails, hammer, muslin (35 x 30cm/14 x 12in), staple gun and staples, electrical tape, scissors, waste paper, water, mixing bowl, potato masher, washing up bowl, petals, soft cloth, newspaper.

1 Ask an adult to help you make two wooden frames. Staple muslin tightly over one of the frames. Cover the stapled edges with electrical tape to make the screen, as shown above.

2 Put some scraps of paper into a bowl of water and leave the paper to soak overnight. Then mash the paper into a pulp with a potato masher. The pulp should look like porridge.

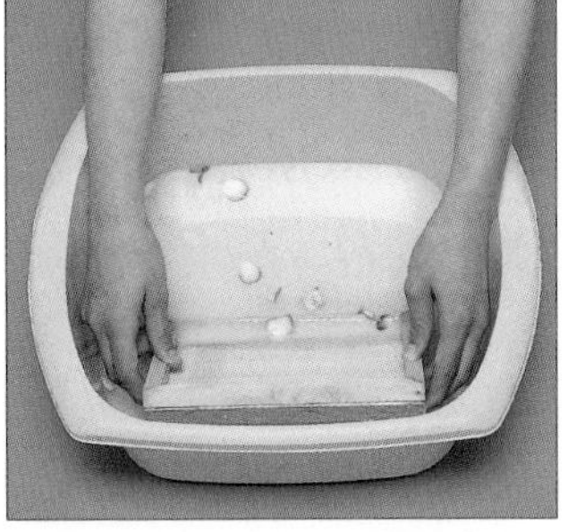

3 Tip the pulp into a washing up bowl and half fill with cold water. Mix in some petals. Place the open frame on top of the screen, put it in the bowl, and scoop some pulp into it.

4 Pull the screen out of the pulp, keeping it level. Gently move it from side to side over the bowl, to allow a layer of pulp to form on the screen. Shake off the excess water.

5 Remove the frame. Lay the screen face down on a cloth placed on layers of newspaper. Mop away the excess water. Peel away the screen and leave to dry for at least 6 hours.

Peel away the cloth to reveal your paper. This heavily textured paper is suitable for painting on.

Japanese ikebana

Although the word *ikebana* roughly translates as 'flower arrangement', the Japanese incorporate all sorts of other organic things in their designs. Driftwood, rocks and shells can all be brought into use. In an ikebana arrangement, the vase or pot represents the Earth, and the plants set in it should be arranged as if they are growing naturally.

This idea is carried through to Japanese gardens, which are often small but create a miniature landscape. Each rock, pool or gateway is positioned where it forms part of a balanced and harmonious arrangement. Japanese designers create gardens that look good during all the different seasons of the year. Zen gardens sometimes have no plants at all – just rocks, sand and gravel.

◂ The art of elegance
Japanese flower arrangements are often very simple. Flowers have been appreciated in Japan for hundreds of years. In the 8th century AD, thousands of poems were collected together in one book. About a third of the poems were about plants and flowers.

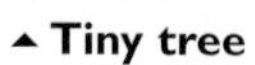

▴ Tiny tree
Bonsai is the Japanese art of producing miniature, but perfectly formed, trees such as this maple. This is achieved by clipping the roots and branches of the tree, and training it with wires.

YOU WILL NEED

Twig, scissors, vase filled with water, raffia or string, two flowers (one with a long stem; one shorter), branch of foliage, two stems of waxy leaves.

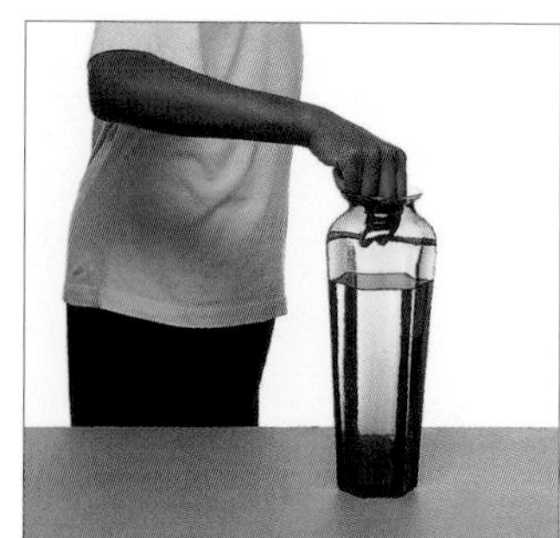

1 Cut the twig so that it can be wedged into the neck of the vase. The twig will provide a structure to build on, and will also control the position of the flowers.

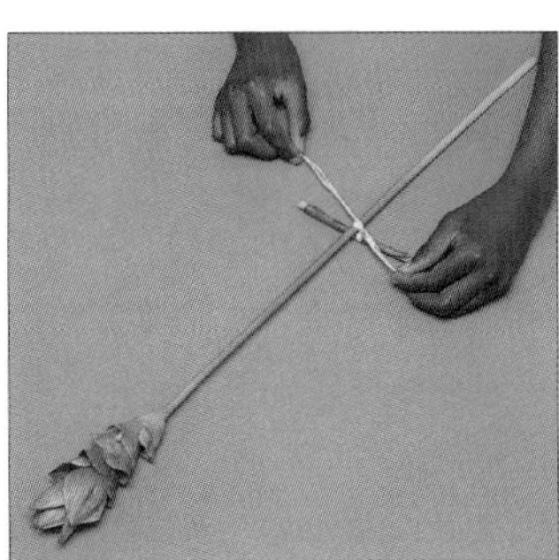

2 Remove the twig from the vase. Next, using a piece of string or raffia, tie the twig tightly on to the stem of the longest flower. Make the knot about halfway down the stem.

3 Place the flower stem in the vase. As you do this, gently slide the twig back into the neck of the vase, so that it is wedged into the same position as it was before.

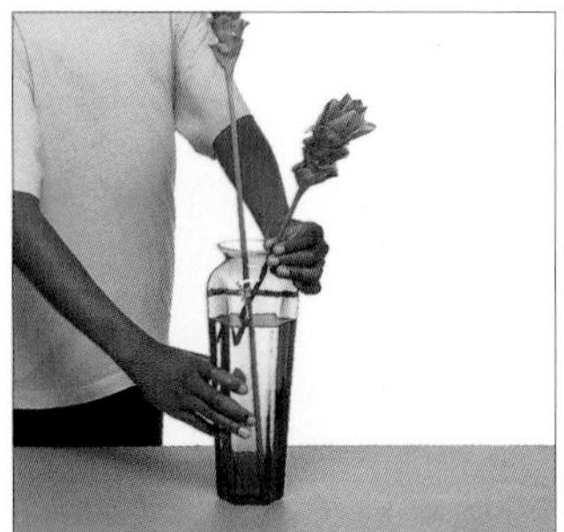

4 Add the flower with the shorter stem to the vase. Position this flower so that it slants forwards and to one side. Carefully lean this flower stem towards the longer one.

5 Slip the branch of foliage between the two stems. It should lean outwards and forwards. The foliage should look as if it is a naturally growing branch.

6 Position some waxy leaves at the neck of the vase. Ikebana is the arrangement of anything that grows, so the foliage is just as important as the flowers in your vase.

7 Add a longer stem of waxy leaves at the back of the vase to complete the arrangement, which is typical of the kinds that Japanese people use to decorate their homes.

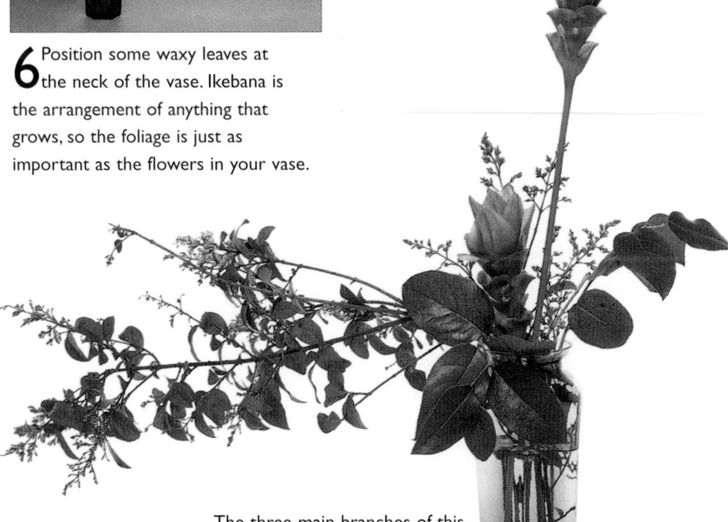

The three main branches of this arrangement represent heaven, the Earth and human beings. Even the leaves and other material are arranged in a carefully balanced way.

Celtic manuscript

By around AD1, the Celtic lands of mainland Europe were part of the Roman Empire. Over the next 400 years, Celtic languages and artistic traditions were gradually absorbed into the Roman Empire.

In the British Isles, the situation was different, as they were more isolated, and many parts were never conquered by Rome. Languages and traditions survived, creating a final flowering of Celtic culture, particularly in the Christian monasteries. There, the monks were making careful copies of sacred Christian texts. They decorated their manuscripts with plaited and spiralling Celtic designs in rich colours. In this way, the new and quite distinctive form of Celtic illumination was developed. Some manuscripts had notes scribbled in the margins such as 'The ink is bad ... the day dark.'

▲ **Irish saint**

A missionary called St Patrick took the Christian faith to Ireland. Irish monks made beautifully illuminated manuscripts. Their love of nature was obvious in their lively pictures of animals and birds.

▲ **Beautiful border**

The *Book of Durrow* is a Christian book decorated with Celtic designs. It was made on the Scottish island of Iona.

▲ **Stone marker**

Celtic standing stones were often turned into Christian crosses to mark burials, preaching places or holy ground.

YOU WILL NEED

Piece of thin card measuring 60 x 40cm/24 x 16in, ruler, pencil, felt-tipped pen, selection of paints and paintbrushes, water pot, eraser.

1 Draw a 57 x 37cm/ 22½ x 14½in rectangle on the thin card. Draw lines 1cm/½in in from the long sides and 1.5cm/⅝in in from the short sides. Draw lines 9.5cm/3¾in in from each end.

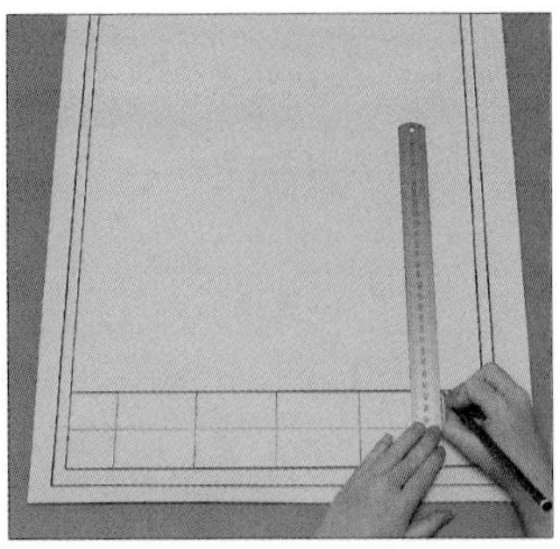

2 Divide the border at the top of the card into two horizontal sections. Mark vertical sections 3.5cm/1⅜in in from each end. Then add three more vertical lines 7cm/2¾in apart.

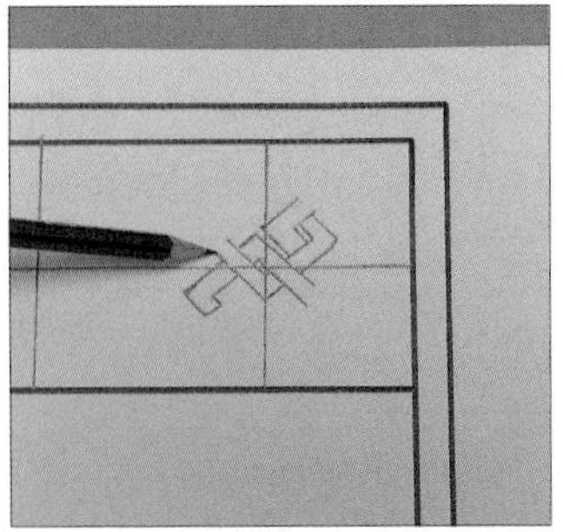

3 Begin at the top right-hand corner of the top section of the border. Place your pencil at the intersection of the first four squares. Draw a design similar to the one shown above.

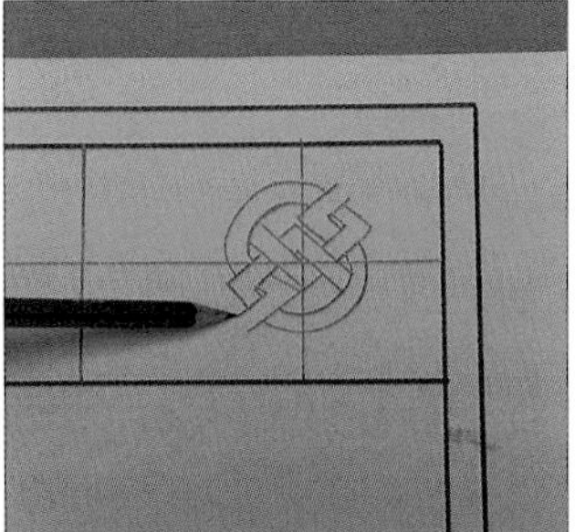

4 Add two outer circles to your design, as shown above. Join the circles to the open ends of your Celtic border to create a design known as an endless knot.

5 Add two even larger circles and the corner designs to your endless knot, as shown above. Extend the open ends on the left of the design to begin a second knot.

6 Create a row of endless knots. Repeat these steps to create an endless knot design in the border along the bottom of the card.

7 Paint the different strands of knot using typical Celtic colours, such as green and red. When the border is completely dry, carefully rub out the pencil grid.

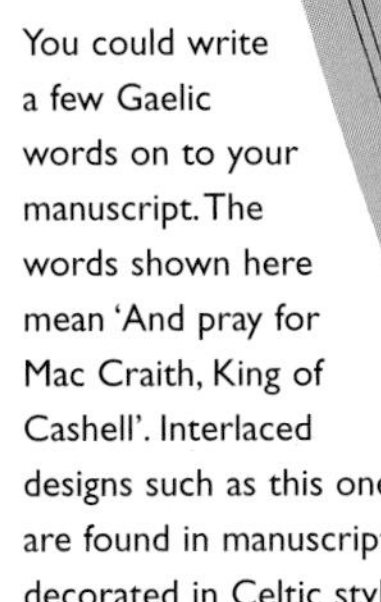

You could write a few Gaelic words on to your manuscript. The words shown here mean 'And pray for Mac Craith, King of Cashell'. Interlaced designs such as this one are found in manuscripts decorated in Celtic style.

Inca tumi knife

The whole region of the Andes had a very long history of metalworking. Incas often referred to gold as 'sweat of the Sun', and to silver as 'tears of the Moon'. These metals were sacred to the gods, and also to the Inca rulers and priests – the gods on Earth. At the Temple of the Sun in Cuzco, there was a whole garden made of gold and silver, with golden soil, golden stalks of corn and golden llamas. Imagine how it must have gleamed in the sunlight! Copper, however, was used by ordinary people. It was made into cheap jewellery, weapons and everyday tools. The Incas' love of gold and silver eventually led to their downfall, for it was rumours of their fabulous wealth that lured the Spanish to invade the region in the 1400s.

▲ **Copper ore**

The Incas worked with copper, found in rocks like this one, and knew how to mix it with tin to make bronze. The Incas also used gold, silver and platinum, but not iron or steel.

YOU WILL NEED
Card, pencil, ruler, scissors, self-hardening clay, cutting board, rolling pin, modelling tool, white glue and glue brush, toothpick, gold paint, paintbrush, water pot, blue metallic paper.

▲ **Tumi knife**

A ceremonial knife with a crescent-shaped blade is known as a tumi. Its gold handle is made in the shape of a ruler.

▲ **Precious blade**

The handle of this Inca sacrificial knife is made of wood inlaid with gemstones, shells and turquoise.

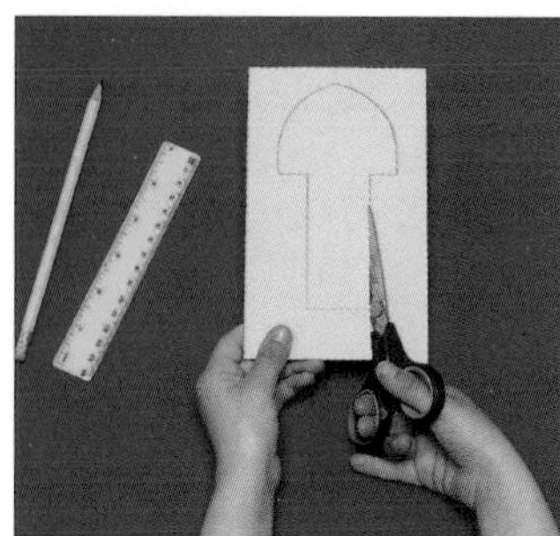

1 Draw the shape of the knife blade on a piece of card and cut it out. The rectangular part measures 9 x 3.5cm/ 3½ x 1⅜in. The rounded part is 7cm/ 2¾in across and 4.5cm/1¾in high.

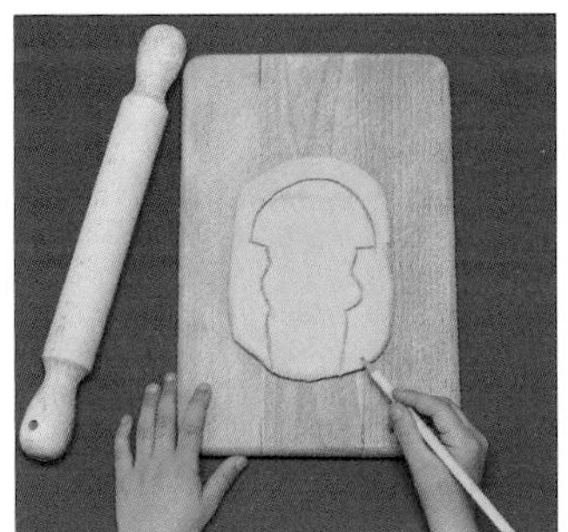

2 Roll out a slab of clay to a thickness of 1cm/½in. Pencil in a tumi shape. It should be about 12.5cm/4⅞in long and measure 9cm/3½in across the widest part at the top.

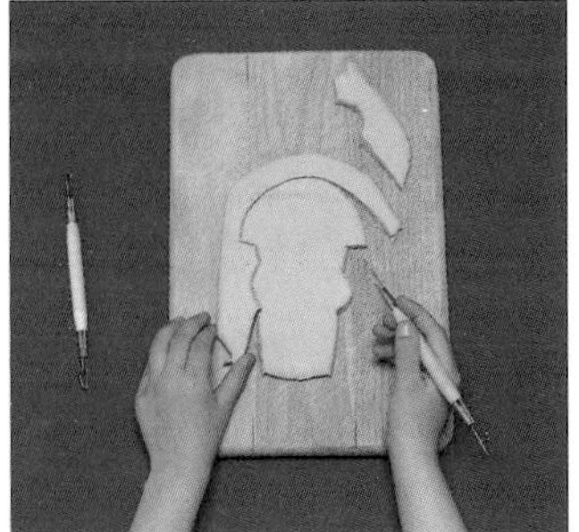

3 Use the modelling tool to cut around the clay shape you have drawn. Put the leftover clay to one side. Make sure the edges of the tumi handle are clean and smooth.

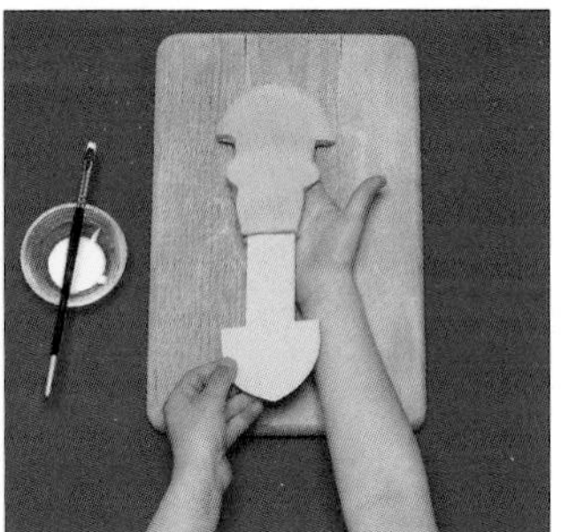

4 Use the modelling tool to cut a slot in the bottom edge of the tumi handle. Lifting it carefully, slide the card blade into the handle. Use glue to join the blade and the handle firmly.

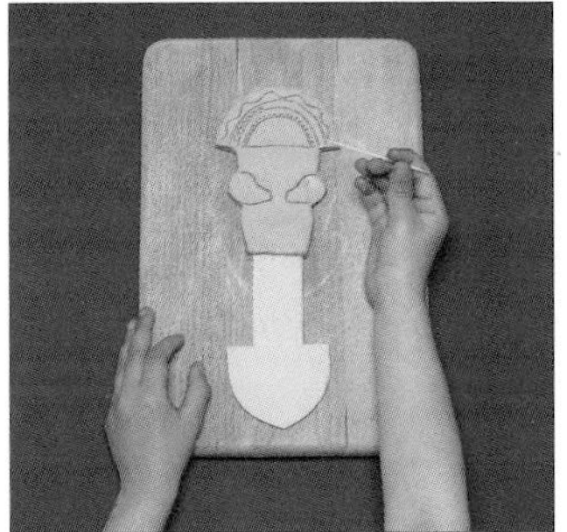

5 Use a modelling tool to mark on the details of the tumi. Use a toothpick for the fine details. Look at the finished knife (*right*) to see how to do this. Leave everything to dry.

6 When the clay is dry, give one side of the tumi and blade a coat of gold paint. Leave it to dry completely before turning it over and painting the other side.

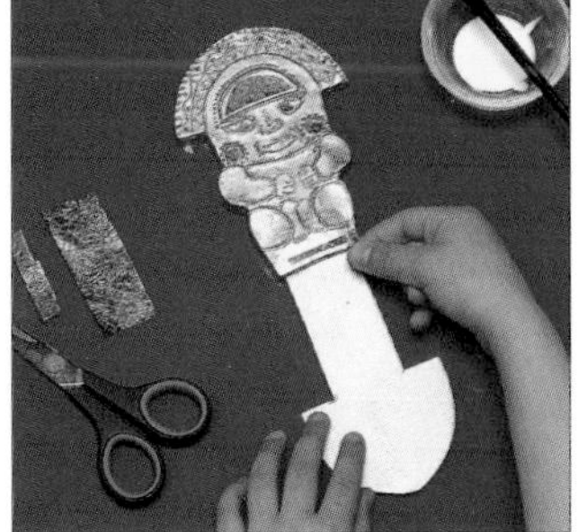

7 The original tumi knife would have been decorated with pieces of turquoise. Glue small pieces of blue metallic paper on to the handle for turquoise, as shown in the picture.

The Chimú gold and turquoise tumi was used by priests of the Chimú people at religious ceremonies. It may even have been used to kill sacrifices for the gods.

Customs

▲ **Urn for ashes**
In some ancient societies, people cremated their dead by burning the bodies on a funeral pyre. The ashes, and sometimes the bones, of the dead person were placed in pottery urns such as the one above. The urn was then placed in a burial chamber.

Today, many aspects of life are similar from one side of the world to the other. People wear the same sort of clothes, drive similar cars, and live and work in the same sort of houses and apartment blocks. This has not always been the case. For thousands of years, customs and lifestyles varied greatly between different continents, and even between countries and regions. There were differences in how people dressed, what they ate and how they greeted each other.

Many customs are very closely related to religion, such as Ramadan (a Muslim period of fasting) and the barmitzvah (a coming-of-age ceremony for Jewish boys). Some ancient customs are still practised today, but a great many have been forgotten and lost forever.

▲ **Crying a river**
Osiris was the Egyptian god of farming. After he was killed by his jealous brother Seth, Osiris became a god of the underworld and the afterlife. The ancient Egyptians believed that the yearly flooding of the River Nile marked the anniversary of Osiris's death, when his queen, Isis (*above*), wept for him.

Symbol of hope ▸

The water lily, or lotus, is a symbolic flower in Buddhism. It represents enlightenment, which can come out of suffering just as the beautiful flower grows from slimy mud.

◂ Elephant god

The elephant god Ganesh is the Hindu lord of learning and remover of all obstacles. His parents were Shiva and Parvati. According to Hindu mythology, Shiva mistook his son Ganesh for someone else, and beheaded him. Shiva realized his mistake and replaced his son's head with one from the first creature he saw – an elephant.

▴ Gateway to beyond

Many people in Japan practise the Shinto religion. Every Shinto religious shrine can only be entered through a gate called a *torii*. The torii separates the holy shrine from the ordinary world outside. It can be some distance from the shrine itself.

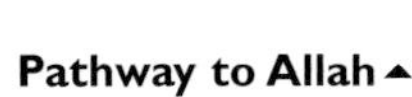

Pathway to Allah ▴

Islamic law schools like this one are found all over the world. Islamic law is known as the *Shari'ah* – an Arabic word meaning a track that leads camels to a waterhole. In the same way, Muslims who obey the Shari'ah will be led to Allah (God).

Stone Age wooden henge

The first stone monuments were built in Europe, and date back to around 4200BC. They are called megaliths, from the Greek word meaning 'large stone'. Some of the first megaliths were made of a large flat stone supported by several upright stones. They are the remains of ancient burial places, called chambered tombs. Others are called passage graves. These were communal graves where many people were buried. Later, larger monuments were constructed. Stone or wood circles called henges, such as Stonehenge in England, were built. No one knows why these circles were made. They may have been temples, meeting places or giant calendars, since they are aligned with the Sun, Moon and stars. The monuments were sometimes altered. Some stones were removed and others were added.

YOU WILL NEED

Card, ruler, pair of compasses, pencil, scissors, self-hardening clay, rolling pin, cutting board, modelling tool, 1cm/½in- and 5mm/¼in-thick dowel, acrylic paint, paintbrush, water pot, fake grass, white glue and glue brush, scissors, sandpaper, varnish, brush.

▲ Stone circle
The megalithic monuments of Europe have stood for thousands of years, but they have not always looked the same. Archaeologists have found many holes in the ground where additional stones and wooden posts once stood. These sites were once even more complex than they are today.

▶ The heavy work
Stonehenge in Wiltshire, England, was built with the simplest technology. The builders probably used sleds or rollers to move the stones, each weighing about 40 tonnes/44 tons, about 25km/15½ miles to the site. Ropes and levers were then used to haul them into place.

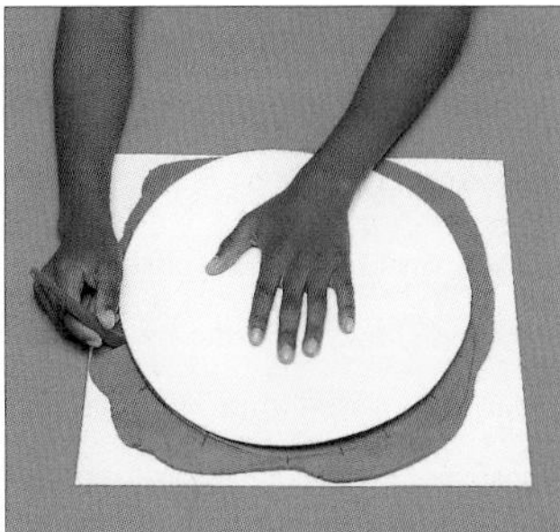

1 Cut out a card circle 35cm/14in in diameter. Roll out the clay, place the card circle on top and score around the card. Use a modelling tool to mark about 18 points around the circle.

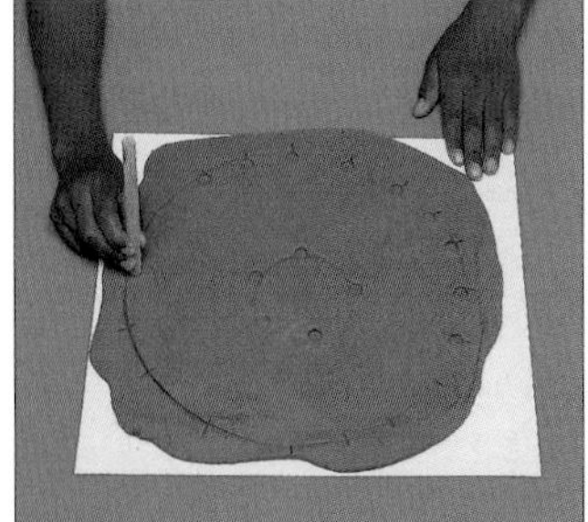

2 Mark another circle, 10cm/4in across, inside the first circle. Mark five points around it for posts. Press a 1cm/½in-thick stick into each point. Repeat for the outer circle.

3 Make sure all the holes for the posts are evenly spaced. When you have finished, leave the clay base to dry. Then smooth over the base with fine sandpaper and paint it brown.

4 Roughly cover the clay base with pieces of fake grass. Glue them into position, as shown above. Be careful not to cover up the holes for the posts you made earlier.

5 Cut seven long and 16 short sticks from the 1cm/½in-thick dowel. These will make the posts. Cut 17 short pieces from the 5mm/¼in-thick dowel for the lintels. Varnish the sticks.

6 When the sticks are dry, glue them in place using the post holes and the picture above as a guide. Then glue the lintels on top of the outer posts to complete your wooden circle.

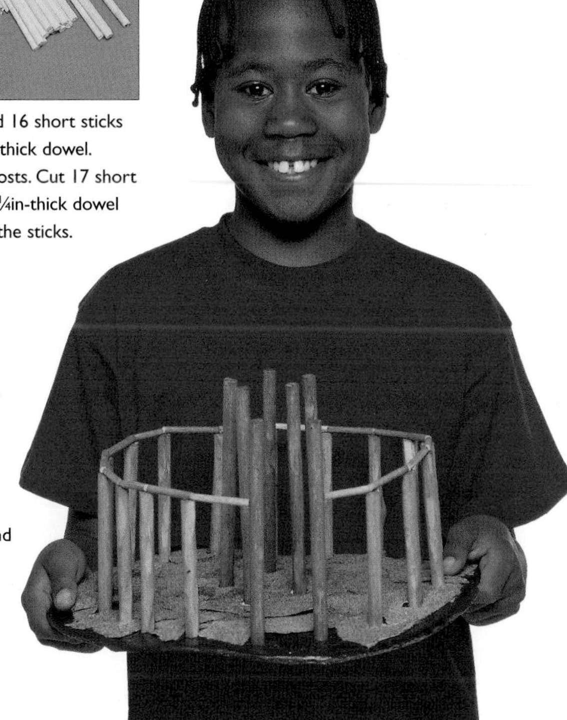

Wood henges had up to five rings of timber posts increasing in height towards the centre. People started building wooden henges around 3000BC. They became centres of religious and social life.

Egyptian canopic jar

Mummy-makers in Egypt removed the body's internal organs and stored them in containers called canopic jars. There was one jar each for the lungs, intestines, liver and stomach. A jackal-headed jar such as the one you can make in this project would have held the stomach. Organs could not be thrown away, because people believed they might be used by an evil magician in a spell. Some mummy-makers filled the space where the organs had been with fragrant herbs and spices, clay, sand, salt, cloth or straw.

YOU WILL NEED

Ruler, pencil, thin white card, black marker pen, scissors, masking tape, old newspaper, sheet of paper, mixing bowl, flour, water, fork, three paper cups, fine sandpaper, cloth, white emulsion paint, acrylic paints, gold paint, paintbrushes, water pot, clear wood varnish.

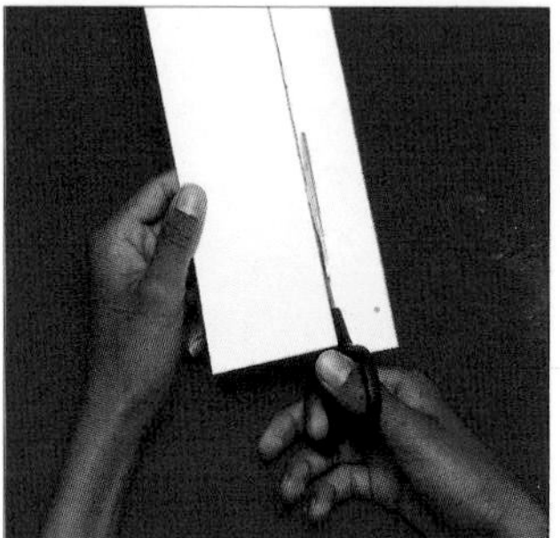

1 Use a ruler and pencil to draw a rectangle measuring 26 x 6cm/10¼ x 2½in on to the thin white card. Trace over the outline with a black marker pen and then cut out the rectangle.

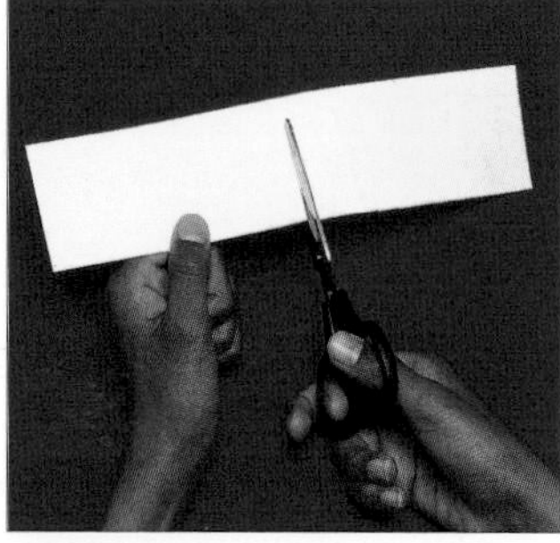

2 Use a ruler and pencil to lightly mark 1cm/½in spaces along one of the longer sides of the rectangle. Make a cut at each mark about 4cm/1½in into the card. This will make a row of tabs.

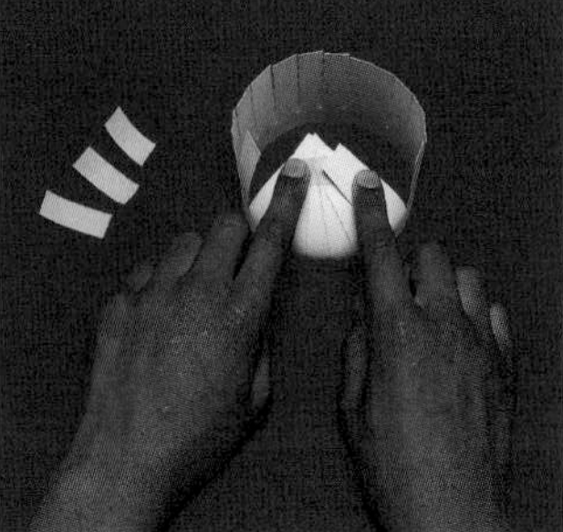

3 Tape the ends of the card together and bend the tabs inwards to make a dome shape, as shown above. Stick each tab to the next one using small fingertip-sized pieces of masking tape.

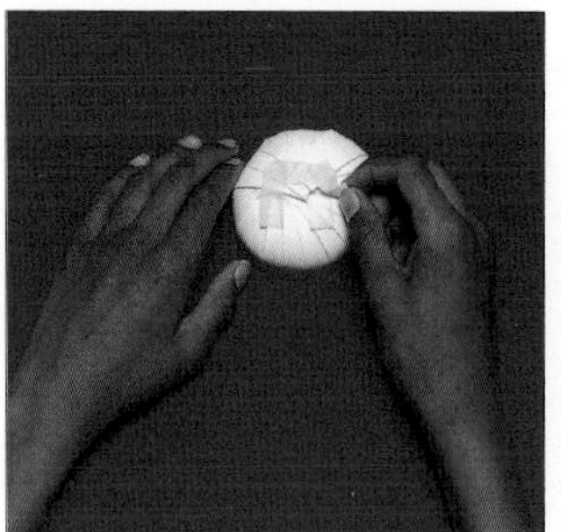

4 When you have bent and stuck all the tabs down to make the dome shape, secure the top of it using some more masking tape. This dome will form the lid of your canopic jar.

5 Take a piece of old newspaper and tear it into small strips. Scrunch them up into a ball with a diameter of 4cm/1½in (about the size of a golf ball). Cover the ball with masking tape.

6 Cut out small card triangles for ears, about 4 x 2.5cm/1½ x 1in. Roll a strip of newspaper into a tube to make the muzzle. Then use pieces of masking tape to fix these pieces to the head.

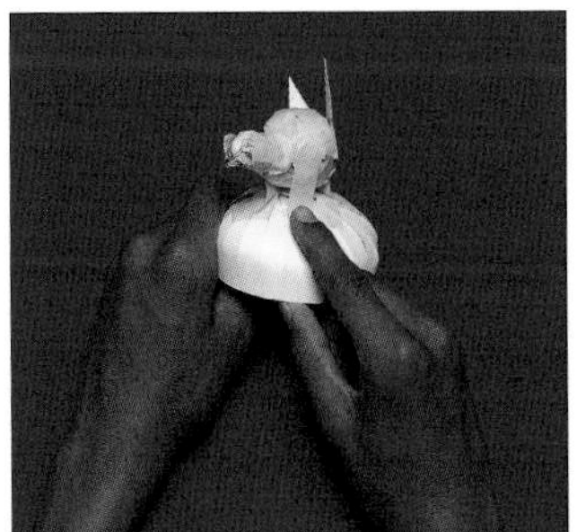

7 Hold the base of the lid firmly in one hand. With the other hand, stick strips of masking tape over the head and dome. The jackal's head is now ready for pasting.

8 Cover the work surface with some paper. Put 250g/9oz of flour into a bowl. Pour in some water to make a paste, stirring with a fork as you pour. Tear some more newspaper into strips.

9 Dip the newspaper into the paste. Cover the jackal's head with three layers, leaving it to dry between layers. Then stack three paper cups together, and cover them with the papier mâché.

10 When both the jar and jackal's head lid are completely dry, sand the outsides down with fine sandpaper until the surface is smooth. Dust them both with a cloth.

11 Paint the inside and outside of the lid and jar with white emulsion. When dry, paint the outside of the jar with cream acrylic paint, leaving a white rim of emulsion at the top.

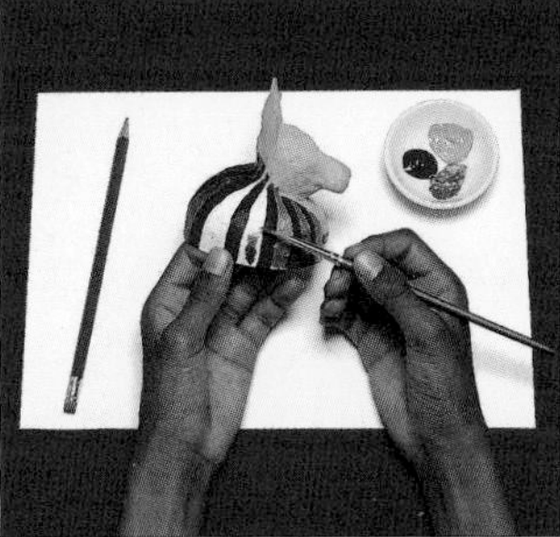

12 Mix up some green, blue and white paints to make turquoise. Use this to paint the head. Paint blue and gold stripes on the dome of the lid. Then draw a face on the head.

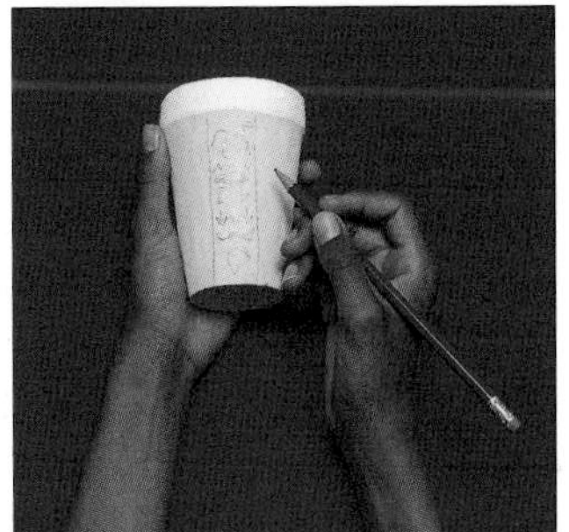

13 Draw a spell on the body of the jar, using a pencil. You can copy the design shown here, or you can look for references to other spells in books about Egypt.

14 Paint over your pencil design in black, and paint the face of the jackal in black and white. Paint the top rim gold and leave it to dry completely. Then varnish the jar and lid.

Jars with different shaped lids were used to store the body's organs. For example, human-headed jars held the liver.

Egyptian udjat eye

When pharaohs died, everything possible was done to make sure that they completed their journey to the gods in safety. During the New Kingdom, the ruler's coffin, containing his mummy, would be placed on a boat and ferried from Thebes to the west bank of the River Nile. The funeral procession was spectacular. Priests scattered milk and burned incense, and women wept. After the ceremony, the coffin was placed in the tomb with food, drink and charms such as the udjat eye you can make in this project.

YOU WILL NEED

Rolling pin, self-hardening clay, cutting board, modelling tool, sandpaper, soft cloth, acrylic paint, paintbrush, water pot.

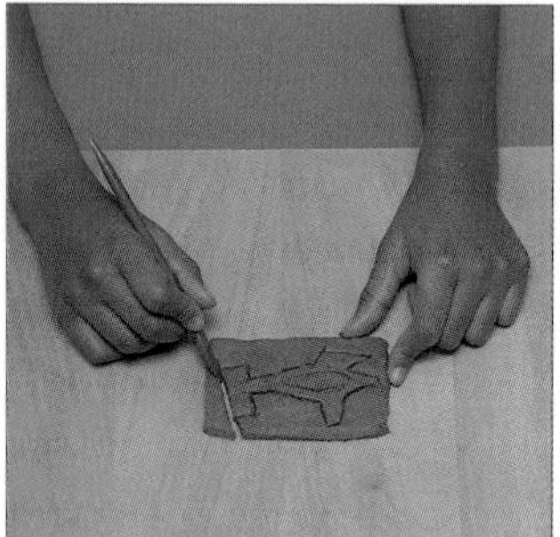

1 Use a rolling pin to roll out some clay on to a cutting board. Use the modelling tool to cut out the pattern of the eye pieces. Refer to Step 2 for the shape of each piece.

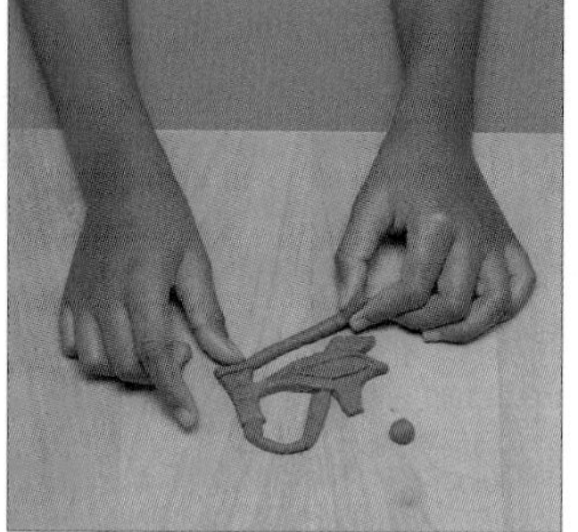

2 Remove the excess clay from the eye pieces and arrange them on the cutting board. The eye is meant to represent the eye of the falcon-headed Egyptian god called Horus.

3 Now press the pieces together until you have the full shape of the eye. You may need to use the modelling tool to secure all the joins. When you have finished, leave the eye to dry.

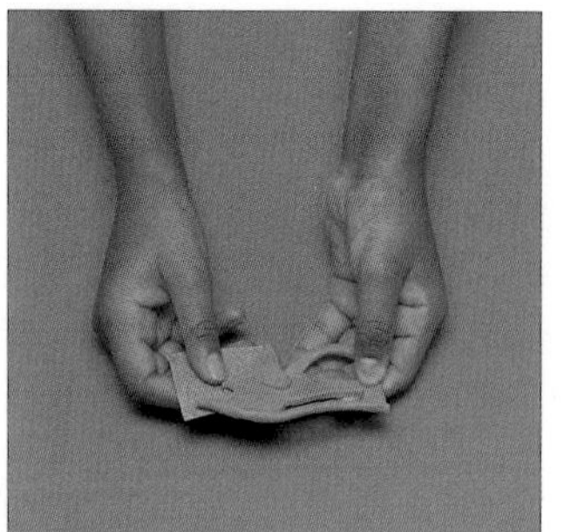

4 When it is dry, smooth the surface of the eye with fine sandpaper. Then wipe it with a soft cloth to remove any dust. The eye of Horus is now ready for painting.

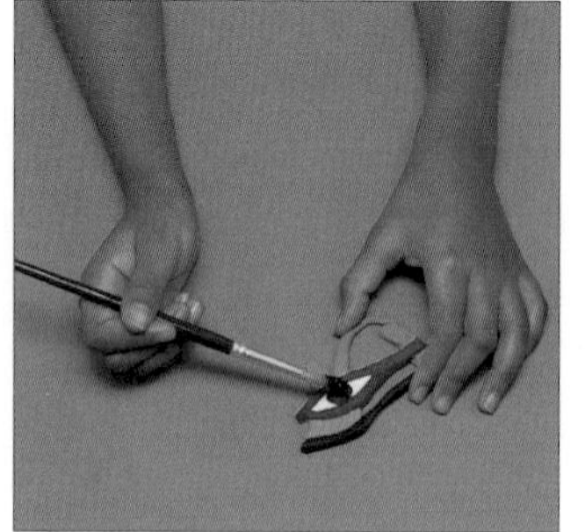

5 Paint in the white of the eye and add the eyebrow and pupil. Next paint in the red liner. Finally, paint the rest of the eye charm blue. Let each colour dry before adding the next.

Horus lost his eye in a battle with Seth, the god of chaos. Udjat eyes were thought to be lucky in ancient Egypt.

Roman temple

Many splendid temples were built to honour the gods and goddesses of the Roman Empire. The Pantheon in Rome was the largest of these. Special festivals for the gods were held during the year, with processions, music and animal sacrifices. The festivals were often public holidays. The mid-winter celebration of Saturnalia lasted up to seven days. It honoured Saturn, the god of farmers. As the Empire grew, many Romans adopted the religions of other peoples, such as the Egyptians and the Persians.

YOU WILL NEED

Thick card for the template pieces, pencil, ruler, pair of compasses, scissors, newspaper, balloon, white glue and glue brush, thin card, masking tape, drinking straws, non-hardening modelling material, acrylic paints, paintbrush, water pot.

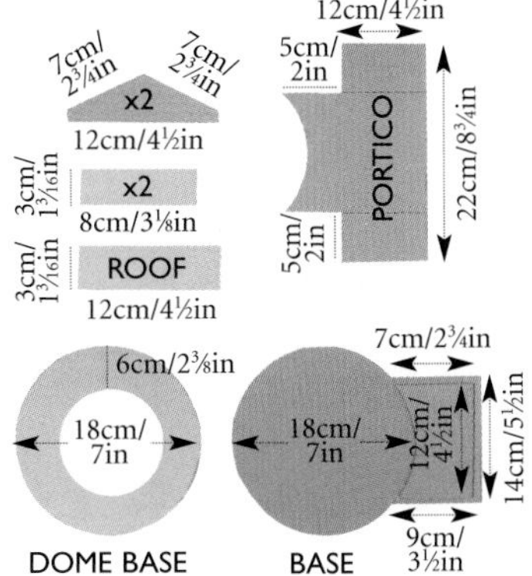

▲ **Templates**
Cut the templates out of thick card.

1 Glue layers of paper to half of a balloon. When dry, burst the balloon and cut out a dome. Make a hole in the top. Put the dome on its card base. Bind the pieces together, as shown.

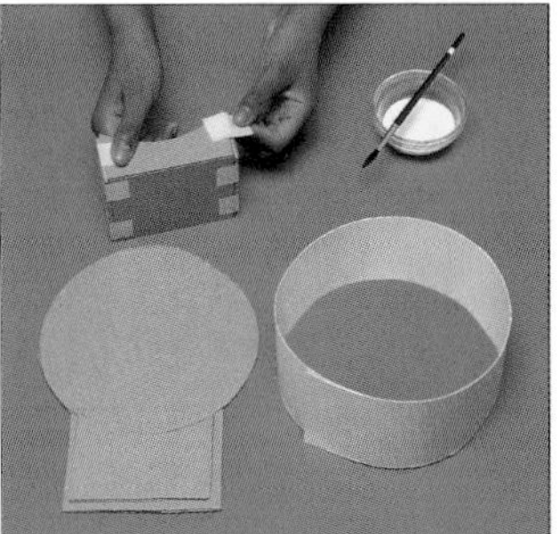

2 Cut a 12cm/4¾in-wide strip of thin card, long enough to fit around the base circle. Secure it with masking tape, and then glue it to the base. Tape the portico section together, as shown.

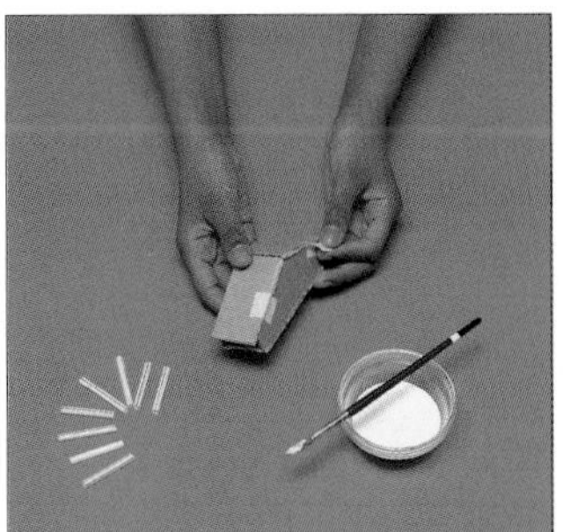

3 Cut some straws into eight pieces, each 6cm/2½in long. These are the columns for the entrance of the temple. Glue and tape together the roof pieces for the entrance to the temple.

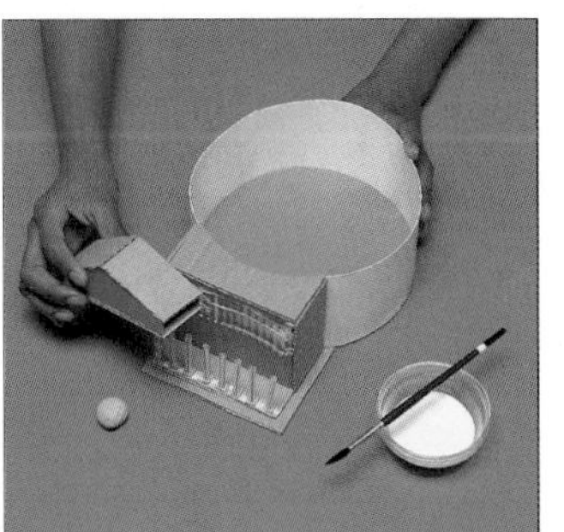

4 Glue everything together, as shown, and secure with tape. Fix each straw column with a small piece of modelling material at its base. Glue on the roof and the dome. Paint the model.

The Pantheon in Rome was built from AD118 to AD128. It was a temple to all the Roman gods. The Pantheon was built of brick and then clad in stone and marble. Its high dome, mosaic floor and interior columns remain exactly as they were built.

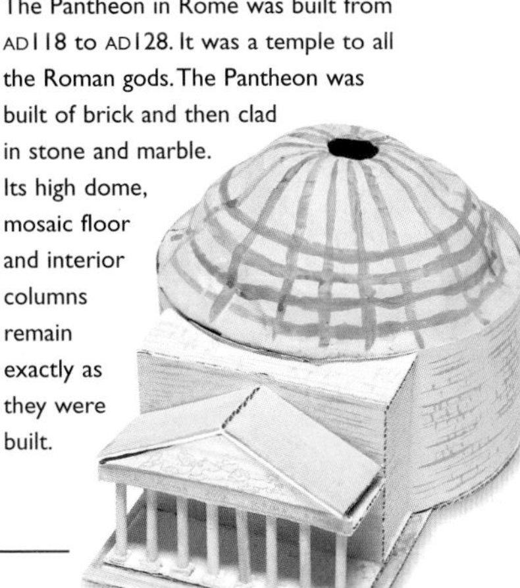

Hindu flower garland

Buddhism was the dominant religion in India until about AD200. Gradually, Hinduism became more widely practised. Hinduism has remained the dominant religion in India ever since.

Hindus have many festivals to honour the gods. At many, garlands of leaves and fresh flowers are used to decorate the body and hair. Garlands are also used to decorate images of Hindu gods in the practice of puja (worship).

Flowers have been very important in India throughout its history. During the Mughal Empire (1526–1758), wealthy nobles created courtyards and gardens filled with pools and flowering plants. The Mughal rulers were Muslims. Their gardens often had a symbolic significance, because they were viewed as a miniature map of paradise. Mughal kings divided their gardens into four parts, called charbhags. Each part was separated by water channels that represented the rivers of paradise.

▲ Nowhere to hide
Brahma is the Hindu god of creation. After he created the first woman, he fell in love with her. She hid herself away, so Brahma grew three more heads so that he could see her from every angle.

▲ Hindu wanderer
Wandering priests or holy men are called sadhus. They give up worldly pleasure, and wander from place to place begging for food.

Priestly caste ▶
Brahmin priests were one of three castes (social classes) that made up the native Aryan people in India. Each caste played a different role in important Aryan ceremonies. The Aryan customs and writings formed the basis of the Hindu religion.

YOU WILL NEED
Tissue paper (orange, yellow, red, blue, pink and white), pencil, scissors, white glue and glue brush, length of string, darning needle.

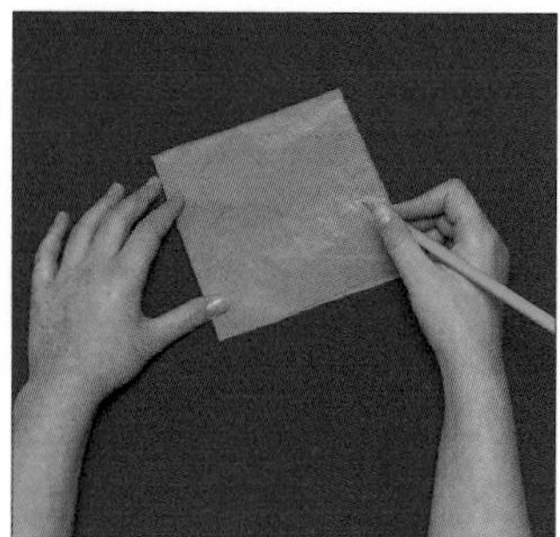

1 Draw simple flower shapes on to the sheets of coloured tissue paper. If you like, you can put the sheets of coloured paper in layers, one on top of the other.

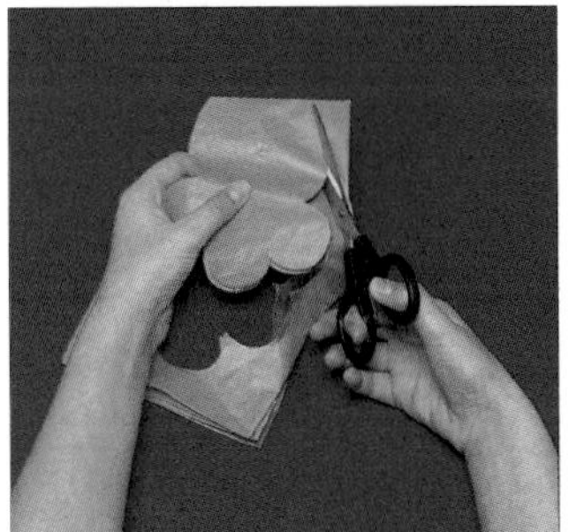

2 Carefully cut out the flower shapes, using a pair of scissors. Take care not to tear the tissue paper as you cut around the outline. Cut the same number of flowers in each colour.

3 Scrunch up the tissue flower shapes with your hands to make them creased. Uncrumple each flower, as shown, making sure not to smooth the flower out too much.

4 Glue the separate flower shapes together in loose layers to make larger, single flowers. Use eight layers of different coloured tissue paper for each finished flower.

5 When each flower is dry, gently fluff up the layers of tissue paper with your fingers. Try not to tear the paper as you go. Your flowers will now look much more realistic.

6 Measure a length of string to fit around your neck and hang down to the level of your waist. Start to thread each flower on to the string using the darning needle.

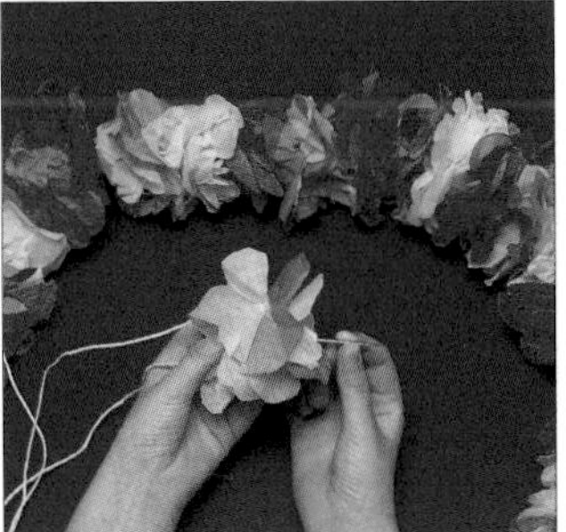

7 Thread all the tissue flowers on to the length of string. When you have finished, firmly tie a double knot in the string to secure the flowers. Your garland is now ready to wear.

Indians are fond of flowers such as mango blossom, ashoka flower and jasmine. They use them in many garlands. Another favourite flower is the lotus (water lily), a symbol of spirituality.

Viking lucky charm

The Vikings believed the universe was held up by a great tree called Yggdrasil. There were several separate worlds. Niflheim was the snowy, cold underworld. The upper world was Asgard, home of the gods.

There were many Viking gods. Odin, the father of the gods, rode through the night sky, and his son, Baldr, was god of the summer Sun. Thor, the god of thunder, carried a two-headed hammer. Vikings were superstitious, and wore lucky charms, such as one in the shape of Thor's hammer, to protect themselves from evil.

▲ Pick me, Odin!
Vikings believed that after a battle, Odin and his servants, the Valkyries, searched the battlefield. They carried dead heroes to a Viking heaven called Valholl, or Valhalla.

▲ Take it with you
Vikings were buried with the weapons and treasures that they would need for the next life. Even poor Vikings were buried with a sword or a brooch.

YOU WILL NEED

Thick paper or card, pencil, scissors, self-hardening clay, cutting board, rolling pin, modelling tool, felt-tipped pen, fine sandpaper, silver acrylic paint, paintbrush, water pot, length of cord, piece of wire.

1 Draw the outline of Thor's hammer on to thick paper or card, using the final project picture as your guide. Cut it out. Use this card hammer as the pattern for making your lucky charm.

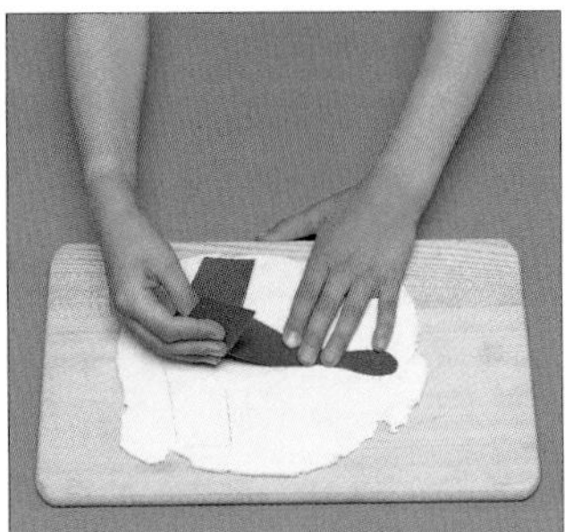

2 Roll out a piece of clay to a thickness of 5mm/¼in on the cutting board. Press the card hammer pattern into the clay, so that it leaves the outline of the hammer in the clay.

3 Remove the card. Use the modelling tool to cut around the imprint. Mark lines around the edge of the hammer, and draw on a pattern. Make a line at the end of the hammer for a handle.

4 Pierce a hole through the end of the handle. Cut off the handle end and turn it upright. Then join the handle back up to the main part of the hammer. Make the join as smooth as possible.

5 Use the end of a felt-tipped pen to make some more impressions on the clay hammer, as shown above. When you have finished, leave the clay to dry and completely harden.

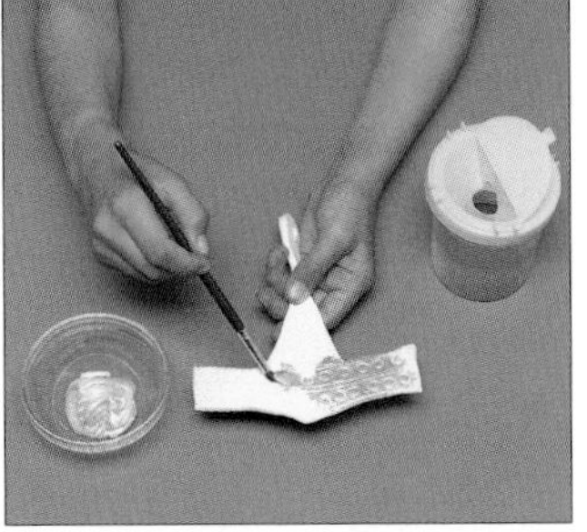

6 When your lucky charm is dry, smooth any rough edges with the sandpaper. Then paint one side silver. Leave it to dry before painting the other side of the lucky charm.

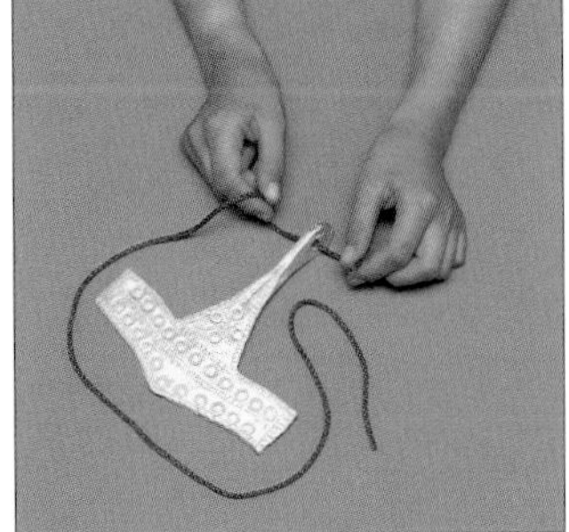

7 When the paint is dry, take a length of cord to fit around your head. Thread the cord through the hole in the hammer. Cut off any excess with the scissors, and tie a firm knot.

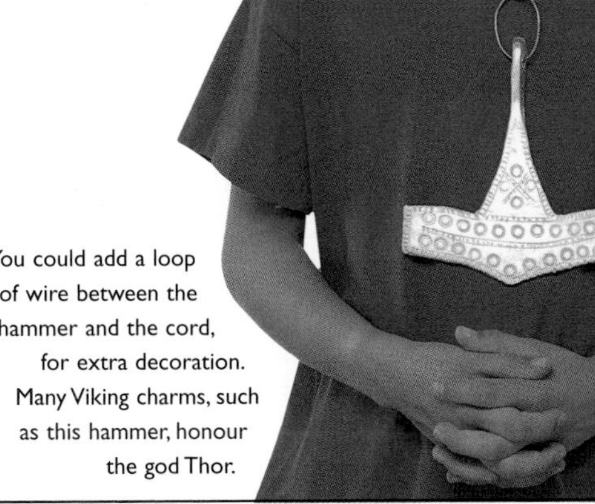

You could add a loop of wire between the hammer and the cord, for extra decoration. Many Viking charms, such as this hammer, honour the god Thor.

Tribal dance wand

Dancing was an important part of Native American life. Some of the sacred dances were performed before or after great events such as births, deaths, marriages, hunts or battles, but the occasion was more than just a big party. The Green Corn Dance was held at the Creek New Year and celebrated agricultural growth, and the Arikara Bear Dance aimed to influence the growth of corn and squash crops. Dancers often wore costumes. Cheyenne Sun dancers painted their upper body black (for clouds), with white dots (for hail). Assiniboine Clown dancers often danced and talked backwards, and wore masks with long noses.

▲ Fierce dance
This is a member of the Huron tribe. He dances in his feathered headdress, brandishing his tomahawk.

▲ Winter help
This Woodlands tribe is performing a Snowshoe Dance. Winter was a hard time and food was scarce, with few animals available to hunt. The dance asked the spirits for help to survive.

▲ Mourning dress
A ghost-dance shirt worn by the Sioux during a dance to mourn their dead. European settlers mistakenly saw the dance as provocation to war.

YOU WILL NEED

White paper, pencil, ruler, scissors, acrylic paints, paintbrush, water pot, eight 20cm/8in lengths of 3mm/⅛in-thick balsa wood, white glue and glue brush, pair of compasses, thick card, red and orange paper, 75cm/2½ft-long stick (1cm/½in thick), string.

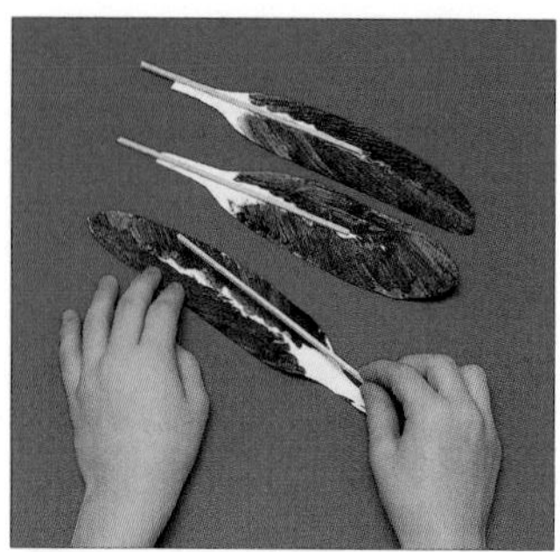

1 Cut out eight 29cm/11⅛in-long feather shapes from white paper. Make cuts on the top edges, and paint the tips of the feathers black. Glue sticks 12cm/4¾in from the top of the feathers.

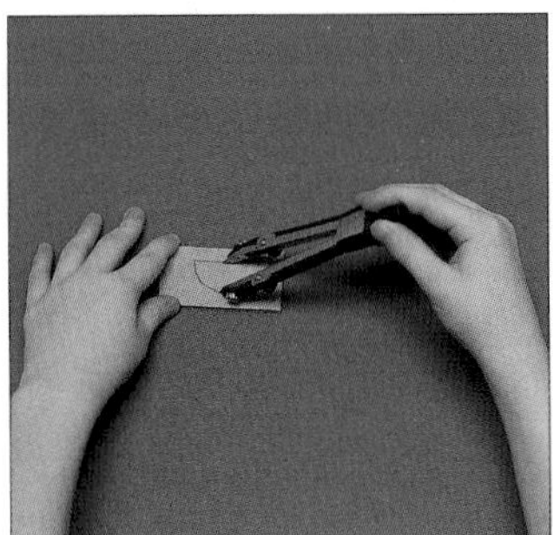

2 Use the compasses and a ruler to measure and draw two semicircles, each with a diameter of 5cm/2in, on to the thick card. Use a pair of scissors to cut out both shapes.

3 Hold the feathers by the sticks. Glue the bottom end of each of the feathers between the two card semicircles. Arrange them around the curved edge of the card, as shown.

4 Draw and cut out twelve 6cm/2½in-long feather shapes from the red and orange paper. Make another eight red feathers, each 2.5cm/1in long. Make feathery cuts along the top edges.

5 Divide the 6cm/2½in-long feathers in two, and glue them to each end of the 75cm/2½ft-long stick. Secure them with a piece of string tied around the bottom of the feathers, as shown.

6 Paint the semicircles cream, and then leave them to dry. Bend back the two straight edges. Place the flaps either side of the centre of the stick. Glue the flaps firmly in place.

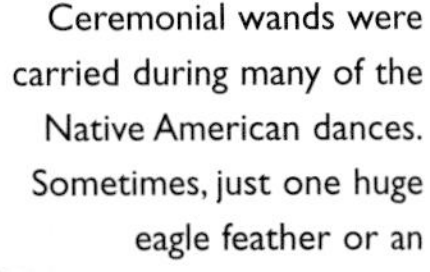

Ceremonial wands were carried during many of the Native American dances. Sometimes, just one huge eagle feather or an animal tail hung from the top.

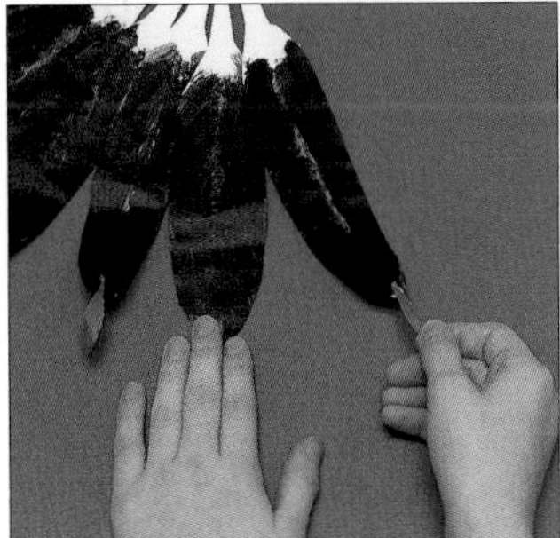

7 Glue the 2.5cm/1in-long red feathers to the outside tips of each black feather. Leave the dance wand to dry completely. Your wand will then be ready, so let the dance begin!

Chancay doll

Archaeologists have found many burial sites in the Andes Mountains. As early as 3200BC, Andean peoples had learned how to mummify (preserve) bodies. Respect for ancestors was an important part of the civilizations in the Andes. The Chancays were an ancient people who lived on the coast of central Peru. They were conquered by the mighty Incas in the 1500s. Dolls such as the one you can make in this project were placed in the graves of the Chancays to help them in the afterlife.

Final resting place ▸
The body of an Inca noble wrapped in cloth is carried to a *chulpa* (tomb). Chulpas were tall stone towers used to bury important people in ancient Peru.

YOU WILL NEED
Cream calico fabric, pencil, ruler, scissors, acrylic paints, paintbrush, water pot, black wool, white glue and glue brush, wadding, 20 red pipe cleaners, red wool.

1 Draw two rectangles 16 x 11cm/6¼ x 4⅜in on calico fabric to make the body. Draw two shield shapes 7 x 8cm/ 2¾ x 3⅛in for the head. Paint the body and one head, as shown. Cut them out.

2 Cut 35 strands of black wool, each measuring 18cm/7in in length. These will make the doll's hair. Glue each wool strand evenly along the top of the unpainted head shape, as shown above.

3 Cut a piece of wadding slightly smaller than the head shape. Glue the wadding on top of the hair, and the headpiece below. Then glue the painted face on top, as shown. Leave to dry.

4 For each arm, take five pipe cleaners and cut each one 11cm/4¼in long. Twist the pipe cleaners together to within 1.5cm/⅝in of one end. Splay the open end to make the doll's fingers.

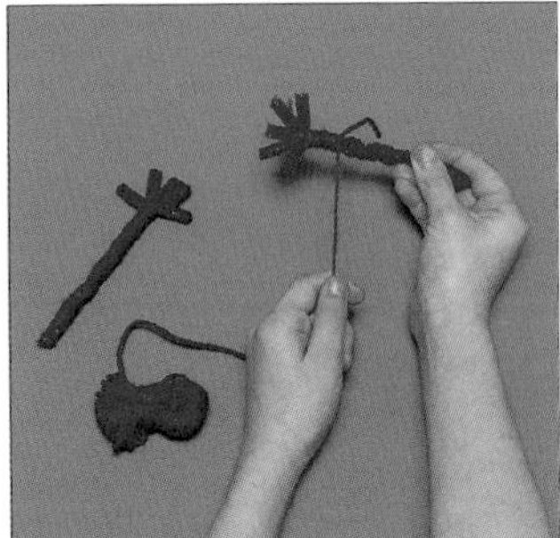

5 Make the legs for the doll in the same way, but this time twist all the way down and bend the ends to make feet. Wind red wool around the doll's arms and legs, to hide the twists.

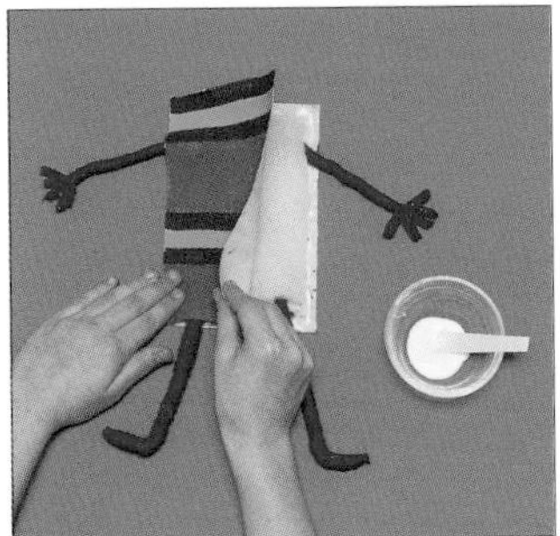

6 Assemble the pieces of the doll using the picture above as your guide, using glue to fix wadding between the pieces. Then glue the front piece of the doll's body in place, as shown.

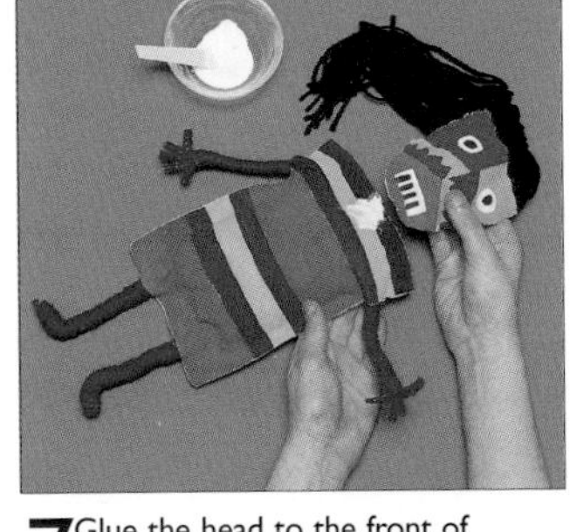

7 Glue the head to the front of the doll's body, making sure the hair does not become caught in the join. Leave the doll to dry completely before picking it up.

▲ **Inca mask**

This face mask is made of beaten gold, and dates back to the 1100s or 1200s. It was made by a Chimú goldsmith, and was laid in a royal grave.

Dolls such as these were placed in the graves of the Chancay people of the central Peruvian coast. The Chancay believed that grave dolls such as these would serve as helpers in the life to come.

Theatre and Entertainment

▲ Poets' corner

Poets such as Tao Yuanmin were highly respected in ancient China. Poetry dates back over 3,000 years in China. It was sung rather than spoken.

Throughout history, people from every country and culture have enjoyed listening to music, reading stories and poetry, and watching dance, drama and shows. Artistic styles vary in different parts of the world, but representing important events and rituals in human society has always been a big part of our lives.

Many arts aim to entertain their audience by bringing an event or story vividly to life. The arts are also an excellent way of introducing people to new ideas. They are sometimes used to influence the audience's thoughts and beliefs.

◀ Festive times

Festivals were an important part of Inca society. This one is Situa, which was held in August to ward off illness. Music and dance played a large role during these occasions. People would play musical instruments such as drums, whistles and rattles all day.

An actor's disguise ▶

The ancient Greeks enjoyed music and art, and went to the theatre regularly. The actors wore special masks during a performance. The top mask was used in tragedies, and the one at the bottom in comedies.

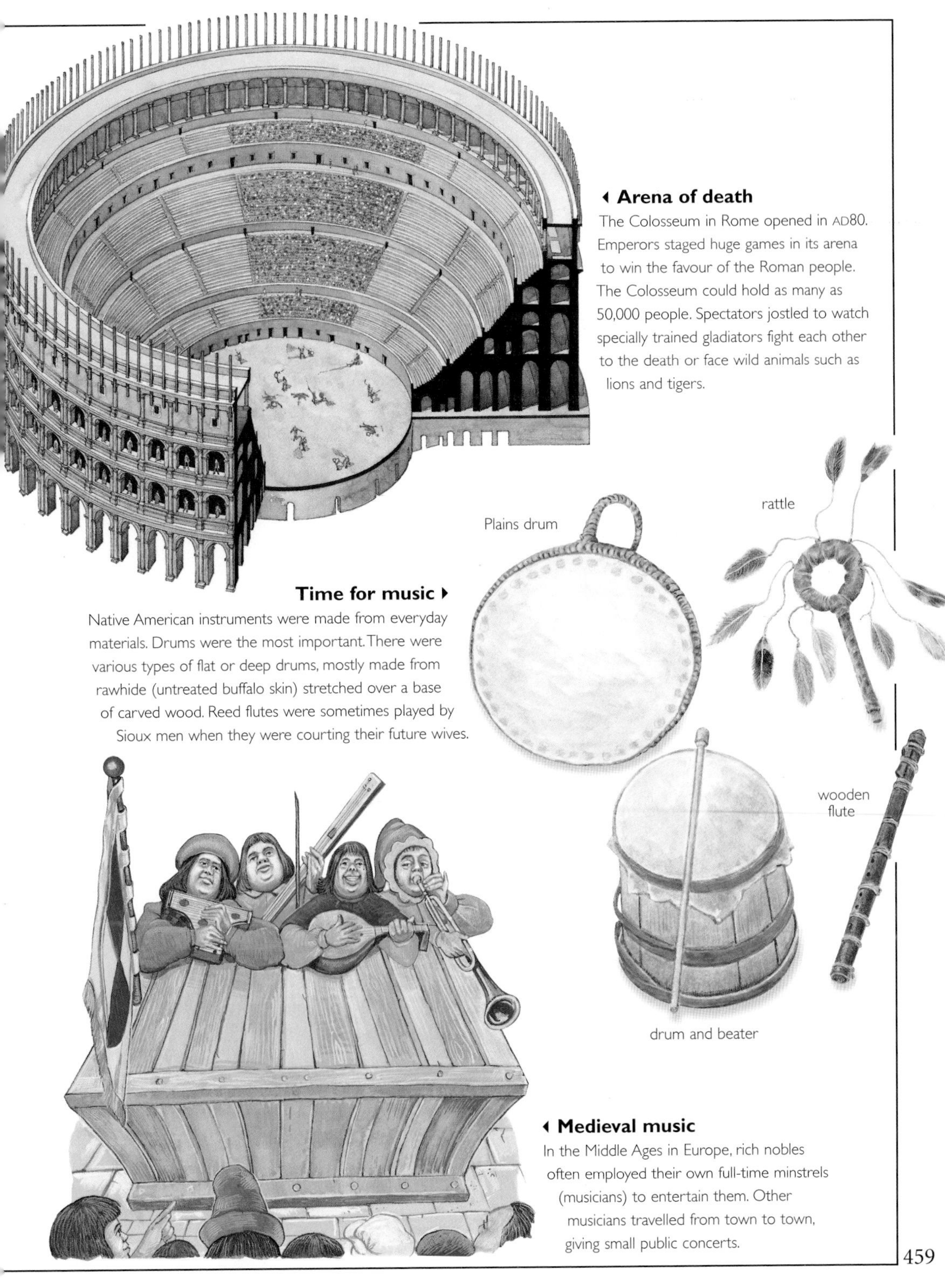

◂ Arena of death

The Colosseum in Rome opened in AD80. Emperors staged huge games in its arena to win the favour of the Roman people. The Colosseum could hold as many as 50,000 people. Spectators jostled to watch specially trained gladiators fight each other to the death or face wild animals such as lions and tigers.

Time for music ▸

Native American instruments were made from everyday materials. Drums were the most important. There were various types of flat or deep drums, mostly made from rawhide (untreated buffalo skin) stretched over a base of carved wood. Reed flutes were sometimes played by Sioux men when they were courting their future wives.

◂ Medieval music

In the Middle Ages in Europe, rich nobles often employed their own full-time minstrels (musicians) to entertain them. Other musicians travelled from town to town, giving small public concerts.

Greek Medusa's costume

In ancient Greek mythology, the Gorgons were three sisters called Stheno, Euryale and Medusa. They were the daughters of two sea monsters, and had writhing, living snakes instead of hair, tusks like boars, gold wings, and hands of bronze. Two of the Gorgons were immortal, but the youngest sister, Medusa, was killed by the Greek hero Perseus. He cut off her head and gave it as a present to his guardian goddess Athene. She wore it ever after like a monstrous brooch on the front of her cloak.

YOU WILL NEED

2 x 2m/2 x 2yd green fabric, soft-leaded pencil, ruler, scissors, white glue and glue brush, sheet of thick card, pair of compasses, dark green acrylic paint, paintbrush, water pot, pair of green tights, 40 pipe cleaners, red card, needle and thread.

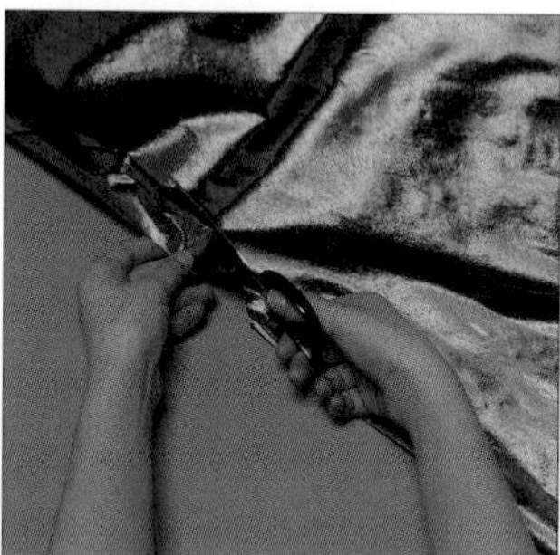

1 Fold the green fabric square in half. Along the centre of the fold, mark a narrow crescent shape 20cm/8in long, using a soft-leaded pencil. Cut out the crescent of fabric.

2 Make small cuts along the centre of the hole, to create a series of flaps. Fold each flap over and glue it down, as shown above. This gives the neck hole a neat, even edge.

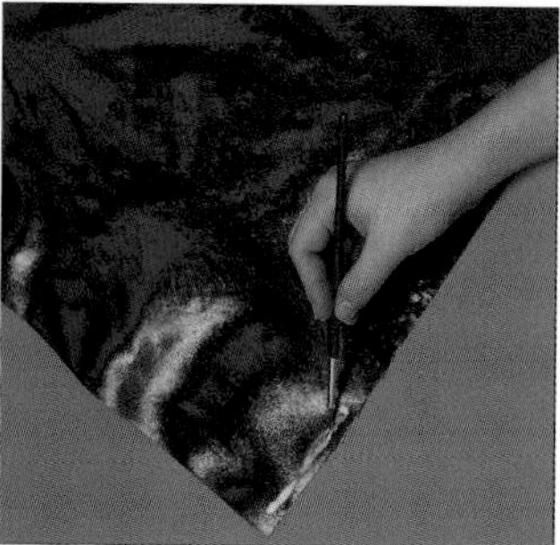

3 Fold over and glue down any frayed edges of fabric to complete your gown. Leave it to one side to dry completely while you make the rest of the Medusa's costume.

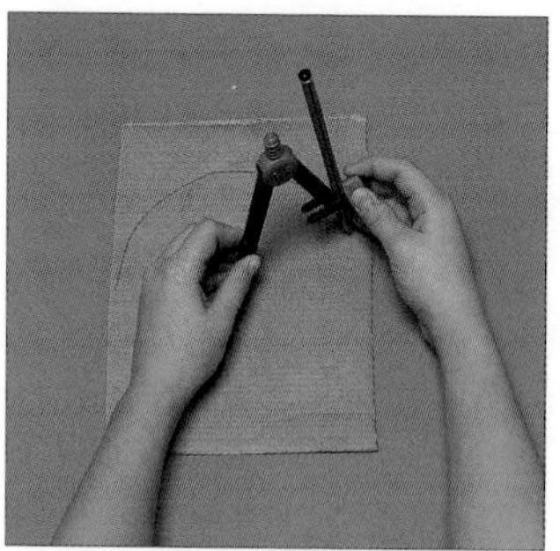

4 Use the compasses and ruler to measure and draw a circle with a radius of 7cm/2¾in (diameter 14cm/5½in) on to the sheet of thick card. Carefully cut out the card circle.

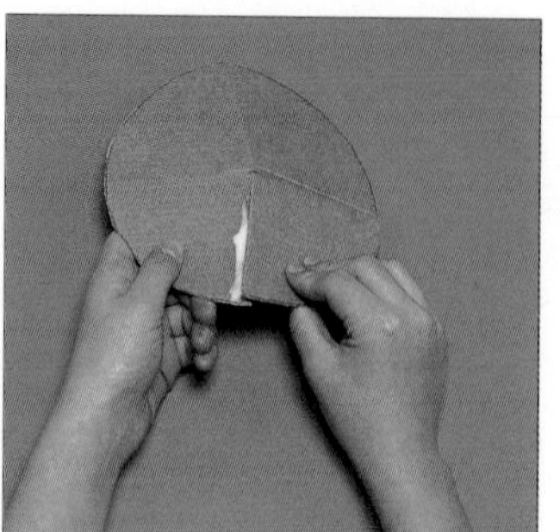

5 Cut into the centre of the circle. Bend the card slightly, overlapping the two edges, and glue them into position, as shown above. Leave to dry, then paint the card dark green.

6 Cut the foot and an extra 20cm/8in of the leg from a pair of green tights. Stretch the foot over the card circle so that it lies over the centre of the card, as shown above.

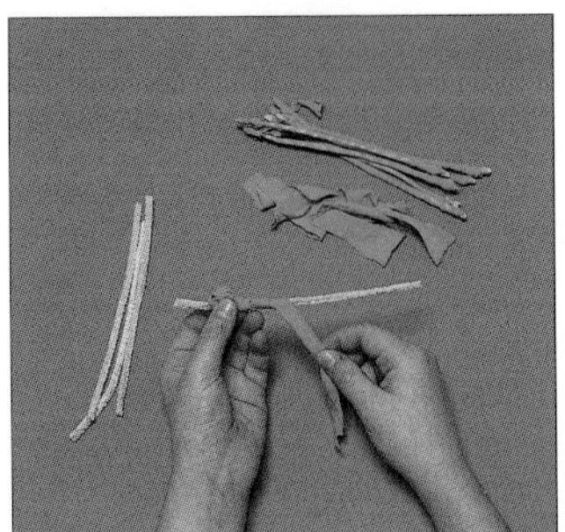

7 Cut the remainder of the tights fabric into small strips, and wrap them around 40 pipe cleaners, as shown above. Dab a spot of glue on each end to secure the strips in place.

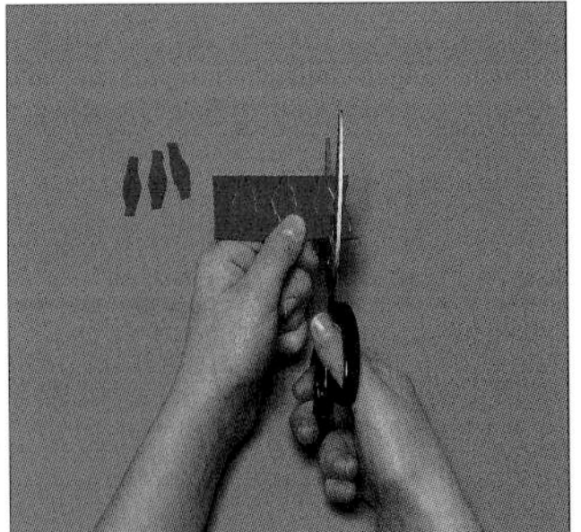

8 Draw small snake head shapes on the red card. Make 40 heads about 2.5cm/1in long and 1cm/½in wide at the ends. Cut them out. (You could fold the card over and cut out two at a time.)

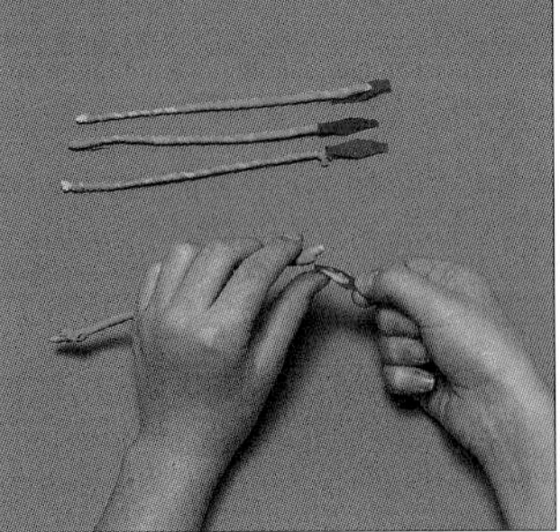

9 Glue the snake heads on to the ends of the pipe cleaners. Leave the snakes to one side until the glue is completely dry. You are now ready to fit the snakes to the headpiece.

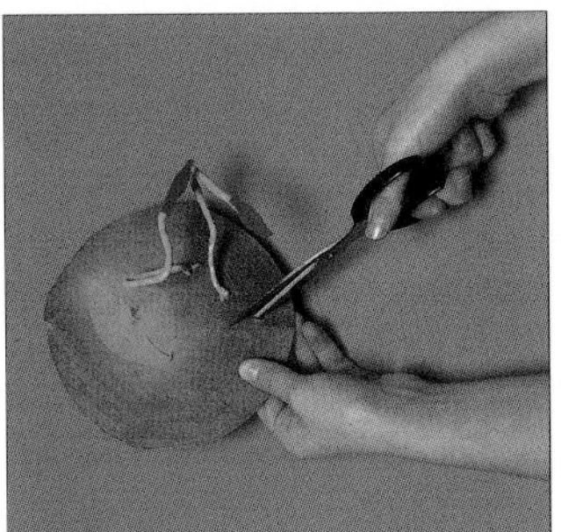

10 Using the pointed end of a pair of scissors, carefully pierce 20 small holes through the headpiece you made earlier. Take care to space the holes out evenly.

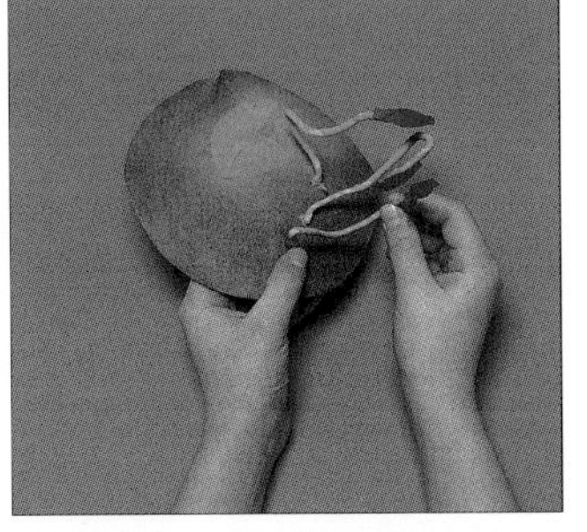

11 Poke a pipe cleaner through each hole. Bend the ends on the inside of the headpiece to hold them in position. Form the pipe cleaners into twisted snake shapes.

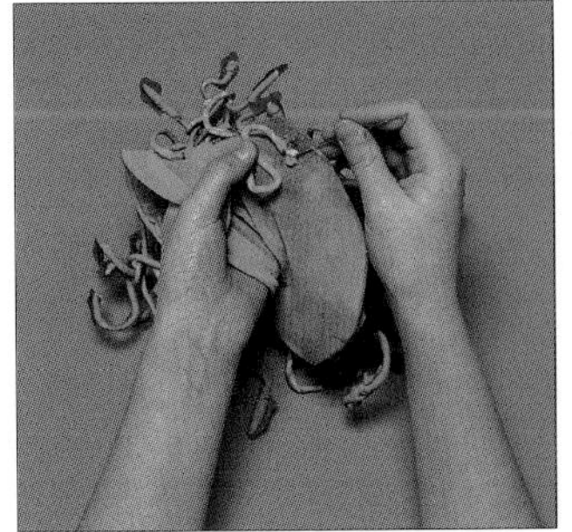

12 Curve the unused pipe cleaners into twisty snake shapes. Use a needle and thread to sew them over the excess tights fabric that hangs around the card headpiece, as shown.

To complete the gown, tie a green cord around your waist. If you have any extra fabric, make a scarf for your neck. Paint your face green to add to the scary effect. The only way to see a Gorgon without being turned to stone was to look at their reflection on a shiny surface. Clever Perseus, who defeated Medusa, used his shield.

Greek bird mask

The first Greek dramas were performed at temples in honour of the gods and goddesses. The stories they told were a mixture of history and myth. They featured the adventures of famous Greeks, as well as the exploits of gods, goddesses and other legendary heroes. The all-male cast was backed up by a chorus of masked singers and dancers, who provided a commentary on the action.

Drama became so popular in Greece that large open-air theatres were built in major cities and at sacred places such as Delphi. Prizes were awarded to the best dramatists. Over 30 plays by Aeschylus, Sophocles and Euripides have survived, although they wrote many more than this. Some are still performed in theatres today. The works of another 150 known writers have been lost.

▲ Playing many parts
Actors in Greece used masks to represent different characters. The same actor could play different roles in one drama by changing his mask.

◀ Beware of the Minotaur
One popular Greek legend told of the Minotaur. This monster, half-bull and half-man, lived in a maze called the labyrinth. The hero Theseus took a sword and a ball of string into the maze. He unwound the string as he walked. After killing the Minotaur, he followed the string back to the entrance, so he didn't lose the way.

YOU WILL NEED
Balloon, petroleum jelly, papier mâché (newspaper soaked in one part water to two parts white glue), black pen, scissors, acrylic paints, paintbrush, water pot, two pieces of ochre card (20 x 10cm/8 x 4in), glue stick, pencil, pair of compasses, ruler, two pieces of red card (20 x 20cm/8 x 8in), cord.

◀ Straight in the eye
Odysseus was the hero of *The Odyssey,* a story by the poet Homer. Here, with the help of his friends, he gouges out the eye of the Cyclops, a vicious one-eyed giant.

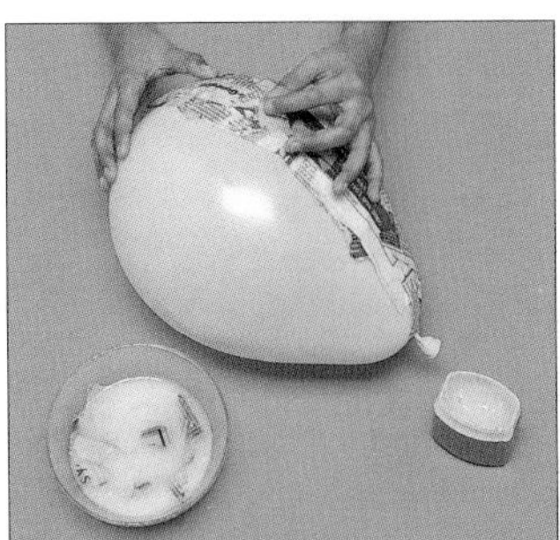

1 Blow up a balloon to slightly larger than your head. Cover half of the balloon in petroleum jelly, and add layers of papier mâché to cover this. When it is dry, pop the balloon.

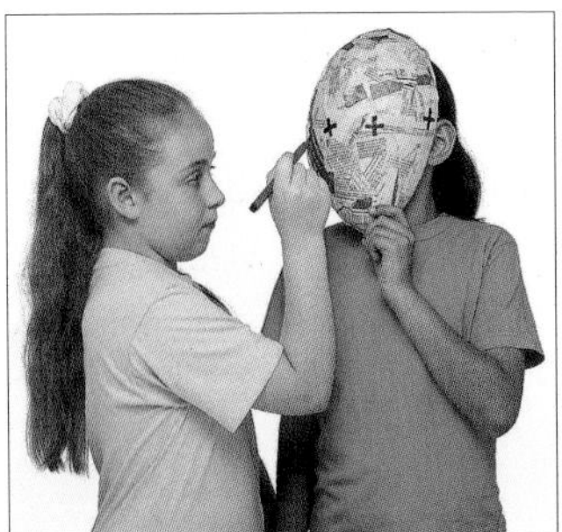

2 Ask a friend to mark the position of your eyes and the top of your ears on the mask. Cut out small holes at these points. Paint the mask, using turquoise acrylic paint.

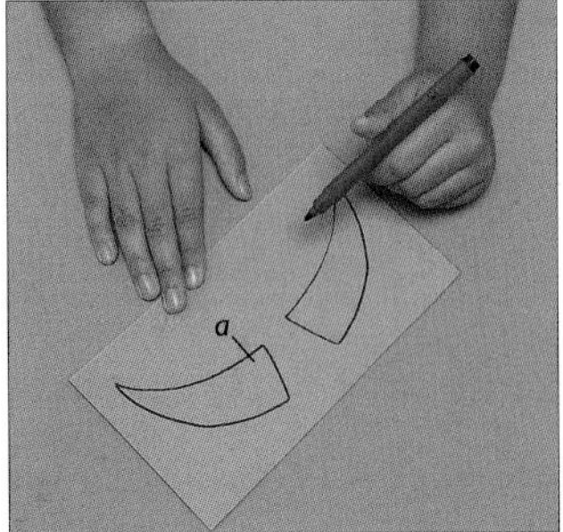

3 Draw and cut out four identical beak shapes, two on each sheet of ochre card. Mark a point 1cm/½in along on the bottom of each pair (the edge marked *a* on the picture above).

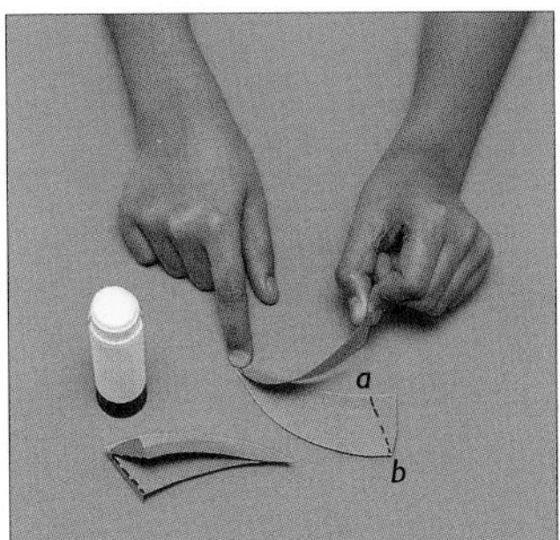

4 Draw a line from *a* to top edge *b* on identical beak shapes. Fold back the line. Glue the two shapes along the top edge, as shown above. Repeat for the other pair of beak shapes.

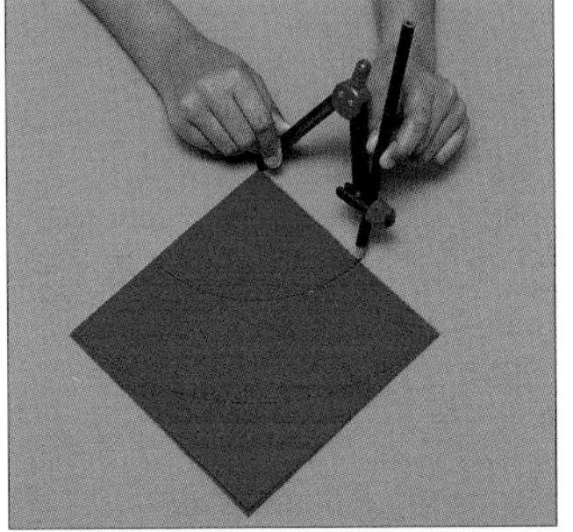

5 Put the point of the compasses on the corner of the red card. Draw two arcs, one with a 10cm/4in radius and one with a 20cm/8in radius. Cut along each line you have drawn.

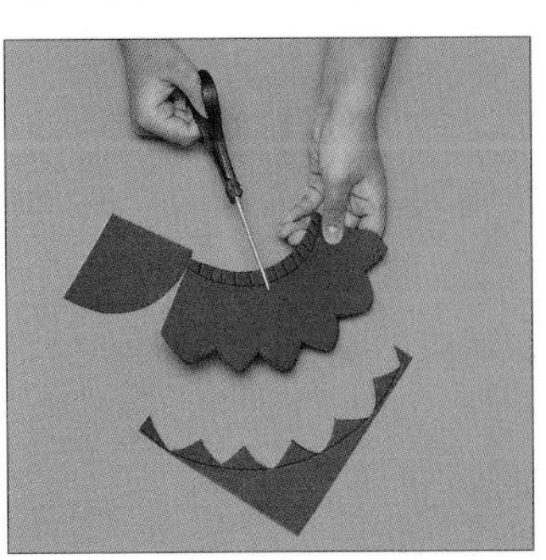

6 Cut a wavy feather shape into the top of the red card. Draw an arc 1.5cm/⅝in from the bottom. Cut out 14 tabs, as shown above. Repeat Steps 5 and 6 for the other piece of red card.

7 Glue the two pieces of red card together at the top. Glue the tabs down to the top of the mask, as shown. Glue the beak pieces to the mask. Then draw on a pair of eyes.

To wear your mask, thread a piece of cord through the holes on each side of the head. Tie the two ends together at the back. This mask is modelled on an original worn by the chorus in Aristophanes' comedy *The Birds*.

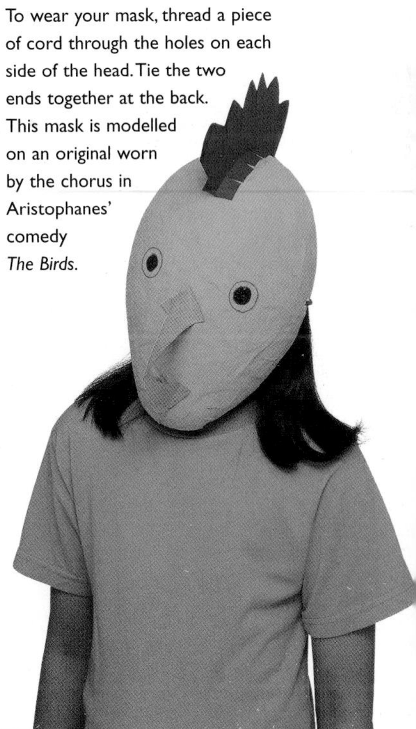

Chinese mask

The earliest Chinese poetry was sung rather than spoken. *Shijing* (the 'Book of Songs') dates back over 3,000 years, and includes the words to hymns and folk songs. Music was an important part of Chinese life, and models of musicians were often put into tombs to provide entertainment in the afterlife.

Musicians were frequently accompanied by acrobats, jugglers and magicians. Such acts were as popular in the markets and streets of the town as in the courtyards of nobles. Storytelling and puppet shows were equally well loved. Plays and opera became popular in the 1200s, with tales of murder, intrigue, heroism and love acted out to music. Most of the female roles would be played by men. Elaborate make-up and fancy costumes made it clear to the audience whether the actor was playing a hero or a villain, a princess or a demon.

▲ New Year dragon
Dressing up is a popular part of Chinese religion, with everybody joining in events such as Chinese New Year. Dragons symbolize happiness and good luck, and represent the generous spirit of New Year.

▲ Energetic opera
Some ancient Chinese plays are still performed today. Modern theatre companies try to recreate how plays would have looked to their original audience.

YOU WILL NEED

Tape measure, self-hardening clay, cutting board, modelling tool, petroleum jelly, newspaper, white glue and glue brush, water, bowl for mixing glue and water, thick card, pencil, ruler, scissors, masking tape, two large white beads, acrylic paints, paintbrush, water pot, wood glue, needle, black wool, string.

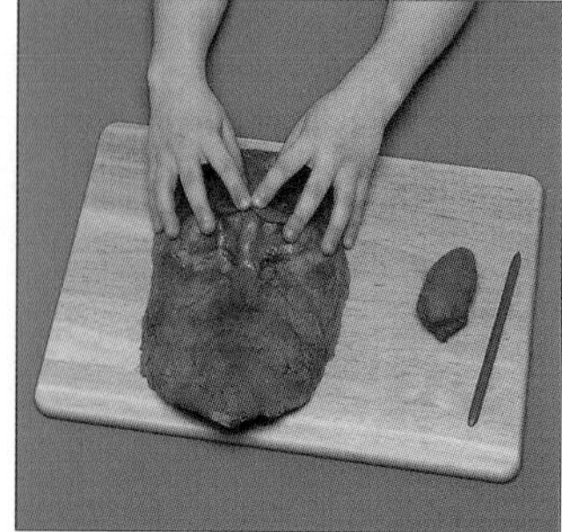

1 Measure the dimensions of your face, using a ruler or tape measure. Mould a piece of clay to fit the size of your face. Carve out eye sockets and attach a clay nose. Leave to dry.

2 Smear the front of the mask with petroleum jelly. Apply six layers of papier mâché, made by soaking strips of newspaper in two parts white glue to one part water. Leave the mask to dry.

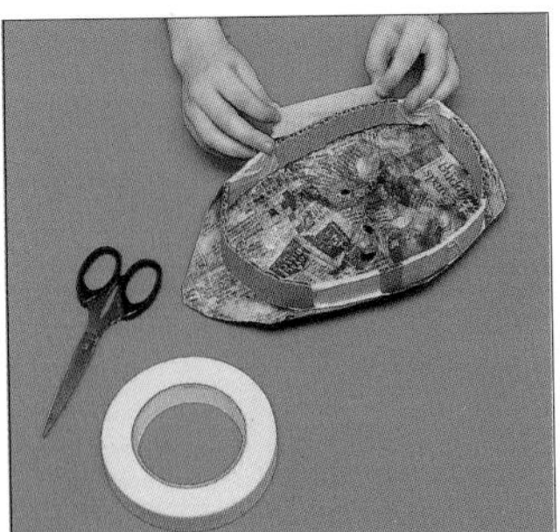

3 When it is dry, remove the mask from the clay mould. Cut a 2.5cm/1in-wide strip of card long enough to fit around your face. Bend it into a circle. Tape it to the back of the mask.

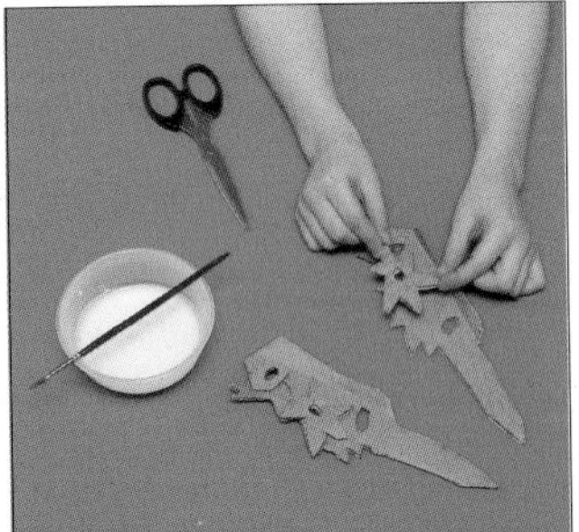

4 Cut two pointed ear shapes, as shown. Fold the card at the straight edges to make flaps. Cut out and glue on decorative pieces of card. Glue the ear flaps to the sides of the mask.

5 Glue two large white beads on to the front of the mask for the eyes. Cut out more small pieces of card. Glue these on for eyebrows. Glue on another piece of card for the lips.

6 Paint the entire mask in a dark blue-grey. Leave it to dry. Paint on more details using brighter colours. When the mask is dry, varnish it with wood glue.

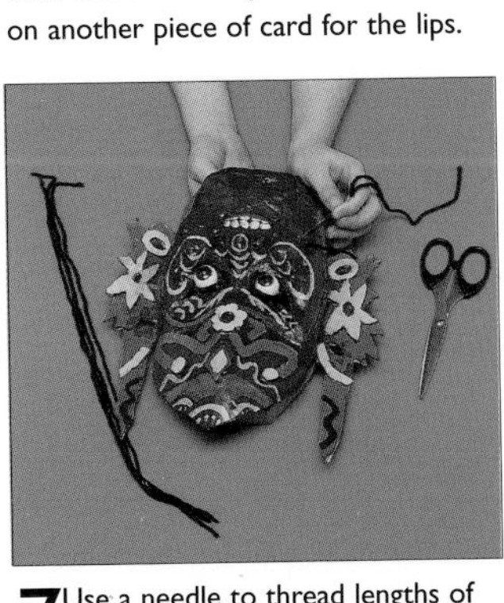

7 Use a needle to thread lengths of black wool through for the beard. Tape the wool at the back. Then thread string through the sides of the mask behind the ears to tie it on.

Highly decorative masks such as this one were worn to great effect in the Chinese opera. Folk tales were acted out to the dramatic sound of crashing cymbals and high-pitched singing.

Japanese Noh mask

Going to the theatre and listening to music were popular pastimes in ancient Japan. There were several kinds of Japanese drama, all of which developed from religious dances at temples and shrines, or from slow, stately dances performed at the emperor's court.

Noh is the oldest form of Japanese drama. It developed in the 1300s from rituals and dances that had been performed for centuries before. Noh plays were serious and dignified. The actors performed on a bare stage, with only a backdrop. They chanted or sang their words, and the performance was accompanied by percussion and a flute. Noh performances were traditionally held in the open air, often at a shrine. Kabuki plays were first seen around 1600, and were a complete contrast to the tragic Noh style. In 1629, the shoguns (military governors) banned women performers, and so male actors took their places. Kabuki plays became very popular in the new, fast-growing towns.

▲ Wooden expression
This Noh mask represents a warrior. Noh drama did not try to be lifelike. The actors moved very slowly, with stylized gestures to show their feelings.

◄ Plays made fun
Kabuki plays were very different to the more serious Noh-style theatre. They were fast-moving, loud, flashy and very dramatic. Audiences admired the skills of the Kabuki actors as much as the cleverness or thoughtfulness of the plots of these plays.

YOU WILL NEED

Tape measure, balloon, petroleum jelly, mixing bowl, newspaper, white glue, water, pin, scissors, felt-tipped pen, self-hardening clay, bradawl, acrylic paints, paintbrush, water pot, piece of cord.

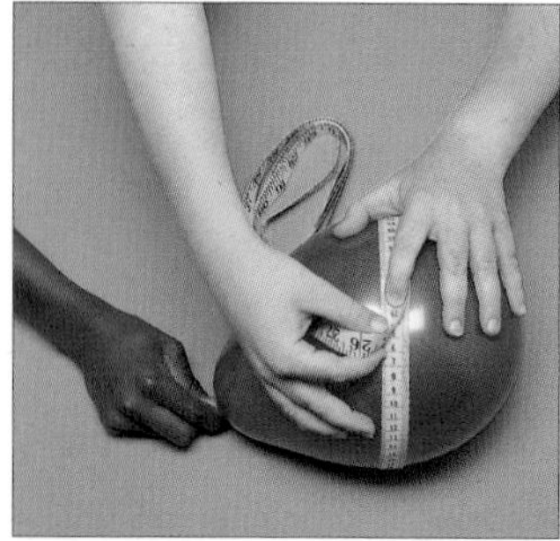

1 Ask a friend to measure around your head, above the ears, with a tape measure. Blow up a balloon to the same size. This will act as the mould for the papier mâché mask.

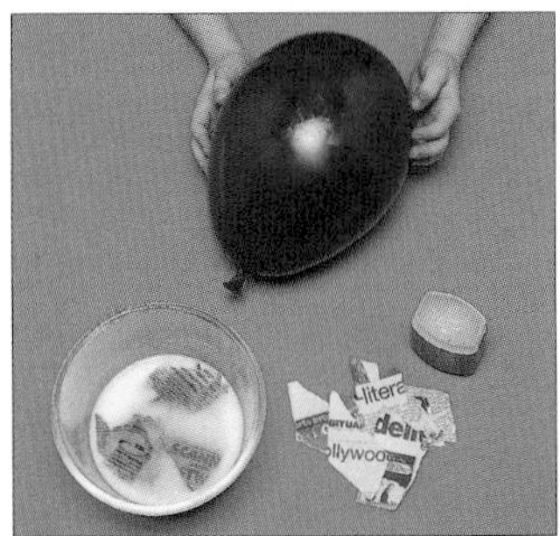

2 Smear the balloon with a layer of petroleum jelly. Then rip up strips of old newspaper and soak them in a bowl containing a mixture of two parts white glue to one part water.

3 Cover the front and sides of the balloon with the papier mâché. You will need to add three or four layers of papier mâché. When the mask is dry, pop the balloon.

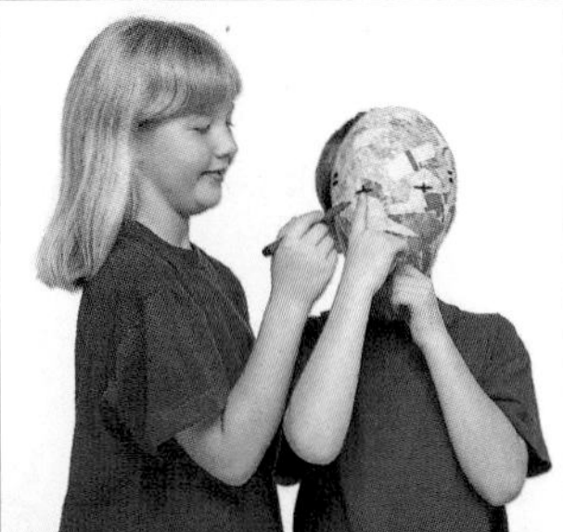

4 Trim the papier mâché to tidy up the edges of your mask. Then ask a friend to mark where your eyes and mouth are when you hold the mask to your face.

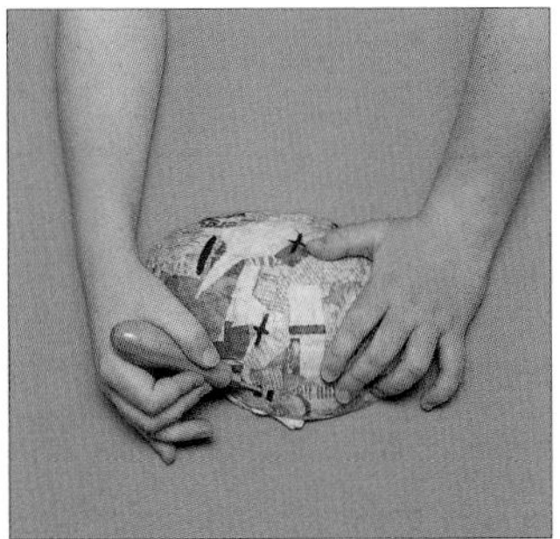

5 Cut out holes for the eyes and mouth, using scissors. Then put a piece of clay either side of the face at eye level. Use a bradawl to pierce two holes on each side of the face.

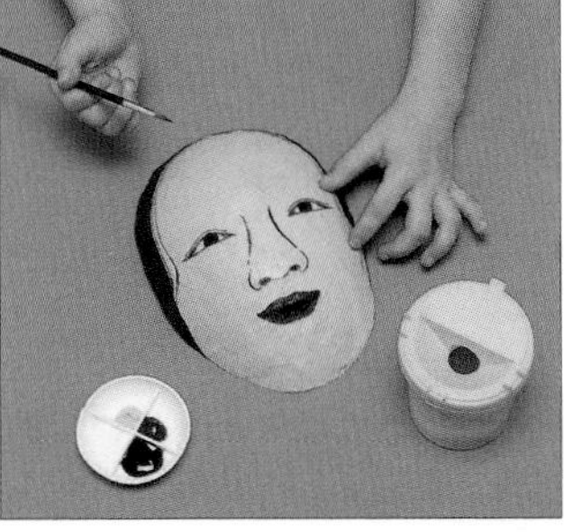

6 Paint the face of a calm young lady from Noh theatre on to your mask. You can use the picture above as your guide. In Japan, this mask would have been worn by a man.

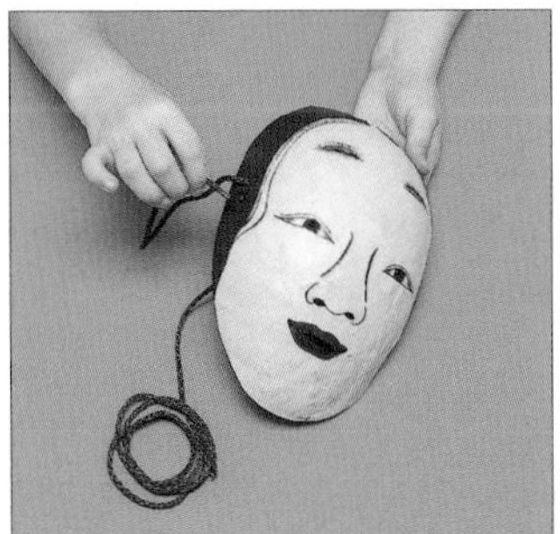

7 Fit a length of cord through the holes at each side of the mask. Tie one end of the cord. Once you have adjusted the mask to fit your head, firmly tie the other end of the cord.

Put on your mask and feel like an actor in an ancient Noh play. Noh drama was always about important and serious topics. Favourite subjects included death and the afterlife, and the plays were often tragic.

Celtic harp

The Celts enjoyed music, poems and songs as entertainment, and for more serious purposes, too. Music was played to accompany Celtic warriors into battle, to help them feel brave. Poems praised the achievements of a great chieftain or the adventures of bold raiders, and recorded the history of a tribe. Dead chieftains and heroes, and possibly even ordinary people, were mourned with sad laments.

On special occasions, and in the homes of high-ranking Celts, poems and songs were performed by people called bards. Roman writers described the many years of training to become a bard. Bards learned how to compose using all the different styles of poetry, and memorized hundreds of legends and songs. They also learned how to play an instrument, and to read and write. Becoming a bard was the first step towards being a druid (priest).

▲ Making music
Instruments such as this stringed lute have been played by humans as far back as 3500BC – long before the age of the Celtic civilization.

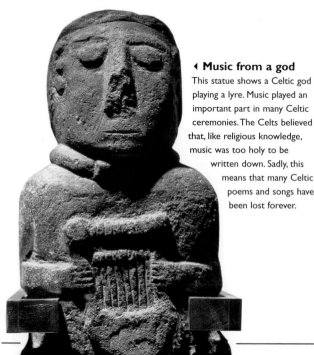

◀ Music from a god
This statue shows a Celtic god playing a lyre. Music played an important part in many Celtic ceremonies. The Celts believed that, like religious knowledge, music was too holy to be written down. Sadly, this means that many Celtic poems and songs have been lost forever.

YOU WILL NEED

Thin card (49 x 39cm/19¼ x 15½in), pencil, ruler, scissors, thick card (49 x 39cm/19¼ x 15½in), felt-tipped pen, white glue and glue brush, acrylic paint, paintbrush, water pot, bradawl, coloured string, 16 brass split pins.

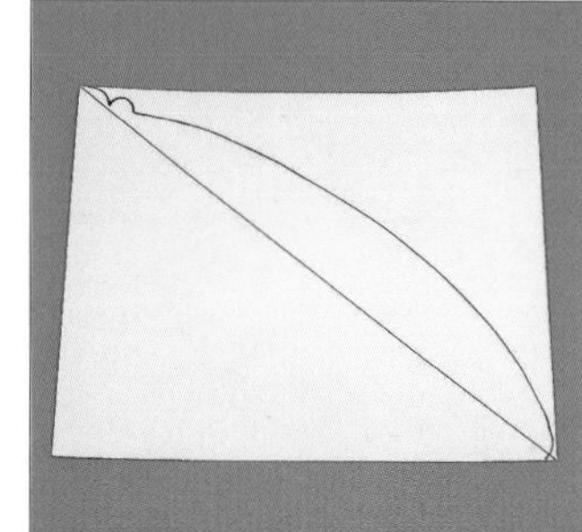

1 Draw a diagonal line, from corner to corner, on the rectangle of thin card. Then draw a gently curving line, with a shape at one end, using the picture above as your guide.

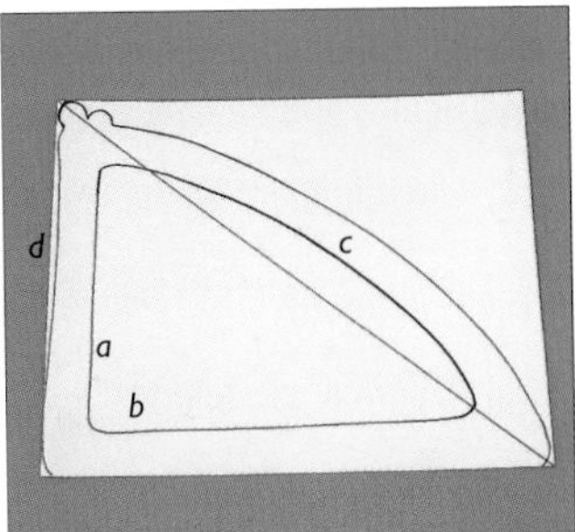

2 Using the picture above as your guide, draw two lines – *a* and *b* – 4.5cm/1¾in in from the edge of the card. Join them with a curved line *c*. Finally, add a curved line *d* parallel with *a*.

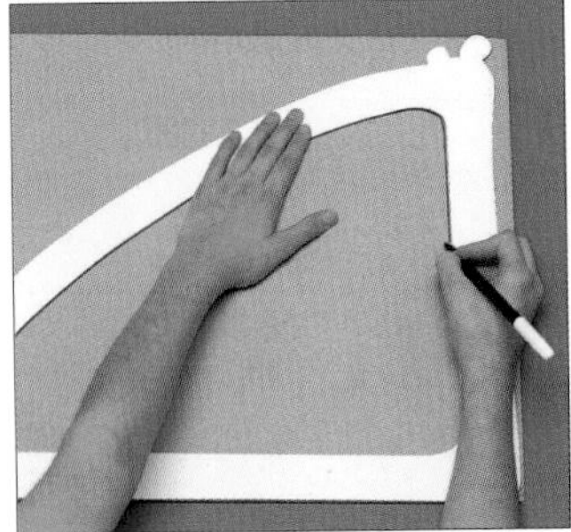

3 Cut out the harp shape you have drawn, and place it on the rectangle of thick card. Draw around it, inside and out, with a felt-tipped pen. Cut out the harp shape from the thick card.

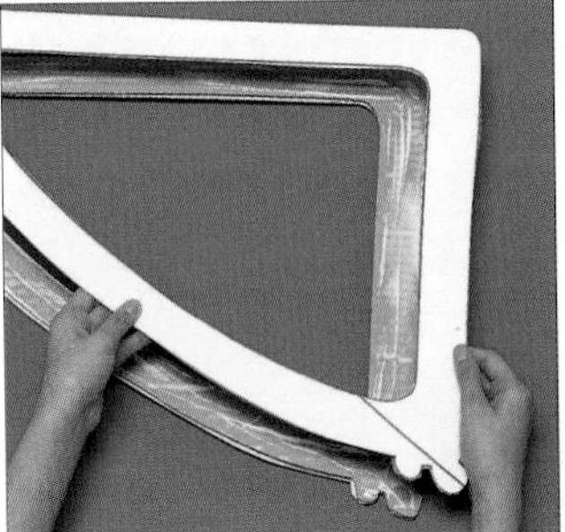

4 Glue one side of the thin card harp shape to one side of the thick card harp shape. Apply two coats of dark brown paint, leaving the harp shape to dry between each coat.

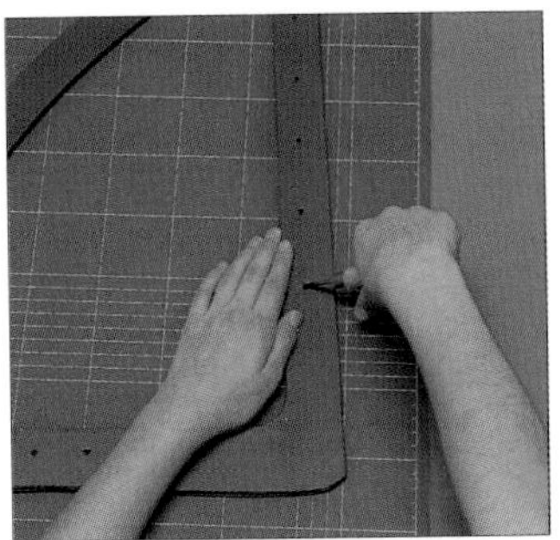

5 Use a bradawl to pierce a series of seven holes approximately 5cm/2in apart along the two straight sides of the frame of your harp. These will be the holes for the strings.

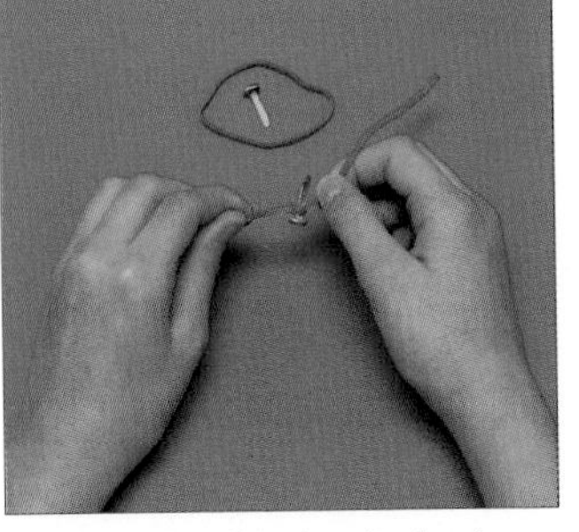

6 Cut a 40cm/16in length of string. Then cut six more pieces of string, each one 5cm/2in shorter than the last. Tie a brass split pin to both ends of all the pieces of string.

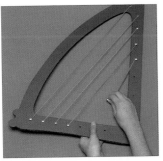

7 Push the split pins into the holes you made earlier, so that the strings lie diagonally across the harp. Adjust each string so that it is stretched tightly across the frame.

Most Celtic poetry was not spoken, but sung or chanted to the music of the harp or lyre. Bards used the music to create the right atmosphere to accompany their words, and to add extra dramatic affects, such as shivery sounds during a scary ghost tale.

Inca hand drum

Music and dance were very important to the Incas. Instruments, such as rattles, flutes, large drums, hand drums and panpipes, were made from wood, reeds, pottery and bone. At festivals, such as the Inti Raymi (Sun Festival), musicians would play all day without a break. Large bands walked in procession, each panpipe player picking out a different part of the tune. The Spanish influenced these festivals after the conquest, and they became known by the Spanish term, *fiesta*. However, many of the fiestas celebrated had their dances or costumes rooted in an Inca past.

▲ **Traditional music**
A modern street band plays in Cuzco, the ancient capital of the Inca Empire. Ancient tunes and rhythms live on in the modern music of the Andes.

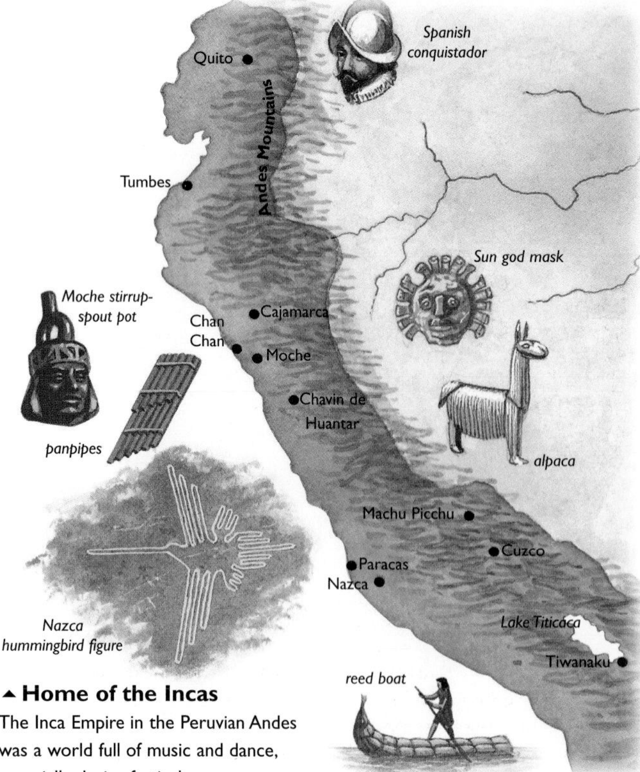

▲ **Home of the Incas**
The Inca Empire in the Peruvian Andes was a world full of music and dance, especially during festivals.

YOU WILL NEED

Pencil, ruler, thick card (100 x 20cm/39½ x 8in), scissors, masking tape, cream calico fabric, white glue and glue brush, acrylic paints, paintbrush, water pot, wadding, 30cm/12in length of thick dowel, coloured wool.

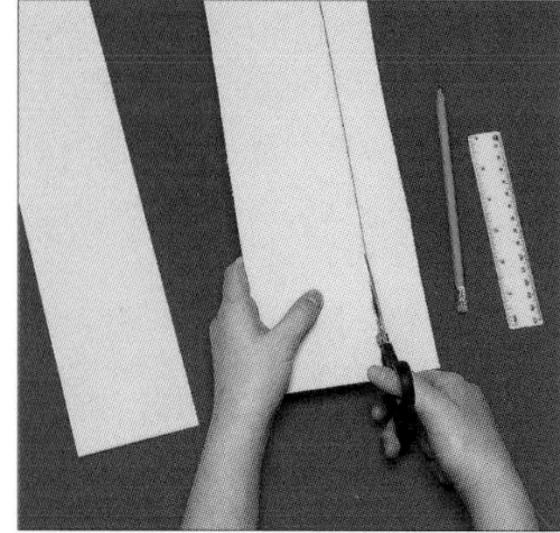

1 Use a pencil and ruler to mark two rectangles on the thick card, each measuring 85 x 9cm/33½ x 3½in. Cut the rectangles out carefully. They will form the sides of your Inca hand drum.

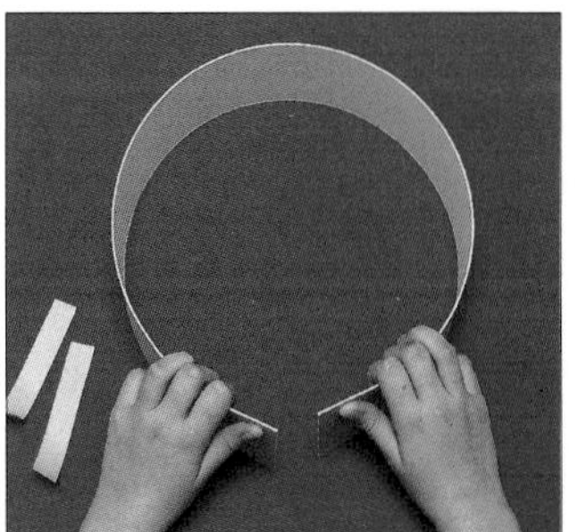

2 Bend one rectangle into a circle, as shown above. Use strips of masking tape to join the two ends of the card ring together. It may be easier to ask a friend to help you do this.

3 Lay the ring on top of the cream calico fabric. Draw around the card ring on to the fabric, leaving a gap of about 2cm/¾in, as shown. Remove the ring and cut out the fabric circle.

4 Paint glue around the edge of the fabric circle. Turn the fabric over. Carefully stretch the fabric over the card ring. Keep the fabric taut, and smooth the edges as you stick.

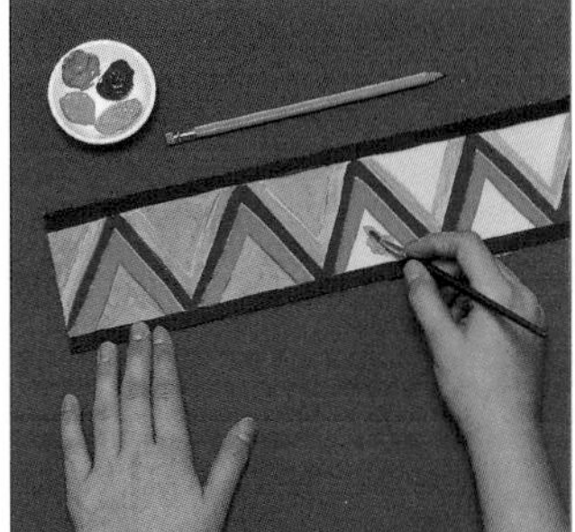

5 Draw a geometric Inca-style pattern on the second strip of card. Use bright colours to decorate the card, as shown above. Lay the card flat and leave it to dry.

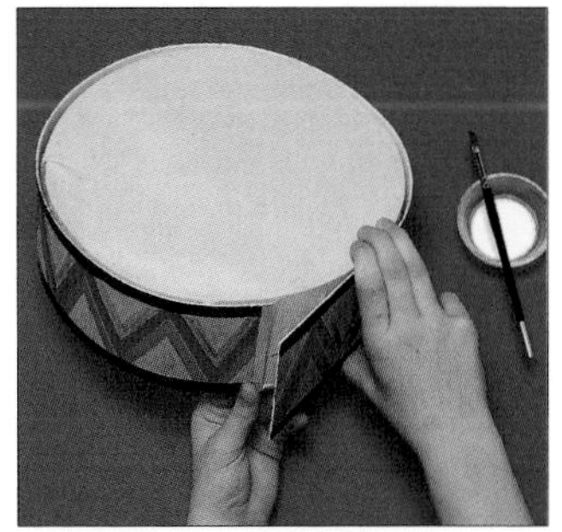

6 When the painted strip is dry, wrap it around the drum, as shown. Use masking tape to fix one end of the ring to the drum. Then glue the rest of the ring around the drum. Leave to dry.

7 Cut out a 20cm/8in-diameter circle of calico fabric. Make a drumstick by wrapping a piece of wadding and the calico circle around one end of the dowel. Tie it with wool.

Women played hand drums like this one at festivals during Inca times. Some festivals were held in villages and fields. Others took place at religious sites or in the big Inca cities.

Playing the fool

Noble families often employed jesters full-time, so that they could be cheered up whenever they wanted. It was rather like having their own private comedy act. Jesters dressed in silly costumes with bells, and played the fool. However, they were often skilled jugglers and acrobats, too. They sang songs and told funny stories and jokes, which were often very rude. They often made fun of their audience, and were great at passing on top-secret gossip that no one else would dare mention.

▲ Roll up for the fair
In the Middle Ages, jesters were often found entertaining merchants and traders at the local markets and fairs.

Juggling

YOU WILL NEED

Juggling: Juggling balls.

Jester's rattle: Pencil, yellow card (24 x 19cm/9½ x 7½in), polystyrene ball, scissors, white glue and glue brush, 40cm/16in length of dowel (1cm/½in in diameter), acrylic paints, paintbrush, water pot, seven bells, two 45cm/18in lengths each of red and yellow ribbon.

1 Take a juggling ball in each hand. Throw both of the balls up into the air together in straight lines, and catch them when they fall. This is the easy part of juggling!

2 Throw both juggling balls up together so that they cross in front of you. The trick is to make sure that they do not bump into each other. Catch each ball in the opposite hand.

3 Now try throwing both balls up together in straight lines again. This time, however, cross your hands over to catch the balls as they fall. You may have to practise this one a lot.

4 Throw the juggling ball in your right hand diagonally across your body. Just as it is about to drop, throw the other ball diagonally towards your right hand. Keep practising!

5 Catch the first ball in your left hand but keep your eye on the other ball still in the air. Catch this one in your right hand. Remember – practice makes perfect.

Jester's rattle

1 Use a pencil to draw a hat shape on to the piece of yellow card. Use the picture above to help you. Draw around the ball to make sure the curve at the bottom is the same diameter.

2 Cut out the hat shape. Put a strip of glue around the curve at the bottom of the hat. Press the ball into the glued section and hold it in place until it is firmly stuck down.

3 Use the pointed ends of a pair of scissors to make a hole in the bottom of the ball. Ask an adult to help you, if necessary. Fill the hole with glue, and insert the piece of dowel.

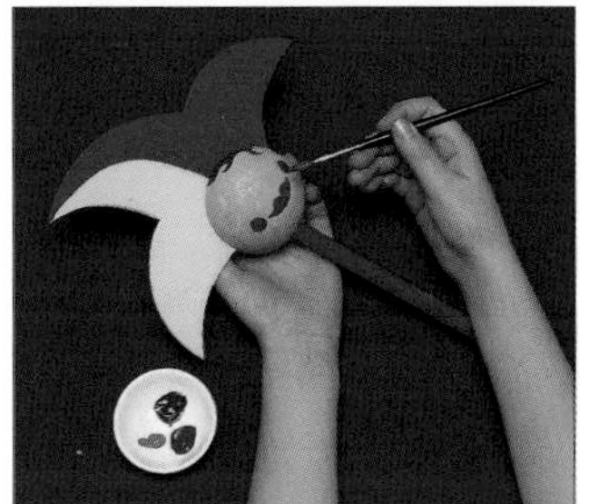

4 Paint the stick bright red. When it is dry, paint some eyes, a mouth, cheeks and hair on the ball to make a cheerful face. Then paint one half of the jester's hat red.

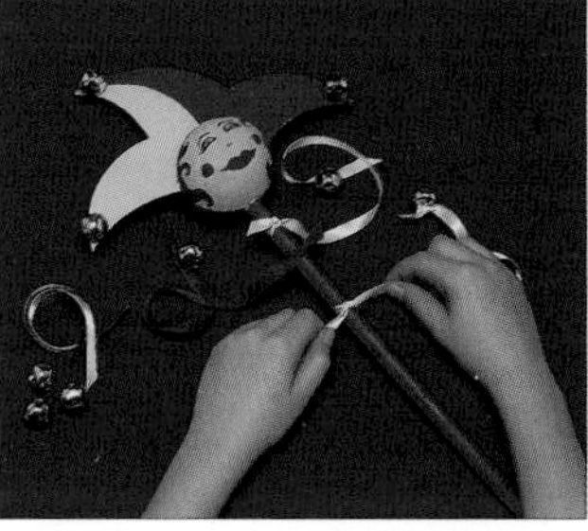

5 Glue three bells to the corners of the hat. Then tie four bells to the lengths of coloured ribbon. Tie the ribbons around the stick, using a simple knot to secure them.

Once you know how to juggle two balls, try to master the three-ball juggle. Professional jugglers who were not employed full-time travelled from castle to castle.

Important people often carried sticks in the Middle Ages, which they banged loudly on the floor to attract attention. The jester's small stick made fun of these.

Monster mask

Myths and legends involving beasts, ghouls and witches have captured the imaginations of people worldwide. Such scary stories have passed through the generations, at first by word of mouth, and then through books, plays, films and now via the Internet. The tale of Frankenstein's monster, created by the English writer Mary Shelley, is one such spine-chilling story. The monster was an ugly creature brought to life by a young scientist called Frankenstein. In this project, you can make a mask of Frankenstein's monster.

YOU WILL NEED

Balloon, newspaper strips, water, white glue and glue brush, pin, scissors, thick card (29 x 14cm/11½ x 5½in, 22 x 12cm/8¾ x 4½in, 29 x 9.5cm/11½ x 3¾in and scraps), ruler, pencil, pair of compasses, brown gum tape, masking tape, two 3cm/1³⁄₁₆in lengths of thin balsa dowel, acrylic paints, paintbrushes, water pot, string.

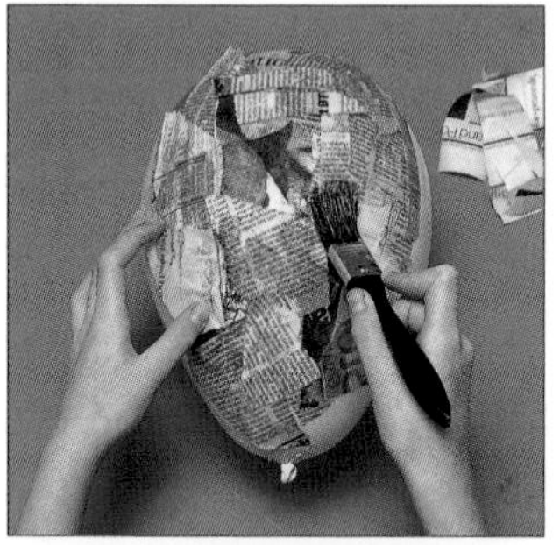

1 Blow up the balloon. Soak strips of newspaper with half measures of glue and water to make papier mâché. Cover one side of the balloon with five layers of papier mâché. Leave it to dry.

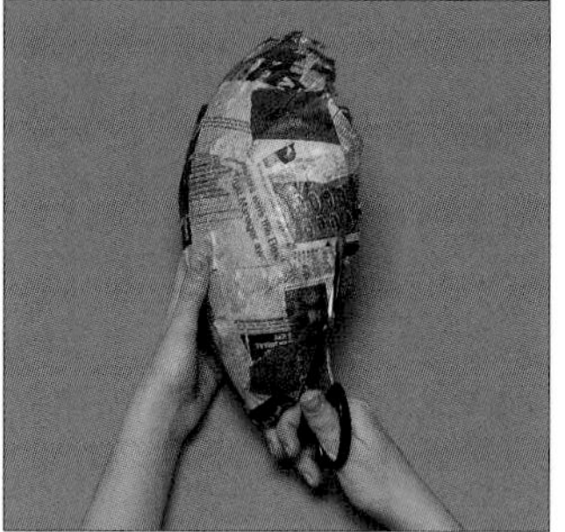

2 When the mask is completely dry, carefully burst the balloon using a pin. Take the papier mâché mask and trim off the excess to produce a rounded face shape.

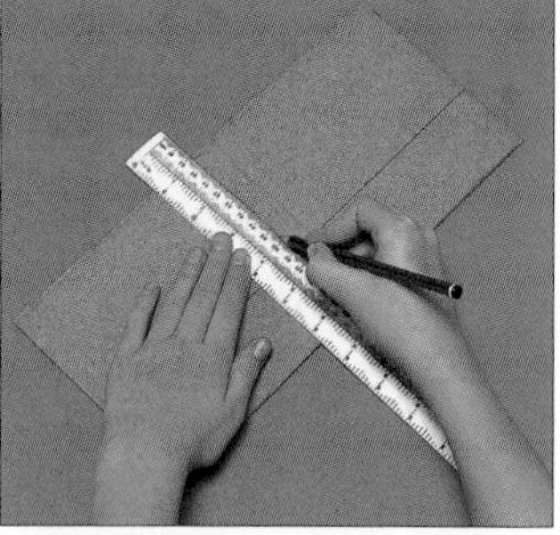

3 Take the piece of card measuring 29 x 14cm/11½ x 5½in. Use a ruler and pencil to draw a line 5cm/2in in from one long edge. Draw a pencil line across the middle, as shown above.

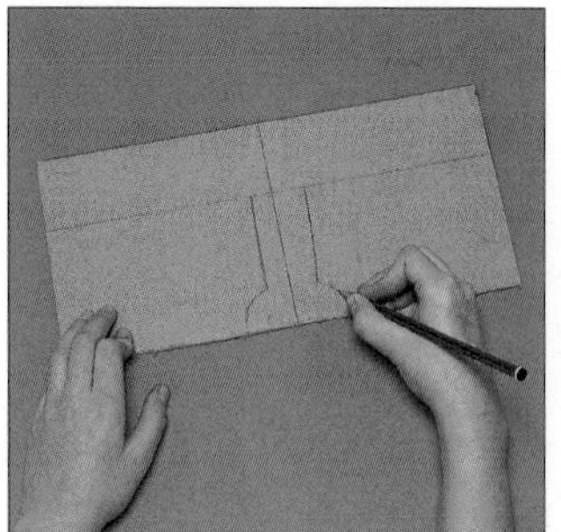

4 Draw the shape of the nose, using the centre line in the middle as a guide. Make the nose 3cm/1³⁄₁₆in wide on the bridge and 4cm/1½in at the nostril. Cut out the nose and the brow.

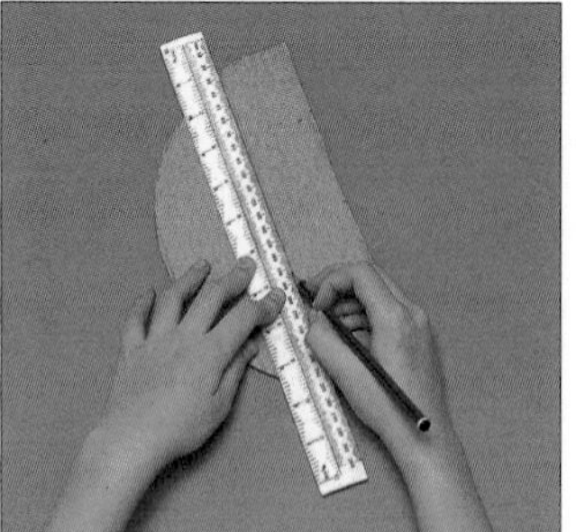

5 Set the compasses to 11cm/4⅜in. Draw a semicircle on to the 22 x 12cm/8¾ x 4½in card. Cut it out. Draw a pencil line 5cm/2in from the straight edge. Cut this 5cm/2in piece off.

6 Line the edges of the semicircle with white glue. Stick it to the top edge of the nose piece, as shown above. Hold the pieces together until the glue has dried.

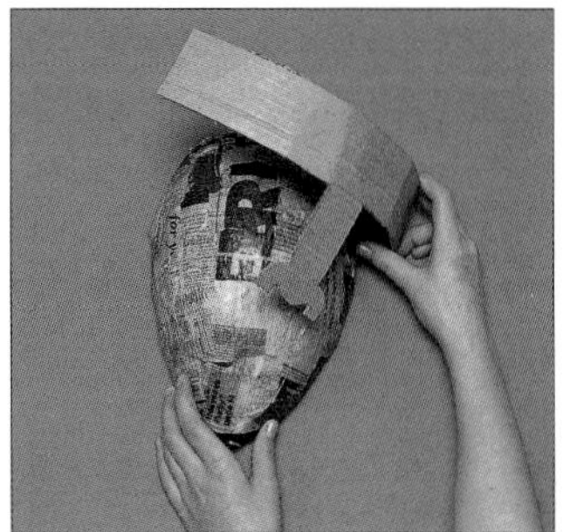

7 Cover the back of the head and nose piece with white glue. Stick this piece in position on top of the papier mâché face mask you made earlier. Leave the mask to one side to dry.

8 Draw a line in the centre of the 29 x 9.5cm/11½ x 3¾in card. Draw a 10 x 4cm/4 x 1½in rectangle at the centre of the line, touching the bottom edge. Cut the smaller rectangle out.

9 Cover the back of the card jaw piece with glue. Stick it over the lower part of the mask. Cover the gaps between the stuck-on face parts and the mask with brown gum tape.

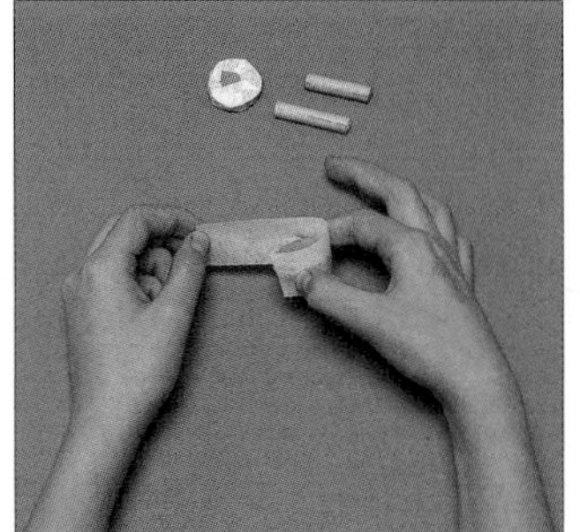

10 Set the compasses to 1cm/½in and draw two circles on a scrap piece of card. Cut out the two circles and cover them with masking tape. Take the balsa dowel.

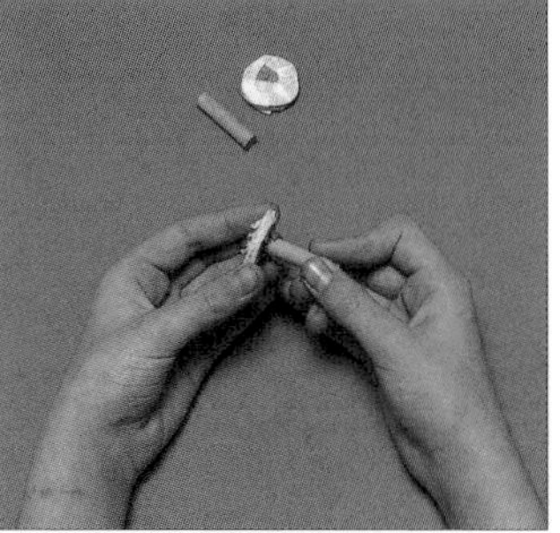

11 Make a hole in the centre of each card circle, using your scissors. Push the balsa dowel through the middle. Glue into position and paint the pieces black.

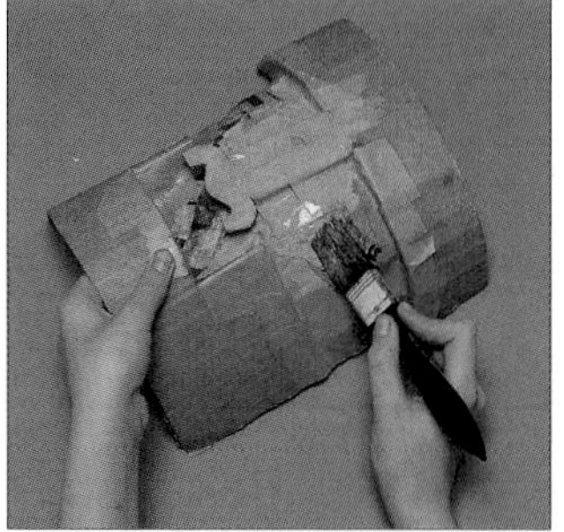

12 Paint the mask with a base colour – grey or green, for example. Wait for the base coat to dry before painting in the details of the face with other colours. Leave to dry.

13 Push the bolts through the sides of the mask. Glue them into position. Put the mask over your face and mark eyeholes. Take the mask off. Make eyeholes with the scissors.

To finish your monster mask, tie or tape string on to either side of the mask. If you can find old clothes, such as a shirt and dinner jacket, you could decorate them as well, perhaps with gruesome blood stains made with red paint.

Toys and Games

People have always played with toys and games. Our early Stone Age ancestors played with small doll-like figures made of clay, and whistles carved from bone. Toys dating from 5000BC have been found in China. Many games from the ancient world are still familiar to us today. Hopscotch and hide-and-seek were played in the ancient civilizations of Egypt, Greece and Rome. There were toys, too, such as rattles, yo-yos, dolls and spinning tops.

As well as being fun, games provided mental and physical challenges. Board games, in particular, showed children different ways of thinking and planning, and prepared them for the adult world.

▲ **Game players**
Archaeologists have found board games and toys among the remains of the great cities of the Indus Valley civilization. These people grew up nearly 5,000 years ago in the area occupied by present-day Pakistan.

◀ **Martial arts**
Kendo, and several other martial arts that are popular today, developed from the fighting skills of samurai warriors from ancient Japan. In kendo, combatants fight one another with long swords made of split bamboo. Players score points by managing to touch their opponent's body, not by cutting or stabbing them.

Royal game ▸

This beautifully made board game was found in the Royal Graves of Ur, an ancient city of Mesopotamia. The board game was made of wood covered in bitumen (tar), and decorated with a mosaic of shell, bone, blue lapis lazuli (a kind of gemstone), red glass and pink limestone. The game may have been a bit like ludo, with two sets of counters and four-sided dice, but the rules have not been found.

◂ Ancient athletes

Sport was important to the ancient Greeks. In fact, it had religious significance. The first-ever Olympic Games were held in 776BC in honour of the Greek god Zeus. Sports included throwing the discus and javelin, boxing, wrestling and the long jump. The games were only open to men – women were not even allowed to watch. They held their own games in honour of Hera, goddess of women.

Dangerous sports ▸

Wrestling was a favourite sport as long ago as 1000BC. Many kings in ancient India had the title *malla* (wrestler). They had to keep to strict diets and physical training programmes in camps known as *akharas*. Wrestling could be a highly dangerous activity. One inscription tells of a malla who was accidentally killed during a match.

Egyptian snake game

Board games such as mehen, or the snake game, were popular from the earliest days of ancient Egypt. In the tomb of the Pharaoh Tutankhamun, a beautiful gaming board made of ebony and ivory was discovered. It was designed for a board game called senet. Players threw sticks to decide how many squares to move at a time. Some of the squares had gains and some had forfeits. Senet was thought to symbolize the struggle against evil.

Another favourite pastime for the ancient Egyptians was sport. Armed with bows and arrows, sticks, spears and nets, they hunted wild animals for pleasure as well as for food. Wrestling was a popular spectator sport at all levels of society. Chariot racing, however, which was introduced around 1663BC, could only be afforded by the nobility.

▲ Tomb raider
A thief breaks into a pharaoh's tomb. Inside are the treasures that were important to him, including game boards and counters.

▲ Games in the afterlife
The walls of many Egyptian tombs were covered with everyday scenes. They were designed to show how life should carry on in the afterlife. In this tomb painting, an official of the Pharaoh Rameses II is playing the board game of senet with his wife.

YOU WILL NEED

Self-hardening clay, rolling pin, cutting board, ruler, modelling tool, acrylic paint, paintbrush, water pot, cloth, varnish, 12 counters (six blue and grey, and six gold and orange), two large counters, dice, pencil.

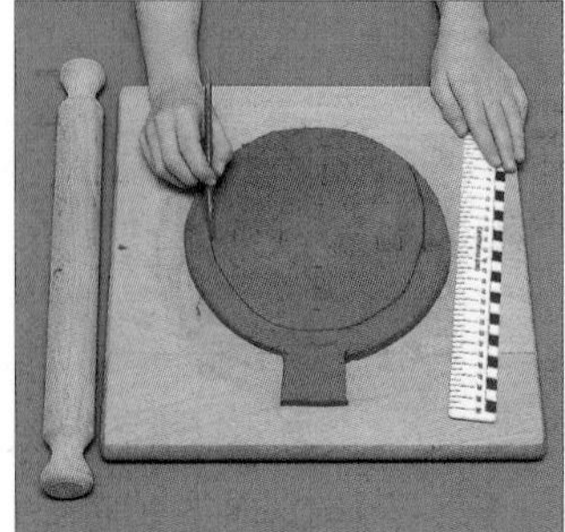

1 Roll out the clay on to a board and cut it into the shape shown above. Score on a snake shape and score lines across the body at intervals. Use the final project picture as a guide.

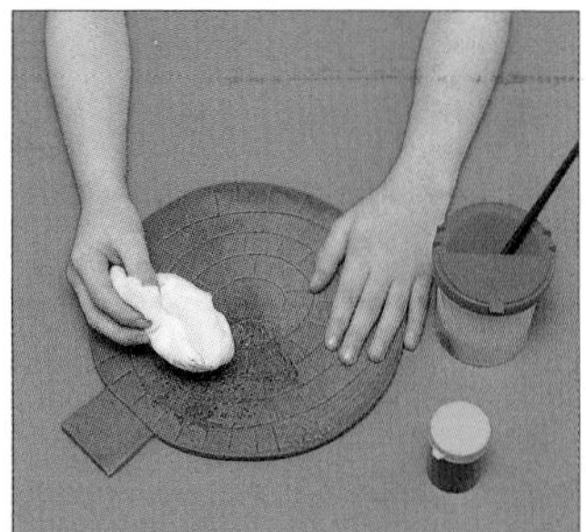

2 When the clay is completely dry, rub the board with diluted green paint to stain the lines. Wipe away the excess paint with a cloth. Leave the board to dry, and then varnish it.

3 Each player takes six counters of the same colours, plus one large piece called a 'lion'. Place the counters so that the same colour faces up. Throw the dice. You need a '1' to start each counter.

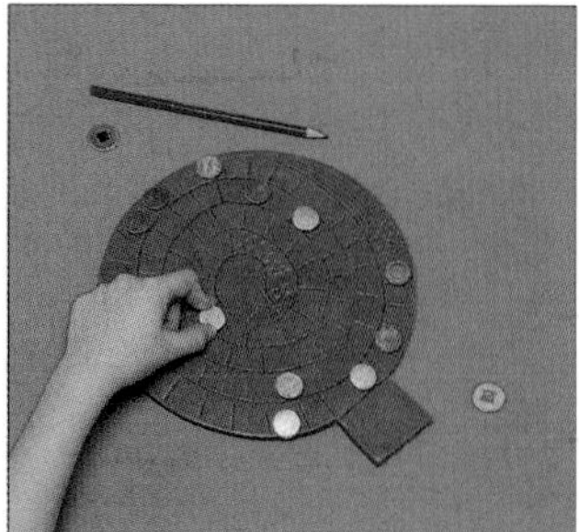

4 Your go ends if you throw another '1'. If it's another number, advance a counter that number of squares towards the centre of the board. Only move counters that have started on the board.

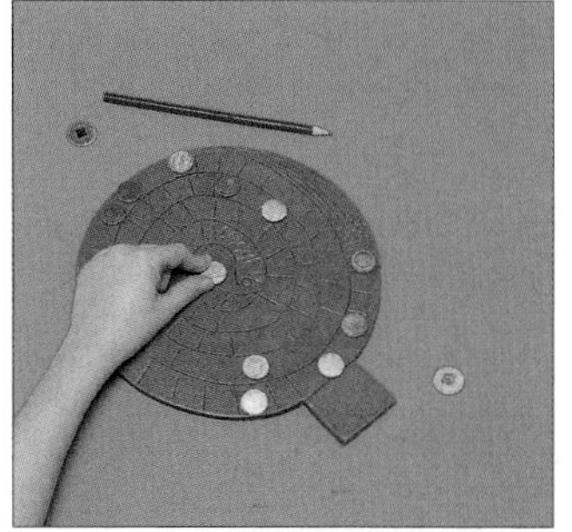

5 Throw exactly the right number to reach the centre. Then turn the counter over so that it can start the return journey. As soon as your first counter gets home, the lion piece begins.

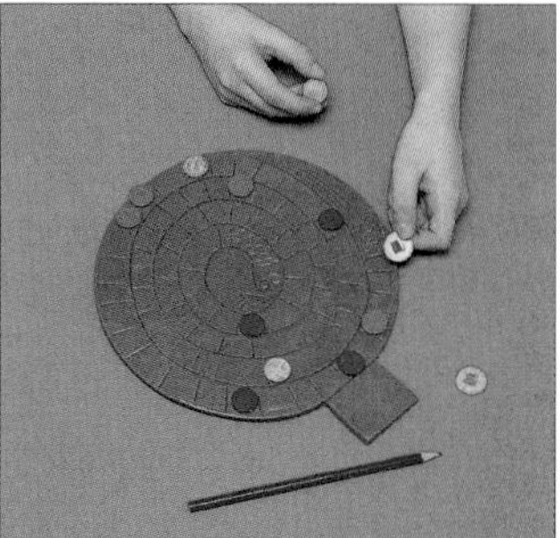

6 The lion counter moves to the centre of the board in the same way as the other counters. On its return journey, it can eat the opponent's counters if it lands on them.

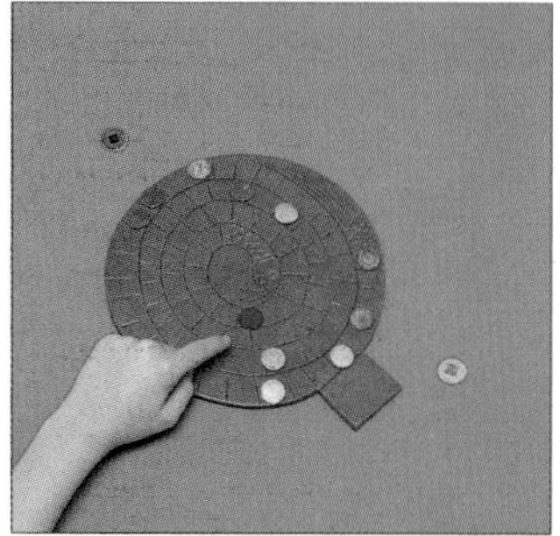

7 The winner is the person whose lion has eaten the largest number of counters. Work out the number of counters you got home safely, and see who has the most counters left.

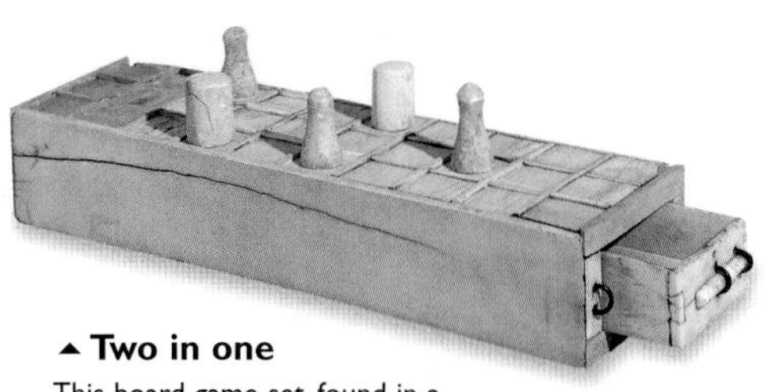

▲ Two in one

This board game set, found in a pharaoh's pyramid, could be used to play senet and another game called tjau. It has a built-in drawer that contained all the loose pieces, such as counters, for the two games.

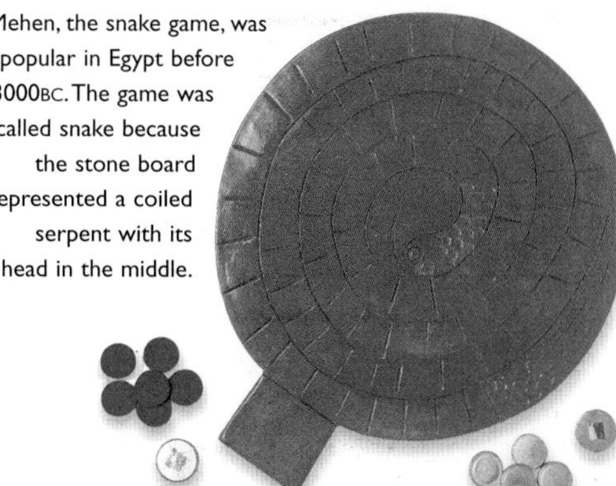

Mehen, the snake game, was popular in Egypt before 3000BC. The game was called snake because the stone board represented a coiled serpent with its head in the middle.

Egyptian lion toy

Wall paintings and goods found in Egyptian tombs have provided plenty of evidence that the ancient Egyptians enjoyed toys and games, such as spinning tops and rattles. Children had only a few years before serious education and work began. However, we know that they played with balls made from rags, linen and reeds. They also played with rattles and spinning tops made of glazed stone, and little wooden models of horses and crocodiles. Toy cats were especially popular, because cats were regarded as holy animals in ancient Egypt. A game called tip cat was also a favourite. In this game, players tried to hit a small oblong piece of wood, called a cat, over a large ring in the ground.

Many ancient Egyptian artefacts have been preserved and are kept in museums throughout the world. In the *Staatliche Museen* (National Museum) in Berlin, Germany, there is a toy crocodile with a moving jaw, dating from more than 3,600 years ago. Equally remarkable are the hedgehog and lion on wheels dating from the same period, which were found in the Persian town of Susa.

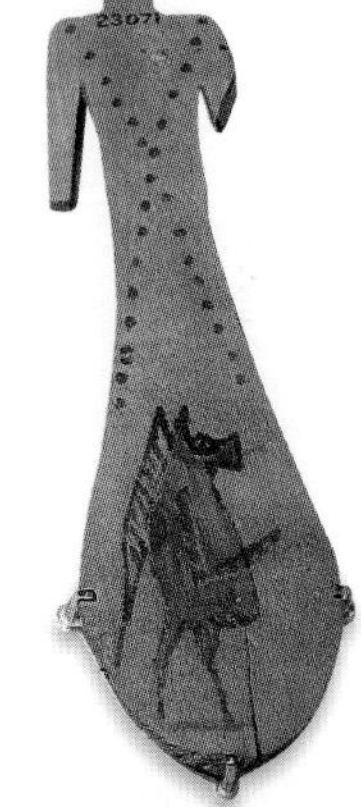

▲ **Paddle dolls**
Egyptian children often played with a paddle doll. The hair of the doll on the left is made from dried mud. Both dolls date from c.1900BC.

YOU WILL NEED
Self-hardening clay, rolling pin, cutting board, modelling tool, piece of card, skewer, balsa wood, fine sandpaper, acrylic paints, paintbrush, water pot, masking tape, string.

▲ **On guard**
The Great Sphinx has the body of a lion and the head of a man. This massive stone statue guards the pyramids of Giza on the edge of modern Cairo. They were built for the Pharaoh Khufu, his son Khafre and the Pharaoh Menkaure.

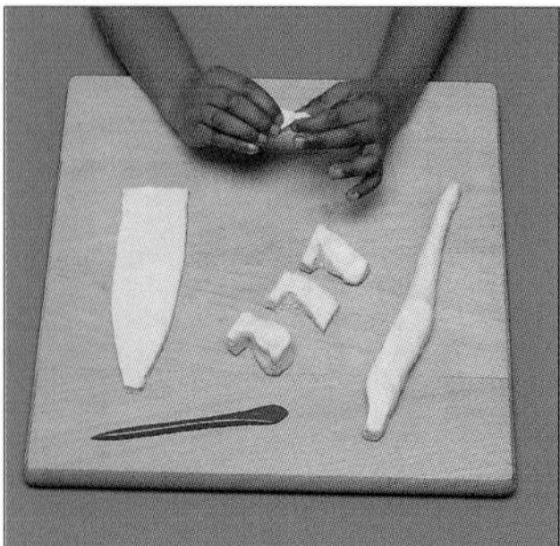

1 Begin by rolling out the clay. Cut the clay into the shapes shown in the picture above. Mould the legs on to the body and the base. Leave the bottom jaw piece to one side.

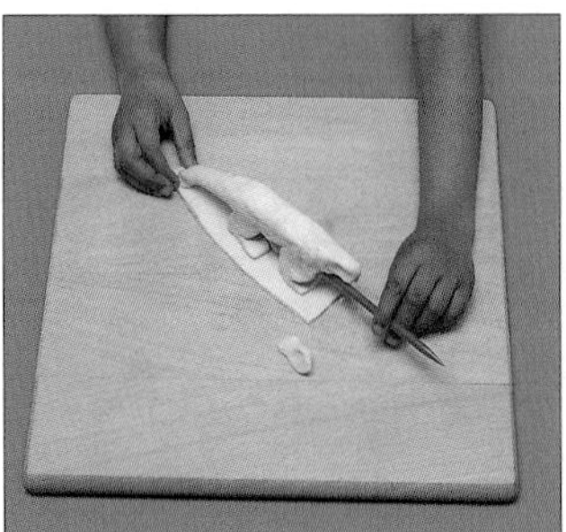

2 Use the modelling tool to make a hole between the upper body of the lion and the base section, as shown above. The lower jaw of the lion will fit into this hole.

3 Insert the lower jaw into the hole you have made, and prop it up with the piece of card. Then use the skewer to make a hole in the upper and lower jaws of the lion's head, as shown above.

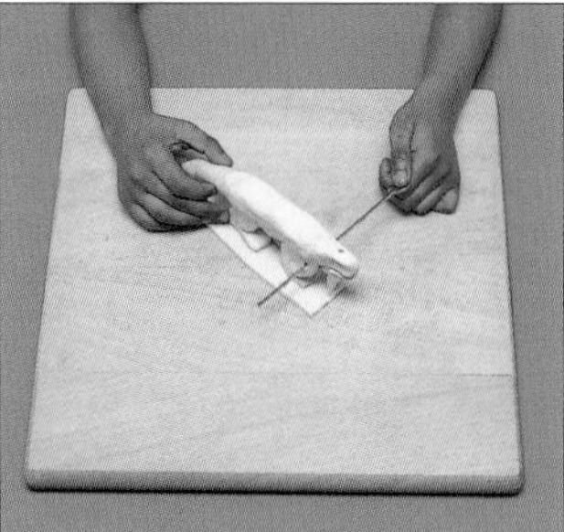

4 Now use the skewer to make a hole from left to right through the lion's upper body and lower jaw. When the figure is dry, you will thread the string through these holes.

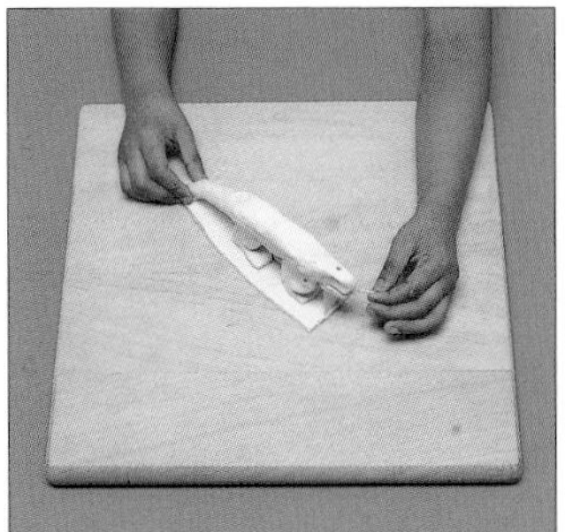

5 Push a small piece of balsa wood into the mouth of the lion. This will form the lion's tooth. Leave the clay lion to dry. Sand down the surface of the figure with fine sandpaper.

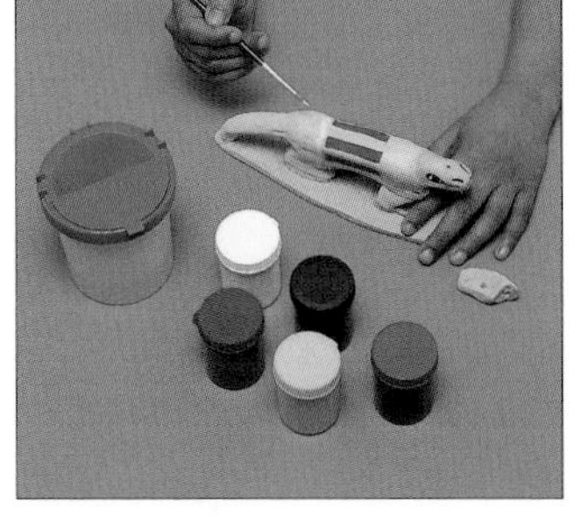

6 Paint the lion using bright colours, as shown above. Use masking tape to ensure that the lines you paint are straight. Leave the lion in a warm place for the paint to dry.

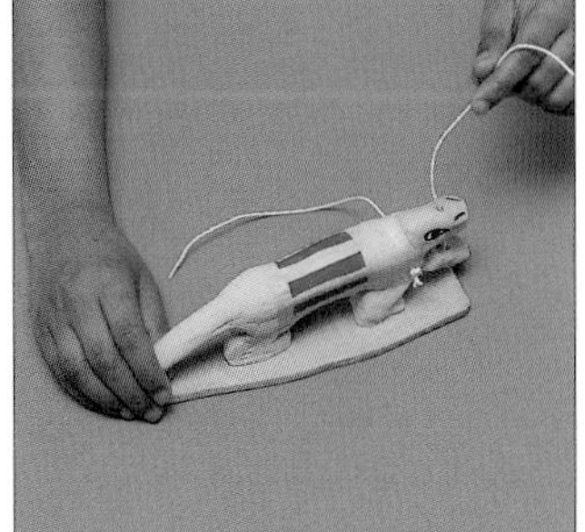

7 Thread the string through the holes in the upper body, and tie it to secure. A second piece of string should then be threaded through the lower and upper jaws of the lion.

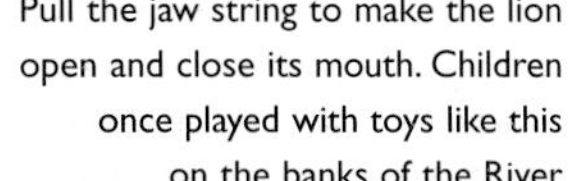

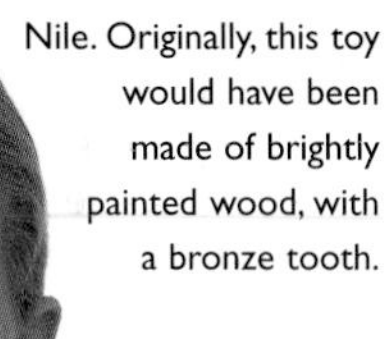

Pull the jaw string to make the lion open and close its mouth. Children once played with toys like this on the banks of the River Nile. Originally, this toy would have been made of brightly painted wood, with a bronze tooth.

Greek knucklebones

The game of knucklebones played in ancient Greece is rather like the more modern game of jacks. It was not a game at all to begin with. The way the bones fell when they were thrown was interpreted to predict the future. The knuckles – little anklebones of a sheep or cow – were called *astragalos* by the Greeks. Girls tended to play the game of knucklebones, while boys preferred to cast the bones like dice in a game of chance. Each of the four distinctively shaped sides of the bone was given a different numerical value.

One of the most popular board games in ancient Greece was a game of siege called *polis* (city). Another was the 'game of the five lines', in which the central, sacred, line had special significance. The exact rules are not known, but it is thought that it may have been rather like the later game of checkers. Board games, picture games and toys have all been found in the tombs of children. Many archaeological finds have unearthed evidence of toys that are still played with today, such as hoops, rattles, dolls, spinning tops and balls.

▲ Fit for life
A Greek athlete lifts weights, perhaps to get himself fit for battle, or for a sports competition. The Greeks were keen on sport for its own sake. Many cities had a public gymnasium, and games were a feature of religious festivals.

▲ Knockout punch
Boxing was one of the sports included in the Olympic Games soon after they began in 776BC. Other sports included weights, discus, javelin, running and wrestling.

YOU WILL NEED

Self-hardening clay, rolling pin, cutting board, modelling tool, cream acrylic paint, paintbrush, water pot.

1 Divide the clay into five small pieces. Then roll each piece into the shape of a ball. Press each ball of clay into a figure-of-eight shape, as shown in the picture above.

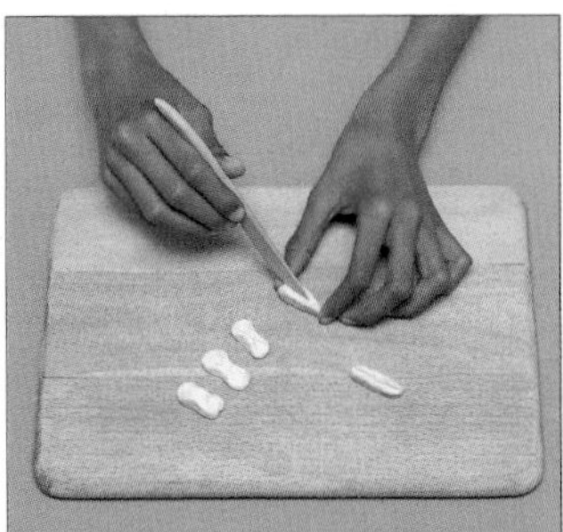

2 Use the modelling tool to carve out a ridge in the middle of each figure-of-eight. Then make small dents in the end of each piece with your finger. Leave the five shapes to dry.

3 When they are dry, give the pieces two coats of paint. Use cream paint so that the pieces look like bone. When the paint is dry, you and a friend can play with them.

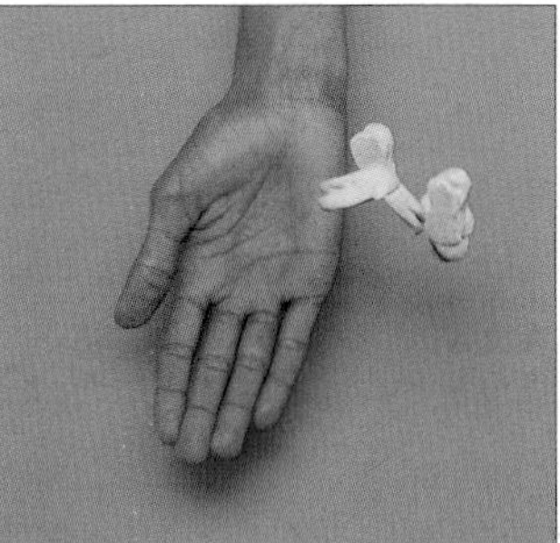

4 To play knucklebones, gather the five pieces in the palm of one of your hands. Throw all five pieces into the air at once, as shown above. Then quickly flip your hand over.

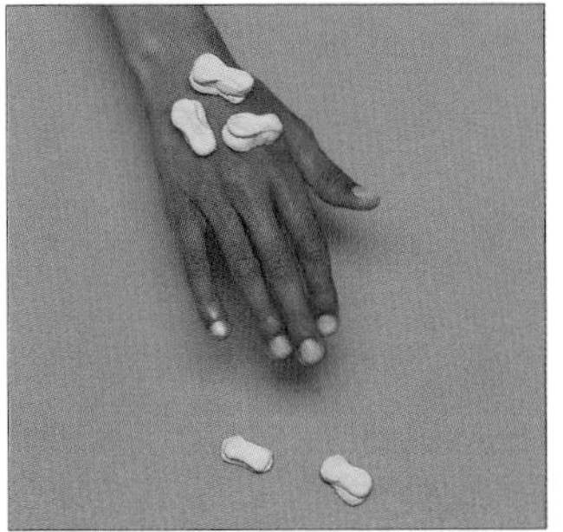

5 Take turns to try to catch as many of the pieces as you can on the back of your hand. If you or your friend catch them all, that person wins the game. If not, the game continues.

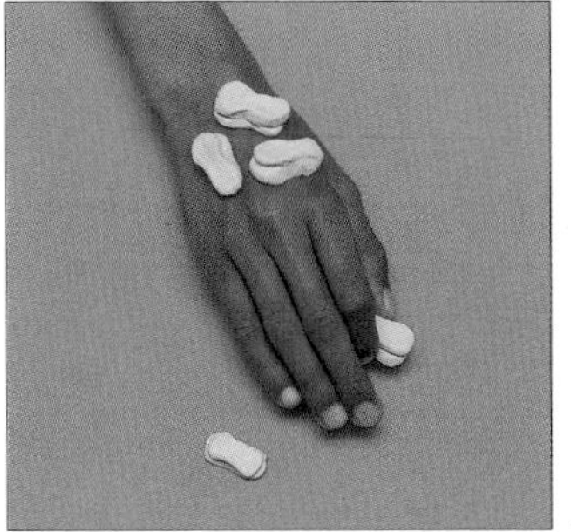

6 If you drop any of the pieces, try to pick them up with the others still on the back of your hand. Throw them with your free hand and try to catch them again.

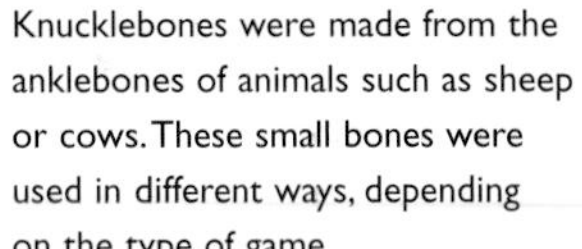

Knucklebones were made from the anklebones of animals such as sheep or cows. These small bones were used in different ways, depending on the type of game. The Greeks also used knucklebones as dice.

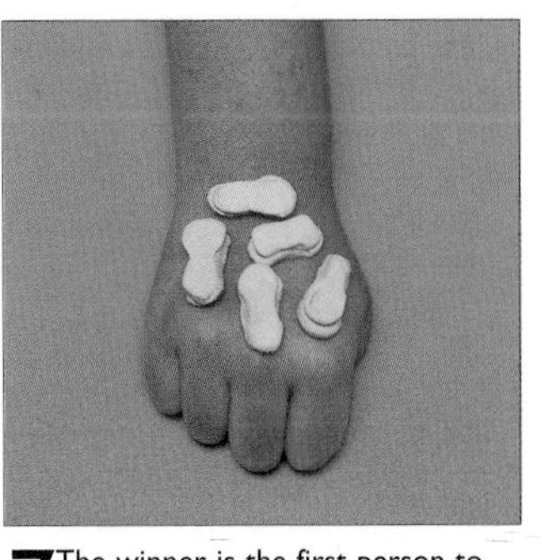

7 The winner is the first person to catch all the knucklebones on the back of their hand. It may take a few goes to get the hang of the game. But remember, practice makes perfect!

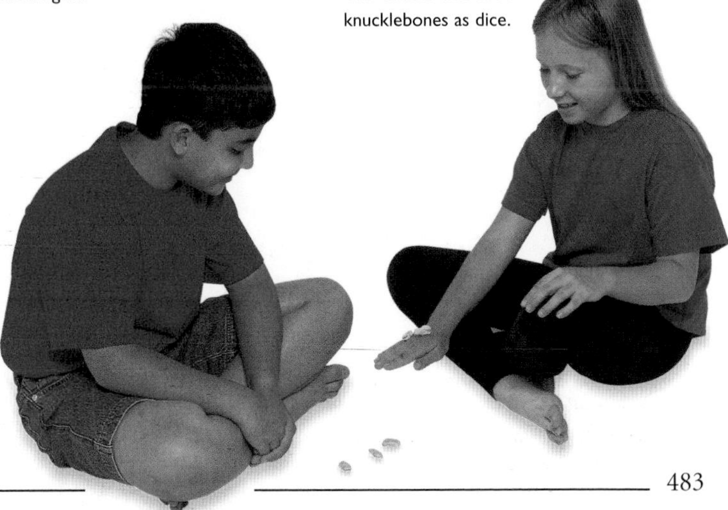

Roman dux game

The Roman game of dux was a little bit like the game of checkers. In terms of difficulty, it comes somewhere between the very simple games that Romans enjoyed playing, such as tick-tack-toe, and more complicated games, such as chess. In some games, a die was thrown to decide how many squares they could move at a time.

Knucklebones was popular at public baths. The Romans learned how to play the game from the Greeks. Each player would throw the small anklebones of a sheep up into the air and try to catch them on the back of the hand. Knucklebones could also be played like dice, with each side of the bones having a different score.

Roman children played games such as hide-and-seek and hopscotch, and had dolls and toy animals made of wood, clay or bronze. A child from a wealthy family might be given a child-sized chariot that could be pulled by a goat.

▲ Playing games
This mosaic dates from around the 1st century AD. It shows three Roman men playing a dice game. The Romans were such great gamblers that games of chance were officially banned. The one exception was during the winter festival of Saturnalia, when most rules were relaxed.

▲ Counter culture
Plain, round gaming counters like these were made of bone or ivory. The Romans sometimes used counters that had been carved into the shape of animals' heads or decorated with a picture in relief (raised from the surface).

YOU WILL NEED

Self-hardening clay, rolling pin, cutting board, ruler, modelling tool, two different colours of glass mosaic tiles (16 of each), two glass beads (two colours; the same as your tiles).

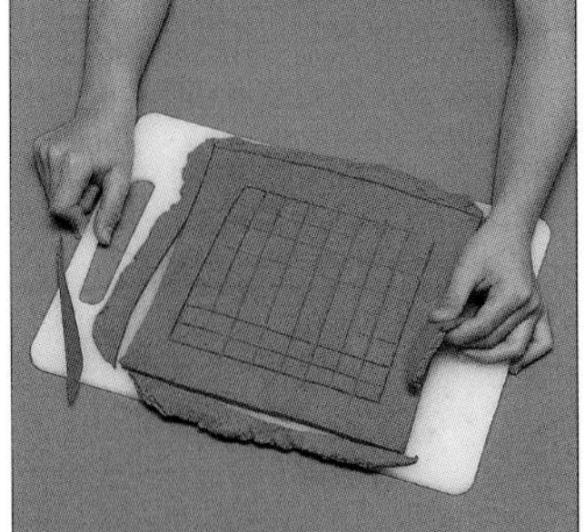

1 Roll out the clay, and trim it to 25cm/10in square. Use the ruler and modelling tool to mark out a grid eight squares across and eight squares down. Leave room for a border.

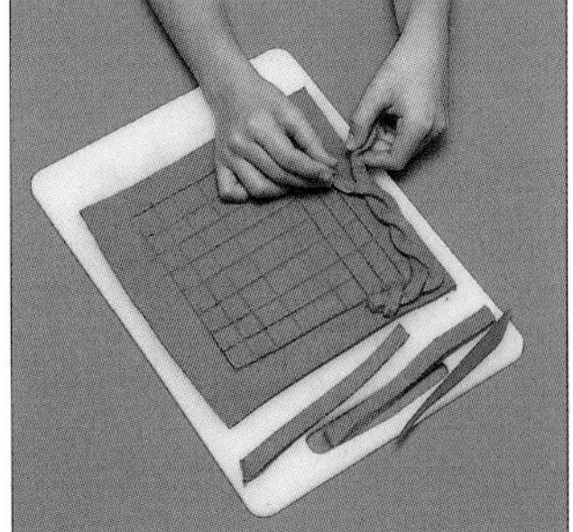

2 Decorate the border using the excess clay, as shown. Leave the gaming board to dry. Each player then chooses a colour, and has 16 tiles and a bead. The bead is the dux, or leader.

3 Players take turns to put their tiles on the squares, two at a time. The dux is put on last. Players now take turns to move a tile one square forwards, backwards or sideways.

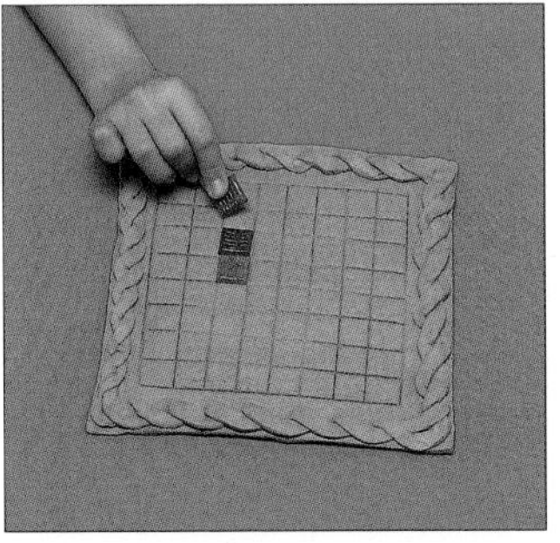

4 If you sandwich your opponent's tile between two of your own, his or her tile is captured and removed. You then get an extra go. The dux is captured in the same way as the tiles.

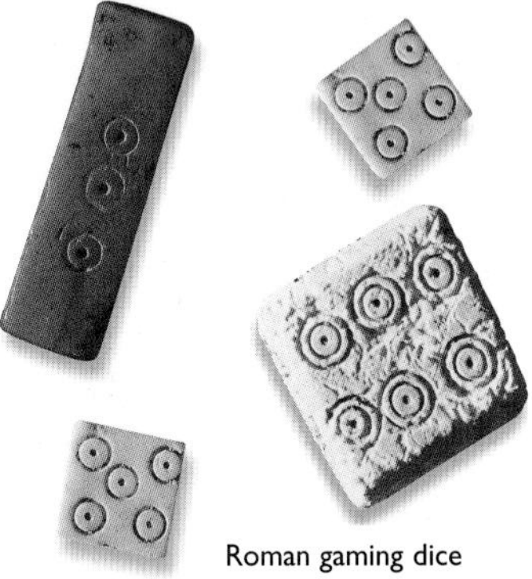

Roman gaming dice

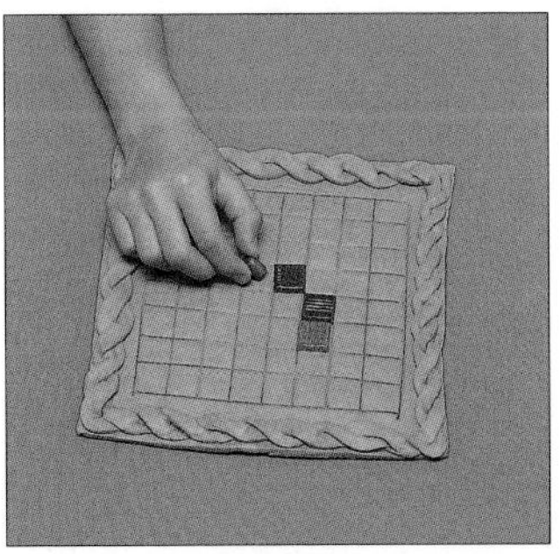

5 The dux can also jump over a tile on to an empty square, as shown. If your opponent's tile is then trapped between your dux and one of your tiles, his or her tile is captured.

During the game, you must move a tile or a dux if it is possible to do so – even if it means being captured. The winner is the first player to capture all of the other player's tiles and dux.

Chinese kite

The earliest kite-flying in China was recorded during the Han Dynasty (206BC–AD220). These early kites were made of silk and bamboo. They were flown high in the sky during battles to scare off the enemy. Gradually, kites were flown during festivals. In the Qing Dynasty (1644–1912), a festival called Tengkao (Mounting the Height) was introduced by the Manchu emperors. People flew kites from high ground in the belief that this would bring them good luck.

Ever since ancient times, the Chinese have loved to play games and watch displays of martial arts and acrobatics. The nobility also invited acrobats and dancers into their homes to amuse their guests. Performances often lasted for hours, especially during festivals and ceremonies. Sports, such as polo and football, were also enjoyed by the wealthy. One emperor, Xuanzong, enjoyed polo so much that he failed to keep up with his official engagements.

▲ **Battleboard**
The traditional game of xiang qi is similar to chess. One army battles against another, with round discs used as playing pieces. To tell the discs apart, each is marked with a name.

YOU WILL NEED

Thirteen barbecue sticks measuring 30cm/12in long, ruler, white glue and glue brush, masking tape, scissors, white paper, pencil, acrylic paints, paintbrush, water pot, 10m/30ft length of string, piece of wooden dowel, small metal ring.

▲ **Training for war**
This figure shows an ancient Chinese polo player. Polo was originally played in India and Asia. It was invented as a training game to improve the riding skills of soldiers in cavalry units.

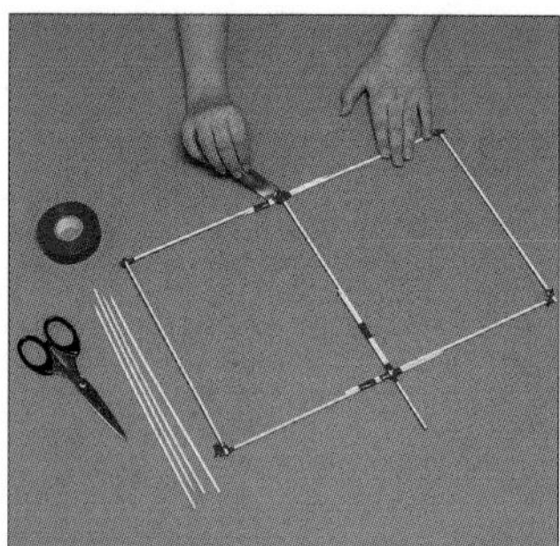

1 Make a 40 x 30cm/16 x 12in rectangle by gluing and taping sticks together. Overlap the sticks for strength. Join two sticks together to make a central rod that sticks out on one side.

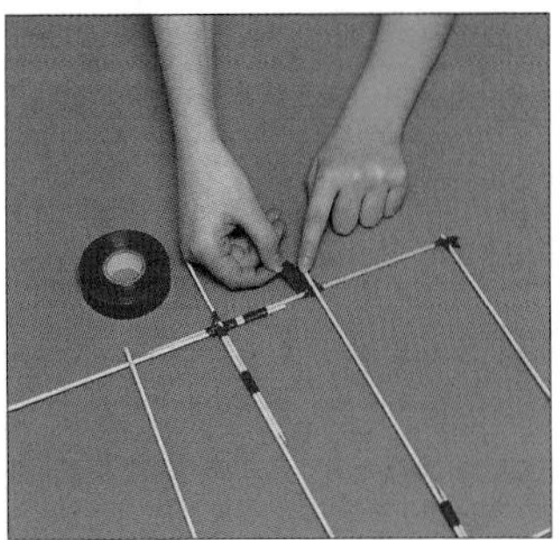

2 Use the last five sticks to make a rectangle 40 x 15cm/16 x 6in. Lay this rectangle on top of the first one at a right angle. Tape the two rectangles together, as shown in Steps 2 and 3.

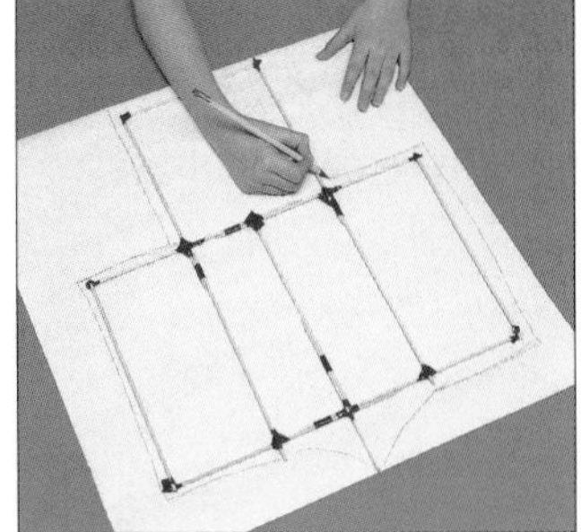

3 Place the frame on to a large sheet of white paper. Draw a border around the outside of the frame, 2.5cm/1in out from the edge. Add curves around the end of the centre rod.

4 Cut out the kite shape you have drawn. Using a pencil, draw on the details of the dragon design shown in the final picture on this page. Paint in the design and leave it to dry.

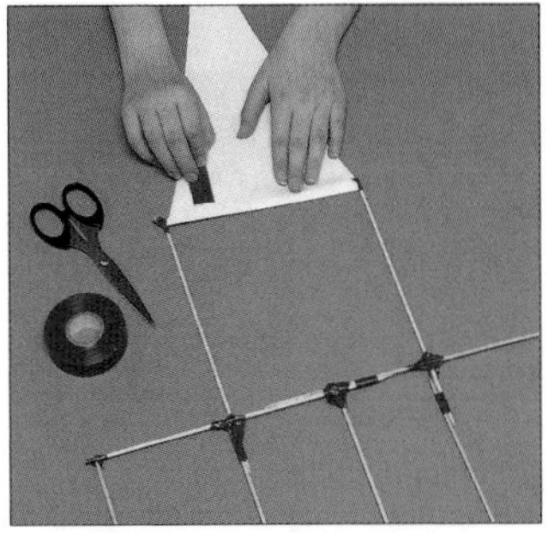

5 Cut a triangular piece of paper to make a tail for the end of your kite. Paint it and let it dry. Fold the tail over the rod at the bottom of the kite, as shown. Tape the tail into position.

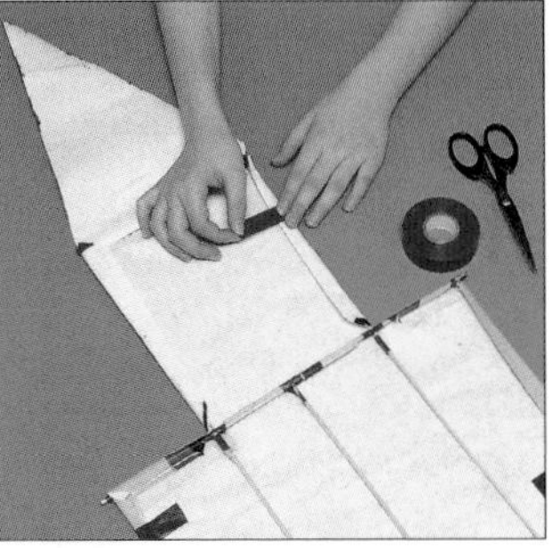

6 Carefully tape and glue your dragon design on to the frame of the kite. Fold the border over the frame and tape it on to the back of the kite, as shown above.

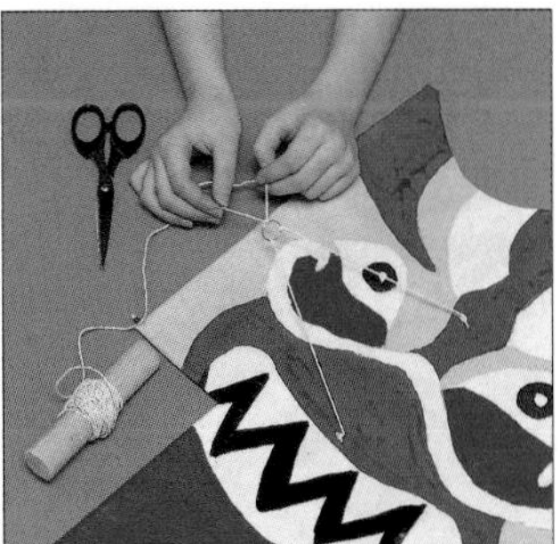

7 Wrap the string round the dowel and tie the end to a ring. Tie two pieces of string to the central rod of the frame. Make two holes in the kite, pass the strings through and tie to the ring.

Kites were invented in China around 3,000 years ago. They were often made into the shapes of animals or mythical creatures such as dragons. Today, Chinese children still play with home-made paper kites.

Japanese shell game

Perhaps one of the reasons why the Japanese invented the shell game was because shellfish have always been an important ingredient in Japanese food. Japan has a rich cultural history, and many pastimes have been handed down through the generations.

A game called menko, which has been played since the 1700s, involves throwing cards on the ground. Players try to flip their opponent's cards over by throwing their card on top of them. Karuta, another card game, has been popular since the 1600s. Karuta cards have pictures, words and poems written on them. In one version, known as iroha karuta, a player acts as the reader and keeps one set of karuta cards with sayings on them. The other players gather around a spread-out set of cards with the first letter or few words of the saying and a picture on them. When the reader starts reading a saying, the players try to find the matching karuta card. Whoever finds the card keeps it, and the player with the most cards at the end of the game wins.

▲ Counters from the sea
The Japanese often ate shellfish and kept the prettiest shells afterwards. They could then use them to play games such as this one.

YOU WILL NEED

Fresh clams, pan, water, bowl, selection of acrylic paints, paintbrush, water pot.

▲ Playing to win
Three court ladies play a card game, probably using karuta cards. These cards often included popular sayings from everyday Japanese life.

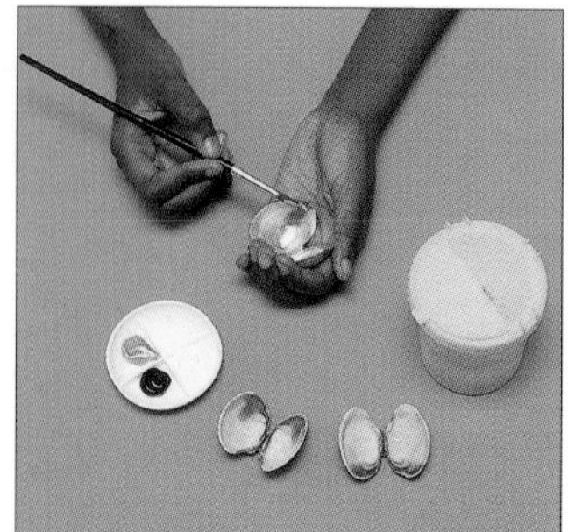

1 Ask an adult to boil the clams. Leave them to one side to cool, and then remove the insides. Wash the shells and leave them to dry. When they are dry, paint the shells gold.

2 When the gold paint is dry, carefully pull each pair of shells apart. Then paint an identical design on to each shell of the pair. Start by painting a round, white face.

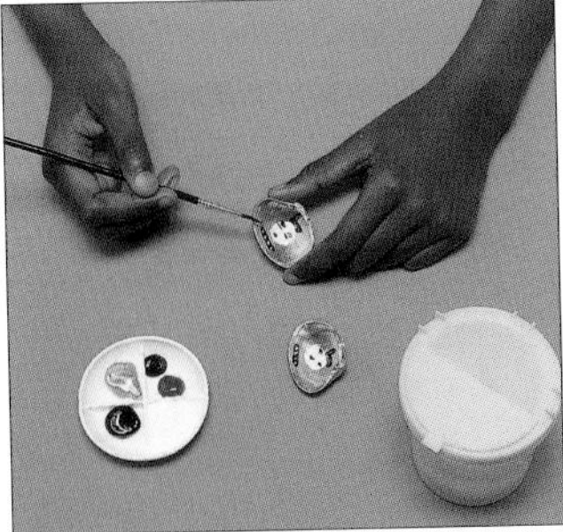

3 Add more features to the face, such as a mouth, hair and eyes. In the past, popular pictures, such as scenes from traditional stories, were painted on to the shell pairs.

4 Paint several pairs of clam shells with a variety of designs. Copy the ones here or make up your own. Make sure each pair of shells has an identical picture. Leave the painted shells to dry.

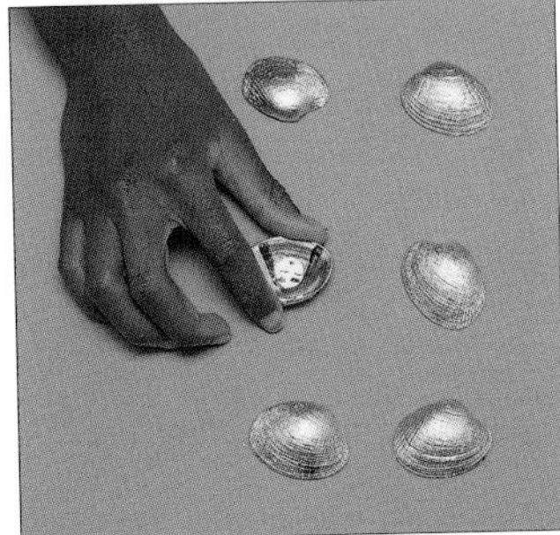

5 Now it is time to play the game. Turn all your shells face down and jumble them up. Turn over one shell and then challenge your opponent to pick the shell that matches yours.

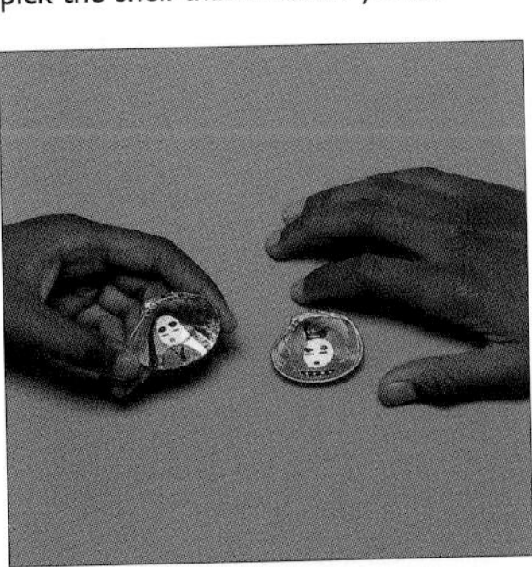

6 If the two shells do not match, turn them over and try again. If they do match, your opponent takes the shells. Take it in turns to challenge each other to find the matching pair.

The player with the most shells at the end of the game wins! Noble ladies at the imperial court enjoyed playing the shell game. This is a simplified version of the game they used to play.

Japanese streamer

There are thousands of local festivals in Japan each year. Most are based on ancient celebrations of the natural world, marking the yearly planting, growing and harvesting cycles. Each festival involves parades, dances, feasts and contests such as tug-of-war and kite-flying.

Boys' Day, held on the fifth day of the fifth month each year, was originally a festival to prepare farm labourers for the hard work of transplanting rice seedlings. This festival was once known as the Sweet Flag Festival, named for the sweet flag plant that people hung outside their homes to keep evil spirits away. Gradually, the meaning of the festival changed to symbolize manliness and courage. Today, paper carp streamers hang from flagpoles above the houses of Japanese families on Boys' Day.

▲ **Swimming for boys**
Carp streamers such as these fly on Boys' Day. The carp swims against the current of a stream, and therefore symbolizes strength and perseverance.

▲ **Festival fun**
This woodblock print shows celebrations during the New Year's festival. Kites filled the sky, and traditional toys and games were enjoyed by everyone in Japan.

YOU WILL NEED

Pencil, two sheets of A1/34 x 22in paper, felt-tipped pen, scissors, acrylic paints, paintbrush, water pot, white glue and glue brush, picture or garden wire, masking tape, string, garden cane.

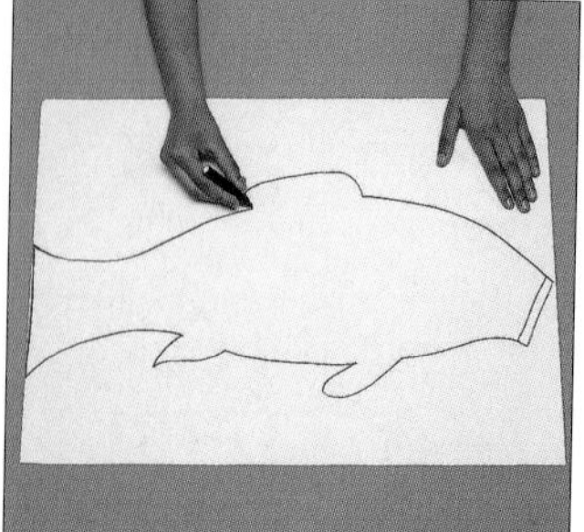

1 Take the pencil and one sheet of paper. Draw a large carp fish shape on to the paper, like the one shown above. When you are happy with it, go over it in felt-tipped pen.

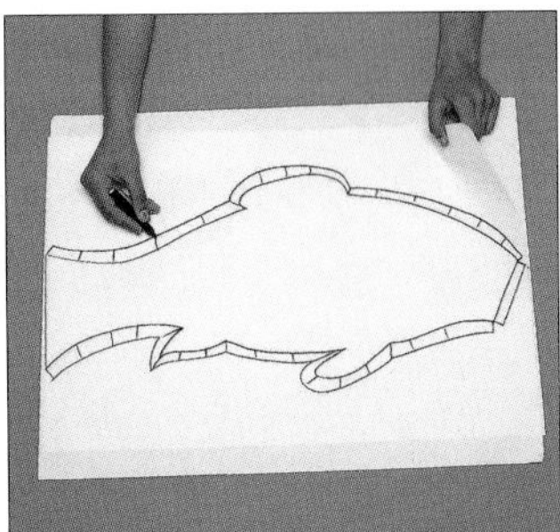

2 Put the second piece of paper over the first. Trace the outline of the fish shape on to the top sheet. Draw a narrow border around this fish shape and add tabs, as shown above.

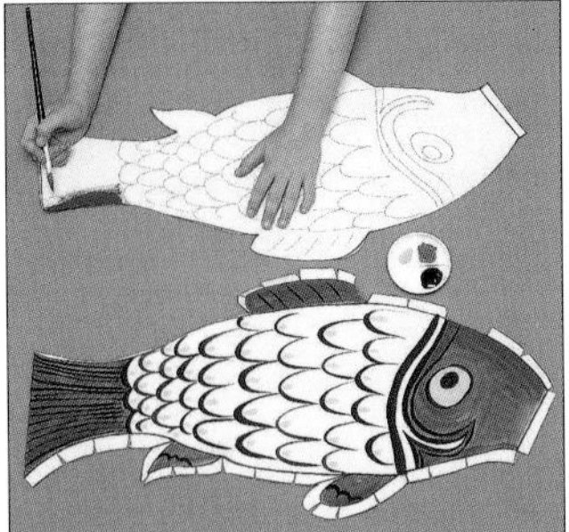

3 Add scales, fins, eyes and other details on both fish shapes, as shown above. Cut the shapes out, remembering to snip into the tabs. Paint both fish in bright colours.

4 Put the two fish shapes together with the painted sides facing outwards. Turn the tabs in and glue the edges of the fish shapes together. Do not glue the tail and mouth sections.

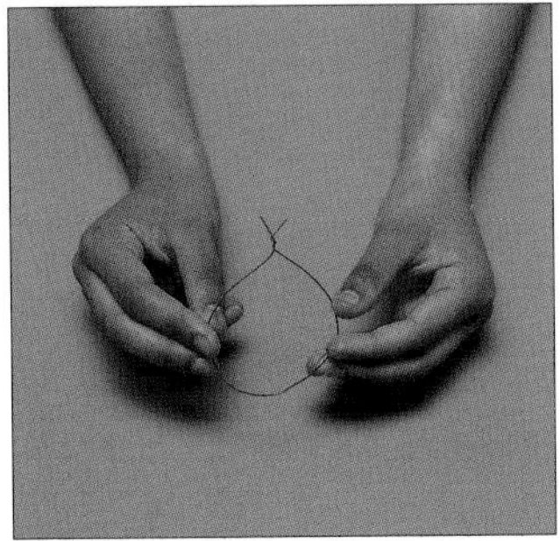

5 Use a small length of picture wire or garden wire to make a ring the size of the fish's mouth. Twist the ends together, as shown above. Then bind them with masking tape.

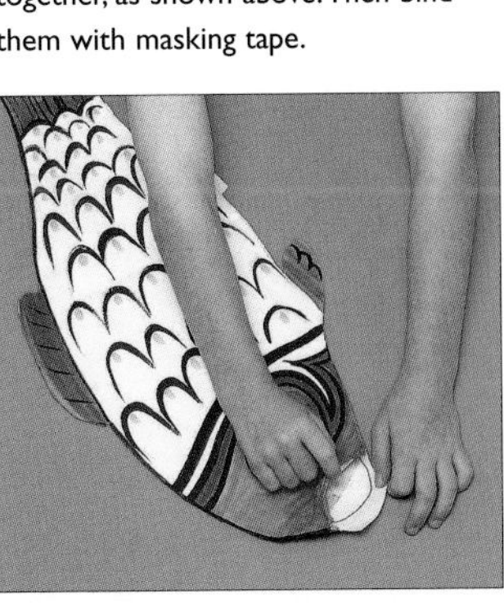

6 Place the ring inside the fish's mouth. Glue the open ends of the mouth over the ring. Tie one end of a length of string on to the mouth ring and the other end to a garden cane.

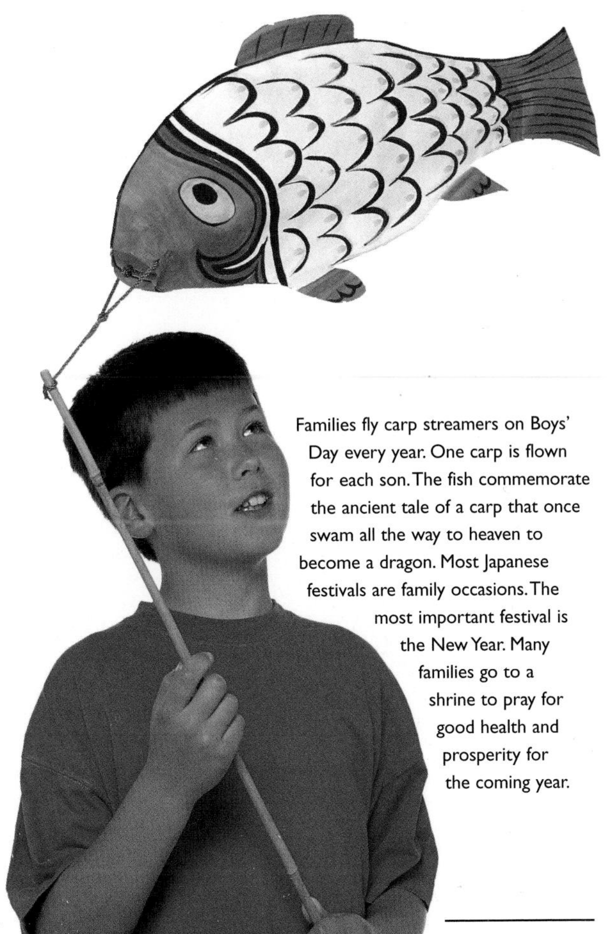

Families fly carp streamers on Boys' Day every year. One carp is flown for each son. The fish commemorate the ancient tale of a carp that once swam all the way to heaven to become a dragon. Most Japanese festivals are family occasions. The most important festival is the New Year. Many families go to a shrine to pray for good health and prosperity for the coming year.

Native American lacrosse

Between hunting expeditions and domestic tasks, Native Americans found time to relax and entertain themselves. Ball and stick games, such as lacrosse, were popular. There were also games of chance, gambling and tests of skill. Games of chance included guessing games, dice throwing and hand games where one person had to guess in which hand his opponent was hiding marked bones or wooden pieces. Archery, spear throwing and juggling were all fun to do, and also helped to improve hunting skills.

Children loved to swim and take part in races. In the north, Native American girls and boys raced on toboggans. Active pastimes such as these helped to develop the skills a Native American needed to survive, such as strength, agility and stamina. Ritual foot races were also of ceremonial importance, helping the crops to grow, to bring rain and give renewed strength to the Sun.

▲ Twice the fun

The ball game some Native Americans played used two sticks, although otherwise it was similar to lacrosse. The Cherokees called the game 'little brother of war'.

YOU WILL NEED

Thick card, ruler, pencil, scissors, masking tape, pair of compasses, barbecue stick, white glue and glue brush, bamboo stick (to reach your waist from ground level), string, brown paint, paintbrush, water pot, light ball.

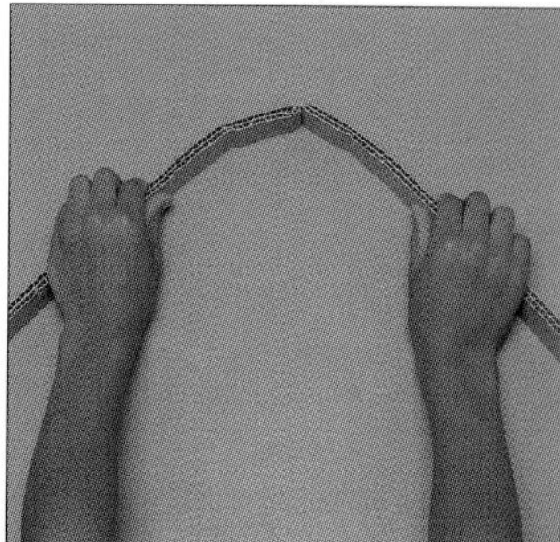

1 Measure and cut a strip of card 120 x 3cm/47¼ x 1 3/16in. Fold it gently at the centre to make a curve. You could also cut two pieces of card 60 x 3cm/ 24 x 1 3/16in and tape them together.

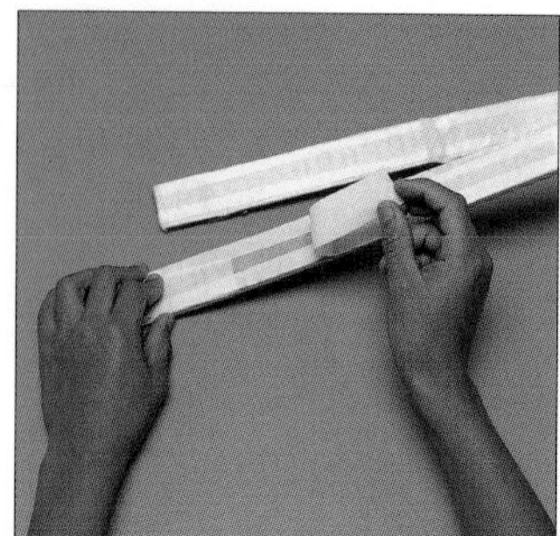

2 Completely cover the card strip with masking tape. Start from the edges and work your way around the strip, keeping the bent shape. Make sure you cover both sides of the card.

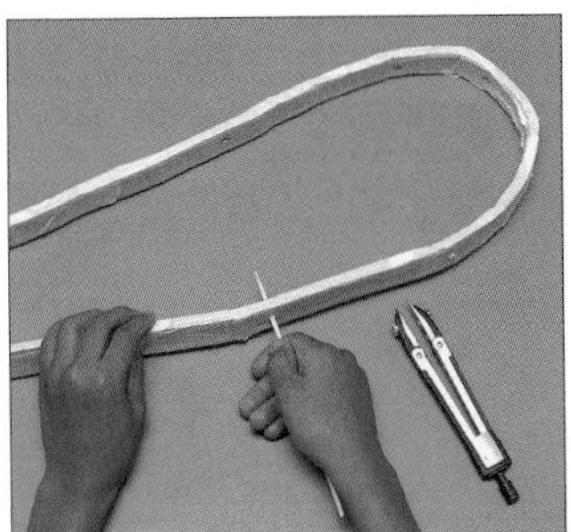

3 Use compasses to make two holes at the top of the bend, 10cm/4in apart. Make two more holes 10cm/4in from these, and then two more 10cm/4in further still. Enlarge with a barbecue stick.

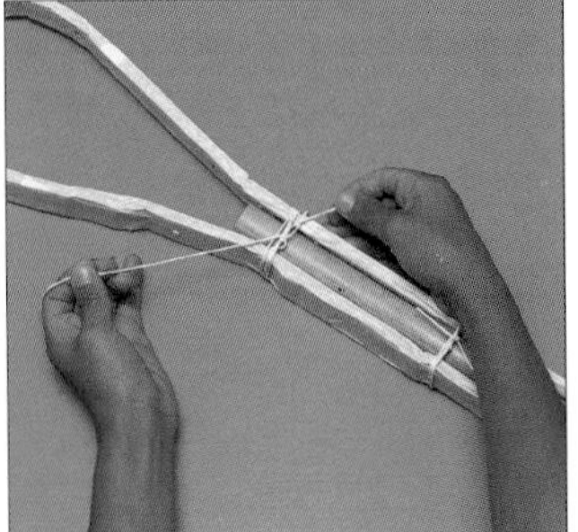

4 Glue the ends of the card strip to the top of the bamboo stick, leaving a loop of card at the top, as shown above. Tie a piece of string around the outside, to keep it in place.

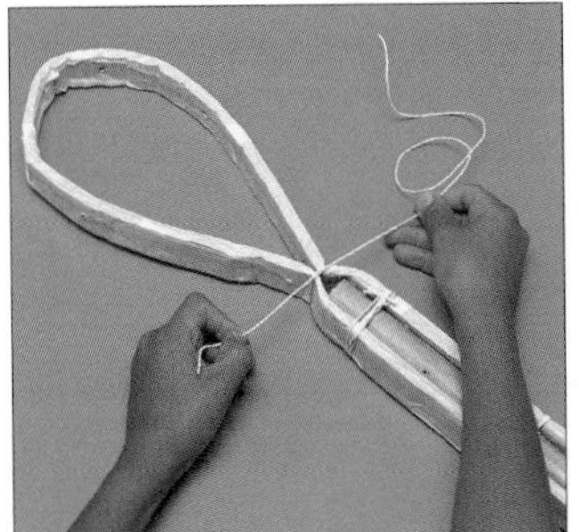

5 Pinch the card together where the loop meets the end of the stick. Tie it tightly with a piece of string, as shown above, and trim off the excess. Now paint the stick brown.

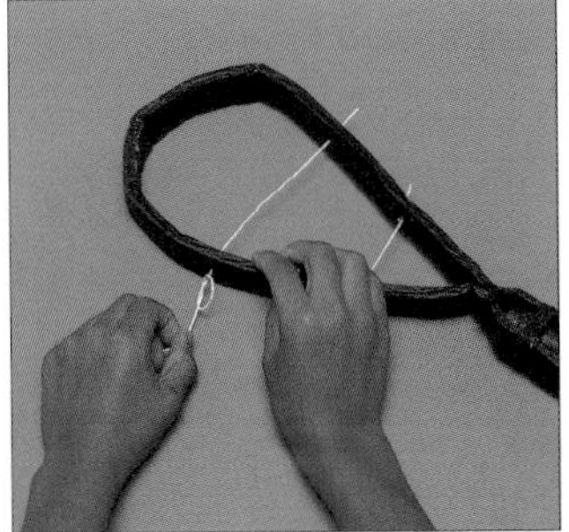

6 When the stick is dry, thread two pieces of string horizontally between the two sets of holes on the sides of the loop. Knot the pieces of string on the outside.

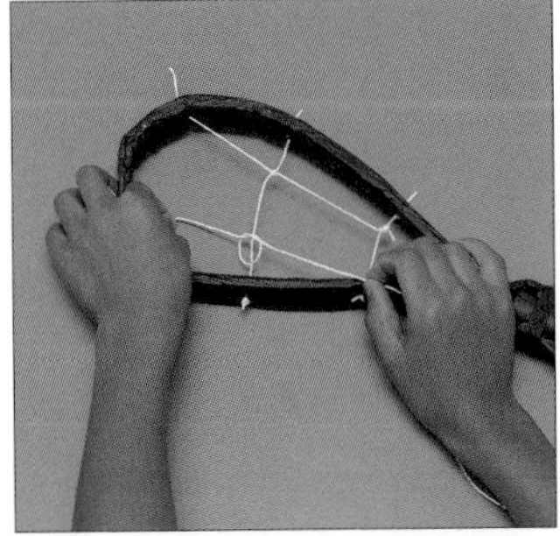

7 Now thread the vertical strings. Start at the holes at the top of the frame and tie the string around both horizontal strings. Tie the ends. Then try scooping up a ball with the stick.

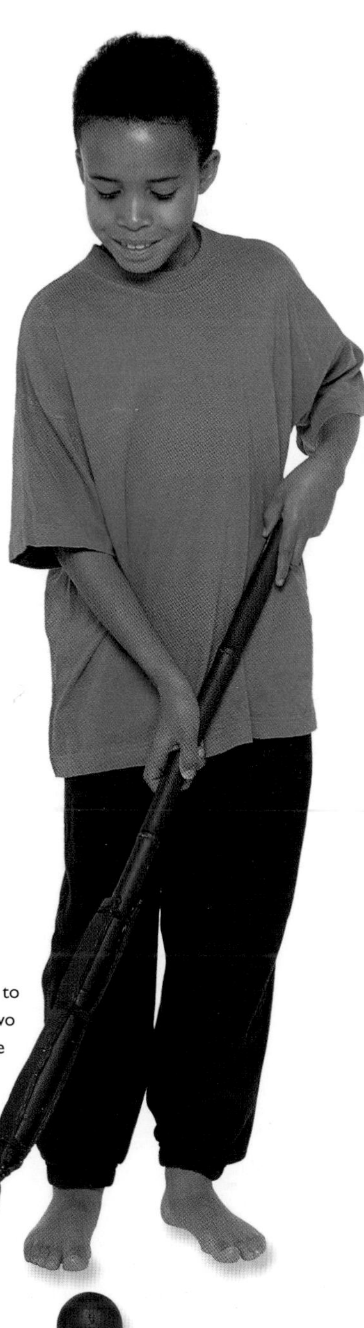

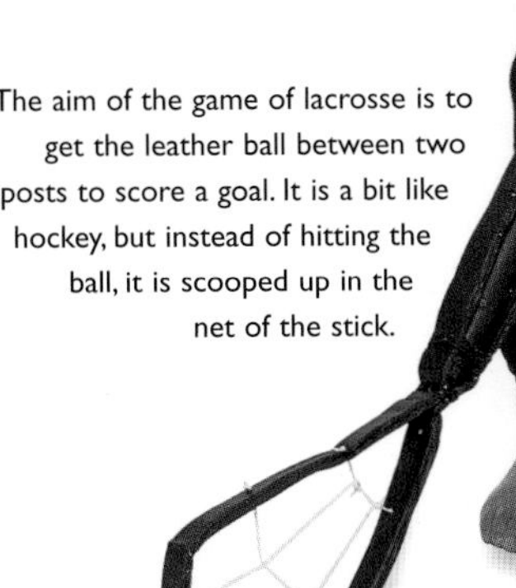

The aim of the game of lacrosse is to get the leather ball between two posts to score a goal. It is a bit like hockey, but instead of hitting the ball, it is scooped up in the net of the stick.

Mesoamerican patolli

Sports and games were enjoyed by Mesoamerican people after work and on festival days. Two favourite pastimes were tlachtli, a ball game, and patolli, a board game. Tlachtli was played in front of huge crowds of onlookers, while patolli was a quieter game enjoyed by two or more players.

Mesoamerican games were not just for fun. Both tlachtli and patolli had religious meanings. In the first, the court symbolized the world, and the rubber ball stood for the Sun as it made its daily journey across the sky. Players were meant to keep the ball moving to give energy to the Sun. Losing teams were sometimes sacrificed to the Sun god. In patolli, the movement of counters on the board represented the passing years.

▲ Playing the game
A group of Aztecs playing patolli. This board game was played by moving dried beans or clay counters along a cross-shaped board with 52 squares. It could be very exciting, especially if players had bet on the result.

YOU WILL NEED

Light fabric, ruler, black marker, acrylic paints, paintbrush, water pot, several sheets of differently coloured paper, scissors, white glue and glue brush, five dried broad beans or butter beans, self-hardening clay.

▲ Sacred circles
Volador is a ceremony performed on religious festival days. Four men, dressed as birds and attached to ropes, jump off a high pole. As they spin around, falling towards the ground, they circle the pole 13 times each. That makes 52 circuits – the length of the Mesoamerican holy calendar cycle.

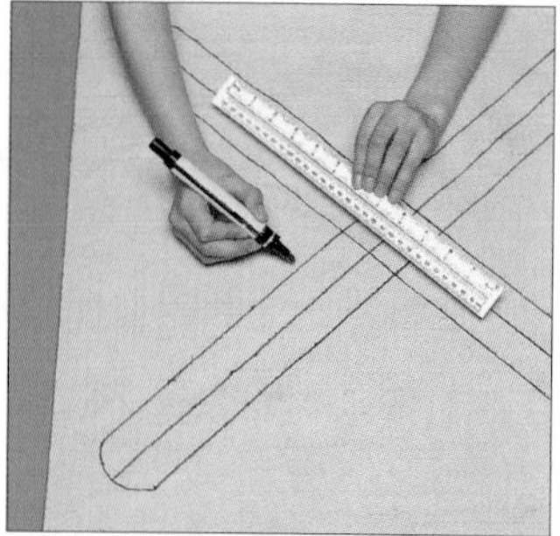

1 Measure a square of fabric about 50 x 50cm/20 x 20in. Using a marker pen and ruler, draw six diagonal lines from corner to corner to make a cross shape, as shown above.

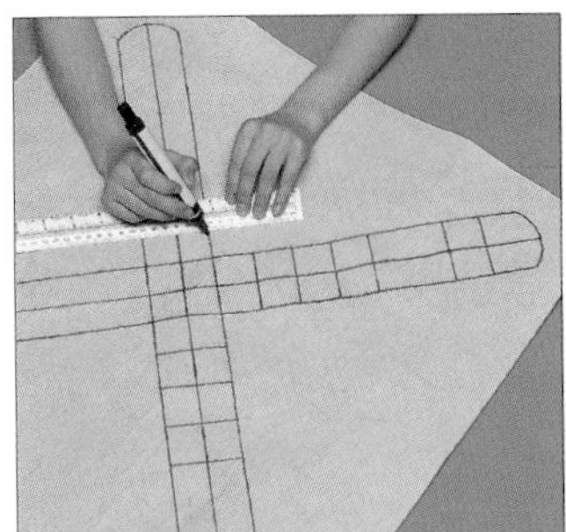

2 Draw six lines along each arm of the cross, to give seven pairs of spaces. The third space in from the end of the cross should be a double space. Paint triangles in the double space.

3 Draw the heads of eight jaguars, and then draw eight marigolds on sheets of coloured paper. Cut them out. Paint the face of the Sun god in the centre of the board.

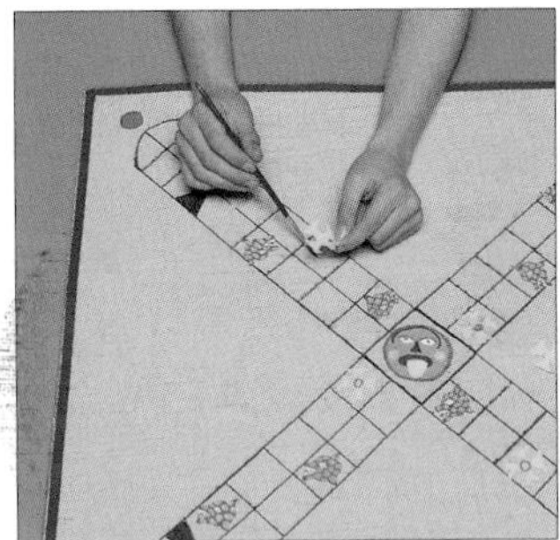

4 Stick the jaguar heads and marigolds on to the board. Paint a blue circle at the end of one arm, and a crown at the opposite end. Repeat in green at the ends of the other arms.

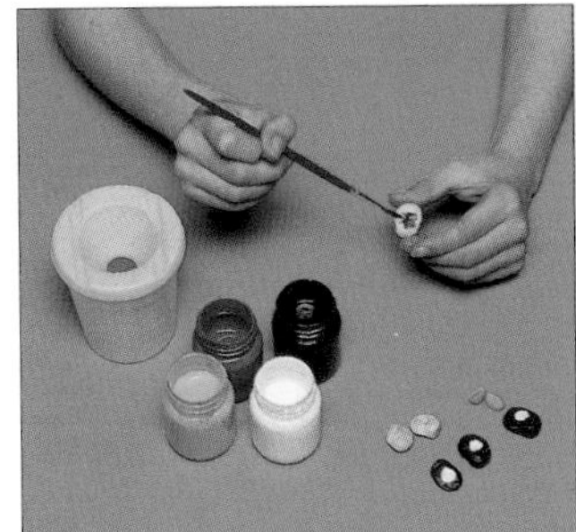

5 Paint the dried beans black with a white dot on one side. These will be used as dice. Finally, shape two small pieces of clay into counters. When they are dry, paint one green and one blue.

Most of the original rules for patolli have been lost. In this version, start each counter on the circle of the same colour. The aim is to move your counter to the crown of the same colour and back. Lose a turn if you land on a jaguar, and get an extra turn if you land on a marigold.

ARCTIC WORLD
ARCTIC WORLD
North Sea
VIKING LANDS
North America
CELTIC LANDS
AZTEC AND MAYA EMPIRES
Gulf of Mexico
Atlantic Ocean
Caribbean Sea
Central America (Mesoamerica)
Pacific Ocean
INCA EMPIRE
Andes Mountains
South America
N
Cape Horn

ARCTIC WORLD
ARCTIC WORLD
Baltic Sea
Europe
ROME
Black Sea
Caspian Sea
ANCIENT GREECE
Mediterranean Sea
Asia
ANCIENT EGYPT
MESOPOTAMIA
CHINA
Sea of Japan
JAPAN
Persian Gulf
ANCIENT INDIA
Red Sea
Arabian Sea
South China Sea
Bay of Bengal
Africa
Indian Ocean
Australia
Cape of Good Hope

Glossary

A

acupuncture A part of traditional Chinese medicine that involves the insertion of fine needles into the body to relieve pain or to cure illness.
aerodynamics The way in which objects move through the air.
aerofoil (airfoil) An object, shaped like a wing, that creates lift in the air.
afterlife Life after death, as believed by people of many world religions.
aileron A moving flap on the trailing (rear) edge of an aircraft wing.
air pressure The force with which air presses on things. Changes in air pressure make air move and cause different weather conditions.
alabaster A type of white stone used to make ornaments.
alloy A material, usually metal such as bronze or brass, that is made from a mixture of other materials.
alpaca A llama-like animal native to South America, which is valued for its fine, silky wool.
amphitheatre An oval, open-air stadium surrounded by seats and used for public entertainment, such as for gladiator fights.
amphora A large, narrow-necked Greek or Roman jar with a handle on either side. Amphorae were used to store liquids such as wine or oil.
ancestor A member of the same family who died long ago.
Anno Domini (AD) A system used to calculate dates after the supposed year of Jesus Christ's birth. Anno Domini dates in this book are prefixed AD up to the year 1000, for example, AD521. After 1000, no prefixes are used.
anvil A heavy iron block on which objects can be hammered into shape.

aperture A hole behind the lens of a camera, which can be adjusted to let more or less light on to the film.
APS Advanced Photographic System. A camera that allows you to change the format for individual shots.
aqueduct A channel for carrying water over long distances.
archaeologist Someone who studies ancient ruins and artefacts to learn about the past.
archaeology The scientific study of the past, which involves looking at the remains of ancient civilizations.
Arctic A vast, frozen area surrounding the North Pole.
aristocracy A ruling class of wealthy, privileged people, or government by such people.
armour A suit or covering worn by people or horses to protect them against injury during battle.
artefact An object that has been preserved from the past.
artificial Describes something that is not created as part of a natural process or with naturally occurring materials.
Assyrian An inhabitant of the Assyrian Empire. From 1530–612BC, Assyria occupied east of the Mediterranean Sea to Iran, and from the Persian Gulf to the mountains of eastern Turkey.
astrolabe A device invented by the Arabs, which consisted of a flat disc with a rod that could be pointed to the stars. Astrolabes helped sailors to navigate when travelling on water.
astrology The belief that stars, planets and other heavenly bodies shape the lives of people on Earth.
astronomy The scientific study of stars, planets and other heavenly bodies. In ancient times, astronomy was the same as astrology.
atmosphere The layer of air that surrounds a planet and is held to it by the planet's gravity.
atom The smallest part of an element that can exist. It is made up of many other smaller particles, including electrons, neutrons and protons.
autofocus A feature on a camera that automatically adjusts the lens position to ensure that a scene is in focus.
auxiliaries Foreign troops that help and support another nation that is engaged in war.
Aztec Mesoamerican people who lived in northern and central Mexico. The Aztecs were at their most powerful between 1350 and 1520.

B

bacteria Simple living organisms, usually consisting of single cells. Many bacteria are parasites and cause disease.
barter An exchange of goods that does not involve money.
battery A container of chemicals holding a charge of electricity.
Before Christ (BC) A system used to calculate dates before the supposed year of Jesus Christ's birth. Dates are calculated in reverse. For example, 2000BC is longer ago than 200BC.
binary code The digital code computers use, made up of two numbers, '0' and '1'.
bow The front end of a ship.
brahmin A Hindu who belongs to the highest of four social classes.
brake A pad or disc that slows a moving surface down by pressing it.
brake van A carriage at the back of trains used in the mid-1800s. A guard riding in the brake van applied the brakes on instructions from the driver in the locomotive.

Bronze Age A period in human history, between 3000BC and 1000BC, when tools and weapons were made from bronze.
Buddhism World religion founded in ancient India by the Buddha in the 6th century BC.
burin A chisel-like tool made from flint.

C

CAD Computer-aided design.
camouflage The adoption of colours, patterns or texture in order to merge with the environment, and so be hidden or disguised.
camshaft A device that creates a regular, rocking movement, such as the opening and shutting of a valve on a car cylinder head.
carbon dioxide A colourless, odourless gas containing the elements carbon and oxygen, which is a part of air.
cargo Goods carried in a ship or other vehicle.
cartouche An oval border used in Egyptian hieroglyphs to show that the name it contains is royal or a god.
caste One of four social classes that divide the followers of Hinduism.
catapult A large wooden structure used to fire stones and iron bolts at the enemy during medieval sieges.
caterpillar The larva of a butterfly or moth.
cavalry Soldiers on horseback.
CD-ROM Compact disc read-only memory. A portable computer disc, similar to an audio CD, that stores information.
Celt A member of one of the ancient peoples that inhabited most parts of Europe from around 750BC to AD1000.

century A unit of the Roman army, numbering up to 100 foot soldiers.
ceramics The art and technique of making pottery.
chainmail Flexible armour for the body, consisting of small rings of metal, linked to form a fine mesh.
chaps Over-trousers worn by cowboys to protect their legs.
chariot A lightweight, horse-drawn cart. Chariots were used in warfare and for sport.
chemical A substance used by scientists, in industry or at home.
chemical reaction The process by which one or more substances react together and change into one or more different chemicals.
chinampa An Aztec garden built on the fertile, reclaimed land on the lake shore. Layers of twigs and branches were laid beneath the surface of the water and weighted down with stones.
chiton Long tunics worn by both men and women in ancient Greece. Chitons were draped loosely over the body and held in place with brooches or pins.
chlorophyll The green pigment of plants that absorbs light energy from the Sun.
circa (*c.*) A symbol used to mean 'approximately', when the exact date of an event is not known, e.g. *c.*1000BC.
citizen A Roman term used to describe a free person with the right to vote.
city-state A city, and the area surrounding it, which is controlled by one leader or government.
civil servant Official who carries out administrative duties for a government.
civilization A society that makes advances in arts, sciences, law, technology and government.
clan A group of people related to each other by ancestry or by marriage.
climate The typical weather pattern of an area.
cocoon A silky, protective envelope such as that secreted by silkworms and other insect larvae, to protect the developing pupa.
codex An ancient manuscript bound and folded into a book.
colonies Communities or groups of people who settle in another land but keep links with their own country.
compass An instrument containing a magnetized strip of metal, used for finding direction.
compressed air Air that has been squashed into a smaller volume than usual.
condensation The process by which water vapour becomes a liquid.
conductor A material through which heat or electricity can travel.
conscription A mandatory term of service to the State whereby people have to work as labourers or soldiers.
continental drift The generally accepted theory that continents move slowly around the world.
continental shelf The zone of shallow water in the oceans around the edge of continents.
convection The rising of hot air or fluid, caused by the fact that it is lighter than its surroundings.
coracle A small boat made of leather tightly stretched over a wooden frame.
counterweight A weight that balances another weight.
coupling A connecting device that joins a locomotive to a carriage to make a train.
coupling rod A link that connects the driving wheels on both sides of a locomotive.
crankshaft An axle that has parts of it bent at right angles so that up-and-down motion can be turned into circular motion.
crossbow A mechanical bow that fires small arrows called bolts.
crusades Eight holy wars from 1096 onwards, which were fought by Christians to recover the Holy Land (modern Israel) from the Muslims.

crystal A mineral or other substance that forms in a regular, 3-dimensional shape.
cubit An ancient unit of measurement equal to the length of a forearm.
cuirass Armour that protects the upper part of the body.
cultivate To prepare and use land or soil for growing crops.
cuneiform A type of writing that uses wedge-shaped figures, carved with a special tool. Cuneiform was developed by the Sumerians, and also used by the Babylonians and Assyrians.
currency Form of exchange for goods, such as money.
cylinder A hollow or solid tube shape.

D

daimyo A nobleman or warlord from ancient Japan.
data Pieces of information.
database An organized store of information.
deciduous Describes trees and shrubs that shed their leaves at the end of each growing season.
democracy A form of government in which every citizen has the right to vote and hold public office.
density A measure of how tightly the matter in a substance is packed together.
deposition The laying down of material, particularly of material eroded from the Earth's crust and carried by rivers, sea and ice.
depth of field In photography, the distance in focus between the nearest and farthest parts of a scene.
dictator A ruler with complete and unrestricted power.
digital camera A camera that takes electronic images that are downloaded on to a computer to be viewed.
dish antenna A large, dish-shaped aerial used to receive signals in radar, radio telescopes and satellite broadcasting.
disk drive The device that holds, reads and writes on to a computer.
dowel A thin cylindrical length of wood. Dowel is available from hardware stores.
drag A force that acts in the opposite direction to motion, and creates resistance.
driving wheel The wheel of a locomotive that turns in response to power from the steam engine.
dugout canoe A canoe made by hollowing out a tree trunk.
dynasty A successive period of rule by generations of the same family.

E

Earth's crust The outermost, solid rock layer of the planet Earth.
ecosystem A community of living things that interact with each other and their surroundings.
edict An order issued by a ruler or by government.
effort The force applied to a lever or other simple machine to move a load.
electricity A form of energy caused by the movement of electrons (charged particles) in atoms.
electrum A mixture of gold and silver used for making coins.
element A substance that cannot be split by chemical processes into simpler parts.
elevator In aircraft, a movable flap on the tailplane or rear wing that causes the nose to rise or fall.
emperor The ruler of an empire.
empire A group of lands ruled or governed by a single nation.
engine A device that uses energy in fuel to make movement.
engrave To carve letters or designs on stone, wood or metal.
environment The external conditions in which people, animals and plants live on Earth.
epicentre The region on the Earth's surface that lies directly above the focus of an earthquake.
Equator The imaginary circle around the middle of the Earth between the Northern and Southern Hemispheres, where day and night are equal in length, and the climate is constantly hot and wet.
erosion The gradual wearing away of the land by agents of erosion such as ice, rain, wind and waves.
escape velocity The minimum speed that a body must have to escape from the gravitational force of a planet.
evaporation The process by which something turns from liquid to vapour.
evergreen Describes plants that bear leaves all the year round.
excavation A place where archaeologists dig up the ground to learn about past civilizations.
exoskeleton Outer skeleton – the hard case that protects an insect's soft body parts.
exposure time The time it takes for a camera to take a picture.
exposures Photographs on a film.

F

fault A break in the Earth's crust that causes one block of rock to slip against an adjacent one.
fax machine A machine that photocopies and electronically sends and receives written words and pictures over a telephone line.
fertilization The act or process of the male part of a plant or a male animal that enables a female's egg or eggs to produce young.
fiesta A religious festival with dancing and singing, especially common in Spain and South America.
firing The process of baking clay or glass paste in a kiln, to harden it and make it waterproof.

focal plane The area at the back of a camera where the exposed film is held flat.
force A push or a pull.
fossil The remains, found preserved in rock, of a creature that lived in the past.
freight Goods transported by rail, road, sea or air.
fresco A picture painted on a wall while the plaster is still damp.
friction The force caused by the two surfaces rubbing together. This results in the slowing down of movement, and heat being produced.
fumarole An opening in the ground in volcanic regions, where steam and gases can escape.

G

galley A warship powered by oars.
garrison A fort or similar place that is guarded by a group of soldiers. The word garrison can also refer to the group of soldiers themselves.
gauge The width between the inside running edges of the rails of a train track. In Britain, the USA and most of Europe, the gauge is 1,435mm/4ft 8½in.
gear A toothed wheel designed to interact with other toothed wheels to transfer motion in a controlled way.
geisha A Japanese woman who entertains men with song and dances.
gem A precious or semi-precious stone or crystal, such as diamond or ruby. Gems often decorate jewellery or other ornaments.
generate To produce energy such as electricity.
geology The scientific study of the origins and structure of a planet and its rocks.
geothermal energy The energy created by the heat of the rocks underground.
germination The point at which a plant seed or an egg in an animal is fertilized and begins to grow.
geyser A fountain of steam and water that spurts out of a vent in the ground in volcanic regions.
gilding The process of applying a thin layer of gold to metal or pottery.
gladiator A professional fighter, slave or criminal in ancient Rome, who fought to the death in arenas for public entertainment.
glyph A picture symbol used in writing.
government The way in which a country or state is ruled.
gravity The pulling force that exists between large masses.
greaves Armour worn to protect the shins.
groma An instrument used by Roman surveyors to measure right angles and to make sure roads were straight.
guilds Groups of skilled workers or merchants who checked quality standards, trained young people and looked after old and sick members.

H

haft The handle of an axe.
hard drive A computer's main storage area, which holds the operating system and application files.
hardware All the equipment that makes up a computer – hard drives, monitor, keyboard, mouse etc.
harpoon A spear-like weapon with a detachable head fastened to a rope.
hemispheres The top and bottom halves of the Earth, divided by the Equator, and known as the Northern and Southern Hemispheres.
hibernation A period when many animals save energy by remaining inactive in order to survive the winter.
hieroglyph A picture symbol used in ancient Egypt to represent an idea, word or sound.
hilt The handle of a sword.
Hinduism A world religion characterized by the worship of several gods and a belief in reincarnation.
hominid Humans and their most recent ancestors.
Homo sapiens The Latin species name for modern humans. The words *Homo* and *sapiens* together mean 'wise man'.
hoplites Greek fighting force made up of middle-class men. Their armour and weaponry were of the highest standard.
hot spot A place where plumes of molten rock in the Earth's mantle burn through the Earth's crust to create isolated areas of volcanic activity.
hot springs Water that has been heated underground and bubbles to the surface in volcanic regions.
hull The frame or body of a ship or aircraft.
humidity The amount of water, or moisture, in the air.
hunter-gatherers People who hunt wild animals for their meat, and gather plants for food as a way of life.
hydraulics The use of water or other liquids to move devices such as pistons.
hydrometer An instrument for measuring the density of liquids.
hygrometer An instrument for measuring humidity.

I

Ice Ages Several periods in Earth's history when the average temperature of the atmosphere decreased and large parts of the Earth's surface were covered with snow and ice. The most significant Ice Age occurred between 30,000BC and 12,000BC.
igloo A dome-shaped Inuit shelter built from blocks of firmly packed snow.
igneous rock A rock that forms when magma (hot, molten rock) cools and becomes solid. It is one of three main types of rock, the others being sedimentary and metamorphic rock.

ikebana The ancient Japanese art of flower arranging. The word ikebana means 'living flowers'.
immigrant A person who travels from his or her native country to live in another land.
Inca A member of an indigenous South American civilization living in Peru before the Spanish conquest.
indigenous Native or originating from a certain place.
infrared Electromagnetic radiation with a wavelength between the red end of the visible spectrum and microwaves and radio waves.
inlay To set or embed pieces of wood or metal in another material, so that the surfaces are flat.
inro A small, decorated box that is worn hanging from the sash of a Japanese kimono.
inscribed Lettering, pictures or patterns carved into a hard material such as stone or wood.
insulate To cover or protect something to reduce the amount of heat or electricity entering and/or leaving it.
Inuit The native people of the Arctic and regions of Greenland, Alaska and Canada.
Iron Age The period when iron became the main metal used for producing tools and weapons. The Iron Age began around 1200BC.
iron ore Rock that contains iron in a raw, natural form.
irrigation Using channels dug into the earth to bring water to dry land, so that crops can grow.
Islam A world religion founded in the 7th century AD by the prophet Mohammed.

J

jet engine A type of engine that propels a vehicle, such as a car or a plane, by the forceful expulsion of hot gases.
jet propulsion Reactive movement to a jet of fluid or gas.

K

kanji The picture symbols based on Chinese characters that were used for writing Japanese before about AD800.
kayak A one-person Inuit canoe powered by a double-bladed paddle. The wooden or bone frame is covered with sealskin.
kendo A Japanese martial art that involves fighting with bamboo swords.
keystone The central stone in the arch of a bridge or curved part of a building.
kiln An oven or furnace used for firing bricks or pottery.
kimono A loose wide-sleeved robe, worn by both men and women in Japan.
knucklebones A favourite game of the Greeks and Romans. Knucklebones involved flipping small animal bones from one side of the hand to another, without dropping them.

L

larva The immature stage in the life of many insects, amphibians and fish.
lava Hot, molten rock emerging through volcanoes, known as magma when underground.
leading wheel The wheel at the front of a locomotive.
legion The main unit of the Roman army made up only of Roman citizens.
legislation Making laws.
lens A transparent object, such as glass, that is curved on one or both sides. A lens bends and directs beams of light to form or alter the view of an image.
lever A long bar that moves around a pivot to help move a heavy object.
lift The force generated by an aerofoil (airfoil) that counters the force of gravity and keeps a flying object in the air.
light spectrum The colours that light can be split into.
lithosphere The rigid outer shell of the Earth, including the crust and the rigid upper part of the mantle.
load The weight moved by a lever or other machine.
locomotive An engine powered by steam, diesel or electricity, and used to pull the carriages of a train.
loom A frame used for weaving cloth.
lyre A harp-like, stringed musical instrument common in ancient Greece.

M

magistrate A government officer of justice, similar to a local judge.
magma Hot, molten rock in the Earth's interior, known as lava when it emerges on the surface.
magnetism An invisible force found in some elements, but especially in iron, which causes other pieces of iron to be either pushed apart or drawn together.
mantle The very deep layer of rock that lies underneath the Earth's crust.
mass The amount of matter there is in a substance or object. Mass is measured in kilograms/pounds, tonnes/tons etc.
Maya An ancient civilization native to Mesoamerica.
medieval A term describing people, events and objects from a period in history known as the Middle Ages.
megalith A large stone, either standing on its own or used as part of a tomb, stone circle or other monument.
Mesoamerica A geographical area made up of the land between Mexico and Panama in Central America.
Mesopotamia An ancient name for the fertile region between the Tigris and Euphrates rivers in the Middle East. This area is now occupied by Iraq.
metamorphic rock Rock that has been chemically changed by heat or pressure to form a different rock.

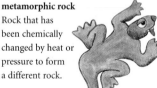

metamorphosis Change, as in the life cycles of some animals, that involves a complete change of form, appearance and other characteristics.
meteorologist A person who studies the science and patterns of weather and climate.
Middle Ages Period in history that lasted from around AD800 to 1400.
migration The movement of people to other regions, either permanently or at specific times of the year.
mineral A naturally occurring substance found in rocks.
missionary A member of a religious organization who carries out charitable work and religious teaching.
molten Something solid that has been melted, such as lava, which is molten rock.
monarchy A form of government in which the head of state is a king, queen or other non-elected sovereign.
monochrome Shades of black and white, with no other colours.
monorail A train that runs on a single rail.
mould A kind of fungus in the form of a woolly growth that is often found on stale or rotten food.
mummy An embalmed or preserved human or animal body.

N

Native Americans The indigenous peoples of the Americas.
navigation The skill of plotting a route for a ship, aircraft or other vehicle.
negative In photography, the image on the developed film from which photographic prints are made. The colours in a negative are reversed, so that dark areas appear to be light and light areas appear to be dark.
neolithic The new Stone Age. The period when people began to farm, but were still using stone tools.
netsuke Small Japanese toggles that are carved from ivory, and used to secure items from the sash of a kimono.
New Kingdom The period in ancient Egypt between 1550BC and 1070BC.
nomads A group of people who roam from place to place in search of food or better land, or to follow herds.

O

Old Kingdom The period in ancient Egypt between 2686BC and 2181BC.
oligarchy Government by a group of rich and powerful people.
oppidum A Latin word meaning town.
orbit In astronomy, the curved path followed by a planet or other body around another planet or body.
order A major grouping of animals, larger than a family.
organism Any living thing, such as a plant or animal, that is capable of growth and reproducing itself.
osmosis The movement of a solvent, such as water, from a more dilute solution to a more concentrated one.

P

palaeontology The study of fossils.
papier mâché Pulped paper mixed with glue, moulded into shape while wet, and left to dry.
papyrus A tall reed that grows in the River Nile, once used to make paper.
patolli A popular Aztec board game.
pharaoh A ruler of ancient Egypt.
photosynthesis The process by which plants make food using energy from sunlight.
piston A cylindrical device that moves up and down a cylinder in response to the application and release of pressure from liquid or gas.
pivot A central point around which something revolves, balances or sways.
plastic A durable, synthetic material that is easily moulded or shaped by heat.
plate armour Protective clothing made out of overlapping plates of solid metal.
plumbline A string with a weight at one end that is used to check whether a wall or other construction is vertical.
points Rails on the track that guide the wheels of a locomotive on to a different section of track.
porcelain The finest quality of pottery. Porcelain is made with a fine clay called kaolin, and baked at a high temperature.
precipitation Any form of water (rain, hail, sleet or snow) that comes out of the air and falls to the ground.
prehistoric The period in history before written records were made.
priest An official who performs religious rituals, such as prayers, on behalf of worshippers.
primary colours Red, blue and green, or magenta, cyan (blue) and yellow. These colours are the basis for all other shades and colours.
prism Specially shaped glass used to split white light into the spectrum, or to refract light rays away from their normal path.
propellant The fuel or force that causes something to go forward, such as the fuel in a rocket.
propeller A device, with blades, that rotates to provide thrust for a vehicle such as a ship or plane.
prototype The first working model of a machine from a specific design.
pupa Inactive stage in the life cycle of many insects, such as butterflies and moths.
pyramid A huge four-sided stone tomb built to house the mummy of an Egyptian pharaoh.

Q

quipu Knotted, coloured cords tied together and used by the Incas to record information.

R

RAM Random access memory. Computer memory that holds data temporarily until the computer is switched off.
ramparts The defensive parapets on the top of castle walls.
reflecting telescope A telescope that uses mirrors.
refracting telescope A telescope that uses lenses.
refraction The bending of light rays.
regent Someone who rules a country on behalf of another person.
relic Part of the body of a saint or martyr, or some object connected with them, preserved as an object of respect and honour.
relief A sculpture carved from a flat surface such as a wall.
republic A country that is ruled by an assembly of representatives elected by citizens rather than by a monarch or an emperor.
ritual A procedure or series of actions often performed for a religious purpose.
rolling stock The locomotives, carriages, wagons and any other vehicles that operate on a railway.
ROM Read-only memory. Computer memory that holds information permanently.
rudder A device for controlling the direction of a ship or plane.

S

Saami The ancient people of Lapland in Scandinavia.
sacrifice The killing of a living thing, or the offering of a possession, in honour of the gods.
sadhu A nomadic Hindu.
samurai Members of the Japanese warrior class. Samurai were highly trained, and followed a strict code of honourable behaviour.
sari A traditional garment worn by Indian women. A sari consists of a long piece of fabric wound round the waist and draped over one shoulder and sometimes the head.
satellite A celestial or artificial body orbiting around a planet or star.
savanna Tropical grassland.
scabbard The container for the blade of a sword. It is usually fixed to a belt.
scribe A professional writer, clerk or civil servant.
sediment Solid particles of rock or other material.
sedimentary rock A rock made up of mineral particles that have been carried by wind or running water to accumulate in layers elsewhere, most commonly on the beds of lakes or in the seas and oceans.
seismology The study of earthquakes.
Senate The law-making assembly of ancient Rome.
shield boss A metal plate that is fixed to the centre of a shield to protect the hand of the person holding it.
shinden A single-storey Japanese house.
Shinto An ancient Japanese faith, known as the way of the gods, and based on honouring holy spirits.
shogun A Japanese army commander. Shoguns ruled Japan from 1185 to 1868.
shrine A place of worship, or a container for holy relics such as bones.
shutter Camera mechanism that controls the amount of time light is allowed to fall on to the lens.
siege A long-lasting attack to capture a fortified place or city by surrounding it and cutting off all supplies.
Silk Road The ancient overland trading route between China and Europe, used mainly by merchants travelling on camels.
smelt To extract a metal from its ore by heating it in a furnace.
society All the classes of people living in a particular community or country.
software Applications that enable computers to carry out specific tasks.
Solar System The family of planets, moons and other bodies that orbit around the Sun.
soldered Something that is joined together with pieces of melted metal.
solution A mixture of something solid and the liquid into which it has been completely dissolved.
sound wave Energy that transmits sound.
space probe A spacecraft that works in deep space.
space shuttle A vehicle designed to be used for at least 100 space flights.
space station A large artificial satellite in which astronauts live and work.
species A group of animals that share similar characteristics and can breed successfully together.
spindle A rod used to twist fibres into yarn for weaving.
staple food The major part of the diet. For example, rice was the staple food of people from ancient India.
steam traction Pulling movement achieved through the conversion of water to steam.
Stone Age The first period in human history in which people made their tools and weapons out of stone.
streamlined A shape that moves through air or water in the most efficient manner, with the least resistance from drag or friction.

subject A person who is ruled by a monarch or government.
surcoat A long, loose tunic worn over body armour.

T

tachi The long sword that was carried by Japanese samurai.
tax Goods, money or services paid to the government or ruling state.
tectonic plates The 20 or so giant slabs of rock that make up the Earth's surface.
tectonics The study of the structures that make up the Earth's surface.
template A piece of card cut in a particular design and used as a pattern when cutting out material. You can use a photocopier to enlarge the templates in this book. Alternatively, copy the templates on to a piece of paper, using a ruler to make sure the size follows the measurements given in the book.
temple A building used for worship or other spiritual rituals.
tepee A conical tent made up of skins stretched over a framework of wooden poles. Tepees are still used by some Native American tribes today.
tesserae Coloured tiles made of stone, pottery or glass, and pressed into soft cement to form mosaics.
textile Cloth produced by weaving threads, such as silk or cotton, together.
thermometer An instrument for measuring temperature.
thorax The part of an insect's body between the head and the abdomen, which bears the wings and legs.
thrust The force that pushes a machine such as an aircraft forwards.
tidal wave A huge ocean wave.
toga A loose outer garment worn by the upper classes in ancient Rome. A toga consisted of a large piece of cloth draped around the body.
tomb A vault in which the bodies of dead people are placed.
torii The traditional gateway to a Shinto shrine.
trading post General store where people from a wide area traded or swapped goods.
transpiration The process in the water cycle by which plants release water vapour into the air.
treadwheel A wooden wheel turned by the feet of people or animals, and used to power mills or other machinery.
tribe A group of people who shared a common language and way of life.
tribute Goods given by one person or nation to another as a form of taxation.
trident A three-pronged spear.
trireme A warship used by the ancient Greeks. Triremes were powered by men rowing in three ranks.
tropical A climate that is very hot and humid.
tropics Part of the Earth's surface that is between the Tropic of Cancer and the Tropic of Capricorn.
tundra A treeless area where the soil is permanently frozen under the surface.
turbine A propeller-like device driven by fast-moving gas currents, wind or water.
turbulence Air or water movement that consists of eddies in random directions, with no smooth flow.

U

umiak A rowing boat used by peoples native to the Arctic. Umiaks are made from whalebone, covered with walrus hide, and waterproofed with seal oil.
underworld A mysterious place to which the spirits of the dead were believed to travel after death and burial.
upthrust The force that makes a ship float, or an aircraft take off.

V

valve A device that controls the flow of a liquid.
Viking One of the Scandinavian peoples who lived by sea-raiding in the early Middle Ages.
villa A Roman country house, usually part of an agricultural estate.
volador A religious Aztec ritual in which four men spun round and round a tall pole.

W

water wheel A simple water-driven turbine used to drive machinery.
weather The condition of the atmosphere at any particular time and place.
weathering The breakdown of rock and other materials when exposed to the weather.
weightlessness In Space, a state in which an object has no actual weight because it is not affected by gravitational attraction.
wind Air moving in relation to the Earth's surface.
windmill A machine for grinding or pumping, driven by vanes or sails that are moved by the wind.

Z

Zen A branch of the Buddhist faith that was popular among Japanese samurai warriors.
ziggurat A pyramid-shaped temple built by the ancient Babylonians, with a broad, square base and stepped sides.

Index

L

M

N

O

P

Acknowledgements

This edition is published by Armadillo
an imprint of Anness Publishing Ltd
Blaby Road, Wigston
Leicestershire LE18 4SE
info@anness.com

www.annesspublishing.com

If you like the images in this book and would like to investigate using them for publishing, promotions or advertising, please visit our website www.practicalpictures.com for more information.

A CIP catalogue record for this book is available from the British Library.

Publisher: Joanna Lorenz
Senior Editor: Felicity Forster
Editors: Rebecca Clunes, Gilly Cameron Cooper, Caroline Davison, Rasha Elsaeed, Leon Gray, Louisa Somerville, Sarah Uttridge and Elizabeth Woodland
Contributing Authors: Stephen Bennington, John Farndon, Ian Graham, Jen Green, Peter Harrison, Robin Kerrod, Peter Mellett, Al Morrison, Chris Oxlade, Steve Parker, John Roston and Rodney Walshaw
Consultants: Rachel Halstead, Chris Oxlade and Struan Reid
Designer: Sandra Marques/Axis Design Editions Ltd
Jacket Design: Oakley Design Associates
Photographers: Paul Bricknell, John Freeman, Don Last, Robert Pickett and Tim Ridley
Illustrators: Rob Ashby, Julian Baker, Cy Baker/Wildlife Art, Andy Beckett, Mark Beesley, Stephen Bennington, Mark Bergin, Richard Berridge, Peter Bull Art Studio, Vanessa Card, Rob Chapman, James Field, Wayne Ford, Chris Forsey, Mike Foster, Terry Gabbey, Roger Gorringe, Jeremy Gower, Peter Gregory, Simon Gurr, Stephen Gyapay, Richard Hawke, Nick Hawken, Ron Hayward, Gary Hincks, Sally Holmes, Richard Hook, Stuart Jackson-Carter, Rob Jakeway, John James, Kuo Chen Kang, Aziz Khan, Stuart Lafford, Michael Lamb, Ch'en Ling, Steve Lings, Rob McCaig, Kevin Maddison, Alan Male/Linden Artists, Janos Marffy, Shane Marsh, Chris Odgers, Alex Pang, Helen Parsley, Terry Riley, Andrew Robinson, Chris Rothero, Eric Rowe, Martin Sanders, Peter Sarson, Mike Saunders, Rob Sheffield, Don Simpson, Guy Smith, Donato Spedaliere, Nick Spender, Clive Spong, Stuart Squires, Roger Stewart, Sue Stitt, Ken Stott, Steve Sweet/Simon Girling and Associates, Mike Taylor, Alisa Tingley, Catherine Ward, Shane Watson, Ross Watton, Alison Winfield, John Whetton, Mike White, Stuart Wilkinson and John Woodcock
Stylists: Ken Campbell, Jane Coney, Marion Elliot, Tim Grabham, Konika Shakar, Thomasina Smith, Isolde Sommerfeldt and Melanie Williams
Production Controller: Mai-Ling Collyer

The publisher would like to thank Scallywags and all the children modelling in this book.

Previously published in two separate volumes, *150 Great Science Experiments* and *120 Great History Projects*

PUBLISHER'S NOTES
Bracketed terms are intended for American readers.
Although the advice and information in this book are believed to be accurate and true at the time of going to press, neither the authors nor the publisher can accept any legal responsibility or liability for any errors or omissions that may have been made nor for any inaccuracies nor for any loss, harm or injury that comes about from following instructions or advice in this book.

Manufacturer: Anness Publishing Ltd, Blaby Road, Wigston, Leicestershire LE18 4SE, England
For Product Tracking go to: www.annesspublishing.com/tracking
Batch: 3363-22480-1127

Picture Credits

b=bottom, t=top, c=centre, l=left, r=right
Bruce Coleman Ltd: 91cl. Bryan and Cherry Alexander: 327bl, 332bl. Ancient Art & Architecture Collection Ltd/R.Sheridan: 480tr, 484tr. The Art Archive: 338tr, 352t/Oriental Art Museum Genoa/Dagli Orti, 386tr/Dagli Orti, 454cl, 468bl/Conseil Général Saint Brieuc/ Dagli Orti, 478bl/Eileen Tweedy, 479bl/ British Museum/Jacqueline Hyde, 482tr/ Museo Provinciale Sigismondo Castromediano Lecce/Dagli Orti, 484b & 485cr/Musée Alésia Alise Sainte Reine France/Dagli Orti, 488bl/Private Collection/Dagli Orti, 492bl/Chateau de Blerancourt/Dagli Orti. The Bridgeman Art Library: 280cl/Christie's Images, 486bl/Oriental Museum/Durham University, 490bl/Victoria & Albert Museum. Christie's Images: 352b. Corbis: 432cl/Dave G. Houser, 464bl/Dean Conger, 466tr/Werner Forman, 482bl/Dave G. Houser. Frank Lane Picture Agency: 91bl, 100bl, 100bc, 100br. The Hutchison Library: 337t/Robert Francis, 338b/Liba Taylor, 470tr/H. R. Dönig, 490tr/ Jon Burbank, 494bl, 494tr. Japan Information and Cultural Centre: 273t, 280b. Nature Photographers Ltd: 80bc. South American Pictures/Diego Rivera: 337b.

Every effort has been made to trace the copyright holders of all images that appear in this book. Anness Publishing Ltd apologizes for any unintentional omissions and, if notified, would be happy to add an acknowledgement in future editions.